Encyclopedia of Corporate Names Worldwide

A Dictionary of Art Titles:
The Origins of the Names and
Titles of 3,000 Works of Art (2000)

A Dictionary of Music Titles:
The Origins of the Names and
Titles of 3,500 Musical Compositions (2000)

Dictionary of Pseudonyms and Their Origins,
with Stories of Name Changes, third edition (1998)

Placenames of the World: Origins and Meanings
of the Names for Over 5000 Natural Features, Countries,
Capitals, Territories, Cities and Historic Sites (1997)

Literally Entitled: A Dictionary of the Origins
of the Titles of Over 1300 Major Literary Works
of the Nineteenth and Twentieth Centuries (1996)

African Placenames: Origins and Meanings
of the Names for Over 2000 Natural Features,
Towns, Cities, Provinces and Countries (1994)

The Naming of Animals: An Appellative Reference to
Domestic, Work and Show Animals Real and Fictional (1993)

Encyclopedia of Corporate Names Worldwide

ADRIAN ROOM

McFarland & Company, Inc., Publishers
Jefferson, North Carolina, and London

Library of Congress Cataloguing-in-Publication Data

Room, Adrian.
Encyclopedia of corporate names worldwide / Adrian Room.
p.   cm.
Includes bibliographical references and index.

ISBN 0-7864-1287-9 (illustrated case binding : 50# alkaline paper)

1. Business names—Encyclopedias.
2. Trademarks—Encyclopedias.
3. Brand name products—Encyclopedias.
4. Corporations—Encyclopedias.
I. Title.

HD69.B7 R66   2002   929'.7—dc21   2002004605

British Library cataloguing data are available

Cover photograph ©2002 Corbis Images

Manufactured in the United States of America

*McFarland & Company, Inc., Publishers
Box 611, Jefferson, North Carolina 28640
www.mcfarlandpub.com*

Contents

Introduction

This reference book aims to give the stories behind, or origins of, more than 3,500 commercial names, from major corporations, such as *Anheuser-Busch* and *McDonnell-Douglas*, to patent drugs and medicines, such as *Allonal* and *Ritalin*. It encompasses automobiles such as *Amilcar*, whiskey such as *Buena Vista*, sauces such as *Durkee's*, harmonicas such as *Hohner*, baskets such as *Longaberger*, childrenswear such as *OshKosh*, movie theaters such as *Roxy*, artificial fiber such as *Tricel*, and publishers such as *Van Nostrand Reinhold*. Here are the products and services of a whole range of manufacturers and entrepreneurs, many of them American or British, but a number originating in other countries such as France, Germany, Italy, and Japan. The services range from travel agents and business consultancies to banks and Internet search engines. All human commercial life is here.

The names themselves are basically of two types: what one might loosely call "name names," such as those of companies and corporations named after their founders or benefactors, and "word names," where a product or service has a more or less (and often less) meaningful name based on a standard word. Examples of the latter are the many brands of petfood, such as *Bounce*, *Chappie*, *Pal*, and *Pedigree* for dogfoods, and *Choice*, *Friskies*, *Top Cat*, and *Whiskers* for cat foods. Such transparent names are in fact mostly missing from the book, since their meaning is clear, and the entry for each would simply confine itself to the product's date of launch and the name of its manufacturer(s).

As mentioned, however, the aim is to give more than this, and to identify the original makers or inventors who made the "name name" famous, or to elucidate the origin of the "word name."

Let us take a broader sweep of well-known brand names to illustrate the scope of the subject. The following 50 domestic products were published in *Marketing* magazine's "Top 50 British Brands"

1. *Coca-Coca*; 2. *Walkers*; 3. *Nescafé*; 4. *Stella Artois*; 5. *Müller*; 6. *Persil*; 7. *Andrex*; 8. *Robinsons*; 9. *KitKat*; 10. *Pepsi*; 11. *Carling*; 12. *Pampers*; 13. *Cadbury's* "Dairy Milk"; 14. *Ariel*; 15. *Ribena*; 16. *Whiskas*; 17. *Walls'* ice cream; 18. *Heinz* canned soup; 19. *Lucozade*; 20. *Heinz* baked beans; 21. *Felix*; 22. *PG Tips;* 23. *Pringles;* 24. *Flora;* 25. *McCain* chips; 26. *Huggies;* 27. *Bold;* 28. *Colgate;* 29. *Bell's* 8-year-old whisky; 30. *Tetley;* 31. *Birds Eye* frozen poultry; 32. *Mars Bar;* 33. *Budweiser;* 34. *Lurpak;* 35. *Chum;* 36. *Dairylea;* 37. *Foster's;* 38. *Comfort;* 39. *Ernest & Julio Gallo;* 40. *Smirnoff* "Red Label"; 41. *Mr Kipling;* 42. *Sunny Delight;* 43. *Velvet;* 44. *The Famous Grouse;* 45. *Tropicana;* 46. *Jacob's Creek;* 47. *Birds Eye* frozen ready meals; 48. *Birds Eye* frozen vegetables; 49. *Kleenex* "Facial"; 50. *Celebrations* (Source: *The Times*, August 11, 2001).

Although a British listing, many of the names are of American origin, *Coca-Cola*, *Pepsi*, *Pampers*, *Heinz*, *Colgate*, *Budweiser*, *Tropicana*, and *Kleenex* being among the most familiar. But the names represent a good cross-section of "name names" (*Walkers*, *Robinsons*, *Walls*, *Heinz*, *Birds Eye*, etc.) and "word names" (*Coca-Cola*, *Pepsi*, *Whiskas*, *Huggies*, *Velvet*, etc.), and most are so well known that no indication of the product(s) associated with the name is necessary. (It is given here in a few cases to differentiate between products or to specify a particular brand.) The listing also illustrates the different types of names that exist. There are proprietorial ones for proud products (*Walls* regard their name brand ice cream as superior to others, *Smirnoff* see their vodka similarly), homely names for homely products (*Pampers*, *Huggies*, *Comfort*), "exotic" names for "special" products (*Stella Artois* as a "star" beer, *Tropicana* as an exotic juice drink), and bright and cheerful names to imply an enjoyable or tasty product (*Sunny Delight*, *Celebrations*). There are also the rather baffling names. How come *KitKat*, a chocolate cookie, has a name like a cat food? Who or what is the "PG" of *PG Tips*? Who is *Mr Kipling*? What is the language of origin of *Lurpak*? What type of bird is *The Famous Grouse*?

The creation of a product name or brand name can be a hazardous business, especially if of the "word name" type and involving a foreign (non-English) language. Chevrolet found that its *Nova* model failed to find popularity in Mexico, where its name was understood as Spanish *no va*, "does not go," while English-speaking consumers are unlikely to take to the French orange drink marketed in its home country as *Pschitt*, any more than they will welcome a make of Turkish cookies called *Bum*! (In British English this has a deeper downside than in American English.) David A Ricks, in *Blunders in International Business* (1993), recounts further such *faux pas*. Rolls-Royce learned their lesson when they attempted to promote their luxury *Silver Mist* model under this name in Germany, not realizing that *Mist* is German for "dung." Sometimes a name is not in itself an embarrassing malapropism but for one reason or another is deemed unsuitable by the public or simply fails to catch on. In the early 1960s, General Mills spent over $1.4 million advertising their *Betty Crocker* cake mixes in an attempt to enter the British market. The costly promotion did not achieve

the desired objective, however, since the British could not identify with the exotic names given to each. Finally, at least for our purposes here, the Australian brewers Castlemaine changed their plans to market their popular *XXXX* ("four X") beer under this name in the United States, where *Fourex* is more familiar as a make of condom.

Some of the names listed above have long been in existence. *Coca-Cola*, for example, dates from 1886, while *Heinz* was founded ten years earlier and *Lorillard* more than a hundred years before that. In the latter years of the 20th century, many of the old familiar "name names" were gradually abandoned in the supposed interests of creating a more modern and sophisticated image. In May 2001, the revered British bank name *Salomon and Schroder* morphed into the bland *Citigroup*, so joining other such names consigned to oblivion in the previous 15 years, among them *Morgan Grenfell*, *Hill Samuel* and *Kleinwort Benson*. (Some of these names, even so, appear in the present book, as they enshrine their respective firms' founders.) Brand consultants claim that such name changes or "makeovers" are necessary for the refurbished image of the company or corporation in question. But the process has produced some inconsistencies. Why should one of Britain's best-known banks, *Midland Bank*, rebrand itself as *HSBC*, which to 90 percent of customers is a meaningless (and hard to remember) initialism? Why should the *FI Group* rename itself as *Xansa* on the basis that this supposedly Sanskrit name emphasizes the firm's global role? What is to be gained by the US firm *Andersen Consulting* in rechristening itself as *Accenture*? In some cases, a name is not changed but instead a distinctive device or diacritic is added to it. This happened with the US investment bank *Morgan Stanley*, who retained their name but revamped their logo by placing a little blue triangle over the "n" of "Morgan." Their logic for this? "The graphic element of the signature is a 'directional triangle.' It points toward the northeast, the general direction of financial success. As a delta, the triangle symbolizes change and the inclination to innovate. The three points symbolize the three groups served by the firm: clients, shareholders and employees." But who could possibly deduce this subtle hidden meaning from simply seeing the logo?

The creation of a company or product name is often straightforward. Most "name names" evolved naturally, offending no one and breaking no copyright laws, even if we now forget (if we ever knew in the first place) who *Jack Eckerd* was or when *Singer* first made his sewing machine. One legal hazard has been mentioned already. But there is another, more insidious than the promotion of an unsuitable name in a foreign language. The danger is that as a product becomes increasingly familiar, especially if first in the field or long dominant over its rivals, it will become generic. The *UK Press Gazette* of July 9, 1979, thus reminded its readers that the following names, among others, are registered trademarks, and must thus be written with a capital letter: *Ansafone, Band-Aid, Cellophane, Coke, Day-Glo, Dictaphone, Hoover, Jeep, Kleenex, Levi's, Polaroid, Sellotape, Thermos, Vaseline.* The following are unregistered, however, and can be written with a small initial: *aspirin, cornflakes, escalator, gramophone, hovercraft, shredded wheat* (but not *Welgar Shredded Wheat*). (Legislation may differ across the Atlantic, so that in the USA *Thermos* is no longer a registered name, but *Shredded Wheat*, owned by Nabisco, still is.)

The "name name" entries that follow can be quite detailed, since they outline not only the founding or creation of a company but the early years of its founder, youthful years that can in retrospect be seen as the burgeoning of entrepreneurial talent. Thus the computer company *Dell* was founded by Michael Dell, who began his business "career" by selling his stamp collection at the age of 12. Again, the history of some companies may well intertwine with that of others, and in certain manufacturing enterprises, such as the automotive industry, several other

related names may be involved. Thus the history of *David Brown* relates directly to that of *Massey-Ferguson*, and in turn engages *Aston Martin* and *Lagonda* and interacts with *Vosper Thornycroft*. (All such names are printed in bold in the text, to serve as cross-references.) Further, a commercially successful corporation or company is invariably involved in mergers, acquisitions, takeovers, buyouts, sellouts, and the like, most of which are too numerous to include in their history here. But the more important or influential such milestones will need to be mentioned, since they can affect the original name. A merger, for example, will often bring two names together, or result in an entirely different name that reflects neither of them. Sometimes, as happened with *Ralston Purina*, a "name name" may combine with a "word name" to create a company's regular established name.

While every endeavor has been made to give the origin of the many "word names" entered below, in some cases this has been impossible, if only because the name was never intended to be meaningful. Computer-generated names are often resorted to, and as long ago as the early 1970s names such as BABA, DOLA, GIMO, LAHU, SODI, and TIXY were being churned out by a computer programmed to fulfill certain criteria (260 such names are quoted in Casper J. Werkman, *Trademarks: Their Creation, Psychology and Perception*, 1974). Many modern drugs and medicines bear such names, and who is to say what meaning, if any, lies behind *Adifax, Brasivol, Clinoril, Dialar,* or *Semprex*? One may hazard a reasonable guess at the etymology of *Antabuse, Betaferon, Duragel,* and *Medinol*, but most such names remain indecipherable. On a less specialized level, the names of food products can often be decoded, such as *Almarz* marzipan, *Butta-Crest* cheeses, *Cloverkist* butter, *Delisha* ice cream, or *Kiddiekandee* cookies. But where a "word name" has been blended with a "name name," interpretation is often impossible. Who could guess that *Danoxa* meat extract combines the name of the manufacturers, S. Daniels & Co., with generic *ox*, or that *Frenlite* self-rising flour blends the makers' name, J.W. French & Co., with a respelled *light*?

The above examples are from *The Food Trade Directory of Trade Marks and Brand Names* (*see* Bibliography, p. 565), which reminds trademark creators that in order to be registrable in the ordinary way, a trademark must consist of at least one of the following:

1. The name of a company, individual, or firm represented in a special or particular manner;

2. The signature of the applicant for registration or of some predecessor in business;

3. An invented word or words;

4. A word or words having no direct reference to the character or quality of the goods and not being according to its ordinary signification a geographical word or a surname;

5. Any other distinctive mark, but a name, signature, word or words other than such as fall within the descriptions above (1 through 4) shall not be registrable except upon evidence of distinctiveness.

The same reference source shows that certain words are perennially popular in the names of food products, the most frequently favored being *Gold* or *Golden*, *Silver*, and *Sun* or *Sunny*. *Golden Sun* wheat flour thus has the best of both worlds. Similar preferences exist for other types of goods.

The registering of the name of a new company, product, or service is obviously an important step, since it signifies unique ownership of the name. Many of the entries below thus include particulars of the registration of the name in question, either in the *Official Gazette* of the US Patent Office or the *Trade Marks Journal* of the British equivalent. The latter was first issued in 1876, its first entry being that for *Bass* beer.

The present book has two appendices: one on the naming of *nylon*, which although not a registered trademark is nevertheless a familiar name with an interesting history, and one as a selection of advertising slogans designed to reflect the name of the product or service in question. A bibliography follows, and the book concludes with an index of the men and women whose enterprise or specialist knowledge created the product, and perhaps its name, in the first place.

Adrian Room
July 2002

Corporate Names Worldwide

A&C Black *(publishers)*

The Scottish publishing house, famous for annually issued reference works such as *Who's Who* and *The Writers' and Artists' Yearbook*, was founded in 1807 when Adam Black (1784–1874), the son of an Edinburgh master builder, opened his own bookshop in the city at 57 South Bridge. After acquiring the copyright of the *Encyclopaedia Britannica* in 1827, the publishing side of his business gained momentum, and in 1834 he brought into partnership his nephew, Charles Black (1807–1854), with the firm assuming its present name that year. The company is now based in London, still owned by the Black family, and in 2000 was acquired by **Bloomsbury**.

A&P *(grocery stores)*

The story of A&P begins with George Huntington Hartford (1833–1917), born in Augusta, Maine, the son of a farmer and merchant, who at the age of 18 sailed to Boston, Massachusetts, and took a job as a clerk in a dry-goods store. Around 1858 he went to New York, where he met George F. Gilman, a leather merchant, who advised him to go to St. Louis, Missouri. There he set up shop to represent Gilman's business. The flow of hides was irregular, however, so Hartford installed a retail selection of coffee, teas, and spices in his shop. When he returned to New York two years later, Gilman was already established in the grocery business. Hartford joined him as partner, and in 1869 the two men opened a series of stores with the name of Great Atlantic and Pacific Tea Company, as the grandiose original of what is today simply A&P. They soon undersold the competition and had grown to 100 stores when Hartford's son, George, Jr., joined them in 1880 at the age of 15. By 1900 A&P had 200 stores, by 1912 400, and in 1913 they started selling products under their own name, finding that they could undersell name products like Cream of Wheat, which had won a suit preventing A&P from selling "Cream of Wheat" at wholesale prices. In 1916 Hartford turned the company over to his sons.

A&W *(restaurant chain)*

Root beer and hot dogs have long been buddies on the American roadside, and in 1919 Roy W. Allen, an Illinois native who bought and sold old hotels, opened a walk-up root-beer stand in Lodi, California. In 1922, Frank Wright, one of Allen's employees, became a partner, and they named their enterprise simply "A&W Root Beer." In 1923, the company opened its first (and possibly America's first) drive-in, in Sacramento, California, and from 1925 Allen expanded the business, retaining the "A&W" name after Wright sold out in 1924, to build the nation's first system of franchise roadside restaurants. By the mid-1930s, about 200 outlets displayed the chain's familiar "bull's-eye and arrow" logo, and in 1996, with the company headquartered in Livonia, Michigan, there were 778 A&W restaurants worldwide.

Abarth *(automobiles)*

Carlo Abarth (1908–1979) was an Austrian-born Italian who had to wait until after World War II to gain real fame in the motor industry. In 1950 he launched his firm as a tuning concern specializing in the Fiat marque. He produced his first car in 1955, using **Fiat** parts, and went on to build a number of successful Fiat-based racing cars. It was Abarth's racing activities that pushed the company into liquidation in 1971, however, when it was taken over by Fiat for its own competition purposes.

Abbey *(life insurance)*

The British company Abbey Life was founded in 1962 by Mark Weinberg (b.1931), born in Durban, South Africa, the son of a life insurance agent. He followed in his father's footsteps but immigrated to Britain in 1961 following the Sharpeville massacre that year. He first of all "studied the opposition" then set about choosing a name for his enterprise, as follows (Kay 1985; *see* Bibliography p. 566):

"It had to be old and respectable, but unused," Weinberg pointed out. "I had several rejected by the Registrar of Business Names because they had been used back in the eighteenth century. Thames Life was one. The theory is that there might be some people holding policies with the old company, and a new one would cause confusion." Eventually he tried a different approach. He returned to the pavement and walked around with five names to see how people reacted. Two were the names of existing and well-known insurance companies. But more people Weinberg spoke to said they recognized the name of Abbey Life as a respectable company they were sure they had heard of. It was one of Weinberg's inventions, and it was the name he chose for his new company.

Abbey National *(building society)*

The British building society (savings and loan association) was formed in 1944 on the merger of the Abbey Road Building Society, founded in 1874 as a self-help group in a Baptist church schoolroom in Abbey Road, London, and the National Building Society, established in 1849. Abbey National became a public limited company in 1989 and is now a major retail bank.

Abbot Ale *(beer)*

The beer by the British brewers **Greene King** is named for the last abbot of Bury St. Edmunds, Suffolk, the brewery's home town. Bury St. Edmunds had 33 abbots down to 1539, when its abbey was abolished under the Suppression of Religious Houses Act.

Abbott *(iron and steel)*

The Abbott Iron Company took its name from Horace Abbott (1806–1887), born in Sudbury, Massachusetts, a farmer's son. In 1822 he was apprenticed to a blacksmith in Westborough, Massachusetts, and after completing his five-year term, spent the next two years as a journeyman blacksmith. He then returned to Westborough and set up his own blacksmith shop. In 1836, Abbott moved to Baltimore, Maryland, where together with a partner, John J. Ferguson, he bought a spade factory and converted it into an ironworks. With the purchase of the Canton Iron Works of East Baltimore in

1847, Abbott became established as a leading iron manufacturer. His company became the Abbott Iron Works and, after the American Civil War, the Abbott Iron Company.

Abbott *(pharmaceuticals)*

Abbott Laboratories were founded in north Chicago in 1888 by Wallace Calvin Abbott (d.1921), a farmer's son who began his career as a family doctor in Ravenswood, Illinois, but who discovered that he preferred selling drugs to practicing medicine. In 1887 he began buying alkaloid pills from a Chicago company as a new form of treatment (superseding liquid extracts) for fever reduction, but being dissatisfied with their quality, turned to manufacturing them himself in his kitchen the following year. In 1900 he set up the Abbott Alkaloidal Company, the germ of today's "Abbott Labs."

ABC *(teashops)*

The former chain of teashops in London, England, took their name from the Aerated Bread Co., a bakery firm who made "aerated" bread, meaning bread that has been raised by introducing carbon dioxide into the water used for the dough. The ABC opened their first teashop in 1861, and hundreds followed over the next century. They are now all closed.

ABC *(television networks)*

ABC is one of the few US corporations started by government order. In 1941 the Federal Communications Commission forced NBC to sell two of their radio networks, called the Red Network and the Blue Network. NBC kept the more profitable Red Network, while in 1943 the Blue Network was bought by Edward J. Noble (1882–1958), heir to the **Life Savers** candy fortune, who the following year renamed it the American Broadcasting Company (ABC). In 1953 ABC merged with United Paramount, the movie theater business of **Paramount** Pictures.

Abercrombie & Fitch *(fashionwear)*

In 1892, David T. Abercrombie, a former trapper, prospector, and railroad surveyor, and a keen devotee of "the great outdoors," opened a small waterfront shop and factory in downtown New York City, selling camping, fishing, and hunting gear. One of his early clients was Ezra H. Fitch, a lawyer in Kingston, New York, a like enthusiast of the natural world, who enjoyed trekking the slopes of the Adirondacks or casting flies in the Catskills. In 1900 he convinced Abercrombie to let him buy out the business, and four years later the shop, now on Broadway, became Abercrombie & Fitch. Both men were stubborn individualists, however, and the partnership dissolved, with Abercrombie resigning in 1907. Even so, the trade did well, even after Fitch's retirement in 1928. But the firm went bankrupt in 1977, when it was bought by Oshman's Sporting Goods. In 1988 they in turn sold it to the Limited, Inc., since when it has thrived as never before, so that by the end of the 20th century there were over 250 Abercrombie & Fitch stores, some ("abercrombies") devoted exclusively to teenage fashions.

Abraham & Straus (department store)

The New York City store originated in Brooklyn in 1865 as a small dry-goods shop called Wechsler and Abraham, the former being Joseph Wechsler, the latter 22-year-old Abraham Abraham. When the Brooklyn Bridge was completed in 1883 the two men foresaw that a new shopping district would evolve at its eastern terminus, so moved their business to a five-story building on Fulton Street that by 1889 was the largest dry-goods store in New York State. In 1893 Abraham joined with Isidor Straus (1845–1912) and his brother Nathan to buy out Wechsler's share of the business and gave the store its present name. With 15 stores, Abraham & Straus was the second-largest department store in the metropolitan chain until 1995, when Federated Department Stores, of which it had become a division in 1949, announced plans to discontinue the name. Isidor Straus was the head of **Macy's** until he and his wife met their deaths in the sinking of the *Titanic* in 1912.

Abrams *see* **Harry N. Abrams**

Abricotine (liqueur)

The name of the apricot brandy liqueur, from French *abricot*, "apricot," and the common commercial suffix *-ine*, although no longer proprietary in the USA, was entered by the French firm of A. Garnier, of Enghien-les-Bains, in the US Patent Office *Official Gazette* of September 11, 1906, and by "Caroline Henriette Garnier, trading as Veuve A. Garnier" in the *Trade Marks Journal* of June 8, 1921, with a claim of use since January 31, 1895.

Absolut (vodka)

The brand of vodka owes its existence to Lars Olsson Smith, a Swedish distiller on the island of Reimersholmen, Stockholm, who in 1879 introduced a method of producing a very pure form of spirit from potatoes. He described his product as *absolut rent*, Swedish for "absolutely pure," and this gave the name, although today the vodka is made from grain, not potatoes.

AC (automobiles)

The origins of the British cars date back to 1904, when engineer John Weller and partner John Portwine, who owned a chain of butchers' shops, formed Autocars and Accessories Ltd. in West Norwood, London. They introduced three-wheeler trade carriers in 1907, when they renamed their business Auto Carriers. A passenger version called the AC "Sociable" was launched in 1908, and the first AC four-wheeler arrived in 1913. In 1922 Auto Carriers Ltd. became AC Cars Ltd. The AC "Ace" sports car was launched in 1954 and in 1962 the classic AC "Cobra."

AC *see* **Champion**

Accenture (business consultants)

The US firm was originally part of **Arthur Andersen** and as such was known as Andersen Consulting. It broke away from its sibling in 2001 and adopted the new name "Accenture" (properly spelled with a musical stress mark over the "t") to denote its "accent on the future." The firm took 80 days to devise the name, and reduced more than 5,000 names to a "shortlist" of 500 before selecting the winner.

Acrilan (synthetic fiber)

The synthetic acrylic fiber, used for carpets, furnishing, and clothing, derives its name from a blend of "acrylic" and Latin *lana*, "wool." It was entered by the Chemstrand Corporation, of Philadelphia, in the US Patent Office *Official Gazette* of May 8, 1951: "For Yarns, Threads, and Yarn and Thread Filaments."

Action Man (toy doll)

The doll for boys was launched by **Hasbro** in the USA in 1964 as GI Joe, a figure in military costume with a scarred cheek. His manly visage, according to Hasbro, was based on the faces of 20 real soldiers who had won medals of honor. He was a huge success, and **Palitoy** quickly secured the UK rights. But the US soldier had to be anglicized and needed a new name. One suggestion was "Ace 21," because the doll had 21 moving parts. This was rejected, however, and in 1966 Action Man hit Britain's stores, his name entered by Palitoy in the *Trade Marks Journal* of August 3, 1966 for: "Dolls in the form of men, incorporating means of performing movements." In the late 1960s, anti-Vietnam War feeling severely affected the US sales of GI Joe but his British cousin went from strength to strength. By the 1970s it was estimated that there was more than one Action Man for every boy in Britain. By the time production ceased in 1984, over 350 outfits had been created and Action Man had been everything from a deep-sea diver to an astronaut to a footballer. The doll was relaunched in 1993 and again in a nonmilitary role in 2001, his face remodeled with the features of some of Hollywood's best-known actors and his dress focusing on street gear, extreme sports, or other adventures far removed from war.

Adams *(transportation)*

Alvin Adams (1804–1887), born in Andover, Vermont, and orphaned as a child, began working at odd jobs at age 16. In 1840 he founded Adams & Company in New York City as an express package business between Boston and New York. The company prospered, buying routes in New England and as far south as St. Louis. In 1849 Adams opened 35 offices in California. In 1854 the Adams Express Company was incorporated and expanded to Europe.

Addis *(brushes and housewares)*

The British firm was founded in 1780 when William Addis (1734–1808) set up business as a "stationer and rag-merchant" in premises at 64 Whitechapel High Street, London. The same year that he started in business he devised a new style of toothbrush for his personal use, and realizing its commercial potential began manufacturing the brush and selling it in his own shop. At that time many stationers also retailed patent medicines, so there was no incongruity in such an outlet for Addis's new implement, which enabled the teeth to be cleaned both horizontally and vertically. His invention caught on, and from that moment he devoted himself to manufacturing toothbrushes, which

were initially crafted from bone and horsehair. *See also* **Wisdom**.

Adecco *(recruitment)*

The world's largest recruitment company was formed in 1996 through the merger of the Swiss group Adia and Ecco, founded in Lyon in 1964 by the French entrepreneur Philippe Foriel-Destezet (b.1936). The present name blends the two former names.

Adelphi *(publishers)*

The Italian publishing house was founded in Milan in 1962 on the basis of a plan prepared by the literary scholar and editorial consultant Roberto "Bobi" Bazlen (1902–1965), who did much to influence Italian culture in the 1950s and 1960s.

Adidas *(sportswear)*

The firm was founded in 1948 in the small Bavarian mill town of Herzogenaurach, near Nürnberg, when Adolf Dassler (1900–1978) left the family sports business to set up on his own after a violent quarrel with his brother Rudolf (the founder of **Puma**). He formed the name of his new business from his own pet name, Adi, and the first three letters of his surname, making it additionally individual by spelling it "adidas," with a lowercase "a." The first samples of Adidas footwear appeared at the Olympic Games in Helsinki in 1952, and the sales drive led at the 1956 Olympics in Melbourne, Australia, by Adi Dassler's son Horst Dassler (1936–1987) helped to establish the reputation of the company among leading athletes. Horst Dassler became chairman of the company in 1985.

Adler *(typewriters and automobiles)*

The German company Adlerwerke ("Eagle Works") was originally known by the name of its founder, Heinrich Kleyer (1854–1932), who had been employed by a machinery-importing business in Hamburg. In 1879 he resigned his position and went to the USA, where he found work in various factories. In 1880 he returned to Germany and began to make bicycles in Frankfurt am Main. He soon became interested in typewriter production and in 1896 acquired the patent of Wellington Parker Kidder's "Empire" machine. By this time he had turned his business into a limited company and his factory had become known as the Adlerwerke. Kleyer produced his first automobile in 1900, and success was such that by 1914 one car in every five in Germany was an Adler. Production stopped with the advent of World War II in 1939, although the company continued to make motorcycles until 1957.

Adnams *(beer)*

The long-established Sole Bay brewery in Southwold, Suffolk, England, was bought in 1872 by George and Ernest Adnams, two brothers from Berkshire. George did not stay long, but Ernest Adnams formed a partnership with his brewer, Thomas Sargeant, and together with him formed Adnams & Co. Ltd. in 1890. In 1901 a stake in the business was acquired by Pierse Loftus, a brewer of Irish origin, and at the close of the 20th century members of the third and fourth generations of the Loftus and Adnams families were still running the brewery and managing its East Anglian pubs.

Adolph's *("Meat Tenderizer")*

In the 1940s Adolph Rempp (b.1911) owned popular steakhouses in Los Angeles and Santa Barbara, where juicy steak dinners could be bought at hamburger prices. The secret behind the dish was his own papaya extract tenderizer, which transformed inexpensive, tough cuts into soft slabs that could almost pass as filet mignon. One day in 1947, two struggling World War II veterans, Larry Deutsch and Lloyd Rigler, visited Rempp's Los Angeles eatery. They were so impressed with their steaks that they bought the rights to sell Rempp's tenderizer to the retail grocery market. Billed as "Adolph's Meat Tenderizer," the product was introduced at the 1949 Los Angeles Home Show and went on to make Deutsch and Rigler's fortune. Adolph Rempp himself, however, remained in the restaurant business.

Adriamycin *(antibiotic)*

The antibiotic, used in the treatment of cancer, was isolated in 1967 in the Farmitalia Research Laboratories (from 1978 **Farmitalia-Carlo Erba**, and from 1993 part of the Swedish group Procordia-Kabi Pharmacia). Hence its name, from the Adriatic Sea and the "-mycin" element denoting a compound derived from fungi (Greek *mukēs*, "fungus"). The name was entered in the *Trade Marks Journal* of September 22, 1976 and the US Patent Office *Official Gazette* of February 14, 1984.

AEG *(electronics and electrical equipment)*

The German company was founded in Berlin in 1883 when the industrialist Emil Rathenau (1828–1915), with financial support from **Siemens** and Halske, another leading German electrical company, founded the Deutsche Edison Gesellschaft für Angewandte Elektricität ("German Edison Company for Applied Electricity"). (*See* **Ediswan**.) In 1887 the company was renamed the Allgemeine Elektricitäts-Gesellschaft ("General Electricity Company"), giving the present abbreviated name. In 1966 Telefunken AG was integrated into AEG, changing the company name the following year to AEG-Telefunken, but in 1983 most of the company's Telefunken operations were sold off, in 1984 it was reorganized, and in 1985 it again became AEG. It then passed to **Daimler**.

Aeolian *(mechanical pianos)*

The British manufacturers of the **Pianola** and the **Vocalion** took their name from their home at the Aeolian Hall, New Bond Street, London, a concert hall that was formerly the Grosvenor Art Gallery. The firm was originally the Orchestrelle Co. and under this name opened the Aeolian Hall with a recital in 1904. (The orchestrelle was a type of mechanical organ.) The Aeolian Hall itself ultimately took its name from Aeolus, the Greek god of the winds. (Hence the Aeolian harp, Aeolian mode in music, etc.) It was taken over by the BBC as a broadcasting studio in 1941 and closed in 1975.

Aer Lingus *(airline)*

The national airline of Ireland consists of two companies: Aer Lingus Teoranta ("Air Fleet Limited"), incorporated in 1936 and operating air services between Ireland and Britain and continental Europe, and Aerlinte Eireann Teoranta ("Airlines of Ireland Limited"), incorporated in 1947 and operating services between Ireland and the USA and Canada. *Cp.* **Aeroflot**.

Aeritalia *(aircraft)*

The government-financed Italian aerospace company was founded in 1969 with the backing of **Finmeccanica**, Aerfer, and **Fiat**, and in 1976 passed entirely to the first of these. After playing its part in the Ariane project and the production of the Tornado fighter-bomber, it merged with Selenia in 1990 to form the new company Alenia.

Aero *(chocolate)*

The chocolate bars are "aerated" with hollow "bubbles," and this presumably gave the name, which in its day would also have evoked the still glamorous aeroplane (airplane). The candy was first marketed in 1935 by **Rowntree**, who entered the name in the *Trade Marks Journal* of August 28, 1935.

Aerobie *(toy rings)*

The name of the thin plastic rings, spun through the air as a catching game, is based on "aero-" and the latter half of **Frisbee**. It was entered in the US Patent Office *Official Gazette* of May 7, 1985, with a note of first use on March 8, 1984, and in the *Trade Marks Journal* of March 26, 1986.

Aeroflot *(airline)*

The national airline of Russia was founded in 1928 as the Soviet state airline Dobroflot, this name being short for Dobrovol'ny Flot ("Volunteer Fleet"), and itself growing out of two earlier lines: Dobrolyot ("Volunteer Air Fleet"), founded in 1923, and Ukvozdukhput', or Ukrainian Airways, founded in 1925, the latter's name combining *Uk*raina ("Ukraine"), *vozdukh* ("air"), and *put'* ("way"). Dobroflot was reorganized as Aeroflot ("Air Fleet") in 1932.

Aertex *(cotton cellular fabric)*

The British company of this name was formed in 1888 by Lewis Haslam (1856–1922), a former Member of Parliament for Newport, Monmouthshire, and two doctors, Benjamin Ward Richardson and Richard Greene. Within three years the firm was manufacturing women's underwear in the new, light fabric, and it has remained popular for undergarments and sportswear. The name alludes to the "airy texture" of the fabric and was entered by The Cellular Clothing Company, London, in the *Trade Marks Journal* of September 23, 1896.

Aetna *(insurance)*

Aetna Life & Casualty trace their origins to 1850, when Eliphalet A. Bulkeley (d.1872), a Hartford, Connecticut, businessman, formed The Annuity Fund as a subsidiary to the Aetna Fire Insurance Company, itself founded in New England in 1819. The Annuity Fund sold life insurance to New Englanders until 1853, when Bulkeley and some other investors branched off and made the Fund into a separate company, naming it after their parent. "Aetna" is a classical spelling of the name of Etna, Europe's highest active volcano, in northeastern Sicily, whose own name is popularly derived from Greek *aithō*, "I burn." Hence the connection with fire insurance.

After Eight *(chocolates)*

The mint chocolates by **Rowntree Macintosh** were introduced in 1963, an age "when children weren't supposed to be awake after early evening, the name 'After Eight' being adopted to suggest something rather sophisticated and adult for the grown-up members of the household" (Mark Robinson, *Channel 4/The Sunday Times 100 Greatest TV Ads*, 2000).

Aga *(cooking stoves)*

The solid-fuel cooker was invented in 1924 by the blind Swedish physicist Nils Gustaf Dalén (1869–1937), president of the company that originally manufactured it and that gave it its acronymic name, from Svenskaa Aktiebolaget *Ga*sackumulator ("Swedish Gas Accumulator Company"). His aim was to design a stove that would be efficient, clean, and attractive-looking, simple to manage by the visually impaired, and economical in fuel consumption. The Aga was introduced to Britain in 1929 through a branch of the newly formed Allied Ironfounders Ltd. and its name was entered by Bell's Heat Appliances Ltd., London, in the *Trade Marks Journal* of July 15, 1931. It was first made in Slough, Buckinghamshire, but in 1947 a manufacturing unit was opened at the Coalbrookdale foundry near Telford, Shropshire. The Swedes ceased producing Agas in the 1950s when electric cookers caught on, so the Coalbrookdale foundry was the only place in the world where they were still made. *See also* (1) **Glynwed**; (2) **Rayburn**.

Agence France-Presse *(news agency)*

The roots of the French news agency go back to the translation bureau set up in 1832 by Charles Louis Havas (1783–1858) to translate news reports and distribute them to Paris and provincial newspapers. It took the name Agence Havas in 1935, and its information branch, "nationalized" by Pierre Laval in 1940, became Agence France-Presse ("France Press Agency") in 1944. Havas still exists in its own right as a company involved in advertising, media, publishing, and tourism. *See also* **Vivendi**.

Agene *(baking agent)*

The commercial name for nitrogen trichloride derived from its former wide use in bread-making to improve, stabilize, and artificially *age* the flour. It first found general application in the 1930s but was discontinued in the mid-1950s.

Agfa-Gevaert *(photographic goods)*

The name is that of the 1964 merger of two companies: the German Agfa and the Belgian Gevaert. Agfa, its name an abbreviation of Aktiengesellschaft für Anilinfabrikation ("Corporation for Aniline Manufacture"), was founded as a dye company in 1867 at Rummelsburger See near Berlin, and began producing film in 1908. The history of Gevaert dates from 1890, when Lieven Gevaert (1868–1935) began manufacturing photographic paper in Antwerp. In 1920 the company he founded became Gevaert Photo-Producten.

Agilent *(electronics)*

Although the US company Agilent Technologies split off from **Hewlett-Packard** only in 1999, it is a giant in its own right, conducting business worldwide in semiconductors, chemical analysis, test and measurement devices, and healthcare products. Its name is based on "agile" (in the dictionary sense "nimble and coordinated; mentally quick and resourceful"), alluding to its focus on providing products and services with agility, speed, and commitment to its customers.

Agusta *(aircraft)*

The Italian firm was founded in 1923 by the titled Italian Agusta family, and only five years later passed to the founder's son, Count Domenico Agusta, who built it into a successful enterprise, diversifying into helicopters. His real ambition, however, was to build racing motorcycles, and accordingly in 1946 he set up MV Agusta (from Italian *motoveicolo*, "'motor vehicle'"). His machines dominated the tracks in the 1950s and 1960s, but financial difficulties led to the closure of the firm in 1980. The name was subsequently bought by **Cagiva** in 1991.

Air Canada *(airline)*

The national airline of Canada was established by act of the Canadian Parliament in the Trans-Canada Air Lines Act of April 10, 1937 and was originally known as Trans-Canada Air Lines. It assumed its present name in 1965.

Air France *(airline)*

The national airline of France was formed in 1933 on the merger of four independent airlines: Société Centrale pour l'Exploitation de Lignes Aériennes (founded 1919), Compagnie Internationale de Navigation (1920), Air Union (1923), and Air Orient (1929). A few months later, on August 30, the combine merged with Compagnie Générale Aéropostale (founded in 1919) to form Air France.

Air-India *(airline)*

The national airline of India was founded in 1932 as Tata Airlines, taking its name from Jehangir Ratanji Dadabhoy Tata (1904–1993), a member of the Tata family of Indian industrialists. In 1946, after World War II, Tata Airlines was converted into a public company and took its present name.

Airbus Industrie *(aircraft manufacturers)*

The European consortium was formed in 1970 with the aim of competing with American aircraft manufacturers. It is now is a four-nation corporation, comprising the UK, France, Germany, and Spain, but the original partners were France and West Germany only. Hence the name, with "airbus" referring to the planned series of wide-bodied airliners to be built (the first entered commercial service in 1974), and "Industrie" the French and German word for "industry."

Airey *(houses)*

The type of British house, constructed from precast concrete sections, takes its name from Sir Edwin Airey (1878–1955), born in Leeds, Yorkshire, who at the age of 14 became an apprentice joiner in the builders firm of Wood & Airey, in which his father, William Airey, was a partner. In 1895, William Airey set up on his own and in 1902 took his son into partnership. After William Airey's death in 1905, Edwin assumed control of the business and gradually won a number of construction contracts. By the early 1930s, William Airey & Son ranked among the top 1 percent of builders in the UK and employed over 800 men, almost a tenth of the workforce in the local building industry. It was in 1946, after World War II, that the famous two-story "Airey house" was designed for the Ministry of Health to supplement traditional construction in rural regions. It was based on precast piers and panels that could be erected quickly without bricklayers or plasterers, and the company built some 20,000 houses on this system between 1945 and 1950 under government guarantee.

Airfix *(model construction kits)*

In 1939, Hungarian-born Nicholas Kove, a World War I veteran originally named Kovacs, formed a company in the UK to exploit the growing thermoplastics industry and provide the public with cheap toys and synthetic household products. He began by making rubber toys filled with air. He liked words ending in "-ix," but also believed that any reputable company should have a name that stood out in a listing. He hit on "Airfix," which covered both these points while also denoting the type of product he was making. That same year his firm launched its first kit, a scale model of the new Ferguson tractor, produced as promotional material for the vehicle's manufacturers, the future **Massey-Ferguson**. Airfix then had mixed fortunes until after World War II, when John Gray, a former armorer in the British Army, and German-born Ralph Ehrmann, a Royal Air Force bomb aimer, became partners and saw the potential of injection-molded construction kits. They launched their first such kit, of Francis Drake's ship, the *Golden Hind*, in 1952. They then turned their attention to aircraft, and produced the first Airfix *Spitfire* in 1953. More kits were gradually added, from veteran cars to historical subjects, and were bought as much by adult enthusiasts as by model-making schoolboys. In 1981 the company went into receivership, however, hard hit by the growing recession. It was bailed out for a time by **Palitoy**, then in 1986 was taken over by **Humbrol**. The name was entered in the *Trade Marks Journal* of October 2, 1946.

AJS *(motorcycles)*

The initials are those of Albert John Stevens, son of the British owner of an engineering works in Wolverhampton, who with his brothers Harry, George, Jack, and Joe began experimenting with gas engines as early as 1897. At first the five sold engines to early makers of motorcycles, automobiles, and cyclecars. In 1909 they produced their first own motorcycle, setting up the AJS company at the same time. Financial pressures following World War I resulted in the takeover of the firm by their arch rivals, Matchless, who called the combined enterprise Associated Motor Cycles (AMC). Many more famous names were acquired, but the entire group ended its days in 1966, when it passed to Manganese Bronze Holdings. The AJS name continued until 1974, however, under Norton-Villiers (*see* **Norton**).

AJW *(motorcycles)*

The British company was founded in Exeter, Devon, in 1926 by Arthur John Wheaton, whose initials gave the firm's name. He sold the business off in 1945 to Jack Ball, who transferred it to Wimborne, Dorset, where it remained until its demise in 1957.

Aladdin *(oil heaters and lamps)*

Aladdin kerosene lamps and heaters were popular in Britain from the 1920s. The name, obviously referring to the *Arabian Nights* hero and his magic lamp, was entered by Jack Imber of Holborn, London, in the *Trade Marks Journal* of May 12, 1920 for: "Kerosene Lamps and Parts thereof."

Alar *(growth retardant)*

The proprietary name for daminozide, a growth-regulating chemical used as a spray on fruit trees, is apparently of arbitrary origin. It dates from the mid-1960s.

Albertsons *(supermarkets)*

The American company, whose supermarkets are found mainly in the Western and Southern states, takes its name from A. Joseph "Joe" Albertson (1906–1993), a former district manager of **Safeway**, who opened his first store in Boise, Idaho, in 1939.

Albucid *(eye ointment)*

The proprietary name for the sodium salt of suphacetamide, used to treat eye disorders, appears to have no actual meaning, despite a suggested blend of Latin *albus*, "white," and *lucidus*, "light," "bright," "clear." It was entered in the *Trade Marks Journal* of November 23, 1938.

Alcan *(aluminum)*

The Canadian multinational company traces its origins to 1902, when the Northern Aluminum Company was incorporated as a Canadian subsidiary of the **Aluminum Company of America** (Alcoa). In 1925 the name was changed to Aluminium Company of Canada, Ltd., using the British spelling of "aluminum" and giving the Alcan trademark. In 1928 it was renamed Aluminum, reincorporated, and separated from Alcoa, which then transferred to it almost all of its own assets held outside the USA.

Alclad *(aluminum material)*

The composite material, consisting of sheets of aluminum alloy coated with pure aluminum to increase corrosion resistance, derives its name from the first syllable of "aluminum" and "clad." It was entered in the US Patent Office *Official Gazette* of July 19, 1927 for: "Duplex aluminum and aluminum-base alloys."

Alcoa *see* **Aluminum Company of America**

Aldis *(lamp)*

The hand-held lamp for signaling in Morse code takes its name from its British inventor, Arthur Cyril Webb Aldis (1878–1953). The lamp was first in use in World War I.

Alenia *see* **Aeritalia**

Alessi *(kitchenware)*

The Italian family business, famous for its unusually designed kettles and other kitchenware, was founded in 1921 in Omegna, a lakeside suburb in the foothills of the Italian Alps, by Giovanni Alessi, a latheturner from the nearby Valle Strona. He moved into design proper in the 1930s with his eldest son, Carlo, who had trained as an industrial engineer, and in the 1950s became chief executive. By the end of the century, under Alberto Alessi, the firm was employing 500 people worldwide, exporting to 60 countries, and moving into new sectors such as bathroomware, cameras, watches, and textiles.

Alexbow *(ice plow)*

The device for breaking and parting Arctic sea ice, shaped like the bow of a ship, takes its name from Scott Alexander, the Canadian who invented it in the 1960s.

Alexon *(fashionwear)*

The British firm was founded by Alexander Steinberg, born near Warsaw in 1886, who came to England in 1900 and four years later set up in London as a master tailor, his three sons joining him in the 1920s. The resulting limited company of Steinberg & Sons was formed in 1929, and began marketing its products under the name by which it is known today, with Alexon standing for *Alex*ander Steinberg & *Son*s. The name was entered in the *Trade Marks Journal* of January 6, 1943.

Alfa-Laval *(milking machines)*

The firm derives its name from that of the Swedish engineer Gustaf de Laval (1845–1913), inventor in 1877 of a cream separator. De Laval patented his machine in 1878 and started a firm to manufacture it. In 1883 the business was incorporated as AB Separator. Six years later, De Laval acquired the patent rights to the "Alfa" disk, a conical insert, which improved the efficiency of the separator, its own name meaning simply "alpha." The parent company, based in Tumba, Sweden, adopted the name Alfa-Laval in 1963, and subsequently merged with **Tetra Pak** to become Tetra-Laval.

Alfa Romeo *(automobiles)*

The first half of the Italian name represents the initials of Società Anonima Lombarda Fabbrica Automobili ("Lombardy Motor Works Limited"), the company that manufactured its first autos in 1910 in Milan, having assembled lightweight **Darracq** cars for four years previously. In 1915 Nicola Romeo (1876–1938) became manager and added his surname to the existing name. In 1954 the essentially romantic association of his name was exploited in the launch of the elegant new Giulietta model. In 1973 Alfa Romeo became part of **Fiat**.

Alfred A. Knopf *see* **Knopf**

Alitalia *(airline)*

The Italian international airline was founded in 1946 as Aerolinee Italiane Internazionali ("International Italian Airlines"). In 1957 it merged with Italy's other airline, LAI, or Linee Aeree Italiane ("Italian Airlines"), and adopted its present name, Al- standing for *aerolinee* ("airlines").

Alka-Seltzer *(analgesic)*

The preparation is alkaline, or antacid, and when in solution effervesces like Seltzer water, or medicinal mineral water from Niederselters in Germany. The name derives from these two key attributes. The name was entered in the *Trade Marks Journal* of September 28, 1932 for: "Medicated preparations in tablet form for use in making seltzer water for the purpose of treating acidity.".

All-Bran *(cereal)*

The high-fiber cereal was launched by **Kellogg's** in 1919, its name implying that it was pure and simply "all bran" and nothing else. The fiber comes from wheat bran, which is removed from the outer layers of wheat grains as they are milled to produce flour.

All Nippon *(airline)*

The largest domestic airline in Japan was founded in 1952 and at first was restricted to carrying passengers and freight on domestic routes, unlike **Japan Air Lines**, which monopolized the country's overseas service. In the late 1980s, however, All Nippon began regular service on major international routes. It takes its name from *Nihon*, "sun origin," the Japanese name of Japan. Hence "land of the rising sun" as a descriptive name of Japan and the symbol of the sun as a red disk on the national flag.

Allard *(automobiles)*

Sydney Allard (1910–1966), born in London, England, quit school to become director of the family-owned Adlard [*sic*] Motors Ltd in Putney, south London. (The name came from Roberts Adlard, a building firm that Allard's father had acquired.) Allard was fascinated by racing bikes and cars and was a keen trials participant in the 1930s. He built a number of **Ford**-engined cars before World War II and after it, in 1945, formed the Allard Motor Co. to build saloons, tourers, and sports cars, many of which became popular on the American market. The company faltered after his death but in the 1980s was reborn in Mississauga, Ontario, Canada, selling a **Chrysler**-engined model in limited numbers.

Allders *(department stores)*

The British company had its origins in the two adjacent shops opened in 1862 at 102 and 103 North End, Croydon, Surrey, by Joshua Allder (1839–1904), who described himself as a "linen draper and silk mercer," and who would become one of Croydon's leading businessmen and a Salvation Army sponsor. The head office of the company is today on the original site in North End, and the Croydon store is now the third largest department store in the UK after **Harrods** and **Selfridges**.

Allen *(screw)*

The name is that of various tools, notably a screw with a hexagonal recess in the head and a key (an L-shaped hexagonal rod) to turn it, produced by the Allen Manufacturing Co. of Hartford, Connecticut. The name was entered in the *Trade Marks Journal* of May 3, 1972 and the US Patent Office *Official Gazette* of May 9, 1978. The tools themselves date from at least the 1920s.

Allen, W.H. *see* **W.H. Allen**

Allen & Hanbury *(medicines)*

The British business had its ultimate origin in that of the pharmacy set up in London in 1715 by Silvanus Bevan, who later took his brother Timothy into partnership. In 1775 Timothy retired in favor of his third son Joseph, who in 1792 engaged William Allen (1770–1843) as his confidential clerk. In 1808 Daniel Bell Hanbury entered the firm, and after a number of changes of name the business became stabilized as that of Allen and Hanbury in 1818. Both Daniel Hanbury and his wife Rachel were noted Quakers, while William Allen was the first president of the Royal Pharmaceutical Society, founded in 1841. In 1958 the firm was acquired by **Glaxo**.

Allen & Unwin *(publishers)*

The British publishing house owes its origin to George Allen (1832–1907), who after a brief period as a joiner, apprenticed to his uncle in Clerkenwell, London, studied drawing under Ruskin and gradually devoted more and more time to working for him, first as general assistant, then as engraver, and finally as publisher. Allen set up in this last capacity in 1871 at Keston, near Bromley, Kent, subsequently moving to London in 1890. His firm got into difficulties after his death, however, and soon became bankrupt. It was then bought up, just before World War I, by Stanley Unwin (1884–

1968), a London printer's son who had learned the art of publishing from 1904 under T. Fisher Unwin, his father's younger stepbrother, and who now wanted to set up his own publishing firm. In 1986 Allen & Unwin merged with another publisher, Bell & Hyman, to form Unwin Hyman, so that Allen's representation disappeared (as did Bell's), although Allen & Unwin still flourishes in Australia.

Allen Lane (publishers)

The founder of the British firm was born Allen Williams (1902–1970), the son of a Bristol architect. In 1919 he changed his name to Lane (his mother's maiden name), by which time he was employed at the **Bodley Head** publishing house under the tutelage of its founder, John Lane, a distant cousin. Allen Lane rose to a prominent position within the company, and on John Lane's death in 1925 became its managing director. Ten years later, together with his two younger brothers, Lane founded **Penguin** Books, in turn becoming its managing director. Towards the end of his life he set up a separate imprint within Penguin Books under the name Allen Lane to publish King Penguins, and subsequently hardbacks, as distinct from the standard Penguin paperbacks.

Alliance & Leicester (building society)

The British building society (savings and loan association) dates from 1852, when the Leicester Permanent Benefit Society was founded in Leicester. In 1929 it started an expansion program with the Brighton & Sussex Equitable Building Society, which gradually merged with other societies to became the Alliance Building Society in 1945. In 1975 Leicester Permanent combined with the Leicester Temperance & General Building Society as the biggest ever building society merger to date, becoming the Leicester Building Society. In 1985 the two societies, Leicester and Alliance, merged as the Alliance & Leicester. In 1990 the **Girobank** became part of the Alliance & Leicester, which itself became a public limited company and major retail bank in 1997.

Allied Breweries see **Lyons**

Allied Domecq see **Domecq**

Allied-Lyons see **Lyons**

Allied Signal (aerospace systems and components)

The American corporation's name arose in 1985 from the merger between Allied Chemical, itself the result of earlier mergers (hence "Allied"), and Signal Companies, an aerospace and engineering firm.

Allinson (bread)

The name behind the British bread is that of Thomas Richard Allinson (1858–1918), a Cumberland chemist who studied medicine at Edinburgh University and qualified as a doctor in 1881. He established his own practice in London in 1888, having by this time become specially interested in the role of diet and exercise in promoting good health. In 1892, becoming increasingly dissatisfied with the quality of bread as it was usually baked, he bought his own flour mill in Bethnal Green, London, and opened a bakery, calling it the Natural Food Company. The essential ingredient of his bread was pure wholemeal flour, as it is today for the bread that bears his name. Although a North countryman, it seems unlikely that he spoke with a broad accent, so that he would hardly have uttered the slogan "Bread wi' nowt taken out" that appears on the loaf wrapper.

Allonal (sedative)

The sedative and hypnotic drug, a derivative of barbituric acid chemically known as 5-allyl-5-isopropylbarbituric acid, forms its name by combining the first part of "allyl" with the suffixes "-o" and "-al" and inserting "n." It was entered in the *Trade Marks Journal* of October 11, 1922.

Allsopp's (beer)

The noted English brewery in Burton-on-Trent, Staffordshire, famous for its India Pale Ale, was founded in 1708 by Benjamin Wilson, father-in-law of Samuel Allsopp (d.1838), who gave his name to the business that became known as Samuel Allsopp & Sons Ltd.

Aloha Airlines (airline)

The Hawaiian airline was founded in 1946 as the charter operator Trans-Pacific Airlines. It became a certificated scheduled airline in 1949 and took present name in 1958. As anyone who has been to Hawaii knows, "Aloha" is the Hawaiian word used when greeting or parting from someone. As such, it is eminently suitable for an airline that both brings people to Hawaii and takes them from it.

Alpo *(dog food)*

The story goes that the pet food was originally called "All-Pro," presumably meaning "all professional" (or possibly "all protein"), but that when the name ran into trademark complications the "l" and the "r" were dropped to give "Alpo."

AltaVista *(Internet search engine)*

In the spring of 1995, three employees of Digital Equipment Corporation, based in Palo Alto, California, began talking over lunch about DEC's new Alpha 8400 computer, nicknamed "TurboLaser," which promised to run database software 100 times faster than any other. They realized that such a computer could be used to host a searchable full-text database of the World Wide Web, and resolved to develop it to this end. Back in their lab, a researcher had created a precise e-mail index to track bulletin board conversations posted over the previous ten years, mainly to settle heated technical debates, and this tool became the framework of their venture. The name for their enterprise was prompted by a whiteboard that had not been fully wiped and that showed the word "Alto" (of "Palo Alto") beside the word "vista." Someone said, "How about AltoVista!" This was good, but better still was "AltaVista," interpreted as "the view from above." In 1999, AltaVista was acquired by **Compaq**.

Altman, B. *see* **B. Altman**

Altoids *(peppermint lozenges)*

The British-made lozenges were first sold in the second half of the 19th century, when "-oid" was a fashionable suffix for patent medicines. When they were originally introduced as a "curiously strong" peppermint, they were intended for the druggist trade. They were accordingly promoted as the best or highest "-oid" on the market. Hence the name, from Latin *altus*, "high," entered in the *Trade Marks Journal* of October 29, 1947.

Aluminum Company of America *(aluminum)*

The American corporation, known acronymically as Alcoa, was founded in 1888 as the Pittsburgh Reduction Company by a group of young men who included the industrialist Charles Martin Hall (1863–1914), the first American to develop a cheap method of smelting aluminum. It took its present name on reincorporation in 1907. *See also* **Alcan**.

Alvis *(automobiles)*

The Alvis Car Co. was founded in 1919 in Coventry, England, by T.G. John, formerly of Armstrong-Whitworth (*see* **Armstrong-Siddeley**) and G.P.H. de Freville, importer of the French DFP cars (*see* **Bentley**). The name is generally said to have no meaning but to have been adopted because it sounded good in any language. Inevitably, there are countertheories. One claims that it combines the first two letters of "aluminum" with Latin *vis*, "force." Another suggests it is based on the name of a woman, Avis, with "L" inserted to give the name symmetry when displayed on the car. There may be a grain of truth in the former, since the name is first found on a piston manufactured by Aluminum Alloy Pistons Ltd., founded in London in 1914. Alvis were taken over by **Rover** in 1965.

Amaretto di Saronno *(liqueur)*

The Italian almond and apricot liqueur is said to have been created by the model for the Madonna depicted in Bernardino Luini's *Adoration of the Magi* fresco (1525) in the Santa Maria delle Grazie sanctuary in Saronno, Italy. "Amaretto" is a generic term meaning "slightly bitter," but the rest of the name is a registered trademark of the manufacturers, ILLVA. The company emphasizes the name by referring to the liqueur as "Di Saronno Amaretto" on the bottle labels, not "Amaretto di Saronno."

Amazon *(Internet bookselling service)*

The Internet service, claiming to be the "biggest bookstore in the world," was launched in a garage in Seattle on July 16, 1995 by Jeffrey P. Bezos (b.1964), a New York banker. The story behind the name was told in *Time* (December 27, 1999), who voted him Person of the Year:

> Bezos called a lawyer who specialized in start-ups. What do you plan to call your company, the lawyer asked. Bezos liked the sound of Abracadabra, but the word was a little long. "So I said, 'Cadabra,'" he recalls. "Cadaver?" repeated the lawyer. A few weeks later, Bezos changed the name

to Amazon Inc., after the seemingly endless South American river.

AMAX *(coal, metal, and mineral mining)*

The US corporation has roots going back to 1700, when the Jewish banking house of Liebmann Cohen in the kingdom of Hanover became the fiscal agent of the Hanover court and later financed mining in the Harz Mountains. The business flourished, and in the 19th century set up a branch in Frankfurt, where Philipp Abaham Cohen acted as sales representative for the minerals extracted in Hanover-Braunschweig. Cohen's daughter, Sara Amalie, married Rafael Moses of London, England, who anglicized his name to Ralph Merton, and in due course Merton's son, Henry, established the London metal-trading company of Henry R. Merton & Co. The English and German branches of this company grew and added other associates, and in 1880 the Ladenburgs, a Frankfurt family related by marriage to the Mertons, opened a private banking firm in New York City. In 1884 Berthold Hochschild came from Germany to join the New York company, which was already active in the international trading of metals. In 1887 the London and Frankfurt companies joined with the New York company to establish a new body, the American Metal Company, to be active in the treatment and trading of metals, but not the mining, as that was considered too risky. In World War I the English branch of this threefold combine went out of business, and in 1920 the US government sold the German interest to a group of investors, leaving the American company to stand on its own. Meanwhile the Climax Molybdenum Company was formed in 1918 to develop mining claims in Colorado, taking its name from Climax, Colorado, the site of its main mine. In 1957, American Metal and Climax Molybdenum merged, forming American Metal Climax, and in 1974 finally shortened their name to AMAX.

AmBev *(beer)*

The world's third-largest beermaker after **Anheuser-Busch** and **Heineken**, based in Brazil, was formed in 1999 when the Brazilian brewery Brahma merged with its next-largest competitor, Antarctica. The name is short for Companhia de Bebidas das Américas, "Drinks of the Americas Co."

Ambre Solaire *(suntan lotion)*

The first mass-market suntan lotion was launched by **L'Oréal** in 1936, with a French name meaning "solar amber," suggesting the color of both the sun and of the skin following application of the lotion. The association of *ambre* with a color descriptive is familiar to the French, who use the term *ambre jaune*, "yellow amber," for amber proper (the resin) and *ambre gris*, "gray amber," for ambergris.

Ambrosia *(rice pudding)*

The name, originally that of a US company, was appropriated in 1917 by two men, an American named Hatmaker and an Englishman named Alfred Morris, when they set up a creamery in the village of Lifton near Launceston, Devon, England, on discovering ways of drying milk in order to produce rice puddings commercially. The name represents the ambrosia that was the "food of the gods" in classical mythology, and that was felt to be appropriate for a delectable foodstuff.

Ambu *(resuscitator)*

The Ambu bag, a type of resuscitator, consists of a face mask connected by a valve to a self-inflating bag which, when squeezed, inflates the patient's lungs with air or oxygen. Its name, a shortening of "ambulance," was entered in the *Trade Marks Journal* of April 22, 1959 and the US Patent Office *Official Gazette* of July 12, 1960.

AMC *see* **American Motors**

Amdega *(conservatories)*

The British firm was founded in Darlington, Co. Durham, as W. Richardson & Co. in 1874. In the 1970s the business was acquired by a family company, who gave it a snappier name, representing an acronymic encapsulation of their commercial creed: "*Am*bition, *de*termination, and *ga*in." The name was entered in the *Trade Marks Journal* of November 16, 1988.

Amé *(health drink)*

The nonalcoholic drink, containing fruit juices, spring water, and herbal extracts, has a name (pronounced "Ah-may") representing Japanese *ame*, "rain," or as the British manufacturers, Orchid Drinks, interpret it, "refreshing gentle rain." The name was entered in the *Trade Marks Journal* of April 14, 1993.

Orchid Drinks also produce **Aqua Libra** and **Purdey's**.

America Online *see* **AOL**

American Airlines *(airline)*

The major American airline evolved over the years from the union or merger of some 85 other companies. Two core companies were Robertson Aircraft Corporation, founded in 1921 in Missouri, and Colonial Air Transport, which first flew mail between New York City and Boston in 1926 after developing from a charter service called The Bee Line, formed in 1923. In 1929 these airlines were combined under a holding company, The Aviation Corporation, which was reorganized as an operating company and renamed American Airways in 1930. The company took its present name on reincorporation in 1934.

American Brands *(tobacco and other products)*

The American industrial conglomerate was formed in 1969 as the parent company for the American Tobacco Company and various associated companies engaged in a wide range of goods and services. American Tobacco itself traces its history to the post-Civil War period in North Carolina, when a Confederate veteran, Washington Duke (1820–1905), began trading in tobacco. In 1874 he and his sons, Benjamin N. Duke (1855–1929) and James Buchanan Duke (1856–1925), built a factory and in 1878 formed the company of W. Duke, Sons & Co. They soon entered the "cigarette war" and eventually, in 1890, established the American Tobacco Company, with James as president.

American Chicle *(chewing gum)*

The brand of gum owes its origin to Thomas Adams, Jr. (1846–1926), born in Brooklyn, New York, the son of a photographer. When in 1866 a friend sent young Thomas a sample of chicle, a reddish-brown gum that coagulated from the sap of the sapodilla tree, his father noted its elastic properties and thought of using it to make a substitute for commercial rubber. One day soon after, however, a customer entered his father's shop chewing something vigorously. It turned out that what he had in his mouth was chicle. That night Adams and his two sons rolled their chicle into small balls and persuaded a New York drugstore to offer them to customers with each piece of candy purchased. In 1869 Thomas and his father formed Adams & Sons as a pioneer chewing gum company, patenting the process for making it. Other firms started making chicle-based gum, using the Adams patent, and in 1899 Adams merged with five of them to form the American Chicle Company. *See also* (1) **Chiclets**; (2) **Tutti Frutti**.

American Cyanamid *see* **Cyanamid**

American Express *(insurance and banking)*

The original company of this name was founded on March 18, 1850, as a consolidation of three companies active in the express transport of goods, valuables, and specie between New York City and Buffalo and points in the Midwest: (1) Livingston, Fargo & Company (formerly Western Express), founded in 1845 by Henry Wells and William G. Fargo (*see* **Wells, Fargo**); (2) Wells & Co (formerly Livingston, Wells & Co), cofounded by Wells in 1846; and (3) Butterfield & Wasson, founded by John Butterfield (1801–1869) and James D. Wasson. On Fargo's death in 1881, his younger brother, James Congdell Fargo (1829–1915), became president and introduced the American Express Money Order (1882) and American Express Travelers Cheque (1891). American Express introduced its credit card in 1958, and the name was entered in the US Patent Office *Official Gazette* of August 25, 1959: "for credit card plan for extension of credit to customers who patronize subscribing establishments and making collections from said customers through a central billing system," with a note of first use on September 23, 1958. The company was reincorporated in 1965. *See also* **Diners Club**.

American Home Products *(proprietary and prescription drugs)*

American Home Products (AHP) produce a wide range of products that include "Preparation H" hemorrhoid ointment, **Anadin** analgesic tablets (under the name "Anacin"), and **Chef Boy-ar-dee** canned spaghetti and meatballs, to name just three. The company was incorporated in 1926 as an amalgam of nostrum makers, among them one firm that had marketed "Hill's Cascara Quinine," another that that made a medicine called "Petrolagar," and a third that made "Freezone" (still an AHP brand). The strategy was to buy up small companies and add them to the corporate body. One of their major acquisitions was Wyeth, one of America's oldest drug companies, which went to them in 1932.

American Motors *(automobiles and automotive products)*

The American Motors Corporation (AMC) was created in 1954 and descended from two pioneering auto manufacturers: Nash Motors Company (*see* **Nash-Kelvinator**) and **Hudson** Motor Car Company. In 1970 AMC purchased the **Jeep** Corporation and in 1987 became a subsidiary of **Chrysler**.

American Standard *(plumbing)*

The corporation dates from 1881, when American Radiator was formed in Buffalo, New York, to make equipment for steam and hot water heating of buildings. In 1899, two plumbing supply companies, Ahrens & Ott of Louisville and Standard Manufacturing of Pittsburgh, joined forces to form Standard Sanitary, who in their turn combined with American Radiator in 1929 to form the American Radiator & Standard Sanitary Corporation, a name subsequently shortened to American Standard

American Stores *(food and drug stores)*

One of the largest mergers in US retailing took place in 1979, when American Stores, founded in 1891, combined with the Skaggs Companies of Salt Lake City (*see* **Safeway**). The result was a giant that operates over the country under a variety of names, among them Acme and Super Saver supermarkets in the eastern states, Alpha Beta supermarkets in Arizona and California, Skaggs drug stores in a range of states, and Rea & Derick and Hy-Lo stores in Pennsylvania, New York, and Maryland. Although American Stores was the larger unit, it was Skaggs that did the actual acquisition and that emerged as the larger stockholder. The merger agreement stipulated that the new company would be named American Stores and have its headquarters in Wilmington, Delaware.

American Tobacco Company *see* **American Brands**

Amex *(insurance and banking)*

The name was entered by **American Express** as an official abbreviation in the *Trade Marks Journal* of August 12, 1970 and in the US Patent Office *Official Gazette* of December 25, 1973. American Express had earlier entered the name Amexco on March 21, 1950. The name should not be confused with Amex as an abbreviation for the American Stock Exchange.

Amfac *(sugar and french fries)*

The corporation traces its history to November 28, 1848, when the brig *Wilhelmine* cast off from Bremen, Germany, and set sail for Hawaii. Some eight months later it docked in Honolulu, where its owner, a merchant named Heinrich Hackfeld, set up business as an agent for sugar growers and Hawaiian merchants. He also set up retail stores and sold imported building materials. Following the anti-German hysteria of World War I, the Alien Property Custodian seized the company in 1918 and its assets passed to major competitors such as **Castle & Cooke**, Alexander & Baldwin, and C. Brewer. The new owners changed the name from Hackfeld to American Factors (a factor being an agent) and concentrated their attention on the sugar business. The name was subsequently shortened to Amfac.

Amilcar *(automobiles)*

The French sports car derives its name from its original backers, Émile Akar and Joseph Lamy, who formed the company in 1921 and became its respective managing and sales directors. (The name happens to suggest that of Hamilcar, the 3d-century BC Carthaginian general and father of Hannibal, whose name is alternately spelled Amilcar in French.) Akar and Lamy left the company in the late 1920s, when the firm was taken over by **Hotchkiss**, and the last Amilcars were made in the late 1930s.

Amoco *(petroleum)*

The American company was founded in 1889 by the **Standard Oil** Trust as the Standard Oil Company (Indiana) to direct the refining and marketing of oil in mid-continental states. The trust was dissolved in 1911 and the company became independent. Following various acquisitions, in 1954 it acquired the entire assets of American Oil Company, founded in 1910, and in 1962 created a subsidiary, American International Oil Company, subsequently Amoco International Oil Company. In 1985 Standard Oil Company (Indiana) itself adopted the name Amoco. In 1998 Amoco was taken over by **British Petroleum** to form BP Amoco, whose own acquisition of **Atlantic Richfield** in 2000 made it the world's second largest producer of natural oil and gas.

Ampex *(audio and video tapes)*

The tapes take their name from the Ampex Corporation, the Californian company named from the initials of its founder in 1944, Alexander Mathew Poniatoff (1892–1980), born in the Kazan district of Russia, who immigrated to the USA in 1927 and became a US citizen in 1932. The final "-ex" of the name is stated to stand for "excellence." In 1946 Poniatoff turned to the production of audio tape recorders developed from the German wartime Telefunken Magnetophon machine. The commercial production of video recorders began in 1956 following a broadcasting exhibition in Las Vegas.

Amphicar *(automobiles)*

The vehicle, a cross between a boat and a car, was the invention of the German engineer Hans Trippel, who had built amphibious vehicles for the Wehrmacht in World War II. The prototype, known as the "Alligator," was displayed at the Geneva motor show in 1958 and most of the 3,000 Amphicars that were subsequently sold ended up in American hands. Formal production ceased in 1963, and later cars were assembled from the vast stock of parts at the works. The name is of obvious origin.

Amplex *(deodorants)*

When under development in the laboratory, the complex of chlorophyll compounds forming the basis of the product was designated by the code name "Plex." The story goes that when the finished product was first marketed, the letters "a.m." were added, since the deodorant was designed to be applied first thing in the morning. The name was entered in the *Trade Marks Journal* of June 6, 1945.

Amstel *(beer)*

The different Dutch beers so named are produced by **Heineken**, who took over the Amstel brewery in Amsterdam in 1968 and kept the name, which is that of the river on which Amsterdam stands.

Amstrad *(consumer electronics)*

The name of the British company developed as a short name for A.M.S. Trading, which in turn bears the initials of its founder in 1968, Alan Michael Sugar (b.1947). He hails from Hackney, in London's Cockney East End, and on quitting school at 16 tried a number of jobs before starting up his own enterprise selling car aerials from the back of a van. His business prospered, so that by 1980 he was dealing in audio and television products, always adhering to his policy of "no frills" in order to exploit the consumer market by offering goods at affordable prices. In 1985 he had a major breakthrough when he introduced a word processor for the then absurdly low price of £399. The following year he shook the electronics market again when he produced a home computer for a third of the price of the one marketed by **IBM**, with which it was compatible. "Amstrad" happens to be an anagram of "smart ad." The name was entered in the *Trade Marks Journal* of March 19, 1975 for: "Apparatus and instruments, all for receiving, tuning and amplifying radio signals, and for reproducing and amplifying sound."

Amtrak *(passenger trains)*

The federally supported National Railroad Passenger Corporation was set up by Congress in 1970 and took over control of passenger service from America's private rail companies the following year. Its popular name is an abbreviation of "*Am*erican *Tra*vel and Trac*k*." The name was entered in the US Patent Office *Official Gazette* of March 20, 1973, with a note of first use "on or about Apr. 21, 1971."

Amvescap *(investment management)*

The American company, one of the world's largest investment houses, was founded by Charles W. Brady (b.1935), who early in his career became manager of investment operations at the Citizens and Southern Bank, Atlanta, Georgia. In 1978 he led a management buyout of the bank's investment department, naming the resulting business Invesco ("Investment Company"). The present name was adopted in 1996 following a merger with the AIM Management Group. The names "Invesco" and "AIM" remain as brand names.

Amytal *(sedative)*

The sedative and hypnotic drug is a form of amylobarbital and bases its name on this generic term. The name was entered by its manufacturers, **Eli Lilly**, in the *Trade Marks Journal* of March 26, 1930. The "-t-" is simply for ease of pronunciation.

An Cnoc *(whisky)*

The Gaelic name means "The Hill," referring to the Knockdhu ("Black Hill") Distillery, Knock, Banffshire, Scotland, where it is blended. The distillery was established in 1893 on a favorable site with water available from nearby Knock Hill, barley from the surrounding farmlands, and a rich supply of local peat. The whisky was itself previously known as "Knockdhu."

An Gúm *(publishers)*

The Irish publishing house was established in 1925 as the Irish language publications branch of the Department of Education and Science. Its name means "The Scheme," referring to its aim to supply textbooks and reading matter required by the state policy of reviving the Irish language. It now produces general reading, textbooks, and dictionaries in Irish.

Anacin *see* **Anadin**

Anaconda *(copper and aluminum mining)*

The story of Anaconda goes back to 1856, when Marcus Daly (1841–1900), born near Ballyjamesduff, Ireland, the son of poor peasant farmers, emigrated to New York. He tried his hand at a number of jobs before sailing in 1861 to California, a move that enabled him to gain experience working in various mines in the West. He eventually became acquainted with the mining tycoon George Hearst, father of the newspaper publisher William Randolph Hearst. Daly persuaded Hearst that he should buy the Anaconda vein of silver ore in Montana and set him (Daly) up with one-fourth of the business for extracting the ore. As it turned out, the mine was rich in copper ore rather than silver. In 1883 Daly built a huge new smelter on the site of what is now the town of Anaconda, Montana, to refine the metal, and by 1895 the enterprise had become the world's top producer of copper. In 1899 **Standard Oil** bought Anaconda and formed a new company out of it, but retained the name, which was further kept when **Atlantic Richfield** in turn bought the company in 1977. The original copper mine was so named from a report that General Grant was encircling General Lee "like an anaconda."

Anadin *(analgesic tablets)*

The product originated in the United States, where in 1918 it was invented by a Wisconsin dentist and sold as "Anacin," the name by which it is still marketed in many countries of the world today. A modification of this had to be used in the UK, where it was introduced in 1931, as the name "Anacine" already existed in the Trade Mark Register. "Anacin" itself probably derives from the Greek prefix *an-* meaning "not," as in "analgesic" ("no pain"), plus an apparently arbitrary *-cin*. The name "Anadin" was entered in the *Trade Marks Journal* of April 6, 1932 for: "An analgestic medicine for human use."

Anaglypta *(wallpaper)*

The type of thick embossed wallpaper, designed to be painted over, dates from the 19th century. Its name represents the Latin word (from Greek) meaning "work in low relief" and was entered by Thomas John Palmer in the *Trade Marks Journal* of October 12, 1887 for: "Decorative Material in the Nature of a Covering, sold in the Piece, for Application to Walls, Ceilings, or other Surfaces."

Anchor *(butter)*

The name was first used in New Zealand in 1886 by Henry Reynolds, an emigrant Englishman from Cornwall, who had taken up dairy farming on the Waikato plain, south of Auckland in North Island. The reason for his choice of name for the butter he first churned on November 3 that year is not recorded, but it was doubtless an appropriate one for use by a settler seeking a safe arrival in a new country. As applied to butter, or indeed any foodstuff, it suggests reliability and stability. The first wrapped packs of Anchor butter were introduced in 1924 and the brand was first marketed in the UK in 1929 by Empire Dairies, renamed Anchor Foods in 1978. The name was entered in the *Trade Marks Journal* of August 22, 1923.

Andersen *see* **Arthur Andersen**

Anderson Clayton *(foods)*

The American company, with headquarters in Houston, Texas, takes its name from William L. Clayton (1880–1966) and his brother-in-law, Frank E. Anderson, who in 1904, with Frank's brother Monroe, formed a cotton brokerage, Anderson, Clayton & Company, in Oklahoma City. When World War I threatened, Clayton realized the potential for American cotton and in 1916 moved his warehouses to Houston, a plan that paid off handsomely and that enabled him to sell direct to European textile interests. Rising to be the world's largest supplier of cotton, however, the company subsequently moved out of cotton in the 1960s and began to build up its expertise in consumer foods, especially margarines and salad dressings.

André Deutsch *see* **Deutsch**

Andrews *("liver salts")*

"Andrews Liver Salt" was registered as a trademark in 1909 when the British firm of Scott & Turner, originators of so-called "health salts" (laxatives) adopted the name for the product from the church of St. Andrew near their offices in Newcastle upon Tyne. Mr. Scott and Mr. Turner had first sold their "health salts" in 1893, and their expanding business was partly due to the popularity of their product among sailors visiting the port of Newcastle. St. Andrew's was at one time believed to be the city's oldest church.

Andrex *(toilet paper)*

The British product was originally made in 1945 by a small firm in St. Andrews Road, Walthamstow, London, and sold as "Androll." This name was changed to "Andrex" in 1954. The road itself is named for St. Andrew's church here, so that the name is similar in origin to that of **Andrews**. The name was entered in the *Trade Marks Journal* of October 17, 1934 for paper handkerchiefs, and in the *Journal* of January 1, 1938 for medicated toilet paper and medicated paper handkerchiefs.

Anectine *(relaxant)*

The proprietary name of the drug suxamethonium chloride, a derivative of curare, used to "soften" electroshock treatment in psychotherapy, is apparently arbitrary in origin. It was entered in the *Trade Marks Journal* of August 30, 1950.

Angel Delight *(instant dessert)*

The creamy, strawberry-flavored dessert, made by adding milk to the packeted powdered preparation and stirring the outcome, was launched by **Bird's** in 1967, its name hinting at lightness and sweetness. It was initially aimed at adults, but became a favorite with children, who were specifically targeted ("Instant Dessert for Little Angels!") when it was relaunched by the parent company, **Kraft**, in 2001.

Angelina *(chocolates)*

The famous French chocolate house was founded in Nice in 1870 by Austrian-born Antoine Rumpelmayer, who expanded his business to Paris in 1903. His son René eventually took over, and gave the enterprise his wife's name. The Angelina shop on the Rue de Rivoli became a place of fashionable resort, and after René's death was visited by George V of England, Marcel Proust, and Coco **Chanel**, among other notables.

Anglepoise *(desk lamps)*

The jointed desk lamp or reading lamp was designed in 1932 by George Carwardine, a British motor engineer of Bath, Somerset, who specialized in car suspension systems and shock absorbers. His design used hinges that mimicked the action of a human arm, making the lamp flexible and balanced and able to hold a pose at any angle. He approached the firm of Herbert Terry & Sons of Redditch, Worcestershire, experts in spring manufacture, and production began in 1933. Carwardine had originally wanted to patent his lamp as the "Equipoise," with reference to its balancing springs, but this name was disallowed by the Patent Office as it was a standard English word. Instead, "Anglepoise" was entered by the manufacturers in the *Trade Marks Journal* of June 22, 1949 for: "Electric lamps embodying adjustable brackets or supports." The company subsequently gave away the rights to manufacturing in continental Europe and the United States to Jac Jacobsen, a Norwegian entrepreneur, who in turn launched the lamp in the USA as the "Luxo" (from Latin *lux*, "light") in 1951. After the US patent expired in 1953, Luxo's operation reached a turnover of $1 million in eight years. In 1971 Herbert Terry & Sons was acquired by the Associated Spring Corporation of the USA, but the Terry family bought back the Anglepoise part of the business in 1975. The lamp thus remains British, although the design has been imitated under different names all over the world.

Angostura *(bitters)*

"Angostura Bitters" is the proprietary name of a kind of aromatic bitters or tonic made in the Venezuelan town of Angostura, now Ciudad Bolívar. It was not, however, made from the bark that was exported from Angostura. The bitters were actually produced by J.G.B. Siegert & Sons Ltd., a British firm founded in 1825 by the German physician Johann G.B. Siegert, who in 1820 settled in Venezuela to study the medical benefits of tropical plants. The success of the carminative bitters that he made prompted him to begin manufacture on a commercial scale. The name was entered in the *Trade Marks Journal* of April 13, 1910, with a facsimile of the signature of Johann Siegert.

Angus & Robertson *(publishers)*

The Australian publishing house had its origin in a small bookshop at 110 Market Street, Sydney, which opened for business in 1884 under David Mackenzie Angus (1855–1901), a red-bearded Scot who had arrived in Australia 18 months earlier. Two years later he took into partnership George Robertson (1860–1933), a fellow Scot (albeit black-bearded) who had been a colleague of his when he had worked in the Sydney branch of the Melbourne bookseller George Robertson & Co., with *his* George Robertson (1825–1898), although also a Scot, no relation to his namesake. The publishing side of the business soon developed, and the two men brought out three books in 1888. Robertson subsequently continued and expanded the business alone after Angus's early death. In 1981 Angus & Robertson became part of the News Limited Group

Anheuser-Busch *(beer)*

The American company had its origins in a small brewery opened in St. Louis, Missouri, by George Schneider in 1852. The ailing enterprise was bought in 1860 by the soap manufacturer Eberhard Anheuser, and the following year Anheuser's daughter, Lilly, married Adolphus Busch (1839–1913), a German brewery supplier who had immigrated to the United States in 1857. In 1875 E. Anheuser & Company's name was changed to Anheuser-Busch Brewing Association, and in 1876 the company introduced a new, light-colored beer called **Budweiser**. And thereby hangs a tale.

Ann Summers *(sex shop and lingerie chain)*

The British business takes its name from Annice Goodwin, girlfriend of the firm's founder in the 1960s, Kim Caborn-Waterfield, who adopted her stepfather's surname, Summers. Its first shop opened in London in 1970. The company owes its current status to Jacqueline Gold, a 21-year-old office junior who watched women giggling over lingerie and sex toys at a party in 1981. Why not, she reasoned, get Ann Summers to organize **Tupperware**-style lingerie parties for women too embarrassed to go into stores? The men on the board were not convinced, but Gold persisted and, by her early 30s, her enterprise had made her a millionaire. At the end of the 20th century Ann Summers herself was living as a recluse in Italy. The name was registered in the *Trade Marks Journal* of June 6, 1990 for: "Articles of underclothing; sleeping garments; lingerie; stockings and tights; all included in Class 25."

Anne Klein *(fashionwear)*

Anne Klein (1923–1974) was born Hannah Golofski in Brooklyn, New York, where she showed a natural gift for design as a young girl. By the age of 15 she had already obtained work as a freelancer preparing sketches for a wholesale fashion house, and only a year out of school accepted a post at Varden Petites, where she virtually invented a whole new set of sizes in women's ready-to-wear clothing, a category of sophisticated clothes for young women later known as "Modern Miss." In 1948 she married Ben Klein, a prominent manufacturer of womenswear, and together they founded Junior Sophisticates. By 1960, however, Anne had left this firm and divorced Ben. Two years later she remarried and established her own freelance design studio, incorporated as the Anne Klein Studio in 1965. In 1968 she founded Anne Klein and Company, an independent sportswear business, leading her to be credited with essentially inventing sportswear as an integral part of the fashion scene.

Ansafone *(telephone answering system)*

The system "answers the phone." Hence the

name, entered in the US Patent Office *Official Gazette* of June 11, 1963 by the Ansa Fone [*sic*] Corporation of Inglewood, California, and in the *Trade Marks Journal* of November 11, 1970 by Ansafone Limited of Camberley, Surrey. The generic term "answerphone" evolved from the proprietary name.

Ansaldo *(electrical goods)*

The Italian company was founded at Genoa in 1853 by Giovanni Ansaldo (1815–1859), initially to built railroad locomotives. It then turned to shipbuilding, but this activity ceased in 1966. It now operates in the field of electro-mechanics, transport, and energy.

Ansells *(beer)*

Joseph Ansell began production as a maltster in Birmingham, England, in 1857. Seven years later he was joined by his eldest son William and in 1869 by another son, Edward, with the partnership formed that year under the name of Joseph Ansell and Sons. On his father's death in 1885, William Ansell assumed the position of senior partner and four years later the firm became a limited company. The brewery closed in 1981 but its dark beer lives on, brewed by **Carlsberg-Tetley** at Burton-on-Trent.

Ansett *(airline)*

The Australian company takes its name from Reginald Myles Ansett (1909–1981), born in Inglewood, Victoria, the son of a garage proprietor. He was educated at Inglewood state school and Swinburne Technical College, and in 1931 set up an automobile passenger service in the Western District of the state of Victoria. In 1936 he founded the airline company Ansett Airways Pty., renamed Ansett Transport Industries Ltd. in 1946. In 1993 the company became Ansett Australia, following the Australian government's "One Nation" statement of February 26, 1992, according to which all airlines, rather than just **Qantas**, were allowed to fly internationally, while Qantas was permitted domestic routes. In September 2001 Ansett went into receivership, although a buyer was expected to emerge.

Antabuse *(alcohol abuse deterrent)*

The name is a proprietary term for disulfiram, a synthetic compound used in the treatment of alcoholics. If taken after drinking alcohol, it produces highly unpleasant side effects, such as nausea and headaches. Hence its name, from "anti-" and "abuse," entered by Ayerst, McKenna & Harrison Ltd., New York, in the US Patent Office *Official Gazette* of May 16, 1950.

Antoinette *(aircraft)*

The French aircraft took their name from the Société Antoinette, headed by Jules Gastambide and named for his daughter. In 1902 the electrical engineer Léon Levasseur (1863–1922) was appointed technical director of the firm and originally designed Antoinette aeroengines. In 1908 he produced a tractor monoplane, the Gastambide-Mengin I. It crashlanded, however, but was rebuilt and improved to become the Antoinette II. Levasseur then produced a series of monoplanes of the name, but the series came to an end soon after 1911, the year that Hubert Latham flew an Antoinette across the Golden Gate at San Francisco.

Antron *(nylon fiber)*

The type of strong, light, nylon fiber, used in the manufacture of carpets, upholstery fabrics, and the like, has a name of apparently arbitrary origin, although the final "-on" probably comes from "nylon." It was entered in the *Trade Marks Journal* of June 29, 1960.

Anturane *(anticoagulant)*

The drug, used to treat gout and (experimentally, in the 1960s) to prevent the formation of blood clots, stimulates the excretion of uric acid. Hence probably its name, from "anti-" ("against"), the first element of "uric," and the chemical suffix "-ane."

AOL *(Internet service provider)*

America Online (AOL) was the creation of Stephen M. "Steve" Case (b.1958), born in Honolulu the son of a corporate lawyer. On graduating in 1981 from William College, Williamstown, Massachusetts, with a degree in political science, Case held marketing positions with **Procter & Gamble** and **Pizza Hut** before buying his first computer and discovering the world of online computing. In 1983 he took another marketing position, this time with Control Video Corp., a start-up company that planned to offer video games via telephone lines. The plan failed, but the company regrouped under the name Quantum Computer Services and began providing an online network for users of Commodore 64 computers. Case saw that the service could be made more widely available. Using a graphical interface originally developed by **Apple**, Quantum became America Online in 1991 and gradually outgrew all other online service in number of subscribers. In 2000 AOL acquired **Time Warner** in the largest corporate merger in history

Apollinaris *(table water)*

The sparkling mineral water was discovered in the mid-19th century when the German farmer Georg Kreuzberg was digging an irrigation system in his vineyard at Bad Neuenahr, south of Bonn. The spring from which the water came was named "Apollinaris" after a nearby chapel, itself presumably so called from some pagan connection with Apollo, and the name was then transferred to the water itself, first distributed in England by one of Kreuzberg's cousins. The name is often affectionately abbreviated as "Polly," and is found as such in Dickens. The British-owned Apollinaris Natural Mineral Water Co. was founded in 1872.

Apple *(computers)*

Apple Computer, Inc., had its origins in a garage in Palo Alto, California, where the enterprise was started on April 1, 1976 by the computer hobbyists Steve Jobs (b.1955) and Steve Wozniak (b.1950). Jobs was a Beatles fan, and he admired the famous pop group's Apple Records (itself part of the punningly named Apple Corps.) Hence the "user-friendly" name. There may be rather more to it than this, however, for the company motif of a multicolored apple with a bite taken out of it is a reference to the biblical story of Adam and Eve, in which the apple (though not identified as such) represents the fruit of the Tree of Knowledge. The company launched its popular **Macintosh** model in 1984.

Appleton *(publishers)*

The American publishing house takes its name from Daniel Appleton (1785–1849), born in Haverhill, Massachusetts. He opened a general store in Haverhill in 1813, then moved with his family to Boston in 1817, where he opened a wholesale dry goods store. In 1825 Appleton moved to New York City, where he opened a store in Water Street, at the center of the fash-ionable retail district. Much of his business was devoted to the sale of books, and in 1831 he published his first book, *Crumbs from the Master's Table*, a selection of biblical texts. He now turned to publishing full-time, and in 1838 took his son into partnership, changing the name of the firm to D. Appleton & Co.

Aqua Libra *(health drink)*

The drink is based on a mixture of mineral water and fruit juices with various herbal and other natural flavorings and is promoted by its British manufacturers, Orchid Drinks, as an aid to good digestion and alkaline balance. The name, entered in the *Trade Marks Journal* of February 18, 1987, apparently derives from Latin *aqua*, "water," and *libra*, "balance," perhaps with an implicit quasi-mystic reference to the two astrological signs Aquarius and Libra. Orchid Drinks also produce **Amé** and **Purdey's**.

Aquapulse *(device to measure shock waves)*

The Aquapulse gun is a compressed-air device used in undersea exploration to measure shock waves reflected off the seabed as an indicator of rock structures below the surface. It was first exploited in the 1970s and derives its name from "aqua-" ("water") and the "pulse" of the shock waves.

Aquarobics *(fitness program)*

The program is essentially a form of aerobics carried out in a swimpool, devised in the USA in 1980 by Georgia Kerns and Judy Mills and registered as a trademark. The name itself is a blend of "aquatic" and "aerobics."

Aquascutum *(raincoats)*

The name is a combination of Latin *aqua*, "water," and *scutum*, "shield," and was first used in 1853 for a chemically treated rain-repellent fabric patented in 1851 by the British firm of Bax & Co., London. The firm of Aquascutum Ltd. was subsequently incorporated in 1901, and in World War I introduced the trench coat for British army officers on active service in France. The name was entered in the *Trade Marks Journal* of April 10, 1895 for: "A waterproof raincoat."

ARA *(fast-food services)*

The company was formed in 1959 by the merger of two small vending companies, one in

Chicago and the other in Los Angeles. Their original name was Davidson Automatic Merchandising, after one of their founders, Davre J. Davidson, but they soon changed this to Automatic Retailers of America, subsequently abbreviated to ARA. They entered the food-service business in 1961 when they acquired Slater Systems of Philadelphia.

Araldite *(adhesive)*

The epoxy resin was developed in the 1930s by the British firm of Aero Research Ltd. of Duxford, Cambridgeshire, a company colloquially known as ARL, and this probably gave the first part of the name, with "D" for "Duxford" and the common commercial suffix "-ite." The name was entered in the *Trade Marks Journal* of October 2, 1946, and the product was introduced commercially in 1950 as a credible rival to the various types of superglue.

ARBED *(steel)*

The full name of the Luxembourg company is Aciéries Réunies de Burbach-Eich-Dudelange ("Burbach-Eich-Dudelange United Steelworks"). It was formed in 1911 through the merger of Les Forges d'Eich, Le Gallais, Metz et Cie, established (under a different name) in 1838, La Société Anonyme des Mines du Luxembourg de Sarrebruck, founded in 1856, and La Société Anonyme des Hauts Fourneaux et Forges de Dudelange, established in 1882. All the proper names are placenames.

Archer-Daniels-Midland *(soybean processing)*

Archer-Daniels-Midland (ADM) had its origins in a group of small midwestern companies that processed farm products, the earliest being Daniels Linseed, founded in 1902 to make flax seed into linseed oil. Members of the original Archer and Daniels families came to be represented on the board of directors, and give the first two parts of the name. The last part refers to the location of the company's headquarters, in Decatur, Illinois, a city in the middle of the Midwest farm belt.

Arco *see* **Atlantic Richfield**

Ardath *(cigarettes)*

The American tobacco company, manufacturers of **State Express**, was founded in the late 19th century by Sir Albert Levy (d.1937) as "La Casa de Habana" (Spanish, "The House of Havana"). In 1895 he gave the firm its new name from the 1889 novel *Ardath* by Marie Corelli, who herself took it from the Apocrypha: "So I went my way into the field which is called Ardath ... and there I sat among the flowers, and did eat of the herbs of the field, and the meat of the same satisfied me" (2 Esdras 9:26). It was an apt name for its day if one considers the tobacco plant as a "herb of the field" furnishing a "meat that satisfies."

Arden, Elizabeth *see* **Elizabeth Arden**

Ardente *(hearing aids)*

The British company of this name arose from the business set up in 1919 by a family named Dent, who in their Wigmore Street, London, premises, "R.H. Dent for Deaf Ears," sold hearing aids imported from continental Europe. Their firm later went on to manufacture its own hearing aids, but continued trading under the original name until 1937, when the name was changed to "Ardente" (for "R. Dent"). The suggestion of "ardent" is not inappropriate for a keen commercial business.

Argo *(corn starch)*

The starch, launched in 1892, has a name of uncertain origin. A connection with the *Argo*, the ship of classical mythology on which Jason sailed in search of the Golden Fleece, seems unlikely. It may have simply been selected to place the starch higher in the alphabet than **Kingsford's**, then a rival brand.

Argyrol *(antiseptic)*

The name is a brand name for vitellin of silver, a dark brown powder whose aqueous solution is used as a local antiseptic to treat infections of the eye and throat. It was the invention in 1902 of the American pharmacologist Albert C. Barnes (1872–1951), and its name, based on Greek *arguros,* "silver," was entered by Barnes and his German business partner, Hermann Hille, in the US Patent Office *Official Gazette* in April 1908.

Ariel *(motorcycles)*

The British company was founded in 1907 by Charles Sangster, taking its name from the fairy in Shakespeare's play *The Tempest*. At first the firm flourished, but went bankrupt in 1932, when the rights to the Ariel name passed to Charles's son, John Young Sangster (1896–1977), who soon set up the new business of Ariel Motors (J.S.) Ltd. In 1943, as chairman of **Triumph**, he sold Ariel to **BSA**, at the same time assuming a place on the latter's board. (He became chairman in 1956.) Sales began to slump in the 1960s, and the last Ariel model was produced in 1971.

Aristoc *(stockings)*

The name, a blend of "aristocratic" and "stocking," was suggested to Albert Ernest Allen, a director of the British hosiery company Robert Rowley & Co. of Leicester, by a business acquaintance who had no connection with the hosiery trade. Allen is said to have applied to register the name on the afternoon of the day in 1924 when it was offered him, although it was two years before it was actually used. The company was itself renamed Aristoc Ltd. in 1934. The name was entered in the *Trade Marks Journal* of March 9, 1932 for: "Underclothing made wholly or principally of silk or artificial silk."

Arm & Hammer *(baking soda)*

The famous brand dates back to the days when James A. Church ran a mustard and spice business in Brooklyn. Over the door of the Vulcan Spice Mill swung a sign depicting the symbol (an arm and a hammer) of the mythological Vulcan, the hammer-wielding god of fire and metalworking. In 1867 Church closed his spice factory to go into the baking soda business, taking the sign along with him for old times' sake. Sales were sluggish, however, until Church realized that the old Arm and Hammer sign would make a perfect symbol for his baking soda. After all, it took power to raise that hammer as it took power to leaven baked goods. Church immediately had a supply of paper bags printed with the "Arm & Hammer" label and rushed them to the local stores. His hunch was right, and the label was an outstanding success. The international entrepreneur Arm and Hammer (1898–1990), chairman of **Occidental Petroleum**, was so named punningly by his father, a Russian-born pharmacist. In consequence, it was popularly supposed that he owned Church & Dwight, as the firm became in 1896. An article about Hammer by Daniel Yergin in the June 1975 number of *At-*

lantic Monthly says that at one time Hammer thought about buying the business, and still thought about it occasionally. Hammer related: "I used to have a boat and my boat had the arm and hammer on it. Every place I went people would say that he must be the Soda King and finally I said to my brother—we were in the distilling business—let us buy it so we do not have to apologize."

Armalite *(rifle)*

The first rifle by the American manufacturers of the same name was the AR-10, a 7.62-millimeter gas-operated weapon. The name, properly "ArmaLite," is based on "arm" and a respelled "light" and was entered in the US Patent Office *Official Gazette* of March 4, 1938 for: "Small bore weapons comprising pistols, rifles, and carbines." The British firm Sterling Aramament Company produces a Sterling-Armalite AR-18 rifle that resembles and operates like the American AR-15.

Armco *(steel)*

The American corporation was founded on December 2, 1899, in Middletown, Ohio, by a group of investors led by George Matthew Verity (1865–1942). Its original name, as a manufacturer of iron and steel, was the American Rolling Mill Company. In 1948 an acronym from this gave a new name, Armco Steel Corporation, and in 1978 this in turn became simply Armco Inc. The abbreviated name was entered in the *Trade Marks Journal* of August 11, 1920 and the US Patent Office *Official Gazette* of October 19, 1920 for a soft iron of high purity manufactured by the company, and later in the *Gazette* of November 21, 1961 and *Journal* of May 16, 1962 for a crash barrier for a motorway or racing track made by the company.

Armitage Shanks *(plumbing fixtures)*

The origins of the British firm lie in a ceramic pottery founded in about 1817 in the village of Armitage, near Rugeley, Staffordshire. In 1861, this was bought by the Rev. Edward Johns, a hygiene-conscious entrepreneur as well as a clergyman, who traded as Edward Johns & Co. In the meantime, the Scots plumber John Shanks had founded his own sanitary fitting business in Paisley, Scotland, in 1851, and much of his ware was promoted by Edward Johns in export markets. Finally, the two concerns combined in 1960 as Armitage Shanks, adopting the name by which Edward Johns' products had been familiarly known. Popular linguists sometimes like to derive "john" as a term for a toilet from the name of John Shanks or Edward Johns, but the word in this sense has been current only since the 1930s and originated among US college students, who are hardly likely to have even heard of the men. Armitage Shanks has been a subsidiary of **Blue Circle** since 1980.

Armor *(risk management)*

The US company was founded in 1969 as American Body Armor & Equipment, a maker of bulletproof vests. With headquarters in Jacksonville, Florida, it expanded to provide security risk-management services to multinational corporations and government agencies through its ArmorGroup Service division, while also manufacturing security products for military and law enforcement agencies and private security companies. By 2001 the company, floated in 1999, was operating on five continents.

Armour *(canned meat and fish)*

The American firm bears the name of Philip Danforth Armour (1832–1901), born in Stockbridge, New York, the son of a farmer. Following education at the Cazenovia Academy, he left the farm in 1852 to mine gold in California, returning in 1856 several thousand dollars richer. In 1859 he went into the provision business with Frederick B. Miles in Milwaukee, and when the partnership ended, formed Plankinton, Armour and Company in 1863 in that city with John Plankinton, a grain dealer and meatpacker, making his money by buying pork at depressed rates and selling it for much more in New York. In 1868 he added a pork-packing plant to the grain commission house managed in Milwaukee by his brother, Herman Ossian Armour (1837–1901). He subsequently promoted new slaughtering methods, the sale of canned meat, and the establishment of refrigerated distributing plants, as well as the export of meat products to Europe. In 1892 he founded the Armour Institute of Technology (now the Illinois Institute of Technology) in Chicago.

Armstrong *(floors and carpets)*

The American flooring company, originally known as Armstrong Cork, after its original product, takes its name from Thomas Morton Armstrong (1836–1908), who bought a cork business in Pittsburgh, Pennsylvania, in 1860. In 1902 the company began making cork insulation for cold-storage rooms, and in 1907 took to the manufacture of linoleum, which in those days was made with finely ground cork powder. This was how Armstrong Cork got into flooring and interior furnishings. In 1980 the company dropped the "Cork" and renamed itself as Armstrong World Industries.

Armstrong-Siddeley *(automobiles)*

The first name is that of Sir William George Armstrong (1810–1900), an English engineer who set up a business in Newcastle upon Tyne in 1847 that would subsequently manufacture automobiles. The second name is that of John Davenport Siddeley (1866–1953), later Lord Kenilworth, who progressed from being a draftsman in the bicycle works owned by Thomas **Humber** to becoming an auto manufacturer, initially as general manager of **Wolseley** Motors when Herbert **Austin** left in 1905, then afterwards in partnership with Major Henry Hugh Peter Deasy (1866–1947) in Coventry. Armstrong, meanwhile, had formed his own partnership with Sir Joseph Whitworth to form the company of Armstrong-Whitworth, and in 1919 a merging of all these interests produced the first Armstrong-Siddeley car. In 1935, however, Siddeley sold control of the company to Harry Hawker's firm of aircraft manufacturers, from which **Hawker Siddeley** was formed. The latter firm continued to manufacture the Armstrong-Siddeley car until 1960, when production ceased after Hawker Siddeley itself merged with Bristol Aircraft.

Arndale *(shopping malls)*

The British malls arose from the business set up in Bradford, Yorkshire, in 1931 by Samuel Chippindale (1909–90), an estate agent (realtor) specializing in shops. This grew into the Arndale Property Trust, taking its name from a blend of Chippindale's own name and that of his partner, Arnold Hargenbach. The first Arndale Centre opened in Leeds in 1967, its architecture based on an American design. The bulldozing of various town centers to make way for the malls horrified many, although the later buildings regained some of the panache of Victorian glass and wrought-iron shopping arcades. Manchester's Arndale Centre, derisively dubbed "the longest lavatory in Europe" for its expanses of yellow tiling, was destroyed in 1996 by an IRA bomb but reopened in 1999.

Arnet *(sunglasses)*

The name is that of US designer Greg Arnette (b.1960), who set up Arnet Optic Illusions in San Clemente, California, in 1992, catering mainly for snowboarders. His early line of "Raven" glasses, produced in silver, failed to take off, but suddenly became sought after when relaunched in gold.

Arnold, E.J. *see* **E.J. Arnold**

Arnold, Edward *see* **Edward Arnold**

Arnold, Wallace *see* **Wallace Arnold**

Arnolt *(automobiles)*

Chicago dealer S.H. "Wacky" Arnolt introduced a sports-racing car in the early 1950s. He was best known for the Arnolt Bristol, manufactured from 1954 to 1964, when all production ended. Arnolt himself died in 1960.

Arriflex *(cinecameras)*

The cameras are made by the Arriflex Corporation, which takes its name from its German parent company, *Ar*nold and *Ri*chter Cine Technic of Munich. The forerunner of the lightweight and relatively small Arriflex 35mm camera was introduced in 1935.

Arrow *(shirts)*

The firm of Maullin and Blanchard in Troy, New York, began manufacturing detachable shirt collars in the 1860s. In 1889 they merged with Coon & Company and soon after launched the "Arrow" trademark for the collars, referring to the collar points. The company subsequently became **Cluett**, Peabody & Co. "Arrow" shirts, with attached collars, were not introduced until the 1920s.

Artaria *(music publishers)*

The Austrian firm of music publishers was founded in Mainz in 1765 with a name apparently based on Latin *ars*, *artis*, "art," and Italian (now also English) *aria*. It was equally renowned as an art and map publisher, and issued many of Mozart's works. The firm closed in 1858.

Artex *(decorative plaster)*

Artex is a type of decorative plaster applied to walls and ceilings to give a textured finish, typically in decorative patterns. The name, a blend of "art" and "texture," was entered by the British firm of Artex (Decorations) Ltd., of Rustington, Sussex, in the *Trade Marks Journal* of May 7, 1952 for: "Distemper in powder form for use in the manufacture of water plastic paint," with a claim of use since 1945. The name "Artex Ax" was entered by the same company, now Artex Ltd., of Newhaven, East Sussex, in the *Journal* of August 1, 1984 for: "Paints and decorative texturable coatings (in the nature of paint)."

Arthur Andersen *(accountants)*

The US firm of accountants takes its name from Arthur Andersen (1885–1947), born in Plano, Illinois, the son of a foundry foreman. Soon after his birth, the family returned to their native Norway, where they lived for several years before immigrating again to the United States and taking up residence in Chicago. Andersen began his career as an office boy at the Fraser & Chalmers Company in Chicago, his father's employer. In 1907 he decided to become an accountant, and that same year joined Price Waterhouse & Co. in Chicago, where he remained until 1911. In 1913, together with Clarence M. DeLany, Andersen purchased the Audit Company of Illinois. His firm was originally known as Andersen, DeLany & Co., but in 1918 adopted the name Arthur Andersen & Co. after the withdrawal of its cofounder. In 2001 "Arthurs" dropped "Arthur" from its name to become plain Andersen, on the basis that "Arthur Andersen" sounded "too much like a boring Swedish accountant." *See also* **Accenture**.

Arthur Murray *(dance studios)*

The chain of dance studios for those who wanted to learn "dancing in a hurry" took its name from Arthur Murray (1895–1991), born Murray Teichman in New York City, the son of an immigrant baker. Murray quit high school to work at a variety of jobs but was already dancing at an early age, winning a waltz contest at a local settlement house in 1912. He originally taught dancing in evening classes at the Georgian Terrace Hotel in Atlanta, Georgia, and opened his first dance studio there in

1920. In 1924 he returned to New York, where he married Kathryn Kohnfelder (1906–1999) and established a studio on Forty-third Street. By 1943 the Murrays were operating studios in 47 American cities, and when Murray sold his business in 1965, there were 350 franchised studios. Today there are still 275.

Arzoo *(Internet shopping service)*

The service, facilitating online shopping, was launched in 2000 by Sabeer Bhatia, the Indian founder of **Hotmail**. The name represents Hindi *arzu*, "keen desire," "yearning," epitomizing the "must-have" syndrome of the 21st-century shopaholic.

Asahi *(beer)*

The name, Japanese for "morning sun," is used by several breweries in Japan. The main one was founded as the Osaka brewery in 1889. In 1906 it became part of the Dai Nippon brewing company, which was subsequently split into Nippon (later renamed Sapporo) and Asahi. The latter was originally the small of the two, but in 1987 launched its successful "Super Dry" brand and is now Japan's second-largest brewing group.

Asarco *(metal ore refining)*

The American company dates its founding from 1814, when the Gunpowder Copper Works, the ancestor of Asarco's Baltimore refinery, was supplying copper to the company started by Paul Revere in colonial days. It gradually grew into a network of mining and metal-processing concerns as the American Smelting and Refining Company, or fully and formally, International Miners and Refiners of Antimony, Asbestos, Bismuth, Cadmium, Coal, Copper, Gold, Limestone, Silver, and Zinc. The former name was officially abbreviated acronymically as now in 1975.

Ascot *(gas water heaters)*

The British company was founded in London by a German, Dr Bernard Friedman, as an agency for marketing the heaters made by **Junkers** in Germany, and the Junkers name was originally used for the product. Friedman changed the name of the firm to Ascot Gas Water Heaters in 1933, when a more specifically English name seemed desirable. (Hitler came to power in 1933.) He also needed a shorter name to fit into the inverted blue triangle that until then had contained "Junkers." The name is purely prestigious, from Ascot, the site of a famous annual race meeting attended by royalty. The name was entered in the *Trade Marks Journal* of April 10, 1935.

Asda *(supermarkets)*

The British chain was set up in 1965 by *As*sociated *Da*iries, an amalgamation of various regional dairy farmers formed to proved outlets for milk, butter, and other farm products. Its name was both an acronym and an allusion to one of the three founders, Peter *A*squith, a butcher who together with his brother, Fred, had started and sold a store in Pontefract, Yorkshire. He then wished to expand beyond butchery and to this end had formed a partnership with Noel Stockdale, vice chairman of Associated Dairies. (The third member of the team was Eric Binns, chief executive officer of Associated Dairies.) The company diversified, buying first Allied Carpets, then in 1985 **MFI**. The arrangement was not a success, however, and in 1987 MFI managers bought the business out, spinning the dairy business off as Associated Fresh Foods and leaving Asda to stand alone. In 1999 Asda was acquired by **Wal-Mart**.

Ashley, Laura *see* **Laura Ashley**

Ask *(restaurants)*

The British restaurant chain, based in St. Albans, Hertfordshire, takes its name (in full Ask Central) from the initials of its founders in 1993, brothers Adam and Samuel Kaye (b.1968 and 1972), the sons of Phillip Kaye (b.1932), a long-time restaurant owner. By 2000 the group, specializing in pizzas, had more than 100 restaurants, with a further 28 planned.

Askit *(analgesic powder)*

The product was originally sold without a name in Laidlaw's Pharmacy, Glasgow, Scotland. The story goes that one day in 1919, Mr. and Mrs. Laidlaw heard two girls whispering together in their shop in a repeated exchange: "You ask it," "No, you ask it." The Laidlaws decided to adopt "Askit" as a brand name for their powder and the Askit Company (later Askit Laboratories) was formed. In 1959 the product was acquired by **Aspro**-Nicholas, who were still marketing it at the close of the 20th century. The name was entered in the *Trade Marks Journal* of September 24, 1924.

Asprey (jewelers)

The London, England, jewelry firm takes its name from William Asprey, an immigrant Huguenot who set up in Mitcham, Surrey, as a seller of fine leathers and silver goods in the 18th century. In 1847 his grandson, Charles, moved the business to Bond Street, London, where he began advertising "articles of exclusive design and high quality for personal adornment or personal accompaniment," and it is in New Bond Street today that the firm still has its head office. The business became a limited company in 1909 and remained a family concern until 1995, when it was hard hit by recession and bought by Prince Jefri, brother of the Sultan of Brunei.

Aspro (aspirin)

The name has its origin in Australia. When that country's supply of aspirin from the German firm of **Bayer** was cut off at the start of World War I, the Australian Attorney-General suspended the German patent and trademark rights in the name (now generic in Britain and many other countries) and granted them to any native manufacturer who could meet the required standards. An Australian chemist, George Nicholas, set out to make his own aspirin, assisted by a fellow chemist, Harry Shmith [sic]. On June 12, 1915 they had succeeded in manufacturing the product to the required standard and hurried to take over the Bayer trade name "Aspirin," itself first used in 1899 as a shortened form of German *acetylierte Spirsäure* ("acetylated spiraeic acid"), with the chemical suffix *-in*. (Spiraeic acid is the old name for salicylic acid.) Permission to do so was granted. Sales, however, were not good, mainly as a result of hostile associations with the product, which still bore its German name. Nicholas therefore decided to change the name and did so in 1917 by combining the last two letters of his own name with the first three of "product," so stressing that it was a "Nicho*las* *pro*duct" and not a German one. At the same time, the name still strongly suggested the nature of the product. Sales later picked up, and were helped by the ending of the war. The name was entered in the *Trade Marks Journal* of April 6, 1921.

Associated Press (news agency)

The oldest and largest news agency in the USA traces its beginnings to 1848, when six New York daily newspapers combined their resources to finance a telegraphic relay of foreign news brought by ships to Boston, the first US port of call for westbound transatlantic ships. In 1856 the service took the name New York Associated Press, and in 1892 the modern AP was set up under the laws of Illinois.

Aston Martin (automobiles)

The first half of the name is that of the village of Aston Clinton, near Aylesbury, Buckinghamshire, England, where shortly before World War I motor enthusiast Lionel Martin (the second half of the name) took part in a famous speed hill climb at the wheel of a finely tuned **Singer**. In 1914, together with an engineer colleague, Robert Bamford, Martin built the first Aston Martin automobile, and despite several changes in ownership, the brand is still in production today, both as a racing car and as a standard road car. The famous DB range that emerged after World War II took its name from the initials of **David Brown**, who acquired the company in 1947.

AstroTurf (artificial grass surface)

The name was created by the American sports executive Roy M. Hofheinz (1912–1982), born in Beaumont, Texas, the son of a truck driver. Hofheinz is best known for the building of the Astrodome at Houston, Texas, the first covered, air-conditioned baseball stadium in the world. It opened in 1965 and originally had a playing field of Bermuda grass. The grass died, however, so Hofheinz replaced it with an artificial surface being tested by the Chemstrand Corporation and named it "Astroturf." The name was entered in the US Patent Office *Official Gazette* of December 3, 1968 and the *Trade Marks Journal* of December 11, 1968.

Atabrine (antimalarial drug)

The proprietary name for quinacrine (also known as mepacrine) is of uncertain origin. The British equivalent is "Atebrin," suggesting a possible source in the chemical suffix "-ate" as in "acetate" plus "brine" (present in many marshes and swamps). The name was entered (as "Atebrin") by **Bayer** in the *Trade Marks Journal* of March 12, 1913, for: "Chemical Substances Prepared for Use in Medicine and Pharmacy," but was not applied specifically to the antimalarial drug discovered by the German chemists H. Mauss and F. Mietzsch in 1930 (when it was known by the laboratory name of "Erion") until 1932.

AT&T *(telecommunications)*

The American company traces its origins to 1875, when Alexander Graham Bell signed an agreement with two investors, Gardiner C. Hubbard and Thomas Sanders. The following year Bell's experimental telephone gave its first wire transmission of intelligible speech and in 1877 the three members of the agreement formed the Bell Telephone Company. This underwent various reorganizations and renamings over the rest of the 19th century but in 1885 the American Telephone and Telegraph Company was formed as a subsidiary to handle long-distance service and in 1900 became the central organization of the **Bell System**. The word "Telegraph" in their full name has essentially been superfluous since 1913, when AT&T sold their **Western Union** stock. AT&T's "Bell" symbol dates from 1888, when Angus S. Hibbard drew a rough sketch of a bell, printing "Long Distance Telephone" across its face. The symbol was thus at first used solely for advertising the location of a long-distance telephone, but in 1895 the wording was altered to read "Local and Long Distance Telephone." The blue bell made its appearance in the early years of the 20th century, and was accompanied by the words "Bell System." The name is also preserved in that of "Ma Bell," a popular nickname for AT&T. In 1995, just 12 years after the breakup of the old Bell System, AT&T voluntarily split itself into three publicly held companies. One, specializing in communications services, retained the AT&T name. The second, devoted to systems and technology, became **Lucent**. The third, dealing in business computing, readopted the old **NCR** name.

Atari *(video games)*

In 1972, Nolan Bushnell, an **Ampex** Corporation engineer, found a way of harnessing the might of a microprocessor to the electronic games long played in amusement arcades. Others had experimented with video games before him, but the equipment was always too large and too expensive to be a commercial proposition. Now Bushnell was able to bring the leisure-time activity within the reach of millions. Together with two colleagues, Ted Dabney and Larry Brian, he set about marketing his concept. First they needed a name. The original choice of the enthusiasts was "Syzygy," a word they found defined in a dictionary as "the straight-line configuration between three celestial bodies." But the name was already taken. They then considered "BD Inc." and "DB Inc." (for their initials), but the first was too close to **Black & Decker** and the second to **Dun & Bradstreet**. A new tack was needed. Bushnell and Dabney often played go, the Japanese game of territorial possession, and realized that a term from the game could provide the answer. They considered "Sente" (literally "forestalling"), the term used for having the upper hand, "Atari" (literally "hit"), a term equivalent to English "check" in chess, and "Hanne" (literally "half-price"), an acknowledgement of an overtaking move. They then submitted all three to the Office of the Secretary of State, and "Atari" was the name approved.

Atco *(motor mowers)*

The British-made mowers were originally manufactured by Charles H. Pugh Ltd. in 1921. The directors were looking for a short and catchy name for their product, and took it acronymically from the full name of a firm within the group that made bicycle chains, the Atlas Chain Co. The name was entered in the *Trade Marks Journal* of February 9, 1921.

Atebrin *see* **Atabrine**

Atlantic Richfield *(petroleum)*

The American corporation, formally known as Atlantic Richfield Company and commercially as Arco, was created in 1966 by the merger of Richfield Oil Corporation, founded in 1911 as the product of several mergers, and Atlantic Refining Company, earlier Atlantic Petroleum Storage Company, founded in 1866 by Charles Lockhart, James S. Wright, and other pioneers of the Pennsylvania oil industry. "Richfield" means what it says and denotes the rich oil fields that the corporation has from the first been successful in exploring and exploiting. In 2000 Atlantic Richfield was acquired by BP **Amoco**.

Atora *(shredded suet)*

The name dates from 1893, when Gabriel Hugon, a French immigrant to Britain, founded a suet-making firm in Manchester. At that time, the beef fat that went to make up shredded suet came from South America, and the exporters there were said to have referred to the fat as *a toro*, Spanish for "from (a) bull." This is one of the more plausible explanations of the name. The name was entered in the *Trade Marks Journal* of February 6, 1895.

Au Bon Marché *(department store)*

The oldest department store in Paris, France, was founded in 1852 by Aristide Boucicaut (1810–1877). At that time, many Paris stores had names such as *Le Diable Boîteux* ("The Lame Devil"), *Les Deux Magots* ("The Two Magots"), or *La Belle Fermière* ("The Beautiful Farmer's Wife"). But Boucicaut and his wife called their enterprise *Au Bon Marché* ("The Bargain"), emphasizing their wide range of goods at reasonable prices. (The French phrase literally means "at a good market," and to a Parisian ear would evoke the many street markets for which the city is famous.) On Boucicaut's death, his widow sold the business to the store's employees and guided its expansion until her own death ten years later, after which Au Bon Marché was run cooperatively by its own employees. It remained the "greatest department store in the world" for many years, reaching over $30 million in sales by 1897.

Auburn *(automobiles)*

The first Auburn automobile was built in 1900 by Frank and Morris Eckhart in Auburn, Indiana, and named after their home town. The Eckhart Carriage Co., as their business was called, produced its first proper production model in 1903, but the Eckharts sold out to a group of Chicago businessmen in 1919. Auburns continued to be manufactured until 1937, when the company went into liquidation. *See also* **Cord**.

Audi *(automobiles)*

In 1899 the German engineer Dr. August Horch (1868–1951) founded the company of A. Horch & Cie. He originally manufactured cars under his own name but in 1909 left the company after a row and for legal reasons could not give his name to another car. He therefore ingeniously translated his surname, as if German *horch!*, "hark!", into Latin *audi* and in 1910 founded the Audi Automobilwerke GmbH in Zwickau. The name disappeared in 1939 at the start of World War II and reappeared in 1965. The rings in the Audi badge represented the four auto companies, Audi, **DKW**, Horch, and Wanderer, that amalgamated in 1932 to form Auto Union. Audi alone survived as an independent marque. It is presumably fortuitous that Horch chose a name which also happens to suggest "auto."

Audio-Animatronics *(robot modeling technique)*

The name describes a technique of constructing robot models in accurate likenesses of humans or animals and programming them to perform lifelike bodily movements in synchronization with a prerecorded soundtrack. It derives from "audio," referring to the soundtrack, and a blend of "animated" and "electronics," and was entered by Wed Enterprises, Inc., of Glendale, California, in the US Patent Office *Official Gazette* of February 14, 1967, with a note of first use about July 1, 1961. (Wed Enterprises, unsurprisingly, takes its name from the initials of Walter Elias Disney.) "Audio-Animatronic" was subsequently entered in the *Trade Marks Journal* of February 8, 1978. "Audio-Animatronics" gave "animatronics" as a more common general name for the technique.

Augener *(music publishers)*

The British firm of music publishers, employing German immigrant printers, began as music importers in 1853, becoming Augener & Co. in 1855, Augener Ltd. in 1904, and eventually part of Galliard Ltd., which was subsequently absorbed by **Stainer & Bell**.

Aunt Jemima *(pancake mix)*

The story of "Aunt Jemima" began in 1889 in St. Joseph, Missouri, where Chris L. Rutt, a local newspaperman, had the idea of a self-rising pancake mix and accordingly, with two associates, started experiments with various combinations of ingredients. Within a year they had produced a mix to their satisfaction and then began searching for a name and package design for it. Inspiration came when a vaudeville team called Baker and Farrell came to St. Joseph. Baker's hit song was "Aunt Jemima," and Rutt immediately decided that this was the name for the new pancake mix since it naturally made one think of good cooking. Rutt and his assistants could not afford to promote their product, however, and they sold their interests to the David Milling Company, who risked their whole future on it with a lavish promotion at the World's Columbian Exposition in Chicago in 1893. They constructed the world's largest flour barrel to house displays and receive customers, while "Aunt Jemima" herself was personified by Nancy Green, a famous Negro cook born in Montgomery County, Kentucky, whose specialty happened to be pancakes. Her talent and friendliness helped make "Aunt Jemima" pancake mix a household name, and by 1910 it was known in all 48 states. The Aunt Jemima Mills were purchased by **Quaker Oats** in 1925 and the mix still ranks as one of the most popular in the USA.

Aurum *(liqueur)*

The Italian orange liqueur was the creation of the distiller Amedeo Pomilio, who invited the famous poet Gabriele d'Annunzio (1863–1938) to choose a name for it. He at first considered modern Latin *aurantium*, a word suggesting classical Latin *aurum*, "gold," but actually based on English "orange." This was regarded as somewhat ponderous, however, so the word for "gold" itself was decided upon.

Austin *(automobiles)*

The British name is that of Herbert Austin (1866–1941), who started making automobiles in 1898 when he was with the **Wolseley** Sheep-Shearing Company in Birmingham, England. He had originally intended to pursue a career as an architect. After a brief apprenticeship with his uncle, however, he instead turned from architecture to his first love, engineering, which he studied with honors in Australia. It was his engineering experience in that country that brought him in touch with Wolseley, and in the early 1890s he returned to England when that company removed its sheep-shearing operations to his homeland, with himself as its manager. Although his first cars were thus built under the Wolseley name, Austin did not break from the company until 1905, when he set up his own plant at Longbridge, now a district of Birmingham. The famous Austin Seven or "Baby Austin" was first on the road in 1922, and remained in production until 1939. In 1952 Austin became part of the British Motor Corporation (*see*

BL), and that same year the **Austin Healey** was launched. *See also* **Mini**.

Austin Healey *(automobiles)*

In 1952, British automobile engineer and racing driver Donald Healey (1898–1988), founder of the Donald Healey Motor Company in 1945, launched a new Healey 100 model with **Austin** engine and transmission to replace the old **Riley**-engined Healeys. Leonard Lord, chairman of the British Motor Corporation (*see* **BL**), was so impressed that he immediately agreed to take it over, renaming it the Austin Healey 100 and making it in large numbers. The first cars were delivered in 1953, and the last were built in 1970, most of them finding a ready market in the USA.

Austin Reed *(menswear)*

Austin Leonard Reed (1873–1954) was born in Reading, Berkshire, England, the son of a tailor and outfitter. On leaving school he joined his father's business, and in 1893 went to the United States to gain experience in the trade, working in one of the leading stores of the day, **Wanamaker** of Philadelphia. On his return in 1898 he aimed to put into practice what he had learned, and persuaded his father to invest in a new branch of Reed & Son at 167 Fenchurch Street, in the City of London. It was there that in 1900 Austin Reed established his own business, with the first Austin Reed branch being the one he opened the following year across the road at 13 Fenchurch Street. It is still there, and continues to be known to the firm's employees as "Branch No. 1."

Autobianchi *(automobiles)*

In 1885 the Italian engineer Edoardo Bianchi (1865–1946) began to make bicycles in Milan. He progressed to motorcycles, then to automobiles, mainly small-size models. In 1955 the firm was acquired by **Fiat**. The marque disappeared in 1996, when subsequent cars were badged **Lancia**.

Autocue *(television prompting device)*

In its simplest form, the Autocue is a device that projects the enlarged image of a script in front of a person speaking on television (or in public) in such a way that the speaker can read the words while seeming to look directly at the television viewers (or public). The name, dating from the 1950s, combines "auto-" (in the sense "self-") and "cue." It is often generically but is properly proprietary, and should be written with a capital "A." The US equivalent is the **Teleprompter**. The name was entered in the *Trade Marks Journal* of May 19, 1976.

Automat *(cafeteria)*

After opening their first lunchroom in Philadelphia in 1888, Joseph V. Horn and Frank Hardart incorporated their business as a commissary and catering service in 1898 and four years later opened their first Automat at 818 Chestnut Street, Philadelphia. The equipment for the coin-operated compartments providing self-service ("automated") meals was imported from Berlin, where a similar restaurant of the same name had been successful. The profitability of the Automats finally declined, however, and the last remaining one, in New York City, closed its doors on April 9, 1991.

Aveda *(cosmetics)*

The brand of natural cosmetics was the creation of Austrian-born US hairdresser Horst Rechelbacher, who opened his first chain of salons, Horst of Austria, in Minnesota in 1965. His fast-lane lifestyle and drug dependence caused liver and kidney failure, however, whereupon his mother nursed him back to health with herbs. After hitting the hippie trail to India, where he learned yoga and meditation, Rechelbacher returned to Minnesota and began concocting "little goodies," the first buds of Aveda, for his customers. In 1978 he switched entirely from hairdressing to the manufacture of natural cosmetics, calling his business "Aveda," partly from Sanskrit *veda*, "knowledge," and *a*, "all," and partly as a token of his keen interest in traditional systems of medicine such as the Indian ayurveda, "knowledge of long life." In 1997 Rechelbacher's ever-expanding enterprise was acquired by **Estée Lauder**.

Avery *(scales and balances)*

The ultimate origin of the British firm lies with John Barton, a blacksmith who made steelyards near Birmingham in the 18th century. He died in 1760, when he was succeeded in the business by his son. In 1782, however, after the son's own death, the concern was taken over by one Thomas Beach. Beach had a clerk named John Avery, whom Beach's sister Mary married, and one of their sons was

William Avery, who in turn married and had two sons, William and Thomas. When Thomas Beach died in 1813 his own two sons were still minors. Their cousin, William Avery, therefore took over, but as he knew nothing about the business, he brought in his brother Thomas, renaming the firm as W. & T. Avery. William Avery continued to run the business alone when his brother died in 1824, and on his own death in 1843 the firm was taken over by *his* sons, William (d.1874) and Thomas (1813–1894). The full name of the company, now based at Smethwick, near Birmingham, is still W. & T. Avery Ltd.

Avery *(self-adhesive labels)*

The name is that of R. Stanton Avery (b. 1905), born in Oklahoma, who graduated from Pomona College, California, in 1932. In 1935 he set up the Kum-Kleen Adhesive Products Co. in Los Angeles to make and market self-adhesive price-marking labels. The company later changed its name to Avery International and pioneered many industrial breakthroughs, including manual and automatic dispensers for self-adhesive labels. By 1980 the sales of Avery International, now based in Pasadena, California, made it one of America's 500 largest corporations.

Avis *(car hire)*

The American company owes its origin to Warren E. Avis (b.1917), who as a US Air Force officer in World War II frequently found that on landing at an airport there was no convenient transport link to the nearest town except by means of an expensive taxi ride. Avis therefore resolved to remedy this by setting up a car rental business, basing his enterprise on the already established **Hertz**, who offered cars for travel round the country but who had not yet exploited the link with airports. Immediately after the war, therefore, when he was still in his 20s, Avis started up his airport rent-a-car business, beginning with the Willow Run Airport, Detroit, and then moving to the one at Miami. Within seven years, his company had become the world's second largest international car rental system, proving not only that the need had been there, but that he had more than successfully exploited it.

Avon *(cosmetics)*

The American company, familiar from its

door-to-door selling, was launched by David H. McConnell (1858–1937), born in Oswego, New York, who at the age of 16 had himself been selling books in this way. In his rounds, McConnell found that he was not always welcome with his goods, so hit on the idea of giving each prospective customer an "enticer" in the form of a small flask of perfume. He soon found that his lady customers preferred the perfume to his books, and in 1886 founded The California Perfume Company, named in honor of a friend who came from California and who had been the first to invest in his business, or according to another account, for its evocation of clean, fresh air. The firm prospered, engaged female door-to-door sellers of the perfume and expanded. Mrs. P.F.E. Albee (d.1914) was the first "Avon lady," selling the "Little Dot" perfume set in 1886 in New York. As a Shakespeare lover, McConnell chose "Avon" for its literary associations, with Shakespeare's Stratford-upon-Avon also suggesting McConnell's hometown, Suffern-on-the-Ramapo, New York.

Avon *(tires)*

The British company was founded in a former cloth mill at Limpley Stoke, Wiltshire, in 1885, was acquired by Browne & Margetson Ltd. soon after, and in 1889 was transferred to larger premises, also a former cloth mill, at Melksham, Wiltshire. The company name was changed to Avon India Rubber Co. in 1891, and shortened to Avon Rubber Co. in 1963. Both cloth mills were on the same Avon River. Hence the name.

Avon Books *(paperbacks)*

The American firm of paperback publishers was founded in New York in 1941 by pulp publisher Joseph Meyers, the name alluding to Stratford-upon-Avon, the English birthplace of William Shakespeare. The firm was at once sued for imitating the format of **Pocket Books**, but won their case.

Avro *(aircraft)*

The firm of A.V. Roe & Co. was formed in 1910 by the English aircraft designer Alliott Verdon Roe, later Sir Alliott Verdon Verdon-Roe (1877–1958), born a doctor's son at Patricroft, near Manchester. He made and studied flying model aircraft as a young man while studying engineering and tried out experimental models at Brooklands motor-racing circuit,

Surrey. His name thus gave that of both the original company and the aircraft it manufactured. The name lacks the final "E" because Roe ended up short of space when painting the company name on the top gable of a shed at Brooklands. In 1928 Roe sold his interest in the company and joined forces with Saunders Ltd. of Cowes, Isle of Wight, to form Saunders-Roe. "Saro," as it was known, went on to produce a series of flying boats. In 1962 the firm became an integral part of **Hawker Siddeley**.

Avruga *(caviar substitute)*

The quasi-caviar, made from golden herring roe, not sturgeon roe, is a product of the Spanish firm Pescaviar, founded in Madrid in 1997. Its name blends letters from "caviar" with "sevruga," a species of sturgeon valued for its caviar. The firm, whose own name combines Spanish *pescado*, "fish (as food)" and *caviar*, also produces Lobsviar (from "lobster" and "caviar"), or lobster roe, and Anchoviar ("anchovy" and "caviar"), or anchovy roe, as well as Moluga (apparently from Spanish *mollas*, "soft" and *beluga*, another type of sturgeon), made from imperial herring roe.

Ayer's *(proprietary medicines)*

Ayer's Cherry Pectoral appeared in 1841 as a proprietary medicine made by James C. Ayer (1818–1878), born in Ledyard, Connecticut, the son of a mill operator. In 1836 Ayer went to live with his uncle in Lowell, Massachusetts, and two years later took a job in the apothecary shop of Jacob Robbins, learning the apothecary's skills and becoming a practical and analytical chemist. In 1841 he bought the shop and produced his first medicine. It was followed by Ayer's Sarsaparilla (1848), Ayer's Cathartic Pills (1854), Ayer's Ague Cure (1857), and Ayer's Hair Vigor (1858), among others, and lavish advertising brought his preparations to the attention of America and countries worldwide.

B. Altman *(department store)*

The famous New York City store owed its origin to Benjamin Altman (1840-1913), born in New York City. He had little formal education, but in 1865 set up a small dry-goods store on 3d Avenue. The business gradually expanded and in 1906 Altman founded B. Altman & Co., which became one of the country's most stylish department stores. In 1987 the company was bought by L.J. Hooker, a firm owned by the Australian corporate raider George Herscu, and in 1989 ceased operation.

B. Dalton *see* Dayton Hudson

B&Q *(do-it-yourself stores)*

The initials are those of the British firm's two founders, Richard Block and David Quayle, who in March 1969 opened their first do-it-yourself self-service store in Portswood Road, Southampton, where it remained until 1986. Block left the business in 1976, but Quayle remained until 1980, when the firm became a public company. By this same year the first supercenter had spawned 25 more, and by the end of the decade there were 280 stores nationwide. In 1998 B&Q merged with the French company Castorama to become the largest DIY retailer in Europe.

Babcock & Wilcox *(engineering plant)*

The US company dates from 1867, when George H. Babcock and Stephen Wilcox set out to pioneer the production of water-tube boilers, which raised steam without the necessity of heating a large quantity of water as in the older shell-type boiler. In 1881, based in New York, the partners established a branch office in the UK, choosing Glasgow, Scotland, as their European headquarters, and it was in that city, at the plant of the **Singer** Sewing Machine Co., that they manufactured their first boiler. By 1890 the European side of the business had grown to such an extent that the New York company had outrun its viable capital. In 1891, accordingly, a completely independent British firm, Babcock & Wilcox Ltd., was formed to acquire from the American business the patents, goodwill, and rights to manufacture throughout the world outside the USA and Cuba. Following a series of acquisitions and the formation of branches in other countries, the company finally became Babcock International plc.

Baby Ruth *(candy bar)*

The famous candy bar takes its name not from baseball player Babe Ruth but from "Baby Ruth" Cleveland, the popular eldest daughter of US President Grover Cleveland (1837-1908), born in 1891 between his two administrations (1885-9, 1893-7). The nut-roll bar was the creation in the 1910s of a Chicago confectioner,

Otto Schnering, who originally called it "Kandy Kake." The candy was rechristened in 1921 when one of Schnering's employees suggested "Baby Ruth" in a contest.

Babybel *(cheese)*

The small, round, wax-coated cheese, somewhat similar to Edam, is made by the French company of Bel and was first produced in 1931. The same cheese is manufactured under license in Kentucky, USA, under the name "Albany."

Babycham *(perry)*

The brand of sparkling perry made by **Showerings** was introduced in 1949, after a series of experiments in the fermentation of fruit juices, by Francis Showering, a great-grandson of the founder, also Francis Showering. The drink won many awards, so was nicknamed a "baby champ," and this is the origin of its name, which now appears on the label accompanied punningly by a stylized young chamois, as if "leaping" in the mouth. A suggestion of "baby champagne" is also present in the name.

Babygro *(babywear garment)*

The all-in-one stretch garment for babies, serving as pajamas or sleepers (or overalls), was designed by Walter Arzt, an American father frustrated with dressing his child. It is intended to adapt to the baby's increasing size as the child grows. Hence the name, which was entered by the manufacturers, Lisle Mills, Inc., of New York, in the US Patent Office *Official Gazette* of October 13, 1959.

Bacardi *(rum)*

The Bacardi family of distillers were established in Spain in the 17th century. In 1830 Don Facundo Bacardí y Masó (1816-1886) came from Spain to Cuba, where he settled in Santiago. He found work with a local merchant and later opened his own wine shop. In his spare time, Bacardi experimented with different techniques of making rum, selling it to friends and favored customers from a room in the back of his shop. In 1862 he purchased a small local distillery and set up what would become the world's largest rum company. He was searching for a suitable trademark for the new product when his wife, Doña Amalia, inspired by the colony of bats that inhabited the rafters of the distillery's tin roof, suggested the now famous black bat. The company's head office is now at Hamilton, Bermuda. The name was entered by the Compania Ron Bacardi, of Santiago de Cuba, Cuba, in the US Patent Office *Official Gazette* of December 26, 1933. In 1993 Bacardi took over **Martini** & Rossi to become Bacardi Martini. *See also* **Daiquiri**.

Badedas *(bath additive)*

The product, in full known as "Badedas Vita Bath Gelee," originated in Germany in the 1950s near Baden-Baden, and the name of that city, blended with German *Bad*, "bath" (which gave the town's name in the first place), formed the base of the name. The final "-das" is perhaps intended to represent German *das*, "the," so that by reversing the elements one has *das Bad*, "the bath."

Badger *see* **Hall & Woodhouse**

Baileys *("Irish Cream")*

The liqueur, made from Irish whiskey and dairy cream, was introduced in the 1970s by the firm of R. & A. Bailey & Co., of Dublin, Ireland, who promote it as the "Original Irish Cream" (as opposed to crème, as for crème de menthe, crème de noix, etc., meaning a liqueur with a particular flavor).

Bailie Nicol Jarvie, The *(whisky)*

The whisky is blended by Macdonald and Muir of Leith, Edinburgh, Scotland, a distillery founded in 1893 by Roderick Macdonald and Alexander Muir. The Bailie Nicol Jarvie, known to its aficionados as simply "The Bailie" or "BNJ," takes its name from the fictional magistrate (bailie) and merchant in Walter Scott's novel *Rob Roy* (1817).

Baixas *(chocolates)*

The Spanish firm had its beginnings in the pâtisserie started in Barcelona by Francisco Baixas (d.1987) and his wife Conxita in 1958. By 1968 he had added chocolates to his repertoire, and was subsequently joined in the family business by his son Joan in 1982 and daughter Nuria in 1987.

Bakelite *(synthetic resin)*

The early form of plastic, formed from the chemical combination of phenols and formaldehydes (*cp.* **Formica**), was invented in 1909 by the Belgian-born US chemist Leo Hendrik Baekeland (1863-1944) as a substitute for shel-

lac and is named after him. (The suggestion of "bake" for a hard, heatproof plastic is purely coincidental, as is that of the equally apt "light.") Baekeland patented his invention in 1907, two years before the publication of his article "The Synthesis, Constitution, and Uses of Bakelite" in the *Journal of Industrial and Engineering Chemistry*. The company he founded, later the Bakelite Corporation, was acquired by **Union Carbide** in 1939. The name was in danger of becoming generic, a hazard for many popular products alluded to in the following passage from the Foreword to Patrick Cook and Catherine Slessor's *Bakelite: An Illustrated Guide to Bakelite Objects* (1992):

> A word of caution about the use of the word "Bakelite". As we have seen, it was the trade mark coined by the inventor. It was also used as the company name, that is the Bakelite Corporation and Bakelite Limited. Further complications arose when the giant Union Carbide Corporation of America acquired Baekeland's business. Recognizing the tremendous value of the mark ... they used it to sell other types of plastics such as polyethylene and PVC.
>
> So successful was the trade mark and so dominant did it become that, like Hoover and Sellotape, it became generic. In other words, many mouldings described as "Bakelite mouldings" might well be made from phenolic materials made by another manufacturer unconnected with the Bakelite organization.

Baker's *(chocolate)*

The story behind the name starts in 1764, when Dr. James Baker befriended a young Irish immigrant chocolate maker named John Hannon. Hannon complained that there was no chocolate mill in the New World. Baker decided to help. He leased a mill on the banks of the Neponset River in Dorchester, Massachusetts, obtained a run of mill stones and a set of kettles, and supplied the necessary capital. The new industry prospered, and by 1777 Hannon was widely advertising his product. In 1779, however, misfortune struck. Hannon started off for the West Indies to buy cocoa beans but never reached his destination. He was presumed lost at sea, and Dr. Baker himself continued the business. It was his grandson, Walter Baker, who in 1824 gave the company the name by which it is known today. The brand is now marketed by General Foods (*see* **Bird's**).

Baldwin (pianos)

In 1840 Dwight H. Baldwin (1821-1899) en-rolled at the Oberlin College divinity school, Ohio, with the aim of becoming a Presbyterian minister. Poor health obliged him to end his studied after only a year, however, and he moved to Cincinnati, where he became a music teacher. He left his teaching job in 1862 and invested his life savings of $2,000 in a piano store. Baldwin's store might never have grown into a major manufacturing firm if he had not sold an interest in his business to his book-keeper, Lucien Wulsin, 24 years his junior, who took the firm into manufacturing in the late 1880s when **Steinway** dropped it as a dealer-ship. Wulsin and various more recent partners developed large markets for the firm's Hamilton reed organ and Baldwin piano, the latter introduced in 1891.

Balenciaga (fashionwear)

The House of Balenciaga dates back to 1916, when the Spanish designer Cristóbal Balenci-aga (1895-1972) opened a dressmaking and tai-loring establishment in San Sebastián. By the early 1930s he had gained a reputation as Spain's leading couturier, and in 1937 he moved to Paris, France, where his classically designed garments soon became instantly iden-tifiable. He retired in 1968, whereupon his label lost direction. The haute couture business closed, and continued as a fragrance operation only. In 2001 Balenciaga was acquired by **Gucci**, providing it with a much needed sales boost.

Balkan Sobranie *see* **Sobranie**

Ball (fruit jars)

The five Ball brothers became partners in various businesses, but all their ventures came to nothing until Edmund Ball (1855-1925) and Frank Ball (1857-1943) set up a can company in 1880 in Buffalo, New York. A short while later they were joined by George, Lucius, and William, and together devised a method of closing cans that eliminated a previously re-quired patent royalty. In 1886 the Balls branched out into glass fruit jars, and eight years later, after relocating to Muncie, Indiana, were making 31 million jars annually. The fam-ily business soon became one of the world's leading producers of fruit jars, turning out 90 million jars in 1910.

Ballantine (whisky)

The Scottish company traces its origins to George Ballantine (1809-1891), a farmer's son born in Peebles. At the age of 18 he set up as a grocer in Edinburgh, and developed a special interest in the wine and liquor trade, and par-ticularly in that of whisky. His son, George Ballantine, Jr., then joined the family firm and became established as a wine and liquor mer-chant independently in Glasgow, at the same time setting up a bonded warehouse for the whisky. In 1919 he sold his Glasgow business to another whisky company, Barclay and McKin-lay, which in turn adopted the Ballantine name for its particular blend of whisky. Today the company's main distillery and head office are in Dumbarton, where a blending and bottling complex was opened in 1938.

Ballantine *see* **Bantam Books**

Bally (footwear)

Carl Franz Bally (1821-1899) began the commercial manufacture of shoes in Switzer-land in 1851, with the firm's first factory open-ing three years later in the village of Schönen-werd, near Aarau. Sales were initially poor in Switzerland itself, and the firm was saved from bankruptcy only by export sales to South America. Business contracts with Britain were established in 1881, and on the founder's death the concern passed to his two sons under the style of C.F. Bally Söhne. The name is pro-nounced approximately "Buy-ee."

Bally (slot and pinball machines)

The US company dates its origins from 1931, when a business known as Lion Manufacturing made a wooden slot machine called the "Bal-lyhoo." The firm subsequently changed their name in honor of this machine, and in 1963 launched the first electromechanical slot ma-chine. By the 1980s Bally had moved into casino ownership and were supplying 80 per-cent of the slot machines in Nevada, the only state where gambling is legal everywhere.

Balmain (fashionwear and cosmetics)

When Pierre Balmain (1914-1982) left his native Savoie, France, in 1933 to study archi-tecture at the École des Beaux-Arts in Paris he took with him letters of introduction to several leading couturiers. The following year he sold some sketches to couturier Robert Piguet, and his choice of career was decided. He rapidly gained experience and in 1945 open the Maison Balmain in Paris. His first perfume, *Élysées 64 83*, was launched a year later, and in 1951 he opened a salon in New York. The business was bought by **Revlon** in 1960.

Bandai *(toys)*

The Japanese firm was founded in 1950 by Naoharu Yamashina (?1918-1997) in the town of Bandai. Among the many popular figures and toys it has produced are the Mighty Morphin Power Rangers and the cyberpet **Tamagotchi**.

Band-Aid *(adhesive plasters)*

The American make of elastic adhesive plaster, similar to British **Elastoplast**, was the invention in 1920 of Earle E. Dickson, a cotton buyer in the purchasing department of **Johnson & Johnson**. Dickson had recently married, and had come up with the idea of putting a small gauze pad in the middle of a thin strip of surgical tape to provide a ready self-stick bandage for his wife, who was prone to burning and cutting herself in the kitchen. After seeing the dressing, James Johnson decided to market it under a name that soon became one of the most familiar in America, combining "bandage" and "first aid." It was entered in the US Patent Office *Official Gazette* of November 4, 1924 and the *Trade Marks Journal* of February 22, 1933.

Bang & Olufsen *(electronic sound systems)*

The Danish company, noted for its home recording and playing systems, owes its name to Peter Boas Bang (1900-1957) and Svend Andreas Grøn Olufsen (1897-1949), who met as electrical engineering students, in Bang's case after a short spell working with radio in the USA in 1924. Both men had developed an early interest in the technical side of radio receivers, and founded the firm of Bang & Olufsen in 1925 to develop their skills, basing themselves in the village of Quistrup. Their enterprise flourished, and by the 1950s they were producing televisions and tape recorders as well as radios, marketing them under names that began with "Beo-" (for "Bang & Olufsen"), as "Beosystem."

BankAmerica *(holding company)*

The American corporation, owner of and named after Bank of America National Trust and Savings Association, was incorporated on October 7, 1968. Bank of America NT & SA itself resulted from the merger of two earlier banking systems, both founded by Amadeo Peter Giannini (1870-1949), who on October 17, 1904, opened a small neighborhood bank in San Francisco called the Bank of Italy. In 1927 he began assembling another banking system which after various mutations became known as the Bank of America of California. On November 3, 1930, in a complex merger, he incorporated the Bank of America NT & SA and Bank of America, and in 1934 the latter was absorbed by the former. *See also* **VISA**.

Banlon *(synthetic fabric)*

The US firm of Joseph Bancroft & Sons introduced a process to texturalize yarn by adding crimp and stretch to synthetic fabrics. The result blended the first part of their name with the last part of "nylon." Banlon fiber was popular in the 1960s, made up into socks, sweaters, and dresses.

Bantam Books *(paperbacks)*

The American firm of paperback publishers was founded in 1945 by Ian K. Ballantine (1916-1995), previously manager of the US branch of **Penguin**. The name of the new firm was selected by Bernard Geis, at the time a young editor for **Grosset & Dunlap**. The bantam is a pugnacious bird, and was at least partly selected as a name and pictorial symbol in order to "do combat" with the already established **Pocket Books**, who sported Gertrude the Kangaroo. The bird name also went well with Penguin and its association with paperbacks. In 1952 Ballantine resigned from Bantam to start his own Ballantine Books, another paperback firm, now an imprint of the Ballantine Publishing Group, a division of **Random House**. The first Bantam Book to be published was Mark Twain's *Life on the Mississippi* (1945), while the first Ballantine Book was Cameron Hawley's *Executive Suite*, published in cooperation with **Houghton Mifflin**. (Both publishers' names were listed on the cover.)

Baratti & Milano *(chocolates)*

The Italian chocolates, sold in specialist gourmet stores, take their name from Ferdinando Baratti and Eduardo Milano, who founded their Turin-based business in 1858. A presentation of the Italian royal family's coat of arms in 1875 authorized the firm to use the prestigious device as part of their logo.

Barbie *(dolls)*

The progenitor of the curvaceous blonde doll was the German toy manufacturer Rolf Hausser, who launched her on the market on August 12, 1955, basing her on a cartoon character called Lilli, the svelte and sexy creation of the German cartoonist Reinhard Beuthien, who first appeared in the German newspaper *Bild Zeitung* in 1952. In 1956 Ruth and Elliot Handler, cofounders of the toy manufacturers Mattel, were on holiday in Lucerne, Switzerland, with their daughter Barbara and son Ken when 15-year-old Barbara pointed out the Lili doll in a shop window. Mrs. Handler bought one and took it home. A manufacturer (*Mattel*) for a clone was found, and on March 9, 1959, Barbara Millicent Roberts, alias Barbie, named for the young girl who had spotted her prototype, was launched at the American Toy Fair in New York. In 1961 she was joined by a "boyfriend," Ken, named after Barbara's brother. Other friends followed, including one with a disability, Share A Smile Becky, introduced in 1997. By 1998 the average young girl in the USA owned nine Barbies. The name was entered in the *Trade Marks Journal* of February 6, 1963. Ruth Handler died in 2002, aged 85.

Barbour *(waterproof clothing)*

The British firm's history begins with John Barbour (1849-1918), a Scottish farmer's son who did not, however, follow in his father's footsteps but set up as a traveling draper in Newcastle upon Tyne in about 1870, together with his cousin, also named John Barbour. In about 1880 the two cousins parted company, and by 1894 the original John Barbour had moved to South Shields, where he opened a draper's shop in the Market Place. The town was a prosperous North Sea port, and Barbour found that he had a lucrative business supplying "wet weather wear," or oilskins, to the seamen who came to the port and the dockers who worked there. After Barbour's death, the company came to be associated with fashionable yet practicable clothing for country gentlefolk, as typified by the "Barbour" itself, a distinctive green-colored waterproof and thornproof jacket.

Barclaycard *(credit card)*

The combined credit card and cheque guarantee card was issued in the UK by **Barclays** Bank in 1966. The name was entered in the *Trade Marks Journal* of June 28, 1989.

Barclays *(bank)*

The British bank was created in 1896 as Barclay & Co. Ltd. as a merger of the banking business of Barclay, Bevan, Tritton, Ransom, Bouverie & Co., Gurney & Co., and various other private concerns. The name ultimately derives from David Barclay (1682-1769), an English Quaker merchant of Cheapside, London. He was not the actual "founder of Barclays," as sometimes stated, but his sons James, David, and John were important early partners in the bank, and the mercantile fortune he had built up was a major source of capital for it from the 1770s. The bank traditionally traces its origin to 1690, when John Freame (1665-1745), a leading Quaker banker, and his brother-in-law, Thomas Gould, set up a goldsmith's business in Lombard Street, London. They were joined in 1736 by James Barclay, who three years earlier had married Freame's daughter, Sally.

Barigo *(motorcycles)*

France's only motorcycle manufacturer for most of the 1990s takes its name from Patrick Barigault, who founded the firm in 1992 at La Rochelle, originally producing "supermoto" competition bikes. Road-legal models followed soon after.

Barilla *(pasta and sauces)*

The Italian company owes its existence to Pietro Barilla (1845-1912), who in 1877 opened a bread-and-pasta shop in Parma, turning out 100 lbs. of pasta a day. In 1910 the firm opened its first factory, on the Via Veneto, with 80 workers producing 8 tons of pasta a day. In 1971 the US multinational W.R. **Grace** bought a majority holding of the Barilla family shares, but eight years later the family reacquired their controlling interest. Meanwhile, in 1975, Barilla had introduced its first cookies, called "Mulino Bianco" ("White Mill"). In 1992 Barilla acquired the **Pavesi** cookie company, and increasingly worked to strengthen their international presence.

Baring Brothers *(investment bank)*

The British bank dates from 1763, when it

was founded by Francis Baring (1740-1810), the grandson of a Lutheran pastor from Bremen, Germany, and his brother John Baring (1730-1816), as the John & Francis Baring Co., acting initially as merchants trading internationally in commodities. In 1801 the name became Sir Francis Baring & Co., and Baring Brothers & Co. from 1807. The bank weathered a liquidity crisis in 1890, but a century later went into administration in 1995 when its leading trader in Singapore, Nicholas Leeson, lost around £250 million of its assets in unauthorized transactions. It resumed trading later that year when it was acquired for just £1 by a Dutch company, ING (Internationale Nederlanden Groep), now ING Barings.

Barker & Dobson *(confectioners)*

The British company's logo shows a tête-à-tête between a bonneted young lady and a handsome young man, together with the company name and the date 1834. This summarizes the founding of the firm, for the young lady is Miss Dobson, the young man is Mr. Barker, and the year is the one in which the couple married and went to Dublin for their honeymoon. They intended to settle in London on their return, but as their ship was making its way up the Mersey into Liverpool, they decided instead to set up home in that city. They opened a small candy store in Paradise Street, making a modest living from their sales. Towards the end of the century, the Dobsons moved to another shop in Hope Street, where they began to make their own candy, and a few years later the business moved again to larger premises in Whitefield Road, outside the city center, where the company remained until the 1980s, when it moved to Bury, near Manchester.

Barker's *(department store)*

The former British department store, in Kensington High Street, London, was founded as a small drapery shop in 1870 by John Barker (1840-1914), formerly a salesman employed by William Whiteley at his emporium in Westbourne Grove (*see* **Whiteley's**). Almost from the start, Barker had envisaged expanding his shop into a large store that would sell a wide range of goods. He therefore seized every opportunity to acquire new premises, and by 1880 was trading in 15 shops in Kensington High

Street and Ball Street. The single building that housed John Barker's famous department store was constructed in the early years of the 20th century, and is now a leading **House of Fraser** store.

Barnes & Noble *(booksellers and publishers)*

The US company dates from 1873, when Charles M. Barnes set up a small book business in Wheaton, Illinois. In 1917 his son, William, went by train to New York, where he negotiated with G. Clifford Noble to form a partnership. That same year the two men opened the first Barnes & Noble bookstore. In 1932 the firm opened what would be its flagship store on Fifth Avenue, New York, and trade did well. Business later fell off, however, and in 1971 the faltering company was acquired by Leonard Riggio, who succeeded in turning the New York store into "The World's Largest Bookstore," housing 150,000 textbook and trade titles. In 1985 Barnes & Noble set up a publishing division, selling books by mail order, and other bookselling chains were subsequently acquired.

Baron *(cigarette-making machines)*

Bernhard Baron (1850-1929) was born in Brest-Litovsk, Russia, of French descent. At the age of 17, unable to speak a word of English, he emigrated to New York, where he worked in a tobacco factory for a few cents a week. Using some tobacco lent him by a factory foreman, he started to manufacture hand-made cigarettes. He then moved to New Haven, Connecticut, where he found customers for his wares among Yale students. After a spell of insolvency following the failure of a New York bank, Baron picked himself up and moved to Baltimore, where he began manufacturing cigars. Sales were good, and in 1890 a group of financiers persuaded him to join in a enterprise aimed at challenging the powerful tobacco trusts of the day. For the next five years, Baron was managaing director of the National Cigarette Tobacco Co. of New York. Meanwhile, in 1872, Baron had parented his first invention, a machine for making cigarettes with a tobacco cover, and in 1895 he visited England with the intention of selling the rights to his machinery. On arriving, however, Baron saw excellent opportunities to manufacture his cigarette-making machines himself, for rental to cigarette manufacturers, and he formed the Baron Cigarette Machine Co. Ltd. His machine did well, and was taken up by **Players**, who were keen to challenge **Wills** in the expanding market for machine-made cigarettes. Baron later sold his patent to the United Cigarette Machine Co. and decided to settle in England and make his own cigarettes, using his Baron machine and other patent machines of his own invention. His opportunity came with the formation of **Carreras** Ltd. in 1903, and the rest of Baron's career was devoted to that company.

Barratt *(shoes)*

The man behind the British company name is Arthur William Barratt (1877-1939), born in Northampton the son of a shoe machine operator and former silk weaver. The son followed in his father's footsteps, working part-time in the business from the age of ten, and nine years later becoming manager of his father's third shoe shop in Gold Street, Northampton. When his father's business failed in 1902, however, Arthur Barratt purchased it from him as a going concern, taking his elder brother David into partnership. Having successfully survived further financial difficulties, the company was eventually registered as W. Barratt & Co. Ltd. in 1907. Its head office is now in Bradford.

Bartholomew *(publishers)*

Noted for its maps and atlases, the Scottish publishing house was founded in 1826 by John Bartholomew (1805-1861), an Edinburgh engraver who had taken up the craft of his father. But whereas his father engraved artwork, John Bartholomew specialized in the engraving of maps, otherwise cartography, and while George Bartholomew worked for the firm of Lizars, John was freelance. He was thus in a position to build up a personal reputation, which he rapidly did after his initial apprenticeship. The year of 1826 is given as that of the company's founding because it was the year when John Bartholomew issued his first work, a Directory Plan for Edinburgh.

BASF *(chemicals and plastics)*

The world's biggest chemical company, with more than twice as many employees as **Dow** Chemical, the largest US chemical company, was founded in Mannheim, Baden-Württem-

berg, Germany, in 1865 as the Badische Anilin-und Soda-Fabrik ("Baden Aniline and Soda Factory"), giving the letters that form the present name, adopted in 1973. The principal founder was Friedrich Engelhorn (1821-1902), a former goldsmith and manufacturer of coal-tar dyes. From 1925 to 1945 it was part of **IG Farben**. It was then refounded in 1952 as one of the successor companies.

Baskin-Robbins *(ice cream)*

The names are those of two California brothers-in-law, Burton Baskin (1913-1967) and Irvine Robbins (b.1917). They first entered the ice-cream business in late 1945 and early 1946 respectively, when Chicago-born Baskin opened Burton's Ice Cream in Pasadena and Robbins launched the Snowbird Ice Cream store in nearby Glendale. The two became partners in 1947, and by the following year owned eight ice-cream stores. They then introduced a franchising plan that saw a total of 43 stores by the end of 1949, as yet all in California. They made their first move outside the state in 1959, and a year later the number of stores in the chain passed the 100 mark. In 1967 Baskin and Robbins sold their thriving empire of 500 stores to United Fruit (now **United Brands**).

Bass *(beer)*

The brand of British beer came about because William Bass (1717-1787), a carrier by trade, of Burton-on-Trent, decided in 1777 to make the goods that until then he had been carrying. He therefore transferred his carrier business to **Pickfords**, and set up his own brewery in Burton. The reputation of his beer soon became known, and his son, Michael Thomas Bass (1760-1827), subsequently developed a thriving export side to the business, especially in eastern Europe and Russia. The firm had the unique privilege of acquiring the first registered trademark, filed on January 1, 1876, and entered in the *Trade Marks Journal* of May 3, 1876, where it appeared in the form of the label on the bottle, with the words "Bass & Co.'s Pale Ale" and the well-known red triangle. The trademark is clearly visible on the bottles of beer in Manet's 1882 painting *The Bar at the Folies-Bergère*, the original of which is now in the Courtauld Institute Galleries, London. (A more appropriate repository would surely be the Bass Museum, Burton-on-Trent.) In 2000, Bass sold off its traditional brewing operations to the Belgian company Interbrew and the following year changed its name to Six Continents to denote its self-proclaimed global importance in the area of hotels, leisure, retail and branded drinks.

Bass (footwear)

Henry Bass (1843-1925), a cobbler from Wilton, Maine, began making shoes in 1876, his first product being a 14-inch-high farmer's shoe. This was followed by other utilitarian shoes such as the National Plow Shoe, Bass Guide Shoe, and Bass Best. Henry's sons, John and Willard, joined the business in the early 1900s, when it was adding moccasins to its line. The outcome was the famous **Weejuns**. In 1978 Bass was acquired by **Chesebrough-Pond's**.

Bassett (furniture)

John D. Bassett (1866-1965) began his career peddling the Appalachian oak lumber of his native Blue Ridge Mountains to furniture makers in Grand Rapids and other northern cities. He then decided that he could build tables and chairs equal to those of his clients, and that his proximity to the source of raw material would enable him to price them favorably. In 1902, together with three partners, he accordingly set up the Bassett Furniture Co., and his long life enabled him to see his company become the world's largest maker of wooden furniture.

Bassett (licorice candy)

George Bassett (1818-1886) was born in Derbyshire, England, the son of a woolcomber turned small landowner and farmer. His father died when he was only 12, and two years later it was another man, one George Smith, who put up the money to apprentice George to a Chesterfield confectioner and fruiterer, William Haslam. George spent seven years with him, plus another three years working for his employer. Then, probably in 1842, he bought a retail business of his own at 30 Church Street, Sheffield, specializing in candy and wines. By 1859 he was running a substantial confectionery works in Portland Street, Sheffield, making a wide range of toothsome candies. The famous "Liquorice Allsorts," however, did not

materialize until 1899. The story goes that one Charlie Thompson, a "Bassett Traveler," knocked over his individual sample boxes in the course of a "presentation" to a Leicester candy wholesaler. The buyer had not been much impressed with the individual selections but like the look of the "mix," with its varied shapes and colors. Bassetts decided to market them in this way and they soon caught on with the public. The firm has now merged with **Trebor**.

Bassett-Lowke (model railways and ships)

Wenman Joseph Bassett-Lowke (1877-1953) was born in Northampton, England, the son of an engineer and grandson of the founder in 1859 of Bassett & Sons, a boilermaking business. While apprenticed to his father's firm of J.T. Lowke & Sons, Bassett-Lowke became increasingly frustrated by the difficulties he experienced in obtaining the components he needed for his hobby of model-making. He therefore decided to manufacture them himself, and with the help of his father and a friend, Harry Franklin, as cashier, set up his own mail order business in the 1890s, issuing the first of his famous catalogs in 1899. From then on, his models of railroad, ships, and engineering equipment became world famous, with his customers, according to the *Daily Mail,* ranging "from small boys to oriental princes, from millionaires to kings."

BAT Industries (tobacco products)

The British conglomerate of this name was formed in 1976 in the merger of Tobacco Securities Trust (TST) with British-American Tobacco (BAT). The latter company was incorporated in 1902 to handle international trade in tobacco products, while TST was incorporated by BAT in 1928 as an investment trust. In the 1976 merger, TST changed its name to BAT Industries and the old BAT became a wholly owned subsidiary. In 1994 BAT Industries acquired American Tobacco (*see* **American Brands**).

Bata (footwear)

The company was founded in 1894 in the Czech town of Zlín by Tomáš Bata (1876-1932), which under his family grew into an almost self-sufficient factory community. On the founder's untimely death in an air crash, the business passed to his son, Thomas J. Bata, a Canadian citizen living in Ontario, where the company's international headquarters are located today. After World War II the Bata industries within Czechoslovakia were nationalized and renamed Svit.

Batchelor's *(foods)*

The British firm was founded in the 1890s by William Batchelor (1860-1913), a Sheffield tea salesman. Batchelor was particularly interested in packing tea effectively and cleanly, and on building up a successful business selling packets of tea bearing his name. He extended his packing principles to other products, notably dried peas, which until the early 20th century had been sold loose over the counter from sacks. In 1912, when he had become a city counselor, Batchelor devised a method of grading and packing good quality dried peas. His site for this operation was the basement of a Methodist chapel in Sheffield's Stanley Street. Sadly, William Batchelor died suddenly the following year at the age of 53 leaving a daughter barely out of her teens and two young sons, and it was they who built up the embryo business into the large food-producing concern it is today. The company's head office remains in Sheffield.

Bath Travel *(travel agents)*

The British company had its beginnings in a firm of estate agents (realtors) in Bournemouth, Hampshire, founded in the early 1920s as Allan & Bath. The latter name was that of Reginald Bath (d.1957), who in 1924 introduced a passenger shipping department to the business and who later set up a separate travel concern in Albert Road, Bournemouth. Bath became specially interested in Bermuda after escorting a party of vacationers there in the early 1950s, and liked the island so much that in 1953 he made his home there, handing over the company to his son Peter, founder of **Palmair Express**.

Batsford *(publishers)*

The British publishing house takes its name from Bradley Thomas Batsford (1821-1904), a Hertfordshire tailor's son, who after the death of his father in 1835 set out, aged 14, for London. There he obtained work in a Leicester Square bookshop run by his cousins, the Bick-

ers family. He was formally apprenticed to Henry Bickers at age 16. In 1843, aged 21, he married his cousin, Letitia Bickers, and opened a bookshop of his own in High Holborn, at first selling mainly general and medical books. The present company dates its founding from the latter year, although it was not until 1874 that Batsford published his first book, J.K. Colling's *English Mediæval Foliage and Coloured Decoration*. In 1999 the firm was acquired by the **Chrysalis** Group.

Bausch & Lomb *(optical instruments)*

In 1849, Henry Lomb (1828-1908), born in Burghaun, Germany, immigrated to Rochester, New York, and several years later invested his meager savings in an eyeglass business started in 1853 by John Bausch (1830-1925). The young partners had to work hard to keep their enterprise solvent, even repairing windows for a while, but business then began to pick up and in 1866 Bausch and Lomb enjoyed considerable success making optical instruments from vulcanite. In 1875 they began the production of microscopes, and later became the main supplier of lenses for **Eastman Kodak**. At the time of Lomb's death, the firm was producing over 20 million lenses annually, making it the largest company of its kind in the world. *See also* (1) **Luxottica**; (2) **Ray-Ban**.

Baxter's *(soups)*

The Scottish Highland business of W.A. Baxter & Sons, acclaimed for its soups, had its beginnings in 1868 when George Baxter opened a grocery shop in Fochabers, Morayshire. His wife Margaret made jams and jellies in the back of the shop, and they soon became popular with visitors. The expansion into soups was the work of Baxter's son, William Alexander Baxter (d.1973), who together with his wife, Ethel, introduced a whole range of new recipes and products, among them "Cock-a-Leekie," "Poacher's Broth," and the famous "Royal Game Soup." His is thus the name borne by the firm today. His own son, Gordon Baxter (b.1918), began his career developing explosives for **ICI** but returned to the family business as production director in 1946, becoming managing director the following year and chairman in 1973. The firm, still in Fochabers, is now run by Gordon's daughter, Audrey (b.1961).

Bayer *(chemicals and pharmaceuticals)*

The German company was founded in 1863 as Friedr. Bayer et comp. by Friedrich Bayer (1825-1880), a chemical salesman who had started a dye works at Elberfeld in 1850. In 1912 the chemist Carl Duisberg (1861-1935) became Bayer's general director and initiated the move that resulted in the consolidation of Germany's chemical industries as **IG Farben** in 1925. An independent Bayer was reconstituted in 1951 as Farbenfabriken Bayer Aktiengesellschaft and the current name, Bayer AG, was adopted in 1972.

BBD&O *(advertising agency)*

The American advertising agency, in full Batten, Barton, Durstine & Osborne, had its beginnings in the firm of Barton, Durstine & Osborne, formed in 1919 by Bruce F. Barton, Roy S. Durstine, and Alex F. Osborne. In 1928 their business merged with the older George Batten & Co. to become the fourth largest and the best-known advertising agency in the country.

Beale's *(department store)*

The Bournemouth, England, department store owes its name to John Elmes Beale (1848-1928), the Dorset-born son of a ship's captain who was lost at sea when the boy was only a few years old. After an apprenticeship with a Weymouth draper, John Beale served for eight years in a draper's shop in that town before deciding that it was time for him to set up on his own. In 1881 he moved to Bournemouth and rented a shop in a terrace close to Old Christchurch Road, near the commercially attractive Bournemouth Arcade. By the early years of the 20th century, with Beale now mayor of Bournemouth, something like the present store had already opened on its central site, and by the time of his death the family business reportedly employed a staff of 700.

Beamish *(beer)*

The Irish brewery is named for William Beamish, one of two Scottish-Irish Protestant landowners who exported local butter and beef and who became involved in brewing in 1792. The firm, based in Dublin, is now part of the Scottish **Courage** group.

Bean, L.L *see* **L. L. Bean**

Beanie Babies *(toys)*

The soft, bean-filled toys were launched in 1994 by the American toymaker H. Ty Warner (b.1944). They exist in about 200 different types of animals and characters and soon became an all-consuming craze for collectors, first in the USA, then in the UK. Each type has a different name, such as Quackers the Duck, Chilly the Polar Bear and Waddle the Penguin, and collectors attended regular Beanie Fairs or traded their toys on the Internet. In 1999 Walker halted production for three months until customers "voted" to replace Beanies on the shelves. They returned with a new white bear called The Beginning.

Beatrice *(dairy products)*

The US company was started in 1894 by George E. Haskell (d.1919) and William W. Bosworth, who formed a partnership in Beatrice, Nebraska, adopting the town's name for their enterprise. They bought butter, eggs, and poultry from farmers, graded them, and shipped them. They then set up skimming stations where farmers could deliver their milk to have the cream separated off, but when this did not produce enought cream, supplied the farmers with hand cream separators on credit. The Beatrice Creamery did so well that by 1899 they were churning over 900,000 pounds of butter a year. They called their butter "Meadow Gold," trademarked the name in 1901, and later used it on other products. In World War II Beatrice moved into nondairy products such as candy, snack foods, and soft drinks.

Beazer *(houses)*

British housebuilders C.H. Beazer (Holdings) plc take their name from Cyril Henry George Beazer (d.1983). His son, Brian Cyril Beazley (b.1935), joined the company in 1958 and became chief executive on the death of his father. In 2001 Beazer was taken over by their great rivals, **Persimmon**.

Bechstein *(pianos)*

The name is that of Friedrich Wilhelm Carl Bechstein (1826-1900), born in Gotha, Germany, who after working in piano factories in Germany, France, and England, founded his own firm in Berlin in 1853. His first grand piano was inaugurated in 1856 by Hans von Bülow with a performance of Liszt's B minor sonata. The Bechstein Hall in London, England, was built in 1901 as a recital hall but in 1917 renamed the Wigmore Hall after the street in which it stands.

Bechtel *(construction and engineering)*

The US company, famous for its giant-sized projects, notably power plants and pipelines, takes its name from Warren A. Bechtel (d. 1933), who left his Kansas ranch in 1898 and set out with his team of mules to grade a stretch of railroad in Oklahoma. He followed the line to Oakland, California, where he built up contracts for railroad construction and for new enterprises such as irrigation canals and pipelines. Together with his three sons, Warren, Jr., Steve, and Kenneth, he finally incorporated the company in 1925, by which time it was one of the largest construction concerns in the West. In 1931 Bechtel organized a consortium of six companies to build Hoover Dam, the biggest in history.

Beck's *(beer)*

The German beer, one of the most familiar on the international market, dates from 1874, when the Beck family began brewing in the northern port of Bremen. In 1917 the brewery merged with Saint Pauli, its main export rival in Bremen. The latter's Saint Pauli Girl brew, with a picture of a barmaid on the label, is popular in the USA.

Beecham *(pharmaceuticals)*

The English founder of the company that gave the world "Beecham's Pills" was Thomas Beecham (1820-1907), born in Curbridge, Oxfordshire, the son of a farm laborer. At the age of eight, Thomas worked as a shepherd. As he grew older he became interested in the medical properties of herbs, and before he was out of his teens was making herbal remedies for animals and humans and selling them at Oxfordshire markets. In 1842 he moved to Wigan, Lancashire, where he became established as a "Chemist, Druggist and Tea Dealer," with a stock that soon included the famous Pills. In 1858 he moved to the new township of St. Helens, where in 1866 he was joined by his son Joseph (1848-1916), and together they built up a good overseas market. The original firm of Beechams Pills Ltd. became the Beecham Group Ltd. in 1945. In medicinal terms, "Beecham's

Pills" are a brand name for aloin (a stimulant laxative), "Beecham's Coughcaps" for dextromethorphan (a cough suppressant), and "Beecham's Powders," introduced in 1926, for paracetamol (an analgesic) and pseudoephedrine (a decongestant). *See also* **SmithKline Beecham**.

Beechcraft *(aircraft)*

In 1923, Walter H. Beech (1892-1950), a World War I army veteran, became general manager of the Swallow Airplane Co. in Wichita, Kansas. After helping the firm lead the way in the light aircraft field, Beech resigned in 1925 to pursue his own design projects. He then joined with Clyde **Cessna** and Lloyd Stearman to form the Travel Air Manufacturing Co., but the partnership was marred by disputes over aircraft design. Beech resigned in 1932 and formed the Beech Aircraft Company, this time taking his wife, Olive Ann Beech (1903-1993), as a more congenial partner. With Olive as secretary-treasurer and Walter as president, the firm introduced its famous Beechcraft biplane in 1934. Four years later its sales exceeded $1 million, and the plane dominated the general aviation market in its class. Following Walter's untimely death, control of the company passed to Olive, who became both president and chairwoman. In 1980 Beechcraft was bought out by **Raytheon**.

Beefeater *(gin)*

The British firm of distillers was apparently founded in London in 1820, although records for the early years are rather vague. In 1898, following the death of **James Burrough**, two of his three sons formed the business into a company and sought a trademark that was symbolic of London and synonymous with tradition, prestige, and quality. They chose "Beefeater," the popular name of a member of the Yeomen Warders of the Tower of London, so called from the former nickname for a well-fed servant. The name was entered in the *Trade Marks Journal* of September 10, 1958.

Beer Seller *(drinks distributor)*

When in 1987 British banker Paul Horsley decided he wanted a change of scene, he bought the Somerset soft-drinks maker Dawes Ltd., founded in 1888, for £125,000. He changed the family name to a pleasantly punning "The Beer

Seller" and disposed of the manufacturing side to concentrate on distributing drinks. In 2000 the flourishing enterprise was bought by the drinks giant **Bulmer**.

Beetle *(automobiles)*

The nickname for the **Volkswagen** saloon car first in production after World War II was suggested by the vehicle's compact, rounded body. The name translated German *Käfer*, additionally a word for an attractive girl or young woman, something like English "chick." A "new look" Beetle was launched in 1999. Volkswagen entered the name in the US Patent Office *Official Gazette* of May 16, 1972.

Beetle *(synthetic resin)*

The first white molding powder in the world was produced under this name in 1925 by tbe British Cyanides Company, a concern that in 1936 became British Industrial Plastics and that in 1961 was acquired by Turner & Newall. The name was entered in the *Trade Marks Journal* of June 24, 1931. The following account is given in Cyril S. Dingley, *The Story of B.I.P.* (1963):

> For years it had been the custom for chemical manufacturers to attach a trade mark to their products. The British Cyanides Company Limited used a beetle to designate chemicals of its own make and, as far as one can recollect, the choice fell on this insect as being a symbol of activity and industry. All the cases of cyanide, the barrels of prussiates of soda and potash had the outline of a beetle with the words 'Beetle Brand—registered' stencilled upon them.
>
> For the Wembley Exhibition [1925] all exhibitors has small adhesive labels which bore the stand number and advertised the Exhibition. These were used on outgoing correspondence. The British Cyanides Company Limited had designed attractive coloured labels which carried a beetle as the Company's trade mark.
>
> At the Exhibition the demand for samples of the new colourless resin was great. These were sent out in small glass bottles appropriately labelled and, by way of salesmanship, the portion of the exhibition label showing the beetle was also stuck on to the bottle. As a result, the customers often referred to the material as 'that Beetle resin of yours'.
>
> The name 'Beetle' so took root that the Company saw no advantage in calling it by any other name. Thus 'Beetle' the resin became, and 'Beetle' it remained; the moulding powders subsequently made from it, and the many other types of resins, all became 'Beetle', too.

Tableware made from Beetle molding powders in 1926 was named "Beatl", ostensibly meaning "beat all" but actually altered from "Beetle" to avoid an undesirable association with the insect. Later the Streetly Manufacturing Co. Ltd., acquired by the British Cyanides Company in 1929, took up the molding of tableware for **Woolworths** and registered the name "Beetleware" for this.

Beiersdorf *(healthcare and cosmetic products)*

The German company was founded in Hamburg in 1882 by Paul C. Beiersdorf, the inventor of a new method of manufacturing medical adhesive dressings. In 1890 the laboratory he had set up was purchased by Dr. Oskar Troplowitz, who in 1911 introduced the firm's flagship product, **Nivea**. (Beiersdorf later set up a factory in England to make this hand cream, diplomatically changing their name in World War II to Herts Pharmaceuticals Ltd.) In 2000 Beiersdorf bought British **Elastoplast**. *See also* (1) **Eucerin**; (2) **Tesa**.

Bejam *(frozen food centers)*

The origins of the British firm lie with the businessman John Apthorp (b.1935), who in the mid-1960s bought a home freezer and installed it in his kitchen. Freezers were rare in private homes then, and were mostly found in commercial premises, such as hotels. Apthorp filled the freezer full of market produce and joints of meat, and offered to store his neighbors' food there as well. In 1968, Apthorp realized that there must be a better way of packaging food for freezer storage. He therefore went to the United States to study methods of preparing frozen foods. Back in England a few months later, he set up the firm of Bejam in an old banana warehouse in Burnt Oak, Middlesex, offering his customers a wide range of frozen products from two cold stores. Demand increased, and he soon moved his operation to the High Street, setting up frozen food centers in different towns. (Seeing the unfamiliar large white freezers, many people at first mistook them for **Laundromats**.) "Bejam" represents John Apthorp's genuine "freezer food family": the letters *ja* are his initials, while *B* is Brian his brother, *e* is Eric his father, and *m* is both Mildred (Millie) his mother and Marion his sister. The name was entered in the *Trade*

Marks Journal of April 16, 1975. In 1989 Bejam was acquired by **Iceland**.

Bekins *(movers and carriers)*

The American company dates from 1891, when Martin and John Bekins set up a moving business in Sioux City, Iowa. In 1895 they transferred their enterprise to Los Angeles, growing as the state of California grew. The firm soon became the state's largest mover and storer of household goods, and by the 1980s had a fleet of around 5,000 vehicles making an average of 1,000 moves a day.

Bel Paese *(cheese)*

As its name implies, the rich, white, mild, creamy cheese was originally made in Italy, where it was introduced in the north of the country in 1906 by Egidio **Galbani**. The name means "beautiful country," and although this obviously applies to the northern Italian landscape, the actual source was the title of a popular book describing it, *Il bel paese* (1875), by the Italian cleric and geologist Antonio Stoppani (1824-1891). The cheese is sold in small wheel shapes with a distinctive wrapper featuring the head of the Abbot Stoppani and a map of Italy. (The Bel Paese made in the USA has what appears to be the same wrapper but closer inspection reveals the map to be of the Americas.)

Bell *(aircraft)*

The American aircraft take their name from Lawrence Dale Bell (1894-1956), born in Mentone, Indiana, the son of a lumber mill operator. When Bell was 13, his family moved to Santa Monica, California, where after graduating from high school he secured his first job in aviation as an aircraft mechanic for his brother, George E. Bell, and Lincoln Beachey. In 1914 Bell took up a mechanic's position in the Glenn L. Martin Aircraft Company in Santa Ana, California, where he rapidly rose to become superintendent at the young age of 20. He left Martin Aircraft in 1925 and three years later was offered the post of sales manager with Consolidated Aircraft Corporation in Buffalo, New York. Bell was increasingly keen to set up his own company, and finally did so on July 10, 1935, when with two partners, Ray Whitman and Bob Woods, he incorporated the Bell Aircraft Corporation. The company designed and

built its first aircraft, the twin-engine *Airacuda*, in 1938.

Bell & Howell *(photographic equipment)*

The two Americans behind the name are Donald J. Bell (1869-1934) and Albert Summers Howell (1879-1951), who first met at the Crary Machine Works in Chicago in 1905. Bell, born in Jamestown, Ohio, in 1869, had begun his career as a chief usher at the Schiller Theatre, Chicago, where he had come in 1896. He soon rose from usher to projectionist at this same movie theater. His interest in the construction and design of film projectors took him to the Crary Machine Works, where projector parts were manufactured. Meanwhile, Howell had been born a farmer's son near West Branch, Michigan, in 1879. His earliest work involved the repair and maintenance of farm and lumbering machinery. In 1895 his family moved to Chicago, where one of his many jobs was with a firm that built and repaired projectors. This particular link explains his visit to the Crary Machine Works, which gave him the knowhow to produce his first patent, a framing device for projectors. Having made each other's acquaintance, Bell and Howell pooled their different talents and formed their new company, hitching their star to the rising movie industry. Bell, the dominant partner of the two, was chairman. Howell, with his practical flair, was secretary. The two worked together for ten years after which, as a result of Bell's increasing absences on business, Howell continued alone until his death.

Bell Laboratories *see* Bell System

Bell Punch *(ticket recording punch)*

The Bell Punch Company was set up in Britain in the early 1880s to manufacture a device for recording tickets issued by bus conductors. A ticket was inserted into the machine, known as a "pistol punch," which rang a bell as it punched in the particular destination stage. The punch was first used by the London Road Car Company, then from 1891 by the London General Omnibus Company.

Bell System *(telephones)*

The former American telephone system, governed by **AT&T** and including **Western Electric** and Bell Laboratories, takes its name from Alexander Graham Bell (1847-1922), Scottish-born American inventor of the telephone in 1876 and founder in 1877 of the Bell Telephone Company, which then began a race with **Western Union** to develop the country's telephone service. The Bell company underwent a number of reorganizations and renamings over the years from 1875 to 1900, and at first AT&T was a subsidiary building long lines. In 1900 it became the central organization of the Bell System, and in 1925 Bell Telephone Laboratories was incorporated as as a research and development company. Bell System was dismantled in 1983, when the 22 operating companies were divested by AT&T under court order. *See also* (1) **Lucent**; (2) **NCR**.

Bellanca *(aircraft)*

The name is that of Giuseppe Mario Bellanca (1886-1960), born in Sciacca, Sicily, the son of a flour mill owner. Bellanca's interest in aviation emerged while attending school in Milan, and during his third year, with help from friends, he designed and built his first aircraft. In 1911 Bellanca immigrated with his family to Brooklyn, New York, where he built another aircraft and taught himself to fly. In 1912 Bellanca incorporated the Bellanca Aeroplane Company and Flying School, where his career as an aircraft manufacturer literally took off. A second Bellanca Aircraft Company was formed in Farmingdale, Long Island, in 1924.

Belling *(stoves)*

Charles Reginald Belling (1884-1965) was a Cornish-born Englishman who began his career as an electrical apprentice with the firm of **Crompton** in Chelmsford, Essex. After three years he joined **Ediswan** at Ponders End, Middlesex, where he was in charge of the department that produced arc lamps, transformers, and electric heaters. After a further three years, he felt ambitious enough to set up on his own as a manufacturer of electric heaters, and to this end acquired an empty shed in Lancaster Road, Enfield, where with a former Ediswan colleague and a local boy he made a start one Monday morning in 1912. Later that year, Belling patented his new invention, a resistance wire wound round a strip of fireclay to give out heat when a current was passed through it. This was the first firebar, and when six such firebars were attached to a cast-iron frame with heating con-

trol knobs, the result was marketed as the "Standard Belling Fire." It was also the debut of the company of Belling & Co. Belling then turned his attention to other types of heaters and cookers. The "Modernette" cooker appeared in 1919, and the familiar "Baby Belling" cooker in 1929.

Bell's *(whisky)*

Bell's goes back to 1825, when Thomas Sandeman, a Scottish wine and whisky merchant, opened a shop in Kirkgate, Perth. In due course he was joined by James Roy, and in 1851 Arthur Bell entered the firm. By 1865 Bell had gained control of the business and in 1895, when he took his two sons into partnership, the firm became known as Arthur Bell & Sons. Bell died in 1900, and he was succeeded by Arthur Kinmont Bell, who became chairman and managing director in 1922, when the firm was converted to a limited company. Since 1942, when Arthur Kinmont Bell died, there has been no Bell on the board. The company's head office remains in Perth today. The name "Bell's Extra Special Old Scotch Whisky Estd. Perth 1825" accompanied by the signature "Arthur Bell & Sons" was entered in the *Trade Marks Journal* of March 15, 1995.

Ben & Jerry's *(ice cream)*

The creators of such delights as "Chunky Monkey," "Cherry Garcia" (a punning tribute to rock musician Jerry Garcia), "Chubby Hubby," and "Wavy Gravy" are Bennett R. "Ben" Cohen (b.1950) and Jerry Greenfield (b.1951), who launched their premium ice cream business in 1978 in a converted gas station in Burlington, Vermont. By 1990 they had five owned and 80 franchised outlets in 18 states. Company mythology has the folksy partners starting with a $5.00 mail-order course in ice-cream making from Pennsylvania State University and a rock-salt ice cream machine. In 2000 Ben & Jerry's was taken over by **Unilever**.

Bendicks *(chocolates)*

The British firm of Bendicks (Mayfair) Ltd., noted for its peppermint chocolates, was founded in the late 1920s by a Colonel *Ben*son and a Mr. *Dick*son. The elements from the two names were perhaps intentionally combined to suggest the aristocratic English name Bentinck, that of the dukes and earls of Portland. The firm is actually based in Winchester, Hampshire, but has "Mayfair" in its official name as another prestigious association, that of the fashionable and opulent London district of Mayfair. The recipe for the firm's noted chocolate mints was apparently created by Benson's sister-in-law. The company is now owned by the German-based confectionery manufacturer August Stork KG.

Bendix *(automotive components)*

The American corporation was founded in 1924 to make automobile brake systems by the inventor and industrialist Vincent Bendix (1881-1945), who in 1907 had organized the Bendix Company of Chicago to manufacture automobiles. Over 7,000 were produced but the company failed in 1909 and Bendix concentrated on developing the starter drive instead. Bendix himself was the son of a Swedish Methodist minister whose original family name was Bengtson.

Benedictine *(liqueur)*

The liqueur of brandy and herbs is said to have been originally made in the early 16th century by Dom Bernardo Vincelli, an Italian monk who lived in the Benedictine abbey at Fécamp, northern France. In 1862 a local merchant, Alexandre Le Grand, discovered the recipe among some old manuscripts and set to work to re-create the elixir. A year later, he announced that his efforts had met with success, and began to make the liqueur commercially, calling it "Bénédictine" after its creator and reinforcing its ecclesiastical origins by printing "DOM" (both for Dom Vincelli and as the Latin abbreviation of *Deo Optimo Maximo*, "To God, the best, the greatest") on its label.

Benelli *(motorcycles)*

The Italian make of motorcycle takes its name from the six Benelli brothers, Tonino, Francesco, Giovanni, Giuseppe, Filippo, and Gino, who founded their firm in Pesaro in 1911. Tonino Benelli, the team's star rider, was killed in an accident in 1937 after retiring from racing. Financial troubles forced the Benelli family to sell up in 1971. The name remained under their new owner, Alessandro **De Tomaso**, but never regained its former glory.

Benetton *(fashionwear)*

The many Benetton fashion shops found in Britain and elsewhere developed from the business built up in Italy after World War II by the children of Leone Benetton, a truck driver from Treviso, near Venice, who died of malaria in 1946. His eldest son, Luciano (b.1935), quit school at age 14 to work in a clothing store, while the youngest child, 13-year-old Giuliana, worked in a garment shop, knitting sweaters by night to sell to individual customers. Her sweaters sold so well that her brothers pooled their money to buy her a secondhand knitting machine. Orders started coming in from knitwear shops, and by 1965 the four siblings (Luciano, Carlo, Gilberto, and Giuliana) had enough money to start a firm of their own. The company remained exclusively Italian until 1982, when expansion began into other countries both in and beyond Europe and extended to interests in property, Formula One racing, and motorway trading. The business remains a family concern, and a famous "United Colors of Benetton" ad showed all 15 Benetton family members: Christian, Carlo, Massimo, Andrea, Sabrina, Gilberto, Barbara, Carlo, Giuliana, Paola, Daniela, Mauro, president Luciano, Rossella, and Alessandro. In 2001, in a controversial takeover, Benetton joined forces with **Pirelli** to acquire **Olivetti** and hence telecommunications giant Telecom Italia, in which Olivetti held the controlling stake.

Ben-Gay *(ointment)*

One day in 1898, on a trip to Europe, Thomas Leeming, Jr., the co-owner of a small New York pharmaceutical firm, paid a visit to the noted French pharmacist Jules Bengué. Leeming left Bengué's office with the American rights to manufacture several of the Frenchman's preparations, including an analgesic pain reliever containing menthol, salicylate of methyl, and lanolin. He tried to market it as "Baume Bengué" ("Bengué Balm"), but sales were slow until he simplified the doctor's name as "Ben-Gay." The balm quickly found a place on drugstore shelves, helping Leeming's company emerge as a leader in its field. Ben-Gay liniment was subsequently acquired by **Pfizer**.

Benn *(publishers)*

The British publishing house of Benn Brothers was founded in 1880 by John Williams

Benn (1850-1922), a former commercial traveler for a furniture company, to publish his new trade journal, the *Cabinet Maker*. His subsequent career was in politics, and he admitted that although his journal was the cornerstone of the business, "the bricks for the House that Benn built have been well and truly laid by my eldest son." This was Ernest John Pickstone Benn (1875-1954), who quit school at 15 and went to work for his father, spending six years selling advertising space in the *Cabinet Maker*, and eventually becoming its manager. In 1900 Ernest Benn took over the *Hardware Trade Journal* as well, buying the periodical from the printers. In 1923 Sir Ernest Benn, as he now was, started an independent book publishing company, Ernest Benn Ltd, which became a direct subsidiary of Benn Brothers in the 1930s. Benn Brothers itself was built into one of the leading postwar publishers of trade and technical magazines by Sir Ernest's second son, Glanvill Benn (1905-2000), who for a short time in the 1950s was chairman of both Ernest Benn and Benn Brothers.

Benson & Hedges *(tobacco)*

Information on the two Englishmen behind the familiar name is rather sparse. It is known, however, that Richard Benson and William Hedges opened a small tobacconist's and gift shop at 13 Old Bond Street, London, in 1873, sharing the premises with Truefitt's, the court hairdresser. Until that time, tobacco had been sold by weight. Mr. Benson and Mr. Hedges decided that their tobacco should be prepared beforehand as a blend or mixture and dispensed in a sealed tin. In this way the tobacco would remain fresh for the smoker. In 1885 Richard Benson left the partnership, and William Hedges continued alone until his son Alfred was old enough to take over in turn. The shop remains at 13 Old Bond Street, although the manufacture of cigarettes was transferred from the small premises to a new factory elsewhere at the end of World War I.

Bentalls *(department store)*

The British store in Kingston upon Thames, Surrey, originated from the draper's shop run at 31 Clarence Street by Frank Bentall (1843-1923), a local man. Bentall was both energetic and enterprising, and under his management the shop expanded from its initial small premises with a staff of just five in 1867, to half a dozen shops, subsequently unified in a single department store, with a staff of over 100 when Bentall retired in 1909. His son Leonard (d. 1942) then took over, expanding the premises further and converting the business into a private limited company in 1925.

Bentley *(automobiles)*

The prestigious British car takes its name from Walter Owen Bentley (1888-1971), born in London into a family with a Yorkshire background. On quitting school, young Walter became a railroad apprentice in Doncaster, thus achieving a childhood ambition. He soon decided, however, that railroads offered little prospects of promotion, so turned his attention to the internal combustion engine, and to driving race cars. In 1912, Bentley joined forces with his brother to run the London agency of three French car makes, Buchet, La Licorne, and Doriot, Flandrin et Parant (the DFP). The premises were at New Street Mews, off Upper Baker Street, and seven years later, after World War I, the first engine designed by Bentley roared into life. The first complete Bentley car soon followed, undergoing its road tests in January 1920. Full-time production then started in Cricklewood, and the age of the "Bentley Boys" was born, that of the rip-roaring, scarf-flying young men who drove Bentley's cars. In 1931, to Bentley's chagrin, the company was bought by its great rival, **Rolls-Royce**, and in 1935, his contract expired, Bentley moved to **Lagonda**.

Benz *see* **Mercedes-Benz**

Benzedrine *(stimulant drug)*

The proprietary name for amphetamine was entered by Smith, Kline & French (now **SmithKline Beecham**), of Philadelphia, Pennsylvania, in the *Trade Marks Journal* of May 22, 1935 for: "A medicated preparation consisting of benzyl-methyl-carbinamine, oil of lavender and menthol." The first part of the name is based on "benzyl," while the rest is from "ephedrine," an alkaloid drug used to relieve hay fever, asthma, etc.

Beretta *(firearms)*

The Italian company traces its origins to Bartolomeo Beretta, a *maestro da canne* (master gun-barrel maker) for the republic of Venice as early as 1526. His son Giovannino inherited his father's work, but the present firm was founded commercially in 1680 by Pietro Beretta. The business has since been handed down in an unbroken chain from father to son, so that in the late 20th century it was in the hands of Pier Beretta (1906-1993), who inherited control of the company in 1957. In 1988, **General Motors** adopted the Beretta name for one of its **Chevrolet** models. The Berettas saw this as an insult to the family name, and hit the automotive giant with a $250 million trademark infringement lawsuit. Within months, GM appeased Beretta and settled the matter by donating $500,000 to the family's Foundation for Cancer Rearch and Treatment in exchange for being allowed to continue using the name on its cars. The full formal name of the Italian company is Fabbrica d'Armi Pietro Beretta SpA ("Pietro Beretta Arms Works Limited"), and its headquarters are at Gardone Val Trompia, near Milan.

Bergan (rucksacks)

The name is sometimes used loosely for any rucksack on a frame, but properly it is that of the original manufacturing company. It was entered by Sverre Young of Christiania (now Oslo), Norway, in the US Patent Office *Official Gazette* of June 19, 1923, with a claim of use since 1911. The name itself suggests Germanic *berg*, "mountain," or the well-known Norwegian seaport of Bergen.

Bergdorf Goodman (fashion store)

The New York City store began its life as Bergdorf and Voight, a ladies' tailoring and fur shop opened on Fifth Avenue in 1894 by a Frenchman, Herman Bergdorf, and Herman Voight, his American business partner. In 1901 the store became Bergdorf and Goodman, the latter being Edwin Goodman (1878-1953), who bought out Bergdorf but kept the name. Bergdorf subsequently retired to France. In 1927 Goodman was joined by his son Andrew (1907-1993), who became president of the company in 1951 and on the death of his father two years later sole owner and chairman. In 1955 Goodman opened the phenomenally successful Miss Bergdorf Goodman shop, and in 1966 he added "Bigi" (from "BG") as a contemporary "mod" department. In 1967 Bergdorf Goodman began a major expansion which nearly doubled the store's size. Two years later,

it was the only large high-fashion specialty store in the United States to remain privately and independently owned. In 1972, however, Goodman sold the company to Los-Angeles-based **Broadway-Hale** and in 1987 it passed to the **Neiman-Marcus** Group.

Berger (paint)

The British company that eventually became Berger, Jenson & Nicholson takes its primary name from Lewis Berger, a German color chemist from Frankfurt, who in 1760 set up a business manufacturing dry pigments in Shadwell, London. In 1780 he moved to Homerton, Hackney, London, and by 1790 was producing 19 colors. The business was subsequently managed by Berger's three sons and two grandsons, and in 1879 was incorporated as Lewis Berger & Sons Ltd. In 1960 it merged with Jenson & Nicholson Ltd, a firm of coach-paint manufacturers founded in 1821, and adopted its longer name.

Berlei (women's underwear)

The Berlei story begins in Sydney, Australia, where in 1907 a Mr. Grover and a Miss Mobberly set up Grover & Co. to make corsets. In 1910 their business was taken over by Fred R. Burley, who soon started his own firm and in 1912, joined by his brother Arthur, formed a limited company. This expanded rapidly, becoming Berlei Ltd. in 1917, at the same time adopting a more "stylish" spelling of Fred's own name. Fred Burley subsequently went to England, and established Berlei (UK) Ltd. in 1919 as a subsidiary company with its head office in Slough, Berkshire. The name was entered in the *Trade Marks Journal* of February 23, 1955 for: "Corsets, corselettes, girdles (corsets), brassieres, bodices, panties and suspender belts."

Berlitz (language courses)

The name is that of the German-born American educator Maximilian D. Berlitz (1852-1921), who in 1878 pioneered a way of teaching foreign languages by the so-called "direct method," that is, entirely in the language being studied. Establishments where languages were taught in this way were known as the Berlitz Schools. In recent years the Berlitz name has been popularized by Charles Berlitz, Maximilian's grandson, who has written books on such arcane subjects as the Bermuda Triangle. From 1967, however, Charles Berlitz dissociated himself from his grandfather's Berlitz Schools.

Bermaline *(bread)*

The once popular make of so-called "fancy bread" has a name of uncertain origin. According to a former managing director's secretary, who had been with the makers since 1926, one John Montgomery, a Scot from the Hebrides, had sailed as a young man on commercial ships and had been impressed with a group of South Pacific islands called the Bermalinos. On his return to Glasgow, he needed a name for the malt loaf that was his specialty, and gave it that of the islands, setting up his business in 1868. But no such island name appears to exist, so maybe Montgomery misremembered it. Since 1972 the company has specialized in malting, rather than producing Bermaline bread. The Bermaline Mills themselves were set up in Haddington, East Lothian, Scotland.

Bernachon *(chocolates)*

The French firm of Bernachon et Fils, based in Lyon, owes its origin to Maurice ("Papa") Bernachon, who began his craft as a 14-year-old apprentice pâtissier. In 1955 he started his own business in the Cours Franklin Roosevelt, where it remains today, with a staff of 50 artisan *chocolatiers.*

Bernard Matthews *(meat products)*

The Norfolk, England, farmer who gained fame for his tasty turkeys began his career as a trainee auctioneer. Then one day in 1950, Bernard Matthews (b.1930) bought 12 turkey eggs and a paraffin incubator for £2.10s.0d. at a livestock auction. Three years later he had developed his hobby sufficiently to quit auctioneering and take up breeding turkeys fulltime. In 1955 he bought the company's present head office, Great Witchingham Hall, near Norwich, for £3,000. It was then a run-down but not quite derelict Elizabethan manor. It served well enough, however, for Matthews' new enterprise, enabling him to hatch the turkeys in the dining room, rear them in the bedrooms, and slaughter them in the kitchens. This rather unsalubrious state of affairs ended in 1958, when Matthews bought a disused airfield and erected turkey houses on the runways. In the 1970s Matthews began cutting up turkeys into individual portions. The turkey sausage arrived in 1980, closely followed by the "crispy-crumb" turkey steak and the awardwinning turkey "drummer," shaped like a drumstick.

Berni *(restaurants)*

The ultimate origin of the popular British steakhouses lies with Francesco Berni, an immigrant Italian who in the late 19th century opened a chain of temperance bars in England. He was joined in the business by his son Louis, although World War I forced most of the bars to close. In 1931 two of Louis' sons, Frank (1903-2000) and Aldo (1909-1997), opened their own restaurant in the High Street, Exeter. It paid its way, and by 1939 they had opened two more restaurants, one in Plymouth and another in Bristol. Then World War II once again halted business, and their Bristol premises were destroyed by fire. After the war they resumed their enterprise by buying Hort's, a famous restaurant in Broad Street, Bristol, and in 1948 Horts Restaurants Ltd. was floated as a public company. Marco, Louis' third son, had meanwhile branched out as an independent restaurateur. Aldo and Frank were aware that they needed a more distinctive image, and after a visit to the United States and an examination of American limited menu specialty eating houses, they decided to introduce the steak bar to the British public. The plan worked, with the first such bar opening at The Rummer restaurant, All Saints Lane, Bristol. Finally, in 1961, Horts Restaurants was renamed Berni Inns Ltd.

Be-Ro *(self-rising flour)*

Some time around 1880, Thomas Bell opened a grocery in Newcastle upon Tyne, England, where two of his top-selling products were "Bell's Royal" baking powder and self-rising flour. After the death of Edward VII in 1910, however, it was illegal to use "Royal" in a commercial name, so Thomas Bell & Son, as the business became, shortened their brand name to "Be-Ro." The first Be-Ro cookbook, designed to promote the novelty of self-rising flour, was produced in 1923 and is still available today.

Berol *(pencils)*

The man behind the name is Emil Berolzheimer, born in the Bavarian town of Fürth in 1862. From an early age, Emil helped out in his father's office at the Berolzheimer & Illfelder pencil factory, right next door to the family home. At the age of 16, Emil was sent by his father to work in a bank in Frankfurt. He did well there, and three years later moved to the large Banque de Paris in Brussels. Meanwhile, his father had moved to the United States and had set up a pencil factory there. In 1883, Emil was invited to come over and manage it. Although still only 21, Emil was wise for his years, and the business prospered, becoming the Eagle Pencil Company and, within a few years, the largest pencil factory in the world. The company subsequently developed into the Berol Corporation, and became well known for its "Venus" brand pencils.

Berry Bros. & Rudd *(wine and liquor merchants)*

The British firm began when George Berry, who had come from Exeter to London in 1803, took control of the firm of his grandfather, John Clark, at No. 3 St. James's Street. In 1920 Hugh Rudd, a member of an old East Anglian family with a wine business in Norwich, Norfolk, joined the firm after leaving the army, but his name did not appear in the title of the firm until 1940, when it became a limited company. The firm is best known for its **Cutty Sark** whisky.

Bert Grant's *(beer)*

Scottish-born Bert Grant gained fame as a leading American expert on hops and was a pioneer of micropubs and brewpubs in the USA. He founded the Yakima Malting and Malting Co. in Yakima, Washington, in 1982 and his portrait appears on all bottle neck labels.

Bertelsmann *(publishers)*

The German publishing house was founded in Gütersloh in 1835 by Carl Bertelsmann (1791-1850). It is the biggest mass media multinational in Europe and the second biggest in the world, with offices in over 30 countries. It gained a significant hold on the US market in 1987 when it acquired interests in **RCA** and **Doubleday**, and in 1994 gained control of **Ricordi**. In 1998 it acquired **Random House** and in 2000, following diversification into other areas, merged its television interests with **Pearson**.

Bertone *(automobile design)*

The Italian automobile-design company dates from 1912, when Giovanni Bertone founded a *carrozzeria* (body factory) in Turin. The firm produced models for such famous manufacturers as **Fiat**, **Alfa Romeo**, and **Lamborghini**, and was steered through its greatest era, from the 1950s, by Giovanni's son, Giuseppe "Nuccio" Bertone (1914-1997), regarded as one of the most influential figures in the car world.

Best *see* **Pabst**

Bestfoods *(food products)*

Until 1997 the American company was known as CPC International, after its original core business, Corn Products Co., founded in 1908. It owes its ultimate origin to Thomas Kingsford, who gave the name of **Kingsford's** corn starch. In 1899 the firm that he founded, T. Kingsford & Sons, merged with two competitors to become the United Starch Co. Further mergers led to the amalgamated Corn Products Co., which in 1958 acquired the Best Foods Co., known mainly for its own-brand mayonnaise and peanut butter, and this gave the name of the present concern.

Betacam *(videocameras)*

The cameras are produced by **Sony** and base their name on the earlier **Betamax** video format. The name was entered by Sony in the *Trade Marks Journal* of March 1, 1989.

Betamax *(videocassettes)*

The video format was introduced by **Sony** in the 1970s but soon lost out to **Matsushita**'s VHS (Video Home System). The name derives from Japanese *betabeta*, "all over" (not the Greek letter beta) and the abbreviation of "maximum," referring to the condensed format in which the signal was recorded. The name was entered in the US Patent Office *Official Gazette* of September 2, 1975, with a note of first use on October 9, 1974, and in the *Trade Marks Journal* of January 19, 1977.

Bethlehem *(steel)*

The Bethlehem Steel Corporation was first incorporated on December 10, 1904, for the purpose of consolidating Bethlehem Steel Company (of Pennsylvania), the Union Iron Works, and various smaller manufacturing and shipbuilding companies. It traces its history to 1857, when a group of railroaders and investors of the city of Bethlehem, Pennsylvania, founded the Saucona Iron Company to make railroad rails. In 1899 the facilities were acquired by a newly formed enterprise, the Bethlehem Steel Company. The major founder of the corporation was Charles M. Schwab (1862-1939), who bought control of the Bethlehem Steel Company in 1901 and who later launched Bethlehem Steel Corporation.

Bettendorf *(railroad cars)*

William Peter Bettendorf (1857-1910) was born in Mendota, Illinois, the son of a schoolteacher. After a rudimentary education, mainly resulting from the moves made by his family, he obtained a position in 1872 or 1873 as an apprentice machinist for a plow-manufacturing company in Peru, Illinois. This spurred Bettendorf to study mechanical engineering, and in 1878 he invented a sulky plow, that is, a plow with wheels and a seat for the driver. Further inventions followed, including new types of wheels for use in wagons and other farm vehicles, until in 1886 he and his brother, Joseph William Bettendorf, founded their own wheelmaking business in Davenport, Iowa, as the Bettendorf Metal Wheel Company. In 1895 the Bettendorf Axle Company was incorporated, and the manufacture of parts for rolling stock eventually led to the production of whole railway cars. Bettendorf's final years were spent working and living in the little city in Iowa, formerly Gilbert, that in 1903 was renamed after him.

Betty Crocker *(baking products)*

When "Gold Medal" flour became a **General Mills** product, it was advertised by means of a picture puzzle in a national magazine. More than 30,000 people sent in their solutions, with some women adding everyday questions on home baking, such as "How do you make a single-crust cherry pie?" The advertising staff did their best to answer such queries, sending each writer a personal reply on the lines of: "In answer to your inquiry about a single-crust cherry pie, I suggest you try [etc.]. Sincerely," But sincerely who? Clearly a woman's signature was needed. They found a surname, Crocker, as that of the popular secretary-director of the company who had just retired. Now a suitable

first name was needed, one that sounded friendly and cozy. The answer was "Betty." The replies could now end: "Sincerely, Betty Crocker." In due course a team of women was engaged to answer queries about cooking sent to "Betty Crocker," and her name now appears on a range of General Mills products.

Bettys & Taylors *(tea and coffee)*

The British company dates from 1886, when Charles Taylor set up as a tea and coffee merchant in a small warehouse in Leeds, Yorkshire, his firm duly becoming C.E. Taylor & Co. In 1907, a Swiss citizen, Frederick Belmont, came to England to seek his fortune. Arriving in London and unable to speak English, he caught the wrong train and found himself in Harrogate, Yorkshire, where in 1919 he opened a tea room, as it happened opposite the Café Imperial, owned by Charles Taylor. Belmont called his tea room "Betty's," but the reason for the name is uncertain. It may have been a compliment to Elizabeth Bowes-Lyon, the mother of Queen Elizabeth II, born in 1900. Or perhaps it was for Betty Lupton, manageress of the Harrogate Spa. A more homely tale tells how the firm was discussing its new name at its first board meeting, when a little girl called Betty stumbled into the room by mistake. Both businesses continued in friendly rivalry until 1962, when Taylors was acquired by Bettys and the present joint name was adopted.

Bevan Funnell *(furniture)*

Britain's largest manufacturer of traditional English furniture had its beginnings in 1945, when Pamela Bevan Funnell (1920-2000) and her husband Barry started a reproduction furniture company in a garage in Hove, Sussex. The couple already dealt in antiques, but felt that good reproductions would be welcome, so began making small items in oak. By 1951 business was booming, and they began to develop foreign markets. In 1961 the Hove factory suffered a major fire, prompting a move to nearby Newhaven, where the company headquarters remain today. Bevan Funnell furniture can now be seen not only in private homes, but in hotels, embassies, and palaces around the world.

BHP *(mining)*

The Australian company, formally the Broken Hill Proprietary Co. Ltd., takes its name from the mining city of Broken Hill, New South Wales, where a rich silver, lead, and zinc lode was discovered in 1883. The company was registered in Victoria in 1885 and began to exploit Broken Hill's silver deposits, the richest in the world. In 1900 it started its transfer to steel and soon became responsible for almost all the iron and steel production in Australia. BHP began searching for petroleum and gas in 1954, but began active drilling only after 1964, the year when it entered into formal collaboration with **Esso** Exploration Australia. In 2001, "The Big Australian," as Australians know it, merged with **Billiton** to become BHP Billiton, one of the world's largest mining concerns

Biba *(fashion stores)*

The first store of this name was opened in 1964 in Kensington High Street, London, England, by Barbara Hulanicki (b.1936), born in Palestine of Polish parents. She had used the name earlier for Biba's Postal Boutique, a mail order fashion business aimed at teenagers, calling it after her youngest sister, Biruta, known within her family as Biba. The three London stores closed in 1973 and Hulanicki and her family moved to Brazil. In 1978, however, Biruta herself opened a Biba boutique in Conduit Street, London, and two years later Barbara opened a new boutique, "Barbara Hulanicki's."

Bibby *(livestock feed and soap)*

Although not the founder of the British company, the man behind the name is Joseph Bibby (1851-1940), the Lancashire-born son of James Bibby, a corn miller and farmer. Quitting school at 14, Joseph joined his father in the milling trade and was entrusted with the running of a small warehouse in Lancaster. After a brief visit to North America in 1872, Joseph Bibby gradually took over his father's concern. In 1878 James took Joseph and his younger brother, also James, into partnership, trading as J. Bibby & Sons. By the 1890s, the firm was producing not only animal feed but soap, and in 1914 it was registered as a private limited company with Joseph Bibby's younger brother James as chairman and Joseph himself as vice chairman. James died in 1928, and Joseph, although by then aged 77, succeeded him as chairman. He remained in the post until his own death at the age of 89.

Bic *(ballpoint pens)*

The pen was the invention of two men, Marcel Bich (1914-1994), born in Turin, Italy, to French parents, and his brother Gonzalve, who after World War II set up a manufacturing company near Paris to produce a new type of ballpen that was both cheap and disposable, unlike earlier types. The concern was so successful that in 1957 it took over the **Biro** Pen Manufacturing Co. The following year, the company introduced the first successful "throwaway" ballpen to Britain, the "Bic Crystal." It sold in millions, and had a "throwaway" price of just one shilling, incredibly cheap for its day. In 1993 the company was producing 15 million pens a day and has extended its production to razors and lighters. The name was entered in the *Trade Marks Journal* of December 5, 1951.

Bicycle *(playing cards)*

The United States Playing Card Company registered the name "Bicycle" for its playing cards in 1886 in order to compete with another make of cards called "Tally-Ho." "Tally-Ho" was a name with aristocratic overtones that rather limited its appeal to the general public. "Bicycle," on the other hand, was a much more homely name, for a form of transport that anybody could ride. Even so, at the time of registration, the bicycle itself was still the old-fashioned high-wheel type that could mean a dangerous fall for its rider. It thus took some time for the new name to establish itself, and it only became popular on the invention of the smaller-wheeled safety bicycle some five years later. The company registered the illustration of a safety bicycle in 1893, and the picture of the king from a deck of cards riding a bicycle, depicted on the joker, is also a registered trademark.

Big Mac *(hamburger)*

The name of the largest in a range of hamburgers sold by **McDonald's** was entered in the US Patent Office *Official Gazette* of November 5, 1974, with a note of first use "at least as early as 1957."

The Big "T" *(whisky)*

The whisky is blended by the Tomatin Distillery at Tomatin, Inverness-shire, Scotland, whose own name provides that of the whisky.

Bigelow *(carpets)*

Erastus B. Bigelow (1814-1879) left his home at West Boylston, Massachusetts, at the age of ten and worked at a number of jobs until 1837, when he invented a power loom to produce lace. He followed this with other noted looms, including several designed to weave carpeting. In 1843 Bigelow and his brother established the Clinton Co. mill near Lancaster, giving rise to what is now Clinton, Massachusetts, and the mill subsequently became the center of the giant Bigelow carpet works.

Bikini *(swimsuit)*

The name is a registered trademark in France for the skimpy two-piece women's swimsuit. The name dates from 1947, the year following the testing of an atom bomb on the atoll of Bikini in the Marshall Islands of the western Pacific. The name was registered by the French fashion designer Louis Réard, who is said to have likened the bomb's explosion to the swimsuit's "explosive" effect on men.

Billiton *(mining)*

The British metal and mineral mining company had its beginnings in 1860, when a group of Dutch businessmen acquired a concession to tin deposits on the Indonesian island of Billiton (now known as Belitung), midway between Sumatra and Borneo. Business developed to include tin and lead smelting in the Netherlands, then, in the 1940s, the mining of bauxite in Indonesia and Suriname. In 1970 Billiton was acquired by **Royal Dutch/Shell** and in 2001 merged with **BHP** to form a giant concern rivaling **Rio Tinto-Zinc** (RTZ) and the **Aluminum Company of America** (Alcoa).

Bimota *(motorcycles)*

The Italian firm was founded in 1973 by Massimo Tamburini, a former heating engineer who had turned to making special bikes. The business took its name from those of the three partners, *Bi*anchi, *Mo*rri, and *Ta*mburini himself, although Bianchi soon left. Bimota gained early success by combining its own manufacturing skills with top Japanese engines from **Suzuki** and **Kawasaki**.

Binatone *(consumer electronics)*

The British firm was founded in 1960 by Gulu Lalvani, born in Karachi, India, but raised in Bombay, who went to Britain as a student. He first made his fortune in the pearl business and then together with his brother, Partap, launched Binatone to import pocket radios from Hong Kong, naming the enterprise after their sister, Bina. In 1989 Lalvani bought out Partap to take sole control of the business.

Binga *(bank)*

The Binga State Bank of Chicago was founded in 1921 by Jesse Binga (1865-1950), born in Detroit, Michigan, the son of a barber. At first Binga worked in the barbering trade with his father, then opened his own barber shop. While in Ogden, Utah, he invested in a land deal on a former Indian reservation that provided him with enough capital to begin building his own empire in Chicago in 1893. He opened his first real estate office there in 1898, and by 1907 was one of the most prosperous African-American real estate agents in the city. A year later he opened the Binga Bank in Chicago as the first private bank in the North to be owned, managed, directed, or controlled by blacks. The opening of Binga State Bank was the high point of Binga's career, which ended ignominiously in 1930 when the bank failed, partly as a result of the Great Depression, but also because Binga was convicted of embezzlement and sentenced to ten years in prison.

Bird's *(custard and jellies)*

The name is that of the English chemist and druggist Alfred Bird (1813-1879), who opened a shop in Bell Street, Birmingham, in 1837. He put his inventive mind to good use when it turned out that his young wife Elizabeth suffered badly from dyspepsia. She was allergic to yeast-based products, and also to eggs, so could not take custard, which was made with eggs. Aiming to make a dish that his wife could enjoy, Bird perfected a yeast substitute in 1843 which he called Bird's Fermenting Powder (later, Bird's Baking Powder). This produced superior bread, with a light texture. Bird had an even greater success when it came to devising an eggless custard. He invented a powder based on cornflour, which was both tasty and popular, as well as easy to make. Moreover, his wife could readily eat and digest it. By 1850 both products, Bird's Baking Powder and Bird's Custard, had achieved nationwide distribution, and caused a move into larger premises in Worcester Street, Birmingham. When Alfred's son, also Alfred (1849-1922), joined the business, the firm soon diversified to further products, such as blancmange powder, egg substitutes, and jelly crystals. In 1947 the firm became part of the US General Foods group, itself dating from 1925, when the Postum Cereal Company (*see* **Post Toasties**) combined with the **Jell-o** Company. In 1967 the British company was renamed after its American parent, and the following announcement appeared in the introduction to a special survey in *The Times* of June 1, 1967:

> Today, to mark its 20-year membership of the international General Foods group, Alfred Bird & Sons is formally changing its name to General Foods. In these four pages the development of the 130-year-old British firm from a small custard manufacturer to a major unit in a worldwide organisation is discussed. The new name gives the company a corporate identity with its increasingly diverse range of products and further strengthens the links with its international associates. But the Bird's name will not disappear.

Birds Eye *(frozen foods)*

The American company takes its name from Clarence Birdseye (1886-1956), who went to Labrador as a fur trader in 1912 and again in 1916. While there he saw natives fishing in temeperatures of 50 degrees below zero. The fish froze solid as they were caught, and when thawed out some months later, some of the fish showed signs of life. This observation, together with the need to feed fresh food to his infant child, let him to make basic experiments with cabbage, rabbits, ducks, and caribou meat. The results proved that various kinds of meat, if frozen very rapidly and kept at low temperatures, retained their freshness. Returning to the United States, Birdseye worked to exploit the process commercially. He helped found the General Seafoods Company in 1924 and five years later began selling his quick-frozen foods in a procedure that involved the rapid freezing of packaged foods between two refrigerated metal plates. In 1929 his company was bought by Postum (*see* **Post Toasties**), which changed its own name to the General Foods Corporation. Birdseye was president of Birds Eye Frosted Foods from 1930 to 1934 and of Birdseye Electric Company from 1935 to 1938.

Birkenstock *(footwear)*

The distinctive-looking orthopedic sandals were invented in 1965 by Karl Birkenstock, the US descendant of a German family of footwear manufacturers. Birkenstocks were first distributed in the USA in 1967, when they were initially favored by "underground" types such as Grateful Dead fans and health-food nuts. In the 1990s they went "overground," and were seen on the feet of many famous designers and celebrities, such as Madonna and Keanu Reeves. According to a report in the *New York Times*, Birkenstock sold more shoes between 1992 and 1994 than it had in the previous 20 years.

Biro *(ballpoint pens)*

The man generally credited with the invention of the ballpoint is László József Biró (1899-1985), a Hungarian painter and civil engineer who with his brother Georg, a chemist, is believed to have registered his first patent for the pen in 1938. Details of Biró's early life are sketchy, but it is known that when editing a magazine in the early 1930s he observed that the quick-drying ink used in the printer's shop had its advantages. He then experimented to see if such ink could be used in a conventional pen, whether with a standard nib or with a ball-bearing. (The latter system had been patented in 1888, for use in marker pens, by an American, John Loud.) In 1942 Biró perfected his pen, by which time he had emigrated to Argentina. There, he found commercial backers for his product, and patented it in 1943. After being manufactured in considerable quantities for use by the British and US armed forces, the pen took off in a big way among the general public, with the name later becoming near-generic for any make of ballpoint, even a **Bic**. The name was entered in the *Trade Marks Journal* of October 29, 1947 for: "Writing instruments and parts thereof, not included in other classes."

Bismag *(indigestion remedy)*

The name refers to the preparation's original main ingredients, *bis*muth and *mag*nesia. Its modern content comprises sodium bicarbonate with magnesium carbonate.

BiSoDol *(indigestion remedy)*

The distinctively spelled name combines elements from the preparation's main ingredient, *bi*carbonate of *so*da (sodium bicarbonate), and Latin *dolor*, "pain."

Bisquick *(baking mix)*

One day in 1930, Carl Smith, a sales executive of the Sperry Division of **General Mills**, went in the dining car of a train long after the dinner hour. He had little hope of getting a hot meal, but to his surprise was served a palatable dish along with a plate of fresh hot biscuits. After the meal, he went into the galley to ask the chef how he had been able to produce the delicious hot biscuits at such a late hour. The chef explained his secret. For just such cases, he always kept blended lard, flour, baking powder, and salt in the ice chest. Then, when an order came in, he could serve piping hot biscuits in five minutes without any need for measuring, mixing, or sifting. Smith was intrigued, and passed his experience on to the research division. The challenge was to blend a mixture of flour and shortening that would not go rancid on the grocer's shelves. The answer lay in sesame oil, which had a special affinity for flour and preserved its sweetness. It has since been replaced by other ingredients, but it enabled America's first prepared mix, "Bisquick," to be launched in 1931, named with a simple pun.

Bisquit *(brandy)*

The French brandy takes its name from Alexandre Bisquit, who in 1819, aged 19, set up his cognac business in Jarnac, near Cognac. The firm is now based in a modern distillery north of Cognac.

Bissell *(carpet sweepers)*

When Anna Bissell (1846-1934) and her husband Melville Bissell (1843-1889) were running a crockery store in Grand Rapids, Michigan, in the 1870s, Melville developed an allergy to the straw dust in which their merchandise was shipped. Hoping to relieve his symptoms, Melville designed a lightweight sweeper to pick up excess dust from the shop floor. His machine worked so well that customers who saw it in action asked where they could buy one. In 1876 the couple formed the Bissell Carpet Sweeper Co., with Anna supervising the production side and her husband handling sales. When Melville died, only 12 years after the business was founded, Anna led it to a position of undisputed leadership in the carpet sweeper industry.

Bisto *(gravy powder)*

The product was introduced to the British public with an advertisement in the *Daily Mail* of February 4, 1910 and is said to derive its name as an acronymic anagram of the slogan "*Browns, Seasons, Thickens In One*." From 1919 it became associated with the "Bisto Kids," the urchin children portrayed on the pack and in advertisements inhaling the gravy's aroma with the approving words "Ah! Bisto." Attempts to link the name with French *bistre* as a term for a brownish pigment are almost certainly speculative, although the "browning factor" of the powder is the first to figure in the slogan. The name was originally entered in the *Trade Marks Journal* of December 11, 1895.

Bitrex *(synthetic compound)*

The name is that of a *bit*ter-tasting synthetic organic compound added to cleaning fluids or other products in order to make them unpalatable, especially to young children. The name was entered in the *Trade Marks Journal* of December 14, 1960.

Bitter *(automobiles)*

The German firm of Bitter-Automobile was founded in 1973 by Erich Bitter, a former racing driver and **Coca-Cola** salesman with no experience as an engineer or even as a businessman. The firm had its times of financial crisis but was still active at the close of the 20th century.

Bitumastic *(asphaltic protective coating)*

The name, a blend of "bitumen" and "mastic," was entered in the *Trade Marks Journal* of January 23, 1889 for: "Asphaltic and Composite Paints for Protecting from Corrosion the interior parts of Iron or Steel Ships ... Bridges, and other structures of Iron and Steel."

BL *(automobiles)*

The former British company was formed in 1968 as British Leyland on the merger of British Motor Holdings and Leyland Motors, the latter being a manufacturer of commercial vehicles formed in 1907 and originating from the steam-driven wagon built by James Sumner of Leyland, Lancashire, in 1884. Leyland first produced automobiles in 1961, when it acquired the **Triumph** Motor Co. In 1966 it merged with the **Rover** Co. to become Leyland Motor Corp. British Motor Holdings had a more complex history, but basically grew out of the three auto manufacturers **Morris**, **Austin**, and **Jaguar**. (Austin had merged with Morris in 1952 to form the British Motor Corporation, and Jaguar's amalgamation with BMC in 1966 in turn formed British Motor Holdings.) British Leyland was taken over by the government in 1975 and became BL in 1979. It was privatized in the 1980s, with Jaguar sold off in 1984 and the remainder, as the Rover Group, going to British Aerospace in 1988.

Black, A & C *see* **A & C Black**

Black & Decker *(power tools)*

The famous partnership takes its name from S. Duncan Black (1883-1951) and Alonzo G. Decker (1884-1956), who in the early 1900s were respectively employed as a superintendent and design engineer in the Maryland office of the Rowland Telegraph Co. In 1907 the two decided to go into business themselves, with plans to make such handy devices as a milk bottle capper, a postage stamp slitter, and a candy dipper. They "struck gold" in 1916 with their newly invented portable electric drill, the first of its kind, moved their workshop from downtown Baltimore to rural Towson, Maryland, and that same year, with a loan from Decker's father-in-law, set up the business that became the power tool giant of today.

Black & White *(whisky)*

The whisky is the standard blend of the company begun in 1884 by James **Buchanan** as a whisky blenders and merchants in London. It was originally sold with a simple white label on a black bottle, and the resulting popular nickname was registered as brand name in 1904. It was subsequently illustrated on the label by a black Aberdeen terrier and a white Highland terrier.

Black Bottle *(whisky)*

The whisky, first produced in 1879 by a family of merchants from Aberdeen, Scotland, takes its name from its distinctive black, pot-shaped bottle, used almost since its first appearance.

Black Death *(vodka)*

The Belgian-made vodka was first imported into the USA in 1991 by the Cabo Distributing Co. of California. The following year, it was banned by the Bureau of Alcohol, Tobacco and Firearms on the grounds that the liquor's name and label, the latter showing a grinning skull in a black top hat, created "the misleading impression of bubonic plague and poison." In October 1992, Cabo won its appeal against the ban in a Federal district court in San Francisco.

Blackie *(publishers)*

The British firm was founded in 1809 by a Scot, John Blackie (1782-1874), born in Glasgow the son of a tobacco spinner. He began his working life when just six years old, as a tobacco boy, becoming an apprentice weaver when he was 11. After five years, he progressed to being a journeyman, so that his apprenticeship was completed. In 1804, the newly married Blackie was offered work as a canvasser and deliverer by the publishers W.D. & A. Brownlie. He became increasingly involved with the firm, and in 1809 set up his own independent partnership as a publisher of books and newspapers, with an office off Gallowgate, Glasgow. Rapid expansion necessitated a move to larger premises in Saltmarket Street the following year. A new company Blackie & Co. was founded in 1999.

Blackwell *(booksellers and publishers)*

The British company originated with Benjamin Harris Blackwell (1814-1855), who began selling books in Oxford, England, in 1846. He died when his son, Benjamin Henry Blackwell, was only six years old, and the business had no member of the family to take it over. However, Benjamin Blackwell refounded it in 1879, when he was just 20. In 1913 his own son, Sir Basil Henry Blackwell (1889-1984), joined the firm and developed its publishing side, succeeding his father as chairman of B.H. Blackwell Ltd. in 1924. In 1939 Sir Basil's son Richard Blackwell (1918-1980) set up Blackwell Scientific Publications (now Blackwell Science). The combination of bookseller and publisher is not common in modern times, although formerly it was the norm. At the close of the 20th century, with the company successfully exploiting the US academic market, the chairman was Richard Blackwell's son Nigel (b.1947).

Blakeys *(boot and shoe protectors)*

The protective metal plates fitted as heelcaps or toecaps to shoes or boots take their name from their British manufacturers, John Blakey of Leeds, Lancashire, "trading also as E. Blakey and Sons," who entered it in the *Trade Marks Journal* of March 9, 1887. The name is no longer proprietary.

Bloodaxe *(publishers)*

Bloodaxe Books, Britain's biggest publisher of new poetry, was founded in 1978 by Neil Astley (b.1953) in Newcastle upon Tyne and named for Erik Bloodaxe (d.954), the last Viking king of York, who is said to have captured the most famous poet of the day and spared his life in return for an epic in his honor.

Bloomingdale's *(department store)*

The famous New York store takes its name from Lyman G. Bloomingdale and his brother Joseph, who in 1872 opened a dry-goods store that came to be known as the "great East Side bazaar." It originally occupied a building at 938 3d Avenue near 56th Street, but in 1886 moved to larger quarters at 3rd Avenue and 49th Street. By 1927 it occupied the entire block bounded by 60th Street, 3d Avenue, 59th Street, and Lexington Avenue, where a huge new building was completed in 1931. Lyman G. Bloomingdale was the grandfather of Alfred S. Bloomingdale, a cofounder of **Diners Club**.

Bloomsbury *(publishers)*

The British publishers were founded in 1986 in the district of Bloomsbury, London, a name associated in the literary world with the Bloomsbury Group, a circle of London writers and artists active in the early years of the 20th century. Among the best known of the group, several of whom lived in Bloomsbury, were E.M. Forster, Lytton Strachey, John Maynard Keynes, and Virginia Woolf. The publishing company's head office is now in Soho Square, not actually in Bloomsbury.

Blue Bell *(jeans)*

The US firm began its existence in 1916 as the Jellico Manufacturing Company, based in Jellico, Tennessee, where it made suspender-bib overalls for field workers. By 1930, after some mergers, it became the Blue Bell Overall Company, the world's largest produces of work clothes, and moved to Greensboro, North Carolina. After World War II the firm followed Levi Strauss, maker of **Levi's**, and moved into Western-style jeans, using cowboy stars to promote its **Wrangler** brand.

Blue Circle *(cement)*

The story behind the British name is perhaps in part apocryphal, but runs as follows. Soon after World War I, a unifying name was needed for Associated **Portland** Cement Manufacturers and British Portland Cement Manufacturers, two companies that manufactured cement, and the Cement Marketing Company, who sold it. The matter was considered at a high-level board meeting at which, after lengthy discussion, one of the directors, Alfred Critchley (1890-1963), drew a blue circle around all three names with a large blue pencil that he affected. Thus the name and its accompanying logo were created, the design itself symbolizing a seal of quality achieved under the British Standard Specifications of 1920. The company name was modified to Blue Circle Industries in the 1970s and in 2001 the company itself was acquired by **Lafarge**.

Blue Nun *(wine)*

In 1927, Walter Sichel, of the German wine and liquor distribution company H. Sichel Söhne, blended a new sweet white wine. He envisaged a label showing a nun in a brown habit against a bright blue sky. When the artwork was sent to the printer, however, there was a mixup over the colors, and *braun* ("brown") became *blau* ("blue"). Rather than reject the labels and reprint, Sichel decided to use them. Hence the now familiar picture of a single, alluring nun in a blue habit for the popular brand.

Bluetooth *(digital communication system)*

The system enabling electronic devices to communicate with ("talk to") one other without the need for wired connections was launched in 2001 by a consortium of communications companies that included **Ericsson**, **IBM**, **Intel**, **Lucent**, **Microsoft**, **Motorola**, **Nokia**, and **Toshiba**. They named it after King Harald Bluetooth (*c.*910-*c.*985), said to have united the warring tribes in Denmark and Norway.

Blu-tack *(adhesive)*

The British-made blue adhesive material, used to attach notices, posters, and the like to walls, derives the first part of its name from its color and the second part from a blend of "attach" and "tacky." The name was entered in the *Trade Marks Journal* of April 23, 1981.

Blüthner *(pianos)*

The firm was founded in Leipzig, Germany, in 1853 by Julius Blüthner (1824-1910). In 1874 Blüthner patented the so-called "aliquot scaling," whereby the weaker upper notes of a piano are provided with a fourth "sympathetic" string to strengthen the register.

BMW *(automobiles)*

The initials of the German company stand for Bayerische Motorenwerke ("Bavarian Motor Works"), an automaking concern founded in 1929 in Munich, the capital of Bavaria. It arose from an earlier company formed in 1916 as Bayerische Flugzeugwerke ("Bavarian Aircraft Works"). BFW originally made aero engines, but in 1923 branched out into motorcycles and in 1928 launches its first car on taking over the Fahzeugfabrik Eisenach ("Eisenach Vehicle Factory"). The latter firm had the previous year begun to make the British **Austin** Seven car under license, calling it the "Dixi." The car was renamed BMW on the takeover.

Bobcat *(motorized digger)*

The bobcat is a North American lynx and the Bobcat, named after it, is an American vehicle, capable of working in the sort of terrain that the animal itself inhabits. The name was registered by the Clark Equipment Company of Woodcliff Lake, New Jersey, in the *Trade Marks Journal* of July 18, 1984.

"Do you know what a Bobcat is?" Louise asked fiercely. She is a formidable woman in her late twenties ... She was talking about Bobcats because she was trying to explain why the bill for cleaning up farms with foot-and-mouth has been so spectacularly huge. A Bobcat is a small digger weighing around a tonne, ideal for cleaning out sheds and narrow passageways, and ... she has had a great deal to do with them ... "Bobcats are highly manoeuvrable, but dangerous in the wrong hands. They bob all over the place."

(*The Times*, August 4, 2001)

BOC *(industrial gases)*

The British company was originally formed in 1886 as Brin's Oxygen Co. by the Brin Brothers and Henry Sharp, producing oxygen by the barium oxide method for use as "limelight" in theaters and for medical purposes. Their factory was in Horseferry Road, London. Other companies were licensed to produce oxygen, and were taken over by the firm, which in 1906 became the British Oxygen Co. In 1975 the name became BOC International Ltd., or simply BOC. The story goes that whereas other abbreviated names omitted the "C" for "Company," BOC kept it, since to call themselves "BO" would suggest the popular euphemistic abbreviation for "body odor" (not the sort of gas they wanted). BOC now manufactures the many other gases required by modern industry and science.

Boddington's *(beer)*

The original brewery from which the British firm of Boddington's developed was the one founded in Manchester by Caister and Fray in 1778. In 1832, Henry Boddington, then a young man of 19, was engaged by them as a clerk. Within a few weeks Henry gained the first of several promotions on the discovery that a more senior clerk had been diverting a proportion of the firm's funds into his own pocket. Eventually, Henry Boddington was appointed a partner in 1848 and four years later became the company's sole proprietor. By 1876, Boddington's was the biggest brewery in Manchester.

Bodley Head *(publishers)*

John Lane, a remote relative of **Allen Lane**, was a Devon man whose career begun in 1869 as a junior clerk in the Railway Clearing House, London, England. Long ambitious to become a publisher, he chanced on premises in Vigo Street, London, in 1887 and set up business there in partnership with Charles Elkin Mathews, a fellow Devonian who was an established antiquarian with a readymade clientele. The two men named their enterprise after a third Devonian, Sir Thomas Bodley (1545-1613), founder in 1602 of Oxford's famous Bodleian Library. He was therefore their "tutelary genius," and as such the partners hung a sign with his head portrait outside their premises. Bodley Head was taken over by **Random House** in 1987, along with its partners Jonathan **Cape** and **Chatto & Windus**, but the unusual name remains as an imprint.

Body Shop *(cosmetics stores)*

The British cosmetics stores owe their origin to Anita Roddick (b.1942), born Anita Lucia Perella in Brighton, Sussex, the daughter of an Italian immigrant cafe owner, who died when she was ten. Perella did well at school and took up a career as a teacher of English and history. In 1970 she married Gordon Roddick, and in 1976 the couple opened a shop in Brighton to sell cosmetics made from natural materials and "stripped of the hype." The name was not original, but had been suggested by an automobile bodywork repair shop called "The Body Shop" that Roddick had seen in the USA. Following the opening of the shop, two undertakers (funeral directors) with premises in the same street, Kensington Gardens, sent Roddick a legal letter claiming her enterprise would adversely affect their business. The local paper ran a story that she, a defenceless woman, was being harassed, and the incident served instead as welcome start-up publicity. Roddick started by selling 25 hand-mixed products produced in various sizes to make the range seem larger. One of her gimmicks was to sprinkle scent on the sidewalk close to the shop to lure customers in. Body Shop soon had stores in London and started opening others elsewhere in Europe. By the end of the century it was operating more than 1,600 outlets in 47 countries and making 400 products.

Boeing *(aircraft)*

The American company was founded in 1916 as Pacific Aero Products Company by William E. Boeing (1881-1956) a few months after he and a US Navy officer, G. Conrad Westervelt, had developed their "B&W seaplane," a two-seater with twin floats. In 1917 the company was renamed the Boeing Airplane Company and in 1961 dropped "Airplane" to reflect its expansion into fields beyond aircraft manufacture, such as missiles, hydrofoil boats, and municipal railway cars.

Boilerine *(radiator tablets)*

The British company of this name was founded in 1886 as a firm of "hydrological chemists" with the aim of producing tablets that would remove and prevent incrustation in boilers, steam wagons, and the like, and subsequently in the cooling systems of automobiles, tractors, and other vehicles.

Bollinger *(champagne)*

The original name behind the champagne is not Bollinger at all. Admiral Comte Athanase Louis Emmanuel de Villermont (1726-1840) was the descendant of a Flemish family who settled in the Champagne region of France in the 14th century. Following a naval career, he returned to his ancestral estates and, with little money, began selling wine anonymously from his vineyards. His business was not a great success. It was boosted, however, in his latter years, when he was joined by a young German, Joseph Bollinger, the youngest son of a noblewoman and a legal officer in Württemberg, who wished to make a name for himself in the French wine trade. All began to go well. Joseph gallicized his first name to Jacques and in 1829 married the admiral's daughter, Louise Charlotte. Later, in 1854, he became a naturalized Frenchman and was known as Jacques Bollinger de Villermont.

Bollom *(dry cleaners)*

Long familiar in Britain as the local dry cleaners, the name of the firm is that of its founder, Ivor Bollom (1896-1965), a Bristol tailor. Bollom's father-in-law was manager of the dry cleaning department at **Harrods**, and Bollom himself became interested in methods of dry cleaning. He decided to switch from tailoring to dry cleaning when the Great Depression of the 1920s caused a falling off in demand for new clothes, and accordingly in 1924 opened his first shop in Redcliffe Hill, Bristol. The dry cleaning was not actually carried out there, but was subcontracted to a London firm. Bollom's staff thus pressed and finished the cleaned garments when they came back a week later to Bristol. In 1932 Ivor Bollom bought a dry cleaning machine of his own, and opened a new shop in Jamaica Street, Stokes Croft, Bristol, where the whole process could be carried out. Three years later he opened his first factory in Horfield Road, refurbishing a former army riding school for the purpose. Bollom and his director brothers retired in 1955 when the company was taken over by **Johnsons**.

Bols *(liqueur)*

The name is that of the Dutchman Lucas Bols, who in 1575 founded his business in Schiedam, originally making gin. Now a district of Rotterdam, Schiedam became one of the great distillery centers of the world, and of the four there today, three are owned by Bols. The firm built up its reputation by making *genever,* otherwise Dutch gin or schnapps, later diversifying into a range of crèmes and liqueurs. The present full name of the company is Erven Lucas Bols, the first word being Dutch for "heirs." The name of Lucas Bols is thus preserved, but the family itself died out in 1815.

Bombardier *(aircraft)*

The leading aerospace company, based in Montreal, owes its origin to the Canadian engineer Joseph-Armand Bombardier (1908-1964), of Valcourt, Quebec, who built a prototype snowmobile in 1922 when he was just 15 years old. In 1937 he established L'Auto-Neige Bombardier to make tracked vehicles for transportation on snow-covered terrain. In 1967 the firm he had founded became Bombardier Ltd, and several key acquisitions followed, including that of Canadair, Canada's main aircraft manufacturer, in 1986 and the British **Shorts** in 1989. In 1990 Bombardier set up a new subsidiary, **Learjet** Inc., to acquire the assets and operations of the US Learjet Corporation.

Bompiani *(publishers)*

The Italian publishing house was founded in 1929 by Valentino Bompiani (1898-1992), author of the comedy *Albertina* (1945).

Bon Marché *see* **Au Bon Marché**

Bond *(automobiles)*

In 1949 Sharps Commercials Ltd. of Preston, Lancashire, England, started building three-wheeled cars named after their designer, Lawrence Bond. The vehicle was always known as the Bond Minicar and sold steadily until 1963, when the company launched its four-wheel Bond Equipe. In 1969 the business was bought out by **Reliant**, who in 1970 launched the Bond Bug, an unusual sporting three-wheeler, after which all Bond production ceased.

Bond *(helicopters)*

The British firm of Bond Helicopters Ltd. was founded in 1961 by David Bond, who a few years later sold the business to **Fisons**, where Bond became chief aviation manager of the crop-spraying division. In 1968, aware of the potential market for helicopter services, he bought back the helicopters and restarted his own business, at the same time expanding the scope of his activities to include power line patrols and underslung load lifting. Following further expension into helicopters services for the new North Sea oil and gas fields, Bond Helicopters merged in 1994 with Helikopter Service of Norway to form the world's largest civil helicopter operating group, Brokers'.

Bonjela *(oral pain-relieving gel)*

The name was entered in the *Trade Marks Journal* of December 21, 1938, by the British firm of Walfox Ltd., based in Yorkshire. It derives from a combination of French *bon,* "good," and an element suggesting "jelly" or "gel." Bonjela gel is properly choline salicylate, a drug similar to aspirin, while Bonjela pastilles for mouth ulcers contain lignocaine (a local anesthetic) and aminacrine (a skin antiseptic).

Book Tokens *(book purchase vouchers)*

Book Tokens had their origin one Christmas during the 1920s, when Harold Raymond (1887-1975), a partner in the British publishing house **Chatto & Windus**, noticed that out of the 119 family presents exchanged, only three were books. He appreciated that many people were reluctant to give books as presents, since it was regarded as presumptuous to choose a book on someone else's behalf. At the same time he resolved to devise a scheme that would make books more acceptable as presents. He proposed a nationwide book token scheme to his trade colleagues in 1926. Purchasers could give a Book Token as a present which could be exhanged for a book of the recipient's choice. It was six years before the National Book Council launched the idea, and even then mainly to provide work for staff who might otherwise have been laid off in the slump of the 1930s. The first Book Tokens appeared in 1932 in the form of a greetings card with stamps attached to a stated value. The scheme soon took off, and in 1943 the enterprise was formed into Book Tokens Ltd., owned by the Booksellers Association.

Booker McConnell *(health foods and agricultural products)*

Three of the seven sons of John and Ann

Booker of the village of Over Kellet, near Carnforth, Lancashire, were the founders of the original British business. They were Josias Booker (1793-1865), George Booker (1799-1866), and Richard Booker (1801-1838). In 1815 Josias was the first of the three to go from England to Demerara (now in Guyana, South America) to manage a cotton plantation. His brothers joined him soon after, but in 1827 he returned to England and founded his own merchant house in Liverpool, where his brother George joined him and helped found George Booker & Co. in 1832. Two years later his brother Richard also joined in partnership, and the company became Booker Bros. & Co. John McConnell (d.1890) became a clerk in the company in 1846, rising to partner status in 1854. It was Josias Booker who was the "leading light" of the company, and who indirectly gave the name of the prestigious annual literary award, the Booker Prize for Fiction, first sponsored by Booker McConnell in 1968. Since 1986 the company has been known as Booker plc.

Boosey & Hawkes (music publishers)

The British firm of Boosey & Co. was founded in the mid-18th century by a clockmaker's son, Thomas Boosey, the descendant of a family of French origin who had come to England in the early 15th century. Boosey discovered that there was a ready demand for imported musical works, and his sales of continental sheet music and scores brought in steadily increasing profits. In 1816 he decided to switch from selling music to publishing it, acquiring premises in London's West End for the purpose, and appointing his 21-year-old son, also Thomas, as manager. In 1930 the Boosey family concern merged with a similar business originally founded as Rivière & Hawkes in 1865. The latter name was that of William Henry Hawkes, a Liverpool-born musician who had joined forces with Jules Prudence Rivière, a French bandmaster, to publish band music. In 1865, meanwhile, Boosey had purchased the instrument-making firm of Henry Distin, so that they made their reputation both by publishing music and by manufacturing the instruments for playing it.

Booth's (gin)

Booth's Distilleries dates its founding from the year 1740, although the precise significance of this year remains unclear. The Booths were an English Northcountry family, apparently associated with the wine and brewing trades in London since the 16th century. Philip Booth (1745-1818) is the key figure in the company's history, and his distillery, at 55 Turnmill Street, was the cradle of the present business. His son, Sir Felix Booth (1775-1850), is commemorated in the Boothia Peninsula, Northwest Territories, Canada, originally known as Boothia Felix. This came about because Felix Booth, having made his fortune distilling gin, was keen as a man of scientific interests to promote Arctic exploration. He thus sponsored the expedition undertaken in 1829 by Captain John Ross to search for the Northwest Passage. Ross failed, but Booth's name remains on the map as a memorial to his endeavors.

Boots (drugstores and department stores)

Jesse Boot (1850-1931) was born in Nottingham, England, the son of a medical herbalist and Wesleyan preacher. He was only ten when his father died, and soon had to quit school to help his mother and sister in the little herbalist shop in Goosegate, Nottingham. In 1874, the year that the company regards as that of its founding, Jesse Boot changed the shop's profile by selling patent medicines, which were increasingly in demand, instead of just herbal remedies. He had already been manufacturing some of the preparations he sold, and he now broadened this activity, while continuing to sell the medicines produced by other firms. Further shops and branches were opened, and new premises were built in Goosegate in 1883. Five years later, the original J. Boot & Co. Ltd. became Boots Pure Drug Co., a name that lasted many years. The company's headquarters remain in Nottingham today.

Borazon (abrasive)

The industrial abrasive, noted for its resistance to oxidation at high temperatures, is a crystalline form of boron nitride. Hence its name, from "boron" with the insertion of "azo-" (from "azote" as an old name of nitrogen). The product was introduced in the late 1950s.

Borden (cheese and dairy products)

The name is that of Gail Borden (1801-1874), born in Norwich, New York. He began his career as a cartographer and surveyor, making the first topographical map of Texas and surveying the site of Galveston in 1838. In 1851, changing tack somewhat, he invented a new kind of meat biscuit. While returning that same year from England, where he had received a gold medal from Queen Victoria for his invention, he was distressed by the crying of hungry babies on board ship. Four had died from drinking contaminated milk. That determined him to devise a vacuum process to remove water from milk and make it safe and pure for use over a long period. He called his product "condensed milk," received a patent for it in 1856, and set up a company to make it in 1857, initially as the New York Condensed Milk Co., but later becoming the familiar Borden Co.

Borg-Warner *(automotive components)*

The US company was formed in 1928 from a merger of four auto parts companies: Borg & Beck who made clutches, Warner Gear who made transmissions, Mechanics Universal Joint, pioneers of the standard "U-joint," and Marvel Carburetor, the country's leading carburetor manufacturer. They named themselves after the two major components and in due course broadened their base to include chemical and plastics, air conditioning and refrigeration, armored cars, fire and burglar alarms, and security guards, among others. George Borg bought the Bradley Knitting Mills, Wisconsin, in 1947 and the following year invented a fabric that was the precursor of fake fur.

Borgward *(automobiles)*

The first properly new car built in Germany since World War II was the Borgward "Hansa" 1500, launched in 1949 and named for its manufacturer, Carl Friedrich Wilhelm Borgward (1880-1963). The company failed in the year of Borgward's death.

Boringhieri *(publishers)*

The Italian publishing house was founded in Turin in 1958 by Paolo Boringhieri. It acquired a majority holding in the firm of Romilda Bollati in 1987 to become Bollati-Boringhieri.

Borsalino *(hats)*

The type of men's wide-brimmed felt hat takes its name from the Italian hatmaker Giuseppe Borsalino (1834-1900), who started his business in Alessandria in 1857. The firm subsequently passed to his son Teresio (1867-1939), who developed the export side of production.

Bosch *(household appliances)*

The German electrical engineer Robert August Bosch (1861-1942) was born in Albech, near Ulm. He opened a "precision and electrical engineering workshop" in Stuttgart in 1886 and the following year produced his first low-voltage magneto, which he installed in a stationary gas engine. In 1897 he tested the magneto on a **De Dion-Bouton** three-wheeler, and in 1901 opened a factory in Stuttgart to manufacture magnetos. In 1906 the Bosch Magneto Co. opened an office in New York, and that same year the 100,000th magneto left the German Bosch works. The first Bosch factory in the USA was set up in Springfield, Massachusetts, in 1910. Further electrical appliances followed, many of them aimed at the burgeoning automobile industry. The first Bosch headlamp was produced in 1913, an electric starter in 1914, a motor horn in 1921, a windshield wiper in 1926, a diesel fuel injection pump in 1927, and an electric drill in 1932. Production then broadened to launch the first Bosch refrigerator in 1933, first freezer in 1956, first washing machine in 1958, and first dishwasher in 1964.

Boscos *(beer)*

Bosco's Brewing Co., a pioneer of stone beer (German *Steinbier*), was founded as a brewery and restaurant in Germantown, a suburb of Memphis, Tennessee, in 1992, taking its name from Italian *bosco*, "wood." Colorado granite is heated in a wood-burning pizza oven in the making of the firm's Flaming Stone beer. (Italian *bosco* is "wood" as in "group of trees," and maybe the word they really wanted was *legno*.) A branch of the brewery has now opened in Nashville.

Boss *(menswear)*

The company, now owned by the Italian **Marzotto** group, takes its name from the German tailor Hugo Ferdinand Boss, who opened an atelier in 1923. He soon found a ready market for uniforms, notably those of the SA brownshirts, the black uniforms of the SS, and the smart shirts and ties of the Hitler Youth. His business expanded, and he soon won the supply contract for the complete Nazi collection and on April 1, 1931, joined the Nazi Party himself. As demand grew, he needed more seamstresses and cutters, and imported forced laborers and prisoners-of-war to supplement the German workforce. The workers lived in appalling conditions on the fringes of Metzingen, and half a century later, in 2000, Boss finally agreed to pay $800,000 into a compensation fund for slave laborers. The company legend, however, is that Boss himself was a kindly patriarch who treated his workers fairly.

Boss Hoss (motorcycles)

America's biggest bike was launched in 1990 by Monte Warne, who powered it with a **Chevrolet** V-8 engine. Its name denotes a "hoss" that dominates all others on the road. By the end of the decade 1,000 models had been produced.

Bostik (adhesive)

The name has its origin in the Boston Blacking Company, founded in Leicester, England, in 1898, and obtaining its adhesives from the firm of the same name in Boston, Massachusetts. In 1931 the business developed a rubber latex adhesive for the footwear industry and in 1962 accordingly changed and streamlined its name to "Bostik," a blend of "Boston" and "stick." The name was originally entered for the product in the *Trade Marks Journal* of January 30, 1935.

Botox (muscle relaxant)

The muscle relaxant, used both in medicine to control disorders such as strabismus and in cosmetic surgery to remove facial wrinkles, is a dilute form of the toxin that causes botulism. Hence its name, a blend of the first elements of "*Bot*ulin *Tox*in."

Bournville (chocolate and cocoa)

The name directly derives from Bournville, a specially planned housing estate laid out in 1879 near Birmingham, England, by the firm of **Cadbury** for the workers at its factory. The name was originally to have been "Bournbrook," after the small stream here, the Bourn Brook ("Bourn" itself meaning simply "stream"), but "Bournville" was chosen instead for its French associations (*ville*, "town"), as at that time French chocolate was regarded as the best. "Bournville" was subsequently blended with Latin *vita*, "life," to give "Bournvita" as a name for the company's chocolate drink.

Bournvita *see* **Bournville**

Boursin (cheese)

The thick cream cheese, flavored with herbs, garlic, or pepper, takes its name from its French manufacturers, started as a dairy business in Croisy-sur-Eure, northwestern France, in 1957. The firm produced its first "Boursin" cheese in 1964 and is now part of **Unilever**. The name was entered in the *Trade Marks Journal* of September 25, 1968.

Bouygues (construction and public works)

The French company takes its name from Francis Bouygues (1922-1993), who began his career in construction in 1952. Nicknamed *Monsieur Beton* ("Mr. Concrete"), Bouygues (pronounced "Bweeg") expanded his enterprise in the 1960s from construction in the Paris region to oil engineering and water, electricity, and gas distribution. Further diversification followed in 1987, when Bouygues won effective control of France's most popular television station, TF1. He then invested in CIBY 2000, a film production company that became his prime focus after he relinquished control of the construction conglomerate to his son Martin in 1989. Before he died, Bouygues saw the company achieve a number of successes, including David Lynch's *Twin Peaks* (1989), Pedro Almodóvar's *High Heels* (1991), and Jane Campion's award-winning *The Piano* (1993), all far removed from bricks and mortar.

Bovril (essence of beef)

The concentrated beef extract was the invention in 1886 of John Lawson Johnston (1839-1900), a Scot who had studied with a view to entering the medical profession but who instead turned his attention to dietetics. The product was a development of his "Johnston's Fluid Beef," first commercially produced in Canada in 1874, and he named the new food from a combination of Latin *bos, bovis,* "ox," and Vril, a substance described in Lord Lytton's novel *The Coming Race* (1871) as an "electric fluid ... capable of being raised and disciplined into the mightiest agency of all forms of matter." This invented term itself suggests Latin *virilis,* "manly," so that the overall name implies "beefiness." The resemblance of the name to English "brothel" subsequently led to its use as British euphemism for that establishment. The name was entered in the *Trade Marks Journal* of February 16, 1887.

Bowater-Scott *(paper products)*

The present company, named simply Scott Ltd. in the UK since 1986, traces its origins back to 1881, when William Vansittart Bowater (1838-1907) set up as a papermaker's agent in London. In 1887 he was joined by his three sons, and in 1910 the limited company of W.V. Bowater & Sons was formed. Bowater was thus the British half of the company, while Scott represented the American side. The two companies merged in 1956. Scott traces its origins back even further, when in 1867 T. Seymour Scott started his paper jobbing business in Philadelphia with the help of his younger brother, Edward Irvin Scott (1840-1931), who is now regarded as the actual founder of the company. In around 1869 a third brother, Clarence W. Scott (1848-1912), joined the firm. Ten years later the business was reorganized after financial problems, and it is from that year, 1879, that Scott dates its founding. In 1995 Bowater changed its name to Rexam, basing this on the Welsh town of Wrexham. The name was selected from a list of more than 600 suggestions made by Bowater employees. Two rejected proposals were "Hakari," which was too close to "hara-kiri," and "Summus," which had an ambiguous pronunciation.

Bowes & Bowes *(booksellers)*

The former Cambridge bookstore was the oldest in Britain and originally opened in 1581, when one William Scarlett, a "stacyoner," set up in business. It owed its best-known and longest-lasting name, however, to Robert Bowes (1835-1919), a Scot from Ayrshire, who as a young man joined his uncles, Daniel and Alexander **Macmillan**, in their bookselling and publishing business in Cambridge. In 1858 Bowes was appointed manager of the newly opened Macmillan office in London, remaining there until 1863, when Macmillan transferred its whole enterprise to the English capital. Bowes thereupon returned to Cambridge to manage the bookselling business, known until 1907 as Macmillan & Bowes and thereafter as Bowes & Bowes. The second Bowes of

the name was his son, George Brimley Bowes, who eventually succeeded his father as head of the concern. After 400 years of selling books to Cambridge University dons and undergraduates, Bowes & Bowes was obliged to close in 1991 when its landlord, Gonville and Caius College, redeveloped the site for student accommodation.

Bowker *see* **R. R. Bowker**

Bowser *(tankers)*

The tankers used for fueling aircraft or supplying water have a name entered for "oil and petrol pumps" by S.F. Bowser and Co. Inc., of Fort Wayne, Indiana, in the *Australian Official Journal Of Patents* (Canberra) in 1918 and the *Trade Marks Journal* of October 26, 1921. The name is still in use in Australia for a petrol (gasoline) pump. In 1885, Sylvanus F. Bowser, living and working in Fort Wayne, was approached by a local storekeeper, Jake Gumper, after receiving complaints from some of his customers. Gumper had stored kerosene (lamp oil) and butter side by side, and the kerosene cask had leaked and tainted the butter. Instead of recommending the obvious solution, which was to move the containers apart, Bowser set about devising a means of dispensing kerosene in given quantities. He delivered the result to Gumper on September 5, 1885, in the form of a circular tank with a cylinder soldered inside and an outlet pipe attached to the top. A hand-operated piston controlled two marble valves and wooden plungers fitted inside the cylinder. When the handle was raised, a gallon of kerosene flowed from the tank into the cylinder, and when it was lowered, the liquid discharged. Bowser formed S.F. Bowser & Co. to exploit his invention, and in 1905 the company introduced the first self-measuring pump designed specifically for motor spirit.

Bowyer's *(sausages and meat pies)*

The British firm takes its name from Abraham Bowyer, a Wiltshire farmer's son born in about 1793, the family farm being at South Wraxall, near Bradford-on-Avon. Soon after marrying in 1815 he started up as a butcher at Staverton, moving shortly after to Trowbridge where he opened a grocer's and baker's shop in Fore Street. He soon became one of the town's leading provision merchants, while also curing bacon on a commercial scale. The company is still based in Trowbridge. Abraham Bowyer died in 1873 at the age of around 80.

BP *see* **British Petroleum**

Brach's *(candies)*

In 1904, Emil Brach (1859-1947), a German immigrant to the USA, set up a small candy business in Chicago. A year later, he brought his two sons, 17-year-old Edwin and 14-year-old Frank, into the enterprise. Edwin concentrated on building up a mail-order operation for Brach's caramels, the family specialty, while Frank sold the candy wholesale to downtown department stores. As a result of his son's efforts, Brach expanded the business steadily, and by 1921 had earned enough to build a $4-million candy plant. Frank Brach headed the family concern until 1966, when it merged with **American Home Products**.

Bradenham *(ham)*

The type of dark, sweet-cured English ham was originally produced by the Bradenham Ham Company from a recipe dated 1781 apparently made for the last Lord Bradenham, whose family came from Bradenham, Buckinghamshire. The firm was taken over in 1897 by the Wiltshire Bacon Curing Co. Ltd., based in Chippenham, Wiltshire, and when that company closed in turn, production was moved to Yorkshire.

Brains *(beer)*

"It's Brains you want!" is the slogan of this Welsh brewing company, founded in 1713 and based in Cardiff. It takes its name from Samuel Arthur Brain, who acquired the business in 1882, and is still in family hands. One of its best-known brands is **SA**.

Brakspear *(beer)*

The British brewery, based in Henley-on-Thames, Oxfordshire, traces its origin to 1779, when it was founded by the Brakspear family, their name rhyming with "Shakespeare." The firm has a bee as its logo, a papal symbol adopted with reference to Hadrian IV, the only English pope, born Nicholas Breakspear (*c.*1100-1159).

Brand *(beer)*

Brand's is the oldest brewery in the Netherlands, dating from 1341. Frederik Edmond Brand acquired the business in 1871 and his family are still involved, although the firm is now owned by **Heineken**.

Braniff *(airline)*

Braniff is one of the few major airlines named for its founder. He was Thomas E. Braniff (1883-1954), born in Salina, Kansas, the son of a businessman. The family moved to Kansas City, Missouri, where Tom and his younger brother, Paul, enrolled in public school. Braniff's father started an insurance business, and as a teenager, Tom hit the road for him, driving a buckboard through the trails of western Oklahoma's "Indian Territory." In 1902, in partnership with a friend, Braniff opened his own insurance business in Oklahoma City. When his partner retired in 1919, Braniff bought him out, and the T.E. Braniff Company expanded rapidly. Braniff first developed an interest in aviation in the 1920s, and after he bought a share in a single-engine Stinson in 1928, his brother, Paul, who had been a pilot in World War I, convinced him to fly it on a 116-mile passenger run between Oklahoma City and Tulsa. With backing from two oil companies, Paul R. Braniff, Inc., was organized by the two brothers, with Paul as chief pilot. Tom Braniff expanded the airline throughout the Midwest and Texas and into South America, but met his death in a crash in Louisiana while flying as a passenger in a private airplane.

Branston *(pickle)*

The British brand of pickle was first produced in 1922 by **Crosse & Blackwell** at the old machine gun factory in Branston Road, Burton-on-Trent, Staffordshire, and named after its place of origin.

Brasso *(brass and metal polish)*

The name, of obvious origin, was entered by the product's manufacturers, **Reckitt** and Sons, Ltd, in the *Trade Marks Journal* of May 24, 1905.

Braun *(electric shavers)*

The German company was founded in 1921 in Frankfurt-am-Main by Max Braun, a mechanical engineer, with his first product a device he had invented for connecting driving belts. By the early 1930s he was constructing radios, including some of the earliest radiograms. Only in 1940 did Braun progress to the manufacture of electric razors. On his untimely death in 1951 the company was taken over by his sons, Artur and Edwin, the former handling the production side and the latter the marketing. The firm's head office is still in Frankfurt today.

Breathalyzer *(alcohol measurer)*

The device for determining the alcohol content of a breath sample was developed in the USA in the 1940s and derives its name fairly obviously as a shortening of "breath analyzer." *Cp.* **Intoximeter.**

Breck *(shampoo)*

One day in the 1900s, John Breck (1877-1965), captain of the Volunteer Fire Department in Willimansett, Massachusetts, noticed he was beginning to lose his hair. Concerned at the prospect of going bald when only in his 20s, he visited several physicians in nearby Springfield. Every doctor said the same, that there was no cure for baldness. Breck refused to accept this diagnosis, however, and after painstaking research concluded that regular massages at the base of the neck could correct many hair and scalp problems. He developed his own massage preparations, and soon balding friends were calling on Breck for treatment. In 1908, Breck opened a small "scalp treatment center" in Springfield, and within a few years he was shipping his preparations to beauty salons throughout western Massachusetts. Breck gradually expanded his product line, introducing a shampoo for normal hair in 1930, and shampoos for oily and dry hair in 1933. By the end of the decade, Breck had gained national distribution for his hair care products, and at the time of his death was America's shampoo leader.

Breda *(engineering)*

The Italian company was founded in 1886 by Ernesto Breda (1852-1918) to manufacture locomotives, agricultural machinery, and armaments. In the 1950s it became a holding company of the FIM (Fondo per il Finanziamento dell'Industria, "Industrial Finance Fund"), consisting of seven firms, then developed and diversified. It larer became part of **Finmeccanica**, controlling over 70 companies in the defense, steel, and engineering sectors.

Bréguet *(aircraft)*

The French aircraft construction company takes its name from Louis-Charles Bréguet (1880-1955), grandson of Louis Bréguet (1804-1883), a manufacturer of scientific instruments who was himself the grandson of the celebrated watchmaker Abraham Louis Bréguet (1747-1823). Educated at the Lycée Condorcet and Lycée Carnot and at the École Supérieure d'Électricité, Louis-Charles joined the family engineering firm, Maison Bréguet, to become head engineer of its electric service. He built his first airplane in 1909, and two years later founded the Société des Ateliers d'Aviation Louis Bréguet. In World War I he manufactured military planes, and in 1919 founded the Compagnie des Messageries Aériennes, which eventually became **Air France**. Bréguet remained an important manufacturer of military aircraft in World War II and after the war produced a series of four-engined transports.

Breitkopf & Härtel *(music publishers)*

The German firm of music printers and publishers was founded in Leipzig in 1719 by the printer Bernhard Christoph Breitkopf (1695-1777). It gained fame under his son, Johann Gottlieb Immanuel Breitkopf (1719-1794), who was succeeded as director in 1796 by Gottfried Christoph Härtel (1763-1827). The Breitkopf family then severed all connection with the firm, although it retained their name.

Brentano's *(booksellers)*

Long New York City's largest bookstore, Brentano's, Inc., had its modest beginnings in the newsstand set up in front of the New York Hotel on lower Broadway by August Brentano, an immigrant news vendor from Austria, who arrived in America in 1853. His business prospered, and he moved his stand to a hallway of the old Revere House, at Broadway and Houston Street, where he erected a sign reading "Brentano's Literary Emporium." Young Brentano sold bundles of papers at a dollar a piece, and became rich enough to open a real emporium, which in 1870 moved to Union Square, just down the block from **Tiffany's**. His nephew, Arthur, who started in the store in 1873, made Brentano's an institution, and he was soon joined by his younger brothers, Simon and August Brentano. In 1882 the three brothers bought out their elderly uncle, who died in 1886, working humbly at the cashier's desk in the business he had founded.

Brick (beer)

The Canadian brewery, based in Waterloo, Ontario, takes its name from Jim Brickman, who founded the firm in 1984. One of its best-known brands is "Brick Bock," matured for three months.

BridgePort (beer)

The BridgePort Brewing Co. was founded in 1984 in Portland, Oregon, as Columbia River Brewing. It then adopted its present name, for the bridges that unite a city framed by the Columbia and Willamette rivers, both flowing from hop regions.

Bridgestone (synthetic rubber goods and fibers)

The Japanese company was founded as a tire-manufacturing enterprise in 1931 by Shojiri Ishibashi. He gave his firm a European name based on his own name, translating its two elements, *ishi*, "stone," and *hashi*, "bridge," into English, and then reversing them to give what he regarded as a more euphonious result than "Stonebridge." The name also suggested that of **Firestone**, a company that he much admired and which his business would ultimately absorb in 1988. (Their combined operations were consolidated in the Americas in 1990 under the name Bridgestone-Firestone.)

Brigg (umbrellas)

The British firm of Brigg & Sons was founded by Thomas Brigg in St. James's Street, London, in 1836. The business soon became noted for its umbrellas and extended its line of goods to include walking sticks, shooting sticks, and riding crops. St James's Street itself has been reputed for its high-quality shops and gentlemen's clubs since the early 18th century.

Brillo (soap pads)

Soon after the turn of the 20th century, a New York door-to-door salesman called Mr. Brady was traveling around New England selling the new aluminum pots and pans. Following complaints about how difficult it was to clean his utensils, Brady turned to his brother-in-law, a Mr. Ludwig, who made costume jewelry. He had the idea of combining the scouring and polishing properties of steel wool with a special soap container jeweler's rouge. Brady soon found that the new cleaning concoction

was outselling his pots and pans, and with Ludwig he approached the lawyer Milton B. Loeb to help form a company to manufacture and market the product. Loeb did more than providing professional advice. He named the product, allegedly from Latin *beryllus*, "beryl" (rather than English *brilliant*), and went on to become treasurer and then president of the Brillo Manufacturing Co. He remained president until the company was sold to the Purex Corporation in 1963, when he went to oversee its British operation. Brillo produced the special cakes of red soap plus wads of steel wool that were its original Brillo pads in its factory in Brooklyn. They were first sold in 1913 by salesmen like Brady, but they were taken on as a line by **Woolworths** in 1918 and were soon carried by grocery stores all over the country. The product remained virtually unchanged until 1930, when Brillo introduced its steel-wool pads impregnated with soap. After World War II, Brillo became the world's best-selling cleaner, although it was later overtaken by its archrival SOS, which was formed on the West Coast only a few years after Brillo. The name was originally entered in the *Trade Marks Journal* of April 7, 1909. Since 1969, Brillo's two main factories have both been in London: London, Ohio, and London, England.

Brinsmead (pianos)

John Brinsmead (1814-1908) was born at Weir Gifford, Devon, England, the son of a farmer and lime burner. He quit school at 12, and after a year in agriculture was apprenticed to a cabinetmaker in Torrington, where he remained for seven years. In 1835 he set out to walk to London, and once there became a journeyman maker of piano cases. After a brief partnership with his brother, which was not a success, he started his own piano-making business in 1837. Although slow to gain recognition, his business expanded rapidly in the 1870s, and a registered company was formed in 1900, by which time he had overtaken the much better known British piano manufacturer, **Broadwood**.

Bristol (automobiles)

The stylish and expensive cars of this name were first built in 1947 with a **BMW** engine at Bristol, England, by the Bristol Aeroplane Co., founded in 1910, and in many respects the first

Bristols were a development of the BMW itself. The airplane company was divorced from the business in 1960, when the autos continued to be produced by Bristol Cars Ltd.

Bristol Cream *(sherry)*

The style of sweet sherry was introduced by **Harvey's** of Bristol in the late 19th century. The name relates to "Bristol Milk," an existing style of sweet sherry sold in the early 19th century by Harvey's. According to one account, a lady visiting the firm's cellars in 1882, on tasting the as yet unnamed sherry, observed, "If that is Milk, then this is Cream." Other sources, however, attribute the remark to Edward VII (reigned 1901-10), made on one of his visits to Bristol. But this is undoubtedly too late, since the name was entered in the *Trade Marks Journal* of June 23, 1886. "Bristol milk" as a generic name dates from the 17th century, and is mentioned in Thomas Fuller's *The Worthies of England* (1662): "Some will have it called milk, because ... such wine is the first moisture given infants in the city. It is also the entertainment [*i.e.*, provision], of course, which the courteous Bristolians present to all strangers, when first visiting their city."

Bristol-Myers *(pharmaceuticals)*

The origins of the American business lie in the Clinton Pharmaceutical Company, set up in New York in 1887 by two medical graduates, William McClaren Bristol, Sr., and John R. Myers, with the aim of producing drugs in bulk for doctors. The company adopted the Bristol-Myers name in 1900, and in 1928 William Bristol's three sons took over the management, with Henry as president, William, Jr., as chief manufacturing executive, and Lee in charge of advertising. In World War II, when the US government was looking for companies to manufacture penicillin, the Bristols bought a company in Syracuse, New York, changed its name to Bristol Laboratories, and became one of the country's leading manufacturers of antibiotics. In 1989 Bristol-Myers merged with **Squibb** to become one of the world's largest pharmaceutical companies.

Bristow's *(toffee and fudge)*

The British firm's history began in Crediton, Devon, in 1932, when Charles S. Bristow took over the interests of chocolate manufacturer John Cleave & Sons, which had been established in the town for almost 50 years. Charles Bristow had trained as a confectioner in Switzerland, and on acquisition of the Cleave concern he concentrated on the manufacture of butterscotch. His son George joined him that same year, and became chairman on the death of his father in 1951, by which time the firm had moved to a new factory in Mill Street, Crediton. The company naturally exploits one of the best known local products, Devonshire cream (sometimes called clotted cream), in its confectionery.

Britain *(toy soldiers)*

William Britain was a native of Birmingham, England, who moved to London around the middle of the 19th century. He made a wide variety of toys but found they were expensive and appealed only to a limited market. In 1893 he therefore enlarged his scope making miniature model soldiers out of solid lead. His sons and daughters worked with him, the sons doing the necessary research for each model, the daughters painting them. Soon Britain's house in Lambeth Road, Hornsey, was converted into a factory, and literally thousands of toy soldiers were "marching" out each week. Today plastic has taken the place of lead, but each soldier is still produced to the original standard 1/32d scale.

Britax *(car seatbelts)*

The name of the product is a shortening of that of its original manufacturers, British Accessories, founded by one Percy Steer early in the 20th century. The name was entered in the *Trade Marks Journal* of September 3, 1975.

British Airways *(airline)*

The British company was formed in 1974 in the merger of British Overseas Airways Corporation (BOAC) and British European Airways (BEA). Its origins go back to 1924, when four small companies, Handley Page Transport, Instone Air Line, Daimler Airway, and British Marine Air Navigation, merged to form Imperial Airways. Meanwhile, three other airlines, Hillman's Airways, Spartan Air Lines, and United Airways, had merged in 1935 to form British Airways. In 1938 the government decided to merge and nationalize Imperial Airways and British Airways. The result was British Overseas Airways Corporation, formally established in 1939. In 1946 British European Airways, formerly a division of BOAC, was split off to become a state corporation in its own right.

British Caledonian (airline)

The Scottish airline was founded in 1961 as Caledonian Airways by Adam Thomson (1926-2000), a Scot born in Glasgow who was already an experienced pilot. It was named for Caledonia, the Roman name for northern Britain, now usually associated exclusively with Scotland (as for the Caledonian Canal that crosses Scotland from east to west). The airline's first commercial flight took place on November 30, 1961, from Barbados to London. BCal, as it came to be known, gradually extended its services but fell on hard times in the early 1980s and in 1988 was absorbed into **British Airways**.

British Leyland *see* **BL**

British Midland (airline)

Britain's second largest airline started life in 1938 as Air Schools Ltd. at Burlaston, near Derby, where it specialized in flying instruction for Royal Air Force pilots. It became Derby Aviation in 1949, as it began to diversify, then Derby Airways in 1959, British Midland Airways in 1985 (Derby is in the English Midlands), and British Midland in 1985. In 2001 it broke into the transatlantic market and became British Midland International (otherwise bmi british midland), having considered but rejected "Bluebird" and "British Blue," names that would have alluded to one of the three colors in its red, white, and blue livery.

British Motor Corporation *see* **BL**

British Motor Holdings *see* **BL**

British Petroleum (petroleum)

The British petrochemical corporation was formed in 1909 as the Anglo-Persian Oil Company to take over and finance an oil-field concession granted in 1901 by the Persian government to an English investor, William Knox D'Arcy (1849-1917), a solicitor (lawyer) turned prospector who from 1866 had followed legal, pastoral, and mining pursuits in Queensland, Australia, before returning to England in 1889. In 1917 it acquired the British Petroleum Co. Ltd. to act as its marketing subsidiary and in 1935, when Persia was renamed Iran, became the Anglo-Iranian Company. In 1954 it reorganized as British Petroleum (BP) and in 1998 took over **Amoco** to form BP Amoco, which in turn became the world's second largest oil and natural gas producer on its acquisition of **Atlantic Richfield** in 2000.

British Railways (railroads)

The former British railroad system came into existence in 1948 on the nationalization of Britain's private railway companies. Its shorter title, British Rail, was in use from 1965, and it was generally known simply as BR. A process of privatization began in 1992 and in 1997 British Rail ceased to exist. *See also* **Railtrack**.

British Steel (steel)

The British corporation was established as a state-owned concern in 1967, when it assumed control of 14 major steel companies in the UK: Colvilles, Consett Iron Co., **Dorman, Long &** Co., English Steel Corporation, GKN Steel Co. (*see* **Guest, Keen & Nettlefold**), John Summers & Sons, The Lancashire Steel Corporation, The Park Gate Iron and Steel Co., Richard Thomas & Baldwins, Round Oak Steel Works, South Durham Steel & Iron Co., The Steel Company of Wales, Stewarts & Lloyds, and The United Steels Companies. It was privatized in 1988 and in 1999 merged with the Dutch steel producer Koninklijke Hoogovens (founded 1918) to create the international metals group **Corus**.

British Xylonite (plastics)

The company evolved from a business established in around 1862, when Daniel Spill began to use "Parkesine," a type of plastic invented by Alexander Parkes (1813-1890), at his brother George's waterproofing works in Hackney, London. Parkes founded the Parkesine Co. with Spill as works manager in 1865, but it went into liquidation three years later. Spill then founded the Xylonite Co. in 1869 to manufacture "Xyloidine" at the old premises of the Parkesine Co. Both these names are based on Greek *xulon*, "wood." This company was in turn liquidated in 1874 and Spill then founded Daniel Spill & Co. in Homerton, London, where he produced Xylonite (a form of celluloid) and "Ivoride" knife handles, brooches, and decorative trinkets. Following various mergers and acquisitions, in which **Bakelite**,

Halex and **Union Carbide** were involved, among other chemical and plastics concerns, the British Xylonite Co. finally became a dormant subsidiary company of **BP** Chemical Ltd. in 1983.

British-American Tobacco see BAT Industries

Britvic (soft drinks)

The British drinks derives their name acronymically from *Brit*ish *Vit*amin Products, a firm that began life as James MacPherson & Co. but that was renamed on being acquired by one Ralph Chapman in 1938. Chapman changed the name to reflect his introduction of fruit juices to a business that had hitherto manufactured only flavored mineral waters. The shorter name was originally entered in the *Trade Marks Journal* of January 25, 1935.

BRM (racing cars)

The history of the British racing cars goes back to 1934, when English Racing Automobiles (ERA) was launched at Bourne, Lincolnshire, by three motor enthusiasts, Peter Berthon, Raymond Mays, and Humphrey Cooke. The 1500 cc. car was successful, with many international victories, but in 1938 ERA went out of business. After World War II, Berthon rejoined Mays to set up British Racing Motors (BRM), and the first car of the name was displayed at Folkingham Airport, Lincolnshire, in 1949. After some abortive race appearances, the BRM began to win races, but interest in the car waned and in 1952 BRM was bought out by Alfred Owen, of the **Rubery Owen** empire. BRM then hit a winning streak and in 1962 racing driver Graham Hill won the world championship with the marque.

Broadway-Hale (department stores)

The billion-dollar retailing organization had its beginnings in the small dry-good store opened in Los Angeles in 1896 by Arthur Letts, a 34-year-old immigrant merchant from Northamptonshire, England, who began his career at the age of 14 in a drapery store. One day in 1896 he was walking along Broadway and saw a little store on the corner of Fourth Street with a sign "The Broadway Department Store" that had closed through bankruptcy. Letts purchased the stock and took over the store. Hence the first part of the name. The second part represents Hale Bros. Stores, a firm subsequently acquired. Letts, who died in 1923, was responsible for setting up John Bullock of **Bullock's.**

Broadwood (pianos)

John Broadwood (1732-1812) was born in Dunbartonshire, Scotland, into a Northumbrian farming family who had recently settled north of the border. As a young man, he came south to London to seek his fortune as a cabinetmaker, walking all the way, as his fellow artisan, John **Brinsmead**, would do a century later. There in 1761 he found employment with the Swiss-born harpsichord maker Burkhardt Tschudi (1702-1773), who had come to England in 1731 to set up his business in Soho. Broadwood became Tschudi's partner, married his daughter, Barbara, and took over the business when Tschudi retired in 1769. After Tschudi's death, Broadwood formed a partnership for a time with his (Tschudi's) son, but from 1782 had sole charge of the concern, and remained so until 1795, when he took his own son James Tschudi Broadwood (1772-1851) into partnership. By this time he was making pianos, not harpsichords, thus keeping pace with musical advances. The present company of John Broadwood & Sons was formed in 1901.

Brockhaus (publishers)

The German publishing house takes its name from Friedrich Arnold Brockhaus (1772-1832), who founded a book business in Amsterdam in 1805. It was subsequently organized as the printing and publishing firm F.A. Brockhaus and transferred to Leipzig in 1817. Brockhaus' first published work was the encyclopedia *Konversations-Lexikon*, begun in 1796 by R.G. Löbel, from whom the copyright was bought in 1808. The second edition, entitled *Der grosse Brockhaus*, was begun in 1812. Other reference works followed. After Brockhaus' death, the business passed to his sons, Friedrich (1800-1865) and Heinrich (1804-1874), who further expanded the list. In 1889, together with the Russian publisher Ilya Abramovich Efron (1847-1917), the firm of Brockhaus and Efron was set up in St. Petersburg, where its main prerevolutionary work was the great Russian *Entsiklopedicheskiy slovar'* ("Encyclopedic Dictionary"), published from 1890 to 1907 in 82 half-volumes and 4 supplementary half-volumes (43 volumes altogether). Efron's descendants continued the firm after the Revolution until 1930. In 1945 the parent Brockhaus transferred from Leipzig to Wiesbaden.

Brock's *(fireworks)*

The British firm was originally known as Brock's Crystal Palace Fireworks, and was set up some time before 1720 by John Brock, a firework maker's son, who died that year on November 5, significantly enough, in a firework accident. From 1865 through 1936 the firm held spectacular displays at the Crystal Palace, London, which explains its former name. These were colloquially known as a "Brock's benefit," now a standard expression for any striking display. The phrase is said to have originated from a wellwisher who allowed the firm to display an exhibition of fireworks on his estate "for his benefit" when an explosion nearly put Brooks out of business. The firm is now based in Sanquhar, Scotland.

Broken Hill *(steel, minerals, oil, and gas)*

Australia's largest corporation was registered in Victoria on August 13, 1885, taking its name from Broken Hill, a city on a hill range in New South Wales where a rich silver, lead, and zinc lode was discovered by the boundary rider Charles Rasp in 1883. The city takes its own name from the range, so called in 1844 by the explorer Charles Sturt for its humpbacked profile.

Bromo-Seltzer *(sedative)*

The patent remedy for headaches was the invention of Isaac E. Emerson, a former chemistry instructor at the University of North Carolina who took up pharmacy in Annapolis, Maryland. In 1888 he went to Baltimore and began making and selling "Bromo-Seltzer," deriving its name from "bromide" and "seltzer (water)." The Emerson Drug Company, of Baltimore City, was incorporated three years later.

Bronco *(toilet paper)*

The British newsprint firm of Peter Dixon & Son added the manufacture of toilet paper to their main product in the 1930s and one of their mills at Oughtibridge, Yorkshire, was accordingly modified to manufacture hard toilet

tissue. One of its first customers was the British Patent Perforated Paper Co., the makers of "Bronco," a firm subsequently acquired by Peter Dixon in 1955. The name itself is said to have been based on "Bromo," an existing toilet paper said to contain some kind of chemical. If this is so, the "Br-" could also represent the "British" of the company name, with the "-co" as the "Co." At the same time there is also a suggestion of "bronco," the untamed horse, as an image of strength. The name was also said to be imitative, representing the sound made when a sheet of the paper was sharply detached from the roll ("*bronco!*"). The name was entered in the *Trade Marks Journal* of March 20, 1935.

Brook Street Bureau *(secretarial recruitment agency)*

Britain's best-known secretarial recruitment agency was founded in 1946 in Brook Street, London, by Margery Hurst (1913-1989), who after World War II set herself up as a secretary to support her infant daughter. She originally worked at home, in Portsmouth, Hampshire, but also commuted weekly to the small London office, where she provided office services. She soon realized, however, that such work lacked proper potential, so instead concentrated on supplying other businesses with temporary secretaries. Within six months she had 25 temporary staff on her books and a client list that included top companies such as **Shell** Petroleum. After a year she was placing one "temp" per day, on average, and her business gradually expanded, helped by her second husband, Eric Hurst, whom she married in 1948. By the end of the 1960s the Brook Street Bureau was recognized as the largest agency in the world, with a turnover in excess of £2 million.

Brooke Bond *(tea)*

The Brooke of the name is Arthur Brooke (1845-1918), born a tea dealer's son in Ashton-under-Lyne, Lancashire, England. His father at first put him in the cotton trade, but when the cotton mill failed, Arthur Brooke joined the Liverpool branch of a tea merchant, Peek Bros. & Winch. He showed promise, and was transferred to London. He soon returned to his home town, however, to join his father as a tea salesman. In 1869 he felt he had saved enough to start his own business, and that year opened a shop at 29 Market Street, Manchester. He sold tea in packets, a concept that was then a novelty. On the facia of his shop he placed the title "Brooke, Bond & Co." There was no actual Mr. Bond, and Brooke added the name because it seemed appropriate in the overall title. All went well from then on. In 1872 his business had expanded and new branches opened, enabling him to move south to London and take a warehouse and office there. He married in 1875, spending his honeymoon in Paris visiting color printers to order showcards for his flourishing business.

Brooks Brothers *(menswear)*

In 1818, 46-year-old Henry Sands Brooks, the son of a Connecticut physician, opened a clothing store on the corner of Cherry Street and Catherine Street, Manhattan, doing a good trade with the sea captains who visited New York harbor. After his death in 1833, the business was taken over by two of his sons, Henry and Daniel H. Brooks, and in 1850 the company name was changed from H. & D.H. Brooks & Co. to Brooks Brothers. By the time a second, larger store was opened at Broadway and Grand Street in 1858, Henry Brooks was dead, and control of the firm passed to the four younger brothers Daniel H. (already initiated), John, Elisha, and Edward S. Brooks. In 1903 the business was incorporated by Henry S. Brooks's four grandsons and six veteran employees. The name "Brooks Brothers" subsequently caught on as the term for a distinctive businessperson's fashion style, characterized by button-down collars, tailored skirts, Ivy League suits, trenchcoats, and the like.

Brother *(typewriters)*

The name is a relationship, not a surname, and the typewriter evolved from a sewing machine. In 1908 Kanekichi Yasui left his job in the Japanese army's arsenal to start his own business, the Yasui Sewing Machine Company, in Nagoya, repairing sewing machines and making spare parts. He trained his eldest son, Masayoshi, to take over the business and eventually, in 1925, other sons entered the concern, and the name of the company was changed to "Yasui." The type of machine that Masayoshi had mostly been dealing with was the chain stitch machine used to make straw hats, and it was this kind of machine which he launched on

the market in 1928 under the brand name "Brother." All six brothers entered the business and the husbands of the four sisters also joined. A shrewd businessman, Masayoshi realized the importance of diversifying and he entered the field of manufacturing woollen yarn knitting machines. In 1934 the firm's name was changed to Brother Industries, Ltd. During World War II the firm was asked by **Mitsubishi** to manufacture airplane engines. After gaining experience at this kind of work, Masayoshi set about producing electrical goods for the Japanese market. Further diversification took place and in 1954 the firm considered the possibility of adding typewriters to their portfolio. A typewriter is rather more sophisticated than a sewing machine, and Masayoshi took some time to perfect a good, reliable model. Eventually, in 1961, production began, and in 1966 work began on the firm's Mizuho Typewriter plant, which was completed a year later. Today around 90 percent of all Brother typewriters are earmarked for export. In the company logo, the "m" of "machine" is the basis for the design of the initial Chinese ideogram of Yasui's name.

Brough-Superior *(motorcycles)*

The name is that of the British engineer George Brough. He originally formed a partnership with his father, William, who produced his first automobile in 1899 and his first motorcycle a few years later. In 1919 George decided to branch out on his own, and at the suggestion of a friend added "Superior" to his name in order to avoid confusion with his father's business. Many fine models were produced, but World War II then intervened and the last machine of the name left the works in 1940.

Brown, David *see* **David Brown**

Brown, William H *see* **William H. Brown**

Brown & Polson *(cornflour and custard powder)*

John Polson was born in Caithness, Scotland, in the late 18th century. He later moved to Paisley, where he became a weaver, while his two sons, John Jr. and William, built up a thriving muslin-making business in the town. In the early 19th century another firm, William Brown & Son, moved their muslin manufacturing business from Glasgow to Paisley. Where there are textile mills there is a need for starch production, and in 1840 John Polson, Jr., formed a partnership with Brown & Sons to set up a bleaching, scouring, and starching works. Their first product was a "Powder Starch" made from sago, which was put on the market in 1842. Polson began to use maize (Indian corn) as his starch, and in developing his processes discovered that a finely ground corn starch was readily digested. Brown & Polson's edible corn starch was accordingly soon adopted for making blancmanges, custards, baby and invalid foods, and as a thickener for soups and gravies. By the time of John Polson's death in 1900, aged 75, his invention of edible cornflour had made him a millionaire. At the turn of the 20th century Brown & Polson were noted for "Raisley," a raising powder consisting of a combination of cornflour and raising agents. The name itself combined "raising" (powder) and "Paisley" (flour).

Brown 'N Serve *(rolls)*

Joe Gregor, a small-town baker in Avon Park, Florida, was also a member of the Volunteer Fire Department. One day, the fire alarm sounded when his roll were only half baked. He hurriedly removed them from the oven and dashed to the fire station. After the call-out, he returned to his bakery and the half-baked rolls. He felt like throwing them out, but instead slid them back in the oven. The rolls browned in a matter of minutes and were delicious. **General Mills** heard about the half-baked rolls and themselves repeated the process. Once tested and proved, the company presented its own part-baked rolls under the name "Brown 'N Serve," denoting the simple completion process.

Brown-Forman *(liquor)*

The US company owes its origin to George Garvin Brown (1847-1917), a young pharmaceutical salesman, who in 1870, together with his half-brother, started J.T.S. Brown & Brother in Louisville, Kentucky, selling whiskey in sealed glass bottles to preserve its quality, as distinct from the barrels then normally favored. Brown later formed a partnership with his friend, George Forman (d.1901), and in 1890 the name of the business was changed to Brown-Forman & Co. Brown's son, Owsley

Brown, entered the firm in 1904 and took it over on his father's death. In 1956, Brown-Forman purchased **Jack Daniel's** distillery in Lynchburg, Tennessee, and this soon became the firm's best-known brand. The company was still in family hands at the turn of the 21st century.

Brownie *(camera)*

George **Eastman**, the founder of **Kodak**, wanted a cheap, simple camera that anyone, and especially children, could operate with ease. The first model was introduced to the public in 1900, taking its name from the "Brownies," the miniature humanoids that populated the books and poems of the Canadian-born American writer and illustrator Palmer Cox (1840-1924), who based his creations on the brownies of fairy folklore. Cox's Brownies, like their originals, were helpful, cheerful, and efficient, and this was the image that Eastman wanted for his new popular camera, with a name to match. The camera itself was in the USA until 1962 and in the UK until 1967, when it was replaced by the **Instamatic**.

Broyhill *(furniture)*

In 1913, James E. Broyhill (b.1892) left his family's impoverished North Carolina farm to enroll in a teacher's training college, raising his tuition fees by working as a barber. His plans to become a teacher were cut short by World War I, however, when he was drafted in the army. Following his discharge, Broyhill felt he was too old to return to school so instead joined the furniture factory owned by his brother, Tom, in Lenoir, North Carolina. In 1926 Broyhill launched his own furniture business, the Lenoir Chair Co. He built his venture gradually during the Depression, buying bankrupt factories cheaply and specializing in the production of inexpensive furniture. Broyhill went on to prosper in the post-World War II housing boom, and his company grew into the second largest in the industry.

Brunswick *(bowling equipment)*

The Swiss-born cabinetmaker John Brunswick (1819-1890) was disappointed by the poor quality of the tables at local billiard establishments in Cincinnati, where he had moved in the 1840s, and accordingly determined to build a perfect table. By 1845 he had completed work on his ideal table, and it was soon accepted by pool hall owners. Brunswick's business gradually grew, and in the 1870s he merged with two competitors to form what would eventually become the Brunswick Corporation. His son-in-law, Moses Bensinger, added pins and bowling balls to the company's line, and in due course Brunswick diversified into rubber products, including automobile tires. The firm sold its tire business to **Goodrich** in 1922.

Brush *(arc lamps)*

The name is that of Charles Francis Brush (1849-1929), born near Cleveland, Ohio, the son of a woolens manufacturer and farmer, who built his own battery-charged arc lighting system while still at high school. In 1873 Brush became a partner in an iron ore marketing firm, a post that gave him enough time to undertake electrical research. His career as a manufacturer of lighting equipment was launched in 1877, when he put an improved type of dynamo on the market. In 1879 he operated the first electric street lighting system in the United States, in Cleveland, and in 1880, together with a longtime friend, George Stockly, incorporated the Brush Electric Company. It was later eclipsed by the Thomson-Houston Company (*see* **Thales**), who purchased the business in 1889.

Bryant & May *(matches)*

The British partnership traces its origins back to 1839, when William Bryant (1804-1874) of Plymouth, Devon, and Francis May (1803-1885) of London set up in business as general merchants at 133 Tooley Street, London, with blacking as their special initial product. The two men did not always see eye to eye, however, and under an agreement of 1851 Bryant returned to Plymouth, leaving May to manage the London business. But the firm continued to be known as Bryant & May, and included imported Swedish matches among its general stocks. Then in 1861 the concern started making its own safety matches, using Swedish splints (matchsticks), while continuing to import standard Swedish "strike anywhere" matches. They were now established matchmakers, despite the fact that Francis May himself left the partnership in about 1868, so that the firm was in the hands of William Bryant's son, Wilberforce, who seven years previously

had taken charge of the new match factory. The brand name "Brymay," entered in the *Trade Marks Journal* of December 8, 1915, was long current for the safety matches. *See also* **Swan Vestas**.

Brylcreem *(hair dressing)*

The name is a respelled blend of "brilliantine" and "cream." The product was first marketed in 1928 by the County Chemical Co. of Birmingham, England, whose manager, Wilfrid Hill, had asked his chief chemist (druggist) to formulate a new-style hair cream that would be different from the brilliantines, oils, and gums then in use. The new product contained no gum or starch, and was originally sold only to hairdressers. During the early years of World War II, the young officers of the British Royal Air Force were nicknamed "Brylcreem Boys," partly for their dashing, well-groomed appearance, but more specifically from an advertisement showing an RAF officer who had dressed his hair with Brylcreem. Sales of Brylcreem soared after the war, when a New York advertising agency introduced the "Brylcreem Man" (actor Mark Weston) and a jingle, "Brylcreem... a little dab'll do ya!" The brand passed to **Sara Lee** in 1993. The name was entered in the *Trade Marks Journal* of May 30, 1928.

BSA *(motorcycles)*

The initials are those of the Birmingham Small Arms munitions company, a British firm founded by J.D. Goodman in 1861 with the encouragement of the War Office. When government orders fluctuated, BSA decided to diversify. They produced their first safety bicycle in 1880, took a pioneering interest in motorcycles from 1895, and produced their first motorcycle frames in 1903. The company's first actual motorcycle was launched in 1908, and by 1920 BSA motorcycles were a leading make. Production declined in the 1960s, however, and ceased altogether in 1971. The name was subsequently revived for a new company, based in Gloucestershire, which made relatively light models mainly for export until 1973. The BSA name was brought back for a while in the late 1970s by Norton-Villiers-Triumph (*see* **Norton**), but afterwards only sporadically surfaced under license.

BTR *see* **Invensys**

Buchanan *(whisky)*

Scotsman James Buchanan (1849-1935) began his working life as a clerk in a Glasgow shipping office at the age of 14. By the time he was 30 he had moved to London where he became the agent for Charles Mackinlay & Co., a firm of whisky distillers. In 1884 he set up on his own account in Bucklersbury, near the Bank of England. After lean years repaying the money lent him to open his whisky premises, his fortunes began to rise, and he became one of the best known racehorse owners and philanthropists of his time, eventually being raised to the peerage as Baron Woolavington of Lavington. Today, Buchanan's name is intimately linked with the firm's **Black & White** whisky.

Budgen *(grocery stores)*

The British chain stores had their origin in a small grocery shop opened in 1872 in Egham, Surrey, by two brothers, John and Edwin Budgen. In 1897 the Budgens opened their second shop in Maidenhead, Berkshire, and this became their main store where they bottled wines and spirits on the premises. Further stores were opened, but in 1920 the Budgens sold their shops to the retail and wholesale firm of Alfred Button & Sons. Two years later, the Alfred Button group was bought by **Booker McConnell**, who renamed all the stores Budgen and began to convert them to self-service shops. Today most of the Budgen stores are still in London and southeast England.

Budweiser *(beer)*

In 1265, it is said, King Premysl Otakar II founded a brewery in Budweis, now the Czech Republic city of České Budějovice. Naturally, it produced Budweiser beer, or beer made in Budweis. But the "Bud" familiar to most of the Western world, and especially to Americans, is not a Czech beer at all, but produced by the US brewing giant **Anheuser-Busch**. Back in Budweis, it was not until 1895, 600 years after the town brewed its first Budweiser, that the Budvar brewery was founded in Czechoslovakia. By that date, the Americans had already been calling their brew Budweiser for 19 years. The idea was prompted by one Carl Conrad, who had been traveling in Bohemia. He took the recipe over to St. Louis and his friend Eberhard Anheuser, who founded his brewery there in 1860, and his son-in-law Adolphus Busch, who had joined five years later. As a result there are now two sorts of Budweiser, American (in cans) and Czech (in bottles), but with tastes as different as St. Louis and Prague.

A legal wrangle over the rightful ownership of the name began in the 1970s, when both companies started to market their products in the UK. Anheuser-Busch tried to take out an injunction to prevent the Czech brewery from selling its beer as "Budweiser," but after five years of argument, its application was rejected by the Court of Appeal. Following the collapse of communism in Eastern Europe in 1989, Anheuser-Busch then offered to buy a share of the Czech Budweiser brewery in return for the right to the trademark. At first the Czech government was inclined to allow the sale, but was later dissuaded, partly as a result of negotiations from the Campaign for Real Ale, which warned that Anheuser-Busch might want to close the brewery. After several years of negotiation, Anheuser-Busch's offer was thus rejected. The American brewery accordingly resumed its tactic of pursuing its Czech rival through the European courts, with varying success. The dispute then entered another stage in 1999, when in London, England, Anheuser-Busch took out a private criminal prosecution against the distributors of the Czech beer, alleging that, by claiming on their bottles that "Budweiser beer has been brewed in Budweis since 1265," they were guilty of misleading advertising, contrary to the Trade Descriptions Act. The Czech company produced a historian who testified in court that Budweis had been a brewing centre since the 13th century. The magistrate then threw out the case. The affair seems simple. Given that beer was brewed in Budweis for more than three centuries before Europeans settled in America, how could Anheuser-Busch continue to claim that its Budweiser was the "genuine original" and warn drinkers to "beware of imitations"? The answer is that although Anheuser-Busch's beer was based on an already existing Czech beer, the company insists that it was the first to use "Budweiser" as a brand name. The Czechs, for their part, argue that "Budweiser" is a generic term to describe the sorts of beers traditionally brewed in Budweis. By this criterion, the American version of Budweiser is not really a Budweis-style beer at all. The Czech version is a full-bodied lager made entirely from malted barley. The American version may have been so in the 19th century, but it has changed considerably since, and much of the barley has been replaced by rice. Moreover, while the Czech beer is matured for three months, its American namesake is matured for only three weeks. The dispute goes on, but in 2000 the Court of Appeal ruled that both the Czech and the American breweries were allowed to sell their beer as "Budweiser" in the UK.

Buell *(motorcycles)*

American Erik Buell began his career as a motorcycle mechanic in Pittsburgh, where he enrolled at night school for an engineering degree. In due course he found a job as a test engineer with **Harley-Davidson**, and at age 22 began motorcycle racing. He decided he wanted to build his own bikes, and in 1983 left Harley-Davidson to this end. He produced his first sportsbike in 1987, and did so well that Harley bought a 49 percent holding in his business in 1993. In 1998 it took over the whole company, with Buell remaining as chairman and chief technical officer.

Buena Vista *(whiskey)*

When US journalist Stanton Delaplane stopped off at Shannon Airport, Ireland, on a return journey home in 1952, the bartender there prepared him an Irish coffee to keep out the cold. Delaplane was so impressed with the warming concoction that he passed the recipe on to the bartender at his downtown haunt, the Buena Vista cafe at Fisherman's Wharf, San Francisco. To cope with growing demand, the Buena Vista management stuck a deal with the Irish Distillers Co. soon after its formation in 1966 to supply an Irish whiskey to their own specifications. As a result, Buena Vista is now the only blended whiskey supplied on an exclusive basis to anyone in the world, and no other place in the whole of the USA produces Irish coffee in the quantity of the Buena Vista cafe.

Bugatti *(automobiles)*

The distinctive cars owe their origin to Ettore Bugatti (1881-1947), an Italian furniture maker's son who began his career as an engineering apprentice in Milan. Even as a teenager he was designing cars, and in 1901 gained an award for one of the two automobiles he had designed and exhibited in Milan. He was invited to Alsace by Baron de Dietrich to design cars at his plant in Niederbronn, and subsequently worked for one of the Baron's agents in Strasbourg. He fell out with both men, however, and in 1907 moved to being a designer for the important Cologne company of Deutz, which was about to manufacture automobiles. But once again there was a disagreement, and Bugatti eventually produced his own cars two years later at Molsheim, near Strasbourg. The first Bugatti was thus born in 1909, even though its creator's early models were closely based on the ones he had designed for Deutz.

Buick *(automobiles)*

The Buick Manufacturing Company was founded in Detroit in 1902 by the Scottish-born engineer David Dunbar Buick (1854-1929), who was taken to the United States when only two years old and whose first business there was a Michigan company that made plumbing equipment, set up in 1884. The first Buick automobile was successfully road tested in 1903, and mass production followed soon after the company's recapitalization in 1904. Although the automobile was one of **General Motors**' bestsellers, Buick himself became involved in ill-advised business ventures and sank ever deeper into debt, so that at the time of his death he was a mere clerk at a Detroit vocational school.

Buitoni *(packaged foods)*

Now one half of the Princes-Buitoni food manufacturing concern, the original Buitoni Company was founded in 1827 in Sansepolcro, near Arezzo, Italy, by Giovanbattista Buitoni and his wife Giulia Boninsegni, their initial aim being to make pasta. The story goes that Giulia pawned her gold jewelry to start the business, but it was her son, Giovanni Buitoni (1822-1901), who some years later, after his father's death, turned the enterprise into a company, so that in 1880 there were three factories in Italy producing a more sophisticated range of pasta, including a gluten variety that was in effect the first Italian baby cereal. The company was subsequently acquired by **Nestlé**.

Bukta *(sport clothing)*

The British company, with its logo of a stylized leaping buck, takes its name from its founder, Edward Robinson Buck, who in the 1870s set up a clothes-making business in a cellar in Portland Street, Manchester, with plant of around 12 treadle sewing machines. The origin of the "-ta" is uncertain. The name was entered in the *Trade Marks Journal* of July 17, 1985.

Bulgari *(jewelry)*

The Italian company ultimately goes back to 1897, when Sotirio Bulgari, descended from a family of Greek silversmiths who had moved to Rome in the mid-19th century, began making and selling jewelry. The family business eventually passed to Gianni Bulgari, and he chaired the firm for 20 years until in 1984 he was ousted by his nephew, Francesco Trapani (b.1957), who developed the company into the third-largest jeweler in the world. In 2001 Trapani went into partnership with **Marriott** to develop luxury hotels.

Bullock's *(department store)*

The prestigious Los Angeles store takes its name from John Gillespie Bullock (1871-1933), a Canadian of Scottish ancestry born in Paris, Ontario, the son of a railroad employee. At the age of 11, the young Bullock started work delivering groceries for Munn & Co., a small local store. He moved on to Rheder's, a dry-goods store, but at age 25 he was still not earning enough, so when two uncles mining in the West wrote back about the wonders of California, he bought a railroad ticket to Los Angeles with money loaned by his widowed mother. He reached the city in January 1896 and began walking the streets, looking for work. He found it in the future **Broadway-Hale** store run by Arthur Letts on Broadway, where he was given increasing responsibility. A chance to run his own store came in 1906, when Letts purchased a newly-built department store at the corner of Seventh and Broadway and gave Bullock the task of establishing an additional store. It was planned to call it "Bullock's Department Store," but a shorter name seemed desirable and "Bullock's" was adopted. The new store opened in 1907 and business went well, even during the Depression. In 1943 Bullock's merged with I. Magnin & Co., a fashion business founded by Mary Ann Magnin in 1876, and became Bullock's-Magnin.

Bulmer *(cider)*

The British firm originated in 1887 in Here-fordshire, when Henry Percival "Percy" Bulmer (1867-1919) first made cider commercially in the village of Credenhill, near Hereford, where his father was the rector. The Bulmer family were already established as wine merchants, and were experienced in brewing their own cider. Two years later, Percy Bulmer was joined by his elder brother, Edward Frederick "Fred" Bulmer (1865-1941), and the two men embarked in earnest on the cider-making business in the small factory in Ryelands Street, Hereford, that Percy had now opened. The firm was already known as H.P. Bulmer & Co., with Percy's initials, and the company, now HP Bulmer Holdings plc, still has its head office in Hereford. Esmond Bulmer (b.1935) was chairman of the family concern from 1982 through 2000.

Bulova *(watches)*

The watches take their name from Joseph Bulova (1851-1935), an immigrant jeweler's apprentice from Austria-Hungary, who arrived in the United States in the early 1870s. He settled in New York, and by 1875 had saved enough money to start his own jewelry manufacturing business. The firm prospered, and in the 1900s Bulova added watches to his line. The first full line of men's jeweled wristwatches followed in 1919, and women's watches in 1921. Two years later the business was reincorporated in 1923 as the Bulova Watch Company, Inc., with Joseph Bulova remaining president until his death.

Bunnykins *(ceramic models)*

The model ceramic rabbit figures were conceived by an English nun, Barbara Vernon Bailey, daughter of **Doulton** managing director Cuthbert Bailey, who submitted her designs from the convent. The characters, inspired by bedtime stories her father had told her as a child, were launched in 1934 and the first models produced in 1939. The Bunnykins design remains a popular nurseryware pattern today. The name itself is a childish double diminutive for a pet rabbit.

Burberry *(waterproof clothing)*

The name is that of Thomas Burberry (1835-1926), born in the village of Brockham, near Dorking, Surrey, England, and learning the skills of a country draper there on leaving elementary school. In 1856 he opened his own business, T. Burberry & Sons, in Basingstoke, Hampshire, and became particularly interested in developing clothing that was not merely fashionable but practicable, both cool in summer and warm in winter, and, if possible, damp-proof. He examined the linen smocks worn by shepherds and saw that they had many of the advantages he sought. He realized, however, that they could be more cheaply produced from cotton than linen, and that they would need a closer weave to keep out the wet. By a series of tests and improvements he evolved a weatherproof cloth which came to be called "gabardine," after the old word for the smock frock. And from this emerged the Burberry raincoat, both weatherproof and cool and comfortable to wear. Burberry and his two sons moved to London in 1899 and in 1901 took premises in the Haymarket. The Burberry logo is a knight in armour on a galloping steed. The name "Burberrys" was entered by "The Firm trading as Burberrys, 30 to 33 Haymarket" in the *Trade Marks Journal* of October 13, 1909 for: "Cloths and Stuffs of Wool, Worsted and Hair," and the following notice appeared in the *UK Press Gazette* of July 9, 1979:

> Certain competitors of Burberrys Limited have recently made attempts to imitate BURBERRY merchandise. Copies have included the illegal use of our Registered Trade Marks. As a result, legal undertakings have been obtained from those firms that they will not repeat such infringements. The words BURBERRY and BURBERRYS and the Mounted Knight device are the Registered Trade Marks of Burberrys Limited of London. Any unlawful action involving mis-use of our name or Registered Trade Marks or other acts of unfair competition will result in legal action being taken to preserve our rights.

Burger King *(hamburgers)*

The American hamburger chain had its beginnings in the Insta-Burger-King chain founded in 1953 by Matthew Burns of Long Beach, California, and his stepson, Keith G. Cramer, the owner of a Daytona, Florida, drive-in. "Insta" referred to the automatic broiler and milkshake maker of this name that they used. The firm's franchise for Dade County, Florida, was soon after acquired by David R. Edgerton, Jr., and he formed a partnership with James McLamore to improve and expand the business. The name Burger King was adopted in 1957. "King" suggests superi-

ority and size, and the latter quality is even more evident in the quarter-pound "Whopper" hamburger that McLamore introduced. By 1996 Burger King had over 8,000 outlets worldwide, second only to their great rivals, **McDonald's**. Burger King should not be confused with Burger Chef, which was founded in 1958, rose to second rank among hamburger chains in the 1960s, and was sold off to **Hardee's** in 1982.

Burlington *(textiles)*

The US company owes its origins to J. Spencer Love (1896-1962), born in Cambridge, Massachusetts, the son of a college professor. Educated at Harvard, Love attended its business school before receiving a commission in 1917 as a lieutenant in the US Army. Discharged in 1919, he went to work for his uncle in a cotton mill at Gastonia, North Carolina. In 1923 he became its principal owner, and persuaded the inhabitants of Burlington, North Carolina, to sell stock to help him finance a new mill there. On November 6, 1923 Burlington Mills was born. It was renamed Burlington Industries in 1955.

Burmah Oil *(petroleum)*

The Burmah Oil Company was incorporated in 1886 to produce oil in Burma (Myanmar) when it was still a province of India. It has since expanded worldwide and has made several important acquisitions, including **Castrol** (1966), **Rawlplug** (1968), and **Halfords** (1970), but it has retained the 19th-century spelling of the country name with the final "h," if only as a nostalgic (for some) reminder of the days when the British "pukka sahib" made his home in the towns he knew as "Poonah" and "Simlah."

Burns & Oates *(publishers)*

The British Roman Catholic publishing house takes its name from two men who were Protestant converts to Catholicism. James Burns (1808-1871) was born in Bo'ness, near Edinburgh, the son of a Scottish Presbyterian minister. Although his father had wanted him to follow his vocation, James instead went to London in 1832 to work with the publishers **Whitaker**. Three years later he started his own business as a bookseller and stationer in Duke Street, off Manchester Square. He made his dramatic conversion in the 1840s, under the influence of the High Church movement then prevalent, with his business known as Burns & Lambert, the latter name being that of his partner, about whom little is known. Meanwhile William Wilfred Oates (1828-1876) had been born in Yorkshire into an Anglican family. Under the same High Church influence, he likewise became a Catholic (in 1851) and began a career as a teacher. After a spell subsequently as a partner in a Catholic publishing house in Bristol, he came to London in 1866 and there joined James Burns in his own firm. Burns & Oates are now an imprint of The Continuum International Publishing Group, founded in 1999 by a buyout of the academic and religious publishing of **Cassell** and the acquisition of Continuum, New York.

Burpee's *(seeds)*

The name is that of W. Atlee Burpee (1858-1915), who in 1878 set up a catalog mail-order house in Philadelphia to sell purebred livestock and fowl. To provide his customers with the proper feed for their animals, he also included several varieties of farm seed in his catalog. When he found that many of the orders he received were for seeds rather than livestock, Burpee decided to pursue the seed side of his business aggressively. The move paid off and the business flourished, although a limited selection of livestock was included in the catalog until 1917, by which time the company was being run by the founder's son, David Burpee (1893-1980), who marketed the first commercial hybrid seeds, for red and gold marigold, in 1939.

Burroughs *(computers)*

The American company takes its name from William Seward Burroughs (c.1857-1898), born with indifferent health into a poor family in Rochester, New York. His early interest in mechanical things led him to read widely on the subject, and in his first job as a bank teller he dreamed of a machine that could accurately add up figures. However, he lacked any formal mechanical or engineering training, and ignoring his doctor's suggestion that he obtain a job in the open air, instead went to St. Louis, where in 1882 he began employment in a machine shop. There he spent many long hours learning mechanical skills and endeavoring to devise his projected cal-

culator. Success followed two years later, and in 1885 he applied to patent his model. Despite many difficulties, the American Arithmometer Company was set up to produce Burroughs' calculators, and the first machines were assembled in 1888. In 1905 the Burroughs Adding Machine Company was organized in Michigan as its successor. In 1986 Burroughs merged with the Sperry Corporation, formerly **Sperry Rand**, to form **Unisys**.

Burrough, James *see* **James Burrough**

Burton *(outfitters)*

Montague Burton is a name that for most Britons has for decades been synonymous with "tailor and outfitter," with every branch in every town exactly like every other, down to the precise window dressing and distinctive shop-front lettering. Montague Maurice Burton (1885-1952), the founder of the firm, was born Meshe David Osinsky in the small town of Kurkel, Lithuania, the son of a bookseller. After an Orthodox Jewish education, the future Montague Burton (who adopted this name in 1904, possibly from a public house) emigrated on his own from Lithuania to England, as many Jews were doing to escape the pogroms. He arrived in Chesterfield, Derbyshire, where he began learning English while working as a salesman in a draper's shop. By the time he was 19 he felt he was ready to set up on his own, and did so, calling his outfitters' firm the Castle Clothing Company. In 1909 he married and moved to Sheffield, where he lived at Violet Bank Road while carrying on his business at 101-103 South Street, Moor. His stock comprised readymade menswear bought from wholesale clothiers. By 1913 branches in other towns had been opened, and the firm was called Burton and Burton, the second Burton being Montague's younger brother, Bernard. In 1929 his firm became a public company under the name Montague Burton, Tailor of Taste, Ltd. But the year of founding of the present Burton Group is regarded as 1900, the year when its future director first landed in England as a 15-year-old youngster.

Burton Bridge *(beer)*

The British brewery was established in 1982 on Bridge Street in the prime brewing city of Burton-on-Trent, Staffordshire. Hence the name.

Bush (beer)

Belgium's strongest beer derives its name from an English equivalent of its brewery, Dubuisson, based in Pipaix, Hainault. In the USA the beer is sold as "Scaldis" to avoid confusion with **Anheuser-Busch**.

Bushmills (whiskey)

The Irish whiskey takes its name from the town of Bushmills, Co. Antrim, Northern Ireland, where on April 20, 1608, a license was granted by Sir Arthur Chichester, Lord Deputy of Ireland, to Sir Thomas Phillipps, James I's Deputy for the Plantation of Ulster, "for the next seaven yeres, within the countie of Colrane, otherwise called O Cahanes countrey, or within the territorie called the Rowte, in Co. Antrim, by himselfe or his servauntes, to make, drawe, and distil such and soe great quantities of aquavite, usquabagh and aqua composita, as he or his assignes shall thinke fitt; and the same to sell, vent, and dispose of to any persons, yeeldinge yerelie the somme 13s 4d." When in 1891 the Bushmills Old Distillery Company advertised their new blend "Old Glynn Bush," they gave 1784 as their year of founding, but the license justifies their label claim: "From the World's Oldest Whiskey Distillery."

Butazolidin (anti-inflammatory drug)

The proprietary name of the drug phenylbutazone, early discovered to be an effective pain reliever, derives from its generic chemical name with the suffix "-idin" (more commonly found as "-idine"). The name was entered in the *Trade Marks Journal* of September 26, 1951.

Butterfly (adhesive paper products)

The British manufacturers of the products, Samuel Jones & Co., had their premises in Camberwell, London, and took the Camberwell Beauty (mourning cloak) butterfly as their trademark and name. The name was entered in the *Trade Marks Journal* of November 4, 1925.

Butterick (dress patterns)

On leaving school, Ebenezer Butterick (1826-1903), born in Sterling, Massachusetts, began his career working in his brother's village store. He learned the rudiments of business, but did not like the work, so left the store to be apprenticed to a tailor. This suited him better, and he eventually became a merchant tailor in Fitchburg, Massachusetts. He married in 1850, and as he watched his wife tailoring, Butterick felt there must be an easier way to make clothes. He began to experiment. First he cut stiff paper into pieces, then snipped the fabric around them and sewed up the pieces. In 1863 he cut out his first complete pattern, which was for a shirt for his four-year-old nephew, Clarence Butterick. He went on to make patterns of a gingham dress designed by his wife, grading the patterns so that dresses of different sizes could be made. A New York office of E. Butterick & Co. was opened, and by 1879 the firm had set up branches in London, Paris, and Vienna. In 1881 the Butterick Publishing Company was formed to publish patterns for men's, women's, and children's fashions in reviews and magazines, but Butterick himself gradually withdrew from commerce to devote more time to the care of poor children.

Butterworth (publishers)

The British publishing house, which specializes in law books, was founded by Henry Butterworth (1786-1860), born in Coventry the son of a wealthy timber merchant. When he was 15 he left school and went to work in the bookshop managed in London by his uncle, Joseph Butterworth, who had learned the business of a law bookseller and founded a lucrative concern in Fleet Street. In 1818 Joseph set up as a publisher on his own account, and soon became established as the chief London law publisher. Today Butterworth, part of **Reed Elsevier**, still concentrates on law books, but has a growing scientific and medical list.

BVDs (underwear)

The abbreviation has been popularly derived from "babies' ventilated diapers" or "best ventilated drawers," but it actually represents the name of the US manufacturers, Bradley, Voorhees & Day. The garment was originally a type of lightweight, long underwear for men, although the name was entered by Lyman H. Day of New York in the US Patent Office *Official Gazette* June 16, 1893 for: "Suspenders, belts, shirts, and drawers," with a note of use since September 1, 1876. A later entry of January 2, 1906, by Erlanger Bros. of New York, narrows the description to "Undershirts and underdrawers." A broader range of garments is entered in the *Trade Marks Journal* of June 13,

1923, by "The B.V.D. Company Incorporated" of 519, West Pratt Street, Baltimore, Maryland, for: "Shirts, Drawers for Wear, Sleeping Garments and Union Suits for Men and Women." H.L. Mencken (*see* Bibliography, p. 566) relates his receipt of a letter dated March 29, 1935, from P.B. Merry of the B.V.D. Company, Inc., with the following offer (which Mencken did not pursue):

> From the standpoint of business psychology and because of the great public curiosity as to the meaning of our trademark, we would not care to have you publish any information regarding its origin, but for your personal use, if you request it, we will be glad to tell you the history of *B.V.D.*

Byrrh *(aperitif)*

The bitter French aperitif wine owes its existence to two young French brothers, Simon and Pallade Violet, the sons of a mule driver, who in around 1860 were itinerant cloth sellers in the plains of the Roussillon region of southern France. In 1866 they bought a small cellar to make a new kind of quinine-flavored aperitif, and successfully sold it to druggists and doctors. They needed a name for it, however, and found it in the cloth samples that they still traded, each of which was marked with a distinctive letter. Five such samples produced the letters B, Y, R, R, and H, and this produced the answer. The name was acceptable to the local Catalan population, as it sounds like a type of wine. To English speakers, on the other hand, it suggests "beer," which partly explains the problem of exporting Byrrh to English-speaking countries.

C&A *(clothing stores)*

The stores owe their name to two Dutch brothers, Clemens and August Brenninkmeijer, born into a farming family, who started their careers as travelers selling textiles, linen, and other cloths. In 1841 they opened their first shop, in Sneek in the Dutch province of Friesland. They gradually expanded to Amsterdam, Rotterdam, and other towns in the Netherlands, and some members of the family crossed into Germany in 1910 to repeat the pattern there. In 1922 the store C&A Modes opened on Oxford Street, London, England, and further stores followed in other cities. Although obviously standing for the brothers' initials, the abbreviated name was additionally promoted by the firm as short for "Cheap and Artistic." The general public, however, preferred a punning interpretation as "Coats and 'Ats," while less flattering readings also existed, such as "Cheap and Abysmal" or "Common and Appalling." The company never offered aggressive price discounts like other fashion stores, nor did it even stock the latest fashions, and these two key factors led to the closure of all 109 UK stores in 2000.

Cable and Wireless *(communications)*

The British company traces its origins to 1868, when the firm of Anglo-Mediterranean Telegraph was formed to lay a cable under the sea from Malta to Alexandria, Egypt. A global network of cable was in place by the time Marconi (*see* **RCA**) posed a major threat in the 1920s. In 1929 the two enterprises, by then respectively the Eastern and Associated Telegraph Companies group and the Marconi Wireless, Telegraph and Signal Co., merged as Cables and Wireless Ltd. (from 1934 Cable and Wireless Ltd.). A large part of the company was nationalized in 1947, but reprivatized in 1981.

Cacharel *(fashionwear and cosmetics)*

Fashion designer Jean Bousquet was born in 1932 in Nîmes, France, and at the age of 15 was apprenticed to a tailor. In 1951 he became a student at the École Technique, Nîmes, and five years later moved to Paris, where he worked as a cutter and stylist for Jean Jourdan. In 1958 he opened a studio making men's shirts, and booming business enabled him to found the Cacharel company in 1962, making ready-to-wear clothes for women. He named his firm after the local word for a wild duck from the wetlands of the Camargue, near his native Nîmes, and the word soon became almost synonymous with a type of fitted, printed cotton shirt worn by women. Cacharel began making men's shirts in **Liberty** prints in 1967 and in 1978 the company launched its first perfume, *Anaïs Anaïs*. A new range of menswear shops followed in 1998.

Cadbury *(cocoa and chocolate)*

The Cadbury family originates from the West of England. Richard Tapper Cadbury was born in Exeter in 1768, and became a Birmingham draper. He married in 1796 and had ten sons, two of whom were concerned with the subsequent confectionery business. These were Benjamin Head Cadbury, the eldest son, and John Cadbury (1801-1889), the third son. In 1816 John Cadbury was apprenticed to a tea dealer in Leeds. In 1824 he set up on his own account as a tea dealer and coffee roaster in Bull Street, Birmingham, and this year is regarded as the founding of the present company. It was not until 1831, however, that John Cadbury moved to a warehouse in Crooked Lane, Birmingham, to become a maker of cocoa and chocolate. In 1861 John Cadbury's sons, George Cadbury (1839-1922), and his elder brother Richard, took over their father's ailing business and in 1879 moved it out of industrial Birmingham to a site they called **Bournville**, where they introduced a private social security scheme and working conditions well ahead of their time. In 1919 the company absorbed **Fry's** and in 1969 merged with **Schweppes** to form Cadbury Schweppes.

Cadillac *(automobiles)*

The maker of the first automobile so named was Henry Martyn Leland (1843-1932), a small-arms manufacturer who in 1890 set up a precision engineering works in Detroit as the firm of Leland, Faulconer and Norton. The nature of his products made it easy to switch to the motor industry when that arose in the late 19th century, and in 1902 Leland produced his first car. He did not name it after himself, as was the custom, but for Antoine de La Mothe Cadillac (1658-1730), French commander of the fortified village built in 1701 on the narrow strait (French *détroit*) between lakes Huron and Erie. The fort subsequently became the present city of Detroit, and the place where the first Cadillac was produced 200 years after the French commander and colonialist had founded it. His coat of arms, with its distinctive quarterings, was adopted as the car's emblem. *See also* **Lincoln**.

Caffarel *(chocolates)*

The Italian firm so named opened its first chocolate factory near Turin at the turn of the 19th century. The precise date of the launch is uncertain, but a newspaper clipping of around this time confirms (in translation) that: "Caffarel Father & Son have purchased a machine to make chocolate from Bozelli of Genoa." The Swiss firm **Caillers** essentially owe their existence to Caffarel, who inspired the young François-Louis Cailler to start making chocolate in Switzerland.

Cagiva *(motorcycles)*

The Italian firm began as a business making metal ornaments in 1950, taking its name from its founder, *Gi*ovanni *Ca*stiglioni, and the city where it was based, *Va*rese. In 1978 it moved into motorcycles, amd after signing a deal with **Ducati** for its engines, bought the latter company in 1985. Further acquisitions included **Husqvarna** in 1986 and **Agusta** in 1991.

Caillers *(chocolate)*

François-Louis Cailler (1796-1852) discovered Italian **Caffarel** chocolate at a Swiss fair when he was still a teenager. He was so attracted by its smell and taste that he went to work in Italy as a Swiss immigrant laborer. He obtained a job in a Milan chocolate factory for four years, then returned to his native Switzerland to set up his own business as a chocolate maker. In 1819 he opened the first Swiss chocolate factory at Corsier, near Vevey. Cailler's son-in-law was Daniel Peter, of **Peter's** chocolate.

Callanetics *(exercise system)*

The name of the system of exercises designed to improve muscle tone is based on that of its creator, American fitness instructor Callan Pinckney (b.1934), who introduced it to the general public in her 1984 book *Callanetics: Ten Years Younger in Ten Hours*. The second part of the word suggests "athletics," while the name as a whole also evokes the system of gymnastic exercises known as callisthenics. The name was entered in the US Patent Office *Official Gazette* of August 19, 1986 with a note of first use on February 1, 1974 [*sic*].

Callard & Bowser *(candy)*

The British company was founded in 1837 as a combined bakery and confectioner's business in Finchley, London, by Daniel Callard and his brother-in-law James Bowser. The firm flourished, and later in the 19th century moved to larger premises in the Euston area of London, where it expanded its candy lines to include butterscotch and nougat. After World War I, James Callard, son of the founder, sold the concern to his son-in-law, and in 1933 it was bought by a Major A.E. Allott, who moved it to a new factory in west London. Today the company has its head office at Hayes, Middlesex.

Calmann-Lévy *(publishers)*

The French publishing house was founded in 1836 by the brothers Michel and Calmann Lévy, who began in the field of theatrical publishing. In 1856 they launched the "Collection Michel Lévy," a new collection of novels and poetry at the price of only 1 franc a volume, and this rock-bottom promotion formed the foundation of the Lévy empire, which included interests in French and Italian railroads and Bordeaux vineyards. The name Calmann-Lévy was reserved for their publishing activity.

Calor *(gas)*

The first liquefied gas was probably produced by the Riverside Oil Company in Britain, while in the United States the American Gasoil Company was formed, and first used gas to cut steel in 1911. A contract to import French butane into England was agreed in 1934, and in 1935 the Modern Gas & Equipment Company was set up to market it in bottled form. The gas itself was named "Calor," the Latin word for "heat," and the bottled gas was delivered to rural communities by the Calor Gas (Distributing) Co. The name was entered in the *Trade Marks Journal* of June 8, 1938.

Calvin Klein *(jeans)*

Calvin Richard Klein (b.1942) was born in New York City the son of a Bronx grocer. He displayed a flair for fashion early, and in 1962 graduated from New York's Fashion Institute of Technology. In 1968, with Barry Schwartz as partner, he launched his own firm, Calvin Klein Ltd., in a Seventh Avenue hotel suite which served as both workshop and office. Schwartz handled the sales and administrative side of the business, leaving Klein free to devote his energy to designing and sewing their original product, women's coats. Klein began to receive coat orders from New York department stores, and in 1970 expanded his collection to include suits, skirts, blouses, and slacks. In the mid-1970s he played a leading role in raising the modest blue jean into a fashion item, at the same time working on his own blue jean designs. In 1976 he introduced Calvin Klein jeans, which succeeded beyond all expectations, selling at the rate of 250,000 pairs a week by the end of the decade.

Cambozola *(cheese)*

Cambozola is a type of German blue soft cheese with a Camembert-like rind, produced using Gorgonzola blue mold. Hence the name, a blend of "Camembert" and "Gorgonzola" (with an inserted "-bo-"), entered in the *Trade Marks Journal* of June 6, 1984.

Camel *(cigarettes)*

The familiar **R.J. Reynolds** brand made its first appearance shortly before World War I. In 1907 Reynolds himself introduced a pipe tobacco that he called "Prince Albert." Soon after, he decided that the time was ripe to match it with a brand of cigarettes, and with an eye on the then current fashion for exotic names, chose "Camel" for the new product, the name evoking the mysterious Orient and suiting the Turkish tobaccos that the cigarettes would contain. He began his advertising campaign in 1913, taking advantage of a coincidental visit to the company's home town of Winston (now Winston-Salem) by Barnum and Bailey's Circus. The public was "teased" by a series of strange slogans reading "Camels" and "The Camels are coming!", accompanied by a drawing (made from a photograph) of Old Joe, Barnum and Bailey's circus dromedary. The new cigarette pack, with its haughty-looking "camel" and stylized pyramids and palm trees, would become a classic.

Cammell Laird *(shipbuilding)*

When only five years old, John Laird (1805-1874), born in Greenock, Scotland, traveled with his family to Merseyside, England, where his father, William Laird, was setting up a ship-repair yard. In 1824 William established the Birkenhead Ironworks for ship and engine repairs. John became his father's partner, and the business was renamed William Laird & Son, then in 1833 John Laird. In 1861 John retired to pursue a career in politics, and the firm was carried on by his sons as Laird Brothers. In 1902 Laird merged with Cammell, a steel-producing firm based in Sheffield. In 2001, following a string of failed orders, Cammell Laird called in the receivers.

Camp *(instant liquid coffee)*

The coffee of this name was introduced in the late 19th century by a Scotsman, Campbell Paterson, and from the earliest days was associated with a colonial military image. The label on the bottle showed the coffee being savored by a Scots army officer outside his tent with a native Indian manservant in attendance. The imagery thus originated in British colonial days and pertains to that era, the name itself referring to a supposedly typical army camp while punning on the name of Campbell Paterson. The name was entered in the *Trade Marks Journal* of April 24, 1907.

Campari *(aperitif)*

The origins of the Italian drink lie with Gaspare Campari, who in 1842, aged just 14, went to Turin to seek his fortune. There he was apprenticed to a liqueur distiller named Bass. After mastering the art, Gaspare moved to the small town of Novara, near Milan, and went into business on his own account, subsequently transferring his operations to Milan itself. There in 1860 he produced his own brand of what he called *amaro all'olandese,* "Dutch-style bitters," which became the Bitters Campari that his son Davide Campari promoted worldwide in the 1890s. Aside from launching Campari Soda in 1932, Campari remained a monobrand company until the mid-1990s, when it acquired a number of spirits, wines, and soft drinks brands, including **Cinzano** and **Cynar**. By the turn of the 21st century, Campari was the market leader in Italy and the ninth-largest spirits firm in the world.

Campbell's *(soups)*

The man behind the internationally known name was the fruit merchant Joseph Campbell (1817-1900), who with Abram Anderson, an icebox manufacturer, formed a partnership in 1869 to can and preserve fruit and vegetables. They started their operations in Camden, New Jersey, where Campbell's head office remains today. Anderson, however, left the business in 1876, and that same year his place as partner was taken by Arthur Dorrance. Campbell himself retired in 1894, and three years later Arthur's nephew, John Thompson Dorrance (1873-1930), joined the company. He was a talented chemist who in 1899 invented the condensed soup for which the Campbell Soup Company is famous today. It was then effectively the Dorrance family who took over and ran the company, although retaining the Campbell name. Dorrance became the company's vice president in 1900 on Campbell's death, and general manager in 1910. In 1915 he

became its sole owner and in 1922 changed its name from the Joseph Campbell Preserve Company to the Campbell Soup Company.

Camper *(shoes)*

The brand of this name was introduced in 1975 by Lorenzo Fluxa, grandson of the founder of Spain's first footwear company in 1870. Fluxa Snr. had set up his business on the island of Majorca by gathering local artisans and importing shoe-making machines from England. By the end of the 20th century Camper had become internationally known, with stores in all the fashion capitals, the first opening in Barcelona in 1981. The name is Catalan for "peasant," reflecting the shoes' simple style.

Canada Dry *(ginger ale)*

The formula for this brand of ginger ale was devised by J.J. McLoughlin, a Canadian chemist, who after 16 years of experimenting in a small plant in Toronto perfected his product in 1906. The firm of J.J. McLoughlin Ltd. was formed in 1914 and the trademark "Canada Dry" officially adopted. The name was obviously chosen because the product was a dry ginger ale and made in Canada. A selling agency was set up in New York City in 1921 and "Canada Dry" was introduced to the United States.

Candee *(footwear)*

The make of rubber footwear takes its name from Leverett Candee (1795-1863), born in Oxford, Connecticut, the son of a politician. A series of partnerships in the dry goods trade ended in failure in 1842, whereupon Candee began the manufacturing of men's elastic suspenders. A meeting with Charles **Goodyear** led to establishment of the L. Candee Rubber Company to manufacture rubber shoes under the Goodyear patent. The Candee line soon grew in popularity, and in 1852 Candee & Company was formally organized. The firm remained active and profitable until after World War I, when changes in technology caused a decline in sales. In 1928 the firm was sold to US Rubber (*see* **Uniroyal**).

Caneite *(building board)*

The soft type of building board is made from the fibers of sugar cane. Hence the name, entered in 1938 by the Colonial Sugar Refining

Co. Ltd. in the *Australian Official Journal of Patents* (Canberra) for: "Structural materials, including fibre board, fibre laths, fibre tiles."

Cannon Mills *(towels)*

The name is that of James William Cannon (1852-1921), born in Mecklenburg County, North Carolina, the son of a farmer. In 1868 Cannon went to work at the general store part-owned by his brother in Concord, North Carolina, where he purchased an interest in the business and became known as a successful merchant. Concerned about the role of cotton in the southern economy, Cannon decided to improve the situation by establishing cotton mills, thus saving the high cost of purchasing and transporting finished cotton goods from the north. He built his first mill in Concord in 1888 and operated it through the Cannon Manufacturing Company, which he had founded the year before. Instead of merely manufacturing cloth and selling it, Cannon decided to market branded products. "Cannon cloth" acordingly soon became a favorite with southern women for its versatility, and was used for everything from bedding to clothing. A second mill followed in 1892 and others soon after, the whole enterprise being known as Cannon Mills. In 1898, Cannon decided to begin manufacturing the first towels ever produced in the South, and to this end in 1906 established the textile town of Kannapolis, a name that punned on his own while loosely meaning "city of looms" (Greek *kanna*, "cane," "reed"). The company subsequently expanded to become the world's largest manufacturer of towels, with Kannapolis as its headquarters.

Canon *(cameras)*

The name originates in Kannon, the Japanese Buddhist god of compassion and mercy, and this was the name first used (in the spelling Kwannon) for the Japanese make of camera in the 1930s.

Cantors *(furniture stores)*

The British firm was founded in Sheffield in about 1920 by Mrs. Eva Cantor as the retail side of a small manufacturing business started up by her then fiancé A.D. Cantor, on his release from the Royal Flying Corps after World War I. The retail side expanded, while the manufacturing side remained on a limited scale

and ceased altogether when the small factory was destroyed in an air raid in World War II. The company remains based in Sheffield today.

Cape *(publishers)*

The founder of the British firm was Herbert Jonathan Cape (1879-1960), born in London, England, the son of a builder's clerk. After a patchy education, he began his career as an errand boy working for **Hatchards** bookshop, Piccadilly, progressing from this to a post with the US publishers Harper & Brothers (the future **Harper & Row**) in 1899, working as a traveling salesman, first in the provinces, then in London. In 1904 he moved to the publisher Gerald Duckworth, where he soon became manager. After war service in the Royal Army Ordnance Corps he returned to Duckworth, but in 1920 became manager of the **Medici** Society. A colleague there, book designer George Wren Howard, became a friend, and realizing that there was no realistic future for their talents at Medici, the two men decided to start up their own publishing firm. This they did, under Jonathan Cape's name, at 11 Gower Street, Bloomsbury, on New Year's Day 1921, with their first publication a reissue of C.M. Doughty's *Travels in Arabia Deserta* (1888), having convinced T.E. Lawrence ("Lawrence of Arabia") to write a long introduction for nothing. Cape was taken over by the US publishers **Random House** in 1987, together with its partners **Bodley Head** and **Chatto & Windus**.

Caplet *(capsule)*

The name of the coated medicinal capsule was entered in the US Patent Office *Official Gazette* of April 13, 1937, with a claim of use since February 18, 1936. The "-let" suggests a diminutive, as if a "little cap," but the origin is more likely in a blend of "capsule" and "tablet." A registration followed in the *Trade Marks Journal* of April 6, 1955 for: "Pharmaceutical preparations and substances, … but not including preparations in tablet form for the treatment of headaches."

Caproni *(aircraft)*

The Italian aircraft manufacturers take their name from Giovanni Caproni (1886-1957), who founded his business in 1908. He acquired several other aircraft firms, and the big twin-engined, twin-tail-boom Caproni bombers were among the finest of their kind in World War I.

Captain Morgan *(rum)*

The largest-selling dark rum in the world is named for Sir Henry Morgan (?1635-1688), the celebrated Welsh pirate who was appointed lieutenant-governor of Jamaica in 1674. It is thought that Morgan grew sugar cane and made rum on his estate when he retired from buccaneering. The rum has a distinctive Jamaican flavor and is now produced by **Seagram**.

Caran d'Ache *(artists' materials)*

The origins of the name are in Switzerland, where in 1915 Henri Fatio and Gustave Reverdin founded a pencil factory in Geneva. Business was not good, however, and in 1922 the firm failed. Its assets, premises, and personnel were taken over two years later by Arnold Schweitzer (1885-1947), a stockbroker from St. Gallen, who welcomed the commercial challenge. His interest in art and advertising prompted him to select an artistic name for his acquisition, and this was Caran d'Ache, the pen name, based on *karandash,* the Russian word for "pencil," of the Russian-born French caricaturist Emmanuel Poiré (1858-1909). Under Schweitzer, business boomed, so that today the company and its colorful crayons are known worldwide.

Carborundum *(abrasive)*

The Carborundum Company was organized in 1891 in Monongahela City, Pennsylvania, by the American inventor Edward G. Acheson (1856-1931), born in Washington, Pennsylvania, the son of a merchant and ironworks manager. He quit school at 16 to work as a timekeeper at Monticello Furnace, an ironworks operated by his father, where he developed his first invention, a drilling machine for coal mining. Monticello went out of business in 1874, and Acheson then took up a series of jobs, widening his interest in chemistry and electricity. In 1885 he invented an anti-induction telephone wire that eliminated "crosstalk," then in 1890 established a power station for electric lighting in Monongahela. He now returned to an earlier interest in experiments with carbon, and by 1891 had perfected an abrasive second only to the diamond in hardness. He named the chemical compound "carborundum," thinking it a combination of carbon and corundum. Later, however, he found that it was actually silicon and carbon. Even so, he decided not to change the name, which he saw as "phonetic and of pleasing effect in print, even though a trifle lengthy." After founding the Carborundum Company, he entered the name in the US Patent Office *Official Gazette* of June 21, 1892. The word itself is now generic in some countries.

Cargill *(grain trading and soybean processing)*

The US company started in 1865 with a single grain warehouse in Conover, Iowa, operated by William Cargill, the son of a retired Scottish sea captain who had settled his family on a Wisconsin farm. As the western wheatfields opened up with the coming of the railroad after the Civil War, Cargill and his brothers set up grain elevators or warehouses to store the crops. Cargill's eldest daughter married John H. MacMillan in 1895, and the Cargills and the MacMillans have run the company ever since.

Carling *(beer)*

The name behind the long familiar "Black Label" brand is that of Sir Thomas Carling, the Canadian who founded the firm in Ontario in 1840 as the Carling Brewing and Malting Company. The present name of the Canadian business is Carling O'Keefe, the latter half of which is that of the brewery founded in Canada in 1862 by Eugene O'Keefe, an Irishman from Co. Cork who had immigrated to Canada 30 years earlier. Carling was taken over by the Australian brewers **Foster's** in 1987, but that company overreached itself and in 1989 Carling was merged with **Molson**. The "Black Label" name was dropped in 1998 to make a snappier "bar call" for many Britons' favorite pint.

Carl's Jr. *(hamburgers)*

The American hamburger chain takes its name from Carl Karcher, who quit school in Grade 8 to help on the family farm in Ohio. In 1939 he went west to seek his fortune, at first running a series of hot-dog carts. In 1944 he and his wife started a family restaurant in Anaheim, California, and soon after launched a hamburger chain. His brother, Donald, joined the business in 1954 and they ran it together like an extended family. In 1997 Carl's Jr. acquired the flagging **Hardee's** chain.

Carlsberg *(beer)*

In the early years of the 19th century the Danish brewer Jacob Christian Jacobsen began experimenting with German yeast to produce a new kind of bottom-fermented lager. He brewed his beer and aged it in cellars that he had leased, by royal permission, under the city walls of Copenhagen. The new beer was popular, encouraging Jacob to build a new brewery at Valby, on the outskirts of the city. It was located on a hill, and when the first beer was brewed there in 1847 he named it Carlsberg, after his five-year-old son Carl, and *berg*, the Danish word for "hill." Jacob died in 1887, and Carl in 1914, but not before the latter had grown rich from the products of his brewery and, in 1913, donated the famous "Little Mermaid" statue to the city of Copenhagen. In 1970 Carlsberg merged with **Tuborg** to form United Breweries, which in 1987 reverted to the name Carlsberg.

Carnation *(corn caps)*

At the age of 16, Alfred William Gerrard left his native Dorset for London, where three years later he became a dispensing chemist at Guy's Hospital. He rose to be chief pharmacist at University College Hospital, London, and in 1878 founded the pharmaceutical company of Cuxson, Gerrard & Co. A leading product was the alliteratively named "Carnation Corn Caps," so called from the flesh color of the three constituent items of the finished product: the adhesive cloth, the medicated ointment, and the adhesive ring to relieve shoe pressure. The name was entered in the *Trade Marks Journal* of December 12, 1928.

Carnation *(evaporated milk)*

The man behind the somewhat unexpected name is Elbridge Amos (originally Amos Elbridge) Stuart (1856-1944), born in the New Garden section of Guilford County, North Carolina, a farmer's son. In 1864 young Elbridge contracted rheumatic fever, which played a part in his future career decisions. After spells as a day laborer, bookkeeper, railroad line grader, and general store manager, a meeting with an old associate, Thomas E. Yerxa, settled his choice once and for all.

Offered a partnership in an evaporated milk firm in 1899, Stuart and Yerxa purchased an old plant in Kent, Washington, brought in John B. Meyerberg, a Swiss immigrant, and on December 31, 1900 chartered their new firm as the Pacific Coast Condensed Milk Company. The brand name "Carnation" was then chosen for Stuart's product. The story goes that he was looking for a good name to match an as yet undesigned brightly colored label that he intended to put on the cases of milk. On business one day in Pioneer Square, Seattle, he noticed in a shop window a pile of cigar boxes with the incongruous name "Carnation cigars." He bought a box, and decided that he had found the name he was looking for. To this day the can labels portray three red carnations to match the name. The company became the Carnation Milk Products Company in 1916 and simply the Carnation Company in 1929. The town of Kent eventually changed its name to Carnation, while the company itself sold up to **Nestlé** in 1987.

Caron *(perfumes)*

The original house of this name was a small boutique on the rue Rossini in Paris, France. It was bought in 1903 by Ernest Daltroff, a perfumer looking for a French-sounding label for his new products. In 1904 he created his first perfume, Radiant, and a year later moved to the rue de la Paix, where he met dressmaker Félicie Vanpouille. The two became lovers (but did not marry), and in 1922 Daltroff gave Vanpouille a half-share in the business. In 1939, on the outbreak of World War II, antisemitism forced Daltroff, a Jew, to quit France for Canada, leaving Caron in the care of Vanpouille. In 1941, Daltroff died of cancer in New York, and Michel Morsetti took over as perfumer with Vanpouille still sole proprietor. In 1867, Mme. Bergaud, as she now was, retired at the age of 94 and in 1970 Caron was taken over by U.S. pharmaceutical company Robins. The firm is still famous for its perfumes, such as *Nocturnes* (1981), *Le No. 3* (1985), *Eau de Cologne de Caron* (1995), and *Aimez-Moi* (1997).

Carpano *(vermouth)*

The Italian vermouth takes its name from Antonio Carpano, who made the first commercial preparation of the drink in Italy in 1786. *See also* **Punt e Mes.**

Carphone Warehouse (mobile phones)

The British company was founded by Charles Dunsmore, whose retailing experience began as a 16-year-old school student, buying sunglasses and cigarette lighters through an ad in *Exchange and Mart* and selling them on at 100 percent profit to his classmates. In 1989, as a 25-year-old engineer with just £6,000 in the bank, he set up his mobile phone enterprise, turning over a huge £1.5 million by the end of the year and increasing his employees from two to 14. By 2001, Carphone Warehouse was Europe's largest independent retailer of mobile phones, with 433 stores in the UK and 833 in total. The name suggests phones for use in cars (mobile phones for mobile people) from a well-stocked warehouse.

Carrefour (supermarkets)

The French chain, with a name meaning "crossroads," was founded in 1959 by Badin Defforey and members of the Fournier family. The company is credited with inventing the hypermarket concept, and today is the world's second-largest retailer after **Wal-Mart**. In 1999 Carrefour took over the Spanish Promodès supermarket chain.

Carreras (tobacco products)

The name behind the brand is that of José Joaquin Carreras, the son of a Spanish nobleman, Don José Carreras-y-Ferrer, who in 1843 opened his first shop at 61 Princes Street (now Wardour Street), London, England, selling special tobacco blends, cigars and snuff. The firm was taken over by William Yapp just before the turn of the century, and was incorporated in 1903 as Carreras Ltd., when Yapp brought in Bernhard Baron of **Baron** cigarette machines as director. The following year, when Baron became managing director, an allied private company, Carreras & Marcianus Cigarette Co., was formed for the production of cigarettes using Baron's machinery, and that same year the new business launched three brands of machine-made cigarettes, including the popular "Black Cat." In 1912 Carreras & Marcianus ceased to operate as a separate company and its interests were taken over by Carreras Ltd., while in 1919 the Baron Machinery Co. was incorporated as a subsidiary to market Baron cigarette-making machinery. Expansion of the business continued steadily during and after World War I, and Carreras' Black Cat and **Craven "A"** brands were among the most serious competitors of the Imperial brands (*see* **Imperial Tobacco**). In 1928 a new factory was opened at the Arcadia Works, Hampstead Road, London, and each of the 3,000 employees was presented with a medal inscribed "My thanks for all your help, Bernhard Baron, Chairman, Carreras Ltd."

Carrier (air conditioning)

Willis Haviland Carrier (1876-1950), born in Angola, New York, the son of a dairy and fruit farmer, showed an interest and ability in mechanics from an early age. In 1901 he received a degree in electrical engineering from Cornell University, and was offered a post with Buffalo Forge, a major manufacturer of fans, blowers, and industrial heating equipment. The following year Carrier presented his employers with a plan for what was probably the first scientific air-conditioning system. The system soon worked, and in 1907 Buffalo Forge named Carrier vice president of a wholly owned subsidiary, the Carrier Air Conditioning Company of America. In 1915, after an amicable separation from Buffalo Forge, Carrier and six associates launched the Carrier Engineering Corporation, a company that after subsequent mergers became the Carrier Corporation in 1930. Carrier did not invent air conditioning or even name it, but his enterprise and expertise in that area soon earned him popular esteem as "the father of air conditioning," while "Carrier" and "air conditioning" became largely synonymous in the public mind, especially when Carrier's firm improved summer comfort by installing cooling systems in movie theaters.

Carr's (crackers, or biscuits)

Jonathan Dodgson Carr (1806-1884) was born in Kendal, Westmorland (now Cumbria), into an English Quaker family. His father was a wholesale grocer and tea dealer. Carr began his career as baker and biscuit (cracker) maker in Kendal, but in 1831 moved to Carlisle, reckoning that the larger town would offer greater opportunities. He was soon running a profitable factory, flour mill, and bakery and retail shop there, and in 1841 decided to concentrate on crackers alone. Brothers Henry and John Carr had earlier joined Jonathan in the business, although John left in the 1850s to take over the London-based biscuit company **Peek Frean** with his sons Arthur and Ellis Carr becoming managing directors of that firm in 1901.

Carter Hawley Hale *(department stores and booksellers)*

Until the mid-1960s, the company was established as a middle-America chain of department stores based in Los Angeles. But through takeovers of other famous stores and chains the firm now has outlets in many parts of North America. They began from the Hale Bros. department stores that opened in 1876 in San Jose and Los Angeles, the "Bros." being Prentis Hale, Sr., and his brother Marshall. In 1946 Edward Carter took over The Broadway store, Los Angeles, previously run by an Englishman, Arthur Letts, and in 1950 expanded northward to merge with Hale Bros. The third name of the team is that of Carter's deputy, Philip Hawley. Until 1974 the company was known as Broadway-Hale. Carter himself stepped down as chairman in 1977 at the age of 65.

Carter's *("Little Pills")*

The man that gave the formerly familiar name was a Dr. Carter of Pennsylvania, who in the mid-19th century had established a reputation as a maker of "liver pills," which were essentially pills to treat dyspepsia. He formed a partnership for a time with another chemist and druggist, a Canadian named Brent Good, who had moved to the United States and who would subsequently form a further partnership with William Warner, of what is now the company of **Warner-Lambert**. There were differences of opinion, however, and Dr. Carter was obliged to form a separate concern, the Carter Medicine Company, which itself was bought out by Good in 1870, so that he became the sole proprietor of the firm that made the liver pills. Even so, he retained the Carter name, and it continued to sell the "Little Pills" well into the latter half of the 20th century. The name "Carter's Little Pills" was entered in the *Trade Marks Journal* of February 17, 1886.

Carter's *("Tested Seeds")*

The British firm was founded in Holborn, London, in 1830, and it was from here that the famous "tested seeds" were first distributed. The founder was James Carter, an apothecary

and herbalist who had earlier practiced from premises in Drury Lane. On one of his visits to Continental Europe, he bought a small quantity of aster seed to give to his customers as a spring gift. It was so well received that he decided to sell seeds on a commercial scale. Soon herbalism was taking second place, and Carter's seeds became so popular that they were in demand by royalty. The ultimate accolade came in 1886, when the firm was granted the Royal Warrant. The company secretary was so overwhelmed at the honor that he misspelled the firm's name in his entry in the boardroom memorandum book: "Messrs. Cater & Co. appointed Seedsmen by Royal Warrant to Her Majesty the Queen."

Cartier *(jewelry and watches)*

The company dates back to 1847, when Louis-François Cartier (1819-1904) set up business in Paris, specializing in "fantasy jewelry," embellishing gold with colored stones. Soon he was supplying jewelry to the French royal house. His son Alfred Cartier (1841-1925) joined him after the 1870 Revolution, and in 1898, together with his own son, Louis-Joseph Cartier (1875-1942), moved the firm to luxurious premises in the Rue de la Paix. It was Louis-Joseph Cartier who introduced the clocks and watches side of the business, and by the turn of the century he was designing clocks for many royal houses of Europe. Alfred's second son, Pierre Cartier (1878-1964), opened a branch in London in 1902 and followed this with another in New York in 1908.

Carvel *(ice cream)*

The name is that of Thomas Andreas Carvel (1906-1990), born Thomas Andreas Carvelas in Athanassos, Greece, the son of a wine chemist. His family moved to New York City when he was four years old, where he subsequently worked as a mechanic and served as a test driver for **Studebaker** automobiles. In the early 1930s, Carvel contracted tuberculosis and was advised to work outdoors in the countryside. He began selling ice cream from a truck as well as from a handcart he pushed around Hartsdale, New York. One day in 1934 his truck developed a flat tire. Carvel stopped in a vacant parking lot and plugged his freezer unit into a nearby pottery shop so he could go on selling ice cream. The experience gave him the idea of opening his own ice cream store. He soon earned enough money to buy the pottery shop, and the first Carvel ice cream store opened there. Business flourished, and Carvel initiated a franchise system that eventually gave him 100 stores on the East Coast by 1951. In 1989 Carvel sold his Carvel Corporation, by then the third largest ice cream chain in the United States, to Investcorp, an investment bank in Bahrain, and in 1991 the bank relocated the Carvel Corporation's headquarters from Yonkers, New York, to Farmington, Connecticut.

Cash's *(name tapes)*

Two British brothers gave the name, John Cash (1822-1880) and Joseph Cash (1826-1880), the elder sons of a Coventry cloth merchant and leading businessman. The brothers served seven years apprenticed to their father's trade, and in the early 1840s operated a ribbon-making business from a warehouse in Hertford Street, Coventry. In 1846 they built a factory at West Orchard, taking on French designers to create their ribbons. Despite disputes between the "outworkers," who wove the ribbons at home, and those employed in the factory, the business prospered. It was not until after the brothers' deaths, however, that the firm turned to manufacturing the familiar name tapes. These were introduced in the early 20th century, originally as labels for manufacturers who wished to identify their products. The company's head office remains in Coventry today.

Casio *(pocket calculators)*

The Japanese company takes its name from its cofounder, Tadao Kashio (1917-1993), born in Nankoku the son of a poor rice farmer. At the age of six, Tadao moved with his parents to Tokyo, where his father hoped to earn a better living as a carpenter during the rebuilding of the city following its destruction in the 1923 earthquake. Tadao quit school at 13 and entered the workforce to support his family, first as a shopboy in a firm that recycled oilcans, then in a company that made medals for military uniforms. The following year, Tadao began work as a lathe operator at the Enomoto Manufacturing Company, a manufacturer of machine tools. There he acquired further skills, and when the second son of the Enomoto fam-

ily set up his own business, he invited Tadao to work for him. The enterprise had to close in 1936, however, so Tadao started working for Japan Valve, but left it soon after when he was offered a job at the Japan Typewriter Precision Machine Plant. Although by now an experienced technician, Tadao could only advance so far without a college degree. He thus decided to found his own company, installing his first lathe in his parents' home in 1942. After World War II, his business turned to the production of nonmilitary goods, and in 1946, together with his younger brother, he produced a "ring pipe," a cigarette holder worn as a ring. The brothers' next project was a calculator, which after much trial and error was completed in 1954. In 1957, together with two other brothers, Tadao established the Casio Computer Co. Ltd. to develop and manufacture calculators, and business boomed followed the launch in November that year of the popular Casio 14-A calculator. In 1972 Casio led the competition against **Sharp** and Ohi Electronics when it introduced the Casio Mini, the cheapest consumer-oriented pocket calculator. Two years later, Casio produced its first electronic watch, soon to be followed by the first electronic piano keyboard. The way was now clear for pocket televisions, stereo systems, electronic cash registers, and office automation products.

Casseiver *(cassette recorder and radio)*

The combined cassette recorder and radio has a name devised in 1976 by **Rank** Radio International for a new **Bush** radio incorporating a stereo cassette deck. It was entered by Binatone International Ltd. in the *Trade Marks Journal* of May 11, 1983 for: "Electrical and electronic apparatus and instruments, all for recording, reproduing, amplifying and transmitting sound or video." *Cp.* **Cassingle**.

Cassell *(publishers)*

John Cassell (1817-1865) was a Manchester, England, innkeeper's son who began his career as a carpenter in Salford, Lancashire. After a period as a self-taught temperance lecturer, visiting different towns, he went to London in 1836 to seek employment as a carpenter of a more specialized nature. Instead, he was taken on as a temperance lecturer by a Mr. Meredith, and while serving as an agent turned his hand to dealing in tea and coffee and selling patent medicines. In the meantime he had the idea of issuing cheap publications on the theme of temperance. In 1848 he published *The Standard of Freedom* as a weekly newspaper, and acquired a printing office to publish the *Working Man's Friend and Family Instructor,* first appearing in 1850. He broadened his range of publications to include general educational subjects such as history, biography, and science, all with the working man in mind, and in 1852 moved his publishing business to La Belle Sauvage Yard, off Ludgate Hill, where the house of Cassell remained many years. Cassell was bought by **Collier Macmillan** in 1972, but returned to independence in 1986.

Cassella *(chemicals)*

The German company takes its name from Leopold Cassella (1766-1847), who founded it in Frankfurt in 1789. It originally dealt in the import and selling of colored woods and natural dyestuffs, but in 1870 took up the manufacture of dyestuffs. It underwent a number of name changes, but was known as Leopold Cassella & Co. in 1904, when it merged with Farbewerke **Hoechst**. In 1925, when Hoechst joined the new chemical cartel, **IG Farben**, Cassella reasserted its independence, and was not absorbed by the cartel until 1937. Its full name today is Cassella Farbewerke Mainkur Aktiengesellschaft ("Cassella Dyeworks Mainkur Limited Company") and it is now a subsidiary of Hoechst, who purchased a controlling interest in the company in 1970.

Cassingle *(audio cassette)*

A now dated name for an audio cassette containing a single piece of music on each side, as a tape version of the former "single," or record with such pieces. The name, blending "cassette" and "single," was entered in the *Trade Marks Journal* of November 29, 1978 for: "Magnetic tapes contained in cassettes, adapted to play either of the two recordings on each side repeatedly without rewinding."

Castle & Cooke *(fruit)*

The American company takes its name from Samuel N. Castle and Amos S. Cooke, who set sail from Boston harbor in 1836 to carry out missionary work in Hawaii. In 1851 they took over a failing store that supplied the missionaries with flour, calico, and other goods. The business flourished, the two men bought land, and in 1858 they teamed up with a clergyman, the Rev. Elias Bond, to form the Kohala Sugar Company. By 1875 they were suppliers and marketers for the big plantations, and in 1932 they acquired a share in the ailing Hawaiian Pineapple Company. This had been started in 1901 by James D. Dole (1877-1958), born in Jamaica Plain, Massachusetts, a Unitarian pastor's son, who had come to Hawaii in 1899 to grow coffee but who turned instead to canning pineapples. Castle and Cooke reorganized his business, but kept his name on their well-known cans of Dole pineapple.

Castlemaine XXXX *(beer)*

The well-known Australian lager beer, officially described as a bitter ale, takes its name from its brewery, originally established by the Fitzgerald brothers in Castlemaine, Victoria, in 1859. They set up another brewery in Melbourne in 1871 and then expanded across the country to Brisbane, where they are based today. Their main beer, "Castlemaine XXXX," was introduced in 1924 and became an international rival to **Foster's**. The "XXXX" (pronounced "four X") denotes its supposed extra-strong quality, although it is actually an average 4.8% (as compared, say, to the 4.7% of US **Budweiser**).

Castrol *(motor oil)*

The association of the name with "castor oil" is correct, since Castrol originally had castor oil as its base. Initially named Wakefield Motor Oil in 1906, for Charles C. Wakefield (1859-1941), later Viscount Wakefield, founder in 1899 of C.C. Wakefield & Co., a firm dealing in lubricating oils and appliances, the product was renamed Castrol "R" for the first British aero meeting at Doncaster, Yorkshire, in 1909 and Castrol Motor Oil, for car engines, in 1912. Today Castrol motor oils are based on mineral oils. The name was entered in the *Trade Marks Journal* of August 15, 1906.

Caterham *(automobiles)*

The British firm of Caterham Cars Ltd. began its life as a sports car garage business in Caterham, Surrey, called Caterhams Car Sales. It soon took on a **Lotus** dealership, and in 1973 bought the rights to manufacture the obsolete Lotus 7, renaming it the Caterham Super-7.

Subsequent models have been variations on this. A particularly striking sports car was the Caterham 21, launched at the 1994 Motor Show and named for the 21st century.

Caterpillar *(earth-moving and construction equipment)*

In 1864 Charles Henry Holt led three of his brothers to California in response to the gold rush. In 1868 he founded C.H. Holt & Co. in San Francisco, dealing in timber as well as wagon and carriage materials, as did the business left behind in Concord in the care of his youngest brother, Benjamin Holt (1849-1924). In 1883 Benjamin joined the others in California and together they formed the Stockton Wheel Company, with offices in San Francisco and Stockton. The brothers produced their first traction engine in 1890, and in 1904 Benjamin began experimenting with a track-laying machine that ran on continuous metal-belted tracks instead of wheels. The many shoes of the track suggested the legs of a caterpillar as it moved over the ground. Hence the nickname, which Holt entered in the US Patent Office *Official Gazette* of November 28, 1911, with a note of first use in 1904. In 1925 Holt's firm was merged with another equipment company, the C.L. Best Tractor Company, and in 1928 the Caterpillar Tractor Company was incorporated, becoming Caterpillar Inc. in 1986.

Cathay Pacific *(airline)*

Hong Kong's principal airline had its origins in the charter flights first operated by the American Roy Farrell in 1946. The company was officially founded that same year by Farrell and the Australian Sydney de Kantzow, who had met while flying "over the hump" from Calcutta to China during World War II. Cathay is the name by which China was known to medieval Europe. (A form of it survives today in *Kitay*, the modern Russian name of China.) *See also* **John Swire**.

Catseyes *(reflective road studs)*

Catseyes are light-reflecting studs set in rubber pads in the road in order to demarcate traffic lanes when it is dark or foggy. They were the invention in 1934 of the British roadmender Percy Shaw (1889-1976), of Halifax, Yorkshire, who is said to have been inspired with the idea when driving along the Queens-

bury road between Halifax and Bradford in a dense fog. The story goes that he was prevented from crashing through a fence and down a sheer drop when a cat's eyes, gleaming in his headlights, warned him he was about to drive off the road. In April 1934, Shaw laid 50 studs at his own expense at the dangerous crossroads at Drighlington, near Bradford, and in 1935 set up Reflecting Roadstuds Ltd. to produce the studs on a commercial scale. Over 50 million Catseyes have now been installed on Britain's roads, where on average there are around 250 studs in each kilometer of road, if laid in a straight line. The name was entered in the *Trade Marks Journal* of April 30, 1947.

Caudwell *(mobile phones)*

British entrepreneur John Caudwell was born in Stoke-on-Trent in 1953, the son of an engineering-company representative. He quit school in 1970 and after stints in a steel factory and acting as a nightclub bouncer joined **Michelin** as an engineering apprentice. It was while he was working as a car salesman, traveling to auctions to sell to dealers and garages, that Caudwell came across the potentially lucrative mobile phones market, and in 1987 he sold his first mobiles from the trunk of his own car. Today, based in Stoke-on-Trent, the Caudwell Group incorporates a range of companies, as well as the Phones 4U retail chain, with 120 outlets in 2001 and another 80 planned by the end of the year.

CBS *(broadcasting)*

The initials were officially adopted in 1974 as the name of the Columbia Broadcasting Company, incorporated in 1927 as United Independent Broadcasters, Inc. It owes its origin to William S. Paley (1901-1990), born in Chicago, Illinois, the son of a Russian Jewish immigrant cigar manufacturer, who initially went into his family's successful cigar business. In 1927 he became interested in broadcasting when his business began advertising La Palina cigars on WCAU, a Philadelphia radio station. In 1928, when the financially struggling **Columbia** Phonographic Broadcasting System came up for sale, the Paley family purchased it.

Cecil Gee *(menswear)*

Cecil Gee (1903-1980), whose original surname was Goldstein, was a tailor in the tradition made famous by **Moss Bros**. and **Burton**. He initially set up business in the East End of London, England, in 1931, but then moved up-market to the West End in 1938 where he opened a shop in Charing Cross Road, soon gaining a reputation for his fashionable and original clothing. His real fame, however, came in the years of austerity after World War II, when people wanted to express their individuality in what they wore. He first created an "American style," typically with double-breasted suits and wide lapels, but when this became associated with gangsterism, progressed to an "Italian style," with narrow ties and lapels. He opened further stores in the West End in the 1960s, including the one on Shaftesbury Avenue where the company's head office remains today.

Ceefax *(teletext system)*

The name, representing "see facts," is that of a teletext system introduced by the BBC in the UK in the early 1970s. It was entered by the BBC in the *Trade Marks Journal* of June 13, 1973 for: "Telecommunications apparatus for use with television transmitters and receivers and for the transmission and display of data." *Cp.* **Oracle**.

Celador *(television production)*

Following a spell as movie director for **Twentieth Century-Fox** in the USA, British television producer Paul Smith (b.1947) and his wife, Sarah, set up Complete Video Facilities as a provider of production services. His company took its present name (Spanish for "monitor") soon after, and in 1998 devised the hit game show *Who Wants to Be a Millionaire?*, eventually shown in 80 countries.

Celanese *(viscose fabric)*

The firm that first introduced the fabric on a commercial scale was British Celanese, founded in 1916 at Spondon, near Derby, by the Swiss-born brothers Henry Dreyfus (1882-1944) and Camille Dreyfus (1878-1956) as the British Cellulose and Chemical Manufacturing Company, who entered the name in the *Trade Marks Journal* of April 27, 1921 for: "filaments, fibres, threads, and fabrics (being goods … made wholly or principally from cellulose derivatives)." The American Cellulose and Chemical Manufacturing Company was incorporated

in 1918 by Camille Dreyfus and in 1927 became the Celanese Corporation of America. The name itself was devised as the result of a competition by Henry Dreyfus, and is based on "cellulose," with the final "-ese" perhaps intended to suggest "ease" in allusion to the fabric's comfort of wearing.

Celis *(beer)*

The American brewery takes its name from Pierre Celis, born in Belgium next to a brewery. When the local "white" wheat-style beer disappeared, he decided to revive it, setting up the De Kluis ("The Cloister") brewery in Hoegaarden in 1966. It proved so popular that, after expanding the brewery more than once, he sold the business to Belgium's largest brewer, Interbrew, in 1989. He then decided to cross the Atlantic, and in 1992 opened the Celis Brewery in Austin, Texas, to brew his original Belgian-style wheat beer, now called "Celis White." It also proved a success, and was copied by others. In 1995, Celis sold a controlling interest to **Miller**, and in 1996 the company doubled capacity.

Cellnet *(cellular radio service)*

The name of the mobile communications system, using cellular radio, was entered in the US Patent Office *Official Gazette* of February 19, 1985: "For communications services—namely, providing a network for paging and mobile telephone services," with a note of first use on November 11, 1982. The name thus simply combines "cell" (or "cellular") and "net" (or "network").

Cellon *(insulating material)*

The composition of cellulose acetate, used as an insulating material, takes its name from "cellulose" and the arbitrary suffix "-on." It was first in production in the early 20th century.

Cellophane *(transparent wrapping material)*

The material was first made from regenerated cellulose in Zürich, Switzerland, in 1908 by the Swiss chemist Jacques Edwin Brandenberger. He created its name from "cellulose" and the element "-phane" meaning "showing through," and the product began to be made in Paris, France, in 1912. Brandenberger, or rather his American assignee, **Du Pont**, lost his exclusive right to the name in the USA when the courts decided that, on the expiration of the patent, the article had no other general name, so that "cellophane" was descriptive. The name is thus generic in the USA but a registered trademark in the UK, as attested by the following letter in *The Times* of June 30, 1980, from the patent manager of British Cellophane Ltd.:

Sir, On page 18 of *The Times* (June 16) there is an article entitled "ICI's trade mark policemen" in which John Huxley discloses the efforts taken by the staff of ICI to protect the trade marks of their company. We, British Cellophane Limited, also take great pains to protect the status of our marks, including the valuable trade mark "Cellophane" which is registered in the United Kingdom and in a number of principal countries in the world. It was therefore with astonishment that we read in the above-mentioned article that "Cellophane" was an example of a mark which had lost its status and was now used generically. Nothing could be further from the truth. The statement is quite erroneous. The mark "Cellophane" is very much in use in connexion with our products and we would not be happy with its unauthorized use. Yours faithfully, N.H. Hollingsworth.

Centronics *(computer printers)*

The name for various types of computer printers and peripherals was entered in the US Patent Office *Official Gazette* of July 16, 1974: "For data terminals in the nature of high speed printers of the dot matrix type and components and sub-assemblies used therein," with a note of first use in July 1968. The name is presumably a shortening of "central electronics."

Cerebos *(table salt)*

The salt first appeared in 1894 as the invention of a British chemist (druggist), George Weddell (1855-1916), who wanted something to strengthen his baby daughter's teeth and bones. (Its name was entered in the *Trade Marks Journal* of February 22, 1893.) The name is a classical concoction, ostensibly suggesting a bull made of wax, from Greek *kēros*, "wax," and Latin *bos*, "ox." More likely is a connection with Ceres, the Greek goddess of grain, or even, given the intention of the product's inventor, a blend of Latin *cerebrum*, "brain," and *os*, "bone." All these possibilities are mentioned in a piece of doggerel that appeared by way of advertising the product in the early 20th century, two of the verses running as follows:

"Ceres" is Greek for the goddess of grain,

"Cerebrum" stands for the best of the brain,
"Bos" is an ox, and "Os" is the bone—
A rare combination, as critics will own.
Now "Cerebos Salt" is the strength of the grain,
That is needed to nourish the bones and the brain,
Thrown out with the bran, but restored to the food,
Is a salt for the table, rich, dainty, and good.

Cerumol *(earwax remover)*

The name of the preparation alludes to its basic function as an earwax softener, from a blend of modern Latin *cerumen*, "earwax," and classical Latin *mollis*, "soft." The name was entered in the *Trade Marks Journal* of February 27, 1952.

Cessna *(aircraft)*

The popular light aircraft takes its name from the American aviator Clyde Vernon Cessna (1879-1954), born in Hawthorne, Louisiana, who worked as a farmhand, prospector, threshing-machine operator, and automobile salesman until one day he saw a flying circus in Oklahoma and decided to be a flyer. He worked at an airplane factory in the Bronx, New York, for two months and returned to Oklahoma, where he flew his first plane in 1911. In 1917 he produced a monoplane powered by a six-cylinder, air-cooled engine, and in the 1920s teamed up with businessman and air enthusiast Victor Roos to produce Cessna-Roos aircraft until 1927. He then bought out the company, which was closed for four years from 1931 in the Great Depression. A revived Cessna Aircraft Company subsequently came to produce 8,000 planes a year.

Chambers *(publishers)*

The long familiar *Chambers's Twentieth Century Dictionary* arose from the initiative shown by the two Scots brothers William Chambers (1800-1883) and Robert Chambers (1802-1871), born in Peebles, the sons of a cotton trader. (Their father had changed his name to Chalmers as a teenager, but the sons reverted to the original spelling.) As children they read avidly, but their father's business was less of a success, and the family moved to Edinburgh. There in 1814 William was apprenticed to a bookseller. On completing his apprenticeship in 1819 he immediately set himself up, in Leith Walk, as a bookseller in his own right. Robert, meanwhile, had quit school and had also started up as a bookseller, using his old schoolbooks for his original stock. Further, his own writings were gaining acclaim, mostly in the form of historical and biographical works on Scotland. In 1832, the brothers began to publish *The Chambers's Journal,* a weekly publication on subjects such as history, religion, language, and science. It sold so well that the two men moved to new premises, and there established the firm of W.& R. Chambers. In 1861 they published their first dictionary, edited by Arnold J. Colley. This was followed in 1867 by *Chambers's Etymological Dictionary,* compiled by James Macdonald. A larger version of this, *Chambers's English Dictionary,* came in 1872, with a second edition in 1898. Finally, in 1901, the Revd. Thomas Davidson produced a new, compact edition of the English dictionary, *Chambers's Twentieth Century Dictionary,* reissued and retitled in 1988 as *Chambers English Dictionary* and in 1993 as *The Chambers Dictionary.* Chambers subsequently acquired the core business of **Harrap.**

Champion *(spark plugs)*

The name is that of Albert Champion (1878-1927), born in Paris, France, who at about the age of 12 obtained employment as an errand boy for a bicycle manufaturer. In 1894, aged 16, Champion began entering bicycle races. His series of victories made him middle-distance champion and took him to the United States in 1899 to compete with riders there. He participated not only in bicycle races but in automobile and motorcycle races, giving him a valuable insight into the sale of automobile accessories.

In 1905 he started a small plant in Boston, Massachusetts, to manufacture "sparking plugs," and the demand for his products brought such success that he soon opened a second plant in Toledo,Ohio. In 1908 he set up the Champion Ignition Company in Flint, Michigan, to produce ignition devices, spark plugs, and other electrical equipment for **Buick** cars. In 1910 Buick purchased control of the company and it began to operate as a **General Motors** subsidiary, AC Division, with Champion as general manager. AC went on to purchase other spark plug factories in Europe, and soon won acclaim for its products. Thus both "Champion" and "AC" became names associated primarily with spark plugs.

Chanel *(perfume)*

The well-known name is that of Gabrielle "Coco" Chanel (1883-1971), the French daughter of a provincial fairground huckster who sold suspenders and handkerchiefs from a pushcart. Orphaned early, Gabrielle had intended to make a career as a singer, but her voice lacked power. She therefore turned to being a milliner, starting to design hats. She opened a boutique in Deauville, and among other fashions brought out a simple but "chaste" bathing suit to supersede the cumbersome costume hitherto worn by ladies when swimming. After service as a nurse in World War I, "Coco" (so nicknamed from a song she had sung in concert cafés) founded a couture house in Paris, introducing a whole new range of fashions and accessories. In 1921 the famous perfume Chanel No. 5 was created by Ernst Beaux for Chanel while they were staying in Biarritz. There was no Chanel Nos. 1-4, and the story goes that No. 5 was so named because the perfume was launched on May 5, the fifth day of the fifth month. The House of Chanel continued after Chanel's death and flourishes today in Paris.

Chapman & Hall *(publishers)*

The English publishing house, noted for its editions of famous authors such as Dickens, Thackeray, Carlyle, and Kingsley, was founded in 1830 at 186 Strand, London, by Edward Chapman (1804-1880) and William Hall (?1801-1847). Chapman retired in 1864, when his place was taken by his cousin, Frederick Chapman (1823-1895), who had been active in the business for some years. In 1850 the firm moved to Piccadilly, and in 1880 to Henrietta Street, Covent Garden, in which year it was incorporated. In 1836 William Hall initially approached Dickens with the suggestion that the firm publish his *Pickwick Papers,* and this duly appeared in 1837, when Dickens was still only 25. The firm was sold to **Methuen** in 1938.

Chappell *(music publishers)*

The British firm of music publishers, concert agents, and piano manufacturers was founded in 1810 when the pianist and composer Johann Baptist Cramer (1771-1858) joined forces with F.T. Latour and Samuel Chappell (d.1834). The business eventually devolved on Chappell's son William (1809-1888), who was succeeded by his brother Thomas Patey Chappell (1819-

1902). In 1970 the firm merged with Ascherberg, Hopwood & Crew, formed in a merger of 1906, and it is now part of **Philips**.

Charbonnages de France (coal mining)

The French state-owned coal-mining and processing company was formed in 1946 following France's post-World War II nationalization of the country's most productive coalfield, the Nord Pas de Calais, located in the Ruhr region. The French title might be rendered in English as "French Coal Board." Its first word is based on *charbon*, "coal."

Charbonnel et Walker (chocolates)

The British firm arose in 1875 as a partnership between the Englishwoman Mrs. Walker and the Frenchwoman Madame Charbonnel, the latter from the Maison Boissier chocolate house in Paris. The firm has been the victim of many acquisitions and mergers, but in 1989 returned to private ownership.

Charlemagne (chocolates)

The Belgian firm was founded in 1987 by Denise Courant-Bellefroid, an art and culinary historian, and Jean-François Staesbolet, a former endive (chicory) farmer. The couple had dreamed up the idea of making chocolate two years before following a holiday abroad, and set up their enterprise in Herstal, a town noted for its associations with Charlemagne. (His great-grandfather, the Frankish ruler Pepin the Younger, was born there, and it was one of the favorite residences of the Carolingian kings.) The firm operates 20 stores, mainly in Brussels.

Charrington (beer)

The founder of the British company was the London brewer John Charrington (1739-1815). In 1766 he bought one third of the shares in the brewery of Westfield and Moss, at the Anchor Brewery, Mile End Road, and followed his acquisition with another third in 1769 and the remainder in 1783. Two years later he was elected Master of the Brewers' Company. He was succeeded in the business by his son Nicholas, who died in 1827.

Chase Manhattan (bank)

The second part of the name of the American bank derives from the water company set up in New York City in 1799. The company was authorized to engage in other business if it had surplus funds, and within a few months it set up the Bank of the Manhattan Company at 40 Wall Street. In 1808 it sold its waterworks to the city and turned completely to banking. Meanwhile, the first half of the name was represented by a bank founded in New York in 1877 by a former schoolteacher, John Thompson (1802-1891), who named his enterprise after the late US secretary of the treasury Salmon P. Chase (1808-1873). It was not until 1955, however, that The Chase National Bank, then the nation's third largest bank, merged with the Bank of the Manhattan Company, the 15th largest, and The Chase Manhattan Corporation was formed in 1969.

Chatto & Windus (publishers)

The British publishing house was founded in 1855 on the site of the present Ritz Hotel, Piccadilly, London, by John Camden Hotten (1832-1873), a colorful character who made his name as a writer and bookseller. He used to publish the works of Mark Twain without making any payment, even adding chapters of his own. On Hotten's death, the business was sold to one of his colleagues, Andrew Chatto, himself the third son of William Andrew Chatto (1799-1864), a miscellaneous writer from Newcastle. Chatto, whose somewhat indolent partner was W.E. Windus, a minor poet, laid the foundations of the present firm, setting things right with Mark Twain and continuing to publish him, but this time with payment. In 1987 Chatto & Windus were taken over by **Random House**.

Chef Boy-ar-dee (foods)

The man behind the name is Italian-born Hector Boiardi (1897-1985), who began his career as an apprentice chef at the age of nine. After a spell working in European hotel kitchens, Boiardi moved to Manhattan and became a chef at the Plaza, where his brother Richard was a waiter. He left the Plaza in 1929 to start a restaurant in Cleveland, Ohio, where his piquant sauce became so popular with customers that he began retailing his spaghetti dinners in bottles. In 1936, Hector, Richard, and a third brother, Mario, formed a company to market the chef's specialities under the phonetically spelled-out "Chef Boy-ar-dee" label. The brothers sold their company to **American Home Products** in 1946.

Cheney *(locks)*

The founder of the British firm of C.W. Cheney & Son of Birmingham was Charles William Cheney (1875-1959), who after a period as an apprentice with a firm of die-sinkers, started up his own business in 1894 in a small back room in Vyse Street, Birmingham. By 1900 he had done well enough to move to larger premises in York Terrace, and in 1916 started the present factory in Factory Road (named after it), Hockley. From the beginning his firm specialized in locks and fittings for luggage, and he registered his first patent for this type of lock in 1899.

Cherry Blossom *(shoe polish)*

The name was originally used by the Chiswick Soap Company, London, England, for a perfumed toilet soap packed in a tin. After a period of nonuse, the name was revived for similarly packed boot polishes manufactured by the same firm, the name itself being registered in 1903. The company name was accordingly changed to the Chiswick Polish Company. The firm was in due course acquired by the company that became **Reckitt & Colman**. Hence the unlikely connection between an attractive spring flower and a shoe-cleaning preparation.

Cherry Heering *see* **Heering**

Chesebrough-Pond's *(cosmetics)*

The two companies behind the name merged only in 1955, but their respective origins date back a century earlier. Robert A. Chesebrough (1837-1933) was originally a kerosene dealer in Brooklyn, New York. A chance experiment with petroleum residue in 1859 left him with a jellylike substance that turned out to be efficacious for cuts and scratches, and that subsequently became the famous **Vaseline**, making his fortune. He therefore incorporated his company to manufacture the substance in 1880, the year that Chesebrough-Pond's now regards as its "birthday." The other branch of the company tree goes back to Theron T. Pond, a chemist in Utica, New York, who in 1846 brewed a new kind of witch hazel. He called his product "Pond's Extract," subsequently moving his distillery to Connecticut, where he broadened his activities to include other toiletries and cosmetics. Pond's skin cream became popular worldwide in the 20th century,

and was publicly promoted by socially prominent women in a series of advertisements. Chesebrough did not live to see the merger between the two companies, but he did reach the age of 96, attributing his longevity to the daily spoonful of Vaseline that he ate as a "general panacea."

Chesterfield *(cigarettes)*

The brand of this name, manufactured by **Liggett & Myers**, is simply a "prestigious" compliment to Philip Dormer Stanhope, 4th Earl of Chesterfield (1694-1773), who had achieved world fame for his gracious living. (His title also passed to other "quality" objects, such as the Chesterfield coat and the elegant sofa known as a chesterfield.) Liggett & Myers acquired the name, formerly used by the Drummond Tobacco Company, from the American Tobacco Company (*see* **American Brands**) in 1911, and reintroduced it the following year. The name was earlier the subject of litigation when in 1898 Lichenstein Brothers of New York sued Drummond, claiming that they (the Lichensteins) originally used the name on a cigar. The New York Supreme Court ruled against Lichenstein Brothers on the grounds that "Chesterfield" is a geographical name as well as that of an actual person.

Chevrolet *(automobiles)*

Louis Chevrolet (1878-1941) was born at La Chaux-de-Fonds, near Neuchâtel, Switzerland, and began his career as an engineer with a special interest in motor engines. In 1900 he emigrated to the United States and took up motor racing, defeating the famous American driver Barney Oldfield in 1905 in his first race. In 1911, together with William Crapo Durant of **General Motors**, he built the first Chevrolet car. He had little confidence in it, however, and in 1915 sold his interest to Durant, who the following year brought the Chevrolet Motor Company into General Motors. Chevrolet continued to race cars and motorboats, but derived little financial benefit from the company he had founded, and in the last years of his life was not even its chairman but merely a minor employee.

Chevron *(petroleum)*

The American petroleum corporation traces its origins to 1879, when the Pacific Coast Oil

Company was founded. In 1900 this company was purchased by the **Standard Oil** Company, which six years later combined it with its own West Coast marketing operations to form Standard Oil Company (California). In 1911, when the New Jersey-based Standard Oil combine was dissolved by the US Supreme Court, the California-based company gained its autonomy. In 1926 it acquired the properties of Pacific Oil Company and became Standard Oil Company of California, retaining this name until 1984 when, in one of the largest mergers ever, it purchased **Gulf Oil**. The name it then adopted, Chevron, had already long been in use as its logo and appeared on many of its gas stations. The chevron itself symbolizes rank or long service, and on either count Standard Oil of California merits it. In 2000 Chevron merged with **Texaco** to form ChevronTexaco.

Chiclets (chewing gum)

An early form of bubblegum was made at the turn of the 20th century by Frank H. Fleer, organizer in the 1880s of Frank H. Fleer Corporation. Fleer originally called the new bubblegum "Blibber-Blabber," but it was too sticky and did not cohere. Moreover, it produced a "wet" bubble that stubbornly stuck to junior's face. Meanwhile, Frank's brother Henry was experimenting with a form of candy covered in chicle pellets. Results were promising, and one day Henry burst into Frank's office waving a sample of the pellets and crying, "Look, Frank! These little chiclets are coming along just fine!" "That's it!" said Frank. "That's what we'll call them—'Chiclets!'" They were an instant success, and were later sold to the **American Chicle** Co. As for "Blibber-Blabber," in 1928 a way was found of making a gum that produced huge "dry" bubbles, and it was renamed "Dubble Bubble."

Chilprufe (underwear)

The British firm was founded in Leicester in 1906 as manufacturers of children's underwear and subsequently women's nightwear. The garments keep the wearer warm, so are "chillproof."

Chiquita (bananas)

The name, Latin-American Spanish for "Tiny," was adopted by the United Fruit Company (see **United Brands**) for their brand of bananas and was placed on each individual banana by means of pressure-sensitive labels. The name resulted in a popular song, beginning, "I'm a Chiquita Banana, and I'm here to reveal...," and in the 1950s the advertising wizards came up with a sexually suggestive ad showing a banana standing on end with a vertical vector indicating eight inches. The copy read: "What does a banana have to be to be a Chiquita? It's sort of like passing the physical to become a Marine... right height... a good 8 inches along the outer curve... at least 1½ inches across the middle... plump... the peel has to fit tightly. The banana has to be sleek, and firm." The ad ran in several women's magazines before *Life* magazine tumbled to the allusion and refused insertion.

Chivas Regal (whisky)

The origin of the whisky's name is in Aberdeen, Scotland, where in 1801 William Edward opened a grocer's and wine merchant's business at 49 Castle Street. In about 1838 he moved to King Street, and there took on James Chivas (1810-1886), the Aberdeenshire son of a tenant farmer, who had begun his career with a wholesale firm of hat, cap, and shoe manufacturers. The exact date of his entry into Edward's business is uncertain, but on the former's death in 1841, Chivas took over. In 1857 he took his brother John Chivas (1814-1862) into partnership. The firm claims that the name "Regal" had long been used, but it can be specifically dated to 1843, when the Royal Warrant was granted to James Chivas as a purveyor of Scotch whisky to Queen Victoria. Chivas Regal is now part of **Seagram**.

Chivers (jam)

The Chivers family came to England from France, together with other persecuted Huguenots, in the 17th century. One branch settled in Cottenham, near Cambridge, and a member of that branch was John Chivers, a wheelwright at Histon, now a suburb of Cambridge. The village of Histon and the surrounding area were renowned for their fruit trees, and Chivers together with his brother William made the most of such trees on their land. In the 1830s they were joined by John's three sons, and with their help increased their holdings of fruit trees, sending the fruit itself to the London markets. By the late 1860s, Stephen Chivers (1824-1907), the second of the three sons, felt that they should have their own depot, rather than sending fruit to market. Persuading their father to make jam from the fruit, the family business set up a small jam boiling plant in a barn at Impington, near Histon, in 1873. Chivers' own brands of jam were first marketed in Cambridge that year, and in 1874 the family purchased an orchard at Histon, strategically sited near the railroad station. The company still has its head office there today, at The Orchard, Chivers Way, Histon, Cambridge.

Chloromycetin *(antiobiotic)*

The proprietary name for the drug chloramphenicol, discovered in 1947 and used for treating typhoid fever, derives from Greek-based *chloro-*, "green," Greek *mukēs*, *mukētos*, "fungus", and the pharmaceutical suffix "-in", and dates from the late 1940s, when its production and distribution was in the hands of Parke, Davis & Co. (later part of **Warner-Lambert**).

Chock Full o' Nuts *(coffee)*

The founder of the quirkily named corporation was William Black, who was unsure of his age when he died in 1983. Black said he was born in Brooklyn, but he in fact emigrated from Russia when he was four years old. He graduated in engineering from Columbia University, but when unable to find work in that profession saw his opportunity in the long lines that formed outside a discount theater-ticket outlet in Times Square, New York, where in 1922 he set up a nut stand. Within a decade, he owned 18 Chock Full o' Nuts restaurants. During the Depression, nuts became very expensive, so Black converted the stands into lunch counters that specialized in cheap, quick meals. "Chock" began selling coffee in 1953, and eventually the retail coffee overtook the restaurants in sales. The restaurants were at their peak in the 1960s, but soon fell from favor when a younger generation with a liking for hamburgers and pizzas no longer wished to patronize lunch counters where waitresses in hairnets served nutty cheese sandwiches, frankfurters, and pea soup. The company gradually closed the restaurants as their leases expired, then sold the remainder to Riese Bros., Inc., a New York management firm, who converted them into fast-food restaurants. The last lease expired in 1992.

Chopper *(bicycles)*

The type of children's bicycle, with high-rise handlebars and front-wheel fork extended forwards, was introduced in the early 1970s by Leslie Charles (1917-2000), director of factories for **Raleigh**. The design and name were adopted from the 1960s motorcycle, itself so called because it was "chopped" or reduced to the essence, with chrome and extras stripped away and standard parts and fittings replaced with improvisations. (Such bikes were originally customized **Harley Davidson** 74s, favored by Hell's Angels.) The name was entered by Raleigh in the *Trade Marks Journal* of March 31, 1971.

Chris-Craft *(boats)*

Christopher Columbus Smith (1861-1939), of Algonac, Michigan, did not follow his father's trade of blacksmith but instead tried his hand at making boats. In 1881 he began building rowboats and duck boats for hunters on Lake St. Clair, and later moved on to gasoline-powered inboard motorboats. With the backing of promoter and financier John J. Ryan, Smith embarked on a venture to build speedboats. Their boats broke many speed records in the early 1900s, and when Ryan left the firm in 1913, Smith was joined by four sons and a daughter. Beginning in the 1920s, the Smiths introduced a number of production innovations, and by the time Chris Smith retired in 1930 his company's Chris-Craft boats were distributed worldwide by over 200 dealers.

Christian Salvesen *(food distribution)*

Christian Salvesen (1827-1911) was the Norwegian son of the owner of a shipping and ships' agency company. On leaving school, he followed in the footsteps of his elder brother Theodor who had learned the shipping business in Prussia and Scotland and who had set up his own agency in Grangemouth, Scotland. Christian worked in his brother's Scottish office for a time before returning to Norway to widen his experience. In 1851 he came back to Scotland to take charge of Theodor's new agency in Leith, the port for Edinburgh. He remained as a partner until 1872, when he set up under his own name. The company headquarters remain in Edinburgh today. At the close of the 20th century, Alastair Salvesen (b.1941) and his brother Robin (b.1935) retained stakes in the group.

Christian Saunal (chocolates)

The 50 types of chocolates and 20 varieties of chocolate cakes produced by the French pâtissier Christian Saunal (b.1946) evolved from the pâtisserie set up by his father in 1954. Following a three-year degree course in physics and chemistry at Toulouse University, and a stint in the family business, Christian took over the enterprise in 1974 and soon built up a range of seasonal specialties.

Christie's (auctioneers)

James Christie (1730-1803) had for some years pursued a career as a British naval officer before resigning his commission to become an auctioneer. He held his first sale in 1766 in rooms in Pall Mall, London, England, where the premises had been the print warehouse of the painter and engraver Richard Dalton. Christie later went to live at Schomberg House, Pall Mall, where he had rooms next to the famous painter Gainsborough. After his death, his auctioneering business was carried on with increasing success by his son, also James, and it was he who moved the business in 1824 to new premises in King Street, off St. James's Square, where the firm's head office is today.

Christy (hats, towels, bedlinen)

The man whose name lies behind the Turkish towels is Miller Christy, born at Haddington, Scotland, in 1748. By the time he was 25, Christy was in London, where he was apprenticed to a feltmaker. In 1773 he married, and the same year opened a small hatting business in a courtyard off Gracechurch Street. Four years later he was joined by his son, William Miller Christy (1778-1858), who was in turn apprenticed with his father. When Miller Christy retired in 1804, William took over the management of the business, together with his brothers, Thomas and John. In 1826 the Christy family moved to Stockport, Cheshire, where William had acquired a banking business. It was Henry, another brother, who brought back a piece of hand-fashioned cloth from Turkey in the 1840s, and this sample of terry toweling formed the basis for the Turkish towels for which Christy's became prominent. Only in 1955 did the company introduce bedlinen to its range.

Chrysalis (music publishers)

British entrepreneur Christopher Norman "Chris" Wright (b.1944) began his career in 1965 at the University and College Booking Agency in Manchester. Two years later, with business partner Terry Ellis, he formed the Ellis Wright Agency, but punningly changed this prosaic name to the more colorful Chrysalis (Chris + Ellis) in 1968. The firm he founded, now Chrysalis Group, became an international multimedia giant with a range of interests spanning television production, books, and music publishing. It also runs seven British radio stations. In 1992 Wright sold the original Chrysalis record label to **Thorn EMI** but kept the publishing interests, which in 1999 brought him **Batsford**.

Chrysler (automobiles)

Walter Percy Chrysler (1875-1940), the son of a Union Pacific Railroad engineer, was so determined to be a machinist that he had built his own tools before the age of 20. After working as a machinist in several towns, he became a power superintendent in 1908 for the Chicago Great Western Railroad. That same year, using his entire savings of $700 and borrowing a further $4,300 from a bank, he bought his first car, a Locomobile. In 1912 he entered the motor industry, and soon became president of **Buick** Motor Cars and in 1919 manufacturing vice president of **General Motors**. In 1920 he began to build the car of his dreams, a low-priced model with a high-compression engine, eventually creating his fantasy in 1924, when the first six-cylinder Chrysler 50 was built. That same year, around 32,000 Chrysler cars were sold, and a new name joined the motor industry. In 1999 Chrysler merged with **Daimler** to form DaimlerChrysler AG.

Chubb (locks)

Originally in the hardware trade at Winchester, Hampshire, England, Charles Chubb (1772-1845), born in Fordingbridge, Hampshire, moved to Portsea in that county after his younger brother Jeremiah had been granted a patent there in 1818 for a new form of "detector" lock. Charles then went to London, where in 1827 he opened his own premises in St. Paul's Church Yard, moving once again in 1830 to Wolverhampton, where he began to manufacture locks. He patented his first safe in 1835, and by 1846 his firm's safe manufactory was established in Smithfield, London, when the business was in the hands of his executors and his son, John Chubb (1816-1872), who was in turn succeeded by his three sons, John C. Chubb, George Hayter Chubb (created Lord Hayter of Chislehurst in 1927), and Henry W. Chubb. The last Chubb to be in charge of the firm was Sir George Charles Hayter Chubb, 3d Baron Hayter (b.1911), who was managing director from 1941 to 1957 and chairman from 1957 to 1981. In 1984 Chubb was acquired by **Racal**.

Churchill (insurance)

The British company was founded in 1989 by the entrepreneur Martin Long and originally sold car insurance. The name was chosen to reflect its intended qualities of "Britishness, trust, strength, and perseverance," attributes traditionally ascribed to Sir Winston Churchill (1874-1965).

Churchman (cigarettes)

Early details about the British company are scanty, but it is known that the business was founded in 1790 in Ipswich, Suffolk, with the founder's two grandsons, William and Arthur Churchman, succeeding to ownership in 1888, when they were respectively aged 23 and 21.

Church's (footwear)

Information is sparse about the British founders of Church & Co. and about exactly where they lived, although it is certain that they were three brothers, Alfred, Thomas, and William Church, who established their shoemaking business in Northampton in 1873. Although shoemaking at that time was frequently carried out by workers in their own homes, the Church brothers brought all their employees together in a newly built factory, where they could be personally supervised. The company still has its head office in Northampton today and is still in the hands of the Church family. In 1999 Church & Co. became a part of **Prada**.

Church's (fried chicken)

In 1932, Texan George W. Church (1887-1956) became a salesman of chicken incubators. He was increasingly convinced, however, that a restaurant selling quickly prepared food would be what the mobile American customer wanted, and in 1952 accordingly opened "Church's Fried Chicken to Go" in downtown San Antonio. At the time of Church's death, his company operated four restaurants in the area. It continued to grow under the leadership of his sons, Bob and George, Jr., so that by 1968, the year it opened its first location outside of Texas, it had 44 stores. In 1977, the chain operated some 740 stores in 22 states, and was considered a leader among all US companies in profit growth.

Ciba-Geigy (pharmaceuticals)

The company's origins are in Basel, Switzerland, where Johann Rudolf Geigy-Gemuseus (1733-1793) set up a business in 1758 as a trader in chemicals, dyes, and a whole range of drugs, the latter mostly from the East Indies. The year mentioned can thus be regarded as that of the company's founding. "Ciba" represents the initials of Chemische Industrie Basel Aktiengesellschaft ("Basel Chemical Industries Company"), founded in Basel in 1859. The two companies merged in 1970 to form Ciba-Geigy (renamed simply Ciba in 1992), which in 1996 merged with **Sandoz** to form **Novartis** as the world's second largest pharmaceutical company.

Ciment Fondu (cement)

The rapidly hardening high-alumina cement is made by fusing or sintering lime or other calcareous material and alumina or bauxite and grinding the cooled mass to a fine powder. Its name, French for "melted cement," was entered by the Société des Chaux et des Ciments de Lafarge du Teil (see **Lafarge**) in the *Trade Marks Journal* of October 8, 1924.

CinemaScope (film projection process)

The wide-screen film projection process, using an anamorphic lens, was introduced by **Twentieth Century-Fox** in 1953 with its production of *The Robe*. The process itself was based on the work of the Frenchman Henri Chrétien, who had developed a special lens for tanks that allowed a 180-degree field of vision. The name blends "cinema" and "-scope," as in "telescope," "microscope," etc.

Cinerama (film projection process)

The film projection process using three projectors and a wide, curved screen was the creation of the American motion picture technician Frederic Waller (1886-1954), who with the architect Ralph Walker founded the Vitarama Corporation in 1938 to develop it. Cinerama Inc. was formed with Waller as chairman and on September 30, 1952 introduced the invention to the general public in the feature film, *This Is Cinerama*, at the Broadway Theater, New York City. The name blends "cinema" and "panorama," while echoing Waller's "Vitarama." A development of Cinerama was **Todd-AO**.

Cinzano *(aperitif)*

The House of Cinzano dates its founding from the year 1757, when the names of two Italian brothers, Carlo Stefano Cinzano and Giovanni Giacomo Cinzano, are found to have been registered in the records of the Confectioners' and Distillers' Guild of Turin. But the family origins naturally go back further than this, and it is known that the two brothers had opened a spirit merchant's shop in Pecetto, near Turin, by the year 1742, when Carlo Stefano would have been 23 and his brother 17. It was the brothers' descendants who established the company's reputation for vermouth, and the family moved from Pecetto to Turin for good in the early 19th century. The present company was organized in 1922 on the basis of the business begun by Francesco Cinzano (1783-1859). In 1992 control of Cinzano passed to **Grand Metropolitan**.

Cirio *(canned foods and dairy products)*

The Italian company takes its name from its founder, Francesco Cirio (1836-1900), a Piedmontese of humble origin who as a 14-year-old had already taken an interest in the fruit and vegetable market at the Porta Palazzo in Turin. In 1856, aged 20, he had the initiative to adopt growing technology in order to preserving produce that might otherwise have perished. It was then that the first Cirio "enterprise" was born in Turin, his original product being preserved peas. He soon extended his range to other fruit and vegetables as well as meat produce, and in 1867 exhibited his foods at the Universal Exposition in Paris. Cirio then began exporting worldwise, from Liverpool to Sydney, so that by the time of his death, the firm he had founded was one of Italy's leading food companies. It later acquired brands such as Calabrialatte ("Calabria Milk") in 1988 and Latte Sole ("Sun Milk") in 1989 before gaining control of the Cragnotti group, and is now a top producer of canned foods and fresh milk products.

Cisco Systems *(computer networking equipment)*

The alliterative name relates to San Fran*cisco*, California, where the company was founded in 1984 by Sandy Lerner and her then husband. It became a public company in 1990 but Lerner and her former husband sold their shares and left the business. In 1995 Lerner founded the Urban Decay cosmetics firm but sold it the following year. By 2000 Cisco was the third largest company in the world, behind the General Electric Co. (*see* **Ediswan**) and **Microsoft**.

Cisitalia *(automobiles)*

The Italian company was founded in 1946 by racing driver and businessman Piero Dusio, a professional footballer forced to retire early because of injury. He had already built a prototype car of the name in 1939, but the postwar period enabled him to make a fresh start, and his first project was a single-seater racing car. The name itself was the acronym of *Consorzio industriale sportivo Italia* ("Italian Industrial Sporting Consortium"), a conglomerate that sold everything from textiles to sporting goods and racing bicycles. The enterprise was an initial success, but by the end of the 1950s Cisitalia was reduced to "customizing" **Fiat**-based cars and the business finally folded in 1956.

Citibank *(bank)*

The American bank traces its origins to 1812, when some of the shareholders and other investors of the First Bank of the United States secured state corporation of the City Bank of New York. The bank grew, and in 1865 was renamed the National City Bank of New York. In 1955 it merged with the First National Bank of the City of New York, founded in 1863, to become the First National City Bank of New York. In 1967 the holding company Citicorp was created to hold the stock of this bank, now renamed City Bank of New York. In 1968 the bank changed its name yet again to First National City Bank and finally to Citibank in 1976.

Citicorp *see* **Citibank**

Citroën *(automobiles)*

The name is that of André Citroën (1878-

1935), a French engineer who graduated from the École Polytechnique in Paris in 1900 and then worked as an engineer and industrial designer. His great-grandfather was a Dutch Jewish costermonger, Roelof Limoenman (1780-1814), who changed his name, meaning "lemon seller," to Citroen, the Flemish equivalent. When André's father, Levie Citroen, a diamond merchant from Amsterdam, adopted French nationality in 1871 and established himself in Paris, he altered the "e" of the name to "ë" to ensure a French pronunciation. In 1908 André helped the Mors automobile firm increase its production but left the company in 1913 to set up a workshop to make gearwheels. In 1915, during World War I, he built a munitions plant and after the war converted it into a factory to mass-produce a small inexpensive automobile. The first "people's car" came off the assembly line in 1919, the year that the company regards as that of its foundation. The two reversed chevrons of the company's logo represent the double-helical gears that Citroën had first made back in 1913. In 1935, the year of Citroën's death, the ailing company was taken over by **Michelin**, and in 1976 it became part of **Peugeot**.

Clairol *(haircare and beauty products)*

Hair dyes originally had rather dubious associations. All that changed in 1955, when Lawrence M. Gelb, an American chemical broker and manufacturer of specialty chemical goods, promoted a product that he had acquired from a French firm called Mury. It was a color preparation called Clairol, which contained a shampoo base and mild oils that cleansed the hair. Hence its name, from French *clair*, "clear," and the common *-ol* suffix meaning "oil." Gelb's promotion resulted in the memorable "Does she... or doesn't she?" advertising campaign. In 1959 Gelb sold his enterprise to **Bristol-Myers** (now Bristol-Myers **Squibb**).

Clarins *(cosmetics)*

The French company, based in Paris, was founded in 1954 by Jacques Courtin-Clarins.

Clark *(candy bar)*

The name is that of David L. Clark (1864-1939), an Irish immigrant to the United States who set up a candy business in the back of a small house in Pittsburgh, Pennsylvania, when he was still a teenager. When America entered World War I in 1917, Clark contracted to supply confections to the US Army. His chocolate drops went down well, but the candy's heavy shipping cases were difficult for the post exchanges to distribute efficiently. Clark therefore began to manufacture his candy in a more convenient bar size, making a package that was easier to handle. At first the bar was called simply "Clark," but later its name was lengthened to the more familiar "Clark Bar." The five-cent bar became a huge commercial success after the war, and Clark added other bars to his product line.

Clarks *(footwear)*

The British firm was founded in 1825 in Street, Somerset, by Cyrus Clark (1801-1866), a local farmer's son. Cyrus's career began as a tanner, working for a neighbor making sheepskin rugs. Their partnership broke up in 1825 and Clark took over the fellmongering, woolstapling, and rug side of the business, while his new partner, Arthur Clothier, kept the cowhide tanning. Cyrus's younger brother, James Clark (1811-1906), joined him as an apprentice in 1828, although his father had hopes of his becoming a chemist in Bath. In 1833 James went into full partnership with Cyrus, and the firm of C. & J. Clark was formed. The firm nearly went bankrupt in 1863 but a fellow Quaker businessman made a loan which averted collapse and placed William Stephens Clark (1839-1925) in control. The company's head office remains in Street today.

Claude Gill *(bookstores)*

The British bookseller Claude Gill (1902-1993) was born into a family of booksellers, the textbook publishers George Gill & Sons, but initially he was not interested in the profession. Instead, he joined the Merchant Navy, working on tankers and becoming an expert navigator. His first bookselling job was at **Foyle's**, where he was quickly promoted to manager of the technical and scientific department. He served in the Royal Navy in World War II but after the war was asked by Cleaver-Hulme, a group of correspondence colleges, if he would like to set up a bookshop devoting to selling textbooks. He did so, opening it in South Audley Street, London, originally under the rather strange name of "Books and Careers." It soon became Claude Gill Books and moved to larger premises in Oxford Street, where it became one of London's biggest bookstores, with general books added to its large scientific and technical department. Further Claude Gill boosktores followed in due course.

The Claymore (whisky)

The whisky is a popular blend owned by **Whyte & Mackay** of Glasgow, Scotland. It takes its name from the claymore (Gaelic, "big sword"), the two-edged sword used by Scottish Highlanders. A pair of crossed claymores are depicted on the label.

Clement Clarke (opticians)

The founder of the British company was a London-born man, Clement Clarke (1883-1946), who in 1899 was apprenticed to a firm of dispensing opticians in Wigmore Street. He worked well, so that in 1910, when the firm, George Spiller, became a limited company, he was appointed its general manager, and its managing director three years later. His army service in World War I was brief, as he was invalided out in 1916. That same year he purchased the goodwill of another optician in Wigmore Street and set up under his own name there as Clement Clarke, Ltd., subsequently opening branches gradually in other towns. In 1986 the company was acquired by **Boots**, so that the long familiar name began disappearing from the High Street, and "Clement Clarke" is now "Boots Opticians."

Cleocin (antibiotic)

The proprietary name for clindamycin, used to treat infections by anaerobic bacteria, is presumably based on the generic name. The drug dates from the early 1970s.

Clerical, Medical (insurance)

The British company was founded in London in 1824 to provide life insurance and annuities for all, but mainly to the medical and clerical professions. Its full original name was accordingly Medical, Clerical and General Life Assurance Society. A year later it switched the first two categories around to become the Clerical, Clerical and General Life Assurance Society, or today simply Clerical, Medical.

Cliffords (dairies)

The British company dates its founding from 1874, when William Clifford, a market gardener at Mortlake, London, left his family business to set up as a dairyman in Cross Lances Lane, Hounslow. His initial stock and equipment consisted of two cows, a yoke, and two pails, in which he delivered the cows' milk on foot to the surrounding villages. From such modest beginnings arose the present company, now not based in London but in Bracknell, Berkshire, where they acquired a bottling factory after World War II.

Clifford-Turner (solicitors)

The British law firm, based in London and noted for its company and commercial practice, was founded in 1900 by Harry Clifford-Turner with the formal name H. Clifford-Turner & Co. The acquisition of a partner in 1905 brought the new name Clifford-Turner and Hopton, which it retained until 1926. By 1939 the original two partners had grown to nine, with a staff of around 60, the increase reflected in the new names Clifford-Turner, Hopton and Lawrence (1926-34), Clifford-Turner & Co. (1934-75), and simply Clifford-Turner from 1975. Harry Clifford-Turner himself died in 1941 and was succeeded by his son Raymond. By 1961 there were 16 partners and around 160 staff, and in 1962 the firm entered into partnership with a small firm of English solicitors in Paris, France. From 1968 offices have been opened elsewhere in the world, including Brussels, Madrid, Hong Kong, and New York.

Clik-Lok (child-resistant cap)

The rise of consumerism in the USA in the 1960s caused many manufacturers to review the safety of their products. A particular area of concern was the ease with which young children could open their parents' pill containers. In 1971, US glass manufacturer Owens-Brockway introduced its first design to prevent children opening pill bottles. It was called the "Clik-Lok." You pushed down hard on the cap and unscrewed it to open the bottle, then closed it by replacing the cap and turning it tightly. A turn in the reverse direction, such as a child might make, made a click to show the cap was locked. Other designs were introduced by rival manufacturers, but Clik-Lok became the standard and has been licensed to plastics manufacturers worldwide.

Clinton *(greetings cards)*

Britain's biggest card retailer, with 700 outlets, dates from 1968, when Don Lewin (b. 1933) opened a card shop. He sold up but became bored and started the Clinton Cards chain, an Essex-based business that floated on the stock market in 1988. He named it after his son, Clinton, who in due course took his seat on the board.

Clorox *(household cleaners)*

On May 3, 1913, five Oakland, California, entrepreneurs invested $100 each to set up the first American commercial-scale liquid bleach factory on the east side of San Francisco Bay, calling their business the Electro-Alkaline Co. On acquiring a site in Oakland, an engineer for an equipment supplier, Abel H. Hamblet, suggested they name the new product "Clorox," from "chlorine" and "sodium hydroxide," chemicals that in combination form the active ingredient of bleach. The company duly became the Clorox Chemical Co. and progressed to the production of a range of household cleaners. In 1957 Clorox was purchased by **Procter & Gamble**, but in 1969 regained its independence.

Club Med *(holidays and hotels)*

The Club Méditerranée ("Mediterranean Club"), to give it its full name, had its beginnings in a small holiday camp started on the Spanish island of Majorca in 1950 by a Belgian athlete, Gérard Blitz. He invited a Frenchman, Gilbert Trigano (1920-2001) to join him, and in 1963 handed the running of the club over to him. Trigano expanded the enterprise into a global empire which by the early 1970s was the world's second-largest non-American hotel chain, with 100 holiday villages in 26 countries around the world. Trigano retired from the management of Club Med in 1997. The full name was entered in the *Trade Marks Journal* of August 17, 1983 and the shorter name in the *Journal* of July 4, 1984.

Cluedo *(board game)*

This classic "whodunnit" board game was the invention in 1946 of Anthony E Pratt, an English solicitor's (lawyer's) clerk. The object is to discover which of six suspects, using which of six weapons, murdered Dr. Black, found dead after a dinner party, and in which of the nine rooms of his country house the murder took place. In North America the game is known as "Clue" and the victim is Mr. Boddy. When Pratt's game was accepted by **Waddington's**, they based the name on a blend of "clue" and the existing board game "ludo" (Latin for "I play"). The name was entered in the *Trade Marks Journal* of July 19, 1950.

Cluett *(menswear)*

The American company, famous for its **Arrow** shirts, takes its name from George B. Cluett, who in 1885 bought the original firm founded in 1851 in Troy, New York, and gave it his name. The company at first made nothing but starched collars. In 1889, however, Cluett merged with another maker who was already using the trademark "Arrow." At the same time the business became Cluett, Peabody, the latter name being that of a salesman, Frederick F. Peabody, who had bought into the "Arrow "collar manufacturers. In 1921 the company began making shirts with attached collars, two years after Sanford Lockwood Cluett (1874-1968), nephew of George B. Cluett, had joined the firm as director of engineering and research. It was Sanford Cluett who invented the **Sanforized** preshrunk fabric.

Coalite *(smokeless fuel)*

The type of smokeless fuel, made by refining coal, has a name obviously based on "coal," with the mineral or commercial suffix "-ite." The name was entered by Thomas Parker of London, England, in the *Trade Marks Journal* of October 10, 1906, significantly soon after the emergence of the new word "smog," a blend of "smoke" and "fog" reportedly coined in 1905 by Dr. H.A. des Vœux, treasurer of the Coal Smoke Abatement Society, at a meeting of the Public Health Congress in London.

Coats *(thread)*

The Scottish firm of J. & P. Coats was founded in 1826 in Paisley by James Coats (1774-1857), a weaver's son in that town. He built a factory that year for the manufacture of sewing cotton and expanded the business that in the hands of his sons, James and Peter, became established under the name mentioned in 1890. The firm's works at Ferguslie, now a district of Paisley, soon became the largest in the world. In 1961 J. & P. Coats merged with

Patons & Baldwins Ltd. to form the Coats Patons Group, which in turn merged with Vantona **Viyella** in 1986 to form the Coats Viyella Group.

Cobbold *see* **Tolly Cobbold**

Cobra *(beer)*

The "Indian" beer of this name was first brewed in Britain by Indian-born Karan Bilimoria (b.1961), who realized the potential for a distinctive beer when dining in Indian restaurants. Friends would ask him to order but were not happy with the only brand of Indian beer then available. This was Kingfisher, originally imported but later brewed under license in Britain, when it tasted quite different. Bilimoria first thought of importing a beer called Pals, but it did not travel well and had a name that could be confused with a petfood. He thus worked with a head brewer in Mysore to create a new beer and named it after the cobra, the snake popularly associated with Indian snake charmers. It was first brewed in Britain in 1996, by which time its "charm" had already attracted continental consumers. Its popularity soon increased, so that by 2001 Cobra accounted for 16 percent of the British Indian restaurant beer market, with **Carlsberg** on 40 percent and the rest split among other brands.

Coca-Cola *(aerated drink)*

The well-known drink was first formulated in 1886 by an Atlanta pharmacist, John S. Pemberton (1831-1888), at his Pemberton Chemical Company. His bookkeeper, Frank Robinson, chose the name for the drink, basing it on two of its constituents: *coca*ine from the coca leaf and caffeine-rich extracts from the *cola* nut. (But see quote below.) Pemberton sold his syrup to local soda fountains, and it was was soon being widely advertised as an "Esteemed Brain Tonic and Intellectual Beverage." In 1887 the sole rights to Pemberton's original formula were acquired by another Atlanta pharmacist, Asa Griggs Candler (1851-1929), and he formed the Coca-Cola Company in 1890. *Cp.* **Coke**.

Triple (and sometimes quadruple) alliterations were in vogue, particularly in Atlanta, allowing a tongue-twisting tour of the alphabet: Botanic Blood Balm, Copeland's Cholera Cure, Goff's Giant Globules, Dr Jordan's Joyous Julep, Ko-Ko Tulu, Dr Pierce's Pleasant Purgative Pellets, Radway's Ready Relief, Swift's Sure Specific. Robinson later wrote that he created the name "Coca-

Cola" not to indicate the key ingredients, but "because it was euphonious, and on account of my familiarity with such names as 'S.S.S.' and 'B.B.B.'." Robinson and The Coca-Cola Company later had good reason to emphasize the poetic rather than descriptive character of the name. ... By 1959, the president of The Coca-Cola Company was referring to it as a "meaningless but fanciful and alliterative name."
(Mark Prendergast, *For God, Country and Coca-Cola: The Definitive History of the World's Most Popular Soft Drink*, 2000)

Cockburn *(port)*

The Scottish name (pronounced "Co-burn") is that of Robert Cockburn, who founded the firm in 1815 together with George Wauchope. The two men were joined in 1828 by Captain William Greig. The following year, Cockburn's sons, Archibald and Alexander, joined the company and opened an office in London. In 1845, the brothers Henry and John Smithes joined the company, which accordingly became Cockburn Smithes & Co. John Smithes married Eleanor Cobb and both Smithes and Cobb families remained in the firm for many generations. In 1962 Cockburn became an associate company of **Harveys** and subsequently part of the Allied **Domecq** conglomerate.

Codis *(analgesic)*

The name is that of a British brand of aspirin containing codeine, both analgesics. It was entered in the *Trade Marks Journal* of November 2, 1949, and was devised to describe the nature of the product as a form of *co*deine that *dis*solves.

Coffee-Mate *(coffee whitener)*

The powdered coffee "creamer" was introduced by **Carnation** in 1961, its name indicating its role as a direct accompaniment to coffee. It did not actually contain any cream, yet tasted more like cream than **Pream**, its predecessor in this particular line of convenience food. The name was entered in the *Trade Marks Journal* of December 11, 1963.

Coffee Republic *(coffee bars)*

The British chain of espresso bars was founded in 1995 by Bobby Hashemi, a former merchant banker (investment banker), and his sister Sahar. The name was adopted from the nickname for any coffee-producing country, such as Costa Rica or El Salvador in Central

America. By 2001 there were 80 Coffee Republic outlets in the UK.

Cohiba *(cigars)*

The brand of cigar originated in the mid-1960s at the El Laguito factory in Havana, Cuba, when Eduardo Ribera, a local artisan, was asked to create a blend for Cuban president Fidel Castro. At first the brand had no name, but "Cohiba" was eventually chosen when production began in 1968. The name was originally said to be the native Taino Indian word for "tobacco," but is now understood to mean simply "cigar." At first the brand was reserved solely for government and diplomatic use, but in 1982 it was made more widely available.

Cointreau *(liqueur)*

The name goes back to Adolphe Cointreau of Angers, France, who in 1849, together with his brother, Édouard-Jean, began to make *guignolet*, a type of cherry liqueur. But several other firms were producing this, and as an experiment Édouard-Jean's son, Édouard, decided to use bitter oranges imported from the Dutch East Indies (modern Indonesia). He soon came up with the perfect mix, and Cointreau was launched in 1875. Other manufacturers imitated them, but the family did not register its name for the liqueur until after World War I. The business is still in family hands today.

Coke *(aerated drink)*

The name originated as a popular alternative for **Coca-Cola** before World War I. It was to some extent promoted by a rival firm, the Koke Company of America, who produced a similar drink. Fearing loss of identity and the substitution of other drinks under the name, the Coca-Cola Company adopted it in 1920 when the US Supreme Court ruled that "Coke" was the company's exclusive property. As Justice Oliver Wendell declared at the time: "The name now characterizes a beverage to be had at almost any soda fountain. It means a single thing coming from a single source and is well known to the community." In fact the Court had doubts about the name, since "coke" is also a slang word for cocaine, which was originally present in the drink. But the popularity of the drink helped to disassociate its name from this colloquial sense, and anyone who buys a "Coke" today is unlikely to associate it with

cocaine, any more than they would with the fuel called coke. On the other hand, "coke" is used by many Americans for any carbonated soft drink. (Legal aspects of the situation are further considered in: (1) Peter Tamony, "Coca-Cola: The Most-Lawed Name" in Kelsie B. Harder, comp. *Names and their Varieties*, 1986; (2) Thomas E. Murray, "From Trade Name to Generic: The Case of *Coke*" in *Names*, Vol. 43, No. 3, September 1995.) A full-page ad in the *UK Press Gazette* of July 9, 1979 included the text: "The Trade Marks 'Coca-Cola' and 'Coke' are brand names for the same identical product. And like Your Name they should be Capitalised. So when you write about our product *please* use Upper Case 'C.' It will help protect our Trade Marks."

Coleman *(lamps and camping equipment)*

In 1899 William C. Coleman (1870-1957) started work as a traveling typewriter salesman, hoping to earn enough money to complete his education. One dark and rainy night he found himself in the coal-mining town of Brockton, Alabama. As he picked his way through the mud, he noticed an unusually bright light coming from a drugstore window. Entering the store, Coleman learned that the source of the light was a hanging lamp fueled by gasoline. Unlike the wick-type oil lamps normally then in use, the gas model cast a clear, white light that was bright enough to read by. Coleman was so impressed with his discovery that he decided to drop typewriters and instead sell the lamp to store owners in rural areas where electricity was still unavailable. He bought a small supply of the lamps from the manufacturer in Memphis, Tennessee, and headed west to peddle his merchandise. After a slow start, store owners became increasingly interested, and in 1903 Coleman purchased the right to the gas lamp from his supplier and began marketing it as the Coleman Arc Lamp. By the end of the decade, Coleman's lamps had gained such a good reputation that he was able to sell the product direct to the customer. Other lines such as outdoor lanterns and portable gas camping stoves were added in due course to Coleman's lines, and when gas began to give way to electricity in rural areas, the Coleman Company switched its emphasis to oil space heaters and floor furnaces. By the end of the 1960s, Coleman had become the largest manufacturer of camping equipment in the world, and their lamps were strong rivals of **Tilley** lamps in the outdoor and camping market. In Europe, Coleman now own the French firm of Camping-Gaz, makers of portable butane gas stoves.

Colgate *(toothpaste and soap)*

In 1795, William Colgate (1783-1857), born in Hollingbourne, Kent, England, the son of a gentleman farmer, emigrated with his family to the United States when his father, an outspoken critic of King George III, was forced to flee England to escape prosecution for treason. At first William's father tried to farm and mine coal in West Virginia. This did not work out, however, and in 1800 the family moved to Baltimore, where father and son went into business with Robert Mather, a soap and candle maker. The partnership dissolved two years later, and while his family relocated to Ossining, New York, William remained in Baltimore and opened his own soap and candle works. In 1803 he closed his business and moved to New York City, where he entered the employ of John Slidell & Company, still making soap and candles. In 1806 he resigned to form his own business, William Colgate & Company, concentrating on the manufacture of high-quality soap. The company became Colgate & Company when William's son Samuel joined the business in 1838, but the first toothpaste was sold, in jars, only in 1877, after William's death. After World War I the firm joined up with another soap manufacturer, B.J. Johnson, who introduced **Palmolive** soap. A third manufacturer then joined the Colgate concern, in the form of the firm founded by the Peet brothers in Kansas City in 1872. The resulting combine took the name of Colgate-Palmolive-Peet, shortened in 1928 to Colgate-Palmolive.

Colibri *(cigarette lighters)*

The British firm of this name was founded in 1927 by Julius Lowenthal, who the previous year had invented a lighter enabling the user to light the flame without touching the flint wheel directly with his thumb. The name was chosen to give the new lighter an image of elegance, lightness, and swiftness, attributes associated with the humming bird so called. The name was entered in the *Trade Marks Journal* of May 4, 1932.

Collier *(publishers)*

The name behind the long famous *Collier's Weekly* is that of Peter Fenelon Collier (1849-1909), an Irishman from Co. Carlow who went to America when he was 17, attending Mount St. Mary's Seminary, Cincinnati, Ohio. He entered publishing in 1877, and in 1896 founded the magazine that bears his name to promote his installment plan for selling books. It soon became a well-known illustrated literary and critical journal, as well as a noted "muckraking" publication. Collier's son Robert Joseph Collier (1876-1918) succeeded to the presidency of the firm and editorship of the magazine in 1906. It hit hard times in the 1950s, however, and ceased publication in 1957.

Collins *(publishers)*

Scottish publisher William Collins (1789-1853) was born in Eastwood, Renfrewshire. A weaver by trade, he opened a private school for the poor in Glasgow in 1813. In 1819 he quit teaching to become a publisher instead. His motives were evangelistic, and he particularly wished to promote the books and ideas of his friend, leading Scottish churchman Thomas Chalmers (1780-1847). For seven years he was in partnership with Chalmers's brother, Charles, but things did not work out and in 1826 Collins broke away, still determined to publish religious books. His son, William Collins II, joined him as partner in 1843 and provided paper mills for the growing business, which he converted into a company. The firm went on to become the largest independent publishing house in Britain, remaining under family control until 1979. In 1990 William Collins Sons & Co., as the company had become, was acquired by News International and merged with **Harper & Row** of the USA as HarperCollins.

Collis Browne, J *see* **J. Collis Browne**

Colman *(mustard)*

Colman's mustard ultimately goes back to Jeremiah Colman (1777-1855), an English flour miller from Norfolk, who in 1814 set up on his own in a watermill at Stoke Holy Cross, near Norwich, with the aim of grinding mustard seed. His business prospered, and as he had no sons of his own he took one of his nephews, James Colman, into partnership in 1823, and

James in turn subsequently took his own son, Jeremiah James Colman (1830-1898) into partnership in 1850. Jeremiah James' great-uncle died in 1851, and his father three years later, so that he effectively built the business up from then on, moving it to a site at Carrow, now a suburb of Norwich. The firm became a private company in 1896, and in 1913 set up a joint company named Atlantis with starchmaker **Reckitt** & Sons to pool the activities of the two businesses in South America. This led to the formation of Reckitt & Colman Ltd. in 1938 to manage the trading activities of the two companies, and a full merger followed in 1954 under the name Reckitt & Colman Holdings Ltd.

Colonel Sanders *("Kentucky Fried Chicken")*

The bringer of "finger lickin' good chicken" to the world was Harland Sanders (1890-1980), born near Henryville, Indiana, and working in a variety of jobs before opening Sanders' Café in the back of a service station in 1929. He offered family-type dinners, and his approving clientele affectionately dubbed him "Colonel" soon after, mainly for his military appearance. It was about this time that he perfected his recipe for his special kind of chicken, using a secret blend of 11 herbs and a pressure cooker to seal in the flavor. He sold his restaurant, as it had become, and took to the road with his recipe. At first few restaurants were interested, but by 1964 he had built up a total of 600 franchises. That same year he signed over his successful business to John Brown of Kentucky and Jack Massey of Tennessee on condition he receive $2 million immediately, an annual salary of $40,000 for life (he lived to be 90), and a seat on the board of directors. He died in Shelbyville, Kentucky, in the state whose name has become intimately linked with his own. The name "Kentucky Fried Chicken" was subsequently abbreviated to "KFC," a name change explained by much popular speculation.

Why did Kentucky Fried Chicken alter its name to just KFC? Ask around, and you'll hear:
• They developed a mutant four-legged chicken, and now the government won't allow them to use the word "chicken" for the creature.
• Colonel Sanders had a rule that as long as the company kept the word "Kentucky" in its name, they could never refuse service to someone who

lacked money, and too many homeless people were taking advantage of the free food.
• A psychic advised the company that the old name had bad vibes.
Or is it just because the word "fried" carries negative health connotations? Yes, probably, but that isn't nearly as interesting as the rumors.
(Jan Harold Brunvand, *Too Good to Be True: The Colossal Book of Urban Legends*, 1999)

Colston *(washing machines)*

The man behind the name was Charles Blampied Colston (1891-1969), an English schoolmaster's son born at Gerrards Cross, Buckinghamshire. After serving in the Royal Engineers in World War I, Colston joined the newly formed **Hoover** company in 1919, subsequently becoming its managing director and chairman. He built the company up to a highly profitable and successful concern, with diversification into other appliances besides vacuum cleaners, and in particular into washing machines in 1948. In circumstances that have not been satisfactorily clarified, Colston resigned from Hoover in 1954, and the following year set up his own dishwasher business as Charles Colston Ltd., together with his son Michael. The company continued to manufacture dishwashers, washing machines and other appliances until 1979, when Michael Colston sold the domestic appliances division to the Italian company Merloni.

Colt *(heating and ventilation equipment)*

The founder of the British company in 1924 was a German technician named Wilhelm Harald Gleischner (1887-1947), who came to England before World War I to sell calculating machines. On arrival, he adopted the name Colt, the maiden name of his English wife, anglicizing his first names to William Harold. He was an internee during the war, and while so confined took the opportunity to learn carpentry. After the war he used this knowledge to make and sell large poultry houses, incorporating a special form of ventilation under the eaves to keep the wind out whatever the weather. In 1924 he set up a partnership in the construction of cedarwood poultry houses with one I.J. O'Hea, who had a similar interest in ventilation and heating methods. The two men decided to call their firm "W.H. Colt Ltd." rather than "O'Hea & Colt" as the first name was unfamiliar to many and frequently had to be spelled out on the telephone. The partnership lasted only to 1932, when there was an amicable separation, and it was then that Colt Ventilation was formed, at first selling vehicle ventilators invented by a Bremen, Germany, engineer named Heinrich Kuckuck. From this developed the Colt Cowl that remains one of the company's best known products.

Colt (revolver)

The name is that of Samuel Colt (1814-1862), born in Hartford, Connecticut, the son of a textile manufacturer. In 1832 the young Colt took ship as a deckhand on a voyage to India, and the concept of the revolver is said to have come to him while watching the ship's wheel. On returning to the USA he described his idea to the US Patent Office, but did not register it until four years later, having meanwhile taken out patents in Britain and France during a visit to Europe in 1935. Colt formed a company to manufacture his invention, but it failed in 1842. Note had been taken of his weapon, however, and in 1846, on the outbreak of the Mexican War, the US Government placed an order for his invention that was executed by the Eli Whitney arms factory in his native Hartford.

Columba Cream (whisky liqueur)

The whisky cream liqueur, produced by John Murray & Co. of Calgary on the Isle of Mull, Scotland, takes its name from St. Columba, the Irish missionary who converted the Picts to Christianity.

Columbia (records and recordings)

The Columbia Phonograph Company first made phonograph records in the 1890s, when its headquarters were in Washington, DC (District of Columbia). Hence its name, which ultimately gave that of **CBS**. It is not related to **Columbia Pictures**.

Columbia Pictures (motion pictures)

The motion picture studio was founded by Harry Cohn (1891-1958), born in New York City, the son of German and Russian immigrants. His father was a tailor, and with his parents, four siblings, and two grandmothers, he shared four rooms in abject poverty on 88th Street. Cohn quit school at 14 to appear in the chorus of a popular play, *The Fatal Wedding*,

produced by Al Woods. In 1913, after a succession of jobs, ranging from fur salesman to trolley conductor, Cohn and his brother Jack made a low-budget film called *Traffic in Souls*. He was drafted into the army in 1917 and after leaving it the following year became personal secretary to pioneer moviemaker Carl Laemmle at IMP Studios, later Universal Studios. Ever ambitious, Cohn left Laemmle, and in 1920, together with his brother Jack and a friend named Joseph Brandt, formed CBC Film Sales, from the initials of the three principals. The low-budget company became known in the industry as "Corned Beef and Cabbage," which may explain the change of name to Columbia Pictures in 1924. The company is not related to **CBS**.

Comme des Garçons (fashionwear)

The nontraditional fashion style, with its torn or crumpled garments, has a French name meaning literally "Like Boys," alluding to the frequently "deconstructed" state of boys' clothes as they scrap and play. The label was created in 1969 by the Japanese fashion designer Rei Kawakubo (b.1942). Her company was formed in 1973, originally to design women's clothes. Men's fashions followed in 1978.

Commer (trucks)

The name is short for "commercial," and originated with the British firm Commercial Cars Ltd., founded in London in 1905. It later made its base at Luton, Bedfordshire, as Commer Cars Ltd. and subsequently became part of **Chrysler** UK, although that company does not use the name on any of its vehicles.

Commercial Union (insurance)

On June 22, 1861, a serious fire destroyed a number of warehouses in Tooley Street, London, England. The resulting fire insurance claims caused many companies to raise their premiums dramatically, prompting a group of merchants to form their own commercial union on September 28 to undertake insurance. A life department was established in 1862 and a marine department in 1863. In 2000, following a merger with General Accident and a consequent name change to CGU, Commercial Union merged with **Norwich Union** to become CGNU.

Commerzbank *(bank)*

The German bank was established in 1870 as the Commerz- und Disconto-Bank ("Commercial and Discount Bank") in Hamburg. After two name changes, the bank split into three separate firms in 1951: Commerzbank Bankverein, Commerz- und Credit-Bank, and Commerz- and Disconto-Bank. These were then reunited under the present name in 1958.

Compaq *(computers)*

The US company was founded in Houston, Texas, in 1982 by Rod Canion, Jim Harris, and Bill Murto, three senior managers at **Texas Instruments**, who invested $1,000 each to set up their own firm. Their first product, sketched on a paper placemat in a Houston pie shop, was a portable personal computer able to run all of the software then being developed for the **IBM** PC. The three presented their idea to Ben Rosen, president of the venture capital firm Sevin-Rosen Partners, and he agreed to fund the new company, becoming chairman of its board of directors. In 1999 Compaq, its name suggesting both "computer package" and "compact," acquired **AltaVista**, and in 2001 merged with **Hewlett-Packard**.

Comptometer *(calculator)*

The Comptometer, invented and named in 1887 by Dorr E. Felt (1862-1930) of Chicago, Illinois, was a key-operated machine for performing the four basic mathematical operations. Its name, apparently deriving from French *compter*, "to count," and "-ometer," denoting a measuring device, was entered by the Felt & Tarrant Manufacturing Co. of Chicago in the *Trade Marks Journal* of October 9, 1935.

Cona *(coffee machines)*

The British company takes its name from one of its founders, Alfred Cohn (1859-1944). However, it originally developed from a partnership formed from a firm that was itself founded in 1850. Alfred Cohn's elder brother married the daughter of one of the partners, and Cohn himself then joined the firm in about 1880. The company has been producing its distinctive all-glass coffee makers since 1910, choosing a name that reflects Cohn's own, with the final "a" of "Cona" representing "Alfred." The name was entered in the *Trade Marks Journal* of August 17, 1938.

Condé Nast *(publishers)*

The American publishers derive their name from their founder, Condé Montrose Nast (1873-1942), born in New York the son of a German father and French mother. After graduating from Georgetown University, Washington, DC, and taking a law degree at Washington University, Nast became advertising manager, then business manager, for **Collier** publications. In 1904 Nast organized his own firm, the Home Pattern Company, and in 1909 bought *Vogue* magazine, itself founded in 1892, making it under his direction one of the world's leading fashion journals. In 1913 he purchased two more magazines, *Dress* and *Vanity Fair*, combining them under the latter title, and in 1915 *House and Garden*. By 1922 all of Nast's companies were combined into Condé Nast Publications. In 1936 the depression forced Nast to close *Vanity Fair*, although some of its features were continued in *Vogue*.

Conoco *see* **Continental Oil Company**

Conrail *see* **Consolidated Rail Corporation**

Consolidated Rail Corporation *(railroads)*

The publicly owned American railroad company, also known as Conrail, was established in 1973 to take over to six bankrupt northeastern railroads. It commenced operation on April 1, 1976 with major portions of the Central Railroad Company of New Jersey, Erie Lackawanna Railway Company, Leigh & Hudson River Railway Company, Lehigh Valley Railroad Company, Penn Central Transportation Company, and Reading Company.

Constable *(publishers)*

The British publishing house was originally founded by the Scottish bookseller Archibald Constable (1774-1827), born a land steward's son in Fife. In 1789 he was apprenticed to an Edinburgh stationer and bookseller, and six years later set up his own business in a small shop in the High Street. At first he specialized in selling antiquarian books, then began publishing pamphlets, mainly on theological and political subjects. In 1801 he became the proprietor of the *Scots Magazine,* and the following year brought out the first issue of the prestigious *Edinburgh Review.* In 1805 he published Walter Scott's first original work, *Waverley,* and two years later gave the famous author £1,000 for *Marmion*. But financial problems were increasing, his London agents and prints became bankrupt, and he ended his days, still only 53, a sick and ruined man. Constable's grandson, Archibald, refounded the firm as Archibald Constable in 1890, with the name changing to Constable & Co. in 1909. In 1999 Constable merged with Robinson Publishing, founded in 1983 by Nick Robinson, as Constable & Robinson.

Contac *(decongestant capsules)*

The capsules, used to alleviate the "stuffiness" of a cold, were launched in 1960 using the newly developed **Spansules**. Their name, referring to their *cont*inuous *a*ction over a period, was entered in the *Trade Marks Journal* of March 11, 1970.

Continental *(cans and packaging)*

The American company, earlier the Continental Can Company, was incorporated in 1913 to acquire three can-making companies. It went on to acquire a number of other can and paper companies, and in 1976 changed its name to the Continental Group to reflect its diversification into forest products and insurance. "Continental" originally implied the American continent but was later applicable to any major land area, even the continent of Europe, where the company has been operating since 1930.

Continental Oil Company

(petroleum)

The company in its present form owes its origins to Ernest W. Marland (1874-1941), born in Pittsburgh, Pennsylvania, the son of an English-born industrialist. After private education, Marland graduated from the University of Michigan School of Law in 1893. Too young to be admitted to the bar, Marland went off to the oil fields, eventually arriving in Oklahoma in 1908. After drilling several wells that turned up dry, Marland hit a gusher in 1911 near Ponca City, a strike that touched off the Oklahoma "black gold" rush and that made Marland's company, formed in 1920, one of the area's biggest producers. By 1928 the red triangle that designated Marland Oils appeared on more than 5,000 service stations. Marland, however, was now unable to repay the $30 million he had borrowed from J.P. **Morgan** to finance his company's continuing growth. Morgan and his bankers took over his stock, dismissed Marland, and finally merged his company with a small Colorado firm, Continental Oil Company, itself founded in Ogden, Utah, in 1875 as the Continental Oil and Transportation Company, "Continental" referring to mainland America. Overnight, "Conoco" replaced Marland's name on thousands of red triangles. In 1981 Conoco was acquired by **Du Pont** and became Continental Group.

Converse *(baseball sneakers)*

Marquis M. Converse (1861-1931) was born in Lyme, New Hampshire, and educated at the Thetford Academy in Vermont. In the mid-1880s he was working as a superintendent at the Houghton & Dutton department store in Boston, Massachusetts, when an illness forced him to resign. He recovered in 1887 and cofounded a rubber shoe sales agency. Despite setbacks resulting from spells of ill health, Converse and his business prospered, and in 1908 he launched the Converse Rubber Shoe Co. as his own manufacturing firm. Within two years his plant at Malden, Massachusetts, was producing 5,500 pairs of rubber shoes a day. Demand for his product subsequently declined, however, and the firm was forced into receivership in 1929, when Converse sold out to an investor.

Conway Stewart *(pens)*

The British fountain pens were first made by a business started in 1905 at 13 Paternoster Row, London, by Thomas Howard Garner, formerly with **De la Rue**, and Frank Jarvis. According to Andreas Lambrou, *Fountain Pens: The United States and the United Kingdom* (2000), the two men may have used the names Conway and Stewart while traveling incognito in Scotland. The names themselves were those of two comedians appearing at Collins' Music Hall, Islington, London. Arguably, "Conway Stewart" is a more mellifluous (though less memorable) name than "Garner Jarvis."

Cook, Thomas *see* **Thomas Cook**

Cooper, Frank *see* **Frank Cooper**

Coopers *(beer)*

Thomas Cooper, a shoemaker from Yorkshire, England, emigrated to Australia in 1852 with his wife Alice. She was the daughter of a publican, and when she fell ill, asked her husband to make her some beer as a tonic, giving him the recipe from her sickbed. According to family legend, the brew was so successful that Thomas Cooper decided to go into brewing full-time in 1862. As a devout Wesleyan, however, he regarded pubs (but not beer) as evil, so restricted his trade to making deliveries to private houses. The brewery moved to its present site in Upper Kensington, Adelaide, in 1880 and is still run by the Cooper family.

Coopers & Lybrand *see* Pricewaterhouse Coopers

Coors *(beer)*

The American beer takes its name from Adolph Herman Joseph Coors (1847-1929), born in Barmen, Prussia, a German brewer's apprentice who came to the USA in 1868 to avoid the draft. After working at various odd jobs in the East, he started a brewery with a partner named Joseph Schueler in Golden, Colorado, in 1873. Coors bought out Schueler in 1880, and over the next ten years enjoyed a lucrative trade selling beer in the mining towns that emerged along the Front Range. The first articles of corporation, in 1914, listed Adolph, Sr., as president and treasurer, Adolph, Jr., as vice-president and secretary, and Grover Coors as general manager of the plant at Golden, Colorado, where the company is based today.

Copydex *(adhesive)*

The British firm of this name was founded in London in 1946 as an office supplies business, selling among other things carbon paper (used for copying), typewriter ribbons, and adhesives. The firm began specializing in adhesives when a salesman, by chance, found that the firm's particular brand was effective in repairing holes in potato sacks at home. Hence the unlikely association between a name that denotes copying and a main product that is an adhesive. The "-dex" may be arbitrary or designed to suggest "dexterity." The name was entered in the *Trade Marks Journal* of March 3, 1948.

Coral *(betting agents)*

Coral Racing, one of Britain's leading bookmakers, takes its name from Joe Coral, born Joe Kagarlitski (1904-1996), who became a bookmaker's runner while working in a Lon-

don lighting factory. He used £5 that he had been given for his bar mitzvah to set up his first book, and opened his first premises in Stoke Newington, London, in 1926. After World War II he established himself in Londn's West End, and with legalized bookmaking founded the Coral Leisure group. The company established a large chain of betting shops and diversified into casinos and hotels. In 1981 Coral was acquired by **Bass**, who in 1998 wanted to sell it to **Ladbrokes**. The deal was blocked by the Monopolies and Mergers Commission, however, and instead Coral Racing went to the **Morgan Grenfell** bank.

Corby *(trouser presses)*

The British presses take their name from John Corby, of Windsor, Berkshire, who started his business in the 1930s with a simple "valet stand" on which to hang a jacket. A pressing section for trousers (pants) was added in the 1950s.

Cord *(automobiles)*

Errett Lobban Cord (1894-1974) was born in Warrensburg, Missouri, the son of a storekeeper. As a teenager he showed great interest in automobiles, rebuilding old cars and racing them on dirt tacks in California, where he had moved with his family. After various spells of employment, including one as sales manager for the Moon Automobile Agency, Cord was impatient to start his own auto company. In 1924 he was approached by the **Auburn** Automobile Company of Indiana to help put the ailing business back on its feet. After negotiating a bonus-for-profits deal, he joined Auburn and soon made it profitable again. Within a year he had taken control of Auburn, and soon enlarged his empire by buying the **Duesenberg** Automobile and Motors Corporation of Indianapolis. He was now making Auburns in Auburn and Duesenbergs in Indianapolis, and decided to build a new marque, called the Cord, at both those plants. In 1929 he accordingly created the Cord Corporation, which comprised the Auburn, Cord, and Duesenberg automobiles. The Great Depression halted the company's momentum, however, and in 1937 Cord sold the entire Cord Corporation to a group of Manhattan bankers.

Cordiant *(marketing services)*

The name is that of the former Saatchi & Saatchi group, founded in 1970 in London,

England, by the Iraqi-born brothers Charles
Saatchi (b.1943) and Maurice Saatchi (b.1946),
and soon becoming the world's largest advertising company. The new name, introduced in
1995 when the brothers left to form M&C
Saatchi Ltd., derives from Latin *cor, cordis*,
"heart," implying that the company (to quote
its own literature) is "at the heart of the world's
leading communications groups." When the
brothers' success story first hit America's Ad-
land, the quip doing the rounds was that their
name was not a name at all but an acronym for
"Single Ad Industry Takes Control of Half the
Industry."

Cordtex *(detonating fuse)*

The detonating fuse, consisting of a core of
high explosive in a textile and plastic covering,
derives its name from a combination of "cord"
and "textile." It was entered by Nobel's Explosive Company Ltd. in the *Trade Marks Journal*
of February 13, 1935.

Corfam *(synthetic fabric)*

The type of artificial leather by **Du Pont** is
said to have a computer-generated name picked
from 153,000 offered, presumably each in pronounceable syllables.

Corgi *(paperbacks)*

The paperbacks of this name were first published in 1951 by Transworld Publishers, a
British subsidiary of **Bantam Books** set up the
previous year by Ian Ballantine of the latter
company. At the time of this organization, the
Bantam name and trademark were unavailable
in Britain, so "Transworld" was chosen as the
company name ("across the world" from Bantam in the USA) and the corgi dog was selected
for the name from a list of more than a hundred animals, birds, and pocket-sized articles.
The corgi is a companionable and "compact"
dog, just as paperbacks are. The name also had
royal connotations, since the corgi was the favorite pet dog of the future Queen Elizabeth II.

Corgi Toys *(toys)*

The miniature vehicles made of diecast metal
were introduced by **Mettoy** in 1956. The name
was chosen in late 1955 as the result of a competition. Around 70 suggestions were made,
but in the end "Corgi" was the name selected
by Henry Ullman, a senior staff member. There
were various reasons for this particular choice.

The company's largest manufacturing base was
at Swansea, South Wales. They therefore named
the toys after the corgi, the well-known Welsh
dog breed that was also the favorite of the
British royal family. Finally, the name itself was
short and snappy, like that of the popular
Dinky Toys.

Corning *(glass)*

The Corning Glass Works takes its name not
from its founder, who was Amory Houghton
(1837-1909), but from the city of Corning,
New York, where the business was set up in
1868, having moved there from Brooklyn. The
town itself was named for the American businessman Erastus Corning, promoter of a railroad here connecting Pennsylvania coal mines
with the Chemung Canal.

Corona *(beer)*

The Mexican beer, its name Spanish for
"crown," is produced by Grupo Modelo, a
company that evolved from the simple brewing
business started in 1935 by a poor Basque immigrant to Mexico. The founder's son, Pablo
Aramburuzabala Ocaranza, made a fortune in
Corona beer and died in 1995 aged 63 leaving
no male heirs. The business was taken over by
his elder daughter, María Asunción Aramburuzabala (b.1964), who set the ailing company
on its feet and became vice chairman in 1996.
In 1998 **Anheuser-Busch** purchased a 50%
noncontrolling stake in the company.

Corona *(cigars)*

The familiar brand of cigar takes its name
from Spanish *La Corona*, "the crown," meaning the best. The latter name was entered by
Manuel Lopez and Company of Havana, Cuba,
in the *Trade Marks Journal* of November 14,
1877, and subsequently by The Havana Cigar
and Tobacco Factories Ltd. in the *Journal* of
November 23, 1904. Manufacture of the original brand was transferred from Havana to
Trenton, New Jersey, in the 1930s, and the
name is no longer proprietary.

Corona *(soft drinks)*

The generally prestigious name, from the
Latin word for "crown," was adopted in the
1920s by the Welsh grocer William Evans
(1864-1934) as a brand replacement for his
"Welsh Hills" mineral water which his firm,
Thomas & Evans, had first produced in 1903.

In the 1950s the business was taken over by **Beecham** Ltd., and they now market the drinks. The name was entered in the *Trade Marks Journal* of August 16, 1933.

Cortina *(automobiles)*

The **Ford** model, for many years Britain's top-selling car, was introduced in 1962 with a name adopted from the northern Italian resort of Cortina d'Ampezzo, site of the 1956 Winter Olympics.

Corus *(metals)*

The name was adopted for the company created from the 1999 merger of **British Steel** and the Dutch firm Koninklijke Hoogovens. According to company literature issued at the time of the merger, the name was created to be "distinctive, fresh, modern and easily recognisable." It is "easily pronounced in all languages" and "will clearly differentiate us from our competitors." As to its meaning, it "does not actually have a literal definition, nor is it an abbreviation."

Costain *(houses)*

The British building business was founded by Richard Costain (1839-1902), a joiner who moved in 1865 from the family farm on the Isle of Man to Blundellsands, near Liverpool, where he set up as a small local builder with his brother-in-law, Richard Kneen, as partner. When the two men parted amicably in 1888, Costain was joined by his three sons, Richard, William, and John Kneen Costain, and from then on the firm's building activity extended in scope and area, spreading from Liverpool to regions outside Lancashire. The private limited company of Richard Costain, however, was not formed until 1923, a year after the London branch had been established.

Cotta *(publishers)*

The noted firm of German publishers, formally J.G. Cottasche Buchhandlung, was founded in Tübingen in 1659 by Johann Georg Cotta (1631-1692). His great-grandson, Johann Friedrich Cotta (1764-1832), took over the business in 1787, printing works by Schiller, Goethe, Herder, and other classic writers. His own son Johann Georg Cotta (1796-1863) expanded the business with a number of important acquisitions. In 1889 the firm was sold to Adolf and Paul Kröner.

Coty *(cosmetics)*

The name is that of François Coty (1874-1934), born in Ajaccio, Corsica, with the original name of Francesco Giuseppe Spoturno. He came to Paris when in his 20s to sell ostrich feathers, then fashionable. The job was limited, however, and when he met a young chemist he suggested to him that they form a partnership to make and sell artistically presented perfumes. The chemist declined, and Coty moved to Grasse in the south of France, an already established center for the manufacture of perfumes. He spent two years there, then after a brief return to Corsica came again to Paris where he started a small business in the Rue de La Boétie, packing and selling perfumes. By 1900 his modest business was becoming very profitable, and when Paris began to go "Coty mad," soon after, his fortune was assured.

Courage *(beer)*

The British brewery is named for John Courage, born in about 1760 in Aberdeen, Scotland, where he was a shipping agent before he came south to London in 1787 to purchase a brewhouse at Horselydown, Southwark. When Courage died in 1793, his widow, Harriet, continued the business until her own death four years later. The management was then taken over by the senior clerk, John Donaldson. The brewery was subsequently acquired by a series of international companies until in 1995 Scottish & Newcastle Breweries, a company formed in 1960 as a merger of Scottish Brewers and Newcastle Breweries, bought it from **Foster's** to form Scottish Courage, now Britain's largest brewing group. (Scottish Brewers was formed in 1931 by the merger of the William McEwan and William Younger breweries in Edinburgh; *see* (1) **McEwan's**; (2) **Younger's**. Newcastle Breweries, based in Newcastle upon Tyne, England, resulted from the merger of five local firms.) The Scottish Courage logo is a cockerel, in allusion to the Huguenot origins of John Courage.

Courtaulds *(synthetic textiles)*

The name of the British company ultimately derives from the family of Huguenot descent who were wine merchants and silversmiths in the 18th century. The first member of the family to be concerned with textiles was George Courtauld (1761-1823), who having been apprenticed to a silk weaver in 1775, set up as a silk throwster in London. In 1785 he made the first of a number of visits to the USA, where he farmed in New York State and married Ruth Minton, an Irishwoman. Their eldest son, Samuel Courtauld (1793-1881), set up a small mill to spin silk in Essex, England, in 1816. In about 1830 the partnership of Courtauld, Taylor, and Courtauld began to make mourning crêpe. The crêpe trade waned in the silk industry in the late 19th century, and in 1904 the company, now known as Samuel Courtauld & Co., bought the British rights to the process of manufacturing viscose. In 1913 a new company was formed as Courtaulds Ltd., from which today's Courtaulds plc has directly descended. In the 20th century the company name became particularly associated with its chairman, art patron Samuel Courtauld (1876-1947), founder of the Courtauld Institute, London, and the great-nephew of his identically named Essex ancestor.

Courtelle *(synthetic fiber)*

The synthetic acrylic wool-like fiber is named for its manufacturer, **Courtaulds**. The "-elle" suffix is presumably intended to represent a French diminutive or feminine adjectival ending (as in *nouvelle*). The name was entered in the *Trade Marks Journal* of February 6, 1935.

Courts *(furniture)*

The British firm was founded in 1850 in Canterbury, Kent, by William Henry Court, who took a small shop and started a tinker's trade in Butchery Lane, making kettles and selling oil that was brought to the city by barge. The firm was taken over in 1863, after William Court's death, by his identically named son, a mere 11-year-old at the time. Despite his youth, William Henry Court, Jr., did his best to support his family by extending the range of the business to include mats, lamp glasses, and paints, among other goods. By the end of the century Court's of Canterbury was producing furniture and furnishings. In 1932 the younger William Henry Court died, aged 80, but not before he had formed the business into a family company. The various branches of Courts that now trade in other towns, however, developed only after World War II.

Courvoisier *(brandy)*

Promoted as "Le Cognac de Napoléon," the brandy takes its name from Emmanuel Courvoisier, the wine merchant who is said to have specially selected the blend for the former emperor when the latter abdicated in 1815 and planned to sail to America, although in the event giving himself up to the British. Courvoisier is said to have taken the brandy from Jarnac, a town a few miles east of Cognac.

Coutts *(bank)*

The British bank that became Coutts was founded in 1692 in the Strand, London, by John Campbell, a Scottish goldsmith banker, and it underwent various changes of name as partners came and went until 1755. In that year, the niece of George Campbell, the founder's son, married James Coutts, a member of the Scottish banking family of the same name, and Campbell made Coutts a partner, so that the firm became Campbell & James Coutts. George Campbell died in 1760, and the following year James Coutts took his younger brother Thomas as partner, so that the firm was now James & Thomas Coutts. Eventually, on the death of Thomas Coutts in 1822, the firm became known as Coutts & Co.

Cow *(gum and rubber solution)*

The familiar Cow Gum owes its name to Peter Brusey Cow (1815-1890), son of a master boat-builder at Woolwich Dockyard, London. In 1830, when he was 15, Peter was apprenticed to a linen draper in Chelsea. He learned quickly, and in 1836 became manager of the Cheapside works owned by Charles Macintosh, inventor of the waterproof cloth named after him. There he made waterproof fabrics and garments. In 1851 his business, trading as P.B. Cow, Ltd., opened a factory at Deptford, Kent, and he and his family moved there from Cheapside. He retired in 1888, but the firm he had founded went on to produce the popular gum and a range of other rubber-related products.

Cow & Gate *(dairy products)*

The British company had its beginnings in a grocery store opened some time in the latter half of the 19th century in Guildford, Surrey, by Charles Gates. When Gates died in 1882, he was succeeded by his two sons, Arthur and Leonard, who the following year were advertising themselves as tea and coffee merchants. They must have also introduced dairy products at this time, since they changed the name of the business from Gates Groceries to The West Surrey Dairy. The firm bought local milk, installed a milk separator, and in 1885 introduced a label or logo depicting a cow looking over a gate. Presumably the latter punned on the brothers' name, or may have been suggested by it. The company went on to open creameries elsewhere in southern England, and in 1888 it became the West Surrey Central Dairy Co. "Cow & Gate" milk was soon after marketed specifically as a babyfood, and the company finally became Cow & Gate Ltd. in 1929. In 1959 the firm was acquired by United Dairies to form **Unigate**.

CPC *see* **Bestfoods**

Crabbie's *(ginger wine)*

The name is that of John Crabbie, who is known to have been a grocer and wineseller in Leith, Scotland, in the mid-18th century. The firm was not incorporated until 1801, however. Crabbie's is now a whisky distillery, an activity into which it broadened under George Crabbie (1849-1929) in the latter half of the 19th century.

Cracker Barrel *(cheese)*

The cheese produced by **Kraft** has a name that suggests its role as an accompaniment to a barrel of crackers. At the same time, it alludes to "cracker-barrel" as applied to a plain or simple philosophy, giving it a homely touch.

Crane *(plumbing supplies)*

The American company owes its name to Richard Teller Crane (1832-1912) and his brother Charles, who began their career casting couplings for lightning rods in a small foundry in Chicago in 1859. Their business boomed in the 1890s when Chicago's new skyscrapers required large quantities of cast pipe for central heating, and the firm became the largest maker of plumbing fixtures in the United States, a position it held until the 1950s. It was Crane's son, Richard Teller Crane, Jr., who branched out into bathroom fittings and who to a large extent is responsible for the layout of the modern bathroom today.

Cranium *(board game)*

The game was the invention of Scottish-born Richard Tait (b.1963), a former **Mi-**crosoft employee in the USA. In 1998, together with a colleague, Whit Alexander, he approached retailers with his idea for a game "that exercised all parts of the brain" (hence its name), but none were interested. The two then approached Howard Schultz, head of **Starbucks**. He had been looking for game to market for two years, and took Cranium on. By the end of the century half a million sets were sold in the USA and in 2000 the game was launched in the UK.

Crapper *(sanitaryware)*

The British firm of Thomas Crapper & Co., manufacturers of baths, sinks, lavatories, toilet cisterns, and much more, was founded by the sanitary engineer Thomas Crapper (1837-1910), credited with patenting the flush toilet to be sold in Britain, the "Valveless Water Waste Preventor." He was born in Thorne, near Doncaster, Yorkshire, and came to London at the age of 11 in 1848 to be employed by a plumber in Chelsea. In 1861 he set up on his own account in Marlborough Road and expanded his business into a large works. The site of the firm's head office at 120 King's Road, Chelsea, is now occupied by **Dorothy Perkins**. Crapper's name is popularly but erroneously connected with "crap," but the link between his sanitary specialty and the bodily function is purely coincidental. (His name is actually a variant of "Cropper," one who gathers fruit.)

Craven "A" *(cigarettes)*

The long familiar cigarette name derives from "Craven Mixture," a special blend of tobacco made up exclusively in the 1860s for the 3d Earl of Craven (d.1883) by José Joaquin **Carreras**, with "A" indicating the prime quality of the cigarettes.

Crawford's *(crackers, or biscuits)*

The British firm was founded in 1813 in a small shop in Leith, the port for Edinburgh, Scotland, by William Crawford, who first made and sold crackers there that year. His identically named son gave the firm the company name of Wm. Crawford & Sons, and the company, best known for its "cream crackers," is still based in Edinburgh today.

Cray *(computers)*

The computers take their name from the American electronics engineer Seymour R.

Cray (1925-1996), born in Chippewa Falls, Wisconsin. After graduating in 1950 from the University of Minnesota, Cray went to work for the leading digital computer company Engineering Research Associates (ERA). He left in 1957 when ERA was taken over, and helped to found Control Data Corp., which became a major computer manufacturer. Eager to pursue his ambition of building the world's fastest computer, Cray left Control Data in 1972 to found Cray Research, Inc. His company's first supercomputer, the Cray-1, came out in 1976, and was ten times faster than any other computer on the market. Even faster and more powerful designs followed as the Cray-2 (1985) and Cray Y-MP (1988). In 1989 Cray established Cray Computer Corp, which in 1995 was obliged to file for bankruptcy. Undaunted, in 1996 Cray started another company, SRC Computer Inc., only two months before his death from head injuries sustained in a car crash.

Cream of Wheat *(breakfast cereal)*

The story of the cereal goes back to the Panic of 1893, when the little flour mill operated by Emery Mapes, George Bull, and George Clifford in Grand Forks, North Dakota, was struggling to survive. Head miller Tom Amidon came up with an idea to save the situation by selling "middlings" (the best part of the wheat berry) as breakfast cereal. He packed a few boxes of the new cereal, which he named "Cream of Wheat," and shipped them to the mill's New York brokers, together with the regular carload of flour. Within a short time of the shipment's arrival in New York, the brokers telegraphed: "Forget the flour. Send us a car of Cream of Wheat." The mill promptly abandoned flour production and turned over its entire facilities to the manufacture of "Cream of Wheat." By 1897 the demand for the cereal had completely outgrown the capacity of the small plant at Grand Forks and the business was moved to Minneapolis, then the best source for raw materials. The cereal is now marketed by **Nabisco**.

Creda *(domestic appliances)*

The British name, associated with electric water heaters, arose as a shortening of "Credenda," a company that in 1919 joined with Simplex, Accles and Pollock, and Tubes Ltd. to form Tube Investments. "Credenda" is Latin

for "things to be trusted," just as "agenda" is "things to be done," serving as a suitable name for a firm that wished to emphasize the reliability of its products. The name was entered in the *Trade Marks Journal* of May 2, 1917.

Crimplene *(synthetic fiber)*

The British-made fiber, a modified **Terylene** yarn manufactured by **ICI**, has a name apparently denoting its "crimped" quality. At the same time, it is probably no coincidence that there is a stream called Crimple Beck near Harrogate, Yorkshire, where ICI Fibres has its headquarters. The name was entered by ICI in the *Trade Marks Journal* of November 11, 1959.

Crisco *(vegetable fat)*

The cooking fat, introduced by **Procter & Gamble** in 1911, was made from hardened cottonseed oil and intended to serve as an alternative to animal fats and butter. Its name was perhaps meant to suggest "crisp cook."

Crittall *(windows)*

The British name that is always associated with metal window frames is that of Francis Henry Crittall (1860-1915), born at Braintree, Essex, the son of an ironmonger and plumber. On leaving school at 15, Francis joined his father and elder brother, Richard, in his father's shop, and for the next five years learned the trade. His father died in 1879, leaving most of his estate to Richard, and as there was little love lost between the two brothers, Francis left for Birmingham in 1881. There he worked as a clerk for a firm of bedstead makers, but the following year, having married, he moved to Chester to open a small ironmonger's shop. When Richard Crittall left Braintree for London in 1883, however, Francis returned to the town to take over the business. After trading problems, he realized he needed to concentrate on a single line, and hit on the idea of a metal window. From then on he never looked back, setting up a manufacturing company in 1889.

Crock-Pot *(cooker)*

The large electric cooking pot, used to cook stews and other dishes slowly, dates from 1970, when the American firm Rival acquired the assets of Naxon Utilities Corporation. Included in the package was the old-fashioned "Beanery," a simple bean cooker with a glazed brown crockery liner, white steel housing, and aluminum lid. An improved model was created that would cook other vegetables and also stews, and in 1971 it was given a catchier name as the "Crock-Pot," associating the crockery liner with its pot-like shape. The name is popularly written "Crockpot," especially in cookbooks.

Croda *(chemicals)*

The British firm of Croda International Ltd. had its beginnings in 1925, when George W. Crowe set up the Crowe Manufacturing Company "for the manufacture of grease" at a disused waterworks in the village of Rawcliffe Bridge, near Goole, Yorkshire. He was approached by a Mr. Dawe, who claimed to have a special process for making lanolin, and the men combined their operations. The name of their enterprise was subsequently shortened as now, from a blend of both their names. The company is still based at Goole today. The name was entered in the *Trade Marks Journal* of September 13, 1939.

Croft's *(sherry)*

The Croft family who gave the name trace their origins back to the north of England, with the present family tree descending from Henry Croft of Yorkshire, who died in 1579. It was his great-great-grandson, John Croft, who in 1736 became a partner in the port shipping partnership of Phayre and Bradley, founded in 1678, and this is the year that Croft's now regards as that of its founding. Croft died unmarried in 1762, but the family business was successfully continued by his younger brother Stephen and his sons. The firm has been known as Croft and Co. since 1769.

Crombie *(coats)*

The distinctive style of overcoat or jacket takes its name from its Scottish manufacturers, as detailed in its entry in the *Trade Marks Journal* of January 17, 1951: "Men's and boys' coats, suits, jackets ... all made from piece goods wholly or substantially of wool, worsted or hair. J. & J. Crombie Limited, Grandholm Works, Woodside, Aberdeen, Scotland; Manufacturers and Merchants;—7th September, 1949." The firm itself was founded by John Crombie in 1806.

Crompton *(light bulbs)*

Rookes Evelyn Bell Crompton (1845-1940) was born near Thirsk, Yorkshire, the son of a retired English diplomat. On leaving the army in 1875 he bought shares in an agricultural and engineering firm in Chelmsford, Essex, with the aim of developing his interest in transport. His attention was diverted, however, to the new technology of electric lighting, and he decided to pursue that science. In 1879 he acquired the Chelmsford firm and turned it into Crompton & Co., electrical engineers. He soon became closely associated with Joseph Swan, of **Ediswan**, and with him developed the filament lamp. As a result of this partnership, he became involved in the formation in 1882 of the Swan United Electric Light Co. His name was now principally associated with the manufacture of electric lamps, despite the fact that he eventually lost control of his company as a result of a vote of no confidence by its directors, who protested at Crompton's ever-increasing absences abroad.

Crookes *(pharmaceuticals)*

The British company that became Crookes Products Ltd., of Nottingham, was founded in 1912 in London by a chemist, Henry Crookes, with financial backing from his famous father, Sir William Crookes (1832-1919), inventor of the Crookes radiometer and Crookes tube. Henry was trained in his father's laboratory, and when he set up his new business off Tottenham Court Road, London, he aimed to develop what he called "collosols," that is, metallic colloidal solutions that could be safely injected into the bloodstream. The first name of his company was thus Crookes Colloids Ltd. This later became British Colloids Ltd. and eventually Crookes Laboratories Ltd. in 1946, by which time the firm's name had become popularly associated with the halibut liver oil that it first marketed in the 1930s. Crookes Laboratories was acquired by **Boots** in 1971, but the Crookes name was retained for the specialist company of Crookes Products Ltd.

Crosse & Blackwell *(foods)*

The origins of the British company go back to 1706, when at 11 King Street, London, a firm by the name of West & Wyatt started trading as "oilmen," making and selling sweet oils and the foods preserved in them, such as pickles. In 1819 the firm took on a pair of 15-year-old apprentices, Edmund Crosse and Thomas Blackwell. Although they had never met before, the two got on well, both as buddies and as enterprising businessmen, so that in 1830, after initial opposition from Thomas's family, they bought William Wyatt's firm. They lived above the shop for the next nine years, at the end of this time transferring the business to Soho Square, where it remained for at least the next 100 years. Naturally, they extended their range of foods, although even today people still popularly associate the Crosse & Blackwell name with sauces and pickles, its original products. *See* **Branston.**

Crosville *(bus transport)*

The Crosville Motor Company was formed in 1906 as a British automobile manufacturing and engineering business, taking its name from George Crosland Taylor, the son of a Yorkshire mill owner, and Georges Ville, a French auto engineer. The plan was for the British company to build cars to Ville's design in Chester, Cheshire. In the event only five cars were built, and in 1910 the firm instead started a bus transport service in this part of west central England. The name is apt for a service operating across the region through town (French *ville*) and village.

Crown Zellerbach *(paper)*

The American company was founded in 1870, two years after Anthony Zellerbach, a middle-aged immigrant from Bavaria, arrived penniless in San Francisco after failing to make his fortune in the gold fields of the Sierra Nevada mountains. He decided to sell paper, the least expensive commodity. He was soon pedaling paper out of a small room and pushing his cart to printers about town. His business gradually grew, and in 1927 his company merged with the nation's second largest paper manufacturer, Crown Willamette, founded in 1889, to became the Crown Zellerbach Corporation.

CSX *(railroads)*

The CSX Corporation was formed in 1980 as a merger of the Chessie System, Inc., and Seaboard Coast Line Industries, Inc. The Chessie System was created in 1973 as a holding company for the Chesapeake and Ohio Railway Company, founded in 1868, taking its name from the latter's nickname ("Chessie" for "Chesapeake"). The "CS" of CSX thus stands for Chessie System, and "X" for "extra."

Cuaba *(cigars)*

The Havana cigar was launched in 1996 by the **Romeo and Juliet** factory in Cuba. Its name derives from an old Taino Indian word for a type of bush that still grows on the island today. The bush burns readily and was used for lighting cigars at religious ceremonies. Hence the local Cuban Spanish idiom, *Quemar como una cuaba*, "to burn like a cuaba."

Cuarenta y Tres *(liqueur)*

The name of the Spanish herb liqueur is Spanish for "forty-three," representing the number of ingredients that make up the liqueur's formula. It is also known as "Licor 43."

Cuba *(chocolates)*

The Italian firm, a family-run business started by Pietro Cussino (b.1917), presumably takes its name from the chocolate cigars that are one of its specialties.

Cubs *(breakfast cereal)*

The name was first registered in 1938, although the actual product, a small-sized **Shredded Wheat** cereal, was not marketed until 1957. The name was intended to indicate a "junior" version of the "grown-up" Shredded Wheat, such as might appeal to children.

Cuervo *(tequila)*

The name is that of José Cuervo, who in 1758 was given full territorial rights to extensive lands in the the Mexican state of Jalisco, where Tequila is itself located as the town where the drink was first produced. (Like champagne, tequila is a designated drink, and properly originates only from the town and district that gives it its name.) A year later, another member of the Cuervo family was granted the rights to production, and today the name remains one of the liquor's best-known brands.

Cuesta-Rey *(cigars)*

The American firm takes its name from Angel La Madrid Cuesta and Peregrino Rey, who started their business in Tampa, Florida, in 1884. They specialized in "clear Havanas," i.e. cigars made in the United States from Cuban tobaccos. The firm was subsequently presided over by the Newman family, owners of the last of the great Tampa cigar houses.

Culligan (water softeners)

Emmett J. Culligan (1893-1970) began his career as a farmer and land developer in Porter, Minnesota. He was hit by a farm recession in 1921, however, and moved with his family to St. Paul. One day soon after their relocation, Culligan came across an old friend who was selling a conditioning machine that used zeolite to filter the hard minerals from water. Culligan was impressed with the action of the zeolite, which he tested at home, and launched his own water softener firm in 1924. His business failed, however, and he moved again to La Grange, Illinois, to take a job with the National Aluminate Corporation. Culligan still had dreams of running his own firm, and decided to try again, this time marketing a water softening service instead of selling conditioning equipment direct to the customer. He started his new venture in 1936, and despite initial hardships the business grew quickly. In 1965, at the time of Culligan's retirement, there were over 1,000 dealers beginning their sales presentations by saying, "Hello, I'm your Culligan Man."

Cumberland (pencils)

The first pencil to be documented was in England in 1565, following the discovery of graphite by shepherds under an overturned tree in the Cumbrian Hills. In 1832 a pencil factory opened in the small town of Keswick, Cumberland (now Cumbria). It was originally owned by one A. Wren, but in 1875 was taken over by the local firm of Hogarth and Hayes and with business growing healthily became the Cumberland Pencil Co. in 1916. The familiar "Derwent" range of color pencils first appeared in 1930.

Cummins (truck diesel engines)

America's leading manufacturer of truck diesel engines takes its name from Clessie L. Cummins, a Columbus, Indiana, chauffeur who was convinced he could improve on Rudolph Diesel's "oil engine." He first put his theories into practice in 1919 with a loan of $27,400 from his banker boss. After little initial success he came up in the mid-1920s with a diesel that was both economical and reliable, and after numerous publicity stunts and tests, Cummins Engine showed its first eventual profit in 1937.

Cunard (shipping line)

The greatest shipping line of the steam age took its name from Samuel Cunard (1787-1865), born in Halifax, Nova Scotia, Canada, the son of a merchant. He had early success as a merchant and shipowner and emigrated to Britain in 1838, where he joined up with George Burns of Glasgow and David McIver of Liverpool to found the British and North American Royal Mail Steam Packet Company (later Cunard Line) for the new mail service between Great Britain and the USA. The first passage was on July 4, 1840, when the *Britannia* left Liverpool for Boston, arriving 14 days later.

Cunningham (automobiles)

There are two quite unrelated US firms of this name, one specializing in the manufacture of high-class carriages and cars, the other building competition sports cars. The first was James Cunningham, Son & Co., of Rochester, New York, who first built carriages in 1842 and who launched their first, electrically powered car in 1907. Gas-driven cars followed until the company closed in 1937. The second was the enterprise of the sportsman Briggs Swift Cunningham (b.1907), who produced his first prototype sports car in 1951. In 1955, after successes in several races, including the 1953 Sebring 12-hour race in Florida, Cunningham decided to call it a day, and the manufacture of his cars came to an end.

Currys (electrical and electronic goods)

Familiar as a chain store in many British towns, Currys was at first long associated with bicycles before the present electronic age brought diversification into radio and television. Henry Curry (1850-1916) was born in Leicester the son of a chain maker. On leaving school he trained as a mechanic in a local hosiery factory. He augmented his income by making fireguards, repairing penny-farthing bicycles, and similar types of work, and when the new "safety" bicycles appeared in the mid-1880s, he turned his attention to the assembling of such machines, hand building one a week in his little workshop. Encouraged by his wife, he converted the front room of his house in Painter Street, Leicester, into a shop, displaying the fireguards, bicycles, mangles and so on that he had made. In 1888 he opened a second, larger shop in Belgrave Gate, whereupon business boomed, with a factory opened and with his four sons taken into the firm at the end of the century. By the time he retired in 1910, Curry already had seven branches in towns outside Leicester, the forerunners of the hundreds that exist today.

Curwen *(music publishers)*

The British firm owes its origin to John Curwen (1816-1880), a Congregational minister who in 1864 resigned his ministry to promote the tonic sol-fa system of naming the notes of the musical scale devised by Sarah Glover as a means of teaching the rudiments of music. His work was carried on by his son, John Spencer Curwen (1847-1916), whose wife, Annie Curwen (1845-1932), applied tonic sol-fa principles in her piano teaching methods, published as *The Child Pianist* (1886) (but popularly known as *Mrs. Curwen's Pianoforte Method*). Their nephew, John Kenneth Curwen (1881-1955), ran the publishing firm, which continued under the direction of John Christopher Curwen (b.1911). In 1971 the list was taken over by Faber Music (*see* **Faber & Faber**) and Roberton Publications.

Cusinier *(liqueur)*

The noted French liqueur takes its name from Eugène Cusinier, who first produced his drink in Ornans, in the Jura Mountains, in 1857. A distillery was later set up in Paris in 1889. The firm went on to produce various types of liqueurs and was taken over in 1976 by **Pernod Ricard**.

Cussons *(soap)*

The name behind the soap is that of Alexander Tom Cussons (1875-1951), an English chemist's son who appears to have been born in Ossett, West Yorkshire. In 1895 his father moved from Ossett to Swinton, near Manchester, and that same year Alexander began to make and sell a range of chemist's sundry goods. In 1907 he opened a factory at Kersal, now a district of Salford, forming his company there the following year. He first began to make soap at Kersal in 1920, and his famous **Imperial Leather** toilet soap was produced there in 1938.

Cutex *(nail varnish)*

The name and the product, now made by **Chesebrough-Pond's**, both originate with Northma Warren, a Congregational minister's son who had graduated from the University of Kansas and then studied at the Detroit College of Pharmacy. In 1911, aged 32, he began marketing a liquid cuticle remover. Five years later he introduced America's first liquid nail varnish, calling it "Cutex" after the cuticle remover, the suffix "-ex" meaning "out." Warren had opposition from a foreign manufacturer, who duplicated the name and packaging of Cutex for his own product, defending himself in court on the grounds that "cutex" was a generic term for nail varnish. He lost his case. The name was entered in the *Trade Marks Journal* of January 31, 1917.

Cuticura *(skincare products)*

The name dates back to the 19th century and derives from Latin *cutis*, "skin," and *cura*, "care." The product itself was originally an ointment designed for Newfoundland fishermen, whose hands became chapped and sore in the course of their work. The name was entered in the *Trade Marks Journal* of March 10, 1886.

Cutty Sark *(whisky)*

The blend of whisky by **Berry Bros. & Rudd** of London, England, traces the origins of its name to a day in 1923, when the Scottish artist James McBey was entertained to lunch in the firm's head office. After the meal, Francis Berry asked his guest for his suggestions for the whisky that he planned to put on the US market after the end of Prohibition. McBey came up with the name of the famous clipper ship, launched at Dumbarton, Scotland, in 1869, and now preserved in dry dock at Greenwich, London. The ship's own name came from the garment worn by the witch Nannie in Robert Burns's poem *Tam o' Shanter* (1790), itself Scots dialect for "short shirt."

> Her cutty sark, o' Paisley harn [coarse fabric],
> That while a lassie she had worn,
> In longitude tho' sorely scanty,
> It was her best, and she was vauntie [proud of it].

A couplet near the end of the poem specifically relates the garment to drink:

> Whene'er to drink you are inclin'd,
> Or cutty-sarks rin [run] in your mind.

Cyanamid *(chemicals)*

The American company owes its origin to Frank S. Washburn (1860-1922), born in Centralia, Illinois, the son of a politician and banker. After receiving a degree in civil engineering from Cornell University in 1883, he went to work for the Chicago and North Western Railroad. He resigned from this post in 1887 and over the next two decades became involved in a number of civil engineering ventures. In 1899 Washburn organized the Crescent Coal Company and moved to Tennessee, where he became increasingly interested in hydroelectric power production, as well as the possibilities of applying such power to the atmospheric production of nitrogen fertilizers. He had heard of a German process for extracting nitrogen from the air and combining it with lime and carbide to form cyanamide, a basic element in fertilizer. Such a process, Washburn was pleased to note, demanded a large supply of electricity. He went to Germany, bought the American rights for the process, then set up American Cyanamid on July 22, 1907 to use the electricity generated by dams for the production of fertilizers.

Cyanamide itself is alternately known as cyanogen amide, and its name blends these two words.

Cydrax *(cider)*

The brand of cider is produced by **Whiteway's**, who have always used the spelling "cyder," evoking a rustic or "healthy" image. This particular cider is nonalcoholic, so the final "-ax" is presumably a form of "-ex" in its sense of "out," meaning no alcohol. Whiteway's also produce the similarly-named "Peardrax," a nonalcoholic perry. The name was entered in the *Trade Marks Journal* of June 1, 1921 for: "A sparkling, non-alcoholic beverage prepared from Devonshire apples."

Cynar *(liqueur)*

The brand of Italian liqueur is flavored with artichoke hearts. Hence its name, from botanical Latin *cynara*, "artichoke."

Cyril Lord *(carpets)*

Cyril Lord (1911-1984) was born in Manchester, England, the son of a Co-op stores clerk. On leaving school, his father got him a job with the Co-operative Wholesale Society bank, where it was hoped he would make his career. Cyril found it boring, however, so left after only a fortnight and became an apprentice with a local spinning and weaving firm. In

1935 he joined the London laboratories of a firm of wholesalers and converters (who bought unfinished goods for finishing), and four years later started his own converting firm, Hookin & Lord. A year later, he sold it and joined the Cotton Board as an adviser on the best way to exploit the low supplies of cotton yarn available in wartime. After World War II, Cyril Lord started another textile firm, this time in Belfast, Northern Ireland. Realizing that the textile industry was facing increasing competition in its traditional role, he decided to specialize, and for his new activity chose carpets. Cyril Lord Carpets Ltd. was founded in 1955. Business did well, and he himself gained fame, hobnobbing with showbiz personalities, and even appearing (all 5'3" of him) in a Batman film as the "Karpet King of Europe," the "Holy Matman." Alas, textile weaving declined, and his business crashed in 1968, so that all the familiar Cyril Lord carpet showrooms closed for good.

Cytrel *(tobacco substitute)*

The British tobacco substitute, made from cellulose and used in cigarettes, appears to have an arbitrary name. The product dates from the mid-1970s.

Cytrynówka *(vodka)*

The Polish lemon vodka has a name denoting its distinctive flavoring, from *cytryna*, "lemon."

D. Lothrop *(publishers)*

The noted American publisher of children's books takes its name from Daniel Lothrop (1831-1892), born in Rochester, New Hampshire. He quit formal schooling in 1845 when one of his brothers asked him to take charge of his drugstore. He did so, and when his brother offered him an equal share of the profits, named the business "D. Lothrop & Co." Lothrop decided to sell books in his shop, then a novelty but now commonplace in American drugstores, and in 1850 bought a popular bookstore in Dover, New Hampshire. In 1856 Lothrop opened a bank and a second drugstore in St. Peter, New Hampshire, but both enterprises quickly failed, victims of the 1857 financial panic. Dejected, Lothrop decided to concentrate on his bookstore, and then made plans to start a publishing house. In 1867 Lothrop opened D. Lothrop & Co. in Boston, Massachusetts, targeting the Sunday school market. His success in this field inspired others to follow him, and a wave of religious-moral literature for children began to sweep across the country. Despite charges of mawkish sentiment and tedious pedanticism, Lothrop had many supporters, and he helped establish a genre and set a standard for his chosen field. Subsequent acquisitions brought about the present name of the firm as Lothrop, Lee & Shepard Books.

D. C. Thomson (comics)

Britain's leading comics publisher dates from 1886, when William Thomson, Scottish founder of the Thomson line of steamships to Canada, took over a local paper. His son, David Couper Thomson (1861-1954), succeeded him in the newspaper business, and the low-key Thomson family still runs the firm that became famous for the boys' "adventure papers" *Adventure* (launched in 1921), *Rover* (1922), *Wizard* (1922), *Skipper* (1930), and *Hotspur* (1933), and the more widely popular children's comics *Dandy* (1937) and *Beano* (1938). It is purely a coincidence that Thomson's initials duplicate the name of the US comic-book publishing company DC Comics, where "DC" is "Detective Comics."

D. F. S. (furniture)

Britain's leading retail furniture retail group was founded in 1969 by Graham Kirkham, a coalminer's son, its first store opening in a converted billiard hall near Doncaster, Yorkshire. Further stores were opened, and the company was floated in 1993. The initials are said to have no actual meaning.

D. H. Evans (department store)

The London, England, store takes its name from Dan Harries Evans, a Welsh farmer's son from Llanelli, who in 1879 moved from his small draper's shop in Westminster Bridge Road, London, to 320 Oxford Street, where his business expanded spectacularly into the present department store, just as it had done for a fellow Welshman and draper, **Owen Owen**. The store building as it now stands was built in 1937.

Dacron (synthetic fabric)

The synthetic polyester, the equivalent of British **Terylene**, was first made by **Du Pont** in the late 1940s under the code name "Fiber V." Its eventual name, perhaps based on "D" for "Du Pont" and a blend of "acrylic" and "nylon" (although the former word is not scientifically valid for it), was entered in the US Patent Office *Official Gazette* of November 13, 1951 and the *Trade Marks Journal* of September 17, 1952. *Cp.* **Orlon**.

Daewoo (automobiles)

The South-Korean-produced automobiles evolved from the textile trading business founded in 1967 by Kim Woo Choong (b. 1936) as the Daewoo Industrial Co. Ltd. with just five employees. It grew to be an industrial giant, with cars at first forming only a thin strand of its output. By the 1980s it was starting to modify **General Motors** designs for the home market, and then began an extensive export operation. The first automobile engineered by Daewoo was the 1997 Lanos, but two years later the group suffered a financial collapse, when a number of auto manufacturers began bidding for it, including **General Motors**, **Fiat**, **Ford** and **DaimlerChrysler**.

DAF (automobiles)

The name is an acronym of that of the Dutch manufacturers, Van *D*oorne's *A*anhangwagen*f*abriek ("Van Doorne's Trailer Works"). Brothers Huub and Wim van Doorne set up their workshop in Eindhoven in 1928 and built their first trailer that same year. They then progressed to the manufacture of trucks, military vehicles, and buses. Their first prototype car was produced in 1957.

Daihatsu (automobiles)

The Japanese firm was founded in 1904 as the Hatsudoki Seizo ("Motor Manufacturing") Company to make and sell internal combustion engines. It produced its first three-wheelers in 1930, and in 1951 changed its name to the Daihatsu Motor Company, "Dai-" meaning "large," "great." Daihatsu has always specialized in small cars, and in 1965 was the first Japanese marque to be exported to Europe.

Daimler (automobiles)

The Daimler is the oldest British car name, originating in the Daimler Motor Company, founded in 1890 by the Württemberg-born German mechanical engineer Gottlieb Daimler (1834-1900). His firm went on to produce the famous **Mercedes** in 1899, and in 1926, after his death, joined forces with the firm founded in 1885 by his compatriot and fellow engineer, Karl Benz (1844-1929), to form Daimler-Benz. The first cars powered by Daimler engines arrived in Britain from Germany in 1895, and the first "native" Daimlers were those built in Coventry in 1897. In 1960 Daimler was acquired by **Jaguar** from the **BSA** group and in 1999 merged with **Chrysler** to form DaimlerChrysler AG.

Daiquiri *(cocktail)*

The cocktail was created in 1896 by Jennings Cox, an American mining engineer working in Cuba, when he mixed light **Bacardi** rum with lime juice. His colleague, one Pagliuchi, suggested naming it after the nearby village of Daiquiri. The name is not proprietary.

Daks *(men's trousers)*

The self-supporting trousers, with their distinctive sharp creases, were introduced in 1934 by Alexander Simpson, son of Simeon Simpson, founder of the British menswear firm of **Simpson**. The name was selected by Sir William Crawford, a close friend of Alexander, from several that had been proposed, and is said to denote a shortening of "Dad's slacks," as Alexander's compliment to his father. The name was entered in the *Trade Marks Journal* of October 4, 1933.

Dalkon Shield *(interuterine device)*

The notorious Dalkon Shield, so called from its shield-like shape, was launched by the A.H. Robins Company in 1970 but caused severe and even fatal infections among its users. It was developed by Dr. Hugh Davis at the Johns Hopkins University from 1963 to 1967, at first alone, then with Irwin Lerner. The name presumably comes from letters in these names. Robins suspended sales of the Dalkon Shield in 1974 and filed for bankruptcy in 1985.

Dalton, B. *see* **Dayton Hudson**

Damard *(lacquer)*

The tough lacquer, used for protecting polished metal, was patented in 1907 by its inventor, the Scottish electrical engineer James Swinburne (1858-1958), who named his preparation "Damard" because it it set "damn hard." In 1916 Leo Baekeland, the inventor of **Bakelite**, visited England to establish a subsidiary.

He met Swinburne, acquired his Damard Lacquer Company, and made him chairman of the new Bakelite Ltd. Swinburne served as chairman until his retirement in 1948, aged 90.

Damart *(thermal underwear)*

The special type of underwear was the creation in the 1950s of three French brothers named Despature, who had a weaving business in the town of Roubaix. They experimented with a new type of chlorofiber that had good insulation and water-repellent properties and that also generated triboelectricity, a form of static electricity generated when fibers rub during wear. This latter attribute was believed by some to have therapeutic value in the treatment of rheumatism, arthritis, and muscular complaints generally. They called their new material **Thermolactyl**, while the product itself is said to take its name from the Rue Dammartine, where the three sat in a café discussing their breakthrough. The red "lightning flash" through the "D" of the name represents a charge of triboelectricity.

Dan-Air *(airline)*

Britain's second largest airline took its name from the initials of *D*avies *a*nd *N*ewman Ltd., a London shipbroking company that entered the aircraft broking market in the early 1950s. It established its own commercial airline, based at Southend Airport, Essex, in 1953. Following subsequent financial troubles, its fleet and some of its crews were acquired by **British Airways** in 1992.

Dancercize *(dance exercise program)*

The program of organized physical exercise incorporating moden dance rhythms, popular with children, derives its name as a more or less straight blend of "dance" and "exercise." The system was devised by Debbie Drake of New York, author of *Dancercize* (1967), who entered the name in the US Patent Office *Official Gazette* of June 8, 1971 for: "Instruction in dancing and physical conditioning." The term is now used generically, often with an "-ise" spelling (properly the correct one, given "exercise"). *Cf.* **Jazzercise**.

Daniel's, Jack *see* **Jack Daniel's**

Dannon *see* **Danone**

Danone *(dairy products, cookies, and drinks)*

The French company traces its origins to 1966, when two glass manufacturers, Souchon-Neuvesel and Glaces de Boussois, merged as Boussois-Souchon-Neuvesel (BSN). In 1969 BSN acquired **Evian**, and in 1973 merged with the Gervais Danone food group to become BSN Gervais Danone. Gervois Danone was itself the result of a merger between the cheese export business founded by Charles Gervais, the inventor in the mid-19th century of Petit Suisse cheese, and Danone, a yogurt-making company founded in Barcelona in 1919 by Isaac Carasso and named after his young son, Daniel. In 1994 BSN Gervais Danone shortened its name to Danone, and that same year adopted its logo of a little boy gazing up at a star, partly to promote its baby foods, partly as a tribute to Daniel Carasso. Stateside, the Danone name is familiar in the form Dannon.

Danskin *(fashionwear)*

The story of Danskin begins in 1882, when Joel and Benson Goodman founded a dry goods business in Manhattan, New York, selling hosiery, leatherwear, and clothes for women and children. In 1923 the Goodman sons took over and set up Triumph Hosiery Mills in Philadelphia,Pennsylvania. In the 1930s the firm specialized in the production of theatrical hosiery. The name "Danskin" was created in the 1950s when the company produced its first leotards and dance tights. The aim was to make clothes suitable for dancing that did not go baggy at the knee and ankle. Hence the name, as if "dance skin." The leotard subsequently became popular as fashionwear and often replaced the swimsuit on the beach.

Darracq *(automobiles)*

The automobiles take their name from the Frenchman Alexandre Darracq (1855-1931), born in Bordeaux, who had early experience as a draftsman in the Tarbes Arsenal before founding the Gladiator Cycle Company in 1891. He sold the company in 1896 and for a time manufactured electric cars. His first output of autos in any quantity was in 1898, when he began building Léon Bollée voiturettes under license. He went on to build racing cars, but his firm merged with **Sunbeam** and **Talbot** in 1920 and was dissolved in 1952.

Dart Industries *(containers)*

Famous for products such as **Tupperware**, West Bend pots and pans and **Duracell** batteries, Dart Industries takes its name from Justin Whitlock Dart (1907-1984), born in Evanston, Illinois. On graduating from Northwestern University, he married Ruth **Walgreen**, daughter of Charles R. Walgreen, founder of the Chicago-based drugstore chain. Dart began his career in a Walgreen drugstore, and by 1932 had risen to be head of store operations. Seven years later Ruth Walgreen divorced Dart, and in 1941 he left the company to join a Boston based drug company founded in 1902 and called United Drug. Two years later Dart took it over, and in 1945 moved its headquarters to Los Angeles. In 1980 Dart agreed to a merger with **Kraft**.

Dassault *(aircraft)*

In World War I the Frenchman Marcel Bloch (1892-1986) worked on military aircraft and developed a successful propeller. In 1917, with Henri Potez as partner, he produced a two-seater aircraft which was ordered but cancelled when the war ended. Bloch then engaged in real estate, but returned to aviation in 1930, producing a bomber and several airliners. In World War II Bloch and his brothers were active in the French Resistance. He was captured by the Nazis but survived, although one of his brothers was executed. After the war he changed his name to Dassault, his brother's code name in the Resistance. (It probably came from *char d'assaut*, French for "tank.") In the 1950s, the firm of Avions Marcel Dassault grew rapidly to beome Europe's top producer of jet fighters, the best known being the "Mirage." In 1967 Dassault's company merged with Breguet Aviation, manufacturers of transport aircraft, to become Avions Marcel Dassault-Breguet Aviation. The company has been state-controlled since 1981 and is now known as Dassault Systèmes.

Datsun *see* Nissan

David & Charles *(publishers)*

"The name suggests nice young men who sell antiques but D&C was always sturdy Middle England, a publisher that traded in nostalgia for steam engines and trams" (*The Writer's Handbook 2002*, 2001). The British company was founded in 1960 by David St. John Thomas (b. 1929) and Charles Hadfield (1909-1996), the two men unusually choosing to adopt their first names for the partnership rather than their surnames. Both were members of the Railway and Canal Historical Society, with Thomas a railroad enthusiast and Hadfield keen on canals. Each had written books on his subject, and in 1958 Thomas suggested they set up a publishing business together. They made a start two years later, initially part-time, working from their respective homes in Devon and London. Their first publications were on railroad subjects, which long occupied an important position on the firm's general list. Appropriately, the company's original premises were in the railroad station at Newton Abbot, Devon, and have remained in that town ever since. The firm was acquired by **Reader's Digest** in 1990 but a management buyout led to a takeover by F&W Publications, a US company with a similar profile.

David Brown *(gears and tractors)*

British engineer David Brown (1904-1993) was born into a well-established Yorkshire family whose future had been assured by his grandfather's success in the gear manufacturing industry. Brown's father, Frank Brown, passed on to his son an astute awareness of big business, and as a schoolboy young David was already determined to make money. At the age of 17 he joined the family firm in Huddersfield, Yorkshire, where he was an enterprising apprentice. In 1932 he started a new bronze and steel foundry in Penistone, Yorkshire, producing engine components for aircraft and heavy components for electrical plants. He then turned his attention to tractor production, and in 1936 collaborated with Harry Ferguson (*see* **Massey-Ferguson**) to produce a revolutionary type of tractor that was the first to incorporate the now common hydraulic lift principle. The association ended in disagreement, but Brown pursued his interest in tractors and came up with the first all-British tractor, first shown at the 1939 Royal Agricultural Show. Brown's other great passion was cars, and he had competed in motor races at an early age. In 1947 he acquired the ailing **Aston Martin** business for a mere £20,000, and the following year **Lagonda**. In 1951 Brown merged his parent company with its many subsidiaries to form the David

Brown Corporation. Following subsequent management differences, Brown sold the tractor business off to a Houston, Texas, company in 1972, and his beloved Aston Martin the same year. In 1978 Brown's shipbuilding company, **Vosper Thornycroft**, was nationalized, and Brown left Britain in disgust to settle in Monte Carlo, where in 1980, as his third wife, he married his former personal assistant, Paula Benton Stone, 47 years his junior.

Davidoff *(cigars)*

The name is that of Zino Davidoff (1906-1994), born in Kiev, Ukraine, whose family fled the pogroms to settle in Geneva, Switzerland, where they opened a tobacco shop. After traveling widely in the tobacco lands of Central and South America, young Zino ended up in Cuba, where he made his base. After World War II Davidoff found himself with a fine selection of Havana cigars from Vichy France, and in 1947 he first set up his specialist selection based on Cuban cabinets. In 1963 he was was granted the accolade of a Havana brand from the Cuban industry, and in 1970 formed a partnership with Ernst Schneider, a local Swiss cigar importer. Following a dispute between Cuban manufacturers Cubatabaco and Schneider's Swiss-based Oettinger Imex company, Davidoff cigars ceased to be produced in Havana from 1990, when their manufacture was transferred to the Dominican Republic.

Davis, Godfrey *see* **Godfrey Davis**

Day-Glo *(fluorescent paints and colors)*

The name, from "day" and "glow," is of American origin and was entered by Dane & Co., Ltd. of London, England, in the *Trade Marks Journal* of October 3, 1951 and by Switzer Brothers, Inc., of Cleveland, Ohio, in the US Patent Office *Official Gazette* of January 15, 1952. The US parent company later became the Day-Glo Color Corporation.

Dayton Hudson *(booksellers)*

The Minneapolis-based company takes the first half of its name from George Draper Dayton (d.1938), a former banker, who started a department store in that city in 1902. Meanwhile in Ionia, Michigan, an Englishman named Joseph Lothian Hudson (1846-1912) had opened a small dry goods store in 1866. His business crashed, but he started a menswear and boyswear store with greater success in Detroit in 1881. The resultant businesses merged as the Dayton Hudson Corporation in 1969. The B. Dalton bookstores are owned by the corporation, and take their name from Bruce Dayton, one of George Dayton's grandsons, who deliberately altered one letter of his surname to provide the chain name.

De Beers *(diamonds)*

The prestigious name derives from two South African brothers, Nicolaas and Diederick De Beer, who in 1860 bought a farm for £50 in the Orange Free State near what is now Kimberley. In 1870 a large diamond mine was discovered on their land, and the De Beers were besieged by claimants. They sold up for the princely sum of £6,300 and had no further connection with the mine, although the company formed in 1888 by Cecil Rhodes and others to exploit this and other mines was named after them, as De Beers Mining Company. The discovery of the mine led to the founding of the town of Kimberley itself in 1871. The mine produced a glittering stream of diamonds right until 1990, when its supply ran out and it was closed down.

De Dion–Bouton *(automobiles)*

The French industrialist Count (from 1901 Marquis) Albert de Dion (1856-1946) went into partnership with Georges Bouton (1847-1938) and his brother-in-law, Trépardoux, makers of steam tricycles, in 1883. Their first vehicles were mainly commercial, but they built a car that set the fastest time in the 1894 Paris-Rouen Trials. Trépardoux was against experimentation with gas engines, however, and resigned from the partnership that year, when the De Dion-Bouton name was established. Despite many successful models, ranging from economy cars to luxury vehicles, the firm closed in 1927, although a brief revival by the French government continued production until 1932.

De Havilland *(aircraft)*

Geoffrey de Havilland (1882-1965) was born near High Wycombe, Buckinghamshire, England, the son of a local clergyman. After attending St. Edward's School, Oxford, in 1900 he took a three-year course in mechanincal engineering at the Crystal Palace Engineering School, followed by an apprenticeship with a firm in Rugby. In 1905 he obtained his first post as a draftsman with the **Wolseley** Tool and Motor Car Company in Birmingham. In 1908, inspired by the Wright brothers' example, he designed his own airplane and engine, and in 1910 taught himself to fly a second version. In 1914 de Havilland was engaged by the Aircraft Manufacturing Company to create and lead a design team, and in World War I he designed and flew eight military aircraft. In 1920, together with F.T. Hearle, C.C. Walker, W.E. Nixon, and F.E.N. St. Barbe, he founded the de Havilland Aircraft Co. Ltd. and began to pioneer the manufacture of civil aircraft, one being the famous Tiger Moth trainer (1931). The company was taken over by **Hawker Siddeley** in 1959 and eventually became part of British Aerospace.

De Kuyper *(gin and cherry brandy)*

It was in Rotterdam, Holland, that Johannes de Kuyper first began making alcoholic drinks in 1695. The family business then came to concentrate on making Geneva gin using grain and spices imported from the Baltic and Dutch East Indies (modern Indonesia). The family distillery prospered and the concern broadened its production to include liqueurs. In 1911 the company had no further space to expand in Rotterdam, so moved to a new plant at Schiedam, west of the city, where it remains today with direct descendants of the De Kuyper family still in control.

De la Rue *(printers)*

The name is that of the British company's founder, Thomas de la Rue (1793-1866), a Guernseyman who was apprenticed young to a printer named Chevalier. After further printing experience, Thomas went to London and in about 1821 set up his own business there. At first he seems to have been involved in the manufacture of straw hats, but later turned to making paper hats, that is, bonnets made of embossed paper. They led him to expand into the production of ornamental paper, and especially the manufacture of fine quality cards, such as playing cards, business cards, and visiting cards. In 1839 he invited his son, Warren de la Rue (1815-1889), to join him as partner, and it was the latter who imaginatively developed the firm's production capability to include postage stamps and currency notes, for which the company is famous today.

De Lorean *(automobiles)*

The rise and fall of the De Lorean Motor Company made one of the major media stories of the last quarter of the 20th century. The name is that of the engineer John Z. De Lorean (b. 1925), born in Detroit, Michigan, who from 1956 to 1973 enjoyed a highly successful career in the **Pontiac** and **Chevrolet** divisions of **General Motors**. In 1974 he founded DMC (as it was known) and persuaded the British government to back the building of a factory near Belfast, Northern Ireland, for the manufacture of his first model. It turned out to be his last. The DMC-12, a rear-engined sports coupé with a striking door articulation, was launched in 1981 and by the end of the year 80 cars a day were being produced. But the business was well short of financial viability, and in 1982 suddenly collapsed, while De Lorean himself was arrested and subsequently convicted on drug trafficking charges.

De Soto *(automobiles)*

The low-priced car was launched in 1928 by Walter P. **Chrysler**, who named it after the Spanish conquistador and explorer Hernando de Soto (*c.*1500-1542), discoverer of the Mississippi in 1541. Sales held up well until the 1950s, when there was no longer a demand for a medium-sized car in America, and in 1960 Chrysler decided to cease production of De Soto models. *See also* **Plymouth**.

De Tomaso *(automobiles)*

In 1956, Alejandro de Tomaso, born in Buenos Aires, Argentina, in 1928, set up shop as a maker of sports cars in Modena, Italy. In 1967 he embarked on the production of passenger cars, and in 1976 had done well enough to acquire **Maserati**. The firm is best remembered for the exotic-looking De Tomaso Pantera, first produced in 1970. The model lasted into the mid-1990s and was scheduled for re-launch in 2003.

Debenhams *(department stores)*

The ultimate origin of the British stores was in the draper's shop which Messrs. Flint and Clark opened for business in Wigmore Street, London, in 1778. The shop later became Clark & Debenham, then Debenham & Freebody, as it remained until it closed in 1981. Thomas Clark had gone into partnership with William Debenham in 1813, when the latter, a former farmer's apprentice from Suffolk, bought out the owner, William Franks. In 1818 Clement Freebody married William Debenham's daughter, so that when the latter's sons, William and Frank, joined their father in 1851, the name became Debenham, Son and Freebody. By the 1980s there were more than 70 department stores using the Debenham name, including, in London, the former **Marshall & Snelgrove** and the now closed **Swan & Edgar**, while the flourishing **Harvey Nichols** and **Hamley's**, operating under their own names, are also former Debenhams acquisitions. In 1985 Debenhams became part of the **Burton** Group, and by the mid-1990s there were 88 Debenhams stores.

Decca *(phonograph records)*

The British name was first used in 1913 for a portable phonograph manufactured in London by Barnett Samuel & Co. According to a family descendant, the name was chosen to match the names of other products beginning with "D," in particular "Dulcet." The advantage of the name, it was thought, was that it would be pronounced reasonably accurately in all European languages, whereas "Dulcet" was liable to corruption, especially by Italians. But this origin has not been authenticated. Nor has the more plausible explanation, that the name represents the musical notes D-E-C-C-A. The name was entered in the *Trade Marks Journal* of May 27, 1914 for: "Records for phonographs."

Deeko *(household paperware and plastic utensils)*

The British name derives from a partnership formed in 1899 in Islington, London, between a Mr. Dailley and a Mr. Wilkinson to manufacture paper doyleys and ornamental paper for mantel shelves. Wilkinson left the partnership in 1907 and the firm of Dailley & Co. was then set up. Hence the name, with "Dee-" for the initial of Dailley's name and "-ko" a variant of "Co." The name was entered in the *Trade Marks Journal* of March 9, 1932 for: "Doyleys, serviettes, soufflé cases, table cloths; all made of paper."

Deely-bobbers *(novelty headgear)*

The children's novelty headgear, usually in the form of a pair of ornaments (such as balls) on "antennas" attached by springs to a headband, became all the rage in 1982. It took its name from an earlier type of construction toy, comprising a number of interlinking blocks, entered by Behavioral Sciences, Inc., of San Jose, California, in the US Patent Office *Official Gazette* of July 1, 1969 as "Deelie-bobbers [*sic*] for building toys." The later name was entered by the Ace Novelty Co., Inc., of Bellevue, Washington, in the *Gazette* of November 29, 1982: "For Novelty Item—Namely, a Head Band with Springs Carrying Ornaments," with a claim of use since December 4, 1981. The origin of the name is uncertain, although "bobbers" is presumably from "bob."

Deere *(agricultural machinery)*

Deere & Company take their name from John Deere (1804-1886), inventor of the first steel plow that could till American Midwest prairie soil without clogging. Deere was born in Rutland, Vermont, a tailor's son. His formal education was limited, and he became an apprentice blacksmith at age 17. He then went on to work for various blacksmiths until he opened his own shop when in his mid-20s. In 1836 he headed for Grand Detour, Illinois, where he found plenty of work as a blacksmith. The rich soil of the region was so thick and sticky that plows were unable to turn it without considerable effort. Farmers had to stop frequently to scrape the mud from the moldboards (the large, curved parts that actually turned the soil) of their horse-drawn plows. Deere recognized the problem, and after a period of trial and error devised a plow with a polished steel moldboard that "scoured" itself clean as it moved through the soil. In 1837 Deere set up a business to manufacture and market the plow, and his company was incorporated as Deere & Company in 1868.

DEKALB *(hybrid seed)*

The US company, familiar from its winged corn signs in the Midwest, was founded by Thomas Roberts in DeKalb, Illinois, in 1912 and takes its name from the town.

Del Monte *(fruit canning)*

The American corporation, engaged primarily in processing, canning, and distributing food, especially bananas and pineapples, dates back to 1899, when 11 of California's biggest canners merged as the California Fruit Can-

ners Association (CFCA). In 1916 CFCA drew in two more canners and a food wholesaler, J.K. Armsby, and incorporated itself as the California Packing Corporation (Calpak), marketing its products under the brand Del Monte, a name that had been used by a predecessor company for 25 years. Literally, it is Spanish for "of the mountain," suggesting prestige and purity.

Delage *(automobiles)*

The French engineer Louis Delage (1874-1947), born in Cognac, set up his auto manufacturing business at Levallois-Perret in 1905. In 1911 he moved his works to Courbevoie, where he began specializing in luxury models. After World War I he concentrated on racing cars, but in 1935 overreached himself and was obliged to sell out to **Delahaye**.

Delahaye *(automobiles)*

At one time Delahaye was considered one of the most famous auto makers in France, on a par with **Bugatti**, **Talbot**, and **Delage**. The name is that of Émile Delahaye (d. 1905), who until 1890 had been chief engineer of a Franco-Belgian railroad rolling-stock concern before taking over a brick-making machinery factory in Tours, where he produced his first car in 1894. In 1898 he moved his business to Paris, and in 1935 the firm took over Delage. It then sold out to **Hotchkiss** in 1954, and car production ceased.

Delco *(automotive parts)*

The name is an acronym of *D*ayton *Eng*ineering *L*aboratories *Co*mpany, set up in Dayton, Ohio, in 1909 by Charles F. Kettering (1876-1958), an electrical inventor employed by **NCR**, and Edward A. Deeds, an NCR executive. Their first major product was an auto ignition system, then an electric self-starter. By 1914 Delco boasted a quarter of the American automotive starting, lighting, and ignition market. In 1916 it was acquired by William Crapo Durant, founder of **General Motors**, as part of United Motors, which itself became part of General Motors in 1919.

Dell *(computers)*

The American company takes its name from Michael Dell (b. 1965), who showed early business flair at the age of 12 when he sold his stamp collection for $2,000. Two years later he devised a marketing scheme to sell newspapers, an enterprise that earned him almost ten times as much. He first dabbled in electronics at the age of 15, when his father gave him a calculator, and became interested in computers when he was given an **Apple** 2. While attending a computer convention in Austin, Texas, he became aware of the huge markups on computer hardware, and this set him thinking about finding a way to bypass the retailer. Dell began a pre-med course at the University of Texas in 1983, but realized that his future lay in computers. He decided to go it alone, so quit college and in 1984 set up Dell Computer Corporation. It soon became the industry's fastest-growing company and in 2000 was the USA's largest computer seller.

Dell Books *(paperbacks)*

The American firm of paperback publishers, launched in 1943, grew out of the Dell Publishing Co., a pulp house founded in 1922 by 28-year-old George Delacorte, Jr., basing its name on his own. Dell began by publishing mysteries, but then expanded its list to include other genres, and by the end of the 1950s was grossing more than any other paperback publisher. Its first million-seller, in 1955, was Françoise Sagan's *Bonjour Tristesse*. Its second, Grace Metalious' *Peyton Place*, followed in 1957.

Delta *(airline)*

The American airline began its life as a a crop-dusting service in Louisiana in the 1920s. In 1928 the operation was sold to a group of local businessmen headed by Collett E. Woolman, an agricultural entomologist, and became Delta Air Service, taking its name from the Delta region of the Mississippi River. A passenger service was inaugurated the following year and in 1930 the business was incorporated as Delta Air Corporation. It adopted its present name, Delta Air Lines, in 1945.

Demerol *(analgesic)*

The proprietary name for pethidine, a painkilling drug used especially for women in labor, is apparently of arbitrary origin. It was entered in the US Patent Office *Official Gazette* of July 2, 1940 and the *Trade Marks Journal* of October 21, 1942.

Dennis *(commercial vehicles)*

The name is that of two English brothers,

John Cawsey Dennis (1871-1939) and Herbert Raymond Dennis (1878-1939), the sons of a Devon farmer. As the elder brother, John Dennis showed an early interest in machinery, and on leaving school was apprenticed to an ironmonger in Bideford, where he learned to repair all kinds of implements and machinery. In 1894 he moved away from his native Devon to be an ironmonger's assistant at a shop in Guildford, Surrey, where in his spare time he built a bicycle, selling it by displaying it in a tailor's window. The following year he opened his own bicycle shop in the High Street, and when his models gained commercial acclaim, successfully persuaded his brother Raymond to join him, which he did in the late 1890s. At about this time the brothers began to experiment with motorized tricycles, and from the turn of the 20th century progressed to commercial vehicles. Their first such vehicle was a van sold to **Harrods** in 1904, and soon after, as a special line, they started manufacturing fire engines, selling the first to the City of Bradford in 1908. The London fire brigade converted to Dennis engines two years later, and it is now usual to see the name Dennis on all British fire engines.

Dent *(publishers)*

The full name of the British publishing house is J.M. Dent & Sons Ltd., representing the founder and his family. He was Joseph Malaby Dent (1849-1926), born the son of a house painter in Darlington, Co. Durham. Joseph quit school at 13 and was apprenticed to a printer and bookbinder in turn. In 1867 he went to London to complete his training, and soon set up his own bookbinding business in Hoxton. After a series of misfortunes, including the death of his wife and the burning down of a new factory he had built, he achieved his ambition of becoming a publisher when in 1888 he issued the first two books in the "Temple Library," Charles Lamb's *Essays of Elia* and *The Last Essays of Elia*. The firm of J.M. Dent & Sons was eventually established in 1909. The "Sons" of the name were Hugh, his "right hand," Paxton, and Austin. The latter were by his second wife, Alexandra Main, whom he married in 1890, and were both killed on active service in World War I, wherupon Hugh's brother John took their place.

Dents (gloves)

John Dent (1751–1811) was born in Worcester, England, and at the age of 14 was apprenticed to James Perkins, a master glover in that city. He completed his apprenticeship in 1772 and set up his own glove-making business around 1777, the year that the company regards as that of its founding. Dent's sons, John and William, ran the business after his death, and when they retired in 1845, the firm of J. & W. Dent, as it had become, was bought by John Derby Allcroft. In 1852 the firm accordingly became Dent, Allcroft & Co., and although the Dent family ceased to be involved in the business following the brothers' retirement, "Dents" remains as the name by which the company's fashionable gloves have come to be known worldwide.

Dequadin (throat lozenges)

The name denotes the dequalinium that the lozenges contain, as an antibacterial compound used against mouth infections. The lozenges were first marketed in 1955 and the name was entered in the *Trade Marks Journal* of February 9, 1955.

Derry & Toms (department store)

Information is rather thin on the original Mr. Derry and Mr. Toms who gave their names to the famous London store. However, it is known that Charles Derry was the original founder of the Kensington High Street firm which began in about 1854 as a "Toy and Fancy Repository." Six years later he was joined by C.W. Toms, so that 1862 was the founding of the partnership. Derry's two sons, Arthur and Alfred, subsequently joined their father in the business, followed soon after by Toms' sons, Charles and Stanley. Charles Derry died in 1917 at the age of 97, his son Alfred having retired two years earlier. Although the store was acquired by John Barker (of **Barker's**) in 1920, the old name lasted until 1971, when the store closed, to be reopened a few months later by **Biba**. Today the Derry & Toms premises are divided between **Marks & Spencer** and BhS (British Home Stores).

Dettol (antiseptic and disinfectant)

When this British product was about to be marketed in the early 1930s, there was a debate as to whether it should be promoted as a disinfectant, perhaps called "Disinfectol," or as an antiseptic. It was finally decided that it should be introduced as a disinfectant through doctors for medical uses, and that the name should not be "Disinfectol" but something that had a medical flavor without giving any misleading idea regarding the nature of the product. The name that was adopted, although based on "Disinfectol," was thus "Dettol," which says little or nothing about the product's purpose or contents. (It actually contains chloroxylenol, a skin antiseptic.) The name was entered by **Reckitt** & Sons Ltd. in the *Trade Marks Journal* of February 25, 1931.

Deutsch (publishers)

The founder of the British firm was André Deutsch (1917–2000), born in Hungary the son of a dentist. He came to London in 1939 meaning to enroll at the London School of Economics, but instead worked through a variety of jobs until 1942, when he entered publishing as an employee of Nicolson & Watson. He was detained as an "enemy alien" for the remainder of World War II but in 1946 started his own publishing venture under the imprint (and arbitrary name) of Allan Wingate (Publishers) Ltd., bringing out a good deal of American fiction. His financial budget proved too tight, however, and the firm had to be written off. In 1951 he started again, this time publishing under his own name, gathering many famous authors under his wing and remaining resolutely independent while other publishers merged or were taken over. Deutsch was unmarried, so there were no sons or daughters to take over the business, which eventually fell prey to the forces of commercialism. In 1984 Deutsch stepped down from the firm he had nurtured and it subsequently became a division of the Carlton Publishing Group.

Devenish (beer)

The British firm, based in Dorset, traces its origins to 1742, when a Weymouth widow, Mrs. Mary Fowler, purchased a 1000-year lease on a site near the town where a brewhouse stood. Her heir and only surviving son was Jonathan Fowler, a maltster, who in 1773 conveyed part of the property to a brewer named Robert Flew and to his wife, Grace, Mary

Fowler's daughter. The brewery then passed to Robert Flew's son, John Flew, from whom it was purchased in 1824 by William Devenish (1772-1853), a local landowner's son. In 1843 William Devenish admitted the eldest of six sons, James Aldridge Devenish, into partnership, and it is the latter's name that gave the full name of the company for many years from 1889 as J.A. Devenish & Co. Ltd. The company is still based in Weymouth today.

Dewar's *(whisky)*

The blend takes its name from John Dewar (1806-1880), a Scottish crofter's son born near Aberfeldy, Perthshire. He moved to Perth as a young man to join the wine and spirit business of a relative, and worked with him until 1846, when he started his own business. The subsequent success of the firm owes much to his two sons, John Arthur Dewar (1856-1929) and Thomas Robert Dewar (1864-1930), who joined it in 1879 and 1881 respectively, with John as the administrator and financial manager and Thomas ("Tommy") as the seller and promoter. The company's head office remains in Perth.

Dexedrine *(stimulant drug)*

The proprietary name for dexamphetamine derives from the first syllable of this word and the latter part of the name **Benzedrine** and was entered by Smith, Kline & French Laboratories (now **SmithKline Beecham**) in the *Trade Marks Journal* of November 4, 1942 for: "Pharmaceutical preparations and substances for human use and for veterinary use."

DHL *(express parcel deliveries)*

The express service was the brainchild of Larry Hillblom (1943-1995), born in Kingsburg, California, the son of a farmer. After graduating from high school in California, Hillblom attended Fresno State University and Berkeley, where he studied law. Legal studies for him were a practical means to an end, however, and they led to the setting up of DHL in 1969, the initials standing for the surnames of his two partners, Adrian Dalsey and Robert Lynn, with his own name sandwiched between them. The service began modestly, carrying ships' lading bills by hand on scheduled air services to deliver them in port ahead of the ships. The range of services expanded, with Hillblom

fighting to overcome postal monopoly in both America and Britain. He was killed in an airplane accident in the South Pacific.

Diageo *(drinks and foods)*

The name was created for the British merger in 1997 of **Guinness** and **Grand Metropolitan** with the aim of reflecting their corporate identity as an international company. It combined the classical Greek prefixes *dia-*, "through," and *geo-* "earth," in other words "worldwide," but many regarded it as awkward and meaningless. One UK City analyst claimed the name sounded remarkably like a "small foreign hatchback," while according to a writer in the London *Times*: "It called to mind more an Italian footballer than a worldwide empire spanning everything from burgers to stout" (February 10, 1998).

Dial *(sedative)*

The proprietary name for diallylbarbituric acid is a shortened form of the generic name. The name was originally registered in Switzerland in 1918.

Dialaphone *(automatic dialing device)*

The name of the device for automatically dialing a telephone dates from 1957 and represents "dial a phone." It appears to have been this name that spawned the subsequent "dial-a-" formula for various telephone services, many of them registered trademarks, such as "dial-a-bus" or "dial-a-chat."

Diamond *(matches and playing cards)*

Diamond International dates back to 1881, when the owners of America's largest match manufacturers banded together to form Diamond Match, adopting a generally prestigious name that suggests quality and "sparkle." They now operate stores in several states called Diamond Building Supply Home Centers, selling hardware, tools, lumber, and other home-building materials.

Dickins & Jones *(department store)*

The present store in Regent Street, London, England, has its origins in the draper's shop opened in 1790 at 54 Oxford Street by a Mr. Dickins and a Mr. Smith. In 1830 the shop's name became Dickins, Sons and Stevens, and five years later the business moved to the newly built Regent Street, with the draper's shop subsequently supplied with material from a silk manufactory set up by the Dickins family in Manchester in 1884. In around 1890 the store adopted its present name, when John Pritchard Jones joined the business. The store became part of the **Harrods** group in 1914, although retaining its previous name.

Dictaphone *(dictating machine)*

The type of cassette recorder used to record speech arose as a development of the phonograph. Its name, from "dictate" (or "dictation") and "-phone" as in **Gramophone** (or "phonograph") was entered by the **Columbia** Phonograph Company in the *Trade Marks Journal* of May 15, 1907.

Dictograph *(internal telephone)*

The Dictograph, an American invention dating from the early 20th century, is an instrument for transmitting speech from room to room in a building, with or without the speaker's knowledge, by means of a small concealed microphone. Its name, from "dictate" (or "dictation") and the "-graph" of "phonograph", was entered by Dictograph Telephones Ltd., of London, England, in the *Trade Marks Journal* of April 27, 1921.

Digia *(computer software)*

The Finnish company, with a name based on "digital," was founded in 1997 by a former journalist, Pekka Sivonen (b. 1962), to create applications for the Symbian mobile data platform. Symbian (a Greek-based name meaning "living together") was created that year by the equipment rivals **Nokia**, **Motorola**, **Ericsson**, **Matsushita**, and **Psion** with the aim of building and licensing a mobile operating system that would prevent **Microsoft** from extending its control of the personal computer to the wireless world.

Digitron *(cathode display tube)*

The cold-cathode character display tube derives its name from a blend of "digit" and "electron," entered by **Ericsson** Telephones Ltd. in the *Trade Marks Journal* of June 18, 1958.

Dilantin *(anticonvulsant)*

The proprietary name of the drug phenytoin, used as an anticonvulsant in the treatment of epilepsy, derives from the prefix "di-" and letters from "hydantoin," a compound used in its manufacture, with an inserted letter "l." It was entered in the US Patent Office *Official Gazette* of May 24, 1938.

Dillons *(bookstores)*

The best-known British bookstore of the name is the London one, in Gower Street, where it has long been familiar as the bookshop of the University of London, located nearby. The name behind the store is that of Una Dillon (1903-1993). After graduating from Bedford College, London University, where she had studied physics, Dillon became attracted to the world of bookselling and publishing. As a first step, she organized supplies of books for the Central Association for Mental Welfare, the charity where she worked. She eventually realized her ambition one day in 1936, when walking along Store Street, off Tottenam Court Road, she saw a bookshop that looked as if it were about to go bankrupt. She went in and talked to the owner, asking him if he would like to sell her the shop. He said he would for £800. Borrowing £600 from her father and the balance from her friend, she bought it. She knew next to nothing about bookselling but worked hard to attract custom from London University, just across the road. Her assiduity was beginning to pay dividends when World War II came and the university was evacuated. She persevered after the war, however, and at last in 1956 won the official partnership with London University that she had dreamed of. She retired as manager of the bookstore in 1967 but continued on the board until 1977, when the university sold Dillons to Pentos. At the time of her death there were 117 Dillon bookstores in Britain. In 1995 the chain went into receivership, but was rescued by **Thorn EMI**.

Dimple *(golf balls)*

The type of golf ball, so named for its pits or "dimples," which give truer flight, was the invention of the English mechanical engineer and metrologist William Taylor (1865-1937), better known as the originator of standard screw threads for lens mountings.

Dimple *(whisky)*

The de luxe blend of **Haig** whisky takes its name from its famous dimpled bottle, which made its first appearance at the turn of the 20th century. It immediately attracted attention, and

Haig were involved in a number of prosecutions against imitators. The design was registered in 1919, and eventually in 1952 Haig were awarded the concept of exclusivity by the Scottish Court of Session. Since a dimpled bottle of this type is known as a pinchbottle in the USA, the whisky itself is known there as "Pinch."

Dimplex *(electrical appliances)*

The firm was founded in 1947 by the Irishman Martin Naughton, who named his business from the "dimpled" design of the first oil-filled electric radiators. The name was entered in the *Trade Marks Journal* of December 3, 1947. The company now owns such other well-known names in the electrical and heating world as **Morphy Richards** and **Belling**.

Diners Club *(credit card)*

The first universal credit card, usable at a variety of establishments, owes its origin to three American entrepreneurs: the theatrical agent Alfred S. Bloomingdale (1916-1982), his friend Frank McNamara, then head of an unsuccessful finance company, and McNamara's attorney Ralph Schneider. In 1949 the three men met for lunch in New York City to discuss the debt-collecting problems being experienced by McNamara. They decided to set up a new enterprise, and to finance it McNamara contributed his company and its debts, while Bloomingdale contributed $5,000 in cash. Bloomingdale then returned to California, and the new venture was launched by McNamara and Schneider. In the first three weeks of operation, they purchased a mailing list of 5,000 sales managers for $75 and found 100 who were interested, while they also located about a dozen interested restaurants. The two then borrowed an additional $35,000 from a finance company. Bloomingdale rejoined them, and the enterprise grew to include a collection agency, a credit-checking firm, and a travel bureau, thus meeting the challenge posed by **American Express**. As the *New York Times* reported on January 6, 1952: "Anyone who can sign his name and pay his bills can charge his way through some of the better hotels, restaurants and night clubs of the country under a new credit card system known as the Diners Club." The name was entered in the US Patent Office *Official Gazette* of June 19, 1956 by "Hamilton Credit Corporation, New York ...

now The Diners' Club, Inc. ... For extension of credit to customers who purchase at subscribing retail establishments and making collections from such customers through a central billing system." Alfred S. Bloomingdale was the grandson of Lyman G. Bloomingdale, the founder of **Bloomingdale's**.

Dinky Toys *(miniature toy vehicles)*

In 1932 **Meccano** Ltd. produced six miniature vehicles as accessories to their **Hornby** train sets. The little cars were so popular that the range was relaunched in 1933 as "Dinky Toys," adopting this name from the Scots dialect word meaning "small," "neat," "dainty." The name was entered in the *Trade Marks Journal* of July 5, 1950, but production ceased in 1979.

Dinty Moore *(canned beef stew)*

Dinty Moore was not the name of the stew's creator, who was Jay Catherwood Hormel (1892-1954), son of George A. **Hormel**, founder of the US company that produced it. The 24-ounce cans of stew were originally known by the company name, as Hormel Beef Stew. In 1936, however, Hormel entered into an agreement with C.F. Witt & Sons, a large grocery and meat firm in Minneapolis, to sell and distribute its meat products under the Dinty Moore trademark, which C.F. Witt already owned. Witt, in turn, was granted the right to sell all other food products that were not canned goods under the Dinty Moore name. But Hormel's use of the name was soon challenged. It turned out that Dinty Moore was the name of a character in the gag strip *Bringing Up Father*, an epic comedy of husband-and-wife strife first appearing in 1913. Hormel thus appeared to be infringing the rights of the strip's creator, George McManus (1884-1954). Legal advice was taken, and it was declared that there was no direct competition between Dinty Moore the stew and Dinty Moore the cartoon character, so that Hormel had not violated McManus' rights or those of his publishers, King Features. McManus later revealed that he got the name of the corner saloon owner Dinty Moore from that of a bellhop in a St. Louis hotel.

Diocalm *(antidiarrheal)*

The name suggests a preparation (actually

containing attapulgite and morphine) that "calms diarrhea." It was entered in the *Trade Marks Journal* of August 18, 1965.

Dior *(fashionwear)*

The prestigious French fashion house takes its name from Christian Dior (1905-1957), born in Granville, Normandy. Dior abandoned his political science studies to take up music but instead spent his time running an art gallery and traveling. In 1935 he began earning a living in Paris selling fashion sketches to newspapers, and three years later joined the designer Robert Piguet, who had founded his own house in 1933. In 1942 Dior moved to Lucien Lelong, where he worked alongside Pierre Balmain until in 1947 cotton magnate Marcel Boussac offered him the opportunity to open his own house. Dior's first collection was the influential New Look.

Disprin *(analgesic tablets and powders)*

The British name, denoting a *dis*solvable as*pirin*, was first entered by Roy Vickers of Liverpool in the *Trade Marks Journal* of July 18, 1945. The product later passed to **Reckitt & Colman**.

Dixie *(disposable cups)*

The disposable cups for ice cream or drinks trace their origin to 1908, when Hugh Moore founded the imposingly named American Water Supply Company of New England. His product was simply a drink of water, for which he had developed a special vending machine. For the price of one penny, the machine would dispense a pure drink of cool water in an individual paper cup. Soon Moore was altering the emphasis of his business from supplying drinking water to manufacturing paper cups, and by 1910 his firm had accordingly become The Individual Drinking Cup Company. He could see that the cups themselves needed a catchy brand name, and at first tried marketing them as "Health Kups." The name did not catch on, however, so in 1919 he changed it to "Dixie Cups." He took the name from the Dixie Doll Company, the business run by his neighbor in the downtown New York loft building in which his own firm was located. Moore liked the name "Dixie" and the way it rolled off the tongue. It also had a historical background, since Dixieland was said to be named for the

$10 notes with the French word *dix* ("ten") printed on them that circulated in Louisiana before the Civil War. He therefore asked the doll maker if he could adopt the name. His neighbor did not object, and from that moment "Dixie Cup" became one of America's best-known brand names.

Dixons *(cameras and electronic goods)*

The British company, with its numerous High Street stores, was not founded by a Mr. Dixon. The firm originated in a small photographic studio started up in 1937 in Edgware, London, by East End resident Charles Kalms. He soon after acquired another studio in Southend, Essex, and for his new business adopted the name Dixons from a former department store there, preferring this to his own name, with its rather tricky spelling. His business flourished in World War II, unlike many, because people wanted to send photos of themselves to their friends and relatives (and lovers), and could not easily take their own photos as there was a shortage of film. Charles Kalms, who died in 1978, aged over 80, was joined by his son Stanley (b. 1931) in 1948. The Kalms family still own the company today.

DKW *(automobiles)*

The company dates from 1916, when a Danish engineer, Jorgen Rasmussen, was producing steam-powered engines in Zschopau, near Chemnitz, eastern Germany. Three years later a German engineer from Berlin offered Rasmussen the production of a small 30cc toy two-stroke engine, and in 1921 Rasmussen produced an enlarged version of this to power a normal bicycle as a basic type of motorcycle. In 1928 he built his first car. The initials stand for Deutsche Kraftfahrzeug Werke ("German Motor Vehicle Works"), although the motorized bicycle was familiarly known as Das Kleine Wunder ("The Little Wonder"), just as the toy engine had been dubbed Des Knaben Wunsch ("The Boy's Wish"). The last DKW model appeared in 1966, and the car is now remembered as the predecessor of the modern **Audi**.

Dobro *(guitar)*

The acoustic steel guitar with a metallic resonator, laid flat on the knee to play and particularly associated with country music, derives its name from its inventors, the Czech-American *Do*pera *bro*thers. The name, which also (probably intentionally) represents Czech *dobro*, "good," was entered by the Valco Manufacturing Company of Chicago in the US Patent Office *Official Gazette* of February 26, 1952, with a claim of use since November 1929.

Doc Martens *see* **Dr. Martens**

Doctor Martens *see* **Dr. Martens**

Dr. Martens *(footwear)*

The famous Dr. Martens boot, with its "Air-Wair" sole, seized on by British skinheads from the 1960s and subsequently by other youthful tribes, derives its name from Klaus Maertens, a German doctor who in 1945 had an accident while skiing and damaged his foot. The injury caused him considerable pain, especially when walking in conventional footwear. As a result of this discomfort, he and an old student friend, Herbert Funck, developed an air-cushioned sole. By 1947 the first such shoes were being produced in a run-down factory in Seeshaupt, near Munich, Germany. News of the product spread across Europe and by the mid-1950s the shoes were having a moderate success. In the late 1950s the right to manufacture Dr. Maertens' shoes was offered to a number of UK manufacturers. Only one, however, saw the potential. This was the firm of R. Griggs & Co. Ltd., founded by William Griggs in 1901 at Wollaston, near Wellingborough, Northamptonshire. They secured the contract to use the "AirWair" concept for a new range of working men's boots, and the first Dr. Martens boot came off the UK production line in 1960. By the end of the decade they had become something of a cult in Britain, being accepted as both functional workwear and a street fashion. The anglicized name "Dr. Martens" was entered in the *Trade Marks Journal* of March 23, 1977 with the description: "Soles for boots and for shoes. Ing. Herbert Funck and Klaus Maerten ... Munchen-Pasing, Haidelweg 20, and Seeshaupt (Oberbayern), An der Ach, Federal Republic of Germany," with the note, "Use claimed from the year 1965." The boots are colloquially known as "Doc Martens" or "DMs."

Dr Pepper *(sparkling fruit-flavored drink)*

The name derives from a real Dr. Pepper who owned a drug store in Virginia. A young soda fountain assistant at the store fell for the doctor's beautiful daughter and began courting her. Her father was not amused, however, and sacked the young Romeo, who duly removed himself to the Old Corner Drug Store in Waco, Texas. There he continued the concoction of new fountain flavors that he had begun for the girl he left behind him. One day he hit on a combination that he thought was his best yet. It quickly became a favorite at the fountain, and having learned of the short-lived romance that had bloomed in Virginia, customers nicknamed the new drink "Dr Pepper." Meanwhile, a patron of the Old Corner Drug Store, R.S. Lazenby, had become interested in the "Dr Pepper" flavor, and began extensive research on the drink at his Artesian Bottling Works. In 1885, after two years of careful testing, he put "Dr Pepper" on sale at soda fountains in and around Waco. The drink's popularity spread, and by 1910, "Dr Pepper" syrup had become one of the principal freight items hauled from Waco by the **Wells Fargo** Express. In 1922, Mr. Lazenby's daughter married J.B. O'Hara, an army officer from Pennsylvania. O'Hara saw great prospects for "Dr Pepper" and set up an extensive sales and distribution program. The program was successful, and the company moved to larger quarters in Dallas, Texas. By 1930, the business had grown to such an extent that a modern, three-story syrup plant was constructed. "Dr Pepper" is not a cola but a special blend of many flavors, rightly earning its reputation as the "friendly pepper-upper." The success story is complete when it is known that the original genius of the soda fountain was reunited with his Virginia belle and finally won her hand.

Dr. Scholl *see* **Scholl**

Dodge *(automobiles)*

The name is that of the brothers John Francis Dodge (1864-1920) and Horace Elgin Dodge (1868-1920), born in Niles, Michigan, the sons of a foundry and machine shop operator. The family subsequently moved to Port Guron, Michigan, where the brothers worked with their father for the Upton Manufacturing Company, makers of farm machinery. In 1886 the family moved to Detroit, where John and Horace found work building boilers and repairing boats. After a spell making bicycles for the Dominion

Topography Company in Windsor, Ontario, Canada, the two men returned to Detroit and set up their own machine shop. The Dodge Brothers' business expanded, producing auto parts for Henry **Ford**, and John became vice president of the Ford Motor Company in 1907. Concerned that Ford might face a business decline, or develop on its own the parts they supplied, John and Horace decided to manufacture their own car. In 1914 they incorporated their new firm, and the first Dodge car rolled out of the factory in November that year. The company was taken over by **Chrysler** in 1928.

Dodg'em *(electric car)*

The small electric car, a standard funfair entertainment, derives its name fairly obviously from its role, which is to avoid the other cars being driven about the enclosure (dodge 'em) while its steerer does his best to bump them. The cars first came into their own in the 1920s. The name is not proprietary in British use, where the cars are simply known as dodgems (or bumper cars).

Do-Do *(decongestant)*

The name was entered by Harry Pickup (*see* **Harpic**), owner of the product's manufacturing company, in the *Trade Marks Journal* of March 13, 1940. He derived it from the first letters of the names of two previously unsuccessful tonic products, "Dovim" and "Dovite," respectively sham Latin for "I give strength" and "I give life."

Dolby *(sound recording systems)*

The name is that of the American electronics engineer Ray M. Dolby (b. 1933), born in Portland, Oregon, who was employed by **Ampex** Corporation from 1949 to 1957 and in the latter year received a degree in electrical engineering from Stanford University. In 1965 he established the Dolby Laboratories in London, England, to develop systems to reduce background noise in tape recordings and the following year introduced Dolby A for professional tape and film formats. Dolby B was developed in 1968 and soon found use in the **Philips** compact cassette, the new consumer medium for music. The name "Dolby System" was entered in the US Patent Office *Official Gazette* of March 3, 1970, with a note of first use on October 30, 1966.

Dolce & Gabbana *(fashionwear)*

The name is that of the Italian fashion designers Domenico Dolce (b. 1958), born in Polizzi Generosa, Sicily, and Stefano Gabbana (b. 1962), born in Milan, who opened a fashion consulting studio in Milan in 1982. In the 1990s they became one of Italy's most important and innovative companies.

Dolcelatte *(cheese)*

The cheese, a toned-down version of Gorgonzola, is made at the **Galbani** factory in Pavia, Italy, and has a name literally meaning "sweet milk."

Dole *see* **Castle & Cooke**

Dollond & Aitchison *(opticians)*

The English partnership started with John Dollond (1706-1761), born at Spitalfields, London, into an immigrant Huguenot family. He began his career in the family trade of silk weaving, but had a special interest in astronomy and optics, on which he read widely. His eldest son Peter Dollond (1730-1820) was also destined for the silk-weaving trade, but had inherited his father's interests and in 1750 set up as an optician in the Strand, whereupon his father abandoned his own silk weaving and joined him. The other member of the partnership, James Aitchison (1860-1911), began his career as an optician's apprentice in High Holborn in about 1875 and set up his own business in Fleet Street in 1889. It was not until 1927 that the two businesses combined. At first it was planned to call the new firm Aitchison & Dolland, but when it was realized that "Aitchison" was difficult to pronounce, the order of names was reversed.

Dolmar *(chainsaws)*

The name is that of Mt. Dolmar, Thuringia, Germany, on whose wooded slopes in 1927 Emil Lerp demonstrated the first petrol-engine sawing machine for forestry work. Dolmar GmbH of Hamburg are now one of the leading manufacturers of chainsaws in the world, selling in over 100 countries.

Dom Pérignon *(champagne)*

The name is that of the Benedictine monk and cellarer Dom Pérignon (1639-1715), said to have invented champagne. In 1936 the firm of **Moët et Chandon** launched the first prestige cuvée (blend of champagne) and named it after him. The name was entered by the Chandon Champagne Corporation, New York, in the US Patent Office *Official Gazette* of June 19, 1956, with a note of first use in November 1936, and by Moët et Chandon in the *Trade Marks Journal* of February 17, 1965.

Domecq *(sherry)*

The firm of Domecq was founded in 1730 by a sherry producer in Jerez de la Frontera, Spain, the town whose name gave the word "sherry" itself. The founder was an Irish sherry producer, Patrick Murphy, who was succeeded on his death in 1762 by a Frenchman, Juan Haurie, whose nephew, Jean Charles Haurie, gained the concession to supply Napoleon's army with wine when the emperor's troops invaded Spain in 1808. Jean Charles Haurie's nephew in turn was Pierre de Domecq, and he, with two English partners, took over his uncle's business in 1813, subsequently adopting Spanish citizenship and changing his name to Pedro Domecq. When he died in 1839 he was succeeded by his brother, Juan Pedro Domecq, and when the latter himself died, childless, in 1869, he left the firm to his adopted son, also named Juan Pedro. In 1930, to mark their bicentenary, Domecq produced what is still one of its most popular brands of sherry, "Double Century." In 1994 the company became part of Allied Domecq.

Domes of Silence *(castors)*

The somewhat poetic name, alluding to the soundless swiveling and turning of the small wheels on the legs or base of heavy furniture when moved, was entered for "Metal Castors for Furniture" in the *Trade Marks Journal* of March 12, 1924.

Domestos *(liquid bleach)*

The product was introduced by **Unilever** in 1930 and was being distributed nationally in the UK by 1952. Its name is a blend of "domestic" and "Chloros," the brand name of a bleaching chemical.

Dominic, Peter *see* **Peter Dominic**

Domino's *(pizza chain)*

America's second largest pizza chain (after **Pizza Hut**) dates from 1960, when Thomas S. Monaghan (b. 1937) and his brother James took over a pizzeria in Ypsilanti, Michigan, called Dominick's. There were setbacks in the early years, including the loss of the firm's headquarters in a fire in 1969 and a lawsuit in the late 1970s from Amstar, the owner of Domino Sugar, for infringement on the name "Domino's." But the 1980s were boom years, so that by 1993 there were 2,200 units in the USA and 5,500 worldwide in 1996. Domino's strong suit has always been its rapid home delivery service.

Donna Karan *(fashionwear)*

Donna Karan International was launched in 1984 by the American fashion designer Donna Karan, née Faske (b. 1948), a tailor's daughter, who began her fashion career at the age of 14. She married boutique owner Mark Karan, but founded her enterprise with her second husband, Stephan Weiss. Her subsidiary DKNY (Donna Karan New York) label followed in 1988. In 2001 Karan and Weiss sold their privately held fashion company to the French luxury goods group LVMH (*see* **Louis Vuitton**).

Doona *(duvet)*

The Australian make of quilted eiderdown or duvet is said to base its name on Swedish *dun*, "down." It was entered by its manufacturers, Kimpton Feather Mills Pty. Ltd., in the *Official Journal of Patents, Trade Marks and Designs* of March 1, 1973.

Doritos *(tortilla chips)*

The chips of this name were introduced by Frito-Lay (*see* **Lay's**) in 1966. The name itself is a diminutive of Spanish *dorado*, "golden," rendered by the manufacturers as "a little bit of gold."

Dorling Kindersley *(publishers)*

Peter Kindersley (b. 1941), the son of a sculptor, had a traditional English "arts-and-crafts" background. He originally intended to become a painter, but to make a living worked as a designer with the publisher Thomas **Nelson**, and then joined **Mitchell Beazley** as design director. He became convinced that there was a market for well-illustrated educational books, and in 1974 set up his own business to further this, taking as partner Christopher Dorling. For the first few years he concentrated on producing books for other publishers, but introduced his own imprint in 1982, after which he carved out a distinctive niche in the children's market. In 2000 Dorling Kindersley was bought by **Pearson**, and Kindersley himself resigned from publishing to take up organic farming.

Dorman, Long *(steel)*

The British steel manufacturers took their name from Arthur John Dorman (1848-1931), born in Ashford, Kent, the son of a currier, and Albert de Lande Long, who in 1876 formed a partnership to manufacture iron bars and angles for shipbuilding at the port of Stockton-on-Tees, Co. Durham. The firm gradually grew, especially in World War I, but its fortunes waned financially and managerially in the 1920s until saved by a revival in the late 1930s. In 1967 it became part of **British Steel.**

Dormobile *(motor caravan, or trailer)*

The vehicle, essentially a trailer with sleeping accommodation, has a name blending "dormitory" and "automobile" that was entered by its original British manufacturers, Martin Walter Ltd., of Folkestone, Kent, in the *Trade Marks Journal* of October 22, 1952.

Dorothy Perkins *(fashion stores)*

The original English shop from which the chain developed was the one built in the style of a cottage, with a red-tiled gabled roof. Dorothy Perkins is the name of a well-known rambling rose (*Rosa wichuraiana*, also known as Memorial Rose), and the wife of one of the partners of the store's founder, Samuel Farmer, felt the name would be suitable for the shop, to match its cottage-like appearance. The rose itself was named in 1901 for the daughter of George C. Perkins and the granddaughter of Charles H. Perkins, founder of the American rose nursery Jackson and Perkins.

Double Century *see* **Domecq**

Double-Crostics *(word puzzles)*

The word puzzle, in which the text of a well-known quotation or literary passage is built up in a crossword-like grid from the letters of answers to cryptic clues, was the invention of the American Elizabeth S. Kingsley. The first such puzzle appeared in the *Saturday Review* of March 31, 1934, taking its name from "double acrostic," perhaps with a deliberate hint of "double-cross." The name was entered in the US Patent Office *Official Gazette* of December 3, 1946.

Double Diamond *(beer)*

The beer of this name was first sold in 1876 by the British brewery **Ind Coope**. The allusion is to the brand's logo, now two interlinked diamonds, but originally the two diamond shapes discernible between the first and second X, and the second and third, of a triple X ("XXX"), denoting its strength.

Doubleday *(publishers)*

The American publishing house was founded in New York in 1897 by Brooklyn-born Frank Nelson Doubleday (1862-1934). Frank had begun his career in publishing at the age of 15 when he quit school to work for the company of Charles **Scribner's** Sons, becoming manager of *Scribner's Magazine* when it first started in 1886. In the year stated he formed his own publishing house together with the Irish-born editor and publisher Samuel Sidney **McClure** (1857-1949), founder of *McClure's Magazine*, so that at first the business was called Doubleday & McClure. The partnership lasted only three years, however, so that from 1900 Frank Doubleday ran the company himself, becoming what is now regarded as the first of the truly business-oriented publishers. In 1920 Doubleday obtained a controlling interest in the British publishing house William **Heinemann**, becoming its owner in 1922.

Douglas *(aircraft)* *see* **McDonnell Douglas**

Douglas *(axes)*

Now a generic term in Australian slang for an ax, the name is properly that of the Douglas Axe Manufacturing Co., of East Douglas, Massachusetts, who entered it in the US Patent Office *Official Gazette* of July 13, 1926. The company had earlier announced their "axes, hatchets, adzes, picks, etc." in the US Centennial Commission *International Exhibition: Official Catalog* of 1876.

Douglas *(motorcycles)*

The story of the British company began in the opening years of the 20th century, when one J.F. Barter made a single-cylinder machine in Bristol. He then produced a twin model, using parts from the local Douglas Foundry Company. He soon joined the company himself with the aim of designing them a motorcycle, and the resulting models took their name. Despite a number of financial vicissitudes, the firm continued making motorycles until 1957, by which time it was owned by **Westinghouse**, who that year decided not to produce any more two-wheelers.

Doulton *(pottery)*

Commonly regarded as the greatest potter of the 19th century, Henry Doulton (1820-1897) was born in Lambeth, London, the son of a potter who produced mainly blacking and oil bottles and Toby jugs. On leaving school at 15, Henry joined his father in the pottery, soon becoming an expert "thrower" and producing glazed sanitary pipes from 1846. It was this stoneware that brought his name to the attention of the public, and by the time that Henry Doulton came to produce his distinctive "art pottery" in 1870, the firm of Doulton was famous. The factory he founded in Lambeth remained in operation there until 1956, when it transferred to Devon. The present company's head office remains in Lambeth, however. The pottery it produces is known as "Royal Doulton," from the royal warrant presented to the company in 1901 by Edward VII, together with the authority to use the word "Royal" to describe its products.

Dover *(publishers)*

Dover Publications, famous for its softback reprints of out-of-print titles, especially classics and reference works, was founded in New York City in 1941 as a mail order business for remaindered books by Hayward F. Cirker (1917-2000) and his wife Blanche, taking its name from the building where they lived.

Dow *(chemicals)*

The American company takes its name from Herbert Henry Dow (1866-1930), born in Belleville, Ontario, the son of a master mechanic. He spent his early life in Connecticut, but in 1878 his family moved to Cleveland, Ohio, where in 1888 he graduated from the Case School of Applied Science. During his studies he became interested in the possibility of extracting bromine from the brines (salt-impregnated waters) often associated with oil and gas wells. By 1889 he had devised an electrolytic process for doing this and the following year formed the Midland Chemical Company, moving his operations to Midland, Michigan. In 1894, when the backers of Midland Chemical

withdrew their support for Dow's plans to diversify into chlorine and bleaching powder production, he resigned as general manager, and with new investors formed the Dow Process Company. He eventually built a plant to extract chlorine from Midland Chemical's waste brine, and in 1897 incorporated the Dow Chemical Company, which soon initiated commercial production of chlorine bleach. In 1900 the two companies were combined and grew to become the present Dow Chemical Company.

Dow Jones *(newspapers)*

The name behind the American company is probably most familiar as that of the Dow Jones Industrial Average, the stock market barometer whose figures are announced daily by the media. But figuring out "the Dow" is only a small part of what the company does. Its main activity is publishing the prestigious *Wall Street Journal*. It also brings out a number of smaller provincial newspapers. The name itself is that of two young newspapermen from Providence, Rhode Island, Charles Henry Dow (1851-1902) and Edward D. Jones (1856-1920), who came to New York independently in about 1880. They both got jobs as financial reporters in the Wall Street area, and in 1882 started their own financial news service, Dow, Jones & Company, setting up shop in a basement on Wall Street, behind a soda fountain. Dow went out and covered the news, while Jones stayed in the office as the "desk man." Jones edited and dictated the stories to a small group of clerks, who wrote them out by hand in books of tissue paper interleaved with carbon paper, making up to 24 copies a time. Messenger boys would then deliver the bulletins to the news service's clients throughout the day. The young men's enterprise grew and became increasingly sophisticated, until they were publishing a daily summary of the bulletins. This eventually became the *Wall Street Journal*, the first number of which left the presses on July 8, 1889.

Dralon *(synthetic textile)*

The name of the textile, made from acrylic fiber, was entered by **Bayer**, its German manufacturers, in the *Trade Marks Journal* of December 21, 1955. It is said to be a blend of German *Draht*, "wire," "thread," referring to the manufacturing process, and "nylon." The suggestion of English "drapery" is also appropriate for a fabric used for curtains and uphol-stery.

Dramamine *(travel sickness drug)*

The proprietary name for the drug dimen-hydrinate is apparently based on letters from the generic name with "-am-" repeated. It was entered by the US company G.D. Searle & Co. in the *Trade Marks Journal* of June 7, 1950 for a: "Pharmaceutical preparation consisting of dimenhydrinate for use in the prevention and treatment of motion sickness, nausea and vom-iting, and as antihistaminics."

Drambuie *(whisky liqueur)*

The Scottish manufacturers relate the origin of their liqueur and its name as follows. After the Jacobite rebellion of 1745 (the "Forty-Five"), the Young Pretender ("Bonnie Prince Charlie") fled for his life to the island of Skye. On leaving for France the following year, he gave to John Mackinnon of Strathaird, who had rowed him to a safe hiding place, the se-cret formula of his personal liqueur. For nearly 150 years the Mackinnons kept the secret to themselves. Then in 1906, following the regis-tration of the name by James Ross of Broad-ford, Skye, in the *Trade Marks Journal* of Sep-tember 20, 1893, Malcolm Mackinnon decided to produce the liqueur commercially as "Dram-buie," deriving the name from Gaelic *dram*, "drink," and either *buidheach*, "satisfying," "pleasing," or *buidh*, "yellow," "golden." The adjectives are equally appropriate in their re-spective subjective and objective senses.

Drene *(shampoo)*

The first soapless shampoo to be marketed in the United States was launched in 1933 by **Procter & Gamble**. It is so called as it is a dry shampoo, so the name effectively represents "dry-ene."

DRG *(stationery and paper products)*

The British company traces its origins to John Dickinson, the "D" of the name, who in 1804 set up as a stationer in the City of Lon-don. Five years later he developed a process for making paper by machine, and acquired a mill near Hemel Hempstead, Hertfordshire, for this purpose. The firm was known as John Dickin-son & Co. and went on to acquire further mills, including Croxley Mills near Watford. (This is the origin of the firm's "Croxley" paper.) The

second letter of the name is the initial of E.S. & A. Robinson, a stationery manufacturer founded in 1844 that John Dickinson & Co. acquired in 1966. The company was then re-named as Dickinson Robinson Group Ltd., giving all three letters of the subsequent ab-breviated name.

Drinamyl *(stimulant)*

The drug is named from its main ingredients, dexamphetamine and amylobarbitone, with the first part of the name also based on the last part of **Dexedrine**. The name was entered in the *Trade Marks Journal* of December 13, 1950.

Dry Fly *(sherry)*

The sherry produced by **Findlater Mackie Todd** was originally known as "Findlater's Fino." As its name indicates, it is a dry type, and is so called from the method of fishing in which an artificial fly floats lightly on the sur-face of the water, so is "dry," unlike other flies, which sink below the surface. And if some take "fly" in its sense of "stylish and fashionable," Findlater's are hardly likely to object.

DSFX *(risk management)*

The US firm was formed in 1997 with the merger of *D*ecision *S*trategies International and The *Fairfax* Group. Bart M. Schwartz, a former **Kroll** director, founded Decision Strategies in 1991 and Michael J. Hershman, a former gov-ernment investigator, founded Fairfax in 1983. In 2001, with Schwartz as president and Her-shman as chairman, the group agreed to a takeover by SPX Corporation.

Du Maurier *(cigarettes)*

The British brand of cigarettes, produced by **Gallaher** until 1979, took its name from the English actor Sir Gerald du Maurier (1873-1934), who in the 1920s had asked Peter Jack-son Ltd., a subsidiary of the International To-bacco Company, for "a cigarette less irritating to my throat" than the ones he normally smoked. An advertising campaign for the new brand named for him was launched in 1930, with the actor taking part in the promotion and touring the country in special presentations sponsored by the manufacturer. Gallaher ac-quired the brand when it took over the Inter-national Tobacco Company in 1934, and it then passed to **BAT Industries**.

Du Pont *(chemicals)*

The leading American chemical company takes its name from Eleuthère Irénée du Pont de Nemours (1771-1834), born near Paris a French nobleman's son, who worked in his father's printing plant until it was closed by French radicals. (His unusual first names were suggested by his godfather in honor of peace and liberty, from Greek *eleutheria*, "liberty," and *eirēnē*, "peace.") In 1800 he and his family immigrated to the USA. At first it was uncertain what the family business would be, but du Pont was keen to manufacture gunpowder, a venture that was bound to be profitable. His father reluctantly agreed, and sent Irénée back to France to secure the necessary equipment and financing. Surprisingly, du Pont received enthusiastic backing from the French government, who saw his enterprise as a way of breaking the British monopoly of supplying gunpowder to the USA. The business was duly set up in Paris on April 21, 1801, as E.I. du Pont de Nemours & Company. Three years later, du Pont's mill for manufacturing gunpowder began operating on the Brandywine River near Wilmington, Delaware.

Dubble Bubble *see* **Chiclets**

Dubonnet *(aperitif)*

It was in 1846 that Joseph Dubonnet first blended wine with quinine to produce his distinctive aperitif in his wine shop in the Opéra district of Paris. At first the product was sold without any special name, but it soon came to be called quinquina Dubonnet, and was further improved when Joseph was joined in the business by his two sons, Marius and Paul. The popularity of the aperitif enabled the Dubonnet family to move to new premises in the Rue Mornay, Paris, in 1895, and the firm became a registered company in 1908. Early publicity of the wine came in 1894 with Jules Chéret's poster of the actress Lise Fleuron brandishing a bottle of Dubonnet while sitting with a cat on her lap. The famous slogan "Dubo, Dubon, Dubonnet," suggesting "beautiful good Dubonnet," first appeared in the 1920s. The name is entered for "The Best Appetizer in the World" in the *Trade Marks Journal* of June 25, 1913.

Ducati *(motorcycles)*

In 1926, Italian architect Bruno Cavalieri Ducati (1904-2001), together with his two physics student brothers, Adriano and Marcello, set up the Società Scientifica Radio Brevetti Ducati ("Ducati Patent Scientific Radio Society") in Bologna to make radio receivers. Bruno concentrated on management, finance, and marketing, while Adriano was the technical innovator and Marcello specialized in manufacturing. After the launch of their first product, the Manens condenser, the business soon expanded into optics and mechanics, as well as electronics, but was commandeered by the Germans in World War II. Government funding was provided after the war, and in 1948 Ducati was brought back to life as a motorcycle manufacturer, beginning modestly with a 48cc, four-stroke, 1½ horsepower microengine, the *Cucciolo* ("Cub"), that was attached to a bicycle frame. Under the inspirational engineer Fabio Taglioni (1920-2001) it then entered the world of motor sport, in which it had a glittering career, especially in the 1950s, 1960s, and 1970s, but then fell into steady decline until an American consortium acquired the company in 1996 and turned its fortunes around. Thereafter, Ducati won a string of superbike championships and in 2000 sold an entire year's production of the 904cc MH900 *Evoluzione* motorcycle within a few hours in an Internet sale.

Dudle *(chocolates)*

The Swiss firm of this name was started in 1872 by Karl Habereli-Eizholzer. He was succeeded by his son, Édouard Dudle, who had first come to work as an apprentice in 1914. Dudle then traveled the world to research chocolate manufacture, finally settling in the USA. In 1934 he returned to Switzerland, however, to take over the business, and in 1964 passed it on in turn to his son Max. The firm, based in Lucerne, is now run by Max's son Martin.

Duesenberg *(automobiles)*

The cars owe their name to Frederick Samuel Duesenberg (1877-1932), born in Lippe, Germany. In 1885 he immigrated with his family to the United States, adopting Iowa as his home state. After building and racing bicycles, together with his brother August he designed the Mason car in 1903, then the Maytag, before starting to build engines for racing cars. Duesenberg racing cars followed, and grew in prestige after World War I. To build Duesenberg road cars, the brothers then set up the Duesenberg Automobile Company in Indianapolis, Indiana, launching the Model "A" in 1921. It was technically advanced, and a brilliant design, but the brothers were not good businessmen and in 1926, after fewer than 500 cars had been built, the company was purchased by Errett Lobban **Cord**. Duesenbergs continued to be produced until the entire Cord empire collapsed in 1937.

Duffer *(menswear)*

The British menswear firm was cofounded in 1985 by two East Londoners, Eddie Prendergast and Marco Cairns, who had spotted a gap in the London fashion market. At first they sold vintage clothing, but after a couple of years, when good-quality secondhand garments became harder to find, started making their own clothes in a "quintessentially English" style: tweed jackets, shirts, brogues, club ties, and blazers. They chose the name, in full Duffer of St.George, from a 1950s issue of *Boy's Own Paper*, in which "Duffer" was the nickname of the incompetent schoolboy hero, and "St George" the posh school he attended. By 2001 there were three Duffer outlets in London, including one in prestigious Savile Row, while the company's wholesaling division was selling to some 80 stores in the UK, including **Harrods**, **Harvey Nichols**, and **Selfridges**, and around 600 stores overseas.

Dumpster *(trash receptacle)*

The large container for the collection and conveyance of trash, the equivalent of the British "skip," derives its name both from a blend of "dump" (to deposit) and the suffix "-ster" (as in "roadster") and as a rhyming jingle on the name of the US manufacturers, Dempster Brothers, Inc., of Knoxville, Tennessee. The container is thus properly a "Dempster Dumpster," and this name was originally entered in the US Patent Office *Official Gazette* of November 2, 1939 for "hoisting units and detachable buckets and containers therefor." A subsequent registration of September 29, 1953 was for "Storage and transporting containers for use in carrying and dumping materials—namely, refuse, trash, garbage, scrap, dirt, and rock."

Dun & Bradstreet *(publishers)*

The American publishing company, specializing in business credit rating and financial services, traces its origins to the credit-rating agency R.G. Dun & Co., founded some time before 1861 by Robert Graham Dun (1826-1900), a partner from 1854 in Tappan & Douglass, the first mercantile agency in New York City. In 1933 Dun's firm merged with the Bradstreet Co. to form Dun & Bradstreet, Inc.

Duncan *(yo-yo)*

The name is that of Donald Franklin Duncan (1899-1971), born in Huntington, West Virginia, who began his career in the candy business. He then worked for a time in the automobile industry before trying to create a franchise network that would sell **Good Humor** ice cream. Unable to interest ice cream companies in this venture, he changed tack to promote a toy called a "spinning top" or "yo-yo," which he had seen on a business trip to San Francisco in 1929. (It may have been one made by the Flores Yo-Yo Company of Los Angeles.) With the aid of vigorous advertising, yo-yo contests, and teams of demonstrators touring the country, his enterprise at last took off, and for some 30 years the Duncan Yo-Yo Company had a virtual monopoly in the sale of yo-yos, while the toy itself became known as the "Duncan yo-yo." The company went into involuntary bankruptcy in 1965, and was eventually sold to its plastic supplier, the Flambeau Products Company. *See also* **Yo-Yo**.

Duncan Hines *(cake mixes)*

Duncan Hines (1880-1959), born in Bowling Green, Kentucky, the son of a former Confederate army captain, was originally known for much more than cake mixes. He was first and foremost a noted publisher of travel and restaurant guidebooks for motorists, and enjoyed a reputation as a pioneer in this field until 1948, when Roy H. Park, a New York businessman, approached Hines with a view to using his name to endorse food products. Hines initially resisted the idea, but in the end agreed to form Hines-Park Foods to license the Duncan Hines name, which soon appeared on a wide range of items, from bread and jam to canned fruit, ice cream, and cake mix. In 1956 **Procter & Gamble** purchased all of the Ducan Hines interests, including the guidebooks, and Hines went into semi-retirement. In 1962 Procter & Gamble discontinued the book series and later dropped most products bearing the Duncan Hines name, with the notable exception of the cake mixes. For these, therefore, the Duncan Hines name now lives on, rather than for guidebooks or restaurant recommendations.

Dunhill *(pipes and tobacco)*

The British company takes its name from Alfred Dunhill (1872-1959), the son of a London harness-maker. He served his apprenticeship with his father from the age of 15, and in 1897 took over the running of the harness-making shop altogether. By then, like many young men, he was taking an interest in motoring, and started to broaden his business by selling the accessories that many early motorists needed, such as mats, lamps, horns, and goggles. He then opened up two shops in Conduit Street that specialized in clothing for motorists. In 1902, however, financial restraints obliged Dunhill to abandon these lines, and he tried other activities. After an unsuccessful spell as an architect and builder, he gained an interest in new styles of pipes for tobacco smokers. This prompted him to open his own small tobacconist's shop in Duke Street, St. James's, where in 1907 he first specialized as a tobacco blender before launching the first pipe made to his specifications in 1910. By the time World War I was over, his reputation was secure. The firm's fortunes gradually flagged, however, and when the association with cigarettes and smoking took a negative turn in the late 1990s, Dunhill opened a new store in Old Bond Street and re-branded itself as a luxury retailer of travel accessories and clothing.

Dunlop *(tires)*

The name is that of the Scottish inventor of the pneumatic tire, John Boyd Dunlop (1840-1921), a farmer's son who trained as a veterinary surgeon. In 1867 he moved with his young family to Belfast, Ireland, and there developed his discovery in 1888. Although Dunlop's new kind of tire was exactly right for the rising bicycle and automobile industry, he felt unable to develop his product on his own. In 1889, therefore, he joined forces with William Harvey du Cros (1846-1918), an amateur athlete and keen cyclist, to establish the Pneumatic

Tyre & Booth's Cycle Agency Co. Ltd. to exploit his invention commercially. There were problems, however, when Dunlop's patent was invalidated by an earlier patent for such a tire taken out in 1845 by Robert William Thompson. This obliged Dunlop to resign his directorship in 1895. The following year du Cros formed a new company to continue the business, and recognizing that Dunlop's name was already associated in the public mind with the pneumatic tire, named it the Dunlop Pneumatic Tyre Co., even though he himself was the actual founder of the firm. After his resignation, Dunlop moved from Belfast to Dublin and became the chairman of Todd, Burns & Co., a large draper's store. Dunlop subsequently became part of BTR (*see* **Invensys**).

Dunn *(men's headwear)*

George Arthur Dunn (1865-1939), born in Birmingham, England, opened his first hat shop in Shoreditch, London, in 1887. He soon built up a thriving business, so that by 1897 he had opened no less than 60 branches in London and elsewhere in the country. Dunn claimed to have invented the name "Trilby" for soft hats when they were in vogue in the 1890s, taking it from a hat of this type that one of the characters, Little Billee, is seen wearing in George du Maurier's illustration to his novel *Trilby*, published in 1894. The name itself is that of the artist's model, Trilby O'Ferrall, who is the book's central character.

Duracell *(batteries)*

In the 1940s, the US firm of P.R. Mallory & Co., Inc., founded in 1916 by Philip Rogers Mallory (d. 1975) as a manufacturer of tungsten filament wire, developed a new type of alkaline battery for consumer use, aided by the young scientist Samuel Ruben. In 1960 they produced their first commercial alkaline battery, naming it "Duracell" four years later for its durability by comparison with traditional batteries. In 1979 P.R. Mallory was acquired by **Dart Industries** and became Duracell, Inc. In 1991 Duracell became a publicly traded company which in 1997 merged with **Gillette**.

Duraglit *(metal polish)*

The British name was originally entered by the Duraglit Polish Company in the *Trade Marks Journal* of February 22, 1928, and in the late 1950s passed to **Reckitt & Colman**. It is thought to suggest the *dura*ble *glit*ter that the product gives.

Duralumin *(alloy)*

The hard, light aluminum alloy containing copper perhaps derives its name from Latin *durus*, "hard," and "aluminum." At the same time, it seems to suggest Düren, the name of the town near Cologne in western Germany where such alloys were first produced by the Dürener Metallwerke Aktiengesellschaft. The name was entered by the Electric and Ordnance Accessories Company of Aston, Birmingham, England, in the *Trade Marks Journal* of December 7, 1910.

Durex *(condoms)*

The name of the contraceptive was devised by A.R. Reid, chairman of the British manufacturers, the London Rubber Company (later LRC International), to whom it is said to have occurred one evening in 1929 on his usual train home from London to Southend-on-Sea, Essex. The basis is "durable," a word appropriate both for the specific application of the product and for its long-term future on the market. (According to some sources the name is a blend of "*dura*bility," "*re*liability," and "*ex*cellence.") The name was entered in the *Trade Marks Journal* of November 16, 1932 with the description: "Instruments, apparatus, and contrivances, not medicated, for surgical or curative purposes, or in relation to the health of men or animals, but not including surgical adhesive tape." In Australia the name "Durex" is used for a make of adhesive tape similar to **Sellotape** or **Scotch** Tape, and so a source of potential embarrassment for an Australian visitor to the USA or UK who asks for such tape by name. At the turn of the 21st century, production of Durex was in the hands of SSL International, a firm originating as Seton Healthcare which merged with **Scholl** in 1998 and soon after acquired the London International Group (LIG), as LRC International had become.

Durkee's *("Famous Sauce")*

Eugene R. Durkee (1825–1902) first peddled spices door to door in Buffalo, New York, in 1850. In 1857 he introduced what was probably the world's first commercially packaged salad dressing, soon to be known as "Durkee's Famous Sauce." Durkee promoted his dressing by packaging it in decorative bottles, and from the 1870s he embossed a gauntlet trademark on the bottles as a sign of integrity. When Durkee retired in 1884, he was succeeded as president of the company by his son, Eugene W. Durkee. The business was acquired by Glidden Paint in 1929 and some 40 years later was merged into the SCM Corporation.

Duryea *(automobiles)*

The automobiles bear the name of the brothers Charles Edgar Duryea (1861–1938), born near Canton, Illinois, and Frank Duryea (1869–1967), born near Washburn, Illinois, the sons of a farmer. Charles Duryea entered the rapidly growing bicycle business and showed an original talent in designing and making bicycles. In 1886, at the Ohio state fair, he saw a stationary gasoline engine that seemed to him powerful enough to propel a carriage or wagon. By 1891 he had completed a design, and with his brother constructed a car and engine in a rented loft in Springfield, Massachusetts. The Duryea Motor Wagon Company was duly organized in Springfield 1895 as America's first automobile company.

Dutton *see* E.P. Dutton

Duvel *(beer)*

The celebrated Belgian beer is brewed by the Moortgat brewery in Breendonk, north of Brussels. After World War I, the brewery wanted to brew a Scottish ale. The Moortgat brewers examined bottles of **McEwan's** ale from Edinburgh and made a dark ale using McEwan's yeast. One taster is said to have exclaimed, "It's a devil of a taste," and the name "Duvel" was coined in 1923.

Duvetyn *(dress material)*

The soft material of worsted and silk with a fine downy nap, used for women's dresses and coats, has a name based on French *duvet*, "down," entered in the *Trade Marks Journal* of September 10, 1913.

Duxeen *(bookbinding material)*

The type of strong paper used for covering books, made in imitation of bookbinders' cloth, derives its name from its British manufacturers, the Dux Chemical Solutions Co, of Bromley-by-Bow, London, who entered it in the *Trade Marks Journal* of November 24, 1920.

DYC *(whisky)*

The blend of Spanish whisky takes its name from the main initials of its manufacturers, Destilerías y Crianza del Whisky, S.A. ("Whisky Distilleries and Ageing, Ltd."). The company was set up in Segovia in 1959 and the brand was launched in Spain in 1963.

Dynel *(synthetic fiber)*

The fiber, used to make a wool-like fabric, is a copolymer of vinyl chloride and acrylonitrile. Its name appears to have been devised from letters in "vi*nyl* chlori*de*," but may be entirely random. It was entered by the **Union Carbide** & Carbon Corporation in the *Trade Marks Journal* of December 20, 1950 for: "Yarns and threads, all of synthetic textile materials."

Dyson *(vacuum cleaners)*

The Dyson "dual cyclone" vacuum cleaner takes its name from the British engineer James Dyson (b. 1947), a former designer and manufacturer of high-speed landing craft, who one day in 1978 noticed how the air filter in the finishing room for one of his products was always clogging with powder particles, just as a vacuum cleaner clogs with dust. The following year he founded Dyson Research Ltd. to solve the problem, and between 1979 and 1984 experimented continuously, building prototype cleaners that needed no bag. He launched the first commercial model, the "G-Force," in 1983 and followed this in 1993 with the successful DC01 ("Dual Cyclone 01"), which went on to outsell its nearest competitor, **Hoover**, by nine to one.

E&J *(brandy)*

The top-selling brand of brandy in the USA is produced by the **Gallo** brothers, producers of the top-selling brand of wine in the UK. Its name thus represents the initials of Ernest and Julio Gallo.

E. J. Arnold *(educational equipment)*

The British firm of E.J. Arnold, specializing in educational books, was founded by Edmund James Arnold (1840-1918), born in Sherborne, Dorset. He was apprenticed to the stationery trade in London, and at the age of 23 set up his own business in Barnstaple, Devon, when he bought the stationery, bookshop, and jobbing printing side of the *North Devon Journal*. Within the year, Arnold was printing and publishing on his own account, as well as selling "School Stationery and Books, Copy Books, Ciphering Books, Slates of Various Sizes, Slate Pencils and Writing Ink by the Best Makers." In 1870 he sold his Barnstaple business and moved north to Leeds, where he continued his trade in new premises in Briggate. He soon acquired a factory and warehouse, and in 1878 his first printing plant, so becoming a specialist educational supplier rather than simply a general stationer.

E. P. Dutton *(publishers)*

The US publishing house dates from 1852, when Edward Payson Dutton (1831-1923), born in Keene, New Hampshire, opened a shop with Lemuel Ide selling schoolbooks and maps in Boston, Massachusetts, as Ide & Dutton. By 1855 the firm had expanded into publishing, with an emphasis on religious titles. Dutton bought out Ide's share in the business in 1858 and formed E.P. Dutton & Co., with himself as president. In 1864 Charles Clapp was taken on as junior partner, and that same year the shop moved to the Old Corner Bookstore in Boston, which remained the firm's headquarters when Dutton opened a branch office at 726 Broadway, New York City, in 1868. The Boston base closed the following year, when Dutton moved the entire business to 713 Broadway at Washington Place. Following moves to West 23rd Street in 1882 and to 5th Avenue in 1911, the firm entered educational publishing in 1913. In 1975 E.P. Dutton was sold to **Elsevier**, who in 1981 sold it to the Dyson-Kissner-Moran Corporation, which had no publishing background. In 1985 Dutton was purchased by the New American Library, a paperback publisher that was itself acquired in 1989 by **Penguin**, who in turn subsequently amalgamated with **Putnam**.

Ealing Studios *(motion pictures)*

The English company, famous for its witty comedies that reflected life in post-World War II Britain, was founded in 1929 by the producers Basil Dean and Reginald Baker with the support of the **Courtauld** family at studios in Ealing, west of London. In 1944 most of the stock in the company was sold to the **Rank** Organization, and in 1955 the studio ceased production and was sold to the BBC.

Earex *(ear drops)*

The product was originally named "Aurex," but this classical form was objected to by a company who were using the name "Orex" for a brand of aspirin. A change was thus necessary, and the plain English "ear" was adopted instead. The "-ex" presumably means "out," referring to the removal of the wax, although the name as a whole could be taken to denote the earaches that the drops ease. (*Cp.* **Hedex**.) The name was entered in the *Trade Marks Journal* of December 31, 1975.

Earl Grey *(tea)*

The variety of scented tea takes its name from Charles Grey, 2nd Earl Grey (1764-1845), who is said to have been given the recipe for it in the 1830s by a grateful Chinese mandarin whose life had been saved by a British diplomat. The blend is now marketed commercially by **Twining's**.

Eastman *(photographic materials)*

The name of Eastman is essentially synonymous with **Kodak**. The parent company, in Rochester, New York, is Eastman Kodak, and the name "Kodak" was devised by the firm's founder, George Eastman (1854-1932), himself born in Rochester. At 15 he became an office boy for an insurance company, and five years later progressed to working in a bank. Photography entered his life in 1877, when a friend suggested he take photographs on a holiday trip. Soon he was experimenting at home with chemicals and pans, trying to find a way of making a photographic plate that could be exposed when it was dry, unlike existing plates, which were wet. After many trials, he perfected his plate, and in 1880 leased part of an old building in Rochester to construct a laboratory for his research. One of his aims was to reduce the cumbersome photographic equipment of his day to manageable size. In 1884 he produced films in rolls, following this four years later with his famous Kodak camera. But 1880 was the year when the Eastman Dry Plate and Film Company, as it was originally known, was founded, and Eastman's name is commemorated in the sophisticated products of Eastman Kodak today.

EasyJet *(airline)*

The "no-frills" British airline was founded by the Cypriot serial entrepreneur Stelios Haji-Ioannou (b. 1967), who began his career at the age of 22 as chief executive of his father's shipping company, Troodos Shipping. In 1992, with capital provided by his father, Loucas, he started his own shipping company, Stelmar Tankers, which soon became profitable. Two years later, Stelios, as he is known, was ready for a new challenge, and in 1995 he set himself up at a desk next to the toilets at Luton Airport, England, where he launched EasyJet, a discount airline modeled after America's Southwest Airlines. Its name referred to its uncomplicated, passenger-friendly operation. Further "Easy" enterprises followed, such as EasyRentacar, a discount car-rental company, EasyValue, an online shopping guide, and EasyEverything, a chain of the world's largest cybercafes, including the 800-seat megacafe in New York City's Times Square.

eBay *(Internet trading community)*

The web site was created in 1995 by the American software developer Pierre Omidyar (b. 1968) so his fiancée (later wife), Pamela, could trade her collection of Pez candy dispensers with other Pez enthusiasts in the San Francisco Bay area. Hence the name, with "e-" as in "e-mail" or "e-commerce." By 2000 eBay was the leading online auction house.

Ecosse *(film and television productions)*

The British film and television production company Ecosse Films was founded in 1988 by Douglas Rae (b. 1946), a Scottish television presenter, who named it with the French for "Scotland" as copyright laws would not have permitted the use of an English country name and a Gaelic name could have caused pronunciation difficulties. The choice of a French name is in the event not inappropriate, for France and Scotland enjoyed a special relationship at the time of the "Auld Alliance," an offensive and defensive pact against England that existed from the 13th through 16th centuries. In 1997 Rae was named Scottish filmmaker of the year for his movie *Mrs. Brown*, the story of Queen Victoria's relationship with her gillie (Highland servant), John Brown. Rae had conceived the film in the 1960s.

Eddie Bauer *(sporting goods)*

Eddie Bauer (1899-1986) was born on Orcas Island, Washington, the son of a gardener-caretaker. He held various jobs as a boy, then became a retail clerk at a Seattle sporting goods store. He promoted himself as an outdoorsman, winning numerous hunting and fishing competitions, and successfully attracted custom to his employer. He then developed such skill in stringing tennis rackets that he was put in a store window to draw crowds. Realizing that he could put this to better use, Bauer quit his job, rented space in a nearby shop, and strung tennis rackets fulltime. Less than a year later, in 1920, he had earned enough to open his own store, Eddie Bauer's Tennis Shop. He then began to diversify, changed the store's name to Eddie Bauer's Sports Shop, and took to carrying high-quality gear for fishing and hunting. His business expanded further, becoming Eddie Bauer's Sporting Goods and finally, in 1968, Eddie Bauer, Inc., collecting $1 million annually from mail-order sales. The company continues under that name, although **General Mills** purchased it in 1971 and then sold it in 1988 to Spiegel, Inc.

Eddie Stobart *(transport)*

Britain's largest private haulage company, based in Carlisle, Cumbria, was founded in 1976 by Edward Stobart (b. 1954), who now runs the business with his brother William (b. 1962). Stobart's green and red liveried trucks have attracted a 35,000-strong fan club, and a separate enterprise, Eddie Stobart Promotions, sells toys, T-shirts, and the like.

Ediswan *(electric lamps)*

The name was first used by the Edison and Swan United Electric Light Company, and is a blend of the names of Thomas Alva Edison (1847-1931), the American inventor, and Joseph Wilson Swan (1828-1914), the English physicist and chemist who developed the incandescent light independently of him. Edison, of Menlo Park, New Jersey, patented his lamp in 1879, having set up the Edison Electric Light Company the previous year to back his experiments. Swan, in Newcastle upon Tyne, produced his first true filament lamp in 1880, after demonstrating a basic bulb the previous year. The first commercial production of electric lamps took place in the United States in 1880, when the Edison Lamp Works was established at Menlo Park. In Britain, commercial production was begun early in 1881 by the Swan Electric Light Company at Benwell, near Newcastle upon Tyne. The companies merged in 1882, when the two men agreed to end their transatlantic rivalry and to collaborate with each other rather than compete. In 1892 the Edison Electric Light Company merged with Thomson-Houston (*see* **Thales**) to form the General Electric Company. *See also* **RCA**.

Éditions de Minuit *see* **Minuit**

Éditions du Seuil *see* **Seuil**

Editola *(film editing machine)*

The name, from "edit" and "-ola" (as in **Moviola**), was entered by the Photographic Electrical Co. Ltd. of Wardour Street, London, England, in the *Trade Marks Journal* of July 31, 1935 for: "Apparatus included in Class 8 for reproducing motion picture films and sounds simultaneously."

Editori Riuniti *(publishers)*

The Italian publishing house, with a name meaning "United Editors," arose in 1953 in the merger of Edizioni di Cultura Sociale ("Social Culture Editions") and Edizioni Rinascita ("Revival Editions").

Edsel *(automobiles)*

The relatively inexpensive car of this name was launched by **Ford** in the USA on September 4, 1957. It was not popular, however, and manufacturing ceased in 1959. The name was chosen after a great deal of market research, when all manner of unsuitable names were suggested. In the end it was decided to adopt the first name of Edsel Bryant Ford (1893-1943), son of Henry Ford, father of Henry Ford II, and president of the Ford Motor Co. from 1919 to his death. The name was perhaps no better than any of the others, especially as it happened to suggest German *Esel*, "donkey" (both the animal and as a term for a stupid person).

Edward Arnold *(publishers)*

The founder of the British publishing house, Edward Arnold (1857-1942), was not only the grandson of the famous headmaster of Rugby School, Thomas Arnold (1795-1842), but the nephew of the poet and critic Matthew Arnold

(1822-1888) and the younger brother of the novelist Mrs. Humphry Ward (1851-1920), whose maiden name was Arnold. After gaining publishing experience, Edward Arnold set up his own business in Bedford Street, London, in 1890, starting with a general publishing list but in due course including a high proportion of educational titles, from schoolbooks to scientific and medical works. He retired in 1930. In 1987 Edward Arnold merged with **Hodder & Stoughton**.

Eidos *(computer games)*

The British firm, famous for the feisty, busty adventuress Lara Croft, has a name that is Greek for "form." It was cofounded in 1990 by Stephen Streater (b. 1966), who abandoned work on a Ph.D. on artificial intelligence when he was advised he could either finish his Ph.D. or become a millionaire. Streater's work on video compression prompted him to leave the company in 1999 and start a new firm, Forbidden Technologies, to develop ways of watching television programs on a home computer.

Einaudi *(publishers)*

The Italian publishing house was founded in 1933 by Giulio Einaudi (1912-1999), son of Luigi Einaudi (1874-1961), first president of the Italian Republic (1948-55).

Ekco *(radios and televisions)*

The British make of radio, popular in the 1930s, derived its name acronymically from the electrical engineer Eric Kirkham Cole (1901-1966), born at Prittlewell, near Southend-on-Sea, Essex, the son of a dairyman. After attending a technical school, he served a three-year apprenticeship with a local electrical firm, then went into partnership as an electrical engineer with his father. After his father's retirement in 1922, Cole began trading as E. Kirkham Cole from a single room in nearby Westcliff, manufacturing two-valve radio receivers and selling them under the brand name "Ekco." In 1926 he formed E.K. Cole Ltd. and production of radios steadily grew, most of them in molded plastic **Bakelite** cabinets. Televisions were added in due course, as well as profitable diversification into military equipment in World War II. After the war, however, the company's financial fortunes flagged fol-

lowing the failings of top management, and in 1960 a merger with **Pye** led to the formation of British Electronics Ltd. and the effective demise of the "Ekco" name, with its apt evocation of "echo."

Ektachrome *(film)*

The make of color-reversal photographic film derives the first part of its name from the initials of its manufacturers, **Eastman Kodak**, and the last part from the Greek word for "color." The name was entered in the *Trade Marks Journal* of November 26, 1947. *See also* **Kodachrome**.

El Al *(airline)*

The Israeli airline was founded in November 1948 after the establishment of the new nation. Its name was devised by David Remez, Israeli first transport minister, who took it from the Hebrew version of a phrase in the Old Testament: "though they called them to the most High" (Hosea 11:7). The Hebrew version of this reads literally "though they called them to 'Al'," this last word or title meaning "him on high." The more prosaic suggestion of "Air Israel," made by some top men in Israel's Southern Bomber Command, was rejected in favor of a more meaningful name for the new airline.

El Dorado *(rum)*

The brand of rum produced by Demerara Distillers Ltd. of Georgetown, Guyana, takes its name from the fabulous South American city ("The Gilded One") that was long believed to abound in gold. The name equally applies to the liquor itself, blazoned on the bottle's label as "The Golden Rum."

El Rey del Mundo *(cigars)*

The brand of this name, Spanish for "The King of the World," was launched in 1882 by the Cuban-based Antonio Allones company. The cigars are produced by the **Romeo and Juliet** factory in Havana.

Elastoplast *(adhesive plaster)*

The British make of elastic adhesive plaster, similar to US **Band-Aid**, has a name of obvious origin that was entered by its original German manufacturers, Luscher & Bomper Aktiengesellschaft, in the *Trade Marks Journal* of August 29, 1928. The product then passed to **Smith & Nephew**.

Elbrewery *(beer)*

Poland's largest brewing company was founded in 1872 in what was then the Prussian port of Elbing as the Brauerei Englisch Brunnen Elbing ("Elbing English Springs Brewery"). The name demonstrates the early influence of English merchants in the Baltic beer trade. Elbing is now Elbląg in Poland.

Elders IXL *(beer)*

The Australian company, famous for its **Foster's** beer, owes its name to a Scots brewer, Alexander Elder, who in 1839 set sail from Kirkcaldy to Australia to found his beermaking business. The latter half of the name represents "I excel," implying "I excel in everything I do." This was the maxim of a Tasmanian jam-maker, one Henry Jones, whose business was acquired by Elders in 1972. The company also bought up breweries such as **Courage** of England and **Carling** of Canada but after overreaching itself and struggling under heavy debts was eventually reconstructed as Foster's Brewing.

Eldridge Pope *(beer)*

Sarah Eldridge started a brewery in Dorchester, Dorset, England, in the 1830s. Her lawyer, Alfred Pope, became involved in 1879. The owning families were friendly with the Dorset poet and novelist Thomas Hardy (1840-1928), a beer called "Thomas Hardy's Ale" was launched in 1968 on the 40th anniversary of his death, and in 1996 the brewery was itself renamed Thomas Hardy after a management buyout. Hardy wrote admiringly of Eldridge Pope's beer in *The Trumpet-Major* (1880): "It was of the most beautiful colour that the eye of an artist in beer could desire; full in body, yet brisk as a volcano; piquant, yet without a twang; luminous as an autumn sunset."

Electrolux *(domestic appliances)*

The British company, dating from 1921, grew out of the small Swedish firm AB Lux, founded in 1910 to manufacture paraffin lamp mantles. Its name represents Latin *lux*, "light." In 1919 the same Swedish firm changed its name to AB Elektrolux to reflect its diversification into electrical domestic appliances. In 1924 a salesman from the Swedish company introduced the first canister (tank-type) vacuum cleaner to the United States.

Eley *(cartridges)*

Information about the original Eley brothers who founded the British business is rather sketchy, but it is known that their names were William and Charles Eley and that in 1828 they owned an "extensive manufactory" for patent cartridges at 14 Charlotte Street, London, where they would have made a range of gunmakers' accessories. The firm that manufactures the familiar Eley Cartridge is thus deemed to have been founded this year. Of William Eley little is known except that he was born in 1795, shot snipe in Battersea Park, and blew himself to pieces at the age of 46 when experimenting with fulminate of mercury, the compound that is used in detonators.

Elf Aquitaine *(petrochemicals and mining)*

The French corporate group was formed in 1976, a major interest being owned by a government company, Entreprise de Recherches et d'Activités Pétrolières ("Enterprise for Petroleum Research and Activity") (ERAP), known by its oil trademark, Elf. This last name was chosen by computer and is applied internationally except in Austria, where "Elan" is used instead, as German *elf* ("eleven") gives a misleading connotation for an oil product. (An association with English "elf" is equally misguided.) In Germany itself "Elf" was retained, since the name was already well known before the company began operations there. The other half of the name derives from the Société Nationale des Pétroles d'Aquitaine, formed in 1941, which the group also controls. The name came about following the discovery of natural gas at Saint-Marcet in the historic region of Aquitaine, southwestern France, in 1939. Elf subsequently merged with TOTALFINA (*see* **Total**) to form TotalFinaElf.

Eli Lilly *(pharmaceuticals)*

The name is that of Eli Lilly, a former colonel with the Union army's Ninth Indiana Cavalry in the Civil War, who in 1876 opened a small laboratory in downtown Indianapolis to make drugs, including those typical of his day, such as pills and elixirs. He was one of the first druggists to develop gelatin-coated capsules to hold medicines, and even today Eli Lilly is one of the largest manufacturers of empty capsules.

Colonel Lilly died in 1898, and his business was taken over by his son, Josiah Kirby Lilly (1861-1948). The company's head office remains in Indianapolis today.

Elizabeth Arden *(cosmetics)*

Elizabeth Arden (*c.*1878-1966) was born in Woodbridge near Toronto, Canada, the daughter of a Scot, William Graham, and a Cornishwoman, Susan Pearce Tadd, who had emigrated to Canada in the latter half of the 19th century. Elizabeth's baptismal name was Florence Nightingale Graham, and she began her career as a dental surgeon's secretary. Finding the work unrewarding, however, she began to train as a nurse, possibly influenced by her own name. When even this did not provide the satisfaction she sought, she decided to move to New York, where she felt there would be more opportunities for whatever her final career should be. There she joined a modest beauty salon run by two Englishwomen. They offered her a partnership, but Graham felt she should set up her own salon, if only to put to practical use the creams and lotions she had developed. So in 1909 she opened her own skin treatment salon at 509 Fifth Avenue, at the same time changing her name to Elizabeth Arden, adopting this, it is said, from a book she had been reading, *Elizabeth and Her German Garden* (1898), and Tennyson's poem *Enoch Arden* (1864), which she admired. Further American salons followed, with the first in London opening in 1922. Arden's estate was mostly liquidated by taxes, and to take care of death duties the business she had founded was sold for $37.5 million to **Eli Lilly**.

Elsan *(chemical toilet)*

The transportable chemical toilet was invented in 1920 by Ephraim Louis Jackson, a British chemical manufacturer, and the initials of his first two names, plus the "san-" of "sanitation," gave the name of the product and the company, the Elsan Manufacturing Co., that produced it. The name was entered in the *Trade Marks Journal* of January 9, 1924.

Elsevier *(publishers)*

The Dutch publishing house traces its origins to 1880, when Jacobus George Robbers started a publishing business in Rotterdam. He took the name of his firm from the famous El-sevier (or Elzevir) family of Dutch booksellers, publishers, and printers founded in Leiden in 1581 by Louis Elsevier (*c.*1546-1617), a printer from Louvain. That business gained a near legendary reputation for the excellence of its typography and design, and lasted until 1712. The present Elsevier company was established in New York in 1937 through a joint venture and in 1993 merged with the UK **Reed** International to form Reed Elsevier.

Elva *(automobiles)*

The British sports cars, marketed in the 1950s and 1960s, took their name from the Elva Engineering Co. that manufactured them, the name itself romantically derived from French *elle va*, "she goes." They were the enterprise of Frank Nichols, a former specialist in sporting machinery, who after World War II decided to design a car of his own. The original company went into voluntary liquidation in 1961, to be replaced by Elva Cars (1961) Ltd., and the last cars of all were produced in 1968.

EMC *(computer hardware)*

The "E" is the initial of the American computer engineer Richard Egan (b. 1936), who after working at **Honeywell**, **Lockheed**, and **Intel** founded EMC in 1979 as a supplier of add-on memory boards for minicomputers. The "M" is his cofounder and former college buddy Roger Marino (b. 1938). The "C" is "Company."

Emerson *(electrical equipment)*

Formerly familiar as the Emerson Electric Co., the US company was founded in St. Louis, Missouri, in 1890 as a manufacturer of electric motors and fans. Its originators were two Scottish-born brothers, Charles and Alexander Meston, who developed and patented an alternating current motor and persuaded John Wesley Emerson, a former Union Army colonel, judge, and lawyer, to be the principal investor in their business. New products were added, such as dental drills, player pianos, and hair dryers, and in World War II the company was the world's largest manufacturer of aircraft gun turrets. Emerson has diversified from the 1950s to become a leading player in the field of telecommunications, electronics, heating, ventilating and air-conditioning systems, and process controls.

EMI *(records and television)*

The British company was formed as Electric and Musical Industries in 1931 by the merger of the London-based **Gramophone** Company and **Columbia**. The merger brought together many of the best-known labels, including Columbia itself, Parlophone, and the Gramophone Company's **HMV**. From the start the new company took a leading role in the development of television and its 405-line system was adopted by the BBC. In 1979 EMI was taken over by Thorn Electrical Industries as **Thorn EMI**.

Emva *(wine)*

The sweet fortified wine, at one time classified as "sherry," is mainly exported to the UK from Cyprus. Its name is short for "Empire Vat," referring to the former British tradition of taking sherry from the British colonies (of which Cyprus was one) and placing it in vats to carry to England. The name "Emva" was entered in the *Trade Marks Journal* of December 12, 1930 and that of "Emva Cream" in the *Journal* of February 19, 1975.

Encarta *(reference works)*

The name is used by **Microsoft** for two major reference resources: the online *Encarta Encyclopedia* (1993) and the conventional *Encarta World English Dictionary* (1999), the latter published by **Bloomsbury**. The name is strictly speaking meaningless but suggests the "en-" of "encyclopedia" and a word meaning "map" (English "chart," French *carte*, Italian *carta*).

Energen *(dietetic foods)*

The British name was originally used for a type of biscuit (cookie) produced by a baker in southwestern England in 1908. It was marketed by Richard Maurice, founder of a firm called Energen Foods, its name based on "energy" and "-gen" implying "generate," as for **Sanatogen**. The name was originally printed with thick bars over the first and last letters, "E" and "N", with the capital lowered to accommodate this. In World War I, however, this device was abandoned in case it seemed to suggest a name of German origin. The name was entered in the *Trade Marks Journal* of February 7, 1912.

England, John *see* **John England**

England, Peter *see* **Peter England**

England's Glory *(matches)*

The brand of matches by **Bryant & May** has a label portraying a ship. "England's Glory" was her epithet, not her name, which was HMS *Devastation*, a twin-screw iron-turret battleship of 1871, sold in 1908. The particular depiction was originally used in the 1870s by another match manufacturer, Thomas Gee of Gloucester. When Gee's business closed in 1891, it was taken over by a second matchmaker, Moreland, also of Gloucester, and in 1972 eventually passed to Bryant & May.

Enkalon *(artificial fiber)*

The first part of the name derives from the initials of the fiber's original Dutch manufacturers, Nederlands Kunstzijde Fabriek ("Netherlands Artificial Fiber Factory"), founded in 1911, with "NK" pronounced in the Dutch fashion ("en ka"). The second part derives from "nylon." The name was registered in the *Trade Marks Journal* of March 1, 1950.

Enodis *(kitchen equipment)*

The British company dates from the mid-19th century, when a small food merchant named S. & W. Berisford started up in the north of England. It was incorporated as a company in 1910 and gradually diversified, one of its major acquisitions being that of a retail kitchen and joinery business called Magnet in 1994. In 2000, still known as Berisford, it decided to update its image and adopted its present name, from Latin *enodis*, "clear," "plain" (literally "without knots"), interpreted by the company as "solving," since it aimed to provide solutions to customers throughout the world.

Enos *("Fruit Salt")*

James Crossley Eno (1820-1915) was born in Newcastle upon Tyne, England, as the son of a general shopkeeper. After serving an apprenticeship with a local druggist, he was appointed dispenser at the Old Infirmary, Newcastle, where he dealt with prescriptions and also did some dental work. In 1852 he bought a chemist and druggist business in Groat Market, where he continued his dentistry as well as selling medicines. He began adding products of his own, one of which was the famous "Fruit Salt," basically a mixture of tartaric and citric acids with sodium bicarbonate, which effervesced healthily in water. The "Salt" sold well, so that in 1876 its inventor left his pharmacy to set up its production on a commercial scale. To this end he moved to London, and there, in a factory at New Cross, "Eno's Fruit Salt" began its health-giving journey to all parts of Britain and to the world at large, with Eno himself living in a large and comfortable house in Dulwich. His "Fruit Salt" still sells well today, although it is now marketed by **Beecham**. The name "Eno's Fruit Salt" was entered in the *Trade Marks Journal* of September 30, 1908 for: "A medicinal preparation, for human use," while "Eno" alone was entered in the *Journal* of May 12, 1920.

Entero-Vioform *(antidiarrheal)*

The proprietary name for a preparation of Clioquinol, formerly used to prevent and treat diarrhea, especially among tourists and travelers, derives its name from Greek *entero-*, "intestine," and presumably Latin *via*, "way," and *forma*, "form." "Vioform" was entered by the Basle Chemical Works, Switzerland, in the *Trade Marks Journal* of August 15, 1900. The complete name was entered by Ciba Pharmaceutical Products, Inc. (*see* **Ciba-Geigy**), in the US Patent Office *Official Gazette* of May 7, 1957, with a note of first use on April 1, 1955, and by CIBA Ltd. in the *Trade Marks Journal* of June 25, 1958: "For use in the treatment of intestinal complaints."

En-Tout-Cas *(hard tennis court)*

The patent on the British court was taken out in 1910, its French name meaning literally "in any case," indicating that its new type of surface could be used equally in wet or dry weather, meaning soon after rain. The phrase was already in existence for a type of combined umbrella and parasol, and legend has it that a lady from Paris with such an umbrella was present at the opening ceremony of the first court of this type. The name was entered in the *Trade Marks Journal* of October 17, 1928, not for the court itself but for "marking tapes, and pins used … for marking out hard lawn tennis courts." The En-Tout-Cas Co. Ltd. was originally based at Syston, Leicestershire.

Entryphone *(intercom)*

The type of intercom at the entrance to a building such as an apartment block has a name obviously derived from "entry" and "phone" that was entered in the *Trade Marks Journal* of July 28, 1976 by its manufacturers, the Entryphone Co. Ltd. of London, England, incorporated in 1958.

Epson *(computers)*

The name derives from that of the firm's parent company, the Japanese-based Seiko Epson Corporation, which takes the first word of its name from the earlier Suwa Seikosha, a company making men's watches. In 1968 Suwa Seikosha produced the first commercially successful computer printer, the EP-101, and in 1975 created the name "Epson," based on this (as if "son of EP"). *Cp.* **Datsun**.

Equitable Life *(insurance)*

The world's oldest and formerly most revered life insurance company was founded in England in 1762 as the Society for Equitable Assurances on Lives and Survivorship. Its creation was inspired by the radical scientific work of James Dodson, who first used mortality tables and probability studies to calculate the premium that needed to be paid to guarantee an amount of money payable on death. Early policy holders included such famous names as Sir Walter Scott, William Wilberforce, and Samuel Taylor Coleridge. The company began selling life pensions in 1913, and in 1957 launched its "Retirement Annuity," a flexible pension for the self-employed. The latter led to Equitable's downfall in 2000 when it was obliged to close following the revelation that it was breaking its contract with customers by cutting bonus rates on pensions. The scam effectively ended the firm's 238-year history.

Erasmic *(shaving cream)*

The name was originally registered in 1886 by a British firm of household and washing soap manufacturers, Joseph Crosfield of Warrington, Lancashire, with the aim of entering the toilet soap market. In 1898 they formed the Erasmic Company to launch a full range of products including perfumes, brilliantines, talcum powders, and toilet soaps. The familiar Erasmic Shaving Stick was introduced in 1900, and in 1915 the Crosfield and Erasmic companies became part of **Unilever**. In 1989 the Erasmic brand was sold to Dep Corporation of Los Angeles, but in 1994 the British firm Keyline

Brands purchased the Erasmic business and trademark from Dep, thus repatriating them to their homeland. The origin of the name is obscure, but an anagram of "is cream" suggests itself.

Ercol *(furniture)*

The name is a shortening of the Italian surname Ercolani, that of the company's founder, Lucian Randolph Ercolani (1888-1976), born in Tuscany, the son of a picture-frame maker and evangelist. Lucian came with his family to England in 1898, sponsored by the Salvation Army, and began his job as a messenger boy for that body before entering its joinery workshops in 1905. He was now attending night school as a design student, and his work and experience soon brought him the offer of a post as a designer for Frederick Parker Ltd., a firm of quality furniture makers in High Wycombe, Buckinghamshire. He took this up in 1910, but three years later moved to join Ebenezer Gomme (*see* **G-plan**) in the same town. By 1920 his work had become so accomplished that his colleagues suggested he form his own company as a furniture manufacturer. He did so, designing a new factory for the purpose in the town. The project was viewed with misgivings by some, and his factory, which was difficult for horse-drawn transport to reach, was even nicknamed "Erkie's Folly." But Furniture Industries Ltd., as his firm was called, got off to a sound commercial start, and by the time its name was changed to Ercol after World War II was one of the leading furniture manufacturers in Britain.

Erector *(toy construction set)*

The child's construction set, designed for making small mechanical models of vehicles, cranes, bridges, and the like, has a name of obvious origin entered by the Mysto Mfg. Co. of New Haven, Connecticut, in the US Patent Office *Official Gazette* of March 9, 1915. A subsequent registration followed in the *Trade Marks Journal* of January 19, 1921, with a claim of use from October 15, 1915.

ERF *(trucks)*

The trucks take their name from the initials of Edwin Richard Foden, who having resigned from his own firm of **Foden** Ltd. in 1932, formed a team the following year with his son

Dennis and another resigned Foden manager, George Faulkner, to build their own oil-engined truck chassis.

Ericsson *(telephone equipment)*

The world's biggest supplier of mobile phone networks takes its name from the Swedish engineer Lars Magnus Ericsson, who opened a repair shop for telegraph equipment in 1876. Soon he was manufacturing telephones, as well as repairing them, following their invention that same year by Alexander Graham Bell (*see* **Bell System**). He then set up offices worldwide to sell telephones to local operators, and in due course Ericsson became one of Sweden's top companies.

Eskimo Pie *(chocolate-coated ice cream)*

In 1919 Christian K. Nelson, a Danish immigrant confectionery store operator in Onawa, Iowa, coated ice cream with chocolate and refroze it as an "I-Scream" bar, coining the slogan "I scream, you scream, we all scream for ice cream." (This later inspired a popular song by Howard Johnson, Billy Moll, and Robert King.) Taking his invention to nearby Omaha, he met ice cream manufacturer **Russell Stover** who established an office in Chicago from which to popularize the new product, renaming it in the process as "Eskimo Pie." The name relates to its "icy" content and in turn gave Russian *eskimos* as a dictionary word for a chocolate-coated ice cream.

Esky *(insulated container)*

The portable insulated container for keeping food or drink cool is of Australian origin. Its name, from "Eskimo," a people associated with cold and ice., was entered by the manufacturers, Malleys Ltd., of Rosebery, New South Wales, in the *Australian Official Journal of Patents* of September 13, 1962 for: "Cooling apparatus and equipment inclusive of portable ice boxes."

Esmark *(processed foods and home products)*

The makers of **Playtex** brassieres, STP motor oil, and Jensen audio equipment take their name from the initial of **Swift**, the American meatpackers, and the word "mark." Swift had begun to diversify in a big way in the 1960s, so in 1973 devised a new name for the expanding business, since its original name was still chiefly associated with meatpacking. They took over International Playtex in 1975, and in 1978 branched out further to buy in STP car products and Pemcor, the makers of Jensen car stereo speakers and other audio equipment.

Essanay *(motion pictures)*

The American film company was organized in 1907 by George K. Spoor and G.M. Anderson and took its name from a phonetic respelling of "S and A," their initials. The company was bought out by **Vitagraph** in 1917.

Esselte *(office supplies)*

In 1913, 13 individual Swedish businesses, all involved in graphics and related operations, joined to form SLT. The group gradually grew, and in 1970 altered the initialism to the single word "Esselte." In 1981 Esselte acquired **Letraset**.

Esso *(petroleum)*

The name represents a spoken form of the letters SO, the initials of **Standard Oil** (New Jersey), who introduced it on the eastern American seaboard in 1926. When they tried to extend this brand name into other territories, however, they were challenged by the other Standard Oil companies, and in 1935 Standard Oil (Indiana) secured a court order keeping Esso out. When in due course Standard Oil (New Jersey) found that they could use the Esso name in only 19 eastern and southern states, they began selling under other names in the rest of the country: "Humble" in Ohio and "Enco" elsewhere. Standard Oil (New Jersey) famously became the **Exxon** Corporation in 1972. As a name in its own right, "Esso" happens to be Italian for "it," while fortuitously suggesting French *essence*, "petroleum." Gas station staff in the 1930s and 1940s interpreted the acronym as "Every Saturday and Sunday Off."

Estée Lauder *(cosmetics)*

The American company has a name now familiar to millions in the fashion world. Josephine Esther Mentzer (b. 1908) was the daughter of poor Hungarian Jewish immigrants to New York, where she grew up in the lower middle-class neighborhood of Corona. In 1930 she married Joe Lauder (d. 1982), and in 1946 launched both the company, Estée Lauder,

Inc., and herself, now also Estée Lauder, as the company's president and chief saleswoman. She soon became known for her role as a supersocialite, an image that became similarly attached to the company, not always to its advantage. Her son Leonard (b. 1934) joined the company in 1958, becoming vice president in 1962, president in 1972, and chief executive officer in 1982.

Etam *(fashion stores)*

The name is an acronymic abbreviation of *Éta*blissement *M*eilleur ("Best Establishment"), the French hosiery company that opened retail outlets in Europe in 1916 and that came to Britain in 1923.

Eucerin *(skin cream)*

A product of the German company **Beiersdorf**, the skin cream and its name evolved from "Eucerit," the first water-in-oil emulsifier, based on wool fat, named by the company chemist, Isaac Lifschütz, to mean "beautiful wax," from Greek *eu-*, "well," "good," and *kēros*, "wax." *See also* **Nivea**.

Eucryl *(toothpaste)*

In 1899 a series of toilet preparations was manufactured by a chemist (druggist) in the north of England who based his products on a mixture of three chemical substances, each of which was some form of antiseptic. The name of the toothpaste is said to derive from the two chief of these, but their identity has not been revealed. (One may have been eucalyptus, as for **Euthymol**.) The name was entered in the *Trade Marks Journal* of August 3, 1898.

Eukanuba *(petfood)*

Paul **Iams** wanted an unusual and memorable name for his superior brand of petfood, so called it "Eukanuba" (pronounced "you can noo' bah"), from an expression used in the 1940s to mean "the best." It was popularized generally by the jazz musician Hoagy Carmichael.

Eurostar *(transport service)*

The name is that of the high-speed passenger train service that links London, England, with mainland Europe via the Channel Tunnel. The service first operated in 1994.

Eurotunnel *(transport service)*

The name is that of the Anglo-French company which owns the Channel Tunnel linking the UK with mainland Europe and which operates its own drive-on services for road vehicles, using specially designed rail wagons. The actual trains are known by the awkward Anglo-French name of "le Shuttle." The service first operated in 1994.

Euthymol *(toothpaste)*

The brand of toothpaste, now owned by **Warner-Lambert**, was first sold in around 1898. The name alludes to two of its constituents, as spelled out in an advertisement in the *Sunday Times* of July 7, 1985: "Which toothpaste contains Eucalyptus and Thymol to keep your teeth and gums healthy?" The name was entered in the *Trade Marks Journal* of November 11, 1925.

Evans, D.H. *see* **D.H. Evans**

Evans Brothers *(publishers)*

The British firm dates from 1896, when Robert Charles Evans left his native Northern Ireland to join the publishing house of **Blackie** in Glasgow. By 1906 he had worked his way up to be manager of Blackie's educational department in London, and was ambitious to start his own business. That year, therefore, he set up an advertising agency in a small room in Newgate Street. He soon attracted custom, and the following year was joined by his elder brother, Edward Evans, then working as a thread mill manager back in Ireland. Both brothers felt they were ready to move into publishing, especially in the field of education, so in 1909 expanded to larger premises in Fleet Street, where they published their first book, the *Evans Recipe Cookery Book*, based on recipes tested by Robert's wife. This was not quite what they had in mind, but they achieved their aim in 1911 with the first issue of *Woman Teacher's World*, subsequently renamed *Teacher's World* and running for many years. In 1912 the firm moved again to a building in Kingsway, adopting the imprint "Kingsway" for many of their later educational titles. Edward Evans died in 1954, and Robert in 1961. In 1990 Evans Brothers acquired **Hamish Hamilton**'s children's nonfiction list and now specializes in educational books for Africa.

Ever Ready *(dry batteries)*

The name is that of the British Ever Ready Electrical Company, formed in 1906 as a renamed American Electrical Novelty & Manufacturing Company, a small firm set up in London in 1901 with William Stern, an American, as chairman. This business already produced electrical novelties powered by batteries named "Ever Ready," for their continuing availability, and the name passed to the new company. By 1927, Ever Ready was the largest battery manufacturer in Europe. In 1978 the company renamed itself Berec, from its initials. This name was already used for the company in foreign countries, with "berec" even adopted as a word for "battery" in some parts of Africa. The reason for the new name was the existence of competitors who were using the "Ever Ready" name in one form or another. Berec later reverted to its original name, and in 1992 was purchased by **Ralston Purina**.

Everards *(beer)*

The British firm traces its history to the brewing business carried on at Southgate Street (now Castle Street), Leicester, by the Wilmot family in the early 19th century. In 1849 the firm was acquired by Thomas Hull, a maltster, together with William Everard (1821-1892) and his son Thomas. William Everard is thus regarded as the founder, although the brewery appeared in directories as "Thomas and William Everard." Thomas Everard died in 1924, but the brewery still has its head office in his father's native village of Narborough, near Leicester, and at the close of the 20th century the company chairman was Richard Everard (b. 1954).

Evian *(mineral water)*

The name is that of Évian-les-Bains, a spa and tourist resort in eastern France on the southern shore of Lake Geneva, where a spring of natural mineral water was discovered in 1789. Bottling began in 1826 and has since become increasingly commercialized. Cynics scoff at suckers who pay high prices for bottles of the product, since if you want to drink water you can get it freely from the faucet. "What does Evian spell backwards? Exactly" (*Sunday Business*, March 18, 2001).

Evinrude *(outboard motors)*

The story goes that the inspiration for the world's first practical outboard motor occurred on a hot summer day in 1904, when Ole Evinrude (1877-1934) of Milwaukee, owner of a small automobile manufacturing business, took his office manager, Bess Cary, out to a picnic on an island in Lake Michigan. After a time, Bess had a craving for a cooling ice cream, and gallant Ove had to row over two miles back to shore to fetch some. When he returned to the island, the ice cream had melted into a gloopy mess. The embarrassing experience prompted the young mechanic to look for a more efficient way of propelling a boat. In 1909 Evinrude patented his new outboard motor and formed the Evinrude Motor Company to manufacture it. The business manager and advertising director of the business was Bess Cary Evinrude, who married Ole two years after their disappointing island picnic. Bess died in 1933 and Evinrude, saddened by her loss, died the following year. The name was registered in 1949.

Evipan *(anesthetic)*

The proprietary name of hexobarbitone sodium, used as a basic anesthetic, is of uncertain origin. In view of the drug's function, it perhaps combines the first letters of Latin *evincere*, "to overcome completely," and Greek *pan*, "all." The name was entered by **Bayer** in the *Trade Marks Journal* of June 8, 1932 for: "A medicine for human use as a hypnotic."

Evo-stik *(adhesive)*

The name of the adhesive is based on that of its British manufacturers, Evode. The forerunner of Evode Ltd. was Spic and Span Shoe Polishes Ltd., founded in 1932. The firm first changed its name in 1938 to Spic and Span Chemical Products Ltd., then later that year to Dove Chemical Products Ltd., then again in 1940 to Evode Chemical Works Ltd. The reason for this last change was that there was a possibility of confusion between the chemical products marketed by Dove Chemical Products and similar goods made by another company, Wailes Dove **Bitumastic** Ltd. "Evode" was thus devised by reversing "Dove" and adding "E." The name was entered in the *Trade Marks Journal* of June 30, 1948.

Excalibur *(automobiles)*

In 1964, the Excalibur Automobile Corporation of Milwaukee, Wisconsin, named after King Arthur's magic sword, first produced au-

tomobiles in the style of the 1920s and 1930s. Their cars were expensive, however, and the business folded in 1990.

Exercycle *(stationary bicycle)*

The stationary bicycle or bicycle frame is designed to be pedaled for exercise. Hence its name, short for "exercise bicycle," entered in the US Patent Office *Official Gazette* of March 31, 1936, with a claim of use since September 1, 1935.

Exide *(batteries)*

The name appears to have been first used by an American company, ESB Inc., in 1900. The origin of the name probably lies in "oxide," with the "e" of "electric" substituted for "o." The initials of the American firm themselves stand for Electric Storage Batteries.

Ex-Lax *(laxative)*

The laxative originated as a preparation with a chocolate flavor devised in 1905 by Max Kiss (1882-1967), a Hungarian-born scientist in New York City, under the name "Bo-Bo" (from "bonbon"). The story goes that Kiss came up with a new name when his brother, Adolf, while reading a Hungarian newspaper, commented, "They have ex lex in Hungary." "Ex lex" (from Latin *ex*, "outside," and *lex*, "law") was a legal term for an unusual condition of stalemate in the Hungarian parliament, when all legislative and governmental functions were blocked. A much more obvious origin, however, is in *ex*, "out," and "laxative," although an abbreviation of "excellent laxative" is an equal possibility.

Exocet *(guided missile)*

The rocket-propelled short-range guided missile, first familiar to the general public from its use by Argentinian forces against British ships in the Falklands War of 1982, is of French manufacture, and its name was entered by the Société Nationale Industrielle Aérospatiale in the *Trade Marks Journal* of November 25, 1970, and in the US Patent Office *Official Gazette* of November 14, 1972. The name itself is the French word for "flying fish," through Latin from Greek *exōkoitos*, literally "out of bed." (The Latin scientific name of the flying fish is *Exocoetus volitans*.)

Explorateur *(cheese)*

The rich cow's-milk French cheese was invented in 1958, soon after the launch of the US spacecraft Explorer 1. Hence the name, French for "explorer." A picture of the space satellite still appears on the wrapper of the cheese.

Express Dairy *(milk retailers)*

The Express Country Milk Supply Co. was founded in 1864 by Sir George Barham (1836-1913), who had started a dairy in Dean Street, London, England, in 1858. Until then, milk for the British capital had either been produced in London itself or within a few miles around. The herds of cows in the town dairies had recently been sharply reduced by an outbreak of foot-and-mouth disease, however, and it was thus necessary to obtain supplied from further afield. Farmers were accordingly persuaded to send milk from the herds in Leicestershire, Buckinghamshire, and other counties around London. The first task was to keep the milk fresh during the journey from the country and stop it turning sour. A form of refrigeration was introduced, and transportation of the milk by rail was arranged as speedily as possible. Hence the company name, which perhaps also implies milk destined "expressly" for London. The firm was reformed as the Express Dairy Co. Ltd. in 1881 and in 1890 it became a public company. In 1969 it was acquired by **Grand Metropolitan**.

Extel *(news agency)*

The name is short for the Exchange Telegraph Co. Ltd., a British company founded in 1872 by Sir James Anderson, the former captain of the *Great Eastern* cargo and passenger liner, and an American, George B. Field. Their aim was to transmit business intelligence, stock and share prices, shipping news, and the like, from stock or commercial exchanges to subscribers to their service. The men leased two adjacent buildings in Cornhill, London, and obtained a license to carry out a sytem of telegraphy within a 900-yard radius of the Stock Exchanges in London and other cities. Captain W.H. Davies, the former first officer of the *Great Eastern*, became managing director. By 1886 the firm had over 500 subscribers to its Financial Service and over 200 to its General Service. The present abbreviated name was adopted in 1980.

Exxon *(petroleum and natural gas)*

The Exxon Corporation dates back to 1882,

when the company was founded by the **Standard Oil** Trust. In 1911 the US Supreme Court broke the Trust up into 34 companies, seven of which retained the name Standard Oil. The largest was Standard Oil (New Jersey), which introduced the brand name **Esso** in 1926. In 1972 Standard Oil (New Jersey) adopted its present name, selected from literally thousands created by computer. It was first tested on American gas stations in September 1971. The name change was domestic only, and "Esso" is still used in other countries. In 1998 Exxon took over **Mobil** in the world's biggest industrial merger to date.

Faber & Faber *(publishers)*

The British publishing house dates its founding from 1929. Its origins, however, go back to 1924, when Geoffrey Faber (1889-1961) was invited to become chairman of the Scientific Press, which specialized in nursing textbooks and other medical works. His brief was to expand the firm's list to include general titles. In 1925 Faber created a new imprint named Faber & Gwyer, the latter name being that of the owners of the Scientific Press, founded by Sir Henry Burdett. (Burdett's daughter, Alsina, had married Maurice Gwyer in 1906.) Four years later the firm was reconstituted as Faber & Faber. The second Faber replaced the Gwyer of the original name, but did not actually exist. A story tells how the writer Walter de la Mare, father of Richard de la Mare, one of the original directors of Faber & Gwyer, had suggested the name "because you can't have too much of a good thing!"

Faber-Castell *(pencils)*

The Germany company arose from the small business set up in 1761 in the German village of Stein, near Nürnberg, by Caspar Faber, a cabinetmaker who also made pencils. The activity remained a "village industry" until 1839, when Caspar Faber's great-grandson, Lothar Faber, expanded and modernized the business. The second half of the name was added in 1898 when Lothar Faber's granddaughter, Ottilie, married Count Alexander zu Castell Rüdenhausen, a member of one of Germany's oldest noble families. By the end of the 20th century Faber-Castell was producing 1.8 billion blacklead and coloring pencils a year and employing 5,500 people worldwide. Heading the operation was Count Anton Wolfgang von Faber-Castell, in the eighth generation of Faber-Castells.

Fabergé (*cosmetics*)

American entrepreneur Samuel Rubin wanted to give his newly formed cosmetics firm an image of elegance in the 1930s, so he borrowed the name of Peter Carl Fabergé (1846-1920), the Russian goldsmith and jeweler, famous for his lavishly jeweled Easter eggs. The choice of name seems to have been a good one, for Fabergé went on to become one of the ten top-selling cosmetics brands.

Fablon (*self-adhesive plastic covering*)

The British product was launched in 1957 and soon became popular for covering shelves, lining drawers and the like. Its name is probably a blend of "fabric" and "-lon" as in "nylon". The name was already entered in the *Trade Marks Journal* of May 3, 1950.

Facel-Véga (*automobiles*)

The French car owed its origin to Jean Daninos (1906-2001), founder in 1938 of Forges et Ateliers de Construction d'Eure-et-Loir (FACEL) ("Eure-et-Loir Forges and Workshops"), a firm originally producing large tools and press dies for the aircraft industry. In 1954 Daninos decided the company should produce its own cars. Although large and ponderous, the first Facel-Végas were modern-looking and speedy, and found ready purchasers. Later models proved unreliable, however, and the firm finally failed in 1964.

Factor, Max *see* **Max Factor**

Fairey (*aircraft*)

The name is that of Richard Fairey (1887-1956), born in Hendon, London, England, the son of a mercantile clerk. At the age of 15, following education at Merchant Taylors' School and Finsbury Technical College, Fairey started work as a trainee with an electrical company in Holloway, London. At 18 he had progressed so well that he was entrusted with the installation of electric lighting at Heysham harbor. He had built and flown model aircraft since schooldays, and in 1910 entered an airplane model competition at Crystal Place, which he won easily. Soon after became acquainted with the aircraft pioneer J.W. Dunne, and so entered the world

of aviation. In 1913 he joined Short Bros. (*see* **Shorts**), and in 1915 set up his own firm, the Fairey Aviation Company. Short Bros. gave him his first contract to build a dozen of their airplanes, and Fairey went on to play a dominant role in the production of British military aircraft. The company name became particularly associated with the Fairey "Fox," the fastest bomber of its day. After World War II Fairey turned to the development of helicopters, including the short-lived **Rotodyne**, but in 1960 was taken over by Westland Aircraft. In 2001 the Fairey name was dropped in favor of the so-called "Euroneutral" Spectris, that of a German company acquired by Fairey the previous year. It was fitting, the company said, with only 10 percent of sales now in the UK, to adopt a new name "that reflects the international focus of the group."

Fairthorpe (*automobiles*)

The initial attempt of Australian-born Air Vice Marshal "Pathfinder" Donald Bennett (1910-1986) to produce a British "people's car" called the "Atom" led to the manufacture of sports cars. The firm he set up for this purpose took its name from that of his home, Fairthorpe, at Denham, Buckinghamshire. The enterprise finally closed its doors in the late 1970s.

Famel (*cough linctus and pastilles*)

The product was first marketed around 1916 and was formulated by a Frenchman named Famel, of Paris. The name was registered in the UK in 1931.

Famous Amos (*cookies*)

The man behind the name is Wally Amos (b. 1936), who in 1975 forsook his career as a talent scout with the William Morris Agency to open a chocolate chip cookie store in Los Angeles. Within five years, his business had become a national cookie company, selling its products to top-rank department stores. Amos had acquired his taste for chocolate chip cookies growing up in Harlem, where his Aunt Della baked them for the family.

Famous Grouse (*whisky*)

Scotland's most popular blend of whisky was introduced at the end of the 19th century by Matthew Gloag & Son of Perth, founded in 1814. The grouse of the name, pictured on the label, capitalizes on the fashionable Victorian and Edwardian sport of grouse-shooting.

Fanny Farmer (*candy*)

In 1919 John Hayes, founder of Canada's Laura Secord candy store chain, opened a store in Rochester, New York, in order to expand his market. He decided to call his American outlet by a different name, and settled on "Fanny Farmer," after Fannie Merritt Farmer (1857-1915), a noted American cooking school director and cookbook author, famous for her recipes. Hayes is said to have chosen Farmer's name because he admired her courage in overcoming a paralytic stroke she had as a teenager.

Fanta (*sparkling orange drink*)

The drink, now marketed by **Coca-Cola**, was launched in Germany during World War II. Its name derives from German *Fantasie*, "fantasia," as considerable imagination was needed to create a palatable drink from the limited resources available during those years of austerity. The name was entered in the *Trade Marks Journal* of November 21, 1956.

Farah (*men's pants*)

The name is that of two American brothers, James Farah (*c*.1916-1964) and William Farah (b. 1919), who in 1937 inherited a small clothing factory from their father. In the early 1960s, the brothers capitalized on the boom in moderately priced apparel by introducing Farah slacks. The business went downhill after James's untimely death, but sales picked up again in the 1980s when higher priced menswear was introduced.

Farberware (*kitchenware*)

In 1905 Simon W. Farber (*c*.1881-1947), a young Russian-Jewish immigrant to America, moved his growing metalworking business from cramped quarters in Manhattan's Lower East Side to a more spacious location at Broadway and Grand streets. Together with his wife, Ella Sachs, he built it into one of the most innovative companies in the housewares industry. The first line of Farberware, silver-and-nickel-plated serving accessories and giftware, was introduced in 1910. In 1966 the firm they had founded was acquired by Walter Kidde & Co., Inc.

Farley's (*babyfoods*)

The name is that of the English family who originally ran a small bakery in Plymouth in 1880. It was a local doctor, however, Dr. William Penn Eales, who devised the distinctive cereal cookies for babies. He named them after the family who baked them, and who originally sold them as "Farley's Feeding Biscuits." In 1912 the business was sold by Edwin Farley, who that year emigrated with his family to Canada. The bakery passed to one William Bolitho Trahair, who after World War I formed a new company, not under his own name but that of the original owners, so that the business became known as Farley's Family Foods. The infant cookies later became familiar as "Farley's Rusks."

Farman (*aircraft*)

The aircraft take their name from the Paris-born Frenchman Maurice Farman (1877-1964), who began his career as a champion bicyclist and racing driver. In 1909 he built his first airplane, his early craft being modifications of the Voisin biplane. By the beginning of World War I, his "Longhorn" model, first built in 1912, was one of the standard trainers in France and Britain. Farman and his brother Henri pooled their resources that same year and in 1917 produced the "Goliath," the first long-distance passenger plane. Its regular flights between Paris and London did much to stimulate commercial aviation in both France and the rest of Europe.

Farmitalia-Carlo Erba (*pharmaceuticals*)

The Italian company was formed in 1978 on the merger between Carlo Erba, a firm formed in 1853 and named for its founder, and Farmitalia (from *farmaceutici*, "pharmaceuticals", and *Italia*, "Italy"), created in 1935, both of the **Montedison** Group. In 1983 it became part of the holding company Erbamont, together with which it passed in 1993 to the Swedish company Procordia-Kabi Pharmacia, a world leader in oncological products.

Farola (*wheat-based pudding*)

The name was registered in 1885 and is based on Latin *far*, "corn," with the then popular suffix "-ola" as in **Granola**.

Fassbender (*chocolates*)

The German firm dates from 1910, when one Herr Fassbender opened a konditorei in Siegburg, near Bonn, serving coffee, cakes, and chocolates. The business remained in the family, and eventually passed to Fassbender's grandson, Hans-Werner Fassbender, who in 1982 opened a second shop in Cologne.

Fauchon (*chocolates*)

The French chocolates take their name from Normandy-born Auguste Fauchon (1856-1938), who quit school at an early age to seek his fortune in Paris. There he set up a stall selling fruit and vegetables, and at the age of 30 bought a small corner shop in the Place de la Madeleine. It proved such a success that he soon opened two more shops, and by 1925 his business boasted a delicatessen, a pâtisserie, wine cellars, and a restaurant. World War II hit the firm badly, but it was rescued and taken over by Joseph Pilosoff, who remained faithful to the creative ideas of Auguste Fauchon and preserved his name. In 1986 the firm was taken over by Pilosoff's granddaughter, Martine Premat, and Fauchon is now represented in specialty stores worldwide.

Feculose (*gelatine substitute*)

The preparation of acetylated starch, made by heating dry starch with glacial acetic acid, was formerly used as a substitute for gelatine and vegetable gums. Its name comes from "fecula" (the sediment from an infusion of vegetable substances) and the chemical suffix "-ose," and was entered by the firm of William Wotherspoon, at the Glenfield Starch Works, in the *Trade Marks Journal* of July 29, 1903.

Federal-Mogul (*automotive components*)

Federal-Mogul Corporation was founded in 1899 as the Muzzy-Lyon Company by J. Howard Muzzy and Edward F. Lyon, who sold mill supplies and rubber goods on Woodward Avenue in Detroit, Michigan. That same year, the partners set up the Mogul Metal Company as a subsidiary to manufacture new bearing alloys. At that time it was usual to sell one type of bearing metal for all types of uses, but Muzzy and Lyon reckoned that bearing metals for different speeds and different loads required correspondingly different qualities and structures. Accordingly, they blended two babbit metals and sold them under the brand names "Duro" and "Mogul." Duro was made using a purchased formula, but the Mogul formula was developed by Muzzy and Lyon themselves. In the early 1900s, bearings were made by pouring molten babbit metals directly onto the motor block and shaping the metal to fit, so that to replace a bearing, a mechanic had to gouge out the old one and pour in new metal. Muzzy and Lyon believed that metals could be die-cast directly into replaceable metals. Experiments with an old printer's type-casting machine were so successful that they stopped selling mill supplies and instead began selling automotive bearings and metal projects. In 1910, **Buick** placed an order for 10,000 connecting rod bearings for their Buick 10 model, and business took off. The Mogul Metal Company became Federal-Mogul in 1924 when the company merged with Federal-Bearing Bushing, a manufacturer of engine bearings and bushings. In 2001 soaring asbestos liabilities forced Federal-Mogul into administration.

Federated Department Stores *see* **Lazarus**

Felix (*cat food*)

The name was originally that of Felix Cat Food Ltd., a British firm that had been manufacturing dry cat foods since before World War II and that was acquired by **Quaker Oats** in 1970. The name not only alludes to Felix the Cat, the famous cartoon cat created by Pat Sullivan in the 1920s for the silent screen, but also hints at Latin *Felis*, the name of the cat genus, and Latin *felix*, "happy," "fortunate."

Feltrinelli (*publishers*)

The Italian publishing house was founded in 1954 by Giangiacomo Feltrinelli (1926-1972), founder in 1950 of the Feltrinelli Institute for the History of International Socialism and the Working Men's Movement. He was killed while preparing a terrorist attack.

Femidom (*contraceptives*)

The name of the make of female condom, blending "feminine" and "condom," was entered by the Medic Group of Scandinavia, of Copenhagen, Denmark, in the *Trade Marks Journal* of October 4, 1989, with the note: "Date claimed under International Convention. 5 November 1987 (Denmark)."

Fendi (*fashionwear*)

The Italian company was founded in 1918 by Adele Fendi (1897-1978) to produce leather handbags. Since 1954 the business has been run by the founder's five daughters, Paola (b. 1931), Anna (b. 1933), Franca (b. 1935), Carla (b. 1937), and Alda (b. 1940), together with their husbands and children. In the 1960s Fendi moved into furs.

Fenwicks *(department stores)*

The British stores owe their origin to John James Fenwick (1846-1905), son of a provision merchant in Richmond, Yorkshire, who began his working life helping his father before being apprenticed to a draper in Stockton-on-Tees. Aiming higher, he left for Newcastle upon Tyne in 1868, where after a few weeks as a draper he obtained a post as a buyer for a firm of silk dealers, Charles Bragg & Co. He rose to be manager, at the same time taking up insurance as a sideline. This activity led to his temporary downfall, and Braggs dismissed him for working with insurance while officially engaged in silk buying. Fenwick's dismissal was a blessing in disguise, and enabled him to start up his own business, which he did in 1882 as a "Mantle Maker & Furrier" in Northumberland Street, Newcastle. The flagship Fenwicks store in New Bond Street, London, was opened in 1891 by Fenwick himself. The business is still in family hands, and Mark Fenwick (b. 1948) became chairman in 1997.

Ferguson *see* **Massey-Ferguson**

Ferodo *(brake linings)*

Car brake linings were the invention of the Englishman Herbert Frood (1864-1931), born in Balby, Yorkshire, who in the 1890s pioneered the manufacture of woven cotton brakes for horse-drawn carts. With the advent of the "horseless carriage," he realized that more hardwearing and heavier-duty brakes were needed, and in 1897 set up his business to make them. Soon after he won his first big contract, supplying brake linings to the London General Omnibus Company for their first motor buses. He based the name of his invention and business on his own name, with "Fero-" also suggesting the powdered iron (Latin *ferrum*) present in brake linings. The name was entered in the *Trade Marks Journal* of November 7, 1906.

Ferragamo *(footwear)*

The name is that of Salvatore Ferragamo (1898-1960), born in the tiny village of Bonito near Naples, Italy. He was apprenticed as a shoemaker from the ages of nine to 14, and when he was 16 joined his brothers in Los Angeles, California, where he made shoes by hand for the American Film Company. He built up a clientele of wealthy customers and movie stars, but in 1927 returned to Italy to set up a workshop in Florence. After his death, the company grew under the guidance of his son Leonardo into an empire that produces not only shoes but men's and women's fashions, fragrances, and sunglasses.

Ferranti *(electronic equipment)*

The founder of the British-based firm was Sebastian Ziani de Ferranti (1864-1930), born in Liverpool. His father, Cesar Ziani de Ferranti (1831-1901), was a photographer who had come to England from Ostend, Belgium, to set up a photographic partnership in Liverpool with his father-in-law, William Scott, a North of England portrait painter. Sebastian's mother, Juliana Szczepanowski, was a Polish concert pianist, but her son did not follow in her musical footsteps. Instead, on leaving school, he went to London University to study engineering. He left after two terms, however, as his father was too sick to support him. Ferranti therefore joined the laboratories of **Siemens**, where he put his interest in electricity to good use. In 1882, still only 18, he set up his own company of Ferranti, Thompson & Ince Ltd., the latter being Alfred Thompson, a photographer, and Francis Ince, a solicitor (lawyer), whom he had persuaded to join him in making electrical equipment. His subsequent specialization in electric meters and transformers ensured his future reputation and that of the company.

Ferrari *(automobiles)*

The founder of the Italian marque was Enzo Ferrari (1898-1988), born in Modena the son of a metalworker. Enzo's father wanted him to be an engineer, but instead the boy pursued a different ambition, that of car racing. After an unpromising start in World War I, he settled down to converting military vehicles into passenger cars. In 1919 he was asked to compete in a car race in Sicily. He did not win, but was successful in becoming a racing and test driver for **Alfa Romeo** the following year. In 1929 he decided to run his own racing team, and to this end formed the Scuderia ("racing stable") Ferrari in Modena. This was the germ of his auto business, founded in 1939 in Modena as a machine-tool works under the name Auto-Avio Costruzioni. The two first Ferrari cars of the name entered the Mille Miglia in 1940. In 1988 Ferrari passed to **Fiat**.

Ferrero (*chocolates*)

The Italian chocolates take their name from Pietro and Giovanni Ferrero, who in 1946 founded a confectionery company in Alba.

Ferruzzi (*finance and industry*)

The Italian conglomerate, founded by the grain merchant Serafino Ferruzzi (1908-1979), engages in a wide range of commercial activities, from cereals (1948) to cement (1957). In 1979, under the general guidance of Raul Gardini (1933-1993), who had married Ferruzzi's daughter in 1957 and taken control on the death of his father-in-law, it acquired the sugar manufacturers Eridania, founded in 1899, and the French paper manufacurers Béghin-Say, who joined forces in 1992 as Eridania Béghin-Say. In 1987 it acquired **Montedison**. Arturo Ferruzzi succeeded Gardini as president in 1991 and in 1993 a financial crisis in the company led to the intervention of various banks to regularize matters. That same year, Gardini shot himself during an inquiry into the corruption scandal surrounding his unsuccessful attempt to take over Enimont, a company set up by Montedison in 1989 as a joint venture with the state-owned ENI petrochemicals group.

FI Group *see* Xansa

Fiat (*automobiles*)

The name of the Italian car is an acronym of Fabbrica Italiana Automobili Torino ("Italian Automobile Works Turin"), a firm founded in Turin in 1899 by a native of that city, Giovanni Agnelli (1866-1945), who attended the military school in Modena but quit the army in 1892. The name fortuitously represents the Latin word meaning "let it be done," itself the source of English "fiat" as a term for an authorization or decree. In 1986 Fiat acquired **Alfa-Romeo**, and in 1988 **Ferrari**.

Fibro (*synthetic fiber*)

The name (from Latin *fibra*, "fiber") of the viscose rayon staple was entered by **Courtaulds** Ltd. of London, England, in the *Trade Marks Journal* of August 11, 1926. *Cp.* **Fibrolane**.

Fibrolane (*synthetic fiber*)

The series of wool-like synthetic fibers made from protein derive their name from Latin *fibra*, "fiber," (*cp.* **Fibro**) and *lana*, "wool." It was entered by **Courtaulds** Ltd. of London, England, in the *Trade Marks Journal* of August 7, 1946.

Fields (*soap and candles*)

The British firm of J. C. & J. Field traces its origin to the 16th century, when records of the Worshipful Company of Wax Chandlers show that Thomas Field, a London chandler, retired in 1581. In 1655 his descendant, Thomas Field, likewise retired, and was succeeded by Abraham Field, who in turn claimed his pension in 1670. His own descendant, Thomas Field, was apprenticed in 1697 and his son, also Thomas, born in 1707 or 1709, was apprenticed in 1729. This last Thomas Field died in 1769, but contemporary records show that from 1747 through 1779 the business was carried on in the name of Sarah Field & Son. Thomas's son John succeeded to an interest in the business in 1769 and his second wife, Sarah, bore him a son, also John. John Field Sr. died in 1790, when his widow, Sarah, took the eldest son into partnership and carried on the business as Sarah and John Field. In 1800 the name of the firm was John and Charles Field, but in 1820 John, the eldest son of the then senior partner, was admitted. This finally gave the 20th-century name of the firm, J.C. & J. Field. John Sr. died in 1837, and his son, also John, in 1845, in which year Charles became sole partner, with John Kingsford Field, his son, and John Lyon Field, the son of John Field, Jr., as apprentices. In 1847 the firm began to make stearine candles, and in 1850 nightlights. Charles Field, the only surviving partner, died in 1854, and his son John Kingsford Field, together with John Lyon Field, formed a partnership. In 1855 the firm first produced paraffin (wax) candles, as well as various types of fancy candles. John Lyon Field retired in 1866, and John Kingsford Field admitted his two brothers, Frederick and Arthur, as partners. John Kingsford Field died in 1875, and his brother Arthur in 1879. The business was continued by Frederick Field together with his nephew, John Kingsford Field, while Edmund Field, another son of Charles Field, became a partner. John Kingsford Field retired in 1881, and the business was then carried on by the brothers Frederick and Edmund Field, John Nicholson, and E.J. Stephens. (These last two had earlier been partners in another firm of chandlers, Messrs. Ogleby & Co., which John Kingsford Field had acquired in 1869. The two firms at first operated separately but merged in 1880.) John Nicholson died in 1882 and the following year Leopold Field, son of Frederick Field, the senior partner, was admitted into partnership. Frederick Field died in 1885 and his brother, Edmund, a year later, leaving E.J. Stephens and Leopold Field to carry on the business. In 1887 the Ogleby business was withdrawn from the partnership and the Field business converted into a limited company. In 1910 the Field company appointed Henry Charles Green, the 26-year-old manager of a large soap works in Scotland, as its own general manager. Thus one of Britain's oldest companies was handed down from generation to generation to be finally managed by an appointee from outside the family.

Fiesta *(automobiles)*

The **Ford** model so known was given the code name "Bobcat" in 1972, three years before it came into production. This particular name was chosen both because it began with "B" (for a "Class B" car, i.e. a small car like the **Fiat** 127, **Renault** S, and **Volkswagen** Polo) and also because the bobcat is a sturdy and speedy animal, as the model was itself intended to be. The original plan was to retain the name, but it was already in use for a model of the Ford "Mercury," so had to be changed in any case. The search was therefore on for a name that was short, easy to pronounce, preferably European in flavor, easy to combine with "Ford," understood in most countries, of identical meaning in many languages, original and pleasant, simple, credible and apt (i.e. evoking a small, economical, but lively and sound car), and of course not in use by anyone else. Of the suggestions offered, a shortlist of 50 was made, then a final list of 13, as follows: "Amigo," "Bambi," "Bebe," "Bolero," "Bravo," "Cherie," "Chico," "Fiesta," "Forito," "Metro," "Pony," "Sierra," and "Tempo." Of those questioned, around one person in ten confused "Sierra" with "siesta," European interviewees thought

"Pony" too specifically British (and the British did not like it anyway), "Amigo," "Fiesta," and "Sierra" seemed too Spanish, and the Germans were not too keen on "Bambi." Despite such adverse comments, these five formed the final choice, in order of preference: "Fiesta," "Amigo," "Bambi," "Pony," and "Sierra." At this point a further factor was considered. Apart from the "Escort," launched in 1968 (and withdrawn from production in 2000), all Ford cars up to then had been named for a town or region (like the **Cortina**). Thus the name "Nice" was proposed, but then rejected, since for Germans this should be "Nizza," which for many people would be unattractive and meaningless. Here Henry Ford II himself put his word in. He felt that "Bravo" was not a good name for a car. It was meaningful in Spanish or Italian, but virtually meaningless in English. He did, however, like the alliteration of "Ford Fiesta." This was therefore the final choice, although "Fiesta" had formerly been used by **Oldsmobile** and permission had to be obtained by Ford from **General Motors** for its use. The official "christening" took place on September 22, 1974. Other proposed names for the car, such as "Adonis," "Sonata," "Gato," "Piccolo," and "Ischia," were thus nonstarters.

57 Varieties *(food products)*

The familiar number in the **Heinz** name is arbitrary. It was devised by Henry Heinz himself, when riding one day in 1896 on an elevated train in New York City. He saw an advertising card in the train for a brand of shoes offering "21 Styles." As he told it (quoted in Lambert; *see* Bibliography, p. 566):

> I said to myself, "We do not have styles of products, but we do have varieties of products." Figuring up how many we had I counted 57, and "57" kept coming back into my mind. Seven, seven— there are so many illustrations of the psychological influence of that figure and of its significance to people of all ages and races, that "58 Varieties" or "59 Varieties" did not appeal at all to me as being equally strong. I got off the train immediately, and went down to a lithographer's where I designed a street-car featuring the phrase "57 Varieties" and had it distributed throughout the United States.

The name "57 Varieties" was adopted in 1896 and registered in 1907.

Fig Newtons *(cookies)*

James Henry Mitchell, a Philadelphia inventor, devised a machine that could make a cookie and fill it with preserves or jam at the same time. It was tried out for the first time in 1892 at the Kennedy Biscuit Works in Cambridgeport, Massachusetts. The bakery had a tradition of naming cookies and crackers after towns around Boston, among them Beacon Hill, Shrewsbury, Brighton, and Melrose. The cookie with jam was called the Newton, after that town. As figs subsequently became the most common filling, the cookies were renamed Fig Newtons.

Filene's *(specialty store)*

The world's largest specialty store, in Boston, Massachusetts, takes its name from William Filene (1830–1901), born in Poznań, Poland, the son of a ribbonseller. In 1848, a year of revolution in Europe, Filene renounced his Jewish faith and emigrated, first to England, then to the United States. At age 18 he went to work as a tailor in Boston. Three years later he opened a tiny shop on Washington Street, stocking dry goods. During the Civil War, Filene left retailing for an unsuccessful venture in New York, moving there in 1863. In 1870 he returned to Lynn, Massachusetts, where he launched two small stores. In 1881, Filene and his sons, Edward Albert Filene (1860–1937), and Abraham Lincoln Filene (1865–1957), opened a store on Winter Street in Boston, and this is the date of founding of the present business. In 1891, suffering from a heart ailment, William turned the management over to his two sons and they inherited the store on his death.

Filofax *(loose-leaf notebook)*

The Filofax was the invention of Grace Scurr (1894–1987), an Englishwoman who in 1921 was a temporary secretary with Norman & Hill Ltd., a London firm of printers and stationers. The firm imported personal filing systems from the United States, and Miss Scurr persuaded the company to manufacture the systems itself. In 1925 she coined the name "Filofax" (repesenting "file of facts"), and it was entered in the *Trade Marks Journal* of May 6, 1931. Initial demand for the product came from the clergy, scientists, and certain army regiments, and during World War II Filofaxes were standard issue at the Royal Military College, Sandhurst. Grace Scurr rose to became company chairman, a post

she held until 1955, but it was only in the 1980s that the Filofax became a cult yuppie accessory. In 2001 Filofax was acquired by **Letts**.

Findlater Mackie Todd *(wines and spirits)*

In 1822 Alexander Findlater (1797–1873), a Scottish farmer's son, set sail across the Irish Sea for Dublin. He already had some experience in the wine trade, and was successful in opening a business in the Irish capital. He soon set up wine shops in other cities, with the first in London opening its doors in the Strand in 1850. By this time he had formed a partnership with Ivie Mackie, so traded as Findlater, Mackie & Co. Within five years of opening his first London store he had expanded to another branch, in Tooley Street, where he now traded as Findlater Mackie Todd & Co. The third name was that of another partner, Bruce Beveridge Todd, who acquired the firm after Findlater's death, and who himself died in 1893. The firm is now noted for its **Dry Fly** sherry.

Findus *(frozen foods)*

The company owes its origin to two Scandinavian chocolate firms, Marabou and Freia, who in 1941 acquired a fruit and vegetable canning factory in the small town of Bjuv, southern Sweden. The name itself is a shortening of *"Fruit Indu*stries." In the UK, Findus became part of **Nestlé**.

Finmeccanica *(diversified industries)*

The name is that of the holding company of the Italian group IRI (Istituto per la Ricostruzione Industriale, "Industrial Reconstruction Institute"), a public company set up in 1933 to handle the crisis in the country's industry and banks. Finmeccanica operates in the aerospace and energy sectors, among others, and was constituted in 1948 as the Società Finanziaria Meccanica ("Engineering Holding Company") with the aim of uniting a number of companies separated from the IRI in the engineering and shipbuilding sectors, such as **Alfa Romeo** and **Ansaldo**. The shipbuilding side of the business was hived off in 1959 as Fincantieri (*cantiere*, "shipyard"), a company that in 1986 took control of **Isotta Fraschini**, the same year that **Fiat** acquired Alfa Romeo. Selenia (*see* **Aeritalia**) became part of Finmeccanica in 1990, and in 1993 the group took over various aerospace and defense companies that belonged to the liquidated Efim (Ente per il Finanziamento dell'Industria Manifatturiera, "Manufacturing Industry Finance Corporation"), set up as a holding company in 1962, among them **Agusta** and **Breda**.

Fiorucci *(fashionwear)*

The Italian firm takes its name from its founder, the fashion designer Elio Fiorucci (b. 1935), born in Milan. In 1962 he inherited a shoe store from his father, and in the mid-1960s began traveling to London, England, to bring miniskirts and other fashionable garments back to his shop in Milan. In 1967 he opened a larger store, selling clothes from London's youth-oriented designers. His name gained worldwide fame in the 1970s, with his creations finding a ready response in a mainly young market. In 1990 his business was taken over by the Japanese company Edwin.

Firestone *(tires)*

The American company takes its name from Harvey Samuel Firestone (1868-1938), born in Columbiana County, Ohio, the son of a farmer. After briefly working as a bookkeeper and patent medicine salesman, Firestone joined the Columbus Buggy Company in Detroit. In 1896 the business went bankrupt and Firestone moved into mounting solid-rubber tires on wheels in Chicago. In 1900 he went to Akron, Ohio, where he joined the engineering firm of Whitman and Barnes as manager of the tire department. That same year he founded the Firestone Tire and Rubber Company. His entry into manufacturing in 1902 made him one of the principal beneficiaries of the new automobile era and in 1906 Firestone captured a major contract for the **Ford** Model N, for which he devised a new type of cheaper tire. Like Ford's own company, Firestone's has been family-controlled ever since. In 1998 it was acquired by **Bridgestone**.

Fireworks by Grucci *(fireworks)*

The US company owes its fame to Felix Grucci (1905-1993), born in Brooklyn, New York, the son of a grocer and the grandson of Angelo Lanzetta, who in the mid-19th century founded the firm that was the eventual ancestor of Grucci's own business. Lanzetta came from Bari, Italy, to Long Island, New York, in the 1870s, and started the Suffolk Novelty Fireworks Company, named for Long Island's Suffolk County. His son, Anthony, Felix's mother's brother, carried on the business after Lanzetta died, and Grucci joined his uncle as a young man. In the 1920s, Grucci organized his own firm, the New York Pyrotechnics Company, and gradually expanded his business and his family. In the 1970s he was joined by his two sons, James and Felix "Butch" Jr., and his daughter, Donna. The firm was subsequently renamed as the New York Fireworks Company and, following a successful display at the 1974 International Fireworks Competition in Monte Carlo, Monaco, Fireworks by Grucci.

Firmin *(buttons and badges)*

The small British button factory in Birmingham dates back to 1677, when it was founded by Thomas Firmin (1632-1697), born in Ipswich, Suffolk. At an early age he was apprenticed to a fabric merchant, subsequently setting up his own shop in London selling belts and silk fabrics. He was a noted philanthropist, providing welcome local employment for the poor, and when his London factory burned down in the Great Fire of London (1666) he built better and larger premises for linen manufacture, so that by the late 1670s he had 1,700 employees as spinners, flax-dressers, weavers and buttonmakers at what he called his "workhouse" close to St. Bartholomew's Hospital. The business subsequently transferred to Birmingham, and today specializes in the manufacture of buttons for uniforms, badges, and accoutrements.

First Tuesday *(e-commerce networking)*

The Internet enterprise was the brainchild of Julie Meyer (b. 1966), an American from Sacramento, California, who went to London in 1998 and initiated a plan whereby a group of net entrepreneurs seeking funding, and venture capitalists seeking to invest, would meet on the first Tuesday of each month. Cofounders were Nick Denton, Adam Gold, John Browning, and Mark Davies. By 2000 the group had spread to 55 cities across five continents and in 1999 made Meyer a small fortune when she sold her business to Yazam, an Israeli technology investment group. In 2001, however, a cash-strapped Yazam was forced to sell First Tuesday to a group of 11 London businessmen in a bid to raise funds.

Fischer *(music publishers)*

The US firm of music publishers derives its name from Carl Fischer (1849-1923), a German immigrant to the USA in 1872 who began in business as a music retailer in New York. He eventually became the chief publisher of Sousa and other important figures in the band world, and in 1885 started a journal for bandleaders, *The Metronome*. His son, Walter S. Fischer, took over the firm on his father's death, and it remains a family concern, still preeminent as a publisher of band music.

Fish Eagle *(brandy)*

As the label explains on bottles of this South African brandy: "This remarkable Natural Brandy is a tribute to the African Fish Eagle which possessively guards over the wild waterways of our continent." A picture of the bird accompanies the hype. The brandy is produced by the Distillers Corporation.

Fisher *(automobile bodies)*

The name is that of six American brothers: Frederic John Fisher (1878-1941), Charles Thomas Fisher (1880-1963), William Andrew Fisher (1886-1969), Lawrence P. Fisher (1888-1961), Edward Francis Fisher (1891-1972), and Alfred Joseph Fisher (1892-1963), born in Ohio the sons of a blacksmith. They all grew up in Norwalk, Ohio, where they worked for their father in his blacksmith and carriage shop. After further experience with various carriage companies, the brothers formed the Fisher Body Company in 1908. They planned to make closed "all-weather" automobile bodies, as distinct from the open bodies that until as late as 1919 were the norm for American cars. At first they met with resistance from automobile manufacturers, who believed that motorists would not like being confined behind glass and would enjoy driving only in the open air. Cars with closed bodies, moreover, were much more expensive. But the Fisher brothers persisted, and by 1927 85 percent of automobiles had closed bodies, representing a major transformation of the American automobile industry.

Fisher-Price *(toys)*

One of the world's largest manufacturer of infant and preschool toys had its origin in 1930, when three western New Yorkers converted an old house outside Buffalo, New York, into a small factory. One of them, Herman G. Fisher (1898-1975), was a veteran toy salesman. Another, Irving L. Price (1884-1976), was a retired chain store executive. The third, who missed out on the company name, was Helen Schelle, the former operator of the Penny Walker Toy Shop in Binghamton, New York. In their first year, the three introduced a line of 16 toddler toys. Despite the Depression, their imaginative creations appealed to preschool youngsters and were snapped up by their parents. By 1936 their business turned its first real profit, and ten years later their annual net sales were $1.6 million.

Fisherman's Friend *(throat lozenges)*

In 1865 James Lofthouse, born in Lancaster, Lancashire, England, opened a pharmacy and chemist's (druggist's) shop in the fishing port of Fleetwood, Lancashire, where he determined to develop a remedy to bring relief to local trawlermen, many of whom suffered from bronchial ailments. At first he came up with a liquid preparation, but the bottles were easily broken on the tossing fishing boats, and instead he created menthol-enriched lozenges. They proved to be an effective and welcome remedy for the throat and chest complaints suffered by the fishing folk, and customers were constantly coming to Lofthouse's store and asking for "a bag of fisherman's lozenges" or "an ounce of friends." The brand name thus invented itself. The product remained a secret in the local community until 1963, when Doreen Lofthouse (b. 1930), wife of Tony Lofthouse, the founder's grandson, took to the road with the lozenges, selling them to retailers outside Lancashire. She now runs the company, and all the shares are owned by her family. The name was entered in the *Trade Marks Journal* of November 25, 1987.

Fisons *(fertilizers)*

Fisons manufactures much more than fertilizers, but this is the product with which the British firm is still chiefly associated, and it was the one originally made by Joseph Fison, a village baker, when he set up his business in East Anglia in 1847. The first fertilizer works was built by Fison's son James at Two Mile Bottom, Norfolk, in 1856, while the original firm of Joseph Fison & Co. opened a similar factory at Bramford, Suffolk, two years later. The company name eventually became simply Fisons Ltd. in 1942, and Fisons still has its registered office in Ipswich, Suffolk, Joseph Fison's birthtown.

Fitch Lovell (*wholesale grocers*)

The British company name is that of two men, not one. James Fitch (1762-1818) was born into a family of cheesemongers, and in 1784 opened his own cheesemongery in Leadenhall Street, London. His business took various partners over the next few years, and broadened its range of foods. In 1828 the firm moved to larger premises around the corner in Bishopsgate, where it remained until 1929, when it moved again to St. Martin's Lane. Meanwhile, back in 1856, a partnership had been formed elsewhere in London between William Lovell, a Somerset farmer's son, and Charles Christmas, a retail cheesemonger. They traded as Lovell & Christmas at their shop near Smithfield Market, not far from Fitch Lovell's present head office. In 1958 the two concerns merged under their present name, losing that of Charles Christmas in the process.

Flammarion (*publishers*)

The French publishing house was founded in 1876 by Ernest Flammarion (1846-1936), his first major publication being the *Astronomie populaire* (1880) of his brother, the astronomer Camille Flammarion (1842-1925). The firm went on to publish a wide range of medical, scientific, geographical, and historical works, and still flourishes as a family concern.

Fleer *see* **Chiclets**

Fleischmann (*yeast*)

Charles Louis Fleischmann (1834-1897) was born near Budapest, Hungary, the son of a distiller and yeast maker. Following education in Vienna and Prague, he began his career at age 19 as a general store clerk in Tasgendorf, Austria. He then emigrated to the United States. While eating at his sister's wedding in New York in 1866, he realized that the inferior liquid yeast used in baking gave a poor quality bread, and so resolved to create a better, solid yeast. In 1868, working with his brother Maximilian and James W. Gaff in a Cincinnati bakery, he persuaded his partners to include baker's yeast as one of their products. The new process was duly patented in 1870 and gained the at-

tention of restaurants. In 1883 the name of the business was changed to Fleischmann and Company, and by 1900 it operated the world's largest yeast plant at Charles Point in Peekskill, New York, with branch offices in cities across the country.

Flexowriter (*typewriter*)

The name for a kind of electric typewriter incorporating a tape punch and a tape reader was entered in the *Trade Marks Journal* of September 21, 1955 for: "Appliances consisting of a typewriter and a duplicator in one unit for office use." The name itself blends "flexible" and "typewriter."

Flextime (*timing device*)

The device used to time the hours worked by an employee derives its name from a combination of "flexible" and "time" and was originally introduced as a translation of German *Gleitzeit*, literally "sliding time." It was entered in the *Trade Marks Journal* of February 9, 1972, and the US Patent Office *Official Gazette* of January 8, 1974, and came to be an alternate general term for the more common "flexitime," meaning the arrangement whereby employees, although working a contracted number of hours, are free to vary their starting and finishing times within prescribed limits.

Flit (*insecticide*)

The name was first entered by the **Standard Oil** Company (New Jersey) in the US Patent Office *Offical Gazette* of November 27, 1923, with a claim of use since May 17 that year. A subsequent registration by Standard Oil in the *Trade Marks Journal* of March 17, 1926, was for: "Chemical substances used for Agricultural, Horticultural, Veterinary and Sanitary purposes," while that in the *Journal* of November 10, 1926, was for: "Sprayers, Squirtguns and Atomizers." The name itself was the invention of C.A. Straw, patent attorney for Standard Oil, who after a long search for a suitable name suggested "Flit" as a word associated with flies, which both flit (fly fast) and would be made to flit (disappear fast) when hit with "Flit" (in due course by a "Flit gun").

Floatel (*floating hotel*)

The term for a floating hotel, especially a boat operating as a hotel, is a straightforward blend of "float" and "hotel" on the lines of "boatel" ("boat" and "hotel") or especially "motel" ("motor" and "hotel"). Although also spelled "flotel," and almost always written with a small initial, the name is actually proprietary in the UK, and was entered in the *Trade Marks Journal* of November 16, 1983 for: "Buildings adapted to float and frameworks therefor; all made wholly or principally of metal." But the general word was already in use as early as the 1950s.

Floris *(perfume)*

The aptly named family business of J. Floris in Jermyn Street, London, England, originated in 1730 as a barbershop owned by Juan Famenias Floris, a Spaniard from Menorca. He built up a fashionable clientele, making individual perfumes to the recipes of his customers. The fragrances were soon in such demand that he gave up his barber's business and used the shop to display his perfumery. Mary Ann Floris later married J.R.D. Bodenham, and they continued the family ownership, now in the seventh generation, from the 1870s.

Flowers *(beer)*

The British brewery, based in Cheltenham, Gloucestershire, was founded in 1831 by Edward Fordham Flower (1805-1893) in Brewery Street, Stratford-upon-Avon. Flower was born in Hertfordshire the son of a brewer, banker, farmer, and sheepbreeder. When he was 12 he went with his father to the United States, but returned in 1824 and after marrying a young lady from Leamington Spa settled in Stratford, where he opened his brewery seven years later. It did so well that after 30 years he was able to retire and leave the management to his sons, one of whom, Charles Edward Flower, founded the Shakespeare Memorial Theatre in Stratford. Brewing continued in the town until 1969, when the business moved to Cheltenham. It was subsequently taken over and closed by **Whitbread**, who now use the name for their Cheltenham brewery.

Fluevog *(footwear)*

The Canadian company was founded in Vancouver, British Columbia, in 1970 by John Fluevog (b. 1948) and Peter Fox. The partnership split up in 1980, when Fox went on to become a mainstream designer while Fluevog found fame for his revival of the platform shoe.

The shoes themselves were made in England, often with **Dr. Martens** soles, and after their adoption in the 1990s by celebrities such as Deee-Lite pop singer Lady Miss Kier (b. Kierin Kirby) were widely available in boutiques and a chain of self-named stores nationwide.

Fluon *(plastic)*

The proprietary name for polytetrafluoroethylene, a plastic with non-adhesive surface properties, derives from the chemical name. The name was entered in the *Trade Marks Journal* of March 9, 1949.

Fluor *(construction and engineering)*

The Fluor Corporation, now a world-class engineering and construction firm, takes its name from John Simon Fluor, a Swiss-born carpenter, who founded the company in California in 1912. The company owed its initial growth mainly as a builder for the petroleum industry, and Fluor's original customers included Southern California Edison and Richfield Oil.

Flymo *(lawnmower)*

Swedish engineer Karl Dahlman was fascinated by the idea of a lawnmower that needed no wheels, floating instead on a cushion of air like a hovercraft. He spent a long time researching and developing the necessary technology, and finally in 1963 came up with his first hover-mower model, which he called the "Flymo," the "flying mower." The name was entered in the *Trade Marks Journal* of April 8, 1964. The Flymo company became part of **Electrolux** in 1969, based in the UK, and has since become Europe's largest manufacturer of powered lawnmowers.

Focke-Wulf *(aircraft)*

The German aircraft company was founded in Bremen in 1924 by Heinrich Focke (1890-1979) and Georg Wulf, who between 1911 and 1914 had built a monoplane. They designed and constructed various civil and military aircraft, but in 1935 Focke resigned from the partnership to concentrate on helicopter development. The following year his researches resulted in the construction of the first practical helicopter, the Fw-61. In World War II the Fw-190 fighter aircraft of Nazi Germany was second in importance only to the Me-109 produced by **Messerschmitt**.

Foden *(trucks and buses)*

The name is that of the company's English founder, Edwin Foden (1841-1911), born near Sandbach, Cheshire. In 1856 he became an engineering apprentice with a firm that made agricultural machinery and portable steam engines, which attracted Edwin for their possible exploitation in an increasingly mechanized world. He was made a works foreman in 1860, and subsequently became a partner in the firm, so that its original name of Plant & Hancock became Hancock & Foden. In 1875 Mr. Hancock retired, and Edwin Foden was left in sole control. He now branched out, patenting the first compound (as distinct from single-cylinder) steam engine in 1880. In 1887 he formed a new company, with himself as managing director and his sons, William and Edwin Richard Foden, as partners. Production of steam and traction engines boomed from then on. The two sons took over the firm on their father's death, with Edwin Richard Foden subsequently setting up his own diesel lorry business in 1933 as **ERF**, while William continued with the main company, now Foden Trucks and still based at Sandbach.

Fodor *(publishers)*

The popular travel guides take their name from the Hungarian-born American writer Eugene Fodor (1905-1991), the son of a businessman, who began his career studying political economy in Czechoslovakia, France, and Germany. He then went to work for a French shipping company, writing articles in his spare time about exotic places and life aboard ship. He submitted these to French and Hungarian newspapers and his obvious love of adventure and flair for writing, coupled with his knowledge of foreign languages, brought him work in 1930 as a travel correspondent and editor in Prague and then, in 1934, in London. His first book, *1936—On the Continent* was a bestseller in Europe and the United States. In 1938, when in America on business, he decided to stay there, becoming a naturalized citizen in 1942. In 1949 he settled in Paris and founded Fodor's Modern Guides, Inc., to publish informative but readable guides to particular countries. His first three guides, published in 1951, covered France, Switzerland, and Italy.

Fokker *(aircraft)*

Dutch airman Anthony Fokker (1890-1939) built his first airplane in 1910 and taught himself to fly. In 1912 he set up a small aircraft factory at Johannisthal near Berlin, and in World War I produced more than 40 types of planes for the German High Command. After the war he set up a factory in the Netherlands. In 1922 Fokker emigrated to the USA where he became president of the Fokker Aircraft Corporation in New Jersey. He then concentrated on the development of commercial aircraft. In 1993 the Dutch Fokker company became a subsidiary of Daimler-Benz (*see* **Daimler**), but went bankrupt in 1996 after the Dutch government terminated further credit. In 1998 a new Dutch company, Rekkof Restart (spelling the name backward), was negotiating to resume its regional aircraft production.

Folger *(coffee)*

In 1849 three American brothers, Edward, Henry, and James Folger, left Nantucket, Massachusetts, for San Francisco. While the older men went off to the mountains soon after they arrived, young James Folger (1835-1889) stayed behind and started a coffee business, eventually building it into a prosperous trade selling roasted and ground beans to miners. In 1859 he became a partner in a coffee and spice mill. When the mill failed during the 1865 recession, Folger bought out his partner and convinced the creditors to let him continue operating the business. Soon all of the firm's debts were paid and its name changed to J.A. Folger & Co. Folger's son, James II, succeeded him as head of the firm in 1889.

Food Fair *(supermarkets)*

The American chain of supermarkets was founded in the 1920s in Harrisburg, Pennsylvania, by Samuel Friedland (1896-1985), a Russian immigrant to the United States. Their number grew, until there were some 450 Food Fair supermarkets along the Eastern Seaboard. But competition was also growing, and eventually, in 1978, the company filed for protection from creditors under Chaper 11 of the United States Bankruptcy Act. The Friedland family gave up control of the business, which took a new name, Pantry Pride, and moved to a new base in Fort Lauderdale.

Force (*breakfast cereal*)

Force Wheat Flakes originated in Canada, from where they were exported to Britain in 1902. The origin of the name is obvious, but the cereal itself became memorably associated with an advertising campaign centering on a sprightly character, "Sunny Jim," sporting a monocle and dressed in Regency clothing. He was shown jumping over a fence with the accompanying jingle: "High o'er the fence leaps Sunny Jim, / 'Force' is the food that raises him." Sunny Jim himself is said to have been the creation of an American schoolgirl named Ficken, while the jingle was written by Minnie Hanff. "Sunny Jim" was entered in the *Trade Marks Journal* of March 30, 1904 by "Cereal Food Products. The firm trading as the 'Force' Food Company, 6, Holborn Viaduct, London, E.C.; Manufacturers." *The Story of Sunny Jim*, published at this time by the Force Food Co., included the following doggerel:

Jim Dumps was a most unfriendly man,
Who lived his life on a hermit plan,
He'd never stop for a friendly smile,
But trudged along in his moody style.
Till 'Force' one day was served to him.
Since then they call him Sunny Jim.

Ford (*automobiles*)

The story of Henry Ford (1863-1947) is one of the most famous in commercial history. He was born a farmer's son near Dearborn, Michigan, and from an early age was fascinated by farm machinery, especially steam engines. The interest led him to train as a machinist and craftsman in his own right, and in 1896, as chief engineer of the Edison Illuminating Company, Detroit, he manufactured his first automobile, a 2-cylinder, 4-horsepower, 3-kilowatt model. In 1903 he founded the company that bears his name, producing the world's most popular car, the Model T, or "Tin Lizzie," in 1908, and mass-producing it from 1913. The Model A followed in 1928, and the V8 engine in 1932. Ford's son, Edsel Bryant Ford (1893-1943), was president of the Ford Motor Co. from 1919 to his death, when his elderly father reassumed the presidency, with Edsel's son, Henry Ford II (1917-1987), as vice president. The Ford family name is still prominent in the company boardroom. *See also* **Edsel**.

The one thing to remember about the Fords is that their name is on the building and they never forget it. If you get the chance to run the Ford Motor Co. and your name isn't Ford, you're likely to get pushed out at some point. This is history going back to Old Henry, who started the company in 1903 (*Forbes Global*, March 19, 2001).

Foremost-McKesson (*dairy products and drugs*)

The second half of the name is that of John McKesson (d. 1891), a descendant of an old colonial family, who opened a drugstore in Manhattan in 1833. In 1840 he took another New Yorker, Daniel Robbins, as partner, and changed the name of his enterprise to McKesson-Robbins. The men's respective families continued the business, but the McKessons split off in 1924 to form the New York Quinine & Chemical Works, and three years later the Robbins family sold McKesson & Robbins (as it had become) to the infamous crooked entrepreneur F.D. Coster, whose real name was Philip Musica. After a scandal, involving large-scale embezzlement, Coster (Musica) shot himself in 1939. The McKesson-Robbins firm kept a low profile after the humiliation, but continued in business, and in 1967 was taken over by the dairy company Foremost, itself founded as a merger between **J.C. Penney**'s Foremost Dairy, founded in Jacksonville, Florida, in the 1920s and named for Penney's prize bull, and Ferndale, California's Central Creamery, founded in 1905.

Formica (*plastic laminate*)

The hard, smooth, durable material, used to make objects such as tabletops and wallboards, has a name devised in 1913 by two young **Westinghouse** engineers, Herbert A. Faber and Daniel J. O'Conor, Jr., who were instrumental in discovering a natural resin substitute *for mica* as an insulation material for electrical wiring. The italicized words are said to have given the name of the company they founded that same year. On the other hand, Formica itself is made from formaldehyde resins (similar to **Bakelite**), and "formaldehyde" derives from a blend of "formic (acid)" and "aldehyde," so ultimately goes back to Latin *formica*, "ant." The name was entered by the Formica Insulation Company of Cincinnati, Ohio, in the US Patent Office *Official Gazette* of January 10, 1922, and subsequently in the *Gazette* of March

12, 1946: "For laminated sheets of wood, fabric, or paper impregnated with synthetic resin and consolidated under heat and pressure, for use on table tops, furniture, and wall panelling."

Forte *(hotels and restaurants)*

The British company evolved from Trusthouse Forte (THF), formed in 1970 (as Trust Houses Forte) in a merger between Trust Houses Group Ltd. and Forte Holdings Ltd. The former enterprise was founded in 1903 as the grandly named Hertfordshire and Essex Public House Trust Company with the aim of reviving the standards of the old coaching inns of Britain, many of which had declined with the coming of the railways. Over the years the company developed into a nationwide group of hotels, with "Trust" implying that these were managed by, or in the trust of, the company itself, as distinct from hotels that were privately run or owned by breweries. Forte is the name of Sir Charles Forte (b. 1908), the direct descendant of a family of Italian immigrants who had set up ice-cream parlors and cafés, the first in Dundee, Scotland, in the early 1880s. Forte was himself born in Italy, but taken to Scotland by his father at the age of eight. On completing his education he went to Rome to perfect his Italian, then returned to Britain to join his father's catering business, founded in 1935, and start a chain of milk bars in London. Catering led to the acquisition of restaurants and hotels, including the prestigious Café Royal in 1954 and Waldorf Hotel in 1958. Lord Forte's son, Rocco Forte (b. 1945), took over from his father as chief executive in 1983 and the company name became Forte in 1991. In 1996 the company left Forte hands in a takeover by **Granada**. Rocco Forte then set up a new hotel group, RF Hotels.

Fortnum & Mason *(food and department store)*

The famous London, England, store was started in 1707 by William Fortnum, a footman in the household of Queen Anne, together with his friend Hugh Mason, a grocer. It seems that the enterprising Mr. Fortnum had been selling cut-price candles to the staff of the royal household before this, and it is likely that the two men's first business was little more than in used candles, plus a few groceries, from a stall in a doorway in Piccadilly. This trade then progressed to that of a grocery, with the business being handed down to successive generations of Fortnums and Masons until about 1800, since when there have been no members of either family connected with the firm. The elegant premises of Fortnum & Mason, however, remain in Piccadilly today, and figures of Mr. Fortnum and Mr. Mason appear on the hour on the clock over the main entrance and bow to each other.

Foster Brothers *(menswear)*

The British company had its origins in the draper's shop opened in 1876 in Pontefract, Yorkshire, by William Foster. There was no actual "brother" as Foster did not have one. He maintained the illusion, however, by having two photographs of himself in his advertisements, one full-face, the other profile. Eight years after opening, Foster moved his business to Birmingham, where the company's head office remained until 1967, when it moved to Solihull. Foster died in 1914, and his wife remained as chairman with his son as managing director. The menswear stores subsequently bore the simple name "Fosters," but in 2001 Fosters Menswear, as it had become, was merged with a similar company, Jeans for Sale, to become d2, a new casualwear retail chain with 86 outlets in the UK and Ireland.

Foster's *(beer)*

The internationally famous name derives from two individuals about whom little is known. In 1886, W.M. and R.R. Foster came to Australia from New York to set up a brewing business. They lived in George Street, Fitzroy, now a Melbourne suburb, having brought with them a Mr. Sieber, a German-American who had studied brewing in Cologne, and Frank A. Rider, a New York refrigeration engineer. Between them the men built a brewery in Rokeby Street, Collingwood, just south of Fitzroy. Brewing started in 1888, and the following year the Melbourne public had its first taste of ice-cool Foster's beer. But the business soon faced keen competition from cheaper imported beers, so that within the year the Foster brothers sold their brewery to a local syndicate and returned to the United States, never to be heard from again, at least in Australia. But their names lives on in the Foster

Lager Brewing Company Ltd., and is now as familiar in their native America as it is in the country where they first arrived over a century ago.

Foulsham *(publishers)*

Not much information is available about William Foulsham, who founded the present British company in 1819, as the firm's records were destroyed by German air raids in World War II. It is known, however, that Foulsham was a friend of the astrologer Edwin Raphael and that when the latter published *Raphael's Prophetic Almanac and Year Book* in the year stated, Foulsham decided to set up as publisher to issue this publication annually. The venture was a success, and Foulsham published a variety of astrological and occult works over the next few years, some written by Raphael, others by himself. W. Foulsham & Co. is now best known for *Foulsham's Old Moore's Almanac*. The firm first published this popular astrological work in 1919, having acquired it from The Stationers Company, who had originally brought it out in 1697 and named it after its founder-author, the astrologer Francis Moore. Foulsham is one of the few remaining family companies in the UK to survive takeover.

Four Roses *(whiskey)*

In 1865, at the end of the War Between the States, Paul Jones, a young officer from the Virginia regiment of the Confederate Army, and his 66-year-old father, Colonel Paul Jones, went into the distilling business, and soon established a reputation for fine whiskey. By 1886 the business had outgrown its facilities, so the Jones family decided to move to Louisville, Kentucky, and it was there that Four Roses whiskey was born. The origin of the name is uncertain. According to one account, it refers to the four red roses worn as a corsage by a Southern belle at a cotillion in antebellum days as a sign that she would marry the young Paul Jones. According to another, the four roses were the four red roses worn by four girls dressed alike when they visited the mansion owned by the R.M. Rose family of distillers in Atlanta. When this account appeared in an Atlanta newspaper, however, a descendant of the Rose family said that the name in fact referred to an early ancestor, Rufus Rose, who established the distillery. He was thus the first rose, while his wife and two children were the other three.

4711 *(eau de Cologne)*

The unusual name for the toilet water is said to owe its origin to the gift of a scrap of paper made by a monk to the man who had given him refuge. This was Ferdinand Mühlens, the Cologne banker who founded the firm that first made the fragrance. The paper simply contained the figure 4711, an allegedly secret formula for making "Aqua mirabilis," the "miracle water" that was genuine eau de Cologne. Six years later, in 1794, when the French occupied Cologne, the soldiers had difficulty reading names in the Gothic script and chalked this number on the wall of the original factory building on the Glockengasse by way of an address. The number was adopted by Mühlens as a brand name, but could not be registered in Germany until 1915 because of a regulation in the German Trademark Act which excluded the registration of marks consisting of numbers or letters. Only when the firm pointed to the lengthy use of the name, established as its characteristic symbol, was registration allowed. The name was registered internationally in 1923.

Fox *see* **Twentieth Century-Fox**

Fox's *(cookies, or biscuits)*

The British firm is based in Batley, Kirklees, where Michael Spedding opened a small confectioner's shop in 1853. His sweet biscuits (cookies) and especially his brandy snaps, soon became commercially popular, so that in 1864 he moved to larger premises, although still in Batley. He retired in 1897, when his business was taken over by his son-in-law, Fred Ellis Fox, who added further appetizing lines to the existing cookies, such as ginger buttons. After World War I, Fox began a programme of expansion, and his firm became known simply as Fox's Biscuits, as which it remains today, still in Batley.

Fox's *("Glacier Mints")*

The British company began life as a wholesale grocery and confectionery business, set up in the 19th century in Leicester, England, by Walter Richard Fox. He made his own confectionery, and liked to devise new lines with attractive names, such as "Cupid's Flavours," "What Ho," and "Ocean Wave." He did not devise the company's best known line, however, the "Glacier Mint." This was the creation of Fox's son, Eric, who by the end of World War I had discovered a potential market for a type of clear, smooth peppermint. The result was the familiar Fox's Glacier Mint, with the picture of a polar bear standing on an ice floe (rather than a glacier, to be precise).

Foyle's *(booksellers)*

The full name of the London bookstore is W. & G. Foyle Ltd., after the two brothers who founded it, William Foyle (1885-1963) and Gilbert Foyle (1886-1971), the sons of a Shoreditch grocer. On failing their Civil Service examinations, they advertised their unwanted textbooks for sale. They met with an unexpectedly large response, so realized that there was a demand for books of this type. In 1903 they accordingly set up their own bookselling business, making their first base off the City Road. Four years later they moved to Charing Cross Road, taking larger premises to broaden their stock, which at this stage was still all secondhand. New books duly followed in 1912. William was the dominant brother in the business, and it was his daughter, Christina Foyle (1911-1999), who gained fame for her "literary luncheons," first held in 1930, enabling book lovers to see and hear famous writers.

F-Plan Diet *(diet)*

The type of high-fiber diet was devised by Audrey Eyton and introduced in her book *The F-Plan* (1982). The "F" stands for "fiber," meaning food material such as bran and cellulose that is not broken down by digestion. The name (as "F Plan Diet") was entered by P. Leiner Nutritional Products, Inc., of Torrance, California, in the US Patent Office *Official Gazette* of May 1, 1984.

Frame's Tours *(travel agents and coach tours)*

The British company was started in 1881 by John Frame (1848-1934), a Scottish-born tailor who lived in Preston, Lancashire. In his spare time he organized temperance and Sunday school outings, and this provided the motivation for him to enter the tourist business. At first he was an agent for railroads and shipping lines, developing the firm internationally. Early in the 20th century he then started to op-

erate sightseeing coaches for tours in London. He also began to open up hotels, one of the best known being the Bonnington Hotel, in Southampton Row, which first received guests in 1911. The company is still owned by the Frame family, although all except one of the travel agencies were sold to **Thomas Cook** in 1985 to allow for the development of the other side of the business, coaching and hotels.

Francis-Barnett *(motorcycles)*

The first half of the name is that of Gordon Francis, son of Gordon J. Francis, cofounder of **Lea-Francis**, who made both automobiles and motorcycles. The second half is that of Francis's father-in-law, Arthur Barnett, who together with Gordon Francis Sr. provided capital for the new enterprise, which produced its first machine in 1920. The company was taken over by Associated Motor Cycles (*see* **AJS**) in 1947 and the last of the "Fanny-Bs," as their fans called them, left the factory in 1966.

Frank Cooper *("Oxford" marmalade)*

Frank Cooper (1844-1927) was an English grocer with a shop at 84 High Street, Oxford. There in 1874 his young wife, Sarah Cooper, made 74 pounds of marmalade from an old family recipe on her kitchen range. Such an amount was too much for the family to consume, so Frank offered to package the surplus in earthenware jars and sell it in his shop. It sold so well that Sarah could not produce enough of it in the kitchens behind the shop. In 1900, therefore, production moved to a "manufactory" in Park End Street, and later still to a factory on the site of the former Oxford Ice Rink and Majestic Cinema. Today Frank Cooper products, which extend beyond mere marmalade, are manufactured at a factory in Redditch, Worcestershire, while Frank's original shop in Oxford is a museum. *See also* **Oxford**.

Franklin Mint *(collectibles)*

The Franklin Mint is a multinational company with headquarters in Pennsylvania. It is named for the famous American statesman and inventor, Benjamin Franklin, who although born in Boston came to settle in Philadelphia. The company was actually founded in 1964 by one Joe Segal, who left it in the early 1970s. It originally aimed to produce commemorative coins and ingots, a specialty which explains its acquisition in 1969 of John Pinches, a British firm of medalists. The latter business originated as a private mint in the early 19th century, taking its name from John Pinches (1825-1905), the first of his family to conduct the firm. Its effective founder, however, was the medalist William Joseph Taylor (1802-1885). The firm was sold off to Franklin Mint when no further member of the Pinches family remained to continue the concern.

Fran's *(chocolates)*

Fran is the US chocolate maker Fran Bigelowe, who graduated as an accountant and only became interested in cooking and pastry-making after her two children were born. She studied with the legendary Josephine Araldo in San Francisco, then enrolled in the newly-opened California Culinary Academy in 1976. All the time her children were growing up, Fran was determined to start her own business, and this finally happened after the family moved back to Seattle in 1980. In 1981, Fran invested her life savings and opened her shop in the Madison Park neighborhood, where her dark chocolate truffles soon found an enthusiastic clientele. Fran's chocolates are now sold in US retail stores and are equally available by mail order.

Fraser, Gordon *see* **Gordon Fraser**

Fraser, House of *see* **House of Fraser**

Fray Bentos *(meat products)*

The products take their name from what is now the city and port of Fray Bentos, in western Uruguay, founded in 1859 and subsequently becoming important when the first large-scale meatpacking plant in Uruguay was established there in 1861. The town was originally named Independencia but was renamed for an 18th-century religious hermit of the region, his name meaning "Brother Benedict."

Frazer Nash *(automobiles)*

There has been much debate whether the name of the British auto manufacturers should have a hyphen or not. Whatever the case, there was one in the name of its founder, Captain Archibald Frazer-Nash (d. 1965), who began production of the racing cars and sports cars at Kingston upon Thames, Surrey, in 1924. The factory moved to Isleworth, north London, in

1926 as A.F.N. Ltd., and remained there until 1956, when production ceased.

Frederick's *(underwear)*

The man who introduced the crotchless panty to America was Frederick Mellinger (1914-1990), born on the Lower East Side of New York City. At 14, he got his first job with a firm that specialized in "intimate apparel." While there, he learned the art of mail-order merchandising, and began to evolve his own concepts of style. He came to the conclusion that women's clothes and in particular underwear needed to be more "romantic," and in 1946 opened his first mail-order business, Frederick's of Fifth Avenue, to remedy this deficit. The following year he moved his business to Hollywood Boulevard, where he began to market a range of underwear, from see-through nighties to panties with emboidered messages. His mail-order firm then branched out into shops across America, in towns such as Dayton, Ohio, and Omaha, Nebraska. The enterprise was such a success that by the time of Frederick's death there were 100 stores, proving the truth behind their creator's slogan, "Sex never goes out of fashion."

Freefone *(toll-free telephone service)*

The name for the service whereby a subscribing organization pays for incoming telephone calls derives fairly obviously from "free" and a respelled "phone" and was entered in the US Patent Office *Official Gazette* of May 8, 1984, with a note of first use on September 2, 1975. The service was in operation in the UK in the late 1950s, but the term is not proprietary and is also spelled "freephone.".

Freeman Hardy Willis *(footwear)*

The British company with its long familiar triple name dates back to 1870, when Edward Wood (1839-1917) began making boots and shoes in Leicester, trading as Edward Wood & Co. In 1876 he turned his business into a limited company, appointing as its directors Arthur Hardy, an architect, William Freeman, his factory manager, and Frederick Willis, his traveler. Wood himself was the chairman, and he now named his company, somewhat self-effacingly, as Freeman, Hardy & Willis Ltd. Trading began in 1877 from 39 Portland Street, Leicester, and the first retail outlet opened that same year in Wandsworth, London, followed by shops in other towns and cities. By 1921 the company owned 428 shops. Freeman and Willis did not remain long as directors, but Hardy was succeeded by his son, and the Hardy family were connected with the company until 1953, when Hugh Hardy resigned his directorship. The "and" of the name was dropped in about 1960, when the company was extensively modernized. Apart from anything else, it was found that its omission allowed bolder lettering for the triple name on shop facias. In 1982, by which time it had changed its name to the British Shoe Corporation, the company was the largest retail footwear store chain in Europe, with 551 outlets.

Freeman's *(mail order house)*

Hardly any information is available about the Mr. Freeman who gave the British company its name, and even his initials are not known. What is known is that the firm arose from a tailoring business started in 1905 at a house in Lavender Hill, London, by four people. They were A.G. Rampton, his son S.C. Rampton, one W.E. Jones, and the shadowy Mr. Freeman, who may have been related in some way to the Ramptons. In 1922 the business expanded to premises in the old Gem Cinema in southwest London. In 1936 it finally moved to 139 Clapham Road, London, where it has remained ever since, now with a staff of several thousand.

Freeserve *(Internet service provider)*

Europe's biggest Internet service provider was the creation in 1998 of the British entrepreneur John Pluthero (b. 1963), then an employee of **Dixons**. His innovation, backed by Dixons boss Sir Stanley Kalms, offered "free" access to the Internet, and was thus the first UK service provider not to charge a monthly subscription. In 2000 the business was acquired by the French company Wanadoo.

Freightliner *(rail transport system)*

The British name, combining "freight" and "line," is that of a special train used for transporting freight that has been loaded from road vehicles. The system was developed by **British Railways** from 1963, the first such train running the following year. In 1969 the system was transferred to a separate company, Freightlin-

ers Ltd., but in 1978 was returned to direct British Railways control. In 1988 the activity was merged with Speedlink to form Railfreight Distribution, but in 1995 once again became a separate business, in preparation for privatization.

French Connection *(fashionwear)*

The British firm was founded in 1972 by Stephen Marks (b. 1945), a hairdresser's son who quit school at 16 to become a tennis professional but who had to opt out for lack of money. Although implying a link with French fashion, the name rode on the back of the popular movie *The French Connection*, released the previous year. In 1997 Marks launched the notorious "fcuk" logo, ostensibly standing for "French Connection United Kingdom." It at least gave the brand instant recognition in the UK, and a similar *succès de scandale* soon followed in the USA. Today French Connection is the best-known British High-Street fashion brand in the world, with 1,500 outlets across the globe.

French's *("Cream Salad Mustard")*

Robert T. French (1823-1893), born in Ithaca, New York, spent much of his adult life working as a salesman for a New York City wholesaler of coffee, tea, and spices. In 1880 he started his own business, and was soon joined by his sons, George and Francis. In 1883 the firm was moved to Rochester, New York, where it produced spices and other products, including bird seed. It was French's sons who introduced the famous mustard in 1904. Up to that time, American mustards were mostly hot and fiery, but the French brothers believed there was a market for a milder, creamy variety. French's Cream Salad Mustard was a success from the first, and in 1912 the company built a new Rochester plant to meet the demand. Ten years later, a second factory was built and national advertising begun. In 1980, when the R.T. French Company celebrated its centennial, the firm was selling 500,000 jars of mustard a day. French's mustard must not be confused with French mustard, which like its namesake is a milder form of mustard by comparison with strong English mustard.

Freon *(refrigerant)*

The aerosol refrigerant, dating from the

1930s, contains fluorine and perhaps bases its name on this or else on "freeze." The name was entered by **Du Pont** in the *Trade Marks Journal* of February 25, 1959 for: "Fluorinated hydrocarbons being chemical substances for use as propellents for aerosols."

Fribourg & Treyer *(cigarettes)*

The British firm arose from the shop opened by a Mr. Fribourg in 1720 at 33 Haymarket, London, to sell tobacco. He was joined at the end of the 18th century by Gottlieb Augustus Treyer, a Dutchman with an English wife. Cigarettes seem to have been added to the shop's stock of tobacco, cigars, and other smokers' requisites in the mid-19th century. The shop was patronized by royalty and other notable figures, and remained open until 1981. Fribourg & Treyer cigarettes, however, continue to be manufactured by the House of Bewlay.

Friends' Provident *(insurance)*

The Friends' Provident Institution was established in Bradford, Yorkshire, England, in 1832 to provide life insurance for the Society of Friends (Quakers). In 1915 the Friends' Provident Institution Act was passed, incorporating the institution as a mutual life office. In 1918 it acquired the Century Insurance Co. (founded in 1885) and changed its name to the Friends' Provident and Century Life Office. In 1974 it adopted its present name, formally Friends' Provident Life Office, and the following year sold the Century Insurance Co. to the Phoenix Assurance Co., after which it specialized as a life and pension office.

Frigidaire *(refrigerators)*

The name is said to have been devised from "frigid air" by the founder of **General Motors**, William Crapo Durant, in 1918, when he privately purchased a small company called the Guardian Refrigerator Co. The following year he sold his acquisition to General Motors, when the company became the Frigidaire Corporation. The name began as pseudo-French, but became a genuine word in French itself for a refrigerator, as if from Latin *frigidarium*, the term for a cooling room in a Roman bath. The Frigidaire Corporation remained a division of General Motors until 1979, when the company's name and assets, with the exception of the original plant at Dayton, Ohio, were sold to White Consolidated Industries. The name was entered in the *Trade Marks Journal* of December 16, 1931.

Frisbee *(toy disks)*

The plastic disks, sailed between players by a flick of the wrist, take their name from the Frisbie Pie Company, Bridgeport, Connecticut, founded by William R. Frisbie in 1871, whose pie tins could be similarly used. In 1948 Frederick Morrison, a 28-year-old Los Angeles building inspector, produced a plastic version. He originally called it "Morrison's Flyin' Saucer," but later changed the name to "Frisbee," altering the spelling of the company name to avoid legal problems. In 1957 the rights to the Frisbee were acquired by the Wham-O Manufacturing Co., San Gabriel, California. (The well-known novelty firm was so named from the slingshots they made, which when fired made a sound like "wham-o!") Frisbie's itself went out of business in 1958. The name was entered in the US Patent Office *Official Gazette* of May 26, 1959 for: "Toy Flying Saucers for Toss Games in Class 22."

Frisby's *(footwear)*

All of the British shoe shops named Tandem in the 1980s were earlier named Frisby's. The name is that of Joseph Frisby, born in about 1840 into a Leicestershire farming family. He seems to have made shoes in Leicester from about 1860, selling them in Chesterfield market place. Shops later opened in Leicester and Chesterfield itself, as well as elsewhere in the region. Frisby married the daughter of a Leicester hosiery manufacturer in the 1880s, and they lived in Rutland Street with a warehouse nearby, close to Halford Street (*see* **Halfords**). The business moved to larger premises in Leicester in the early 20th century, and it was during the actual transfer that Joseph Frisby died, leaving the firm in the hands of his son, also named Joseph. Precise dates are unknown, as all of the Frisby family records were destroyed in a fire.

Frito-Lay *see* **Lay's**

Frog *(model aircraft kits)*

In 1932 two British brothers, Charles and John Wilmot, founded International Model Aircraft Ltd., marketing their flying models with the promotional tag "Flies Right Off the

Ground." The initials of this gave "FROG," a name soon adopted by the manufacturers themselves. Their models were marketed exclusively by Lines Brothers of **Tri-Ang**. The name was entered in the *Trade Marks Journal* of November 1, 1933.

Fruehauf *(truck trailers)*

The American corporation takes its name from August Charles Fruehauf (1868-1930), who ran a sizeable blacksmith shop in Detroit. One day in 1914 a local lumber merchant, Frederic M. Sibley, Sr., came to Fruehauf and asked him if he could help transport his pleasure boat to his summer place in upper Michigan. He didn't want to take the boat by horse and wagon as the journey would take too long. Could perhaps Fruehauf devise a contraption to hook to Sibley's Ford Model T roadster so that he could haul the boat? Fruehauf came up with a "semi-trailer," as he called it, and it worked so well that Sibley commissioned more for his lumberyard. Business boomed, and four years later, in 1918, Fruehauf incorporated the Fruehauf Trailer Company. The company continued to prosper, first under Fruehauf himself, then under his son, Harvey Charles Fruehauf (1896-1968). The company became the Fruehauf Corporation in 1963.

Frye *(boots)*

The heavy leather boots, reaching to the calf and adapted from traditional Western boots, derive their name from their US manufacturers, who introduced them in the 1970s.

Fry's *(chocolate)*

Fry's claims to be Britain's oldest chocolate manufacturer. The firm dates back to 1748, when Joseph Fry (1728-1787), a Quaker apothecary, came to Bristol and began to make chocolate. In 1759 he bought a shop which had been opened in 1728 by one Walter Churchman to make and sell chocolate, and this gave him the patent rights to produce chocolate on a commercial scale. On Fry's death, the business was continued by his wife and son, Joseph Storrs Fry (1767-1835), as Anna Fry & Son, and when the latter's own three sons, Joseph, Francis, and Richard, joined their father in the business, the firm became J.S. Fry & Sons, as which it was familiar for many years. In 1919 Fry was taken over by **Cadbury**, but the name

remains for certain candy lines, such as Fry's Cream Sticks, introduced in 1853 (renamed Fry's Chocolate Creams in 1866), the first bars to be sold that consisted of something other than just chocolate. Fry's Turkish Delight followed in 1914.

Fuji Bank *(bank)*

The Japanese bank originated in a money-lending operation established in the 1860s by Yasuda Zenjiro, the founder of the Yasuda business combine. In 1880 it became the Yasuda Bank, and when the business combine was broken up after World War II, the bank was reorganized in 1948 under its present name. It is that of Mt. Fuji, Japan's highest mountain, southwest of Tokyo, whose own name is thought to be of Ainu origin, meaning "everlasting life." The mountain is regarded as the sacred symbol of Japan and thus occurs in a number of commercial names, such as that of the Fujica camera, manufactured by the Fuji Film Company, where it is combined with the "ca-" of "camera."

Fuller *(brushes)*

The Fuller Brush Company owes its origin to Alfred Carl Fuller (1885-1973), born in Welsford, Nova Scotia, Canada, a farmer's son. In 1903 he went to Boston, Massachusetts, where his siblings already lived, and there found work for a time as a streetcar conductor. Following further short-lived jobs, Fuller started work in 1905 as a salesman with the Somerville Brush and Mop Company, a business begun by one of his brothers. He proved to be an effective brush salesman, readily winning the confidence of housewives, and the following year went into the business himself, setting up a brush-making workshop in the basement of his sister's house. Within a few months Fuller had moving his enterprise to Hartford, Connecticut, and by 1910 he had 260 dealers and a nationwide business. In 1921 the *Saturday Evening Post* coined the term "Fuller Brush Man," introducing an American icon that became the subject of cartoons in the national press. Alfred remained chairman of the Fuller Brush Company until 1968, when it was sold to Consolidated Food Corporation.

Fuller's *(beer)*

The British company traces its ultimate history to an Elizabethan brewery in Chiswick,

London. In 1685 it passed to the Mawson family, who leased it to Wiliam Harvest in 1740. In 1782 it was acquired by John Thompson and David Roberts. On Roberts's death Thompson was joined by his son, Douglas Thompson, who ran the brewery after his father died and in 1816 named it the Griffin. In 1821 Philip Wood, brother of Matthew Wood, Lord Mayor of London in 1815, was called in to reorganize the business and in 1829 was joined by John Fuller. When Fuller died in 1839 he was succeeded by his son, John Bird Fuller, who was joined in 1845 by Henry Smith and John Turner to form Fuller, Smith and Turner Ltd. The present company dates its founding from the latter year, and in 1995 launched a special "Strong Ale" to celebrate its 150th anniversary. "ESB" ("Extra Special Bitter"), launched in 1969, is now well known both sides of the Atlantic.

Fullers *(cakes)*

The British company originated in the visit of a party of American cake and confectionery manufacturers to London in 1889, with the aim of exhibiting their products. A member of the group was William Bruce Fuller, from Buffalo, New York, whose goods were so popular that he decided to stay on in Britain. He opened a shop in London's Oxford Street, and ran it himself until 1895 when he was joined by Arthur Burdett, who set up a limited company the following year and became its managing director. Burdett was keen on the latest technology then available, and when Fuller opened a new factory and bakery in Hammersmith in 1900 it was one of the first in Britain to be lit by electricity. Fuller died in 1909 leaving the company in the capable hands of the Burdett family, who expanded the range of cakes and confectionery and opened many Fuller shops around the country.

Fulton *(umbrellas)*

Arnold Fulton, born in the Polish town of Częstochowa in 1931, was a Jewish Holocaust survivor originally named Arnold Frucht. After World War II, like many East Europeans, he made his way to Britain, where he hoped to become an engineer. He changed his name to Fulton, after the American submarine pioneer Robert Fulton (1765-1815), and in 1955 spotted a business opportunity when visiting his sister in Stockholm, Sweden. She and her husband made umbrellas, but used an archaic production method with almost everything done by hand. Fulton designed some machines to do the work faster and better, then thought he could use them to build a business in London. The result was the A. Fulton Company Ltd., founded in 1957. At first Fulton struggled. He approached **Selfridges** but was told the chief buyer was too busy to see him. Fulton persisted, and at last managed to see the buyer only to be told he did not know what he was doing and that his product would never sell. He pleaded with the buyer, saying he was desperate, and would be bankrupt if he did not get into Selfridges. The buyer relented, and took two dozen umbrellas on sale or return. That was on a Saturday morning. In the afternoon it poured with rain, and Selfridges sold out. On Monday the buyer phoned to say he needed 240 umbrellas urgently. Fulton had broken through the barrier. Repeat orders followed, and he was soon supplying **House of Fraser**, **John Lewis**, and **Marks & Spencer**.

Funk & Wagnalls *(dictionary publishers)*

Isaac Kauffman Funk (1839-1912) was born near Clifton, Ohio, the son of a farmer. He graduated from Wittenberg College in 1860 and from its theological seminary the following year, after which he held pastorates at various Lutheran churches. In 1872 he took up religious journalism, and gradually expanded into general publishing, taking as partner Adam Willis Wagnalls (1843-1924), a lawyer and college friend. In 1891 they incorporated their enterprise as the Funk & Wagnalls Company, and in 1893 produced their first dictionary, *A Standard Dictionary of the English Language*, a work soon regarded as definitive and noted for its emphasis on ease of use and current usage.

Fuzzy-Felt *(toy)*

While cutting gaskets in England in World War II as her contribution to the "war effort," Lois Allan (1905-1989), born in Morristown, New Jersey, found that offcuts from the gaskets (the "felt") would adhere to the felt backs of table mats (the "fuzzy") to make pictures that could be arranged and rearranged and so amuse the children of the working mothers. After the war she and her husband, Peter Allan, decided to market her idea for "Fuzzy-Felt." Launching a new product was not easy, but eventually, in 1950, production began in a factory at Farnham Common, Surrey, where Lois went on to devise around 40 different titles for her toy. Later, memories of Fuzzy-Felt were often associated with Sunday school, where it was adopted as a pleasant pastime that would not harm Sunday-best clothes.

> "Little girl," he began, then he caught sight of the Fuzzy Felt.
> "What's that?"
> "Daniel," I answered.
> "But that's not right," he said, aghast. "Don't you know that Daniel escaped? In your picture the lions are swallowing him."
> "I'm sorry," I replied, putting on my best, blessed face. "I wanted to do Jonah and the whale, but they don't do whales in Fuzzy Felt. I'm pretending those lions are whales."
> (Jeanette Winterson, *Oranges Are Not the Only Fruit*, 1985)

Fyffes *(bananas)*

Bananas were a rarity in Britain until the last quarter of the 19th century, when Edward Wathen Fyffe (1853-1935) did much to change the situation. He was born in Gloucestershire into a tea-trading family, with a business set up some time in the 18th century. At first Fyffe tried farming, but soon abandoned it to join his father in importing tea, taking over the business on the latter's death in 1882. He married in 1884, but his wife was not strong and developed a form of tuberculosis. Fyffe was advised to take her to the Canary Islands for the benefit of her health. The family spent most of 1887 there, during which Mrs. Fyffe completely recovered and Fyffe himself realized the economic potential of the islands, especially with regard to their bananas, which sold very cheaply. He investigated the possibility of shipping bananas from the Canaries to London, and after setting up an import agency there was able to organize this on a regular basis, with the first consignment arriving in 1888. By 1897 the venture had proved so successful that the growers' syndicate in the Canaries decided to buy out the agency. Fyffe himself retired the same year and took no further part in the industry.

Fynnon *("health salts")*

The British preparation, a laxative, was evolved by Evan Jones, a Welsh chemist (drug-gist) with a shop in Caerphilly. Its name is Welsh accordingly, from *ffynnon*, "fountain," "well," "spring," suggesting a bubbling curative water. The "health salts" are actually crystalline sodium sulphate. The name was entered in the *Trade Marks Journal* of January 27, 1937.

Gaggia *(espresso coffee machines)*

The name is that of the Italian engineer Achille Gaggia, who developed a new type of coffee machine in the 1930s. His secret lay in the sprung-piston system, by which hot water was forced at high pressure through finely-ground coffee beans held in a filter. This avoided the need for steam, which produced an inferior brew. The espresso machines were first produced commercially in 1938, and were imported to the UK by an emigrant dental mechanic who was appalled at the quality of English coffee. By the 1990s 35 percent of all espresso machines were still being made by Gaggia, whose original design has been adapted to a wide range of models.

Gak *(toy)*

The malleable purple-colored substance of uncertain composition (perhaps a water-based blend of acrylic and silicone) followed in the footsteps of **Silly Putty** when it was launched by **Mattel** in 1992. Around 8 million units or "splats" were sold in 1993 at $3 each, and bans in some schools failed to halt the spread of the stretchy, bouncy toy, whose name suggests a blend of "gunk" (*see* **Gunk**) and "yuk."

Galalith *(celluloid substitute)*

The product resembling celluloid, made from the casein of milk with the addition of other substances, was used a substitute not only for celluloid but also for horn and ivory. Hence its name, from Greek *gala*, "milk," and *lithos*, "stone," entered by the German manufacturers, Vereinigte Gummiwaaren-Fabriken ("United Rubber Goods Works"), of Harburg-Wien, "in the United Kingdom, c/o Haseltine, Lake, & Co." of London, in the *Trade Marks Journal* of March 20, 1901 for: "Goods, included in Class 50 ..., made of Celluloid-like Material consisting of an Animal Substance (viz., Dried Curds) Hardened by means of Formaldehyde."

Galbani *(cheese)*

The Italian cheese company takes its name from Egidio Galbani (1858-1950), its founder in 1920. After World War II it diversified into dressed pork products, yogurts, desserts, and the like, and is now part of **Danone**. *See also* **Bel Paese**.

Galeries Lafayette *(department store)*

The fashionable Paris, France, store takes its name from the rue Lafayette, where a tiny haberdasher's was founded in 1893 by Théophile Bader. It expanded its premises in 1896 and restyled itself *Galeries Lafayette*, "Lafayette Galleries." It is now in the Boulevard Haussmann. The street was itself named for the French soldier and revolutionary Marie-Joseph de Lafayette (1757-1834).

Gale's *(beer)*

"Gale's Ales" are well known in the south of England, and especially in Hampshire. The company's history dates from 1847, when Richard Gale acquired the Ship and Bell public house at Horndean, near Portsmouth, Hampshire, together with its brewery. By 1855, when the management had passed to his son George Alexander Gale, the business had expanded to include the sale of wine and liquor, and this activity was formed into a registered company as George Gale & Co. in 1888. George Alexander Gale retired in 1896, but the firm was still family controlled a century later. *See also* **Hale's**.

Gallaher *(tobacco and cigarettes)*

The founder of the British company was Thomas Gallaher (originally Gallagher) (1840-1927), a farmer's son born at Templemoyle, Co. Londonderry, Ireland (now Northern Ireland). When still only 17, Tom Gallaher started a small business in Londonderry making and selling pipe tobacco. His tobacco was superior to the adulterated product then commonly sold in Ireland, and his enterprise prospered, enabling him to transfer his activity in 1863 to Belfast, where commercial possibilities were greater. Gallaher also began traveling to the United States to buy leaf, as well as replacing the old single-handed spinning tools, used to twist tobacco, with power-driven machinery. By the end of the 1880s, Gallaher had opened branches in both Dublin and London, and a decade later his business became a limited company, with "Park Drive" as its first successful brand. On Gallaher's death at the age of 87, his empire was taken over by his nephew, John Gallaher Michaels, but he was merely a year at the helm before control passed to a company headed by Edward de Stein, a London financier.

Galliano *(liqueur)*

The Italian herb liqueur in its distinctive slim bottle was created in 1896 by Armando Vaccari and named in honor of Giuseppe Galliano, the heroic Italian soldier who that same year had defended a fort for 40 days during the Italian invasion of Abyssinia. The fort in question, Enda Jesus, is depicted on the bottle's label. Galliano gained a high profile from the 1970s from its use as a key ingredient in a Harvey Wallbanger cocktail. (The story goes that the favorite drink of a Californian surfer named Harvey was a screwdriver with added Galliano. He downed several of these after losing an important contest, and on quitting the bar banged into furniture and collided with walls.)

Gallimard *(publishers)*

The French publishing house, noted for its editions of works by major contemporary writers such as Gide, Camus, Malraux, and Sartre, takes its name from Gaston Gallimard (1881-1975), who in 1911, together with the novelists André Gide (1869-1951) and Jean Schlumberger (1877-1968), set up a firm to publish the works of the contributors to the *Nouvelle Revue Française*, founded in 1909. The house was run from 1919 by Gallimard alone, and subsequently by his son, Claude.

Gallo *(wines)*

The name has long been synonymous with low-cost "pop" wines in the United States, although in recent years the firm has begun to improve its image and has become the producer of the top-selling brand of wine in the UK. The name behind the enterprise is that of Julio Gallo (1910-1993) and his elder brother Ernest (b. 1909). They were born near Modesto, California, the sons of Italian immigrants from Piedmont, and grew up working their father's smallish vineyard during Prohibition. On their father's tragic suicide in 1933, the brothers took their small inheritance and set up their own commercial bulk wine business. By 1940 they had grown sufficiently to buy bottling companies in Los Angeles and New Orleans, and that year marketed the first wine under their own name, mostly in the forms of sherries and muscatels. In 1983 a third brother, Joseph, Jr., started a cheese factory under the Gallo name, prompting the winery to sue him for trademark infringement. His countersuit charged that he had been cheated out of a one-third interest in the family business. The court ruled, however, that Julio and Ernest had started their own concern when Joseph was only 13 years old. *See also* **E&J**.

Galloway's *(cough syrup)*

The name behind the British brand is that of Philip Henry Galloway, born in Leeds in 1857. On leaving school, he was apprenticed to a Bradford chemist until 1880, when he went to London. There he worked for a number of different firms over the next ten years, eventually opening a pharmacy in Deacon Street, Walworth, in 1890. He soon added a retail department and opened another shop in Kennington, where his packing factory was located. It was not until 1905, however, that Philip Galloway began to market "Galloway's Cough Syrup" on a national basis. He retired from his flourishing business in 1930 and died soon after, leaving control of the company in the hands of his son, Jack Ellwood Galloway.

Gamage's *(department store)*

The London, England, store took its name from Albert Walter Gamage (1855-1930), born in Hereford the son of a glazier and plumber. On leaving school he was apprenticed to a draper in Winslow, Buckinghamshire, and in 1874 came to London to work with two drapery businesses, one retail, one wholesale. Four years later he and a young colleague, Frank Spain, opened a small hosiery shop in Holborn, obtaining stock on credit. Their business began to prosper when they started selling the newly popular hair brushes with wire bristles set in rubber, which they sold for ninepence less than other shops. In 1891 Gamage bought out Frank Spain and went ahead on his own, expanding his lines to include toys and games, among other things. Within a few years he had a full-blown department store on his hands, or a "People's Popular Emporium," as he called it. When he died his body rested in the Motoring Department of his great store, which continued in business until 1972, when it was pulled down and the site redeveloped.

Gambrinus *(beer)*

The Czech brewery of this name was founded in Pilsen (now Plzeň) in 1869. Its name is a corruption of the name of Jan Primus, otherwise John I (*c*.1251-1294), first Duke of Brabant and Lower Lorraine. He was born in Burgundy, and ruled what is now mostly Belgium, but is famous in many countries as the legendary King of Beer. Through marriage between royal houses, one of his descendants was king of Bohemia, the Czech state in which Pilsen stands. Around the time of World War I, the brewery moved to a site adjoining **Pilsner Urquell** and became part of that group.

Game Boy *(video game device)*

The hand-held electronic device, used to play computer games loaded in the form of cartridges, was first marketed by **Nintendo** in 1989 following its invention by the Japanese entrepreneur Gumpei Yokoi (1941-1997). Its name is of obvious origin, although "Boy" may allude not only to young males, the product's chief users, but to the device itself as something small and handy, or performing a specific function (like a liftboy who works a lift, newsboy who delivers papers, ballboy who retrieves tennis balls, and the like). There may also be a suggestion of "homeboy." The name was entered in the *Trade Marks Journal* of June 19, 1991.

Gamgee *see* **Robinson & Sons**

Gammexane *(insecticide)*

The product is so called after its chemical name, gamma-hexachlorocyclohexane. The name was entered by **ICI** in the *Trade Marks Journal* of November 7, 1945 but then re-entered as "Gammexan" in the *Journal* of October 3, 1951.

Gannett *(newspapers, radio and television stations)*

The American newspaper and broadcast chain takes its name from its founder, Frank Ernest Gannett (1876-1957), who began his career as a reporter for the *Buffalo Gazette* while still at high school. He also served as a correspondent for the *Ithaca Journal* and the *Syracuse Herald* in his junior year at Cornell University. In 1906 he bought his first newspaper, the *Elmira* (New York) *Gazette*, merging it with three other upstate New York papers to form the Gannett Company. By the time of his death, Frank Gannett had accumulated 30 newspapers and a whole range of radio and television stations.

Gannex *(raincoats)*

The name became familiar from the British firm's most famous customer, prime minister Harold Wilson, who regularly sported a Gannex coat in the 1960s. The firm that made them was founded by the unusually long-lived Benjamin Kagan (1879-1988), born Benjamin Kaganas into a prosperous Lithuanian family, with textile interests in that country. Kagan realized that he would have to take his textile business out of the country if he was to survive, so came to Britain in 1940 and set up his industry in Elland, Yorkshire, where he soon became the chief employer. It was his son Joseph Kagan (1915-1995) who started the Gannex raincoat side of the business in 1951, choosing a name that combined his own with "textile." The name was entered in the *Trade Marks Journal* of June 22, 1955.

The Gap *(fashionwear)*

The Gap was founded by Donald G. Fisher (b. 1928) and his wife Doris (b. 1931), who opened their first store in 1969 near San Francisco State University, naming it after "the generation gap" that was the phrase of the day. At first they sold mainly **Levi's** and records, and the store soon became a hangout for hippies. Expansion was slow, so that by 1970 there were only six Gap stores in the USA, but things picked up after 1990, when stores were set up in other countries, gaining special favor in the UK. By 2001 there were 3,700 Gap stores worldwide, although only 525 of these were international.

Garrard *(jewelry)*

The British London-based firm, famous as the Crown Jewellers since 1843, was founded not by a Garrard but by George Wickes (1697-1760), a goldsmith who in 1735 set up a business in Panton Street. In 1760 his activity was taken over by Edward Wakelin, a baker's son, with John Parker as partner. The firm supplied plate to the nobility, and in 1792 was joined by a new partner, Robert Garrard (1758-1818). Garrard had earlier been employed by Wakelin's son John, so was no stranger to the business. Garrard appears to have run the firm from 1812 until his death, when his eldest son, also Robert, took over and set about making the business the largest goldsmiths' and jewelers' concern in the West End. The Garrard name became dominant from then on, and remains one of the West End's prestige names still.

Garzanti *(publishers)*

The Italian publishing house is named for Aldo Garzanti (1883-1961), who in 1938 took over the firm of Fratelli Treves and gave it his name. He was succeeded by his son, the novelist and short-story writer Livio Garzanti (b. 1921).

Gateway *(computers)*

The direct-marketing personal-computer group was launched by the American engineer Theodore Waitt (b. 1964) and his brother Norman (b. 1954) on his father's Iowa cattle farm in 1985. By the end of the century he had amassed a fortune of $4.3 million and was running the world's sixth-largest computer group, No. 1 in the American consumer market. Its name is all about "access," both between the company and its customers, whom it deals with directly, and by its customers to the Internet. There is also a hint of farm imagery, as gates and ways are important in farm management. (The Gateway black-and-white spot corporate identity was actually inspired by the family's Holstein dairy cows.) In 1991 Norman fell out with his brother and quit Gateway to found Gold Circle Entertainment.

Gatorade *(soft drink)*

The soft drink, containing glucose, citric acid, sodium bicarbonate, and the like, is used by athletes instead of water to replenish their rapidly lost body fluids and salts. The drink was named in 1967 by James Free, a colleague of J. Robert Gade, the inventor of the drink, because it was an "aid to the Gators," the University of Florida football team. The "-ade" suffix is properly based on "lemonade."

Gauloise *(cigarettes)*

The familiar brand of French cigarettes has a name meaning "Gallic," denoting anything or anyone characteristic of France. The name "Cigarettes Gauloises" was entered in the *Trade Marks Journal* of March 17, 1920, and "Gauloises" alone in the *Journal* of August 23, 1933, the latter by the Service d'Exploitation Industrielle des Tabacs ("Tobacco Industry Promotion Board") of the Finance Ministry.

Gaumont *(movie theaters)*

The British cinemas owned by the **Rank** Organization take their name from the French motion picture pioneer Léon Ernest Gaumont (1864-1946), who in 1901 developed a method of synchronizing a film projector with a phonograph. He went into business in France in the 1890s and was soon also active in the UK. In 1909 the Gaumont Company was formed in Britain to manage the UK side of the business, and this company was acquired in 1927 by the Gaumont-British Picture Corporation, specifically formed to bring about the acquisition. In 1942 Gaumont-British became part of Rank. The use of the initials "GB" by Gaumont-British, especially in their newsreels, fortuitously suggested "Great Britain," a patriotic association welcomed by beleaguered British moviegoers in World War II.

Gayant *(beer)*

The French brewing company was formed in 1919 in the town of Douai, near Lille, from a merger of four family breweries. Its full name is Les Brasseurs de Gayant, "The Brewers of Gayant," referring to the two giants who are traditionally said to have protected the town. The firm is best known for its powerful "Bière du Démon" ("Demon Beer").

Gaymer's *("Olde English Cyder")*

The English family business had its origins in the village of Banham, near Diss, Norfolk, where in the mid-18th century Robert Gaymer, a farmer, made his first batch of cider. It was his grandson William Gaymer (1842-1936) who in 1870 developed the enterprise from a cottage craft into the commercial business it is today, with the company's head office at Attleborough, Norfolk, only five miles from where Robert Gaymer made his first vatful of cider.

GAZ *(trucks and automobiles)*

The major Soviet vehicle manufacturing plant was founded in Gorky (now Nizhny Novgorod) in 1932, its name being the abbreviation of Gor'kovsky Avtomobil'ny Zavod ("Gorky Automobile Works"). (Fortuitously, Russian *gaz* also happens to mean "gas.") Initially, trucks were given priority over cars, but

both types of vehicles were steadily produced, two of the best known car models being the "Pobeda" ("Victory"), launched after World War II, and the "Volga" (the river Gorky is on), first out in 1955. The "Chayka" ("Seagull") followed in 1959. The company is still in production.

Gazprom *(natural gas)*

The Russian natural gas company, the largest in the world, has a name that is short for *Gazovaya prom*yshlennost', "Gas Industry," or formerly in full Gosudarstvenny proizvodstvenny komitet po gazovoy promyshlennosti, "State Production Committee for the Gas Industry." This was the old Soviet gas ministry, which in 1989 became the Gazprom State Gas Concern. Its privatization was led by gas minister Viktor Chernomyrdin, who was suceeded in 1992 by Rem Vyakhirev. (Following corruption scandals, the latter was replaced by Aleksei Miller in 2001.) Gazprom now employs 340,000 workers across Russia and owns the world's largest pipeline system. Its subsidiaries include the influential NTV television station, and its bank, Gazprombank, is the fifth largest in Russia.

GEC *(electrical goods)*

The General Electric Company (GEC), Britain's largest manufacturer of electrical goods, traces its origin to an enterprise set up in London in 1886 by two young men, Hugo Hirst (originally Hirsch) (1863-1943), who had immigrated to England from his native Bavaria in 1880, and Gustav Byng (originally Binswanger) (1855-1910), a fellow Bavarian. At first they sold other people's products, but were soon making light fittings, bells, and lamps. Television sets were added when the the the BBC launched its service in 1936. GEC expanded greatly under its managing director from 1963, Lord Weinstock, one of Britain's greatest modern industrialists, who made a series of acquisitions that included English Electric and Marconi (*see* **RCA**). In 1999 GEC was itself renamed Marconi and was transformed into a full-blooded high-tech company. *See also* **Cable and Wireless**.

Gee, Cecil *see* **Cecil Gee**

Gee's *(cough medicine)*

The British-made medicine takes its name

from Samuel Jones Gee (1839-1911), born in London the son of a businessman. On leaving school he studied medicine at London University and in 1865 was appointed house surgeon at the Ormond Street Hospital for Sick Children, subsequently becoming a doctor at St. Bartholomew's Hospital. The medicine named for him is said to have been devised by the "lady bountiful" of a village who used it to cure the cough of one of Dr. Gee's hospital patients. Its official name in the *British Pharmacopeia* is *Linctus Scillae Compositus*, or a linctus based on squill, the dried roots of which were used as an expectorant. Dr. Gee claimed that if he had taken to selling his medicine commercially, he would have been a far richer man than he was as a hospital doctor.

Geest *(bananas)*

The founder of the British company was the Dutchman Jan van Geest (b. 1906), the son of a fruit and vegetable grower near The Hague. After helping his father at an early age, Geest studied horticulture, and by the time he was in his 20s was keen to put his knowledge of growing fruit and flowers to the test. He decided to try England, paying his first visit in 1930. The region where he settled, appropriately enough, was Holland, in Lincolnshire, where the intensive tulip-growing business convinced him that he could profitably set up a company. This he did in 1935, calling it Geest Horticultural Products, with a head office in Spalding. After World War II Geest wanted to expand his activities and in particular to ship bananas to Britain. But **Fyffes** already appeared to have a monopoly in that field, importing bananas from the Canary Islands. Geest therefore went to the West Indies, and in particular the Windward Islands. By the mid-1950s his new enterprise was well under way, but in 1996 the company sold off its banana business to concentrate on chilled prepared foods.

Genatosan *see* **Sanatogen**

General Dynamics *(armaments and defense equipment)*

The American company, one of the nation's top three military contractors, had its beginnings in the Electric Boat Company, founded in 1899, which built the first submarine purchased by the US Navy. The firm was incor-

porated under its present name in 1952, "dynamics" implying the use of force or forces, in both the military and scientific senses. In 1959 General Dynamics merged with Henry Crown's Material Services Corporation, the world's largest cement distributor.

General Electric *see* (1) **Ediswan**; (2) **GEC**; (3) **RCA**; (4) **Thales**

General Foods *see* **Bird's**

General Mills *(packaged foods)*

The American company was incorporated in 1928 to acquire Washburn Crosby Company, a flour-milling company formed in 1866, and four other milling companies. It could thus hardly be called anything other than General Mills. Familiar products include **Wheaties** and "Cheerios" breakfast cereals, "Gold Medal" flour, and **Bisquick** baking mix.

General Motors *(automobiles)*

The General Motors Corporation (GMC), one of the world's largest industrial corporations, was founded in 1908 by the industrialist and financier William Crapo Durant (1861-1947) to consolidate various automobile companies, and initially the firms that produced **Buick**, **Oldsmobile**, **Cadillac**, Oakland (later **Pontiac**), Cartercar, and Elmore autos, as well as Reliance and Rapid trucks. It acquired its present name on reincorporation in 1916.

Genesco *(footwear and menswear)*

The US company has its origins in the Jarman Shoe Company, founded in 1924 in Nashville, Tennessee, by James Franklin Jarman, previously a partner in the J.W. Carter Shoe Company. In 1932 the company became the General Shoe Corporation, and when Jarman died in 1938 he was succeeded by his son, Walton Maxey Jarman (1904-1980), who shortened the name to Genesco in 1959.

Genny *(fashionwear)*

The Italian ready-to-wear company was founded in 1961 by Arnoldo and Donatella Girombelli, its name devised from their own. Their Complice line is designed by **Dolce & Gabanna**.

Gentleman Jack *(whiskey)*

The blend of this name was introduced by **Jack Daniel's** in 1988, as the first whiskey from that distillery in over a hundred years. The formula was based on early work carried out by Daniel himself. The name thus has an obvious application, and is line with similar nicknames such as "Gentleman Jim" for the US heavyweight boxing champion James J. Corbett (1866-1933). Earlier, "Gentleman Jack" was itself current as a nickname of the British actor John Bannister (1760-1836).

Gentleman's Relish *(savory paste)*

The make of savory paste or "potted meat" dates from the 19th century. Its typically English "aristocratic" name was entered (for **Patum Peperium**) by Charles Augustus Osborn, son of its originator, John Osborn (d. 1865), in the *Trade Marks Journal* of April 17, 1907 and again by C. Osborn & Co. Ltd. on December 6, 1950 for "Food pastes consisting principally of anchovy extracts."

Gerber *(baby foods)*

The name of the American company ultimately goes back to Frank Gerber (1873-1952), born in Douglas, Michigan, who 1901 helped found the Fremont Canning Company in Fremont, Michigan. In 1927 his daughter-in-law, Dorothy Gerber, complained how tiresome it was to strain peas for her newborn baby. Frank's son, Daniel Gerber (1898-1974), had the cannery do it, and soon found himself as a major manufacturer of baby foods. His original five products were peas, spinach, prunes, carrots, and vegetable soup, introduced to the public through advertisements in such magazines as *Good Housekeeping, Children,* and the *Journal of the American Medical Association.* By 1941 baby food sales at Fremont Canning exceeded adult food sales, leading the Gerbers to change the company name to Gerber Products Company. Two years later they ceased to produce anything but baby food.

Germolene *(antiseptic ointment)*

The ointment was originally produced by the British **Veno** Drug Co., basing its name on the germs that it banished, with "-ol-" from Latin *oleum,* "oil," in the sense of an emollient or soothing substance. Veno was subsequently acquired by **Beecham**. The name was entered in the *Trade Marks Journal* of March 12, 1913.

Gervais *(cheese)*

The soft, creamy cheese takes its name from the French cheesemaker Charles Gervais (1830-1892).

Gestetner *(office equipment)*

The name is that of a Hungarian, David Gestetner (1854-1939), who quit school at 13 to be apprenticed to an uncle who made sausages. In 1871 he worked for another uncle, this time a stockbroker in Vienna. After a financial crisis in that city, however, he immigrated to the United States, where he had a job selling Japanese paper kites in New York before going to Chicago to have a go at running a laundry. He had little success, so returned to Vienna, where he joined yet another uncle, who made glue and gelatin, the latter for hectographs. When the business failed, Gestetner went to London, England, obtaining employment with a firm of stationers in Shoe Lane. Here at last he found his niche. He took out a patent to develop the hectograph copying process, and in 1881 patented his most important invention, the cyclostyle, a pen with a toothed wheel at its tip. His early experience with sausage skins stood him in good stead when he later made stencils. *See also* **Roneo**.

Ghirardelli *(chocolate)*

The name is that of Domingo Ghirardelli, an Italian confectioner with South American links who was originally in business in Lima, Peru. He befriended James Lick, an American cabinetmaker who in 1847 moved from Lima to San Francisco, taking a large supply of Ghirardelli's chocolate with him. Foreseeing the product's potential in satisfying the daily needs of the goldrush pioneers, Ghirardelli followed, and set up a business in San Francisco importing and selling not only chocolate but also sugar and coffee. By 1856 the enterprise was known as Ghirardelli's California Chocolate Manufactory, and the original factory buildings have become a well-known San Francisco landmark in Ghirardelli Square. In 1963 the company was bought by the Golden Grain Macaroni Co., which in turn was acquired as a subsidiary of **Quaker Oats** in 1983.

Ghost *(fashionwear)*

The British company was founded in 1984 by Tanya Sarne (Ms. Tanya Gordon) (b. 1945). Its ethereal name is appropriate for the loose, flowing clothes in which the firm specializes.

GI Joe *see* **Action Man**

Gibbons, Stanley *see* **Stanley Gibbons**

Gibbs *(toothpaste)*

The name ultimately goes back to the De Guibbe family of Scotland, who in 1712 turned from making bonnets to being maltsters and chandlers, making candles and soap. One member of the family went down to London, where he changed his name to Gibb and set up as a candlemaker in 1768. This was Alexander Gibb, two of whose descendants, David and William Gibb, started making candles and soap under the name of D. & W. Gibbs. They were soon making more soap than candles, and in 1906 the firm's French agent, a Monsieur Thibaud, suggested they try producing a solid tablet of tooth cleaner instead of the powder or "tooth soap" that they had been making hitherto. This "French dentifrice," as they called it, was a success, especially with British troops in World War I. Eventually, in 1936, Gibbs came to manufacture their first toothpaste in a tube, the familiar "Gibbs SR," with the initials standing for "Sodium Ricinoleate," the important cleaning agent it contained.

Gibbs Mew *(beer)*

The British brewery originated in 1838, when George Bridger Gibbs and Sydney Fawcett, two brewers in Salisbury, Wiltshire, set up a partnership in Endless Street. One of their employees was Gibbs' nephew, Bridger Gibbs. He subsequently left and worked at a pub in Catherine Street before taking over the long established Anchor Brewery in Milford Street. In 1898 his firm, by now called Bridger Gibbs & Sons, merged with another brewery, Herbert Mew & Co. of Castle Street, shortening the firm's joint name subsequently as above. Gibbs Mew is still based at the Anchor Brewery.

Gieves *(menswear)*

The British company, based in Portsmouth, Hampshire, originated in that city in 1785, when one Melchisedek Meredith opened a tailor's shop in the High Street. Meredith had a great interest in uniforms, so his business was just right for the officers and men of the Royal Navy based in Portsmouth. By the time of his death in 1814, Meredith had built up a prestigious trade in naval uniforms, with both Nelson and Hardy among his customers. His business should have been taken over by his son, but Augustus Meredith, then 17, was a reluctant tailor and eventually sold the shop in 1841. It was bought by Joseph Galt, who reinvigorated the flagging concern and who in 1852 took as partner James Gieve (1820-1888), a Westcountryman who had built up business as a cordwainer. The firm expanded from there, with the London branch trading as Gieves & Hawkes from 1975 to 1985 (Thomas Hawkes being a further tailor partner) and giving the present name of the company.

Gilbern *(automobiles)*

The only British company to design and build complete cars in Wales took its name from *Gil*es Smith, a local auto enthusiast, and *Bern*ard Frieze, a German-born automobile engineer who decided to branch out on his own. Their factory at Llantwit Fardre, near Pontypridd, produced its first cars in 1966, and at first all went well, but sales subsequently fell off and the company finally folded in 1974.

Gilbey's *(gin)*

The first Gilbey to be associated with the British wine and liquor trade was Henry Parry Gilbey, partner in a wholesale wine merchants' concern in the City of London in the early 19th century. Henry had two brothers just retired from the Army Pay Department in the Crimea, and convinced them to join him in the business. They were Walter (later Sir Walter) Gilbey (1831-1914) and Alfred Gilbey. On Henry's advice, they took cellars at the corner of Oxford Street and Berwick Street and started trading there in 1857. Despite economic setbacks, their business flourished, so that in 1872 W. & A. Gilbey, as they now styled themselves, were able to open a gin distillery. The company's distillery is today in Harlow, Essex, the very town where the Gilbey family originated.

Gilera *(motorcycles)*

The Italian firm was founded by Giuseppe Gilera in 1909, when he was only 22. The company grew quickly, and in 1920 moved to a large new factory at Arcore, near Milan. The firm declined after the early death of Gilera's son, Ferruccio, in 1956, and it was sold to **Piaggio**, who closed the factory in 1993 but reintroduced the name on a range of motorscooters.

Gillette *(razors and razor blades)*

The inventor of the first safety razor, King Camp Gillette (1855-1932), was born in Fond du Lac, Wisconsin, the son of a hardware wholesaler. After his family lost all their possessions in the disastrous fire of 1871, he had to make a living somehow, so got work as a traveler in hardware. He liked "tinkering," and was keen to develop something that would be really useful. He realized his ambition in 1895, when working as a bottle-cap salesman with the Baltimore Seal Company. After repeatedly trying to put an edge on his straight razor, Gillette had the idea of putting a thin, double-edged blade between two plates, holding it there with a "T" handle. Despite initial problems, he finally enlisted the help of a Boston machinist, William Nickerson, to produce his new razor. In 1901 the idea became a commercial reality, and the two men formed the American Safety Razor Company, soon renamed the Gillette Safety Razor Company. Made wealthy by his enterprise, Gillette retired from active management in 1913 and spent much of his time investing in real estate and traveling abroad.

Gilsonite *(asphalt)*

The pure, shiny black, brittle form of asphalt, also known as uintaite, used in making inks, paints, and varnishes, takes its name from the American mineralogist Samuel H. Gilson, who discovered it in the Uintah Mountains, Utah, in the late 19th century. The name is the trademark of the asphalt's manufacturers, the American Gilsonite Company.

Gimbel's *(department stores)*

The stores owe their modern development to Bernard Feustman Gimbel (1885-1966), born in Vincennes, Indiana, the son of Isaac Gimbel (1856-1931), who had founded department stores in Milwaukee (1887) and Philadelphia (1894). He was himself the son of Adam Gimbel, a German immigrant who had opened "The Palace of Trade" in Vincennes in 1842. Bernard Gimbel went to work in the Philadelphia store in 1907 and became its vice president in 1908. He then persuaded his father to open a New York City store and became head of it when it opened in 1910. A block from **Macy's,** the two stores engaged in a legendary retailing competition. In 1927 Gimbel took over from his father as president and chief executive of the Gimbel's corporation. The Gimbel's chain suffered during the Depression, but recovered subsequently, and after World War II the Gimbel's Company pioneered the development of suburban shopping malls. At the time of Gimbel's death, the chain had 27 Gimbel's department stores and 27 Saks Fifth Avenue outlets, the latter taking their name from the Saks Company, which Gimbel's had absorbed in 1923. Gimbel's was itself subsequently acquired by British-American Tobacco (*see* **BAT Industries**).

Ginetta *(automobiles)*

In 1957 the British company Ginetta Cars Ltd. was set up by the brothers Trevor, Ivor, Douglas, and Bob Walklett, at Woodbridge, Suffolk. The four had earlier run an agricultural and construction-engineering business, and all were keen motor-racing enthusiasts. The name of the firm and its cars is of unknown origin. No member of the Walklett family has ever explained it, and one can only assume it is the female forename. The company was still in active production at the turn of the 21st century.

Ginn *(publishers)*

The American publishing house, specializing in primary schoolbooks, takes its name from Edwin Ginn (1838-1914), a farmer's son from Orland, Maine. Towards the end of his schooldays, Edwin roomed with a friend whose father published textbooks. This link enabled him to obtain work with various publishers on graduating from college, at first selling books on commission. He became increasingly keen to set up his own publishing concern, and his chance came in 1867 when a publisher at Crosby & Ainsword, where he was working, suggested he consider purchasing George L. Craik's *The English of Shakespeare* (1856), then on their list, and use it as a nucleus for his own business. Ginn, already a Shakespeare lover, accepted the offer enthusiastically, buying the book as the basis for his business, at first called Edwin Ginn, then Ginn Brothers, then finally Ginn & Company. Ginn's London office opened in 1887 to "meet the needs of schools and colleges of the British Empire."

Girobank *(bank)*

British Labour prime minister Harold Wilson set up the National Giro in 1968 as a bank operating through the Post Office. It soon became associated with the weekly social security payments made by giro check, and "giro" entered the language as a term for such payment, especially unemployment benefit. (The word derives from Italian *giro*, "circulation," i.e. of money.) In 1972 the National Giro became a separate business within the Post Office, and in 1978 was renamed the National Girobank. It became a public limited company (as Girobank) in 1985, and in 1990 became part of the **Alliance & Leicester** Building Society. This was the first time a building society had bought a clearing bank.

Gitane *(cigarettes)*

The brand of French cigarettes has a (feminine) name meaning "Gypsy," and specifically "Spanish Gypsy." The name was entered by the Service d'Exploitation Industrielle des Tabacs ("Tobacco Industry Promotion Board") in the *Trade Marks Journal* of September 3, 1933.

Givenchy *(perfume)*

The House of Givenchy dates from 1952, when Hubert de Givenchy (b. 1927) opened a fashion salon in Paris. His family came from the region of Beauvais, where the company has its head office today. Givenchy's father was an army officer in World War I, then a pilot in the French Air Force. On his death in 1930, Hubert and his elder brother Lucien were raised by their mother and grandfather, the latter being director of the famous Beauvais tapestry business. Givenchy sold his firm in 1988 but continued to head the company until 1996, when he retired from couture.

GKN *see* **Guest, Keen & Nettlefold**

Glas *(automobiles)*

Hans Glas GmbH was a long-established manufacturer of agricultural machinery in Dongolfing, Bavaria, when it started making the Goggo scooter in 1951. The four-wheeler Goggomobil appeared in 1955, while the first family-sized Glas, a one-liter model, was launched in 1962. **BMW** took over the firm in 1966 and closed down all Glas manufacture by 1969.

Glaxo *(industrial holding company)*

The present company evolved from a small import-export business founded in Welling-ton, New Zealand, in 1873 by Joseph Nathan (1835-1912), a tailor's son who had emigrated from London, England, in 1853. In around 1900 Nathan bought a milk-drying process and began to export dried milk from Australia. Originally, it seems, he tried to register the name "Lacto," from Latin *lac, lactis,* "milk," but for some reason this was rejected by the Registrar of Companies. He therefore offered other names, among them "Glaxo," based on Greek *gala, galaktos,* "milk," and copying the recent example of **Oxo**. It was accepted, and entered in the *Trade Marks Journal* of December 12, 1906. Glaxo subsequently made many acquisitions, including the veteran **Allen & Hanbury** in 1958 and the prestigious **Wellcome** in 1995. In 2000 the combined Glaxo Wellcome merged with **SmithKline Beecham** to form the UK's third-largest company (after **Vodaphone** and BP **Amoco**) and the world's biggest drugs group by market share, Glaxo-SmithKline (GSK).

Glayva *(whisky liqueur)*

The liqueur was originally created by Ronald Morrison & Co. of Edinburgh, Scotland, a firm experienced in the production of flavors and bouquets. Its name is a phonetic respelling of Gaelic *glé mhath,* "very good," said to be a spontaneous comment of one of the tasters when different formulations were being tested in the creation of the brand soon after World War II. The name was entered in the *Trade Marks Journal* of November 12, 1975.

Glen Grant *(whisky)*

The Scottish distillery that gave its name to the whisky was founded in 1840 in the village of Rothes by two brothers, James and John Grant, sons of a farmer in Inveravon, Banffshire. They chose the site carefully, taking advantage of the water in the small stream that joins the Spey River at Rothes. James Grant became a prominent businessman, and on his death in 1897 Glen Grant passed to his son, Major James Grant. Rothes is now a small town with several distilleries. This particular distillery was given a name to match those of other glens (valleys) in Scotland, such as Glen Coe, although a glen is normally named for the river that flows through it. The firm of J. & J. Grant, Glen Grant Ltd. was formed in 1932 and amalgamated with George and J.G. Smith of The

Glenlivet in 1953 to form The Glenlivet and Glen Grant Distillers. This in turn merged with the Edinburgh blending firm of Hill Thomson in 1970 to form The Glenlivet Distillers. Glen Grant is now part of **Seagram**.

The Glenlivet *(whisky)*

The well-known blend of Scotch whisky takes its name from the distillery founded by George Smith in the village of Glenlivet, Banffshire, in 1824, as the first of the distilleries licensed under the reforming Distillery Act of 1823, which put an end to the hundreds of illicit stills in the district. (Glen Livet is itself the name of the valley of the Livet Water, or River Livet.) The whisky became so popular that other distillers adopted the name, and a resultant legal case and settlement allowed the Smiths to use the prefix "The" in their whisky's name, while others were permitted to use it as a hyphenated suffix. *See also* **Glen Grant**.

Glico *(motor spirits and lubricants)*

The name was current in the early years of the 20th century for a range of motor-related products by the Gas Lighting Improvement Co. Ltd., a British company formed in 1888 to carry out improvements in the carbureting of gas. When the automobile industry came into being, it was one of the first companies to engage in the refining and distribution of motor spirit (gasoline) in Britain. The name is an acronym of the company name.

Gloy *(adhesive)*

The name was originally owned before 1930 by the British firm of A. Wilme Collier Ltd, who based it on Greek *gloia*, "glue."

Glynwed *(engineering and manufacturing)*

The British company takes its name from two earlier firms, Glynn Bros. and the Wednesbury Tube Company, founded respectively in 1890 and 1921. Wednesbury is a town in Staffordshire. Glynwed became a public company in 1941 and soon gained fame for its manufacture of **Aga** cookers, although these now form only about 5 percent of its operation. In 2001 Glynwed sold the engineering business that went along with the Aga manufacture and to mark the change restyled itself as Aga Foodservice.

Goblin *(vacuum cleaners)*

In 1900 Herbert Cecil Booth attended a demonstration at St. Pancras Station, London, England, of a device to clean railroad coaches by blowing the dust from one side of the coach into a dustbox on the other. The device was hardly effective, but it gave Booth an idea. On returning home, he wetted a piece of cloth, placed it over the arm of a chair, and sucked air through it. The result was a visible patch of dirt on the cloth. In Booth's own words, he had invented the "vacuum cleaner." He patented his invention in 1901, forming the Vacuum Cleaner Co. Ltd. to manufacture and market it. The company went on to produce more sophisticated models, and in 1921 brought out their first upright bag model. The first cylindrical model, called the "Turbinet," was produced a few years later. It was then decided to put the whole range of vacuum cleaners under the name of "Goblin." The name is said to have been suggested by the managing director's wife, who observed that the cleaner was "gobblin' up the dirt." Goblin Electrical Appliances, part of the British Vacuum Cleaner & Engineering Co., as it became, were subsequently noted for their automatic teamaker, the **Teasmade**.

Goddard *(silver polish)*

Joseph Goddard (d. 1877) was born in Market Harborough, Leistershire, England, the son of a local banker. He went to London to train as a chemist (druggist) and on his return in 1829 opened a shop in Leicester, where he made and sold a range of his own medicines. Goddard soon realized that the new silver-plated cutlery which people were using, instead of the old steel spoons and forks, would not stand up to the abrasive polishes then current, since these would simply remove the silver coating. He therefore devised a new type of plate powder that did not contain the mercurial element which caused the damage. Although it needed complex mixing, his invention was a success, and was widely adopted for the new type of cutlery. It was only about 100 years later, however, that the Goddard firm managed to find a way of preparing the polish with the plate powder already mixed. In 1969 Goddard's became a wholly owned subsidiary of **Johnson Wax**.

Godfrey Davis *(car hire)*

Godfrey Davis (1890-1961) was an English

Westcountryman who after serving as a pilot in World War I bought two cars in London and in 1923 started up a car hire service with them, basing his office in Albermarle Street. Extensive advertising brought him good business, so that by the mid-1930s he had a fleet of around 350 cars, most of them **Vauxhalls**. In many ways the history of Davis' business parallels that founded in the USA by Walter Jacobs, now familiar under the name of **Hertz**.

Godiva *(chocolates)*

The Belgian chocolate manufacturers date from 1926, when Joseph Draps opened a candy store in Brussels. He named his shop after the English noblewoman Lady Godiva (d. 1080), wife of the Earl of Mercia, who according to a 13th-century legend agreed to ride naked through the streets of Coventry if her husband would reduce unpopular taxes in return. Her feat has been commemorated in many art and literary forms, and it is doubtless this prestigious association, as well as the sexual symbolism of the story itself, that inspired Draps to adopt the name for his enterprise. The business was bought outright by **Campbell's** Soups in 1966, and is now a vast industrial concern, with 1,400 branches worldwide.

Golden Grahams *see* **Graham**

Golden Wonder *(potato chips)*

The British crisps were given their name in around 1947 by William Alexander (d. 1963), the son of a Scottish baker. The name may have been suggested by the potato variety so called, although these are in fact unsuitable for making crisps. In the latter half of the 1970s a brief history of the name was printed on the crisp packets for the edification of consumers.

Goldenlay *(eggs)*

Goldenlay Eggs was formed in the UK in 1970 by four egg businesses from around the country in a bid to prevent an egg price war following the imminent demise of the British Egg Marketing Board. The name is of obvious origin, alluding to an ideal egg's deep yellow yolk, but also hints at the proverbial "goose that laid the golden eggs."

Goldman Sachs *(investment bank)*

In 1869, Marcus Goldman (d. 1904), a former schoolteacher who had arrived in the USA from Germany in 1848, set himself up as a credit broker in lower Manhattan, New York. His youngest daughter, Louisa, married Sam Sachs (d. 1934), a Bavarian immigrant like Goldman himself, and in 1882 Goldman invited his son-in-law to join him and changed the name of the firm from Marcus Goldman & Co. to M. Goldman and Sachs. In 1885 Goldman's son Henry joined the business and it adopted its present name, Goldman Sachs & Co. In 1894 Sachs's son Harry also entered and in 1896 the firm joined the New York Stock Exchange. Through the enterprise of these men and their families, Goldman Sachs became the largest dealer of commercial paper in the USA.

Gollancz *(publishers)*

The founder of the British publishing house was Victor Gollancz (1893-1967), born in London the son of a Pole who ran a small jewelry business. On leaving school and then graduating from Oxford as a classics scholar, Gollancz served in the army in World War I, subsequently entering publishing in 1921 with the firm of **Benn** Brothers. Two years later he was appointed manager of the new firm of Ernest Benn Ltd., but personality clashes with Sir Ernest led him to quit in 1927 and start a business of his own, his stated aim being to steer a course between "the Scylla of preciousness and dilettantism and the Charybdis of purely commercialized mass production." His initial list consisted of histories, biographies, and fiction, and the business soon established itself on a sound commercial footing, its editions drawing the eye with their distinct bright yellow dust jackets. It attracted authors such as Daphne du Maurier, A.J. Cronin, Dorothy Sayers, and George Orwell and began to specialize in socialist and pacifist books, a development that led to the formation of the Left Book Club. From the mid-1940s many of its authors were Americans such as John Updike, Vladimir Nabokov, James Agee, and John Cheever, and in the 1960s it became noted for its science-fiction titles.

Gomer Press *(publishers)*

The leading Welsh publishing house has evolved from the printing business set up in 1892 by John David Lewis (1859-1914) in Llandysul, Carmarthenshire. By 1908 the firm had come to be named Gomerian Press, from

Lewis's admiration for the writer Joseph Harris (1773-1825), known as Gomer. (His name came from the chapel where he preached, Capel Gomer, itself named for the wife of the biblical prophet Hosea.) The firm is still in the hands of the Lewis family and has published many important modern Welsh authors.

Gonk (doll)

The name of the egg-shaped doll, in vogue in the mid-1960s, was entered by Daniel Buckley Enterprises, of London, England, in the *Trade Marks Journal* of February 26, 1964. The name is probably arbitrary, but may have been suggested by "conk" as a slang term for the head.

Gonzalez Byass (sherry)

The company traces its origins to 1783, when José Antonio González y Rodríguez, a 25-year-old Spanish courtier, was appointed to manage the royal saltmarshes at Sanlucar de Barrameda, near Cádiz. He died young, however, and his widow moved to Seville with his five young sons to give them a university education. The youngest, Manuel María González Angel, was not strong, and not a potential scholar. He therefore went to work in a Cádiz wine merchant's office. He developed an interest in the trade, and on a visit to Jerez, already famous for its sherry (named after it), bought a small bodega there. On marrying in 1833 he and his wife went to live in Jerez, and two years later González shipped his first consignment of sherry to England. Byass was Robert Blake Byass, González's London agent, who became a partner in 1855. The company remained in the hands of the two families until 1988, when the González family financed the purchase of the 45 percent of shares held by the Byass family, later placing most of these with IDV, the British drinks subsidiary of the conglomerate **Grand Metropolitan**. In 1997, however, the family bought the shares back from IDV. A well-known Gonzalez Byass brand of sherry is **Tio Pepe**.

Good Humor (ice cream)

In 1920, Harry Burt, a Youngstown, Ohio, confectioner, was already marketing a novelty he called the "Good Humor" sucker when he hit on the idea of putting ice-cream bars on sticks. On his death, the Good Humor trademark was bought by a Cleveland investor group who turned to franchising. The name, implying a contented consumer, was given a boost in the Los Angeles area following **Columbia Pictures**' release of *The Good Humor Man* (1951), starring Jack Carson. Good Humor trucks were ubiquitous until the 1980s, when they disappeared from America's streets. The brand name remained, however, attached to ice-cream novelties available to customers from supermarket freezer chests.

Goodrich (tires)

The American company was founded in 1870 by Benjamin Franklin Goodrich (1841-1888), a New York doctor who had gone into business with the aim of improving his income so as to support his wife. The story of his founding of the company that bears his name is legendary. Goodrich and his wife were on a train journey to Chicago to consult a relative on how best to relocate the Hudson River Rubber Company, which Goodrich had bought the previous year. As they were nearing Akron, a stranger told him about that town's great business potential, as it was served by two railroads with a third planned to join them. The young doctor turned to his wife, saying, "Mary, get your bonnet on." They alighted at Akron, far from Chicago, and within weeks Goodrich had relocated his company as the first of the firms that would make that city the "rubber capital of the world." In 1986 Goodrich merged its tire operations with those of a rival tire manufacturer, **Uniroyal**, to form the Uniroyal-Goodrich Tire Company. The combined business was in turn acquired by **Michelin** in 1990.

Goodyear (tires)

The American company was not founded by a Mr. Goodyear but by Frank Seiberling (1859-1955), son of an Ohio manufacturer of agricultural machinery, and his brother Charles, who in 1865 moved with their family to Akron, where their father established the Empire Mower and Reaper Works. His enterprise failed in 1898, however, whereupon the brothers set up the Goodyear Tire and Rubber Company, naming it for Charles Goodyear (1800-1860), discoverer of vulcanized rubber. (The story goes that one day in 1839 Goodyear accidentally dropped some India rubber mixed with sulfur onto a hot stove, so making his discovery.) Goodyear thus acquired their name by way of a commercial tribute, much as the British tire manufacturers **Dunlop** did. The "Wingfoot" (winged foot of Mercury) that appears in the trademark version of the name was added to distinguish Goodyear from **Goodrich** and Goodyear, the tire company, from its other concerns, such as the manufacture of raincoats and other rubber products.

Google *(Internet search engine)*

Based in Mountain View, California, America's most popular search engine, famous for its speed and accuracy, was founded in 1998 by two Stanford Ph.D. candidates, 27-year-old Larry Page and his friend, Sergey Brin, who between them had developed a technologically advanced method for finding information on the Internet. They named their brainchild after the googol, the number equivalent to 10 raised to the power of 100 (10^{100}), referring to the vast number of queries and sites they reckoned to be handling. By 2001 Google's three huge servers were handling 100 million inquiries daily, with its 10,000 computers trawling the web to pick 1,000 pages a second from its index of 1.3 billion entries.

Gorbatschow *(vodka)*

The German vodka takes its name from the Russian Gorbatschow (Gorbachev) family, official distributors to the Imperial Court of St. Petersburg, who arrived in Berlin from Russia in the wake of the 1917 October Revolution. In 1921 they established a distillery in Berlin to make vodka for their fellow émigrés, and in the early 1990s their brand was one of the fastest-growing in the world.

Gordon Fraser *(greeting cards)*

The British company is named for its founder, Gordon Fraser (1910-1981), a Leeds man with a Scottish grandfather. As a young man, Fraser ran a bookshop and art gallery in Cambridge, where he hit on the idea of using reproductions of some of the paintings for Christmas cards. He started to produce such cards, and first put them on sale in 1938, taking care over the quality of the reproductions and the paper they were printed on. The cards were very popular, and although World War II slowed production, Fraser added other kinds of cards after it, first birthday cards in 1955, then Easter cards, then gradually the whole

range as it exists today. The company, now based in Bedford, is still in the hands of the Fraser family.

Gordon's *(gin)*

Information is scant about Alexander Gordon, the Scot who set up a distillery in Goswell Road, Finsbury, London, in 1769, although it is known that he was given permission by the Huntly family to use their device, a boar's head, as his trademark. It still appears, together with his own name, on bottles of Gordon's gin. The distillery that now produces the brand is located only a few hundred yards from the site where Gordon founded his business.

Gore-Tex *(synthetic fabric)*

The synthetic waterproof fabric, permeable to air and water vapor and used in outdoor and sport clothing, takes its name from Wilbert L. Gore, who as a young chemist in 1945, just a few years out of the University of Utah, landed a job at **Du Pont**. He rose to be head of operations research and worked on a team to develop applications for a chemical known as PTFE (polytetrafluoroethylene) in scientific abbreviation and to the world at large as **Teflon**. One night, after hundreds of hours in the lab, attempting to develop a PTFE-coated cable, he explained the problem to his 18-year-old son, Bob, who remembered seeing some PTFE-coated sealing tape made by **3M**. Why couldn't the tape be bonded to the PTFE-coated cable, Bob wondered. Gore said he would be laughed out of the lab if he suggested that PTFE could be bonded to itself. Bob went to bed, but Gore stayed in the basement, deciding to tinker with the absurd idea. At around 4 a.m., Bob awoke startled to see his father standing over him and grinning broadly as he waved a tiny piece of cable. "It works! It works!" he shouted. For months, Gore tried to convince Du Pont managers of the significance of the development. But this would have meant a radical switch of resources, a risk they were not prepared to take. Accordingly, on January 1, 1958, the night of his 23d wedding anniversary, Gore and his wife, Genevieve, founded W.L. Gore & Associates in Newark, Delaware, to pursue their discovery. It was not long before their enterprise was known for a household name to rival Teflon, "Gore-Tex." Wilbert Gore died of a heart attack while backpacking in Wyoming in

1986, and Gore & Associates are now based in Elkton, Maryland.

Gor-Ray *(skirts)*

The firm that makes the skirts was set up in Britain in the late 1930s by two brothers, C. Joseph Stillitz and Louis Stillitz, who traded as C. Stillitz Ltd. They sold pleated skirts in the so-called gored and sunray styles, the former shaped with tapering or triangular pieces of material, the latter having pleats that were narrower at the top than the bottom. The business was later renamed for the two styles.

Göschen *(publishers)*

The German firm arose from the bookselling and publishing business set up by Georg Joachim Göschen (1752-1828) in Leipzig in 1785. The firm was acquired by **Cotta** in 1838, but regained its independence in 1868. In 1919 it merged with Walter de Gruyter & Co.

Gossard *(corsets and brassieres)*

The name is that of Henry Williamson Gossard, who in 1901, following a visit to France to observe current fashions, founded the H.W. Gossard Company in Chicago. Gossard opened an office in London, England, in 1921 and their first British factory at Leighton Buzzard, Bedfordshire, in 1926. In 1959 the company was acquired by **Courtauld**, and in 1968 introduced the revolutionary **Wonderbra**.

Goya *(perfumes)*

The British company only coincidentally bears the name of the famous Spanish painter. When the firm's founder, Douglas Collins (1912-1972), devised the name in the 1930s, he wanted a name that would work internationally. He liked "Loya," but could not use it as there was already a firm named "Loy Products." Collins changed the "L" to "G," and although he was advised that "Goya" was a proper name, so could not be registered, he went ahead anyway and adopted it. The new company began its advertising campaign with a showcard depicting a reclining nude, but chemists refused to display it, so Collins had to overprint a sort of nightdress to satisfy them. This artistic debut happened to associate the name with the Spanish artist Goya, and in particular his two paintings *Naked Maya* and *Clothed Maya.* The name was eventually registered in 1936.

G-plan *(furniture)*

The stylish, mass-produced furniture of this name came into vogue in the UK in the late 1960s. The manufacturers were E. Gomme Ltd., named for their founder, Ebenezer Gomme (1858-1931), the son of an Oxfordshire chairmaker, who started making furniture on his own account in 1898. The brand name, based on his initial, was devised in 1953 by the firm's advertising agents, **J. Walter Thompson**, and was entered in the *Trade Marks Journal* of September 23, 1959.

Grace *(chemicals)*

The American company, one of the largest chemical manufacturers in the country, was founded in Peru in 1854 by William Russell Grace (1832-1904), an emigrant Irishman from Queenstown (now Cóbh) who sailed to South America as a ship's candlemaker and who went on to charter ships to transport guano (bird droppings used as fertilizer). He invested in Peruvian land and resources, but bad health forced him to leave, and in 1865 he reestablished his business in New York, buying ships to engage in South American trade. The shipping side of the business gradually declined until it ceased altogether in 1977, leaving the production of chemicals as the company's main business today.

Graham *(crackers)*

Sylvester Graham (1794-1851) was born in West Suffield, Connecticut, the son of a clergyman. He entered Amherst College in 1823, but was forced to drop out through mental collapse. By 1826 he had recuperated and become a Presbyterian minister. In the 1830s he traveled about the East preaching on the evils of meat, alcohol, and processed flour. His disciples, "Grahamites," followed a strict vegetarian diet, drank only water, and always slept with the windows open, even in winter. In 1837 Graham published a treatise urging the faithful to bake their own brown bread instead of buying bread from commercial bakers. At first many bakers opposed his discrimination, but later decided it might make good economic sense to capitalize on his popularity. They accordingly applied his name to a variety of wholewheat baked goods, including the graham cracker. **General Mills'** breakfast cereal "Golden Grahams" also borrows the name.

Gramophone *(phonograph)*

The name was patented on November 8, 1887, in Washington, DC, by the German-born US inventor Émile Berliner (1851–1929) as a name to distinguish his machine for reproducing sound recordings from its predecessors. (His used disks, as distinct from the cylinders of the earlier machines.) He is said to have devised the name by reversing the two parts of "phonogram," an existing instrument that in turn based its name on that of the phonograph. The latter was invented by Thomas Edison earlier in 1887 and patented on July 30 that year. The "phone" ("phono") in all three names represents the Greek for "sound," while both "gram" and "graph" derive from the Greek for "to write." *See also* **HMV**.

Granada *(media and hotels)*

The British group, its name familiar from a regional television station, was founded by Sidney Bernstein (1899–1993), the son of a Swedish father and Russian immigrant mother. His father owned quarries in Wales and was a property dealer who built some of the first movie theaters in London's East End. Sidney quit school at 15 to follow his father into the cinema business, and at age 22 inherited the family's four theaters. From this base he developed the Granada cinema chain, naming them thus in 1930 after a walking holiday in Spain, when he was particularly impressed with the city of Granada and its magnificent Alhambra Palace. The name was subsequently extended to the group's other activities, among them television, motorway services, and publishing. In 1987 Bernstein was given a silver pomegranate by the governor of the Spanish province of Granada, Juan Hurtado, in recognition of the company's achievement in "putting Granada on the map." (The city's name, which passed to the historic kingdom and present province, comes from Latin *granatum*, "pomegranate.") In 1996 Granada took over the **Forte** hotel chain.

Granat *(publishers)*

The Russian publishing house was founded in Moscow by the brothers Aleksandr Naumovich Granat (1861–1933) and Ignaty Naumovich Granat (1863–1941). They began in 1892 by securing the publishing rights to an encyclopedic dictionary that had started to appear from the Moscow firm of A. Garbel & Co.

the previous year. Granat continued to publish after the Revolution until 1939, when the business merged with that of the state publishing house Soviet Encyclopedia.

Grand Macnish *(whisky)*

The blend of whisky produced by Macduff International of Glasgow, Scotland, was first established in 1863, in the early days of whisky-blending, by Robert McNish. Hence its name.

Grand Marnier *(liqueur)*

The orange-flavored liqueur, a curaçao based on brandy, originated with a family headed by J.A. Lapostolle in 1827. Louis-Alexandre Marnier subsequently married into the family business and it was he who in 1880 conceived the liqueur that bears his name after encountering the bitter oranges of Haiti on a grand tour. The name was entered in the *Trade Marks Journal* of August 1, 1923.

Grand Metropolitan *(drinks and hotels)*

The former British conglomerate, now merged with **Guinness** to form **Diageo**, originated as Grand Metropolitan Hotels Ltd., as the merger in 1962 of the two London-based companies Mount Royal Ltd. and Grand Hotels (Mayfair) Ltd. By 1965 Grand Metropolitan Hotels claimed to be the largest hotel group in the world by profits, while Trust Houses (*see* **Forte**) was probably the largest in the number of rooms. Following the takeover of various breweries, the company dropped "Hotels" from its name. "Metropolitan" is a suitable name for a company based in a country's metropolis, or capital, and the word equally has associations of industry and commerce, as certainly applied in this case. The whole enterprise was the creation of Sir Maxwell Joseph (1910–1982), who began his career in property.

Grand Ole Opry *(country music radio program)*

The first of the weekly country music radio programs so named began almost by chance in November 1925, when the new Nashville, Tennessee, station WSM put on an hour-long program featuring the 85-year-old country fiddler Uncle Jimmy Thompson. The program happened to follow a broadcast of Walter Damrosch's music appreciation hour from New York, so announcer George B. Day began by saying:

"For the past hour you've listened to grand opera; now you're going to hear some grand *ole opry*." The program was originally known as the "WSM Barn Dance," but gained its familiar name, a dialect form of "Grand Old Opera," in 1926, and this was entered by WSM in the US Patent Office *Official Gazette* of April 18, 1950: "For radio program broadcasting services."

Granola *(breakfast cereal)*

Early in his career as a sanitarium superintendent, Dr. John Harvey Kellogg (*see* **Kellogg's**) had noticed his patients' dissatisfaction regarding their monotonous diet. Enlisting the support of his wife, he was determined to change this. Kellogg was convinced that the cereal grains basic to the diet he favored were more easily digested after prolonged baking. A slow-baked, multigrain biscuit was thus developed. These biscuits were then coarsely ground into granules and named "Granola," the name itself being based on "Granula," that of a biscuit created in the early 1860s by New York health reformer James C. Jackson, and registered in 1876 as "cooked granulated wheat" by Austin Jackson & Co. of Dansville, New York. "Granola" was entered in the *Trade Marks Journal* of March 24, 1886 (as "a product for food") and by the Battle Creek Food Company in the US Patent Office *Official Gazette* of November 8, 1928. The trademark was then cancelled, and "granola" returned in the 1960s as the generic name of a similar breakfast cereal or cereal-type snack. In 1975 **General Mills** introduced high-fiber "Nature Valley" Granola Bars in coconut, cinnamon, and oats 'n' honey flavors.

Granstrem *(publishers)*

The Russian firm of children's publishers was set up by Eduard Andreevich Granstrem (1843-1918), his wife and daughter, in St. Petersburg in 1881, producing gift editions of foreign literature in their own translations from English, French, German, Swedish, and Italian, among them works by Frances Hodgson Burnett, Louis Boussenard, Lewis Carroll, and Zachris Topelius. Major publications included the Finnish *Kalevala* (1881), *Along Russia's Polar Limits* (1885), and *A Hundred Years of Discoveries by Famous Seafarers and Conquerors of the 15th and 16th Century* (1893). The firm closed in 1916.

Grant & Cutler *(booksellers)*

The London, England, bookstore, specializing in foreign books, takes the second part of its name from Frank Cutler (1911-1999), born in Cambridge. He began his bookselling career with **Bowes & Bowes**, where he worked in the foreign department alongside an older colleague, Geoffrey Grant (d. 1965). The two men became friends, and in 1936 decided to go into business together by founding a private library devoted to European literature. Their venture became known as the International Book Club, and soon built up a reputation as the place to go for those with an interest in foreign literature. World War II then intervened, and although the business kept going, it was decided in the late 1940s to turn the library into a shop, as subscription libraries were rapidly becoming a thing of the past. The firm steadily expanded, and in 1971 began publishing under its own imprint.

Grant's *(whisky)*

The name is used for a blend of whisky produced by William Grant & Sons at their Glenfiddich distillery in Dufftown, Scotland. William Grant (1839-1923), the firm's founder, was a village tailor's son who worked as a cowherd and shoemaker's apprentice before joining a local distillery. He remained there 20 years, and in 1886 built his own distillery at Glenfiddich, subsequently converting nearby Balvenie Castle into a second distillery in 1892. The company dates its founding from 1887, the year when the Glenfiddich distillery first produced its whisky. In 1962 the firm built a large new distillery at Girvan, Ayrshire, where it produces the blends "William Grant's Family Reserve" and "Grant's 12 Years Old."

Grape Nuts *(breakfast cereal)*

The cereal was the invention in 1897 of Charles William Post (of **Post Toasties**), who two years earlier had developed the "food-cum-drink" that he would market as "Postum" cereal beverage. It was made of baked wheat and malted barley, and so named for its "nutty" flavor and for the "grape" sugar or dextrose that Post (mistakenly) believed was formed in the baking process. The name was entered in the US Patent Office *Official Gazette* of June 14, 1898 and the *Trade Marks Journal* of April 18, 1956.

Grasset *(publishers)*

The French publishing house, noted for its promotion of young writers in the interwar years, was founded in 1905 by Bernard Grasset (1881-1955), who himself published a book about publishing called *Remarques sur l'édition* (1928).

Grasstex *(tennis court surface)*

The tennis court surface does not actually have a "grass texture" but a top layer of natural fibers that provides a "soft" or cushioning effect similar to that given by grass by comparison with a hard surface. The name dates from the late 1970s.

Grattan *(mail order house)*

The British company, based in Bradford, was founded by John Enrico Fattorini, a local jeweler, who in 1912 had the idea of branching out into the mail order business. He was joined by two partners, and built up his new business so successfully that in 1920 he needed to expand. He moved to Grattan Road, Bradford. Hence the name. It was only in 1935, however, two years after the Grattan Road buildings had burned down, that the name was officially registered. The company was thus obliged to move to Ingleby Road, where it is still based today. John Fattorini was the youngest son of Antonio Fattorini, an Italian immigrant to Britain whose family also founded Empire Stores in Bradford in 1910, where it remains today as an equally well-known mail order house.

Great Universal Stores *(mail order house and clothing stores)*

The British company, familiarly known as GUS, owes its success to Isaac Wolfson (1897-1991), the son of a Russian Jewish immigrant who settled in Glasgow, Scotland, to work as a cabinetmaker. On quitting school young Isaac at first helped in his father's workshop. His fortune changed one day in 1926 while selling clocks and mirrors at a stall in Manchester's exhibition hall, when he met George Rose, who had founded a mail order company in 1900. Rose was impressed by Wolfson's commercial talent and took him on as a buyer. Rose's firm, Universal Stores, carried on a style of business known as "club trading," whereby agents formed clubs into which members paid a nominal amount each week. When the subscrip-

tions amounted to £1, the members chose goods from the company catalog. In 1930 the firm, with its already grand name, was renamed even more imposingly as Great Universal Stores, and two years later Rose was bought out by Wolfson. GUS severed its connection with the Wolfson family in 1998, and in 2001 the company appointed brand consultants to devise a new name.

Great White Shark Enterprises *(golf equipment)*

When Australian golfer Greg Norman (b. 1955) burst onto the scene at the 1983 Masters, he was soon dubbed the "Great White Shark" for his aggressive playing. In 1994 he launched his own company to market golf equipment, naming it with his sobriquet. By 2001 it had grown into an estimated $142 million private enterprise, mainly from golf-related businesses such as golf-course design and residential development, golfing events, and golfing apparel, but also from diversified activities such as wines, casual wear, restaurants, and yachts.

Green Giant *(canned vegetables)*

The American company was founded as the Minnesota Valley Canning Company by 14 merchants who met one evening in 1903 in the back of James A. Cosgrove's harness shop in Le Sueur, Minnesota. Their first product was canned white cream-style corn, packed from corn grown in the Minnesota valley where Le Sueur is located. They first packed peas in 1907, concentrating on a large English variety called "Prince of Wales." These were unfamiliar to American private label customers (stores that put their own names on products supplied by processors), who refused to stock them. Minnesota Valley accordingly marketed the peas under their own label, boasting about the size by calling them "green giant." When the company tried to trademark the name, they were advised that descriptive names were not admissible. They therefore invented the "giant" as a symbol that could be trademarked. The first giant appeared on a label in 1925, and was originally dwarf-like and white. Later he became taller and green, and subsequently added the word "Jolly" before his name. Finally, in 1950 Minnesota Valley Canning became the Green Giant Company.

Green Shield *(trading stamps)*

The name of the former British company was devised by its founder in 1958, Richard Tompkins (d. 1992), who was aware that the trading stamps of the American company Sperry & Hutchinson were known as "green stamps" in the USA and so reasoned that if they wished to enter the UK market they would want to retain the same name there. With a view to forestalling this, he looked for a name that combined "green" with some other favorable word. The color already had popular associations with spring, the countryside, youth, "go," and the like, and he felt that the other half of the name would be best embodied in "shield," a word with the right associations of security and strength. The name was registered in 1957, but not before the rights had been bought from a north London company already using it. The stamps are no longer issued but the Green Shield Trading Stamp Company still exists.

Green Spot *(whiskey)*

The blend of Irish whiskey, produced by Mitchell & Son of Dublin since at least the 1920s, was originally known as "Pat Whiskey," with a picture of an imbiber apparently bursting through the label. Behind him was dark green shading, and this gave the nickname "Green Spot," later adopted officially. The whiskey is a five-year blend, and its popularity subsequently resulted in a seven-year-old "Blue Spot," 12-year-old "Yellow Spot," and 15-year-old "Red Spot.".

Greenall Whitley *(beer)*

Little information is available about the men who founded the British brewery. It is known, however, that in 1762 Thomas Greenhalgh (1735-1805), who later changed the spelling of his name to Greenall, built a brewery in St. Helens, Lancashire, and that he and his descendants developed the brewing business elsewhere in the region. The second half of the name is that of John Whitley, a nephew of Greenall's grandson Gilbert. He joined the business some time in the 1850s. The company now has its head office in Warrington, where Greenall had acquired a brewery in 1786. The Greenalls Group, as it later became, was one of Britain's top major brewers until 1990, when it closed its breweries to become purely a pubs, restaurants, and low-cost hotels operator. In 1999, at the end of a difficult year, it sold these in turn to Scottish & Newcastle to become a hotels and leisure group. Its non-executive chairman at that time was Sir Peter Greenall, 4th Baron Daresbury (b. 1953), who joined the brewery in 1980 when it was still a family-controlled business. In 2000 the long-standing Greenalls name was abandoned in favor of De Vere, the name of Lord Daresbury's hotel group.

Greene King *(beer)*

The first part of the familiar British brewery name is that of Benjamin Greene (1780-1860), a draper's son. He served an apprenticeship with **Whitbread** in London before coming to Bury St. Edmunds, Suffolk, where in 1804 he opened a brewery in Westgate. Business remained modest until 1836, when Greene formed a firm of sugar merchants in London. The brewing business passed to his third son, Edward (1815-1891), who greatly expanded it. In 1887 Edward Greene merged the brewery with that of his neighbor, Fred King, which was literally next door. This brought the second part of the name. The company's head office remains at the Westgate Brewery in Bury St. Edmunds today, and the firm punningly displays the figure of a "green king" as its logo. Descendants of the Greene family include the writer Graham Greene (1904-1991) and BBC director-general Hugh Carlton Greene (1910-1987).

Greyhound *(buses)*

Greyhound Lines, Inc., traces its origin to 1914, when a Swedish miner, Carl Wickman, provided transport to take miners to and from Hibbing and Alice, Minnesota, a distance of four miles, using a seven-seater **Hupmobile**. The following year he extended the service, using bigger vehicles, to make America's first long-distance coach run, from Hibbing to Duluth, Minnesota, a distance of 90 miles. In these early days he painted the buses battleship gray because of the dusty road conditions, and the addition of extra seats in the vehicles made them look long and slim. One day, goes the story, an innkeeper commented to Wickman that the buses looked "just like greyhound dogs streaking by." Wickman adopted the name, and introduced the slogan "Ride the Greyhounds." In around 1925 he combined forces with another long-distance travel operator, Orville S. Caesar, to merge various bus companies into the

Motor Transit Management. In 1930 this firm became Greyhound Corporation, with the already familiar "running dog" as its trademark.

Gro-bag *(plant bag)*

The British name is a proprietary form of "growbag," as the term for a bag containing potting compost in which plants such as tomatoes can be grown. The name was entered in the *Trade Marks Journal* of February 5, 1975.

Groceteria *(self-service grocery store)*

The name, based on "cafeteria," was entered by Lutey Bros., of Butte, Montana, in the US Patent Office *Official Gazette* of March 25, 1913, but is now used generically and written with a small "g."

Grolier *(publishers)*

In 1895 a group of men in Boston, Massachusetts, headed by Walter M. Jackson (d. 1923), set up the Grolier Society with the aim of creating and publishing good books in fine bindings, naming their enterprise for the French bibliophile and patron of bookbinders, Jean Grolier de Servières (1479-1565). (A "Society" then was similar to a "Company" now.) The firm moved to New York in 1900 and in 1908 purchased the rights to Arthur Mee's *The Children's Encyclopaedia*. Grolier editors americanized the text and published it in the fall of 1910 as *The Book of Knowledge*. The reference work was soon established as a Grolier flagship publication, another being the *Encyclopedia Americana*. The company moved its headquarters to Danbury, Connecticut, in 1970 and in 1988 was purchased by **Hachette**.

Grolsch *(beer)*

The Dutch brewery, with its distinctive bottles, was founded in 1676 by Peter Cuyper in Grolle, now Groenlo, a small town in the southeastern Netherlands. The name thus simply means "of Grolle."

Grosset & Dunlap *(publishers)*

In 1898 Alexander Grosset (1870-1934) and George T. Dunlap opened a bookshop on East 16th Street, New York City. When Dunlap left in 1899 to work for **Rand McNally**, the name of the business was changed to Alexander Grosset and Company, but became Grosset & Dunlap on his return the following year. The first books published by the firm were pirated editions of Rudyard Kipling. Dunlap became president following Grosset's death, and in 1945 the firm joined with the Curtis Company, a nationwide book distributor, to form **Bantam Books**.

Grumman *(aircraft and arms)*

Grumman Aerospace Corporation takes its name from Leroy Randle Grumman (1895-1982), the son of a New York carriage shop owner. He enlisted in the navy in 1917 but resigned his commission three years later to join the Loening Aeronautical Engineering Corporation of New York as a test pilot. When in 1929 the Loening company relocated to Pennsylvania, Grumman and several of his fellow employees descided to strike off on their own. On December 6, 1929, they formed the Grumman Aircraft Engineering Company, opening for business in a converted garage in Baldwin, New York. The company prospered during the Great Depression, and in 1937 moved to new premises at Bethpage, New York. Grumman went on to develop the business into a major defense contractor, and during World War II produced such well-known Navy fighters as the Wildcat and Hellcat as well as the Avenger torpedo bomber.

Grundig *(tape recorders)*

The firm was founded by the German electronics pioneer Max Grundig (1908-1989), born in Nürnberg. He quit school at 14 and by the age of 22 had opened a radio shop in nearby Fürth, doing repairs, charging batteries, and repairing customers' sets. In 1946 Grundig hit on an idea to get around the Allied authorities requirement that defeated Germans must have a license to buy a radio set. He produced a "toy" kit, supposedly for children, but really containing parts which their fathers could use to assemble a proper radio. Grundig named the kits "Heinzelmann," from "Heinzelmännchen," the name of a helpful brownie in a well-known fairy tale, starting production in 1947 in a barracks on the outskirts of Nürnberg. ("Heinzelmännchen" means "manikin Heinzel," the latter being a pet form of the male name Heinz. The folk belief is that it is best to call brownies by their pet name to make them helpful rather than harmful.) By 1956 he had a workforce of 11,000, and had expanded spectacularly from toy radios to real radios, television sets, and the famous tape recorders. Grundig continued to run his concern single-handedly until 1984, when Japanese competition forced him to merge with **Philips**.

GSK *see* **Glaxo**

GTE *(telephones)*

The initials are those of the former General Telephone and Electronics Corporation, which arose from Associated Telephone Utilities, founded in 1926 by Sigurd Odegard, a Wisconsin telephone company owner who wanted to acquire smaller companies of this type. His business went bankrupt during the Great Depression but was reorganized in 1934 as General Telephone. In 1950 this company bought the Automatic Electric Company, a manufacturer of telephone equipment, and in 1958 merged with Sylvania Electronics. Words from these names gave that of General Telephone and Electronics in 1959, and in 1982 the corporation adopted its initialism as its formal name.

Gucci *(fashion accessories)*

The company name, with its cachet of quality, is that of Guccio Gucci (1881-1953), a young Florentine craftsman, who in 1904 set up a business as a saddlemaker. His workshop produced high-quality leather goods, and soon increased its range to include luggage and shoes. Later, the distinctive "GG" initials were added to embellish the firm's products. Gucci's family and descendants have been closely involved in the expansion of the business, and it was his son, Aldo Gucci (1905-1990), who came up with the concept of the famous Gucci handbag with detachable gold chain. Recent internecine strife has tarnished the company's reputation somewhat, but the Gucci name still popularly retains its connotation of luxury and status. In 1993 the business was purchased by an investment firm.

Guerlain *(perfumes)*

In 1956, 19-year-old Jean-Paul Guerlain took over the international perfumery business that had begun life three generations earlier as a tiny shop in Paris, France. He had been trained in the business by his grandfather, Jacques Guerlain, who retired that same year, and in 1964 Jean-Paul in turn handed over the reins to Philippe Guerlain. The company is now owned by LVMH (*see* **Louis Vuitton**).

Guest, Keen & Nettlefold
(engineering)

The British company was established in 1900 as Guest, Keen and Company on the merger of two older firms. In 1902 it assumed the name Guest, Keen & Nettlefold (later usually abbreviated to GKN) on the acquisition of J.H. Nettlefold & Sons, a screw- and wire-manufacturing business founded in Birmingham in 1854 by John Sutton Nettlefold (1792-1866), the father of Joseph Henry Nettlefold (1827-1881), who gave his name to the ultimate firm. The Guest name is that of Ivor Guest, Viscount Wimborne (1835-1914), eldest son of Sir Josiah John Guest (1785-1852), owner of the Dowlais Iron Company, the leading iron producer in South Wales, founded by Ivor's grandfather, John Guest. The Keen name is that of Arthur Keen (1835-1915), who in around 1856 formed a partnership with Francis Watkins, an American who had come to Britain to sell a patent nut-making machine. Their company was floated as Watkins & Keen in 1864, and in 1900 Keen himself became the first chairman of the newly formed Guest, Keen and Company. In 1967 GKN Steel became part of **British Steel**.

Guinness *(beer)*

The name derives ultimately from Arthur Guinness (1725-1803), an Irishman who in 1756 leased a small brewery at Leixlip, Co. Kildare. In 1759 he acquired a brewery at St. James's Gate, Dublin, at an annual rent of £45 on a 9,000-year lease. At first the brewery produced standard ale and table beers, but in 1799 it began making the porter that became the Guinness of today. Guinness' enterprise soon grew to become the largest porter brewery in the world. Much of the expansion, however, was due to Arthur Guinness' sons, Arthur, Benjamin, and William, who inherited the brewery after their father's death. In the 1820s the second Arthur Guinness (1768-1855) perfected an extra stout porter which eventually became known simply as stout. His son, Benjamin Guinness (1798-1868), turned St. James's Gate into the largest brewery in the world, and a completely new brewhouse was built under Edward Guinness (1847-1927). The business became a public company in 1886, as Arthur Guinness, Son & Co. Ltd., a name shortened to Arthur Guinness & Sons plc in 1982 and further to simply Guinness plc in 1986. In 1997 Guinness merged with **Grand Metropolitan** to form **Diageo**.

Gulf + Western *see* **Paramount**

Gulf Oil *(petroleum)*

The American petroleum company was originally incorporated in 1907 but has roots going back to the tapping in 1901 of a huge oil gusher on Spindletop Hill, near Beaumont, Texas. The development of the well was funded by the **Mellon** banking family, and Thomas Mellon built the Gulf refinery in Port Arthur, Texas. "Gulf" thus means the Gulf of Mexico. In 1984 Gulf Oil was acquired by **Chevron**.

Gumption *(cleanser)*

The smooth paste cleanser, used for cleaning bathtubs and the like, derives its name from the standard word meaning "spirited initiative and resourcefulness." The name was entered in the *Trade Marks Journal* of June 25, 1924.

Gunk *(detergent)*

The product was launched in 1932 by the Curran Corporation of Malden, Massachusetts, and its name was entered in the US Patent Office *Official Gazette* of August 23, 1932 for: "Liquid Soaps and Liquid Cleaners for Hard Surfaced Materials or Articles." The name itself is expressive but apparently arbitrary, and gave the standard slang term "gunk" for any unpleasantly sticky or messy substance.

GUS *see* **Great Universal Stores**

Gus Carter *(betting agents)*

The British bookmaker was founded in 1958 by a Mr. Carrick and a Mr. Porter, who combined the first first and last parts of their respective surnames and prefixed the result with the forename Gus. A third partner, Bryan Trewhitt, became involved in the company in the 1960s and eventually bought it. In 1996 Gus Carter was acquired by **Stanley Leisure**.

H. Samuel *(jewelers)*

To discover the identity of H. Samuel, one must go back to Liverpool, England, in 1821, where two brothers, Moses and Lewis Samuel, ran a clockmaking business. On their death the family concern passed to Moses Samuel's son. But he survived his father by only 18 months, and it was left to the widow, Harriet Samuel, to continue the concern. So she provided the initial of the present name. Harriet Samuel moved to Manchester where she traded as a mail order company. Her wares were not the jewelry and watches for which the company is famous today, but ironmongery, brassware, and furniture. The retail side of the business was developed by her son, Edgar Samuel, who changed his surname to Edgar also and opened the first retail branch of the new concern in Preston, Lancashire, in 1890. In 1912 the head office of the firm moved from Manchester, then the "capital" of the mail order business, to Birmingham, so as to be near the center of the jewelry manufacturing industry. The company still has its head office there today, while the retail branch in Market Street, Manchester, holds a portrait of "H. Samuel" herself.

H. Upmann *(cigars)*

The name is that of Hermann Upmann, member of a European banking family and a lover of good cigars, who in around 1840 volunteered to open a branch of the bank in Havana, Cuba. The cigars he sent home proved so popular that in 1844 he invested in a cigar factory. The firm traded as both bankers and cigar manufacturers until 1922, when first the bank failed, then the cigar business. A British firm, J. Frankau & Co., saved the cigar brand and ran the factory until 1935 when it was sold to the newly founded Menendez y Garcia company. In 1944 a new H. Upmann factory was opened in Havana to mark the centenary of Upmann's enterprise, and the brand is still produced there. Cigars bearing the Upmann name are now also made in the Dominican Republic. (The label on non-Havana Upmanns is "H. Upmann 1844," while the Cuban version is "H. Upmann Habana.") The name H. Upmann was entered by "Henry Upmann and William Rocholl, trading as H. Upmann and Co., Havana, Cuba" in the *Trade Marks Journal* of January 16, 1878, and by "H. Upmann & Co., Habana, Cuba" in the US Patent Office *Official Gazette* of October 15, 1912.

Häagen-Dasz *(ice cream)*

The name originated in New York City, where it was registered by Reuben Mattus in 1961. It is said to be intentionally meaningless but designed to give an impression of reliable Scandinavian tradition long before the brand fell into British hands. Stories explaining the name abound, even so. (One claims it was taken at random from a phone book and is Norwegian for "outside toilet door.") The Häagen-Dazs chain was launched in Buffalo, New

York, in 1970, and at first sold only soft ice cream. By 1984, after being acquired by **Pillsbury**, it had grown to over 300 outlets featuring hard ice cream. It was later sold to **Grand Metropolitan**, and in 1990 the chain was pared down to 260 shops in 20 states.

Habitat (furniture)

The British chain of stores selling stylish modern furniture was started by the designer Terence Conran (b.1931) when he opened the first store in Fulham, London, on May 11, 1964. The name implies furniture that is suitable for one's home or "habitat," while at the same time suggesting a "natural" environment. In 1982 Habitat merged with **Mothercare** and in 1986 the two joined British Home Stores (BhS) to form the Storehouse group. The latter sold Habitat to **Ikea** in 1992.

Hachette (publishers)

The French publishing house was founded by Louis Hachette (1800-1864) when he bought the Paris bookstore Librairie Brédit in 1826, renaming it after himself. He went on to produce a range of educational books and reference works, including Émile Littré's famous *Dictionnaire de la langue française* (1863-72) and that of the Académie Française. In 1983 Jean-Luc **Lagardère**, president of **Matra**, took control of Hachette, which itself acquired **Grolier** in 1988. In 1992 Hachette merged with Matra to form Matra Hachette and become Lagardère's lead company.

HAG (decaffeinated coffee)

The inventor of a process for manufacturing decaffeinated coffee was the German industrialist Ludwig Roselius (1874-1943), who in 1906 founded a company to market the new product, Kaffee-Handels-Aktiengesellschaft ("Coffee Trading Company"). The first word and letters from the other two words gave the German name of the product, Kaffee-HAG, or simply HAG. Roselius was also the creator of **Sanka**.

Haggar (slacks)

The name is that of Joseph M. Haggar, born Maroun Hajjar in 1892 in the village of Jazzin, Syria. He left his family's one-room home in 1905, when he immigrated to Mexico. Three years later he moved to the United States, where he worked at a variety of menial jobs, anglicizing his name in the process. He gradually

built up enough savings to start a garment factory in Dallas, Texas, in 1925. Business grew, and in 1938 his son Ed Haggar joined him. It was the junior Haggar who transformed the company into a giant by using national advertising to create a brand identity.

Haig (whisky)

The Haigs trace their family tree back to a 12th-century Norman knight, Peter del Hague, who came from La Hague, the cape near Cherbourg, France. He traveled north through Britain and built a castle in Bemersyde, on the banks of the Tweed, where the Haigs still live today. The first Haig to be involved in whisky distilling was Robert, a 17th-century Stirlingshire farmer, who was rebuked by his local kirk session for distilling his whisky on a Sunday. Robert's son, Alexander Haig, is on record as distilling whisky in 1699. But it is a late member of the family, John Haig, with whom the present blend is associated. He built a distillery at Cameronbridge, Fife, in 1824, with the family firm's headquarters at nearby Markinch. A contributor to the *British Medical Journal*, December 24-31, 1983, pointed out that the Gaelic phrase *uisge beatha* ("water of life"), from which the English word "whisky" derives, is an anagram of "best Haig eau."

Halas and Batchelor (cartoon films)

The names are those of the British husband-and-wife team John Halas (1912-1995), born in Budapest, Hungary, and Joy Batchelor (1914-1991), born in Watford, Hertfordshire. Halas was educated in Hungary and Paris and moved to England as an animator in 1936. After art school, Batchelor became a commercial artist and while working on *Music Man* (1936) in London met and married Halas. In 1940 they established Halas and Batchelor Animation, Ltd., which became the largest cartoon studio in Britain. In 1982 they produced *Dilemma*, the first fully digitized cartoon.

Hale, Robert *see* **Robert Hale**

Hale's (beer)

"Hale's Ales" take their name from Mike Hale, a young American who in 1981 spent a brief spell as an "apprentice" at the similarly-named **Gale's** brewery in Hampshire, England. Inspired by his experience, he fired his own kettles in Washington State in 1983, opening an

English-style microbrewery in Spokane and a brewpub in the Seattle suburb of Fremont.

Halex *(table tennis balls)*

The name has its origin in a business arrangement made in 1877 between a British industrialist, Charles Pierce Merriam, and a chemist and inventor, Alexander Parkes (1813-1890), whose company had pioneered the manufacture and marketing of celluloid. (Parkes gave the name of "Parkesine," a substance more or less identical to cellulloid, based on pyroxylin and castor oil or camphor. *See also* **British Xylonite**.) For 20 years Merriam's firm worked alongside Parkes's business making colored celluloid play balls from his materials. The balls were made in sizes of one inch, one and a half inches, and two inches, with the one-inch ball the forerunner of the table tennis ball as it is known today. At the end of the 19th century the two firms decided they must respectively move to larger premises. Merriam's company move to a site at Hale End, Essex, just north of London, and the products made there were given the name "Halex," derived from it.

Halfords *(bicycle shops and accessories)*

The British company with its many retail branches was founded by Frederick William Rushbrooke (1861-1953), born in Willenhall, Staffordshire, the son of a miller and confectioner. On leaving school he was apprenticed to an ironmonger, then worked with a hardware firm in Wolverhampton. In 1892, with a loan from his father, he set up a hardware shop himself in Birmingham, trading as Rushbrooke & Co. A keen cyclist from boyhood, he sold not just the usual hardware but also bicycle parts, such as tubing and frames. In 1902 he opened a warehouse in Halford Street, Leicester, aiming to sell the parts to cycle dealers. Trade was poor, however, so Rushbrooke closed the warehouse and sold off the stock at retail prices. To his surprise, he found there was a great demand for bicycle parts, so he restocked the warehouse as a fulltime store, calling his business the Halford Cycle Shop, after the street. Hence the ubiquitous Halfords of today.

Halifax *(building society)*

Long Britain's biggest building society (savings and loan association), the Halifax was founded in the Yorkshire town of this name in 1853 as the Halifax Permanent Benefit Building and Investment Society. In 1997 it became a public limited company and a major retail bank, and in 2001 merged with the Bank of Scotland to become HBOS and Britain's fifth-biggest bank.

Hall & Woodhouse *(brewery)*

In 1777, 26-year-old English farmer's son Charles Hall began brewing beer in the Dorset village of Ansty. His son, Robert, took George Woodhouse into partnership in 1847, when the latter married one of Charles's granddaughters. In 1875 the brewery adopted the badger as its trademark, from the abundance of these animals locally, and its beers subsequently became known as "Badger" beers. In 1899 the brewery moved to new premises in the village of Blandford St. Mary and itself became popularly known as "Badger," after its beers, one of the best-known brands being **Tangle Foot**.

Hallmark *(greetings cards)*

The American company takes its fortuitously prestigious name from its founder, Joyce Clyde Hall (1891-1982), born in David City, Nebraska, the son of a lay preacher. He lost his father at an early age and went to work at the tender age of nine as a door-to-door saleman for the California Perfume Company, the future **Avon** Products. Two years later his family moved to Norfolk, Nebraska, where his older brothers, Rollie and William, bought a book and stationery store. Their shop also sold picture postcards, imported from Germany and England, which were often sent from one person to another much as greetings cards are today. Hall quit school at 15 and went to Kansas City to seek work. In 1910 he started his wholesale business there, taking on Rollie to help sell his beginner's stock of imported postcards under the name Hall Brothers. When a fire destroyed their whole stock in 1915, the brothers bought an engraving company and produced their own cards as Hall Brothers Paper Craft. Hall Brothers Company was incorporated in 1923, with all three brothers as equal shareholders. That year they began using the name "Hallmark" to identify their line, and by 1928 the name was printed on the back of every card. It was registered as a trademark in 1954.

Haloid *see* **Xerox**

Hambros *(merchant bank)*

The British bank was founded in 1839 by Carl Joachim Hambro (d.1877) as the London branch of C.J.Hambro & Son, merchants and bankers of Copenhagen, Denmark. The Hambro family had its origin in Calmer Levy, a German Jew, who in 1779 applied for a license as a tradesman. He had intended to change his name to "Hamburg," his native city, but the authorities became confused over the spelling so he opted for "Hambro," a simpler version. In 1920 the relatively new British Bank of Northern Commerce merged with C.J. Hambro & Son as Hambros Bank of Northern Commerce, and the following year became simply Hambros Bank.

Hamilton, Hamish *see* **Hamish Hamilton**

Hamish Hamilton *(publishers)*

The founder of the British company was born James Hamilton (1900-1988), but he changed his first name to Hamish as there was already another publisher named James Hamilton. Our Hamilton was born in Indianapolis the son of an American mother and Scottish father. He was taken to Britain when only three, and on completing his education at Rugby and Cambridge took up a publishing post with **Cape**. After a further spell as the London manager of Harper & Brothers (later **Harper & Row**) he set up his own publishing business in 1930, using his private means for the venture. His reputation was assured with the publication of John Gunther's *Inside Europe* in 1936, despite warnings that Hitler or Mussolini might sue him. Hamish Hamilton is now an imprint of **Penguin**.

Hamleys *(toy store)*

The London, England, store takes its name from William Hamley, who came to London from Bodmin, Cornwall, in 1760 and opened a toy shop in High Holborn. In 1830 a descendant, also William Hamley (b.1803), opened a branch of this shop in Regent Street, specializing in the sale of imported dolls, chemistry sets, and model steam engines. In 1906 Hamley Brothers, as they now were, moved further up Regent Street to premises at 200-202, where they remained until 1981. They are now almost next door in larger premises, at 188-196. In 1994 Hamleys became a public company, and other, much smaller shops have been opened elsewhere in London.

Hamlyn *(publishers)*

The British publishing house takes its name from Paul Hamlyn (1926-2001), born Paul Hamburger, who came to England with his family as a German Jewish refugee in 1933 at the age of seven. He changed his name to Hamlyn (because he was tired of being called "Sausage" at school) and in 1948 used a £350 inheritance from his grandfather to start his own bookshop in Camden Town, London. His shop did well, and he was soon able to start as a publisher by setting up Books for Pleasure, selling remaindered books at affordable prices. The venture was equally successful, enabling him to enter real publishing with the establishment in 1950 of Spring Books and Hamlyn Books. By 1960 these enterprises were widely known, and tempted Hamlyn to cast his cultural net wider. Together with **EMI**, he accordingly founded Music for Pleasure, which sold records for 12 shillings and six pence while rivals were charging 32 shillings. By 1964 Hamlyn had made his first fortune when he sold Hamlyn Books for £2.2 million to IPC (International Publishing Corporation). From 1972 he then built up a second empire, Octopus Books, which became a conglomerate, swallowing up imprints such as **Heinemann**, **Secker & Warburg**, **Methuen**, and his own original Hamlyn Publishing. This last purchase gave Hamlyn particular pleasure, as he had long been embarrassed by the widespread belief that he still controlled the ailing company that bore his name.

Hammer *(horror movies)*

Hammer Films owes its notorious name to one of its cofounders, Will Hammer (real name William Hinds) (b.1887), a former British film producer, who in 1948 set up Hammer Film Productions at Bray, near Windsor, Berkshire, together with his partner, Sir James Carreras (1909-1990). Much of the writing and direction of the movies was by Hammer's son, Anthony Hinds, and Carreras's son, Michael. After its production of *The Curse of Frankenstein* in 1956 the company became, in financial terms, the most successful in the history of the British cinema. In 1968 Hammer Films won the Queen's Award for Industry for its earnings in foreign currency, and Carreras was knighted the following year for his contribution to this. The last Hammer movie was made in 1978, when the company passed into the hands of the receiver. Carreras then had the idea of selling the "Hammer House of Horror" series to television, and this was repackaged as video cassettes in the late 1980s.

Hammick's *(bookstores)*

The British bookstore chain was founded by Charles Hammick (1927-1990), born in Weybridge, Surrey. His first career was as a Grenadier Guardsman. When engaged in strenuous commercial activity in 1967, however, he had a severe heart attack, and was advised by his doctors to avoid undue exertion. Encouraged by his second wife, the writer Georgina Heyman, he opened a bookshop in Farnham, Surrey. His business attracted good trade, and in 1973 he decided to start a chain of bookshops, acting as his own wholesaler. He built up a chain of 30 such stores, some becoming well known, such as the one in Windsor, with a café, and the one in Norwich which supplied the students of the University of East Anglia. He later sold off the chain to **John Menzies**.

Hanes *(hosiery and underwear)*

The two products of the name were called after two brothers, Pleasant H. Hanes (1845-1925) and John Wesley Hanes (1850-1903), of Winston, North Carolina, who were partners in a plug tobacco firm in 1900 when they sold out to **R.J. Reynolds**. Although they had worked well together, they decided to strike out independently. Pleasant launched the P.H. Hanes Knitting Co. in 1902 to manufacture men's and boys' underwear, while John started what would become Hanes Hosiery Mills to produce men's stockings, and subsequently women's. The separate paths were distinct until 1965, when the two companies merged to form the Hanes Corporation. In 1979 Hanes was acquired by Consolidated Foods Corporation of Chicago.

Hang Ten *(surfwear)*

Hang Ten was founded in San Diego, California, in 1960 by a surfer, Duke Boyd, who passed it on to an employee, Doris Boeck, soon after. The company's hooped T-shirts with embroidered footprint logo, introduced in 1962, became familiar on beaches and playgrounds in the 1960s and early 1970s, and when relaunched in the early 1990s were known as "Bobby Brady" shirts, after the *Brady Bunch* character. The company name, represented graphically by the logo and familiar to many beside surfers, comes from surfing jargon, in which "to hang ten" is to ride a surfboard with all ten toes curled over the board's front edge.

Hanson *(industry and finance)*

The British company, specializing in the takeover of other companies, had its beginnings in 1964, when a public company, Wiles Group, bought a truck business and put its two owners, James Hanson (b.1922) and Gordon White (1923-1999), on the board. The following year the two men gained control of Wiles, which then became their takeover vehicle. Its name was changed to Hanson Trust in 1969. In 1973 White set up the American side of the business, and in 1987 Hanson Trust became simply Hanson. In 1991 it tried, but failed, to gain control of **ICI**, and a similar raid on **Rank Hovis McDougall** was frustrated in 1992. In 1996 the company demerged but the name still exists for Hanson Capital, Ltd., among other firms, run by Hanson's son Robert (b.1960).

Hapag-Lloyd *(shipping and airline)*

In 1847, a group of businessmen in Hamburg, Germany, founded the Hamburg-Amerikanische Packetfahrt-Actien-Gesellschaft ("Hamburg American Packet Travel Company Limited") (HAPAG) to transport passengers and mail between Germany and North America. The service was inaugurated in 1848 when the sailing ship *Deutschland* set sail from Hamburg. In 1857, Norddeutscher Lloyd ("North German Lloyd") (NDL) was founded by Hermann Heinrich Meier in Bremen to operate a similar service, adopting "Lloyd" as a name that symbolized the quintessence of merchant shipping, from Edward Lloyd (d.1726), the owner of the London coffee house where Lloyd's List was started in 1731 and Lloyd's Register of Shipping in 1760. The service began in 1858 when the steamship *Bremen* left Bremerhaven for New York. In 1970 the two companies ended their rivalry by merging as Hapag-Lloyd. The first Hapag-Lloyd airline operated in 1972.

Harcourt Brace Jovanovich
(publishers)

The American publishing house takes the first word of its name from Alfred Harcourt (1881-1954), the son of a New York fruit farmer, who began his career in publishing in 1904, when he joined **Henry Holt** and Company, first as a salesman, then as an editor. In 1910 he became a director of the firm, but becoming frustrated with the conservative attitude of his aged employer, decided to set up his own business. On July 29, 1919, he accordingly founded Harcourt, Brace and Howe, his partners being Donald Brace, head of manufacturing at Holt, and Will D. Howe, chairman of the Indiana University English department. When Howe left in 1920, the company was renamed Harcourt, Brace and Company. Their first success came that same year when they published John Maynard Keynes' *The Economic Consequences of the Peace*, now regarded as a standard work. They built up a specialist line in textbooks, while also broadening their list to include fiction and poetry. In 1947 they were joined by William Jovanovich (1920-2001), first as head of the house's school textbook department, then as president of the company overall. The present name evolved only in 1970, after being known for many years as Harcourt, Brace & World, the last name indicating the merger with World Books. Jovanovich was proud of his Yugoslav origins, and it is said he altered the company name so people would have to make the effort to get his own name right.

Hardee's (hamburgers)

The American chain takes its name from Wilbur Hardee, the owner and fry cook of a restaurant in Greenville North Carolina, who began his hamburger business in 1960. Hardee's Drive-Ins were bought out the following year by J. Leonard Rawls, Jr., and James Carson Gardner, and by 1996, when they were based in Rocky Mount, North Carolina, Hardee's had over 4,500 outlets.

Hardys (wines)

The Australian company was formed in 1992 in a merger between the family-owned Thomas Hardy & Son and the Berri-Renmano cooperative group. Thomas Hardy began making wine in McLaren Vale, South Australia, in 1850 and was the country's biggest wine producer by 1894. The Berri-Renmano cooperative was formed in the Riverland wine region of South Australia in the 1920s.

Hardys & Hansons (beer)

The story behind the British brewery name is one of rivalry between two brewing families in Kimberley, Nottinghamshire. The firm dates back to 1832, when the original brewery of Samuel Robinson opened in Kimberley. In 1857 it was acquired by Thomas Hardy (1832-1897) and his brother William. In 1847 another brewery started up in Kimberley, this time owned by Stephen Hanson (1800-1861), a former farm manager. In 1861 the Hardys built a new, enlarged brewery downhill from their original site, so that it stood right opposite the Hanson brewery. That same year Hanson himself died, leaving the brewery to be taken over by his wife and 18-year-old son. The two continued as (fairly) friendly rivals until 1930, when they sank their differences, doubtless over a pint or two, and agreed to amalgamate.

Harland and Wolff (shipbuilders)

The Northern Ireland firm of shipbuilders takes its name from Edward James Harland (1831-1895), born in Scarborough, Yorkshire, the son of a physician, and Gustav Wilhelm Wolff (1834-1913), born in Hamburg, Germany, a merchant's son. In 1857 Wolff was appointed personal assistant to Harland, then manager of Robert Hickson's shipyard on Queen's Island, Belfast. In 1858 Harland purchased the yard, renaming the business Edward James Harland & Co., and in 1861 the two men formed a partnership as Harland and Wolff.

Harley-Davidson (motorcycles)

The "H-D" story starts in 1902, when Walter Davidson (1876-1942), a Milwaukee machinist, in Kansas on a railroad job, got a letter from his brother, Arthur Davidson (1881-1950), inviting him to ride a "motorized bicycle" that he and a friend William S. Harley (1880-1943), had just designed. Later, Walter returned to Milwaukee expecting to take his brother up on the offer, but was informed that before he could go for a ride, he must use his skill as a machinist to help Arthur and Harley build a prototype of their machine. Walter agreed, and soon another Davidson brother, William Davidson (1870-1937), was convinced to join the venture. The foursome completed their first machine in 1903, and the Davidsons' father donated a backyard shed to serve as their factory. Only 61 machines were made by the partners in the first four years, but they steadily increased production, and by the mid-1910s Harley-Davidson was America's third largest motorcycle maker. The Harley family were originally from Manchester, England, and the Davidsons from Scotland.

Harp *(beer)*

The lager beer is produced by **Guinness**, an Irish company that adopted the traditional Irish harp as its pictorial trademark in 1862, registering it in 1876. The lager itself was developed in 1959 to mark the bicentenary of the firm and was launched in 1960. The name was entered in the *Trade Marks Journal* of July 21, 1926.

Harper & Row *(publishers)*

The story goes that 15-year-old James Harper (1795-1869), born in Newtown, Long Island, New York, the son of a farmer and carpenter, was inspired to become a printer after reading Benjamin Franklin's unfinished *Autobiography*. True or not, he and his brother John (1797-1875) were apprenticed to a printer and in 1817 set up their own firm as J. & J. Harper, Printers, on Dover Street, New York. Soon they were joined by their other brothers, Joseph Wesley Harper (1801-1870) and Fletcher Harper (1806-1877), and all four worked well together. In 1825 James and his brothers decided to be publishers rather than merely printers. They carefully divided their responsibilities in their premises at 82 Cliff Street and by 1830 their firm was the biggest book publisher in the United States. In 1833 they became Harper & Brothers, and if one of the brothers was asked who the "Harper" was, he would say that any one of them was Mr. Harper and the other three were his brothers. Under James's leadership the firm weathered many storms and by 1853 Harper & Brothers was the biggest publishing business in the world. In 1867 Fletcher Harper established the magazine *Harper's Bazar*, regularly selecting its contents himself. The business passed out of the Harper family hands in 1900. In 1962 Harper merged with the textbook publisher Row, Peterson & Co., of Evanston, Illinois, founded in 1906 by R.K.

Row and Isaac Peterson, to become Harper & Row, and following News International's acquisition of the British publishers **Collins** in 1990 joined forces with them in turn as Harper-Collins.

HarperCollins *see* **Harper & Row**

Harpic *(toilet cleanser)*

The cleanser takes its name from Harry Pickup, the man who invented its formula and first sold it in London in the 1920s. The name was entered by the Harpic Manufacturing Company in the *Trade Marks Journal* of February 9, 1921, and was acquired by **Reckitt & Colman** in 1943.

Harrap *(publishers)*

The British firm was founded by London-born George Godfrey Harrap (1866-1938), who for 19 years worked with the publishing house of Isbister before starting his own business in 1901. He was enabled to do so through the generosity of the American educational publishers D.C. Heath, who entrusted the British Empire representation of their lists to Harrap, an arrangement that lasted 70 years. The company was subsequently acquired by **Chambers**.

Harrington's *(babywear)*

The British firm was founded in the early years of the 20th century by two partners, H. Lewis and B.C. Niner, who formed a limited company in 1915 under the name of Harrington's (London) Ltd. There was no Mr. Harrington. It seems they selected the name simply because of its connotations of "Britishness," suggesting a long-established family.

Harris *(paint brushes)*

Britain's leading producer of paint brushes takes its name from Leslie George Harris (1905-1995), born in Bournville, near Birmingham, where his father had bought one of the houses on the estate developed by George **Cadbury** for workers at his chocolate factory. Leslie left school at 16 to work in a newly opened shipping office in Birmingham. In 1925 he set up a packing case business with a friend as a sideline, operating it from his home. In 1928 he became an independent agent selling paint brushes for the German firm of Unger & Co. Three years later he started making his own brushes in premises on Constitution Hill, Birmingham, with a foreman and 15 local young women. The business flourished, and after expansion moved in 1936 to Stoke Prior, near Bromsgrove, Worcestershire, where the company's head office and works are today, as L.G. Harris & Co. Ltd.

Harris Tweed *(handwoven cloth)*

The story of Harris Tweed begins in the 1840s, when the Countess of Dunmore, wife of the owner of Harris, the southernmost part of the island of Lewis and Harris in the Outer Hebrides, Scotland, decided she must help her tenants financially. Aware that there was an important potential market for Hebridean cloth among the Scottish aristocracy, she started to sell samples of the islanders' cloth to her friends on the mainland. The cloth was soon sought by the Scottish nobility, and its social prestige spread its popularity generally. As demand grew, merchants set up to represent the fragmented cottage industry. In 1909 a group of such merchants, together with representatives of the producers and weavers, formed the Harris Tweed Association. From that time on, all Harris Tweed cloth and knitwear has carried the familiar trademark of the Orb and the Maltese Cross, taken from the Countess's coat of arms, as a guarantee of the material's authenticity. The main centre of production is now Lewis rather than Harris.

Harris Queensway *(carpets and furniture)*

The British firm originated with Charles William Harris, an army officer in World War II, who owned a carpet shop in Peckham, London. In 1957 he died, still only in his 40s, not long after the death of his wife. This meant that his son, Philip Harris (b.1942), then only 15, was left to run the business or sell it. Although an orphan, he carried on, with the help of a guarantor, and soon opened two more shops that his father had planned. The business flourished and made several acquisitions, one of which, in 1977, was that of Queensway Discount Warehouses, giving the second word of the company name. In 1985 Philip Harris was knighted, and in 1987 he was elected chief executive. The following year he was forced out of the chain when profits collapsed, however, but immediately started a new venture named Carpetright, which was floated on the market in 1993.

Harrison *(printers)*

The British firm is well known for its printing of both postage stamps and security documents. It has its origins in James Harrison, of Reading, who followed his brother Thomas to London, completed a printing apprenticeship in 1750, and became a partner (and son-in-law) of his employer soon after. In 1756 the partnership was printing the *London Gazette* for the government of the day, and has acted ever since as confidential or security printers to a number of national bodies, from the Royal Household to the Post Office, receiving the first stamp contract with the latter in 1881.

Harrods *(department store)*

The man who gave the name of the famous London store was Charles Henry Harrod (1800-1885), a tea merchant of Eastcheap who had married a pork butcher's daughter. In 1849 he bought a small grocery shop in Brompton, continuing his tea trading there. In 1861 he handed the shop over to his son, Charles Digby Harrod (1841-1905), on the understanding that it was not an inheritance but a business deal, for which he must pay in instalments. Charles worked hard. He paid off the purchase price in three years, running the shop on a strictly cash basis, without the "tick" or credit that other shops granted. His enterprise did well and expanded, and when the premises were destroyed by fire in 1883 he opened an even bigger and better store the following year. Thus was created the present department store, which despite its Knightsbridge address is still geographically in Brompton.

Harrogate *(toffee)*

"Farrah's Original Harrogate Toffee" was already being made in Harrogate, Yorkshire, England, in the late 19th century, and the name "Farrah's Harrogate Toffee" was entered by John Farrah Ltd. in the *Trade Marks Journal* of December 28, 1910.

Harry N. Abrams *(publishers)*

The American publishers, noted for their art books, take their name from Harry Nathan Abrams (1905-1979), born in London, England, the son of a shoeshop proprietor. In 1913 the family moved to New York City, where Abrams studied at the National Academy of Design and at the Art Students League. In 1926 he took a nonsalaried post with the advertising firm of Schwab and Beatty, supporting himself by working at his father's shoe store. In 1936 he was taken on as art director of the Book-of-the-Month Club, and came to appreciate the attractiveness of high-quality art reproductions with commentaries. In 1949 he founded his own company, Harry N. Abrams, Inc., and was the first American publisher to devote himself exclusively to art books.

Harry Ramsden's *(fish and chip restaurants)*

Fish and chips as a main meal are a popular British institution, not least thanks to their promotion by Harry Ramsden (1886-1963), a Bradford, Yorkshire, fish frier. His restaurant was the first in the area to offer a sit-down fish-and-chip meal, and he attracted both local people and visiting celebrities. His wife fell ill, however, and was advised by her doctor to move out of industrial Bradford into the country. Harry was dismayed at having to close his beloved restaurant, but resolved to continue his profitable business elsewhere. Accordingly, on December 20, 1928, Harry borrowed £150 to open a fish-and-chip shop in Guiseley, then a small town near Leeds. He happened to have chosen an ideal location, for Guiseley was the terminus for Leeds and Bradford trams (streetcars) and also the gateway to the beautiful Yorkshire Dales and Lake District. The word soon spread, and Harry was increasingly visited by day trippers. Trade was so good that Harry resolved to build the largest fish-and-chip emporium in the country. It duly opened to much publicity in 1931 and there are now Harry Ramsden's restaurants in many other British towns.

Hart Schaffner & Marx *(menswear)*

The American name, almost synonymous with men's suits, originated with Harry Hart (b. 1851) and his brother Max (b.1854), who in 1872, six months after the great Chicago fire, opened a clothing store on State Street. Two brothers-in-law, Levi Abt and Marcus Marx, then joined the business, which was renamed from Harry Hart and Brother to the somewhat awkward-sounding Hart, Abt & Marx. In 1887 Joseph Schaffner replaced Abt, and the present name was adopted. The company remains based in Chicago today.

Hartley's *(preserves)*

William Pickles Hartley (1846-1922) was born in Colne, Lancashire, England, the son of a whitesmith. He wanted to become a chemist, but instead helped his mother in her grocery shop, which soon moved to large premises in the town's main street. At the age of 16 he took charge of the shop, adding dried salted foods to standard groceries. In 1871 he became a jam manufacturer by accident. A local grocer failed to supply him with the jam he had ordered, so he was obliged to make his own. His new product prospered, and in 1874 he took the business out of Colne to Bootle, building a new factory not far from Liverpool, which was the port that imported the oranges he needed. In 1885 he formed the company of William Hartley & Sons Ltd., and the following year moved to Aintree, just outside Liverpool, where the British jam manufacturer still has its main office and works today.

Har-Tru *(tennis court surfacing)*

The artificial surface for tennis courts, made from crushed greenstone, was regarded by its US manufacturers as giving an area that was both hard (as distinct from grass, which is soft) and true, in the sense of level. The name dates from the 1970s and was entered in the *Trade Marks Journal* of March 7, 1984.

Harvey *(hotels and restaurants)*

Fred Harvey (1835-1901) was born in London, England, the son of English-Scottish parents. He emigrated to the United States in 1850, where he found immediate employment at the Smith and McNewill Café, New York City, earning two dollars a week as a busboy and pot scrubber. He had a yearn to travel, however, and in 1862 was hired as a postal clerk to sort mail in a specially designed post office railcar on the Hannibal and St. Joseph Railroad, based in St. Joseph, Missouri. While riding on the system's trains, Harvey discovered how poor the food was for travelers. Believing he could improve conditions, he built three eating houses along the route of the Kansas-Pacific Railroad in 1873. In 1876 Harvey approached the superintendent of the Atchison, Topeka and Santa Fe Railroad. Although eating facilities existed in some of the railroad's stations, the food quality was bad and the service poor. Harvey was taken on to operate eating houses for passengers along the railway. In 1883 he first hired women to serve as waitresses in his eating houses, and the "Harvey Girls," as they were known, gained repute for their wholesome image. Soon Harvey's company was famed as one of the largest and most scientifically managed businesses in the world. At the time of his death, Harvey's empire controlled 47 restaurants, 15 hotels, 30 railroad dining cars, and several elegant resorts along the Santa Fe railroad in the southwestern United States.

Harvey Nichols *(department store)*

The London, England, store traces its origins to 1813, when Benjamin Harvey opened a small linen shop on the corner of Sloane Street and Lowndes Terrace. On his death in 1850, the business passed to his daughter, Elizabeth, on the condition that she take into partnership one Colonel Nichols, a silk buyer. Harvey Nichols & Co. Ltd. was incorporated in 1873. Although now owned by **Debenhams**, "Harvey Nicks" has retained its original name and its original site, in what is now better known as Knightsbridge. A mystery remains. Did Elizabeth marry the colonel? The fact that the name became Harvey Nichols, not Harvey & Nichols, suggests she probably did.

Harvey's *("Bristol Cream" sherry)*

The ultimate history of the English firm goes back to the 18th century, when a wine merchant named William Perry came to live in a house in Bristol that is now the main Harvey's shop in the city. In 1796 he took a baker's son named Thomas Urch into business, partly to help him compete against two rivals, father and son wine merchants both named Thomas Harvey. The son married Urch's sister, Anne, and it was their son, John Harvey (1806-1879) who gave his name to the present Harvey's of Bristol. He joined the partnership in 1822, and after a period of apprenticeship to his uncle, and a spell of around ten years in the wine trade in Kidderminster, Worcestershire, took over the business. The famous **Bristol Cream** sherry was introduced later in the 19th century.

Harvey's *(sauce)*

The English sauce is named for Peter Harvey, owner of the Black Dog Inn in Bedfont, Middlesex, who in 1760 invented a new type of thin sauce. It was entered in the *Trade Marks Journal* of June 28, 1876 for: "Harvey's Sauce for Fish, Game, Steaks etc. Prepared from the Original Receipt, only at E. Lazenby's Fish Sauce Warehouse." A note adds: "Caution: The admirers of this celebrated Sauce ... are requested to observe that each bottle bears the well-known Label signed 'Elizabeth Lazenby.'" The lady in question was Harvey's sister, the wife of a London grocer, a Mr. Lazenby, who had wanted to buy the sauce's recipe. Harvey had originally refused, but in the end gave it to his daughter as a wedding present in 1776. After Lazenby's death in 1807, his widow carried on the business. The sauce is mentioned by Dickens in *Household Words* (1856) ("The grocer's hot pickles, Harvey's Sauce, Doctor Kitchener's Zest") and in *The Mystery of Edwin Drood* (1870) ("A condiment of a profounder flavor than Harvey"). Harvey's was taken over by **Crosse & Blackwell**.

Hasbro *(toys)*

The American company dates from 1923, when two brothers, Henry and Helal Hassenfeld, opened a small shop in Providence, Rhode Island. As Hassenfeld Brothers, they originally sold textile remnants, but went on to making pencil boxes and school supplies. In 1943 Henry's son, Merrill, became president of Hassenfeld Brothers and widened production to include toys such as paint sets, wax crayons, and doctor and nurse kits. In 1968 the firm became a public company and changed its name to Hasbro Industries, Inc. It remains in family hands today.

Hasselblad *(cameras)*

The camera owes its name to the Swedish inventor Victor Hasselblad (1906-1978), born in Göteborg, who in 1941 developed a new type of camera for the Swedish Air Force. It was the world's first 2 × 2 inch single-lens reflex camera, with interchangeable lenses and magazines, first appearing commercially seven years later. Hasselblad was chairman of his own company for 22 years to 1966 when he sold it to a Swedish industrial group.

Hatchards *(booksellers)*

The London, England, bookstore is named for John Hatchard (1769-1849), who after serving an apprenticeship with a Mr. Ginger of College Street, Westminster, and working for a Mr. Payne of Mews Gate, opened his own business in Piccadilly in 1797, both as publisher and bookseller, as was then customary. His shop soon became a fashionable rendezvous, and for many years was as much a club as a bookshop. Following his death, the business was taken over by his second son, Thomas Hatchard (d.1858), and in due course by his grandson, Henry Hudson Hatchard. After various changes of ownership in the 20th century, Hatchards was acquired by **Thorn EMI** in 1995.

Havas *see* (1) **Agence France-Presse**; (2) **Vivendi**

Hawker Siddeley *(aircraft)*

The first part of the British name is that of Harry Hawker, who in 1910 was chief test pilot to Thomas Sopwith (1888-1989), designer of many of the aircraft used in World War I, including the famous Sopwith Pup and Sopwith Camel. The Hawker Aircraft Company was formed after the war to manufacture aircraft, such as the Hawker Fury of 1929, a classic biplane. (Hawker was later killed testing a racing plane.) The second part of the name is that of John Davenport Siddeley (1866-1953), later Lord Kenilworth, who before World War I had started an auto manufacturing business, the Siddeley Autocar Company, which in 1919 merged with another firm initiated by Sir W.G. Armstrong to form **Armstrong-Siddeley**. The Hawker-Siddeley Aircraft Company (later Hawker Siddeley Group) was formed in 1935 to merge many famous names of early flying and motoring, such as Hawker Aircraft itself, Gloster Aircraft, A.V. Roe & Co. (see **Avro**), Armstrong Whitworth Aircraft, Air Service Training, and High Duty Alloys. In 1991 the company was taken over by BTR (*see* **Invensys**).

HBOS *see* **Halifax**

Head *(sports equipment)*

In 1947 Howard Head (b.1914) decided he needed a break from his job as an aerospace engineer in Boston, so he went to Stowe, Vermont, to indulge in a little skiing. He put up a bad performance on the slopes, and attributed his failure to his poor equipment. The hickory skis were particularly awkward, and Head determined to design a lighter alternative made of aluminum. After two years of research, Head developed a prototype of his invention, and by the early 1960s it was the best-selling ski in America. In 1969 Head sold his company to AMF, but he was soon back, forming another business to manufacture the "Prince," an oversize aluminum tennis racket he had invented.

Healey *see* **Austin Healey**

Heals *(department store)*

The London, England, bedding and furniture store took its name from John Harris Heal, who in 1810 set up business in Rathbone Place, between Tottenham Court Road and Oxford Street, selling bedding. On his death in 1833, Heal's wife Fanny kept the shop going, and seven years later it was taken over by their son, also John Harris Heal. It was he who moved the shop to its familiar site in Tottenham Court Road itself, where it was gradually extended and rebuilt. In 1893, aged 21, Ambrose Heal (1872-1959) entered the family firm after serving an apprenticeship as a cabinetmaker, becoming managing director in 1907 and chairman in 1913. In 1983 the store was bought by **Habitat Mothercare**, so continuing the link with bedding and furniture, if not the name.

Heath *(candy bar)*

The candy bar takes its name from Lawrence S. Heath (1869-1956), who began his career as a schoolteacher and principal. In 1914 he opened a small confectionery on the west side of the public square in Robinson, Illinois. Heath was joined in the business by his four sons, and together they sold fountain drinks, ice cream, and home-made candy, the latter including a distinctive English toffee. The store's products soon attracted a wider following, and the Heaths started selling candy to merchants in other cities. In 1931 the former teacher and his sons moved to a larger building, where they produced a five-cent Heath Toffee Candy Bar (later simply a Heath Bar). Within a few years, the Heath family was obliged to mechanize its facility to keep up with demand for its bar.

Heaton, Wallace *see* **Wallace Heaton**

Hector Powe *(menswear)*

Hector Powe, the man behind the British firm's name, began his career in his father's tailoring business in Fleet Street, London, in about 1908, and apparently opened his own first shop in Bishopsgate around two years later, when he was 20. World War I put a temporary halt to further development, and Powe served in the army. On demobilization in 1919 he returned to his business and, joined by his two brothers, Herbert Lungley Powe and John Leslie Powe, soon gained fame for his stylish products. In 1922 he opened two more London branches, and a third the following year. Expansion continued to the 1950s, when Hector Powe retired for health reasons and the company was taken over by Hope Brothers. It has now been incorporated into the **Burberry** group and no longer trades.

Hedex *(analgesic)*

The prime purpose of the proprietary preparation (actually paracetamol) is to ease headaches. Hence the name, entered in the *Trade Marks Journal* of March 3, 1976.

Hedges & Butler *(wines)*

The British wine merchants have been known under their present name since 1844. The business originated in 1667, when Edmund Harris (b.1635), an Oxfordshire wine merchant, opened a shop in Hungerford Street, off the Strand, London. In 1733 his activity was taken over by another Oxfordshire merchant, William Hedges, who knew the Harris family well and who in 1739 married Edmund Harris' great-granddaughter, Katherine Killingworth. Hedges lived until 1767, when he was succeeded by his nephew, Killingworth Hedges, who in 1798 brought his son, also William Hedges, into the business when the latter was 21. This William Hedges took his son, William Killingworth Hedges, into partnership in 1835, and his son-in-law, James Butler, in 1844. He himself lived to be 95, dying in 1872. It was under the ownership of the second William Hedges that the firm moved to Regent Street, where the company's head office remains today at No. 153.

Heering *(cherry brandy)*

Familiar for its "Cherry Heering" brandy (originally "Copenhagen Cherry Brandy"), the Danish company was founded in Copenhagen in 1818 by Peter Frederik Husfuhm Heering (1792-1875), a grocery assistant. He had come across cherry brandy through a recipe given

him by his employer's wife, and when he started his own business, his liqueur was so popular among visiting sailors that he decided to promote it at the expense of traditional grocery products. The distilleries and cherry orchards that now produce the liqueur are at Dalby, some 40 miles south of Copenhagen, where they were moved in the 1940s by the founder's great-grandson, another Peter Heering.

Heffer's *(booksellers)*

The Cambridge, England, bookstore was founded in 1876 by William Heffer (1843-1928), who opened his first bookshop in Fitzroy Street. In 1896 the business moved to Petty Cury, and when the premises there were demolished in 1970, together with the former Red Lion hotel and other buildings on the site, the firm made a third move, to its present location in Trinity Street.

Heidsieck *(champagne)*

The name ultimately goes back to Florenz-Ludwig Heidsieck, who founded the firm that bears his name in 1785. The house did not establish its identity, however, until 1834, when Henri-Louis Walbaum, the first of the nephews brought into the original business by Florenz-Ludwig, started up in business as Walbaum, Heidsieck & Co. The Charles Heidsieck brand of champagne did not appear until 1851, when Charles-Camille Heidsieck, one of Florenz-Ludwig's great-nephews, born in Reims, France, in 1822, established himself as a champagne shipper in this city. (According to some accounts he was the original "Champagne Charlie" of the Victorian music-hall song, popular in England in the late 1860s. Various English lords named Charles have also claimed the title, however.) Ever since the foundation of the firm, all male members of the Heidsieck family have had hyphenated names, with one half always "Charles." The name "Charles Heidsieck" was entered in the *Trade Marks Journal* of January 29, 1877, and that of "Heidsieck" alone by Kunkelmann et Compagnie, the legal title of **Piper-Heidsieck**, in the *Journal* of August 26, 1959. In 1985 Charles Heidsieck was sold to **Rémy Martin**.

Heineken *(beer)*

The Heineken family have been brewing

beer in Amsterdam since the 16th century. But the member of the Dutch family who is regarded as the founder of the present concern is Gerard Adriaan Heineken, who on December 16, 1863, aged 22, bought a brewery in the city, moving it to its present site in 1868. He went on to open a second brewery in Rotterdam in 1874, and the business has been managed by his descendants ever since.

Heinemann *(chocolates)*

The German firm dates from 1932, when Hermann Heinemann opened a konditorei in München-Gladbach, serving pastries and confectionery. The business grew slowly at first, and came to a complete standstill in World War II, but revived in 1953, when Heinemann started making his own chocolates. Demand gradually grew, so that by 1966 he had six shops in four different cities, and was obliged to introduce a large, modern production unit to meet his shops' needs. Heinemann's two sons joined him in the firm, although Bernd Heinemann met an untimely death in 1992. By the end of the century, Heinz Richard Heinemann had 11 shops and business was increasing healthily.

Heinemann *(publishers)*

The founder of the British firm, William Heinemann (1863-1920), was born in Surbiton, Surrey, the son of Louis Heinemann, a naturalized German. As a young man, William intended to become a musician, and went to Germany to this end. However, realizing he lacked the necessary talent, he turned instead to another artistic field. He was a good judge of books, not only for their content but as works of art in their own right. He therefore chose to make his career in publishing, receiving his initial training with the London firm of Trübner, later to be acquired by **Routledge**. He was then set to start up his own business, which he did in 1890, soon gaining a reputation for his ability to "sniff out" a good book and building up an impressive fiction list, which included works by such well-known writers as Rudyard Kipling and R.L. Stevenson. William Heinemann is now an imprint of **Random House**.

Heinkel *(aircraft)*

The name is that of Ernst Heinkel (1888-1958), a German tinker's son who designed and built his first airplane in 1910, as a student at the Stuttgart Institute of Technology. He flew it the following year, but it crashed and burned. Continuing his work, however, he became chief designer for the Albatros Aircraft Company in Berlin before the beginning of World War I, and during the war was responsible for the design and construction of around 30 different types of aircraft for the Austrian forces. In 1922, after the war, he founded the Ernst Heinkel Flugzeugwerke in Warnemünde, and between then and the overthrow of Nazi Germany around 100 different types came from his works, among them the He 111 and He 162, widely used by the Luftwaffe in World War II. After the war Heinkel's firm was dissolved, and in 1950 he began a new company to manufacture bicycles, motorcycles, and midget cars. At the time of Heinkel's death there were reports that he and Willy **Messerschmitt** had agreed to team up and develop new aircraft.

Heinz *(baked beans)*

Henry John Heinz (1844-1919) was born in the Birmingham section of Pittsburgh, Pennsylvania, to two German immigrants to America, Henry Heinz, a brick manufacturer, and his wife Margaretha. He started his commercial career early, selling fruit and vegetables from the family garden when he was only eight, and acquiring a horse and cart for this enterprise when he was 12. In 1869 Heinz formed a partnership with a neighbor, L. Clarence Noble, to sell food in bottles, choosing horseradish sauce as its first product, and this year is regarded as the founding of the company. In 1872 E.J. Noble joined Heinz, Noble, and Company and the firm set up its headquarters on the south side of Second Avenue in downtown Pittsburgh. After successfuly overcoming financial problems, Heinz moved from strength to strength in the food industry. With his brother John and his cousin Frederick as partners, Heinz established F. and J. Heinz Company in 1876 and served as the firm's manager. Pickles and other foods were added, and progressed to the famous baked beans, which were haricot beans in tomato sauce. The first ten varieties, including the initial horseradish sauce, were sour gherkins (1870), sour mixed pickles (1870), chow-chow pickle (1870), sour onions (1870), prepared mustard (1870), sauerkraut in crocks (1870), Heinz and Noble catsup (1873), vinegar (1873), and tomato ketchup (1876). In 1888 the H.J. Heinz Company was established when Heinz acquired the shares of his brother and cousin and became president of the new business. In 1896 came the familiar **57 Varieties**, indicating the wide range of products the firm was now turning out. Despite the continuing variety of products, Heinz baked beans remain a regular staple.

Helanca *(artificial fiber)*

The wool-like artificial fiber and fabric appears to derive its name, at least in part, from its Swiss manufacturers, Heberlein & Co., of Wattwil, near St. Gallen, who entered it in the *Trade Marks Journal* of November 15, 1944.

Helena Rubinstein *(cosmetics)*

Helena Rubinstein (1870-1965) was born in Kraków, Poland, with her father an art lover in the import business and her mother the descendant of a long line of bankers. As a girl, Helena wanted to be a doctor. But when she was 18 her parents sent her to Australia to stay with her uncle on his sheep farm. Helena was bored here in the outback, and making her way to the local town offered her services to an elderly pharmacist, who agreed to take her on and let her help prepare his products. Despite the hot Australian sun, Helena had managed to keep her complexion fresh and smooth, thanks to the jars of face cream she had brought with her. Australian women asked her if they could buy some of her cream. She began selling, and when her jars ran out, sent home for some more, eventually setting up her own business in Melbourne. In 1908 she returned to Europe, but to England, not Poland. She opened a beauty salon in London's fashionable Mayfair, and soon gained the fame for her cosmetic products that her name retains to this day.

Hellmann's *(mayonnaise)*

In 1912, Richard Hellmann (*c.*1876-1971), the German-born owner of a Manhattan delicatessen, decided that Americans needed a premixed mayonnaise, since many homemakers did not have the necessary knowledge or equipment to produce the sauce. He accordingly began selling mayonnaise packaged in one-pound wooden "boats." One year later he put the product in glass jars and delivered it to other stores in a pushcart. In due course the cart was replaced by a truck, and Hellmann opened a small plant. In 1927 Hellmann's business was acquired by Postum (*see* **Post Toasties**), but he continued to serve on the board. It later passed to the Best Foods Co., itself acquired in 1958 by **CPC** International.

Henkel *(chemicals)*

The German company, based in Düsseldorf and noted for its cosmetics, toiletries, and detergents, was founded in 1876 by Fritz Henkel and today remains in the control of his descendants. In 2000 Henkel put in a bid for **Clairol**.

Hennessy *(brandy)*

The name is that of an Irishman, Richard Hennessy (1720-1800), from Cork, who in 1735 left Ireland for France to fight for the French king. He was wounded in battle, and when invalided out made his home in Cognac, where many of his former comrades-in-arms were stationed. He soon became aware of the famous local product, named for the town itself, and was so impressed by its curative properties that he sent a cask back to Cork. His family liked it and asked for more, their admiration for the brandy being all the greater as it was the product of a country which, like Ireland, was an enemy of England. This inspired Hennessy to enter the brandy trade in full force and to set up his own business, which he did in 1763. Today the Franco-Irish links have been maintained, and Hennessy's brandy supplies a large percentage of the Irish market.

Henry Clay *(cigars)*

The brand of Havana cigar dates from the 19th century, when it was named after US Senator Henry Clay (1777-1852), who had business interests in Cuba. Its manufacture was transferred in the 1930s from Havana to Trenton, New Jersey, and the brand is now made in the Dominican Republic.

Henry Holt *(publishers)*

The US publishing house owes its origin to Henry Holt (1840-1926), born in Baltimore, Maryland, the son of an oyster dealer. He was a bright boy, studying Latin at eight and taking a prize in Greek at age 11. After attending General Prosser's school in New Haven, he entered Yale with the class of 1861, but did not settle there. He wanted to devote himself to literature, but wary of the precarious life of a writer, enrolled in the Columbia University School of Law, graduating in 1864. He then began to think of publishing books as a worthwhile profession, and in 1866 formed a partnership with a German immigrant publisher, Frederick Leypoldt (1835-1884). As Leypoldt and Holt, they published translations of the works of famous European authors, and in 1870 added foreign-language grammar texts to their list after buying out a publisher of French, German, and Italian dictionaries. Leypoldt retired in 1873, when the firm became Henry Holt & Co. and continued as a major publisher of school and college texts.

Hepworth *(menswear)*

Joseph Hepworth (1834-1911) was born near Huddersfield, England, a shoemaker's son. At the age of ten he began working in a local woolen mill, and after gaining further experience in another mill became a traveling salesman for a woolen manufacturer, packing his samples up every night and rising before five each morning to catch the early train. In 1864 he set up his own business in Briggate, Leeds, taking on his brother-in-law, James Rhodes, as partner. The following year he began to operate as a wholesale clothier in Bishopgate Street, taking advantage of the rise in the clothing trade. He did not open the first of his shops, however, until the early 1880s, when he was in the excellent position of making and supplying clothing for his own stores. Hepworth stores became familiar in most British towns, until in the 1980s all of the shops were renamed as **Next**, and the century-old name disappeared from the High Street.

Hermès *(fashion accessories)*

The French company derives its coincidentally classical name from its founder, Thierry Hermès, who in 1837 set up a business in Paris making saddles. In 1920 his grandson, Émile Hermès, began designing garments made from deerskin. Although now mainly producing handcrafted leather goods, the company has become famous for its equestrian motif headscarves and its "Kelly bag." The latter, launched in 1935 and based on a saddlebag, was named in 1955 after the actress Grace Kelly (1928-1982), who was often seen carrying one.

Heron *(gas stations, property, and insurance)*

The British company of this name was founded by Gerald Ronson (b.1939), born in London the son of a cabinetmaker of Russian immigrant origin. He quit school at 14 to work in his father's furniture business and was soon running it jointly with him. In 1956 they decided there was little future in furniture so switched into property, naming their new enterprise "Heron," a contraction of Ronson's father's name, Henry Ronson. In 1965 they expanded into housebuilding, then into automobile dealing and insurance. In 1976 Ronson successed his father as chairman of Heron Corporation plc (from 1983, Heron International plc).

Heron Parigi *(drawing boards)*

In 1964, the Italian designer Paolo Parigi (b.1936) unveiled his first mass-produced project, the "Heron" drawing table, so called because of its long legs and expectant attitude. It was an immediate success, and suggested the company name, Heron Parigi.

Hershey *(candy and chocolate)*

The chocolate candy bar, a virtual American institution, takes its name from Hershey, Pennsylvania, the town itself being named for the company's founder, Milton Snavely Hershey (1857-1945), who was raised in the Pennsylvania Dutch country of Mennonite farmers. He was apprenticed to a candy maker in Lancaster when he was 15. At 19 he began touring major cities, such as Denver, Chicago, New Orleans, and New York, all the while practicing the candy trade. Back penniless in Lancaster before he was 30, he began making caramels there, building up his business to become a very rich man. In 1900, two years after marrying, he sold his thriving Lancaster Caramel Company for $1 million to the rival American Caramel Company, but retained exclusive rights as its supplier of dipping chocolates. The turn of the century marked another milestone in the Hershey annals, and in February 1900 Hershey's company began marketing its milk chocolate Hershey Bar. Meanwhile, in 1897, he had purchased his birthplace, the family homestead in Derry Church, Dauphin County, Pennsylvania, 30 miles from Lancaster. His original intention was to reunite his parents on the old farm, but he then realized that the rich land surrounding the homestead was an ideal location for his new chocolate plant. Not only did the area provide an abundant supply of fresh milk, but there was plenty of water for cooling purposes in the factory as well as land for expansion. The factory was completed in 1905, when the village of Derry Church was renamed Hershey, and in 1908 the Hershey Chocolate Company was incorporated.

Hertz (car rental)

The American company was founded in Chicago in 1918 by Walter L. Jacobs (1897-1985), son of a ladies' clothing salesman. After a variety of jobs, Jacobs began selling **Ford** cars, first for the manufacturers, then as a used car salesman. He was soon renting out the cars for $10 a day, thus establishing America's first car rental firm. Meanwhile John Daniel Hertz (1879-1961), a Czech brought to the United States as a young boy, had also become involved in the auto business, starting work in an automobile sales agency in 1909. The agency ran taxicabs, and Hertz determined to do likewise. In 1915 he thus came to found the Yellow Cab Company in Chicago, in the process raising the status of cabs and their drivers. His enterprise spread outside of Chicago, but it was in that city that Walter Jacobs bought Hertz's business in 1923. Hertz remained as chairman, but it was Jacobs who ran it, and who was its president until his retirement in 1960. He kept Hertz's name, however, which is why the "rent-a-car" concept is associated with his name, not Jacobs'.

Heublein (liquor and wines)

The American company is famous for its vodka, with **Smirnoff**, Popoff, and Relska accounting for about one third of all vodka drunk in the United States. The name is that of Gilbert and Louis Heublein, who in 1875 set up a distilled spirits business in Hartford, Connecticut. By 1892 the brothers were bottling the first prepared cocktails, and when Vladimir Smirnov fled from Russia after the 1917 Revolution, and the rights to his vodka formula were acquired by an American, it was John Martin, grandson of Gilbert Heublein, who renegotiated the rights in 1939.

Hewitts (whiskey)

The blend of Irish whiskey takes its name from Thomas Hewitt, a merchant of Cork, who with two other entrepreneurs founded the Watercourse Distillery in 1782. In 1868, when the distillery was entirely owned by the Hewitt family, it amalgamated with the city's three other distillers, North Mall, The Green, and Daly's of John Street, as well as the Midleton Distillery, 12 miles from Cork, to form the Cork Distilleries Co.

Hewlett-Packard (electronic measurement equipment, computers, and computer printers)

The US company takes its name from William R. Hewlett (1913-2001) and David Packard (1912-1996), who became partners under the present name in 1939. (According to company legend, the toss of a coin decided the order of their names.) Hewlett was born in Ann Arbor, Michigan, the son of a professor of medicine. He attended Stanford University, California, where as an engineering student he first met Packard, born in Pueblo, Colorado. The two became close friends, and formed their partnership in the year they both graduated with an electrical engineering degree. The partners set up their business in nearby Palo Alto, initially in a small rented garage, their first product being a resistor capacity audio oscillator that Hewlett had designed when in graduate school. HP is still in Palo Alto, and the founding site is an official state landmark and "the birthplace of Silicon Valley."

Hilfiger, Tommy *see* **Tommy Hilfiger**

Hill, William *see* **William Hill**

Hill Samuel (investment bank)

The British firm of M. Samuel and Co. was established in 1831 and built up a merchanting business with the Far East, especially Japan. In 1897 the firm's oil business was hived off as **Shell** Transport and Trading, but the trading side of the business then gradually declined, especially after World War I. In 1920 M. Samuel and Co. was incorporated as a private company and in 1965 merged with Philip Hill, Higginson, Erlangers Ltd. to form Hill Samuel and Co. The former business had evolved as an amalgamation of Philip Hill and Partners, established in 1932, Higginson and Co., founded in 1907, and Erlangers Ltd., dating from 1870.

Hillards *(food stores)*

The founder of the British company was John Wesley Hillard (1857-1935), born in Barrington, near Ilminster, Somerset. On leaving school, he became apprenticed to a tea merchant, and after seven years with him managed grocery stores in Paris and Tralee, Ireland. In 1885 Hillard went up north and bought a grocery shop in Cleckheaton, West Yorkshire. The milling town proved fruitful for his business, and by 1890 he had opened four more stores there. In 1922, when he had been joined by his sons, Jack and Charles, Hillard acquired a local rival chain of 13 stores. Further acquisitions followed after his death, with the first Hillards supermarket opening in Wakefield, Yorkshire, in 1968. In the mid-1980s, however, the long-established Hillards name began to be phased out as the stores were gradually taken over by **Tesco** Foodstores.

Hillman *(automobiles)*

The last of the British-made Hillmans became **Chryslers** from 1976, but the Hillman Hunter was still being assembled in Iran in the mid-1980s, so Hillmans remain on the road. They are named for William Hillman (1847 or 1848-1929), born at Stratford, Essex, a shoemaker's son. Nothing is known about his early life, but he was trained as an engineer and was later employed at the Coventry Sewing Machine Company, where he helped make early "boneshaker" bicycles. In 1875 he set up his own business in Coventry as the **Premier** Cycle Co., making nuts, bearings, and cycle parts, soon progressing to add bicycles themselves. In 1905 he decided to set up a motor company, building a factory in the grounds of his home, Abingdon House. There, helped by the French engineer Louis Coatalen, the Hillman-Coatalen Car Company was formed in 1907. All seemed set for a firm partnership, but Coatalen sold out to Hillman in 1909, leaving his cofounder to continue alone. His company peaked in the 1930s with the production of the popular Hillman Minx.

Hills Brothers *(coffee)*

The brothers of the name are Austin H. Hills (1851-1933) and Reuben W. Hills (1856-1934), born in Maine. They moved with their parents to California in 1873 and took their first steps in the food business by selling eggs and butter from a stall in San Francisco's Bay City Market. With the profits they made from their stall, they bought the Arabian Coffee and Spice Mills in 1878 and roasted coffee, tea, spices, and other products. In 1900 the brothers were the first to sell vacuum-packed coffee in cans, and by 1923 they had dropped all other products to concentrate on coffee.

Hillsdown *(foods)*

The British foods group Hillsdown Holdings was founded in 1975 when Harry Solomon, a solicitor (lawyer), got together with the more entrepreneurial David Thompson (b.1936), a racehorse owner and breeder. They struck out on a string of acquisitions to build up a sizeable conglomerate, naming their enterprise after Hillsdown Court, a house owned by Thompson in Totteridge, Hertfordshire. In 1998 Hillsdown was taken over by **Unigate**.

Hilton *(hotels)*

The famous hotel chain owes its name to Conrad Nicholson Hilton (1887-1979), born in San Antonio, New Mexico. As a boy he helped his father turn the family home into an inn for traveling salesmen, charging $1 a night. On leaving school he went into banking, then served as an army officer in France in World War I. One day in 1918 he went to Cisco, Texas, to negotiate the purchase of a bank. The seller was asking too high a price, however, so Hilton had to stay overnight to contemplate his next move. He started talking to the hotel owner, who told him there was money in the local oilwells. The consequence was that Hilton bought the hotel, not the bank. This was the cornerstone on which he gradually built his empire, with the first "custom-built" Hilton hotel opening in Dallas, Texas, in 1925.

Hine *(brandy)*

The name is Westcountry English, that of Thomas Hine (1773-1822), born in Beaminster, Dorset. In 1792 Hine went to France to complete his education, staying with a friend near Cognac. When England went to war with France in 1793 Hine was imprisoned for a time, but two years later was free to join a brandy company that had been set up in 1763. Hine married the company manager's daughter,

Françoise Elisabeth Delamain, and eventually took the company over, renaming it Thomas Hine & Co. in 1817. Ever since, the firm has been under the management of the English Hine family.

Hingley (anchors and cables)

In the 19th and early 20th centuries, the British firm of Noah Hingley & Sons was the largest anchor and cable manufacturer in the world, serving many famous passenger ships, such as White Star Line's *Olympic* and *Titanic*, **Cunard**'s *Mauretania* and *Aquitania*, Holland American Line's *Sfatendam*, and Hamburg Amerika Line's *Vaterland*. It was founded in Netherton, near Dudley, Worcestershire, in 1838 by Noah Hingley (1796-1877), who began life as a chainmaker on the banks of the Stour River. His elder sons Hezekiah (1825-1865) and George (1829-1901), joined him in the business, which passed on the early death of Hezekiah to his youngest son, Benjamin (1830-1905). In 1890 the firm became a limited company and remained under Benjamin's control to his death. The last family member to be involved in the business was Martin Hingley (1913-2001), Noah's great-grandson. The firm disappeared in 1960, when it was subsumed into F.H. Lloyd, manufacturers of high precision forgings, which soon after merged with **Triplex** Lloyd.

Hires (root beer)

Charles Elmer Hires (1851-1937) was born on a farm near Roadstown, New Jersey. After a meager early education, he moved away from his parents' farm and in 1863 began a four-year apprenticeship in 1863 with a view to becoming a pharmacist. Hines first tasted the drink that brought him fame while staying at a New Jersey boardinghouse during his honeymoon in 1875. During their stay, the couple sampled a pitcher of herb tea, made from a family recipe by the innkeeper's wife. Hines recognized its potential, and after conversations with various chemist friends and experiments with sarsparilla root and other ingredients, he concocted what became known as root beer. (At first he had thought of calling his drink a tea, but decided against this when realizing that miners would never drink it if it was called tea.) In 1876 Hires Root Beer made its debut at the Philadelphia Centennial Exposition. It met a

ready response, its reputation spread, and in 1890 Hines reorganized his business and named it the Charles Elmer Hires Company.

His Master's Voice *see* **HMV**

Hispano-Suiza (automobiles)

The name, Spanish for "Spanish-Swiss," is that of the company founded in Barcelona, Spain, in 1904 by Marc Birkigt, a Swiss-born engineer who had already designed the first Spanish-built car. During and after World War I Hispano-Suiza produced aircraft engines, but after the war, in 1919, the French-designed Hispano-Suiza H6B was launched at the Paris Salon and immediately set new standards in automotive design. In 1938 the factory of Hispano-Suiza France at Bois-Colombes stopped building cars to concentrate on aircraft engines again, and the marque was never revived.

Hitachi (electrical and electronic appliances)

The Japanese company traces its origins to 1904, when an engineer, Fusanosuko Kuhara, organized a mining company in the hills near the fishing village of Hitachi, northeast of Tokyo. He was joined by an engineer friend, Namihei Odaira, who set up a repair shop at the mining site for imported machinery. In 1910 the two men established their own machinery building company, naming it after the village. In 1920 the business was incorporated and began expanding its product line. The company moved rapidly into the communications boom of the 1970s with its computers and electronic equipment, and the private citizen soon became familiar with the name on televisions and other home-based appliances and instruments.

HMV (music stores)

The world's oldest record chain takes its name from the abbreviation of "His Master's Voice," entered by the **Gramophone** Company of London, England, in the *Trade Marks Journal* of October 5, 1910 for: "Talking machines, talking machine needles, talking machine records and other talking machine accessories." The name itself is properly the title of a picture of a dog listening to an old-fashioned phonograph with a brass horn. The picture was painted in 1898 by the photographer and artist Francis Barraud, and the dog himself, named

Nipper, belonged to his brother. In 1899 Barraud visited the Gramophone Company, formed in London in 1897 as an offshoot of the American Berliner Gramophone Company, and left a photograph of his painting. The company bought the picture on condition that Barraud paint out the phonograph and replace it with a gramophone. The picture was duly altered and assigned to the Gramophone Company on January 31, 1900 together with its title, "His Master's Voice," which was duly adopted for commercial use. HMV's "dog and trumpet" logo is still current, with Nipper represented by a modern Jack Russell terrier. The Victor Talking Machine Co. acquired the North American rights to the logo in 1901 and used it on all **Victrola** phonographs and "Victor" records. When **RCA** purchased Victor in 1930, the logo passed to them in turn. In 1998 the HMV record stores merged with the **Waterstone** and **Dillons** book chains to form HMV Media.

Hoare's *(bank)*

The discreet and upmarket London bank, specializing in serving the English landed gentry, was founded in 1672 by Richard Hoare (1648-1718), the son of a yeoman and "dealer of horses" who became a goldsmith and, in 1712, lord mayor of London. The bank has been at its present address, 37 Fleet Street, since 1690 and is still in family hands. Its present chairman is Henry Hoare (b.1931) and all but one of the directors are Hoares.

Hobbs *(fashionwear)*

The British women's clothes retailer, with 37 outlets across the UK, was founded by Marilyn Anselm (b.1945), a sculpture student, who began designing her own clothes in the early 1970s on failing to find any clothing of quality. A keen horsewoman, she took the name of her London-based business from the maker of her favorite horse boxes, and the "equestrian look" is one of Hobbs's most successful lines. Anselm runs the company with her Israeli-born husband, Yoram (b.1942).

Hobbs, Russell *see* **Russell Hobbs**

Hodder & Stoughton *(publishers)*

The British publishing house takes its name from Matthew Henry Hodder (1830-1911) and Thomas Wilberforce Stoughton (b. 1840). Hodder was born a chemist's son in Staines,

Middlesex. At the age of 14 he joined the London publishers Jackson & Walford, rising to become partner in 1861, when the firm became Jackson, Walford & Hodder. Mr. Jackson and Mr. Walford were both elderly, and Hodder realized he could soon acquire the whole business. He therefore began looking for a partner. The man he chose was Thomas Stoughton, a Norfolk Nonconformist minister's son, whom he had previously met, doubtless socially, in London publishing circles. Mr. Jackson and Mr. Walford retired, as Hodder had predicted, and the new partnership between Stoughton and himself was set up in 1868, when the two men moved the business to new premises in Paternoster Row, where it remained until 1906. In 1993 Hodder & Stoughton merged with Headline Book Publishing to become Hodder Headline.

Hoechst *(chemicals)*

The German company was founded in the Höchst quarter of Frankfurt-am-Main in 1863 by Wilhelm Meister and Eugen Lucius, and was accordingly at first known as Meister, Lucius & Co. Two years later it became Meister, Lucius & Brüning, adding the name of another founder, Adolf Brüning. In 1880 it was converted into a limited liability company and in due course became known as Farbwerke Hoechst Aktiengesellschaft ("Hoechst Dyeworks AG"), from its place of origin. From 1925 to 1945 it was part of **IG Farben** but was reestablished in 1951 as Farbwerke Hoechst AG. The first word of this was dropped from the name in 1974. In 1987 the company's American subsidiary, the American Hoechst Corporation, acquired the **Celanese** Corporation.

Hoepfner *(beer)*

The name is that of the German priest who founded a brewery in Karlsruhe in 1798. The firm is now in the sixth generation of the family, whose name happens to mean "hop farmer."

Hoffmann–La Roche *(pharmaceuticals)*

The manufacturers of **Valium**, **Librium**, and **Rohypnol** were founded in Switzerland in 1896 by Franz Hoffmann-La Roche (1868-1920), born Franz Hoffmann in Basle into an old established merchant family. (Following Swiss custom, Hoffmann added his wife's maiden name to his own on marrying Adele La

Roche.) As a young man, he had the idea of supplying and selling drugs in standardized packages, unlike the rough and ready mixtures that pharmacists usually dispensed. At the same time he wanted to concentrate on specialist drugs, and to aim his products not just at the sick man in the street but the doctor who treated him. He put his concept into practice with excellent results, and within a few years Hoffmann-La Roche had pharmaceutical plants in around a dozen countries. His first specialist drug was a cough remedy called Thiocal, and this led the way to other important drugs, although Valium, Librium, and Rohypnol were not introduced till the 1960s.

Hogg Robinson (travel agents and insurance brokers)

Not a great deal is known about the two Britons who founded the original company in 1845. Francis Hogg was a wine merchant who formed a partnership with Augustus Robinson, an insurance broker and merchant. The pair thus pooled their mercantile and insurance interests. The present travel company of the name is a recent development, arising only in the 1970s as the result of a series of acquisitions.

Hohner (harmonicas)

The original mouth-organ maker who gave his name to the German company was Matthias Hohner (1833-1902), a clockmaker of Trossingen, not far from the Swiss border. In 1857 he gave up making clocks and took to harmonicas instead. Until then, such instruments had been produced laboriously by hand, using basic tools such as knives and chisels. Hohner wanted to "automate" the process, cutting the parts by machine, while improving the instrument's quality overall by using brass for the reed plates instead of the usual lead. In his first year of production, Hohner, his wife, and two other workers turned out 650 harmonicas, and production gradually increased and speeded up from then on. In 1879 Hohner was elected mayor of Trossingen in token of his unique achievement. The firm's head office and works remain there today.

Holden (automobiles)

In 1856 James Alexander Holden set up a saddle-making business in Adelaide, South Australia. For many years he concentrated on making saddles for horses and bicycles. By 1910, as Holden and Frost, his business had started to produce components for motorcycles. In 1914 the firm was commissioned to produce the first custom-made car body, and by 1924 had evolved into Holden's Motor Body Builders Ltd.(HMBB). A contract was now signed for the company to become the local car-body supplier for **General Motors**, who had opened a new factory in Woodville, South Australia. GM established its own base in Australia in 1926 and in 1931 acquired HMBB, merging the two businesses. Production still largely centered on car bodies, but in 1946 a prototype Holden car emerged and the first production Holden automobile rolled off the line in 1948.

Holeproof (hosiery)

The history of the name ultimately goes back to 1872, when Carl Freschl founded the Kalamazoo Knitting Works in Kalamazoo, Michigan, to make stockings with a crude knitting machine. In 1882 he moved his factory to Milwaukee, and gradually developed a new type of durable fabric. To denote the wearing qualities of the new product, Freschl chose the name "Holeproof", meaning that the stockings would not develop holes. The name suggested not only durability but dependability. In 1904, the Holeproof Hosiery Co. was incorporated and took over the business of the Kalamazoo company, and in 1906 "Holeproof" was registered as a trademark. The Holeproof Hosiery Co. has always vigorously defended its name and prevented the use by others of such names as "No-Hole," "Sta-Hole," "Hole-Less," "Hole-Shy," and "No-Mo-Hole."

Holiday Inns (hotels)

The inspiration for the world's largest hotel chain came to Kemmons Wilson in 1951, when taking his family on holiday to Washington, DC. Depressed by the succession of seedy roadside tourist courts and motels that they stayed in, he returned to Memphis determined to create a chain of clean, moderately priced, family-centered motor hotels that American families would flock to on holiday. He opened his first Holiday Inn on the outskirts of Memphis in 1952, naming it after the movie *Holiday Inn* (1942) starring Bing Crosby and Fred Astaire. It was quite different from other local hotels, with a swimming pool, free ice, free parking, and a dog kennel. Moreover, children under 12 could stay without charge in their parents' room. Within a week all the hotel's 120 rooms, each with private bath, were filled nightly as motorists welcomed an alternative to the poorly equipped and randomly run tourist courts. Holiday Inns soon started to appear along roadsides, and the first non-United States Holiday Inn opened in Montreal in 1960.

Holland & Holland *(rifles and sporting guns)*

The London, England, firm derives its name from Harris John Holland (1806-1896) and his nephew, Henry Holland (1845-1930). Harris Holland was an organ builder's son who set up as a tobacconist in Holborn in 1835. He was a good rifle shot, and belonged to a pigeon shooting club, where he met James **Purdey**, among others. His sporting interests led him to take up gunmaking, and his rifles sold so well that by 1857 he had abandoned his tobacco business entirely in favor of that craft. He had two daughters, but lacked a son to take into partnership, so instead he apprenticed his 15-year-old nephew. After a move in about 1866, the business acquired its present name in the 1870s, showing that uncle and nephew had become full partners by then. The last of the Holland family died in 1958.

Holloway's *(pills)*

The patent British pills, used principally for laxative purposes, were the creation of Thomas Holloway (1800-1883), born at Plymouth Dock (now Devonport), Devon, the son of a retired militia warrant officer-turned-baker and innkeeper. At first Holloway drifted from job to job, but the turning point in his career came in 1837, when he was a merchant and foreign commercial agent in London. An Italian client, one Felix Albinolo, asked for Holloway's help in marketing his patent ointment in Britain. Holloway introduced him to the authorities at St. Thomas's Hospital and obtained testimonials of the ointment's efficacy on his behalf. The experience showed Holloway how profitable patent medicines could be. He quickly produced a competing product of similar composition, and announced "Holloway's Family Ointment" for sale that same year. Soon after, Holloway began producing pills, and by dint of wide advertising and a network of foreign agents,

their name was made known internationally. Both "Holloway's Pills" and "Holloway's Ointment" were entered in the *Trade Marks Journal* of November 18, 1885.

Holsten Pils *(beer)*

The well-known German beer takes its name from the Holsten brewery, Hamburg, where it was first brewed in 1829. The brewery's own name means "of Holstein," referring to the former duchy in which Hamburg was at one time located, while "Pils" means a beer similar to a Pilsner.

Honda *(motorcycles and automobiles)*

The name is that of Soichiro Honda (1906-1991), born in Tenryu, a village in central Japan, the son of a blacksmith and bicycle repairer. He was fascinated by mechanical things from an early age, and when he was 16 quit school to become an apprentice in a motor repair shop. In 1931 he opened his own garage, concentrating on the development of a new type of piston ring, which he began manufacturing in 1936. The rings did not sell well, however, and Honda was advised by analysts that they lacked the necessary silicon to form a satisfactory alloy. He had never heard of silicon, so enrolled at the Hamamatsu Institute of Technology to improve his patchy technical knowledge. Then came World War II, during which Honda made piston rings, and in 1946 he set up what he called the Honda Technical Research Institute, really just a small shed on a bombsite, to conduct research and development into internal combustion engines. It became Honda Motor Company two years later, originally building motorcycles by fitting surplus military engines on to bicycles. These were very popular, and became known as *bata-bata*, the Japanese equivalent of "phut-phut." Within a few years Honda was producing his "My Dream" range of fully-fledged motorcycles, and in 1957 the first Honda cars were launched.

Honeywell *(electronic control systems and computers)*

In 1883 a Minneapolis inventor, Albert M. Butz, produced an automatic temperature controller by connecting a thermostat to a motor. In 1885 he set up his first plant in a shed and called it the Consolidated Temperature Controlling Company. Ten years later the business had become the Minneapolis Heat Regulator Company, and was expanding rapidly. Meanwhile, in Wabash, Indiana, Mark Honeywell, a young engineer, was perfecting a heat generator as part of his plumbing and heating business, and in 1906 he set up the Honeywell Specialty Company, specializing in hot water heating generators. In 1927 the Minneapolis Heat Regulator Company and Honeywell Specialty Company merged to form the Minneapolis-Honeywell Regulator Company. It adopted its present name, Honeywell Inc., in 1964, and in 1999 merged with **Allied-Signal**.

Hoover *(vacuum cleaners)*

The year 1901 saw the invention of the vacuum cleaner simultaneously in Britain and America. The Briton was H.C. Booth, who had discovered that suction, even by the mouth, removed dust from upholstery. (*See* **Goblin**.) In the United States, a lady named Corinne Dufour invented a device that successfully sucked dust onto a wet sponge by means of an electric motor. The embryo vacuum cleaner was thus already in existence when in 1907 James Murray Spangler, a 71-year-old janitor at Zollinger's Dry Goods Store in Canton, Ohio, devised a machine that retained the dust it sucked from carpets and the like in a rudimentary bag like a pillowcase. His invention worked so well that the following year he patented it, forming the Electric Suction Sweeper Company. He lacked funds, however, so sold his enterprise to a saddler, William Henry Hoover (1849-1932), who was shrewd enough to realize that vacuum cleaners had a brighter commercial outlook than saddles. Later that year he became president of the company, with Spangler as superintendent. The Electric Suction Sweeper Co. became the Hoover Suction Sweeper Co. in 1910 and the Hoover Co. in 1922.

Horch *see* **Audi**

Horlicks *(powdered malted milk drink)*

William Alexander Horlick (1846-1936) was born in Ruardean, Gloucestershire, England, the son of a saddler. Following education in local schools, he was apprenticed to a harness maker before opening his own shop. In 1869 he immigrated to the United States, settling in Racine, Wisconsin, where he worked for James A. Horlick, a relative who had lived there since 1844. In 1873 Horlick moved to Chicago, where

he was later joined by his chemist brother, James Horlick (1844-1921), and together with him set up the business of J. & W. Horlick, obtaining a US patent the following year for their "New Food for Infants, Dyspeptics, and Invalids." They made the food by soaking wheat flour and malted barley in water, then extracting the water and pulverizing the residue. The product was popular, and in 1876 the brothers built a factory in Racine, Wisconsin, to make it in larger quantities. It was then that William proposed they extend their range by selling "Malted Milk," a drink made from a powdered extract of malted barley and wheat mixed with milk. This was the germ of the Horlicks of today, and in 1883 Horlick's Food Company was incorporated to manufacture it on a full-time basis. James returned to London in 1890, opened a British office that same year, and entered "Horlick's" in the *Trade Marks Journal* of August 19, 1891 for: "A dessicated and granulated preparation of malt extract and milk as a food for infants and invalids."

Hormel *(canned meat)*

George Albert Hormel (1860-1946) was born in Buffalo, New York, the son of a tanner. His parents were German immigrants. He held several menial jobs before leaving home at the age of 17 for Chicago, where he found employment first in his uncle Jacob Decker's meat market and then at the Philip D. **Armour** meatpacking house. While at Armour he met Edward A. Cudahy and Gustavus F. **Swift**, who like himself had learned their trade at Armour before creating meat companies of their own. Following his tenure at Armour, Hormel worked a number of jobs in the meatpacking business until 1891, when he opened a small slaughterhouse in Austin, Minnesota. Although it was a time of depression, Hormel's enterprise flourished, so that by the end of the following year he and his handful of employees had slaughtered 610 pigs. The business went on to produce the first canned ham, which went on sale in 1926 as "Hormel Flavor-Sealed Ham." Hormel's son Jay C. Hormel became president in 1928 and subsequently introduced two of the company's best-known products: **Dinty Moore** beef stew and **Spam** luncheon meat.

Hornby *(model railways)*

The name known to generations of model-loving schoolboys (and adults) is that of Frank Hornby (1863-1936), born in Liverpool, England, the son of a provision merchant. On leaving school at 16, Frank worked for seven years as a clerk in his father's office before taking a job with a meat importer, where he became managing clerk. Having a love of mechanical things, he increasingly turned his attention to toys and before World War I set up a business to make **Meccano** kits. In 1920 he expanded his business to include clockwork trains, doing so at a time when the Germans, who traditionally produced such toys, were in a weak position because of the war. In 1925 he introduced the famous Hornby electric trains. These were originally known as gauge "0," but later the smaller gauge "00," or Hornby "Dublo," was the one that took the fancy of most fanatics. In 1932 Hornby went on to produce the equally well-known **Dinky Toys**. After Hornby's death, the company passed to his two sons, Roland and Douglas, but production was suspended in World War II when the Liverpool factory became a munitions line. When the sons tried to upgrade their production lines after the war, the cost effectively bankrupted them, and in 1964 they sold out to their competitors, **Tri-Ang**.

Horniman's *(tea)*

The founder of the British tea business was John Horniman, father of Frederick John Horniman (1835-1906) who founded the Horniman Museum, London. John Horniman was born in Bridgwater, Somerset, and some time after about 1844 set up a tea-packing business in Newport, Isle of Wight. In 1852 he moved his activity to Wormwood Street, London, and continued with it until 1868 when he retired. The firm was registered as W.H. & F.J. Horniman & Co. in 1889 when his sons, William Henry and Frederick John, acquired their father's interests. The Horniman Museum arose out of the artifacts collected by Frederick John Horniman during his travels to different parts of the world over a period of 40 years, with these first displayed in his private home, Surrey House, Forest Hill, in 1890.

Horrockses *(cotton clothes and sheets)*

The British company's founder was John Horrocks (1768-1804), the son of a quarry owner at Edgworth, near Bolton, Lancashire. He first worked himself as a quarryman, making and selling millstones. In 1791 he started a yarn manufacturing business in Preston, taking his brother Samuel as partner, the latter outliving him and dying in 1846. In 1885 the firm amalgamated with Hollins, Brothers & Co., with further amalgamations following. Today the company, still based in Preston, is simply Horrockses Ltd.

Hoseasons *(holiday agents)*

Hoseasons Holidays is best known for its boating holidays and self-catering holiday homes. The British firm was launched in 1945 by W.B. "Wally" Hoseason, a retired harbormaster at Lowestoft, Suffolk, and Oulton Broad, the latter being a fashionable suburb with a lake that is the southernmost of the Norfolk Broads (though actually in Suffolk). The enterprise began as a fairly modest boat rental business. Wally Hoseason fell ill, however, and was helped out part-time by his son James (b.1928), then a civil engineer lecturing in mathematics and engineering at Lowestoft Technical College. In 1950 Wally Hoseason died, leaving his son wholly in charge.

Hotchkiss *(automobiles)*

The name is that of Benjamin Berkeley Hotchkiss (1826-1885), American inventor of the Hotchkiss machine gun (1872) and Hotchkiss magazine rifle (1875). The firm that he founded to build these weapons opened as a workshop in the French town of Saint-Denis, now a suburb of Paris, in 1867. When the demand for weapons was reduced in 1903, the firm turned to making cars. Its auto business was always at a low level, and the company found it a struggle to get going again after World War II. The answer was to merge with another firm, and this came about in 1954, when Hotchkiss, **Delahaye**, and **Delage** combined forces to make trucks and military vehicles.

Hotmail *(Internet e-mail facility)*

The company was founded in 1996 by Sabeer Bhatia (b.1969), an Indian immigrant to the USA, and Jack Smith to provide free e-mail over the Internet, and resulted when Bhatia and Smith wanted to e-mail each other at work without their bosses knowing. The name indicates its purpose and immediacy of function, with "hot" as in "hotline." In 1997 Bhatia sold Hotmail to **Microsoft**.

Hotpoint *(domestic appliances)*

The name now seems incongruous for the refrigerators with which it is usually associated. This is because the manufacturer's original product was electric irons, which became hot at the point. The firm was founded by Earl H. Richardson, plant superintendent of a power company in Ontario, California, who designed the iron in 1903 so his wife could use its tapering point to iron frilly ruffles and pleats. In 1904 he formed the Pacific Electric Heating Company, which became the Hotpoint Electric Heating Company in 1911. In 1918 this company merged with General Electric, while its British branch was formed in 1920 as the Hotpoint Electrical Appliance Company.

Houghton Mifflin *(publishers)*

Henry Oscar Houghton (1823-1895) was born in Suffolk, Vermont, the son of a former tanner and farmhand, and spent his early years in the poverty of a large family in the hill country of northern Vermont. At age 13 he was apprenticed to the Burlington Free Press in return for room, board, and clothing and was encouraged by his brother Daniel to follow him to the University of Vermont. He duly entered in 1842 and on graduating found work in Boston as a compositor and later as a proofreader in the printing house of Freeman and Bolles. In 1849 Houghton entered the first of many partnerships and in 1852, with borrowed capital, bought out the remaining partner, Bolles, and founded H.O. Houghton and Co. In the same year he also established the Riverside Press on the banks of the Charles River in Cambridge, Massachusetts. Following further partnerships, some more successful than others, in 1880 he formed Houghton, Mifflin and Co., the latter name being that of George Harrison Mifflin (1845-1921), a young Boston blueblood whom Houghton had reluctantly taken into the business in 1868 but who had proved his worth. On Houghton's death, Mifflin succeeded him as senior partner of the house the older man had built before him.

House of Fraser *(department stores)*

The British group developed to what it is today through four generations of Frasers, all named Hugh, the first being a Scot who set up a draper's shop in Glasgow in 1849. His son, Hugh Fraser (1861-1927), consolidated the business. The effective founder of the present company, however, was his son, Lord Hugh Fraser (1903-1966), who brought the thriving business south to London's Knightsbridge in 1959. He had gone more or less straight from school into his father's Glasgow business, becoming managing director of the parent company, Fraser Sons & Co. Ltd., in 1927. In 1941 he was appointed chairman, and in 1947 also managing director, with the company then acquiring its present name, House of Fraser Ltd. His son in turn, Hugh Fraser (1936-1987), became group chairman in 1966, and modernized many of its retail outlets, including **Harrods**. He was dismissed from the chairmanship in 1981, however, for his controversial financial connection with Roland "Tiny" Rowland of the **Lonrho** Group.

Hovis *(brown wholemeal bread)*

The British name ultimately goes back to Richard Smith (d.1900), born into a milling family at Stone, Staffordshire. He conceived the idea of baking a new type of wholemeal bread by lightly cooking the wheatgerm in steam so as to preserve its nourishing qualities, and then putting back into flour many times more wheatgerm that it would normally contain. He patented his process in 1887, and the finished product became known as "Smith's Patent Germ Bread." It was marketed by S. Fitton & Son Ltd., millers of Macclesfield, Cheshire, who organized a national competition to find a better name for their increasingly popular bread. The winner was one Herbert Grimes, a university student, who took the Latin words *hominis vis*, "strength of man," and contracted them to "Hovis." The name was entered by "Richard Smith, Corn Flour Mills, Macclesfield, Cheshire" in the *Trade Marks Journal* of November 16, 1890, and in 1898 Fitton & Son duly became the Hovis Bread Flour Co. Ltd. In 1918, by special resolution, the company name was shortened to Hovis Ltd. In its early years the name appeared in advertisements with a tilde over the "o" ("Hõvis"), to indicate that the word was an abbreviation. It is not clear if Mr. Grimes' Latin phrase was a quote from an actual classical author. In 1957 Hovis merged with **McDougall** to form Hovis McDougall, and this company in turn joined **Rank** in 1962 to become Rank Hovis McDougall (RHM).

Howard Johnson's *(restaurants and ice cream)*

Howard Dearing Johnson (1896-1972) was born in Boston, Massachusetts, the son of a cigar wholesaler. He quit school at 16 to work in the family business, but following the sudden death of his father in 1922, discovered that it was badly in debt. He struggled for a time to restore it to prosperity, then decided to look for better prospects. In 1925 he bought a local drugstore, expanding its stock and services, including the sale of ice cream, to include a restaurant in 1929. By 1935, when he had more than a dozen outlets, and the ice cream business was still growing, a friend approached him about building another Howard Johnson's Restaurant in Orleans, a village catering for the tourist trade. Johnson lacked the funds, but instead suggested the friend, Reginald Sprague, open a Howard Johnson's Restaurant himself, with Johnson providing his name and training in return for receiving the exclusive right to supply Sprague's restaurant. The franchising venture was a success, and by 1939 there were 107 Howard Johnson's. In 1959, when Johnson retired, there were over 550 Howard Johnson Restaurants and Motor Lodges, with their trademark "28 Flavors of Ice Cream" and distinctive orange-and-blue color scheme.

Howard Miller *(clocks)*

Howard Miller (b.1905) came to Zeeland, Michigan, as a boy after his father became manager of a local clock factory there. In 1925 the senior Miller started his own business, the Herman Miller Furniture Co. One year later, he branched out into clocks, and with his son founded the Herman Miller Clock Co. The two similar names caused confusion, even in a small town such as Zeeland, so the clock business was renamed the Howard Miller Clock Co. The firm initially made only wall and mantel clocks, but in 1948 developed its popular grandfather clocks.

HP *(sauce)*

The British brand of sauce dates from the 1870s. The initials that form its name are popularly said to stand for "Houses of Parliament", a picture of which appears on the label. However, the name was adopted by the Midland Vinegar Company, its original manufacturers, from that of another firm's product, "Garton's H.P. Sauce," and it was thus ready-made, whatever the letters themselves might have actually meant. The name was entered by Edwin Samson Moore, "trading as 'The Midland Vinegar Company', 'The Trade Malt Vinegar Company', and as F.G. Garton and Co." of Aston Cross, Warwickshire, in the *Trade Marks Journal* of May 22, 1912.

HRG *(automobiles)*

In 1935 three English engineers, E.A. "Ted" Halford, Guy Robins, and H.R. "Ron" Godfrey, joined forces to set up a tiny sports car business at Norbiton, Surrey. The result was the birth of the HRG, known affectionately as the "Hurg," a car somewhat similar to the **Frazer Nash**. (The initials were also those of Godfrey himself.) After 1956 the firm concentrated on general engineering. Godfrey died in 1968 aged 81, after a long illness.

HSBC *(bank)*

The British bank was founded in Birmingham in 1836 by Charles Geach, an official at the Bank of England's branch in that city, as the Birmingham and Midland Bank. After absorbing several banks in the Midlands, it entered London by merging with the Central Bank of London in 1891 to form the London and Midland Bank. It then spread nationwide by a process of expansion and amalgamation, eventually merging with the London Joint Stock Bank in 1918 to form the London Joint City and Midland Bank. The name Midland Bank was adopted in 1982. In 1992 the Midland was taken over by the Hong Kong and Shanghai Banking Corporation (HSBC), itself founded in 1864 on the initiative of Thomas Sutherland (1834-1922), superintendent and later chairman of **P&O**, and a group of Hong Kong merchants. In 1999 Midland was itself renamed HSBC.

Hudson *(automobiles)*

The American company was founded in 1909 by Howard E. Coffin (1873-1937) and Roy D. Chapin (1880-1936), respectively chief engineer and sales manager at the Olds Motor Works (*see* **Oldsmobile**), who named the cars they produced after their principal backer, Joseph L. Hudson, one half of the future **Dayton-Hudson**. The final Hudson car was produced in 1954, when the firm merged with

Nash (*see* **Nash-Kelvinator**) to form **American Motors**, and by 1957 the Hudson name had disappeared.

Hudson's (*booksellers*)

Hudson's of Birmingham, England, is one of the best-known bookstores in the Midlands. It was founded in 1906 by E.F. Hudson and Percy Woolston, two young assistants at an existing bookshop. In 1909 Percy Woolston left to set up on his own in Nottingham, after which the Birmingham shop became a family business run by the Hudsons, who formed it into a limited company in 1926. Unlike many bookshops, Hudson's has not diversified, and has no branch in any other town or city.

Hula Hoop (*toy hoops*)

The plastic hoops for spinning around the body were launched in 1958 by the Wham-O Manufacturing Co., San Gabriel, California, makers of the **Frisbee**. When the hoop is in use, the movements of the body resemble those of someone dancing the hula, the dance performed by Hawaiian women, with its characteristic undulation of the hips. Hence the name, given by Wham-O's Arthur K. "Spud" Melin. Although the name became the company's exclusive trademark, the product spawned a host of imitators, including "Spin-A-Hoop," "Wiggle-A-Hoop," "Hoop-Zing," "Hooper Dooper," and "Whoop-De-Do." "Junior Hula Hoop" was entered in the US Patent Office *Official Gazette* of July 1, 1969.

Humber (*automobiles*)

Like many other motor businesses, Humber began by manufacturing bicycles. It takes its name from Thomas Humber, who first made bicycles in Nottingham, England, in 1868. By the end of the 19th century he was building motor vehicles in that city, as well as in Coventry, and when his company was officially formed in 1909 he had already moved his entire production plant to Coventry, continuing to produce bicycles as well now as motorcycles and cars. Humber and **Hillman** combined their forces in the 1930s, so that cars with the Humber name often resemble Hillmans. Humbers were still being produced in the 1970s, and are still found on the roads today.

Humbrol (*brush and spray enamels*)

The British company was founded in Hull, Yorkshire, by a Mr. Barton in 1919, and originally made oil products. It took its name from the Humber, the river on which Hull lies, and "oil" (or the chemical suffix "-ol" that derives from Latin *oleum*, "oil"). The brand name was first used in 1935. In the mid-1940s the original company name of The Humber Oil Co. was changed to Humbrol, and this was entered in the *Trade Marks Journal* of March 7, 1945. Local people came to refer to the company as "Humbroil," blending its old and new names.

Hummel (*figurines*)

Berta Hummel (1909-1946), born in Massing, Bavaria, began her artistic training when she enrolled in the Munich Academy of Fine Arts as a girl. On graduating in 1931, she entered the convent of Siessen, where she developed her artistic skills as Sister Maria Innocentia. Her sketches of bright-eyed children at play became a popular subject of German postcards. In 1933 her work came to the attention of Franz Goebel, a porcelain manufacturer, who wanted to reproduce the illustrations in a series of figurines. Goebel introduced the first Hummel figurines at the Leipzig Fair in 1935 and they soon became collectors' pieces. Many of the sketches left by Sister Maria Innocentia when she died of tuberculosis aged 37 are still being converted into figurines by the Goebel company today.

Humvee (*military vehicle*)

The name of the American **Jeep**-style vehicle, launched in the early 1990s, is a phonetic representation of the initials of "*h*igh-*m*obility *m*ulti-purpose *v*ehicle." The name was entered by the AM General Corporation, Delaware, in the *Trade Marks Journal* of December 23, 1992.

Huntley & Palmer (*cookies, or biscuits*)

The British pairing represents Thomas Huntley (1803-1857) and George Palmer (1818-1897). Huntley's father had opened a confectionery shop in London Street, Reading, in 1822, with many of his customers waiting to board coaches on their way to or from London. Thomas Huntley took over the shop, extending its range to include biscuits (or cookies). In 1841 he was joined as partner by George Palmer, a Somerset farmer's son who had been apprenticed to his uncle, a miller and confectioner in Taunton. Palmer had been fascinated by the process of making cookies, and decided to try it for himself. Who better to join than Thomas Huntley, not only a fellow Quaker but a cousin by marriage. The partnership prospered, with the firm taking over a disused silk mill next to the river and the railway in 1846. Cookie-making became mechanized and continued at the same factory, long a favorite landmark for rail travelers, until 1977. In 1982 Huntley & Palmer, who had earlier amalgamated with **Peek Frean** and **Jacobs** in the Associated Biscuit Manufacturers Ltd. (later Huntley & Palmer Foods plc), were acquired by **Nabisco**.

Hupmobile *(automobiles)*

The cars take their name from two American brothers, Louis and Robert Hupp, who in 1908 formed the Hupp Motor Car Corporation. The company never recovered after the Depression, and the last Hupmobiles were made in 1941.

Hush Puppies *(footwear)*

The story goes that Jim Muir, sales manager of the Wolverine Shoe and Tanning Corporation of Rockford, Michigan, was on holiday in one of the Southern states of the USA when he came across a local food made from small fried corn dough balls, called "hush puppies." He asked why they were so called, and was told that the farmers used the food to quieten their barking dogs. Muir saw this as a great name for a new style of shoe his company was producing, since tired or sore feet are colloquially known as "barking dogs" and a person whose feet are hurting may say "My puppies are barking." It follows that "Hush Puppies" must be soft and comfortable. The new lightweight shoe was launched nationally in 1958, and its name was entered in the *Trade Marks Journal* of November 15, 1961.

Husqvarna *(motorcycles)*

The Swedish firm arose in the 19th century as armaments manufacturers. In 1903 they diversified into motorcycles, taking their name from their town of origin, Husqvarna (now usually spelled Huskvarna), in the south of the country. The marque was not well known outside Scandinavia until 1930, when Husqvarna produced the first of their racing bikes. The company was acquired by **Cagiva** in 1986.

Hutchinson *(publishers)*

The British publishing house takes its name from George Thompson Hutchinson (1857-1931), who after being apprenticed at the age of 16 to Alexander Strachan, a London publisher, joined the newly formed firm of **Hodder & Stoughton** as a traveling salesman, the "rep" of today. He set up on his own in 1887, publishing his first books two years later, and becoming well known for his popular publications and pioneering partworks. His success was rewarded when in 1912 he was awarded the first knighthood in British publishing, on the firm's 25th anniversary. In 1985 Hutchinson merged with another publisher, Century, to form Century Hutchinson, and this in turn merged with **Random House** in 1989 to form Random Century. Hutchinson is now an imprint of Random House.

Hutchison Whampoa *(shipping, food retailing, property development, and telecommunications)*

The Hong Kong conglomerate dates back to 1828, when a small dispensary named A.S. Watson opened in Canton (Guangzhou), China. In 1841 it extended its operations to Hong Kong, where in 1863 the Hong Kong and Whampoa Dock Co. was established to acquire docks and ship-repair yards at Whampoa (Huangpu), on China's Pearl River. In 1887 a young Briton, John Duflon Hutchison, joined Hong Kong's small community of expatriate merchants as an employee of Robert Walker and Co. His expertise soon enabled him to take the business over and form John D. Hutchison and Co. In the 1960s Hutchison International, as the company was now known, began an acquisition program that included A.S. Watson and Co., Davie, Boag and Co., the Hong Kong and Whampoa Dock Co., and the China Provident Co. Hutchison Whampoa was finally formed in 1977 in a merger between the Hutchison International Co. and the Hong Kong and Whampoa Dock Co.

Hyatt *(hotels)*

The American hotel chain owes its existence to Abram N. Pritzker (1896-1986), born in Chicago, Illinois, the son of a Russian Jewish immigrant who had come to Chicago from Kiev in 1881. Abram graduated from Harvard

University with a law degree in 1920 and then went to work in the law firm his father had founded. In 1936, however, he and his brother Jack N. Pritzker (1904-1979) left the firm to try their hand at real estate. In the 1950s Abram Pritzker gave increasingly important roles to his sons Jay A. Pritzker (1922-1999) and Robert A. Pritzker (b.1926), and in 1957 Jay bought the Hyatt House hotel in Los Angeles, which a third son, Donald Pritzker (1933-1972), built into a chain of over 150 hotels in the USA and abroad. Control of the family empire passed in 1981 to Jay and Robert, and by the mid-1980s the Pritzker family owned not only the Hyatt Corporation but **Braniff** Airlines and *McCall's* magazine, while their largest business interest was the **Marmon** Group, which at Abram Pritzker's death had at least 265 companies under its umbrella.

Hygena *(kitchen furniture)*

The free-standing kitchen cabinet arrived in Britain in the 1920s. Seeing the potential, the British furniture manufacturer Len Cooklin established Hygena Cabinets Ltd. By the end of the decade the company was producing cabinets equipped with a range of fittings such as a pull-out ironing board. The company name is obviously based on "hygiene," with a simplification of the spelling. There is also something of a classical reference, as Hygieia was the Greek goddess who personified health. The name was entered in the *Trade Marks Journal* of June 29, 1932. In 1987, after acquisition by Humber Kitchens, a firm set up in 1976, the Hygena name was sold to **MFI**.

Hypercard *(computer programming system)*

The programming system uses symbols resembling index cards to represent the content and structure of an onscreen database, and permits the creation of hypertext links. Hence the name, entered by **Apple** Computer, Inc., in the *Trade Marks Journal* of November 29, 1989.

Hypospray *(jet injector)*

The type of medical jet injector, used for "blasting" a minute quantity of medicinal fluid into the body tissues, derives its name from a blend of "hypodermic" and "spray," entered by the R.P. Scherer Corporation of Detroit, Michigan, in the US Patent Office *Official*

Gazette of September 7, 1948: "For Hypodermic Injection Devices."

Hytrel *(synthetic fabric)*

The name of the strong, flexible synthetic resin, used in shoes and sports equipment, is probably of arbitrary origin, although the first syllable suggests (and is pronounced) "high." It was entered by **Du Pont** in the *Trade Marks Journal* of September 13, 1972.

Hyundai *(automobiles)*

The creation of South Korea's largest company began when Chung Ju-Yung (1915-2001), born a poor farmer's son in North Korea, realized that reconstruction after World War II presented him with a golden economic opportunity. In 1946 he established the Hyundai ("Modern") Auto Service in Seoul, and the following year the Hyundai Land and Construction Company. In 1952 this became the Hyundai Engineering and Construction Co., participating in postwar restoration work and national land development projects. In 1967 the Hyundai Motor Company was founded, producing a version of the **Ford Cortina**. Its first all-new car was the Pony, launched in London, England, in 1974. By the mid-1990s Hyundai was Korea's biggest car manufacturer, producing over a million cars a year.

I-Scream *see* **Eskimo Pie**

I. W. Harper *(whiskey)*

In 1848, 19-year-old Isaac W. Bernheim landed in New York from Germany with four dollars in his pocket. He made his way to Wilkes-Barre, Pennsylvania, where he sold assorted merchandise, known as "Yankee notions." Business was brisk, and Bernheim was soon able to buy a horse and wagon. The horse died unexpectedly, however, so Bernheim accepted a job offer from his two uncles who ran a general store in Paducah, Kentucky. Three months later Bernheim became a bookkeeper with a wholesale liquor firm in Paducah, and soon saved enough money to bring his brother Bernard to the United States. Two years later the brothers decided to go into business for themselves, and with the purchase of one barrel of whiskey, set up shop in the back room of the wholesale grocery store. One of their salesmen, named Harper, was so popular with his customers that they referred to the whiskey he sold as "Mr. Harper's whiskey." In 1872, when the Bernheims wanted a name for their choice blend, they combined the initials of Isaac's first two names with the surname of their star salesman. Thus the famous I.W. Harper brand was born.

Iams *(petfoods)*

The name is that of Paul Iams, an animal nutritionist who started making dog food in a small feed mill near Dayton, Ohio, in 1946. He was joined in 1970 by Clay Mathile, who purchased the business in 1982. In 1999 it was acquired by **Procter & Gamble**. One of the company's best-known products is **Eukanuba**.

Ibcol *(aromatic disinfectant)*

The name of the product is an abbreviation of its original British manufacturers, the *Ib-betson Company Ltd.* In 1955 Ibcol was acquired by **Jeyes**. The name was entered in the *Trade Marks Journal* of September 9, 1942.

IBM *(computers)*

The American computer manufacturer, formally known as the International Business Machines Corporation, owes its existence to Thomas J. Watson (1874-1956), born in East Campbell, New York, the son of a farmer and lumberman. He started work in 1892 as a bookkeeper for a butcher but soon became a traveling salesman, selling pianos, organs, and sewing machines and later stock in a building and loan association. In 1899 he went to work for the National Cash Register Company (**NCR**) and rose through its ranks to become general sales manager in 1908. He left in 1913 and was soon hired as general manager of the recently-formed Computer-Tabulating-Recording Company (CTR), whose main business was selling an electrical punchcard system based on the technology developed in the 1880s by the American-born German engineer Herman Hollerith (1860-1929) for the 1890 US census. In 1924 IBM took its present name, and Watson's considerable marketing skill built the business up into the giant of today, becoming chairman in 1949. Watson and IBM are frequently cited as the archetypal American business success story.

Iceland *(frozen food stores)*

The British stores were the brainchild of Malcolm Walker (b.1946), born in Wakefield,

Yorkshire. He quit school in 1963 with minimal qualifications and became a trainee manager at the Wrexham, Wales, branch of **Woolworths**. In 1970, together with a friend and Woolworths colleague, Peter Hinchcliffe, Walker started an enterprise selling strawberries to tourists from a roadside site. Later that year the two men invested £30 each to set up the first Iceland store in Oswestry, Shropshire, near the Welsh border, selling to housewives who had no freezers at home so who simply bought enough food for the family's evening meal. By 1980 there were 38 Iceland stores, and in 1989 the firm took over its much larger rival, **Bejam**. There were now some 770 stores. Hinchcliffe resigned in 1996 and Walker in 2001. The name is an obvious one for a business in which ice predominates.

ICI *(chemicals)*

The giant British corporation, with formal name Imperial Chemical Industries plc, was founded in 1926 to amalgamate four major companies: Brunner, Mond & Co. Ltd., Nobel Industries Ltd., United Alkali Company, Ltd., and British Dyestuffs Corporation, Ltd. The first of these had been founded in 1873 as a soda factory in Winnington, Cheshire, by John Tomlinson Brunner (1842-1919) and Ludwig Mond (1839-1909), father of Alfred Mond (1868-1930), later chairman of ICI. The new company's name reflected the British Empire, then almost at its apogee. In 1993 ICI split itself into two. Commodity chemicals, paints, and explosives remained with the existing company, while a new company, Zeneca, took over the specialty chemicals, drugs, agrochemicals, and seeds businesses. The latter name is arbitrary but nevertheless suggests "zenith."

Icy-pole *(frozen confection)*

The make of flavored water ice takes its name from its frozen content and shape, with a punning allusion to the ice in the polar regions. It was entered by the Australian manufacturers, Peters American Delicacy Company (Vic.) Ltd., in the *Australian Official Journal of Patents* (Canberra) in 1952 for: "Ice cream, ice-cream sherbert [*sic*], water ice and frozen fruit juices."

Idem *(carbonless copying paper)*

The paper of this name was originally produced under licence for **NCR**, and was thus formerly known as "NCR paper." In 1970 its manufacturers, **Wiggins Teape**, changed the name to "Idem," Latin for "same," and this was entered in the *Trade Marks Journal* of August 23, 1972. The name was chosen partly to reflect the fact that the product remained the same, even though renamed, and partly as a reminder that the paper was used to produce copies which were identical to one another.

Idemitsu Kosan *(chemicals)*

The Japanese company takes its name from Idemitsu Sazo, who founded it in 1911 in Moji, now a part of Kita-Kyushu, as a general trading company, dealing in the distribution of various goods such as grain, fuel, and lubricating oils. Its original name was Idemitsu Shokai, the latter word meaning "company." It was reorganized under its present name in 1940.

Idris *(soft drinks)*

The British firm, famous for its ginger beer, was founded in 1873 by a Welshman, Thomas Howell Williams Idris (1842-1925). He was born Thomas Howell Williams, but in 1893 adopted the additional surname Idris, that of the legendary Welsh giant said to have given the name of the mountain ridge Cader Idris ("Chair of Idris"). This came about following a move from his native Pembrokeshire to Dôl-y-cae, a locality just south of Cader Idris in Merionethshire. The brand name was entered in the *Trade Marks Journal* of November 18, 1885.

IG Farben *(chemicals)*

The world's largest chemical concern, or cartel, was founded in Germany in 1925 and existed until 1945, when it was dissolved by the Allies at the end of World War II. The name is short for Interessengemeinschaft Farbenindustrie Aktiengesellschaft ("Syndicate of Dyestuff-Industry Corporations"), denoting an Interessengemeinschaft, literally "community of interests," of manufacturers of chemicals, pharmaceuticals, and, notably, dyestuffs (Farben). Its main members were the companies known today as **BASF**, **Bayer**, **Hoechst**, **Agfa-Gevaert** and **Cassella**.

IKEA *(furniture)*

The make of self-assembly furniture, giving a semblance of stability and style at a reasonable cost, was first produced in 1947 by the Swedish manufacturer Ingvar Kamprad. The name is a blend of his initials and those of the farm where he was born, Elmtaryd, and his village, Agunnaryd. Cynical Germans interpret the acronym as *Idioten kaufen eben alles*, "Some fools will buy anything."

Ilford *(films and photographic materials)*

The name is due to Alfred Hugh Harman (1841-1913), a British bootmaker's son who by 1863 had started a photographic business partnership in Peckham, London, with a Frenchman called Dage. He set up on his own the following year, and in 1879 decided to manufacture the newly-invented photographic dry plates. To this end, he sold his photographic business and moved to what was then the small village of Ilford in Essex, setting up a firm that he called the Britannia Works. To meet the growing demand for his product, a special factory was built on the site in 1883 and two years later he changed the name of his products from "Britannia" to "Ilford." The firm itself retained the former name until 1900, when it in turn became the Ilford Co.

IMAX *(film projection system)*

The system of wide-screen film projection was developed in Canada by the Multiscreen Corporation, Ltd., of Galt, Ontario, and first introduced in 1969. It employs the largest film frame in motion-picture history, 65mm film running horizontally through the camera, giving an image approximately ten times larger than that from standard 35mm film and three times larger than the regular 70mm frame. Its name blends the first syllables of "image" and "maximum," with the initial "I" perhaps also intended to suggest "eye."

Immortal Memory *(whisky)*

The blend of whisky by Gordon and MacPhail of Elgin, Morayshire, Scotland, has a label bearing a portrait of Robert Burns. This gives a clue to the name, from the toast "The Immortal Memory," traditionally proposed at the end of a Burns Supper, a meal held on or near Burns Night (January 25, the anniversary of the poet's birth).

Imperial *(whisky)*

The blend of whisky takes its name from the Imperial Distillery that produces it, at Carron,

Morayshire, Scotland. The distillery was founded in 1897, the year of Queen Victoria's Diamond Jubilee. Hence its patriotic name.

Imperial Chemical Industries *see* **ICI**

Imperial Leather *(toilet soap)*

The soap made by **Cussons** is said to derive its name from a perfume with an aroma of leather that was specially devised in the 1780s by a London, England, parfumier, Bayley's of Bond Street, for a Russian count Orlov. The name chosen for the fragrance was "Eau de Cologne Imperial Leather Russe," "Imperial" denoting Russian royalty and "Leather" the aroma. In 1938 this name was used a basis for the new fragrant toilet soap produced by Alexander Cussons.

Imperial Tobacco *(cigarettes and tobacco products)*

The British company, manufacturing **Player's** and "Embassy" cigarettes, as well as beer, prepared foods, and packaging, was founded in 1901 by a consortium of 13 tobacco manufacturers led by William Henry Wills, the son of William Day **Wills**, in reponse to an attempt by James Buchanan Duke, president of the American Tobacco Company (see **American Brands**), to take over the British tobacco industry. The word "Tobacco" was dropped from the company name in 1973 to reflect the diversification that had taken place, and in 1981 it reregistered as a public limited company and became the Imperial Group. In 1986 it was purchased by the **Hanson** Trust and subsequently reverted to the name Imperial Tobacco.

Inchcape *(goods and services)*

The British company was formed in 1958 to bring together varoious enterprises, most of which had been established by Scottish merchants in the 18th and 19th centuries to trade with the East. Several of them had been merged or molded by James Mackay, Earl of Inchcape (1852-1932). Hence the name. The group's business is the worldwide marketing and distribution of goods and services.

Inco *(nickel)*

The US company traces its origins to 1877, when nickel mining operations began in North America with the founding of Orford Copper in New Jersey. In 1902, J.P. **Morgan** and US Steel interests bought Orford and subsequent companies to form a new trust, International Nickel Company, based in New Jersey. (*See also* **Monel**.) The name was subsequently abbreviated as now. *Cp.* **Inconel**.

Inconel *(alloys)*

The various alloys containing nickel, chromium, and iron are used for their strength and resistance to corrosion and oxidation at high temperatures. They derive their name from their manufacturers, the International Nickel Company, Inc. (*cp.* **Inco**), who entered it in the US Patent Office *Official Gazette* of September 12, 1933: "For Nickel Alloys and Alloys of Nickel, Chromium, and Iron," with a claim of use since November 25, 1932. *See also* **Nimonic**.

Ind Coope *(beer)*

The name is that of two British brewers, Edward Ind, who purchased the Star Inn and its brewery in Romford, Essex, in 1799, and W.O.E. Coope and his brother George, who joined him in 1845. In 1961 Ind Coope became part of Allied Breweries, and merged with **Carlsberg** in 1993 to become Carlsberg-**Tetley**.

Indanthrene *(vat dyes)*

The various vat dyes derive from (or contain) the blue compound indanthrone. Hence their name, entered by **BASF** in the *Trade Marks Journal* of October 23, 1901. (The "-one" ending in the generic name denotes the compound's ketonic nature.)

Indesit *(refrigerators)*

The name derives from that of the Italian manufacturing company, *Ind*ustria *E*lettrodome*s*tici *I*talia ("Italian Electric Household Appliances Industry"), now based in Turin and Naples.

Indian *(motorcycles)*

The motorcyle of this name was developed in the early 20th century by two Americans, Oscar Hedström, an engineer who had built a motorized two-wheeler in 1899, and George Hendee, a bicycle manufacturer and former cycle racer. They named their machines after the American Indian, and launched their first model, the Indian Single, in Springfield, Massachusetts, in 1904. The company fell into decline after producing the Indian Chief in 1947, although the name continued for the rest of the century under various owners.

Inditex *(fashionwear)*

The Spanish company, its name short for Industria de Diseño Textil ("Textile Design Industry"), owes its origins to Amancio Ortega Gaona (b.1936), born in León, who came with his family to Galicia as a teenager in the 1950s. In 1963 he quit his clerk's job with an apparel retailer in La Coruña, and with 5,000 pesetas ($25) in hand, started a business manufacturing lingerie, pajamas, and nightdresses. In 1975 he branched out into retailing, opening a store that he called Zara in La Coruña in 1975. In 2001 there were 1,080 Inditex stores in 33 countries, 450 of them under the Zara name, selling 10,000 men's, women's, and children's apparel models created every year under Ortega's personal supervision at the Inditex headquarters in Arteixo-La Coruña. Lesser brands than the flagship Zara include Massimo Dutti apparel for older men and women, Pull & Bear youthwear, and Bershka fashions for young women.

ING Barings *see* **Baring Brothers**

Ingersoll *(watches)*

Robert Hawley Ingersoll (1859-1928) was an American who began to make his name in 1892 when he set up a business that produced goods for only $1 each, including typewriters, cameras and, in particular, watches. He judged that mass-produced watches should sell well if the price was right. His first watch, however, sold for $1.50, and was produced for him by the **Waterbury** Company, Connecticut. Ingersoll's intuition proved correct. Production volumes rose, costs fell, and four years later he produced the first $1 watch, called the "Yankee," marketed with the slogan "The watch that made the dollar famous." By 1898 Ingersoll had sold a million watches and made his name famous. In 1904 he went to England with his brother Charles, set up an office in London, and began selling watches to wholesalers. He now offered the "Crown" as well as the "Yankee," the former appropriately named for its price of five shillings. Only in 1911, however, did Ingersoll first start assembling watches in England.

Initial *(office linen supply)*

The British firm supplying linen to office premises arose from the initiative of Canadian-born Arthur P. Bigelow (*c.*1880-1941), whose first job as a soap salesman in New York brought him in contact with the new industry of office linen supply, then virtually unheard of in the UK. Aware of the prospects, therefore, Bigelow and his wife set sail for England, where they arrived in 1903. On reaching London, Bigelow purchased a supply of hand towels and obtained a laundering contract with the King's Cross Laundry. His wife then embroidered each towel with the customer's initial. Bigelow soon built up a good reputation for his delivery service in the City of London and the West End, and within two years was employing three routemen, who collected dirty linen and delivered clean linen by box tricycle. The business gradually grew, and in 1910 Bigelow formed the Initial Tea Cabinet Co., adding tea-making apparatus to his deliveries. The name came from the initial that his wife originally embroidered on the towels. The Initial Carrier Co. was set up soon after, and by 1928, when Initial Services Ltd. was formed, the firm was the largest of its kind in Europe.

Innocenti *(motorscooters)*

The Italian company takes its name from Ferdinando Innocenti (1891-1966), born in Pescia, near Lucca, the son of a hardware store owner. His career began at the age of 16 when he was taken on in a small workshop in the town. Two years later he set up his own mechanical workshop and in 1922 moved to Rome to experiment in the relatively new field of steel pipes. In 1932 he founded a steel pipe company in Milan, and this was the basis of his expansion into other industrial areas. His first plant, in the district of Lambrate, was virtually wiped out by aerial bombardment in World War II, but immediately after the war Innocenti began reconstruction on the same site, naming his new company Innocenti società generale per l'industria metallurgica e meccanica ("Innocenti Steel and Engineering Industry Company"). In the 1950s he launched the **Lambretta** motorscooter, a worthy rival to the popular **Vespa**.

In-Sink-Erator *(waste disposal unit)*

The unit is installed in the outlet pipe of the kitchen sink. Hence the name, which puns on "incinerator" as another type of waste disposal device. The name was entered by **Emerson** in the *Trade Marks Journal* of March 8, 1961.

Instamatic *(self-loading camera)*

The make of camera was launched by **Kodak** in the 1960s to take over the role hitherto enjoyed by the **Brownie**. Its main advantage was that the film could be instantly loaded in a cartridge instead of being wound from one spool to another. The name, blending "instant" and "automatic," was entered in the *Trade Marks Journal* of September 19, 1962 and the US Patent Office *Official Gazette* of December 11, 1962.

Instant Whip *("instant" dessert)*

The dessert of this name was introduced by **Bird's** in Britain in 1954 as the equivalent of the American **Jell-o** Instant Pudding, and was so called as it was prepared simply by brisk stirring or "whipping." It was originally launched in three flavors (strawberry, vanilla, and butterscotch), although the range was later extended to ten.

Intal *(antiasthmatic drug)*

The proprietary name for cromolyn sodium, used for preventing attacks of bronchial asthma, derives from "*int*erference with *al*lergy." The drug itself dates from the late 1960s.

Intel *(microprocessors)*

The US corporation, originally called N.M. Electronics, was founded in 1968 in Santa Clara, California, by Robert N. Noyce (1927-1990) and Gordon E. Moore (b.1929), who in 1957 had been two of the founder members of the Fairchild Semiconductor Company, the firm that came to form the nucleus of the region later known as Silicon Valley. Noyce had invented the integrated circuit in 1959, and the men's initial aim was to develop this "chip," which they saw as having an almost limitless application to bring intelligence (hence the name) to hitherto "dumb" machines. They launched their 4004 microprocessor in 1971, the first "computer on a chip," so called as it processed four bits of information at a time, and in 1978 the 8088 microchip, which was chosen by **IBM** for use in its first personal computer. The flagship **Pentium** processor followed in 1993. By 1997, Intel controlled 85 percent of the world's PC chip market.

Interco *(footwear)*

In 1911 two shoe manufacturers in St. Louis, Missouri, merged to form the International Shoe Company. The business thrived until the 1960s, when it ran out of steam. A new president, Maurice R. Chambers, revived its fortunes, however, and streamlined both its operations and its name to become the Interco of today, making clothes as well as shoes and operating various retail chains.

Interflora *(flower delivery service)*

The name is properly that of the Florists' Telegraph Delivery Association, an international agency set up in 1946 to organize the delivery of flowers to order. The name, blending "international" and "flora," also serves as that of the British branch of the association.

International Harvester *(farm machinery and trucks)*

The US corporation was formed in 1902 as a merger of five leading harvester manufacturers: the McCormick Harvesting Machine Company, founded in Chicago in 1847 by Cyrus Hall McCormick (1809-1884), inventor of the reaper in 1831, the Deering Harvester Company, founded as William Deering & Co. in 1883 by William Deering (1826-1913), and three smaller machinery makers, Plano, Champion, and Milwaukee. In 1985 Harvester disposed of most of its farm equipment line to the J.I. Case subsidiary of Tenneco Inc. Under the terms of the agreement, it was obliged to change its name, which it did in 1986 to Navistar International Corporation, the new name being formed from letters in the old.

International Paper *(paper)*

The International Paper Company, now one of the largest private holders of timberland in the world, traces its origins to the merger in 1898 of 20 New England and New York paper mills. Its name reflects its wide-ranging self-image.

Intourist *(travel agency)*

The Russian travel agency was set up in 1929 jointly by the People's Commissariat for Foreign and Domestic Trade, the People's Commissariat for Ways and Communications, and the Soviet Merchant Fleet. The name is a shortening of Russian *inostrannyi turist*, "foreign tourist."

Intoximeter *(alcohol measurer)*

The device for measuring the amount of alcohol in the blood of a person who breathes into it derives its name from "intoxication" and "-meter." It was entered in the US Patent Office *Official Gazette* of August 1, 1950: "For apparatus for determining the alcohol-carbon dioxide ratio in the alveolar air of a person," with a claim of use since June 22, 1946. *Cp.* **Breathalyzer**.

Intropin *(heart stimulant)*

The proprietary name for the drug dopamine hydrochloride, used to stimulate the action of the heart, is apparently of arbitrary origin. The drug dates from the 1970s.

Invar *(alloy)*

The alloy of iron and nickel, used in the manufacture of clocks and scientific instruments, derives its name from the abbreviation of "invariable," referring to the fact that it expands or contracts only minimally when the temperature changes. The alloy was discovered in 1896 by the Swiss-born French physicist Charles Édouard Guillaume (1861-1938). *Cp.* **Perminvar**.

Invensys *(electronics and engineering)*

The British company began its life in 1924 as the British Goodrich Tyre Co. (*see* **Goodrich**), with tires as its main product. In 1934 the firm's name was changed to the British Tyre and Rubber Company (BTR), and the initialism was subsequently adopted as the official name. (In 1957 it was stated that the same three letters stood for British Thermoplastics and Rubber.) In 1985 BTR acquired **Dunlop**, and in 1991 **Hawker Siddeley**. In 1999 BTR merged with Siebe plc to become BTR Siebe, a concern that later the same year was renamed Invensys. The name was chosen from a selection of over 3,000, and was stated by the company chairman, Lord Marshall, to be "suggestive of innovation and inventiveness and our drive towards systems solutions."

Invicta *(automobiles)*

The vintage-style British sporting cars were first made in 1925 in Cobham, Surrey, by Noel C. Macklin, with financial backing from Sir Oliver Lyle (of **Tate & Lyle**). The name came from Latin *invictus*, "unconquered," referring to their sporting image. Production ceased on the outbreak of World War II and although a new model was launched after the war it was very costly and resulted in the closure of the firm in 1950.

Irn-Bru *(soft drink)*

The carbonated soft drink, popular in Scotland, is said to be a hangover cure. It originated in Glasgow in 1901 as "Iron-Brew" under the impetus of the temperance movement, and derived some of its inspiration from the tradition of tonics and health drinks prepared by herbalists. The name is something of a misnomer, as the drink often contained no iron and was not a "brew" in the traditional manner. The commercial brand, produced by A.G. Barr (makers of **Tizer**) and promoted as "Scotland's other drink" (the main one being Scotch whisky), does contain iron in the form of 0.002% ammonium ferric citrate. The first part of the name represents "eye-rin" as a Scots pronunciation of "iron." The name was entered in the *Trade Marks Journal* of October 1, 1947.

Ishikawajima-Harima *(heavy machinery and ships)*

The Japanese company was founded in 1853 by the Mito branch of the Tokugawa family as a shipbuilding yard in Edo (modern Tokyo), taking its name from Ishikawa-jima. (Ishikawa is a common placename meaning "rocky river"; *jima* means "island.") It was incorporated in 1889. The Harima Dock (later Harima Shipbuilding and Engineering) was established in 1907 in Kobe and similarly adopted a geographical name. (Kobe is a port in southern Honshu, and the Harima Sea lies between Honshu and Shikoku.) The merger of the two shipyards in 1960 gave the present name.

Isolette *(infant incubator)*

The name, from "isolation" with the diminutive suffix "-ette," was entered by Air Shields Inc., of Hatboro, Pennsylvania, in the US Patent Office *Official Gazette* of June 7, 1949. A subsequent registration was made in the *Trade Marks Journal* of February 21, 1951.

Isopon *(autocare products)*

The name was entered in the *Trade Marks Journal* of January 2, 1957, for a range of home repair and construction products, from "Liquid Rubba" and "Zinc Anti-Rust Coat" to aluminum mesh and repair paste kits. The name was coined from an earlier trademark belonging to Bernhard David, a German chemist who in 1908 founded a business in Hamburg to manufacture chemical products under the name "Isolament," based on German *isolieren*, "to insulate." In 1938 David son's, Walter David, sought refuge in England for political reasons and served six years in the British Army. After his demobilization, he started his own manufacturing business in an old stable near King's Cross, London, making polyester body-fillers to repair dents in auto bodies. He based his trade name, "Isopon," on the one adopted by his father, hoping this would bring him luck.

Isotta Fraschini *(automobiles)*

The Italian firm of this name was founded in 1898 by car enthusiast Vincenzo Fraschini and opulent lawyer Cesare Isotta, initially to import **Renault** and **De Dion-Bouton** cars into Italy. Two years later they officially named their partnership Società Milanese d'Automobili Isotta, Fraschini & Cia., and began building their own cars. Both Fraschini and Isotta left the company in 1922 and in 1933 it effectively went into liquidation. It was rescued by aircraft manufacturer **Caproni**, however, and survived to pass over the years from one owner to another. At the end of the century its main products were engines and industrial drivetrains, made at its two bases in Trieste and Bari.

Isuzu *(automobiles)*

The Japanese company traces its origins to 1916, when the Tokyo Ishikawajima Shipbuilding and Engineering Company (*see* **Ishikawajima-Harima**) merged with the Tokyo Gas and Electric Company to manufacture motor vehicles. In 1918 the company signed an agreement with **Wolseley** in the UK to produce and market their cars in the Far East, and the first Japanese-built Wolseley appeared in 1922. In 1929 an independent company was set up to build cars to original designs. It was initially called the Ishikawajima Automotive Works Company, then the Automobile Works Company, using the trade names "Sumida" and "Chiyoda." It subsequently abandoned these in favor of "Isuzu," for the Japanese river. In 1937 Automobile Industries became known as the Tokyo Automobile Industries Company, and in 1949 it changed identity again to become Isuzu Motor Ltd.

Italcementi *(cement)*

The Italian company was founded at Bergamo in 1865 by Giuseppe Piccinelli and gained a leading role as a cement manufacturer through its acquisition of other cement makers. The name combines *Italia*, "Italy" and *cementi*, "cements." In 1946 it set up the holding company Italmobiliare, through which it gained shares in several other Italian and overseas businesses. In 1980 Italmobiliare itself, under the Pesenti family, headed by Carlo Pesenti (1907-1984), acquired a majority interest in Italcementi.

ITT *(telecommunications)*

The International Telephone and Telegraph Corporation was formed from several Caribbean telephone and telegraph companies in 1920 by Sosthenes Behn (1882-1957) and his brother Hernand, born in the Virgin Islands, the name being patterned on that of **AT&T**. In 1925 IT&T purchased AT&T's foreign manufacturing subsidiary, International Western Electric, and renamed it IT&T Standard Electric Corporation. IT&T is now usually referred to as ITT.

Iveco *(trucks)*

The name is an acronym for *I*ndustrial *Ve*hicles *Co*rporation, based in Amsterdam, Netherlands, as the English-language commercial vehicle wing of **Fiat**. It was formed in 1975 by amalgamating Fiat's truck-making business, then 75 years old, and its subsidiaries OM and French-based Unic, with Magirus Deutz, the commercial vehicle subsidiary of the West German group Klöckner Humboldt Deutz (KHD).

Ivory *(soap)*

The soap made by **Procter & Gamble** was "launched" in both senses in 1878, when a worker in the firm's plant at Cincinnati accidentally let a machine introduce minute bubbles of air into a batch of soap, so producing a soap that floated. The new soap, dead white in color, proved very popular, but remained without a name until the firm's senior partner,

Harley T. Procter, heard an Old Testament reading in church one Sunday in 1879 that included the verse: "All thy garments smell of myrrh, and aloes, and cassia, out of the ivory palaces, whereby they have made thee glad" (Psalm 45:8). There was the name of the new fragrant soap, "Ivory," matching its existing color.

Izal *(disinfectant and toilet tissue)*

The British disinfectant was first formulated in the 1890s, and the story goes that it was named anagrammatically for a lady named Liza, the sister of the young English chemist who helped produce it, Jason Hall Worrall. However, such archive material as exists appears to indicate that he had no sister, let alone one named Liza, and that the name was simply an invented one chosen by the product's advertising agent, T.B. Browne. Izal products are now made by **Newton Chambers.** The name was entered in the *Trade Marks Journal* of July 26, 1933.

J. Arthur Rank *see* **Rank**

J.C. Penney *(clothing stores)*

The New York-based stores were founded by James Cash Penney (1875-1971), born near Hamilton, Missouri, the son of a Primitive Baptist minister. After graduating from Hamilton Public High School in 1893, Penney wanted to attend college, but his parents could not afford the extra expense. Instead he made money as a boy by raising pigs, but two years later got a more permanent job with J.M. Hale & Bros., a small dry goods store in Hamilton. He stayed there three years, and after a series of similar jobs, in 1898 became a sales clerk at the Golden Rule Store, a Longmont dry goods and clothing store owned by Thomas M. Callahan. Its name alluded to the biblical "Golden Rule" equating to "Do as you would be done by," a precept that accorded well with Penney's own religious convictions. His work for Callahan was a turning point in his life. Callahan and W. Guy Johnson, his partner in a Golden Rule Store in Wyoming, were impressed with Penney's work, and offered him a position in their Evanston, Wyoming, Golden Rule Store. The stores themselves were popular for having good quality merchandise that was less expensive than at other merchants. Sales for cash only, rather than credit, made the stores even more popular and their owners wealthy. They were thus keen to open more stores. On April 14, 1902, Johnson, Callahan, and Penney became partners in a new Golden Rule Store in Kemmerer, Wyoming, and this small outpost of the Golden Rule Store chain was the "Mother Store" of the J.C. Penney Company, Inc.

J. Collis Browne *("Mixture" and "Tablets")*

The British patent medicines are now marketed by International Laboratories, and are mainly intended for "tummy upsets" rather than the many ills they were once claimed to treat. The man behind the name was Dr. John Collis Browne (1819-1884), born in Maidstone, Kent, a British army captain's son. In 1842 he qualified as a surgeon and in 1845 as a physician, in which year he joined the Army Medical Service and was posted to India. He saw service in that country at a time when cholera was rife, and his experience as a doctor led him to devise a medicine to combat the disease. What he used was chlorodyne, a narcotic and anodyne drug containing mainly chloroform and morphia. His medicine was widely adopted, both in India and elsewhere, and it was probably because of its commercial success that he decided to leave the army in 1856 and go into partnership with a chemist, who would make a patent mixture based on it. He died at a house in Victoria Road, Ramsgate, where a plaque may be seen commemorating his achievements.

J.M. Dent *see* **Dent**

J.R. Cigars *(cigar stores)*

The initials are those of Jack Rothman, whose son, Lew Rothman, built up J.R. Tobacco of America as a mail-order, retail, and wholesale empire that by the turn of the 21st century was handling 40 percent of all premium cigars sold in the United States.

J. Walter Thompson *(advertising)*

The American advertising agency grew out of one of the first such agencies, Carlton and Smith, founded in 1864 by William J. Carlton, who four years later hired James Walter Thompson (1847-1928), born in Pittsfield, Massachusetts, the son of a contractor and builder, as a bookkeeper. In 1877 Carlton announced his retirement and commissioned Thompson to find a new purchaser. To his surprise, that purchaser was Thompson himself, who renamed the company accordingly. In 1980 the agency became a subsidiary of JWT Group, Inc., a Delaware-based holding company.

J&B *(whisky)*

The initials stand for Justerini & Brooks, the names of the firm's founders. The British house of wine and liquor merchants goes back to 1749, when Giacomo Justerini, a lovesick Italian from Bologna, followed an opera singer, one Signorina Belloni, to London. He came to set up a wine business there, taking an Englishman, George Johnson, as partner. The latter was killed, however, when a runaway horse overturned his sedan chair, and his son, who inherited his father's side of the business, sold it in 1831 to Alfred Brooks, a "gentleman of fashion." Justerini and Brooks was selling whisky by the end of the 18th century, and although the name is still chiefly associated with whisky, especially as J&B, the firm continues to operate as general wine merchants, with premises in St. James's Street, London, and George Street, Edinburgh. Noted J&B blends include J&B Jet, J&B Rare, and J&B Ultima, the latter so named as an "ultimate blend" or unique creation.

Jacaranda *(publishers)*

The Australian publishing house Jacaranda Press was founded in 1952 by Brian Clouston to produce material by Australian writers, initially for Queensland schools. It is based in Milton, Queensland, and takes its name from the state's famous flowering jacaranda tree. Since 1977 it has been known as Jacaranda Wiley, from its merger with the US publisher John **Wiley** & Sons, but keeps the Jacaranda Press imprint for school and general books.

Jack Daniel's *(whiskey)*

The American blend bears the name of Jasper "Jack" Daniel (1846-1911), born into a family of old English colonial stock near Lynchburg, Tennessee. At the age of 12 Jack started working for Dan Call, a local distiller and strict Lutheran churchman. Call's dual vocation left him in a dilemma: should he serve God, or Mammon? To solve the quandary, he

sold his business to Daniel in 1860 as soon as the latter was old enough. It is not known whether Call regretted his choice, but either way Jack Daniel did well out of it, and by 1866 he had bought a large plot of land nearby, with a pool, where he built a new distillery, using water from his own source. On that same site today, in a "dry" county in which the sale of liquor is forbidden, the distillery produces Jack Daniel's special Tennessee Sour Mash Whiskey.

Jack Eckerd *(drugstores)*

Jack Eckerd drugstores are mostly in the American sunbelt, although some stores can be found as far north as New Jersey. Their founder's first job was during the Great Depression in his father's drugstore in Erie, Pennsylvania. Times were hard, but Eckerd worked equally hard, and in 1952 he bought three drugstores in Tampa and Clearwater, Florida, attracting trade by cutting prices. In 1961 he bought a number of southern-based drug chains, and in 1977 acquired Eckerd Drugs of Charlotte, North Carolina. The name was not a complete coincidence: Milton Eckerd had started the chain and sold it in the late 1930s to his son-in-law, Edward M. O'Herron. It was the latter's son, Edward M. O'Herron, Jr., who sold the company to Jack Eckerd, his half-uncle.

Jack in the Box *(hamburgers)*

The American hamburger chain began in San Diego, California, in 1950. Its name presumably alludes to the box in which the hamburgers were served and to the speediness of the service itself, as well as creating an image of youthful pleasure. By 1996 it had over 1,000 outlets worldwide.

Jackson-Stops and Staff *(estate agents, or realtors)*

The British firm originated with Herbert Stops (1884-1949), of Northamptonshire, who on leaving school was articled to a local firm of auctioneers and valuers. In 1907 he qualified as an associate of the Surveyors Institution and the Auctioneers Institute. The following year he opened his office in Towcester, offering his services as estate agent, auctioneer, valuer, architect, and civil engineer. By 1919 his business had moved to Northampton, and he had added the family name of Jackson to his original surname. In 1921 his standing was enhanced when he was entrusted with the sale of the estate of Stowe House, near Buckingham, and three years later he opened an office in London. The "Staff" is not a surname but a tribute to the important role of the company's employees.

Jacobs (crackers, or biscuits)

The story of Jacob's "Cream Crackers" began not in England but in Ireland, where in 1825 William Beale Jacob was born a baker's son in Waterford. When still in his teens, William was left in charge of the business after his father's death. He took his younger brother Robert into partnership, trading as W. & R. Jacob. The bakery already produced ship's biscuits, and it was in 1850 that William Jacob introduced what he called "fancy biscuits," advertising them in the local paper. The crackers sold well, and the following year William Jacob acquired a vacant coach works in Dublin and converted it into a proper factory. Robert Jacob, meanwhile, stayed home in Waterford to run the business. William's crackers (or biscuits) were now selling well in both Ireland and England, and in 1885 he introduced the familiar "Cream Crackers," so named as they were designed to be eaten with butter and cheese, which are "cream" or dairy products.

Jacuzzi (whirlpool baths)

Candido Jacuzzi (1903-1986) was born in Casarsa della Delizia, northeastern Italy, the son of a farmer. In 1920, after quitting school to work on the family farm, he immigrated to the United States with his two oldest sisters to join five of his six brothers already there. His parents and other siblings emigrated in 1921. They settled in Berkeley, California, where the brothers operated a machine shop. Jacuzzi started work as an apprentice machinist as soon as he arrived at the Jacuzzi Bros. Co., and was promoted to sales manager in 1933, by which time the firm's main business was making water pumps for irrigation. Jacuzzi's youngest son, born in 1941, developed rheumatoid arthritis as a toddler, and when he was about seven his doctor recommended hydrotherapy. Such facilities were not readily available, so in 1949, using his business experience, Jacuzzi developed a new pump that created a swirling whirlpool in a bathtub. When his son's suffering was temporarily eased by this treatment, Jacuzzi

patented his invention and assigned it to the family business. The pump system that evolved was subsequently incorporated into specially large baths, known as "hot tubs." The name was entered in the US Patent Office *Official Gazette* of June 13, 1978.

Jaeger (knitwear)

The name is that of Gustav Jaeger (1832-1917), a German naturalist who was professor of zoology and physiology at Stuttgart University. He published a book called *Gesundheitskultur* ("Health Culture") in which he promoted his theory that as humans are animals they should wear animal clothing, that is, clothing made of natural animal hair or wool, and avoid vegetable fibers such as cotton and linen. The book came to the attention of Lewis Tomalin, an English accountant, who resolved to open a London shop to sell such clothing, for which there was a growing public demand. He did so in the late 1870s, obtaining the sole right to retail Dr. Jaeger's "sanitary underwear" and knitwear, made from undyed animal fabrics, and especially Merino sheep wool. In 1883 the business was incorporated as Dr. Jaeger's Sanitary Woollen System Co. Ltd. Jaeger remains popular for its knitwear today, although its clothing does now include nonanimal fabrics. The name was entered by The Jaeger Co.Ltd., of London, in the *Trade Marks Journal* of October 7, 1925 for: "Cloths and stuffs of wool, worsted or hair."

Jaffa Cakes (sponge cakes)

The chocolate-coated sponge cakes are named for their center of concentrated Jaffa orange juice. They were first made in the 1940s by the Scottish firm of **McVitie & Price** at a factory built in 1917 in Manchester, England. The name is not proprietary, and there are other makes.

Jaguar (automobiles)

The name "Jaguar" appeared on a British car for the first time in 1935, with the introduction of the SS Jaguar. The "SS" came from the Swallow Sidecar Company, a firm founded in 1922 by William Lyons (1901-1985) and William Walmsley to produce sidecars for motorcycles. In 1931 the company progressed to the manufacture of cars, a move reflected in its change of name to SS Cars Ltd. in 1934. But why

"Jaguar"? It is on record that Lyons had a list of over 500 fast-moving animals from which to choose a name. It was that of the jaguar that appealed to him, as particularly apt for the car's low lines and powerful performance. Not surprisingly, the "SS" prefix was hardly advantageous during World War II and was dropped soon after it. In 1966 Jaguar merged with the British Motor Corporation to form British Motor Holdings (*see* **BL**). It became independent again in 1984, and was acquired by **Ford** in 1989.

JAL *see* **Japan Air Lines**

James *(motorcycles)*

The British make of motorcycle owes its name to Harry James, who set up quite late in life when already established as works manager of a Birmingham engineering company. His James Cycle Company originally made bicycles, and in 1902 produced its first motorcycle. In 1951 his firm was taken over by Associated Motor Cycles (*see* **AJS**) but ceased production in 1966.

James Burrough *(gin)*

The English founder of the firm of distillers that makes **Beefeater** gin was James Burrough (1834-1897), born in Ottery St. Mary, Devon. On quitting school Burrough trained as a pharmaceutical chemist, and following completion of his apprenticeship spent six years in North America, gaining experience. On his return to England in 1863 he acquired the long-established gin distilling business of John Taylor & Co. in Chelsea, London. Burrough changed the name of the firm to his own, and soon gained fame for the gin he produced. It was only after World War II, however, that the company became internationally known, and this happened when Beefeater gin was introduced to the American market by Eric Burrough, a direct descendant of the founder.

James Wellbeloved *(petfoods)*

The British company, based in Yeovil, Somerset, and specializing in additive-free petfoods, was founded in 1992 by Christine Priest, Robin Cook, and Michael Newsum, who based its name on that of George Cyril Wellbeloved, Lord Emsworth's pigman in the novels of P.G. Wodehouse. By the end of its first year, the business had realized sales of £125,000 and had sold nearly 400 tonnes of its seaweed-enhanced dogfood. Ten years later, the firm was on track for sales of £10 million.

Jameson *(whiskey)*

The story behind the famous brand of Irish whiskey has been told differently by different writers. It seems that the original John Jameson was a Scotsman from Alloa who had married into the **Haig** distilling family and who while still in his 30s was appointed Sheriff Clerk of Clackmannanshire. He subsequently sought his fortune in Ireland, arriving in Dublin some time in the 1770s. His two sons, John and William, became acquainted with a distiller named John Stein operating in Bow Street, Dublin, and John, the elder of the two, married Stein's daughter, Isabella. John Jameson, Sr., took over the Bow Street distillery around 1780, the year the firm now gives as that of its founding, and was later succeeded by his son John. Brother William, meanwhile, ran a second distillery in Marrowbone Lane which later bore his name when he took over. Between them, John and William Jameson established the biggest distilling family in Irish history. The firm became a private limited company in 1891 and a public company in 1902. In 1966 Jameson merged with **Power's** and the Cork Distilleries Co. (*see* **Hewitts**) to form the Irish Distillers Company. The Jameson name was entered by "William Robertson, on behalf of self and partners, William Jameson and James Jameson, trading as Wm. Jameson and Co." in the *Trade Marks Journal* of February 28, 1877, and more recently by "John Jameson & Son Limited" in the *Journal* of March 24, 1965.

Jandal *(footwear)*

The type of flip-flop sandal with a thong between the big toe and the other toes has a name presumably based on "sandal." The name itself is a New Zealand registered trademark.

Jane's *(publishers)*

The founder of the British military yearbooks and related reference volumes was John Frederick Thomas Jane (1865-1916), usually known simply as Fred T. Jane. He was born a vicar's son in Devonshire, and from an early age had an interest in the sea and ships, taking a boy's delight in reenacting naval battles with model ships on the village duckpond. On leaving school, however, Jane went to London with the aim of earning a living by journalism and drawing. He lived a precarious existence in a Chelsea attic until a break came in 1889, when he was appointed the special artist of an illustrated magazine to cover the Spithead Review that year, when all the ships of the Royal Navy were assembled off Portsmouth. Jane went on from there to become a regular contributor and writer on naval affairs, and specialized in drawing battleships. It was the latter craft that led to the publication of the first edition of *Jane's Fighting Ships* in 1898. A subsequent interest in airplanes resulted in the first issue of *Jane's All the World's Aircraft* in 1909. The present Jane's Information Group is part of the Thomson Organization (*see* **Thomson Travel**).

Janet Reger *(underwear)*

It was a case of mistaken identity that set businesswoman Janet Reger (b.1935), born Janet Phillips in London, England, on her career. She spent many years as a freelance designer anonymously creating underwear for major chainstores, but only managed to secure her first order because buyers at **Harrods** and **Fenwicks** mistook her name, that of her German husband, Peter Reger, for the fashionable Rabi label. Janet Reger Creations Ltd. was set up in 1967, the business steadily grew, and the lingerie and nightwear that the firm's founder designed are now worn around the world.

Jantzen *(swimwear)*

The name is that of Carl Jantzen (1883-1939), born in Aarhus, Denmark, who in 1913 invented a rib-stitch method of making bathing suits. At the time he was a partner in a small knitting mill in Portland, Oregon, and his fellow partners, brothers John and Roy Zehntbauer, were so pleased with the lightweight suits resulting from the rib-stitch process that they decided to market the product nationally. In order to do this, they needed a a more meaningful trade name than the "PK" the firm had been using since its founding in 1910. For obvious reasons, the brothers felt that their own name lacked the necessary marketing appeal, but Jantzen was equally opposed to lending his name to the product. The answer was subterfuge. In 1916 John Zehntbauer secretly arranged to have his partner's name printed on the firm's stationery, so presenting Jantzen with

a fait accompli. Accepting the inevitable, Jantzen helped build the product that bore his name into a national and, by 1925, international line of swimwear.

Japan Air Lines *(airline)*

The Japanese airline, often known as JAL, was founded in 1951 and was a private company until 1953, when it was reorganized as a semigovernmental public corporation. It was at first a domestic carrier but became an international airline in 1954, when it inaugurated flights to San Francisco. Its Japanese name is Nihon Koku, corresponding to the English. *See also* **All Nippon**.

Jardine Mathieson *(diversified industries)*

The British company, with interests chiefly in the Far East, evolved from the trade with China established by two Scottish merchants, William Jardine (1784-1843) and Nicolas Mathieson (1796-1878), who set up business in Canton (Guangzhou) in 1832. Their early success was based on smuggling opium into China in collaboration with the East India Company.

Jarrold *(calendars and books)*

The English firm traces its origins to 1770, when John Jarrold (1745-1775), an Essex grocer's son, set up his own grocer's and draper's business in Woodbridge, Suffolk. On his untimely death, the business was continued by a family friend until 1797, when his son, also named John, took it over, while continuing to run his farm nearby. In 1814 he was joined by his brother-in-law, Benjamin Smith, who had learned printing, and after a period of apprenticeship with him John Jarrold took his new activity to the farm. In 1823 he moved to Norwich, and there set up a printing business in London Street, together with his four sons, John, Samuel, William, and Thomas. From this the wider activity of stationery and publishing gradually developed. In 1840 the business moved to larger premises in London Street, and has remained there ever since.

Java *(computer programming language)*

The computer programming language, used to create networking applications, derives its name from Java coffee, a favorite drink of many American computer programmers, and was chosen to suggest the richness and strength of the language. It was first developed in 1990 by software engineers at Sun Microsystems as a control language for consumer electronics products, and launched by them in 1995.

Jawa *(motorcycles)*

The name of the Czech make of motorcycle is an abbreviation of *Ja*nacek-*Wa*nderer, from the arms industrialist F. Janacek and the German Wanderer motorcycle to which he bought the rights. The first model appeared in 1929. The firm was nationalized after World War II.

Jazzercise *(physical exercise program)*

The program of physical exercises carried out in a group to jazz (or other) music was devised in 1969 by the American jazz-dance instructor Judi Sheppard Misset. The name, blending "jazz" and "exercise," was entered in the US Patent Office *Official Gazette* of September 13, 1977: "For educational services—namely, conducting a class in dance and exercise," with a note of first use on November 1, 1974. *Cp.* **Dancercize**.

JCB *(backhoe loaders)*

The initials, now almost generic in Britain for a mechanical digger or earthmover, are those of the manufacturing company's founder, Joseph Cyril Bamford (1916-2001). Bamford grew up in the market town of Uttoxeter, Staffordshire, the son of an agricultural engineer. He was always interested in mechanical things, and in 1945, aged 30, set up a welding business in a lock-up garage with a hacksaw and a second-hand welding kit. His first product was a farm trailer, fashioned from recycled metal parts, which he sold in Uttoxeter market. In 1948 he produced the world's first two-wheeled hydraulic tipping trailer, and later that same year the first hydraulic loader in Europe. Demand for his machines grew, and the turning point came when, in 1953, on a visit to Norway, he came on a rudimentary backhoe. He took it back to Britain, and by equipping a tractor with a digger at the front and the backhoe at the rear created the prototype of the first JCB backhoe loaders. Bamford stepped down as chairman of J.C. Bamford Excavators Ltd. in 1976. The business is now run by his son, Sir Anthony Bamford (b.1945). The initialism was entered by "J.C. Bamford (Excavators) Lim-

ited, Lakeside Works, Rocester, Uttoxeter" in the *Trade Marks Journal* of June 29, 1960 for: "Power-operated loaders and excavators, all for handling, transporting and loading earth, minerals and similar materials, and parts and fittings therefor."

JD Wetherspoon *(public houses)*

When British entrepreneur Tim Martin (b. 1956) was a student in Nottingham, he started visiting a pub called Marler's, run by Andrew Marler. One day, Marler told Martin he was tired of running the pub and asked him if he would like to buy it. Martin jumped at the chance, and with a loan from **Watney's** and an undertaking to stock their beer, took over Marler's three weeks before the New Year, in 1979, changing the name from Marler's to Martin's. On New Year's Eve, Martin politely asked a drunk customer to leave, whereupon the drinker hurled a blackboard through the window. This led Martin to change the name to Wetherspoon, after one of his teachers in New Zealand who could not control his class. The initials JD came from Jefferson Davis "Boss" Hogg, the mayor in the 1980s television series *The Dukes of Hazzard*. By 1983 Martin was running 7 pubs, and by the close of the century 500, with a staff of 12,000 and sales of a million barrels of beer a year.

Jeep *(utility vehicle)*

The usual explanation offered for this well-known American name is that it derives from the letters "G.P.", standing for "general purpose." But things are not quite so simple. The vehicle was designed in July 1940 by Karl K. Pabst, consulting engineer of the Bantam Car Company of Butler, Pennsylvania, in response to a request from the US Army for a military general-purpose vehicle. Both **Ford** of Detroit and **Willys-Overland** Motors submitted a prototype vehicle in November 1940, and the following summer the Willys model was accepted as the standard, with orders being placed with both firms. The Ford vehicle had the code letters "GPW," standing for "General-Purpose Willys," and Ford, therefore, claim the name derives from this. Sources at the Jeep Corporation, however, express doubt about the validity of this, since the name existed in the 1930s. They claim it was suggested by "Eugene the Jeep," a versatile cartoon character with a cry of "Jeep!" "who could do almost everything," introduced in 1936 by Elzie C. Segar in his "Thimble Theatre" comic strip. A quite different story claims that the name came from "Jeepers creepers!", an exclamation made by Major General George Lynch, US Army chief of infantry, when he first rode in a prototype of the vehicle at Fort Myer, Virginia, in 1939, and accordingly adopted by the vehicle's designer, Charles H. Payne. Whatever the case, the experimental models were known by a number of names in the early days, among them "Bantam," "Peep," "Blitzbuggy," "Jitterbug," "Beetlebug," "Iron Pony," "Leaping Lena," and "Panzer Killer." The name "Jeep" finally came to stay in 1941, and was entered by Willys-Overland in the *Trade Marks Journal* of August 22, 1945.

Jell-o *(gelatin dessert)*

In 1845, Pearl B. Wait, a cough medicine manufacturer in LeRoy, New York, patented a new type of gelatin dessert. His wife, Mary, coined a name for it, from "jelly" or "gelatin" and the "-o" suffix then common for names of food products. It was first produced commercially in 1897. It was Jell-o (the firm) and Postum (*see* **Post Toasties**) that formed the nucleus of General Foods Corp. in 1925. The name was entered by the Jell-o Company of Canada in the *Trade Marks Journal* of July 11, 1934 as a "Brand of Jelly Powder" that "can be placed in the refrigerator as soon as dissolved."

Jelson *(builders)*

The British company, founded in 1889 by James Jelley as a small undertaking and shop-fitting business, is now a construction firm building 350 houses a year in a 60-mile area around its Leicester headquarters. It is a family-owned business with Jelley's grandson Ronald (b.1927) as its chairman and his great-grandson, Robert, as a director. Hence the name, as if "Jelley & Sons."

Jeno's *(frozen pizzas)*

In 1954, Jeno Francisco Paulucci (b. 1918), born in Minnesota the son of Italian immigrants, founded the canned and frozen Chinese food company ChunKing. In 1967 he sold this company to **R.J. Reynolds** and switched from egg rolls to pizza rolls when he formed Jeno's Inc. His business boomed, but after losing out

to **Pillsbury** in the late 1970s, when that company developed a new frying process, soon bounced back with its own type of fried pizza crust.

Jensen *(automobiles)*

British brothers F. Alan and Richard A. Jensen, based in West Bromwich, Staffordshire, were originally known to the motoring public from their attractive car body designs of the late 1920s and 1930s. The first Jensen car was launched by Jensen Motors Ltd. in 1936. The brothers moved to the manufacture of light commercial vehicles after World War II, but the company closed in 1976.

Jergens *(lotion)*

Andrew Jergens (1852-1929), a Dutch immigrant to the United States at the age of seven, had already done well for himself in the lumber business when in 1880 he met Charles Geilfus, a Cincinnati soapmaker. Geilfus was looking for a financial backer, so a partnership was struck to manufacture fancy toilet soap. The new firm was originally called the Western Soap Company, but in 1882 changed its name to the Andrew Jergens Company. Jergens remained president of his company to his death, when he was succeeded by his son, Andrew Jergens, Jr. (1881-1969).

Jerome Russell *(glitter hairspray)*

English entrepreneur Alan Marcus was born in London in 1952 the son of an army sergeant major. On quitting school, with no qualifications, he went to work in his brother's hairdressing salon and soon after opened a salon of his own. In 1978 he launched his first company, Jerome Russell, manufacturing glitter and color hair sprays and home bleaching. The name was a combination of his own middle name and that of his brother and business partner, David. The products created by Marcus were at the heart of 1980s trash fashion, and were soon accompanied by a brand of nail-varnish remover and temporary tattoos. In 1998 the brothers sold their enterprise to an American company, Pro Style, by which time they had established JR Universal Inkjet, making a universal ink compatible with over 300 computer printer cartridges.

Jerry's *(home furnishings)*

Jerry's Home Store was founded in 1993 by

British entrepreneur Jeremy Sacher (b. 1956), great-grandson of Michael Marks, cofounder of **Marks & Spencer**, Sacher's first employers. He joined the company straight from school and worked for them for 17 years, rising to take charge of home-furnishings development, a position that took him worldwide in search of new products and ideas. A visit to the Crate & Barrel home-furnishings store in Chicago opened his eyes to a new way of retailing, and he returned to Britain determined to bring the best of the US store to the British high street, but under his own steam. At first he specialized in American goods such as Waring blenders, old-fashioned diner furniture, oversized plates, and American food, but went on to offer products from around the world, including Swedish lighting and Italian corner sofas. Sacher's favorite product was the "Chandler" reclining chair, named for the character in the hit TV show *Friends*. His first store was a **Laura Ashley** outlet in west London, and by 2001 he had six shops, including a concession in **Harvey Nichols** and a new store on London's Tottenham Court Road.

Jessops *(photographic equipment)*

Frank Jessop (1905-2001) was born to a family of pharmacists in Walsall, Staffordshire, England. On quitting school, he studied pharmacy at Birmingham University and opened a pharmacy in Leicester in 1935. He was already a keen photographer, and that side of the business gradually expanded, so that soon his store was the first of a network of photographic stores trading as Jessops of Leicester. At first his firm sold and hired 16 mm. cinefilm, but by the time Frank's son, Alan, joined the business in 1960 it was a specialist photographic store. Alan Jessop decided to cut prices right down and advertise nationally in the *Amateur Photographer*. This proved a great boost, and the store was so popular that lines formed outside. Ten years later Jessops moved to spacious new premises in Leicester, winning it a place in the *Guinness Book of Records* as the world's largest photographic store. By the time of a management buyout in 1996, Jessops had grown to more than 70 stores with a workforce of over 500. Today the company that Frank Jessop founded has more than 200 stores with over 2,000 staff.

Jetfoil *(watercraft)*

The type of passenger-carrying hydrofoil, with a stabilization and control system based on that of an aircraft, was launched (literally) by **Boeing** in the early 1970s. Its name, combining "jet" and "hydrofoil," was entered in the US Patent Office *Official Gazette* of February 17, 1976.

Jewel *(foods and drugs)*

The American company, in full Jewel Companies, Inc., traces its origins to 1899 when Frank Vernon Skiff and his brother-in-law, Frank Ross, founded the Jewel Tea Company as a mobile "store" to supply coffee, tea, spices, and extracts to the Chicago area from horse-drawn wagons. As the automobile gained in importance, the firm moved from wagons to trucks to deliver its good across the Midwest. It incorporated in Illinois in 1903 and took its present name in 1966.

Jeyes *("Fluid")*

The name is that of John Jeyes (1817-1892), a pharmacist's son born in or near Northampton, England. When still at school, John Jeyes had shown a keen interest in botany, and on completing his education went into partnership with a local nurseryman. He married, and on the birth of his sixth child (of nine) went with his family to London, where in about 1871, after a series of jobs and changes of address, he settled in Plaistow. He began experimenting with new kinds of disinfectants, and eventually evolved the type he had been seeking, a preparation consisting of creosote dissolved in water. He patented this as his "Fluid" in 1877, setting up Jeyes' Sanitary Compounds Co. Ltd. to market it. His product sold well in the unhygienic London of his day, and Jeyes Fluid remains a household name when it comes to disinfectants. The name was entered in the *Trade Marks Journal* of July 18, 1888, with the recommendation: "[In] sickness always use Jeyes' disinfectants."

Jiffy *(padded bag)*

The British make of padded bag, typically used for mailing books, is presumably so named because it obviates time-consuming wrapping and sealing. The item can thus be packed "in a jiffy," or in a moment. The story goes that the bag was invented in the late 1950s by George

Gerard after reading a story to his young son about a mouse that made itself a nest by tearing old newspapers to shreds. The name was entered by the Jiffy Packaging Company of Winsford, Cheshire, in the *Trade Marks Journal* of July 2, 1969 for: "Padded paper bags, cushioned paper pads and padded paper in sheet or roll form, all being wrapping and packaging materials for industrial use, for protecting goods in transit." *Cp.* **Jiffypot**.

Jiffypot *(plant propagating pot)*

The special type of plant pot, made of peat and wood pulp through which plant roots can grow, presumably derives its name from "jiffy" since the pots enable plants to grow much more quickly. The name "Jiffypots" was entered in the *Trade Marks Journal* of March 27, 1968 for: "Flower, planting and transplanting pots made of peat" by "Odd Smaaberg Melvold and Leif Fraas Koxvold, trading as Me-Kox Industri Melvold & Koxvold, Østre Akers Vei 210 Grorud, near Oslo, Norway; manufacturers and merchants." An earlier registration in the *Journal* of December 4, 1957 gives the name as "Jiffapot" for: "Hormonal peat in the form of propagating pots for plants."

Jim Beam *(bourbon)*

The name on the bottle is that of Colonel James B. Beam (1864-1947), the great-grandson of Jacob Beam, who founded a distillery in north central Kentucky in 1795. Jim joined the family business at the age of 16 and renamed what had become the D.M. Beam & Sons Distillery after himself to celebrate the end of Prohibition following the repeal of the Eighteenth Amendment in 1933.

Jim Walter *(building materials)*

The story goes that when truckdriver Jim Walter was building his own house in Tampa, Florida, a passerby offered him a good price for the unfinished building. Walter realized the potential market for prefabricated house shells and began selling them. On his first day in business, in 1946, he sold 27 shells, and before long the Jim Walter Corporation was producing a whole range of accessory building materials, from pipes and plumbing to concrete and insulation.

JJB Sports *(sports goods stores)*

Britain's largest sports retailer takes its name from J.J. Bradburn, a Wigan, Lancashire, sports shop bought in 1978 by David Whelan (b. 1937), a former footballer and market trader in toiletries. At the time its leading line was fishermen's maggots, but Whelan refashioned it and by 2001 had transformed it into a growing chain of 450 stores.

Joe Bloggs *(fashionwear)*

The British brand name is that of clothing made by the immigrant Manchester businessman Shami Ahmed (b.1963), who began his career on the family stall in nearby Burnley while still at school and who founded his fashion empire in 1986. Joe Bloggs is a nickname for an average Briton, corresponding to the American Joe Blow.

John Deere *see* Deere

John England *(mail order firm)*

The name of the British firm sounds almost too good to be true. It is, for there was no John England as the founder of the firm, and the name was chosen simply to suggest what later came to be regarded as "the best of British," with John a typical "solid" and reliable English name. It dates from 1933, when the business was first started. For two similar names, compare **John Noble** (who actually existed) and, although not a mail order house, **Peter England**.

John Lewis *(department stores)*

There are two John Lewises behind the British name, father and son. The elder John Lewis (1836-1928) was born a cabinetmaker's son in Shepton Mallet, Somerset. Orphaned at only seven, he and his four sisters were brought up by an unmarried aunt, Ann Speed. John quit school at 14 to be apprenticed to a draper in Wells, Somerset, left four years later to join another draper in Bridgwater in the same county, and in 1856 came to London to work as a salesman for **Peter Robinson**. In 1864 he set up on his own as draper and haberdasher in Oxford Street, where his business flourished. In 1884 he married, and in due course came to live with his family in Spedan Tower, a large house on the edge of Hampstead Heath, named near anagrammatically for the aunt who had raised him. His elder son, John Spedan Lewis (1885-1963), joined him in the business in 1904. In 1906, noting that they earned more than the rest of their employees put together,

John Spedan Lewis began devising a way of sharing the benefits of ownership. He conducted his initial experiments at the ailing **Peter Jones** store which his father had bought that year. By 1929 he had inherited both shops, and transferred his ownership to his employees, so founding the present unique John Lewis Partnership. Today employers and employees alike share in the profits and responsibilities of company ownership.

John Menzies *(newsagents)*

John Menzies (1808-1879) was a Scotsman born and bred, as his name suggests. After completing his education in Edinburgh in 1822, he was apprenticed to a bookseller in the city before being taken on as an employee by a bookseller in London in 1831. Two years later Menzies' father died, and the young man returned to Edinburgh to provide for the family as best he could. He set up his own bookselling business on the corner of Princes Street and Hanover Street, and began to build up contacts with the publishing world. (He was an agent for **Chapman & Hall**, and sold the works of Dickens throughout eastern Scotland.) This laid the foundation for the railway bookstalls that the firm set up just before World War I, and for the nationwide chain of newsagents that eventually developed. The company was in family hands to 1997, with John Maxwell Menzies (b.1926) its chairman from 1952 to that year. In 1998 John Menzies sold its 230 retail stores to **W.H. Smith**.

John Murray *see* **Murray**

John Noble *(mail order firm)*

The present British company of the name was incorporated in 1893. The name of John Noble itself, however, can be traced back earlier than this, to a calico manufacturing business founded in Piccadilly, Manchester, in 1870. A contemporary account tells how "Mr. John Noble was amongst the first producers on a large scale to introduce dealing direct with the consumers," so that "ladies in the country … will soon find the pleasure and convenience of purchasing at the wholesale price from large selections of patterns without the trouble and annoyance of shopping excursions." Mail order was then hardly known as a commercial concept in Britain, but this is what John Noble's enterprise essentially was.

John Robert Powers *(modeling agency)*

John Robert Powers (1896-1977) was born in Easton, Pennsylvania, the son of a farmer. After graduating from Easton Academy, Powers went to New York City, where he aspired to be an actor. He landed some small parts, but was not encouraged to pursue a life on the stage or the screen. One day, having seen a photographer's request for eight models to pose for a magazine advertisement, he decided to respond by rounding up suitable people, and that gave him the idea of assembling a catalog of readily available models for just such occasions. He made and distributed catalogs to advertising agencies, where they were an instant success. Thus in 1923 was born the world's first modeling agency, John Robert Powers, Inc., which by the 1930s had become the largest and most famous such agency in the world.

John Smedley *(knitwear)*

The British firm has its head office and mill on exactly the same site today, near Cromford, Derbyshire, as the one where it was founded in 1784 by John Smedley (1764-1840). The region has historic links with spinning and John Smedley's mill was quick to take up the business, also making calico as well as spinning cotton. The business is still in the hands of the Smedley family.

John Smith's *(beer)*

The English town of Tadcaster, Yorkshire, has two well-known breweries with similar names, John Smith's and **Samuel Smith's**. The two Smith families were directly related, but Samuel's brewery arose through a family quarrel, not a fraternal partnership. John Smith was a young farmer and brewer who in 1847 purchased the brewery of Backhouse and Hartley, founded in 1758. It was rather run down by the time Smith acquired it, and its new owner undertook extensive modernization and expansion, basing his experience on the thriving breweries of Burton-on-Trent. John Smith left the brewery to his brothers Samuel and William, the latter of whom had been in partnership with him.

John Swire *(shipping and transport)*

The British company John Swire and Sons traces its origins to 1816, when John Swire set up as a merchant in Liverpool. He extended his business in 1832 to include his sons, John Samuel Swire (1825-1898) and William Hudson Swire, who inherited the general trading house on his death in 1847. By 1865 the firm, under John Samuel Swire ("the Senior"), had moved the emphasis of the trading business from Liverpool to the Far East, where the family had had shipping interests from the earliest years. In 1914 the firm was incorporated as John Swire and Sons Ltd., and by the late 1940s had acquired Far Eastern agencies for a number of airlines. In 1948 John Kidston Swire (1893-1983), grandson of John Samuel Swire, purchased a controlling share in the recently founded **Cathay Pacific** Airways, and built the Hong Kong airline up into an international enterprise. His own elder son, John Anthony Swire (b. 1922), was company chairman from 1966 through 1987, when he was succeeded by his younger brother, Adrian Christopher Swire (b. 1932).

John West *(canned foods)*

Little is known about the man who gave his name to the products. John West was probably of Scottish origin, and according to one account was the first person to make a commercial success of salting salmon in the mid-19th century. With this as his specialist line, he is known to have opened his own salmon cannery at Westport, Oregon, in 1873. Today John West Foods Ltd. markets not just canned salmon but meat, fruit, and vegetables. Its head office is in Liverpool, England.

Johnnie Walker *(whisky)*

"Johnnie Walker, born 1820, still going strong," runs the slogan. That year, however, was not the one in which the young Scot John Walker was actually born, but the one in which he bought a grocery, wine, and liquor business in Kilmarnock, Ayrshire, Scotland. His enterprise did well, with his son, Alexander, soon joining his father and doing much to open up the export side of the business by setting up retail outlets in ports such as Glasgow. It was Alexander's son, also named Alexander, who in 1908 hit on the idea of incorporating a portrait of the original John Walker, his own grandfather, in the advertising. He commissioned an artist to depict the founder as he might have looked in 1820, so he could be seen striding out as a "walker" in conjunction with the slo-

gan. The device worked well, and the congenial combination of words and portrait helps sell the brand today. There are now various "colored label" blends. Black Label and Red Label were created by the younger Alexander in the early 1900s, while Blue Label was added as recently as 1992.

Johns-Manville *(asbestos and fiberglass)*

For many years Johns-Manville was the USA's leading manufacturer of asbestos. In recent years, however, its reputation has been rocked by the many lawsuits brought against it by the families of workers whose lives have been brought to a painful and premature close by inhaling the lethal dust of the product. Today most of the company's activity is concentrated in fiberglass, not asbestos. The business arose in 1858, when Henry Ward Johns (d.1898) started a roofing business in West Stockbridge, Massachusetts. In 1868 he obtained his first patent for an asbestos compound to make roofing fire resistant. In 1886 Charles B. Manville started a similar venture in Milwaukee, the Manville Covering Company. He and his three sons made pipe coverings and other (nonasbestos) insulations. Manville obtained his asbestos supplies from Johns, and soon became his western distributor. The two firms merged three years after Johns' death, itself the result of a chronic lung disease caused by inhaling the very material that made his living.

Johnson & Johnson *(health care products)*

The origins of the company, well-known for its baby toiletries and **Band-Aid** plasters, go back to 1885, when in New Brunswick, New Jersey, Robert Wood Johnson (1845-1910), a former retail pharmacist and drug broker, formed a partnership with his two brothers, James Wood Johnson (1856-1932) and Edward Mead Johnson (1852-1934), to make antiseptic surgical dressings and medicinal plasters, realizing their advantages over the unhygienic cotton swabs then used for sterilization procedures in hospitals. They soon developed a cotton and gauze dressing that could be packaged for hospitals and doctors alike. Edward left the partnership in 1897 to form his own drug company, but the two remaining brothers evolved increasingly effective sterile bandages, achieving wide sales. Robert Wood Johnson was company president from the year of founding to his death.

Johnson Products *(cosmetics)*

The name behind the American company is that of George E. Johnson, a former door-to-door salesman in Chicago for Fuller Products, a black cosmetics firm. He left in 1954 to make and sell a new hair straightener called "Ultra Wave," and three years later introduced the "Ultra Sheen" line, which enabled him to break through into the beauty shop market.

Johnson Wax *(polishes)*

The name is that of Samuel Curtis Johnson (1833-1919), born in the small town of Elyria, Ohio. When he was only three his family made the first of many moves before settling in Grafton, Wisconsin, where his father started a sawmill. On leaving college, Samuel Johnson became an office boy with the Milwaukee & La Crosse Railroad in Milwaukee, staying with them several years before moving to other different railroad construction companies. Eventually in 1882 he moved to Racine, Wisconsin, becoming a salesman for the Racine Hardware Company, selling parquet flooring. In 1886 he started his own business, the S.C. Johnson Co., buying the flooring from the firm. His enterprise grew, but he had an increasing number of letters from customers asking how best to treat the flooring they bought. Soap and water, the traditional method, simply loosened and warped the wooden parquet blocks. To satisfy his customers, Johnson developed a paste-wax product that would protect the floor, and was soon sending tins of "Johnson's Prepared Wax" with every new floor he sold. By the end of the century, sales of his polish were outstripping sales of his floors, and from then on wax polish was his main product.

Johnsons *(cleaners)*

The British dry-cleaning company was founded by William Johnson (1787-1851), a dyer in Leeds. When the business ceased to be profitable, he left for Liverpool, where in 1829 he bought a silk-dyeing concern. Johnson enlarged its scope, adding woolen and general dyeing to that of silk. In 1843 he handed the business over to his daughter-in-law, Eliza Johnson, and four years later she opened the firm's first receiving shop in her Bold Street home. Johnsons first began dry cleaning only in the latter half of the 19th century, after William Johnson's death, and on the introduction of this service the number of Johnson branches increased considerably.

Johnsons *(photographic materials)*

The British company of Johnsons-HPL (Holdings) Ltd. developed from the goldsmith's business established in Maiden Lane, London, in 1743 by one Richard Wright. His apprentice, John Johnson, eventually took over, becoming London's first private assayer. In 1829 the business moved to Basinghall Street, and in 1831 George R. Johnson, John's grandson, became assayer to the Bank of England and the Royal Mint. The firm soon began to manufacture silver and gold chemical salts for the photographic process pioneered by the English physicist W.H. Fox Talbot. In 1873 the firm moved again to Croft Street and in 1882 was incorporated as Johnson & Sons, Manufacturing Chemists. The assay business was meanwhile formed into a separate company. By the end of the century the popularity of photography was assured, as also was the profitability of Johnson's business, with military photography in World War I bringing greater demand.

Johnsons *(seeds)*

The British firm was founded by William Wade Johnson (1803-1880), born near Lincoln the son of the village squire. On completing his education at the age of 17 he discussed with his father what career he should pursue, but failing to reach agreement left home for the market town of Boston, Lincolnshire. There he bought ten acres of land and began to grow produce which he sold from a stall in Boston market place. He was something of a botanist, and was interested in developing the seed side of his business, saving the best plants from each crop, letting them go to seed, and then harvesting the seeds themselves. The high quality of his seeds brought him increasing business, so that by the time of his death the firm of W.W. Johnson & Co. Ltd., still based in Boston, had acquired much of its current high reputation. It is said that Johnson had five wives but only one son.

Jokari *(game)*

The game, dating from the 1950s and of

American origin, consists in batting a ball which is attached to the bat with a long length of rubber cord, so that it rebounds. The name presumably derives from Italian *giocare*, "to play," or its source, Latin *jocari*, "to jest." The British firm of R. & J. Travis Ltd, of Berkhamsted, Hertfordshire, entered it with a wider application in the *Trade Marks Journal* of April 4, 1973, for: "Games (other than ordinary playing cards), playthings, gymnastic and sporting articles (other than clothing)."

Jolly Time *(popcorn)*

The American Pop Corn Company was formed in 1914 by Cloid H. Smith, an Iowa farmer's son, and his family helped him prepare and package the product. They called it "Jolly Time," to evoke associations of festivity, and their carboard packages showed laughing urchins gleefully wolfing handfuls of popcorn from a huge bowl. The brand-name popcorn was an instant success, and by the end of the first year Smith's company had sold more than 75,000 pounds of popcorn. The enterprise moved into larger premises, and the American Pop Corn Company incorporated in Iowa in 1926.

Jones, Peter *see* **Peter Jones**

Jordans *(breakfast cereals)*

The British maker of specialist breakfast cereals was founded in 1855, when the Jordan family founded a mill at Biggleswade, Bedfordshire. By the 1960s many of the old mills were closing, but a public interest in health foods was growing, and two of the family's descendants, Bill and David Jordan, switched from producing ordinary white flour to wholemeal flour. Their product caught on, and by the late 1970s Jordans was selling its cereals to the supermarkets and once again flourishing.

Joseph, Michael *see* **Michael Joseph**

Joseph Schmidt *(chocolates)*

US confectioner Joseph Schmidt, born in 1939 to Austrian parents, was raised in Palestine and trained as a baker. In 1983, together with his partner, Audrey Ryan, he opened his first shop, and booming trade soon obliged him to expand his 16th Street, San Francisco, premises. His 150 personnel are mainly women, on the basis that adult female hands are cooler than male, and so more suited to a craft where temperature fluctuations of just one or two degrees can be critical.

Jowett *(automobiles)*

British brothers Benjamin and William Jowett launched their first car near Bradford, Yorkshire, in 1910. They ceased to have any connection with their company after World War II and production flagged, so that in 1954 the remnants of the business were sold off to **International Harvester**.

Juan Clemente *(cigars)*

The Dominican Republic cigar brand was founded in 1982 by the Frenchman Jean Clément, who hispanicized his name for the purpose.

Jubilee clip *(hose clip)*

The handy little hose clip tightened by a worm drive was invented in 1921 by Commander Lumley-Robinson, founder of the British firm of L. Robinson & Co. of Gillingham, Kent. The success of the clip owed much to the inventor's indomitable wife, Emily Lumley-Robinson, who sold their house to raise the capital necessary for the original tooling and material of the enterprise. After her husband died in 1939, she took control of the firm and ran it with great energy and success. During World War II, Jubilee clips were used at the rate of a million a month in military aircraft alone. In 1948, John Lumley-Robinson, the couple's son, became managing director of the firm, but his mother worked on until 1982, when she was forced to retire because of ill health at the age of 97.

Jumeau *(dolls)*

Although French *jumeau* means "twin," the name is actually that of the 19th-century French dollmakers Pierre François and Émile Jumeau, who entered the words "Bébé Jumeau" in the US Patent Office *Official Gazette* of November 27, 1888, with a note of use since 1840. The dolls, with their well-modeled heads, lifelike eyes, and movable joints, are still sought after by collectors.

Juncal *(chocolates)*

The Spanish firm dates from the late 19th century, when Dr. Zaragueta began making chocolates as a hobby. The first proper shop was opened in 1950 in Irún, adopting the name of the town's patron saint, the Virgin of Juncal. In 1953 the business moved to Madrid, where at the close of the 20th century it was run by the founder's great-grandson, Jesús-Maria Zaragueta Elgorriaga, together with his three daughters, Marta, Susana, and Juncal.

Jungle Gym *(children's climbing frame)*

The name, alluding to a "jungle" where young children can climb and swing, was entered (as "Junglegym") by the Chicago firm of this name in the US Patent Office *Official Gazette* of January 30, 1923 for: "Playground Apparatus, in Particular Climbing Frames." The now generic name gave that of Jungle Jim, the American comic-strip character created by Alex Raymond in the 1930s.

Junkers *(aircraft)*

The German aircraft are named for Hugo Junkers (1859-1935), who patented a flying-wing aircraft in 1910, the year he set up an aircraft factory at Dessau. His Ju-1 Blechesel ("Metal Donkey") monoplane of 1915 was the first successful all-metal airplane. Many Junkers aircraft had a corrugated sheet-metal skin copied by several US manufacturers, including **Ford**. The Ju-87 dive- bomber (*Sturzkampfflugzeug*, or "Stuka") and Ju-88 all-purpose bomber were notorious in World War II.

JWT *see* **J. Walter Thompson**

K *(footwear)*

The British make of footwear takes its name from the Lake District town of Kendal, Westmorland (now Cumbria), where in 1842 a London leather merchant, Robert Miller Somervell (1821-1899) set up a business making uppers for the bespoke shoemakers of the district. In 1848 he was joined as partner by his brother John (1814-1887) and they began making shoes themselves, but the business made only modest progress until the second generation, the five sons of the founding partners, joined in the 1870s. For identification they branded their products with the letter "K" when sending them to outworkers for finishing, and the increasingly familiar name was registered in 1875. K Shoes Ltd. was established as a holding company in 1949.

Kaiser Aluminum *(aluminum)*

The name is that of America's last great self-made industrialist, Henry John Kaiser (1882-1967), born to German immigrants in Sprout Brook, New York. He quit school at 13 and got a job in a dry goods store in Utica. He later became a photographic salesman, and at 23 had his own photographic studio and supply store. He went on to find another job in a hardware store in Spokane, Washington, where in turn he became involved in the construction industry, notably in British Columbia, Washington, California, and Cuba. During World War II he moved into the shipbuilding industry, and after it augmented his construction business and began producing automobiles, notably **Jeeps** and Henry J. cars. In short, business boomed, and so did the Kaiser Aluminum & Chemical Corporation, which dates its founding from 1931.

Kalamazoo *(business systems)*

The British company originated as Morland and Impey, a firm of Birmingham jobbing printers. So how come the name of the Michigan city? The story goes that one of the company founders visited Kalamazoo and brought back a loose-leaf binder so named. The firm then obtained the sole right to manufacture and sell this outside the USA. The new name Kalamazoo was adopted in 1943.

Kalydor *(skin tonic)*

The skin tonic based on almond oil was on sale in England from the early 19th century. Its name was entered by "Henry Edward Rowland and George William Rowland, trading as Alexander Rowland and Sons" of "Hatton Gardens, Middlesex" in the *Trade Marks Journal* of December 13, 1876 for: "Rowland's Kalydor for improving and beautifying the complexion. Eradicates all cutaneous eruptions." The name presumably derives from Greek *kallos*, "beauty," and *dora*, "skin."

Kango *(power tools)*

The name is especially associated with a make of mechanical hammer. It may derive from Australian "kanga," a slang word for a pneumatic drill, itself from "kangaroo," with reference to the animal's jumps. The name was entered in the *Trade Marks Journal* of April 1, 1925.

Kangol *(headwear)*

The range of headwear, safety harnesses, and seat belts had its origins with the Polish-born British beret manufacturer Jacques Spreiregen (d.1982) and his nephew, Jo Meisner, who in 1937 set up a factory at Cleator, near Whitehaven, Cumbria, to make berets for schoolwear, Girl Guide uniforms, and fashionwear. They devised the name from the three original raw materials used for the headgear, sil*k*, *ang*ora, and wo*ol*, and after World War II extended their range to military berets and subsequently to related fabric-based items. The Kangol "Kangaroo" was introduced in the 1970s when Kangol headwear became popular with Afro-American males, who asked for a "Kanga," and the company name on the front of the hat was accompanied by a stylized kangaroo. In the 1980s, the headgear was visibly popularized by black US rappers such as Run DMC, Doug E. Fresh and, in particular, LL Cool J. The name was entered in the *Trade Marks Journal* of March 12, 1952.

Kardex *see* **Sperry Rand**

Kardomah *(coffee houses)*

The British chain of coffee houses has its origins in a grocery business specializing in tea and coffee set up by Samuel and Christopher Vey in James Street, Liverpool, in 1844. The Liverpool China & India Tea Co. was incorporated in 1868 to acquire the business, when the grocery side was discontinued in favor of concentrating on tea and coffee. By 1894 the company was marketing its own brand of tea, "Kardomah," and an exhibition cafe was opened up in Liverpool to advertise it. (The name was already entered in the *Trade Marks Journal* of October 25, 1893.) This pattern was repeated with later branches, and by 1898 the firm was established as cafe and restaurant proprietors. By 1926 the company had 26 branches, and in 1936 changed its name to that of its brand of tea. In 1963 Kardomah Ltd. was taken over by **Forte**, who changed its exotic name to bland Fortes Popular Restaurants. It was then purchased from Forte in 1966 by **Cadbury Schweppes**, and its name was changed back to Kardomah. The origin of the name remains uncertain. In the USA, Khardomah [*sic*] Lodge in Grand Haven, Michigan, now a hotel, was built by the shores of Lake Michigan in 1873 as a private residence by a Grand Rapids entrepreneur, James Brayton. The name here is said to be that of an Indian chief, or to mean "happy home" in some Indian language. But this may not be the same name, and one would have expected an Asian Indian origin for the tea rather than an American Indian one.

Karo *(corn syrup)*

In 1902 the Corn Products Refining Company of New York and Chicago was founded and introduced "Karo" light and dark corn syrup. The origin of the name is disputed. One theory traces it to Caroline, wife of the chemist who formulated the syrup, while another derives it from an earlier table syrup called "Kairomel," itself perhaps from Greek *kairos*, "proper time," and Latin *mel*, "honey."

Kasha *(fabric)*

The soft, napped fabric of wool and hair, now produced in the United States, is of French origin, with a name apparently devised by its Parisian manufacturers, Rodier Frères. The name itself may be random, or possibly based on Kashan, the Iranian city noted for its woolen and silk carpets.

Kaufman & Broad *(houses)*

Literally throusands of American families live in homes built by Kaufman & Broad. The names are those of Donald Kaufman and Eli Broad, who started out in 1957 with $25,000 and a few small lots on the outskirts of Detroit. Their enterprise grew rapidly, and by 1969 they were second only to **Levitt**. In 1964 the company offices were moved from Detroit to Los Angeles, and Kaufman & Broad now has developments in Europe as well as North America.

Kawasaki *(transportation equipment)*

The Japanese company Kawasaki Heavy Industries, Ltd., arose as a shipyard enterprise founded by Shozo Kawasaki at Tsukiji, Tokyo, in 1878. In 1886 Kawasaki established another shipyard in Kobe, and when the two merged in 1896, formed the Kawasaki Shipyard Company. The business adopted its present name in 1939, after expanding into the manufacture of railroad equipment, aircraft, and machinery. A subsidiary, the Kawasaki Steel Corporation, was incorporated in 1950 as a separate company. After World War II the name became generally associated with automobiles and motorcycles, and the Kawasaki Z1 became the outstanding superbike of the 1970s.

Kayser Bondor *(stockings)*

The British firm began its career in 1928 as The Full-Fashioned Hosiery Co., registering its first brand name, "Fulfa," the following year. In 1931 the new brand name "Bondor" was registered, its origin in sham French *bon d'or*, "good as gold." In 1936 The Full-Fashioned Hosiery Co. joined forces with the US firm Julius Kayser & Co. as Kayser-Bondor Ltd. In 1946 The Full-Fashioned Hosiery Co. changed its name to Bondor Ltd. Kayser Bondor acquired the Kayser name from Julius Kayser & Co. in 1955, and was itself taken over by **Courtaulds** in 1966.

Kearley & Tonge *(foods)*

The British paired name derives from those of Hudson Ewbanke Kearley (1856-1934), later 1st Viscount Devonport, and his partner G.A. Tonge (d.1927). Kearley was born in Uxbridge, Middlesex, a plumber's son. He quit school at 15 and worked for a while, without pay, for a London coffee merchant before obtaining a post with **Tetleys**, the tea merchants. He rose to be company salesman, operating a profitable sideline buying tea in bulk from Tetleys and selling direct to shopkeepers who were too small to deal with Tetleys themselves. He set up on his own in 1876, taking first a Mr. Heseltine as partner, then G.A. Tonge, who had also worked for Tetleys. His business expanded, so that by 1886 he had ten shops, trading as the International Tea Company's Stores. He later became a pioneer in the retailing business, establishing multiple grocery stores to cater for the mass market. For his work in this field he was made a baronet in 1908 and became Baron Devonport two years later.

Keating's *(insect powders)*

The long familiar British household name is that of the chemist and druggist Thomas Keating (c.1787-1870), born in Homerton, Middlesex, the son of an attorney. An early proprietary preparation was his patented cough lozenges, introduced in around 1820. The famous insect powders came later, and "Keating's Persian Insect-Destroying Powder" was awarded a medal at the 1862 International Exhibition. This same name was entered in the *Trade Marks Journal* of October 11, 1876. "Keating's Insect Powders" continued to be produced until 1981 by LRC Products Ltd. (the former London Rubber Company).

Keds *(sneakers)*

The name was entered by the manufacturers, US Rubber, now **Uniroyal**, in the *Trade Marks Journal* of November 14, 1917. They had wanted to call the shoes "Peds," from Latin *pes*, *pedis*, "foot" (or related English "pedal"), but this was found to be close to existing names. They therefore opted for "Keds," choosing the incisive letter "K" instead, in the process producing a name that aptly enough happened to suggest "kids."

Keedoozle *(self-service stores)*

The American stores were the invention of Clarence Saunders, pioneer of the **Piggly Wiggly** chain. Saunders had the idea of an automatic, electrically operated type of retail grocery store in which the customer selected merchandise by using a special key. Hence the name, a fanciful respelling of "Key Does All." The mode of operation was as follows. The customer placed the key into a slot beside the desired item and pushed a button. This perforated a tape inside the key. On completing the shopping trip, the customer handed the tape to a clerk who ran it through a machine that added up the bill. Saunders's first attempt at the Keedoozle in 1937 failed due to mechanical difficulties. A plan to revive the idea was revived in 1945, but it was only in 1948 that an improved Keedoozle was unveiled. Although Saunders sold 12 franchises, the automatic device proved too complicated and too expensive to compete with the lower costs of normal grocery stores, and he ended the experiment in 1949. Even so, it was a worthy attempt at what was essentially an early equivalent of the modern EFTPOS (electronic funds transfer at point of sale) or "card swipe".

Keiller's *(marmalade)*

The Scottish firm has roots going back to the 18th century. The story goes that the wife of John Keiller, a Dundee grocer, made some marmalade one day by adding sugar to bitter Seville oranges, just as she usually added sugar to quinces to make jam. The resulting preserve was so popular that she and her son James decided to make it commercially. Thus the firm of James Keiller & Sons was founded in 1797. The firm's head office remains in Dundee today, and Keiller's also now makes candy and chocolate.

Keith Prowse (ticket agency)

The name is not that of one Englishman, but two. Their partnership dates from 1780, when Robert W. Keith was making musical instruments off Oxford Street, London, specializing in flutes and clarinets. He moved his business to Cheapside in about 1800, and soon after took one William Prowse into partnership. At that time they were mainly concerned with making musical instruments and publishing music. They began to sell theater tickets in about 1847, presumably when there was an increase in demand for them. The company later claimed to be the largest theater ticket agency in the world, with the famous slogan, "You want the best seats, we have them."

Kellogg's (breakfast cereals)

The American company was founded by Will (originally Willie) Keith Kellogg (1860-1951), born in Battle Creek, Michigan, the son of a broommaker, who began his own career selling brooms and at 19 was the manager of a broom factory in Dallas, Texas. Returning to Michigan in 1880, he went to work for his brother, Dr. John Harvey Kellogg (1852-1943), at the Battle Creek Sanitarium, where Dr. Kellogg was the chief surgeon and superintendent. Dr. Kellogg was a vegetarian, as were his patients, and the brothers began experimenting to find ways of making the patients' meatless diet more interesting. One day in 1894, when the Kelloggs had placed some boiled wheat on a baking tin, Dr. Kellogg was called to an emergency. When the brothers returned the following day, they ran the wheat through rollers, expecting it to come out in sheets. But it actually came out in individual flakes, in other words, as prototype corn flakes. The patients loved them and asked for more. Soon friends were asking for the tasty food, and to meet the demand Dr. Kellogg started the Sanitas Food Company, producing wheat flakes, rice flakes, and corn flakes, basically using the same process. Will Keith Kellogg then bought the

rights from his brother, and in 1906 started the Battle Creek Toasted Corn Flake Company. Since then, Kellogg's has snapped, crackled, and popped up a whole variety of breakfast cereal for the world market.

Kelly Services (employment agency)

The American employment agency was founded in 1946 by William Russell Kelly (1905-1998) with the aim of providing businesses with "temps," or temporary secretaries. The few "Kelly Girls" who were available for such employment in the early years grew to the more than 700,000 employees who found placement in 1997.

Kelly's (directories)

Kelly's Directories ultimately derives from the historic London directories of the 17th century. In 1734 one Henry Kent began to produce such directories annually. In 1799 His Majesty's Inspectors of Letter Carriers compiled a new annual directory, with a view to making life easier for the "letter carriers," or postmen of the day, as they hunted out this or that address. The first edition of this directory appeared in 1800 as the *Post Office London Directory*. In 1837 Festus Frederick Kelly was appointed Her Majesty's Inspector of Letter Carriers, and he continued publication of the Directory, still purely an alphabetical list of names and addresses. In 1844 Kelly introduced a new system of compilation, with information for the directories provided by special agents. Four years later the first of the familiar county directories appeared. In 1894 the name of the firm became Kelly's Directories Ltd., and has remained as such ever since.

Kelvinator *see* **Nash-Kelvinator**

Kennecott (copper)

The Kennecott Corporation dates from 1915, when the Guggenheim family joined their copper holdings into a single corporation to finance the Copper River and Northwestern Railroad in order to reach a rich copper find they had made in 1898 in Alaska. The corporation took its name from the mine, so called after a nearby glacier that was itself named for the US naturalist and Arctic explorer Robert Kennicott (1835-1866). The mine closed down in 1938 but Kennecott flourishes.

Kenning *(automobile dealerships and travel agents)*

The Kenning Motor Group, with its car showrooms, auto shops, and tire service depots, ultimately sprang from the hardware store started in 1878 in Clay Cross, Derbyshire, England, by Francis Kenning. Part of the business of the store was selling kerosene and other petroleum products. By the end of the century, Kenning's activity had developed into a distribution business from the different petroleum products, at first through agencies, then through road vehicles. He died in 1905, leaving his son George (later Sir George) Kenning (1880-1956) to develop the firm into the multifaceted company it is today. The group's head office is now in Chesterfield, Derbyshire, where it moved, through expansion, in 1923.

Kensitas *(cigarettes)*

The British make of cigarettes ultimately derives its name from Kensington, the upmarket London district where Julius Wix, an immigrant from continental Europe, started a business in 1898 to manufacture cigarettes for **Barker's** department store. The reason for this particular alteration of the placename is uncertain. One account claims that one of Wix's foreign employees telephoned a broken English order for "John Barker of Kensitas." Another traces the name to "Ken Bar," an abbreviation used to designate articles manufactured by John Barker. But the origin may really have been in the classical Latin suffix *-itas* (as for **Sanitas**) added to the first part of the name. J. Wix & Sons was acquired by **Gallaher** in 1961. The name was entered in the *Trade Marks Journal* of November 25, 1914.

Kent *(cigarettes)*

The brand of cigarettes by **Lorillard** take their name from the manufacturers' former president, Herbert A. Kent, under whom the company had made some of its greatest progress. The "Kent Micronite" filtered cigarette was launched in March 1952.

Kentucky Fried Chicken *see* **Colonel Sanders**

Kenwood *(kitchen appliances)*

The name behind the British food mixers and blenders is that of Kenneth Maynard Wood (1916-1997), born in Lewisham, Kent. His father died when he was 12, and at 14 the boy decided to go sea. In his four years in the Merchant Navy the teenager became interested in electrical equipment, and back in England at age 19 enrolled in evening classes to study accountancy and electrical engineering. He found work in a radio repair shop, then build up a radio business of his own. In World War II he was with the Royal Air Force, working with electronic equipment. After the war, in 1946, he set up a company with a partner to manufacture electric toasters. The partner's name was Roger Laurence, and but for the timely intervention of an accountant, what is now the familiar name of Kenwood might well have been "Woodlau." The company started life in modest premises next door to a fish shop in Woking, Surrey, but thanks to shrewd marketing gradually grew into the international concern it is today.

Kenzo *(perfumes)*

The name is that of Kenzo Takada, born in Himeji, Japan, in 1939. Despite protests from friends and family, he quit art school to become a fashion designer, and in 1965 sold his car to visit Paris, France, where he managed to sell five of his fashion sketches to the designer Louis Féraud. Kenzo soon found work after that, first with a designer, then with a textile company, and his designs were so well received that in 1970 he was able to open his own fashion boutique. By the mid-1970s Kenzo had opened boutiques all over the world and in 1988 he presented his first perfume, called simply "Kenzo," a delicate blend of oriental flowers. More fragrances followed, among them the 1990s "Jungle" series.

Kepone *(pesticide)*

The proprietary name for chlordecone, a highly toxic chlorinated hydrocarbon developed by the Allied Chemical Corporation and formerly used as a pesticide, is apparently of arbitrary origin although suggesting "ketone" (which gave the "-one" of the generic name). The name dates from the 1970s.

Kerr *(jars)*

In 1902 Alexander H. Kerr (1862-1925), a grocery wholesaler of Portland, Oregon, resolved to give a tenth ("tithe") of whatever he earned in his remaining years to church charities. That same year he purchased a fruit jar patent and formed the Kerr Glass Manufacturing Company. By 1914 his business had grown into one of the most successful in the country. True to his word, Kerr gave a tenth of his fortune to missions, churches, homes, hospitals, and similar institutions.

Kerr-McGee *(uranium)*

The American company drilled the world's first offshore oil well in 1947. In 1952 it was the first to expand into the uranium business. And in 1979 it was the first to be tried for its safety record, in the famous Karen Silkwood case. The first half of its name is that of Robert Samuel Kerr (1896-1963), born in a log cabin in Indian territory, near present-day Ada, Oklahoma, the son of a farmer, clerk, and politician. After graduating from high school, Kerr taught while earning a two-year degree from East Central State Normal School in Ada. He then studied law for a time at the University of Oklahoma but was forced by poverty to drop out in 1916. He was commissioned as a second lieutenant in the army in 1917, when the United States entered the world war, but never saw combat. Kerr's subsequent personal and business fortunes were mixed until 1929, when he and his brother-in-law, James L. Anderson, bought an Oklahoma oil-drilling company. In 1936 Anderson retired and the following year Kerr hired Dean A. McGee, former chief oil geologist for **Phillips Petroleum**. Eventually, in 1946, McGee's name was added to Kerr's to form Kerr-McGee Oil Industries, Inc.

Kevlar *(synthetic fiber)*

The synthetic fiber, noted for its stiffness and tensile strength, is mainly used as a reinforcing agent in composite materials and as a constituent of ropes and cables. Its name, probably partly based on the earlier **Mylar**, was entered in the US Patent Office *Official Gazette* of February 12, 1974, with a note of first use on April 6, 1973. Kevlar itself was the invention in 1963 of Stephanie Louise Kwolek (b.1923), a **Du Pont** scientist specializing in textile fibers.

Kewpie *(doll)*

The American celluloid doll, designed by Joseph Kallus and made by George Borgfeldt, evolved from the drawings by the illustrator and writer Rose C. O'Neill (1874-1944) of chubby, top-knotted cherubs, first appearing in 1909 in the *Ladies' Home Journal*. The name comes from Cupid, with perhaps a hint of "cute." It was entered by O'Neill (under her married name of Rose O'Neill Wilson) in the US Patent Office *Official Gazette* of May 13, 1913, and subsequently (as "The Kewpies") in the *Gazette* of June 15, 1937: "For Cartoons in Periodical Publications," with a claim of use since December 21, 1912, and (as "Kewpie") by Cameo Doll Products Co., Inc., of Port Allegany, Pennsylvania, in the *Gazette* of August 30, 1960.

Kia-Ora *(soft drinks)*

The name is Maori for "good health." The drink was first produced as a lemon squash by an Australian farmer's son, John Dixon, of Sydney, who had started a business as a seller of ice and soft drinks in 1896, and who entered the name in the *Trade Marks Journal* of December 18, 1901. In 1913 the drink was first marketed in the UK by a partner, A.H. Gasquoine, and the company of the name was formed in 1929.

Kikkoman *(soy sauce)*

The Japanese company dates from the 17th century, when the Mogi and Takanashi families began to make soy sauce along the Edo River in Noda, east central Japan. In 1917 eight family firms merged to form Noda Shoyu Ltd., a company that was renamed Kikkoman Shoyu in 1904 and Kikkoman Corporation in 1980. ("Shoyu" is Japanese for "soy," and gave the English word.) "Kikkoman" represents Japanese *kikko*, "tortoise shell," and *man*, "ten thousand." In Japanese folklore the tortoise is said to live for ten thousand years and is a symbol of longevity, which every company hopes for. The hexagonal logo on Kikkoman products thus represents a tortoise shell with the Chinese character for "ten thousand" inside.

Kilner *(jar)*

The Kilner jar, used for preserving fruit, takes its name from its British manufacturers, Kilner Brothers of London, who entered it in the *Trade Marks Journal* of November 19, 1930.

Kimball *(pianos and organs)*

William Wallace Kimball (1828-1904), of Rumford, Maine, began his career selling real estate and insurance in the Midwest. One day in 1857, while living in Chicago, Kimball met a musical instrument salesman and traded him four lots in Decorah, Iowa, for four pianos. He sold the pianos, bought more with the profits, and soon opened a retail music store on Lake Street, Chicago. His company began making its own pianos and organs in the 1880s, and by the time of his death it was the largest manufacturer of keyboard instruments in the world. The firm remained in the hands of Kimball and his descendents until 1959, when it was acquired by the Jasper Corporation of Jasper, Indiana, founded in 1950 by Arnold P. Habig (1908-1999), which in turn adopted the Kimball name when it went public in the 1970s. The company is now also known for its office furniture and electronic goods, including the "Kimball tag," a punched tag detached from retail goods when sold and used as computer output for information on sales, stock control, and the like.

Kimberly-Clark *(paper tissues)*

The US company has always been based in the small town of Neenah, Wisconsin, where in 1872 four young men each invested $7,500 to set up a business making newsprint from linen and cotton rags. The partnership was named for two of them, John A. Kimberly (1838-1928) and Charles B. Clark (d.1891). Kimberly was elected president when the company was incorporated in 1880 and held the post until his death at the age of 90. The group's activities expanded from mere newsprint and wrapping paper to include the well-known paper-based sanitary napkin **Kotex**, which they first produced in 1920. The business passed down the Kimberly family to John Robbins Kimberly (1903-1992), John A. Kimberly's grandson, who joined Kimberly & Clark, as it was then known, in 1924, and rose to the presidency in 1953. He remained at the helm until 1970, when a new president, Darwin E. Smith, masterminded the company's rise to prominence and its steady growth. Today, John A. Kimberly's name lives on both in that of the company and in the small mill town of Kimberly, near Appleton, Wisconsin.

Kinemacolor *(color film system)*

The first commercial color film system was developed in 1906 by two Englishmen, Edward R. Turner and George Albert Smith, and finan-

cially supported by an American, Charles Urban. Its first public demonstration was in 1908, and it became memorable from its use in the feature-length film *The Durbar at Delhi* (1912). The name combines "kinema," an earlier form of "cinema," recalling its origin in the Greek word for "movement," and "color," and was entered by Charles Urban (as "Kinema Color") in the *Trade Marks Journal* of May 19, 1909 for: "Kinematographic apparatus and photographic films bearing finished pictures in natural colours for use therewith." (The spelling with "c" arose under French influence.)

Kinescope *(television tube)*

The name was devised by the US physicist Vladimir Zworykin (1889-1982) for the cathode-ray tube that he applied to television and that he patented in 1928. It derives from Greek *kinēsis*, "movement," and the common "-scope" element meaning "looking at" (as in "telescope"), and was entered by the **RCA** Victor Company of Camden, New Jersey, in the US Patent Office *Official Gazette* of May 17, 1932. The registration was cancelled in 1950, however, by which time the word had come into generic use for a film recording of a television broadcast.

Kingsford's *(corn starch)*

The name is that of Thomas Kingsford (1799-1869), an English immigrant to the United States, who in 1842 developed a wet milling process by which starch could be isolated from corn. In 1846 he set up his business as T. Kingsford & Son in Bergen, New Jersey, calling his starch "Maizena." The firm that Kingsford founded ultimately led to the multifaceted **Bestfoods** company of today.

Kinney *(footwear)*

George Romanta Kinney (1866-1919), of Candor, New York, the son of a general store owner, left home at 17 to seek better opportunities in the nearby city of Binghamton, where he landed a job as a stock clerk with the Lester Shoe Company. He worked his way up to become manager of the firm's outlet in Waverly, New York, but lost his position when the firm went bankrupt in 1894. Scraping his savings together, he bought a portion of his former employer's inventory and opened his own retail store in Waverly. The business started modestly with just one employee, Milner Kemp, an English cobbler. Thanks to Kinney's policy of selling footwear for men, women, and children under the same roof, his store did well, and within a year he had opened another store in Corning, New York. By 1899 he had eight retail outlets, by 1909 24, and by 1917 the G.R. Kinney Co. was operating 49 stores in 13 states. Finally, between 1917 and 1920 the company acquired four shoe factories to began manufacturing its own products.

Kir *(drink)*

The alcoholic drink, made from dry white wine and blackcurrant liqueur, takes its name from Canon Félix Kir (1876-1978), a World War II French Resistance hero who was also mayor of Dijon. He may have actually devised the drink, which is also known generically as *vin blanc cassis.*

Kirbigrip *(bobby pin)*

The Kirbigrip, in the form of a U-shaped piece of springy metal with one side ridged to prevent slipping, takes its name from the original manufacturers, Kirby, Beard & Co. Ltd. of Birmingham, England. The company was founded in Gloucester in 1743 by William Coucher, who after moving his business to London took Robert Kirby into partnership in 1803 and later George Beard and William Tovey. The business must have prospered, for in 1816 Robert Kirby was elected a sheriff of London. The firm subsequently moved to Birmingham, where it merged with Newey Brothers, a business making hooks and eyes that had been started by Richard Newey in the 18th century. Kirby, Beard & Co. entered the name in the *Trade Marks Journal* of January 6, 1926. This was the "Roaring Twenties," the era of the Eton crop and bobbed hairstyle, when there was a sharp drop in the demand for bobby pins, but a sudden increase in the demand for a grip that would suit the new short hairstyle. Kirbigrips are sprung, unlike traditional hairpins. The successor company to Kirby, Beard is the Newey Group, who now produce a wide range of dressmaking and fashion products at their headquarters in Tipton, West Bromwich, a town just west of Birmingham.

Kitemark *(emblem)*

The official symbol or emblem of the British

Standards Institution is in the form of a kite, based on the initials BSI. The mark is an official seal of approval for manufactured goods and was first carried by streetcar rails in 1901, the year after the BSI itself was founded.

> The British Standards Mark (known as the Kitemark) is a registered certification trade mark owned by BSI. Manufacturers may apply to BSI to use the mark on their products when their quality control arrangements are considered satisfactory and they have agreed to comply with a Scheme of Supervision and Control involving ... inspection, sampling and testing.
> *British Standards Yearbook*, 1971.

KitKat *(chocolate-coated wafer)*

Britain's bestselling confectionery brand was originally named "Chocolate Crisp" when launched by **Rowntree** in 1935. Two years later the name was changed as now. Although London had a famous 18th-century Kit-Kat Club, said to have been called after Christopher (Kit) Katt, a pastrycook, the name does not appear to allude directly to this but instead probably represents a soft cracking sound, like that of breaking a crisp cookie in two or biting off a piece. The two-bar chocolate-coated wafer has long been advertised by the slogan, "Have a break, have a Kit-Kat."

Kiwi *(shoe polish)*

The polish was originally marketed in 1906 in Melbourne, Australia, by William Ramsay, who named it as a compliment to his wife, née Annie Elizabeth Meek, who was born in Oamaru, South Island, New Zealand, and who was thus a "Kiwi." (New Zealanders are so nicknamed for the indigenous flightless bird so known.) The brand name, with accompanying illustration of a kiwi, was entered in the *Trade Marks Journal* of February 18, 1925.

Klaxon *(electric horn)*

The name soon became generic for the loud electric horn formerly found on motor vehicles. It began life in the early 20th century as the name of the US manufacturing company, and derives from Greek *klaxein*, "to make a loud sound," a word related to English "clang." The name was entered in the *Trade Marks Journal* of June 23, 1909.

Kleenex *(paper tissues)*

The tissues first appeared on the market in

the United States in 1924, when they were produced by **Kimberly-Clark**, who as with **Kotex** assigned them to International Cellucotton Products Co. They were originally promoted as a substitute for the "cold cream towel" used in the bathroom to remove cosmetics. Customers did not think much of this, however, and instead wrote in to say what great disposable handkerchiefs they were. When the tissues were accordingly advertised as disposable handkerchiefs, sales doubled. The basic function of the tissues is wiping or cleaning. Hence the name, with a respelling of "clean" and the common commercial suffix "-ex." The name ties in with the earlier Kotex not simply in form and identity of manufacture but because some women had discovered that the cellulose layers of Kotex pads were useful in removing cold cream and cosmetics, a function specifically assumed by Kleenex. The name was entered in the *Trade Marks Journal* of July 15, 1925 for: "Absorbent pads or sheets (not medicated) for surgical or curative purposes or in relation to the health."

Klein, Calvin *see* **Calvin Klein**

Kleinwort Benson *(investment bank)*

The British bank had its origins in Cuba in 1792, when the firm of Kleinwort & Sons was founded. Alexander F.H. Kleinwort (d.1886), originally from Hamburg, came to London in 1855 and set up his own firm. On his death the firm passed to his two sons, Herman Greverus Kleinwort (1856-1942) and Alexander Drake Kleinwort (1858-1935). In 1961, under Alexander's son, Ernest Greverus Kleinwort (1901-1977), the firm, Kleinwort Sons & Co., merged with Robert Benson, Lonsdale Ltd. to become Kleinwort, Benson Ltd.

Klischograph *(engraving plate)*

The German make of electronic engraving plate, used in printing, takes its name from German *Klischee*, "stereotype," "electronic plate" (English "cliché"), and the Greek element "-graph" meaning "writing." It was entered by the manufacturers, Dr. Ing. Rudolf Hell of Kiel, in the *Trade Marks Journal* of March 16, 1955.

KLM *(airline)*

The Dutch airline, in full Koninklijke Luchtvaart Maatschappij ("Royal Dutch Air Travel Company"), was founded on October 7, 1919 by a group of banking and business interests led by a former Dutch pilot, Albert Plesman (1889-1953), who headed the company for the rest of his life. In 1928 he also founded Koninklijke Nederlandsch-Indische Luchtvaart Maatschappij ("Royal Netherlands-East Indies Air Travel Company") (KNILM), which merged with KLM in 1945.

K-Mart *(discount stores)*

The initial is that of Sebastian Spering Kresge (1867-1966), born in Bald Mount, Pennsylvania, the son of a poor farmer. Eager to escape the grind of farm life, Kresge persuaded his parents to finance his education in return for his entire income until he reached the age of 21. This arrangement enabled him to attend the Fairview Academy in Brodheadsville and the Gilbert Polytechnic Institute. After a period as teacher and grocer's deliveryman, in 1892 he became a traveling salesman for a company in Wilkes-Barre that specialized in tinware and hardware. Among his customers who prospered despite the widespread depression were Frank W. Woolworth (*see* **Woolworths**) and John G. McCrorey, founders of the two earliest dime store chains. After being rebuffed when he tried to buy his way into Woolworth's company, Kresge struck a deal with McCrorey, who agreed to train him and take him as a partner in new stores. In 1897 the two opened a store in Memphis, Tennessee, which Kresge managed, and later one in Detroit, managed by George C. Murphy, McCrorey's cousin. By the time they incorporated in Michigan in 1916 as the S.S. Kresge Company, the firm owned 150 dime stores with annual sales of over $12 million. When Kresge retired as president in 1929, his company had almost 600 stores in the United States, and sales of $156 million. The "K-Mart" concept was evolved by Harry B. Cunningham (1907-1992), a former Kresge store manager who became company president in 1959. He built the first K-Mart in Garden City, near Detroit, in 1962. By the time Kresge himself died, aged 99, 162 of the company's 915 stores were K-Marts. The company name was changed to K-Mart Corporation in 1977, despite protests from Stanley Kresge, son of the founder, who at the annual directors' meeting that year said he "was not pleased with the change" and who later told the *Wall Street Journal* that "the company name should relate to the founder." But the directors won the vote, with 89.4 million shares to 11.3 million.

Knight-Ridder *(newspapers)*

The American newspaper publishing company derives its combined name from two wealthy newspaper families, the Knights and the Ridders. John Shively Knight (1894-1981) was born in Bluefield, West Virginia, the son of Charles Landon Knight, a lawyer and the publisher of the *Akron Beacon-Journal.* John began work in 1920 as a reporter for his father's paper and became its managing editor the following year. In due course, age and illness forced his father to make Knight publisher of the paper, and on his father's death in 1933 he assumed leadership of the family business. Knight's brother James had now joined him in the enterprise, and between them they added several newspapers to their armoury. In 1974 Knight Newspapers, as it had become, merged with the Ridder Group, a chain of newspapers owned by a German-American family descended from Herman Ridder (d.1915), who had bought the *Staats-Zeitung,* America's leading German language newspaper, in 1892. The combined concern, Knight-Ridder Newspapers, Inc., consisted of 35 dailies with 4 million subscribers, and the numbers of each grew until Knight's death, whereupon his newspaper empire passed to his only suviving son, Charles Landon Knight II.

Knight's *(Castile soap)*

The name is that of the soap's original British manufacturers, John Knight Ltd., founded in 1817 by John Knight, a Hertfordshire farmer's son. After starting his small-scale soap-making operation in London's East End, Knight presided over it until his death in the 1860s. His reputation originally rested on a soap called "Royal Primrose," advertised widely from the 1840s. The now much better known Castile soap was not introduced by the firm until 1919, with "Castile" a standard name for any white or mottled soap made with olive oil and soda, as such soap was originally made in Castile, Spain. In 1920 Knight's was taken over by Lever Brothers (*see* **Unilever**).

Knirps *(umbrellas)*

German umbrella manufacturers Knirps GmbH were involved in a legal dispute in 2001 when the name "Knirps" was registered by an insurance company as a domain name on the Internet. The case, Knirps GmbH v. Kay Tomforde, came before the WIPO (World Intellectual Property Organization) Arbitration and Mediation Center, who outlined the history of the name as follows:

> The word Knirps was carefully chosen by its inventors, due to its original background. At the time when the KNIRPS® umbrellas were invented, back in 1927, the word "Knirps" was used in every day language to mean little boy, baby and equivalent meanings for very small people. Following the intentions of the founders of Knirps®, the word Knirps was chosen to illustrate the extremely small size of the umbrellas that were produced. The trademark KNIRPS® was registered in Germany for the first time in 1929 under registration No. 3985270.

According to the manufacturers: "The word is not a typical generic or descriptive word that can be used by anyone. The word has changed from meaning 'little boy' to a fixed expression in the German language for all kinds of fixed umbrellas." However, WIPO ruled that the domain name "Knirps.com" had been adopted in good faith and should not be transferred to the complainant. (Adjudication of March 20, 2001.)

Knockando *(whisky)*

The Scotch whisky takes its name from that of the village near Aberlour, Banffshire, where a distillery was built on the left bank of the Spey River in the 1890s. The firm is now owned by International Distillers and Vintners (IDV).

Knogo *(antishoplifting tag)*

When Arthur J. Minasy was growing up in Astoria, Queens, New York, he frequently pocketed marbles and tennis balls from the local **Woolworths** five-and-ten. By the early 1960s he was working as a consultant for the New York City Police Department, trying to tackle the growing problem of shoplifting. In 1964 he created in his garage an electronic tag that would deter shoplifting. The tags, fastened to items in a store, would set off an alarm when they passed through a security system by the door. He called his invention the "Knogo," since it meant "no go" for the item and it would "know" when the shoplifter made to "go" with it. The Knogo Corporation was founded on the basis of Minasy's device.

Knopf *(publishers)*

The eponymous founder of the prestigious American publishing house Alfred A. Knopf (1892-1984) was born in New York City the son of an advertising executive and financial consultant. He enrolled in Columbia University, New York, in 1908, graduating in 1912, and after working for a short time at the publishing house of **Doubleday**, Page, and Company, started his own firm in 1915. In 1966 the Knopf concern became a subsidiary of **Random House**, which was in turn acquired by S.I. Newhouse and Sons in 1980.

Knorr *(powdered soup)*

The name is that of the company's founder, Carl Heinrich Knorr, who traded in cereals and who set up his business in Heilbronn, Germany, in 1838. He was later joined by his two sons, one of whom, Eduard, had already come across soup powders when visiting France. The brothers saw the potential, and produced their first dehydrated product in about 1880 as a "sausage" of dried peas which made pea soup when placed in boiling water. The Heilbronn factory was destroyed in World War II, after which the Swiss affiliate represented the company's main production interests until the Heilbronn headquarters were re-established in the late 1950s.

Knox *(gelatin)*

Rose Markward Knox (1857-1950), born Helen Rosetta Markward in Mansfield, Ohio, was the daughter of a druggist. She attended public schools in Mansfield, then in her 20s moved with her parents to Gloversville, New York. She found work sewing gloves, a job that introduced her to a glove salesman, Charles Briggs Knox, whom she married in 1883. In 1890 the Knoxes decided to invest their savings in a gelatin business in Johnstown, New York. Their first challenge was to promote different ways of using the substance, which they did by vigorous advertising and sales trips. Knox's husband died in 1908, when she announced her intention of continuing to run the business alone until her two sons came of age. Her elder son, Charles, also soon died, but by 1913, when James joined the business, she had no intention of retiring. Knox now promoted her gelatin primarily to women, running ads titled "Mrs. Knox Says." Her industry paid off, and by 1915

the value of Knox Gelatin had tripled. In 1916 the company acquired a half interest in a former supplier, Kind and Landesmann, of Camden, New Jersey, which was renamed Kind and Knox. In 1930 Knox became vice president. T.J. Lipton, a unit of **Unilever**, bought Knox in the early 1970s, while in 1994 RJR-Nabisco (*see* **R.J. Reynolds**) acquired the American rights to Knox gelatin to add to its Royal Desserts line. Kind & Knox became a wholly owned subsidiary of DGF Stoess, a German-based gelatin producer, and it now operates the world's largest gelatin factory at its headquarters in Sergeant Bluff, Iowa.

Kodachrome *(color film)*

The process of color photography and make of color film evolved from the patent filed in 1912 by George **Eastman** of the Eastman **Kodak** Company for "plate or film for color photograph." The name itself combines "Kodak" with "-chrome" (from the Greek word for "color") and was entered in the *Trade Marks Journal* of September 22, 1926. Kodachrome film was commercially introduced in 1935 following its development by the American musicians and photographers Leopold Godowsky, Jr. (1900-1983) and Leopold Damrosch Mannes (1899-1964), whose work contributed to the subsequent appearance of **Ektachrome**. "Kodacolor" followed in 1942 as the first color roll film designed for making color prints.

Kodacolor *see* **Kodachrome**

Kodak *(cameras, films, and photographic equipment)*

George **Eastman** introduced the first Kodak camera in 1888 and patented its name on September 4 that year. He later detailed its origin in an interview (quoted in Lambert; *see* Bibliography, p. 566):

I devised the name myself. A trade-mark should be short, vigorous, incapable of being misspelled to an extent that will destroy its identity, and—in order to satisfy trade-mark laws—it must mean nothing. If the name has no dictionary definition, it must be associated only with your product and you will cease to be known as producing a "kind" of anything.

The letter "K" had been a favorite with me—it seemed a strong, incisive sort of letter. Therefore, the word I wanted had to start with "K." Then it became a question of trying out a great number of combinations of letters that made words, starting and ending with "K." The word "Kodak" is the result. Instead of merely making cameras and camera supplies, we make "Kodaks" and "Kodak" supplies. It became the distinctive word for our products.

Aside from any linguistic considerations, "K" was doubtless also favored by Eastman as it began his mother's maiden name, Kilbourn. "Kodak" as a word also has the "snap" of a camera shutter. The name was entered by the Eastman Dry Plate and Film Company in the *Trade Marks Journal* of September 26, 1888. A small type of Kodak camera, the "Kodet," was launched in the 1890s.

Koff *(beer)*

This is an abbreviated name for a range of beers from Finland's oldest brewery, Sinebrychoff, founded in Helsinki, then under Russian rule, by a Russian merchant, Nikolai Sinebrychoff, in 1819. (Today his name would be spelled Sinebryukhov.) Koff has brewed porter from the start, aside from a period of prohibition in Finland in the early part of the 20th century.

Kohler *(bathtubs and sinks)*

The American company had become the country's largest manufacturer of air-cooled engines by the 1980s, but has long been associated with bathtubs and domestic plumbing fixtures. It takes its name from John Michael Kohler, Jr. (1844-1900), who came from his native Austria to the United States at the age of 10. In 1871 he moved to Sheboygan, Wisconsin, and two years later started a foundry and machine shop to make agricultural implements. He added the manufacture of enamelware and a few years later abandoned the production of implements. In 1888 his original business was incorporated as the Kohler, Hayssen and Stehn Manufacturing Company and devoted itself to the manufacture of enamel bathroom fixtures and kitchenware. On his death, the company was taken over by his son Robert, but when he in turn died unexpectedly in 1905 at the age of 31, the presidency of the Kohler Company, as it had become, was assumed by Robert's younger brother, Walter Jodok Kohler (1875-1940), who held the post until 1937. The company was still in family hands at the end of the century, with Herbert Kohler (b.1939) as its third-generation head.

Kolynos *(toothpaste)*

The name was coined around the turn of the 20th century by (or for) one Dr. N.S. Jenkins, who developed the toothpaste's original formula. He based it on Greek *koloúō*, "I limit," "I check," and *nosos*, "sickness," "disease." The name was entered in the *Trade Marks Journal* of September 30, 1908.

Konica *(cameras)*

The Japanese make of camera dates from 1873, when Rokusaburo Sugiura began selling photographic and lithographic materials at Konishiya Rokubeiten in Kogimachi, Tokyo. His store was renamed Konishi Honten ("Main Konishi Store") in 1879, and in 1882 it began making cameras. The first brand-name camera was the "Cherry" hand camera, launched in 1903. Konishi Honten was registered as a public corporation in 1936, and the business was renamed Konishiroku Photo Industry Co. in 1943. In 1948 the company released its first brand-name 35mm camera, the Konica 1, the final two letters standing for "camera."

Korvettes *(discount stores)*

The business of this name had its beginnings in a small second-floor luggage store in New York opened in 1948. Its founder was Eugene Ferkauf, born in Brooklyn in 1920, who on graduating from high school went directly to work in his father's two small luggage shops near Grand Central Station. After World War II service as a sergeant in the Signal Corps, Ferkauf returned to his father's stores but soon became restless. He wanted to prove his theory that he could increase sales substantially by cutting the conventional 40 percent markup by half. He thus rented a walkup on East Forty-sixth Street and began selling luggage at a discount. He called his store "E.J. Korvette": "E" for his first name, "J" for an early business associate, Joseph Zwillenberg, and "Korvette" for the small warships known as corvettes, respelled with a "k." By plowing all the profits back into Korvette, Ferkauf was running a $2-million business only two years after he started. In 1951 there were three stores, in 1955, eight. Business continued to boom, but slumped in 1966, when Korvettes were obliged to merge with Spartans Industries, a clothing manufacturer and retailer. In 1968, Ferkauf resigned from all his associations with Korvettes and Spartans to start a group of giftwear boutiques, and in 1980, as a result of poor hiring practices, undercapitalization, and ill-planned expansion, Korvettes closed the last of their stores.

Kosset *(carpets)*

The British carpet company chose a respelled "cosset" as its brand name, evoking the "pampering" afforded by a rich carpet. The logo of Kosset Carpets Ltd. was a picture of a white chinchilla cat, reinforcing the intended image of luxury, softness, and domesticity. The name was entered in the *Trade Marks Journal* of October 11, 1967.

Kotex *(sanitary napkins)*

The napkin was introduced to consumers by **Kimberly-Clark** in 1920, who discreetly set up a separate sales company, International Cellucotton Products, to market it. Unlike **Kleenex**, Kimberly-Clark's other main product, the name appears to be arbitrary, although "Kot-" suggests "coat" and "-tex" hints at "texture," perhaps with reference to the newly invented "cellucotton," a creped cellulose wadding made from bagasse as a substitute for surgical cotton. On the other hand, the name also suggests German *Kot*, "filth," and the Latin *ex-*, "out," implying a product that disposes of excreted matter. The name was entered in the *Trade Marks Journal* of July 19, 1922.

KP *(nuts)*

The founder of the British company was Simon Heller (1907-1989), a Lithuanian immigrant to England as a child, whose father supplemented his income by selling candy and peanuts from a tray in London's East End. Simon helped his father, and became interested in the origin and type of nuts he sold. As the boy grew, so did his knowledge of nuts, until in 1948 he acquired Kenyon, Son & Craven, then a small candy firm in Rotherham, Yorkshire. The firm expanded to employ over 1,200 people and made the name KP nuts (from Kenyon Products) known throughout the world. Heller himself became a world authority on nuts, traveling widely to purchase entire crops. In 1968 his lucrative enterprise was acquired by United Biscuits.

Kraft *(cheese)*

The name is that of James Lewis Kraft (orig-inally Krafft) (1874-1953), born in Fort Erie, Ontario, Canada, a farmer's son. He was raised in a strict Mennonite environment characterized by hard work and strict discipline. After graduation from high school he left the farm to become a clerk in a Fort Erie general store. In 1903 he moved to Buffalo, New York, where he attended a business college while working as a janitor and selling eggs, cheese, and ice. The following year he moved to Chicago, where he entered the cheese business by purchasing it in bulk from wholesalers and delivering it in small quantities to local grocers packaged in tinfoil and glass jars. His four brothers, Fred, Charles, Norman, and John, soon joined him in the enterprise, and in 1909 J.L. Kraft and Brothers was formed. By 1914 his business was doing so well that he was selling over 30 varieties of cheese in many parts of the United States. From then on, it was a matter of mergers and expansions, although the Kraft Cheese Company, as it was renamed in 1924, did not diversify much, and was still mainly associated with dairy products, above all cheese. New lines that gained favor with the public were "Velveeta" in 1928, "Miracle Whip" (1933), "Kraft Macaroni and Cheese Dinner" (1936), and "Parkay Margarine" (1937). Later, salad dressing, caramels, marshmallows, and ice cream toppings were added, and in 1945 the firm changed its name to Kraft Foods to reflect this product mix. *See also* **Angel Delight**.

Krakus *(vodka)*

The Polish rye vodka takes its name from Krakus, the legendary founder of Kraków, the Polish capital. The name is also found for other Polish products.

Krilium *(soil improver)*

The product added to soil to improve its structure consists of synthetic polymers. Hence its name, from "kril-," an altered form of "-cryl-" in "polyacrylonitrile" (a polymer of acrylonitrile), with the suffix "-ium." The name was entered in the US Patent Office *Official Gazette* of July 8, 1952: "For synthetic resin materials in the form of powders, granules, emulsions, dispersions, and solutions."

Kriziamaglia *(fashionwear)*

The Italian company was founded in 1954 in Milan by Mariuccia Mandelli (b.1935), born in Bergamo, who adopted the professional name Krizia. She had trained as a teacher but then switched to the world of fashion and began selling skirts and dresses. In 1967 she branched out into knitwear (*maglia*) design, and later into complete ranges of ready-to-wear clothes.

Kroger *(supermarkets)*

The American supermarkets take their name from Bernard Henry Kroger (1860-1938), born in Cincinnati, Ohio, the son of immigrant German dry-goods vendors. At age 13 Barney, as he was known, found a job as a clerk in Rheum's drugstore in downtown Cincinnati. He then worked for a spell on a farm near Pleasant Plain, Ohio, about 30 miles outside of Cincinnati. He contracted malaria, however, and returned to Cincinnati, where he looked for a job that could lead to the successful career he envisioned. At age 16 he found employment with the Great Northern and Pacific Tea Company, selling coffee and tea door-to-door. He would take orders one day and deliver them the next by horse and cart. Next, at age 21, he became manager of the ailing Imperial Tea Company. Two years later, in 1883, with one B.A. Branagan as partner, he formed his own business in Cincinnati, the Great Western Tea Company. By 1885 he had four stores, by 1893 17, and by 1902 40. That same year he changed the company name to the Kroger Grocery and Baking Company and began expanding to other Ohio cities such as Hamilton, Dayton, and Columbus. In 1928 Kroger sold all his holdings, just before the crash, and soon after retired to Florida.

Kroll *(risk management)*

It was in 1972, in the wake of Watergate, that Jules Kroll founded what is now the biggest group of its kind in the world. Kroll did not invent the term "risk management," but he could see that it had a key role to play in the corporate world, providing bodyguards for businessmen, teaching them kidnap and ransom drill, and enabling them to discreetly monitor their rivals and beat the competition. Kroll started on his own, but by the end of the century had a worldwide network of intelligence staff, accountants, researchers, economists, and IT specialists. His firm almost doubled in size with the 1997 merger with O'Gara, a maker of armored vehicles.

Kronenbourg *(beer)*

France's best-known beer takes its name from the Cronenbourg district of Strasbourg, Alsace, where a brewery opened in 1664. The company grew after World War II by selling its premium Bière d'Alsace across France in small bottles, at a time when most lagers were low in strength and sold in liter bottles. In 1960 a new brewery was opened at Obernai, and soon after the company became part of BSN. In 2000 it was acquired by Scottish & Newcastle. The firm adopted the original German form of the name as more appropriate, as beer is popuarly seen as a Germanic drink. The actual name of the Strasbourg district means "crown castle," from an early 13th-century fortress nearby, destroyed in 1246, and has provided a historically "strong" name for the beer.

Krug *(champagne)*

The firm of Krug et Cie. was founded in the city of Reims, France, in 1843 by Johann-Josef Krug (usually known as Joseph Krug), born in Mainz, Germany. The name Krug & Co. was entered by Paul Krug, Joseph's son, "of and on behalf of the firm of Krug and Co." in the *Trade Marks Journal* of September 6, 1876, and by 1893 the firm occupied its current modest cellars, where the Krug family still live around the courtyard.

Krug *(wines)*

Charles Krug (1825-1892) came to San Francisco from his native Germany in 1852 as a newspaper editor. After one or two vineyard ventures, he was employed as a winemaker in the Napa Valley, California, in 1858 and settled there two years later. In 1861 he founded a winery near Saint Helena and soon became the most eminent winemaker of his day. The winery he founded was acquired by the Mondavi family in 1943, and in the immediate postwar years they became a leading maker of premium wines under the Krug label, as well as producing popular wines under their own name.

Krupp *(steel and alloys)*

The history of the German Krupp empire is essentially that of the Krupp family. In 1811 Friedrich Krupp (1787-1826) founded a plant in Essen to produce English cast steel and associated products, calling the works Gusstahlfabriek ("Cast-Steel Factory"). In the course of the 19th century, under his son, Alfred Krupp (1812-1887), the company gained a worldwide reputation, introducing not only the Bessemer steel-making processes but a cast-steel cannon. Under the direction of Alfred's son, Friedrich Alfred Krupp (1854-1902), the business underwent considerable expansion, and he in turn was succeeded by his elder daughter, Bertha Krupp (1886-1957), who gave "Big Bertha" as the nickname of the 42cm howitzer. The family concern was meanwhile incorporated in 1903 as Fried. Krupp Grusonwerk AG, taking this name from its founder. In 1968 the firm became a corporation wholly owned by a foundation called Alfried Krupp von Bohlen und Halbach-Stiftung, taking the name of Bertha Krupp's son, the last member of the Krupp dynasty, born in Essen in 1907 and found dead there in 1967. (Stiftung means "foundation.")

Kruschen *("health salts")*

The product was first marketed in the late 19th century and was originally made by E. Griffiths Hughes. The "health salts" (laxative) were based on the medicinal properties of creosote, and the name appears to derive from some form of that word, such as German *Kreosot*, with the German diminutive suffix *-chen*. Until World War II the name was spelled with an umlaut ("Krüschen"). The name was entered in the *Trade Marks Journal* of October 16, 1940.

Krystal *(hamburgers)*

The American hamburger chain was founded in Chattanooga, Tennessee, by Rody B. Davenport, a hosiery mill owner, and J. Glenn Sherill, a banker, in 1932. Its name ties in with its slogan: "Clean as a whistle and clear as a crystal."

Kwells *(travel sickness tablets)*

A dose of the tablets quells travel sickness, claim the manufacturers, **Aspro**-Nicholas. Hence the name. The preparation itself is actually hyoscine. The name was entered in the *Trade Marks Journal* of May 3, 1950.

Kwik Save *(supermarkets)*

The British chain of discount food stores, with a name of obvious reference, was formed in 1959 by Albert Gubay, a Welsh-born entrepreneur who began his career selling candy

from the back of a truck. Gubay sold up in 1973 and went to New Zealand and America to continue in retailing, but returned in 1983 and started a chain of health and fitness clubs. Following falling sales, Kwik Save was taken over in 1998 by Somerfield, formerly Gateway, itself formed from the Dee Corporation owned by Alec Monk, chief executive officer of Linfood.

Kwik-Fit *(tires and automotive parts)*

At the age of 23, Tom Farmer (b.1940) was selling motor tires from a van in eastern Scotland. When for the third time he did not get the bonus owed him he left his job and decided to go it alone. He found a shop in a good location in Edinburgh and in 1964 set up Tyres and Accessory Supplies, offering cheap tires to beat competitors. He soon had a small chain but later sold out to Albany Tyre Services and retired, aged 30, to San Francisco. Boredom prompted him to return to Scotland, however, and he started another company, selling out once more, this time to a G.A. Robinson, who gave him a seat on the board. When the firm ran into difficulties in the economic crisis of 1974, Farmer responded by taking control, renaming it Kwik-Fit, a name of obvious meaning if unconventional spelling. By the end of the century it had grown into a highly profitable company, and was taken over by **Ford** in 1999.

Kynoch *(cartridges)*

The name was formerly familiar on British rifle cartridges, although now it is rarely seen. This is because the original Kynoch company, started in 1862 by a Scotsman, George Kynoch (1834-1891), in two wooden sheds at Witton, Birmingham, merged in 1928 with **Eley**. At first the Kynoch name was prominently used and promoted. But Eley was the older company, with a name that had been associated with sports guns and shooting since 1828. So that was the name that prevailed.

L. L. Bean *(sporting goods)*

The man behind the name, an embodiment of Yankee virtue and value, was Leon Leonwood Bean (1872-1967), born in Greenwood, Maine, the son of a farmer. Lennie Bean worked in his brother's retail store in Freeport and in an Auburn clothing store from 1892 to 1907, when he moved to Freeport, his wife's hometown, to take over his brother Ervin's retail store. Bean gained fame in 1911, when he invented the leather-top, rubber-bottom Maine Hunting Shoe, and more importantly discovered the lucrative sporting goods business that resulted from selling these shoes by direct mail to holders of hunting licenses outside Maine. In 1917 Bean opened a retail store in Freeport and added other hunting and camping gear. He soon built up a loyal clientele, and in the course of time his rambling Freeport store became a tourist attraction, while the L.L. Bean Company, founded in 1912 as a small specialty retail and mail-order catalog company, was operated in later years by Bean's grandson, Leon A. Gorman.

Labatt *(beer)*

The major Canadian brewery takes its name from John K. Labatt (1803-1866), who in 1847 invested in the brewery operated by his friend, Samuel Eccles, in London, Ontario. In 1854 Eccles retired and Labatt gained control of the brewery, guiding it through a period of steady growth for the rest of his life. The brewery remained under the control of the Labatt family until 1964, and in 1995 was taken over by the Belgian brewing company Interbrew.

La Corona *see* **Corona**

Lacoste *(sportswear)*

French tennis star René Lacoste (1904-1996) was nicknamed "Le Crocodile" for his tenacious playing style following his admiration of an alligator suitcase at a Boston store in 1923. After his retirement from tennis in 1929, Lacoste founded La Société Chemise Lacoste ("The Lacoste Shirt Company"), and its polo shirts with a "crocodile" emblem on the chest were long a status symbol.

Lada *(automobiles)*

The Russian car is manufactured in Tolyatti (formerly Stavropol) on the Volga River. The latter is reflected in the vehicle's logo, which depicts a boat. The name derives from the folk word *lada*, "spouse," "dear one." In Russia itself the car is known as a Zhiguli, so called from the hills that border the Volga. The name Lada is preferred for the foreign market as it is simpler in most languages. Moreover, the native name could have undesirable connotations for non-Russians, since in many European languages it suggests "gigolo."

Ladbrokes *(betting agents)*

The British name dates from 1886, when Harry Schwind and a Mr. Pennington set up a partnership at Schwind's home, Ladbroke Hall, Warwickshire, to act as "Commission Agents and Bookmakers to the Aristocracy." In 1892 the business was bought by the entrepreneur Arthur Bendir, who moved it to London. It became a public company in 1967. In 1998 the Monopolies and Mergers Commision blocked Ladbrokes' offer to purchase **Coral** Racing, and the following year Ladbrokes adopted the name of its parent company, Hilton Group. By a strange coincidence, the Anglo-Saxon place-name Ladbroke means "stream used for predicting the future" (modern English *lot* and *brook*).

Ladybird *(children's picture books)*

The British children's book imprint traces its origins to 1915, when Wills and Hepworth, a firm of printers in Loughborough, Leicestershire, found themselves short of orders and decided to sell a product of their own. The result was the "Ladybird" picture books. The reason for the choice of name is unknown, but it is not inappropriate for children's books, since the ladybird (ladybug) is a cheerfully colored insect that features in children's rhymes and tales (such as "Ladybird, ladybird, fly away home"). The original books eventually developed into an educational series of early readers, and in the 1970s Wills and Hepworth changed their name to Ladybird Books Ltd. By 1999, when the imprint came to an end, it boasted over 100 fiction and nonfiction series in 60 languages, as well as cassettes, activity packs, and posters. The name was entered in the *Trade Marks Journal* of February 26, 1947.

Ladybird *(knitwear)*

The name for the brand of children's clothing is said to have been chosen as the result of a dream by an ancestor of Eric Pasold (1906-1978), an Austrian knitted goods manufacturer who first visited Britain in 1924 and who settled there to build a knitwear factory at Langley, near Slough, Buckinghamshire, in 1932. The name was entered in the *Trade Marks Journal* of January 18, 1939. In 1957 Pasolds Ltd., by then the largest childrenswear manufacturers in Britain, became a public company. The firm was acquired by **Coats Patons** in 1971.

Laetrile *(anticancer drug)*

The drug, supposed to release cyanide into the body to kill cancer cells, is obtained by hydrolyzing amygdalin (obtained from almonds, apricot pits, and other seeds) and oxidizing the resulting glycoside. The name, from the compound's chemical name, *l*-mand*e*loni*trile*, itself from "*l*evorotatory" (*cp.* **Levonelle**), German *Mandel*, "almond," and "nitrile," is no longer proprietary in the USA, but was entered by the John Beard Memorial Foundation, San Francisco, California, in the US Patent Office *Official Gazette* of March 31, 1953: "For treatment of disorders from intestinal fermentation," with a claim of use since June 2, 1952, and by "Dipix Distributions Limited, Gusta Lodge, Worth, Deal, Kent" in the *Trade Marks Journal* of April 27, 1983.

Lafarge *(building materials)*

The French company goes back to 1749, when the Pavin family purchased the Lafarge domain between Lyon and Marseille, southern France, where limestone was already being extracted. Auguste Pavin decided to start regular lime production, and in 1833 his elder son, Léon, took charge of the enterprise, a small limeworks between Viviers and Le Teil. In 1839 Léon's younger brother, Édouard Pavin de Lafarge, succeeded him. The business developed, and at the turn of the 20th century was known as the Société des Chaux et des Ciments de Lafarge du Teil ("Lafarge Le Teil Lime and Cement Company"). Lime and cement companies elsewhere in France were acquired over the years, and in 1956 Lafarge Cement of North America was founded near Vancouver, Canada. In 1981 Lafarge merged with General **Portland**, and in 2001 acquired **Blue Circle**.

Lagardère *(publishing and automotive)*

In 1963 Frenchman Jean-Luc Lagardère became president and chief executive officer of **Matra**. In 1983 he took control of **Hachette**, which in 1992 merged with Matra as Matra Hachette, making Lagardère the group's leading company. Lagardère is now a major European group in the field of communication and technology.

Lagonda *(automobiles)*

The car owes its name to Wilbur Gunn, an American from Springfield, Ohio, who at first considered a career as an opera singer. In 1897 he went to England, where he built air-cooled motorcycles at Staines, Middlesex. He turned to cars in 1906, calling them Lagondas, from the Native American name of a creek (now known as Buck Creek) near his home town. The company experienced financial problems in 1937, and the receivers were called in. The firm was revived, however, with W.O. **Bentley** as the technical director, and continued in production until 1947, when it ceased its independent existence and became part of the **David Brown** empire, together with **Aston Martin**. There have been no Lagondas since 1990.

Lalique *(jewelry and glassware)*

In 1876, René Lalique (1860-1945), born in Ay, Marne, France, began studying drawing in Paris. He then worked as a goldsmith and spent several years in London before returning to Paris. In 1885 he started his own firm, designing and manufacturing jewelry which he sold to **Cartier** and other French jewelry companies. He then refined his art to designing a wide range of products in glass. As the popularity of his glassware grew, Lalique set up a factory in Wingen, Alsace, where it remained the town's only industry until World War II. In the late 20th century Lalique reinvented itself as a luxury goods business with ambitions to rival such houses as **Louis Vuitton** and **Gucci**.

Lalonde *(chocolates)*

The French firm, based in Nancy, was founded in 1850 by Jean-Frédéric Goddefroy Lillig. In 1901 it was taken over by Albert Lalonde, whose family ran the business until 1970, when it was bought by Fernand Bader. He was joined in 1984 by Jean-Luc Guillevic, who in turn took over in 1994.

Lamborghini *(automobiles)*

Ferruccio Lamborghini (1916-1993), born near Ferrara, central Italy, worked as a mechanic in the Italian army during World War II and after it started a tractor company to build farm implements using recycled parts from Allied army surplus and abandoned German tanks. In 1959, in Sant'Agata Bolognese, near Bologna, he opened an ultramodern factory to manufacture a new type of sports car that would be grander than any he had previously owned, including **Ferrari** and **Maserati**, and the first Lamborghini car was turned out in time to be displayed at the 1963 Geneva Motor Show. By the end of the 1960s, Lamborghini's luxury sports cars were in demand by sports car enthusiasts and celebrities, who admired them for their panache, but in 1973 their designer sold his shares in the business and retired to Umbria to devote his time to winegrowing. In 1987 **Chrysler** bought control of Lamborghini, and in 1998 the company was sold to **Audi**.

Lambretta *(motorscooters)*

The scooter was launched in the 1950s by the Italian firm of **Innocenti**, rebuilt after World War II in Lambrate, Milan, and the district name passed in Italian diminutive form to the vehicle.

Lamb's *("Navy" rum)*

The man who gave his name to the most familiar of the dark ("Navy") rums was Alfred Lamb, born in 1827 the son of a Scotsman who had come down to London from Elgin to start up a wine business. The first recorded mention of the "Navy" blend is in 1849. Unlike **Navy Cut**, the name is not proprietary. It simply indicates a dark rum, such as that formerly issued in the Royal Navy.

Laminex *(plastic material)*

The hard, durable, plastic laminate (hence the name), used as a surfacing material, is of Australian origin and in 1945 was entered in the *Australian Official Journal of Patents* (Canberra) for: "Articles ... moulded, cast or otherwise formed from or incorporating synthetic resin or similar moulding material and including laminated sheets, blocks, tubes, rods, gear wheels and other goods comprising superposed sheets of fabric, paper or other material impregnated with synthetic moulding material."

Lanchester *(automobiles)*

English engineer Frederick William Lanchester (1868-1946) was born in Lewisham, Kent, the son of an architect. Following education at the Royal College of Science, in 1889 he joined T.B. Barker & Co. of Birmingham, gas-engine manufacturers, and became their works manager and designer. In around 1894 he started to develop an automobile on his own account, producing an experimental model the following year. In 1899 he founded the Lan-

chester Engine Company, but financial problems delayed full-scale car production until 1901. In 1905 a new company was formed as the Lanchester Motor Company, although owing to disagreements with the management, Lanchester himself ceased to play any active part. In 1910 he was appointed consultant engineer to **Daimler**, with whom he remained until 1930. Meanwhile the Lanchester marque struggled on until the 1950s, after which it became a "shell" company, one of the assets bought by **Jaguar** in 1960.

Lancia *(automobiles)*

The Lancia has a distinctive logo representing a standard mounted on a lance (Italian *lancia*) together with the name. It aptly reflects the name of the car's designer and manufacturer, Vincenzo Lancia (1881-1937), born in Italy the son of a soup merchant. In 1898 he began his career with the firm of Ceirano as an engineering apprentice and two years later was appointed as tester and race driver for **Fiat**. In 1906 Lancia started his own motor manufacturing business in Turin, although he did not produce his first model until two years later, as the result of a fire. All his first models were race cars, and it was only later that standard road cars were produced. The firm flourished after World War II but in the late 1960s suffered a financial crisis and in 1969 was taken over by Fiat.

Lancôme *(perfumes)*

In 1935, Armand Petitjean, former director of **Coty**, founded Lancôme to restore French perfumery to what he regarded as its rightful supremcy. The new company, named after a chateau in Touraine, was launched with a display of no less than five perfumes: *Tropiques*, *Kypré*, *Tendres Nuits*, *Bocages*, and *Conquête*. Petitjean felt that if couturiers could launch designer collections, then so could perfumers.In 1964 the company was taken over by **L'Oréal**.

Land *(cameras)*

The Land camera is named for the man who invented the Polaroid instant-picture process, Edwin D. Land (1909-1991). He was born in Bridgeport, Connecticut, and although he attended Harvard, he never graduated. Instead he devoted his time and interests to experimenting with light waves. The results of his research enabled him to "polarize" light by eliminating those rays in a light beam that were not traveling along a single plane, so reducing glare. It took him nine years to perfect the process, and in 1937 he founded the Polaroid Corporation, which began by making sunglasses. After World War II the firm was ready to diversify. It did so by introducing the instant camera, which first saw the light of day in 1947. Land stepped down as chief executive of Polaroid in 1980, but continued to serve as chairman. The name "Polaroid" was originally entered by the Sheet Polarizer Company, Inc., of Union City, New Jersey, in the US Patent Office *Official Gazette* of May 26, 1936, for the light-polarizing material itself, "comprising suspensions of crystalline particles in a light-transmitting medium adapted to be used in connection with optical devices such as microscope eye-pieces, glare eliminators, [etc.]," with a claim of use since November 19, 1935.

Land O' Lakes *(butter)*

The US farmers' cooperative of this name was set up in 1921 in six upper Midwest states: North Dakota, South Dakota, Nebraska, Minnesota, Iowa, and Wisconsin. Originally the name went on butter alone, but is now on other products such as milk, cheese, turkey, eggs, and canned and frozen food. Geographically the name applies primarily to Minnesota, "The Land of 10,000 Lakes," while Land o'Lakes is also a village in northern Wisconsin, a resort center in a wooded lake region.

Land-Rover *(cross-country vehicle)*

The first Land-Rover, produced in 1948, was designed to provide farmers with a cheap, rugged vehicle that could travel virtually anywhere over their land. Hence its name. Much of the design of the **Range Rover** was based on that of the Land-Rover.The name was entered by **Rover** in the *Trade Marks Journal* of September 29, 1948.

Lane *(furniture)*

The two Americans behind the name are father and son John Lane (1857-1930) and Edward Lane (1891-1973). John was an engineering contractor, cotton mill operator, farmer, and horse breeder before he turned his attention to furniture, and even when the Lane Co. was founded in 1912, it manufactured only

cedar chests until the 1950s, when Edward added tables, chairs, and other wood furniture. The contrast between the varied interests of John Lane and the sole product is notable.

Lane, Allen *see* **Allen Lane**

Lane Bryant *(fashionwear)*

The name that became synonymous with maternity wear and clothes for outsize women in America is that of Lane Bryant (1879-1951), a seamstress originally named Lena Himmelstein who had immigrated from her native Lithuania to New York at the age of 16. In 1899 she married a Brooklyn jeweler, David Bryant, who died of tuberculosis soon after, leaving her a widow at the age of 21. Lena fell back on the only trade she knew, and began making lingerie in her West 112th Street apartment. Her negligees were well received, and within six years she was able to move into a loft in West 38th Street. In 1906 she opened her first bank account at the Oriental Bank on Broadway, Manhattan, where she was so awed by the opulent surroundings that she wrote her first name "Lane" instead of "Lena," misplacing the vowels. Too timid to correct the mistake, she thereafter accepted it. In 1909 Lane Bryant married Albert Malsin, a Lithuanian-born engineer, and he managed the financial side of her expanding business until his death in 1923.

Lanique *(vodka)*

The range of Polish fruit-flavored vodkas take their name from Lańcut, the town in southwestern Poland where the distillery is based, as one of the oldest and largest in the country.

Lanson *(champagne)*

The brand dates back to 1760, when François Delamotte began making and selling champagne in Reims, France. In 1828 his son took on Jean-Baptiste Lanson as a partner, and when Delamotte died in 1837, the firm's name was changed to Veuve Delamotte-Barrachin. Lanson's two nephews, Victor-Marie and Henri, then entered the business. In 1856 Delamotte's widow died, and the Lansons gained full control of the firm soon after, changing its name to Lanson, Père et Fils. The name "Lanson père & fils à Rheims" appears in a figure in the *Trade Marks Journal* of February 1, 1888, and "Lanson" is entered separately in the *Journal* of June 6, 1962.

Lanvin *(fashionwear and cosmetics)*

France's oldest established couture house dates from 1885, when Jeanne Lanvin (1867-1946), born in Paris, opened a milliner's workshop. Business flourished, enabling her to open a childrenswear department in 1908 and a couture house the following year. After her death, the company was taken over by her daughter, Marguerite (later Marie-Blanche), Comtesse de Polignac (1897-1958), and in 1985 the couture house passed to Maryll Lanvin, wife of Jeanne's great-nephew, Bernard. The firm was acquired by **L'Oréal** in 1990, and three years later abandoned couture to concentrate on ready-to-wear clothes. Lanvin's first commercial perfume, *My Sin*, was launched back in 1925.

La Perla *(fashionwear)*

The Italian lingerie firm, with a name meaning "The Pearl," was founded in 1954 when Ada Masotti, a corsetry seamstress, opened a tiny, one-roomed atelier with two assistants in her hometown, Bologna. The business grew to become a global company, and at the turn of the 21st century was still in family hands, with Ada's granddaughter, Anna Masotti (b.1974), as its heiress.

Laphroaig *(whisky)*

The whisky takes its name, pronounced "Lafroig," from the site of its distillery on the island of Islay in the Hebrides, Scotland. The name "Laphroaig Islay" was entered in the *Trade Marks Journal* of March 8, 1916, with the note: "The said Trade Mark has been used ... since 16 years before the 13th August 1875." According to the label on the bottle, the distillery was set up in 1815.

Largactil *(sedative drug)*

The drug derives its name from French *large activité*, "broad activity," indicating the essential feature of its chief constituent, chlorpromazine, noted for the diversity of its applications. The name was entered by its manufacturers, **May & Baker**, in the *Trade Marks Journal* of May 20, 1953.

Lariam *(antimalarial drug)*

The proprietary name of the antimalarial drug mefloquine, consisting of a fluorinated derivative of quinoline, probably derives from letters in "malaria" itself. The name was entered by Roche Products Ltd. (*see* **Hoffmann-La Roche**) in the *Trade Marks Journal* of July 14, 1982.

Larousse *(publishers)*

The French publishing house, based in Paris, was founded in 1852 by Augustin Boyer (1821-1896) and Pierre Larousse (1817-1875), born in Toucy, north central France, the son of a blacksmith. He obtained a bursary to study at Versailles and then returned to Toucy as a schoolmaster. In 1840 he went to Paris, where he led a spartan existence while pursuing his linguistic researches. His first work, a basic vocabulary textbook, was published in 1849. It was followed by a steady stream of grammars, dictionaries, and other textbooks, all of which were brought out by his own publishing house. His financial success provided a firm base for the encyclopedic *Grand Dictionnaire universel du XIXᵉ siècle*, which first began to appear in fortnightly parts in 1863 and was published in 15 volumes from 1866 to 1876. Two supplements followed in 1878 and 1890, making a work of around 100 million words. (It was reissued in 34 volumes in 1976 and from 2000 was available in DVD form.) In 1996 Larousse merged with Bordas, founded in 1944, to become Larousse-Bordas.

Laservision *(video system)*

The system for the reproduction of video signals recorded on a laser disc derives its name from a combination of "laser" and "vision," based on "television." It was entered (as "LaserVision") in the US Patent Office *Official Gazette* of October 30, 1984: "For reflective laser optical video discs, players and components," with a note of first use in April 1981.

Lastex *(elastic yarn)*

The name was created in the early 20th century by US Rubber (*see* **Uniroyal**) for an elastic yarn made of rubber combined with silk, cotton, or rayon that was used in foundation garments and underwear. The name itself, suggesting "elastic textile," was entered by the **Dunlop**-Revere Thread Co. Ltd., of Birmingham, England, in the *Trade Marks Journal* of January 17, 1934 for: "Yarns and threads composed of a mixture of india-rubber and silk, the silk predominating."

Lauder, Estée *see* **Estée Lauder**

Launder-Ometer *(laundry washing machine)*

The machine was devised to make standard laundry tests and consisted of a number of jars clamped to a rotating shaft in which the actual washing was carried out. The name, as a combination of "launder" and "-ometer," was entered in the US Patent Office *Official Gazette* of May 21, 1929, with a claim of use since April 27, 1928. The machine itself was the invention of an American dyestuff manufacturer, Hugh Christison.

Laundromat *(launderette)*

The name was originally used for an automatic washing machine manufactured by **Westinghouse** in the early 1940s, and as such was entered by the company in the US Patent Office *Official Gazette* of July 14, 1943. It soon passed to a launderette, as an establishment with coin-operated washing machines. The name itself blends "launder" and "automatic."

Laura Ashley *(furnishings and fashions)*

Laura Ashley (1925-1985) was born in South Wales the daughter of a civil servant. As Laura Mountney she worked as a secretary before marrying Bernard Ashley (b.1925), a London businessman, in 1949. Laura Ashley was keen to reproduce the Victorian-style prints and designs that she admired. In 1953, operating simply at first, she and her husband printed table mats and scarves on an old kitchen table in the living room of their third-floor apartment in Pimlico, London, selling them to small shops and department stores. After a difficult few years, when Laura Ashley had additionally to cope with a young family, demands for her prints suddenly increased. Bernard Ashley developed a continuous textile printing machine, and soon left his own job to handle the financial side of the booming business. After more than one move to larger homes and premises, the Ashleys finally settled in Wales in 1963, with the first Laura Ashley shop opening in London four years later. The name was entered by Ashley Mountney Ltd. in the *Trade Marks Journal* of August 7, 1974 for: "Dresses, smocks, slacks, blouses, shirts, skirts, aprons (for wear), sleeping garments, capes, jackets, coats and hats, all for women and girls."

Lauren, Ralph *see* **Ralph Lauren**

Lava Lite *(lava lamp)*

The name was registered in 1968 as an alteration of "lava light," a term for a transparent electric lamp containing a viscous liquid in which a brightly colored waxy substance is suspended, rising and falling in constantly changing shapes when the lamp is switched on. Lava lights were more usually known as "lava lamps," with "lava" referring to the resemblance of the shapes to that of molten lava in water. The lamp itself was launched in **Selfridges** in 1963 by its British inventor, Edward Craven Walker (1918-2000), who had left the Royal Air Force at the end of World War II. He named his first model "Astro," for the space age that was then beginning to dominate the public consciousness. In 1990 Walker was bought out by Cressida Granger's **Mathmos** company.

Laverda *(motorcycles)*

The name of the Italian firm ultimately goes back to Pietro Laverda, who set up a factory to build plows and harrows in Breganze, northwest Italy, in 1873. The move from agricultural machinery to motorcycles came only in 1948, when Francesco Laverda built his first bike, mainly for his own amusement. When friends asked him to build replicas, he set up Moto Laverda the following year and went into production. Although under new management, machines of the name were still being manufactured at the end of the century.

Lawrence & Wishart *(publishers)*

The left-wing British publishing house owes its origin to Ernest Edward Wishart (1902-1987), a colonel's son. On completing his education at Rugby and Cambridge, Wishart set up a publishing business, taking as partner his friend Douglas Garman, whose sister he would later marry. He was soon publishing many famous writers of the day, such as E.M. Forster, Robert Graves, and Aldous Huxley. At the same time, like many of his Cambridge contemporaries, he developed Marxist sympathies, although he never joined the Communist Party. In 1936 he took over the firm of Martin Lawrence, trading from then on as Lawrence & Wishart and publishing literature of an increasingly political nature, including translations of the complete works of Lenin, Marx,

Engels, and Stalin. On the outbreak of World War II, however, Wishart lost interest in publishing and retired to Sussex to manage his many farms. Lawrence & Wishart remains an independent publisher.

Lay's *(potato chips)*

Herman W. Lay (1909-1982) began peddling potato chips out of the trunk of his touring car in Nashville, Tennessee, in 1932. Two years later he had six sales routes, and his business expanded steadily until his Atlanta, Georgia, supplier ran into financial difficulties in 1938. Lay acted quickly. He purchased the troubled company, changed the name of his business to H.W. Lay & Co., and introduced "Lay's" potato chips. Meanwhile, also in 1932, Elmer Doolin had founded the Frito Company (Spanish *frito*, "fried") in San Antonio, Texas, to make corn chips, buying his recipe from a Mexican businessman returning to Mexico. In 1961, H.W. Lay & Co. merged with the Frito Co. as Frito-Lay, Inc. Four years later Frito-Lay in turn merged with **Pepsi-Cola** to form PepsiCo., with Lay himself as chairman of the board. Subsequent brands of chips introduced by Frito-Lay include **Doritos** in 1961, "Tostitos" in 1981, and "Wow!" in 1998. *See also* **Taco Bell**.

Lazarus *(department store)*

The Ohio department stores take their name from Fred Lazarus, Jr. (1884-1973), the most famous member of the family that built the Lazarus and Shillito business in Columbus and Cincinnati. From 1946 through 1966 he was chief executive officer of Federated Department Stores, Inc., of which the Ohio stores are model units. The chain had its origins with Simon Lazarus (d.1877), who emigrated from Germany in 1850 because of the Jewish segregation laws of 1848. He opened a one-room menswear store in Columbus, Ohio, in 1851, and it was from that base that he and his family built the leading retail emporium in southern Ohio. It was at F. & R. Lazarus, as the store became, after Simon's two sons, Fred and Ralph, that Fred, Jr., Simon's grandson, began selling collars at the age of 10. In 1930 he joined forces with the owners of **Filene's** in Boston, **Abraham & Straus** in Brooklyn, and **Bloomingdale's** in Manhattan to form Federated Department Stores.

Lea & Perrins *(Worcestershire sauce)*

The names are those of John Wheeley Lea (1791-1874) and William Henry Perrins (1793-1867), both of Worcestershire, England. Lea was a druggist with premises in Worcester, while Perrins had a chemist's shop in Evesham. On New Year's Day 1823 they pooled their resources to develop a chemist and druggist business in Worcester, with their shop a "drugstore" selling cosmetics and groceries as well as medicines. One day in 1835, the story goes, Sir Marcus Sandys, returned to his native England from India, where he had served his country many years as Governor of Bengal, walked into the shop and asked the two men to make him up a sauce from a recipe he had obtained in India. They did so, at the same time preparing a few gallons for themselves in stone jars, as a possible commercial line. On tasting the sauce, however, they found it quite unpalatable, so relegated the jars to the cellar. Opening the jars some months later they tried the sauce again and found it delicious, as it had matured. Thus was Lea & Perrins Worcestershire sauce created.

Lea-Francis *(automobiles)*

English engineers Richard H. Lea and Gordon J. Francis started building bicycles in Coventry, Warwickshire, in 1895. Their first car appeared in 1903, after which they turned to motorcycles until 1920, when auto production was resumed. The firm was then hit by the Depression, and stopped building cars in the 1930s. In 1937 the marque was revived by a new company, Lea-Francis Cars Ltd., but sales again tailed off following World War II and the last production models were built in 1953. Even so, the marque has been subject to repeated if precarious renewal since then, and a prototype Lea-Francis appeared at the 1998 Motor Show. *See also* **Francis-Barnett**.

Learjet *(aircraft)*

The small passenger jet aircraft, popular among the rich and famous, takes its name from its designer, the American electrical engineer William P. Lear (1902-1978), born in Hannibal, Missouri, the son of a carpenter and teamster. After quitting school at the eight grade, Lear found work as a mechanic. A spell in the navy followed in World War I, after which he found employment with a number of electrical and radio businesses. In 1931 he became chief engineer for Galvin Manufacturing Company (later **Motorola**), and that same year founded his own firm, Lear Development Company, which perfected a simplified radio frequency amplifier. In 1934 RCA bought his plans, enabling Lear to organize a completely new research and development company, Lear Avia Corporation, located in Dayton, Ohio. In 1939, on the eve of World War II, he changed the name of his business operations to Lear Incorporated, a diverse electronics and engineering firm that won many wartime contracts. By the end of the 1950s Lear's experience in the executive airplane market had convinced him he could sell a small corporate jet, and the first Learjet was duly launched from his base at Wichita, Kansas, in 1963. It has since come to be regarded as one of the most glamorous aircraft, its name entering the language as a symbol of affluence and power. In 1990 the company became a subsidiary of **Bombardier**.

Lec *(refrigerators)*

The name derives from the initials of the Longford Engineering Company, a British firm set up in 1942 in premises on the Longford Road, Bognor Regis, Sussex. In 1946 the company moved to larger premises in the same town and shortened its name, which fortuitously suggests "electric." The name was entered in the *Trade Marks Journal* of December 30, 1946.

Lee *(jeans)*

The name behind the brand is that of Henry D. Lee (1849-1928), born in Vermont. Lee left home as a young man and started a kerosene distributing business in Galion, Ohio. In 1888 he sold out to **Standard Oil** and moved to Salina, Kansas, where he set up a wholesale grocery firm. In due course his business expanded to distribute hardware, stationery, and work clothes. Lee's eastern workwear supplier was often late in making deliveries, however, so he set up a small plant to produce overalls, jackets, and dungarees. His rugged style of clothing soon caught on, and by 1916 he was operating four garment plants. Lee continued to head the clothing firm until his death.

Lee Cooper *(jeans)*

The origins of the British company go back to the early years of the 20th century, when the firm of M. Cooper (Overalls) Ltd. was set up to manufacture industrial workwear. Their founder was killed in World War I, and immediately after it his son, Harold Cooper, returned to the business and began to change the product line from workwear to blue jeans. He devised the name Lee Cooper for the revived company, as a combination of his wife's maiden name, Daphne Leigh (respelled "Lee" for simplicity), and his own surname. The name was first registered in Britain in 1958 and became known internationally. In the late 1980s, however, the company name was changed to Vivat Holdings plc, although the Lee Cooper name remained for the jeans and other garments.

Lego *(construction toy)*

The toy consisting of interlocking plastic building blocks arose from a business set up in 1932 at Billund, Denmark, by Ole Kirk Christiansen, a master carpenter and joiner, who originally made and sold stepladders, ironing boards, and wooden toys. In 1934 he named the latter "Lego," from Danish *leg godt*, "play well," a name that it was later realized was also Latin for "I study." The business introduced plastic toys in 1947, and began to perfect what were at first known as "Automatic Binding Bricks." The firm's products grew in variety and in 1958 the coupling system for the blocks was patented. In 1960 the company opened Legoland, an entire village made of Lego at Billund. It remained the sole Lego Mecca until 1996 when a second Legoland opened in England at Windsor, near London. A third was added in 1999 at Carlsbad, California. The name was entered in the *Trade Marks Journal* of June 5, 1957 for: "Toy models and sets of parts for constructing such toys, all made of rigid plastics."

Leica *(cameras)*

The well-known camera of this name was first produced by the Leitz Optical Works at Wetzlar, Germany, founded by Ernst B. Leitz (1843-1920). It was not designed by Leitz, however. That privilege fell to the optical engineer Oskar Barnack (1879-1936), who joined the company in 1910 to work on research into microscope design. He was an enthusiastic photographer, and his first construction in this field was a 35mm movie camera, which he used to cover events in and around Wetzlar. He then considered the design of a still camera in which short lengths of film could be tested before shooting. He built a model with a frame size of 18 x 24mm, a simple focal-plane shutter adjustable to 1/500 of a second, and a **Zeiss** Milar lens of 42mm focal length. This was what is now known as the UR-Leica. Ernst Leitz, Jr., was lent the camera for a trip in June 1914 to America, where he was urged to put it into production. World War I halted development, but after the war Leitz took Barnack off microscope work to design prototypes for a commercial model. Leitz's chief optician, Max Berek, designed a new lens for the camera, and they settled on the name Leica, as a blend of "*Leitz*" and "*ca*mera." The first models of the 35mm miniature camera went on show at the Leipzig Spring Fair in 1925, and by the end of the year 1,000 Leicas had been shipped. The name was entered by Ernst Leitz GmbH in the *Trade Marks Journal* of July 23, 1930.

Lemon Hart (rum)

The name is that of Lemon Hart (1768-1845), a wine and liquor merchant of Penzance, Cornwall, England, who conducted a rum importing business from the West Indies, for which Penzance, on the extreme southwest coast, was the nearest port. Lemon Hart was of German origin, with his first name an anglicized form of an original Jewish name such as Lehmann. His father, Lazarus Hart, whose original surname had been Altstader, had come from Weinheim, Germany, to settle in Penzance in the 1750s. On his death in 1803, his son Lemon Hart took over.

Lenox (china)

Walter S. Lenox (1859-1920), regarded as launching America's fine china industry, was born in Trenton, New Jersey. He was the part owner of a small ceramics house when in 1894 he interested his partner in setting up a firm to make porcelain dinnerware modeled on that produced by the Belleek Pottery in Ireland. The fledgling firm's first break came in the early 1900s, when they sold a large china order to **Tiffany's**, and in 1981 Nancy Reagan placed an order for a 4,372-piece dinnerware service with Lenox, Inc.

Lente (insulin)

The form of insulin is metabolized or absorbed only gradually into the body following its introduction. Hence the name, from Latin *lente*, "slowly," registered in Denmark in 1958 (when already in use) and entered by the Novo Terapeutisk Laboratorium A/S, of Copenhagen, in the US Patent Office *Official Gazette* of July 7, 1959. *See also* **Ultralente**.

Lenthéric (perfume)

Guillaume Lenthéric first opened his hairdressing saloon and perfume laboratory in the Rue St. Honoré, Paris, France, in 1875. He had a fashionable clientele, and had become adept at creating exclusive perfumes for many of his aristocratic patrons. He came to concentrate increasingly on the perfumery side of his business, so that growing demand for his products eventually obliged him to move to a larger laboratory at Courbevoie, northwest of Paris. In 1924, 12 years after his death, the House of Lenthéric became a limited company, with a subsidiary formed in London in the 1930s.

Le Roux (chocolates)

The French firm Le Roux Caramelier-Chocolatier, based in Quiberon, Brittany, was founded in 1977 by Henri Le Roux and his wife Lorraine. Their shop at first sold both ice cream and chocolate, but the success of the chocolates prompted them to concentrate on that line alone. Le Roux subsequently gained international renown for his special recipes.

Lesney (toys)

The British firm Lesney Products was founded in 1947 by Leslie Smith, Rodney Smith (no relation), and Jack Odell as a diecasting company, taking their name from the first and last syllables of the first two men's forenames. The toys that they originally produced as a sideline became the famous **Matchbox** series.

Letraset (transfers, or decals)

The product, in the form of a sheet of letters that can be transferred to other surfaces, was the creation of the Scottish-born printer Frederick W. Mackenzie (1912-1987), who first demonstrated his invention at a 1957 national exhibition in Brussels. The name, suggesting a set of letters than can be "set" on a surface, was originally entered by Art and Technics Ltd. in the *Trade Marks Journal* of February 27, 1957, after which it became that of the manufacturing company itself. In 1981 Letraset was acquired by **Esselte**.

Letts *(diaries)*

The link between Letts and diaries stems from John Letts (1782-1851), a stationer and printer in the Royal Exchange, London, who in 1812 published what is now generally regarded as the world's first commercial diary, *Letts Diary of Bills Due Book and Almanack*. In issuing it, John Letts had in mind the needs of merchants and traders in the City of London, who required to know the movements of ships to and from the Port of London and who would have welcomed a book in which they could keep a record of their finances. The diary was thus for future-planning, not simply for a record of the past, as diaries had been hitherto. John Letts was succeeded in the business by his son, Thomas Letts (1803-1873), who offered a free supply of diaries to David Livingstone, in which the explorer recorded his travels and encounters in Africa. Thomas was in turn succeeded by his own son, Charles John Letts (1839-1912), who left the firm to create the company that today produces the whole range of pocket diaries. In 2001 Letts acquired **Filofax**.

Lever *see* **Unilever**

Levi's *(jeans)*

The well-known jeans are named for Levi Strauss (1829-1902), born Loeb Strauss in Buttenheim, Bavaria (now in Germany), the son of a dry goods peddler. His father died in 1845, and two years later Strauss immigrated with his mother and three sisters to America, where they joined his two older half-brothers, Jonas Strauss and Louis Strauss, in New York City. Changing his name to the more pronounceable Levi, the young Strauss began to travel with his brothers, peddling notions and dry goods, such as needles, scissors, buttons, and bolts of cloth. Jonas Strauss opened a small retail shop in 1848, and three years later Louis became his partner. Soon after, Levi Strauss moved to Louisville, Kentucky, where he continued the life of an itinerant peddlar. His sister Fanny Strauss married David Stern, a dry goods peddler from the Midwest, and the couple went to San Francisco, California, drawn by the city's gold boom. Stern established a modest dry goods business and invited Levi to join him.

When he and Stern set up shop, however, they discovered that the bolts of cloth Levi had brought with him were the wrong kind of fabric for tents, as he had intended, but that they could be cut into serviceable work pants, an important commodity among the miners, ranchers, and lumberjacks of the West. Strauss therefore used his canvas to make those garments, selling them from a store opened in 1856 under the name Levi Strauss & Co. It was Jacob W. Davis, a Russian tailor immigrant to Nevada, who really put "Levi's", as the miners nicknamed them, on the market, as he had discovered a new way to repair the ripped pockets on the pants. In 1827, with the help of the local druggist, he drafted a letter to Levi Strauss offering a half share in the right to sell the pants. In his own words, "The secratt of them Pents is the Rivits that I put in those Pockets." That was how Levi denim (not canvas) jeans came to be produced with copper rivets in their pockets. The company did make one adjustment. It moved the rivets from the back pockets to the front when schools complained that students wearing Levi's scratched the furniture. The name was entered in the US Patent Office *Official Gazette* of September 18, 1928.

Levi Strauss *see* **Levi's**

Levitt *(houses)*

The first model village called Levittown was built on Long Island, New York, over the five years 1947-51 by the firm of Levitt & Sons, Inc., founded by William J. Levitt (1907-1994). Levitt's brother, Alfred, designed the houses, his father, Abraham, concentrated on the landscaping, and William Levitt himself dealt with the organizing, financing, advertising, and sales. After the success of the first Levittown, which included more than 17,000 houses, a second Levittown was constructed over the period 1951-56 in Bucks County, Pennsylvania, and a third followed in 1958 in New Jersey. In 1968 Levitt sold his pioneering concern to **ITT**.

Levonelle *(contraceptive)*

The proprietary name for the synthetic steroid hormone levonorgestrel, used as a "morning-after pill," derives from this generic word, itself from "levo-" (as a levorotatory isomer) and "norgestrel" (*cp.* **Norplant**). It was entered by its German manufacturers, Schering Aktiengesellschaft (*see* **Schering-Plough**), in the *Trade Marks Journal* of November 17, 1999.

Lewis, John *see* **John Lewis**

Lewis's *(department stores)*

The British department stores, mainly in central and northern England, owe their origin to David Lewis (d.1885), who in 1856 opened a store selling boys' clothes in Liverpool. The business grew, and girls', men's, and women's clothes were added, as were boots and shoes. A new store opened in Manchester in 1880, and another in Birmingham in 1885. In 1923 Lewis's became the first UK department store to establish a central buying office, and in 1924 it became a public company. Further stores followed in Leeds (1932), Leicester (1936), Bristol (1957), and Blackpool (1964), and other businesses, cafes, and shops were acquired. The head office later moved to Manchester.

Lexan *(thermoplastic)*

The name of the polycarbonate thermoplastic, of high impact strength (and so bulletproof), is apparently of arbitrary origin. It was entered in the US Patent Office *Official Gazette* of August 28, 1956: "For synthetic resinous compositions useful in molding applications and other industrial arts," with a note of first use on November 10, 1955.

Lexicon *(card game)*

The card game, popular in the 1930s and 1940s, was played with cards marked with letters of the alphabet, the aim being both educational, teaching children to spell, and recreational, forming unusual words. The name, from the standard word for a vocabulary or dictionary, was entered by **Waddington's** in the *Trade Marks Journal* of June 22, 1932.

Leyland *see* **BL**

Libby *(canned foods and drink products)*

The company originated in Chicago, where its headquarters remain today. There in 1868 two brothers, Arthur Libby (1831-1899) and Charles Libby (1838-1895), with their friend Archibald McNeil, formed a partnership to produce corned beef in barrels. The business got off to a good start, but took a sharp turn upward in 1875, when the partners began packing corned beef and other compressed meats in

tapering tin cans. In 1902 the company passed into the hands of **Swift,** the USA's largest meatpacker. Swift disposed of Libby in 1920, and the company continued on its own for a while until it was acquired by **Nestlé** in 1976, with the canned range now extending to fruit, vegetables, and fruit drinks as well as meat products.

Liberty *(corsets)*

The formerly familiar "Liberty Bodice," originally worn by young children, was made by **Symington's** in the early 20th century and so called because it allowed the wearer's body to move freely, unlike earlier rigid corsets. It had no connection with **Liberty** of London, although Symington's was able to use the name only by special agreement with that firm. The garment had a unique strapping arrangement, and was so popular in its early days that a number of manufacturers attempted to copy it and as a result were involved in litigation. It was discontinued in the 1960s. The name was entered in the *Trade Marks Journal* of June 23, 1920 for: "Stays for women or children."

Liberty *(fabrics and furnishings)*

The London, England, store takes its name from Arthur Lasenby Liberty (1843-1917), born in Chesham, Buckinghamshire, the son of a draper. When he was eight, Arthur's family moved to Nottingham, where his father began manufacturing lace. At age 16, Arthur was apprenticed to a draper in Baker Street, London, and two years later took up a post at Farmer & Rogers' Great Shawl and Cloak Emporium in Regent Street. By 1864 he had risen to be manager, dealing directly with Pre-Raphaelite painters who sought sensuous silks to drape on their models. In 1876 Arthur Liberty asked to be taken into partnership. This was refused him, however, so with a loan from his fiancée's father he set up his own business, opening a small half-shop at 118A, Regent Street. This was the germ of the present familiar department store with its striking Tudor-style buildings, still located in Regent Street. Over the years the store began to sell furniture, silver, pewter, jewelry, wallpapers, and much else besides, and in 2000, the Stewart-Liberty family, as it now was, agreed to sell it to the Marylebone Warwick Balfour group.

Librium *(tranquilizer)*

The proprietary name of chlordiazepoxide, a drug used to relieve tension and nervousness, relax muscles, and encourage sleep, was entered by **Hoffmann-La Roche** in the US Patent Office *Official Gazette* of March 15, 1960. It is stated to be arbitrary in origin, but in view of the drug's function a suggestion of "liberation" (freedom from anxiety) or "equilibrium" (of mind and body) seems plausible.

Licenciados *(cigars)*

The cigars of this name, from Spanish *licenciado*, "graduate" (in Latin America, "lawyer"), were first produced by Matasa in the Dominican Republic in 1990.

Liederkranz *(cheese)*

The cheese, a type of Limburg, was the invention in 1892 of Emil Frey, a German immigrant to the USA, who named it after a choral group popular at the time. The name means "wreath of songs."

Life Savers *(mints)*

In 1912, Clarence A. Crane, manufacturer of Crane's & Mary Garden Chocolates in Cleveland, Ohio, decided to add a line of hard mints to boost his summer business. He made his mints in the shape of a ring to distinguish them from the square mints of German and Austrian confectioners, and called them "Life Savers" from their resemblance to a ship's life preservers or lifebelts. He then had a label made showing an old salt throwing a life preserver to a young lady with the wording: "Crane's Peppermint Life Savers—5¢—For That Stormy Breath." Soon after, Crane sold his stock and trademark to two young men, Edward J. Noble and J. Roy Allen, who successfully merchandized the mints. They are now marketed by **Squibb** as America's leading hard roll candy. Crane was the father of the poet Hart Crane (1899-1932).

Lifebuoy *(soap)*

The brand of household soap, manufactured by **Unilever**, originally appeared in 1894 as a successor to William Lever's **Sunlight** Soap. It was a carbolic soap containing a germicide, with a name chosen to suggest safety or immunity from disease. A toilet soap variety was introduced in 1933. The name was originally entered in the *Trade Marks Journal* of November 29, 1893.

Liggett & Myers *(tobacco and whisky)*

Liggett began as a snuff-making shop opened by Christopher Fouls in Belleville, Illinois, in 1822. The business moved to St. Louis, Missouri, in 1833, and Fouls' 18-year-old grandson, John Edmund Liggett (1826-1897), entered the firm in 1844. In 1858 John Edmund's brother, William, joined the firm and the name was changed to J.E. Liggett & Brother. In 1873 George S. Myers bought William Liggett's share in the company, and in 1878 the name became Liggett & Myers. From snuff the company moved logically to tobacco, progressing to the production of many famous brands, including the highly popular **Chesterfield**. The company made nothing but tobacco products until 1964 when it began to diversify, first into dog food, then into **J&B** whisky, then into National Oats. In 1968 the corporate name was changed to Liggett & Myers Inc., and again in 1976 to the Liggett Group. In 1980 the company was acquired by the British-based conglomerate **Grand Metropolitan**, but in 1984 ownership reverted to American interests.

Lilia *(sanitary napkins)*

The napkins take their name from their British manufacturers, Lilia-White, a firm formed in 1958 as the result of a merger between Lilia Ltd. and other makers of sanpro products, one of which was Arthur Berton, who produced "Dr. White's" looped napkins. (There was no actual doctor of this name, which was chosen to suggest medical probity and purity.) The Lilia napkin was originally sold by a firm called "Sashena," its name consisting of letters from "desirable" words such as "safe," "secure," "hygienic," etc. This firm was renamed Lilia Ltd. in 1948, a name suggesting "lily," another token of purity. The name was entered in the *Trade Marks Journal* of May 7, 1947.

Lilley & Skinner *(footwear)*

The British firm had its origins in King Street, southeast London, where in 1825 Thomas Lilley started to make shoes on his own premises. He opened a shop, trading as "Thos. Lilley," and business was so good that in 1849 he was able to open factories in

Wellingborough and Irthlingborough, both in Northamptonshire. In 1870 his son, also named Thomas, entered the business, and saw it move the following year to larger premises off Edgware Road. After a disagreement with his father, however, he started opening up his own shops, taking as partner W. Banks Skinner, a sales representative who happened to be his brother-in-law. The two men worked well together, and in 1881 the name "Lilley & Skinner" first appeared over their stores. A reconciliation between father and son followed, and the two firms amalgamated in 1894.

Lilly, Eli *see* **Eli Lilly**

Lillywhites *(department store)*

The London, England, sports store takes its name from a famous cricketing family. Frederick William Lillywhite (1792-1854) played for Sussex in the early 19th century. James Lillywhite, the eldest of his three sons, took a small stand in 1862 at an exhibition in a street off Euston Square, London, where he sold articles connected with cricket. The following year he opened a shop in the Haymarket, gradually increasing his stock to include other sports equipment. By 1925, when Lillywhites moved to its present site, in Piccadilly Circus, the firm was catering for as many as 34 different sports.

Li-Lo *(airbed)*

The type of inflatable mattress, used as a bed or for floating on water, was originally manufactured by the makers of **Cow** Gum, who entered the name in the *Trade Marks Journal* of September 16, 1936 for: "Air-beds, air-pillows and air-pillow-bags, all made principally of india-rubber." The name, from "lie low," is now often spelled generically as "lilo."

Limacol *(skin lotion)*

The skin lotion, popular in the West Indies, has a name of uncertain origin. An anagram of "Camillo" is a possibility. It was entered in the *Trade Marks Journal* of November 25, 1936 and (by the Guyana Pharmaceutical Corporation) in the US Patent Office *Official Gazette* of May 11, 1982, the latter with a note of first use on December 31, 1933.

Lincoln *(automobiles)*

When Henry M. Leland resigned from **Cadillac** in 1917, he immediately set about founding the Lincoln Motor Company, named after the famous US president, to produce Liberty airplane engines. After World War I Leland geared up to produce a new luxury car, and 1920 he and his son Wilfred formed the Lincoln Motor Company of Delaware. He received 1,000 orders for his new V-8 Lincoln car before it even went into production, but the company then faltered, and in 1922 was taken over by Henry **Ford**. Lincolns were still being produced at the turn of the 21st century.

Lindt *(chocolate)*

Quality chocolate makes are often associated with Switzerland, and Lindt is no exception. The name is that of Rodolphe Lindt (1855-1909), founder of a chocolate factory in Berne. In 1879 he produced the first "melting" (fondant) chocolate by a special refining process known as "conching." In 1899 Lindt's chocolate works was bought by the **Sprüngli** family, who had themselves been making chocolate in Zürich since 1845. Today the parent company and main factory of the Lindt & Sprüngli firm are at Kilchberg, right by Lake Zürich.

Linguaphone *(recorded language courses)*

The name combines Latin *lingua*, "language," and the Greek element "-phone" meaning "sound" extracted from **Gramophone**. The firm was founded in London, England, in 1904 by an immigrant Pole, Jacques Roston, as a language-teaching system using gramophone records and textbooks. Originally a phonograph was used, which meant that the learner could not only hear the language spoken but record his voice on the wax cylinder. Roston ran the business until his death in 1947. The name was entered by Roston, "teacher of languages and translator," in the *Trade Marks Journal* of November 4, 1925.

Linguet *(medicinal tablets)*

The name is that of a tablet designed to be held under the tongue so that its active ingredients can be absorbed through the oral tissues. It derives from Latin *lingua*, "tongue," and the diminutive suffix "-et" and was entered in the US Patent Office *Official Gazette* of March 16, 1943.

Linofilm *(photocomposing machine)*

The electronic photocomposing machine, using punched tapes, was developed by the manufacturers of the **Linotype**. The name is based on this and was entered by the Mergenthaler Linotype Company, Brooklyn, New York, in the *Trade Marks Journal* of December 5, 1956 for: "Phototypographic machines and tape perforating machines for use in setting and composing type photographically."

Linograph *(composing machine)*

The US composing machine, casting a line of type at a time, was similar to the **Linotype** but had a vertical rather than a horizontal magazine. The name is based on that of the earlier machine and the Linograph itself first came into regular use in the early 20th century.

Linotype *(composing machine)*

The composing machine, producing lines of words as single strips of metal, was patented in 1884 by the German-born American inventor Ottmar Mergenthaler (1854-1899), then working in Baltimore, USA. It could cast a whole line of type (hence the name) from molten metal, and was controlled by a typesetter operating a keyboard.

Linson *(fabric)*

The name of the tough fibrous paper fabric, used mainly for bookbinding, was entered by the material's manufacturers, R. & W. Watson, Renfrewshire, Scotland, in the *Trade Marks Journal* of February 18, 1948. The name itself perhaps blends "linseed" (used to make oilcloth) and "cotton."

Linux *(computer operating system)*

The freeware version of the **Unix** operating system was developed at the University of Helsinki by the Finnish computer engineer Linus Torvalds (b.1970) with worldwide specialist help. The first version, Linux 1.0, was launched in 1994, while Linux 2.0 followed in 1996. The name combines Torvalds' first name with that of Unix. As freeware, the system can be downloaded free of charge from the Internet, and by 1999 an estimated 7 million computers were running on Linux.

Lionel *(model railways)*

The name is that of Joshua Lionel Cowen (1877-1965), born in New York City, the son of a hatmaker and real-estate dealer. As a child, Cowen was interested in what made toys work, and he would break them apart to find out. He often skipped classes at school, and later dropped out of both the City College of New York and Columbia University. He finally ended up at the Acme Electric Lamp Company, where he developed the skills that would soon stand him in good stead. After inventing then abandoning a new type of flash lamp, in 1900 Cowen and a colleague, Harry C. Grant, filed to conduct their own business as the Lionel Manufacturing Company, its purpose being "the manufacture of electrical novelties." In 1901 Cowen had the idea of fastening the motor from an electric fan to the bottom of a miniature wooden railroad flatcar. This would run on a small circle of miniature railroad tracks made from brass strips mounted on wooden ties. The batteries that powered the train would connect directly to the tracks, and the whole invention, reasoned Cowen, would be ideal for use in shop window displays, where the train would attract customers while carrying featured merchandise. Orders from shop owners followed almost immediately, and the toy trains themselves, as a literal spin-off, soon became a highly popular Christmas gift.

Lipiodol *(radiographic contrast material)*

The liquid, obtained by treating poppyseed oil with iodine, is used as a contrast medium in radiography. Its name derives from the first syllables of Greek *lipos*, "fat," and English "iodine" with the added "oil" suffix "-ol." It was entered by Laurent Lafay of Paris, France, in the *Trade Marks Journal* of May 20, 1925.

Lippincott *(publishers)*

The publishing house owes its origin to Joshua Ballinger Lippincott (1813-1886), born in Juliustown, New Jersey. After receiving a common school education, Lippincott moved in 1827 to Philadelphia to work as a clerk for "Clarke, the bookseller." He did well there, and in 1836 bought the business and renamed it J.B. Lippincott & Company, at the same time expanding into publishing and specializing in Bibles and prayer books. In 1849 he bought Grigg, Elliot & Company, America's largest book distributor and foremost medical publisher, dating back to 1792, and by assuming their "publishing tradition" was able to date his own company similarly. Lippincott's most popular books included the 2,000-page *Lippincott's Pronouncing Gazetteer of the World* (1855) and the 2,300-page *Universal Dictionary of Biography and Mythology* (1870). As Lippincott-Raven, headed by J.W. Lippincott III, the company now specializes in medical books.

Liptons *(tea)*

Thomas Johnstone Lipton (1850-1931) was born in Glasgow, Scotland, the son of an Irish laborer who had emigrated from Co. Monaghan because of the potato famine. In Glasgow, Lipton's father set up a grocer's shop, where Thomas began to work when he was nine years old. In 1865 Thomas Lipton booked a passage to New York, and worked in various parts of the United States, including a New York grocery store, before returning to Scotland four years later. There, on his 21st birthday, he opened his own shop in Stobcross Street, selling mainly "Irish" produce, such as ham, butter, and eggs, as his father had done. Business prospered, and by 1878 Lipton had opened four more Glasgow shops, all known as "Irish markets." It was not until 1889, however, that Lipton began selling the tea that made his name famous. By the end of the century Thomas Lipton was a millionaire from his enterprise, and in 1898 he was knighted for his generous gifts to charity.

Liquid Paper *(correction fluid)*

In order to correct her typing mistakes as a secretary at Texas Bank and Trust in Dallas, Texas, Bette Nesmith Graham used the white tempera waterbase paint that she carried in a bottle with her to work, applying it with an eyebrow brush. When in 1956 the other typists began asking for her "correcting fluid," she began bottling it in a garage with the help of her son Michael (b.1942), later famous as Mike Nesmith of the pop group The Monkees. Bette achieved her fame and fortune with what would be later known as "Liquid Paper," and her enterprise was worth $47 million by the time she sold out to **Gillette** in 1979. The name, of obvious origin, first appeared in a figure in the *Trade Marks Journal* of October 23, 1968, with the note: "Registration of this Trade Mark shall give no right to the exclusive use of the words 'Liquid Paper'." It was subsequently entered in the US Patent Office *Official Gazette* of March 25, 1969, with a note of first use on May 18, 1967.

Listerine *(mouthwash)*

The antiseptic mouthwash takes its name from Joseph Lister (1827-1921), the English surgeon who invented antiseptic techniques in surgery. The product was developed in 1879 by the American pharmacist Jordan W. Lambert, the second half of **Warner-Lambert**, who based his product on Lister's earlier formula, and the name was registered in 1881 by the Lambert Pharmacal Company. It was reported that Lister was not happy about having his name used in that way. His objections were of no avail, however. The name happens to suggest "sterile."

Lite *see* **Miller**

Litek *(light bulbs)*

The fluorescent light bulbs are designed to last up to ten years and consume 70 percent less energy than ordinary bulbs. They appear to take their name from the *Li*ght *Te*chnology Corp., the company set up in the 1970s by their American inventor, Donald D. Hollister, to develop them.

Lithol *(dyestuff)*

The name of the various azo pigment dyestuffs is apparently of arbitrary origin. It was entered by the Badische Anilin & Soda Fabrik (the future **BASF**) of Ludwigshafen, Germany, in the US Patent Office *Official Gazette* of June 16, 1903, with a note of use since June 6, 1901.

Little, Brown *(publishers)*

The American publishing house takes its name from Charles Coffin Little (1799-1869) and James Brown (1800-1855). Little was born a farmer's son in Kennebunk, Maine, and like many young men of his day decided to leave the farm and head for the city. In Boston he first got a job with a shipping company, then in 1821 was hired as clerk with Carter, Hilliard, a bookseller specializing in law books. Meanwhile Brown, also a farmer's son, had been born in Acton, Massachusetts. At 15 he, too, decided to leave the farm and made his way to Cambridge, where he obtained a post as a servant in the home of a law professor. In 1818

Brown was hired as a clerk by the University Bookstore, Cambridge, owned by Hilliard. By 1826 he had become a partner, with an interest in the Boston shop, and the following year Little likewise became a partner in Hilliard, Gray, as it now was. Since the two firms were closely affiliated, Little and Brown were soon close friends. When Hilliard died in 1836, the two decided to form their own partnership and take over the Hilliard, Gray shop. Thus Little, Brown was born, and the company still has its head offices in Boston today.

Littlewoods (department stores)

The Littlewoods Organisation is known not only for its stores but also for its mail order business and its football pools. The British firm was founded not by a Mr. Littlewood but by John (later, Sir John) Moores (1896-1993), born in Eccles, Lancashire, the son of a building tradesman. He quit school at 14 and became a post office messenger, studying telegraphy at night. At 16 he went to work for the Commercial Cable Company and, after spending part of World War I in the Royal Navy, was posted in 1921 to an isolated cable station in Ireland. Back in England in 1923, Moores and two work colleagues set up a football pool business in Liverpool. Because they did not wish their employers to learn of their spare-time activity, they chose the name Littlewood rather than Moores, this being the original surname of one of them, Harry Askham. At first the venture lost money, but John brought in his younger brother Cecil Moores (1903-1989) as manager. Three years later John Moores was able to give up telegraphy to run the football pool enterprise full time. In 1932 he founded the mail order side of the business, and in 1936 organized a division of chain stores. The first Littlewoods store opened in Blackpool the following year, and the firm went on to become the UK's biggest privately-owned retailer, with 135 stores in 2000, while the home-shopping business was by then second only to **Great Universal Stores**.

Litton (microwave ovens)

Litton Industries make office calculators and electronic cash registers, but they are still best known for their microwaves. The founder was not a Litton but was Charles B. "Tex" Thornton (1913-1981), born in north central Texas. As a teenager, he invested money from odd jobs in real estate. At 19 he opened a gas station and started dealing in cars. He developed a system of statistical controls for the US Air Force during World War II, and after the war became assistant general manager of Hughes Aircraft, a Howard Hughes company, in Los Angeles. For reasons that are not clear, Thornton left this concern in 1953 and with a colleague, Roy Ash, started a company called Electro Dynamics. In 1954, with a loan of $1.5 million from Wall Street, the two bought Litton Industries, Inc., a small electron-tube company owned by Charles V. Litton and founded in 1932. The company now bears his name and dates its founding from the year that Thornton and Ash took over the business, the first of many lucrative acquisitions.

Lladró (porcelain figurines)

The name is that of three Spanish brothers, Juan, Jose, and Vicente Lladró, who came from a family of market gardeners living near Valencia. Juan and Jose enrolled at the local school of arts and crafts, and Vicente later joined them to study sculpture. The three soon put into practice the techniques they learned by building a small kiln to make porcelain on the patio of their father's house. In the mid-1950s they started a manufacturing enterprise, making ceramic flowers and selling them to the decorative arts industry. They gradually built up their ceramics business, and the figurines and statuettes they produced began to become collectors' pieces. Today Lladró is a world leader in the manufacture of porcelain, and in 1988 a special Lladró Museum opened in New York.

Lloyd Loom (wicker furniture)

The name is that of Marshall B. Lloyd (1858-1927), born in St. Paul, Minnesota, the son of English immigrants who had originally settled in Canada. At age 14 Lloyd went to work in a country store, the first of a number of jobs that he combined with a string of inventions. A wire doormat that he devised in 1890 attracted the attention of the C.O. White Company. In exchange for his patents, Lloyd received an interest in the firm, becoming its president in 1894 and eventually purchasing it in 1900, when he renamed it the Lloyd Manufacturing Company. His inventions continued, one of the most notable being a mechanized process for producing wicker carriage bodies and later furniture. His successful Lloyd Loom line was finally introduced in 1922, and by 1940, ten million pieces of Lloyd Loom wicker furniture had been sold in the USA and UK.

Lloyds *(bank)*

The British bank with its logo of a prancing black horse and the date 1677 is named for its founder, Charles Lloyd, a Welshman born in Dolobran, Meifod, Montgomeryshire, in 1637. After studying at Jesus College, Oxford, Lloyd settled in Birmingham, where he became an ironmaster and founded his bank in the year stated. In its present form, however, the bank was established in Birmingham in 1765 by John Taylor (1711-1775), a Unitarian button maker, and Sampson Lloyd (1699-1779), a Quaker ironmaster, as Taylor and Lloyd's. The bank changed its name to Lloyds & Company in 1853 and eventually to Lloyds Bank Ltd. in 1889. The Sign of the Black Horse was originally that of a 17th-century London goldsmith, Humphrey Stokes, and although goldsmiths were the forerunners of modern bankers, Lloyds did not adopt the Black Horse for its own symbol until 1884. In 1995 Lloyds merged with the Trustee Savings Bank (TSB) to become Lloyds TSB.

Locke-Ober's *(restaurant)*

The fashionable Boston, Massachusetts, restaurant, noted for its Old World elegance, was founded in 1880 by Frank Locke and Louis F. Ober. It was originally known as the Winter Place Restaurant, from the alleyway where it is located. It then became Locke's, and finally Locke-Ober's. Custom was flagging at the close of the 20th century, when it was rumored that a well-known woman restaurateur was interested in taking over the former male bastion.

Lockheed *(aircraft and arms)*

The American company traces its origins to June 15, 1913, when two brothers, Allan Haines Lockheed (1889-1969) and his elder brother Malcolm Lockheed (1887-1958), born in Niles, California, the sons of a fruit grower, flew a seaplane of their own construction over San Francisco Bay. (The brothers originally bore the Scottish surname of Loughead, but changed it to Lockheed when people persisted in pronouncing it "log-head" or "loaf-head.") Three

years later they set up an aircraft company in Santa Barbara, working with designer Jack **Northrop**. Malcolm left the company in 1919 to market hydraulic automobile brakes, and Northrop left soon after to form his own company. Allan stayed on, however, to score a success with the Vega plane which Amelia Earhart later used in her solo flight across the Atlantic, and in 1931 he moved the company headquarters to Burbank, a suburb of Los Angeles, where they remain today.

Loctite *(superglue)*

The quick-acting glue was the invention of Dr. Vernon Krieble of Hartford, Connecticut. Working in the laboratories of Trinity College, he developed a liquid bonding resin that hardened in the absence of air. His wife christened the product "Loctite," for obvious reasons, and the new superglue was announced at the University Club, New York, on July 26, 1956. By 1975 sales had reached $67 million.

Loew's *(theaters and hotels)*

The American company, known also for its cigarettes, was founded in 1946 by brothers Laurence and Preston Tisch, on inheriting $125,000 from their father, a clothing manufacturer who ran children's summer camps. The two brothers bought a New Jersey resort hotel, and began adding other hotels to it. In 1959 Laurence Tisch began buying Loew's theaters from their owners, **MGM**, eventually acquiring the whole chain in 1960. The theaters themselves take their name from Marcus Loew (1870-1927), the son of a immigrant waiter from Vienna, who began his formal career as a show business entrepreneur with the opening of a nickelodeon in 1905. He went on to open a theater in Brooklyn in 1908 and then gradually moved from managing vaudeville theaters to owning and operating a string of movie palaces. By 1919 Loew's, Inc., ranked as a $25 million corporation traded on the New York Stock Exchange, and this is the year that the Loews Corporation of today regards as that of its own founding.

Log Cabin *(syrup)*

The brand of syrup, acquired by General Foods (*see* **Bird's**) in 1927, owes its origin to P.J.Towle, a grocer of St. Paul, Minnesota, who aimed to produce maple syrup at a price most people could afford. After experimenting by blending syrup with inexpensive sugar cane, he finally achieved the desired result in 1887. Now came the matter of marketing it. Towle first chose a sealed container to suggest the syrup's cleanliness and purity. Next a good name was needed. He thought of his boyhood hero, Abraham Lincoln, but soon decided against using the former president's name. Then he hit on the solution. Why not name the syrup "Log Cabin," a concept directly associated with Lincoln, and make the container in the shape of a log cabin? The ploy paid off, and the tin log cabin was soon familiar on the American scene.

Y Lolfa (publishers)

The idiosyncratic Welsh publishing house, its name meaning literally "The Lounge" (or more loosely "The Place of Nonsense") was founded by Robat Gruffudd at Tal-y-Bont, Cardiganshire, in 1966. It specializes in the production of books deemed to be too bawdy or too politically extreme to be risked by the more conventional Welsh publishers, but has also issued serious works, such as a series devoted to the works of young poets. Its most notorious publication is the annual magazine *Lol*, which carries satirical or even scurrilous stories about members of the Welsh establishment.

Lomo (cameras and mobile phones)

The Austrian cellphone had its origins in the *Lomo Kompakt*, a simple Russian camera similar to the **Brownie** mass-produced for the Soviet bloc in the Cold War era by LOMO (*Leningradskoye optiko-mekhanicheskoye ob'yedineniye*, "Leningrad Optical Engineering Combine"). In the early 1990s, two Viennese entrepreneurs, 33-year-old Wolfgang Stranzinger and 34-year-old Matthias Fiegl, discovered a stock of Lomos in a used-camera shop while vacationing in Prague. The pair recognized their potential, and in 1995 their Lomographic Society won an exclusive contract to sell up to 540,000 Lomos over 15 years. Together with the Swiss company Uboot, backed by Deutsche Telekom, they then developed it into a wireless mobile phone aimed at the younger consumer, launching in Europe and the USA in 2002.

Londis (supermarkets)

The British supermarket chain was formed in London in 1959 by a group of independent retailers under the full name London Independent Supermarkets. The present name is an abbreviation of this. There are now around 2,000 Londis stores throughout the UK.

Long John (whisky)

The blend of whisky takes its name from "Long" John Macdonald, a statuesque Scotsman who built Ben Nevis Distillery at Fort William, Scotland, in 1825. The Long John company name and the distillery eventually went separate ways, and after passing through several hands and a company name change to Long John International in 1971, the firm is now operated by Allied Distillers.

Longaberger (baskets)

The handmade maple baskets were the enterprise of David Longaberger (1934-1999), born in Dresden, Ohio, the son of a basketmaker. Despite not graduating from high school until the age of 21, as well as suffering from a stuttering problem, Longaberger carried on the tradition begun by his father, J.W. Longaberger, and in 1973 started a business making high-quality baskets. To celebrate the 25th anniversary of his company in 1998, Longaberger opened a new office building in the shape of a market basket, one of his firm's key designs.

Longines (watches)

The name is not that of the company founder but of the village near St. Imier, Switzerland, where Ernest Francillon and Jacques David opened their watch factory in 1867.

Longman (publishers)

The founder of the British publishing house was Thomas Longman (1699-1755), born in Bristol into a family active in the soap trade. Thomas's father died when the boy was only nine. When he was 17, he was apprenticed to John Osborn, a London bookseller, and later married his daughter. On completing his apprenticeship in 1724, Longman bought the business of John Taylor, a bookseller who had been the first publisher of Daniel Defoe's *Robinson Crusoe*. Taylor's premises were at the sign of the Ship and Black Swan in Paternoster Row, and were to remain Longman's head office for many years. (The sign gave the ship that became Longman's logo.) Within a few months, Osborn had joined his former apprentice as partner, and they traded as "J. Osborn and T. Longman" at the Sign of the Ship. On the death of his father-in-law in 1734, Longman became the sole owner of the business. The Longman family headed the firm for seven generations, concluding with Mark Longman (1916-1972). Longman is now an imprint of **Pearson** Education, an enterprise created in 1998 following Pearson's acquisition of **Simon & Schuster**'s educational business.

Longs (drugstores)

The US company, based in Walnut Creek, California, dates from 1938, when Marion Skaggs, founder of the business that became **Safeway**, lent his son-in-law, Joseph M. Long, and Long's brother, Thomas, $15,000 to start a drugstore business. Over the next 40 years, the Longs chain grew from "a hole in the wall in Oakland" to 108 stores in California, a dozen in Hawaii, and one each in Alaska, Arizona, and Oregon.

Lonrho (mining)

The British company originated in 1909 as the London and Rhodesian Mining and Land Company, with the present shorter version of this adopted in 1963. In the 1970s Lonrho expanded to become one of Britain's largest companies, with worldwide interests in manufacturing, agricultural, and service industries.

Lord, Cyril see **Cyril Lord**

L'Oréal (cosmetics)

France's most successful company was founded by the chemist Eugène Schueller, who was asked by a Paris hairdresser to come up with some new coloring products. Schueller quit his job and started a business making hair dyes at home. In 1907 he registered the name L'Oréal, a respelling of French *l'auréole*, "the aureole," from Latin *aureola corona*, "golden crown." Schueller ran the firm until his death in 1957, when his daughter, Liliane Bettencourt, became its major shareholder.

Lorillard (cigarettes)

The oldest American tobacco manufacturer in the country, famous for its "Old Gold" and **Kent** cigarettes, dates its origin to 1760, when a French immigrant, Pierre Lorillard (1742-c.1778), opened a snuff factory in a small rented house on Chatham Street in Manhattan, New York City. After Lorillard was killed by British troops seeking refuge in the house, the business was taken over by his sons Peter and George in 1792. For many years they produced pipe tobacco, cigars, plug chewing tobacco, and snuff, but tobacco for "roll-your-own" cigarettes was introduced in 1860 and cigarettes themselves were being manufactured by the 1880s. From the 1890s to 1911 Lorillard was part of the American Tobacco Company (*see* **American Brands**) but became independent again when the US Court of Appeals dissolved the trust. The firm was bought by the Loews Corporation (*see* **Loew's**) in 1969.

Lot (airline)

The principal Polish airline, founded in 1929, has a name that is simply the Polish word for "flight," although it also occurs as part of the full name, Polskie linie lotnicze ("Polish Airlines").

Lothrop see **D. Lothrop**

Lotus (automobiles)

The man behind the British sports car was Colin Chapman (1928-1982), born in Richmond, Surrey, the son of a licensed caterer. He gained a degree in civil engineering at University College, London, when he already displayed an interest in fast cars and flying. The former won the day when in 1948 he built a two-seater car based on the **Austin** Seven known as the Lotus Mark I. The reasons for the choice of name were always kept private. The first Lotus production car was the Six of 1953 and the first road car was the sleek Lotus Elite, launched in 1958.

Louis Vuitton (luxury leather goods)

Louis Vuitton (1821-1892) was born in Anchay in the Jura Mountains of eastern France. In 1835 he set out on foot for Paris, taking casual work on the way, and arrived in 1837, when he was apprenticed to a packing-case maker. Vuitton gradually gained experience in making and packing custom-built trunks and in 1854 opened his first shop, on the rue Neuve-des-Capucines (now the rue des Capucines). Here he improved on the trunk designs then in use, introducing a flat-top trunk instead of the traditional dome-shaped one. Commissions began to arrive, and in 1875 Vuitton made special trunks, including a bed trunk, for the French explorer Pierre Savorgnan de Brazza, founder of Brazzaville, capital of the Republic of Congo. In 1859 Vuitton moved his workshop to the Parisian suburb of Asnières. His son, Georges Vuitton (1857-1936), took over the business in 1880 and expansion followed. An outlet opened in London, England, in 1885 and travel luggage was first sold at **Wanamaker** in the USA in 1898. The firm has since specialized in luxury leather goods, and in 1987 the Louis Vuitton Group merged with **Moët Hennessy** to form LVMH. The name was entered in the US Patent Office *Official Gazette* of May 18, 1976: "For luggage and ladies' handbags," and in the *Trade Marks Journal* of February 6, 1980 for: "Handbags, suitcases, trunks, umbrellas, pocket wallets, purses, [etc.]."

Löwenbräu *(beer)*

The well-known brewery in Munich, Germany, claims to date from 1383 and has a name translating as "lion brew." There are a number of lesser-known breweries of the same name dotted around the country.

Lowe's *(lumber and building materials stores)*

The US business dates from 1945, when two former GIs, Jim Lowe and his brother-in-law, Carl Buchan, opened a hardware store in North Wilkesboro, North Carolina. In 1949 they bought a lumber yard in nearby Sparta, but in 1952 Lowe sold out to his partner. The company's slogan, "Lowe's Low Prices," appealed to Buchan so much that he decided not to change the name.

Lucas *(lamps and electric batteries)*

The founder of the British company was Joseph Lucas (1834-1902), born in Birmingham the son of a metalworker and plater. At first he followed his father's trade, becoming an electroplater journeyman. In 1860 Lucas set up his own business, buying and selling mainly hollow-ware (pots, kettles, and so on). He also sold kerosene (paraffin) from door to door. In 1869 his name appeared in *White's Birmingham Directory* as "lamp and oil dealer." In the early 1870s, Lucas began specializing in making oil

and candle lamps and lanterns, and within a year or two introduced his first bicycle lamp, "The King of the Road," which was on sale in 1875 for the penny-farthing. The bicycle boom was good for his business, as was the subsequent rise of the motor car. Today the company still has its head office in Birmingham.

Lucent *(systems and technology)*

The US company was formed in 1995 when **AT&T** voluntarily split itself into three publicly held companies. (One retained the name AT&T, while the other reverted to its old name of **NCR**.) The name Lucent was adopted in 1996 from the dictionary word (from Latin *lucens*, *lucentis*, "shining") in its sense of "marked by clarity" or "glowing with light." According to the company's first chairman and chief executive officer, Harry Schacht, the name "suggests clarity of thought, purpose, and vision, and had a technological feel."

Lucite *(transparent plastic)*

The name of the plastic, which is made of the same material as **Perspex**, was entered by **Du Pont**, its manufacturers, in the US Patent Office *Official Gazette* of July 6, 1937. It derives from Latin *lux*, *lucis*, "light," and the chemical suffix "-ite." *See also* **Plexiglas**.

Lucky *(food stores)*

The US company traces its origins to 1931, when the Depression prompted six stores near San Francisco to team up and form a business called Peninsula Stores. Four years later they added a store in nearby Berkeley. By 1947 the chain had 29 outlets and was doing well enough to have changed its name to Lucky.

Lucky Strike *(cigarettes)*

The name was originally used in 1856 by Dr. R.A. Patterson of Richmond, Virginia, for a sliced plug tobacco. The time was that of the Gold Rush, when a "lucky strike" was what all prospectors sought. The American Tobacco Company (*see* **American Brands**) reintroduced the name for their blended tobacco in 1916 and for cigarettes in 1917, the latter in answer to **R.J. Reynolds's Camel**. The name became familiar nationwide from a number of slogans, such as "Reach for a Lucky instead of a sweet," "Luckies are gentle on my throat," "With men who know tobacco best, it's Luckies two to one," "Lucky Strike green has gone to war" (in World War II), "Lucky Strike means fine tobacco." The last of these was so well known that it was shortened to initials: "L.S.M.F.T."

Lucozade *(tonic drink)*

The drink has a name based on "glucose," its chief constituent, with "-ade" a suffix patterned on that of "lemonade" or some similar fruit drink. Lucozade was developed in the 1930s by William W. Hunter, an English chemist (druggist) at the shop of W.W. Owen and Son in Newcastle upon Tyne, opened by William Owen in 1847. Hunter's daughter had contracted jaundice, then a prevalent disease, and he was prompted to formulate a carbonated drink containing as much glucose as possible, flavored with orange and lemon oils. He sold his product to **Beecham** in 1938. The name was entered in the *Trade Marks Journal* of November 12, 1930.

Luden's *(cough drops)*

William H. Luden (1859-1949), born in Reading, Pennsylvania, started making candy in his mother's kitchen in 1881. His first product was moshie, a Pennsylvania Dutch confection made of corn syrup and brown sugar. A few years later, Luden added cough drops to his line, coloring them amber to distinguish them from the many red lozenges then on the market. He promoted his product in magazine ads that announced their effectiveness not only in checking coughs but also in "sweetening the breath and clearing the head." The company is still located in Reading today.

Lufthansa *(airline)*

The German airline, organized in Cologne in 1953, was the successor to the Deutsche Luft Hansa (DLH), founded in 1926, and itself the result of a merger between Deutscher Aero Lloyd, founded in 1924, and Junkers Luftverkehr, formed in 1921. The airline's name represents modern German *Luft*, "air," and Old High German *hansa*, "company," as for the historically famous Hanseatic League, the medieval association of north German cities.

Luger *(pistol)*

The make of German automatic pistol takes its name from George Luger (1849-1923), the Austrian firearms expert who invented it in

1898. It was first manufactured in 1900 for both military and commercial use and from 1908 to 1938 was the standard pistol of the German armed forces. It is also known as the **Parabellum.**

Luminal *(sedative)*

The proprietary name for phenobarbital probably derives from Latin *lumen, luminis,* "light," translating the "phen-" of "phenobarbital" (from Greek *phaino-*,"shining"), and the common pharmaceutical suffic "-al." The name was entered by **Bayer** in the *Trade Marks Journal* of March 20, 1912 for: "A medicine for human use as a sedative and hypnotic."

Lunn Poly *(travel agents)*

The founder of the British firm was Dr. (later Sir) Henry Lunn (1859-1939), born in Horncastle, Lincolnshire. On completing his education, he entered Headingley College, Leeds, to train as a Methodist minister, becoming ordained in 1886. He went to India as a medical missionary, but bad health obliged him to return to England in 1888. He subsequently became involved in arranging conferences in Europe for religious leaders, and this led him to examine the various methods of travel that could be used, especially for parties. In 1892 he began to arrange travel tours in Europe, at first mainly religious or educational in nature, then more generally for holidaymakers. In 1909 the firm of Sir Henry Lunn was formed, and existed until the 1960s, when it merged with another travel organization, the Polytechnic Touring Association, which itself had been founded in 1888 to provide travel facilities for students of the Regent Street Polytechnic, London. The present name of the company results from this merger.

Lurex *(artificial fabric)*

Lurex is a type of yarn or fabric that incorporates a distinctive glittering metallic thread. Its name was entered by the Dobeckmun Company of Cleveland, Ohio, in the US Patent Office *Official Gazette* of October 16, 1945, and although probably arbitrary even so suggests "lurid" or "alluring."

Lurpak *(butter)*

The butter is of Danish origin, and takes its name from the lur, a long, curved Bronze Age trumpet used in Scandinavian countries for calling cattle. A picture of the instrument appears on the pack.

Lux *(toilet soap)*

The name was originally used for the soap flakes introduced in 1899 by the British manufacturer William Hesketh Lever (*see* **Unilever**). At first they were called "Sunlight Flakes," after **Sunlight** soap, but they were soon renamed "Lux," a word that is not only Latin for "light," reflecting the "Sunlight," as it were, while evoking airy cleanliness, but also suggests "luxury." The name was probably proposed by Lever's patent agent in Liverpool, W.P. Thompson.

Luxo *see* **Anglepoise**

Luxottica *(spectacles)*

The Italian firm, with a name based on Latin *lux*, "light," and Italian *ottica*, "optics," was founded in 1961 in Agordo near Belluno, northeastern Italy, by Leonardo Del Vecchio, initially with a staff of just 14. By the end of the century, with a staff of 2,000 and Del Vecchio reputedly the richest man in Italy, Luxottica had made many key acquisitions, including the prestigious **Ray-Ban** name.

LVMH *see* (1) **Louis Vuitton**; (2) **Moët et Chandon**

Lycra *(elastic fabric)*

The artificial fabric was introduced in 1958 by **Du Pont** and became popular for use in underwear and sportswear. Its name, suggesting "acrylic," was entered in the US Patent Office *Official Gazette* of November 18, 1958 and the *Trade Marks Journal* of April 8, 1959. The first garment made of Lycra was the "Little Godiva" step-in girdle, introduced in 1960 by the Warner Lingerie Company. The following year **Berlei** adopted it for their brassieres.

Lydia Pinkham's Herbal Compound *(proprietary medicine)*

The name is that of Lydia E. Pinkham (1819-1883), born Lydia Estes in Lynn, Massachusetts, a farmer's daughter. In 1843 she married Isaac Pinkham, a widower living precariously on the profits of his real estate speculations. When he finally went broke in the panic of 1873, the family hit on the idea of marketing a home remedy developed by Lydia Pinkham to treat "female complaints." In 1876, Pinkham registered the label and trademark for "Lydia Pinkham's Vegetable Compound," a medicine that gained a foothold in the 1880s, largely through Pinkham's imaginative newspaper advertising. Lydia Pinkham's picture in the advertisements and on the label won her a place in American folklore, and the "Vegetable Compound" competed effectively with its rivals. Pinkham heirs sold the company in 1968, but Numark Laboratories acquired the medicine in 1987 and now markets it as "Lydia Pinkham's Herbal Compound." Pinkham's picture still adorns the bottle, although the medicine today bears little resemblance to her original formula.

Lyle & Scott *("Y-Fronts")*

The Scottish knitwear company was founded in 1874 by William Lyle (1833-1903) and Walter Scott (d.1893). Lyle was born in Hawick, the son of a hosiery warehouseman. He began his working career with a local tweed manufacturer before joining the hosiery firm of Wilson and Armstrong, staying 13 years with that company as manager. He then decided to set up business on his own account. His partner, Walter Scott, had similarly been a hosiery manager. By the 1870s there was an increasing demand for woolen underwear, as well as hosiery, and the two men turned this to good account. Their business increased and expanded, but did not become a limited company until 1897, eight years after the retirement of Lyle and five years after the death of Scott. The **Y-Fronts** for which the company is now best known were first produced in the 1930s.

Lymeswold *(cheese)*

The British make of mild blue soft cheese was marketed from 1982 to 1992. Its name, unfortunately suggesting "slime" and "mold," may have contributed to its uncertain reception, although it was apparently intended to evoke "limes" and "wold," as words of rustic imagery. Its actual inspiration may have been the village of Wymeswold, near Loughborough, Leicestershire, a county famous for its cheese. Lymeswold itself was actually manufactured at Aston in Cheshire. The name was entered in the *Trade Marks Journal* of December 30, 1982.

Lyons *(foods and teashops)*

The origins of the British company go back to Montague Gluckstein (1854-1922), son of a cigar dealer in London's East End. Working with his father, tobacconist Samuel Gluckstein (1821-1873), he became interested in the possibilities of running a catering business that was more efficient than the existing catering trade, whose standards were very low. He discussed his idea with his brothers, who agreed to start a catering venture with him so long as the family name was not associated with it. Gluckstein went ahead and secured the catering rights for the Newcastle Jubilee Exhibition of 1887, taking as partner a distant relative to negotiate with the exhibition authorities. The partner was Joseph Nathaniel Lyons (1847-1917), then running an exhibition stall in Liverpool. He himself was the son of an itinerant watchseller, and had begun his career as a watercolor painter. But he was happy both to support Gluckstein and to lend his name for the enterprise. In 1894 Lyons became chairman of the company that was formed in his name to operate restaurants and teashops, and J. Lyons & Co. Ltd. went on to give many familiar names and institutions, such as Lyons' Corner Houses, "Nippies" (the waitresses who served in them, so called from their speed and nimbleness), **Lyons Maid** ice cream, and the group of brewers, vintners, and hoteliers that became Allied-Lyons in 1981 following the acquisition of the company by Allied Breweries, itself formed in 1961 by the merger of **Ind Coope**, **Tetley** Walker, and **Ansells**.

Lyons Maid *(ice cream)*

The name combines that of the manufacturer, J. **Lyons**, with that of their top-selling ice cream in 1955, "Pola Maid," so called as it was made in "pole" lengths before being sliced and packed. But there is also a pun on "polar," of course, just as "maid" puns on "made."

Lysol *(disinfectant)*

The solution of cresol and soap, formerly used as a disinfectant, derives its name from Greek *lusis*, "loosening," and the "-ol" suffix meaning "oil." The name was entered in the *Trade Marks Journal* of December 8, 1909, but was already in use some 20 years before this.

Maalox *(antacid)*

The antacid preparation, for the relief of indigestion, contains dried aluminum hydroxide and magnesium hydroxide. Hence its name, which derives from letters in "*ma*gnesium" and "*al*uminum hydr*ox*ide." It was entered in the US Patent Office *Official Gazette of* June 26, 1951.

M•A•C *(cosmetics)*

M•A•C (Make-up Art Cosmetics) was launched in 1985 from a Toronto, Canada, hairdressing salon by make-up artist and photographer Frank Toskan and his business and life partner Frank Angelo. Its success took off soon after, when the product was adopted by such models and media stars as Linda Evangelista and Madonna, the latter wearing the firm's popular "Russian Red" lipstick. With a global status enhanced by its Canadian drag-queen origins, the brand came to the attention of **Estée Lauder**, who bought a 51 percent stake in 1994 and completed the acquisition in 1998. Toskan then resigned as creative director, saying he no longer wished to be involved in the enterprise he and his partner (who had died after a heart attack the year before) had built together.

M&B *see* **May & Baker**

M&Ms *see* **Mars**

Mac Fisheries *(fish and fresh-food supermarkets)*

The British stores of this name were familiar for much of the 20th century. They owe their origin to Lord Leverhulme, who gave the name of **Unilever**. In 1919, as a philanthropic gesture, he decided to help develop the Scottish island of Lewis and Harris. He bought a herring-drifting firm called Bix and then purchased about 300 shops in which to sell the fish they were supposed to catch. But what to call them? Lord Leverhulme considered several names, among them "Silent Deep," "Island Deep," "Lipsco" (standing for "Lewis Island Preserved Specialities Company"), "Silvascale," "Wavecrest," "Deepcast," "Snack," "Shoal," and "Siren." The basis "Mac" for a Scottish industry was then suggested to him, and he at first considered prefixing each kind of fish with this, as "Mac Herring," "Mac Cod," "Mac Lobster," and the like. Fortunately, he did not take this idea further, but instead used "Mac" alone for the shops. After a short period as "The

Island Fisheries," Mac Fisheries was thus incorporated in 1919 with its headquarters in London. The shops flourished for many years, but by the 1980s were becoming commercially unviable, and Unilever began to close them. The small town and fishing port of Leverburgh on Harris remains, however, as a reminder of Lord Leverhulme's gallant effort to transform the former village of Obbe into a major fishing port.

The Macallan *(whisky)*

The name is both a surname and a place-name, the latter giving the former. The whisky takes its name from the Macallan family, who had a farm of the same name by the Spey River near Craigellachie, Banffshire. There were formerly many illicit stills in the district, but the Macallans registered theirs in 1824, and were one of the first families to do so. The distillery was bought and extended in 1892 by Roderick Kemp, whose descendants owned the company until it was acquired by Highland Distilleries in 1996.

Macanudo *(cigars)*

The brand was founded in Jamaica in 1868 with a name that is colloquial Spanish for "great," "terrific," "dandy," or any similar expression of enthusiastic approval. It is now made by General Cigar in both Jamaica and the Dominican Republic.

Macdonald *(chocolate-coated crackers, or biscuits)*

The British firm takes its name from William Macdonald (1875-1940), who in 1920, when a traveling salesman, set up on his own as a food commission agent, selling candy and similar products for a variety of companies. He first made chocolate-covered biscuits (crackers) in Glasgow in 1927. **Penguins** came after World War II, with other distinctive lines following, such as "Munchmallow" in 1950, "Bandit" in 1959, and "Taxi" in 1960.

Mace *(chemical spray)*

The irritant chemical, sprayed from an aerosol to disable attackers, derives its name from letters in the chemical compound involved, *m*ethylchloroform choro*ace*tophenone, at the same time suggesting "mace" in the sense of a heavy staff or club. It was entered by the General Ordnance Equipment Corporation of Pittsburgh, Pennsylvania, in the US Patent Office *Official Gazette* of November 22, 1966 as "Chemical Mace" with the note and description: "The word 'Chemical' is disclaimed apart from its use with the mark. For Non-Explosive Defensive Weapons in the Nature of Tear Gas Packaged in Aerosol Containers." The name was first filed on November 26, 1965.

Macfarlane & Lang *(crackers, or biscuits)*

In 1817 James Lang, a Scot, opened a small bakery and shop in Glasgow. There he was joined by his nephew, John Macfarlane (1824-1908), who took over the business after his uncle's death in 1841 and called the firm John Macfarlane & Sons. The premises continued to be known as "Lang's Bread Factory," however, so to allow for this, the name was altered to Macfarlane Lang & Co. The company is now part of United Biscuits.

MacGibbon & Kee *(publishers)*

James MacGibbon (1912-2000) was born at Hamilton near Glasgow, Scotland, the son of a Church of Scotland minister. He was educated at Glasgow Academy and Fettes College, but when he was 17 his mother unexpectedly removed him from the latter school and send him to work with the British branch of **Putnam**, where he eventually became managing director. In 1947 he left Putnam to start his own publishing business, taking as partner Robert Kee (b.1919). The two men remained close friends, but Kee soon dropped out of the business and MacGibbon continued to run it alone. In 1965 the firm was sold off to the property tycoon Howard Samuel, when MacGibbon became a literary agent. He later worked with other publishers, including **Gollancz** and **David & Charles**.

Macintosh *(personal computers)*

The popular computer, the first to replace typed commands with a graphical user interface (a mouse for pointing and clicking at icons and windows), was launched by **Apple** Computer, Inc., in 1984, and was so called by Jef Raskin, one of the firm's engineers, for the abundance of apples of this variety in Washington State. The name began as a code name for the project. The apple itself is named for John McIntosh (b.1777), a Canadian from Ontario, who discovered it as a chance seedling in eastern Ontario in 1811. It is is now regarded as Canada's national apple, but not surprisingly has strayed south of the border, which is why it is found in Washington.

Mack *(trucks)*

In 1900 John M. Mack (*c*.1864-1924) and his brothers, William and Augustus, built one of the world's first gasoline-powered buses, which they sold to the operator of a New York sightseeing service. In 1905 the three men moved to Allentown, Pennsylvania, where they formed the Mack Brothers Motor Car Co. with John Mack as president. Soon the Macks were joined by two more brothers, Joseph and Charles, and began manufacturing gasoline-powered trucks. Their business grew steadily, and in 1911 the **Morgan** bank merged Mack Brothers into the International Motor Company, a truck-making holding company. Following the merger, all the Macks except William left the firm and had nothing more to do with the trucks that bore their name. The name was entered by the International Motor Company of New York in the US Patent Office *Official Gazette* of January 4, 1921, with a claim of use since about October 13, 1911.

Mackeson's *(beer)*

England's best-known bottled sweet stout, marketed by **Whitbread**, was first brewed in 1907 by the firm of Mackeson & Co. of Hythe, Kent. At that time it was claimed to be a tonic for invalids, as it contained milk sugar (lactose), and was accordingly known as "Mackeson's Milk Stout." In 1946 the British government banned the use of the term as misleading, although Whitbread maintain the connection by showing a milk churn on the label.

Mackie *see* **White Horse**

Mackinlay *(whisky)*

Charles Mackinlay (1795-1867) set up as a whisky merchant in Leith, near Edinburgh, Scotland, in 1815. It was only in 1850, however, that he produced his own distinct blend, the "Original Mackinlay." The distillery is still in Leith and still in the hands of the Mackinlay family.

Mackintosh *(toffee)*

John Mackintosh (1868-1920) was born in Derbyshire, England, the son of a cotton spinner, with his family moving to Halifax, Yorkshire, only a few months after his birth. He started work as a "half-timer" in a Halifax cotton mill at the age of ten, becoming a "full-timer" at 13. In 1890 his father died, leaving John to support the whole family. Soon after, John married a weaver's daughter who was herself working as a confectioner's assistant. The newly married couple set up a pastrycook's shop, with John still going to the mill while his wife Violet made and sold cakes, pies, and other pastry products. The two decided to settle on a particular line, and chose toffee, the difference being that the Mackintoshes' toffee would be a *blend* of traditional hard, brittle, English butterscotch and soft, imported, American caramel. They sold the result as "Mackintosh's Celebrated Toffee," and advertised free samples. The response to their advertising was so great that they issued a second advertisement: "On Saturday last you were eating MACKINTOSH'S TOFFEE at our expense. Next Saturday pay us another visit and eat it at your expense." The public did, in their thousands, so that in that year, 1890, Mackintosh's toffee was established. Mackintosh merged with **Rowntree** in 1986. *See also* **Quality Street**.

Maclaren *(baby buggies)*

Owen Finlay Maclaren (d.1978) was a retired British aeronautical engineer and former test pilot in the 1960s, when he decided to redesign the heavy and ungainly pushchair in which he wheeled his young grandchild around. He used modern lightweight materials, such as tubular aluminum, to build a structure that could carry even a large child yet fold into a small space. He was granted a patent for his invention in 1965 and the first buggy, manufactured in converted riding stables, went on commercial sale two years later. In 1992 his company, Maclaren Ltd., was chosen as the official supplier of baby buggies to all three Disney resorts.

Maclean *(toothpaste)*

The man behind the coincidentally apt name ("Did you Maclean your teeth today?") was New Zealand-born Alex C. Maclean. After joining a gold rush in Australia, Maclean went to the United States, where he ultimately became a salesman for **Spirella** corsets. He then went to England to set up the Spirella business there, but after a quarrel left the company and in 1919 started his own business making "own-brand" products for chemists. In the course of his work, Maclean and his three sons, with the help of a chemist, decided to market sixpenny tubes of toothpaste, and in 1930 he first produced "Maclean's Peroxide Tooth Paste." This was his own brand of white toothpaste, as distinct from the pink toothpaste, also called "Peroxide," that Maclean was then producing for the chemists. It was sold widely by **Woolworths**, which until then had stocked only **Colgate** toothpaste, and was effectively the launch of Maclean's own brand, which reached the market at the very time when people were becoming increasingly conscious about the care of their teeth. In 1938 the product passed to **Beecham**.

Macmillan *(publishers)*

The UK publishing house takes its name from its founder, Daniel Macmillan (1813-1857), born a farmer's son on the Scottish island of Arran. He quit school at age 11 and was apprenticed to a bookseller and binder in the town of Irvine, where the family had moved. In 1931, on completion of his training, he started work in a Glasgow bookshop. Two years later he went to London, but rejected an offer of employment with the publishers Simpkin & Marshall in favor of a post with a Cambridge bookseller. Macmillan spent three years in Cambridge before returning to London. In 1843 he started his own bookselling business there in a shop in Aldersgate Street. By the end of that year he had earned enough to take over the Cambridge bookshop, and a year later he issued his first publisher's catalog under the name Macmillan & Co., the "Co." being his younger brother Alexander, who now ran the London business. In 1863, after Daniel's death, Alexander moved the business from Cambridge to London, where the manager of the head office was Robert Bowes, of **Bowes & Bowes**. British prime minister Harold Macmillan (1894-1986) was Daniel Macmillan's grandson. In 1995, Verlagsgruppe Georg von Holtzbrinck, a major German publisher, acquired a majority stake in the Macmillan Group.

Macy's *(department store)*

The New York store, with its many branches elsewhere in the USA, was founded by Rowland Hussey Macy (1822-1877), born on Nantucket Island, Massachusetts, the son of a merchant ship captain turned bookstore owner. At the age of 15 he went to sea on a whaler, where he was tattooed with a red star that was later adopted as Macy's distinctive trademark. On his return, he opened a dry-goods store in Boston. It failed, however, so he had to try his luck elsewhere. He eventually had success in 1858, when he persuaded a man to lend him $20,000 and opened a store in lower Manhattan. Business took off, and the store thrived. In 1888 the store passed to the Straus family (*see* **Abraham & Straus**), who ran it until 1968. Macy's now occupies an entire block on 34th Street, New York City, and for many years was physically the largest single store in the country.

Madame C.J. Walker *(hair preparations)*

Madame C.J. Walker (1867-1919) was born Sarah Breedlove in Delta, Louisiana, the daughter of a sharecropper. She was left an orphan at the age of six, when she lived with her sister in Vicksburg, Mississippi. In 1881, at the age of 14, she married Moses McWilliams, but he was killed in 1887 during a race riot, leaving her a destitute 20-year-old with a two-year-old child. Leaving Mississippi, Breedlove headed up to St. Louis, where she became a washerwoman. Toiling daily over hot wash tubs, her body assaulted by the steaming vapors of chemical and fumes, Sarah Breedlove began to lose her hair. She began experimenting with the chemicals she used, hoping to find a preparation that would aid in the care and grooming of the hair and skin of black women like herself. Around the turn of the 20th century, she finally came up with a new hair care formula, which met with some success. In 1905 Breedlove moved to Denver, where she met Charles J. Walker, a newspaperman and publicist, who gave her tips for advertising her product. The two were soon married, and with astute advertising and prominent promotion, it was only a matter of time before "Madame C.J. Walker" was operating the largest black-owned business in the United States.

Maersk *(container ships)*

The Danish shipping company was founded in 1904 by Arnold Peter Møller (1876-1965) and his father, Peter Mærsk Møller, whose middle name came from his mother, born Kiersten Pedersdatter Mærsk (1808-1875) into a family originating in Ballum, southern Jutland. The firm was originally Aktieselskabet Dampskibsselskabet Svendborg ("Svendborg Steamship Company"), but in 1928 the Maersk name was adopted for the liner service Maersk Line. The firm's parent company, AP Møller Group, is now based in Copenhagen and still effectively controlled by the Møller family.

Maggs *(rare books)*

The London, England, firm of rare book and manuscript sellers was founded by Uriah Maggs (1832-1913), a Westcountryman who came to London as a newsagent and bookseller and who opened his first shop in Westbourne Terrace in about 1853. A few years later he moved to Church Street, Paddington, where in about 1870 he issued his first catalog of secondhand books "ancient and modern, in all classes of literature." When he retired in 1894 the business was taken over by his two sons, Benjamin and Henry, and became Maggs Bros., as it still is today, although now with a head office in Berkeley Square.

Magic Eye *(cathode ray tube)*

The name of the miniature cathode ray tube, used as a tuning indicator on a radio receiver, was entered by the **RCA** Manufacturing Company, Inc., in the US Patent Office *Official Gazette* of October 6, 1936: "For radio receiving sets of the type equipped with cathode ray tubes for resonance indication and accessories and parts thereof."

Magic Marker *(marker pen)*

The name of the felt-tipped pen containing a tube of quick-drying ink was entered by its manufacturers, Speedry Products, Inc., of Richmond Hill, New York, in the US Patent Office *Official Gazette* of December 4, 1956 with the following disclaimer, description, and note of first use: "Applicant disclaims the term 'Marker' apart from the mark as a whole. For Felt Nib Marking Pens Comprising Small Containers for Such Ink, Equipped with Caps and having Felt Nibs at their Ends for Mark-ing. First use on or about Sept. 1, 1952." The name was doubtless mainly devised to attract young purchasers, since the marker's distinctive features are not all that unusual.

Magnum *(handgun)*

The gun so called fires cartridges that are more powerful than its caliber would suggest. Hence the name, from Latin *magnum*, "great," entered by **Smith & Wesson** in the US Patent Office *Official Gazette* of March 26, 1935, with a claim of use since December 28, 1934.

Malathion *(insecticide)*

The insecticide, used chiefly in the house and garden, contains diethyl *mal*eate and a *thio*-acid. Hence the name, entered by the American **Cyanamid** Company in the US Patent Office *Official Gazette* of April 14, 1953, but also registered as a generic (nonproprietary) name, enabling it to be spelled with a small initial. The original name proposed was "malathon," but this was not adopted for reasons explained in a statement issued in 1953 by the Interdepartmental Committee on Pest Control, Bureau of Entomological and Plant Quarantine, US Department of Agriculture:

> On January 30, 1952 the Interdepartmental Committee on Pest Control approved the name "malathon" as coined name for O,O-dimethyl diothiphosphate of diethyl mercaptosuccinate. Because of difficulty encountered in the trade-marking of the name selected at first the commercial sponsor, American Cyanamid Co., decided to change the name to "malathion." The American Chemical Society and the American Medical Association are agreeable to the change. Malathion has been registered with the Trade-Mark Division and released for general use. On March 27, 1953, the Interdepartmental Committee on Pest Control approved the name "malathion" as a coined (generic) name for the chemical in question.

Malev *(airline)*

Hungary's principal airline was founded in 1946 as Magyar Légiközlekedési Vállalat ("Hungarian Air Traffic Company") and adopted its present acronymic name in 1954.

Malibu *(liqueur)*

The liqueur, a blend of Caribbean white rum with coconut extracts, gained popularity in the 1980s following the growth of tourism in the Caribbean islands. Its name, however, more readily evokes the beach resort of Malibu, California, noted for its business and entertainment personalities.

Maltesers *(chocolates)*

The malted milk chocolate balls were first marketed by **Mars** in the mid-1930s. Their name is obviously based on "malt" but perhaps was also designed to evoke the dark-brown skin of the Maltese. It also contains the letters of Mars' own name. The name was entered in the *Trade Marks Journal* of October 28, 1959.

Mama's and Papa's *(baby carriages and pushchairs)*

The British company, based in Huddersfield, began after Luisa Scacchetti (b.1951) became pregnant in 1979 and was dismayed at the choice of baby carriages in Britain. She flew to her native Italy to buy one and when she returned it proved so popular that she and her husband, David (b.1952), started a business to import nursery products. Hence the (Italianate) name.

MAN *(trucks)*

The name of the German trucks is the abbreviation of Maschinen Augsburg-Nürnberg ("Augsburg-Nürnberg Machines"), a company founded in 1898 that originally made diesel engines. It built its first diesel-engined trucks in the 1920s and began selling trucks in the UK in 1974 through MAN-VW Trucks and Bus, a division of the **Volkswagen/Audi** auto sales company. The Volkswagen connection was no accident, as a jointly developed range of medium-weight trucks was produced by the two companies.

Mandarine Napoléon *(liqueur)*

The type of curaçao, made with the skins of tangerines, was launched in 1892 by a Belgian distiller, Louis Schmidt, who while pursuing some chemical research came across the correspondence of the French chemist Antoine François de Fourcroy (1755-1809). The latter had found favor with Napoleon, whose nightly indulgence was a liqueur made by steeping tangerine peel in cognac. Hence the name, from French *mandarine*, "tangerine," and the emperor's name.

Mandrax *(sedative drug)*

The drug, containing metaqualone and diphenhydramine hydrochloride, was launched in the 1960s. Its name suggests "mandrake," if only from that plant's former use as a hypnotic, but it may well be arbitrary. It was entered by Roussel-Uclaf of Paris, France, in the *Trade Marks Journal* of April 19, 1963. *Cp.* **Quaalude**.

Manfields *(footwear)*

The founder of the British shoeshop chain was Philip Manfield (1819-1899), born in Bristol a cordwainer's son. He began his career as an apprentice shoe closer in Bristol, learning to "close" boots and shoes by joining their uppers together. In 1844 he came to Northampton with £100 in savings, and finding it hard to obtain employment there, invested his money in a new factory, taking on outworkers, as was the tradition, to do the basic shoe and bootmaking. His business did well enough for him to transfer to a larger factory in Regent Street, Northampton, in 1849, where it remained for 20 years. The first shop to sell Manfield's shoes, however, did not open until the early 1880s. A hundred years later there were over 200 Manfield shoeshops and store concessions throughout the UK, as well as branches in continental Europe, where the first Paris shop had opened as early as 1889. Thus from inauspicious beginnings, Manfield developed one of the dominant footwear manufacturing and distribution firms in both Britain and Europe.

Manischewitz *(matzo and wine)*

When Rabbi Dov Ber Manischewitz (1857-1914) arrived in Cincinnati in the mid-1880s, he was concerned at the paucity of kosher foods in the city. He accordingly started a small matzo bakery in the spring of 1888. Unlike other matzo bakers, the rabbi installed new gas-fired ovens, so gaining control over the baking process. His reputation grew, so that he began supplying Jewish communities in other cities. He was succeeded in his firm by three generations of his family, beginning with his son, Hirsch Manischewitz (1891-1943), and they gradually branched out into other products, including the popular Manischewitz wines.

Mannesmann *(iron and steel)*

The German corporation was founded in Düsseldorf in 1890 as Mannesmannroehren-Werke ("Mannesmann Pipe Works") by Reinhard Mannesmann (1856-1922), and soon became a leading manufacturer of steel tubing. The company subsequently diversified into data processing equipment and precision instruments, and in 1999, as a major telecommunications concern, took over **Orange**.

Manolo *(women's shoes)*

This is the short name in fashion circles for shoes designed by Manolo Blahnik (b.1943), born in Santa Cruz, Canary Islands, to a Czech father and Spanish mother. He studied law and literature at the University of Geneva, Switzerland, before moving to Paris, France, where he spent 1968 studying art at the École du Louvre. On a visit to New York, he showed his portfolio of sketches to a number of fashion editors, including Diana Vreeland, who encouraged him to concentrate on shoe design. Blahnik was put in touch with an Italian shoe manufacturer and in 1973 opened his first boutique in London, England. He has since become one of the world's most famous shoe designers and has contributed to the collections of many dress designers and couturiers. "When you buy a Manolo, you're buying a highly engineered Ferrari for the foot" (*Sunday Business*, April 29, 2001).

Mansion *(floor and furniture polish)*

The name was first entered by the Chiswick Soap Company, of London, England, in the *Trade Marks Journal* of April 1, 1908, and is said to have been suggested by Chiswick House, a mansion near the original manufacturing site. The brand subsequently passed to **Reckitt** & **Colman**.

Maples *(furniture store)*

The founder of the London, England, store was John Maple (1815-1900), born in Sussex the son of a yeoman farmer. At the age of 14 he was apprenticed to a shopkeeper, James Constable of Horley, Surrey. He completed his term six years later in 1835 when, weary of country life, he went to London to seek wider opportunities. His specific search was for a cabinetmaker who could do with an assistant to help market sideboards, wardrobes, and desks to furniture retailers. He soon sold his potential to Martin Atkinson, who had extensive workshops and showrooms in what is now Westminster Bridge Road. There he gained useful experience and in 1841, with a fellow employee, James Cook, as partner, opened his own furniture store at 145 Tottenham Court Road, a street already famed for the trade. By 1851 Cook had left the partnership and Maple continued alone until 1861, when he was joined by his son, John Blundell Maple, who did much to improve and enlarge the concern, and who was its virtual head from about 1880. The elder John Maple, even so, remained actively involved in the business up to his death. A branch of Maples was opened in Paris in 1905. The London store, still on its original site, remains today.

Mappin & Webb *(goldsmiths, silversmiths, and jewelers)*

Now with a head office in Regent Street, London, England, the business was first located in Poultry in 1870 before moving soon after to the West End. Its founder was John Newton Mappin (1836- 1913), the son of a Sheffield cutler and younger brother of the Sheffield cutlery and steel manufacturer Frederick Thorpe Mappin (1821-1910). With his partner, George Webb, Mappin's business was soon firmly established. A branch opened in Oxford Street in 1906, in premises still known as Mappin House.

Marathon *see* **Snickers**

Marconi *see* (1) **GEC**; (2) **RCA**

Marcos *(automobiles)*

The British cars take their name from Jem *Mar*sh, the owner of a small tuning company, and Frank *Cos*tin, an aerodynamicist, who got together in 1959 to develop a lightweight racing-sports car. Their business collapsed in 1972, but Marsh bought back the rights to recommence manufacture in the early 1980s, and the firm was still in active production as the century came to a close.

Marezine *(motion sickness tablets)*

The drug derives its name from Latin *mare*, "sea," and the final syllable of "piperazine," one of its constituents. It was entered by Burroughs **Wellcome** in the US Patent Office *Official Gazette* of December 23, 1952: "For medicinal preparations intended for use in the prevention or treatment of allergies, motion sickness, nausea and vomiting in pregnancy, or nausea due to other causes." In the UK the drug was marketed as "Marzine," and this name was entered by the Wellcome Foundation, Ltd., London, in the *Trade Marks Journal* of March 24, 1954.

Margarita *(sherry)*

The Spanish equivalent of the woman's name Margaret was entered by John Harvey & Sons Ltd. (*see* **Harvey's**) for a "very superior very pale dry sherry" in the *Trade Marks Journal* of December 17, 1924. The name is distinct from the tequila-based margarita cocktail, which is said to have been named in 1948 by Danny Herrera, owner of the Rancho La Gloria restaurant near Tijuana, Mexico, for the US actress Marjorie King, a regular guest who was allergic to most liquor except tequila.

Marie Brizard *(liqueur)*

The French brand of anisette takes its name from the Bordelaise who is said to have been given the drink's recipe in 1755 by a West Indian acquaintance.

Marigold *(rubber gloves)*

The latex rubber gloves, associated domestically with washing up and cleaning, were introduced in 1950 by the J. Allen Rubber Company, a small firm in Gloucestershire, England, that had been making babies' bottle teats and dummies (soothers) since the 1930s. The first such gloves were orange, hence the name, which also suggested a female market (Mary) and a quality product (gold). Two years after the launch of its gloves, the J. Allen Rubber Co. was taken over by United Transport. Sales boomed in the late 1950s, and Marigolds were exported all over the world, especially to the USA, where their main competitor was **Playtex**. The London Rubber Co., famous for its **Durex** condoms, bought the Marigold brand in 1960 and developed the range still further.

Marks & Spencer *(department stores)*

The names behind the British chain are those of Michael Marks (1859-1907), a Jewish refugee from Poland, and Thomas Spencer (1852-1905), from Skipton, Yorkshire. Marks first setting up his stall in 1884 in Leeds market place to sell homewares. He divided his stall into two sections, separating those that cost a penny from the rest. Above the penny goods he hung a notice, "Don't ask the price, it's a penny." His stall did good business, and he was soon able to open similar "Penny Bazaars," as he called them, in other towns. By 1894 his business had become so large that he sought a partner. He found him in Tom Spencer, a cashier at one of Marks' suppliers. By 1900 the two men were operating 24 stalls and 12 shops, mainly still in the Midlands and north of England. But the trend was set, and it only remained to convert the "Penny Bazaars" to national chain stores. This was brought about by Israel Sieff, brother-in-law of Marks' son Simon. *See also* **St Michael**.

Marlboro *(cigarettes)*

The cigarettes go back to **Philip Morris**, who by 1885 was selling tobacco brands named "Blues," "Cambridge," and "Derby" in his Bond Street shop in London, England, as well as cigarettes called "Marlborough" (*sic*). All these names have a common aristocratic or military link, with "Blues" suggesting "blue blood" or the Blues and Royals regiment of the Household Cavalry (or the Oxford and Cambridge University sporting award), and the other three representing the titles of dukes and earls. In 1942 the cigarette was launched in the United States under the shorter name "Marlboro." Its specific promotion was originally as a woman's cigarette (it had a red filter tip, "a cherry tip for your ruby lips") but it was subsequently marketed as very much a man's smoke, with a cowboy, "Marlboro Country" promotion. No actual US placename Marlboro (or Marlborough) is implied.

Marley *(thermoplastic tiles)*

The British company takes its name from Marley Lane, the road in Lenham near Maidstone, Kent, where it was founded in 1948 to make floor coverings and where its main works are located today.

Marmet *(prams, or baby carriages)*

The British company of this name was founded in Letchworth, Hertfordshire, in about 1915 by Edward Thompson Morriss (1870-1947), born in Hitchin in the same county. Until World War I Morriss owned a bicycle and perambulator shop in Finchley Road, London. He devised the name of his business from the initials, surname first, of his wife, Alice Rebecca Morriss, and those of his own name similarly. The company, although subsequently subsumed by **Britax** Restmore

Ltd., itself part of BSG International, still has its head office in Letchworth.

Marmion *(industrial cleanser)*

The name was first registered in 1888 for a type of cleanser called "Stanley's Marmion Flakes." It was reregistered in 1923, and "Marmion Granules" were still being made by **Procter & Gamble** at their factory in Manchester, England, in the 1980s. The name is that of the hero of Walter Scott's poem *Marmion* (1808), about the defeat of the Scots by the English at the Battle of Flodden (1513).

Marmite *(yeast extract)*

The tangy yeast spread, usually eaten on bread or toast, is made from brewers' yeast and was first produced in 1902 in the brewery town of Burton-on-Trent, Staffordshire, England. Its name is the French word for an earthenware cooking pot, a picture of which appears on the label. The name was entered by the Marmite Food Extract Co. Ltd. in the *Trade Marks Journal* of August 25, 1920 for: "A Concentrated Culinary Preparation, being an Article of Food." *See also* **Vegemite**.

Marmon *(automobiles)*

In 1851, E.& A.H. Nordyke was founded in Indianapolis, Indiana, as a firm of millwrights. In 1865 they became the Nordyke & Marmon Co., the latter name being that of Howard C. Marmon, who in 1902 built a car for his own use. The following year the Marmon car was put into production. Sales went into terminal decline in the early 1930s, however, as a result of the Depression and the repercussions of mass production, and the last passenger cars were manufactured in 1933. Earlier, Walter C. Marmon and Arthur W.S. Herrington (1891-1970) had broken away to form the Marmon-Herrington Company, specializing in trucks. The Marmon Motor Car Company later evolved into the Marmon Group, turning out a host of manufactured goods that ranged from brake drums to railway boxcars.

Marplan *(antidepressant)*

The name, used for the drug isocarboxazid, was entered (as "Marplon") in the *Trade Marks Journal* of April 18, 1956 and (as "Marplan") in the US Patent Office *Official Gazette* of December 1, 1959: "For product useful in the treatment of mental depression and angina pectoris." It may have been based on an earlier name, "Marsilid," used for iprioniazid phosphate, and itself entered by Roche Products Ltd. in the *Trade Marks Journal* of May 7, 1952.

Marriott *(restaurants and hotels)*

The American company made its name through its public catering, not only to customers and clients in hotels and bars but to airline passengers in particular. The man behind the name is John Willard Marriott (1900-1985), born in Marriott, Utah, a farmer's son. At 19 he left behind the hard life of farm work to serve as a Mormon missionary in New England, after which he worked his way through junior college and then the University of Utah. In 1927 he decided to enter business for himself. First, together with Hugh Colton, the younger brother of Utah congressman Don B. Colton, he bought the A&W Root Beer franchise for Washington, DC. Then, with his newly-wed wife, the former Alice Sheets (d.2000), he opened a nine-stool 5-cent root beer stand at 14th and Kenyon streets in the northwest section of Washington. When customers tailed off in the winter months, the Marriotts converted their stand into The Hot Shoppe, serving chili con carne and hot tamales, borrowing the recipes from a cook at the Mexican Embassy. Soon the two were running a chain of Hot Shoppes throughout Washington. Marriott soon opened several more such restaurants in Washington, and in 1929 he officially incorporated the business in Delaware as Hot Shoppes, Inc., with plans for expansion beyond the city. The move into the hotel side of the business came in 1957, when Marriott's son, John Willard Marriot, Jr. (b.1932), opened a motel in Washington, and in 1964 the corporate name changed to Marriott-Hot Shoppes, Inc. In 1993 the company split into two: Host Marriott, managing real estate, and Marriott International, managing hotels.

Mars *(chocolate-coated toffee bars)*

The man behind the name is Forrest Mars (1904-1999), born in Tacoma, Washington, the son of a candymaker. His parents divorced when he was six, and Mars was sent to live with his grandparents in Canada. He was reunited with his father after dropping out of the University of California at Berkeley, where he had been studying mining. In 1922, his father's new project, the "Mar-O-Bar," met with lukewarm interest from the public. It was only after buying a malted milk drink one day that Mars suggested his father develop a chocolate bar that tasted like a chocolate-malt drink. The result was the **Milky Way**. In 1932 father and son fell out, and Forrest moved to Europe, taking the rights to the Milky Way with him. At first he worked for **Nestlé** in Switzerland, then moved to England and started a candy operation in Slough, Buckinghamshire. It turned out to be a highly successful development, as the British have a notoriously sweet tooth, so that Mars was able to capitalize handsomely on this predilection. The Mars name also lies behind the bean-shaped sugar-coated chocolates called M&Ms ("Mars and Mars"), which Mars based on the **Smarties** made by **Rowntree Mackintosh**. The name was entered in the *Trade Marks Journal* of October 5, 1932.

Marshall & Snelgrove *(department store)*

The London, England, store had its origins in the drapery shop opened in Vere Street in 1837 by James Marshall and a Mr. Wilson. In 1848, when the firm was trading as Marshall, Wilson & Stinton, the latter clearly a further partner, James Marshall was joined by John Snelgrove, and the name was changed to the familiar form above. By 1871 James C. Marshall, the founder's son, had launched a large mail order business, and the firm's reputation as a fashion house was assured. It was at about this time that Marshall & Snelgrove moved to the newly designed premises in Oxford Street. The business was subsequently acquired by **Debenhams**, who had been their rivals almost from the first.

Marshall Field *(department store)*

The famous Chicago department store, at one time the largest in the world, was founded in 1865 by Marshall Field (1834-1906), born near Conway, Massachusetts, the son of a farmer, and Levi Zeigler Leiter (1834-1904), born in Leitersburg, Maryland. Field left home at 17 to work as a clerk in a dry goods store in Pittsfield, Massachusetts. In 1856 he arrived in Chicago and with the help of his elder brother, Joseph, found employment as a clerk in the wholesale firm of Cooley, Wadsworth and Co., then the city's largest dry goods firm. He was talented and soon rose through the ranks, becoming a junior partner in 1860 and a full partner in 1862. He became ambitious to start his own firm, so dissolved his partnership and formed a new one with Potter Palmer and Levi Z. Leiter, who had himself been taken on by Cooley, Wadsworth in 1856 as a bookkeeper and who had risen to be head bookkeeper and accountant. The new partnership was at first named Field, Palmer, and Leiter, then Field, Leiter and Company, and took its present name in 1881 when the firm was reorganized. Marshall Field department stores are now found in many American cities. In 1982 the company was acquired by BATUS Inc., an American subsidiary of London-based **BAT Industries**. The **Dayton Hudson** Corporation then purchased Marshall Field & Co. from BATUS in 1990.

Marshall of Cambridge *(aerospace engineers)*

The six-company group had its beginnings in the business started by David Marshall (d.1942) in Cambridge, England, in 1909 as a provider of chauffeured cars to wealthy professors and students at Cambridge University. Marshall's son Arthur (b.1903) joined Marshall (Cambridge) Ltd., as it then was, in 1926, and in 1929 moved into the growing aircraft industry by founding the firm that is now Marshall of Cambridge (Aerospace) Ltd. His own son Michael (b.1932) joined the family concern in 1955, becoming managing director in 1964 and chairman and chief executive in 1990.

Marsilid *see* **Marplan**

Marston's *(beer)*

The British brewery, based in Burton-on-Trent, Staffordshire, was founded some time before 1818 by John Marston (1785-1846), a local man whose father, Edward Thompson, had also started a brewing venture but one that had ended in bankruptcy in 1805. In 1825 John Marston took over the malthouse of another small brewery, Coat's, in Horninglow, then a village suburb of Burton. The business expanded from then on to his death, when it was continued by his second son, John Hackett Marston, together with his two brothers. The

Thompson side of the business goes back ultimately to John Thompson, who in 1765 owned the Bear Inn, Horninglow Street, to which a small brewhouse was attached. On his death in 1781 the business passed to his two nephews, also named John Thompson. It stayed in the Thompson family until 1898, when the brewery merged with that of Marston. It later combined with another brewery to form Marston, Thompson and Evershed, and at the end of the 20th century was the last major independent company brewing in Burton.

Martell *(brandy)*

The French firm is still in the hands of the founder's family. He was Jean Martell, from St. Helier, Jersey, Channel Islands, who in 1715 abandoned a life of smuggling to set up a brandy exporting company in the Charente region of France, near Cognac. His first exports were to the Channel Islands, but he later extended his contacts to include the Low Countries, Germany, and Scandinavia. His business did well, so that by 1722 he was exporting 40,000 barrels a year. He died in 1750. The St. Helier coat of arms remains in use as the Martell trademark to this day.

Martens, Doc *see* **Dr. Martens**

Martin *(aircraft)*

Glenn L. Martin (1886-1955) was born in Macksburg, Iowa, the son of a hardware and farm implements salesman. When he was two years old his family moved to Liberal, Kansas, then in 1895 to Salina, where Martin would eventually begin working in carriage and bicycle shops. In 1905 the family moved again to Santa Ana, California, where Martin opened a successful automobile dealership. Martin's aviation career began with gliding in 1907, and two years later he opened an aircraft factory, which by 1911 had been incorporated as the Glenn L. Martin Company. For the next four years he was one of the outstanding barnstorming flyers, and used his experience to develop several types of military aircraft. In 1916 he built a new factory in Cleveland, Ohio, and two years later designed and built a bomber for the US Army, later known as the MB-2. It was launched too late to see action in World War I, but its success in the hands of General William "Billy" Mitchell established Martin as one of America's leading military aircraft manufacturers.

Martin-Baker *(ejector seats)*

Those who have ejected safely from aircraft have every reason to thank Northern Irishman James Martin (1893-1981), founder of the Martin Aircraft Company in 1929 with Captain Valentine Baker. After the death of Baker in 1942 flying one of the firm's prototypes, Martin focused on aircraft safety and in 1945 started work on ejector seats at Denham, Buckinghamshire. The first seat was tested a year later, and at the end of the 20th century the business was in the hands of Martin's twin sons, James and John (b.1943), with 75 percent of the world market and 6,800 lives saved.

Martini *(vermouth)*

The Italian firm of Martini & Rossi, who manufacture the vermouth, was officially founded in Turin in 1863, although in reality it continued the work of an earlier distillery that had been set up in 1847 by Alessandro Martini and Luigi Rossi. The cocktail called the "Dry Martini" is said to have been invented in about 1910 by Martini di Taggia di Arma, head bartender in the former Knickerbocker Hotel, New York. But this is a blend of dry ("French") Martini and gin, and not the same as the dry Martini produced by Martini & Rossi that is now marketed as "Extra Dry." In 1993 Martini & Rossi were taken over by **Bacardi**.

Martins *(newsagents)*

The British newsagent chain developed from the three shops that formed the minichain of H. Goodwin & Co. in Aylesbury, Buckinghamshire, in the early 1930s. In 1934 the three stores were acquired by two London businessmen, W. Harold Martin and Archibald Gedge, who reformed the group as the Retail Trade Co-operative Society Ltd. By the end of their first year the two partners had also acquired a small bakery chain of six shops and other newsagents in London, making 25 shops in all. In 1938 Gedge retired, and Martin took his place as managing director, bringing in his second son, Bernard Martin, as partner. The firm survived World War II, and in 1947 became a limited company as Retail Trades (London) Ltd. In 1963 Harold Martin died and Bernard

Martin (1913-1985) became chairman. The multiple chain now covers much of southeast England, but it was not until 1969 that the company name became "Martin the Newsagent Ltd." to identify it with the name that appeared over the shops.

Mary Jane (shoes)

The style of low-heeled, broad-toed, patent-leather shoe with a single-buckle ankle strap, especially as worn by young girls, dates from the early 20th century, a time when the name itself was regarded as typical of a little girl. During the 1920s the style became popular with women. The name is owned by Pacific Brands and is used in the form "Mary-Jane" as well as "Mary Jane."

Mary Kay (cosmetics)

The woman behind the name is Mary Kay Ash, of Hot Wells, Texas. Mary Kay had originally intended to be a doctor, but her parents could not afford to send her to college. She married a guitar player named Ben Rogers, but was left on her own following a divorce 11 years later, and to support her young family sold cleaning supplies for Stanley Home Products. In 1953 she left Stanley and joined another direct sales organization, but was obliged to resign following complaints that she abused her authority, and for a time she lived in retirement. The idle existence did not suit her, however, and in 1963 she opened a retail cosmetics shop, Beauty by Mary Kay, in a Dallas, Texas, storefront. Soon after, she was joined by her youngest son, Richard Rogers, and working together mother and son transformed the small store into a direct sales company within three years.

Marzine *see* **Marezine**

Marzotto (fabrics and clothing)

The Italian company traces its origins to the wool mill set up in 1836 at Valdagno, northern Italy, by Luigi Marzotto (1773-1859). The enterprise was developed by his son Gaetano (1820-1910), and under Gaetano Marzotto, Jr., (1894-1972) diversified into various areas of fabric production. Following various acquisitions and disposals, including the sale of its household linen department to **Zucchi**, the company took over Hugo **Boss** in 1991. It is now one of the biggest textile companies in the world, and is still in family hands.

Maserati (automobiles)

The name behind the car is that of six Italian brothers, Alfieri, Mario, Carlo, Bindo, Ettore, and Ernesto Maserati. All of these except one (Mario, who was an artist) were involved in the motor industry, with Alfieri (d.1932) first developing the car in 1924 at his sparkplug works in Bologna. The name became known internationally when Alfieri won his class in the first Maserati sports car in the Targa Florio on April 25, 1926. After his untimely death, the company was run by Bindo, Ettore, and Ernesto, Carlo having become ill and died earlier in 1910. Although Maserati cars are still produced today, there has been no family involvement since 1947, when the first road cars were built. Ettore Maserati, the last surviving brother, died in 1990, aged 96.

Masonite (fiberboard)

The type of fiberboard made from wood fiber pulped under high steam pressure takes its name from its manufacturers, the Mason Fibre Company, of Laurel, Mississippi, who entered it in the US Patent Office *Official Gazette* of November 23, 1926 for: "Fiber Board, Insulating Board, Composite Construction Board, Synthetic Lumber, or Artificial Lumber."

Massey-Ferguson (tractors)

The names behind the "Massey-Fergie" are those of Daniel Massey, of **Massey-Harris**, and Henry "Harry" George Ferguson (1884-1960). Ferguson was born an Irish farmer's son in Co. Down. He began by working on his father's farm, but did not like farming and when he was 18 left it to work in his brother's motor and cycle repair shop in Belfast. By 1911 he felt he had become competent enough to set up his own automobile and farm implement business in that city. During World War I he was asked by the Irish Board of Agriculture to find a tractor that would be suitable for food production. He did so, but subsequently designed his own model, which was manufactured by **David Brown** of Huddersfield and sold by a firm that Ferguson had set up specially for the purpose. By 1938 the arrangement with David Brown had lapsed, and instead Ferguson made an agreement with **Ford** in the USA for that company to build tractors to his design. When that and yet another agreement were cancelled, Ferguson finally merged both his British and American companies with the Canadian firm of Massey-Harris in 1953, becoming its chairman.

Massey-Harris *(agricultural implements)*

The Canadian company dates its origins from 1847, when Daniel Massey (1798-1856), born in Vermont, opened a small workshop in Newcastle, Ontario, and began making simple farm implements. By 1852 he had progressed to producing more complex machines, including mowers. In 1857 Alason Harris opened a similar farm machinery workshop in Beamsville, Ontario. Both ventures prospered and expanded, but each operated independently, remaining keen rivals in the field. Eventually, after a world trade recession, Massey and Harris, Canada's two most successful agricultural machinery manufacturers, agreed to merge in 1891. The combined Massey-Harris went on to gain international prestige for its equipment, and in particular its harvesting machinery. Its tractors were never quite in the same league, although the combined name became associated with these vehicles in 1953, when it merged its interests with those of Harry Ferguson to form the threefold combine of Massey-Harris-Ferguson, later known simply as **Massey-Ferguson**.

Master McGrath *(pet food)*

The dog food was originally manufactured at Portadown, Northern Ireland, by Windsor Foods Ltd., a firm taken over by General Foods in 1970. Its name is that of a famous Irish greyhound owned by Lord Lurgan. It raced from 1867 to 1873, was beaten only once, and after winning the Waterloo Cup three years in a row was presented at court by order of Queen Victoria. According to legend, Lurgan rescued the dog when it was a puppy about to be drowned by a drunken tenant farmer, and named it for the orphan boy who raised it.

MasterCard *(credit card)*

Like other credit cards, MasterCard has its roots in the 1940s, when various US banks started giving their customers specially issued paper credit notes that could be used like cash in local stores. In 1951, Franklin National Bank, New York, formalized the practice by introducing the first real credit card. Over the next decade, several franchises evolved whereby a single bank in each city would accept cards as payment with specified merchants. In 1966, one such group formed the Interbank Card Association (ICA), later renamed as MasterCard International. When the arrangement spread to other countries, ICA itself changed its name to MasterCard. The name itself ultimately derives from the master card in card games such as bridge, in which it is the card that commands a suit or that is the highest of all those remaining to be played. MasterCard's world headquarters are (appropriately) in Purchase, New York.

Matalan *(fashion stores)*

On holiday in the USA in the early 1980s, John Hargreaves, a British market trader, was impressed by the discount out-of-town retail concept, whereby a wide range of food and nonfood products could be sold at low prices. He decided to introduce the same system in the UK, and in 1985 opened the first Matalan discount club in Preston, Lancashire. His enterprise succeeded, and in 2000 Matalan opened its 100th fashion store. The name has family connections.

Matchbox *(toy vehicles)*

The story of Matchbox toys starts in Germany in the late 1870s, when Moses Kohnstam founded a toy company at Fuerth, near Nürnberg, and began to produce toys named "Moko," from the first syllables of his two names. The firm survived both world wars but changed its profile in the late 1940s when Richard Kohnstam set about bringing new ideas into the trade. He had been working in England with **Lesney** Products, and in around 1950 they jointly produced a large model of the royal coronation coach with a team of horses. This was effectively the forerunner of the Matchbox range. In 1952, they produced a smaller version of the coach under the "Moko-Lesney" name. In 1953, the year of Queen Elizabeth's coronation itself, well over a million miniature coaches were sold, and Lesney became firmly committed to toys. At about the same time Kohnstam had the idea of manufacturing diecast miniature vehicles, and they were introduced to the trade packed in imitation matchboxes. Hence the name by which the series came to be known. In 1959 Lesney bought out the equity of the Kohnstam business and the firm became the sole property of Lesney Products, floated as a public company in 1960.

Matchless *(motorcycles)*

The British make of motorcycle was one of the first marques in the business. It owed its origin to H.H. Collier, who had been a maker of bicycles until 1899, when he was joined by his two sons, Charlie and Harry, and made his first motorized version. The firm ran smoothly for over half a century, taking over several rivals, but financial problems led to its demise in 1966.

Mateus Rosé *(wine)*

The medium sweet, sparkling rosé wine takes its name from the Mateus Palace near Vila Real, northern Portugal, where it was first made in 1942 by Fernando van Zeller Guedes, whose family owned a property producing vinho verde. The Mateus estate did not belong to the Guedes family, however, and its owners opted for a single payment in return for the use of the name and a picture of the palace on the label, rather than a royalty on each bottle sold. The family later diversified into other areas of the Portuguese wine industry. The name "Mateus" (Portuguese for "Matthew") was entered in the US Patent Office *Official Gazette* of May 24, 1949.

Mathmos *(lava lamps)*

In 1990, the British entrepreneur Cressida Granger (b.1964) set about making a profitable business out of the "Astro" lava lamp invented in 1963 by Edward C. Walker (*see* **Lava Lite**). She named her enterprise "Mathmos," an adaptation of "Magmous," the name of the evil presence something like a lava lamp that surrounds the city in the 1968 movie *Barbarella*.

Matra *(automobiles)*

The French firm of Engins Matra, long familiar in the aerospace and armaments industries, was founded by Marcel Chassagny in 1945 with a name short for *Mécanique-Aviation-Traction*. In due course it diversified into low-volume sports car production and motor racing, and in the early 1970s formed an alliance with **Chrysler-Simca**, but in 1978 Chrysler sold out its European interests to **Peugeot**. In the early 1980s, however, Matra dissolved its links with Peugeot to set up a better deal with **Renault**. The result was an end to Matra's sports car activities. In 1999 Aérospatiale-Matra, as it now was, merged with the defense arm of **Daimler-Chrysler** to become the world's third-largest aerospace company. *See also* **Lagardère**.

Matsushita *(electrical and electronic goods)*

The name behind the Japanese company is that of Konosuke Matsushita (1894-1989). When he was nine years old, Konosuke began working as an errand boy, afterwards becoming apprenticed as a bicycle repair worker. He quit this menial chore at 16 to work for the Osaka Electric Light Company, and in 1918 set up his own company, Matsushita Electric Industrial Co., to make just one product, an electric light socket of his own design. Business was slow to take off, but when he added a second item, an electric attachment plug that sold for 30 percent less than his rivals' products, trade picked up sharply. After a setback in World War II, Matsushita bounced back to broaden the range of his products considerably, and by the time of his retirement in 1973 his company had gained worldwide fame for its home electrical and electronic appliances, sold under such well-known brand names as **Panasonic**, National, Quasar, and Technics.

Mattel *(toys)*

The American company, famous for putting **Barbie** on the US market, had its beginnings in 1945 in a Los Angeles garage workshop, where Harold Matson and Elliot Handler set up a picture-frame business, naming it after letters from Matson's surname and Handler's first name. When Handler found himself with a lot of extra frame slats, he and his wife, Ruth, branched out into doll furniture, whereupon Matson sold out. In 1955 the couple introduced toy burp guns and also registered their brand name, plugging the slogan, "You can tell it's Mattel, it's swell." Barbie was launched in 1959 and was soon joined by other toys, such as the talking doll Chatty Cathy, the Thingmaker series of the 1960s (including Incredible Edibles, Creepy Crawlers, Fun Flowers, and Fright Factory), and Hot Wheels cars in 1968.

Mattessons *(delicatessen products)*

A father and son lie behind the name, familiar in British foodmarkets. They are Richard Mattes (1896-1974) and his son Rolf Werner Mattes. Richard Mattes was born in Neuwied, Germany, near Koblenz. At first he worked in his father's pork butcher's trade, then set up on his own in Frankfurt. His business was closed by the Nazis, however, and in order to escape persecution he went to England in 1936. After being employed by various butchers and meat processors throughout World War II, in 1946 he bought a small meat processing business in London's East End. He changed its name to Richard Mattes & Co. Ltd. and three years later, when trade was picking up nicely, altered this to Mattessons Meats Ltd. to show that his *son* had joined him in the business. Today the company operates from a large factory in West Ham, producing a wide range of products from cooked meats to coleslaw.

Matthew Clark's *(whisky)*

Matthew Clark (1786-1866) was born in London, England, the son of the Inspector General of the Port of London. On completing his education at 16, he was sent to Rotterdam to learn Dutch, and subsequently entered a firm of merchants there, Campbell Bowden & Co. After service with a firm of general merchants and government contractors in London, he was sent to South America, where he managed to persuade many traders that England was a better market than Spain for goods such as hides and beef. He returned again to Britain in 1810, setting up his own business as a broker of foreign wines and liquors near the Tower of London. There he built up the contacts that the company still maintains today, acting as agent for such well-known firms as **Martell**. The company name is familiar to the public from "Matthew Clark's Very Special Scotch Whisky," but the firm's main activity is still in the distribution of wines and liquors.

Matthews, Bernard *see* **Bernard Matthews**

Max Factor *(cosmetics)*

Max Factor (c.1872-1938) was born Max Faktor in Łódz, Poland, where he began his career as a wigmaker's apprentice. At age 14 he was then make-up artist for the Imperial Russian Theatre. At 18 Max joined the Russian army for four years, as the law required. After his release in 1894, he opened a small shop in Ryazan, a Moscow suburb, where he made and sold his own creams, rouges, fragrances, and wigs. His services came to be demanded by the Russian nobility, and he was given the title of cosmetics expert to Alexander Nikolaevich Romanov, uncle of Czar Nicholas II. Seeking to widen his horizons, in 1904 Factor emigrated to the United States and that same year set up a perfume, make-up, and hair goods concession at the St. Louis World's Fair. But the motion picture industry was now developing fast, and to capitalize on this, Factor moved his family to Hollywood, where he formed Max Factor & Company in 1909, with the main aim of creating make-ups specifically for the movies. (*See* **Pancake**.) This was in effect the foundation of the firm of today, with its international status enhanced by the film stars who personally advertised Max Factor products. On Factor's death, the business passed to his son, Max Factor, Jr. (1904-1996).

Maxwell House *(coffee)*

The brand of coffee was not directly named after someone called Maxwell. It owes its origin to an American grocer and coffee blender, Joel Owsley Cheek, who in 1873, at the age of 21, set out from his father's Kentucky farm to seek his fortune. At first he joined a wholesale grocery firm as a traveling salesman, taking goods around to local stores. He was specially interested in coffee, however, and in 1882 quit this routine job to set up on his own with the aim of evolving a new blend of coffee. He finally achieved what he judged to be a particularly fine blend, and took it for sampling to what was then one of the best hotels in the southern states, the Maxwell House, Nashville, Tennessee. The management agreed to give Cheek's blend a trial, and within a week the hotel's fastidious guests were declaring it to be delicious and recommending it to their friends. Thus Maxwell House coffee was born, even though the hotel that gave the name was burned down in 1961. The instant coffee of the name followed this original blend of coffee only in the 1940s.

Maxwell's *(hamburger restaurants)*

The first restaurant so named was opened in London, England, in 1972 by Brian Stein (b.1944), a South African-born photographer, who called it after the Beatles number "Maxwell's Silver Hammer" (1969), still played on the jukebox there. It became so popular that Stein was encouraged to start a chain. In 1978 he accordingly opened a second restaurant in Oxford, and a third followed in London in 1980. Maxwell's is now London's largest privately-owned restaurant chain.

May & Baker (pharmaceuticals)

The names are those of the founders of the British firm, familiar for its "M and B" tablets in World War II, used to treat pneumonia and other infectious diseases of bacterial or viral origin. John May (1809-1893) was born in Harwich, Essex, a ship captain's son. On quitting school, he served an apprenticeship with a chemist and druggist in Ipswich, Suffolk, where his father had retired. In 1830 May went to London, where he attended medical lectures and worked as an assistant to a manufacturing chemist in Battersea, a district noted for its chemical plants. In 1834 he started in the same business, taking on two partners. They both left after only a few years, however, and in 1839 May was joined by William Garrard Baker, then aged 24 and the son of a Chelmsford, Essex, chemist and druggist. The two became formal partners in 1840, and the following year built a new factory in Battersea. This remained the company's headquarters until 1934, when it moved to Dagenham, Kent. The "M and B" tablets themselves, containing sulphapyridine, continued to be manufactured until 1986, when they were discontinued in favor of antibiotics. A symbol representing the letters M and B was entered in the *Trade Marks Journal* of October 30, 1935, and the abbreviated name "M & B" subsequently in the *Journal* of February 18, 1953.

May Company (department stores)

Morton Jay May (1881-1968) was born in Denver, Colorado, the son of a German immigrant who had opened a dry goods store in Irwin, Colorado, shortly before May's birth. Within a few years the elder May, in partnership with his brothers-in-law, had six stores in the Rocky Mountain states, and in 1888 moved the firm's headquarters to Denver. Morton May began learning his father's business early, and on leaving school worked his way up through sales and managerial positions. In 1903, when his father moved the growing com-

pany's headquarters to St. Louis, Morton May left the May Company store in Cleveland and went to work in the family-owned Famous store in St. Louis. In 1910 the elder May dissolved the partnership with his brothers-in-law and incorporated. Morton May became a member of the board, then president in 1917, and finally chief executive officer as well as president in 1927 on the death of his father. By the time of May's death, the family company owned 80 stores in nine states and the District of Columbia, and with annual sales of $1 billion was the fourth largest chain in the United States, rivaling **Sears Roebuck**, **J.C. Penney**, and Federated Department Stores.

Maybach (automobiles)

The name is that of the German engineer Wilhelm Maybach (1846-1929), born the son of a skilled carpenter in Heilbronn. He was orphaned at the age of ten, and at 15 was apprenticed to the Bruderhaus engineering works. From 1883 Maybach was associated with Gottlieb **Daimler** in developing efficient internal-combusion engines, and in 1890 the two men formed the Daimler-Motoren-Gesellschaft, in Cannstatt, to manufacture automobiles. In 1909 Maybach and his son Carl organized a company at Friedrichshafen to build aero engines, but after World War I he again turned to making cars. Automobiles with the Maybach marque were produced from 1922 to 1939.

Maynards (fruit-flavor gums)

The British name is that of Charles Riley Maynard (1857-1926), who in around 1880, together with his wife, Sarah Anne, and brother, Tom, opened a candy store in Stoke Newington, London. Maynard made the candy himself in a special kitchen, while Sarah Anne served in the shop. Their original favored lines were boiled sweets and coconut candy. The business did well, and soon the Maynards acquired another confectionery retailer business based in Brighton, Sussex, where it had been started in 1840. It was coincidentally named G. Maynard, which caused considerable local confusion, leading people to think that 1840 was the year when Charles Maynard's firm had been founded. In 1896 Charles formally established his company, by which time a number of other branches had been opened and the business had developed to take in a fullblown manufacturing, wholesale, and retail operation. The so-called wine gums were added to the range in 1909 by Charles Gordon Maynard. At first Charles Riley Maynard was horrified at the idea, as he was a strict teetotal Methodist. He was assured, however, that despite their name the gums were merely flavored to suggest different wines, and did not actually contain alcohol. The eventual Maynards plc was taken over and broken up in 1986, and the gums are now produced by **Trebor Bassett**.

Maytag *(washing machines)*

Fred Maytag (1857-1937), of Newton, Iowa, was originally a manufacturer of farm machinery. The agricultural industry was seasonal, however, and Maytag and his three associates looked for products that could boost sales during the slack periods. As part of its diversification, the firm introduced a hand-operated washing machine in 1907. It gradually became the company's dominant line, and in 1923, by which time Maytag had resigned, the company dropped all other products in favor of its "gyrafoam" washer. Unlike other machines, which simply pulled clothes through the water, the Maytag used blades to force water through the clothes. The result was cleaner laundry, and a huge increase in profits for Maytag itself, making it the world's biggest washing machine maker by 1925. The firm held this lead position until 1950, when it lost out to **Whirlpool**.

Mazawattee *(tea)*

The Indian tea of this name was at one time very popular in Britain. The name itself was created in the 1880s and derives from Hindi *maza*, "pleasure," "taste," and *vati*, "house," "building." (The double "t" ensures that the second part of the name is not pronounced "weighty.") The name was entered in the *Trade Marks Journal* of May 11, 1887.

Mazda *(automobiles)*

The Mazda Motor Corporation, with its headquarters at Hiroshima, was founded by Jujiro Matsuda, born in 1875 in the Aki district of Hiroshima. He began his career as an engineering apprentice in Osaka, then in 1906 started an ironworks in that city. In 1918 he returned to his native Hiroshima, and two years later joined the Toyo Cork Kogyo Company, a manufacturer of corks for bottle caps. Mat-

suda rose through the ranks and in 1923 switched the firm's production from cork to machines, shortening its name in 1927 to the Toyo Kogyo Company. (The Japanese words mean "Oriental Industry."). He progressed to the production of motorcycles, then in 1931 began manufacturing three-wheeler trucks, which he named "Mazda-Go," mainly after Ahura Mazda, the Zoroastrian god of light, but also after his own name, Matsuda. (The names "Sumeru," that of a Buddhist god, and "Tenshi," that of an angel, were also considered but rejected.) The company entered the passenger car market in 1960 with the production of a coupé model, and over the next two decades the Mazda car marque expanded considerably, both in numbers and in scope and technology. In 1984 the company itself became the Mazda Motor Corporation.

Mazda *(electric lamps)*

The name was first used by the General Electric Company in 1909. It was suggested to them by Frederick P. Fish, a Boston lawyer and ex-president of **AT&T**. After considering "Apollo," "Jupiter," and "Jove," Fish decided that "Mazda," from Ahura Mazda, the Persian god of light, was a more suitable name for the new tungsten incandescent lamp.

Mazola *(corn oil)*

The product was introduced in the USA in 1911 as the first refined corn oil. It takes its name from "maize," known as Indian corn or simply corn in North America, and Latin *oleum*, "oil."

MCA *(entertainment)*

The US company dates from 1924, when the show business entrepreneur Jules C. Stein (1896-1981) founded the Music Corporation of America in Chicago. By the end of the 1930s, when the company had moved to California, he had a flourishing national talent agency. MCA first produced theater films in 1966 when they merged with **Decca**, the company that owned Universal Studios (*see* **Universal Pictures**).

McAlpine *see* **Sir Robert McAlpine**

McCain *(chips)*

The Canadian company now known worldwide for its chips was founded as a French fries business in Florenceville, New Brunswick, in 1957 by Harrison McCain (b.1927) and his brother Wallace, two years his junior. In 1994 Wallace was ousted from the company after attempting to position his son Michael as his successor as co-chief executive officer. Harrison, meanwhile, was believed to be grooming his nephew, Allison, to take over his own role.

McDonald's (fast-food chain)

The founder of what is now the biggest restaurant chain in the world was actually Ray A. Kroc (1902-1984), born in Oak Park, Illinois, the son of a Western Union employee. Kroc dropped out of high school at age 15 and began looking for a way of making money. After various unsuccessful attempts he found a proper position in 1926 as a salesman with the Lily Tulip Cup Company. He enjoyed selling and traveling and understood the restaurant business, but became restless for the elusive big opportunity. He thought he found it in the "multimixer," a multispindled milkshake mixer. He left Lily Tulip in 1937 to set up his own company, Prince Castle, to sell the machine, and despite the restrictions imposed by World War II his business did relatively well, especially in the boom years immediately after the war. But the decline of the soda fountain threatened Prince Castle's future, and Kroc began to seek new outlets for the multimixer. One place that interested him was McDonald's, a little drive-in operated by Maurice "Mac" McDonald (1902-1981) and Richard "Dick" McDonald (1909-1998) in San Bernardino, California. In their business the McDonalds sold milk shakes, using eight of Kroc's machines that could each make six shakes. Kroc was curious to see what sort of a setup it was that needed to make 48 milk shakes simultaneously. He paid the brothers a visit in April 1954 and found a little octagonal building with no indoor seating serving only burgers, fries, and drinks. Meals were produced assembly-line style, and it usually took less than a minute for a customer to place his order and receive his meal. Kroc was sure the place had potential, and asked the brothers whether they would consider franchising the operation. That way they would sell more burgers and he would sell more multimixers. At first they demurred, but eventually agreed, on the condition they had 0.5 percent of all sales. Kroc went ahead and in April 1955 opened his first McDonald's restaurant in a Chicago suburb, with others soon fol-

lowing. In 1961 Kroc bought out the McDonalds for $2.7 million, by which time there were around 250 restaurants throughout the United States. By the end of the decade around 1,500 McDonald's were open worldwide, and by 2001 there were 28,700 restaurants in 120 countries. See also (1) **Big Mac**; (2) **Pret A Manger**.

McDonnell Douglas (aircraft and arms)

The name of the American company came about in 1967 from the merger of McDonnell and Douglas, two of the oldest aviation businesses in the country. The former name is that of James S. McDonnell, Jr. (1899-1980), born in Denver, Colorado, a merchant's son. He graduated from high school in Little Rock, Arkansas, in 1917, graduated from Princeton with a bachelor of science degree in 1921, and then immediately enrolled in the graduate program in aeronautical engineering at the Massachusetts Institute of Technology. While at MIT he enlisted in the army aviation section and received a reserve pilot's wings in 1923. The following year, even before completing his studies, he found work as an aeronautical engineer at the Huff-Daland Aircraft Company in Ogdensburg, New York, but did not stay long and over the next 15 years moved as a roving aeronautical engineer from one aircraft company to another. Eventually he quit his job at the Gleen L. Martin Company in Baltimore in 1938 and on July 6, 1939 organized the McDonnell Aircraft Corporation in Maryland. The latter name is that of Donald Wills Douglas (1892-1981), a Brooklyn banker's son, who graduated from MIT in 1914 with a bachelor of science degree in aeronautical engineering. In 1915 he was taken on as chief engineer by the Martin Aircraft Company, based in Los Angeles, where he rose to be vice president in 1920. That same year he formed a partnership with David R. Davis, a millionaire sportsman and pilot, to form the Davis-Douglas Aircraft Company in the back room of a barbershop. The aim was to build an aircraft that would enable Davis to be the first man to make a coast-to-coast nonstop flight. The aircraft, named the "Cloudster," was produced in 1921 and Davis took off for Long Island. The flight ended over Texas when the engine failed, however, and Davis dissolved the partnership. Undeterred, Douglas continued alone, and persuaded the navy to give his company a contract to build three more Cloudsters that could be used for torpedo bombing. He opened a plant in an old movie studio in Santa Monica and in due course produced the successful DT-1. Further orders and commissions followed, so that by the late 1920s Douglas's firm had grown to over 500 employees.

McDougall *(self-rising flour)*

The origins of the flour go back to the British firm of McDougall Brothers, a chemical manufacturing firm in Manchester in the 1860s. A member of the family, Alexander McDougall, assisted by his son Arthur, discovered a new baking powder, and resolved to sell it to millers so they could make self-rising flour. The millers were not responsive, however, so the McDougalls decided to open their own mill in Manchester and make the flour themselves. They were the first company to do so on a commercial scale, although they did not actually invent self-rising flour, which already existed. In 1957 McDougall merged with **Hovis** to form Hovis McDougall, and this company then combined with **Rank** in 1962 to form Rank Hovis McDougall (RHM).

McEwan's *(beer)*

The Scottish firm of William McEwan and Co., registered in 1889 and famous for its keg and canned beers, was set up to take over the Fountain Brewery in Edinburgh, founded in 1856 by William McEwan (1827-1913), nephew of George Younger, 1st Viscount Younger of Leckie (1851-1929), great-great-grandson of George Younger (1722-1788), the founder of **Younger's**. His uncle's brewing interests, latterly run by his brother, William Younger (1857-1925), were eventually merged with Younger's in 1931 as Scottish Brewers and are now part of Scottish **Courage**. The original Fountain Brewery is still in use, although now rebuilt.

McFarland *(publishers)*

The US publishing house was founded in 1979 and takes its name from the middle name of its founder, Robert McFarland Franklin (b.1943), the son of two librarians in Memphis, Tennessee. The name Franklin already formed part of the corporate names of five or six book-related endeavors and was thus disfavored by the new firm, who are based in Jefferson, North Carolina.

McGraw-Hill *(publishers)*

The two Americans behind the name, James Herbert McGraw (1860-1948) and John Alexander Hill, were both involved in the publication of trade magazines in the 1880s. McGraw was born in Panama, New York, the son of an Irish farmer who had immigrated in 1849 in the wake of the Great Famine. After graduating in 1884 from the free State Normal School in Fredonia, New York, he spent a year as a teacher before joining the American Railway Company, publisher of the *Journal of Railway Appliances*. He disagreed with his partners, however, and broke with them in 1888, buying out the *Journal*. With his father-in-law providing much of his capital, McGraw went on to buy a number of technical magazines, and in 1899 his burgeoning empire enabled him to incorporate his business as the McGraw Publishing Company. By coincidence, Hill, a locomotive engineer, was beginning to contribute to *American Machinist* and *Locomotive Engineer,* and similarly acquired these two magazines. In 1909 the two men merged their interests to form the McGraw-Hill Book Company and publish technical books, while keeping the magazine interests separate. When Hill died unexpectedly in 1917, no heir was interested in taking his magazines on, so his journals were merged with those of McGraw. The business accordingly became the McGraw-Hill Publishing Company and expanded its services.

McKellar Watt *(sausages)*

The Brtish meat company takes its name from Eric McKellar Watt (1920-2001), born Alexander McKellar Watt in Glasgow, Scotland. (He later changed his first name to avoid confusion with his father, who was also in the meat business.) After army service in World War II, when rationing was imposed on the British public, he set himself up as a maker and seller of sausages in a small shop in Parliamentary Road, Glasgow, initially using a mixing bowl discarded from a prison kitchen. Despite the difficult times and the restricted supply of foodstuffs, McKellar Watt's enterprise slowly grew into the present sausage empire, famous for its slogan "McKellar Watt for Meatiness".

McLaren *(automobiles)*

The British supercar ultimately derives its name from the New Zealand-born racing driver and sports car constructor Bruce McLaren (1937-1970), killed testing a prototype. In the late 1980s, Gordon Murray, a chief Formula 1 designer for McLaren, decided the time was right to launch out on his own and build the ultimate car. The company was founded in 1989 and the first supercar was unveiled at the Monaco Grand Prix in 1992. Production began in 1993, and for the rest of the decade the McLaren F1 remained the fastest, most powerful, and most expensive car in the world.

McLean *(transportation)*

Long familiar on US highways from its red diamond emblem, the McLean Trucking Company took its name from Malcolm P. McLean (1913-2001), born in North Carolina a farmer's son. McLean started as a truck driver when still in his teens, and in 1934 scraped together $30 for a secondhand pickup. This allowed him, with two of his siblings, to found a proper trucking business. In 1937, driving a consignment of cotton bales to New Jersey, it occurred to McLean that it would be easier to lift his trailer up and put it right on a ship that way, rather than unloading goods laboriously from small boxes. His scheme led to the introduction of cargo containers, which revolutionized the way in which goods were moved. In 1956, McLean bought the Pan-Atlantic Shipping Company, changed its name to Sea-Land, and started to haul domestic cargo. In 1969 he sold Sea-Land to **R.J. Reynolds** and began dabbling in real estate, but returned to shipping in 1978 when he purchased US Lines and made it part of McLean Industries. Foreign competition began to depress McLean's business, however, and in 1986 US Lines filed for bankruptcy, followed soon after that same year by the McLean Trucking Company.

McVitie & Price *(cookies, or biscuits)*

Robert McVitie (1809-1884) was the son of a Scottish provision merchant with a shop in Rose Street, Edinburgh. Robert's first job was working with his father. He soon moved on, however, to set up his own bakery in 1839 in Charlotte Street (now Randolph Place). He remained there until his death, when his business was taken over by his son and partner, also named Robert. In that same year, 1884, the younger McVitie took as partner Charles E. Price (d.1934), previously a traveler for **Cadburys**, and the name of the business duly changed to McVitie & Price. Price remained with the firm until 1901, when he became the Liberal Member of Parliament for Central Edinburgh. Lines of biscuits (cookies) made by McVitie & Price in the early 1920s included "Digestive," "Osborne," "Butterette," "Royal Scots," "Cream Crackers" (*see* **Jacob's**), "Petit Beurre," "Academy Creams," "Breakfast," "Ginger Nuts," "Rich Tea", "Marie," and "Queen's Shorties." (The "Osborne" was originally made in 1860 by **Huntley & Palmer**, who wanted to name it after Queen Victoria. She said she would prefer they name it instead after her favorite home, Osborne House, Isle of Wight.) The name of the firm is now commercially shortened as "McVitie's." *See also* **Jaffa Cakes**.

Mead *(paper)*

The American company, well-known for its throwaway containers, especially beverage carriers (as for the sixpack), takes its name from Colonel Daniel Mead (d.1891), who in 1846 bought a part interest in a small Dayton, Ohio, paper mill. By 1882 he had bought out his partners, and renamed the firm Mead Paper. The business went bankrupt after Mead's death, but was revived by one of his grandsons, George Mead. The company is still based in Dayton.

Meccano *(toy construction kit)*

The construction set owes its origin to the English inventor Frank Hornby (1863-1936), who had long had an interest in mechanical things and wanted to make some sort of toy for his children that would be more durable than the ones they so frequently discarded. He had the idea of devising a kit that could make different types of models by using thin metal strips perforated at ½-in. intervals. He patented his invention in 1901, at first under the name "Mechanics Made Easy," but later as "Meccano," a name entered in the *Trade Marks Journal* of October 23, 1907. (The form of the name suggests that it may have been influenced by French mécano, "mechanic.") The venture did well, so that in 1908 he formed Meccano Ltd., taking over a former car factory in Liverpool to manufacture his toy. Despite legal wrangles over patents, particularly in the USA, Meccano soon outstripped all competitors to become widely acknowledged as "The World's Most Famous Toy." *See also* **Dinky Toys**.

Medeva *(pharmaceuticals)*

The British company was founded as Medirace in 1987 by Ian Gowrie-Smith (b. 1948). In 1990 it merged with Evans Medical, a company engaged in the development, manufacture, and sales of vaccines, and became Medeva, from *Medi*race and *Eva*ns. In 1999 Medeva was bought by Celltech.

Medici *(greeting cards and calendars)*

The Medici Society, noted for its fine art reproductions, takes its name from the great Florentine family who lived in the 14th and 15th centuries and who encouraged art at the time of the Italian renaissance. The Society dates its origin from 1906, when its British founder, Philip Lee Warner (1877-1925), first produced fine art prints at **Chatto & Windus**, the publishing house where he worked. The prints were made by the so-called collotype process, and were an improvement on the hand-drawn lithographic prints found hitherto. Warner had the prints reproduced in full color by Mr. Hoesch of Milan, with Leonardo da Vinci's *Last Supper* and Botticelli's *Virgin and Child* among the earliest consignment. In 1908 the Society was incorporated as a limited company, and at first actually was a society as such, with subscribers able to join and receive copies of new prints as they were published. This scheme was later abandoned, however, through lack of support, and the prints were sold normally through shops and art galleries.

Medinal *(sedative)*

The proprietary name for the sodium salt of barbital was entered by the German company of Schering (*see* **Schering-Plough**) in the *Trade Marks Journal* of August 12, 1908. The name itself is perhaps based on "medicine," especially as the registration description is for: "Medicines for human use."

Megger *(electric testing apparatus)*

The name of the apparatus for measuring electrical insulation resistance was entered by Evershed and Vignoles Ltd. of London, England, in the *Trade Marks Journal* of September 2, 1903. The name itself is perhaps based on "megohm," the unit of electrical resistance. The abbreviated name "Meg" for a type of Megger was entered by the same firm in the *Journal* of November 11, 1942.

Meggezones *(throat pastilles)*

The pastilles much later made for S-P Consumer Products Ltd. were originally produced by Meggeson & Co. Ltd., so that the brand name is a modification of the personal name. The British firm was founded in 1814 by George Meggeson (1784-1874), a Yorkshireman who came to London to manage the druggists' business of Widow Staveley & Co., of Fenchurch Street. When that failed, he started another business with a partner, trading as Cooke & Meggeson, and specializing in "medicated confectionery," or lozenges for coughs and colds. Meggeson's surname may have been respelled in such a way that the brand name suggested "ozone," in turn implying easy breathing. The name was entered in the *Trade Marks Journal* of September 16, 1936.

Melitta *(coffee filters)*

The name is that of Melitta Bentz, a German housewife who in 1908 devised a new process for making coffee by filtering it instead of simply putting ground coffee into a cloth bag and boiling it in water. The filter she invented was developed from a brass pot with a perforated bottom in which a sheet of blotting paper had been inserted. Within four years the firm was making its own filters, and Frau Bentz's husband had become the manager of the business, naming it for her.

Mellon *(bank)*

The American bank, now the principal subsidiary of Mellon National Corporation, takes its name from its founder in 1870, Thomas Mellon (1813-1908), born near Omagh, Co. Tyrone, Ireland, a farmer's son. In 1818 the family immigrated to the United States, where Mellon's father purchased a farm in Franklin Township, east of Pittsburgh. The family's arrival coincided with the economic depression of 1819, and young Thomas worked a double shift, tending the fields by day and spinning flax by night. In 1823 he made his first trip to Pittsburgh, where the busy factories and homes of prosperous citizens decided him against a life as a farmer. He attended the Western University of Pennsylvania, graduating in 1837, then read law, passing the bar in 1838. His career as a lawyer then took off, and he proved an adept common pleas court judge. He felt stifled by the judicial appointment, however, and left the court at the end of 1869. One month later he opened what would become his most lasting business, the private bank of T. Mellon and Sons, the latter being Thomas A. Mellon (1844-1899) and James R. Mellon (1846-1934). In 1902 the bank was reorganized as Mellon National Bank. The holding company was formed in 1971.

Mellotron *(musical instrument)*

The electronic keyboard instrument, introduced in 1963, is programmed to produce the prerecorded sounds of orchestral instruments. Its name is a blend of "mellow" and "electronic."

Melrose's *(tea and coffee)*

The Scottish company was founded in 1812 by Andrew Melrose, when he left a job as a butcher's assistant in Edinburgh to open his grocery shop in Canongate, then one of the city's chief trading centers. He soon added shops in Princes Street and George Street, and opened a warehouse in Drummond Street. His real expansion, however, came in the importing of tea, and Melrose was the first Scottish merchant to organize such imports outside the Port of London. The first consignment arrived in Leith, the port for Edinburgh, in 1835. When Melrose retired in 1850, the business was continued by his sons, John and William. Andrew Melrose died five years later, having founded a select tea and coffee company that today is still well known for its **Earl Grey** blend.

Melson Wingate *(opticians)*

The British firm takes its name from George Melson Wingate (1848-1901), who was apprenticed to a watchmaker and photographer before emigrating to the United States in 1870. He did not stay long, however, finding the American weather more inclement than clement, and after the birth of his first son in Philadelphia in 1872, returned to England. He settled in Plymouth, Devon, where he started his own business as watchmaker and jeweler. In about 1888 Frank Melson Wingate, George's son, suggested his father turn his attention to sight-

testing and spectacle fitting. At the age of 49, George Melson Wingate took the dioptric grade examination of the British Optical Association, and in 1898 was granted the Freedom of the City of London as a spectacle maker, having also passed the examinations of the Worshipful Company of Spectacle Makers. After his father's death, Frank Melson Wingate continued and expanded the practice, opening a branch in Bournemouth, Hampshire, in 1919 which became the firm's head office two years later.

Meltonian *(shoe polish)*

The polish was originally produced by a firm near Melton Mowbray, Leicestershire, England, and takes its name from that town, famous for its hunting associations. "Meltonian cream" was originally used for polishing the tops of riding boots. The name was entered in the *Trade Marks Journal* of June 17, 1925.

Melville *(footwear)*

The Melville Corporation, with shoe and clothing stores in many American suburban shopping malls, takes its name from Frank Melville, a onetime cowboy, sailor, and stage-coach driver who in 1882 got a job as a shoe clerk in New York. He went on to become a traveling wholesaler, acquired three shoe stores in New York, and set up the Melville Shoe Company in 1892.

Menier *(chocolate)*

The French company takes its name from Jean-Antoine Menier (d.1853), a pharmacist who originally bought a small chocolate factory near the Marne River with the aim of producing chocolate to coat his pills. After his death, the business passed to his son, Émile-Justin, who concentrated on full-scale chocolate manufacture. His own son, Henri, continued the expansionary policy, arranging in 1889 for electricity lines and telephones to be installed in the workers' homes.

Mennen *(toiletries)*

Gerhard Mennen (1856-1902), a German-born drugstore owner in downtown Newark, New Jersey, brought out his first product in 1879, a foot remedy of his own invention that he called Mennen's Sure Corn Killer. Its sales were slight, however, and Mennen looked for a more lucrative product to make in his back-room laboratory. He found it when many of the young mothers who visited his store complained that the chalk-type powders then on the market were ineffective in relieving diaper rash. Mennen devised a talc-based powder, which he first handed out as free samples in 1889. A short time after, contented mothers were reporting that the powder had worked wonders in dealing with the rash. Mennen went into fullscale production of the powder, and incorporated his business in 1892 as the Gerhard Mennen Chemical Company. The firm later diversified into other products, and in 1931 introduced its famous Mennen Skin Bracer.

Menzies, John *see* **John Menzies**

Mercedes-Benz *(automobiles)*

The cars known simply as Mercedes from 1901 to 1926 were **Daimlers** before this period and Mercedes-Benz after it. The Mercedes name is due to Emil Jellinek, a rich and influential Austrian banker who was a Daimler enthusiast and who suggested to the technical chief at the Daimler works in Germany that they design a more modern car than the existing 1899 Daimler Phoenix. Jellinek was not only a banker but also a racing driver, and when he raced his cars (always a Daimler) he drove under the name "Mercedes," that of his young daughter, Mercedes Jellinek (1889-1929). In 1901, Daimler produced a newly designed car for Jellinek to use in the Nice Speed Week, after which all German Daimlers were renamed Mercedes by way of a tribute to him. The name "Benz" was added in 1926 when the two firms of Daimler and Benz combined. The latter's originator was the German engineer Carl Benz (1844-1929), who founded Benz & Cie in 1885 to build stationary internal combustion engines and who in 1887 produced the world's first car to run on an engine of this type. The Mercedes-Benz name is now one of the most glamorous in the world automotive market.

Exactly 100 years ago, Emil put us in the history books by asking us to build him a light, beautiful car that was fast enough to win the Nice race. So we did. He also suggested we name our pride and joy after his pride and joy. His 10-year-old daughter, Mercedes. So we did. Even now, we build nearly every car to the owner's individual requirements. Only please, don't ask us to rename it again. (Mercedes-Benz ad, *Sunday Times*, April 1, 2001.)

Mercer *(automobiles)*

The Mercer Automobile Company was founded in the early years of the 20th century by the Roebling family, famous for John Augustus Roebling (1806-1869), the designer of Brooklyn Bridge, and his son, Washington Augustus Roebling (1837-1926), who took over from his father as chief engineer and saw through construction of the bridge to its completion. The Roeblings were based in Trenton, New Jersey, the seat of Mercer County. Hence the name of their company, which launched the Raceabout, an early type of sports car, in 1911. The limited demand for the firm's cars gradually died away, however, and the last Mercers were sold in 1925. All three of the founding members died before 1918, one tragically in the *Titanic* disaster of 1912.

Merck *(pharmaceuticals)*

The name is ultimately that of Friedrich Jacob Merck, who in 1668 bought an apothecary next to the castle moat in Darmstadt, Germany. His direct descendant, Heinrich Emmanuel Merck, was the originator of the company that now bears the name. This younger Merck, a friend of Justin von Liebig, the well-known chemist, began manufacturing drugs in Darmstadt in 1827, starting with morphine. The result of his work, which aimed to test Liebig's theories on organic chemistry, was the setting up of a company to make further drugs. By 1855, the year of his death, Merck's products were already in use all over the world, including in particular the United States, where in 1899 Heinrich's grandson, George Merck, began manufacturing chemical and drugs. The site of his business, Rahway, New Jersey, remains the company's headquarters today. Merck died in 1925, whereupon his son, George Wilhelm Merck (1894-1957), already in the firm, became president. Under his leadership Merck & Co become one of the foremost American pharmaceutical manuacturers, merging with Sharp & Dohme in 1953.

Meredith & Drew *(cookies, or biscuits)*

The British paired names are those of William Meredith and William George Drew. Meredith set up as a baker in London in 1830, with Drew as his chief assistant. Unfortunately, the two men frequently disagreed, and split up in 1852. In 1891, however, the business reunited under their more harmonious sons, Fred Meredith and Lear J. Drew, who in an agreeable show of amity tossed a coin to decide the order of their names in a new partnership. Meredith, as we now know, was the winner.

Merriam-Webster *(publishers)*

The American publishing house, noted for its dictionaries and reference works, takes its name from the brothers George Merriam (1803-1880) and Charles Merriam (1806-1887), born respectively in Worcester and West Brookfield, Massachusetts, the sons of a newspaper publisher and editor. As young men they joined the family business, but in 1831 set up a printing shop and bookstore in Springfield, Massachusetts, naming their fledgling business G. & C. Merriam and Co. On the death of the lexicographer Noah Webster in 1843, they acquired the copyright of his *American Dictionary of the English Language,* first published in 1828. The Merriams brought out their edition of this in 1847 to great acclaim under their present combined name. Merriam-Webster reference works now carry a notice on the verso of the title page:

> The name *Webster* alone is no guarantee of excellence. It is used by a number of publishers and may serve mainly to mislead an unwary buyer.
>
> A *Merriam-Webster®* is the registered trademark you should look for when you consider the purchase of dictionaries or other fine reference books. It carries the reputation of a company that has been publishing since 1831 and is your assurance of quality and authority.

Merrill Lynch *(securities brokerage)*

The American company, formally known as Merrill Lynch, Pierce, Fenner & Smith, is the world's largest stock brokerage house. The first name is that of Charles Edward Merrill (1885-1956), born in Green Cove Springs, Florida, the son of a physician and drugstore proprietor. As a teenager in Jacksonville, Florida, Merrill did good business selling newspapers at the edge of the red light district to gentlemen wishing to hide their faces on leaving. At age 22 Merrill went to New York City, where he worked in the city office of Patchogue Plymouth Mills, a textile firm that operated its main factory in Patchogue. It was in New York that he had met Edmund C. Lynch (d.1938), at a Young Men's Christian Association facility, and the two become close friends and as-

sociates. In 1914 Merrill set up his own securities firm, Charles E. Merrill & Company, and Lynch joined him.

Merrydown *(cider)*

The British business was founded in 1946 by Ian Howie and Jack Ward. The two men produced the first 400 gallons of cider in the garage of Ward's house in Rotherfield, East Sussex. Having no name for the new enterprise, they adopted the name of his house, "Merrydown," itself suggesting the South Downs that are a famous natural feature of the county. There is also a fortuitous association with archaic English "merry-go-down" as an old term for strong ale. The name was entered in the *Trade Marks Journal* of April 17, 1957.

Merthiolate *(disinfectant)*

The proprietary name of thiomersal, a medical disinfectant and preservative for biological products that inhibits the growth of bacteria and other microorganisms, represents a shortening of the compound's full name, sodium ethyl *mercurithio*salicy*late,* entered by **Eli Lilly** in the US Patent Office *Official Gazette* of November 6, 1928: "For medical or pharmaceutical preparation—viz., sodium mercurithiosalicylate or organic mercury compound solution useful in antisepsis."

Messerschmitt *(automobiles)*

The Messerschmitt 109 was the leading fighter aircraft of the Luftwaffe during World War II and feared by the Allies. It took its name from Willy Messerchmitt (1898-1978), born in Frankfurt am Main, who set up his aircraft manufacturing works in 1932. After the war Germany was forbidden to build aircraft, and Messerschmitt kept his employees together by giving them all kinds of jobs. They were joined in 1952 by Fritz Fend, who had been building single-seater three-wheeler cars for some years, and he convinced Messerschmitt to put the car into production. One car for one person seemed not such a good idea, however, and Messerschmitt introduced a two-seater in 1953. The first four-wheeler appeared in 1958, by which time Messerschmitt had sold the factory to Fend, who continued to build the cars as FMR (Fahrzeug- und Maschinenbau Regensburg, "Regensburg Vehicle and Engine Construction"). *See also* (1) **Focke-Wulf**; (2) **Heinkel**.

Meta *(fuel and slugkiller)*

The name, a shortening of "metaldehyde," is used for a prepared block of this chemical compound serving either as a fuel ("solid spirit") for a portable stove or as pellets for killing slugs. It was entered by the Swiss firm of Lonza Elektrizitätswerke in the former sense in the *Trade Marks Journal* of March 26, 1924, and in the latter in the *Journal* of May 18, 1938.

Metal Box *(packaging)*

In 1869 Edward Barlow (1846-1937) set himself up in the East End of London, England, to make tin boxes, a trade then requiring a simple stock of tinplate and solder, some shears and a soldering iron, and a minimum of skill. By the end of the century his business began to prosper. In 1921, in a separate development, the leading tin-box manufacturers of Britain set up Metal Box & Printing Industries Ltd. as a holding company for a loose association of various family firms. Edward Barlow's enterprise, which had now passed to his son, Robert Barlow (1891-1976), was at first not one of their number, but eventually joined in 1929. Barlow Jr. soon took over the leadership of the firm and in 1930 renamed it as The Metal Box Co. The company rapidly acquired a monopoly in the UK in the supply of metal cans and gradually extended the scope of its activities. In 1988 the simple name was abandoned in favor of a more businesslike CMB Packaging Ltd.

Metallgesellschaft *(mining and metal refining)*

The German industrial company, its name meaning simply "Metal Company," was founded in 1881 by Wilhelm Merton (1848-1916) and originally confined its activities to metal trading. In 1928 it merged with Metallbank and Metallurgische Gesellschaft, established in 1910, and through this and other mergers and acquisitions became one of the largest industrial enterprises in Europe.

Metamec *(clocks)*

The British firm was founded in 1923 by one G.B. Jenkins, presumably as a more general engineering business, since Metamec did not make clocks until 1943. The name comes from "metal" and the first element of "mechanics." The name was entered in the *Trade Marks Journal* of January 21, 1948.

Metaxa *(brandy)*

The name of the dark Greek brandy is that of Spyros Metaxa, who as a young silk trader in the late 1880s began to experiment with a new process of blending muscat wines from the Aegean Islands with aged distilled Greek spirits. He eventually discovered the right proportions of each, and put his new product on the market in 1890.

Methedrine *(stimulant drug)*

The proprietary name for methamphetamine derives from the first part of this word and the last part of **Benzedrine**. It was entered by The **Wellcome** Foundation in the *Trade Marks Journal* of January 11, 1939, and the drug itself was originally used in World War II by the German army to counter fatigue on missions where little sleep was possible.

Methuen *(publishers)*

The founder of the British publishing house was Algernon Methuen Marshall Methuen (1856-1924), whose original surname was Stedman. He was born a doctor's son in Southwark, London, and on completing his education at public school and Oxford worked for two years in a coaching (tutorial) establishment before opening his own school at Milford, Surrey, in 1880. While still a schoolmaster, he wrote a number of Latin, Greek, and French textbooks, at first selling them himself from the school, then having them published by George Bell & Sons. The success of his enterprise prompted him to set up his own publishing business, and in 1889 he opened an office to this end in a room off Bury Street, London, near the British Museum. He named his business Methuen & Co., because he did not wish to mix his teaching with his publishing. In 1896 he gave up teaching altogether, and in 1899 changed his own name from Stedman to Methuen. Methuen & Co. became a limited company in 1910, and six years later Methuen was created a baron. Methuen was owned by **Reed** International until 1997, when it was bought by **Random House**.

Metopirone *(drug for treating hormonal disorders)*

The proprietary name for metyrapone, used to treat Cushing's syndrome, is an adjustment of the generic name, with alteration of "y" to "i" and the insertion of "o." The name was entered by the Swiss firm of CIBA Ltd. (*see* **Ciba-Geigy**) in the *Trade Marks Journal* of February 8, 1961.

Metrazol *(analeptic)*

The proprietary name for leptazol, a drug formerly used in convulsive psychotherapy, is extracted from its chemical name, penta*meth*-ylenete*trazol*, entered by E. Bilhuber, Inc., in the US Patent Office *Official Gazette* of September 11, 1928: "For medicine for the heart and the vascular system."

Metro-Goldwyn-Mayer *see* **MGM**

Mettoy *(toys)*

The British company was set up in Northampton in the mid-1930s by Arthur Katz (1908-1999), born in South Africa to German parents, who had emigrated with his family to England on the coming to power of Hitler in 1933. The firm specialized in metal toys (hence the name), and by 1939 employed 600 people. During World War II production was switched to military components. Pressure diecasting in zinc was introduced in 1955 and in the form of **Corgi Toys** dominated the company's growth and worldwide renown.

MFI *("flatpack furniture" stores)*

The initials of the British company stand for Mullard Furniture Industries, Mullard being the maiden name of Lucy Searle, wife of the firm's founder in 1964, Donald Searle (d.1970). Searle's cofounder was Noel Lister (b.1928) and the two men began their venture by selling "downmarket" furniture and camping gear by mail order. Their business was not a success, however, so in the early 1970s, following Searle's tragic death in a gliding accident, the firm moved out of the High Streets of the north of England towns where it had started up, and transferred to out-of-town sites, setting up warehouses where customers could buy self-assemblable furniture. MFI opened a new store every month over the next ten years, and today it has stores throughout Britain. Like many initialisms, the name has been the butt of mean jokes, in this case enduring an interpretation as "Made For Idiots."

MG *(automobiles)*

The initials of the distinctive sports car stand for "Morris Garages," as the company set up by William **Morris** in Oxford, where the marque was first produced in 1923. Its base did not long remain in Oxford, however, and in 1929 the business moved into its new factory in Abingdon, Berkshire (now Oxfordshire), where the first of the famous "Midgets", the M-Type, was produced. In 1961 the company produced its best-selling sports car, the MGB, the "B" standing for BMC (British Motor Corporation), of which MG was by then a part (*see* **BL**). Production continued until 1980, when the Abingdon plant was closed down. The marque was soon revived, however, though all types were merely modified versions of **Austin-Rover** cars. After mixed fortunes, the smart and stylish MGF was launched in 1996 and became the best-selling sports car in Britain.

MGM *(motion pictures)*

There is no need to be a movie buff to know that these initials stand for Metro-Goldwyn-Mayer. As this triple name implies, the company arose as the merger of three individual businesses. Goldwyn was Samuel Goldwyn (1879-1974), the American motion picture pioneer, born Schmuel Gelbfisz in Warsaw, Poland. He had started a movie company in 1916 with two Broadway producers, Edgar and Arch Selwyn, and, by combining half of his anglicized surname, Goldfish, with half of theirs, created the Goldwyn Corporation. He liked the name so much that he subsequently adopted it himself. Mayer was Louis B. Mayer (1885-1957), born Lazar Meir, probably in the Ukrainian town of Dumier, whose family immigrated to New York City around 1887. In 1915 Mayer created the Metro Pictures Corporation in Boston but three years later left Metro to set up a film production unit in Los Angeles. His success attracted the attention of Marcus Loew, the owner of **Loew's** theaters and Metro Pictures, who was negotiating the purchase of the Goldwyn studio. He needed an experienced executive to oversee the films that would be produced by the combined Metro-Goldwyn company and in 1924 appointed Mayer to serve as vice president in charge of production at the studio. Mayer and Loew decided to rename the studio Metro-Goldwyn-Mayer to honor the new executive. Goldwyn, meanwhile, had been edged out of his own company two years earlier as a result of corpo-

318

rate infighting, and had no affiliation with MGM.

Micarta *(insulating material)*

The laminated electrical insulating material originally consisted of paper, mica, and enamel, but is now composed of layers of paper or fabrics bound by a resin and used in the form of sheets or tubes. The name, deriving from "mica" and possibly Italian *carta*, "paper," was entered by the **Westinghouse** Electric & Manufacturing Co. in the US Patent Office *Official Gazette* of February 10, 1914, with a claim of use since April 4, 1912, and the *Trade Marks Journal* of January 3, 1923.

Michael Joseph *(publishers)*

Michael Joseph (1897-1958), born in London, England, the son of a diamond merchant, was educated at the City of London School and London University. No sooner was his education completed than it was time for him to serve in the army in World War I, which he did in the Wiltshire Regiment, then the Machine Gun Corps. He had already started writing, and had his first book published (significantly, *Short Story Writing for Profit*) when he was still in his 20s. Writing led to publishing, and to a near ideal situation where he could publish his own books, many of which were on his beloved cats. The British publishing house that bears his name was formed in 1935, a potentially difficult time, when several other publishers were closing. But Joseph held on ("by the skin of my teeth," he wrote in *The Adventure of Publishing*) and his name lives on today as an imprint of **Penguin**.

Michelin *(tires)*

The name is that of two French brothers, André Michelin (1853-1931) and Édouard Michelin (1859-1940), the former born in Paris, the latter in Clermont-Ferrand. In 1888 the two men set up the Michelin Tire Company to manufacture tires for bicycles and horse-drawn carriages. They later went on to prove that pneumatic tires could be fitted to automobiles, just as **Dunlop** had done for bicycles in the very year that the Michelins set up their business. The first car to be equipped with Michelin tires of this type, held onto the rim of the wheel by bolts, was the 4 h.p. **Daimler** that Édouard Michelin drove in the Paris-Bor-

deaux road race of 1895. He did not win, but popular interest in pneumatic tires was created as a result. In 1990 Michelin acquired **Uniroyal-Goodrich**, making it the world's largest tire manufacturer.

Michelob *(beer)*

The American lager beer was first brought out in 1896 by Adolphus Busch of **Anheuser-Busch**, who named it (in altered form) after the brewery in the Czech village of Mecholuby. There is no longer a brewer there, so the name is not challenged in the legal dispute over the name **Budweiser**.

Microsoft *(computer software)*

The American corporation was the creation in 1977 at age 19 of William Henry "Bill" Gates (b.1955), born in Seattle, Washington. At age 15 he constructed a device to control traffic patterns in Seattle. In 1975 he dropped out of Harvard to write computer programs, and two years later cofounded Microsoft with Paul Allen. The company name simply refers to the *micro*computer *soft*ware that they produce.

Midori *(liqueur)*

The bright green Japanese liqueur, launched by **Suntory** in the early 1980s, is flavored with green-dyed melons. It is thus hardly surprising that its name derives from Japanese *midori*, "green."

Miele *(domestic appliances)*

The German company, based in Gütersloh, traces its origins to 1899, when Carl Miele (1869-1938) and Reinhard Zinkann (1869-1939) began producing butter churns and cream separators in a former corn mill in Herzebrock. In 1907, when production facilities on the site could no longer be expanded, the business was transferred to nearby Gütersloh, where a large site with its own railroad sidings was available. By this time washing machines were already under production, and with growing diversification a new factory was built at Bielefeld, where the manufacture of bicycles began in 1924. Vacuum cleaner production came in 1927. Miele launched Europe's first all-metal washing machine in 1930, and the first fully automatic washing machines followed in 1956. (The production of bicycles gave way to dishwashers in 1960.) The firm is still in family hands. Control passed in 1939 to Carl Miele, Jr. (1897-1986) and Kurt Christian Zinkann (1904-1985), and in due course was transferred to their respective sons, Rudolf Miele (b.1929) and Peter Zinkann (b.1928).

Midland Bank *see* **HSBC**

MiG *(aircraft)*

The Russian fighter aircraft, familiar in World War II, took its name from the initials of its designers, Artyom Mikoyan (1905-1970) and Mikhail Gurevich (1893-1976), with *i* the Russian for "and." The MiG-1, MiG-3, MiG-5, and MiG-7 were propeller-driven, but the MiG-9, which first flew in 1946, was the first jet-powered aircraft produced by the Soviet Union. Appropriately for a fast plane, Russian *mig* means "instant," "moment," while *migom* means "in a flash."

Miles *(pharmaceuticals)*

The name, familiar from **Alka-Seltzer** packs, is that of Franklin Miles, an American doctor who had a practice in Elkhart, Indiana, in the second half of the 19th century. He was keen to produce home remedies, the first of these being a sedative that he called "Dr. Miles' Nervine." The Dr. Miles Medical Company was formed in 1884 and remained small in its operations until Alka-Seltzer was added to the firm's products in 1931. This great money-spinner was not directly attributable to Miles himself, but to one of the company's chemists. Even so, it might have never evolved without Dr. Miles' groundwork half a century earlier.

Milium *(insulating fabric)*

The fabric was developed by the firm of Deering, Milliken & Co., and appears to derive its name from the latter. (The names are those of William Deering and Seth Milliken, who in 1865 formed a partnership to sell woolens. Deering later manufactured harvesters; *see* **International Harvester**.) The fabric name was entered by the Vadium Corporation, of Wilmington, Delaware, in the US Patent Office *Official Gazette* of September 4, 1951: "For Textile Fabrics of Cotton, Rayon, Nylon, and Mixtures Thereof Having Heat Reflective and/or Heat Retentive Properties," with a claim of use since April 20, 1950.

Milk of Magnesia *see* **Phillips'**

Milka *(chocolate)*

The milk chocolate bar of this name, now familiar throughout Europe, was launched by **Suchard** in 1901. The name takes into account the similarity of the word for "milk" in many European languages, such as German *Milch*, Dutch, Danish, and Norwegian *melk*, Swedish *mjölk*, Russian *moloko*, Polish *mleko*, etc.

Milky Way *(candy bar)*

The chocolate-coated bar with a milk-white filling was launched by **Mars** in 1924. It was given a name to suggest its taste, that of a chocolate-flavored malt drink, while at the same time having an astronomical association with the manufacturer's name and even suggesting "milky whey." The name was entered in the *Trade Marks Journal* of September 13, 1933.

Millelire *(publishers)*

The Italian publishing house was founded by Marcello Baraghini in Rome in 1992. Its name represents Italian *mille lire*, "thousand lire," denoting the extraordinarily cheap price (under a dollar) of its paperbacks. The enterprise revolutionized bookselling in Italy.

Miller *(beer)*

The name is that of a German immigrant to the United States, Frederick Miller (1824-1888), who arrived in New Orleans in 1854 and the following year took over a small brewery already established by the two Best brothers in Milwaukee, Wisconsin. At first the brewery gained a reputation for its conventional "High Life" beer. But when the business was taken over by **Philip Morris** in 1970, it turned to "light" beers, popular among weight-conscious, dieting Americans. Miller purchased the "Lite" trademark from Chicago's failing Meister Brau brewery, who had introduced "Meister Brau Lite" in 1967, and launched their own famous "Miller Lite" in 1975. "Lite" itself, as respelled "light," was entered for "beer with no available carbohydrates" in the US Patent Office *Official Gazette* of November 30, 1971, with a note of first use on May 15, 1967.

Mills & Boon *(publishers)*

A byword for cheaply priced romantic fiction, the name of the British company comes from Gerald Mills (1877-1927) and Charles Boon

(1877-1943). When the two men founded their London publishing business in 1908, they did not specialize in romantic fiction at all, but put out the work of authors such as P.G. Wodehouse, Jack London, and Hugh Walpole. During the depressed interwar years, however, reading became a favorite form of escapism among the British public, and when the "tuppenny" (rental) libraries sprang up to cater for this need, Charles Boon decided to go for hardback romances. The books were a great success, and led eventually to the familiar paperback Mills & Boon fiction of today, with a fresh selection of stories published each month under the "Rose of Romance" label. Charles Boon's sons, Alan (1913-2000) and John (1916-1996), took over the running of the company after their father's death.

Miltown *(sedative)*

The proprietary name for the drug meprobamate, used as a muscle relaxant and as a sedative, was entered by Carter Products, Inc., of New York in the US Patent Office *Official Gazette* of February 27, 1957. It was invented by Dr. F.M. Berger, who appears to have based the name on a placename.

Mimeograph *(duplicating machine)*

The former type of duplicating machine produced copies from a stencil and took its name from Greek *mimeomai*, "I imitate," and the Greek-based element "-graph" meaning "write." The name was proprietary from 1903 through 1948 but the machine itself, now superseded by the photocopier, was invented by Edison in 1870.

Mini *(automobiles)*

One of the most successful designs of all time, the Mini was launched in 1959 by the British Motor Corporation (*see* **BL**). It was small (hence its name), cheap, and held the road well with its front-wheel drive and independent suspension. Initially it was marketed under the **Austin** and **Morris** labels. From 1961, a faster version, the Mini Cooper, was the result of cooperation between Alec Issigonis (1906-1988), designer of the original Mini, and John Cooper (1923-2000), a Formula 1 racing constructor. It was dropped in 1969 but reintroduced in 1990. Two new models, the Mini One and the Mini Cooper, were launched in

the UK in 2001 by **BMW** following its purchase of **Rover**.

Mini-Moke *(utility vehicle)*

The small motor vehicle, something like a **Jeep**, was launched in the early 1960s by the British Motor Corporation (*see* **BL**) and named for a moke (donkey) in allusion to its "workhorse" ability.

Minipiano *(piano)*

The British make of small piano dates from the 1930s. Its name, of obvious origin, was entered by its manufacturers, Brasted Bros. Ltd., of London, in the *Trade Marks Journal* of April 4, 1934.

Minnesota Mining & Manufacturing *see* **3M**

Minolta *(cameras)*

The name derives acronymically from four words: "machine," "instrument," "optical," and "Tajima," this last being Tajima Shoten (the latter word means "warehouse"), a Japanese wholesale firm dealing in silk fabrics run by the father of Kazuo Tashima, the actual founder of the Minolta Camera Company. The name was entered in the *Trade Marks Journal* of September 18, 1957.

Minox *(miniature cameras)*

The name appears to be based on "miniature" (or simply "mini"). It was entered by the German manufacturers of the same name, based in the village of Heuchelheim, near Giessen, in the *Trade Marks Journal* of April 6, 1966.

Minties *(peppermint-flavored candy)*

The name of the Australian candy, of obvious origin, was entered in 1926 by the manufacturers, James Stedman-Henderson's Sweets Ltd., in the *Australian Official Journal of Patents* (Canberra).

Mintoes *see* **Nuttalls**

Minuit *(publishers)*

The French publishing house Les Éditions de Minuit was founded clandestinely in 1942 by Pierre de Lescure and the writer Vercors (1902-1991), original name Jean Bruller, during the German occupation of France. Much of the printing was done at night. Hence its name, from French *minuit,* "midnight." Its first publication was Vercors' novel on the Resistance, *Le Silence de la mer* (1942), and 24 further such novels appeared before the end of the war. In 1948 the firm was taken over and built up by Jérôme Lindon (1925-2001), and is now run by his daughter.

Minute *(tapioca)*

Now marketed by General Foods (*see* **Bird's**), the dessert was originally made by the Minute Tapioca Company, founded in 1908. It arose from an idea that occurred in 1894 to Susan Stavers, a landlady in Boston, Massachusetts, when her lodgers complained of the lumpiness of her tapioca pudding. To obtain a finer texture, she put the raw tapioca through her kitchen coffee grinder before making the pudding. The result was a smoother, creamier tapioca than had hitherto been thought possible. Anxious to capitalize on her discovery, Mrs. Stavers began to grind more tapicoa and pack it in paper bags for sale to her neighbors. The word soon spread, and John Whitman, owner of a newspaper called the *Enterprise & Journal,* bought the rights to use the process and quickly formed the Whitman Grocery Company to make and sell the new product under the name of "Tapioca Superlative." In 1896 he changed the name to "Minute Tapioca" in honor of the famed minutemen of Revolutionary days, who agreed to be ready for military duty "at a minute's warning." Hence the picture of the minuteman as the well-known trademark. The company itself took the name in 1908.

Mipolam *(plastic)*

The name of various plastics composed of polyvinyl chloride, used for chemically resistant piping and containers, is apparently of arbitrary origin. It was entered by the German manufacturers, Dynamit-Actien-Gesellschaft ("Dynamite Joint-Stock Company"), formerly Alfred Nobel Co., of Troisdorf, near Cologne, in the *Trade Marks Journal* of October 24, 1951.

Mira Lanza *(detergents and soaps)*

The Italian company was formed in 1924 following the merger between the Unione Stearinerie Lanza ("Lanza Stearinery Union") and the Fabbrica Candele Steariche di Mira ("Mira Stearic Candle Works"). It was subsequently acquired in turn by **Piaggio, Monte-** dison, and finally **Ferruzzi**, who in 1988 sold it off to the German firm of Benckiser.

Mirex *(insecticide)*

The chlorinated hydrocarbon compound is used especially to control fire ants, suggesting that the name may be based on Greek *murmex,* "ant." The name is not proprietary or a registered trademark, so can be legitimately written with a lowercase initial ("mirex").

Mr Kipling *(cakes)*

The cakes of this name, sold by the British firm of Manor Bakeries, were first produced in the late 1960s. The name is not that of an actual person, and still less of the writer Rudyard Kipling, but was created as that of a fictional "master baker" who baked traditional-style cakes having a homemade appearance. The name itself was thus chosen to suggest a succulent baking process. Manor Bakeries were set up by **Rank Hovis McDougall** to market the named range of cakes, which they have now done for several years with the slogan, "Mr Kipling bakes exceedingly good cakes."

Mitchell Beazley *(publishers)*

The British publishers, noted for their illustrated reference works, were founded in 1969 by James Mitchell (1939-1985) and John Beazley (d.1977), until then respectively editorial and production directors at **Nelson**. Their original plan was to publish a single bestseller a year, which they achieved with their first three titles: Patrick Moore's *Moon Flight Atlas* (1969), the same author's *The Atlas of the Universe* (1970), and Hugh Johnson's *The World Atlas of Wine* (1971). The latter sold one million copies by the end of the decade. Mitchell Beazley then moved away from atlases into other reference works, such as Alex Comfort's bestselling *The Joy of Sex* (1974) and the ambitious ten-volume illustrated encyclopedia *The Joy of Knowledge* (1977-8).

Mitel *(telecommunications)*

The Mitel story began in the summer of 1969, when Welsh electrical engineer Terry Matthews (b.1943) and his wife were on vacation in Canada. A friend introduced him to some senior people at Microsystems International Ltd., which had opened that year in Ottawa as a federally subsidized venture by the

Northern Electric Co. Ltd. into semiconductors. Matthews was taken on as a team member in the new-products division, but soon became frustrated. In 1972, he set up a small
consulting company, Advanced Devices Consultants of Canada, Ltd., but the firm failed to
take off. Instead, with a bank loan of $4,000,
he set up a business with a fellow team member, Michael Cowpland, calling it Mitel, from
the pet forms of their respective first names
(Mike and Tel). Matthews had the marketing
knowhow, and Cowpland the technical talent.
Pioneering electronic switching systems that allowed for operator-free exchanges and touch-
tone phone sets, the company enjoyed an explosive growth, with sales doubling annually
until 1984, when they peaked at $280 million.
A year later, Mitel sold a controlling stake to
British Telecom, whom Matthews had originally joined at the age of 15 when it was still the
telephone arm of the General Post Office.

Mitin (mothproofing agent)

The name of various mothproofing agents,
perhaps based on "mite" (as a term for a para-
site), was entered by the Swiss firm of J.R.
Geigy (see Ciba-Geigy) in the Trade Marks
Journal of August 17, 1938.

Mitsubishi (automobiles)

Automobiles are only one of the items produced by the consortium of independent Japanese companies, which include the Mitsubishi
Bank, Mitsubishi Corporation, and Mitsubishi
Electric Corporation. They all grew from the
Mitsubishi Commercial Company, formed as a
trading and shipping concern in 1873 by
Iwasaki Yataro out of the government-operated
shipping company that he had managed since
1870. The name means "three stones," from
Japanese mitsu, "three," and ishi, "stone," implying three precious stones or diamonds, as
represented graphically by the company's logo
of three equilaterally placed rhombuses.

Mitsui (diversified trading)

The roots of the consortium of independent
Japanese companies go back to 1673, when
Mitsui Takatoshi (1622-1694), the son of a sake
brewer, opened textile shops in Kyoto and Edo
(now Tokyo). His success led him into money-
lending and other financial services, and from
1691 members of the Mitsui family were offi-

cially recognised as chartered merchants. The
present combine dates from 1909, when the
family council established in the early 18th century to oversee operations was replaced by a
family-controlled holding company.

Mixmaster (foodmixer)

The make of electric foodmixer and fruit
juice extractor has a name of obvious origin entered by the Chicago Flexible Shaft Co. in the
US Patent Office Official Gazette of June 11,
1935.

Mobil (petroleum)

The Mobil Corporation, one of the largest
American holding companies, traces its origins
to 1866, when the Vacuum Oil Company was
founded. In 1882 it became part of the **Standard Oil** Trust, which that same year founded
another company, the Standard Oil Company
(New York) (Socony). Both companies became
independent in 1911, when the US Supreme
Court dissolved the Standard Oil combine, but
they then merged in 1931 to form Socony-Vacuum Corporation. This name was changed in
1934 to Socony-Vacuum Oil Company, in 1955
to Socony Mobil Oil Company, and then in
1966 to Mobil Oil Corporation. The Mobil
name began its life in England, where "Mobiloil" was already available in 1899. The source
of the name was probably in "mobile," or in the
Latin mobilis that gave this word. The reference
was to the new motor car, which "Mobiloil" lu-
bricated. The name was registered in the United
States as a trademark for lubricating oils in 1920.

Mobylette (moped)

The French make of moped or motorized
bicycle, manufactured by **Motobécane**, derives
its name from a blend of mobile, "mobile," and
bicyclette, "bicycle." The name dates from 1955.

Moët et Chandon (champagne)

The champagne from Épernay, France, derives its name from Claude Moët (b.1683), who
founded the house in that town in 1743, and
his grandson's son-in-law, Comte Pierre
Gabriel Chandon de Briailles, who took over
the company in 1832. In 1971 Moët et Chandon merged with **Hennessy** to form Moët
Hennessy, which in turn merged with **Louis
Vuitton** in 1987 to form the luxury goods conglomerate LVMH.

Mogadon *(sleeping drug)*

The proprietary name for nitrazepam, a short-acting hypnotic drug given to treat insomnia, was entered by Roche Products (*see* **Hoffmann-La Roche**), of Welwyn Garden City, Hertfordshire, England, in the *Trade Marks Journal* of February 22, 1956. The name appears to be arbitrary, but it happens to be an anagram of "Goodman" (or "good man"), perhaps referring to a person connected with its development. A source in Greek *mogos*, "pain," and *donax*, "dart," has also been suggested.

Moler *(building and insulating material)*

The type of sandy sediment from the fjords of Denmark was first exploited at the turn of the 20th century and named from Danish dialect *mo*, "loose chalky soil," and *ler*, "loam," "clay." The name was entered by the Danish firm of Skarrehage Molervaerk and the British firm Refractulation Ltd. in the *Trade Marks Journal* of June 6, 1963 for: "Insulators and insulating materials."

Molex *(electrical products)*

The US company of this name was founded in 1938 as the Molex Products Co. in Brookfield, Illinois, by Frederick August Krehbiel to manufacture a variety of products from the named material, a form of **Moler**, such as clock cases, flower pots, valve wheels, and salt tablet dispensers. In 1940 one of Krehbiel's sons, John H. Krehbiel, Jr., joined the business, and recognized the importance of the electrical and insulating properties of Molex. The company went on to become the world's second largest manufacturer of electrical and electronic products. The name was entered in the *Trade Marks Journal* of July 12, 1967.

Molson *(beer)*

The Canadian beer takes its name from John Molson (1764-1836), an English immigrant from Lincolnshire, who came to Montreal in 1782 and soon made his fortune trading in meats and other foodstuffs. Not long after, he and a partner set up a small brewery. Molson gained complete control of the business in 1785 and built it into a sucessful brewery by the end of the century. Molson is now based in Toronto, where it became the rival to **Labatt**. In 1989 Molson merged with **Carling**

O'Keefe to make it the largest Canadian brewer.

Monastral *(pigments)*

The name is that of two groups of synthetic pigments of exceptional fastness: Monastral blue and green, derivatives of phthalocyanine, used in paints, printing inks, and plastics, and Monastral red and violet, derivatives of quinacridone. The name was entered by the British Dyestuffs Corporation Ltd. (*see* **ICI**) in the *Trade Marks Journal* of January 2, 1936. The name itself looks meaningful but is perhaps of random origin.

Mondadori *(publishers)*

The Italian publishing house was founded in Milan in 1907 by Arnoldo Mondadori (1889-1971). After World War II they expanded their activities to include newspapers and magazines, and in 1976 founded the daily newspaper *La Repubblica*. In 1989 they acquired the influential weekly *L'Espresso*, but sold both publications off in 1991 to the CIR (Compagnie Industriale Riuniti, "United Industrial Companies") owned by **Olivetti** chairman Carlo De Benedetti (b.1934).

Monel *(alloys)*

The nickel- and copper-based alloys take their name from Ambrose Monell (1874-1921), cofounder in 1902 and first president of the International Nickel Company (*see* **Inco**), following the invention of the first such alloy in 1904 by the American metallurgist Robert C. Stanley (1876-1951), who succeeded Monell as president after his death. The name "Monel Metal," with Monell's surname modified slightly, was entered by the INC in the *Trade Marks Journal* of February 17, 1909. *See also* **Nimonic**.

Monica *(automobiles)*

The short-lived French car, in production from 1973 to 1975, was named after the wife of its designer and constructor, Jean Tastevin, the head of CFPM (Compagnie Française des Produits Metallurgiques), a firm of railroad wagon manufacturers from Balbigny, near Lyon.

Monk and Glass *(custard)*

The brand name and the accompanying illustration of a jolly monk holding a glass punned on that of the British manufacturers, Monkhouse & Glasscock Ltd, a firm based in

London. It was taken over by General Foods (*see* **Bird's**) in 1958 and although the brand name continued to be advertised for a time, the brand itself was eventually withdrawn.

Monkey Brand (*scouring soap*)

The soap and its name were introduced in 1899, when William Lever (of the future **Unilever**) purchased the US soap firm of Benjamin Brooke & Co. of Philadelphia. The image of the monkey was presumably designed to arrest attention. Early ads showed a clothed monkey seated by the roadside in the guise of a sidewalk artist, holding out a frying pan for "My Own Work," while packets of the soap itself showed a monkey admiring its reflection in a brightly scoured pan. A piece of doggerel also promoted the character, whose ad was designed by G.E. Robinson in 1901:

In costume quaint, with pan in hand,
He would appear, in antic pose,
And sing the praise of Monkey Brand,
That brightens homes, but *Won't Wash Clothes*!

Monopoly (*board game*)

The well-known game, based on the acquisition of real estate, was the brainchild in 1933 of Charles B. Darrow, an out-of-work salesman for an engineering firm from Germantown, Pennsylvania. The game's origins date back to the late 19th century, when property games began to become popular, and it in fact bears a close similarity to "The Landlord's Game," invented by Elizabeth Magie in 1904. Magie had developed her game as a piece of anticapitalistic propaganda, with the aim of showing how unscrupulous landlords could charge exorbitant rents. It is thus somewhat ironic that Monopoly evolved to became one of the great symbols of capitalism. In 1934 the game was acquired by **Parker Brothers**, and they soon arranged for foreign editions. In the UK the game was enthusiastically taken up by **Waddington's**, who substituted London streets for the Atlantic City names of the original American version. (Atlantic City was where Darrow and his wife had spent their last vacation before the stock market crashed.) Today, in whatever country the game is sold, the streets correspond to those of the capital city, so that the most expensive property, Atlantic City's Boardwalk, is Mayfair in London, rue de la Paix in Paris, and Paeso del Prado in Madrid. The name was entered by Waddington's in the *Trade Marks Journal* of June 23, 1954.

Monoprix (*supermarkets*)

The French supermarket chain is noted for its relatively inexpensive products which were originally all sold at the same price. Hence the name, from "mono-" ("one") and French *prix*, "price." *Cp.* **Prisunic**.

Monotype (*composing machine*)

The typesetting machine, now little used, cast type in metal one character at a type. Hence its name, from "mono-" ("one") and "-type." The machine was the brainchild of Tolbert Lanston (1844-1913), who patented his invention in 1887 and set up the Lanston Type Machine Company in Washington, DC, to manufacture it.

Monsanto (*agricultural chemicals*)

The American company was founded in 1901 in St. Louis, Missouri, by John F. Queeny (1859-1933), a purchasing agent for a wholesale drug company. Queeny was unable to persuade the firm he was working for to produce its own saccharin, instead of importing it from Germany. He therefore decided to use $1,500 of his own money and $3,500 borrowed from a local Epsom salts manufacturer to start making the low-calorie sweetener himself, calling his enterprise the Monsanto Chemical Works after his wife's maiden name. By 1905 Queeny was producing caffein and vanillin as well as saccharin, and in 1908 he left his part-time job with the drug house and became Monsanto's full-time president. His activity expanded, with the purchase of an Illinois acid company in 1918, but in 1928, on hearing he had an incurable form of cancer, Queeny turned the business over to his only son, Edgar M. Queeny (1897-1968), who directed it from 1933 until 1962, by which time it had become the Monsanto Chemical Company. It is now the Monsanto Company, with headquarters still in St. Louis.

Montblanc (*pens*)

The celebrity pen was first produced by the Simplo Filler Pen Company, founded in Hamburg, Germany, in 1903 by Claus Johannes Voss, Christian Lausen, and Wilhelm Dziambor, a stationer, banker, and engineer, who had noticed that with the coming of department stores selling mass-produced pens, there was a niche for a luxury brand. By 1909 the firm was selling its "Rouge et Noir" pens in London and Paris, and the following year the "Montblanc" was born. It was named after Europe's highest mountain, on the border between France and Italy, represented graphically by the white snowflake on the pen's cap. By the mid-1930s the company had introduced the screwthread piston filter, changed its name to Montblanc to reflect the product, and added "4810," the mountain's (approximate) height in meters, to its nibs, where it remains today.

Montecristo *(cigars)*

The popular brand of Havana cigar was launched in 1935 by Alonzo Menendez and Pepe Garcia, who had just bought the **H. Upmann** brand from the British firm J. Frankau. It was thus originally known as "H. Upmann Montecristo Selection" and was sold through **Dunhill** in New York. The change of name to Montecristo was suggested by another British firm, John Hunter, which was appointed as the British agent. The name was adopted from Alexandre Dumas' swashbuckling tale *The Count of Montecristo* (1845). The name itself apparently means "Mount (of) Christ," so for commercial purposes has an added biblical resonance.

Montedison *(chemicals and energy)*

The Italian conglomerate was formed in 1966 following the merger of the chemicals company Montecatini, founded in 1888, and the Edison electricity company (*see* **Ediswan**), founded in 1884. Control of Montedison passed in 1986 to **Ferruzzi** when they acquired 40 percent of the shareholding. In 1983 Montedison had set up Erbamont as a separate pharmaceutical entity, which in 1993 passed to the Swedish firm Procordia-Kabi Pharmacia together with **Farmitalia Carlo-Erba**. In 1989 it set up Enimont, a joint venture in the chemicals sector with the state-owned ENI petrochemicals group. ENI (Ente nazionale idrocarburi, "National Hydrocarbons Corporation") began to be privatized in 1995.

Montgomery Ward *(mail order firm)*

The American company takes its name from Aaron Montgomery Ward (*c.*1844-1913), born in Chatham, New Jersey, the son of a farmer. When Monty, as the boy was called, was eight or nine, his father sold the family farm and bought what he understood to be a well-stocked general store in Niles, Michigan, a boom town on the St. Joseph River. But when the family arrived in the town they discovered that the store had no merchandise. The elder Ward was thus obliged to work as a clerk in another shop. To support his family, Monty quit school at 14 and worked for a while in a barrel-stave factory. In 1861 he moved to nearby St. Joseph, a larger town on Lake Michigan, and found work in a general store. He made good progress, and three years later became its manager. In the autumn of 1865 Ward moved on to Chicago, where he worked for two years as a clerk at the Field, Palmer & Leiter retail store (*see* **Marshall Field**). He then became a traveling salesman for a succession of employers, and while journeying around conceived of a new type of business that would use the mails and expanding railroad to sell directly to rural people. To put his plan into practice, Ward moved back to Chicago and became a buyer for C. W. & E. Pardridge Company, wholesalers and retailers. The Chicago fire of 1871 destroyed Ward's personal inventory but not his ambition, and in 1872, with George Drake and Robert Caulfield, fellow employees at Pardridge, Ward launched his mail-order business. His firm, incorporated as Montgomery Ward & Company in 1889, was the first national retail business in general merchandise to operate exclusively by mail order. In 1997 Montgomery Ward filed for Chapter 11 bankruptcy protection after losing ground for years to sprightlier department stores such as **Sears, Roebuck**.

Moog *(synthesizer)*

The electronic music synthesizer takes its name from the American audio engineer Robert A. Moog (b.1934), who invented and patented it in 1965 and whose company, Moog Music Inc., of Williamsville, New York, entered the name in the US Patent Office *Official Gazette* of February 5, 1974, with a note of first use on January 1, 1954.

Moosehead *(beer)*

Canada's oldest and largest brewing company was founded in Halifax, Nova Scotia, by Susannah Oland in 1867. It used old family recipes from Britain and then won the contract to supply beer to the Canadian armed forces, so that it became known as the Army and Navy brewery. After a run of misfortune, including the death of brewmaster Conrad Olson in an explosion in 1917 when two ships collided in Halifax harbor, the company moved to St. John's, New Brunswick. In 1931 George Oland renamed his main beer "Moosehead," for the common North American animal, and this proved such a popular innovation that the company adopted the name in 1947.

Mordue *(beer)*

The British brewery was set up in in 1995 in the village of New York near Wallsend, northeastern England, by two young brothers, Matthew and Gary Farson, who named their enterprise after a former brewery that had operated in the building where they started up. In 1997 they won the title Champion Beer of Britain with their ale "Workie Ticket," local slang for a troublemaker.

Morgan *(automobiles)*

The British cars take their name from H.F.S. Morgan (1881-1959), born in Herefordshire the son of a clergyman. He began his career at the age of 18 as a draftsman in the drawing office of the Great Western Railway at Swindon, Wiltshire, but was long undecided whether to specialize in locos or autos. In 1906 he made up his mind and opened a garage and motor works at Malvern Link, Worcestershire. The Morgan Motor Company was formed in 1912 and embarked on the manufacture of three-wheelers. In 1935 it produced its first sports car, the 4/4, so called for its four wheels (as distinct from three) and its four cylinders. The firm has always been in family hands, so that H.F.S. was succeeded by his son Peter (b.1920), who joined in 1947 as "general dogsbody," became managing director in 1958, and was still in charge in 2001 with his own son Charles.

Morgan *(bank)*

The American bank holding company, formally J.P. Morgan and Company, Inc., was formed in 1968 to acquire control of Morgan Guaranty Trust Company, a commercial bank and trust company established in 1959 in the merger of J.P. Morgan and Company, Inc., and Guaranty Trust Company of New York. The former company was founded in 1895 as a reorganization of Drexel, Morgan and Company, a firm in which John Pierpont Morgan (1837-

1913), born in Hartford, Connecticut, son of the merchant banker Junius S. Morgan (1813-1890), became a partner in 1871. In 1861 he had been appointed agent for his father's banking company in New York City and had opened his own foreign exchange office there. J.P. Morgan's son, John Pierpont Morgan, Jr. (1867-1943), succeeded his father as head of the firm on the latter's death.

Morgan, Captain *see* **Captain Morgan**

Morgan Crucible *(industrial materials)*

The British business was founded in 1856 by five Morgan brothers. Its first principal products were crucibles for its nonferrous foundries, and although it now produces a wide range of products, it remains the largest manufacturer of foundry crucibles in the world. The last member of the family to work in the company was Lord Reigate, born John Vaughan-Morgan (1905-1995).

Morgan Grenfell *(bank)*

The Anglo-American bank traces its origins to 1838, when the merchant house of Peabody, Riggs & Company was established by George Peabody of Boston, Massachusetts. The firm was at first located in Moorgate, London, but in 1854 moved to Old Broad Street, when Junius S. Morgan (1813-1890) became a partner. In 1864 Peabody retired and left the firm, which was renamed Junius S. Morgan & Company. With his son, John Pierpont Morgan (1837-1913), founder of J.P. **Morgan** & Company, Morgan developed the firm's banking business, especially in railroad finance and international loans. In 1900 Edward Charles Grenfell (1870-1941), the future Baron St. Just, after making the acquaintance of Walter Hayes Burns, a partner in the firm, was appointed manager of the house. He in turn became a partner in 1904, and in 1909, when the house style had to be changed under the provisions of Junius S. Morgan's will, it was renamed Morgan, Grenfell & Company. In 1989 Morgan Grenfell was taken over by Deutsche Bank.

Morland's *(beer)*

The British brewery, based in Abingdon, Oxfordshire, takes its name from John Morland (1671-1726), a farmer from near Didcot, Berkshire. In 1711 he acquired a maltster's business in his native village of West Ilsley, which on his death passed to his son, Benjamin Morland. He in turn set up a fullblown brewery on the premises, which passed down the family until it came to Edward Morland in the mid-19th century. In 1861 Edward Morland purchased a brewery in Abingdon, acquiring further breweries in the town in due course. It is thus logical for the present company to have its head office there. John Morland was related to the painter George Morland (1763-1804), and the agreeable association between ale and art is represented in the company's logo, which shows an 18th-century artist holding a palette and paint brush in his left hand and a glass of beer in his right. The firm gained fame outside Oxfordshire in the 1990s thanks to its **Old Speckled Hen** beer.

Morley *(hosiery and underwear)*

The name is that of Samuel Morley (1806-1886), born in London, England. His father, John Morley, was a farmer and hosiery manufacturer in Nottinghamshire who in around 1796 moved the family to London to set up a branch of the hosiery business there. On completing his education in 1825, Samuel Morley became a clerk in the firm's counting house. His father died in 1848, and other members of the family gradually retired from the scene, so that in 1855 Samuel was left in sole charge. He immediately began a program of expansion and diversification. The family firm had always been chiefly associated with hosiery, but under Samuel Morley the output was extended to include gloves and, in particular, a wide variety of underwear.

Morny *(perfumes and cosmetics)*

The firm of Morny Frères was founded in London, England, in 1908 by four Englishmen, F.N. Layman, Claud Johnson, Geoffrey Poole, and Walter Hales. They made exclusive perfumes and cosmetics, and combined this business with that of running a pharmacy in Bond Street, with the factory close by in New Burlington Place. They seem to have chosen the French name because of its aristocratic connotations: the Duc de Morny (1811-1865), half-brother of Napoleon III, was a leader of world fashion. The firm changed its name to Morny Ltd. in 1930, the year in which it introduced its "French Fern" perfume. In 1965 Morny was acquired by **Lenthéric**.

Morphy Richards *(electrical appliances)*

The British name is that of William Morphy (1901-1975) and Charles Frederick Richards (1900-1964). Little is known about Morphy's birth or early education, but on leaving Imperial College, London, he was apprenticed to Metropolitan Vickers in Manchester before working for two London electrical companies. He attempted to set up his own business there, but failed. Success eventually came in 1936, when he went into partnership with Charles Richards. The two men started their venture assembling electric fires in a former oasthouse in Kent. As this was only a seasonal product, however, they turned to one with a continuous potential, and started producing electric irons, the appliance with which their name is still primarily associated today. They then went on to manufacture pop-up toasters and refrigerators, with Morphy apparently being the inventive half of the partnership, and Richards handling the marketing. In 1961 the business was taken over by **EMI**, and Morphy retired, leaving Richards to continue alone for a year or so.

Morrell's *(beer)*

The British brewery is the only one left in the city of Oxford, where it was founded by James Morrell in 1782. On Morrell's death in 1855 the business passed to his son, also James, and since 1943 it has been run as a private limited company under the control of the Morrell family.

Morris *(automobiles)*

William Richard Morris (1877-1963), later familiar as Lord Nuffield, was born in Worcester, England, the son of a draper's assistant. He quit school at 15 to be briefly apprenticed to a bicycle trader before setting himself up in his parents' home, now in Oxford, as a bicycle repairer. By 1896 Morris was able to advertise himself as a "cycle-maker," and in 1901 he opened a business at 48 High Street, Oxford. He gradually progressed to making motorcycles and to repairing and servicing automobiles. By 1909 he had moved to new premises in Holywell Street, where he abandoned bicycles altogether and rechristened his business as "Morris Garages." In about 1913 he took the obvious step and began to manufacture cars themselves. The first was the Morris "Oxford," made not in Oxford but outside the city in a new factory at Cowley, which Morris had converted from a former military college. Things took off in a big way after World War I. In 1923 the first of the **MG** sports cars appeared, followed in 1928 by the Morris "Minor," produced as a "counter" to the popular **Austin** Seven. And although the Minor was superseded by the **Mini**, and the MG itself nearly disappeared as a distinctive marque, Morris remains as a prestigious name in British motor manufacturing history, with Morris himself gaining a popular accolade as "Britain's Henry **Ford**." In 1952 Morris merged with Austin to form the British Motor Corporation (*see* **BL**).

Morris, Philip *see* **Philip Morris**

Morrisons *(supermarkets)*

The British supermarket chain dates from 1899, when 24-year-old William Murdoch Morrison, born in Chickenley near Dewsbury, Yorkshire, set up as an egg and butter merchant in Bradford. In 1950 Morrison fell ill and asked his son, then a National Serviceman in Germany, if he would like to come home and take over the business. Kenneth Duncan Morrison (b.1933) did so, and in 1962 opened the first Wm. Morrison supermarket in a disused movie theater in Bradford's Thornton Road. Similar stores followed in other towns, mainly in the North of England, each having a distinctive "Market Street" layout.

Morse *(taper)*

The type of taper on a shank or socket, one of a standard series with specified dimensions and angles, takes its name from the Morse Twist Drill & Machine Co. (later Morse Cutting Tools), of New Bedford, Massachusetts, who entered it in the US Patent Office *Official Gazette* of August 28, 1906, with a note that it had been "used ten years."

Morton *(salt)*

The name is that of Joy Morton (1855-1934), raised on the family's homestead at Arbor Lodge, Nebraska. He quit school at 16 and took up a job as an errand boy at a Nebraska City bank, eventually gaining promotion as a teller. In 1880 Morton used his entire savings to become a partner in E.I. Wheeler & Co., a Chicago salt company. On the death of Wheeler in 1885, Morton gained complete control of the firm, changed its name to Joy Morton & Co., and built it into the nation's largest salt supplier. In 1910 it became the Morton Salt Co. and in 1969 joined forces with the manufacturers of "Norwich" aspirin and "Pepto-Bismol" upset stomach remedy to form MortonNorwich.

Moschino *(fashionwear and perfumes)*

When he was 17, Franco Moschino (1950-1994), born in Abbiategrasso near Milan, Italy, ran away from home rather than join his father's iron foundry. He first worked as a handyman, but in 1972 was taken on by **Versace** as an illustrator. By 1983 he had advanced sufficiently to found his own company, Moonshadow, and that year launched the Moschino label with his first womenswear collection. Menswear followed in 1986, and a year later his first perfume, named after himself. Moschino Parfums was launched in New York in 1991, but only three years later the surrealistic designer, with his anarchic sense of humor, died of complications following an abdominal tumor.

Moskvich *(automobiles)*

The birth of the Moskvich ("Muscovite") goes back to the period of the Russo-German entente before the German invasion of the Soviet Union in 1941, when a Russian **Opel** Kadett called the KM10 was made. The Moskvich proper dates from 1947, when the plant had been removed from Germany to Moscow. The car was produced by the Moskovsky zavod malolitrazhnykh avtomobiley (MZMA) ("Moscow Small-Engined Automobile Factory"), in 1969 renamed the Moskovsky avtomobil'ny zavod imeni Leninskogo komsomola (MAZLK) ("Moscow Automobile Factory Named after the Lenin Komsomol").

Moss Bros *(tailors and clothiers)*

The familiar British name derives ultimately from that of Moses Moses (1820-1894), a bespoke tailor and itinerant secondhand clothes dealer who first set up shop in London's Covent Garden in 1860. He had five sons, George, Alfred, Lewis, Benjamin, and David, of whom only the first two enjoyed their father's confidence. George Moss (1855-1905) and Alfred (originally Abraham) Moss (1862-1937) were set up on the site in 1881, with George in charge. These were therefore the "Bros" (brothers) of the name. On their father's death, George inherited two-fifths of the business, Alfred three-fifths, and the rest nothing. Over the course of the 19th century the name of the shop changed from "Moses Moses," when it originally opened, to "M. Moss," when Moses had anglicized his name, to "Moss Bros" after Moses' death. The dress side of the business, for which the firm became famous, began only after World War I.

Mossimo *(beachware)*

The fashion label was launched in 1987 with a line of volleyball shorts, taking its name from Mossimo "Moss" Giannuli (b.1963), the son of an Orange County, California, landscape architect. The range soon expanded to include sunglasses, belts, backpacks, footwear, and swimwear.

Mothercare *(babywear and childrenswear)*

The British chain of stores selling everything needed by the expectant mother and her child up to the age of eight was founded by a former banker, Selim Zilkha (b.1927), when he opened his first shop in Kingston upon Thames, Surrey, in 1961. The name implies both "care for mothers" and "mothers who care." In 1986 the chain merged with **Habitat** and British Home Stores (BhS) to form the Storehouse group.

Motley Fool *(Internet financial service)*

The service was launched on **AOL** in 1994 by two US entrepreneurs, brothers David (b.1966) and Tom (b.1968) Gardner, successful students who were interested in money management. A motley fool is one in multicolored costume (the "clownish fool" Touchstone in Shakespeare's *As You Like It* is so described by Jaques), and the brothers are said to have named their service thus so that if they "totally screwed up [they] could fall back on the fact that [they're] just Fools." By late 1996 Motley Fool, Inc., had projected annual revenues of more than $3 million.

Moto Guzzi *(motorcycles)*

The foundations of the Italian firm were laid before World War I by two Italian Air Force pilots, Giovanni Ravelli and Giorgio Parodi, and their mechanic and driver, Carlo Guzzi (1889-1964). Ravelli was killed on active service dur-

ing the war, but Guzzi and Parodi went on to set up the company at Mandello del Lario in 1921. Excellent design and quality construction made Moto Guzzi one of Italy's biggest manufacturers. In 1972 they were acquired by Alessandro **De Tomaso**. "Moto" is short for *motocicletta*, "motorcycle."

Motobécane *(motorcycles)*

The French firm produced its first machine in 1923, taking its name from *moto*, short for *motocyclette*, "motorcycle," and *bécane*, "bike" (perhaps from slang *bécant*, "bird," from *bec*, "beak"). The firm's most popular postwar model was the **Mobylette**. The company changed its name to MBK in 1984 and was subsequently taken over by **Yamaha**.

Motorola *(electronics)*

The American firm originated as the Galvin Manufacturing Co., a Chicago-based maker of radio chassis, founded by Paul V. Galvin in 1928. While working for the company, William Lear, creator of the **Learjet**, designed the first workable radio for automobiles. Galvin concentrated its production on this invention and changed its name to Motorola, a blend of "motor" and **Victrola**. It subsequently expanded its manufacture into military equipment and by 2000 was the world's third largest maker of microchips.

Motosacoche *(motorcycles)*

The leading Swiss motorcycle manufacturer was founded in 1905 by two brothers named Defaux. Their first product was a clip-on engine for a bicycle, which they called a *motosacoche*, from French *moto-*, "motor" and *sacoche*, "bag." The "motor in a bag" subsequently progressed to a conventional engine, and the firm, renamed as MAG, became one of the biggest motorcycle engine suppliers in Europe. Motorcycles followed, but were discontinued in 1956.

Moulinette *(food mill)*

The name of the hand-operated rotary device for puréeing food derives from French *moulin*, "mill," with the diminutive suffix *-ette*. It was entered by its French manufacturers, Mantelet & Bouchet of Bagnolet, near Paris, in the *Trade Marks Journal* of December 3, 1936, and subsequently by Mouliware Ltd. of London, England, in the *Journal* of March 7, 1951.

The abbreviated form of the name, "Mouli," was similarly entered in the *Journal* of July 21, 1937. *See also* **Moulinex**.

Moulinex *(food processor)*

The handy kitchen gadget owes its existence to the French entrepreneur Jean Mantelet (1900-1991), born in Paris, who began his career in 1922 as a maker of agricultural pulverizers. His move into kitchen equipment is said to have been prompted by some kind of argument with his wife about potatoes, which Madame Mantelet was mashing either with a wooden pestle or with a sieving machine bought for her by her husband. Neither of the couple thought much of the lumpy outcome. Mantelet accordingly retired to his workshop, not emerging until he had come up with the Moulin-Légumes ("Vegetable Mill"), a kind of hand-operated food processor for puréeing vegetables He launched his invention at the 1932 Paris Fair to great acclaim, and a year later was making 700 Moulin-Légumes a day at Bagnolet on the outskirts of Paris. In 1935 he decentralized production, setting up in Alençon in Normandy. In due course there were 13 factories in the region, turning out variants of his idea, such as the **Moulinette**, all marketed under the brand name Moulinex. The company later diversified into microwave ovens, vacuum cleaners, air conditioners, and hair dryers.

Moussec *(sparkling wine)*

The British wine, popularly regarded as a champagne substitute, has a name combining French *mousse*, "froth," "fizziness," and *sec*, "dry," as if referring to a medium sweet champagne. The name was entered in the *Trade Marks Journal* of May 4, 1932.

Mouton Cadet *(wine)*

The popular Bordeaux wine began its life in 1927, when it was created by Baron Philippe de Rothschild (1902-1988) for the Château Mouton-Rothschild estate in the Bordeaux region of France. It was a poor vintage, however, and its successor in 1930 was named Mouton-Cadet, as Philippe was the youngest (French *cadet*) of the Rothschild family. As Mouton Cadet, the wine went on to become the most successful Bordeaux brand. The first part of the name comes from that of the original estate, Château

Mouton d'Armailhacq, acquired by Nathan de Rothschild in 1853.

Movietone *(sound film system)*

The optical sound system for motion pictures was developed in the 1920s by Theodore W. Case and Earl I. Sponable while working for Western Electric, the research facility of **Bell Telephone**, and purchased by William Fox for Fox Film Corporation (*see* **Twentieth Century–Fox**). It was an improvement on the **Vitaphone** system then being developed by **Warner Brothers**, since picture and sound were recorded on the same film, and Fox's film company first produced some shorts with it in 1927. Movietone made its mark, however, in the newsreels first made that year. The name, combining "movie" and "tone," was entered in the *Trade Marks Journal* of April 4, 1928.

Moviola *(film editing machine)*

The portable film editing machine, once much in use, dates from the 1920s and takes its name from a blend of "movie" and **Pianola**. The name was entered by "Iwan Serrurier, trading as Moviola Company" of Hollywood in the *Trade Marks Journal* of September 20, 1944 for: "Projectors, synchronizing apparatus, film measuring machines, sound reading apparatus, sound amplifiers and re-winding apparatus; all for use in editing cinematographic films." *Cp.* **Editola**.

Mowbray *(booksellers and publishers)*

Long associated with religious books, especially Bibles, prayer books, and theological works, the British firm of Mowbray, now also a general bookseller, owes its name to Alfred Richard Mowbray (1824-1875), born in Leicestershire, although not himself a clergyman. While still at school, Mowbray was attracted to the Oxford Movement, founded in Oxford in 1833 with the aim of effecting a Catholic revival in the Church of England. By the time he was a qualified teacher at the age of 21, Mowbray was thus a High Churchman. His first teaching post was in Bingham, Nottinghamshire, where he developed an interest in stained glass. He then went on to other posts, and was about to go to New Zealand to further the Anglican missionary cause there when he paid a visit to Oxford, intending to bid farewell to his friends. Instead he became involved in social work in the city, and soon realized that the "Catholic cause" could best be promoted if there was a special bookshop in Oxford to sell High Church literature, especially the famous *Tracts for the Times*. In 1858 he leased a shop in Cornmarket to this end, selling not only books but religious prints and cards. That was the foundation of the present bookselling and publishing business, with one of its best known shops in Margaret Street, London, not far from All Saints, one of England's foremost Anglo-Catholic churches. Mowbray was acquired by **Cassell** in 1988 and is now an imprint of The Continuum International Publishing Group (*see* **Burns & Oates**).

Moygashel *(linen)*

The type of Irish linen takes its name from its place of origin, the small village of Moygashel in Co. Tyrone, Northern Ireland. The name was entered by Stevenson & Son, Ltd., of Moygashel Mills, Dungannon, Co. Tyrone, in the *Trade Marks Journal* of November 11, 1931.

Mrs. Smith's *(pies)*

The name is that of Amanda W. Smith (1860-1947), a widow from Pottstown, Pennsylvania, who began baking commercially in 1919 when she supplied pies to the YMCA lunch counter run by her 17-year-old son Robert. In 1922 Robert Smith dropped out of college to work fulltime selling his mother's fruit pies and Pennsylvania Dutch specialties. At first the pies were made at the family home on South Street, but in 1923 Robert moved the operation to a small storefront. Amanda Smith continued to have a hand in making her pies until her semiretirement in 1925, the year the bakery was incorporated as Mrs. Smith's Delicious Homemade Pies, Inc.

Mu-Cron *(decongestant)*

The name of the preparation of phenylpropanolamine (a decongestant) and paracetamol (an analgesic) contains letters from "*mu*cus," "*chr*onic," and "de*con*gestant." The name was entered in the *Trade Marks Journal* of April 13, 1960.

Mueller *(noodles)*

Christian F. Mueller (1839-1926), a German immigrant baker from Württemberg, began making noodles commercially in the kitchen of his home in Newark, New Jersey, at first supplementing his income by selling eggs and cheese. The popularity of his noodles gradually spread beyond his neighborhood, and in 1885 Mueller opened a small factory in Newark. At first he made only egg noodles, but in 1894 he purchased a macaroni press and was soon turning out 500lbs. of macaroni a day. In 1905 the business was incorporated as the C.F. Mueller Co., with Mueller as president, a post he held until his retirement ten years later.

Muji *(supermarkets)*

The Japanese company, famous for its low-key advertising and modest but stylish merchandise, takes its name from *mujirushu ryohin*, "plain quality goods." It was the brainchild in 1980 of three independent consultants who set out to create a subbrand for Seiyu supermarkets, part of Japan's Saison retail group. The first products were household goods and foodstuffs sold through a "shop-within-a-shop." Clothing followed in 1981 when underwear began to be sold in the supermarket. Stationery appeared in 1982, and when the product line began to outgrow the supermarket, the first separate Muji store opened in Tokyo's Aoyama district the following year. Muji was established as a wholly owned subsidiary of Seiyu in 1989, and international expansion followed. The first store in London, England, opened in 1991, and Europe's largest Muji began operating there in 1999.

Mulberry *(luxury leather accessories)*

The British business so named was set up by Roger Saul (b.1950), who as a teenager at school in Bath traveled to London at the weekend to trade old military uniforms from a market stall. He was soon making belts in a garden shed from snakeskin, cutting out designs that his girlfriend stitched together. On quitting school he enrolled on a business studies course but dropped out in 1970 to concentrate on design. His sister thought up the Mulberry name on the basis that the mulberry is a tree of life, bears fruit, and is a good wood. The company is now Britain's top maker of leather accessories and an international brand.

Mullard *(television and radio valves)*

Stanley Robert Mullard (1883-1979) was

born in Bermondsey, London, England, the son of a chemist and druggist. He quit school at 14 and two years later joined his father's firm, which by then included a separate business making electric lamps. By the time he was 23, Mullard had risen to be the firm's director. In 1909, however, it went bankrupt, unable to compete with the technical innovations of other firms. Mullard was thus obliged to find an outlet for his talents elsewhere, and after a period with a Paris lamp factory he joined **Ediswan** at Ponders End, London, where he was put in charge of the lamp laboratory. After World War I Mullard became managing director of a small lamp-making firm at Southfields, London, and arranged with the owners to manufacture wireless valves on the premises under his own name. His tests went well, and in 1920 Mullard set up his own company, the Mullard Radio Valve Co., on the basis of an initial order of 250 valves from the Admiralty. His business met with even greater success when the following year the British Broadcasting Company (now the BBC) was set up. Soon other electric components and products were added, although these were manufactured by **Philips**, who wholly acquired the Mullard business in the mid-1920s.

Multics *(computer operating system)*

The multi-user operating system for mainframe computers derives its name acronymically from "*multi*plexed *i*nformation and *com*puting *s*ervice." It was entered (as "MULTICS") in the US Patent Office *Official Gazette* of June 2, 1981 and (as "Multics") in the *Trade Marks Journal* of December 2, 1981. *Cp.* **Unix**.

Mumetal *(alloy)*

The alloy of iron containing mostly nickel but also copper and chromium takes its name from "mu" (the Greek letter μ, conventionally adopted to denote permeability) and "metal." It was entered by the Telegraph Construction and Maintenance Co. Ltd., of London, England, in the *Trade Marks Journal* of April 16, 1924 for: "Metallic alloys, unwrought or partly wrought."

Mumm *(champagne)*

The firm was founded in 1827 by two Germans, Peter Arnold de Mumm and Frederick Giesler, who together set up Mumm, Giesler &

Co. at Reims. Giesler left ten years later to start his own firm of Giesler & Co. at Avize. In 1920 G.H. Mumm & Co. was purchased by a group of investors, one of whom was **Dubonnet**.

Munsingwear *(underwear)*

The name derives from the American inventor of the union suit, George D. Munsing, who in 1886, with two young graduates from the Massachusetts Institute of Technology, set up The Northwestern Knitting Company in Minneapolis to knit underwear. The partnership was incorporated in 1887 and the new company started labeling its goods "The Munsing." This name was registered as a trademark in 1906. The word "wear" was added in 1911 to make the trademark rather more distinctive and to indicate that it applied to wearing apparel. In 1920, The Northwestern Knitting Company changed its name to The Munsingwear Corporation (subsequently Munsingwear, Inc.).

Muppets *(puppets)*

The glove and rod puppets and marionettes (mostly animals) of this name were originally popularized in the US children's television programme *Sesame Street*, first screened in 1969. They were the creation of Jim Henson (1936-1990), who said that their name, seemingly a blend of "marionette" and "puppet," was simply one that "sounded good to him" (*Time*, December 25, 1978). "Muppet" was entered for the puppets themselves by Muppets, Inc., of New York, in the US Patent Office *Official Gazette* of September 26, 1972, with a note of first use "on or about Sept. 22, 1971," and "The Muppets" for "entertainment services featuring puppets and large animated animals and creatures" in the *Gazette* of October 3, 1972, with a note of "first use August 1954."

Murine *(eye lotion)*

One day in 1890 Otis F. Hall, a banker in Spokane, Washington, was chatting to a friend when he noticed that his friend's horse had a broken shoe. As he bent down to examine it, the horse's tail struck him in the eye, cutting the surface of the cornea. A painful ulcer developed, and Mr. Hall was soon on his way to Chicago to seek treatment from Drs. James B. and George W. McFatrich, two brothers who were prominent ophthalmologists. Under their care, the eye healed completely within a few weeks, part of the treatment being the application of a special eye lotion that the doctors had compounded. Mr. Hall felt it should be made available to the public, but the brothers were reluctant to embark on such a venture. They were finally persuaded, however, and the three men formed a company to market the eye drops. What should they call the preparation? The McFatrich brothers felt the name should reflect the chemical formula of the lotion. This was muriate of berberine, and the first and last syllables of this were combined to form "Murine." "Murine" eyecare products are now marketed by **Abbott**.

Murphy *(radios)*

The name is that of Frank Murphy (1889-1955), born a headmaster's son in London, England. He did well in mathematics at school, and completed his education at age 19 by graduating in electrical engineering. He then entered the research section of the General Post Office, continuing his postgraduate studies at East London Technical College, where his special interest was the cathode ray tube. After World War I, during which he was a wireless operator in the newly formed Royal Flying Corps, he set up an advertising agency, soon gaining important clients such as **Mullard**, **Belling**, **Ediswan**, and Vickers-Armstrong. He left the agency in 1928, however, to found Murphy Radio Ltd. in Welwyn Garden City, taking as partner another radio enthusiast, one Edward Power. With the help of fullpage advertisements in the *Radio Times,* in which the distinctive features of "The Man with the Pipe" soon became familiar nationwide, his business boomed, progressing from just one radio set in the first month of production in 1930, to 80,000 a year in 1935. Although Frank Murphy subsequently severed all connections with Murphy Radio and took to manufacturing furniture instead, it is the radio with which his name is still chiefly associated.

Murphy's *("Irish Stout")*

The name is that of James Jeremiah Murphy (1825-1897), the eldest of 15 children, and the progenitor of nine himself, who in 1856 opened a brewery in Cork, southern Ireland. He was a member of the Royal Cork Yacht Club and donated widely to local hospitals and churches.

Murray *(publishers)*

Britain's oldest privately owned publishing house was founded by John MacMurray (1745-1793), born in Edinburgh. After serving as a lieutenant in the Royal Marines from 1762, he retired on half pay in 1768 to set up business in London as a publisher and bookseller, purchasing the business of William Sandby at the Sign of the Ship, 32 Fleet Street, and at the same time dropping the "Mac" of his name. At first trade was slow, but he managed to bring out several important works of the day. The business really came into its own under the management of his son, also John Murray (1778-1843), who published Byron, making the poet famous, founded the prestigious *Quarterly Review* in 1809, and in 1812 moved the firm to its well-known address at 50 Albemarle Street, where it remains today. In the 20th century the firm was in the hands of the sixth John Murray, born John Grey (1909-1993), who was a Murray on his mother's side and who adopted her name in 1930 on joining the family business. In 2002 Murray was sold to Hodder Headline (*see* **Hodder & Stoughton**).

Murraymints *(peppermint candy)*

The name originated with that of R.S. Murray & Co. Ltd., a small English confectionery business acquired in the 1950s by **Beecham**. "Murraymints" themselves, as wrapped mints, were widely advertised on television at this time in a memorable jingle with the repeated lines: "Murraymints, Murraymints, / The too-good-to-hurry mints."

Muzak *(recorded background music)*

The system of piped music, used in public places such as supermarkets and restaurants, has a name based on "music" that was entered by Rediffusion Ltd., of London, in the *Trade Marks Journal* of May 11, 1938 and by Muzak Corporation in the US Patent Office *Official Gazette* of September 21, 1954. The firm traces its origins to New York City in 1922, when George O. Squier, a retired army officer, had the idea of transmitting news, music, lectures, and advertising directly into private homes by means of electric wires. The result of his plan was Wired Radio Inc., out of which the Muzak Corporation was formed in 1934. By this time wireless radio was widespread in American homes, so Muzak concentrated on selling its prerecorded "functional music" to hotels and restaurants. In 1938 it introduced music for offices and factories. In 1986 Muzak was purchased by the Field Corporation of Chicago and moved from New York to Seattle.

MV Agusta *see* Agusta

Mylar *(polyester resin)*

The form of polyester resin so known is used to make heat-resistant plastic films and sheets. Its name is arbitrary, and was entered by **Du Pont** in the *Trade Marks Journal* of November 3, 1954 for: "Non-mouldable plastics in the form of films for use as a substitute for glass; and electrical insulating mateials."

Myleran *(anticancer drug)*

The proprietary name for busulphan, used in the treatment of myeloid leukemia, was entered by the **Wellcome** Foundation, London, England, in the *Trade Marks Journal* of November 12, 1952. The name itself appears to be based on "myeloid" (referring to bone marrow).

Mysoline *(anticonvulsant)*

The proprietary name for the drug primidone, used to treat epilepsy, is apparently of arbitrary origin. It was entered by Imperial Chemical (Pharmaceuticals) Ltd. (*see* **ICI**) in the *Trade Marks Journal* of October 12, 1949.

MZ *(motorcycles)*

When Germany divided into East and West after World War II, the **DKW** factory at Zschopau was in the East. Many of its personnel relocated in the West, taking the name with them. Production then restarted at Zchopau, where the factory became known as Motorradwerke Zchopau ("Zschopau Motorcycle Works"), or simply MZ, their machines based on DKW designs. MZ bikes were still being produced when East and West Germany were reunited in 1990, but the following year the company went into liquidation. It was resurrected in 1992, however, and in 1996 was taken over by the Malaysian motorcycle manufacturer Hong Leong.

Nabisco *(crackers, or biscuits)*

The US company originated in 1898 from the merger of two large cracker manufacturers, the New York Biscuit Company and the American Biscuit Company, to form the National Biscuit Company. The company grew and diversified into other foods until it was one of the largest manufacturers of packaged foods in the world, one being **Shredded Wheat**. In 1971 it adopted its shortened name, first registered in 1901, and in 1985 was acquired by **R.J. Reynolds** to become RJR-Nabisco. The tobacco company was sold off in 1999, however, leaving Nabisco alone again.

Nalline *(antinarcotic)*

The proprietary name for the drug nalorphine, used as an antagonist for morphine, derives from its chemical description: *N-allyl-nomorphine*. It was entered in the US Patent Office *Official Gazette* of October 28, 1952: "For therapeutic substances useful in counteracting certain undesirable effects … induced by natural and synthetic narcotic drugs."

Napier *(automobiles)*

The name goes back to that of D. Napier & Son Ltd., a small precision-engineering firm set up in London, England, in 1808. Its fortunes declined as the century wore on, however, and in 1898 Montague Napier, the founder's grandson, decided to rectify matters by becoming involved in the fledgling motor industry. He did this by producing a two-cylinder engine for the racing cyclist-turned-motor salesman Selwyn Francis Edge (1868-1940), to serve as a replacement unit for his 1896 **Panhard**. The outcome of this tentative project was that Edge set up a car distribution company, the blandly named Motor Vehicle Co., which became Napier's sole outlet until 1912. Thanks largely to Edge, the Napier became the most famous British car on the road until the arrival of the **Rolls-Royce** Silver Ghost in 1905, but no Napiers were built after 1924.

Napster *(Internet music-exchange service)*

The program, allowing computer users to exchange music tracks stored on the hard disks of their computers, was set up in 1999 by Shawn Fanning, a teenage student at Boston's Northeastern University, who named his enterprise with his high school nickname. The service was free until 2001, when a court ruled that copyright must be respected and payment made to record companies and artists.

Nardil *(antidepressant)*

The proprietary name for the drug phenelzine, given to treat depression, comprises the "nar-" of "narcotic" and a second element of unknown origin. It was entered in the *Trade Marks Journal* of November 18, 1959 and the US Patent Office *Official Gazette* of January 5, 1960, the latter: "For psychic energizer." A "medicinal malt extract" of the same name was entered in the *Gazette* of March 7, 1944.

Nash-Kelvinator *(automobiles)*

Charles W. Nash (1864-1948) was born in DeKalb County, Illinois, the son of a farmer. He worked for a local farmer until he was 12, then escaped this form of child labor to become a farm hand, apprentice carpenter, hay presser, farm foreman, and grocery clerk. Eventually, at the age of 27, Nash become an upholstery trimmer for the Flint Road Cart Company, rising through its ranks to become a vice president of the subsequent Durant-Dort Carriage Company by 1895. In 1910, Nash became president and general manager of the insolvent **Buick** Motor Company, which he reorganized and set on a sound financial footing. In 1912, Nash became president of the nearly bankrupt **General Motors**, and in 1916 purchased the Thomas B. Jeffrey Motor Car Company of Kenosha, Wisconsin, transforming it into Nash Motors. Nash set out to build a "simple car for the average man," and production soon soared. The company was hit hard in the Great Depression, and Nash resigned as president in 1932. In 1937 Nash Motors merged with Kelvinator, a Detroit refrigerator manufacturer, whose name was a blend of "kelvin," the base unit of thermodynamic temperature named after the Scottish physicist Lord Kelvin (1824-1907), and "refrigerator."

Nast, Condé *see* **Condé Nast**

Nastro Azzurro *(beer)*

The Italian lager beer was introduced in 1964 by **Peroni**, the country's leading brewer. Its name means "Blue Ribbon," as a general mark of prestige or token of excellence.

Nathan's Famous *(sandwich chain)*

The man behind the name is Nathan Handwerker (1891-1974), born in Poland. He arrived in New York in 1912 and worked as a roll slicer for Charles Feltman, popularly credited as the creator of the first hot dog in America. In 1916, Handwerker opened a sidewalk stand on Coney Island, selling his hot dogs for a nickel, half of what Feltman charged. His stand grew, and in 1925 he incorporated as Nathan's Famous. The firm went public in 1967 and began selling products to supermarkets in the 1970s. In 1996, based in Westbury, New York, the company had 175 units worldwide. The chain is said to take its name not from Handwerker but from a popular song of the day, "Nat'an! Nat'an! Tel! me for what you are waitin' Nat'an?"

National Benzole *(gasoline)*

The British company was founded in London in 1919 with the aim of selling benzole, a crude form of benzene used as a fuel that had been overproduced by the end of World War I. A huge marketing effort was thus needed to use the excess capacity that had been created. National Benzole vigorously extolled the virtues of the new "motor spirit," as petrol (gasoline) was then often known, with a series of slogans punning on "spirit," such as "National Benzole—The Spirit of the Future," "National Benzole—That's the Spirit," and the like. The play on words was reinforced by a logo in the form of a stylized head of Mercury, the fleet-footed Roman messenger of the gods.

National Westminster *(bank)*

The British bank, familiarly known as "NatWest," was formed in 1970 on the merger of the National Provincial Bank, established in 1833, the Westminster Bank, founded in 1834, and the District Bank, started in 1829. The National Provincial was formed with the specific purpose of creating a network of offices throughout England and Wales. Hence "Provincial." Its first such office opened in Gloucester in 1834. The Westminster was founded as the London and Westminster Bank, serving each of these distinctive neighboring cities. The District Bank was initially the Manchester and Liverpool District Banking Company, but became simply District Bank in 1924.

Nationwide *(building society)*

Currently Britain's largest building society (savings and loan association), with over 10 million members, the Nationwide justifies its name. It was formed in 1987 as the Nationwide Anglia by the merger of the Nationwide Building Society, founded in 1883 as the Co-operative Permanent Building Society but calling itself Nationwide from 1970, and the Anglia Building Society, formed in 1967 when the Northampton Building Society, founded in 1848, merged with the Leicestershire Building Society. The Nationwide is not properly speaking a bank but provides a full range of banking services. In 1987, the year of its formation, Nationwide Anglia introduced its Flex Account, the first British checking account to pay interest.

Naugahyde (upholstery material)

The material consists of a fabric base coated with a layer of rubber or vinyl resin and finished with a leather-like grain. It takes its name from Naugatuck, Connecticut, a town noted for its rubber manufacture, and an altered form of "hide." The name was entered by United States Rubber Products, Inc. (see Uniroyal), in the US Patent Office Official Gazette of December 7, 1937: "For upholstery material, more specifically fabric base which has been treated with rubber and other substances producing artificial leather."

Navistar see **International Harvester**

Navy Cut (cigarettes)

The name was originally that of a make of **Players** tobacco, alluding to the British Royal Navy, and "Player's Navy Cut," with a picture of a sailor wearing a cap with the ship's name "Hero," was entered in the Trade Marks Journal of March 25, 1891. The name was later adopted by other tobacco manufacturers. **Wills**, for example, produced a brand of "Capstan" Navy Cut tobacco and cigarettes.

NCR (cash registers and computers)

The American corporation was founded by John H. Patterson (1844-1922), born in Dayton, Ohio, the son of a wealthy landowner. After army service, he spent 15 years as a mine operator and merchandiser of coal, in partnership with his brother Frank. Their business eventually failed, and at age 40 Patterson was faced with bleak prospects. He saw an opportunity, however, in a machine invented by a Dayton saloonkeeper, James J. Ritty, to keep track of sales in his tavern. This "cash register" was a metal drawer attached to a box with levers

that punched holes in marked columns on a strip of paper every time a clerk added to or took away money from it. In 1884 Patterson founded the National Cash Register Company to manufacture these machines. Sales at first were slow, as the device was resisted or resented by employees, who saw it as a "monitor" of their honesty, but Patterson effectively promoted it as a key tool to record retail sales and soon won many stores over. In 1991 NCR was purchased by **AT&T** and for a time retained its name before becoming Global Information Solutions (GIS). It then resumed its name following the breakup of AT&T in 1995 into three publicly held companies. See **Lucent**.

NCR (copying paper)

The initials, standing for "no carbon required," denote a type of paper that has been chemically treated so that the pressure of writing or typing alone is enough to make duplicate copies, without the use of carbon paper between sheets. The name was entered in the US Patent Office Official Gazette of July 12, 1954.

Necchi (engineering)

The Italian company, noted for its sewing machines, takes its name from its founder, Vittorio Necchi (1898-1975).

Neill (hand tools)

The British firm's history began in 1889 when James Neill (1858-1930), the grandson of a Scottish farmer, decided to quit his job as an accountant and enter the steel industry. He set up his own small steel business in Sheffield, where he lived, melting ingots by the crucible process in rented premises in a back street. By the end of the century, Neill's enterprise had done well enough for him to move to larger premises. These were in Napier Street, Sheffield, where the group's head office and its biggest production unit, Eclipse Tools Ltd., are still located today. In 1911 Neill began making hacksaw blades, and it was these that first brought the "Eclipse" name before the public. After World War I, Neill used the same name for his razor blades. In 1985 Neill Tools took over another famous name, **Spear & Jackson**, so now produce their tools as well.

Neiman-Marcus (department stores)

The prestigious store chain was founded in

Dallas, Texas, in 1907 by 29-year-old Herbert Marcus, his 23-year-old sister, Carrie, and her husband, Abraham Lincoln Neiman. Herbert and Carrie were born in Louisville, Kentucky, and had moved to Hillsboro, Texas, where a brother had a grocery, and from there north to Dallas, where Herbert sold women's shoes. After a spell at Sanger Brothers, then the largest of Dallas stores, Marcus quit and joined Neiman in opening an advertising agency in Atlanta, Georgia. Their business did so well that they sold it after two years and returned to Dallas, where they started Neiman-Marcus. Business boomed, and by the end of the 20th century Neiman-Marcus had branch stores throughout the USA. Herbert Marcus died in 1950, aged 72, and his sister, by then "Aunt Carrie" to many, three years later. Al Neiman outlived both his partners.

Nelson *(publishers)*

Thomas Nelson (1780-1861), whose surname was originally Neilson, was born near Stirling, Scotland, a farmer's son. He quit school at 16 and tried a number of jobs before setting off for London and finding work with a publisher in Paternoster Row. He enjoyed it, and after a year or so took his savings back up to Scotland. In 1798 he opened his own business selling secondhand books in Edinburgh. He soon felt, however, that selling books was not enough, and decided to start publishing them. He particularly wanted to bring out inexpensive educational literature for the ordinary reader. His first publications were selections from his favorite religious authors, such as Bunyan, but he went on to produce cheap editions of the classics, such as *The Vicar of Wakefield* and *Robinson Crusoe*. By 1818 his business was doing so well that he needed to open a bank account, and it was then that he respelled his name as Nelson. ("Like the great naval hero of the name," he quipped, "I have had to sacrifice an 'i' in a good cause.") In 2000 Thomas Nelson & Sons merged with Stanley Thornes (Publishing) Ltd. to become Nelson Thornes Ltd.

Nembutal *(sedative)*

The hypnotic, sedative, and antispasmodic drug, generically known as sodium pentobarbitone, was introduced to medicine in 1930 and takes its name from the first letter of "Na," the chemical symbol for sodium, and the initial letters of "*eth*yl," "*meth*yl," and "*but*yl," elements of the systematic name. The suffix "-al" was added in the United States to denote a barbiturate. The name was entered in the US Patent Office *Official Gazette* of April 21, 1931 and the *Trade Marks Journal* of December 15, 1937.

Neo-Synephrine *(decongestant)*

The proprietary name for the drug phenylephrine derives from Greek-based "neo-" ("new") and "synephrine" (from "syn-" and "epinephrine"). It was entered by Winthrop-Stearns, Inc., of New York, in the *Trade Marks Journal* of August 2, 1950 for: "Vasoconstrictors and antispasmodics being pharmaceutical preparations."

Nescafé *(instant coffee)*

The brand of instant coffee, made by **Nestlé**, was first marketed in 1938, taking its name from that of the company plus French *café*, "coffee." The name is not a complete success in all languages, since in Spanish it suggests *n'es café*, "it is not coffee." The name was entered in the *Trade Marks Journal* of September 4, 1946 for: "Preparations of coffee in powder form."

Nestlé *(dairy products, chocolate, and instant coffee)*

Nestlings nestle in a nest in the company logo. But this is a play on words, or rather on the name of the company founder, Henri Nestlé (1814-1890), born in Frankfurt, Germany, but living in Vevey, Switzerland, from 1843. He was a research chemist, and was keen to devise a satisfactory substitute for mother's milk, since infant mortality in Switzerland was high at that time. In 1867 he tried out his new product, testing it on a premature baby who had refused his mother's milk and gone into convulsions. The two-week-old infant took the milk and thrived on it. (It was basically ordinary milk mixed with specially baked meal.) Nestlé went ahead to make it in large quantities, in 1875 selling his business to a Geneva group who kept the name. In 1878 the Nestlé Company began making condensed milk, thus competing with the existing Anglo-Swiss Condensed Milk Company, set up by two American brothers in 1866. (They called it "Anglo" as they expected their big market to be in Britain.) In 1905 the two companies merged to form the Nestlé and Anglo-Swiss Condensed Milk Company, the largest dairy company in the world. By this time Nestlé was also producing chocolate. **Nescafé** followed later as the firm's first nondairy product.

Nestle *(haircare products)*

The name is that of Charles Nestle (1872-1952), born Karl Ludwig Nessler in Bavaria, a shoemaker's son. After factory work in neighboring Switzerland, Nestle decided to concentrate on his real interest, human hair. He learned to cut and wave hair in salons and in 1899 moved to Paris to study the Marcel wave as the leading technique of its day. His growing fame as a Marcel wave hairdresser led a wealthy English customer to invite Nestle to set up a salon in London. (It was there that he changed his name from Nessler to Nestle.) Nestle was still a German citizen when World War I was declared, and in 1915 he departed for New York, where he opened a salon in Manhattan. By the time his family joined him in 1919, Nestle had founded the Nestle Company, which manufactured and distributed salon equipment and hairdressing supplies. In 1927 Nestle opened on Broadway what was then the largest beauty salon in the world, and the following year his company merged with the LeMur beauty parlor supply firm to become one of the leading manufacturers of permanent wave supplies and haircare products.

Neuhaus *(chocolates)*

The Belgian chocolate company traces its history to 1857, when Jean Neuhaus, a Swiss who had settled in Belgium, opened an apothecary's shop, with his brother-in-law as partner. Certain confectionery lines, such as licorice and squares of chocolate, were sold as an aid to digestion, and after the death of his brother-in-law, Neuhaus decided to concentrate on the chocolate side of the business, which had already acquires an excellent reputation. The first exclusive "Neuhaus-Jerrin" chocolate shop opened in 1895, and the firm passed down the family until 1978, when it was sold and developed into the multinational NV Neuhaus Mondose SA.

Newcastle Brown *(beer)*

The British beer, a brown ale with a distinctive nutty, caramel taste, was launched in Newcastle upon Tyne by Newcastle Breweries in 1927. It is now brewed by Scottish **Courage**.

Newhouse *(newspapers)*

The name of one of America's largest newspaper chains is that of Samuel Irving Newhouse (1895-1979), born the son of a Russian immigrant garment worker in a tenement on Manhattan's Lower East Side, and skipping high school because of poverty. His first job was the one that settled his career. It was as an office boy with judge Hyman Lazarus in Bayonne, New Jersey. Lazarus had taken over the ailing *Bayonne Times* as payment for a bad debt. He told Newhouse, then aged 17, to "take care of it until we get rid of it." But Newhouse instead revived the paper by cutting costs and encouraging local advertising. By 1916 this same paper was bringing Newhouse profits of around $30,000 a year. By 1922 he had bought the *Staten Island Advance,* and this small paper was the one on which Newhouse built his future empire.

Newnes *(publishers)*

It was the Englishman George Newnes (1851-1910), born in Matlock, Derbyshire, the son of a Congregational minister, who founded the popular British magazine *Tit-bits.* Newnes began his career as a fancy goods salesman in London, later transferring to an identical job in Manchester. While he was there, he had the idea of bringing out a magazine that would print intriguing stories and "titbits" (tidbits) of trivial information, which he delighted in himself. He began collecting "bits and bobs" of this kind from the press, and launched his magazine in 1881. It was an immediate success, and was boosted by his imaginative advertising campaigns, one of which got members of the Boys Brigade marching up and down a Manchester street wearing caps with "Tit-bits" on their bands and carrying bundles of the magazine itself. Newnes went on to publish other magazines, including the famous *Strand Magazine,* which contained the first Sherlock Holmes stories, and in 1891, the year this first appeared, he founded his publishing house of George Newnes Ltd.

Newton Chambers *(cleaning fluids)*

The British manufacturer of **Izal** and related products owes its name to George Newton

(1761-1825) and Thomas Chambers (1771-1814), who in 1792 set up a partnership to found the Phoenix Foundry, Sheffield. The following year they bought land nearby at Thorncliffe, and in 1796 had already built two furnaces, with collieries also acquired to smelt the ironstone. The firm's business operations gradually extended to include steel and cast iron fabrications, while chemical works were set up in the 1880s to produce insecticides, antiseptic soaps, and cleaning fluids.

Next *(fashion stores)*

The British chain of menswear, womenswear, and childrenswear stores emerged in the 1980s from the long-established menswear chain that was **Hepworth**. The name dates from 1981, when Hepworth bought the Kendalls chain of womenswear stores with the aim of diversifying away from menswear. The name itself was proposed by John Stephenson, an associate of Terence Conran, the founder of **Habitat**. The introduction of the name is recalled by George Davies (b.1941), the new company's first chairman and chief executive, in Kay 1987 (*see* Bibliography, p. 566):

"Stephenson phoned me up and said 'I think I've got the name you're looking for. Have you got a pencil and paper?' I said, 'OK, I'm waiting.' Then he spelt out N, E, X, T. I said 'Is that it? Next?' But of course he was right. It meant things happening, and not just then but tomorrow. And it was so odd it made people remember it. I got home and asked my daughter, who was about seventeen then. She said 'It's a terrible name, no good at all.' That made me a bit miffed, but I asked her again a few hours later. She said it still sounded terrible, but the point was it had stuck in her mind, and that was what impressed me. Next has set a trend ever since. Before Next, most people called their shops by the name of the owner. We were the first to call it by an idea."

Nextel *(blood substitute)*

The synthetic substance resembling blood, used in plays, films, and the like, appears to have an arbitrary name. It dates from the early 1970s.

Nichrome *(nickel alloy)*

The alloy of nickel with chromium and sometimes iron, used in electrical heating elements, derives its name from a blend of "nickel" and "chrome." It was entered by the Driver-Harris Company of Harrison, New Jersey, in the US Patent Office *Official Gazette* of July 4, 1933.

Nicorette *(nicotine-flavored chewing gum)*

The special chewing gum first became generally available in 1980 as an aid to reducing dependency on tobacco. Hence its name, a blend of "nicotine" and "cigarette," entered the following year in the US Patent Office *Official Gazette* by AB Leo of Helsingborg, Sweden, for: "medications for suppressing, reducing, or eliminating smoking and the urge to smoke," with a note of first use on June 22, 1973, and "in commerce" on October 29, 1973.

Nielsen *(market research)*

The American company, noted for its television rating surveys, owes its name to Arthur Charles Nielsen (1897-1980), born in Chicago, Illinois, the son of an immigrant Danish business executive. He received his early education at the grammar school in Berwyn and Morton High School in Cicero, and went on to the University of Wisconsin, where in 1918 he obtained a bachelor of science degree in electrical engineering with the highest academic average ever recorded there. Four years later he started up a statistical consulting firm with a loan from his fraternity brothers. That year, 1923, was the founding year of one of the biggest names in the ratings business of today.

Nike *(sports shoes)*

In 1962, concerned at the increasing dominance of the sportswear market by **Adidas**, US athlete Philip H. Knight (b.1938) and sports coach Bill Bowerman set up the Blue Ribbon Sports Company, importing lower-cost, higher-tech sports shoes from Japan. They met with moderate success, and opened their first retail outlet in 1966. In 1971 BRS commissioned Carolyn Davidson, an art student, to design a new logo. The result was the familiar "swoosh," resembling a tick or check mark. In 1972 BRS split with their Japanese suppliers, Onitsuka Tiger, and started to make their own trainers, launching them at that year's US Olympic trials and naming them after the Greek goddess of victory, who on vases of the classical period is depicted striding, running, or flying. (The name was already familiar to many from the Nike guided missiles of the 1950s.) The strategy worked, and by 1980 BRS had stolen more than 50 per cent of the US market from Adidas and **Reebok** and sales had soared from $5 million in 1974 to $269 million.

Nikka *(whisky)*

The Japanese blend of whisky owes its origin to Masataka Taketsuru, who introduced whisky production at **Suntory** before establishing a fruit-juice business, Dai Nippon Kaju ("Japan Fruit-Juice Company"), in 1934. His first whisky went on sale in 1940, exactly 20 years after he returned to Japan from a two-year study of whisky in Scotland, bringing his Scottish bride, Rita, with him. In 1952 he renamed his company Nikka, from "*Ni*ppon" and "*Ka*ju." The "Super Nikka" blend was introduced by Taketsuru in memory of his wife after her death in 1961. *See also* **Tsuru**.

Nikkatsu *(motion pictures)*

Japan's oldest motion-picture company, founded in 1912, has an acronymic name deriving from its original title, Nippon Katsudo Shashin (literally, "Japan Moving Photographs"). By 1915 Nikkatsu had captured two-thirds of the viewing market, and despite financial setbacks went on to become one of the country's leading studios.

Nikon *(cameras)*

The name originates from the company founded in Japan in 1917 as Nippon Kogaku KK ("Japan Optics Company"). In 1932 this company produced camera lenses named "Nikkor" and then in 1948 its first 35mm camera named "Nikon." From 1959 Nippon Kogaku became increasingly known internationally by this shorter name, formed from letters in its original name.

Nimonic *(alloys)*

The name of the various nickel-based alloys, similar to **Inconel**, derives from a blend of "nickel" and **Monel** and was entered by Henry Wiggin and Co., of London, England, in the *Trade Marks Journal* of April 9, 1941 for: "Cast and wrought alloys of nickel sold in the form of bars, sheets, rods, ... and other shaped pieces," and in the US Patent Office *Official Gazette* of July 22, 1947.

Ninhydrin *(oxidizing agent)*

The oxidizing agent, used to detect amino acids and polypeptides, has a name entered by the German company of Farbwerke, formerly Meister Lucius & Brüning, in the *Warenzeichenblatt* ("Trademarks Journal") of November 1912. The name itself appears to be based on the chemical formula "triketohydrindene," but the initial "Nin-" is unexplained.

Nintendo *(video games)*

The company was founded in Kyoto, Japan, in 1889 by Fusajiro Yamauchi to manufacture "Hanafuda" (literally "flower cards"), a type of Japanese playing cards. In 1902 the firm began making standard playing cards, and in 1933 took the name Yamauchi Nintendo. The latter word is made up of Japanese *nin*, "office," "duty," *ten*, "the heavens," "sky," and *do*, "way," otherwise: "Work hard, but in the end, it is in heaven's hands." In 1947 the distribution company Marufuku (literally "lucky circle") was set up, and in 1951 this became the Nintendo Playing Card Co. When the company began manufacturing games as well as cards in 1963, the name became simply Nintendo Co. In 1977 Nintendo developed its first video games with the cooperation of **Mitsubishi** Electric, and in 1980 set up a wholly owned subsidiary, Nintendo of America, Inc. In 1981 Nintendo launched its video arcade game "Donkey Kong,"which first introduced its popular character Mario, the dumpy, mustachioed plumber from Brooklyn. In 1949 the original company passed to Hiroshi Yamauchi, great-grandson of the founder, and it is still in the hands of the Yamauchi family today. *See also* **Game Boy**.

Nippon Steel *(steel)*

The Nippon Steel Corporation, Japan's largest industrial concern, was created in 1970 on the merger of two companies, Yawata Iron & Steel Co., first operating at Yawata, northern Kyushu, in 1901, and Fuji Iron & Steel Co. (*see* **Fuji Bank**).

Nissan *(automobiles, trucks, and buses)*

The Japanese corporation originated in two earlier companies, Kwaishinsha Company, founded in Tokyo 1911 by the US-trained engineer Masujiro Hashimoto to produce DAT cars, and Jitsuyo Jidosha Seizo Company, founded in 1919. ("Jidosha Seizo" means "Automobile Manufacturers.") In 1923 these merged to form DAT Jidosha Seizo Company. The car took its name from the initials of three Kwaishinsha backers: K. *Den*, R. *Aoyama*, and A. *Takeuchi*. Later models were called "Datson," intended to mean "son of DAT," but as pronounced in Japanese, "son" suggested the word for "loss" (*cp.* **Sony**), so in 1932 the name was modified to "Datsun." In 1933 the assets of the manufacturing company were taken over by new investors, who established the Jidosha Seizo Company, giving it the name Nissan Jidosha the following year. ("Nissan" is Japanese for "daily output.") The Datsun name continued, however, and the 1969 240Z sports coupé would become the best-selling sports car in the world. The name Datsun was officially dropped at the end of 1983 and since then all of the company's vehicles have been Nissans.

Nitralloy *(alloy steel)*

The range of alloy steels, used for nitriding (heating steel in the presence of ammonia to increase its hardness and corrosion resistance) and containing (among other elements) small proportions of aluminum and carbon, derives its name straightforwardly from a blend of "nitriding" and "alloy." The alloys date from at least the 1920s, and the name was entered by the British firm of Firth Brown Ltd., of Sheffield, in the *Trade Marks Journal* of June 1, 1972.

Nitrochalk *(fertilizer)*

The name of the mixture of chalk and ammonium nitrate, combining the former word with an element from the chemical name, was entered (as "Nitro-Chalk") by **ICI** in the *Trade Marks Journal* of November 4, 1936.

Nivea *(skin cream)*

Development of the flagship brand of the German company **Beiersdorf** was initiated in 1911 by the firm's owner, Oskar Troplowitz. Together with chemist Isaac Lifschütz and dermatologist Paul Unna, he based it on an emulsion similar to his own invention of "Eucerit" (*see* **Eucerin**), taking its name from Latin *nivea*, the feminine of *niveus*, "snowy white." The name would work equally well in Italian, as the feminine of *niveo*, and Nivea is an Italian female forename. (Miss Nivea Giaccardi of Bournemouth, England, was named as a prize crossword winner in *The Sunday Times* of May 21, September 10, and December 17, 2000.) Nivea cream is produced in the UK by **Smith and Nephew**. The name was entered in the *Trade Marks Journal* of January 27, 1909.

Noble, John *see* **John Noble**

Noilly Prat *(vermouth)*

The world's biggest-selling French vermouth takes the first part of its name from Joseph Noilly, inventor of the dry vermouth in around 1800. Prat was the name of his commercial director in the business he set up in 1813 to make it in the town of Marseillan, in the south of France. Prat married Noilly's daughter, and the name of the company, if not the ownership, has been set ever since.

Nokia *(cellular phones)*

The company's roots go back to 1865, when Fredrik Idestam, a Finnish mining engineer, set up a woodpulp mill near the small town of Nokia, west of Tampere in southern Finland, and began manufacturing paper. The business gradually expanded to include chemicals and rubber, until by the 1990s its profile was that of a telecommunications company. This particular development came about following research by the firm's electronics department in the 1960s into radio transmission.

Norplant *(contraceptive)*

The contraceptive implant for women operates through a controlled release of the synthetic hormone levonorgestrel (*cp.* **Levonelle**) via matchstick-sized rods inserted into the upper arm. Hence its name, from a blend of "levo*nor*gestrel" and "im*plant*." The name was entered by The Population Council, Inc., of New York, in the *Trade Marks Journal* of April 6, 1983.

Northern Foods *(food and dairy products)*

One of Britain's most successful enterprises owes its origin to Alec Horsley (1902-1993), born in Ripley, Yorkshire. His father owned a small wholesale dairy business in the north of England, supplying Dutch condensed milk to the confectionery industry. Horsley joined his father as a young man, but left the company in 1937 to start his own condensed milk manufacturing plant in nearby Holme-on-Spalding Moor. Over the years his business, Northern

Dairies, expanded throughout England and into Northern Ireland. In 1970 Horsley was succeeded as chairman by his son, Nicholas, who changed the name of the company to Northern Foods, reflecting its continuing expansion into the cake, cookie, and frozen food markets. By the time of his father's death, the business was the largest fresh-food manufacturer in the United Kingdom.

Northern Rock *(building society)*

The British building society (savings and loan association) dates from 1850, when the Northern Counties Permanent Benefit Building and Investment Society was founded in Newcastle upon Tyne, Northumberland, in the north of England. In 1865, the Rock Permanent Benefit Society was formed in the same city, its name suggesting permanence and reliability. The two societies merged under the present name in 1964 and Northern Rock became a public limited company in 1997. It is now a major retail bank.

Northrop *(aircraft and arms)*

The name is that of John Knudsen Northrop (1895-1981), born in Newark, New Jersey. Soon after his birth, his family moved to Nebraska, where his father worked as a salesman in a Lincoln department store. In 1904 the family moved again to California, where in 1913 Northrop graduated from Santa Barbara High School. He first worked as a garage mechanic, then became an architectural draftsman. In 1916 he was hired by local aviation experts Allan and Malcolm Loughead, who were building a seaplane for exhibition flying (and who later respelled their name **Lockheed**). In 1920 the depressed market forced Loughead out of business, and Northrop worked for his father for a time. He returned to the aviation industry in 1923, when he was hired as draftsman by the **Douglas** Aircraft Company of Santa Monica. In 1926 Northrop left Douglas and joined with Allan Loughead to form the Lockheed Aircraft Company. He left it the following year to found the Avion Corporation, which in 1929 merged with the United Aircraft and Transport Corporation as the Northrop Aircraft Corporation. The company went on to specialize in making aircraft parts for other companies, such as the fuselage and doors for the **Boeing** 747 jumbo jet.

Norton *(motorcycles)*

The name is that of the British engineer James Lansdowne Norton (1869-1925), born in Birmingham, who set up the Norton Manufacturing Company in Wolverhampton 1898, initially to make chains, but who four years later was advertising his first motorcycle, in the form of a bicycle with a motor bolted on. Conventional machines followed, until in 1953 the company was bought by Associated Motor Cycles (*see* **AJS**), a group that was itself taken over in 1966 by Manganese Bronze Holdings. **BSA** and **Triumph** then joined Norton to form the Norton-Villiers-Triumph Group (NVT). NVT eventually collapsed in 1977, but the Norton name was saved and small-scale manufacture of the marque began in the early 1980s. Norton are one of the most successful motorcycle makers in the history of the Tourist Trophy race, first held on the Isle of Man in 1907.

Norton, W.W *see* **W.W. Norton**

Norton Simon *(foods)*

The American conglomerate now markets a disparate family of brand-name products, ranging from Hunt's tomato sauce to **Max Factor** cosmetics. It owes its name to Norton Winfred Simon (1907-1993), born in Portland, Oregon, the son of a department store owner. After receiving his education in his hometown, Simon completed high school in San Francisco, where he moved in 1921 with his sisters following his mother's death and the collapse of his father's business. He began his career while still at high school, wholesaling paper products. He moved to Los Angeles at age 16 and joined an export concern, putting what savings he had into the stock market. In 1927 he was able to start his own steel distribution firm, the Los Angeles Steel Products Company, and by dint of shrewd investment emerged from the 1929 crash not only solvent but $35,000 richer for his efforts. Simon's next business venture came in 1931, when he invested $7,000 in Gold Brands, Inc., an orange juice bottler in Fullerton, California. He wasted little time in effecting a turnaround, renaming the company Val Vita Foods and broadening its product to include tomatoes. He did so well that Hunt Brothers of Fullerton, California, bought Val Vita for $3 million. With his gain, Simon started to buy into Hunt, and by 1943 had enough money to control the company. He then invested in a series of other companies, eventually combining all his enterprises in 1968 into a new corporation, Norton Simon, Inc. To everyone's surprise he thereupon left, naming David Mahoney, who had served as **Canada Dry**'s president since 1966, as his successor.

Norvic (footwear)

The Norvic Shoe Company, based at Norwich, Norfolk, England, took its name from the abbreviation (used by the bishop of Norwich) of modern Latin *Norvicensis*, "of Norwich." The name itself dates from 1846 and was entered in the *Trade Marks Journal* of May 5, 1909.

Norwest (bank)

The American company was incorporated in 1929 as Northwest Bancorporation to control banks, trust companies, and other financial institutions in the north-central United States. It merged with Dial Financial Corporation in 1982 and the following year became Norwest Corporation, as now.

Norwich Union (insurance)

The British insurance company was established in Norwich, Norfolk, in 1797 by Thomas Bignold of Kent, who created two societies: the Norwich Union Fire Office in 1797 and the Norwich Union Life Assurance Society in 1808. They were both formed on the mutual principle but in 1821 the fire office merged with another Norwich insurance company, the Norwich General, and became a proprietary office with its shareholders. The two societies then followed their independent (but parallel) paths until 1925 when all of the share capital of the fire office was acquired by the life society, which continued as a mutual office. In 2000 Norwich Union merged with **Commercial Union** (known as CGU) to become CGNU.

Novartis (pharmaeuticals)

The Swiss pharmaceutical company, formed in 1996 in the merger of **Ciba-Geigy** and **Sandoz**, adoped its name from Latin *novae artes*, "new arts," reflecting (to quote its promotional literature) its "commitment to research and development that lead to innovative medicines and services." Its first president was Daniel Vasella (b.1953), former chief executive officer of Sandoz Pharma Ltd.

Novello (music publishers)

Vincent Novello (1781-1861) was born in London, England, the son of an Italian pastrycook and an English mother. When still a small boy he was sent with his brother Francis to a French school near Boulogne, which he left just as France was about to declare war on England in 1793. On his return, still only 12, he became a chorister at the Sardinian Embassy, London, where he also occasionally filled in as organist, both before and after his voice broke. In 1797, when just 16, he was appointed organist at the Portuguese Embassy, London, where his elder brother Francis was a bass in the choir. Vincent remained in this post until 1822. In the meantime the music that he and his choir performed in the embassy chapel was so popular that he decided to print and publish some of it, and in 1811 a set of two volumes appeared entitled *Selection of Sacred Music as Performed at the Royal Portuguese Chapel*. It was this enterprise that laid the foundation of the music publishing house of Novello & Co., which subsequently did much to make choral singing popular. In 1970 Novello was absorbed by the **Granada** group of companies.

Novocaine (local anesthetic)

The proprietary name for procaine, a drug used as a local anesthetic, especially in dentistry, was created from Latin *novo-*, the combining form of *novus*, "new," and the latter half of "cocaine." It was entered (as "Novocain") by the German manufacturers, Meister, Lucius & Brünning of Höchst, in the *Trade Marks Journal* of November 22, 1905.

Noxzema (skin cream)

George Avery Bunting had been a school principal for six years when he walked away from education and instead enrolled at the University of Maryland's pharmacy school, from which he graduated in 1899. A few years later he opened a modest drugstore in Baltimore, and by 1914 had perfected a skin cream formula for "Dr. Bunting's Sunburn Remedy." His preparation sold well, but he was keen to find a more original name for it. After considering hundreds of names, he was about to give up in despair when one day a customer walked into the store and observed, "Doc, you know your sunburn cream sure knocked out my eczema." From this chance testimony, "Dr. Bunting's Sunburn Remedy" was converted into "Noxzema Skin Cream." The little blue jars containing Doc Bunting's sunburn remedy that "knocks eczema" became a multimillion dollar business, while the manufacturing company that came to produce the cream was in turn named for it as Noxell.

NSU *(automobiles)*

The German marque takes its name from the initials of Neckarsulmer Strickmaschinen Union ("Neckarsulm Knitting Machine Union"), from the town of Neckarsulm, north of Stuttgart, where a firm was set up in 1873 to make knitting machines. It progressed to the manufacture of bicycles, and then to motorcycles in 1901 and automobiles in 1906. The business was modest until the 1930s, when it expanded into a new factory at Heilbronn, a few miles away. It continued the production of all types of road transport until its last and most famous model, the Ro80 saloon, brought about its downfall and was finally discontinued in 1977.

Nujol *(emulsifying agent)*

The type of paraffin oil, used as an emulsifying agent in pharmacy and for making mulls (suspensions of finely ground solids in a liquid) in infrared spectroscopy, has a name entered by the **Standard Oil** Company of Bayonne, New Jersey, in the *Trade Marks Journal* of February 16, 1916. The "Nuj-" of the name presumably represents "New Jersey," while "-ol" is probably "oil."

Nuova Italia, La *(publishers)*

The Italian publishing house, with name meaning "New Italy," was founded in Venice in 1926, at a time when Italy was becoming a Fascist police state. It moved its head office to Florence in 1930.

Nurdin & Peacock *(cash & carry warehouses)*

The history of the British firm dates from 1810, when Paul Augustus Nurdin (d.1854), a French egg merchant from Cherbourg, arrived in London to set up a business importing eggs from France. He made his base in Wardour Street, London, buying the eggs from his brother-in-law in Cherbourg, who sent them to Portsmouth by sailing ship (later, steamship), from where they were taken up to London by carrier. In 1829 Nurdin moved to Berwick Street, where his business expanded. Extra staff were taken on, and among them was John Peacock (1808-1890), who had moved from his native Herefordshire to be with his brother, a dairyman in Mayfair. The two men became friends, and in 1842 formed a partnership. They continued to import eggs, with the transportation from Portsmouth to London now made by rail. In 1848, however, Nurdin became ill, and returned to Cherbourg. On his death, the entire business went to Pocock, as Nurdin was unmarried and had no heirs. The firm then passed down through the Pocock family, until in 1919 Nurdin & Peacock Ltd. was formed to take over the businesses that had meantime been acquired. In 1960, under John Atkins Peacock (1898-1979), the company opened its first cash-and-carry store in Portsmouth.

Nurofen *(painkiller)*

The proprietary name for the analgesic drug ibuprofen presumably comprises a stock respelling of "new" plus the latter part of "ibuprofen." The name was entered in the *Trade Marks Journal* of August 25, 1982.

Nuttalls *("Mintoes" candy)*

William Nuttall first made boiled sweets in the kitchen of his home in Doncaster, Yorkshire, in 1884. The candy was sold by his family from small stalls in the market. He was helped in his work by his son, Harry, who in 1909 developed mint-flavored boiled sweets which he called "Nuttall's Mintoes." That same year a small candy factory was opened in Doncaster, and as the popularity of "Mintoes" spread, three retail shops were opened and the factory extended. Harry Nuttall died in 1948, but his "Mintoes" are still popular in Britain, even though they are now marketed by **Callard & Bowser**, who took over the Nuttall business the year after Harry's death. The name was entered by William Nuttall Ltd., of Doncaster, in the *Trade Marks Journal* of October 16, 1935 for: "Boiled sugar sweetmeats flavoured with mint."

Nutter *(butter substitute)*

The British product, a substitute for butter

made from the oil of nuts, was marketed from the early 20th century. Its name, an obvious blend of "nut" and "butter," was entered by its makers, Mapleton's Nut Food Co. Ltd. of Liverpool, in the *Trade Marks Journal* of May 19, 1920.

Nylex *(nylon)*

The proprietary name for nylon, based on this generic name, was entered by Polymers, Inc., in the US Patent Office *Official Gazette* of September 3, 1957: "For extruded synthetic fibres, particularly adapted for use as brush bristles."

Nylon *see* Appendix, p. 563

Oasis *(foam-based material)*

The make of rigid, water-absorbent, foam-based material, into which cut flowers and other plants are secured for display, takes its name from the oasis that is a fertile spot in the dry and barren desert. The name was entered by the Smithers-Oasis Co., of Cuyahoga Falls, Ohio, in the *Trade Marks Journal* of July 19, 1961.

Occidental Petroleum *(oil and gas)*

The American company was founded in 1920 in Bakersfield, California (hence "Occidental," or western), and for many years remained a small and mostly unprofitable oil driller. In 1957 the international businessman Armand Hammer (1898-1990) bought a controlling share in "Oxy," as it is known on Wall Street, with the aim of using it as a tax shelter, something that would give him a nice loss for his income tax return. Instead, Occidental struck natural gas in the Sacramento Valley, deciding Hammer to come out of retirement and go into the oil and gas business. He quickly increased his holdings, became the company's chief executive officer and president, and transformed it into one of the 12 major US corporations of his time. *See also* **Arm & Hammer**.

O-Cedar *(polishes and mops)*

In 1910, a 32-year-old American, Charles A. Channell, founded a business in Chicago to develop a new kind of floor and furniture polish. At first he called it "Wondermist," but then named it "O-Cedar," presumably because it smelled "o' cedar." However, a somewhat fanciful story behind the name is also told: "He had just finished polishing the bar of a public-house and the proprietor and himself were admiring the glistening surface, when a negro porter came in, and seeing the brilliant shining bar, exclaimed in his vernacular 'O see dar,' and so was born a name that has reverberated around the world" (Beable 2, 1926; *see* Bibliography, p. 565). Yet another theory derives the name from French *Eau cède à air* ("Water yields to air"), but this would apply to the polish as sprayed on in aerosol form, some time after its original application by cloth. (And why a French name for an American product?) O-Cedar became a British product in 1913, and the Channell Chemical Company (of England) Ltd. was soon after renamed O-Cedar Ltd. In the 1980s O-Cedar mops were being marketed by **Bristol-Myers**.

Oddbins *(liquor stores)*

The British chain was set up in the early 1970s and specializes in finding and buying binends, as the odd bottles remaining from a bin of wine, usually sold at a reduced price. Hence the name, entered in the *Trade Marks Journal* of April 22, 1976.

Odeon *(movie theaters)*

The first movie theater of the name was built in 1930 in Perry Barr, Birmingham, England by Oscar Deutsch (1893-1941), born in Birmingham the son of a Hungarian Jewish immigrant general dealer. In 1920, together with two former school friends, Michael Balcon and Victor Saville, Deutsch set up a motion picture distribution company. They soon moved into film production, while Deutsch himself gained control of two movie theaters. In 1928 he helped other Birmingham businessmen build a movie theater at Brierley Hill, Staffordshire, and two years later erected his own Odeon, choosing its name not only because it represented Greek *ōideion*, "theater," but also because it reflected his own initials. In 1935 the Odeon head offices were transferred to London, and by 1937 Deutsch was in control of a circuit of 250 British movie theaters. The apogee of his career was reached in 1939, when Deutsch took over the prestigious Paramount-Astoria circuit, 18 of the largest and most opulent movie theaters in the country. Odeon Theatres subsequently became part of the **Rank** Organization.

Odhams *(publishers)*

Odhams was a familiar name in British magazine publishing in the first half of the 20th century. It ultimately goes back to William Odhams, who in the 1840s set up a partnership with a fellow printer, William Biggar, to print two magazines, the *Guardian* and the *Railway Times,* the latter of which they owned. The partnership was later dissolved, with Odhams keeping the printing side of the business and Biggar taking the magazine. Odhams himself retired in the 1880s, but his printing works off the Strand, London, combined with a branch in Covent Garden in 1898 to form Odhams Ltd. By the outset of World War I, Odhams was one of the largest publishers of monthly and weekly magazines in Britain, taking over *John Bull* in 1920 and subsequently becoming Odhams Press Ltd. In 1961 Odhams was taken over by the Daily Mirror Group.

Oerlikon *(antiaircraft gun)*

The gun takes its name from the suburb of Zürich, Switzerland, where it was first manufactured in World War II. The name was entered in the *Trade Marks Journal* of October 7, 1970, by "Dieter Buhrle and Charlotte Buhrle-Schalk, trading as Werkzeugmaschinenfabrik Oerlikon Buhrle & Co." for: "Guns and parts and fittings therefor … ammunition for cannon; apparatus … for launching rockets; and rockets (missiles)."

Ogilvy & Mather *(advertising)*

The British advertising agency owes its existence to David Ogilvy (1911-1999), whose first job was in the kitchen of the Majestic Hotel, Paris, France, preparing food for the customers' dogs. He returned to the UK as a door-to-door salesman, then in 1935 joined the London advertising agency Mather & Crowther. In 1949, with his employers' financial backing, he set up his own agency, Hewitt, Ogilvy, Benson & Mather, based in Madison Avenue, New York, but in 1964 merged it with his London backers to form a new international company, Ogilvy & Mather. In 1989 the agency was bought by **WPP**, and subsequently became the Ogilvy Group.

Ohrbach's *(clothing stores)*

The firm originated with the store opened in 1923 in Union Square, New York City, by Nathan M. Ohrbach (1885-1972), born in Vienna. His family migrated to America when he was two years old, and he and his three brothers grew up in the Williamsburg section of Brooklyn. At age 20 he became a buyer of the First Co. of Jersey City, and in 1911 opened a small shop selling women's coats in Brooklyn. By 1923 he had saved enough money to set up a new store selling ready-to-wear clothing at low prices. The store was a success from the start, and Ohrbach made handsome profits by selling in bulk for cash and offering minimal sales service. Further stores were soon opened, but in 1962 about half the stock in the corporation was sold to the Brenninkmeijer family of **C&A** and in 1987 the firm ceased operations.

Oil of Olay *see* **Olay**

Olay *(skin care products)*

In the mid-1940s, a South African chemist, Graham Gordon Wulff, developed a topical skin preparation to prevent the dehydration of burn wounds on Royal Air Force pilots in World War II. After the war, he refined it and called it Oil of Ulay Beauty Fluid, the name perhaps intended to suggest that "you lay" it on the skin. In the early 1950s, Wulff and a marketer, Shaun Adams Lowe, founded the Adams Group to sell the product door-to-door in South Africa. It caught on, and was introduced to other countries, including the USA and UK in 1962 and Canada in 1965. In 1967 the Adams Group was acquired by **Richardson-Merrell**, who marketed Oil of Ulay as "Oil of Olay," altering the name to bring it closer to "oil." In 1985 Richardson-Vicks, as the company had become, was acquired by **Procter & Gamble**, who thus also took over the Olay brand, which was gradually extended to other skin care products. Procter & Gamble entered the name "Oil of Ulay" in the *Trade Marks Journal* of August 10, 1980, and "Oil of Olay" in the *Journal* of April 5, 1995.

Olbas *(herbal remedies)*

The present herbal pastilles, inhalers, embrocations, and the like, owe their origin to a chemist in Basel, Switzerland, who devised a herbal oil in the late 19th century. It came to be known by the Latin medical formula *ol. bas.,* short for *oleum basiliensis,* "oil of Basel," and this gave the name. The products are now marketed in the USA by the Penn Herb Co. of

Philadelphia, Pennsylvania. The name was entered in the *Trade Marks Journal* of June 26, 1935.

Old Gold *(cigarettes)*

The cigarettes were introduced by **Lorillard** in 1926, taking their name from the old Southern belt of Virginia where its rich golden tobacco was grown.

Old Parr *(whisky)*

The blend of whisky was first produced in the early 20th century by the Greenlees brothers of Glasgow, Scotland, who aimed it specifically at the southern English market. Hence its name, whose origin is indicated on the label: "Thomas Parr, Aged 152 years, was interred at Westminster Abbey, A.D. 1635." The veracity of this longevity is highly dubious, but great age is a desirable attribute of whisky, even one that is patently modern.

Old Peculier *(beer)*

The rich, dark brand of British beer is brewed by **Theakston** in Masham, North Yorkshire. The town was economically so powerful in medieval times that it had a "peculiar" status, exempt from the jurisdiction of the archdeacon. The name preserves the alternate former spelling of the word.

Old Smuggler *(whisky)*

The blend of Scotch, officially established in 1835, takes its name from the days when "smuggler's" whisky, made illicitly in Scotland in the 18th century to avoid excise taxes, was regarded as superior in quality to legally distilled whisky, which had to be made hastily in large quantities in order to enable the distiller to stay in business.

Old Speckled Hen *(beer)*

The beer, from the British brewery **Morland's** in Abingdon, Oxfordshire, is named not after a farmyard fowl but an old **MG** car made in the town which was speckled black and gold.

Old Spice *(aftershave)*

The men's cologne was created in the USA in the mid-1930s by William Lightfoot Schultz as a fragrance based on the memory (hence "Old") of a jar in which his mother kept cloves, roses, herbs, and spices (hence "Spice"). The product was launched in the UK in 1956.

Oldsmobile *(automobiles)*

The name behind the name is that of Ransom Eli Olds (1864-1950), born in Geneva, Ohio, the son of a blacksmith and machinist. He attended high school in Lansing before dropping out to work in the family business, P.F. Olds & Son, and in 1885 bought out his brother's interest. P.F. Olds & Son had built a few basic steam engines but spent much of the time on repair work. Ransom Olds investigated new uses for the engines, but eventually came to the conclusion that steam engines were not reliable enough to be a source of power for road vehicles. He therefore turned his attention to the motor vehicle, knowing that such European companies as **Peugeot** and **Daimler** were already producing automobiles. On August 11, 1896 he gave the first public demonstration of a carriage powered by an Olds gasoline engine mounted beneath the body. Olds was satisfied with the result, and on August 21, 1897 set up the Olds Motor Vehicle Company. Little public interest was shown at first until in 1900 Olds hit on a small car with a distinctive curved-dash front. This was the first Oldsmobile, which soon became the most popular car of its day.

Olivers *(footwear)*

The man behind the British name is George Oliver (1836-1896), born a village laborer's son near Leicester, and apprenticed at an early age to a local shoemaker. On completing his apprenticeship, Oliver moved to various places in Britain until in 1860 he decided that he had gained sufficient experience to set up his own business, which he did in Willenhall, Staffordshire. With his younger brother, Charles, as partner, George Oliver soon began to open branch shops elsewhere in the country, setting up the first in Neath, Wales, in 1866. By the time of its founder's death Olivers could boast over 150 branches, and was advertising boots and shoes as sold by "the largest retailer in the world." The head office of Olivers Shoes is today in Narborough, near Leicester, with the company still in the hands of the Oliver family.

Olivetti *(typewriters)*

Camillo Olivetti (1868-1943) was born in Ivrea, Italy, into a family engaged in trade and agriculture. On graduating from Turin Polytechnic, he went to London to complete his education, gaining practical experience at an engineering works, as well as improving his English. In 1893 he accompanied his tutor, Galileo Ferrari, to the United States, and there taught at Stanford University, California, for two years, where he met Thomas Edison. On his return to Italy in 1894, Olivetti went into industry with his partners, Dino Gatta and Michele Ferrero. In 1896 they established a small electrical precision instrument plant at Ivrea, the first in Italy, calling it "C.G.S." from the Italian words for "centimeter," "gramme," and "second," respectively the three basic units of length, weight, and time. His firm moved to Milan in 1903 and prospered, but four years later Olivetti decided to return to Ivrea and go into typewriter manufacturing. It was in 1908 that he founded the "Ing. C. Olivetti & C. First National Typewriter Factory," and after a further visit to the USA to study techniques, produced his first typewriter, the M1 (Model 1), in 1910. The machine was of original design, with legible characters, a standard keyboard, two-color ribbon, decimal tabulator, and back-spacer. It was exhibited at the World Fair in Turin a year later, and the Olivetti Company won an order to supply 100 typewriters to the Italian Navy. From then on the company grew into one of Italy's major engineering firms, subsequently diversifying to produce machine tools, teleprinters, and calculators, among other instruments and appliances. The name was entered by Ing. C. Olivetti & C. in the *Trade Marks Journal* of March 23, 1949. In 2001, Olivetti was acquired by **Pirelli** and **Benetton**. The controversial takeover meant that the two companies also won telecommunications giant Telecom Italia, which then held a controlling stake in Olivetti.

Olympia Press *(publishers)*

The English publishing house, specializing in "banned" works that in some cases became classics, was founded in Paris, France, in 1953 by Maurice Girodias, born Maurice Kahane (1919-1990), the son of an English Jewish father, Jack Kahane, and a French mother, Marcelle Girodias. Girodias named his venture partly as an alliterative allusion to the Obelisk Press set up by his father in 1932, partly as a tribute to Manet's famous painting *Olympia* (1863), depicting a naked woman reclining on a couch. The Press went into liquidation in 1970, when it was bought by Mary Donleavy, wife of the writer J.P. Donleavy, but not before it had published Donleavy's *The Ginger Man* (1955), Henry Miller's *Plexus* (1953) and *Sexus* (1957), Vladimir Nabokov's *Lolita* (1955), Samuel Beckett's *Molloy* (1955), William Burroughs' *The Naked Lunch* (1961), *The Soft Machine* (1961), and *The Ticket That Exploded* (1962), and Pauline Réage's notorious *The Story of O* (1954). A New York Olympia Press office opened in 1970 but went bankrupt and closed three years later.

Olympic Airways *(airline)*

The Greek airline was founded in 1957 by the Greek shipowner Aristotle Onassis (1906-1975) but from 1975 was wholly owned the Greek government. It grew out of three predecessors: Technical and Aeronautical Exploitations Company (TAE), formed in 1940, Hellenic Airlines (Hellas), formed in 1947, and Aeroporiki Metafori Ellados ("Greece Air Transportation") (AME). These were amalgamated under the TAE name in 1951, and continued to be so known until acquired by Onassis, who gave the present name, that of the famous plain that was the site of the Temple of Zeus and the place where the original Olympic Games were held. Appropriately for an airline, as a "lofty" business, the name also evokes Mount Olympus, the highest mountain in Greece.

Omega *(watches)*

In 1877 Louis Brandt, a Swiss watchmaker, set up a partnership with his eldest son, Louis Paul, under the name of Louis Brandt et Fils. In 1894 they introduced a new design of watch movement, which Henri Rieckel, banker to the Brandt family, suggested they call "Omega." Omega is the last letter of the Greek alphabet, and as such can be regarded as synonymous with completion, achievement, and perfection, attributes that the Brandts felt applied to their new design.

Omnimax *(film projection process)*

The Canadian technique of widescreen cinematography, in which 70mm film is projected through a fisheye lens on to a hemispherical screen, derives its name from "omni-" ("all") and "maximum." The name itself, based on

IMAX, was entered in the US Patent Office *Official Gazette* of June 11, 1974: "For motion pictures projectors, cameras, optical printers, film editing machines and motion picture screens."

Omnopon *(opium preparation)*

The proprietary name for a mixture of the hydrochlorides of the opium alkaloids derives from Latin *omnis*, "all," the first syllable of "opium," and the arbitrary suffix "-on." It was entered by **Hoffmann-La Roche** in the *Trade Marks Journal* of December 1, 1909 for: "All goods included in class 3" (i.e. chemical substances prepared for use in medicine and pharmacy). Omnopon is the British equivalent of US **Pantopon**.

Omo *(detergent)*

The name was originally registered in 1908 for a water softener. It appears to be arbitrary, designed as simply a memorable word and a bold visual device. English ethologist Desmond Morris makes the following comment in his seminal anthropological study *The Naked Ape* (1967):

Certain products have been given threat-face brand names, such as OXO, OMO, OZO, and OVO. Fortunately for the manufacturers, these do not repel customers: on the contrary, they catch the eye and, having caught it, reveal themselves to be no more than harmless cardboard boxes. But the impact has already worked, the attention has already been drawn to *that* product rather than to its rivals.

Onazote *(rubber)*

Onazote is a type of rubber that has been expanded to a cellular condition by absorbing a neutral gas under pressure during vulcanization. It is used for making lifebelts and floats, and its apparently arbitrary name was entered by Charles Lancaster Marshall, of London, England, in the *Trade Marks Journal* of December 29, 1920 for: "Raw, or partly-prepared, india-rubber, balata and gutta-percha for use in manufacture."

O'Neill *(sportswear and beachwear)*

Early in the 1950s, Californian surfer Jack O'Neill was determined to create a suit that would keep him warm in the icy waters of Northern California while allowing him freedom of movement for sudden surfing maneuvers. He experimented with various materials until one day in 1952, during a plane trip, he came across a foam called neoprene. With it, he created the wetsuit, which kept surfers warm and made surfing a year-round activity in temperate waters. From humble beginnings in a small Santa Cruz surf shop, O'Neill went on to became the largest wetsuit manufacturer in the world, with O'Neill, Inc., spreading its wings and landing in Japan, Australia, and Europe. As surfing engendered other board sports, the market expanded far beyond salt water, enabling O'Neill to move into those sports. In 1988 O'Neill sponsored the first Snowboard Pro World Cup and subsequently became heavily involved in snowboarding.

Opal Fruits *(sweets, or candy)*

The chewy sweets made by **Mars**, long promoted in the UK as "made to make your mouth water," took their name from the opal gemstone, with its small points of shifting color. In 1997 they were renamed "Starburst" to conform to their US counterpart.

Opalware *(tableware)*

The make of heat-resistant tableware, made of opal glass, has a name of obvious origin entered by its British manufacturers, James A. Jobling & Co. Ltd., of Sunderland, Co. Durham, in the *Trade Marks Journal* of April 29, 1964.

Opel *(automobiles)*

The German company dates from 1898, when Wilhelm von Opel (1871-1948) and his four brothers began converting the bicycle and sewing machine factory founded at Rüsselsheim in 1862 by Adam Opel (1837-1895) into the business that before World War II would produce more cars than any other European concern. Adam's grandson, Fritz von Opel (1899-1971), was famous for his experiments with rocket propulsion for automobiles and aircraft.

Optrex *(eye lotion)*

The preparation was originally introduced in France in 1928 by a M. Rosengart, the poor-sighted son-in-law of M. **Famel**. The name, obviously based on *optique*, "optical," was entered in the *Trade Marks Journal* of February 23, 1938.

Oracle *(computer software)*

The US company, one of the biggest software outfits in the world, owes its origin to Larry Ellison (b.1944), born in Manhattan to an unknown father and an unwed mother, who later gave him to an uncle and aunt in Chicago. When in his twenties, Ellison dropped out of the University of Chicago and headed west to Berkeley, California, where he got into computer programming. By the mid-1970s he was designing a database for the CIA, and in 1977 he and his partners, Robert Milner and Edward Oates, founded what became Oracle, a future-focused name with an appropriate suggestion of precognition and prescience. By 2001, Ellison's driving ambition was to oust **Microsoft** as the biggest software company in the world, not just one of the biggest.

Oracle *(teletext)*

The name is that of a teletext system formerly operated in the UK by the Independent Broadcasting Authority (as distinct from the BBC). It was introduced in the early 1970s and is said to take its name from the acronym of "optimal reception of announcements by coded line electronics," while at the same time alluding to the oracle of classical times who served as a medium by which advice or prophecy could be sought. The name was entered by the IBA in the *Trade Marks Journal* of July 17, 1974 for: "Apparatus for the transmission or reception of television signals and apparatus for the transmission of, processing of, or visual display of alphanumeric characters and/or characters for defining parts of diagrams." *Cp.* **Ceefax**.

Orange *(mobile phones)*

The British company was launched in London in 1994 by the German-born telephone engineer Hans Snook (b.1948). Its name, logo, and corporate identity were created by marketing consultants Wolff Olins, who also came up with the slogan, "The future's bright, the future's Orange." The color was presumably chosen for its optimistic sunrise glow. In 1999, Orange was acquired by **Mannesmann**, who sold it to **Vodaphone**, who in 2000 passed it on in turn to France Télécom.

Oreo *(chocolate sandwich cookies)*

Now marketed by **Nabisco**, "Oreo" cookies were first made in 1912. The origin of the name is problematical. According to one theory, the word is simply pleasant to say and easy to pro-

nounce, without having any meaning. Another account derives the name from French *or*, "gold," referring to the color on early packaging designs. A more academic explanation takes the name from Greek *oros*, "mountain," as the first test version of the cookie was rounded or hill-shaped. Finally, an ingenious story claims that the letters "re" in "cream" were sandwiched between the first and second "o" of "chocolate," like the cookie itself. Less attractively, the brand name gave the derogatory nickname for an American black who is regarded by other blacks as wishing to be part of the white establishment. He is thus dark brown outside but white inside, like the "Oreo" cookie.

Orgatron *(electronic organ)*

The type of electronic organ with the tone of a pipe organ has a name deriving from a blend of "organ" and "electronic" that was entered by the Everett Piano Company of Chicago, Illinois, in the US Patent Office *Official Gazette* of July 16, 1935: "For Musical instruments—Namely, Key-Board Instruments for Producing Pipe Organ Tones through Electronic Means." The registration was subsequently cancelled, but was reinstated by GTR Products, Inc., of Cranford, New Jersey, in the *Gazette* of April 1, 1975, with a note of first use on October 29, 1973.

Orimulsion *(fuel)*

The emulsion of bitumen, water, and detergents, used as a fuel, takes the first part of its name from the Orinoco oil belt, Venezuela, where the bitumen was originally extracted. The name was entered in the US Patent Office *Official Gazette* of June 23, 1987, with a note of first use on September 30, 1986.

Orion *(motion pictures)*

Orion Pictures Corporation was founded in 1978 by five former executives from **United Artists**. Hence the name, in allusion to the constellation, with its five prominent stars.

Orlon *(synthetic fabric)*

The synthetic acrylic fiber was first produced by **Du Pont** during World War II under the code-name "Fiber A," and in the 1950s was adopted as a soft, warm fabric for textiles and knitwear. Its name, probably arbitrary but based on "nylon," was entered in the US

Patent Office *Official Gazette* of October 17, 1950, with a claim of use since August 3, 1948, and in the *Trade Marks Journal* of January 9, 1952.

Orville Redenbacher's *("Gourmet Popping Corn")*

Orville Redenbacher (b.1907), of Brazil, Indiana, began his interest in popcorn when he studied popping-corn hybridization at Purdue University, West Lafayette. Following work in agronomy and plant breeding, and employment in various agriculture-related posts, Redenbacher teamed up with Charles Bowman in 1952 to develop a new hybrid yellow popping corn that popped open more widely than ordinary varieties. Redenbacher began packaging his corn and selling it to retail groceries. Despite initial complaints at its high price, the product caught on with popcorn consumers. In 1976 Redenbacher's still growing business was acquired by Hunt-Wesson Foods, now part of **Norton Simon**.

Oscar Mayer *(wieners)*

The American company dates from 1883, when Oscar F. Mayer (1859-1955), a German immigrant who had spent several years in the meat-packing industry, persuaded his two brothers, Max and Gottfried, to join him in setting up a small sausage shop on Chicago's north side. The Bavarian-type sausages went down well, and five years later the brothers bought property at Sedgwick and Beethoven in Chicago and put up a two-story market, now the site of their Chicago plant. Mayer's son, Oscar G. Mayer (1888-1965), joined the company in 1909 and became president when his father retired in 1928.

OshKosh B'Gosh *(childrenswear)*

The US company was founded in the 1890s as a family business in Oshkosh, Wisconsin, making denim work clothes and selling them mainly in the Upper Midwest. Its hometown gave the first part of its name, with an added "B'Gosh" as part of a vaudeville routine. A third-generation family member, Douglas Hyde, diversified production into childrenswear from the 1960s, and by the end of the 20th century the firm was the leading seller of children's branded clothing in the USA.

Osterizer *(electric food mixer)*

The mixer taked its name from its American manufacturer, John Oster, who entered the name in the US Patent Office *Official Gazette* of April 5, 1949.

Ostermilk *(milk preparation for babies)*

Dried milk was introduced in Britain in 1904 by **Glaxo**, who four years later booked an advertisement to promote their product on the entire front page of the *Daily Mail* (May 27, 1908). In 1929 Glaxo changed the name of the dried milk to "Ostermilk" to denote the addition of "Ostelin," a Glaxo vitamin D product (now no longer manufactured), whose own name came from the Greek element "osteo-," meaning "bone." (Vitamin D prevents rickets in children and osteomalacia, or softening of the bones, in adults.) The name was entered in the *Trade Marks Journal* of October 31, 1928.

Otis *(elevators)*

Elisha Graves Otis (1811-1861) was born in Halifax, Vermont, the son of a farmer and state legislator. He left school without graduating to join his brother, Chandler Otis, a builder in Troy, New York. Otis's health broke following a bout with pneumonia, and he turned to transporting goods between Troy and Brattleboro, Vermont. In 1838 he built a gristmill on the Green River in Vermont, but was unable to make a living from it. After a further breakdown in health in 1845, he took a job as a mechanic with Otis Tingley & Co., a bedstead manufacturer, and during his three years there invented a number of labor-saving devices. In 1851 he took a similar job in Bergen, New Jersey, with Josiah Maize, a former partner of Tingley. While moving Maize's business to Yonkers, New York, Otis developed a new type of hoist incorporating an automatic ratchet to hold the platform in place in case the rope broke. Word of his invention spread, and in 1854 Otis went into the elevator business full time. His future was assured after he demonstrated his invention that same year at the American Institute Fair in New York City, and before the year was out he had received orders for his freight elevators from several states. In 1857 he installed an elevator designed to carry people as well as freight in the new five-story china and glassware shop of E.V. Haughwout & Co. in New York City. By 1953, the centennial year of Otis's revolutionary invention, the Otis Elevator Company was still the undisputed leader in the field.

Ouija *(spiritualist seance board)*

The board with signs and letters on it, used with a planchette at spiritualist seances in attempts to receive messages from the dead, derives its name from French *oui* and German *ja*, both meaning "yes." The implication is that whatever language is used to ask the questions, there will always be an answer. The name was entered by the Kennard Novelty Company of Baltimore, Maryland, in the US Patent Office *Official Gazette* of February 3, 1891 for "Toys known as Talking Boards," with a note of use since July 1, 1890. A later entry was made in the *Gazette* of September 20, 1949 by William Fuld of Baltimore, and a third by **Parker Brothers** in the *Trade Marks Journal* of May 22, 1968, this last for: "Board games, being parlour games providing answers to questions."

Outward Bound *(youth organization)*

The British organization, providing naval and adventure training and other outdoor activities for young people, had its origins in the sea school set up in 1941 at Aberdovey in Wales by the German educationist Kurt Hahn (1886-1974), the founder of Gordonstoun School, with the financial backing of the shipowner Lawrence Holt (1882-1961), of the Blue Funnel Line. On the basis of this the Outward Bound Trust was formed in 1946 with the aim of establishing further residential schools. Holt devised the name from the naval term "outward bound" for a ship leaving a home port for a foreign one. The name is the registered property of the Outward Bound Trust, as is the longer "Outward Bound To Serve To Strive and Not to Yield," used for related products. The added words are based on the line "To strive, to seek, to find, and not to yield" from Tennyson's poem "Ulysses" (1842), in which Ulysses describes how following his safe return after the Trojan War he plans to set forth again "to sail beyond the sunset."

Ovaltine *(malt food drink)*

The malt food drink, known originally (and still in many countries) as "Ovomaltine," was the creation in 1904 of Albert Wander, son of the founder of the Wander Company of Berne,

Switzerland, the name alluding to two of its main ingredients, eggs (Latin *ovum*, "egg") and malt. The name was subsequently shortened as now and entered by Wander in the *Trade Marks Journal* of June 13, 1906. A company to make the drink was set up in the UK in 1909 and it became the archetypal soothing nightcap. Its popularity was enhanced by *The Ovaltineys*, a children's radio show sponsored by the manufacturers and first broadcast on Radio Luxembourg in 1935.

Ovomaltine *see* Ovaltine

Owbridges *(cough medicine)*

Now sold in Britain as "Owbridge's Cough Mixture," the original medicinal preparation appeared in 1850 as "Owbridge's Lung Tonic." It was manufactured by Walter Tom Owbridge, a chemist with a small shop in Porter Street, Hull, Yorkshire. His customers were mainly men of the Hull fishing fleet, who found his product beneficial in their work in cold Arctic winters. The reputation of the "Lung Tonic" spread, so that other chemists began to stock Mr. Owbridge's remedy, and in order to meet the demand, he built a factory in Hull in 1895. The preparation of today is still based on the original formula, and the mixture retains its distinctive taste of cloves and capsicum.

Owen Owen *(department stores)*

The name behind the British stores is that of a Welshman, Owen Owen (1847-1910), born near Machynlleth, Montgomeryshire, the son of a tenant farmer. On completing his education Owen, together with his brothers, Thomas and William, was apprenticed to his uncle Samuel Owen, a linen draper in Bath, Somerset. By 1867 he had decided to set up on his own, so moved that year to Liverpool, where another uncle, Robert Owen, had similarly been a successful draper. Within a few weeks Owen Owen had rented suitable premises, only a few doors from his uncle's business, and in 1868, single-handedly, opened his first shop. His venture did so well that five years later he was employing over 100 people and owned several adjoining shops to form his store. By the time of Owen's death, the Liverpool department store was one of the largest and most prestigious in the north of England, and today Owen Owen stores are found throughout England, from north to south.

Oxford *(marmalade)*

The name of the thick-cut marmalade was registered as a trademark by **Frank Cooper** of Oxford, England, in 1908 and again in 1931.

Oxford Instruments *(electronic equipment)*

The British high technology company had its beginnings in a garden shed in Oxford in 1959, when Martin Wood (b.1927), a research officer at the Clarendon Laboratory, University of Oxford, began a small business custom-manufacturing very powerful electromagnets. A breakthrough came in 1961, when developments in the USA led to the availability of new superconducting alloys, making it possible to generate powerful magnetic fields at low cost. The business gradually grew, with Wood's wife Audrey as finance director, and in the 1970s expanded into the medical electronics field. By 1983, when Oxford Instruments was floated on the stock market, it had grown into a company with 1,100 staff worldwide and a turnover approaching £50 million. It is now based in Eynsham, Oxfordshire.

Oxo *(beef extract)*

The British name, entered in the *Trade Marks Journal* of May 24, 1899, is said to have arisen as a colloquial abbreviation for dried meat in granular form that was being exported to Europe from **Fray Bentos**. The product itself was a development of "Liebig's Extract of Meat," first produced by the German chemist Justus von Liebig in Munich in 1847 as a so-called "extractum carnis." The actual origin of the satisfyingly symmetrical name may not simply be the word "ox," and according to one account, the separate consignments of dried meat from Liebig's factory were distinguished by marking the letters O-X-O on crates destined for the liquid product. *Cp.* **Wincarnis.**

Oxydol *(washing detergent)*

Oxydol was first sold in 1914 by the William Waltke Soap Co. of St. Louis, who named it for the oxygen in the bleach. In 1927 the company and its product were purchased by **Procter & Gamble**, who in 1933 used it to sponsor the first soap opera, the radio program *Ma Perkins*, created by Frank and Anne Hummett, a husband-and-wife advertising agency. In 2000 Procter & Gamble sold off Oxydol to a new company, Redox Brands Inc., set up by two P&G executives.

Ozalid *(drawing-office equipment)*

The name derives from the coated materials that are one of the company's products. The precise reference is to the diazo-sensitized coating applied to paper and film for using in drawing-office printrooms. (Diazo is a copying or coloring process using a diazo compound, which contains diazonium. "Diazo" itself denotes the presence of two nitrogen atoms, from Greek *di-*, "two," and *azo-*, "nitrogen.") "Ozalid" is "diazo" reversed with the letter "l" inserted. The first rolls of Ozalid paper were manufactured in 1926, but the name was already entered by the German company of Kalle & Co. of Biebrich, a suburb of Wiesbaden, in the *Trade Marks Journal* of July 16, 1924. A later entry by Kalle in the US Patent Office *Official Gazette* of November 13, 1928 claimed use of the name since March 19, 1923, as did one by the General Aniline & Film Corporation of New York in the *Gazette* of December 23, 1941. The name then passed to the company itself, with a further entry in the *Journal* of April 12, 1944.

P.K. *see* **Wrigley's**

P&O *(shipping line)*

The Peninsular and Oriental Steam Navigation Company, to give the British company its full name, was founded in 1837 by Arthur Anderson (1792-1868) and Brodie McGhie Willcox (1786-1862). Their first regular destination was Portugal and Spain. Hence the "Peninsular" part of the name. "Oriental" was soon added, when steamships began services to the eastern Mediterranean. It was not long before the company had ships in the Indian Ocean, so that passengers and mail, after making the land journey across the Egyptian desert from Alexandria, could continue by sea to India and Hong Kong. P&O's luxury white liners have now become familiar in the ocean cruise market. *See also* **Townsend Thoresen**.

Pablum *(children's breakfast cereal)*

The name, deriving from "pabulum" as a term for anything that feeds or nourishes, was entered by Mead Johnson & Co., of Evansville, Indiana, in the US Patent Office *Official Gazette* of July 13, 1932: "For specially prepared cereal food consisting of a mixture of wheat meal, to which have been added wheat embryo, dried yeast, powdered dehydrated alfalfa leaf and powdered beef bone prepared for human use," with a claim of use since June 4, 1932. The same company entered the name in the *Trade Marks Journal* of February 5, 1941 as: "A food for infants and invalids." The cereal was originally created in 1930 as a strengthener for weakly infants by a Canadian physician, Dr. Alan Brown of the Toronto Hospital for Sick Children, and it was he who devised the name.

Pabst (beer)

Frederick Pabst (1836-1904) began his adult life as a Great Lakes steamship captain, piloting the *Comet* between Milwaukee and Chicago. As he plied between the ports, he became aware of an attractive girl traveling on the boat. She was the daughter of Philip Best, owner of the Empire Brewery in Milwaukee, who used the *Comet* for his regular commute and took Maria along with him. Pabst began courting her, and the two were married in 1862, whereupon Best prevailed on his son-in-law to join the family brewery. He did so in 1864, despite having no experience in brewing beer, and soon learned the trade and the family's commercial secrets. When Philip Best retired in 1866, Pabst took control of the business, together with Emil Schandein, another of the old brewer's sons-in-law. Pabst was the dominant member of the partnership, and in 1873 he turned the family concern into a corporation, Best Brewing Co. His beer gained such renown and won so many awards that in 1889 a group of stockholders voted to rename the firm in Pabst's honor, and in 1892 Pabst was the first American brewery to achieve an annual output of more than 1 million barrels. The name was entered by the Pabst Brewing Co. of Milwaukee, Wisconsin, in the US Patent Office *Official Gazette* of June 26, 1906, with a note that "the name 'PABST' on the upper part of the band" had been used ten years. A later registration by the company in the *Gazette* of June 15, 1920, claimed a use of the name since June 1889 (the date cited above).

Packard (automobiles)

The name is that of James Ward Packard (1863-1928), born in Warren, Ohio, the son of a hardware store, lumber mill, and iron mill owner. After graduating from Lehigh University in 1884 with a degree in mechanical engineering, Packard embarked on a career in the electrical industry. He worked for the Sawyer-Mann Electric Company of New York City and soon became foreman of its incandescent lamp department. His interest in research led to a number of electrical patents, one of which was the Packard lamp, patented in 1889. The Sawyer-Mann Electric Company was sold to **Westinghouse** that same year, and in 1890 Packard returned to Warren, Ohio, where he and his brother, William Doud Packard, incorporated the Packard Electric Company. Early in 1891 Packard persuaded some former New York City associates to invest in a new company, The New York and Ohio Company, set up to manufacture Packard's incandescent lamps and transformers, and this was the base from which the Packard Motor Company was developed. The first car of the Automobile Department of the New York and Ohio Company was shipped in 1900, and that same year the Automobile Department was separately incorporated as the Ohio Automobile Company. Production grew, and in 1902 the company was renamed the Packard Motor Car Company.

Pac-Man (computer game)

The computer game, launched in 1980, is one in which the player attempts to guide a voracious blob-shaped character through a maze while eluding attacks from "enemy" characters, which it may in turn devour. The name presumably alludes to the way the creature attempts to "pack" away or eat everything that gets in its way. It was entered in the US Patent Office *Official Gazette* in September 1983: "For coin and non-coin operated electronic amusement apparatus for playing a game on a video output display," with a claim of first use on October 30, 1980.

Paddy (whiskey)

The story goes that Paddy Flaherty, sales representative in the 1920s for the Cork Distilleries Co., Ireland, so enthusiastically recommended the company's Old Irish Whiskey that repeat orders started to come in for "Paddy Flaherty's whiskey." Cork Distilleries realized they could turn this to good advantage. First, they put the Paddy Flaherty name at the foot of the label to show it was the genuine article.

Then they gradually altered the label until eventually the blend was called simply "Paddy." The name was entered in the *Trade Marks Journal* of December 23, 1925, but is also sometimes used for any Irish whiskey. In 1966 Cork Distilleries joined forces with **Jameson** and **Power's** to form the Irish Distillers Group.

Paddy Power *(betting agents)*

Ireland's biggest bookmaker, noted for its outrageous betting offers and advertising (it once gave odds on the Pope signing for the Protestant Scottish football team Glasgow Rangers), originated in a chain of 10 betting shops run by Stewart Kenny (b.1952) and Vincent O'Reilly. In 1986 it was acquired by **Coral** and two years later teamed up with John Corcoran, of Green Property, and the Powers group to form Paddy Power, a 40-strong chain run by three "Paddys" (Irishmen). The firm has also taken bets on who shot JR in *Dallas*, the O.J. Simpson trial, and Prince Charles's marriage.

Pains *(fireworks)*

The man who started the British company was James Charles Pain (1836-1923). The Pain family had been making fireworks in the 17th century, and a reference in the *London Gazette* is made in 1670 to a "Gunpowder Seller" named Pain. James Pain set up his business in Walworth, London, in about 1860, moving to other addresses in the area after his first address at 20 Albion Place caught fire. In about 1873 he opened a factory in Brixton, but transferred production to another works in Mitcham about five years later. It was at this time that Pain began manufacturing marine distress flares, and this side of the business was gradually built up, as well as that of conventional fireworks. Today, after various mergers, the firm's main business is operated by Pains-Wessex, with a head office near Salisbury, Wiltshire.

Pakkawood *(wooden laminate)*

The name of the heat-resistant wooden laminate, used to make handles for cutlery, cooking utensils, and the like, was entered in the *Trade Marks Journal* of May 4, 1955. The origin of "Pakka-" is uncertain. It may be a form of "pukka" (as in "pukka sahib") in its original sense of "cooked," "substantial," "permanent."

Palantype *(shorthand typewriter)*

The machine derives its name from "type" added to the first part of the surname of Clementine Camille Marie Palanque, of London, England, who entered it in the *Trade Marks Journal* of August 14, 1940 for: "Typewriters and parts thereof, typewriter inks, typewriter ribbons, typewriting paper, and stands for typewriters (not being furniture)."

Palitoy *(toys)*

The name derives from the founder of the British company, A.E. Pallett. When application was first made to register the name around 1934, permission was refused on the grounds that there was an Indian village called Pali and that "Palitoy" could imply that the toys were actually made there. The company persisted in its use of the name, and it was successfully entered in the *Trade Marks Journal* of October 19, 1938.

Pall Mall *(cigarettes)*

The cigarettes were introduced by the American Tobacco Company (*see* **American Brands**) early in the 20th century when the craze for Turkish cigarettes was at its height. They took their name from Pall Mall, a fashionable street in London, England, noted for its exclusive clubs.

Palm Beach *(clothing fabric)*

The make of lightweight clothing fabric, typically found in the Palm Beach suit, derives its name from the famous Florida resort, entered in the US Patent Office *Official Gazette* of October 26, 1915 for: "Woolen piece goods, mohair piece goods, and piece goods of combinations of cotton, wool, mohair, alpaca, camel-hair, silk, and artificial silk." The name originated with William S. Nutter, an expert in textile fabrics, who in 1905 invented a new type of cloth suitable for wearing apparel in warm weather. Walking along the beach near his home in Maine, he first conceived the name "Beach Cloth" for his material. In 1909 this name was changed to "Palm Beach," probably because of the growing popularity of the Florida winter resort. The name was subsequently adopted by the Goodall Worsted Co., the manufacturers and sellers of the product.

Palmair Express *(airline)*

Britain's smallest airline, with just one aircraft, based in Bournemouth, Dorset, was founded in 1957 by Peter Bath (b.1928), son of Reginald Bath of **Bath Travel**, to take vacationers to Palma, Majorca. Hence the name. Despite its diminutiveness, a 2001 survey of 31,000 passengers voted the airline third best in the world, beaten only by Air New Zealand and Singapore Airlines.

Palmer *(champagne)*

The champagne of this name is produced by the *Société Coopérative de Producteurs des Grands Terroirs de Champagne* ("Cooperative Society of the Great Lands of Champagne"), founded in 1947 in Avize, France, but now based on Reims. Its name is something of a mystery. According to one theory, the letters stand for qualities to which the original founders aspired: *précision* (or *poésie*), *assemblage* (or *amour*), *limpidité* (or *légèreté*), *maîtrise* (or *majesté*), *érudition* (or *élégance*), and *recherche* (or *raffinement*). Another explanation derives the name acronymically from the initials of the founders, although there were seven of them, not six. A third account claims that the founders tried to form an acronym from their initials but found it impossible. At a loss what to do, one of them happened to see a packet of **Huntley & Palmer** biscuits (cookies) and took the name from that. This seems unlikely, but it is known that the French, having been deprived of imported foods in World War II, seized on Huntley & Palmer biscuits in the late 1940s and granted them venerated status. The choice of name caused problems, and was objected to by the owners of the Château Palmer in Bordeaux. A heated exchange of letters continued for some time until finally the objection was amicably quashed by the despatch of a case of the champagne in question.

Palmolive *(soap)*

The soap derives its name from the palm and olive oils it contains. Palm oil from the flesh of palm fruits was used for slow lathering soaps, while oil from the nut of the palm fruit gave the kernel fat for quick lathering soaps. Olive oil was used for "soft" soaps. The brand was first manufactured in Milwaukee in 1898 by the soapmaker B.J. Johnson, who after World War I merged his business with that of **Colgate**.

Paludrine *(antimalarial drug)*

The proprietary name for proguanil derives from Latin *palus, paludis,* "marsh," plus the "-rine" ending of **Atabrine** or **Quinacrine**. It was entered by Imperial Chemical (Pharmaceuticals) Ltd. (*see* **ICI**), of Slough, Buckinghamshire, in the *Trade Marks Journal* of March 22, 1944.

Pampers *(disposable diapers)*

The diapers date from the 1950s, when Victor Mills (1897-1997), a chemical engineer working for **Procter & Gamble**, looked for an easier way to diaper his grandson. The result was Pampers, launched in 1961 with a name implying they are kind and gentle to the body, as well as suggesting a typical "baby" word. (It even evokes a blend of "mama" and "papa," and to some extent blends "Procter" and "Gamble.") It was not the original name, and "Dry-Wees," "Winks," "Tenders," "Tads," "Solos," and "Zephyrs," among others, were considered before the final choice was made.

Pan *(paperbacks)*

The ultimate origin of the name of Pan Books is the classical Greek god Pan. Toward the end of World War II, the English writer and illustrator Mervyn Peake gave a small pen-and-ink drawing of the god Pan to Alan Bott (d.1952), managing director of the Book Society and Reprint Society. Bott was thinking of starting a paperback publishing company as soon as the war was over but could not hit on a suitable name. He did not want to have a bird (because of **Penguin**) or an animal (because of Gertrude the Kangaroo on **Pocket Books**), so had to try elsewhere. Sitting at his desk and pondering the problem, he found himself gazing at Peake's little picture. There was the name he had been looking for. Pan Books were founded in 1944 and Pan is now a division of **Macmillan**.

Pan American *(airline)*

Pan American World Airways, popularly known as "Pan Am," was founded by a former World War I navy flyer, Juan Terry Trippe (1899-1981), born in Seabright, New Jersey, the son of a railroad surveyor and banker. Spurred by the transatlantic flight of Charles A. Lindbergh in May 1927, Trippe secured a contract that year to fly mail between Key West, Florida, and Havana, Cuba. The airline's first passenger service began the following year, and by the end of 1929 Pan American had a 12,000-mile route linking the United States with Cuba, Haiti, the Dominican Republic, Puerto Rico, Mexico, British Honduras (now Belize), Panama, and Colombia. Pan Am inaugurated the first transpacific flights in 1936, with the famous *China Clipper*, the first transatlantic flights in 1939, with the *Yankee Clipper*, and the first round-the-world flights in 1947. Trippe adopted the company name from that of a losing contender for the original contract. "Pan" is the Greek word for "all," implying both an "all-American" origin and a service to all parts of North and South America and even to all parts of the world, which in the event was not far from the truth. Pan Am began to suffer financial reverses in the 1960s and 1970s, however, and in 1991 finally went out of business. (A revived Pan Am began scheduling services again in 1996, with just three aircraft, but died once more in 1998.)

Pan Yan *(pickle)*

The name, despite its oriental look, has no actual meaning. It was chosen as the result of a competition among the employees of a British company, Maconochie Brothers, in 1907. The name was entered in the *Trade Marks Journal* of October 19, 1927, and the product itself was acquired by **Rowntree** in 1967.

Panadeine *(analgesic)*

The preparation combines paracetamol with codeine. Hence the name, blending **Panadol** and "codeine," and entered in the *Trade Marks Journal* of March 18, 1964.

Panadol *(analgesic)*

The proprietary name for paracetamol perhaps blends "panacea" and Latin *dolor*, "pain," suggesting an all-purpose remedy or painkiller. It was entered by **Bayer** in the *Trade Marks Journal* of December 14, 1955. *Cp.* **Panadeine**.

Panasonic *(radios and televisions)*

The **Matsushita** brand name was first used in 1955 for audio equipment as a quasi-classical word meaning "sound everywhere" or "all-sounding," from Greek *pan*, "all," and Latin *sonus*, "sound."

Panatrope *(record player)*

The make of electric record player, dating from the 1920s and noted for its comparatively loud reproduction, apparently derives its name from Greek *pan*, "all," implying maximum volume, and *tropē*, "turning." The name was entered by the **Decca** Record Company of London, England, in the *Trade Marks Journal* of September 15, 1954.

Panavision *(film projection system)*

The wide-screen film projection system, and the anamorphic lenses and cameras that produce it, take their name from Panavision, Inc., of Los Angeles. The name itself, combining "panorama" and "vision," dates from the 1950s and was entered in the *Trade Marks Journal* of May 24, 1967.

Pancake *(cosmetic preparation)*

The word is now used generally for any form of compressed make-up. It was originally a trademark, however, entered (as "Pan-cake") by **Max Factor** & Co. of Los Angeles, California, in the US Patent Office *Official Gazette* of July 13, 1937: "For cosmetic in the nature of a solidified cream used for a make-up base." (A note adds: "The word 'cake' is disclaimed apart from the mark.") A subsequent registration (as "Pancake") was made in the *Trade Marks Journal* of May 15, 1946 for: "Cosmetic preparations for toilet use and for use in theatrical, motion picture, television, and photographic make-up." Max Factor had long been associated with Hollywood at this time. *Cp.* **Pan-Stik**.

Panhard *(automobiles)*

In 1891 French engineers René Panhard (1841-1908) and Émile Levassor (1843-1897) produced the first motor vehicle with an internal combustion engine mounted at the front of the chassis rather than under the driver's seat. It was put on sale in 1892 as a racing car, competing successfully in early races, and was the prototype of the modern automobile. The company of Panhard's name produced cars until 1967 when it was acquired by **Citroën**.

Pan-Stik *(cosmetic)*

The type of matt cosmetic in the form of a stick derives its name from a blend of **Pancake** and "stick." It was entered by **Max Factor** &

Company of Los Angeles, California, in the *Trade Marks Journal* of August 10, 1949 for: "Non-medicated toilet preparations, cosmetic preparations and perfumes."

Pantene *(shampoo)*

In World War II, scientists at **Hoffmann-La Roche** developed a new chemical substance called Pantenol, an analog of vitamin B_5 (pantothenic acid), which produced a healing effect when applied to the skin of burns victims. In 1947, the scientists incorporated this into a form of shampoo, calling it "Pantene" after the original chemical name, which itself derived from "pantothenic" and the "oil" suffix "-ol." ("Pantothenic" in turn comes from Greek *pantothen*, "from every side," alluding to the vitamin's widespread occurrence.) The name was entered in the *Trade Marks Journal* of September 14, 1955.

Panther *(motorcycles)*

The name of the British make became so closely identified with that of its manufacturers, Phelon and Moore Ltd., that it was frequently used in place of it. The name is appropriate for a fast and powerful machine, and also partly reflects the name of the makers themselves. (The first name was that of Jonah Phelon, who in 1901 was experimenting with motorized bicycles. The second name was that of his partner, Richard Moore.) Panthers were produced from 1904 to 1966.

Pantopon *(opium preparation)*

The proprietary name for a mixture of the hydrochlorides of the opium alkaloids derives from Greek *panto-*, "all," the first syllable of "opium," and the suffix "-on." It was entered by **Hoffmann-La Roche** in the US Patent Office *Official Gazette* of February 1, 1910 for: "A pharmaceutical preparation containing all the alkaloids of opium in an easily-soluble state and in a form suitable for subcutaneous injections." Pantopon is the US equivalent of British **Omnopon**.

Pantry Pride *see* **Food Fair**

Parabellum *(pistol)*

The alternate name of the **Luger** derives from Latin *para*, the imperative of *parare*, "to prepare," and *bellum*, "war." The words come from the Latin tag *Si vis pacem, para bellum*, "If

you want peace, prepare for war," a popular misquotation of the original by the 4th-century Roman writer Vegetius: *Qui desiderat pacem, praeparet bellum*, "Let him who desires peace, prepare for war."

Parafilm *(thermoplastic)*

The name of the various thermoplastic materials presumably derives from "para-" (in the sense "similar to," as in "paramilitary") and "film." It was entered by the Marathon Mills Co. of Rothschild, Wisconsin, in the US Patent Office *Official Gazette* of September 18, 1934: "For moistureproof, self-sealing flat wrapper," by Lindsay & Williams Ltd. of Manchester, England, in the *Trade Marks Journal* of May 21, 1952 for: "Backing cloth, being piece goods ... consisting of textile material coated with a thermoplastic substance containing rubber, the textile material predominating, for use in the manufacture of boots and shoes," by the same firm in the *Journal* of February 8, 1956 for: "Electrical insulation identification tape," and again in the *Journal* of September 26, 1956 for: "Thermoplastic materials in the form of sheets, ribbons and tapes, none being textiles."

Paramount *(communications and media)*

Paramount Communications, Inc., was founded by Charles G. Bluhdorn (1926-1983), born in Vienna, Austria. In 1942 he came to the United States, where he worked for a cotton broker in New York City. In 1945 he joined the US Army, and on his release got a job with an import-export firm, attending Columbia University in the evenings. In 1949 he formed his own importing firm. His venture was successful, and within five years he was a millionaire. He then purchased a controlling interest in Michigan Plating and Stamping, a small auto bumper manufacturer founded in 1934, and the following year acquired an auto parts replacement firm, Beard and Stone Electric, of Houston, Texas. In 1958 he combined the two as Gulf + Western, his aim being to make auto parts on the Gulf of Mexico (the first part of the name) and ship them west (the second part). Once again, his enterprise took off, and began to expand its holdings in the media and communications fields, at the same time selling its unrelated businesses. In 1989 its name was changed to Paramount Communications, reflecting the new concentration on entertainment and publishing. Among the many businesses owned by Paramount are the film production and distribution company Paramount Pictures, founded in 1914 by the motion picture pioneer W.W. Hodkinson (1881-1971) and acquired by Bluhdorn in 1967, which gave the new name, and **Simon and Schuster**. "Paramount" itself, meaning "supreme," suggests "mount" or "mountain," as in the familiar Paramount Pictures logo, but it actually derives from Old French *par*, "by," and *amont*, "above," which is not quite the same.

Parfait Amour *(liqueur)*

The sweet, spiced liqueur, with a French name meaning "perfect love," is almost certainly Dutch in origin, but has a French name as French is traditionally the language of love. It is produced by the Dutch liqueur specialists **Bols** and by certain French firms, including the makers of **Marie Brizard**. "Parfait Amour" dates from at least the early 19th century and is mentioned in Thomas Moore's *The Fudge Family in Paris* (1818): "A neat glass of *parfait-amour*, which one sips / Just as if bottled velvet tipped over one's lips!" (Letter III).

Paris *(womenswear)*

The American firm of A. Stein & Company, manufacturers of garters, suspenders, and belts, was organized in 1887. They adopted the name "Paris" for these garments, choosing it because of its connotations of style, and registered it as a trademark in 1909. Geographical names are normally difficult to register, but "Paris" was used arbitrarily, and not in its natural sense, so was held to be a valid trademark.

Park *(newspapers)*

The American newspaper chain takes its name from Roy H. Park (b. 1910), from Dobson, North Carolina, who worked his way through North Carolina State University, editing the campus newspaper, then went into public relations and advertising for various farm cooperatives, first in North Carolina, then, from 1942, in Ithaca, New York, where he ran an advertising agency which mainly served GLF, the state's big farm cooperative. His company headquarters later came to be based in the former GLF offices at Terrace Hill, Ithaca.

Parker *(pens)*

The famous pens take their name from George Safford Parker (1863-1937), born in Shullsburg, Wisconsin, of immigrant English stock. While George was still a small child, his parents moved to Fayette, Iowa, where his first job was working on his father's farm. On graduating from Upper Iowa University, Parker considered his future career. He felt he was not suited to be a farmer, so instead enrolled at a nearby school of telegraphy to improve his academic prospects. Within a year he had joined the staff of the establishment, and to supplement his salary he became the local representative of the John Holland Fountain Pen Company. Naturally, he sold pens to his students, who brought them to him when they needed repairing. To carry out the repairs more efficiently, Parker bought his own tools, and soon found that the more pens he sold, the more he repaired. In 1888 he set up the Parker Pen Company in Janesville, Wisconsin, taking as partner a former insurance agent, W.F. Palmer. By the end of the century he was manufacturing his new self-filling pen, and Parker pens were being advertised in England in 1899. The rest is scribal history. The popular "Duofold" pen, with its enlarged ink capacity, was introduced in 1921, to be followed by **Quink** ink in 1931, the "Vacumatic" in 1933, and the Parker "51" pen in 1939, so named to mark the 51st anniversary of the company's founding. The Parker name was entered as "used ten years" in the US Patent Office *Official Gazette* of October 2, 1906, and was subsequently entered in the *Trade Marks Journal* of August 5, 1914, the *Gazette* of January 2, 1923 (with a claim of use "since 1891 on fountain pens; since 1921 on mechanical pencils"), and the *Journal* of June 5, 1935 for: "Fountain pens and propelling pencils (none being of precious metal or of imitation precious metal) and desk stands (not of precious metal or imitation precious metal) for pens."

Parker, Tom *see* **Tom Parker**

Parker Brothers *(board games)*

George S. Parker (1866-1952) of Medford, Massachusetts, invented his first board game, a borrowing-lending contest called "Banking," when he was only 16. After graduating from Medford High, Parker signed on as a cub reporter with Boston's *Commercial Bulletin*. In 1886 a respiratory ailment obliged him to seek a less strenuous occupation, however, so he fell back on game-making. Two years later, he and his brother Charles formed Parker Brothers game company. A third brother, Edward, joined the firm in 1898 and together the trio built the business into an industry leader, producing such classics as **Monopoly**, **Cluedo**, and "Risk."

Parker Knoll *(furniture)*

Parker Knoll chairs and settees owe their name to Tom Parker (1881–1961) and Willi Knoll, a German furniture manufacturer. Parker was himself the son of a London, England, furniture maker, and had been managing his father's firm, together with his three brothers, since about 1920, taking it over entirely when his father died in 1927. The firm had a good reputation for its chairs, and the association with Knoll arose in 1930, when the latter came to England from Stuttgart with the aim of finding a furniture maker who could produce chairs with a new springing device he had patented. One day Parker was visiting **Heals** when he came across one of Knoll's prototype chairs, with its horizontal cable springs across the seat and back. He saw immediately that such a chair frame needed only a seat and a cushion to complete it. He sought out Knoll at his hotel, and soon made an arrangement with him to manufacture chairs with the German's new springing system, subsequently patented as "tension suspension." Parker Knoll Ltd. was formed in 1942.

Parkerizing *(rust-proofing process)*

Parkerizing is a rust-proofing process in which iron or steel is given a protective coating of phosphate by being briefly immersed in a hot acidic solution of manganese dihydrogen phosphate. The process was introduced by the Parker Rust-Proof Co., of Detroit, Michigan, incorporated in 1915, who entered the name in the US Patent Office *Official Gazette* of May 24, 1949, with a claim of use since March 15, 1936. "Parkerized" was subsequently entered by the Pyrene Co. Ltd., of Brentford, Middlesex, England, in the *Trade Marks Journal* of May 20, 1942 for "Hand tools and side arms" and in the *Journal* of December 2, 1942, with regard to: "Small domestic utensils and containers, non-electric instruments for cleaning purposes ... all being goods of common metal."

Parkesine *see* (1) **British Xylonite;** (2) **Halex**

Parkray *(heating equipment)*

The name is a blend of The Park Foundry (Belper) Ltd., who actually manufactured the convector open fire of this name, launched in 1953, and this British firm's parent company, Radiation Ltd., suggesting "ray." The company name was changed to Radiation Parkray Ltd. in 1961 and Parkray Ltd. in 1972. The name "Parkray Coalmaster" was entered in the *Trade Marks Journal* of July 18, 1971.

Parks *(sausages)*

Henry Green Parks, Jr. (1916–1989), was born in Atlanta, Georgia, the son of a domestic laborer. When he was a few months old, Parks's family moved to Dayton, Ohio, where he attended public school and Ohio State University. He worked his way through college, graduating in 1939. The only black in his class, Parks was advised to go to South America, change his name, and return to the USA under an assumed identity if he wished to succeed in business. Parks declined, and instead accumulated managerial experience in a number of different posts. In 1951 he began an entirely new venture in Baltimore, Maryland, opening Parks Sausage Company in an abandoned dairy. At first the business struggled, but with vigorous promotion, not least through the company symbol "Parky the Pig," who gave gifts to children, the enterprise prospered, with Parks sampling the product every day for 20 years. In 1977 Parks sold his interest in the company to the Miami-based Norin Corporation, who were acquired two years later by Canadian Pacific Corporation.

Parmalat *(dairy products)*

The Italian company was founded in Parma in 1961 by brother and sister Calisto and Anna Maria Tanzi. The name, now associated with sports sponsorship, combines that of Parma with Italian *latte*, "milk" (or *latteria*, "dairy").

Parnate *(antidepressant)*

The proprietary name for the drug tranylcypromine was entered by Smith, Kline & French Laboratories (later **SmithKline Beecham**), of Philadelphia, Pennsylvania, in the US Patent Office *Official Gazette* of May 17, 1960, and in the *Trade Marks Journal* of December 29, 1960. The name itself appears to be arbitrary.

Parowax *(paraffin wax)*

The product, used for sealing fruit jars and the like, has a name of fairly obvious origin. It was entered by **Standard Oil** in the US Patent Office *Official Gazette* of December 7, 1909.

Parozone *(household bleach)*

The quasi-scientific name was originally that of the British manufacturers, now part of the **Jeyes** Group. The company was incorporated soon after 1900 with a name designed to connote good health and cleanliness. Analyzed as "par ozone," the name implies "by the ozone," evoking the fresh and invigorating air that blows inshore from the sea, while in a chemical sense, both ozone and bleach have a common property in oxygen. The name was first entered in the *Trade Marks Journal* of June 13, 1888.

Partagas *(cigars)*

The name is that of Don Jaime Partagas, who started his business in Havana, Cuba, in 1845. The name was entered by "Juan Antonio Bances, of and on behalf of the firm of Bances and Co." of Havana, Cuba, in the *Trade Marks Journal* of April 17, 1878, and subsequently by "Cifuentes, Fernandez y Ca.," also of Havana, in the *Journal* of June 3, 1908. The brand is manufactured by General Cigar.

Passport *(whisky)*

The blend of whisky by Chivas Brothers of Paisley, Scotland (*see* **Chivas Regal**), was launched in 1965 with the aim of appealing specifically to a younger, less traditional market. Hence the name, suggesting a "gateway" or introduction to the world of whisky.

Patak *(spices)*

Patak Spices, famous for its sauces, chutneys, pastes, and poppadoms, is based in Wigan, near Manchester, England, where it is run and owned by Kirit Pathak (b.1953) and his wife Meena (b.1957). The business began when Kirit's father came to London from Kenya in 1956 with just £5 and opened a corner shop. Dropped the "h" from their name to ease pronunciation, his family worked 18 hours a day to build up a chutneys and pickles concern. Kirit took over the firm in 1976 and moved it to Wigan, where Meena writes the recipes.

Pathé *(motion pictures)*

The name is that of the Paris-born Frenchman Charles Pathé (1863-1957), who with his brother Émile founded Pathé Frères in 1896 to make and sell phonographs and phonograph cylinders. Using the camera developed by Louis and Auguste Lumière, Pathé Frères went on to film a number of short subjects, many of them sensational criminal adventures or melodramatic love stories, and in 1909 produced their first "long" film, *Les Misérables*, a four-reel screen version of Victor Hugo's novel. That same year Pathé originated the *Pathé Gazette* in France, soon an internationally famous newsreel. After Pathé's death the company continued as a leading film distributor.

Patons *(knitting yarns)*

In 1811, John Paton (1768-1848) set up a spinning mill in Alloa, Scotland. He was eventually joined by his youngest son, Alexander, and the firm became John Paton & Son. The business thrived, and in 1920 merged with J. & J. Baldwin & Partners Ltd., founded in 1785 by James Baldwin (1746-1811) in Halifax, Yorkshire, England, as a wool-washing and cloth-fulling business. In 1961 the combined Patons & Baldwins Ltd. merged with J. & P. **Coats** to form the Coats Patons Group, and this in turn merged with Vantona **Viyella** in 1986 to form the Coats Viyella Group.

Patou *(perfumes)*

Jean Patou (1887-1936) was born in Normandy, France, to a family of wealthy furriers. In 1912 he opened his own boutique, Maison Parry, in Paris, and sold his first collection outright to an American retailer. In 1914, he was called up for military service in World War I, but resumed business after the war and in 1919 presented his first collection at 7, rue Saint-Florentin, Paris. Patou created his first three perfumes in 1925 and in 1930 launched *Joy*, dubbed "the costliest perfume in the world" by society hostess Elsa Maxwell, to cosset his American clients after the Wall Street crash. The business remains in family hands today.

Patum Peperium *(savory paste)*

The original form of **Gentleman's Relish**

derives its name from pseudo-Latin *patum*, "paste," and a genitive plural adaptation of Latin *piper*, "pepper." The product is not actually a pepper paste but an anchovy paste.

Paul Masson *(wine)*

In 1878, Paul Masson (1859-1940), born in Burgundy, France, immigrated to California, where he found work with Charles Lefranc, a local winemaker. Some ten years later Masson married Lefranc's daughter, Louise, and soon became a partner in the winery. He acquired complete control of the business in 1892, changing its name to the Paul Masson Champagne Company. Although he sold his mountain vineyard, La Cresta, in 1933, Masson continued to make champagne in a San José cellar until his retirement in 1936.

Paul Smith *(fashionwear)*

The name is that of Paul B. Smith (b.1946), a former British warehouse errand boy who opened his first women's fashion store in his native Nottingham in 1970. In 1976 he showed his first menswear collection in Paris. Today there are stores worldwide, including over 200 in Japan.

Paulaner *(beer)*

Germany's most famous spring beer comes from a brewery founded in 1634 by monks in the order of St. Francis of Paola (1416-1507), who was born at Paola, southern Italy, and became a hermit near his home town. He is known in German as Franz von Paula. Hence the name.

Pavesi *(cookies)*

The Italian firm was founded in 1937, when Mario Pavesi (b.1909) opened a cookie factory in Novara. In 1948 Pavesi first produced its famous "Biscottini di Novara," soon to be known as "Pavesini," and in 1992 the company was taken over by **Barilla**.

Pavulon *(muscle relaxant)*

The proprietary name for pancuronium, a synthetic drug similar to curare, appears to be loosely based on the generic name, itself dating from the 1960s.

Paxo *(stuffing)*

The British brand of stuffing, so named as one "packs" it into the poultry or meat, was the invention in 1901 of J. Crompton, a Manchester butcher, who used it to add value to the chickens he sold to customers. The product grew in popularity and by 1938 had attracted the attention of **Cerebos**, who bought the brand. It was in turn acquired by RHM (*see* **Rank**) in 1968. The name was entered in the *Trade Marks Journal* of March 8, 1911.

Paxolin *(plastic)*

The type of laminated plastic, made of paper impregnated with a varnish consisting of phenol and formaldehyde and used as an electrical insulating material, has a name (perhaps based on "packs") entered by The Micanite & Insulators Company, of London, England, in the *Trade Marks Journal* of January 23, 1918, and the US Patent Office *Official Gazette* of October 28, 1958.

Peabody Coal *(coal)*

The largest coal producer in the United States takes its name from Francis S. Peabody, who opened a coal yard in Chicago in 1883. In 1896 he went into mining in Illinois, and by the end of the century his firm had four mines in Williamson County. The company sold out to **Kennecott** Copper in 1966, but were sold by them in turn to Newmont Mining in 1978.

Pearce Duff *(custard powder and jellies)*

Two Englishmen were involved in the evolution of the company, famous for its custard. The start was in 1847, when William Pearce, with William Henry Duff as partner, began making baking and egg powder in a private house in Bermondsey, London. It was Duff's job to travel around the country selling the product. Pearce then died, leaving William Duff to take on his youngest brother, Daniel Duff, not as partner but as employee. When William Duff in turn died, he left the business to his daughter, with Daniel as manager. The firm developed from there, with custard powder, blancmange powder, and jellies added to the original products in the years leading up to World War I. The Pearces and the Duffs were by this time related in marriage, and the family interest in the company continued until 1986.

Peardrax *see* **Cydrax**

Pearl *(insurance)*

The British company owes its origin to

Patrick James Foley (1836-1914), a friendly society employee, who together with some friends in the late 1850s became connected with a loan club, the Pearl Loan Co., that met in a London public house. The club developed into the Pearl Life Assurance Association and Sick Benefit Society, registered as a friendly society in 1862, and two years later Foley and his associates founded the Pearl Life Assurance, Loan & Investment Co. Ltd. In 1874 "Loan & Investment" was dropped from the company title. The pearl, prized as a gem secreted within its shell, is an obvious symbol for a hidden benefit or buried treasure.

Pearl & Dean *(movie theater advertising agents)*

The names are familiar to British moviegoers from the advertisements that appear on the screen between one picture and the next. The first name is that of two brothers born at the turn of the 20th century, Charles and Ernest Pearl, both of whom were raised in Swansea, South Wales, with Charles later working for a Cardiff advertising organization, one of whose activities was placing advertisements on bus tickets. Both men came to work for the Screen Advertising Company (now **Rank** Screen Advertising), but left it and set up in London with Robert Dean (1907-1987) from Bristol, founding the business of Pearl & Dean Ltd. in 1953. In the 1970s, however, the Pearl brothers retired and sold off their company.

Pears *(soap)*

The name of Pears is well known in Britain, not only for the familiar brand of soap but for the annual *Pears Cyclopaedia* and "Miss Pears" photographic contests for pretty little girls. It is that of Andrew Pears (d.1838), who after completing an apprenticeship as a hairdressser, left Mevagissey, Cornwall, in 1789 to open a barbershop in Soho, London. He noticed that the products he made, such as rouges, creams, and powders, were often used to repair the damage caused by the harsh soaps of the day. He therefore decided to produce a soap that would treat complexions more kindly. What he came up with was the now famous "transparent" soap, which not only had all the harshness and impurities removed, but was also delicately perfumed. The launch of the soap was the launch of the business, now officially A. &

F. Pears Ltd., the second initial being that of Andrew's grandson, Francis, whom he took as partner in 1835. The popular "Miss Pears" contests, however, were introduced only in 1958.

Pearson *(media and publishing)*

The British media giant began life as quite a different business in 1844, when S. Pearson was set up in Yorkshire to build drainage ditches. The enterprise grew, and by the time it moved to London in 1882 was one of the largest building firms in the world. At the turn of the 20th century it diversified into the oil business, and in 1919 S. Pearson & Co. was established as a holding company. From 1920 Pearson cast its net ever wider into the media market, acquiring the prestigious *Financial Times* and such noted publishers as **Longman**, **Penguin**, **Ladybird**, and **Dorling Kindersley**.

Peek Frean *(cookies, or biscuits)*

The British firm of Peek, Frean & Co. Ltd. was founded in 1857 by James Peek, a London tea merchant, and George Hender Frean, his nephew-in-law, primarily as a way of occupying James' two sons, Charles and Edward. The two brothers were not interested in the biscuit business, however, so the actual running of the company was undertaken by Peek and Frean themselves, together with one of the latter's friends, John Carr, who was the brother of Jonathan Dodgson Carr of **Carr's** biscuits. It was Carr, in fact, who developed the technology of biscuit-baking, and who changed the typical Victorian "hard tack" biscuit into the crisp and crumbly cookie of today. Carr introduced his "Pearl" biscuit, or cookie, in 1865 as an example of the new technology, for it had no "pin holes," unlike earlier biscuits. Peek Frean has also been a pioneer in other well-known types of biscuits, such as the "Garibaldi" (first made in 1861), "Marie" (1875), "Bourbon" (1910), and "Shortcake" (1912). The "Pat-a-Cake" was likewise popular The firm produced the first chocolate cookie in 1899. *See also* **McVitie & Price**.

Pegaso *(automobiles)*

The Spanish company's main commercial concern has always been trucks and motor coaches, but in 1951 it produced a super sports car, the Pegaso Z102, named for Pegasus, the winged horse of Greek legend. The last car was built in 1958, although the marque lives on for commercial vehicles.

Pegity *(board game)*

The children's board game, in which four players in turn place pegs in holes with the aim of completing a row of five pegs, has a name based on "peg" (and presumably the girl's name Peggotty) that was entered by **Parker Brothers** in the US Patent Office *Official Gazette* of March 31, 1925 for: "Game of the Type of 'Go-Bang'. Played with Pegs, for Adults and Children."

Pelican *see* **Penguin**

Penbritin *(penicillin)*

The proprietary name for ampicillin, a penicillin used in treating infections of the urinary and respiratory tracts, was entered by **Beecham** Research Laboratories Ltd., of Brentford, Middlesex, England, in the *Trade Marks Journal* of November 18, 1959, and the US Patent Office *Official Gazette* of July 26, 1960. The name itself appears to blend "penicillin" and letters from the manufacturer's name.

Pendelfin *(ceramic models)*

Famous for its ceramic model rabbit collectables, the British firm was founded in 1953 by Jeannie Todd and Jean Walmsley Heap, their first creation being a wall plaque called "The Pendle Witch." The name comes from Pendle Hill, Lancashire, nicknamed "The Witches' Hill" from its association with a coven of local witches. (Their mass trial in 1612 was one of the most notorious in England.) The second half of the name suggests "elfin."

Pendleton *(menswear)*

The name is particularly associated with the brightly colored checked sports shirt made by Pendleton Woolen Mills, of Pendleton, Oregon, who entered it in the US Patent Office *Official Gazette* of December 28, 1948: "For outer shirts, lounge robes, trousers and slacks, jackets and blazers, and men's coats." The garments were current some years before this, however, as testified by an advertisement in the December 1940 number of *Esquire*: "Wear a Pendleton—then you'll know why Pendleton shirts have been a religion with sportsmen."

Penguin *(biscuits, or cookies)*

The chocolate-covered biscuits of this name were launched by **Macdonalds** in 1946. The name was simply designed to be enjoyably eye-catching and memorable, and was subsequently promoted in a famous slogan which urged potential consumers to "p-p-p-p-pick up a Penguin."

Penguin *(paperbacks)*

The British publishing house was founded in 1935 by **Allen Lane**, the former managing director of **Bodley Head**. The commitment to paperbacks was at the time a revolutionary step in the publishing trade, and clearly a distinctive name was needed. "Penguin" is said to have resulted from a suggestion made by Lane's secretary, Joan Coles. Lane liked the idea of a logo that would have "an air of dignified flippancy" and that would be easy to draw in black and white. "Dolphin" and "Porpoise" were also considered, but it turned out that another publisher, **Faber and Faber**, already owned the latter. The name agreed, Edward Young, of the Bodley Head production department, was sent to London Zoo to start work on devising the logo for the new series of books. One day two years later, Lane was standing by a mainline railroad station bookstall when he heard someone ask for a "Pelican" book. Alarmed at the prospect of a close rival so named, he decided to issue Pelicans himself, reserving this name for factual books, as distinct from the original fiction. (An advertisement in *The Bookseller* of February 3, 1937 described Pelicans as "a new series of popular books on science, astronomy, archæology, politics, economics, history, etc.") These were followed by imprints for younger readers, also named for birds beginning with "P" (for "paperback"): Puffins, Ptarmigans, Peregrines, and Peacocks. When Penguin merged with **Longman** in 1970 they renamed Longman Young Books also with a bird's name, but not one beginning with "P" as they were not paperbacks. Thus Kestrels originated. The name "Penguin" was entered in the *Trade Marks Journal* of December 13, 1939 for: "Printed publications, stationery and bookbinding, but not including publications on birds, or shaped sheets of paper for display purposes." "Puffin" followed in the *Journal* of September 10, 1947 for: "Printed publications, stationery, bookbinding materials, pens and pencils, but not including publications on puffins." "Pelican" was entered in the *Journal* of May 22, 1957 for: "Printed books, being literary, dramatic, musical or artistic works, but not including books relating to pelicans."

Penhaligon's *(perfumes and toiletries)*

The London, England, business was founded in 1870 in Jermyn Street by William Henry Penhaligon, a Cornish barber born in Penzance in 1841. At the back of the shop he made perfumes, toilet waters, and pomades, and soon built up an aristocratic clientele, eventually becoming court barber and supplier of perfumes to Queen Victoria. The shop is now in Wellington Street, off the Strand, and in 1987 the business was acquired by **Laura Ashley** on making its debut in the toiletry and perfume markets.

Penney, J.C *see* **J.C. Penney**

Pentel *(fiber-tip pen)*

The type of pen, something between a felt marker and a ballpoint, was launched on the market in 1960 by the Japanese entrepreneur Yokio Horie, who devised the name as a blend of "pen" and "pastel." The name was entered by the Tokyo manufacturers, Dainihon-Bungu Kabushiki Kaisha, in the *Trade Marks Journal* of March 30, 1966.

Pentium *(computer processor)*

The processor of this name was introduced by **Intel** Corporation in 1993, and was so called because its performance standard was five times (Greek *pente*, "five") that of the Intel 486 processor, introduced in 1986.

Pentothal *(anesthetic)*

The proprietary name for thiopentone, a barbiturate drug used as an intravenous anesthetic, is arbitrarily based on the generic name. The name was entered by **Abbott** Laboratories in the US Patent Office *Official Gazette* of February 11, 1936: "For pharmaceutical product having hypnotic, sedative, and anesthetic properties," with a claim of use since November 15, 1935.

Peperami *(pork salami sausage)*

The make of spiced sausage apparently derives its name from "salami" but with the substitution of "pepper" (or a form of it) for the Latin *sal*, "salt," that begins the original word (and that also ultimately forms the base of "sausage"). The name was entered in the *Trade Marks Journal* of January 17, 1979.

Pepperidge Farm *(bread, cookies, and cakes)*

Margaret Fogarty (1897-1967), born a trucker's daughter in New York City, began her career in a New York brokerage house. In 1923 she married one of the partners in the firm, Henry A. Rudkin. In 1929, using the money Rudkin had made on Wall Street, the couple built a mansion on a 125-acre estate in Fairfield County, Connecticut, naming it "Pepperidge Farm" for its black gum trees. In 1937, to help her asthmatic son, Margaret Rudkin began baking bread using stone-ground whole wheat and other "pure" ingredients. Her son improved, and her allergist suggested she bake for other patients. She set up a mail order business to do so, and by 1938 she was selling 4,000 loaves of Pepperidge Farm Bread a week. Her baked goods line expanded, and she opened bakeries in Pennsylvania and Illinois. In 1960 she sold Pepperidge Farm to **Campbell** Soups for $28 million in Campbell's stock and continued to run Pepperidge Farm as an independent subsidiary.

PepsiCo *see* **Lay's**

Pepsi-Cola *(cola drink)*

The first beverage of this name was created by Caleb D. Bradham (1866-1934), a pharmacist in New Bern, North Carolina, who named it in 1898, incorporated the Pepsi-Cola Company in 1902, and entered the name in the US Patent Office *Official Gazette* of June 16, 1903 as that of a "flavoring-syrup for soda-water." He based the name on that of **Coca-Cola**, with "Pepsi-" implying that his concoction could relieve dyspepsia. The real founder of modern Pepsi-Cola, however, was Charles G. Guth (1876-1948), former president of Loft, Inc., a candy manufacturer and soda-fountain chain founded in 1919, who established a new company under the name in 1931, got a chemist to formulate a better drink, and set up bottling operations. The short form of the name, "Pepsi," became current, just as **Coke** did for Coca-Cola, and was entered by Pepsi-Cola Ltd., of Feltham, Middlesex, England, in the *Trade Marks Journal* of August 17, 1960. PepsiCo (*see* **Lay's**) subsequently entered "Diet

Pepsi" in the US Patent Office *Official Gazette* of November 29, 1966.

Pepsodent *(toothpaste)*

The toothpaste, originating in the USA but acquired by **Unilever** in 1944, derives its name from a blend of "peppermint," "soda," and "dentifrice" (or Latin *dens, dentis,* "tooth"). The name was entered in the *Trade Marks Journal* of November 9, 1921.

Perbunan *(rubber)*

The nitrile rubber of this name was originally made in Germany and called "Buna-N." Hence the present name, from "per-" ("through"), German *Buna*, a blend of "*buta-diene*" (itself based on "butane") and "*natrium*," and "N," the chemical symbol for nitrogen. The name was entered by I.G. Farbenindustrie Aktiengesellschaft (*see* **IG Farben**) in the *Trade Marks Journal* of May 4, 1938 for: "Compositions consisting mainly of reaction products obtained by the polymerisation of butadiene hydrocarbons, sold in the form of sheets, blocks, tubes," (etc.). **Bayer** subsequently entered the name in the US Patent Office *Official Gazette* of August 18, 1959: "For rubber and rubber substitute materials."

Perfecto *(cigars)*

The name, Spanish for "perfect," is mainly found for a type of cigar that is thick in the middle and tapered at the ends. It has also come to be applied to other cigars and to cigarettes, and "Perfectos Finos" was entered for an export brand of cigarettes by the British-American Tobacco Co. Ltd. (*see* **BAT Industries**) in the *Trade Marks Journal* of August 5, 1953.

Pergamon *(publishers)*

The UK company Pergamon Press, specializing in the publication of scientific journals, was founded in 1951 by the Czech-born entrepreneur Robert Maxwell (1923-1991), born Abraham Lajbi (later Jan Ludvik) Hoch, when he bought **Butterworth Springer** from Ferdinand Springer, who had a 49 percent stake in the company. The new name was adopted from the colophon of the Greek goddess Athena which Springer was already using and which passed in turn to Pergamon. Pergamon (now Bergama) was one of the most important of all Greek cities in the Hellenistic Age with a tem-

ple to Athena Nicephorus. Pergamon Press is now an imprint of **Elsevier** Science Ltd.

Pergonal *(hormonal preparation)*

The proprietary name of various hormonal preparations, and specifically for one of human menopausal gonadotrophin, derives its name from the prefix "per-", the initial syllable of "gonadotrophin," and a final "-al" as in **Nembutal**, **Veronal**, etc. The name was entered in the US Patent Office *Official Gazette* of May 14, 1963: "For hormonal preparations used in the treatment of human endocrine conditions," with a note of first use on or before January 1, 1963.

Perkins, Dorothy *see* **Dorothy Perkins**

Perlon *(nylon fabric)*

The type of fabric known as nylon 6, produced by the polymerization of caprolactam, has a name first used in Germany and entered in the US Patent Office *Official Gazette* of January 28, 1958, and the *Trade Marks Journal* of March 12, 1958. The latter part of the name is presumably based on "nylon." The first part suggests German *Perl*, "pearl," but may be arbitrary.

Perminvar *(alloy)*

The name is used of a series of alloys containing nickel, iron, and cobalt that have an approximately constant permeability over a range of field strengths. The name itself, combining "permeability" and "invariable," was entered by the Western Electric Company, New York, in the US Patent Office *Official Gazette* of June 12, 1928: "For ferromagnetic alloys comprising nickel, iron, and cobalt," with a claim of use since August 23, 1927. *Cp.* **Invar**.

Permutit *(water-softening systems)*

The name suggests "permutation," but actually derives from Latin *permutare*, "to exchange," and refers to the process of ion exchange that is used in commercial water softeners to exchange the dissolved ions responsible for the water's hardness with others that do not have this effect. The name was first entered by the German firm J.D. Riedel Aktiengesellschaft of Berlin in the *Trade Marks Journal* of January 12, 1910, and subsequently by The Permutit Company of New York in the US Patent Office *Official Gazette* of November 4, 1913.

Pernod *(aperitif)*

The origins of the aperitif began with a French doctor, Pierre Ordinaire, who fled from France at the time of the Revolution to settle in Switzerland. There he continued to practice medicine, which in those days involved the preparation of elixirs from herbs and other ingredients. He devised an infusion of some 15 herbs including aniseed, camomile, veronica, and other plants, among them wormwood. Dr. Ordinaire found that the effects of the infusion were heightened when it was steeped in alcohol. The resulting potion was called *absinthe,* from the Latin name for wormwood (*Artemisia absinthium*). Before he died, Ordinaire passed his herbal recipe on to his housekeeper, Madame Henriot, who set up a small shop to sell the absinthe. One of her customers was a French major, Daniel-Henri Dubied-Duval (1758-1841). He set great store by the drink, claiming that absinthe acted as an aphrodisiac, and in turn purchased the recipe in 1797. With it, he and his son-in-law, Henri-Louis Pernod (1776-1851), began to manufacture the drink in commercial quantities, opening a factory in Couvet, western Switzerland, and one across the border in France in 1805. It was then that the product became known as "Pernod," to distinguish it from rival herbal concoctions. The firm of Pernod Fils was entered in the *Trade Marks Journal* of October 11, 1876 by "Louis Pernod, on behalf of self and partner, Fritz Pernod, trading as Pernod, Fils, Pontarlier, Doubs, France; manufacturers of absinthe." In 1975 the company merged with **Ricard** to become Pernod Ricard, who the following year in turn took over **Dubonnet Cinzano** (who had similarly merged) and **Cusenier**.

Peroni *(beer)*

Italy's former leading brewing company, famous for its **Nastro Azzurro** lager, was founded in 1846 in Vigevano, near Milan, by Francesco Peroni (1818-1894). It soon concentrated its activities in Rome, but then expanded, taking over breweries throughout the region.

Perrier *(mineral water)*

Louis Eugène Perrier (1835-1912) was born at Domessargues, near Nîmes, France, the son of a local landowner. He left school with good grades in science subjects, and went to Mont-pellier to study medicine with the aim of becoming a doctor. He qualified in 1862, specializing in arthritic diseases, and soon after opened his practice in a village near Domessargues. In 1875 he was appointed manager of a thermal establishment near Uzès, and keen to establish the curative powers of natural spring water, especially in arthritic cases, acquired the lease of the Bouillens ("bubbling") mineral springs at Vergèze, near Nîmes, in 1894. He sought sponsorship for his project, and found it in Sir A.W. St. John Harmsworth, brother of Viscounts Northcliffe and Rothermere, the British newspaper magnates. Harmsworth was impressed by the natural bubbles that gushed from the spring, and after a single tasting agreed to support Dr. Perrier's venture, naming the spring after him. Harmsworth then began to bottle the water, and by 1905 Dr. Perrier had been granted a Royal Warrant for his "champagne of mineral waters," as Harmsworth called it. The name was entered by Harmsworth "trading as Perrier" in the *Trade Marks Journal* of October 30, 1907 for: "Natural mineral water obtained from the spring known as 'Source Perrier' situated at Vergeze in France."

Perrier-Jouët *(champagne)*

The firm was established in Épernay, France, in 1811 by Pierre Nicolas Marie Perrier, and he added his wife's maiden name to his own to create the brand. Perrier was the uncle of Joseph Perrier, the founder of the champagne house named for him in Châlons-sur-Marne (now Châlons-en-Champagne) in 1825. Perrier-Jouët passed to the **Mumm** Group in 1959.

Persil *(detergent)*

The name is French for "parsley." A sprig of parsley was the trademark of a Frenchman named Ronchetti who discovered how to add bleach to soap in 1907. At the same time the name suggests a blend of "perborate" and "silicate," two essential constituents of the discovery. Persil was the first household detergent, manufactured in Germany by Henkel & Co. of Düsseldorf in 1907 and in England by Joseph Crosfield of Warrington, Cheshire, in 1909. Crosfield dubbed his product "the amazing oxygen washer," as it liberated free oxygen in use. Persil is now marketed by **Unilever**.

Persimmon *(houses)*

Britain's biggest firm of housebuilders was founded in 1972 by Duncan Davidson (b.1941), the boss of a building business who had previously worked for **Wimpey**. He and his wife were keen racegoers, and the name they selected for their enterprise was that of the racehorse Persimmon, winner of the 1896 Derby and of the St. Leger, Ascot Gold Cup, and Eclipse Stakes in 1897. His own name, suggesting the persimmon fruit, was a blend of the names of his sire, St. Simon, another famous racer, and dam, Perdita. In 2001 Persimmon acquired their great rivals, **Beazer**.

Perspex *(transparent plastic)*

The name of the tough transparent thermoplastic was entered by the manufacturers, **ICI**, in the *Trade Marks Journal* of January 9, 1935 and the US Patent Office *Official Gazette* of November 13, 1951, the latter with a claim of use since 1934. The origin of the name lies in Latin *perspicere*, "to look through," or more exactly in this verb's perfect tense, *perspexi*, "I have looked through." In the USA Perspex is sold under the names **Plexiglas** and **Lucite**.

Peter Dominic *(wine and liquor stores)*

The formerly familiar British High Street name is actually a pseudonym, that of the firm's founder, Paul Dauthieu. He was born in Perth, Scotland, of French parents, and on leaving school began his career in the wine trade at the Caledonian Hotel, Edinburgh, subsequently moving south to become a wine waiter at Claridge's Hotel, London. In 1939 he opened his first wine shop in Horsham, Sussex, and feeling that his name could cause pronunciation problems, decided to trade under the more manageable name of Peter Dominic, which also happens to suggest monastic vintages. (The resemblance of the name to that of Pedro **Domecq** is curious but possibly coincidental.) In 1940 Dauthieu joined the Royal Air Force for the duration of World War II, and on his return to "Civvy Street" found that his wife, Blanche, had run the Horsham business so successfully that she had increased the number of staff to 11. Other branches followed, and by the time Dauthieu sold his company to International Distillers and Vintners (IDV) in 1963, he had 21 Peter Dominic wine shops. Dauthieu (Dominic) died of cancer in 1967, when he was about to retire.

Peter England *(shirts)*

The original name of the British company was Hogg & Mitchell, a partnership founded in 1889, with Mr. Hogg responsible for the production of shirts and collars in Northern Ireland, and Mr. Mitchell overseeing the selling operation in England. One of the firm's most popular brands was a shirt named "Old England," a double-fronted tunic shirt with two semistiff matching collars. The company of Hogg & Mitchell was formally registered in 1947, but in the early 1960s changed its name to Peter England. This was regarded as being more "modern" for the later collar-attached shirts than the former "Old England" brand. "Peter" was the nickname that Hogg & Mitchell had affectionately used for the small lion that was their patriotic trade mark, so they now incorporated this as well.

Peter Jones *(department store)*

The London, England, store bears the name of Peter Rees Jones (1843-1905), the Welsh son of a Monmouthshire hat manufacturer. He began his working life apprenticed to a Carmarthen draper, but left his home town of Newcastle Emlyn in 1864 to seek his fortune in London. He obtained a position with a draper in Newington, but did not stay long, and after a further period working for another draper in Leicester Square set up his own first shop in Hackney in 1868. After further changes of location, Jones eventually acquired premises in King's Road, Chelsea, in 1877. His business prospered and expanded, so that by the time of his death his firm occupied most of the block. A year later his business was bought by **John Lewis**, who retained his name for the store.

Peter Owen *(publishers)*

The British publisher Peter Owen, described as "of the old and idiosyncratic school," began his literary odyssey in 1951, when at the age of 21, having failed to land a job in journalism, started his business in a one-room London apartment equipped with a just a typewriter and £850 capital. He hired the budding novelist Muriel Spark, then aged 39, as his first editor, and landed his first coup on publishing Herman Hesse's *Siddhartha*, regarded by Henry Miller as a masterpiece. It became a cult book, and Owen was wooed by publishers eager to bid for the paperback rights. Eventually he acquiesced, obtaining from **Pan** the biggest royalty deal ever secured for a paperback. His distinguished list of authors subsequently expanded to include Boris Pasternak, Octavio Paz, Lawrence Durrell, Peter Vansittart, and Yukio Mishima, among others.

Peter Robinson *(department store)*

The former London, England, store, more recently a Top Man shop, took its name from Peter Robinson, a Yorkshire haberdasher's son, who served his apprenticeship in a small draper's shop in Paddington before setting up on his own in 1833 at 103 Oxford Street, not far from the store's subsequent site on the corner of Oxford Street and Regent Street. Robinson also opened a "Court and General Mourning House" in Regent Street, which because of its funeral draperies became known as "Black Peter Robinson's." **John Lewis** was employed at Robinson's store before establishing his own business, also in Oxford Street, in 1864.

Peter Stuyvesant *(cigarettes)*

The brand belongs to **American Brands**, which owns **Gallahers** in Britain, and is that of a familiar figure in American colonial history, Peter Stuyvesant (?1610-1672), the Dutch governor who tried to resist the attempts of the English to seize New York in 1664. After his defeat, he spent the rest of his life on his farm, "the Bouwerie," near New York (then Nieuw Amsterdam), and the farm name in turn gave that of the modern Bowery, New York City's district notorious for its vagrants. Stuyvesant Town is now a district of Manhattan, and Stuyvesant Square one of its parks. The headquarters of American Brands is in nearby Park Avenue, while the Bowery is to the south, in lower Manhattan. Peter Stuyvesant cigarettes are marketed in the UK by **Rothman's** International.

Peter's *(chocolate)*

The name is that of Daniel Peter (1836-1919), a butcher's son working for a woman who owned a grocer's shop in Vevey, Switzerland, where she made candles as a sideline. Madame Clément saw that this activity interested the boy, and let him take over the candlemaking on his own account. But Peter was not just interested in candles. He also had his eye on Fanny Cailler, daughter of François-Louis **Cailler**, who had opened his chocolate factory near Vevey in 1819. Fanny thus paved the way for Peter to move from candlemaking to chocolate manufacture, and in 1875, using the condensed milk made by **Nestlé**, he was the first to make milk chocolate.

Peters *(music publishers)*

The German firm had its origin in the publishing house, printing works, and music shop opened in Leipzig in 1800 by the composer Franz Hoffmeister (1754-1812). The business was bought in 1914 by C.F. Peters (1779-1827) and given his name. The "Edition Peters" publications are distinctive with their light green covers for works out of copyright and pink covers for original publications.

Petri *(wines)*

Angelo Petri (1883-1961) and Louis Petri (1912-1980) were respectively born in Marseilles, France, and San Francisco, California. Angelo was the son of an Italian immigrant to France who came to the United States in 1886, where he operated a hotel in San Francisco while running a small winery on the side. Angelo himself came to the USA in 1895, attended elementary school in San Francisco, and worked for his uncle, Amadeo Petri, making and selling cigars at the Petri-Italian-American Cigar Company. He became president of the firm in 1912 and seemed set to spend his life there, but in 1933, on the repeal of Prohibition, turning his attention to wine-making, his aim being to raise his father's small, local winery into a major wine-marketing corporation. Louis, meanwhile, attended local schools in San Francisco and later enrolled in the medical school at St. Louis University. He left in 1934, however, and took a job in the family winery in San Francisco. He persuaded his father to stop selling wine by the barrel and instead to bottle it under the Petri Wine label. In 1937 Louis was made general manager of Petri Wines and three years later became vice president. Under the guidance of the brothers, the family winery came to produce one of the best-known brands of wine in the country. In 1944 Petri Wines changed its corporate name to United Vintners and went on to acquire several other wine companies.

Petrobrás *(oil and gas)*

The Brazilian monopoly was formed in 1953

to prospect and extract crude oil and natural gas, refine domestic and imported petroleum, and transport oil and gas and their derivatives. Its name is a shortening of its formal title, Petróleo Brasileiro ("Brazilian Petroleum").

Petrofina *(petroleum)*

The Belgian petroleum company was organized in 1920 as the Compagnie Financière Belge des Pétroles ("Belgian Petroleum Finance Company"), its initial interest being in the development of Romanian oil fields and Belgian interests in Africa. It adopted its present name, based on the original, in 1957. The second part of the name thus represents "finance," not "fine." In 1998 Petrofina was taken over by **Total**.

Petrus *(beer)*

The Belgian beer, made at the De Brabandere brewery at Bavikhove, West Flanders, has a name that simply means "Peter," meaning St. Peter. At one time the name aroused the curiosity of the French Château Pétrus, producers of the famous Bordeaux wine, but after discussion they agreed that any confusion of identity was unlikely.

Petter *(engines)*

The name is that of the British engineer Sir Ernest Willoughby Petter (1873-1954), who together with his brother, P.W. Petter, designed and built one of the first internal combustion-engined automobiles made in the UK. His company, based in Yeovil, Somerset, produced mainly oil engines but also manufactured electric lighting plants and related equipment.

Peugeot *(automobiles)*

The name behind the car is that of Armand Peugeot (1849-1915), born at Valentigney, near Belfort, France, into a family involved in the manufacture of hardware and farm equipment. The first Peugeot bicycles were produced by about 1885, and four years later came the first Peugeot steam car. In 1890 Armand Peugeot built his first gasoline-driven car, using a **Daimler** engine. The cars were soon entering races, and in 1895 it was a Peugeot that was the first car to race on **Michelin** pneumatic tires. After such a good start, Peugeot was soon making its own engines. The lion that is the Peugeot logo derives from the rival brand built by Robert Peugeot from 1906. This family rift was

soon healed, however. Peugeot merged with **Citroën** in 1976, and in 1979 acquired the European car- and truck-making units and related finance operations of **Chrysler,** changing the names of these subsidiaries to **Talbot**.

Pfister *(chemicals)*

Alfred Pfister (1880-1964) was born in Zurich, Switzerland. After attending public schools in that city, he entered the Chemical Institute of the University of Basel. Research at the institute was linked to the local industry, which specialized in the manufacture of dyestuffs and pharmaceuticals. After graduating, Pfister worked as a chemist for **Hoffman-LaRoche** in Basel, but in 1906, soon after marrying, immigrated to the United States. By 1908 he had secured employment as a chemist for Nolde and Horst, Inc., a hosiery dyeing business in Reading, Pennsylvania. Two years later, he was head-hunted by another Reading company, Spring Valley Dye Works, where he served until 1914, when he relocated to Passaic, New Jersey, to accept a position as research chemist and general manager for Jacques Wolf and Company. He guided the company to produce many textile chemicals previously available only from European sources, and after gaining further experience decided in 1932 to set up his own concern, Pfister Chemical Company, in Ridgefield, New Jersey, to manufacture dye intermediates. The company went on to produce other organic intermediates, including specialty chemicals used to make animal products, and in 1936 it was incorporated as Pfister Chemical Works. Pfister served as president until his death, by which time the firm produced more than 80 chemicals for commercial sale as well as various custom compounds sold to other chemical manufacturers.

Pfizer *(drugs)*

The American company, noted for antibiotics and eye drops, takes its name from one of its two cofounders, Charles Pfizer and Charles Erhart, who set up in their Brooklyn laboratory in 1849 as makers of iodine preparations, boric and tartaric acids, and the citric acid that Pfizer still makes and sells to soft drink companies.

PG Tips *(tea)*

The initials represent an earlier name, "Pre-Gestee," in turn based on the tea's original name, "Digestive Tea," introduced in the 1940s by what is now **Brooke Bond Oxo** as a counter to **Typhoo**, who in their advertising claimed that Typhoo aided digestion. In World War II the British Ministry of Food asked both companies to drop the reference to a medicinal benefit and as a result Brooke Bond came up with "Pre-Gestee," implying that the tea could be drunk before food was digested. At the same time the name contained the germ of the original "Digestive Tea." "Pre-Gestee" is an awkward name, however, and soon grocers and van salesmen were abbreviating it to "P.G." The company adopted this as the new official name of the tea, adding "Tips" to refer to the tips of the tea leaves that produced the blend's distinctive flavor. (Tea containing a large proportion of teabuds in this way is known by tea blenders as "tippy.") The fact that "tip" suggests the "peak" or best of something gave the name added prestige.

Phenergan *(anti-motion sickness drug)*

The proprietary name for promethazine, a derivative of phenothiazine used to treat the symptoms of allergies and motion sickness, appears to derive from the "phen-" of "phenothiazine" and (possibly) Greek *ergon*, "work." It was entered by **May & Baker** in the *Trade Marks Journal* of June 8, 1949 for: "Pharmaceutical preparations consisting of or containing benzine or its derivatives for human use and veterinary use."

Phensic *(analgesic)*

The proprietary preparation, containing aspirin and caffeine, was originally advertised as a treatment for influenza. It was manufactured by the **Veno** Drug Company, with a name based on the "phen-" element (Greek *phaino-*, literally "showing") found in the names of drugs such as phenobarbital. The name was entered in the *Trade Marks Journal* of May 24, 1933. *Cp.* **Nurofen**.

Philadelphia *(cream cheese)*

The brand-name cheese was originally made by the Phenix Cheese Company, New York, and following that firm's merger with **Kraft** in 1928 became one of the combined company's best-selling products. It was never made in Philadelphia, however, but was so named because that city enjoyed a reputation throughout the East for its fine food.

Philco *(radios, televisions, and electronics)*

The American firm was founded in 1892 as the Philadelphia Company to produce batteries and power supplies. It gradually extended its product range to include radios, televisions, and domestic appliances and in 1961 was acquired by **Ford**.

Phileas Fogg *(packaged snacks)*

The name is that of the eccentric fictional English traveler who goes *Around the World in 80 Days* in Jules Verne's novel of that title (1872), the idea being that snacks are essentially food for travelers. The snacks are marketed by the British company Derwent Valley Foods, founded in 1982, who use the global exploits of Phileas Fogg as part of their distinctive packaging.

Philip & Tacey *(school stationery)*

The founder of the British company was John Tacey, a schoolmaster from High Wycombe, Buckinghamshire, who in the 1820s was appointed headmaster of the British School (a nondenominational Christian-based school) in Cowper Street, London. His school became a meeting place for other teachers, who frequently asked Tacey for an item of school stationery or for school supplies that they themselves lacked, such as slates, pens, or the odd exercise book. Tacey was happy to oblige, but stocking the items and recording transactions proved a tedious task, and it occurred to him that it might be more sensible to run a school shop, rather than an actual school. In 1829, accordingly, he set up a "school supply shop" in the City Road, London, and became a school stationer. His business gained momentum, and soon a small factory was built. In 1902 his enterprise was linked with that of the publishers George Philip & Son, of Fleet Street, and thus Philip & Tacey emerged. After World War I, however, George Philip withdrew from the partnership, as their publishing business made full-time demands on them. But their name remains today as a reminder of their earlier collaboration.

Philip Morris *(cigarettes)*

The American company traces its origins to 1847, when in Oxford, England, one Philip Morris opened a cigar shop, with university students among his chief clientele. The sign over his shop read: "Philip Morris, Esquire, Tobacconist and Importer of Fine Seegars." In 1854 good business enabled him to open a shop in London's New Bond Street, making his own brand of cigarettes on the premises. After Morris' death in 1873, however, the main developments of the business he had founded were continued across the Atlantic, where an agency opened in New York for the importation and sale of Philip Morris cigarettes. Within a few years, Philip Morris was the fourth leading brand of cigarettes in the United States. It was not until 1929, however, that the American offshoot of the original firm began manufacturing its own cigarettes. In 1954 Philip Morris acquired the **Benson & Hedges** cigarette business after launching the **Marlboro** brand.

Philips (electronics)

The name is that of a Dutch mechanical engineer, Gerard Philips (1858-1942), who in 1891 after studying engineering at Delft and chemistry at Leiden started up a small factory in Eindhoven to manufacture electric light bulbs. Three years later he was joined in his enterprise by his brother, Anton Frederik Philips (d.1951), and although Gerard Philips retired from the business in 1921, he had by then established the company, Philips Gloeilampenfabriken, which would soon become the worldwide concern that it is today.

Philishave (electric shavers)

The rotary action shaver so called was pioneered by **Philips** in 1939. Hence its name, which also (perhaps intentionally) suggests Greek "phil-" meaning "liking," "loving."

Phillips' ("Milk of Magnesia")

In 1849, Charles Phillips (c.1820-1882), the English owner of a drugstore in Elizabeth, New Jersey, tired of retailing and decided to become a manufacturer. He moved to Glenbrook, Connecticut, where he set up a small laboratory to make beeswax. The business prospered for a while, but then languished, and Phillips looked for a replacement. He found it in 1873, when he patented a method of converting powdered magnesium hydroxide into a liquid form to serve as an antacid. Calling his creation "Phillips' Milk of Magnesia," he continued to develop a market for the product until his death. Three

years later, his laboratory was incorporated as the Charles G. Phillips Chemical Co. under the management of his four sons. The name "Milk of Magnesia" was entered in the *Trade Marks Journal* of March 3, 1880. ("Milk" simply refers to the white-colored suspension.) In 1923 the patent remedy was acquired by Sterling Products.

Phillips (screw and screwdriver)

The screw with the cross-shaped slot for turning, and the corresponding screwdriver, derive their name from their inventor, Henry F. Phillips (d.1958) of Portland, Oregon. The screws were originally manufactured in the 1930s by the American Screw Company, of Providence, Rhode Island, and the name was entered in the US Patent Office *Official Gazette* of October 18, 1938, with a claim of use since December 15, 1934. In the UK, the name was entered in the *Trade Marks Journal* of February 20, 1952 by **Guest, Keen & Nettlefolds**. A subsequent entry "for screws and allied fasteners" was made by the Phillips Screw Company, of Natick, Massachusetts, in the *Gazette* of October 18, 1966, with a note of first use in 1933. *See also* **Stanley** (tools).

Phillips (tennis balls and footballs)

Alfred William Phillips appears to have started his British business in Nuneaton, Warwickshire, in about 1870. He was one of the first makers of tennis balls to cover the cores with cloth. A circular letter sent out by Phillips to his customers in 1899 seems to indicate that he had shortly before this date left the original firm of A.W. Phillips & Co. to set up on his own as a "Lawn Tennis Ball and Football Manufacturer." The company later traded as Phillips-Tuftex Ltd.

Phillips Petroleum (oil)

Phillips is smaller than such giants as **Exxon** and **Texaco**, but it is no pygmy, despite still having its headquarters in the small Oklahoma town of Bartlesville where the firm began in 1917. The company takes its name from Frank Phillips (1873-1950), born in Scotia, Nebraska, the son of a farmer, county assessor, and judge. His family moved to Creston, Iowa, in 1874, where he attended the local school. He dropped out at age 14, however, and for the next ten years worked in and around Creston as a farmer, ranch hand, and barber. He built up a small chain of barbershops but sold them on marrying in 1897 to become a traveling bond salesman. The money that he made he began investing in oil leases in Oklahoma. In 1903 he set up the Anchor Oil and Gas Company in Bartlesville and began drilling, bringing in his two brothers, L.E. and Waite Phillips, to help with the business. On June 13, 1917 Frank and L.E. incorporated Phillips Petroleum Company to replace Anchor, and in the next few years realized a huge expansion. They opened their first gas station in Wichita, Kansas, in 1927, and the **Phillips 66** filling station soon became a familiar trademark to American consumers.

Phillips 66 *(gasoline)*

There are many stories to explain the name (or rather number) behind the famous brand of gasoline by **Phillips Petroleum**. Six of those most frequently told, all false, are as follows:

(1) Frank and L.E. Phillips had only 66 dollars left between them when they hit their first oil well. They immediately decided that if ever they marketed gasoline they would call it "66."

(2) Frank Phillips was 66 years old when he founded the company. (He was actually 44.)

(3) The first gasoline of the name was 66 octane. (Octane ratings were adopted later.)

(4) When Phillips started service station operations in Wisconsin, a state law required that the gravity of the gasoline be posted on the pumps. Most gasolines then had gravities in the low 60s, but Phillips offered a superior 66 gravity. (Phillips did not actually start marketing in Wisconsin until 1929.The "66" trademark was created in 1927.)

(5) A Phillips official won the company's first refinery in a dice game when he rolled double sixes. (The company's first refinery was actually purchased in 1927.)

(6) When the first Phillips station's opening day came to a close, the dealer noted he had sold 66 gallons of gasoline, so regarded 66 as his lucky number. (The first station actually sold 12,000 gallons of gasoline on opening day.)

The true origin, as filed in the company's records, is as follows. When Phillips was about to market its new gasoline, a special executive committee session was called for the sole purpose of choosing a name. On the very eve of the meeting, a Phillips official was returning to headquarters in a company car being used to road-test the new gasoline. "This car goes like 60 with our new gas," he commented to the driver, who glanced at the speedometer and said, "Sixty nothing! We're doing 66!" At the conference next day, someone asked where this incident had occurred. "Near Tulsa—on Highway 66," was the reply. That decided it. A unanimous vote for "Phillips 66" was cast, and on November 19, 1927, the name was introduced to the public at the company's first service station in Wichita, Kansas.

Phonevision *(television system)*

The name of the pay-as-you-view television system derives from "phone" (i.e. telephone) and "vision." The system was introduced in the USA in the early 1950s, and enabled the owner of a television to phone a special number in order to view a movie that would otherwise remain "scrambled" on the screen. The name was entered by the Zenith Radio Corporation in the US Patent Office *Official Gazette* of September 8, 1953: "For Radio and Television Transmitting and Receiving Operations and Parts Thereof," with a claim of use since June 13, 1947.

Phonofilm *(motion picture system)*

The sound motion picture system was the invention of the US radio engineer Lee de Forest (1873-1961), who entered the name, from Greek-based "phono-" ("sound") and "film," in the US Patent Office *Official Gazette* of November 8, 1921, with a claim of use since January 1, 1921. The system was widely demonstrated in the 1920s but attracted little studio support, mainly because of the poor sound quality. The name is no longer proprietary.

Phonotas *(telephone cleaning service)*

By the time that Basil Becker (1928-2001) became managing director in 1962 of the company founded by his father, George Becker, in 1911, Phonotas operators were part of Britain's office life, with the "women in brown" smiling from advertisements on the sides of buses and elsewhere as they extolled the virtues of "clean speaking." The original telephone cleaning service grew into a sophisticated telecommunications valeting and sanitizing provision and in 1988 was sold to **Initial**. Its name perhaps blends English "phone" (plus "-o-") with Latin *sanitas*, "health" (*cp.* **Sanitas**).

Phosferine *("health tonic")*

The proprietary preparation was originally marketed by the British firm of Ashton & Parsons as a homeopathic product containing phosphorus. Hence the name, entered in the *Trade Marks Journal* of September 5, 1900. The business was acquired by **Beecham** in 1935.

Phosfon *(plant growth retardant)*

The organophosphorus compound, used to retard the growth of chrysanthemums and other plants, takes its name from its basic chemical constituent. The name was entered by the Virginia-Carolina Chemical Corporation of Richmond, Virginia, in the US Patent Office *Official Gazette* of August 22, 1961, with a note of first use on February 25, 1960. A later registration by **Mobil** was made in the *Trade Marks Journal* of December 23, 1969, for: "Chemical substances ... for use in agriculture and horticulture, being or containing compounds of phosphorus."

Phostrogen *(plant food)*

The garden fertilizer was created in 1960 by Bobby Manners, founder of the British firm of the same name, originally based in Barmouth, North Wales. The name represents the product's two main chemical ingredients, *phospho*rus and ni*trogen*, and was entered in the *Trade Marks Journal* of July 17, 1991. In 1997 the company was sold to **Monsanto**.

Photomaton *(automatic camera)*

The type of automatic camera, originating in the USA in the 1920s as the invention of Anatol Josephs, derives its name from a blend of "photo-" and "automaton." The name was entered by the machine's British manufacturers, Cyril Astor Photomaton (London) Ltd., of Rhyl, North Wales, in the *Trade Marks Journal* of May 26, 1963.

Photoradiogram *(radio-transmitted picture)*

The former proprietary name for a picture, diagram, or the like transmitted by radio was entered by the Radio Corporation of America (*see* **RCA**) in the US Patent Office *Official Gazette* of May 26, 1925 for: "Pictures, drawings, and facsimiles transmitted by radio," with a claim of use since November 30, 1924. The name itself combined "photo" and "radiogram" (i.e. radiotelegram).

Photostat *(photocopy)*

The name, originally that of a kind of pho-tocopying machine, was entered by the Commercial Camera Company of Providence, Rhode Island, in the *Trade Marks Journal* of May 24, 1911 for: "Photographic cameras for making photographic copies of the pages of books, drawings, applications for life insurance and the like." It later came to be used for the photocopy itself. The name combines "photo-" and "-stat" as in "static," denoting something made stationary.

Photronic *(photovoltaic cell)*

The type of photovoltaic cell has a name blending "photo" and "electronic" that was entered by the Weston Electrical Instrument Corporation, of Newark, New Jersey, in the US Patent Office *Official Gazette* of March 15, 1932, with a claim of use since September 25, 1931.

Phul-Nana *(perfume)*

The suffocatingly heavy but highly popular perfume was produced in the late 19th century by the British firm of J. Grossmith & Son of Ivy Lane, Newgate Street, London, who entered the name in the *Trade Marks Journal* of November 19, 1890 for: "Perfumed soap; perfumery; essential oils for toilet purposes; cosmetics; hair lotions; preparations for washing the hair; dentifrices." The supposedly exotic name derived from Hindi *phul*, "flower," and *nana*, "several."

Phurnacite *(fuel)*

The type of smokeless fuel, made by carbonizing briquettes at relatively low temperatures, appears to derive its name as a blend of (respelled) "furnace" and "anthracite." It was entered by the British firm Powell Duffryn Associated Collieries Ltd. in the *Trade Marks Journal* of February 10, 1937.

Phyllosan *("health tonic")*

The British homeopathic preparation, originally manufactured by The Natural Chemicals Co., derived its name from a blend of Greek *phyllo-*, "leaf," and Latin *sanitas*, "health." The firm was acquired by **Beecham** in 1936.

Physeptone *(narcotic)*

The proprietary name for the drug methadone hydrochloride, first used in the USA for the gradual withdrawal of heroin addicts, is of uncertain origin. It was entered by the **Well-**

come Foundation, London, England, in the *Trade Marks Journal* of September 15, 1948.

Piaggio *(aircraft and motorscooters)*

The noted Italian vehicle manufacturer was founded at Sestri Ponente near Genoa in 1884 by Rinaldo Piaggio (1864-1938), a timber merchant. It originally specialized in ship furnishings, a line that was extended in around 1900 to the furbishment of rail coaches. In 1915 the firm entered the aviation business, setting up workshops at Finale Ligure, northwest Italy, and in 1924 acquired CMN (Costruzione Meccaniche Nazionale, "National Engineering Works") of Pontedera, near Pisa, but sold it off in World War II. In the 1980s Piaggio designed a new type of executive aircraft, the P180 "Avanti," first produced commercially in the early 1990s. Meanwhile Piaggio Veicoli Europei ("Piaggio European Vehicles") had been set up as a separate business at Pontedera in 1945 by Piaggio's son, Enrico. This was the firm that launched the famous **Vespa** motorscooter in 1946. In 1956 PVE absorbed the motorcycle manufacturer **Gilera** and the bicycle maker Bianchi and from 1987 itself gradually began to come under the control of **Fiat**.

Pianola *(automatic piano)*

The mechanical piano was developed in 1897 by the American inventor Edwin S. Votey and was manufactured by the **Aeolian** Co. Originally it was not an actual piano but a pneumatic machine that was pushed up in front of an ordinary piano and that played on its keys with felt-covered wooden fingers. By 1901 it was incorporated in the piano itself, and such pianos were made by Aeolian up to 1951. The name, apparently created as a diminutive of "piano," was entered by Aeolian in the US Patent Office *Official Gazette* of September 26, 1962, but was already in use as a trademark at the turn of the 20th century. It in turn inspired the names **Moviola** and **Victrola** and gave words such as "payola" and "pluggola."

Pickfords *(furniture and freight removal)*

The British company traces its origins to 1646, when Thomas Pickford, a yeoman farmer, had his lands sequestered for cooperating with the Cavaliers, the supporters of Charles I in the Civil War. By the end of the 17th century the Pickford family were engaged in mending roads. They owned a quarry, moving the stone with a train of packhorses. But instead of returning to the quarry empty, the horses carried goods for others, making Pickfords a carrier. When James Pickford, a London-to-Manchester wagoner, died intestate in London in 1768, his widow, Martha, and two sons, Thomas and Matthew, took over the business. In 1777 William **Bass** sold his own moving business to Matthew Pickford in order to concentrate on brewing beer, and this was what effectively put Pickfords on the map. In 1800 Thomas and Matthew Pickford had 50 wagons, 400 horses, and 28 canal barges, and by 1809 the firm was in the hands of Thomas and Matthew and their sons James and Matthew. Business now began a steady decline, however, and by 1816 the company was on the verge of bankruptcy. The Pickfords saved their firm by severing their connections and selling out to Joseph Baxendale, Charles Inman, and Zachary Langton, who together with Hugh Hornby Burley took over ownership in 1817. After rigorous pruning of unprofitable operations, the company's fortunes began to rise again. Baxendale's grandson, Harry, entered Pickfords in 1879 as the second member of the third generation of the Baxendale family to join the firm. By now, Pickfords' principal business was as cartage and delivery agents to several railroad companies, including the London & North Western Railway. The decision in 1901 to break with the latter triggered a slump in Pickfords' fortunes and a major quarrel among the Baxendales. In 1912, Pickfords was forced into an alliance with its major competitor, Carter Paterson, and in 1920 the company passed to the Hay's Wharf Cartage Co. In 1933 both Pickfords and Carter Paterson were purchased by the four main railroad companies. The two rivals then again teamed up in 1946 to form the Joint Parcels Service. Their combined complement was now 1,150 motor vehicles, 300 horse vans, and a staff of 4,500. In 1947, Pickfords was nationalized to form part of British Road Services, but in 1953 it was reorganized as BRS (Pickford) Ltd. In 1969, Pickfords became part of the National Freight Corporation, owned by the Treasury. An employee buyout was effected in 1982, and in 1999 Pickfords became part of Allied World Wide, the largest moving company in the world.

Picon (aperitif)

The aperitif of bitters, made from a wine and brandy base with added quinine, orange peel, and herbs, was originally known as "Amer Picon," from French *amer*, "bitter," and the name of Picon et Cie., the manufacturers, who entered it in the *Bulletin Officiel des Marques de Fabrique* of January 25, 1917.

Picturephone (videophone)

The type of videophone has a name of obvious origin entered by **AT&T** in the US Patent Office *Official Gazette* of September 27, 1966 for: "See-while-you-talk, sometimes known as visual telephone, services," with a note of first use on April 20, 1964.

Pierce-Arrow (automobiles)

One of America's last great independent automobile manufacturers owes its name to George N. Pierce, who produced his first car in 1901. He launched a Pierce Great Arrow model in 1904, then changed the marque name to Pierce-Arrow in 1909. The pun on his name was visually represented in the car's sculpted mascot, a naked kneeling bowman drawing his bow. By 1938 Pierce was ailing and ready to quit business for a quiet life, so sold his company to **Studebaker**.

Pifco (electrical products)

The name is an acronym of the original company, founded in 1900 by Joseph Webber in Manchester, England, as the Provincial Incandescent Fittings Co. Ltd. The firm first made gas mantles before progressing to electric batteries and pocket torches (flashlights). The abbreviated name was officially adopted by the company in 1949.

Pig Stands (fast-food chain)

The chain had its beginnings in Dallas, Texas, in 1921, when J.G. Kirby, a candy wholesaler, opened a pork barbecue eatery with attendant carhops on the Dallas-Fort Worth Highway. He called it the Pig Stand, and by 1934 there were over 100 Pig Stands claiming to sell "America's Motor Lunch" throughout the Midwest and on both the Pacific and Atlantic coasts. The Pig Stands Company is thus a rival to **A&W** as the oldest roadside chain.

Piggly Wiggly (self-service stores)

The chain of American stores was the brainchild of Clarence Saunders (1881-1953), born in Amherst County, Virginia, the son of a tobacco farmer. He grew up in Clarksville, Tennessee, where he attended school for four years before going to work aged 14 as a clerk at a grocery store. Following further work in various stores, he organized a retail food chain called United Stores in Memphis, Tennessee, while still in his 20s, but sold it a few years later. In 1916, Saunders began to make a name for himself on the national scene when he developed what is believed to be the first modern supermarket. In September of that year the first store, named King Piggly Wiggly, opened its doors in Memphis. When asked by a business associate in Memphis why he had chosen that name, Saunders replied, "So people would ask me what you just did" (*New Yorker*, June 6, 1959). (But surely his Mom had told him the nursery tale how a certain "piggly wiggly went to market"?) By the end of 1919 nine Piggly Wiggly stores were in operation, and by the fall of 1922 the chain consisted of over 1,200 stores in 29 states. Ever the pioneer, Saunders later devised the **Keedoozle**.

Pilkington (glass)

The full name of the British company is Pilkington Brothers plc. The firm's origins date from 1826, when the St. Helens Crown Glass Company was founded by six partners, all living in St. Helens, Lancashire. One of these was William Pilkington, who with his two daughters ran a wine and liquor business, itself started by their father, a doctor and surgeon. By 1831 four of the partners had withdrawn from the venture, leaving William Pilkington and his brother-in-law, Peter Greenall, to keep the concern viable. In 1835 the wine business was sold and the partnership was joined by Richard Pilkington, William's elder brother, with Greenall in turn withdrawing in 1841. These two men are thus the brothers of the present name. By the end of World War I Pilkington had become Britain's leading plate-glass manufacturer, and it is still based in St. Helens today. Sir Alastair Pilkington (1920-1995), who joined the family business in 1947, was the inventor of the float glass process, while the last member of the family to head "Pilks," through five generations, was Sir Antony Pilkington (1935-2000).

Pillsbury (flour)

The American company's original activity was flour-milling, but it has now diversified into pizzas, pastas, canned peas and corns, and a whole host of food products, as well as operating one of the country's largest restaurant businesses. The name is that of Charles Alfred Pillsbury (1842-1899), born in Warner, New Hampshire. In 1851 his family moved to Concord, where he completed his secondary education at age 15. He then spent a year at New London preparatory academy and was accepted to Dartmouth College, where he studied ancient and modern languages, physics, chemistry, and civil engineering. On graduating in 1863, he moved to Montreal, Canada, working in a produce commission company. In 1869 he bought a small flour mill in Minneapolis and within a couple years was a leader in transforming the Minneapolis milling district from a motley collection of mediocre mills to the largest flour producer in the world. The company headquarters remain in Minneapolis today.

Pilsner Urquell (beer)

The Czech lager beer claims to be the world's first genuine Pilsner. It was launched in 1842 in what was then the Bohemian town of Pilsen and is now the city of Plzeň in the Czech Republic. "Urquell" is German for "primary source," denoting a Pilsner from Pilsen itself. (In the Czech Republic, only a brewery in Plzeň may term itself a Pilsner.) The beer's Czech name is Plzeňský Prazdroj, and the former Pilsner Urquell group is now known as World Brew. *See also* **Gambrinus**.

Pimm's (cocktails)

The name of the familiar cocktail, especially "Pimm's Number One," is that of Englishman James Pimm, who invented it in 1840. He ran the Oyster Bar in the City of London, where his gin-based drink became a favorite among his influential customers. In the 1870s Pimm sold his business to Sir Horatio Davies (1842-1912), the future Lord Mayor of London, who began to bottle the "Number One Cup" for other establishments to sell. Gradually, an export business was built up, so that by the time of Sir Horatio's death Pimm's cocktail was known internationally, especially in the outposts of the British Empire. Today it is the original gin-based Pimm's No. 1 that is the best seller. Down to the 1930s, however, there were five other Pimm's cocktails available. These were the whisky-based Pimm's No. 2, brandy-based Pimm's No. 3, rum-based Pimm's No. 4, rye-based Pimm's No. 5, and vodka-based Pimm's No. 6. Their sales were minimal by comparison. The name "Pimms" was entered by Pimms & Co., "restaurant proprietors," in the *Trade Marks Journal* of June 20, 1888.

Pinch see Dimple

Ping-Pong (table tennis)

Table tennis came to be known as "Ping-Pong" in the late 19th century, "ping" representing the sound made when the paddle strikes the ball and "pong" the sound when the ball hits the table. (There is also a suggestion of "ding-dong," and table tennis itself is often a ding-dong affair, with fast and furious exchanges or "rallies.") The game is said to have been invented by one James Gibb, a former English athlete. It was originally sold under various names, such as "Gossima," "Whiff Whaff," and "Flim Flam," and like these, was a proprietary name from the first. The American rights to the name were sold to **Parker Brothers**, who entered it in the US Patent Office *Official Gazette* of October 4, 1949, with a claim of use from August 1, 1900.

Pininfarina (automobile bodywork)

The Italian bodywork designer Giovan Battista Pininfarina (1893-1966) was born in Turin with the surname Farina. He was the youngest of ten children and only five feet tall when fully grown, so was nicknamed *Pinin* ("Kid") and late in life legally adopted the combined name. His *carrozzeria* (body factory) became one of the most prestigious in the world. His son Sergio (b.1926) ran the design center after his death and was president of Confindustria (Confederazione generale dell'industria italiana, "General Confederation of Italian Industry") from 1988 through 1992.

Pinpoint (card-operated machine)

The type of machine that will accept a credit or other card to issue a train ticket or dispense gasoline derives its name from "PIN" (personal identification number) and "point," with a pun on "pinpoint" in the sense "locate exactly." The

British name was entered in the *Trade Marks Journal* of November 30, 1988, although the first such ticket machine went into service on February 23, 1984.

Piper *(aircraft)*

William Thomas Piper (1881-1970) was born in Knapps Creek, New York, the son of a dairy farmer and oilman. He served in the Pennsylvania Volunteer Infantry during the Spanish-American War, after which he enrolled at Harvard College, where he studied mechanical engineering. He graduated in 1903 and for the next 25 years worked at various jobs, none associated with aviation. It was not until Piper was nearly 50 that he became involved in the aviation industry. This came about in 1928 when the Bradford Chamber of Commerce asked him to represent them on the board of a new corporation, the Taylor Brothers Aircraft Corporation, which the chamber was helping to finance. Piper did so, although he knew nothing about airplanes or flying, using his own money to try and keep the troubled enterprise afloat. It went bankrupt even so, and in the reorganization Piper became treasurer of the company, renamed the Taylor Aircraft Corporation. In 1931 the company developed a glider, from which evolved the first Piper Cub airplane, one of its most successful models, called "Cub" to complement its tiny two-cylinder engine, the Brownbach Tiger Kitten.

Piper-Heidsieck *(champagne)*

The name is an integral part of the history of **Heidsieck**. Its separate entity dates from 1834, when Charles Heidsieck formed his own company. Since then, the house has been the only one allowed to use the single brand name "Heidsieck," although its sales are best known under the Piper-Heidsieck label. The first part of the name dates from 1837, when Christian Heidsieck's widow married Henri-Guillaume Piper, her brother-in-law. Under his control, the firm became H. Piper & Co., but continued selling its champagne under the Heidsieck brand. In 1845, however, it began selling its champagne as "Piper-Heidsieck" in deference to its American customers, who regularly knew it by this name. When Henri Piper died in 1870, he left the business to his partner, Jean-Claude Kunkelmann, and the firm's legal title remained "Kunkelmann et Compagnie" until

1988. In 1990 Piper-Heidsieck was sold to Rémy-Cointreau (*see* **Rémy Martin**).

Pirelli *(tires)*

Giovanni Battista Pirelli (1848-1932), born in Varenna, Italy, was educated in Milan, and it was there that in 1872 he started a small rubber factory, Italy's first. Two years before, an Italian ship, sunk in the Adriatic, had taken several months to be refloated because some rubber cables needed for the operation had to be bought abroad. Pirelli decided this should not happen again, and that Italy needed a rubber industry. He built his factory in what was then the outskirts of Milan and called it the "Sevesetto," from a nearby creek, the Seveso. Pirelli's firm pioneered the manufacture of electric cable in 1884 and of automobile tires in 1899. His two sons, Piero (1881-1956) and Alberto (1882-1971), joined the business in 1904 and expanded it into an international concern. Today the creek has long been covered over and the towering Pirelli Building (1955-9), near the Stazione Centrale, stands on the site of the original factory. The writer Giovanni Pirelli (1918-1973) was Alberto's son. In 2001, Pirelli and **Benetton** acquired **Olivetti** and hence the telecommunications giant Telecom Italia, founded in 1994, in which Olivetti held the controlling stake. The controversial takeover was managed for Pirelli by chief executive Marco Tronchetti Provera (b.1948), who married Cecilia Pirelli, daughter of chairman Leopoldo Pirelli, in 1978.

Pitman *(shorthand)*

The name is that of the English shorthand system inventor Sir Isaac Pitman (1813-1897), born in Trowbridge, Wiltshire. After clerking in a textile mill, he became a schoolmaster, first at Barton-on-Humber, Lincolnshire (to 1836), then at Wotton-under-Edge, Gloucestershire, where he published his *Stenographic Sound Hand* (1837). Following his dismissal from Wotton because he had joined the New (Swedenborgian) Church, he established a Phonetic Institute for teaching shorthand at Bath, Somerset. In 1842 he brought out the *Phonetic Journal* and in 1845 opened premises in London. The system is still widely used in the UK and elsewhere. The name "Pitman's Shorthand" was entered in the *Trade Marks Journal* of June 5, 1907.

His [phonetician Henry Sweet's] true objective was the provision of a full, accurate, legible script for our noble but ill-dressed language; but he was led past that by his contempt for the popular Pitman system of shorthand, which he called the Pitfall system.

George Bernard Shaw, *Pygmalion* (Preface) (1916)

Pitney Bowes *(postage meters)*

In 1902 Arthur Pitney (*c*.1871-1933), a clerk at a Chicago wallpaper firm, patented a machine that was capable of stamping envelopes mechanically, but failed to interest the postal service in his invention, despite its obvious advantages. In 1919, a frustrated entrepreneur, Pitney became partners with Walter Bowes (*c*.1882-1957), an English addressing-machine salesman working in Connecticut. Together, the men won official authorization for their postage meters in 1920. Sales took off, and in 1929 Pitney Bowes had a gross income of around $1.5 million from the product. In 1924, however, Arthur Pitney dissociated himself from the firm following a policy dispute with Bowes, and thus never fully profited from the success of his invention.

Pitocin *(pituitary preparation)*

The proprietary name for (an aqueous solution of) oxytocin, a hormone relased by the pituitary gland that causes increased contraction of the womb during labor, derives from the "pit" of "pituitary" and the "-ocin" of "oxytocin." It was entered by Parke, Davis & Co., of Detroit, Michigan, in the US Patent Office *Official Gazette* of January 15, 1929, and the *Trade Marks Journal* of January 23, 1929. *Cp.*(1) **Pitressin**; (2) **Pituitrin**.

Pitressin *(pituitary preparation)*

The proprietary name for (an aqueous solution of) vasopressin, a pituitary hormone that acts to promote the retention of water by the kidneys and increase blood pressure, derives from the "pit-" of "pituitary" and the "-ressin" of "vasopressin." It was entered by Parke, Davis & Co. in the US Patent Office *Official Gazette* of January 15, 1929, and the *Trade Marks Journal* of January 23, 1929. *Cp.*(1) **Pitocin**; (2) **Pituitrin**.

Pituitrin *(pituitary preparation)*

The proprietary name for an aqueous extract of the fresh pituitary gland of cattle, containing the hormones oxytocin and vasopressin, derives from "pituitary" and the pharmaceutical suffix "-in." It was entered by Parke, Davis & Co. in the US Patent Office *Official Gazette* in December 1909, and the *Trade Marks Journal* of September 3, 1924. *Cp.*(1) **Pitocin**; (2) **Pitressin**.

Pixi *(cosmetics)*

The British business was set up in 1998 by three Swedish-born sisters named Strand: makeup artist Petra (b.1966), with 15 years' experience on fashion shoots in London and Los Angeles, dermatologist Sofia (b.1976), responsible for the firm's skincare products, and chief experimenter Sara (b.1982), who also picks the names. They built up contacts with small laboratories in Britain, France, Sweden, and the USA, and by 2001 had their own store in London and two outlets in America, but no plans to take on the cosmetics giants. Their name primarily suggests "pixie" and the implied mission statement "small is beautiful," but it also evokes Latin *pinxi*, "I have painted'.

Pizza Hut *(pizza chain)*

Pizza Hut was the company that originally popularized pizza as fast food. The first Pizza Hut was opened in Wichita, Kansas, in 1958 by Frank and Daniel Carney, the sons of a grocery store owner. Trade was good almost from the start, and many of Carney's employees and investors asked how they could purchase a similar operation. As a result, Pizza Hut began franchising in 1959. A chain was opened in Oklahoma City and the number of outlets grew steadily from 42 in 1963 to 299 in 1968, so that by 1996 there were a total 12,335 units worldwide.

Placidyl *(sedative)*

The proprietary name of the sedative and hypnotic drug ethchlorvynol, used to treat insomnia, derives from "placid" and the chemical suffix "-yl." It was entered in the US Patent Office *Official Gazette* of November 29, 1955.

Plansifter *(sifting machine)*

The "shaking bolt," as it is also known, is a machine used in flour milling for separating and grading the broken grain. Its name, referring to its superimposed flat sieves, was entered by the Barnard & Leas Manufacturing Company of Maline, Illinois, in the US Patent Office *Official Gazette* of December 26, 1905.

Plasmochin *(antimalarial drug)*

The proprietary name for pamaquin, a drug formerly used in the treatment of malaria, derives from "plasmodium" (a parasitic sporozoan that causes malaria) and German *Chinin*, "quinine." It was entered by **Bayer** Products Ltd., of London, England, in the *Trade Marks Journal* of March 17, 1926. *Cp.* **Plasmoquine**.

Plasmon *(foods and drinks)*

The British name was familiar at the turn of the 20th century for a soluble proteinaceous extract of milk used to make various types of biscuit (cookie), chocolate, cocoa, and the like, promoted as nutritious and healthy. The name, clearly based on "plasma," as the colorless part of milk in which fat globules are suspended, was entered by International Plasmon Ltd., of London, in the *Trade Marks Journal* of April 4, 1906. An advertisement on the front cover of a music sheet published around 1905 reads: "Plasmon is the best part of the best milk converted into a tasteless and colourless powder. It greatly increases the nutritive value of a food without affecting the taste or flavour and is a most valuable aid to digestion. Plasmon will make you strong and healthy."

Plasmoquine *(antimalarial drug)*

The proprietary name for pamaquin, a drug formerly used in the treatment of malaria, derives from "plasmodium" (a parasitic sporozoan that causes malaria) and "quinine." It was entered by **Bayer** Products Ltd, of London, England, in the *Trade Marks Journal* of December 22, 1926. *Cp.* **Plasmochin**.

Plasticine *(modeling material)*

The putty-like modeling material was the invention of William Harbutt (1844-1921), born in Newcastle upon Tyne, England, who began his career as an artist. In 1874 he moved to Bath, Somerset, to take over the headmastership of the old Bath School of Art. His progressive ideas met with disapproval from the governors, however, and in 1877 he resigned, establishing his own art school in the city. When his students began to complain that the modeling clay they used was heavy and difficult to mold, and dried too fast for easy working,

Harbutt resolved to create a new material. He eventually evolved a new composition of the right quality and consistency and found that his children enjoyed playing with it. This prompted him to produce it as a teaching aid, and production duly began in 1900 in an old flour mill at Bathampton, near Bath. A limited company was formed to manufacture the material, which was named "Plasticine" for its plasticity. The name itself was first entered in the *Trade Marks Journal* of April 19, 1899.

Platan *(beer)*

The Czech brewery was originally developed by aristocratic landowners in the small town of Protivín, with records dating back to 1598. It takes its name from the plane trees (*platan*) in its parkland home.

Platforming *(petroleum reforming process)*

The name for a process of reforming petroleum using a platinum catalyst suggests "platform" but actually derives from a blend of "platinum" and "reforming." It was entered by the Universal Oil Products Company of Chicago in the US Patent Office *Official Gazette* of January 29, 1952, with a claim of use since August 29, 1947.

Play-Doh *(children's modeling material)*

The name of the modeling compound, now marketed by **General Mills**, is a respelled form of "play-dough," the latter half of the word denoting the material's moldable nature. The name was entered in the *Trade Marks Journal* of June 23, 1976.

Players *(cigarettes)*

John Player (1839-1884) was born in Saffron Walden, Essex, England, the son of a solicitor (lawyer). In about 1859 he left for Nottingham, where he became a draper's clerk. Four years later he had his own general store on Beastmarket Hill, there operating as an agent for lace thread and artificial manure, among other things, with tobacco added to his lines in about 1863. Player came to realize that customers had definite preferences for particular blends of tobacco, so he started to prepack the blends he sold, instead of selling them loose from jars in a "twist" of plain paper, as was then usual. It was not long before his tobacco sideline became his main business, so that in 1877 he decided to purchase a local tobacco company and make his own tobacco. His venture prospered, and Player was soon packing and selling "Gold Leaf," his first named blend of tobacco. From then on, his commercial success was assured, with the familiar sailor's head appearing on his tobacco packets from 1883. (*See* **Navy Cut**.) The following year, however, John Player died of lung cancer, aged only 45, leaving his business to be continued by family friends and senior employees. "Player's Rough & Ready Mixture" was entered in the *Trade Marks Journal* of December 9, 1885, while "Player" alone followed in the *Journal* of March 20, 1889.

Playtex *(corsetry)*

Many women ultimately owe their vital support to Abram Spanel (1901-1985), born in Odessa, Russia, the son of a tailor and a laundress. When he was ten, Spanel settled with his parents in the United States, and it did not take him long to make his first million with the Vacuumizer Manufacturing Company, founded in 1926 to produce his new garment bag. Six years later he founded the International Latex Corporation, later to become the International Playtex Corporation, best known for its bras and girdles. The change of name suggests a lighter style and touch.

Plessey *(electronics)*

The British company was founded in 1917 as a tool-making concern by a small group of businessmen, with an engineer named Bill Heyne as director. In 1920 Heyne was joined by Allen Clark (1898-1962), the American son of one of the original investors, and between them the two men laid the foundations for the present company. The story goes that Heyne and Clark were wondering what to call their new company. They said they would call it after whoever next came into their office. This was a man named Parker, but they regarded that name as too ordinary, so did not adopt it. They did ask Parker, however, if he had another name, and he replied that his middle name was Plessey. They therefore adopted that, encouraged by the coincidence that Heyne's wife came from the small village of Plessey near Morpeth, Northumberland. Heyne retired in 1947.

Plexiglas *(transparent plastic)*

The name of the plastic, which is made of the same material as **Perspex**, was entered by its German manufacturers, Röhm & Haas of Darmstadt, in the *Trade Marks Journal* of April 10, 1935 and the US Patent Office *Official Gazette* of June 30, 1936. The name itself derives from Greek *plexis*, "percussion," and English "glass." *See also* **Lucite**.

Pliofilm *(packaging material)*

The transparent, waterpoof sheeting made of rubber-based hydrochloride, used for packaging and to make raincoats, was first produced in the USA by **Goodyear**, who entered the name in the US Patent Office *Official Gazette* of November 20, 1934, with a claim of use since June 28 that year. The first part of the name probably represents "pliable."

PLJ *(health drink)*

The name is an abbreviation of the drink itself and of the British firm that manufactures it, The Pure Lemon Juice Co. Ltd., acquired by **Beecham** in 1958.

Plumrose *(canned foods)*

The founder of the company, noted for its canned meat products, was a Danish corn exporter, Edvard Ferdinand Esmann (1835-1899), who in 1864 started his business in Odense. Esmann built up a profitable activity importing butter from Russia, and by the turn of the century his firm was the largest import-export business in Denmark. In the 1920s E.F. Esmann, as the firm now was, switched from being a purely trading company to being a producing company, widening its activities to include the marketing of canned milk, cheese, and meats. Other dairy companies were acquired, one of which was P. and S. Plum, a British butter export firm. To mark its new profile, E.F. Esmann decided to change its name, doing so by combining "Plum" with "rose," the latter word suggesting products that were sweet-smelling and appetizing. Hence the more readily acceptable "international" name, with "Plum" itself also implying richness and prime quality.

Plyglass *(glass)*

The British product consists of units of two or more panes of glass enclosing one or more hermetically sealed spaces containing dry air or filled with a translucent material such as glass fiber. The name (misprinted "Plygloss"), with "Ply-" denoting the multiple layers, was entered in the *Trade Marks Journal* of March 2, 1949.

Plymouth *(automobiles)*

In 1928 Walter P. **Chrysler** bought **Dodge** for $170 million, making Chrysler at a stroke one of the largest US automobile manufacturers. In order to broaden his new company's market reach, Chrysler created Plymouth as a cheap Chrysler and **De Soto** as a cheap Dodge. The name of the new low-priced model was suggested by Chrysler manager Joseph M. Frazer. "Plymouth," it was hoped, would remind people of Plymouth Rock, Massachusetts, on to which the Pilgrim Fathers are said to have stepped from the *Mayflower* in 1620. The story goes that Chrysler approved the name because he thought it reminded people of "Plymouth" Binder Twine, a farmers' staple aid. Plymouth cars have remained an integral component of the Chrysler empire ever since.

Plymouth *(gin)*

The gin traces its origins back to the Dominicans, or Black Friars, who built a monastery in Plymouth, England, in 1431. (The Pilgrim Fathers lodged at the former priory in 1620 before setting sail on the *Mayflower* for the New World.) Documents have been found that refer to Coates & Company's Plymouth Dry Gin in 1793, and this is the date now given on the bottle. In 1933 Plymouth won "geographic designation" after a court case against **James Burrough**, the makers of **Beefeater**, who had tried to market their own "Plymouth" gin. This meant that by law Plymouth gin could only be produced in the city of Plymouth and in the Black Friars distillery owned by Coates. The brand was acquired by **Whitbread** in 1975 and was sold to Allied-Lyons (*see* **Lyons**) in 1991. In 1996 it was bought by four private purchasers who started the drink's revival.

Pocket Books *(paperbacks)*

The first paperback to be issued by the American publishing house of this name, James Hilton's *Lost Horizon*, appeared in June 1939, bearing a logo of Gertrude the Kangaroo with a book in her pocket. The founder of the new firm was Robert F. DeGraff (1895-1981), former president of Blue Ribbon Books, a publisher of clothbound reprints who was convinced that cheap books could sell in the mass as well as cigarettes or shaving cream. The original idea was to call the series 20th Century Books and to sell them for 20 cents, but DeGraff decided on the higher price of 25 cents and the name Pocket Books: "I picked this name because I felt it should be made clear that this was a book that could be carried in the pocket and, at the start, we did a good deal of promotion on selling the public on the convenience of a book that could be carried in a man's pocket or a lady's purse" (quoted in Schreuders; *see* Bibliography, p. 566).

Pocket Fisherman *(fishing tackle)*

The Pocket Fisherman was the popular invention of Samuel J. Popeil (1915-1984), the American founder in 1938 with his younger brother Raymond of Popeil Brothers, famous for their handy gadgets and devices. It took the form of a rod complete with reel, hook, line, sinker, and float small enough to fold into a coat pocket, and was devised by Popeil after he nearly had his eye poked out by a boy carrying a standard fishing rod. It was first sold in 1973 and was one of the most profitable products ever marketed on television. Another Popeil Brothers success was the **Veg-O-Matic**.

Pogo *("jumping stick")*

The toy for jumping about on dates from the 1920s and consists of a long, spring-loaded pole with a handle at the top and rests for the feet near the bottom. Its name, of uncertain origin (a connection with "pole" and "go" has been suggested), was entered by Philip de Journo, of Forest Hills, Long Island, New York, in the US Patent Office *Official Gazette* of September 1, 1942, with a claim of use since February 28, 1941.

Poilite *(building material)*

The building material, made of asbestos and cement and used in the form of tiles, sheets, and the like, has a name perhaps based on **Portland** (cement) that was entered by Bell's Asbestos Company, of London, England, in the *Trade Marks Journal* of February 11, 1903.

Pointolite *(lamps)*

The lamp so called contains a small but

bright source of light that is produced by the incandesence of a small knob of tungsten heated by an arc struck between it and a cathode. Its name, presumably representing "point of light," was entered by the Edison Swan Electric Company (*see* **Ediswan**) of London, England, in the *Trade Marks Journal* of July 25, 1923.

Poit Dubh (*whisky*)

The "old-fashioned" vatted malt made by the Praban na Linne ("Shebeen of the Pool") distillery on the Scottish island of Skye has a Gaelic name meaning "Black Pot," referring to the sooty pots formerly used by smugglers in Scotland to make their illicit liquor. The firm was founded in the 1970s by Sir Iain Noble who set up a business studies college nearby where instruction is in Gaelic. All information on the bottle labels is also in Gaelic. *See also* **Te Bheag**.

Pol Roger (*champagne*)

The house of this name was founded by 19-year-old Pol Roger in Épernay, France, in 1849. Roger's sons, Maurice and Georges, took control of the firm in 1899 and the following year changed their surnames to Pol-Roger to preserve the name of their father, with its dialect form of "Paul." The name was entered by "Pol Roger, Albert Roger, and Veuve Julie Roger, trading as Pol Roger & Co." in the *Trade Marks Journal* of September 25, 1889, and 100 years on the company was still in family hands, its directors then being Christian Pol-Roger and Christian de Billy, the founder's great-grandsons, and the latter's son, Hubert de Billy. Jacques Pol-Roger, the founder's grandson, died in 1964, and his wife, Odette Pol-Roger, née Wallace, in 2000.

Pola Maid *see* **Lyons Maid**

Polaroid *see* **Land**

Polly Peck (*food and leisure*)

The British concern Polly Peck International, a former multinational trading group with interests in food, electronics, and leisure, was originally a small, money-losing, rag-trade company when taken over by Turkish Cypriot immigrant Asil Nadir in 1980. Polly Peck herself never existed, and the name was an attempt at "Polytechnic" by Elizabeth Zelkar, the young daughter of the firm's founder, Raymond Zelkar. She was referring to the Regent Street Polytechnic, London, next door to which Polly Peck had its original office. In 1990 the group went into receivership, and Nadir, accused of misappropriating at least £400 million from Polly Peck, fled to northern Cyprus.

Polycell (*house decorating materials*)

The British name was entered in the *Trade Marks Journal* of June 3, 1953, as a word based on the type of material used in the product. This was sodium carboxymethyl cellulose, which consists of long chain molecules of cellulose, i.e., many (Greek "poly-") cellulose units. This in turn gave the name of other products, such as "Polyfilla" (a Polycell "filler"), a type of plaster used to make minor building repairs, such as filling small holes, "Polystrippa," for stripping paint, "Polyfix," for fixing ceramic tiles, etc.

Polyfoto (*photobooths*)

The name became familiar in the UK in the 1960s for a type of booth or kiosk in which a person could pose for a series of photographs, taken automatically. The name rather obviously derives from the Greek prefix "poly-," meaning "many," and an altered form of "photo." It was entered by the manufacturing company of the same name in the *Trade Marks Journal* of February 2, 1938.

Polygram (*records*)

The world's biggest record company was formed in 1962 by the merger of Phonogram Records, owned by **Philips**, and the German record company Deutsche Grammophon, owned by **Siemens**. The name thus combines Greek "poly-" ("many") with the two "gram" elements. Polygram passed to **Seagram** in 1998, merging with its own company Universal to form Universal Music.

Polynosic (*artificial fiber*)

The type of cotton-like fiber, made from regenerated cellulose, has a name variously explained in literature on the subject. It actually derives from French *polynosique*, a contraction of *polymère d'un glucose* ("glucose polymer") plus the ending *-ique* ("-ic"), an etymology substantiated by N. Drisch in *Reyon, Zellwolle u. andere Chemiefasern* ("Rayon, Rayon Staple, and other Synthetic Fibers") (1959). The name was entered by the Association Internationale Polynosic, of Geneva, Switzerland, in the *Trade Marks Journal* of January 16, 1963 for: "Threads made of synthetic or natural textile materials."

Polyox *(resin)*

The abbreviated name of polyethylene oxide resin was entered by **Union Carbide** in the US Patent Office *Official Gazette* of August 6, 1957, with a note of first use on or about March 4, 1957.

Pom *(cooked potato)*

The make of dried and powdered potato presumably derives its name from French *pomme de terre*, "potato." It was entered by the British manufacturers, M.P.P. (Products) Ltd., of Norwich, Norfolk, in the *Trade Marks Journal* of April 23, 1947.

Poma *(ski lift)*

The type of ski lift, in which a pole attached to a moving cable pulls each skier uphill on their skis, takes its name from its French inventor, Jean Pomagalski, of Fontaine-Grenoble, who entered it in the US Patent Office *Official Gazette* of April 14, 1970: "For cable transport or towing apparatus and installations—namely, cable cars, gondola-lifts, chairlifts, ski-lifts."

Pomagne *(cider)*

The brand of cider by **Bulmer** derives its name from a blend of French *pomme*, "apple" and "champagne," the latter implying the product's sparkling quality. **Whiteway's** formerly marketed a similar sparkling cider called "Champagne de Pomme," although such a name today would be inadmissible on the grounds that the product is certainly not champagne. The name was entered in the *Trade Marks Journal* of June 14, 1916.

Pommery *(champagne)*

The house dates back to 1836, when Narcisse Greno took over the firm of Dubois-Gosset in Reims, France. Louis Alexandre Pommery became an associate in 1856, but died two years later, whereupon his widow, Jeanne Alexandrine Louise Pommery, took over the house. Greno retired in 1860 on health grounds. The full name "Pommery & Greno" was entered by Veuve Pommery & Fils in the US Patent Office *Official Gazette* of November 7, 1882, and "Pommery" alone by Pommery & Cie in the *Trade Marks Journal* of July 27, 1887.

Pond's *see* **Chesebrough-Pond's**

Pontiac *(automobiles)*

The company so named was founded in 1907 in Pontiac, Michigan, as Oakland Motor Car, taking its name from the county of which Pontiac is the capital. It was acquired by **General Motors** in 1909 and soon after renamed for the city, itself founded in 1818 by promoters from Detroit, of which it is now a virtual suburb, and named for the Ottawa Indian chief Pontiac (*c.*1714-1769). The six-cylinder Pontiac Six car was introduced in 1926 and displayed an emblem showing the head of Pontiac himself and the legend "Chief of the Sixes." It became so popular that Oakland-badged cars disappeared after 1931.

Pontin's *(holiday camps)*

The British company was founded by Frederick William Pontin (1906-2000), the son of a London cabinetmaker. He began his career as a messenger boy, later becoming in turn a stockbroker's clerk, pools promoter, and turf accountant (bookmaker). After World War II, during which he was engaged in Admiralty welfare work, he decided to turn his hand to something that would offer the public "fun and food" following the austerity of previous years. In 1946, with the help of a bank loan, he acquired a former army training site at Brean Sands, near Burnham-on-Sea, Somerset, and set about transforming it into his first holiday center. Expansion was slow at first, but from the early 1960s business boomed, and the family firm became a public company. In 1963 Pontin turned his attention to continental Europe, especially Spain and Italy, setting up a new company called Pontinental for the purpose. That too was a success. By the time Fred Pontin was knighted in 1976 his company was servicing around a million holidaymakers annually.

Pontocaine *(anesthetic)*

The proprietary name for pantocain, used as a local anesthetic, is simply an altered form of the generic word, itself from Greek *panto-*, "all," and "cocaine." It was entered by the Winthrop Chemical Company, Inc., of New York, in the US Patent Office *Official Gazette* of December 10, 1935, with a claim of use since August 26, 1935.

Pony *(barley wine)*

The wine, produced by the Guernsey Brewery Co., was so named by a founder director of the firm who was an officer in the Hussars and a keen polo player. It should not be confused with the "Pony" that is a type of Pilsner beer produced by the Eichhof brewery in Lucerne, Switzerland.

Popsicle *(ice lollipop)*

The name was entered in the US Patent Office *Official Gazette* of September 25, 1923, with a claim of use since May 28, 1923. The registrar was Frank Epperson, a lemonade vendor at an Oakland, California, amusement park, who had dreamed up the idea of a frozen lemonade lollipop. He originally termed his creation "Epsicle," but then changed this to "Popsicle," presumably blending "lollipop" and "icicle." The product was launched by the Joe Lowe food processing company, who bought the rights from Epperson. Like **Eskimo Pies** and **Good Humor** bars, Popsicles soon found a national market as a branded product.

Pop-Tarts *(pastry cases)*

The jam-filled pastry cases, introduced by **Kellogg's** in the mid-1960s, were designed to be heated up in a toaster. Hence the name, for "tarts" that you "pop" in the toaster and that "pop" up hot (for you to "pop" in your mouth). The name was entered in the *Trade Marks Journal* of November 24, 1965.

Porsche *(automobiles)*

Ferdinand Porsche (1875-1951) was born in Maffersdorf, Austria. He worked first in Vienna, then in 1916 became general director of the Austro-**Daimler** Company in Wiener Neustadt, Austria, where his son Ferdinand "Ferry" Anton Ernst Porsche (1909-1998) had been born. In 1923 Porsche moved to the Daimler Company in Stuttgart, but left in 1931 to form his own firm to design sports and race cars. Porsche became heavily involved in Hitler's project for a "people's car," and together with Ferry was responsible for the initial design of the **Volkswagen** in 1934. During World War II the Porsches designed military vehicles, notably the Tiger tank. It was not until 1947, after the war, that the first Porsche

cars as such were built, in Gmünd, Austria. As production increased, facilities there were found to be inadequate, so in 1950 a return was made to Stuttgart, where Porsche had been based 20 years earlier. Sadly, he did not live to see the first Porsche win at Le Mans in 1951.

Port Salut *(cheese)*

The mild cow's-milk French cheese takes its name from the Trappist monastery of Notre Dame du Port du Salut ("Our Lady of the Haven of Safety") at Entrammes, northwestern France, where it was first produced in around 1815. In 1938 the monks registered its name as a trademark to protect it from imitations. In 1959, however, they sold the name to a commercial producer in Lorraine, so that their own cheese is now known as "Entrammes." Cheese made to the same specifications in other parts of France is called "Saint-Paulin" and is essentially identical to Port Salut.

Portakabin *(portable building)*

The type of portable building, familiar on building sites for use as temporary offices, rather obviously derives its name from a blend of "portable" and a respelled "cabin." It was entered by its British manufacturers, Portasilo Ltd. of York, in the *Trade Marks Journal* of December 4, 1963.

Portaloo *(portable toilet)*

The type of small portable building containing a toilet, typically used on construction sites, derives its name from a blend of "portable" and "loo," with a suggestion of "Waterloo." (A toilet is a water closet.) The name was entered by **Portakabin** Ltd. in the *Trade Marks Journal* of July 20, 1966.

Portland *(cement)*

The name is not that of Portland, Maine. It dates from October 21, 1824, when Joseph Aspdin, an English bricklayer from Leeds, patented a particular type of cement and called it "Portland" because it was the color of Portland stone, quarried in the Isle of Portland, a peninsula on the Dorset coast. The cement itself originated in southeastern England, and was made by calcining a mixture of the clayey mud of the Thames River with a proportion of chalk. Aspdin's product was used during construction of the Thames Tunnel (opened 1843).

The name is not a registered trademark. In 1900, 24 British cement firms amalgamated to form the Associated Portland Cement Manufacturers. A subsidiary, the British Portland Cement Manufacturers Ltd., was formed by a further 33 firms in 1911. (The names of the individual firms are listed in Appendices 6 and 7 respectively in A.J. Francis, *The Cement Industry 1796-1914: A History*, 1977.)

Possum *(electronic device)*

The device to help a disabled person operate a keyboard or other domestic equipment was introduced in the UK in the early 1960s and was officially known as a patient-operated selector mechanism, the initial letters of which, POSM, were reinterpreted as Latin *possum*, "I am able." The name was entered by Reginald George Maling, of Aylesbury, Buckinghamshire, in the *Trade Marks Journal* of July 12, 1961.

Post Toasties *(breakfast cereal)*

The General Foods product owes its name to Charles William Post (1854-1914), born in Springfield, Illinois, the son of a purveyor of agricultural implements. At 14 Post matriculated at the Illinois Industrial University, where he studed engineering for a year. He then joined the Springfield Zouaves, a militia unit that became known as the Governor's Guard. His military experience gave him an urge to travel, and he and a friend explored western Kansas and the Indian Territory (now Oklahoma) as cowhands. In 1874 Post took a job as a traveling salesman for the Climax Corn Planter Company of Springfield, and three years later worked for a while for the B.D. Buford Company of Rock Island, Illinois, developing markets for their farm tools in Kansas, Iowa, and Nebraska. In 1881 he joined other members of the family to form a plow factory, the Illinois Agricultural Works. In 1885, however, he collapsed from nervous exhaustion, and attempts to pursue new business interests hardly helped matters. Accordingly, in 1891, accompanied by his wife and daughter, Post arrived as a patient at the Battle Creek Sanitarium run by the **Kelloggs**. He recovered there, and subsequently made a cream drink that had been served at the sanitarium as a substitute for coffee. He originally called it "Monk's Brew," but in 1895, the year he founded the Postum

Cereal Company, this misleading name was changed to "Postum," and sales took off. Two years later Post produced his famous **Grape Nuts**. Then in 1904 came his *pièce de résistance*, a corn flake cereal that he proudly named "Elijah's Manna." But religious groups in the USA and the UK objected to the name, and in 1908 he rechristened it "Post Toasties." The cereal went on to be a winner and remains popular today. Post entered "Postum" as the name of a "food drink" (a coffee substitute) in the US Patent Office *Official Gazette* of December 3, 1895, "Toasties" in the *Trade Marks Journal* of October 2, 1907, and "Post Toasties" in the *Gazette* of March 31, 1908.

Post-it *(paper stickers)*

The handy little paper rectangles, bearing an adhesive strip that enables them to be stuck to a surface and then easily removed from it, were the brainchild of Arthur Fry (b.1932), a Minneapolis chemical engineer working in product development for **3M**. Singing in his church choir on the Sunday before Christmas, 1974, Fry was vexed that the scrap of paper he used to mark his hymn book kept falling out. He realized that what was needed was a bookmark that would self-attach without falling out, and which would not damage the book. He then thought of a low-tack adhesive that one of his colleagues, Spencer Silver, had developed. He got to work to perfect his idea. Then, one day in 1975, he cut off a piece of his new bookmark, wrote a question on it, and stuck it on a report for his boss. His boss wrote an answer on it and handed it back. The Post-it note was born, but was not commercially available until 1979. Fry's original name for his creation was "Press and Peel Pads," but when the stickers were test-marketed in 1977, no one knew what to do with them. They were reissued with instructions under their present, snappier name, and soon everyone was scribbling sticky notes and wanting to buy more. "Post" in the name is sometimes taken by the British to mean "send through the mail," but it actually means "display," "stick up publicly" (as if on a post). The name was entered in the *Trade Marks Journal* of October 26, 1979.

Postum *see* **Post Toasties**

Posturepedic *(mattress)*

The name of the **Sealy** mattress designed to

give proper support to the relaxed body derives from a blend of "posture" and "orthopedic." It was entered by Sealy, Inc., of Chicago in the US Patent Office *Official Gazette* of October 14, 1952, with a note to the effect that: "The representation of the human figure is fanciful."

Pot Noodle *(fast-food snack)*

Pot Noodles emerged in the late 1980s in the form of a plastic tub filled with flavored noodles over which hot water is poured to make an instant snack or light meal. The self-explanatory name was entered in the *Trade Marks Journal* of June 19, 1985.

Poulain *(chocolate)*

The French company was founded in 1848, when Auguste Poulain set up shop in Blois in the Loire valley, making chocolate in a back room. By 1878 he was producing chocolate in quantity from five different factories, and in 1884 his son, Albert, introduced a chocolate breakfast drink, *Grand Arôme* ("Great Aroma"), still popular among French children today.

Powe, Hector *see* **Hector Powe**

Power's *(whiskey)*

In 1791, James Power, a coaching innkeeper of Thomas Street, Dublin, Ireland, converted his hostelry into a small distillery. By the end of the century he had been joined by his son John and had expanded and moved his premises a short distance to John's Lane. Although the enterprise was called James Power & Son in 1804, by 1809 it had become a limited company under the name John Power, but with James still in charge. The distillery expanded steadily, and by the end of the century its output was so great that Power's ceased malting and began buying in. No one was left on the board with the Power name following the death of Sir Thomas Talbot Power (1863-1930), but the business remained in the family through his sisters. In 1966 Power's merged with **Jameson** and the Cork Distilleries Co. (*see* **Hewitts**) to form the Irish Distillers Group.

Pozidriv *(screwdriver)*

The type of cross-head screwdriver, with a smaller ridge bisecting each quarter of the cross, has a name entered in the *Trade Marks Journal* of August 26, 1965. The name itself presumably blends "positive" and "screwdriver," referring to the plus sign (+) used to indicate an electrical "positive." *Cp.* **Supadriv**.

PPG *(glass)*

The initials were formally adopted in 1968 as the name of the Pittsburgh Plate Glass Company, incorporated in Pittsburgh in 1883 at a time when European manufacturers had a virtual monopoly on the production of glass. The factory constructed that year was the first commercial plate-glass factory in the United States.

Prada *(fashionwear)*

The Italian fashion house was founded in Milan in 1913 by Mario Prada as Fratelli Prada ("Prada Brothers"), originally as a manufacturer of leather goods. The company's fortunes flagged in the 1970s, but were revived when Miuccia Prada (b.1949), Mario's youngest granddaughter, took over in 1978 with her husband, Patrizio Bertelli, and began producing accessories. Prada introduced tote bags and backpacks in 1985 and its first ready-to-wear line in 1988.

Pratt & Whitney *(aircraft engines)*

The famous aircraft engine manufacturers were not founded by a Pratt or a Whitney, but adopted the name because the founder, Frederick B. Rentschler (1887-1956), set the business up in 1925 in the buildings of the former Pratt & Whitney machine tool company, started in 1860 in Hartford, Connecticut, by Francis Ashbury Pratt (1827-1902) and Amos Whitney (1832-1920), who first met at the **Colt** Armory in that city. Whitney was a distant cousin of Eli Whitney (1765-1825), inventor of the cotton gin. In 1901 their business was acquired by the Niles-Bement-Pond Company.

Pream *(coffee whitener)*

The instant powdered coffee "cream" made its first appearance in 1952, its name blending "powdered" and "cream." It was prepared with dehydrated cream, lactose, and nonfat milk solids, and was the product of M. and R. Dietetic Laboratories of Columbus, Ohio. It tasted more like condensed milk than cream, and was not particularly popular, despite its advantages as a convenience food. The name also happens to suggest "premium."

Preludin *(antidepressant)*

The proprietary name for the drug phenmetrazine hydrochloride, an antidepressant and appetite suppressant popular as a "pep pill" in the 1950s, is apparently of arbitrary origin. It was entered by the German manufacturers, C.H. Boehringer Sohn, of Ingelheim am Rhein, in the *Trade Marks Journal* of March 17, 1954 and the US Patent Office *Official Gazette* of September 13, 1955.

Premarin *(drug for treatment of ovarian deficiencies)*

The proprietary name for a mixture of estrogenic compounds, obtained from the urine of pregnant mares, derives from letters in "*pregnant mare*" with the pharmaceutical suffix "-in." It was entered by Ayerst, McKenna & Harrison (United States) Ltd., of Rouses Point, New York (now Wyeth Ayerst, Philadelphia) in the US Patent Office *Official Gazette* of July 21, 1942, and by the same firm (in their native Canada) in the *Trade Marks Journal* of May 2, 1956.

Premier *(bicycles)*

The Premier Cycle Co. was founded in Coventry, England, in 1875 by William **Hillman**, later a noted automobile manufacturer. The "Kangaroo" bicycle, produced in 1884, was particularly popular on account of its geared pedaling apparatus, one of the first of its kind. (The company adopted a stylized kangaroo as its logo.) In 1909 the company brought out the Premier motorcycle, its name justifying its first-rank position in the world of motorcycling. It was withdraw in 1915, however, when the Premier works were commandeered by the Ministry of Munitions for the production of shells and aircraft parts in World War I. The manufacture of bicycles was resumed after the war, and the production of cars increased with the launch of the "Premier super runabout."

Presdwood *(building board)*

The type of building board with water-resistant properties derives its name from "pressed wood." It was entered by the Masonite Corporation of Chicago in the US Patent Office *Official Gazette* of April 5, 1949: "For fiberboard, insulating board, composite board, (etc.)", with a claim of use since October 6, 1926.

Preservene *(soap)*

The soap of this name was the creation in the late 19th century of an Australian, A.E. Whitelaw, who was prompted to formulate it after a weekend visit to an old school friend on a mulberry farm near Melbourne. Whitelaw joined his host in picking mulberries, but could not remove the purple stains from his hands when washing afterwards. His friend advised him that if he squashed green (unripe) mulberries between his hands, the stains would instantly be removed. Whitelaw realized that he had the makings of a washing soap that could dissolve other types of stains, such as grease, ink, blood, and fruit. He consulted a soapmaker on returning to Melbourne, and after a series of experiments found the right kinds of solvents for use with fabrics such as linen, wool, and even silk. He then lost no time in putting his new soap on the market, naming it "Preservene" for its ability to preserve a fabric while washing it. In 1914 Whitelaw took his soap to England, but a potentially promising advertising campaign was cut short by World War I, so that the soap did not reach the shops until 1919. Whitelaw then himself settled in England, opening his office in London in 1924. The name was entered in the *Trade Marks Journal* of September 9, 1925.

Presser *(music publishers)*

The US firm of music publishers was established in Philadelphia, Pennsylvania, in 1883 by Theodore Presser (1848-1925), born in Pittsburgh, the son of a German immigrant glue factory operator. At age 16 he was employed as a clerk in a Pittsburgh music store, where he eventually became manager of the sheet music department. Presser did not receive any formal musical training until age 19, when he began to study piano. In 1874 he was a student at the New England Conservatory of Music, Boston, and while there taught piano at Ohio Wesleyan University in Delaware, Ohio. In 1878 Presser entered the Leipzig Conservatory, then from 1880 taught piano and theory at Hollins College, Hollins, Virginia. In 1883, at nearby Lynchburg, he began publishing the monthly music journal *The Étude*. Its success led him to leave teaching and move to Philadelphia, where he devoted himself entirely to music publishing.

Prestcold *(refrigerators)*

The company of this name was formed in

1934 as a division of what was then the Pressed Steel Co. Pressed Steel pioneered the all-steel car body in Britain, using a technique borrowed from the US company E.G. Budd of Philadelphia. In the 1930s, Pressed Steel felt that they were well placed and well equipped to move into the growing market for domestic refrigerators. If they could press car body-panels, they argued, they could surely press the square cases of a refrigerator cabinet. The company therefore set up a refrigerator production line at their Cowley, Oxford, headquarters and named their product "Prestcold," a blend of "Pressed Steel" and "cold."

Prestel *(teletext system)*

The computerized visual information system, pioneered in the late 1970s by British Telecommunications (BT), enabled data selected from one or more databases to appear on a television screen by dialing the appropriate telephone number. The word presumably combined "press," or possibly "presto," with "telephone" or "television." The name was entered in the *Trade Marks Journal* of December 6, 1978.

Pret A Manger *(sandwich chain)*

The British chain dates from 1986, when Julian Metcalfe (b.1960), a chartered surveyor (architect), together with a partner, Sinclair Beecham (b.1959), opened a store in Victoria Street, London, making sandwiches in the basement with food that they bought at dawn from the Covent Garden fruit and vegetable market. The two saw themselves as providing a healthy alternative to the mass-produced meals of **McDonald's** burger bars, with products that included organic milk, additive- and preservative-free ingredients, and free-range eggs and chicken. The name of their enterprise, French for "ready to eat" (based on fashion's *prêt-à-porter*, "ready to wear"), was similarly wholesome, dispensing with accents (properly *prêt à manger*) and pronounced in a robust English manner. In 2001 there were 106 "Pret" outlets, as against McDonald's 28,700, but that year the founders sold a 33 percent stake to their US rivals in a bid to fulfill their plans for global expansion.

Pretty Polly *(hosiery)*

The British company traces its origins to 1919, when three technicians, Harry Hibbert, Oswald Buckland, and Charles Meadows, set up a contract knitting business in Sutton-in-Ashfield, Nottinghamshire. Although they were mainly concerned with such major brands as **Morley**, the team also had dealings with a wholesaler in Leek, Staffordshire, whose brand name was Pretty Polly, after the famous English filly (foaled 1901) who won 22 out of 24 races in her four-year career, earning more than $130,000. (The wholesaler had adopted this particular name because the company was owned by a sucessful bookmaker.) In about 1926, the Leek firm got into financial difficulties, so the three partners took it over by way of settling their debts, at the same time adopting its name. There was thus no human Pretty Polly, any more than there was for **Polly Peck**.

Prewett's *(health foods)*

The name of the English company comes from Prewett's Mill, a flour mill in Horsham, Sussex, built in 1861 by William Prewett to accommodate steam power for his stone-ground wholemeal flour-milling operations. The mill subsequently came to be powered by electricity, and was operative until the 1970s, when its great grinding stones were dismantled and transported to Yorkshire, where they continued to grind wholemeal flour at the **Allinsons** bakery at Castleford. The mill itself has now been incorporated into office premises for its current owners, United Rum Merchants. But the Prewett name lives on in the health foods marketed by **Booker** Foods.

Price's *(candles)*

There never was a Mr. Price as founder of the British company, and it owes its origins to William Wilson (1772-1860) and his partner Benjamin Lancaster. Wilson came to London in 1812 after the failure of his father's ironworks in Scotland. Together with Lancaster, he started a brokership business importing commodities from Russia. One of these was tallow, and in 1830 the partners purchased a patent for the separation of the solid and liquid constituents of coconut oil by hydraulic pressure, intending to use the fat as a substitute for tallow in the manufacture of candles while keeping the oil for use in lamps. The two men did not wish to engage in this activity under their own names, for fear of "loss of face," so chose another name for the business. This was "E. Price and Company," Price being the name of one of Lancaster's aunts. Later, after Lancaster had retired from the partnership, the name was fleshed out to "Edward Price and Company." The first coconut pressing factory was in Battersea, London.

PricewaterhouseCoopers (accountants)

The company dates from 1849, when Samuel Lowell Price set up business in London, England. In 1854, William Cooper also set up a London practice, to be joined subsequently by his brother Francis as Cooper Brothers. In 1865 Price, Holyland and Waterhouse joined forces as partners, and in 1874 the name of the business was changed to Price, Waterhouse & Co. In 1898, William M. Lybrand (1867-1960), a junior partner with the US public accounting firm Heins and Whelen in Philadelphia, set up his own firm, Lybrand, Ross Brothers and Montgomery, with three other junior partners: Adam A. Ross, Jr., T. Edward Ross, and his brother-in-law Robert H. Montgomery. In 1957, Cooper Brothers & Co. in the UK, McDonald, Currie and Co. in Canada, and Lybrand, Ross Brothers and Montgomery in the USA merged as Coopers & Lybrand. In 1982, Price Waterhouse World Firm was formed, and in 1990, Coopers & Lybrand merged with Deloitte Haskins & Sells in several countries of the world. Finally, in 1998, Price Waterhouse and Coopers & Lybrand merged as PricewaterhouseCoopers (PwC), retaining three key names (though not Lybrand's) from the past.

Primerica (financial services and consumer goods)

The diversified American corporation was founded in 1901 as the American Can Company through the consolidation of various producers of metal cans for the food-canning industry. In 1981 the company began to move out of manufacturing and transformed itself into a financial conglomerate. It assumed its present name, suggesting "prime America," in 1987.

Primula (cheese spread)

The spread owes its creation to Olav Kavli (1872-1962), born near Molde in western Norway, the son of a farmer. At the age of 18 he left home to seek his fortune in the city of Bergen.

At first he just bought and sold cheese, but in 1924, after years of experiment, succeeded in manufacturing a cheese spread with special long-life properties. He named it "Primula," for the flower, and its popularity grew so rapidly that Kavli was soon setting up factories to make it in other countries. The cheese is sold in packaging with a picture of a dairymaid in Norwegian national costume set in a Norwegian landscape. She holds a bunch of primulas or primroses, the first flower of spring, and these represent not only the fresh-tasting spread and its name but her own youth and beauty.

Primus (portable cooking stoves)

The stove of this name was invented in Sweden in the late 19th century by F.W. Lindqvist. In 1889 one B.A. Hjorth opened a tool and engineering shop in Stockholm and acquired the exclusive rights for the sale of Lindqvist's "Primus" stove. In 1893 a young man named Soeren Condrup, a partner in a British firm, was on holiday with his wife in Norway and noted the "Primus" in a shop. He was impressed with it, ordered 100 stoves, and with his partner secured the rights to act as sole selling agents for "Primus" stoves in the UK. The stove's name is Latin for "first," and it was so called as it was the first practical wickless stove. The name was entered by B.A. Hjorth & Co. in the *Trade Marks Journal* of June 22, 1910 and the US Patent Office *Official Gazette* of July 5, 1910.

Prince Albert (tobacco)

The smoking tobacco of this name was introduced by **R.J. Reynolds** in 1907 as a rather belated tribute to Prince Albert (1819-1861), consort to Queen Victoria (1819-1901).

Prince Matchabelli (perfume)

Georges Matchabelli (1885-1935), the eldest son of a noble Russian family, fled his homeland after the Russian Revolution and came to New York in 1923, where he opened an antique shop at 545 Madison Avenue. Here he began making perfumes for his favored customers. Word of his fashionable product spread, and he was soon forced to give up the antiques to keep up with the growing demand for his perfume. Half his art was in his original packaging, and Matchabelli sold his perfumes in crown-shaped bottles and named them after royal women such as the Duchess of York and Catherine the Great. Matchabelli (properly Machabeli, a name of Georgian origin) headed his internationally known firm until his premature death from pneumonia at the age of 50.

Princes *(canned salmon)*

The name is that of a London, England, grocer, to whom a Mr. Simpson and a Mr. Roberts sold 2,000 cases of imported canned salmon and lobster from North America in the 1880s. The name initially applied to canned lobster, but became familiar after World War I when Princes canned salmon became widely known. After many years of increasing the amount of salmon he bought from the Pacific northwest, Roberts eventually persuaded local canneries to adopt Princes' high standards, and today the company remains the biggest UK importer of canned goods.

Pringle *(knitwear)*

Best known for the "Argyle" motif on its socks and sweaters, the Scottish company was founded in 1815 by Robert Pringle (1795-1859), born in Hawick, Roxburghshire, the son of a merchant. Two of Pringle's 11 children joined him in the business. The first of these, Walter Pringle, in turn bore a son, Robert Pringle, who was the last surviving member of the Pringle family to be connected with the business, and who died in 1953. The company is still centered in Hawick, but in 2000 was acquired by the Hong Kong-based Fang brothers, who made their fortunes as suppliers of knitwear.

Pringles *(crispy snacks)*

The snacks are marketed by **Procter & Gamble** and take their name from Pringle Street, Cincinnati, where the firm was founded.

Priscol *(vasodilator)*

The proprietary name for the drug tolazoline, used in the treatment of spasm of the peripheral arteries (those near the surface of the body), is probably of arbitrary origin. It was entered by the Society of Chemical Industry in Basle, Switzerland, in the *Trade Marks Journal* of May 18, 1938. The US registration is now no longer valid. *Cp.* **Priscoline**.

Priscoline *(vasodilator)*

The proprietary name for the drug tolazoline derives from **Priscol** and the suffix "-ine" and was entered by Ciba Pharmaceutical Products, Inc. *(see* **Ciba-Geigy**), of Summit, New Jersey, in the US Patent Office *Official Gazette* of August 22, 1950: "For preparations having an action on the circulation of the blood," with a claim of use since March 15, 1949.

Prisunic *(supermarkets)*

The French supermarket chain, noted for its relatively cheap goods, originally sold all its lines at the same price. Hence the name, from *prix unique*, "only price." *Cp.* **Monoprix**.

Pro-Banthine *(drug for treating peptic ulcers)*

The proprietary name for the drug propantherine derives its name from "propyl" and "Banthine," itself a proprietary name for methantheline bromide. It was entered by G.S. Searle & Co., of Skokie, Illinois, in the US Patent Office *Official Gazette* of March 17, 1953: "For medicinal agent for the treatment of abnormal conditions of the gastro-intestinal system in tablet and ampoule form."

Procea *(bread)*

The bread of this name originated in New Zealand in the early 1930s as "Procera" bread, the name alluding to the special patented process used to extract gluten from flour. The process was taken to Britain by a laboratory under the charge of three doctors named Amos, Kent, and Jones, and it was they who decided to shorten the name slightly to "Procea." In 1958 the range of breads sold by Procea Products Ltd. was extended to include a slimming loaf, and this very soon came to be known as "Slimcea." The company itself eventually became known as Slimcea Ltd. and in 1975 was sold off to **Spillers**.

Procion *(dyes)*

The name of the large class of reactive dyestuffs, covering a wide range of colors, appears to be of arbitrary origin. It was entered by the manufacturers, **ICI**, in the *Trade Marks Journal* of May 23, 1956 for: "Dyes, dyestuffs and colouring matters, none being for laundry or toilet purposes."

Procter & Gamble *(soaps and detergents)*

William Procter probably did not realize

what he had started when together with his brother-in-law, James Gamble, he began to make soap and candles in Cincinnati in 1837. Procter was an English candlemaker, and Gamble an Irish soapmaker, with their partnership sealed by the fact that they had married two sisters. (Legend has it that it was their father-in-law who proposed the joint commercial venture.) The chief ingredient for both candles and soap was animal fat, and this was where Cincinnati came in, as an important hog-butchering center. Procter ran the office, while Gamble supervised the factory. Their business thrived, and went on to produce some of the most familiar household names in the domestic cleaning and washing world, such as **Ivory** soap, introduced in 1879, **Crisco** shortening (1911), **Oxydol** washing powder (1931), "Tide" powdered laundry detergent (1946), and "Joy" liquid laundry detergent (1949). The company went to Britain in 1930, buying up the Newcastle firm of Thomas Hedley & Co., which made only one product, "Fairy" soap, now also in Procter & Gamble's stable. It was William Procter's son, Harley Procter, who named **Ivory** soap. In 1930, his grandson, William Cooper Procter (1862-1934), handed the presidency to Richard R. Deupree, so that neither a Procter nor a Gamble headed the company.

Prolixin *(tranquilizer)*

The proprietary name for fluphenazine hydrochloride was entered by the Olin Mathieson Chemical Corporation, New York, in the US Patent Office *Official Gazette* of March 1, 1960: "For central nervous system depressant preparations," with a note of first use on September 18, 1959. The name itself is presumably arbitrary in origin, and unrelated to "prolix."

Promin *(anti-leprosy drug)*

The name was entered by the manufacturers, Parke, Davis and Co., of Detroit, Michigan, in the US Patent Office *Official Gazette* of June 29, 1937: "For p-amino-benzene-sulfonamide used in treatment of streptococcic infections," with a claim of use since April 16, 1937. The name is probably arbitrary, although the second element suggests "amino."

Prontosil *(antibiotic)*

The first sulfanomide antibiotic, formerly used to treat a wide range of bacterial infec-

tions, has a name of apparently arbitrary origin entered by the German manufacturers, **Bayer** Products Ltd., in the *Trade Marks Journal* of July 15, 1936 for: "A medicated dye preparation for human use in the prevention and treatment of Streptococcus infections."

Propert's *(neatsfoot oil and saddle soap)*

John Propert was an English coachman employed by Drummonds, the London bankers, in the early years of the 19th century. He devised various preparations to care for the leather trappings on the coaches he drove, and his experiments were so successful that in 1835 he left the bank to set up his own works in South Audley Street. There he sold his cleaning and polishing preparations to his fellow coachmen, accompanying them with a "standard blacking for all boots and shoes" and "boot top powders" for the tops of Wellington boots. Together with other well-known makes of boot polish, such as **Cherry Blossom** and **Wren**, Propert's polishes were subsequently manufactured by the firm of Chiswick Products Ltd. until they were acquired by **Reckitt** in the mid-20th century.

Pro-Plus *(stimulant)*

The proprietary name for a form of caffeine implies that the preparation is for (Latin *pro*) more (Latin *plus*) energy in order to combat fatigue. The product was first marketed in 1956, and the name was entered in the *Trade Marks Journal* of August 21, 1963.

Prostigmin *(drug for muscular complaints)*

The proprietary name of neostigmine, used to treat ileus, glaucoma, and myasthenia gravis (a chronic weakness of the muscles), is based on the generic name (with "pro-" meaning "for") and was entered by **Hoffmann-La Roche** in the *Trade Marks Journal* of November 11, 1931. A subsequent registration in the US Patent Office *Official Gazette* of March 19, 1946, claimed the use of the variant form "Prostigmine" since April 29, 1931, and of the "e"-less form since November 8, 1931. "Neostigmine" itself derives from "neo-" ("new") and "physostigmine," a compound that is the active ingredient of the Calabar bean, its own name coming from the genus name *Physostigma* (literally "bladder stigma").

Prozac *(antidepressant)*

The proprietary name of the drug fluoxetine, used to treat depression, was devised by naming consultants Interbrand to be consumer-friendly and was based on a Latin derivative for readiness of international acceptance. The drug was synthesized by scientists at **Eli Lilly** in 1972 and first marketed in 1987 by Dista Products Co., a division of Eli Lilly. The name was entered in the *Trade Marks Journal* of July 10, 1985.

Prudential *(life insurance)*

Britain's largest life insurance company was founded in 1848 and pioneered the sale of life insurance to the industrial working classes through the door-to-door collection of regular premiums by "the man from the Pru," soon an established feature of British life. The name indicates the basic purpose of insurance as the making of prudential provision for the future.

Prudential *(life insurance)*

The American "Pru" was founded in 1873 in Newark, New Jersey, by John Fairfield Dryden (1839-1911), born near Farmington, Maine, a farmer's son. After attending grammar school and high school in Worcester, Massachusetts, he entered Yale College in 1861 but was forced to withdraw during his senior year. It may have been Dryden's physical limitations that prompted him to enter the growing insurance business. The firm he set up was originally known as the Widows and Orphans Friendly Society, selling industrial insurance to working-class families. In 1875 Dryden changed the name to Prudential in imitation of the British insurer of the same name.

Psion *(palmtop computers)*

South African David Potter (b.1943) first began to use computers when he went to England to study natural science at Cambridge. He also studied in Los Angeles at the time Silicon Valley was being established. Returning to London he bought a small office in Maida Vale and in 1979 started to publish computer software, his first success being an early home computer flight simulator. The game was the break he needed to get his enterprise going and he expanded into palmtop personal organizers, calling his business Psion, standing for *Potter Scientific Instruments* with the scientific suffix

"-on," but also suggesting the term for a psi particle. His company grew from then on.

Puffin *(duvet)*

The make of duvet or continental quilt was presumably so called partly from the plump bird, with its "homely" image, partly from "puff" in its sense of something light and airy. The name was entered by the British manufacturers, Arthur R. Davis & Co. Ltd., of Croydon, Surrey, in the *Trade Marks Journal* of February 18, 1959 for: "Fulled bed coverings in the nature of quilts or eiderdowns." The quilt is also known as a "Puffin Downlet."

Puffin *see* **Penguin**

Pullman *(sleeping cars)*

The railroad sleeping car takes its name from George M. Pullman (1831-1897), born in Brocton, New York, the son of a carpenter and mechanic. He left school at 14 to become a clerk in his uncle's general store in nearby Westfield, and in 1848 rejoined his family, who had moved to Albion, to work with his older brothers in a cabinetmaking shop. Following his father's death in 1853, Pullman became a contractor in moving various buildings near the Erie Canal. In the mid-1850s, however, he moved to Chicago, where he worked raising several buildings to new street levels. While traveling between Chicago and New York by rail, Pullman found the fixed-berth sleeping cars crude and uncomfortable, and in 1858, together with a friend, Benjamin C. Field, contracted with the Chicago & Alton Railroad to remodel two day coaches into sleeping cars. He then went to Colorado, where various projects were successful, and on returning in 1863 decided that the sleeping car business would be his life's work. In 1865 the first "real" Pullman appeared as the "Pioneer," with folding upper berths and seat cushions that could be extended to make lower berths. The Pullman Palace Car Company was organized in 1867, with Pullman as president, and to house his employees he built the town of Pullman, south of Chicago. The business expanded and prospered, and dining cars were added to the sleeping cars. The association of the Pullman name with rail travel became so close that many languages adopted the word for a luxury coach, and punsters like to claim that a rickshaw, in full jinricksha, literally "man-strength-vehicle," is the Japanese word-for-word equivalent of "Pullman car."

Pulmotor *(respiratory apparatus)*

The apparatus for forcing air or oxygen into or out of the lungs when breathing has ceased (or is very weak) derives its name from a blend of Latin *pulmo*, "lung" and *motor*, "that which moves" (English "motor"). The name was entered by Dragerwerk, of Lübeck, Germany, in the US Patent Office *Official Gazette* of June 24, 1913 for: "Mechanical respiratory apparatus and devices for administering oxygen", with a claim of use since February, 1909.

Pulsar *(watches)*

Digital watches first came on the scene in 1971, developed by US engineers George Theiss and Willy Crabtree. They presented a light-emitting diode (LED) or visual number display, and were given the name "Pulsar," after the astronomical term for a neutron star that emits regular pulses of radio waves. The name was entered by the Hamilton Watch Co., of Lancaster, Pennsylvania, in the US Patent Office *Official Gazette* of August 31, 1971, with a note of first use on April 27, 1970.

Puma *(sporting goods)*

The German company arose from the shoe-making business established in 1924 as Gebrüder Dassler Schuhfabrik in the small Bavarian mill town of Herzogenaurach, near Nürnberg, by the brothers Rudolf and Adolf Dassler. Their first specialist product was track shoes, named for the puma, an animal noted for its speed and grace. In 1948, following a violent disagreement between the two, Rudolf Dassler launched his first football boot, the "Puma Atom," while Adolf Dassler broke away altogether to found **Adidas**.

Punch *(cigars)*

The cigar brand, currently the second oldest still in production, was launched by Manuel Lopez in Havana, Cuba, in 1840 with the British market in mind. Hence the name, based on the character in the popular Punch and Judy show. (The eponymous British humorous magazine first appeared the following year.)

Punt e Mes *(aperitif)*

The name of the wine-based Italian aperitif is Piedmontese dialect for "point and a half."

The story goes that in 1786 Antonio **Carpano** opened a bar behind the stock exchange in Turin, where he offered his customers the choice of a sweeter or bitterer variation on his basic vermouth. The stockbrokers began to refer to the gradations of bitterness as "points," and a favorite was the one that was "one and a half points" bitterer than the standard. Carpano's "Punt e Mes" itself was launched commercially in 1876.

Purdey *(sports guns and cartridges)*

Although the English firm was founded in 1814, the first Purdey to be a gunmaker was James Purdey, born in 1732, who established a business near the Tower of London. The youngest of his seven children, also named James Purdey (1784-1863), was apprenticed to the gun trade, and after working for a gun-manufacturing firm as manager, started his own business in Leicester Square in the year mentioned. He expanded to larger premises in Oxford Street in 1826, and after his death the business was taken over by his son, also James Purdey, who in 1881 built Audley House in South Audley Street, so extending the premises even further. It is there that James Purdey & Sons Ltd. still has its head offices today. The name was entered in the *Trade Marks Journal* of March 20, 1974 for "Guns, rifles and ammunition."

Purdey's *(health drink)*

The health or sports drink takes its name from John William Purdey, an English can-maker, who in the early years of the 20th century decided to devise a restorative drink for local huntsmen, who often tired in the field. Together with his uncle, a chemist, he developed a brew based on old herbal recipes to revitalize the flagging sportsmen, canning the result himself. Today the drink is produced in the UK by Orchid Drinks, manufacturers of **Amé** and **Aqua Libra**, while the cans in which it is sold differ little from those originally made by Purdey.

Purimachos *(fireproof cement)*

The fire-resisting cement, formerly used for the repair of furnaces and other structures exposed to high temperatures, as at iron and steel works, gasworks, and munition works, was manufactured by the British firm of the same name, founded in 1880 by John Charles Morgan. The name, at one time almost generic for the product, means "fire fighter," from Greek *pur*, "fire," and *makhē*, "battle."

Putnam *(publishers)*

The New York publishing house takes its name from George Palmer Putnam (1814-1872), born in Brunswick, Maine, the son of a Harvard graduate and lawyer. He attended his mother's preparatory school before beginning his apprenticeship, in around 1825, with a Boston carpet dealer. Four years later Putnam left for New York, where he became a clerk in George W. Bleecker's book and stationery store. Putnam's growing interest in the international book trade led to an association with English writers and publishers, and in 1840 he visited London to seek out importation openings. He returned the following year to set up a literary agency on behalf of the firm, and for the next seven years lived with his young family in London. In 1847 he went back to New York and started his own book publishing business, eventually established as G.P. Putnam & Son in 1866, the son being George Haven Putnam (1844-1930), born in London while his father was there. Although suffering financial setbacks, Putnam struggled on, but died suddenly in his New York office as insolvency loomed. George Haven Putnam became head of the firm on his father's death and with his younger brothers, John Bishop Putnam and Irving Putnam, established G.P. Putnam's Sons. In 1975 the company was taken over by **MCA** and subsequently merged with **Penguin**.

Put-U-Up *(divan beds)*

The bed of this type and name was introduced in 1906 by the British firm of Greaves & Thomas of Harlow, Essex, who were taken over by Schreiber Furniture in 1967. The name denotes a sofa or couch that can be converted into a bed to "put you up" for the night. It has tended to be used generically for any divan bed of this kind, and is sometimes seen in the form "Put-You-Up," a variant actually registered by Schreiber in the 1970s. The original name was entered by Greaves & Thomas in the *Trade Marks Journal* of August 20, 1924 for "settees convertible into bedsteads."

Puyricard *(chocolates)*

In 1968, Belgian-born couple Marie-Anne and Jean-Guy Roelandts came from the Belgian Congo to the Provençal village of Puyricard. Without any tradition of chocolate-making in their families, they set about learning a new trade and promoting their wares to their country neighbors, who traditionally regarded chocolate as a delicacy, to be eaten sparingly at Christmas. By the end of the 20th century, Puyricard had grown from a husband-and-wife enterprise to a full-blown commercial operation, with a full-time staff of 70 and 11 shops in France supervised by Madame Roelandts.

Pybuthrin *(insecticide)*

The insecticide is a compound of *pyrethrins* and piperonyl *but*oxide. Hence its name, combining elements of these words, entered in the *Trade Marks Journal* of January 3, 1951.

Pye *(electronic appliances)*

The name is that of William George Pye (1869-1949), born in Battersea, London, England, the son of a man who had turned his hobby of model-making into a livelihood, and who together with a colleague, A.G. Dew-Smith, ran an instrument-making business in Cambridge, where it eventually became known as the Cambridge Scientific Instrument Company. William received a good training under his enterprising father, and in 1892 joined the staff of the Cavendish Laboratory, Cambridge, as an instrument maker. In 1896 he started his own business on a part-time basis, making instruments for schools and laboratories with the help of his wife and brothers. By the end of the century he had left the Cavendish, his father had joined him, and he had moved to larger premises in Mill Lane, Cambridge, called Granta Works. A final move was made in 1913 to a factory in Cam Road, which became the site of the subsequent Pye Telecommunications. It was only after World War I that Pye began making the radios for which it became popular, although this side of the business was sold off in 1928, continuing independently as Pye Radio Ltd., while W.G. Pye & Co. went on making "precision physical and electrical apparatus for teaching commerce and research" at separate premises in Newmarket Road. *See also* **Ekco**.

Pyramidon *(analgesic)*

The antipyretic and analgesic drug derives

its name from elements in its original generic name of dimethyl*amid*ophenyldimethyl*pyra*zolo*ne*. It was entered by the German firm of Farberwerke, formerly Meister, Lucius & Brünning, of Höchst-am-Main, in the US Patent Office *Official Gazette* of December 6, 1898 for: "Remedy for certain named disease," with a note of use since December 1896.

Pyrex *(heat-resistant glass ovenware)*

The first ovenproof glass vessel was not intended as such by the **Corning** Glass Works, but was the base of an electric storage battery. Even so, Mrs. Becky Littleton, wife of Corning's chief physicist, decided to use it for baking. Jesse Littleton was so impressed that that the vessel baked uniformly without breaking that Eugene G. Sullivan and William G. Taylor were assigned to develop a much thinner glass that would be equally heat-resistant. The compound they created was called "Nonex" (a contraction of "nonexpanding"), but it was soon superseded by an improved version, which was named "Pyrex" and first produced in 1915. The name was entered in the US Patent Office *Official Gazette* of August 1, 1916, claiming use since May 20, 1915, and in the *Trade Marks Journal* of January 10, 1917. "Pyrex" is often explained as a blend of Greek *pur*, "fire," and Latin *rex*, "king," but the company has a different account of the name, quoted in *American Speech* (XXXII, 1957):

> The assistant secretary of the [Corning Glass] company wrote me as follows: The word *pyrex* is a purely arbitrary word which was devised in 1915 as a trade-mark for products manufactured and sold by Corning Glass Works. ... We had a number of prior trade-marks ending in the letters *ex*. One of the first commercial products to be sold under the new mark was a pie plate and in the interests of euphonism the letter *r* was inserted between *pie* and *ex* and the whole thing condensed to *pyrex*.

Pyribenzamine *(antihistamine)*

The proprietary name for tripelennamine hydrochloride blends the first part of "pyridine" with "benzo-" and "amine." It was entered by Ciba Pharmaceutical Products, Inc. (*see* **Ciba-Geigy**), of Summit, New Jersey, in the US Patent Office *Official Gazette* of August 27, 1946, with a claim of use since July 12, 1945.

Pyroceram *(heat-resistant glass)*

The name of the strong, heat-resistant glass derives from Greek-based "pyro-" ("fire") and English "ceramic." It was entered by **Corning** in the US Patent Office *Official Gazette* of May 20, 1958, with a note of first use on February 7, 1957.

Pyrotenax *(heat-resistant cable)*

The name of the tough, heat-resistant, copper-sheathed cable apparently derives from Greek-based "pyro-" ("fire") and Latin *tenax*, "tough," "holding fast," from *tenere*, "to hold." It was entered by the British firm of the same name in the *Trade Marks Journal* of February 2, 1949, and by the Société Alsacienne de Constructions Mécaniques of Paris, France, in the US Patent Office *Official Gazette* of May 17, 1960.

Qantas *(airline)*

The Australian airline, the oldest in the English-speaking world, was founded in 1920 as Queensland and Northern Territory Aerial Services Ltd.. The present acronymic name was adopted officially in 1934 and came to be cynically interpreted by some as "quite a nice trip, all survived."

Qiana *(nylon)*

The arbitrary name for nylon was entered by **Du Pont** in the US Patent Office *Official Gazette* of September 3, 1968: "For Yarns of Man Made Fibers," with a note of first use on May 15, 1968.

Q-Tips *(cotton buds)*

The cotton buds so named, manufactured by **Chesebrough-Pond's**, were the invention in the 1920s of a Polish-born American, Leo Gerstenzang, whose wife used a toothpick stuck into a piece of cotton to clean her baby's ears. Gerstenzang saw that a ready-made instrument for the purpose would be more satisfactory, and devised a small stick of nonsplintering wood with a cotton swab on each end. At first he called his creation "Baby Gays," but in 1926 changed this to "Q-Tips Baby Gays," the "Q" standing for "quality." The "Baby Gays" part of the name was later dropped. In 1946, Q-Tips SA was formed in Paris, France, and the company also expanded into Canada. In 1958 the British makers of lollipop sticks, Papersticks

Ltd., was acquired and its machinery taken to America, where it was adapted for the manufacture of Q-Tips with biodegradable paper-and-wood sticks. Q-Tips was the only product of its kind until 1941. Its main competitor, **Johnson & Johnson**'s Cotton Buds, market leaders in the UK and elsewhere, have always had plastic sticks. Q-Tips retained 60 percent of the market in the USA into the 1990s.

Quaalude *(sedative)*

The proprietary name for the drug methaqualone, a hypnotic sedative, is presumably based on the generic name. It was entered by William H. Rorer, Inc., of Fort Washington, Pennsylvania, in the US Patent Office *Official Gazette* of April 12, 1966, with a note of first use on August 6, 1965. The UK equivalent drug is **Mandrax**.

Quaker Oats *(breakfast cereal)*

The company of this name owes its origin to Henry Parsons Crowell (1855-1944), born in Cleveland, Ohio, the son of a wholesale shoe merchant. Ill health obliged him to quit school at 17 and work in the family business, and while so engaged he attended a Dwight L. Moody revival, which inspired him to vow to God that he would make a lot of money and use it to finance Christian evangelism. In 1874 he left for Denver, and spent the next seven years traveling through the West in an effort to regain his health. On returning to Ohio, Crowell became a partner in an oat mill at Ravenna, east of Akron. It was then, in 1881, that he wrote out his plan for creating a worldwide organization that would sell the best quality oatmeal that technology could make. By the mid-1880s the Ravenna Mill's "Quaker" brand oatmeal was well established. It is uncertain how the name originated. According to one account, the owner of the original business, Henry D. Seymour, had searched for a name in an encyclopedia and found nothing suitable until he came across an article on the Quakers. He was struck by the religious group's qualities of purity, honesty, strength, and manliness, and decided that their name could equally apply to high-grade oats. Another account, however, claims that Seymour's partner, William Heston, had seen a picture of William Penn, the famous English Quaker, while walking in Cincinnati, and as he was himself of Quaker ancestry had decided

then and there that the "quality" parallels were right for him to adopt the name. Either way, the original trademark, showing a man in full Quaker dress carrying a scroll bearing the word "Pure," was the first ever registered for a breakfast cereal. It was filed at the US Patent Office on September 4, 1877, and the name "Pure Quaker Oats" was entered by The American Cereal Company, Chicago, Illinois, in the *Trade Marks Journal* of December 5, 1894. In 1915 the Society of Friends (Quakers) tried to stop the company from using the name, but failed in their effort to get Congress to prohibit the manufacturers from using the name of a religious denomination on a product. The Quakers then sought action in various states, but Quaker Oats drew on all the resources they could muster to avert the attack, and the Friends succeeded in only one state, Indiana.

Quality Street *(confectionery assortment)*

The assortment was introduced in 1936 by John **Mackintosh** & Sons. The name was adopted from the title of J.M. Barrie's play *Quality Street* (1902), set in *c*.1805, and the product's identity was based on the play's main characters, a soldier and his young lady, who duly appeared in period dress and pseudo-dated dialogue in the firm's advertisements, named for the purpose Major Quality and Miss Sweetly. The 1937 movie of the play, starring Katharine Hepburn, provided the perfect advertising opportunity, and during World War I the assortment was promoted by association with such British "quality streets" as London's Regent Street and The Pantiles in Tunbridge Wells, Kent. After the war, "Men of Quality" were shown driving tractors with the slogan "Quality Street keeps you going." The assortment is still made at Mackintosh's Halifax factory and it is now the world's bestselling boxed chocolate brand, with exports around the world.

Quantometer *(spectrograph)*

The type of automatic spectrograph, used to analyze alloys, derives its name from "quantity" and the "-ometer" element denoting measurement. It was entered by Francis Cutler Ellis of Chicago in the US Patent Office *Official Gazette* of May 3, 1927 for: "Instrument diagnosis and food and remedy testing by analysis of radiant energies," with a claim of use since September 1, 1926.

Quinacrine *(antimalarial drug)*

The proprietary name for mepacrine, a blend of "quinine" and "acridine," was entered by the Société des Usines Chimiques Rhône-Poulenc ("Society of Rhône-Poulenc Chemical Works"), of Paris, France, in the US Patent Office *Official Gazette* of October 23, 1934, and the *Trade Marks Journal* of March 4, 1936.

Quink *(ink)*

The brand of ink produced by The **Parker** Pen Co. has a name that is a contraction of "quick-drying ink," this being a highly desirable quality, since ordinary ink is liable to linger liquid on the nib of the pen and on the page as one writes. Quink was introduced in 1931, and the name was entered in the *Trade Marks Journal* of July 13, 1932.

Quintero *(cigars)*

The make of Cuban cigar dates from the mid-1920s, when Augustin Quintero and his four brothers started a small cigar workshop in the southern coastal city of Cienfuegos. By 1940 they had gained a suffciently wide reputation to open in Havana and introduce the brand bearing their family name.

Quonset *(prefabricated building)*

The prefabricated building, made of metal and having a semicircular cross section, takes its name from Quonset Point, Rhode Island, where a Naval Air Station was located in World War II. The name was entered by the Great Lakes Steel Corporation, of Wilmington, Delaware, in the US Patent Office *Official Gazette* of November 19, 1946: "For readily erectable buildings, knock-down buildings, portable buildings, and prefabricated buildings," with a claim of use since September 1941. The British equivalent, although not a proprietary name, is the Nissen hut, designed by Colonel Peter N. Nissen (1871-1930) and dating from World War I.

Quorn *(vegetable protein)*

The type of textured vegetable protein, made from an edible fungus and used as a meat substitute in cooking, takes its name from its original British manufacturers in 1984, Quorn Specialities Ltd., of Leicester, whose own name

came from the village of Quorn (or Quorndon), Leicestershire, famous for its hunt. (There is a nice irony in the adoption of a name linked with a blood sport for a vegetarian food, but the firm originally produced baking powder, cake mixes, jellies, and the like, where the aristocratic association would have purely implied quality. On the other hand, the etymological connection of the placename with "quern," a rudimentary mill for grinding corn, is more favorable, albeit for an ersatz foodstuff rather than a natural cereal product.) The name was entered by Marlow Foods, Ltd., of Middlesbrough, in the *Trade Marks Journal* of October 2, 1988.

Quosh *(fruit drink)*

The name is based on "squash" (to which the dictionary word "quash" is linguistically related). The drink is made by the British firm of H.W. Carter & Co., acquired by **Beecham** in 1955.

R. Whites *(carbonated fruit drinks)*

The British firm, famous for its sparkling lemonade, was founded in 1845 by Robert and Mary White, who sold home-brewed ginger beer from a barrow in Camberwell, then a village just outside London. The brand was popularized by a series of TV ads from 1973 starring a "secret lemonade drinker."

R. J. Reynolds *(tobacco)*

R.J. Reynolds Tobacco is strictly speaking a division of the parent company R.J. Reynolds Industries (known familiarly as RJR), although it is cigarettes for which the firm is best known. The name behind the business is that of the founder of the Reynolds empire, Richard Joshua Reynolds (1850-1918), born at "Rock Spring," the family estate near Critz, Virginia, the son of a farmer and tobacco merchant. As a boy Reynolds attended local country schools and worked on his father's farm. He entered Emory and Henry College in Emory, Virginia, in 1868, only to drop out two years later in order to work fulltime in his father's manufacturing concern. While later attending Bryant and Stratton Business College in Baltimore, Maryland, in 1873, he gained additional experience by soliciting orders for his father's factory in his spare time. In 1874, ever restless, he borrowed money from his family to open a tobacco factory in Winston-Salem, North Carolina. His new location not only provided railroad connections but was physically closer to the "Old Bright" tobacco belt of North Carolina. By 1887 Reynolds was marketing 86 brands of chewing tobacco. In 1911 he began the move from chewing tobacco to smoking tobacco, and it was then, just before World War I, that he introduced his famous **Camel** cigarettes, America's first national cigarette brand. Reynolds' nephew, Richard S. Reynolds, went his own way after his uncle's death and set up **Reynolds Aluminum**. In 1985 R.J. Reynolds Industries merged with **Nabisco** to form RJR-Nabisco, but was sold off from the cookie company in 1999.

R. R. Bowker *(publishers)*

Richard Rogers Bowker (1848-1933) was born in Salem, Massachusetts, the son of a manufacturer of barrel machinery. In 1857 he moved with his parents to New York City, where he attended the College of the City of New York, becoming editor of *The Collegian*, one of the country's first collegiate publications. On graduating with a B.A. in 1868, Bowker became the city editor of the *New York Evening Mail*, and soon after literary editor. Having developed a special interest in libraries, in 1876 he founded the *Library Journal*, and that same year helped to found the American Library Association. In 1879 he purchased *Publishers Weekly*, taking editorial control in 1884. Bowker was not simply a publisher, but a broader businessman. From 1890 to 1899 he was first vice president of the Edison Electric Illuminating Company (*see* **Ediswan**) in Brooklyn, and from 1902 to 1931 vice president of the De Laval Separator Company (*see* **Alfa-Laval**). In 1911 Bowker's interests in publishing and industry combined when his publishing business was incorporated as the R.R. Bowker Company.

Racal *(radio communications)*

The British company was founded in 1951 and takes its name from two of its original founders, *Ra*ymond Brown (1920-1991), head of defense sales for four years from 1966, and G. *Cal*der Cunningham (d.1958). Also present from the beginning was Ernest Harrison, who became chairman in 1966, developing Racal into a leading electronics company. In 1984

Racal acquired **Chubb** and the following year launched **Vodafone**. The cellular radio side of the business was floated in 1988 as the separate company Racal Telecom.

Racasan *(toilet cleansers)*

The founder of the British manufacturing company was Robert Alan Chandler, whose initials gave the first part of the name. Its original product was "Sanitary Fluid," whose "San-" gave the last part. The firm ceased trading in 1977, and its employees were taken over by Odex Ltd. The name "Racasan Blue-Flush" was entered in the *Trade Marks Journal* of October 5, 1966.

Radox *(bath powder and liquid)*

The product first appeared on the British market in the 1920s as a foot bath that supposedly "*rad*iated *ox*ygen," and the name was entered in the *Trade Marks Journal* of November 28, 1923 for: "Bath salts for medicinal purposes." In 1957 the name was transferred to a bath powder.

Rael-Brook *(menswear)*

The name is directly that of the one of the British manufacturer's original owners, Harry Rael-Brook. He was born Harold Seabrook, and worked in partnership with Mrs. R.R. Israel as I. Israel & Sons, when he pioneered the drip-dry shirt. In 1955, together with Mrs. Israel's son, Hyman Usher Israel, he changed his name to Rael-Brook (Rael from "Israel" and Brook from "Seabrook"). His company Mr Harry specializes in men's suits.

Rafael Gonzales *(cigars)*

The box of this brand of Havana cigars, originally created for the English market, has the following text to explain the name and the manufacturer's recommendation for use: "These cigars have been manufactured from a secret blend of pure Vuelta Abajo tobacco selected by the Marquez Rafael Gonzalez, Grandee of Spain. For more than 20 years this brand has existed. In order that the Connoisseur may fully appreciate the perfect fragrance they should be smoked either within one month of the date of shipment from Havana or should be carefully matured for about one year." The brand is actually made in the **Romeo and Juliet** factory.

Ragú *(spaghetti sauce)*

The Italian sauce owes its origin to Giovanni Cantisano and his wife Assunta, who left their native Italy for America in the early 20th century. As the couple stepped ashore at New York, they had no idea that the old family recipe for spaghetti sauce they brought with them would form the basis of an enterprise that would eventually become a multimillion dollar business and a household name in kitchens across the USA. The first batch of Ragú (Italian *ragù*, "ragout") was made by the Cantisanos in 1937 in the kitchen of their home in Rochester, New York. They sold the sauce to friends, then door-to-door in the neighborhood. Gradually sales increased and eventually the sauce was so popular that their small operation could not cope with the demand. The Cantisanos accordingly set up the Ragú Packing Company in 1946 to manufacture and distribute the sauce, and distribution quickly expanded through the northeast of the USA. In 1969 the firm was acquired by **Chesebrough-Pond's,** who immediately set about expanding distribution across the USA. By the mid-1970s, Ragú became the first spaghetti sauce to be available in grocery stores nationally.

Railton *(automobiles)*

The name is that of the British racing-car designer Reid Railton (1895-1977), although his contribution was minimal to the firm founded by Noel C. Macklin and L.A.Cushman in Cobham, Surrey, in 1933. The last Railton car was manufactured in 1948. Macklin was earlier responsible for the **Invicta.**

Rajan *(fashionwear)*

The Manchester, England, fashion business is run by Rajan Kumar (b.1962) and is named for him. It was founded in 1967 by his father, Lal, a former market trader. Rajan joined the business in 1981, and his brother, Sanjay, followed ten years later.

Raleigh *(bicycles)*

The name of the make of bicycle is not a personal one, but that of the street in Nottingham, England, where a small shop made bicycles in the 1880s. The actual founder of the company was Frank Bowden (1847-1921). Returning in poor health to England from the Far East in 1886, Bowden had been recommended to take up cycling to improve his fitness. Walking along a London street, he saw a bicycle with a "Raleigh" label. He tracked the machine to its source, the small bicycle business of Woodhead & Angois, in Raleigh Street, Nottingham, and bought one of the models, impressed by its superior design. He rode it on tours in both England and on the European Continent, as a result of which his health improved considerably. He felt that the bicycle could serve well for both leisure and health purposes. In 1887, therefore, he bought the business, renaming it the Raleigh Cycle Company, financing it and controlling it himself. This was thus the launch of the company, with a factory soon built in Nottingham to make the machines. The suggestion of "rally" in the name was a later bonus.

Ralph Lauren *(fashionwear)*

Born Ralph Lipschitz in the Bronx, New York City, Ralph Lauren (b.1939) worked at **Brooks Brothers** and elsewhere while attending nightschool in business studies at City College, New York. In 1967 he joined Beau Brummell Neckwear, where he created the Polo range for men, then in 1971 turned his attention to womenswear. The "Ralph Lauren" label was launched the following year with a complete range of garments for women, and his styles subsequently became famous as the so-called "prairie look" and "frontier fashions."

Ralston Purina *(pet foods and animal feeds)*

The American company was the enterprise of William Henry Danforth (1870-1952), born in Charleston, Missouri, the son of a general store proprietor and bank president. At age 14 he was sent to live alone and attend the Manual Training School in St. Louis, Missouri, but was soon invited to stay with the family of a classmate, with whom he remained until his graduation in 1887. He enrolled in Washington University in St. Louis, where from 1887 to 1892 he majored in engineering. After an unsatisfactory spell as a salesman for a brick company, where work was both seasonal and dependent on the economy, he was told by his father to "get into a business that fills a need for lots of people, something they need all year around in good times and bad." Danforth's response was to open a feed business near the St. Louis levee in 1894, reasoning that horses had to eat daily whatever the economic climate. He bought grains from farmers, mixed them into sacks, then sold them back to farmers as feed for their horses and mules. The feed itself was a blend of crushed oats and cracked corn that horses found more digestible than the ordinary grain normally used, and Danforth soon added special mixes for pigs, poultry, and cows. He called the product "Purina Feed" to emphasize the purity of the ingredients. In 1898 the company expanded into the breakfast cereal business. Hence the first word of the name, that of Dr. Everett Ralston, born Albert W. Edgerly, who ran a leading health club in St. Louis. When Danforth asked him to approve a new wheat cereal, he agreed to do so on condition that his name be included in that of the company. Thus in 1902 the Ralston-Purina Company was formed, and went on to manufacture not only pet food and grocery products, but a range of goods that included batteries and ice hockey equipment. From the late 1980s Ralston Purina underwent a gradual dismantling, and in 2000 the company was acquired by **Nestlé** to become Nestlé Ralston Petcare.

Ramon Allones *(cigars)*

The brand dates from 1837 and bears the name of Ramón Allones, who emigrated to Cuba from Galicia, in Spain, and who was the first man to put colorful printed labels on his cigar boxes. The name was entered for "Havana cigars and Havana cigarettes" by Allones Ltd., of London, England, in the *Trade Marks Journal* of January 22, 1913. The cigars themselves are rolled in the **Partagas** factory.

Rand McNally *(publishers)*

The American publishing house, specializing in maps, atlases, globes, and tourist guides, and the oldest firm of its kind in the country, was founded in 1856 by William H. Rand and Andrew McNally and incorporated in 1873. Its headquarters are in Skokie, Illinois.

Random House *(publishers)*

The American publishing firm was founded in New York in 1927 by Bennett Cerf (1898-1971) and Donald S. Klopfer (1902-86), owners of the Modern Library, to publish their own luxury editions "at random." Hence the name. When they told their artist friend Rockwell Kent about it, he immediately sketched a logo in the form of a "random house," half-cottage and half-mansion. The name and the logo have now stayed unchanged for three-quarters of a century. In 1998 Random House was acquired by the German publishers **Bertelsmann**.

Range Rover *(cross-country and road vehicle)*

The vehicle was first produced in 1970 and was designed by Maurice Wilks, who also originated the **Land-Rover.** Its name was actually based on the latter and reflects the essential design of the vehicle, enabling it to have cross-country ability ("range") while basically being suitable for road use. When still in the planning stage in the late 1950s it was called the "Road Rover."

Rank *(food, films, and copying equipment)*

The name is currently represented by three leading British companies: The Rank Organization, Rank **Hovis McDougall** (RHM), and Rank-**Xerox**. It is ultimately that of Joseph Rank (1854-1943), born in Hull, Yorkshire, a miller's son. He began working in the mill himself at the age of 14, and could well have taken over the business when his father died in 1874. Instead, Rank set up on his own, leasing a small windmill in Hull. In 1885 he had made enough money to build his own mill, after which his business expanded steadily, with new markets for his flour gained in all parts of the country. By the time of his death, Joseph Rank's business was the largest milling concern in Britain. This milling activity was the germ from which grew today's RHM. Rank's third son was Joseph Arthur Rank (1888-1972), the J. Arthur Rank of the film industry (with the "man with the gong" as his symbol). He acquired bakery businesses all over the world, and in 1962 took over Hovis McDougall to form Rank Hovis McDougall. The Rank Organization had meanwhile been formed in 1953, and three years later joined the **Xerox** Corporation of the USA to form Rank-Xerox, marketing copying and related equipment outside the Americas.

Ransome *(mowers)*

The British company takes its name from Robert Ransome (1753-1830), born a Quaker schoolmaster's son in Wells, Norfolk. He was apprenticed to an ironmonger in Norwich, and soon after completing his term started up an iron foundry with a partner, a Mr. Gurney. In 1785 he took out a patent for tempering cast-iron plowshares, but four years later moved to Ipswich, Suffolk, to start another foundry. Here he perfected the cast-iron plowshare, which would remain sharp in use, unlike the former standard wrought-iron share. It is believed that one Edward Budding made the world's first lawnmower in 1830, and two years later Ransome's firm started manufacturing it under license, extending its range to include horse-drawn mowers in 1870 and gasoline-driven machines in 1902. Today Ransome makes not just mowers but a wide range of agricultural and horticultural machinery.

Raphael Tuck *(greeting cards)*

Raphael Tuck (1821-1900) was a German who became a British subject in 1875. He began his career as a London furniture dealer, but in 1866 started up a printing business in the City of London, specializing in color lithographs. Four years later he started producing Christmas cards, which soon became widely popular. In 1879 he won first prize in a Christmas cards exhibition, when one of the judges was the painter Sir John Millais. After moves to different locations in London, his firm eventually made its base at Raphael House, Moorfields, with the foundation stone of the new premises laid in 1896 by Tuck himself. Since then, the business has moved out of London, and in about 1970 was acquired by Fine Art Developments, of Burton-on-Trent. Today Raphael Tuck postcards are as familiar as the firm's original greeting cards.

Ratners *(jewelers and watchmakers)*

The British company owes its origins to Leslie Ratner, the son of a watchmender in St. Albans, Hertfordshire. After army service in India in World War II, Ratner returned to England in 1947 with a young Indian wife and £120 in the pocket of his "demob" suit. Two years later he opened a small jeweler's shop in George Street, Richmond, Surrey, following it with another in Hammersmith, London, a year or two later. He gradually built up a chain of around 100 shops, which were taken over in 1984 by his son, Gerald Ratner (b.1949), who soon increased their number to the hundreds of stores that exist today in the UK and elsewhere in the world, including over 300 in the United States. Gerald Ratner went on to acquire several similar chains, the most prestigious being that of **H. Samuel**, and in 1988 he opened his 1,000th store. Ratner resigned in 1992 under pressure from shareholders, following a controversial speech in which he jokingly referred to his firm's products as "total crap," and the now legendary gaffe so tarnished the company's image that the following year it renamed itself as Signet.

Ratrac *(snow tractors)*

The Ratrac, a tracked vehicle used to impact the surface of a ski run, was a Swiss invention of the 1960s. The vehicle itself is what is known in German as a *Raupenfahrzeug*, "caterpillar tractor," from *Raupe*, "caterpillar," and the name presumably blends the first two letters of this with the first part of English "tractor." (*Cp.* **Caterpillar**.) The name was entered, originally as "RATRAC," in the *Schweizerisches Patent-, Muster- und Marken-Blatt* of November 28, 1969 and the US Patent Office *Official Gazette* of April 22, 1986, with a note of first use in 1973.

Raudixin *(hypotensive preparation)*

The drug to treat hypertension contains the dried root of the tropical shrub *Rauvolfia serpentina*, named after the German botanist Leonhard Rauwolf (d.1596). Hence the first part of the name, to which "-dixin," of uncertain origin, has been added. The name was entered by E.R. **Squibb** and Sons Ltd. in the *Trade Marks Journal* of September 9, 1953, and by the Mathieson Chemical Corporation, New York, in the US Patent Office *Official Gazette* of November 10, 1953. *Cp.* **Rauwiloid**.

Rauwiloid *(hypotensive tablets)*

The drug to treat hypertension contains a number of alkaloids extracted from the tropical shrub *Rauvolfia serpentina* (*see* **Raudixin**). Hence its name, entered by Riker Laboratories, of Los Angeles, in the *Trade Marks Journal* of July 15, 1953. A subsequent registration in the US Patent Office *Official Gazette* of October 13, 1953, claimed use since October 28, 1952. The drug's generic name is alseroxylon.

Rawlplug *(wall fixing device)*

The thin cylindrical fiber or plastic plug, inserted into a hole in masonry to hold a nail or screw, was invented in the years before World War I, when a British architect made strict specifications for a new building, saying that the old "wooden wedge between the bricks" was not good enough to serve as a fixing device in the walls. London building contractor John Joseph Rawlings thus came up with a brass plug in the shape of a cross, and this was the prototype Rawlplug. He later experimented with plugs made from other materials, and eventually evolved a fiber plug, made of jute bonded with animal blood. Its name was entered by "Rawlings Bros., Limited, 82, Gloucester Road, London, S.W.; Electrical engineers" in the *Trade Marks Journal* of October 30, 1912 for: "A wall plug for electric wiring made of fibre." The war then intervened, and the plug was first marketed only in 1919, with the entire front page of the *Daily Mail* taken to advertise it and to list all of the shops where it could be bought. The closeness of "Rawl-" to "wall" served as an apt reminder of the purpose of the plug, but "Rawl" was subsequently entered in the *Journal* of September 29, 1937 as a prefix for other tools, such as "Rawlbolt" and "Rawltool" itself. In the 1960s plastics began to replace fiber as the manufacturing medium for the plugs. The company was acquired by **Burmah Oil** in 1968 and in 2001 the group was sold to the construction firm BPB.

Ray-Ban *(sunglasses)*

The designer sunglasses were originally devised by **Bausch & Lomb** in the late 1920s as antiglare goggles for the US Army Corps to help deflect the sun's rays from pilots' eyes. The lenses became available to the public in 1936 and the following year they were rebranded as "Ray-Ban," a name entered in the *Trade Marks Journal* of June 7, 1967. In the late 1990s Bausch & Lomb sold its sunglass business to **Luxottica** and instead turned to making contact lenses, eyedrops, and surgical lasers.

Rayburn *(cookers)*

The name of the Rayburn, the "little sister" of the **Aga**, was apparently created by Walter Thomas Wren (1902-1971), managing director of Allied Ironfounders Ltd., who first manufactured the British cooker. He took it from an American friend, a Mr. Rayburn, whose name he felt was doubly appropriate for an appliance that both cooked the food and warmed the

kitchen. The name was entered in the *Trade Marks Journal* of August 6, 1952 for: "Cooking or heating stoves, and boilers (not being parts of machines), and parts of and fittings for all such apparatus included in Class 11."

Raynes *(footwear and handbags)*

The full name of the British company is H. & M. Rayne Ltd., referring to the founder, Henry Rayne (1860-1915), and his wife Mary. The firm has its origins in the shop opened by Henry Rayne in Waterloo Road, London, in about 1885, where he sold equipment and accessories for the theatrical business, such as ballet shoes and stage props. This side of the undertaking then faded out, with a more general emphasis on footwear and, subsequently, handbags. The firm was sold off in 1987.

Raytheon *(electronic systems and appliances)*

The American company was founded in 1922 by two former college roommates, Laurence K. Marshall and Vannevar Bush, together with a young scientist, Charles G. Smith, in order to make electrical parts. They called their enterprise the American Appliance Company, but were soon obliged to change this when an Indiana company showed that it held prior claim to the name. They accordingly adopted the name "Raytheon," that of a new type of radio tube, technically a gaseous rectifier, launched in 1925. Its own name combined Old French *rai*, "ray," and Greek *theōn*, "of the gods," which was regarded as apt for its power and performance and thus equally appropriate for the growing company.

RCA *(electronics and broadcasting)*

The RCA Corporation was founded by the General Electric Company in 1919 as the Radio Corporation of America to acquire the Marconi Wireless Telegraph Company of America, formed in 1899 by the Italian "father of radio," Guglielmo Marconi (1874-1937), who earlier that year in London, England, had set up the Wireless, Telegraph and Signal Company (from 1900 Marconi Wireless, Telegraph and Signal Company). In 1929 RCA acquired the Victor Talking Machine Co. (*see* **Victrola**) and began manufacturing radios and phonographs in Camden, New Jersey. RCA adopted its abbreviated name in 1969 and in 1986 was acquired by General Electric, who in 1987 sold it to Thomson CSF (*see* **Thales**). *See also* **Cable and Wireless**.

RCS Editori *(publishers)*

The Italian company goes back to the publishing and printing business founded in 1929 by the Arte della Stampa ("Printing Guild") as Rizzoli and Co., taking its name from the printing firm set up by the publisher and film producer Angelo Rizzoli (1889-1970) in Milan in 1909. (He produced the *Don Camillo* series of the 1950s as well as movies by Rossellini, De Sica, and Fellini.) In 1974 the company gained complete control of the *Corriere della Sera* newspaper. In 1982 Rizzoli and the newspaper ownership called in the receivers, but were rescued by the financial group Gemina, who in 1985 acquired a majority shareholding. In 1986 the company was restructured and assumed its present name, which thus represents the initials of Rizzoli and the *Corriere della Sera*.

REA Express *(ground and air express services)*

The American company was established in 1918 by the US government as the American Railway Express Company, at the same time as it took over the nation's railroads. The domestic express businesses and property of the country's major express carriers, Adams & Company, founded in 1842, **American Express**, founded in 1850, **Wells, Fargo**, founded in 1852, and Southern Express Company, founded in 1861, were expropriated and merged into a single corporation. In 1928, 86 of the nations railroads joined in setting up the Railway Express Agency, which bought the American Railway Express Company and gave it its own name. In 1970 the name was further changed to REA Express, Inc., but following drastic financial losses the company was declared bankrupt in 1975.

Reader's Digest *(publishers)*

Both the familiar monthly magazine and the publishers who produce it owe their origin to DeWitt Wallace (1889-1981), born in St. Paul, Minnesota, the son of an educator. On graduation from high school, Wallace enrolled at Macalester College, a Presbyterian institution where his father was president. His first job was in banking, where he spent his spare time reading widely in current publications, taking notes on anything that interested him. He then worked for a small publisher in St. Paul, and produced a publication of his own, *Getting the Most out of Farming*. Wallace served in the army in World War I but was wounded in France. While recuperating in hospital, he had plenty of time to collect interesting articles from different magazines. He knew that a periodical containing a selection of condensed versions of such articles would find a popular market, and in 1920 put together a prototype. Two years later, Wallace's experience and experiments led to the publication of the first issue of *Reader's Digest* in February 1922, with an initial circulation of 5,000. In 1950, DeWitt Wallace and his wife Lila Acheson, who had shared her husband's enthusiasm from the beginning, started the Condensed Book Club, and this was soon followed by other publishing projects.

Realtor *(real-estate agent)*

The name, from "realty" and the agent suffix "-or," was entered as a "service mark" by the National Association of Real Estate Boards, Chicago, in the US Patent Office *Official Gazette* of September 14, 1948: "For services in connection with the brokerage of real estate," with a claim of use since March 31, 1916. The term was originally introduced by C.N. Chadbourn in the *National Real Estate Journal* of March 15, 1916, as a professional title for members of the National Association of Real Estate Boards (now the National Association of Realtors). The UK equivalent of the realtor is the estate agent.

Rebel Yell *(whiskey)*

William Weller began making bourbon in Louisville, Kentucky, in 1849. He named his whiskey for the "rebel yell" of attacking Confederate troops in the Civil War. The blend long remained a local brand, not even sold north of the Mason-Dixon Line.

Reckitt *(starch)*

Commonly coupled with **Colman**, the name is that of Isaac Reeves Reckitt (1792-1862), a corn factor of Nottingham, England, who went to Hull, Yorkshire, in 1840 and rented a small starch factory in Dansom Lane. At first business was slow, and at one stage Reckitt even took up stockbroking so as to have a second iron in the fire. But thanks to the efforts of his sons, George and Francis, who went out "on the road" selling starch to grocers, his venture ultimately met with success. After Isaac Reckitt's death, the concern was run as a partnership by his sons, eventually being incorporated as Reckitt & Sons in 1879. The long familiar "Reckitt's blue" (the washing blue used in laundries) was not added to the production line until the 1850s, and the *Trade Marks Journal* of February 19, 1877, records that "Reckitt's Blue in squares will be found far more beautiful & much more economical than any other." The entry was made by "Francis Reckitt, of Hull, Yorkshire, on behalf of self and partner, James Reckitt, trading as I. Reckitt & Sons, at ... London, and as Isaac Reckitt and Sons, at Hull, Yorkshire." James Reckitt (1833-1924) was knighted in 1894 and paints himself in *Who's Who* in glowing colors: "Chiefly known from his long and prosperous business career, his interest in most philanthropic and educational work, his gifts of new library, orphan home, convalescent home, new wing to Royal Infirmary, and other gifts to Hull." In 1921 Reckitt and Colman combined their overseas operations and in 1938 created Reckitt & Colman, although it was not until 1954 that the two merged into a single company. "Reckitt's Blue Bag" was entered by "Reckitt & Colman Products Limited, trading as Reckitt & Colman" in the *Journal* of December 1, 1976 for: "Laundry blue for sale in the United Kingdom and for export to the Irish Republic." In 1999 Reckitt & Colman merged with the Dutch household products company Benckiser, founded in 1823, to form Reckitt Benckiser, ranking as the world's number one homecare products supplier.

Recordak *(photographic recording apparatus)*

The type of camera was first launched by **Kodak** in the 1920s as a way of making a photographic record of a series of documents, such as all the checks that pass through a bank. Hence its name from a blend of "record" and "Kodak," entered in the US Patent Office *Official Gazette* of March 31, 1937.

Red Barrel *(beer)*

The brand of English beer, technically a "keg bitter," was introduced by **Watneys** in 1930 and took its name from the firm's "Red Barrel" trademark, itself on the lines of **Bass**'s distinctive "Red Triangle."

Red Bull *(energy drink)*

The product owes its origin to Dieterich Mateschitz (b.1946), an Austrian entrepreneur who when in Thailand on business in the early 1980s stumbled on a health tonic drunk by tuk-tuk drivers, who travel at breakneck speed around Bangkok. After buying a batch of the tonic to fuel his business trips, he realized he had found a very special product, and launched his company in Austria in 1984. The name seems to suggest the sudden surge of power caused by a "red rag to a bull," but the story goes that the original Thai drink was called "Cretin Daeng," meaning something like "red bull-like animal that roams the forest," and that the English name is a simplified version of this. However, the drink contains taurine, which derives its name from Greek *tauros*, "bull," and this may equally play a part.

Reebok *(sportswear)*

Although now based in Massachusetts, the Reebok name and brand originated in England, where in 1895, the athlete Joseph Foster (d.1961) of Bolton, Lancashire, made himself a pair of the first spiked running shoes. He was soon making them for others, and set up the firm of J.W. Foster & Sons for the purpose. The company expanded its line to the manufacture of football and rugby boots, so that by the 1940s many leading English football clubs wore the make. In 1958, Joseph Foster's grandsons Joseph and Jeffrey broke away from the family business and set up their own company, naming it after the reebok, a South African antelope, and a few years later took over the family firm. In 1979 the US sporting goods distributor Paul Fireman negotiated an American license for the brand, backed by the UK firm Pentland. In 1986 US Reebok absorbed the British Reebok, buying out Pentland in 1991.

Reed *(paper)*

The founder of Reed International plc was Albert Edwin Reed (1846-1920), born in Cullompton, Devon, the son of an excise officer, an occupation that caused the family to make many moves in the English West Country. At the age of 13, Reed was apprenticed to a builder in Torquay, but soon had to give this up because of ill health. A year later he was employed as a junior clerk at Lower Wookey paper mill (now St. Cuthbert's), where he rose to be manager in 1867. He went on to be appointed manager of the Trevarno mill (now Bathgate) at Bathford, near Bath, and eventually in 1877 of the larger mill at Ely, Cardiff, making newsprint, printings, and wrappings. He acquired further mills at Dartford and Maidstone in Kent and in 1894 founded the private company of Albert E. Reed & Co. Reed was now established as one of the most experienced producers of newsprint and printing paper in Britain, and he gained the name of "Wizard of the South" for his knack of buying derelict mills and converting them into profitable ones. The parent company became Reed International Ltd. in 1970 and in 1993 merged with the Dutch publisher **Elsevier** to become Reed-Elsevier.

Reed *(publishers)*

The New Zealand publishing house takes its name from English-born Alfred Hamish Reed (1875-1975), who arrived in New Zealand in 1887 to start work digging for kauri gum, found in fossilized form where kauri trees formerly grew and used as a varnish. He taught himself shorthand, and in 1897 became manager of a typewriter firm in Dunedin. He then turned to bookselling, and in 1907 set up the firm that became A.H. & A.W. Reed, the latter initials being those of his nephew, Alexander Wyclif Reed, born in 1908. Both men were prolific authors, mainly of historical books for young readers. The company was extended to Sydney, Australia, in 1963.

Reed, Austin *see* **Austin Reed**

Reese's *("Peanut Butter Cup")*

Harry B. Reese (1879-1956) worked at a variety of menial jobs for the first part of his adult life. In 1917 he moved to Hershey, Pennsylvania, to manage one of the dairy farms owned by the famous confectioner Milton **Hershey**. Soon after, Reese decided to launch his own candy company. He relocated to nearby Hummelstown and began making "Lizzie Bars," a caramel-like confection that met with only moderate success. He thus returned to Hershey, and in 1923 acquired a plant on Chocolate Avenue, where he produced a new candy consisting of specially processed peanut butter

covered with milk chocolate. He called his creation a "peanut butter cup," and initially sold it in five-pound boxes. He introduced individual penny sizes of the candy in the 1930s, and soon his factory dropped all other products to concentrate on the highly popular "Reese's Peanut Butter Cup." In 1963 Reese's company, then run by his descendants, was purchased by **Hershey** itself.

Reeves *(artists' materials)*

Thomas Reeves (1708-1741) was born in Hertford, England, the son of a local tailor. When his father paid a visit to London in 1720 to obtain some samples of better quality cloth, young Thomas went too, and vowed that he would one day work in London. His first job, however, was in his father's shop. In 1723 his chance came when he was apprenticed to his uncle, John Reeves, a London blacksmith and wrought-iron craftsman. In due course Thomas set up his own workshop, having married in 1738. Sadly, he died when still only 33, leaving his wife to raise their two small sons, the elder of whom, also named Thomas, was born in 1736 and the younger, William, in 1739. William was apprenticed to a goldsmith, but soon left to work independently. He obtained a post with a firm that supplied canvases and material for theatrical scenery, where he enjoyed expressing his "artistic temperament." He devised a way of making blocks or cakes of paint that would not crack or dry up, and felt he could make a living selling these to the public. Accordingly, in 1766 he bought a shop in Little Britain, an old winding street in the City of London, and was soon making up and selling his own paints there, adding paint boxes and brushes in due course. The company's founding thus dates from this year.

Regulo *(thermostatic control)*

The thermostatic control for domestic gas ovens, typically followed by a number to indicate heat settings, as "Regulo 7," derives its name from Latin *regulo*, "I regulate." It was entered by Radiation Ltd., of Birmingham, England, in the *Trade Marks Journal* of November 29, 1922.

Reliant *(automobiles)*

The three-wheeled British cars had their beginnings in the Reliant Motor Company, set up in 1935 by T.L. Williams in a workshop in his garden at Tamworth, Staffordshire, to take over production of the Raleigh Cycle three-wheeler van. The first passenger tricar was the Regal, launched in 1953, and this was succeeded in 1961 by a four-wheel sports car, the Sabre. The highly popular Reliant Robin three-wheeler superseded it in 1972 and soon found favour for its cheap road tax and the fact that it could be driven on a motorcycle licence. The "wobbly wheelbarrow" or "yellow wedge," as it was affectionately known, ceased to be produced in 2000.

Remington *(small arms, typewriters, and electric shavers)*

The familiar American name is that of Eliphalet Remington (1793-1861), born a blacksmith's son in Suffield, Connecticut. When he was seven, his family moved to Utica, New York, where his father built a smithy and forge powered by a waterwheel. In 1816 Remington constructed a flintlock rifle in his father's forge. It fired well and accurately, and led to orders for similar guns. Before long, the main business of the Remingtons was manufacturing sports guns and rifle barrels. In 1828 Remington built a large factory by the Erie Canal where the town of Ilion now is, and together with his son, Philo Remington (1816-1889), eventually founded the Remington Arms Company. Philo supervised his father's small arms factory after his death, and in 1873 invented the breech-loading rifle, still known as the Remington today. The following year he put the first commercially produced typewriter on the market. This was a model developed by Christopher L. Sholes (1819-1890), originally produced two years earlier. When Philo Remington first sold it, it was known as the "Sholes & Glidden Typewriter," Carlos Glidden being one of Sholes' assistants. In 1876, it was renamed the "Remington No. 1." It was a cumbersome machine, with all type in uppercase, but in 1878 the improved "Remington No. 2" appeared, as the first typewriter to offer both upper and lowercase type. In 1902 the Standard Typewriter Manufacturing Company became the Remington Typewriter Company, which in 1927 merged with the Rand Kardex Company to become Remington Rand, making office equipment. In 1936, under Remington Rand's vice chairman, Harry Landsiedel, the Remington Electric Shaver division was formed, introducing its first electric dry shaver the following year. In 1955, Remington Rand merged with the Sperry Corporation to become **Sperry Rand**. In 1993 Remington acquired **Clairol**'s personal care appliance business. The Standard Manufacturing Typewriter Company entered "The word 'Remington'" ("used since 1880") for "type-writing machines" in the US Patent Office *Official Gazette* of October 23, 1888, and the name was subsequently entered (now "used ten years") by the Remington Arms Company in the *Gazette* of December 4, 1906 for "Shotguns, Pistols, Revolvers, and Rifles," and by the Remington Typewriter Company in the *Trade Marks Journal* of May 19, 1926 for: "Typewriters, accounting typewriters and portable typewriters and accessories."

Remploy *(furniture and knitwear)*

The British firm of Remploy Ltd. was founded in 1945 as the Disabled Persons Employment Corporation Ltd. following the 1944 Disabled Persons (Employment) Act. The aim was to offer regular employment to the mentally or physically disabled. The first Remploy factory opened in Bridgend, South Wales, in 1946, where workers were engaged in light engineering and the manufacture of furniture and violins. The company adopted its present name (from "re-employ") in 1949 and today its employees work under contract for many of the leading names in British industry.

Rémy Martin *(brandy)*

The name is that of the French vine-grower who founded the cognac house in 1724. A document of 1738, issued in La Rochelle, France, authorizes Monsieur Rémy Martin to replant his vineyards, showing that even at that early date there was official control over wine growers and their business. The firm was virtually dormant when taken over in 1924, exactly 200 years later, by André Renaud, a local vine grower who had married into the Frapin family, owners of large estates in the Champagne districts of the Cognac region. The name, also spelled without the accent, was entered in the US Patent Office *Official Gazette* of February 26, 1963, with a note of first use in 1884, and by "E. Remy Martin and Co." in the *Trade Marks Journal* of April 14, 1976. Rémy Martin has now joined forces with **Cointreau** as Rémy-Cointreau.

Renault *(automobiles)*

Louis Renault (1877-1944), the fourth son of a wealthy Parisian button manufacturer, was as mechanically minded as his brothers, and it was with two of them, Fernand and Marcel, that he established the firm of Renault Frères at Billancourt, Paris, in 1898, the same year that he completed his first shaft-drive prototype voiturette. The following year the Renault brothers began racing, with Marcel becoming the toast of France when he won the Paris Vienna race in 1902. After Louis Renault's death, his company was nationalized. It kept its name, however, as a tribute to one of Europe's best-known automotive industry pioneers. The direct-drive transmission invented by Louis Renault is still basically the type used today. Sadly, he ended his days in prison, accused of collaboration with the Nazis. A planned merger in 1994 between Renault and **Volvo** came to nothing.

Rennies *(antacid tablets)*

The name is that of the British inventor of the tablets, a Yorkshireman called John Rennie. For some reason Rennie had chosen France as his sole marketing area, hence the French wording "Digestif Rennie" on the packets. The tablets thmeslves contain calcium carbonate with magnesium carbonate. The name was entered in the *Trade Marks Journal* of January 29, 1964 for: "Medicated preparations for human use in the treatment of indigestion acidity and similar digestive ailments."

Rentokil *(pest control and timber preservation)*

The British name started out as "Entokil," deriving from Greek *entoma*, "insects," and English "kill." "Entokil Fluids" was thus the name given in the 1920s by Harold Maxwell-Lefroy (1877-1925), professor of entomology at Imperial College, London, to bottles of solution designed by him to exterminate the deathwatch beetle then prevalent in Westminster Great Hall. When application was made to register the name, however, permission was refused, as a similar name already existed. An initial "R" was thus added to produce "Rentokil," fortuitously suggesting "rent-to-kill." The name was entered in the *Trade Marks Journal* of November 12, 1924, and the company was formed in 1927 by a Dane named Anker-Petersen who had come to England to market rat poison.

Resochin *(antimalarial drug)*

The proprietary name for chloroquine derives from a blend of German *Resorcinol*, "resorcinol," and *Chinolin*, "quinoline." It was entered by **Bayer** in the *Trade Marks Journal* of December 12, 1951, and the US Patent Office *Official Gazette* of July 19, 1955.

Reuter *(news agency)*

The British news agency was founded in 1851 by Paul Julius Reuter (1816-1899), born Israel Beer Josaphat of Jewish parentage in Kassel, Germany. He began his career as a clerk in his uncle's bank in Göttingen, then in the early 1840s joined a small publishing concern in Berlin. He became a Christian in 1844, adopting a new name, and in 1848 moved to Paris, where he began translating extracts from articles and commercial news and sending them to newspapers in Germany. In 1850 he set up a carrier-pigeon service between Aachen and Brussels. Moving to London, England, in 1851, Reuter opened a telegraph office near the Stock Exchange, and two years later launched Reuter's Telegram Company. The former year is now regarded as that of the founding of one of the world's leading news services.

Revco *(discount drugstores)*

The present company originated from a conventional drugstore in Detroit in 1947 run by pharmacist Bernard Shulman. He added a second store, and in 1956 converted both of them to discount operation. Their original name, Regal Drugs, was changed in due course to Revco, after the Registered Vitamin Company, a Regal subsidiary. By 1961 the chain had 20 discount drugstores in the Detroit area, and through expansion and acquisition went on to operate in several states.

Revlon *(cosmetics)*

The name combines names of the men who founded the company in 1932 to produce a new kind of nail enamel, made from pigments instead of dyes. They were Charles Haskell Revson (1906-1975), his brother Joseph, and their chemist partner, Charles R. Lachman. The Revlon name is thus Revson's surname with the initial of Lachman's name replacing the "s." Revson was born in Somerville, Massachusetts, the son of a Russian immigrant and cigar roller for the R.G. Sullivan company. He grew up with his brothers Joseph and Martin in a tenement in Manchester, New Hampshire, and on graduating from Manchester Central High School in 1923, left for New York City, where he sold dresses for the Pickwick Dress Company, owned by a cousin. He had risen to the position of buyer when he left in 1930 to take up a job the following year selling nail polish for a firm named Elka in Newark, New Jersey. Soon after, his brother Joseph joined him and they formed Revson Brothers to sell and distribute Elka nail enamel to New York beauty salons. Charles Lachman worked with Dresden, a small chemical company making nail polish in New Rochelle, New York. He heard about the Revson brothers and contacted them. The result is the Revlon International Corporation of today, a world leader in retail cosmetic sales.

Rexall *(drugstores)*

The drugstores so named were founded by Louis K. Liggett (1875-1946), born in Detroit, Michigan, whose first business was a brokerage that sold goods direct from mills to retailers. In 1897 he became a salesman for Charles Kent & Company, promoting their proprietary tonic "Vinol." In 1903 he founded United Drug Merchants to make drugs and sell them through his own drugstores and subsequently adopted the Rexall name for this purpose. One of his early products was "Rexall Cherry Juice Cough Syrup," its name meaning that it was "king of all," or superior to every other. The name itself was devised by Walter Jones Willson, a young Boston man who was later the editor of United Drug's monthly institutional magazine. In 1943 Justin W. **Dart** became chairman of United Drug and in 1978 sold off the last of the Rexall business.

Rexine *(artificial leather)*

The textile fabric was originally manufactured by the British Pluviusin Company in 1899 following a process devised in 1884 to produce "leathercloth" by using a solution of nitrocellulose and castor oil. The actual trademark, however, was the property of the British Leather Cloth Manufacturing Co. of Hyde, near Manchester, founded in 1899, who entered it in the *Trade Marks Journal* of August

18, 1915. Yet another firm making Rexine was New Pegamoid, who first produced it in 1902. By 1925 all three firms had been acquired by Nobel Industries Ltd., who the following year were merged into **ICI**. The name itself was probably based on Latin *rex*, "king," denoting superiority.

Reynolds *see* **R.J. Reynolds**

Reynolds Metals *(aluminum)*

The American company, one of the biggest producers of aluminum in the world, takes its name from Richard Samuel Reynolds (1881-1955), nephew of Richard Joshua Reynolds, founder of the tobacco empire **R.J. Reynolds**. Reynolds was born in Bristol, Tennessee, the son of the owner of a profitable tobacco business. After graduating in 1898 from King College in Bristol, he studied law at Columbia University and then subsequently at the University of Virginia. In 1902, however, his uncle convinced him to leave law school and enter his tobacco business. He did so, and soon became the firm's leading merchandiser. But by 1913 Reynolds had tired of the tobacco world and set off independently. He first tried making household cleaners, but failed when supplies were commandeered for use in World War I. Success came in 1919, when he realized that increasing cigarette consumption during the war had caused a shortage of tinfoil used in packaging cigarettes. He therefore borrowed $100,000 from his uncle's company and set up the U.S. Foil Company in a small building in Louisville, Kentucky. His business boomed almost instantly, and in 1928 he built the first aluminum foil plant in Louisville and formed Reynolds Metals. Today the company is based in Richmond, Virginia, and one of its best-known products is the familiar 0.0007-inch thick foil, "Reynolds Wrap," introduced in 1947.

RHM *see* **Rank**

Rhodoid *(thermoplastic)*

The incombustible thermoplastic, derived from cellulose acetate, has a name of French origin from *Rhodanus*, the Latin name of the Rhône River, and the suffix "-oid." It was entered by the Société Chimique des Usines du Rhône "(anciennement Gilliard, P. Monnet et Cartier)" (now **Rhône-Poulenc**) in the *Trade*

Marks Journal of June 5, 1918 for: "Celluloid in sheets, rods, tubes and similiar forms." A subsequent entry in the US Patent Office *Official Gazette* of May 14, 1957 was: "For raw or partly prepared plastic material and particularly plastic material having a cellulose acetate base in the form of powder, blocks, rods, sheets, leaves, plates, and plaques."

Rhône-Poulenc *(chemicals and pharmaceuticals)*

The French company originated in 1801 as a dyestuffs manufacturer under the name Maison Debai-Extraits Tinctoriaux ("House of Debai Dye Extracts"), and in 1895 became the Société Chimique des Usines du Rhône ("Chemical Society of Rhône Factories"). In 1928 it merged with Établissements Poulenc Frères ("Poulenc Brothers Establishment"), the pharmaceutical house set up by Camille Poulenc (1864-1942), founder of the French pharmaceutical industry, as Société des Usines Chimiques Rhône-Poulenc, a name later shortened to Rhône-Poulenc. The company was nationalized in 1982 but returned to the private sector in 1993.

Rhovyl *(artificial fiber)*

The make of polyvinyl chloride fiber derives its name from a blend of *Rhodanus*, the Latin name of the Rhône River, and "vinyl" and was entered by the Société Anonyme Rhovyl, Paris, France, in the US Patent Office *Official Gazette* of June 7, 1949: "For threads and yarns containing filaments of polyvinyl chloride," and by the same company in the *Trade Marks Journal* of December 21, 1949.

Ribena *(blackcurrant drink)*

The name of the drink comes from the Latin botanical term for the blackcurrant, *Ribes nigrum*. The British product was developed by H.W. Carter & Co. of Coleford, Somerset, in the late 1930s, and is now marketed by the **Beecham** Group. The name was entered in the *Trade Marks Journal* of July 7, 1939 for: "Blackcurrant syrup for making beverages."

Ricard *(aperitif)*

The aniseed-flavored aperitif takes its name from the Frenchman Paul-Louis-Marius Ricard (1909-1997), the son of a Marseille wine merchant, who created the subsequently fashionable pastis in Marseille in 1932. The name

was entered in the *Trade Marks Journal* of July 21, 1965 for: "Aperitif wines containing aniseed for sale in England, Scotland and Wales." In 1975 Ricard's firm merged with **Pernod** to become Pernod Ricard.

Riccadonna *(vermouth)*

Unlike many well-known vermouths, such as **Cinzano** and **Martini**, Riccadonna is a relatively recent name. It is that of Ottavio Riccadonna, who founded his firm in 1921 and subsequently came to locate his headquarters at Canelli, near Asti, Italy. The company's vermouth was exported only after World War II. The family surname, literally translating as "rich lady," is a coincidental commercial bonus for the manufacturers, especially since vermouths are primarily aimed at the female consumer. The name was entered in the *Trade Marks Journal* of October 10, 1906 for "fermented liquors and spirits."

Rice Krispies *(breakfast cereal)*

The breakfast cereal was introduced in 1929 by **Kellogg's**, who entered its name in the *Trade Marks Journal* of September 30, 1936 with the rather bland description, "a food made of rice, for human consumption." As the second word of the name indicates, the cereal is crisp to serve and eat.

Richard Donnelly *(chocolates)*

Famous for his bite-size (1.75 oz.) chocolates, Richard Donnelly at first followed in his lawyer father's footsteps, studying law for a year at Ripon College, Wisconsin. He soon realized that this was not the right path for him, and moved to Europe, where he studied chocolate-making, completing his apprenticeship with the famous **Wittamer** in Brussels. On returning to the USA, Donnelly spent a season as chocolate maker and assistant pastry chef with Jean-Yves Duperret at the Nouvelle Pâtisseries, San Francisco, after which he was determined to set up his own business. In 1988 he made his first chocolate in his mother's kitchen in Boston, Massachusetts, but soon moved west to Santa Cruz, California, where his company is based today.

Richards *(womenswear and fashion shops)*

Formerly familiar as Richard Shops, the

British firm was founded in 1936 by John Sorio, who named it after his brother Richard. Richards later became an associate of the **Habitat/Mothercare** group, itself renamed Storehouse after its merger with British Home Stores (BhS). The change of name from Richard Shops to Richards took place when the company was keen to change its image from that of a simple chain of womenswear shops to a modern fashion house.

Richardson-Merrell *(drugs and home medicines)*

The American drug manufacturing company takes the first half of its name from the Greensboro, North Carolina, druggist Lunsford Richardson (1854-1919), inventor of its best-known product, **Vicks** VapoRub. The second half of the name is the older, however, and represents William Stanley Merrell, a chemist who in 1828 started a company in Cincinnati to supply drugs to doctors in the West. Before that, physicians had to obtain their medicines from Philadelphia. By 1858 the Merrell portfolio included nearly 1,000 products. It was acquired by Vick Chemical in 1938, and the corporate name, Richardson-Merrell, was adopted in 1960. It later became Richardson-Vicks.

Rich's *(department store)*

The Atlanta, Georgia, store, one of the largest south of New York, takes its name from Morris Rich, one of four young men who emigrated to the United States from Kaschau, Hungary (now Košice, Slovakia), just before and during the Civil War. Aged only 20, Morris rode on horseback from Albany, Georgia, to Atlanta, where his brother, William, had started a dry-goods business in 1865. Morris borrowed $500 from him and set up his own small dry-goods store on Whitehall Street. It opened in 1867, and his brothers Emanuel and Daniel joined him as partners a few years later. The store grew steadily, and in 1907 construction of a new building made Rich's the largest store in Atlanta. Emanuel Rich died in 1897 and Daniel Rich in 1920. Morris Rich lived until 1928, but some years earlier handed over his responsibilities to a nephew, Walter Henry Rich, who died in 1947.

Ricordi *(music publishers)*

The Italian firm was founded in Milan in 1808 by Giovanni Ricordi (1785-1853) as a publisher of classical music and became noted for its editions of operatic works. Under his son Tito (1811-1888), a friend of Verdi, grandson Giulio (1840-1912), a composer of salon music (under the pseudonym J. Burgmein), and great-grandson Tito (1865-1933), a pianist, it broadened its activities to include popular music, recording, and graphic art. In 1994 control of Ricordi passed to the German group **Bertelsmann**.

Ridgway's *(tea)*

The British firm was founded in 1836 when Thomas Ridgway opened a tea shop in King William Street, in the City of London. He had earlier been a provincial tea merchant, but in the confusion that followed the ending in 1833 of the monopoly on the tea trade to Britain held by the East India Company, he decided to close his business down. His new London shop was a great success, and when he retired he left it in the hands of his son, Isaac, and the two employees that he had taken on when he first opened it, Samuel Page and Henry Cooper. Isaac Ridgway retired in 1865, and when Cooper died in 1871 a new partnership was formed between Page and Cooper's two sons, Alfred (1846-1916) and James. The Ridgway family thus ceased to be represented in the business fairly early on, and were certainly not involved when it was formed into a limited company in 1896, with Sir (as he now was) Alfred Cooper as chairman. From the late 1970s Ridgway's has had its head office in Liverpool.

Rigby & Peller *(underwear)*

"The name Rigby & Peller is almost guaranteed to provoke a clear divide between the sexes. Neanderthal Man will shrug and think of some fringe comedy act or possibly a gentleman's outfitter filled with ageing, cracked leather and ageing, cracked assistants. Women and New Modern Boyfriends will immediately think of bras and underwear" (*Sunday Business*, September 2, 2001). The British company in fact takes its name from a Mrs. Rigby and a Mrs. Peller, who first sold corsets in London in 1939. The firm gradually built up a high-class clientele, and in 1960 received the Royal Warrant of Appointment as Corsetieres to Queen Elizabeth II. In 1980 it passed to Harold and June Kenton, who were running a market stall at the time, and they expanded and enhanced it further, so that by 2000 each of their shops boasted a stock of over 7,000 bras in sizes ranging from 30AA to 48I.

Riley *(automobiles)*

The Riley family of Coventry, Warwickshire, England, originally made weaving machinery in the 19th century. They then turned to making bicycles before producing their original prototype car in 1898. Motor tricycles followed from 1900, but the first proper Riley car was not sold until 1906. Meanwhile, in 1903, Percy Riley had established the Riley Engine Company to build engines and sell them to the parent company. When his father planned to abandon car manufacture in 1912, however, Percy and his brothers founded Riley (Coventry) Ltd. and took over the existing car designs. The firm was later famed for its sports cars, but the last Riley emerged from the factory in 1969 after the formation of British Leyland (subsequently **BL**).

Rilsan *(synthetic fiber)*

The name of the kind of nylon used as a fiber originated in France, and is based on French *ricin*, "castor oil plant," referring to the castor oil from which it is made. The name was entered by the Rilsan Corporation, Boston, Massachusetts, in the US Patent Office *Official Gazette* of March 27, 1956, and by Organico, of Paris, France, in the *Trade Marks Journal* of October 2, 1963.

Ringtons *(tea)*

The British firm owes its origin to Samuel Smith (1872-1949), born in Leeds, who became a butcher's boy at the age of nine to support his family. When he was ten he entered the tea trade, where he worked his way up from errand boy to salesman and eventually, at age 35, to a senior position. In 1907, to the surprise of his friends, he gave up his job and went to Newcastle upon Tyne, where he formed a partnership with William Titterington to sell and deliver tea. He named his new enterprise "Ringtons," from the latter part of Titterington's name. Business suffered in World War I, but picked up after the war and in 1926 a new factory was opened. Ringtons subsequently introduced motor vans for their deliveries, but housewives often preferred the original horse-

drawn vehicles. It was the vehicles themselves that eventually brought about the company's diversion into coachbuilding, and a subsidiary, Northern Coachbuilders, was formed. At the close of the 20th century, the managing director of Ringtons was Nigel Smith, Samuel Smith's great-grandson.

Rinso *(soap powder)*

The powder was originally manufactured by the British firm of R.S. Hudson, acquired by Lever Bros. (*see* **Unilever**) in 1908. The name, of obvious origin, was entered in the *Trade Marks Journal* of October 21, 1908. Rinso was a bestseller in the UK in the 1930s.

Rio Tinto-Zinc *(mining)*

The Rio Tinto-Zinc Corporation (usually abbreviated RTZ), based in London, England, was formed in 1962 from the merger of the Rio Tinto Company with the Consolidated Zinc Corporation. Rio Tinto had originally operated a copper-pyrites mine near the town of Riotinto (now Nerva) in southwestern Spain, where the river was polluted from the workings of the mines and so called *Río Tinto*, "tinted river" (or "tainted"). The mines were very old, and had initially been leased to a Swede named Wolters in 1725. In 1873 they passed to the Rio Tinto Company, set up that year for the specific acquisition of the mine. The Consolidated Zinc Corporation was established at Broken Hill, Australia, in 1905 to process the residues of silver, lead, and zinc ore that had been discovered there 22 years earlier.

Ripolin *(paint)*

The French make of brightly-colored gloss paint takes its name from its inventor in 1888, one Riep, with "-ol-" from Latin *oleum*, "oil," referring to the linseed oil that formed its base. It was entered in the *Trade Marks Journal* of December 25, 1889 for: "Chemical substances used in manufactures or philosophical research, and anti-corrosives." ("Philosophical" here means "scientific.")

Ritalin *(stimulant)*

The proprietary name for methylphenidate, a drug used to improve mental activity in attention deficit disorders, is apparently of arbitrary origin, and was entered by CIBA Ltd. (*see* **Ciba-Geigy**) in the *Trade Marks Journal* of June 1, 1949, and the US Patent Office *Official*

Gazette of August 16, 1949, some years before the drug itself was introduced in 1954.

Ritz *(hotels)*

The prestigious hotels of this name commemorate their founder, the Swiss hotelier César Ritz (1850-1918), born in Niederwald. In order to learn the restaurant business, Ritz got a job at the finest restaurant in Paris, the Voisin, until the Siege of Paris (1870) brought shortages of food and fuel and put an end to the business. After the Franco-German War, Ritz worked as a maître d'hôtel in the Hôtel Splendide, Paris, where he came into contact with the rich and famous. When fashionable society moved on, Ritz decided to go with them. For the next few years, he worked in hotels in resort areas throughout Europe, and as general manager of the Grand Hotel in Monte Carlo met the great chef Auguste Escoffier. Together they opened a restaurant in Baden-Baden in 1887. The English impresario Richard D'Oyly Carte then invited Ritz to manage the newly opened Savoy in London. Ritz did so, and soon converted London society to the custom of dining out. His Savoy customers urged him to open a hotel in Paris. With a loan from Marnier-Lapostolle (*see* **Grand Marnier**), Ritz purchased a mansion in Paris and spent two years refurbishing it. In 1898 it finally opened to a crowd of approving diners. By this time Ritz had a controlling interest in nine other restaurants and hotels. In 1902 Ritz suffered a nervous collapse, and was thus able to play only a token part in the opening of the London Ritz hotel in 1905. His name soon become synonymous with luxury, and the word "ritzy" is now used to apply to anything smart or stylish, especially ostentatiously so.

Rizla *(cigarette paper)*

The product traces its origins to 1532, when a Frenchman, Pierre de la Croix, began selling paper in exchange for a Périgord version of champagne. By 1660 the business was making paper, and in 1796 began manufacturing "rice paper" for tobacco rolling, although the product was not perfected until the 1860s. The present name, in full "Rizla +," appeared in 1866, representing French *riz*, "rice", and the Frenchman's name as *la* plus a cross (French *croix*). Rizla was acquired by **Imperial Tobacco** in 1997 and at the close of the century was selling

in 110 countries and dominating the UK with 74 percent of the cigarette papers market. The name was entered in the *Trade Marks Journal* of October 7, 1925.

RKO *(motion pictures)*

RKO Radio Pictures, Inc., originated in 1928 as a joint enterprise of the Radio Corporation of America (later **RCA**), the Keith-Albee-Orpheum theater circuit, and the American **Pathé** production firm, so the letters represent three key words in these names. Keith was Benjamin Franklin Keith (1846-1914), a former circus concessionaire, who in 1885 joined Edward Franklin Albee (1857-1930) to establish the Boston Bijou Theater. Albee was responsible for the expansion of the Keith-Albee vaudeville circuit. The Orpheum name goes back to the Orpheum Theater, a combined saloon and music hall in San Francisco owned by Gustave Waters, who hired Martin Beck (1865-1940) to manage it. Beck soon acquired other theaters in California and formed a partnership with Morris Meyerfield, Jr., who had founded the Orpheum vaudeville circuit in the Far West. The two men then created the Western Vaudeville Managers Association, which together with the Orpheum circuit, controlled most vaudeville theaters between Chicago and the West Coast. In 1912 Keith-Albee joined forces with the Orpheum circuit to create the Keith-Albee-Orpheum circuit. "Orpheum" itself presumably blends the name of Orpheus, the famous musician and singer of Greek mythology, with the theater name Lyceum. RKO ceased production in 1953 and was sold to Desilu Productions in 1957.

Robbialac *(enamel paint)*

The paint is ultimately named for the Italian artist Luca della Robbia (1400-1482), who as an apprentice began to model medallions in terracotta and evolved what came to be known as the "della Robbia glaze." In the 19th century a British paint manufacturer, John Charles Nicholson, was asked by one of his agents for a blue-white or off-white paint "as in the della Robbia glaze." Nicholson had actually seen della Robbia's glaze in a church near Florence, Italy, so knew what his agent was after. Some years later Nicholson perfected an enamel paint and, recalling the agent's description, named it "Robbialac," the final "-lac" denoting a lacquer. Nicholson was the cofounder of Jenson & Nicholson, who in 1960 merged with another company, Berger, to become Berger, Jenson & Nicholson.

Robert Hale *(publishers)*

Robert Hale (1888-1956) was involved in publishing after World War I and for a time was a director of **Hutchinson** before founding his own publishing business in 1936. The British company is still in the hands of the Hale family today, with Robert's son John its current chairman and managing director.

Roberts *(radios)*

The Roberts Radio Co. Ltd., specializing in portable radios, was founded in 1932 by Harry Roberts and Leslie Bismead, and in a market dominated by foreign competition is the only remaining British manufacturer. The firm is based in West Molesey, Surrey, and is still in family hands.

Robertson's *(jam and marmalade)*

The founder of the British company, James Robertson, was originally employed in a thread mill in Paisley, Scotland, before leaving to be apprenticed to a local grocer. It was not long before he had opened his own grocer's shop. One day in 1864 a salesman persuaded Robertson to buy a barrel of bitter oranges. He was wondering what to do with them when his wife, Marion, said she would use them to make marmalade. The resulting preserve was so popular that Mrs. Robertson could hardly make marmalade fast enough, and James gave up his grocer's shop to start a small marmalade factory, renting part of a local cloth-finishing works for the purpose. He soon transferred the business to larger premises in Paisley, and from then on it was a matter of healthy expansion, with a further factory opened in 1880 at Droylsden, near Manchester. Marion Robertson is said to have invented the name "Golden Shred" for the clear kind of marmalade that made the firm famous.

Robertson's jam and marmalade was long popularly associated with the "Golly," an innocently grinning black figure that appeared on the jar labels. The character was introduced by John Robertson, a son of the founder, who on a business trip to America in 1910 noticed children playing with a rag doll made from their mother's discarded black skirts and white blouses. In the late 20th century the figure was increasingly viewed as an offensive racial stereotype and was finally abandoned in 2001.

Robinson, Peter *see* **Peter Robinson**

Robinson & Cleaver *(bedlinen)*

The British firm had its origins in 1870 in the shop opened in Castle Place, Belfast, Northern Ireland, by Edward Robinson and John Cleaver. In 1879 they found the premises too small for their linen-making business, so moved to a larger site in the High Street. In 1885 they were obliged to move yet again, and so came to build their factory opposite the City Hall, where the new works was known as "The Royal Irish Linen Warehouse." In 1884 the firm opened a retail branch in Regent Street, London, and this itself expanded so that it soon occupied the whole "island" site from Church Passage to Beak Street, where **Next** and Miss **Selfridge** now are. The firm became a limited company in 1900, but today no longer exists, either in Belfast or London.

Robinson & Sons *(medical products)*

Robinson & Sons of Chesterfield, England, make a wide range of surgical and medical products, such as Gamgee tissue and **Thermogene** medicated wadding. The firm was founded in Chesterfield in 1839 by John Bradbury Robinson, initially with the aim of manufacturing round pill boxes made of pasteboard. In 1854 Robinson's son, William, was taken into partnership, and the following year he initiated the making of surgical lint. In 1858 a second son, Charles Robinson, joined the business, and within a year or two the firm was making its medical and surgical products by doing its own weaving, bleaching, and spinning. Gamgee tissue, named for Joseph Samson Gamgee (1828-1886), the English surgeon who invented it, was patented in 1883, and other products followed, such as gauze tissue in 1885 and sanitary napkins in 1887. In 1893 the firm became a private limited company as Robinson & Sons, and in 1897 the first sterilized dressings were manufactured. In 1949 Robinson & Sons produced the first disposable diapers, made of absorbent pulp paper.

Robinson Rentals *(television rentals)*

The British company, with retail branches

in many towns and cities, owed its name to Sir David Robinson (1904-1987), born in Cambridge, who started in business in 1930 selling bicycles, later progressing to motorcycles and electrical goods. Impressed by the vast television audience for the coronation of Queen Elizabeth in 1953, he decided to set up a business to rent out television sets. When he sold the firm in 1968 he had become a millionaire from his venture, and retired to breed racehorses. Robinson College, Cambridge, was opened in 1981 on funds donated by him, and was named for him. The naming did not meet with his approval, and he was not present for the opening ceremony conducted by the Queen, even though it was her televised coronation that had inspired his business in the first place.

Robinson's *("Barley Water")*

Very little is known about the Mr. Robinson who gave his name to the soft drinks, except that his first name was Matt. The firm of Robinson and Bellville had been making Robinson's "Patent" Barley and "Patent" Groats since 1823, before they amalgamated in 1862 with the firm of Keen & Sons, of London, which made mustard, to form Keen Robinson (later, Keen, Robinson & Co., taken over by **Colman's** for the sake of its mustard in 1903). **Reckitt** & Colman still produce baby foods and cereals as well as fruit drinks under the Robinson's name.

Rochas *(fashionwear and perfumery)*

Marcel Rochas (1902-1955) was born in Paris, France, and originally trained as a lawyer. He became a fashion designer almost by accident, to satisfy the expensive tastes of his first wife, a former model, and in 1925 opened the House of Rochas in the Faubourg St. Honoré, Paris. In 1936 he launched three exclusive perfumes, but one, *Femme*, dedicated to his second wife, Hélène, was the first to be marketed by Parfums Rochas, founded in 1944. When Rochas died young, after closing the couture house to focus on perfumes and accessories, the business passed to Hélène Rochas, then aged 28. The company was taken over by the German cosmetics group Wella in 1987.

Roche *see* **Hoffmann-La Roche**

Rockwell *(computers and aerospace systems)*

In 1915, Willard F. Rockwell (1888-1978), a consulting engineer, was asked by the Torbensen Axle Company to manage their Cleveland plant. Within three years, Rockwell helped to transform the firm into the nation's biggest truck axle manufacturer. He left in 1919, however, and moved to Oshkosh, Wisconsin, to form his own axle business, which became Rockwell-Standard. Meanwhile, as he was building his axle firm, Rockwell was setting up a separate company, later called Rockwell Manufacturing, in an abandoned Pittsburgh auto plant to make gas meters, parking meters, and taxicab meters. Eventually, Rockwell-Standard branched out into automotive parts, aircraft, and materials-handling equipment and in 1967 merged with North American Aviation, founded in 1928 in El Segundo, California, by which time the older firm was represented by the colonel's son, Willard F. Rockwell, Jr. (1914-1992). Rockwell Sr. remained active in both companies until he was in his 80s.

Rodenbach *(beer)*

The first Rodenbach arrived in Belgium under Austrian rule as an army doctor from the Rhineland, and later married into a Flemish family. In 1820 a member of the family bought a brewery in Roeselare, West Flanders, and subsequently founded the present establishment in 1836. The firm was in family hands until the late 1990s.

Roederer *(champagne)*

The origins of the house go back to 1760, when a firm called Dubois Père & Fils was founded in Reims, France. In 1827 it passed into the hands of Nicolas-Henri Schreider, who sought the assistance of his nephew, Louis Roederer, and the latter took over when his uncle died in 1833. The name was entered by Théophile Roederer & Co. in the *Trade Marks Journal* of November 15, 1876.

Rogers *(chocolates)*

Canadian confectioner Charles "Candy" Rogers started his career at the turn of the 20th century as a greengrocer who also sold imported candies from San Francisco. Finding his source of supply unreliable, he decided to try his hand at producing his own confections. The story goes that they were so popular that long lines formed each morning before his Victoria, British Columbia, shop opened, while Rogers himself, clad only in red underwear, stirred copper kettles full of fondant candy in the back of the store. Before long, Rogers had developed a range of chocolate and candies, and his original shop, built in 1903, has been preserved intact. Following his death, Rogers' wife took over the business until the late 1920s, after which it passed to various owners. By the 1990s, the company had expanded from just two stores and three wholesale customers to 300 wholesale and 25,000 mail-order clients.

Rohypnol *(sedative)*

The proprietary name of the so-called "date-rape drug" flunitrazepam, a powerful tranquilizer manufactured by **Hoffmann-La Roche**, is apparently based on the first two letters of "Roche" and the Greek "hypno-" element meaning "sleep." It was entered in the *Trade Marks Journal* of July 14, 1971.

Rolex *(watches)*

The company that became Rolex was founded in Geneva by Hans Wilsdorf in 1905, and the name was entered by Wilsdorf & Davis, watch manufacturers of London, England, in the *Trade Marks Journal* of August 14, 1912. His choice of name was apparently arbitrary, and has no precise meaning. It is quite apt for a watch, however, suggesting "rolling" (as of time, or its own movement), and is short enough to be placed on the dial. "Rolex" is said to be the first watch name to have the suffix "-ex." The famous waterproof Rolex "Oyster" was introduced in 1926.

Rollei *(cameras)*

The German firm Franke & Heidecke of Braunschweig originally made a stereoscopic plate camera called the "Heidoskop," then a roll-film one called the "Rolleidoskop." (The "Heido-" of Heidecke in the former name has been subtly changed to suggest Greek *eidos*, "form," in the latter, while "-skop" is the equivalent of "-scope" in both.) This in turn led to the Rolleiflex and Rolleicord, twin-lens reflex cameras, the Rolleiflex having its name entered in the *Trade Marks Journal* of January 8, 1930. The name was shortened to "Rollei" and in turn entered in the *Journal* of July 29, 1950.

Rollerblade *(in-line skate)*

Rollerblades are like roller skates but with the wheels (rollers) set in one straight line beneath the boot, instead of in pairs, giving an appearance and action similar to ice skates, which have blades. Hence the name, entered (as "Roller Blade") in the US Patent Office *Official Gazette* of January 8, 1985, with a note of first use in March 1983. The boots themselves were developed in 1980 by the Canadian ice-hockey player Scott Olson, later president of Ole's Innovative Sports of Minneapolis.

Rolls-Royce *(automobiles)*

The prestigious British car takes its name from a gifted electrical engineer, Frederick Henry Royce (1863-1933), and a (titled) motoring enthusiast, the Hon. Charles Stewart Rolls (1877-1910). Royce was born at Alwalton, near Peterborough, the son of a farmer and miller. When still young, he moved with his family to London, where he became a newspaper boy working for **W.H. Smith** at the age of ten. Then an aunt paid for him to become an apprentice at the Great Northern Railway Works at Peterborough. But at 17 Henry was job hunting. After a spell with a Leeds toolmaker, he was offered a position with the Electric Light and Power Company, first in London, later in Liverpool. By the time he was 21 he was an experienced electrical engineer. In 1884, with a friend, he started making electrical components in a rented room in Manchester, trading as F.H. Royce & Co. Business thrived, and in 1903 Royce bought his first car, a secondhand Decauville. It constantly gave trouble, however, so he decided to build his own car. His new Royce cars came to the attention of Charles Rolls, an automobile buff and race driver who had just set up as a London motor trader. The two men met in 1904, and Rolls agreed to be the sole selling agent for Royce's cars. They chose the name Rolls-Royce for their partnership because they thought it sounded better this way round, although logically it should have been "Royce-Rolls." The name was entered by "Rolls Royce, Limited, Cooke Street, Hulme, Manchester; Motor car manufacturers," in the *Trade Marks Journal* of February 26, 1908, two years before the death of Rolls in a flying accident. In 1980 Rolls-Royce Motors merged with **Vickers**, and in 1998 **Volkswagen** bought the company only to find that it did not get the rights to the Rolls-Royce name or the famous insignia. (Much to Volkswagen's embarrassment, **BMW** later bought the rights to use the name for only $66 million, then granted Volkswagen the use of it until 2002.)

Rolo *(candy)*

The round chocolate-coated toffees, marketed by **Nestlé**, are so called as they are sold in rolls, their shape emphasized by the final "o" of the name, which was entered in the *Trade Marks Journal* of March 21, 1951.

Rolodex *(index file)*

The rotary index file, used chiefly for names and addresses, derives its name from a blend of "roll" and "index." The name "Rolodex V-File" was entered by **Berol** in the *Trade Marks Journal* of November 2, 1977 for: "Visible card filing device for use on desks and incorporating a loose leaf binder."

Romary *(crackers, or biscuits)*

The name was entered by the British manufacturers, A. Romary & Co. Ltd., of Tunbridge Wells, Kent, in the *Trade Marks Journal* of December 4, 1929.

Rombouts *(filter coffee)*

The firm was founded in 1896 in Antwerp, Belgium, by Franciscus Rombouts (1879-1972), originally as a conventional coffee business. The idea of an individual filter for making coffee was developed in the early 1900s, but met with little success. Metal filters burned the fingers. Porcelain filters broke. So it was left to Rombouts' sons, Louis, Herbert, and Victor, to devise a filter in the form of a plastic holder that contained a measured amount of coffee for the cup. The first Rombouts filters were not introduced until 1959, however, by which time the original factory had been rebuilt and expanded, with the company itself now concentrating on supply catering. The present one-cup disposable filter was originally intended as a sampler to give the Belgian public a taste of Rombouts coffee, but it has now become the product with which the company name is popularly associated.

Romeo and Juliet *(cigars)*

The name, that of the famous lovers in Shakespeare's play, is an English version of the Spanish original, *Romeo y Julieta*, entered by the manufacturers, Rodriguez Argüelles & Co., of Havana, Cuba, in the *Trade Marks Journal* of September 7, 1904 for: "Tobacco, cigars, cigarettes and snuff." The English name is also found in semi-Hispanic form as "Romeo and Julieta" or "Romeo y Juliet." The brand's early success was due to the efforts of Rodriguez Fernandez (d.1954), manager of the Cabanas factory in Havana, Cuba. Unhappy at its imminent takeover by American Tobacco (*see* **American Brands**), he resigned in 1903 to branch out on his own. Using his savings, he bought a little-known factory that had been making cigars called "Romeo y Julieta" since 1875 solely for the Cuban domestic market. "Pepin," as he was known, traveled the world promoting the brand, and within two years, with his 1,400 workers, had to move to a larger factory. Fernandez was obsessed by his brand, naming his racehorse Julieta and even setting up a stand under the famous balcony in the House of Capulet in Verona, Italy, where Shakespeare's play is set. Until 1939 every visitor to the stand was offered a free cigar in honor of the "pair of star-cross'd lovers" who gave the brand its name.

Roneo *(duplicating machines)*

The germ of the name can be seen in the Neo-Cyclostyle, a pen patented in 1888 by David **Gestetner** as an improvement on the cyclostyle, which he had invented seven years earlier. The cyclostyle was a pen with a small toothed wheel at its point that cut minute holes in a sheet of waxed paper, which could then be used as a stencil. The Neo-Cyclostyle or "new cyclostyle" had an inclined wheel, whereas the cyclostyle had a wheel at right angles to the shaft. In the USA the pen came to be called the Neostyle at the request of Augustus David Klaber (1861-1915), Gestetner's agent in New York for products made by him in London. In due course Klaber and Gestetner split, and Klaber registered the Neostyle Co. in New York in 1893. In 1899 Klaber was selling a duplicating machine called the Rotary Neostyle, but the following year he returned to London, where he had been born the son of immigrants from Prague, and sought a simpler name for the duplicator. With his final choice of name uncertain, he registered three names as trademarks on October 23, 1901: "Neoro," "Nero," and "Roneo," this last from *Rotary Neostyle.* Soon after, his company changed its name to the Roneo Co., and the trade name was assured. The Roneo story does not quite end there, however, as a fourth name that Klaber registered in 1901 was "Neostyle." Legally this was a risky thing to do, as although he had devised this name himself in the USA, he had taken it directly from Gestetner's Neo-Cyclostyle. The two names were thus confusingly and misleadingly similar. Not surprisingly, therefore, Gestetner petitioned in 1903 for the removal of "Neostyle" from the Register of Trade Marks. At first he lost his case. On taking the matter to the Court of Appeal, however, the decision against him was reversed and it was ruled that Klaber's mark should be removed from the Register. Some years later, after the 1905 Act of Parliament had revised the law so as to disqualify any descriptive word from use as a trademark, Klaber in turn brought a case against Gestetner and succeeded in having "Cyclostyle" removed from the Register on descriptive grounds. Even so, it was subsequently revived with the restriction that it could not be used for wheel pens, that is, for the very product for which the name had been chosen. Hence the lowercase "c" for the word in this sense today. In 1980 the Roneo business was sold by **Vickers** to Alcatel. The name "Roneo" was entered by the Neostyle Manufacturing Co. for "paper... stationery and bookbinding" in the *Trade Marks Journal* of November 27, 1901, by Roneo Ltd. for "type printing machines, type setting machines, and embossing machines" in the *Journal* of August 13, 1919, by Roneo again for "duplicating apparatus, duplicating machines" in the *Journal* of March 5, 1947, and further in the US Patent Office *Official Gazette* of December 12, 1950 with the note: "Applicant claims ownership of British Registration No. 241,483 dated Oct. 23, 1901, and United States Registration No. 182,682."

Ronseal *(paint and varnish)*

The British products of this name were originally developed as Roncraft by **Ronuk** and the first varnish appeared on the market in 1956. In 1960 the business was acquired by **Izal**, part of **Newton Chambers**, and in 1970 set up as a separate sales division of Izal. In 1973 it became part of the **Sterling** Drug Co., which was acquired by **Eastman Kodak** in 1989. Kodak's DIY businesses were sold again in 1994 to the New York-based investment bank Forstmann Little & Co., where Roncraft finally became Ronseal. In 1997 the firm, based in Sheffield, was acquired by **Sherwin-Williams**.

Ronson *(cigarette lighters)*

The manufacturers of the lighter take their name from Louis V. Aronson, who set up his business in the USA in 1895. The company was incorporated in the UK in 1929 as Ronson Art Metal Co., a name changed two years later to Ronson Products Ltd. The name was entered in the *Trade Marks Journal* of September 11, 1929.

Ronuk *(floor polish)*

The name is something of a mystery. It originated in 1896 as that of a British polish-manufacturing company later acquired by **Newton Chambers**. The actual polish was made by Thomas Horace Fowler, who had an ironmongery (hardware) store in Brighton, Sussex. The story goes that a competition was held to choose a suitable name for the new polish. The winner was a retired army colonel who had served some time in India, and who based his creation on a word said to mean "brilliance" in one of the Indian languages. The name was entered by "Thomas Mottley Fowler and Thomas Horace Fowler, trading as T.M. Fowler," in the *Trade Marks Journal* of April 8, 1896, and in the late 1920s the firm had its head office at Portslade, near Brighton. *See also* **Ronseal**.

Roquefort *(cheese)*

The soft blue cheese made from ewes' milk and ripened in limestone caves takes its name from Roquefort, a village in southwestern France. It is now a proprietary name in the UK, and was entered by the Société Anonyme des Caves et des Producteurs Réunis de Roquefort (Aveyron) in the *Trade Marks Journal* of June 26, 1963.

Rose's *(lime juice and marmalade)*

The British firm of L. Rose & Co. was founded by Lauchlan Rose as a lime and lemon merchant's business in Leith, the port for Edinburgh, in 1865. Rose had abandoned the family shipbuilding concern to concentrate on importing fruit. But the family provisioned ships, as well as building them, and one of the commodities they supplied to ships' crews was lime juice. This had been carried by Royal Navy ships since the 18th century as a means of preventing scurvy, caused by a deficiency of vitamin C. Lime juice was imported from the West Indies, and it occurred to Rose that by sweetening and bottling it he could make an attractive drink. He evolved a method of preparing the drink by adding very small quantities of sulfur dioxide to prevent the fermentation that would otherwise have been caused by the sugar in the lemons. Rose's drink sold well, so that in 1875 he moved the business down to London. After his death in 1885, the lime juice-making was continued by his three sons, and the firm became a limited company in 1898. Rose's first marketed lime marmalade in the mid-1930s.

Ross *(frozen foods)*

The British company takes its name from J. Carl Ross (1902-1986), who began his career after World War I by working as a barrow boy in the docks of Grimsby, Lincolnshire. His fish-selling business gradually prospered, so that by the late 1950s he had built up a trawler fleet of 66 ships based on Grimsby, the largest in the world, and thus came to give the port its biggest period of fishing prosperity for the following 20 years. In the early 1970s "Mr. Fish," as he became known, was Icelandic Consul for a time, despite the Anglo-Icelandic "cod wars."

Rotameter *(rate-of-flow measurer)*

The device has a transparent wall and is fitted into a pipe or tube to measure the rate of flow of fluid through it. Its name, combining "rotation" and "-meter," was entered by the Rotameter Manufacturing Co. Ltd., of Croydon, Surrey, England, in the *Trade Marks Journal* of June 18, 1952 for: "Apparatus for measuring, indicating, or recording the rate of flow of gases or liquids."

Rotavator *(rotary cultivator)*

A rotary cultivator was patented by Chandon Wren Haskyns in 1853, but the present proprietary machine, with rotating blades for breaking up or drilling the soil, dates from the 1930s. Its palindromic name, said to have been deliberately devised to suggest continuous motion, combines "rotary" and "cultivator" and

was entered by the British firm of Rotary Cultivators Ltd. in the *Trade Marks Journal* of July 1, 1936 for: "Ploughs, cultivators, diggers, harrows and hoes, all being agricultural machines," and by Rotary Hoes Ltd., of East Horndon, England, in the US Patent Office *Official Gazette* of March 13, 1951: "For ploughs, cultivators, diggers, harrows, and hoes."

Rothman's *(cigarettes)*

Louis Rothman (1869-1926) arrived in London, England, as an 18-year-old immigrant Ukrainian, from a family who had owned a tobacco factory. In 1890 he bought the lease of a small shop at 55A Fleet Street, and every night made up by hand the cigarettes which he sold the following day to journalists. His cigarettes won him a good reputation among the nobility, including Lord Rothermere and Lord Northcliffe, the newspaper magnates, so that in 1900 he was able to move to premises in fashionable Pall Mall. There he opened a showroom under the Carlton Hotel. (This move gave the familiar "Rothman's of Pall Mall" on the company's cigarette packs today.) In 1905 Rothman was granted a Royal Warrant from Edward VII, and although cigarettes have now long been machine-made, the company still preserves the traditional custom of making a special London delivery by a horse-drawn carriage, as in its founder's day. Rothman's became a public company in 1929.

Rotissomat *(automatic cooker)*

The commercial automatic cooking appliance has rotating spits for cooking meat. Hence its name, from the first part of "rotisserie" plus "-o-" and "-mat" (*cp.* **Automat**), entered by the Rotiss-o-mat Corporation, Astoria, Long Island, New York, in the US Patent Office *Official Gazette* of July 8, 1947. A later registration by the Harley Manufacturing Corporation, New York, was made in the *Trade Marks Journal* of April 9, 1958 for: "Electric installations for cooking poultry and parts of such installations included in Class II."

Rotodyne *(helicopters)*

The British aircraft of this name was first produced by the **Fairey** Aviation Company in 1957. Only two were built, however, and when Fairey was absorbed by Westland Aircraft in 1960, the craft was abandoned. The name, blending "roto-" (for its rotors) and "-dyne" (from the Greek word for "force"), was sometimes used generically for a compound helicopter or so-called "convertiplane," a helicopter that has short wings to provide most of its lift force. It was originally entered in the *Trade Marks Journal* of August 17, 1949.

Rotoscythe *(mower)*

The type of mower has rotating blades for cutting rough grass or vegetation. Hence its name, based on "rotary" and "scythe," entered by the British firm of Power Specialities Ltd., of Slough, Buckinghamshire, in the *Trade Marks Journal* of January 19, 1949.

Rototiller *(cultivator)*

The Rototiller is a machine with rotating blades or prongs used for breaking up or tilling soil. Hence its name, from "rotary" and "tiller," entered in the US Patent Office *Official Gazette* of October 25, 1932, with a claim of use since February 9, 1929.

Rotring *(engineering pencils and pens)*

The distinctive engineering pencil, with its hexagonal body and aluminum casing, owes its existence to the German designer Wilhelm Riepe, who in 1928 developed the world's first nibless fountain pen. His innovation was taken a stage further by his son, who in 1953 launched the "radiograph," the first type of technical pen. His enterprise became Rotring a decade later, and has since grown into a worldwide group of companies. The name means "red ring," referring to the thin red ring at the pencil's top. (A 1967 advertisement for the firm's four-color ballpoint promoted it as *Das Ding mit dem roten Ring*, "The thing with the red ring.")

Routledge *(publishers)*

George Routledge (1812-1888) was born in Brampton, Cumberland (now Cumbria), England, and on leaving school at 15 was apprenticed to a bookseller in nearby Carlisle. In 1833 he came to London, working with another bookseller until the firm failed three years later. In 1836 he set himself up as a bookseller just off Leicester Square, taking as assistant 15-year-old William Henry **Warne**, whose sister he had married. He specialized in remaindering modern books, but in 1843 went into publishing himself, with an office in Soho Square, and five years later took his brother-in-law into partnership. By 1852, when the business had made a further move to Farringdon Street, Routledge had established himself as a publisher of inexpensive novels. In 1911 the firm merged with the publishing house founded in 1877 by Charles Kegan Paul (1828-1902), a clergyman's son from Somerset. As C. Kegan Paul & Co. he became the publisher of Tennyson, among others. The combined firm, after certain other mergers, became known as Routledge & Kegan Paul in 1947, but in 1988, because of further reorganization within the parent company, it became simply Routledge again. In 1998 it became a subsidiary of Taylor & Francis Group, founded in 1798 with the launch of *Philosophical Magazine*.

Rover *(automobiles)*

The British name was originally used for a bicycle produced in 1885 by a firm set up by John Kemp Starley (1854-1901), nephew of James Starley (*see* **Swift**), to manufacture pennyfarthing bicycles and tricycles in Coventry, Warwickshire, in 1878. The business expanded, first to motorcycles, then to automobiles in 1904. The firm became the Rover Company in 1906. The name was suitable for a vehicle that could "rove" the roads and the countryside and that was thus itself a "rover." The basic name later became part of the names of the **Land-Rover** and **Range Rover**. The Rover Company became a constituent member of the new British Leyland group in 1968 and emerged as the sole survivor when the latter (known from 1978 as **BL**) was sold to British Aerospace in 1988. Rover was acquired by **BMW** in 1994 but when profitability became a problem was sold off by them in 2000.

Rowenta *(electrical appliances)*

The name was created by picking letters from the name of the firm's founder, Robert Weintraud (1860-1928), a hosier's son in Offenbach, Germany. At the age of 24, together with two companions, Weintraud started a business manufacturing leather goods and metal accessories, at that stage naming his partnership simply Weintraud & Co. His business did well, so that he introduced other lines, such as fancy goods. By 1909 the original partners had left, so that Weintraud was in sole charge, and that year he joined forces with a Frankfurt manufacturer, Julius Herzberger, to produce an even wider range of products, such as writing utensils, smoking accessories, and various types of household goods, at the same time registering the name "Rowenta." In 1913 Weintraud began to manufacture the products with which this name is chiefly associated today, i.e. cooking and heating appliances and electric lighting. After interruption by World War I, the company had increased its lines still further by 1920 to include electric irons, toasters, kettles, and other household appliances.

Rowney (artists' materials)

The British firm was founded in 1783 by Thomas Rowney, born in 1760 the son of a London lawyer. Rowney became a perfumer with premises at Holborn Hill, producing powder and patches for the law courts at first, then drawing and coloring materials. In 1789 he was joined by his elder brother, Richard Rowney, born in 1756, who had served an apprenticeship as a coach builder. The brothers widened the scope of their artistic products further, and included pencils as a special product. By 1815 they had been joined by Thomas Rowney's son, George, born in 1793, and it was he who in 1817 took the firm over from his father, so that the business became known as George Rowney & Co. Hence the "Geo. Rowney" still found on the firm's products today. In 1983 the company merged with the Daler Board Co., and is now Daler-Rowney Ltd.

Rowntree (chocolate, cocoa, and fruit gums)

The British company traces its origins to 1725, when a Quaker lady named Mary Tuke opened a grocer's shop in Walmgate, York. By 1785 the business was dealing in cocoa, and by 1815 William Tuke & Sons was roasting coffee and making chocolate. In 1862 Henry Isaac Rowntree, another York grocer, acquired the cocoa and chocolate side of the business, and in 1869 Tuke went into partnership with his brother, Joseph Rowntree (1836-1925). The thriving business progressed to making pastilles and gums in 1879, with the familiar Rowntree's Fruit Pastilles introduced two years later. In 1882 the firm acquired a flour mill to make cocoa on a commercial scale, while also producing chocolate. The following year Henry Rowntree died, leaving Joseph in sole charge. In 1893 Rowntree's Fruit Gums were added to the confectionery lines. In 1969 Rowntree's merged with **Mackintosh** to form Rowntree Mackintosh, and in 1988 this company in turn was acquired by **Nestlé**.

Roxy (movie theaters)

Roxy movie theaters ultimately take their name from Roxy Rothafel (1881-1936), born Samuel Lionel Rothapfel in Stillwater, Minnesota, the son of a shoemaker. (The younger Rothafel dropped the "p" from his family name at the end of World War I when names of Germanic origin fell out of favor.) At age 14, Rothafel began drifting from one temporary job to another. In 1905, after three years in the Marine Corps, he played semiprofessional baseball and gained the nickname "Roxy." In 1908 he became a barman at a saloon in Forest City, Pennsylvania, and realized that its back room could be used to exhibit one-reel movies for five cents, as the nickelodeons did in bigger cities. He set up a successful movie theater there and in 1910 was hired by vaudeville mogul B.F. Keith to travel the circuit of his variety houses and smarten up the presentation of short films. Rothafel repeated the conversions in other theaters, and in 1927 built his own "cathedral of the motion picture" in New York, the Roxy Theater. Later Roxy movie theaters took their name from this one, itself demolished in 1960.

Royal Doulton see Doulton

Royal Dutch/Shell (petroleum)

The two companies that combined in 1907 to form the present name originated as rival organizations in the late 19th century. In 1890 a group of Dutch bankers and businessmen formed the Koninklijke Nederlandsche Maatschappij tot Exploitatie van Petroleumbronnen in Nederlandsch-Indie ("Royal Dutch Company for the Exploitation of Oil Wells in the Dutch Indies"). In 1903 Royal Dutch and **Shell** made their first move toward merging by integrating their distributing and sales operations involving Far East sales and East Indies production. The merger became fully effective four years later.

Royal Enfield (bicycles and motorcycles)

The British company evolved out of the Royal Small Arms Factory founded at Enfield, Middlesex, in 1815. It came to produce many well-known weapons, including the Lee-Enfield rifle, with a bolt action designed by the American J.P. Lee (1831-1904). In 1899 it made its frst powered vehicles. The ubiquitous motorized bicycle followed in 1901, and regular motorcycle production began in 1912. In World War I its main product was bicycles, still an important line of business, but in 1970 Enfield Precision, as it now was, dropped its manufacture of motorcycles in favor of military contracts. The original Royal Small Arms Factory at Enfield closed in 1989.

Royal Insurance *(insurance)*

The British insurance company was founded in Liverpool in 1845 by local businessmen, merchants, warehouse owners, and shipowners. Various amalgamations followed, including a merger in 1919 with the Liverpool, London and Globe Insurance Co., and more recently in 1996 with **Sun Alliance**, so that the company is now known as Royal and SunAlliance (RSA).

Royal Lochnagar *(whisky)*

The blend of Scotch whisky had its origins in the distillery built by John Begg in the village of Crathie, Aberdeenshire, in 1845. Three years later neighboring Balmoral Castle became the summer residence of Queen Victoria, and Begg was in due course granted a royal warrant. Lochnagar is a mountain range to the south of Balmoral, and all three placenames have royal associations, the latter following the publication of Prince Charles's popular story for children, *The Old Man of Lochnagar* (1980). An account of the naming of the whisky appears on the label, the first paragraph quoting from John Begg's diary entry for September 14, 1848:

"I asked Prince Albert if he would like to taste a dram. H.R.H. having agreed to this, I called for a bottle and glasses (which had been previously in readiness) and, presenting one glass to Her Majesty, she tasted it. So did His Royal Highness the Prince. I then presented a glass to the Princess Royal, and to the Prince of Wales, and Prince Alfred, all of whom tasted the spirit."

As a result of this visit the Distillery was granted the privilege of calling itself "Royal" Lochnagar, the very first to be accorded this honour by Her Majesty.

Royle *(greeting cards and calendars)*

The British firm was founded by William Richard Royle, dating its origin from 1826, when records show him to have been working as an engraver in London. In 1833 Royle started business as an engraver on his own account, building up his trade to include the making of copper and steel plates for printing letterheads and business documents. In 1865 he took his son, Theodore, into partnership, and about five years later established a separate copperplate printing department. William Royle died in 1885, after which Theodore became the sole proprietor. The firm did not move into greeting cards until after World War II, when a new concern, Royle Publications Ltd., was set up to manage this venture. The calendars followed, as did other lines such as gift wrap and fancy stationery.

RTZ *see* **Rio Tinto-Zinc**

Rubberoid *see* **Ruberoid**

Ruberoid *(building material)*

The name originally applied to a roofing material made of felt impregnated with bitumen. It is based on "Rubberoid," a name entered by The James D. Frary & Son Co. of Bridgeport, Connecticut, in the US Patent Office *Official Gazette* of January 8, 1884 for a "composition as a hard substitute for rubber." "Ruberoid," with one "b" for differentiation, was entered by The Standard Paint Co. of New York in the *Gazette* of May 28, 1901 for "certain named substances of the nature of rubber," and in the *Trade Marks Journal* of May 14, 1902 for "roofing pasteboard or paper and roofing felt." The name was later extended to materials unrelated to felt or rubber, as shown in an entry by the Ruberoid Company Ltd. in the *Journal* of November 21, 1934 for: "Nails; and sectional sheets of ordinary metal for use in building."

Rubery Owen *(automotive components)*

The British firm was founded in Darlaston, Staffordshire, in 1884 by John Turner Rubery, who was joined in 1893 by Alfred Ernest Owen. At first they traded as Rubery and Co., manufacturing light steel roofwork, fences, gates, and bridgework. Orders for factory construction linked the business with the bicycle boom and the early pioneers of the motor trade, whose fortunes the company has followed to the present day. In 1905 the firm was renamed Rubery Owen and Co., and five years later Owen took over the management on the retirement of Rubery. By the time of Owen's death in 1929 the company was established as a major motor vehicle components supplier, and control passed to Owen's eldest son, Alfred George Beech Owen (1908-1975). His own son, David Owen (b.1936), the current chairman, started the motor division, and the company is now also a vehicle distributor.

Rubik's Cube *(cube-shaped puzzle)*

Ernö Rubik (b.1944), a professor of interior design at an art academy in Budapest, enjoyed playing around with geometric cardboard and wooden shapes in his room at his mother's house. In the spring of 1974 he took some blocks of wood, attached them to one another with elastic springs, and started twisting. The elastic eventually broke, but not before he had become fascinated by the changing relationship between the cubes. Then he tried putting differently colored adhesive paper on each of the cubes, and twisted again. The kaleidoscope of colors fascinated him as he worked, and he soon found he could not recover the original pattern. He realized he had the makings of a teasing puzzle on his hands, and took his invention to a small toymaking cooperative in Budapest. Production started on a small scale in Hungary. Then one November day in 1978, Tibor Laczi, a Hungarian émigré, was shown a cube by a baffled waiter in a café. Laczi bought it off him and asked the state trading firm Konsumex is he could sell it in the West. Granted permission, Laczi went to the Nuremberg trade fair and walked around, twisting the cube and returning the 27 cubelets to their original colors. British toy expert Tom Kremer was intrigued and helped Laczi secure an order from Ideal Toy Company for a million cubes. The puzzle was named Rubik's Cube and registered as such in the UK and USA. The cube and its 43 billion possible combinations became a world craze in the early 1980s, familiar to the French as *le cube de Rubik*, to the Italians as *il cubo di Rubik*, and to the Russians as *kubik Rubika*.

Rubinstein, Helena *see* **Helena Rubinstein.**

Ruddles *(beer)*

The ultimate origin of the British firm goes back to the brewery that Richard Baker owned in the mid-19th century in the village of Langham, near Oakham, Rutland. After his death

in 1861 the brewery passed through various hands until it was acquired in 1911 by George Ruddle (1875-1923). He was a Hertfordshire farmer who had served an apprenticeship in a brewery near Baldock, and who had come to be manager of the Langham brewery from 1896. The family firm lost its independence in 1986 when **Watneys** bought up the brewery in Langham, and since 1992 it has been owned by **Grolsch.**

Rudge-Whitworth *(bicycles)*

The name of one of Britain's oldest bicycle makers goes back to 1869, when Daniel Rudge, a bicycle manufacturer of Wolverhampton, produced a "boneshaker." Further information about Dan Rudge is hard to come by. In 1880 his business was purchased by George Woodcock of Coventry, with the Coventry Tricycle Co. incorporated at the same time. In 1887 the firm became known as the Rudge Cycle Co. Ltd., and in 1894 it amalgamated with the Whitworth Cycle Co., founded by Charles Vernon Pugh and his brother John in 1891, to form Rudge-Whitworth. There does not seem to have been an actual Mr. Whitworth. Unlike other bicycle makers, Rudge-Whitworth did not go into car manufacture but it did make motorcycles from 1910 to 1939. In 1943 Rudge-Whitworth was acquired by **Raleigh.**

Rufflette *(curtain-heading tapes)*

The British product is a form of tape that can be sewn to the top edge of a curtain. It has slits or loops at regular intervals by which curtain hooks can be attached, and cords threaded through that enable the tape and the curtain to be gathered or "ruffled." Hence the name, which was entered in the *Trade Marks Journal* of November 18, 1931, with use claimed from September 28, 1922.

RU486 *(abortion pill)*

The proprietary name for mifepristone, a synthetic steroid used to induce abortion in early pregnancy by inhibiting the action of the hormone progesterone, derives from the initials of its manufacturers, the French pharmaceutical company Roussel Uclaf, who first marketed it in 1988. The figures are simply a numerical code.

Rumbelows *(television and electronics stores)*

The man who gave his name to the British High Street stores was Sydney Charles Rumbelow (1909-1974), born a painter's son in Hatfield, Hertfordshire. When still at school he showed musical talent, and on completing his education ran a dance band for some time, touring with the players to different towns. He gained experience in the radio business when working for **Murphy** at its factory in Welwyn Garden City, and began to set up his own group of radio and music shops, opening the first in Hatfield in 1946. However, at some stage he appears to have become disillusioned with the way the radio and television side of the business was going, and left the running of the shops to his two sons, Mark and Paul. In 1962 the four Rumbelow shops then existing (two in Hatfield, one each in Hertford and Welwyn Garden City) were acquired by the Tucana Finance Company, which was set up that year to take over a number of small chains and businesses. In 1971 the decision was taken to give all the retail shops the Rumbelow name, which by the time of Sydney Rumbelow's death numbered over 300. In 1995 the company failed, and all of its 311 stores closed for the last time.

Russell Hobbs *(coffee makers)*

The two men behind the British name are William Russell (b.1920) and Peter Hobbs (b.1916). Russell, a factory machinery inspector's son, was raised in High Wycombe, Buckinghamshire, and served his apprenticeship at the Rheostatic Company which had been founded by Leonard **Satchwell**. On completing his apprenticeship, he joined the assembly management team in the factory, becoming involved in the production of gyrocompass motors in World War II. Peter Hobbs, whose father managed various electric power supply companies in southeast England, was raised in Tunbridge Wells, Kent, and shortly before World War II was appointed district engineer of the Kent Electric Power Company. By 1951 both men were employed by **Morphy Richards**, where Russell was chief development engineer and Hobbs was sales manager of the industrial division. However, a disagreement developed between Hobbs and Charles Richards with regard to sales policy, and Hobbs resigned

to run his own small business manufacturing domestic appliances to a German patent. A few months later Russell similarly quarreled with Donal Morphy about the design constraints that the latter imposed on him. As a result, Russell Hobbs Ltd. was formed in 1952, with its first product an electric coffee percolator. The "automatic" coffee pot was a success, and the two partners followed it with an automatic electric kettle, which would switch itself off when the water had boiled. In 1962 the partners sold their enterprise to Tube Investments Ltd., and it is the TI Group that still produces Russell Hobbs coffee makers and electric kettles today.

Russell Stover *(candies)*

Russell Stover (1888-1954), of Hume, Saskatchewan, Canada, had been married just over a year in 1912 when he came home with some secondhand equipment and announced to his wife, Clara, that they would start up a candy business. Although neither of them had any experience, their chocolate won local approval. World War I rationing then made sugar scarce, and in 1919 the Stovers moved to Chicago, where they set up another candy enterprise. The business did not go well, however, and the couple closed shop in 1920 so Russell could take a job with a Des Moines confectioner. In 1921 Russell helped develop **Eskimo Pie**, which greatly improved his affairs. He sold his interest in the product for $30,000 and in 1923 the Stovers moved to Denver, where they launched the company that today is Russell Stover Candies, Inc. Clara succeeded her husband as head of the firm on his death, and when she sold the company in 1961 it was producing 22 million pounds of candy annually.

Ryanair *(airline)*

Ireland's first wholly independent airline, famous for its competitive fares, was founded in Dublin in 1985 by Tony Ryan (b.1934) and was floated on the stock market in 1997. At the end of the decade, Ryan's family, which included his three sons Cathal (b.1960), Declan (b.1964), and Shane (b.1972), were the third-richest business group in Ireland.

Ryvita *(rye crispbread)*

The name, from "rye" and Latin *vita*, "life," was entered in the *Trade Marks Journal* of February 18, 1925 by John Edwin Garrat of London, England, the first importer to Britain of Swedish crispbread. The name then passed to the manufacturers, The Ryvita Company Ltd., who entered it in the *Journal* of March 22, 1967 for: "Bread, crispbread and biscuits (other than biscuits for animals)."

S&A Foods *(Indian foods)*

The British company was founded by Perween Warsi (b.1957), the daughter of a civil engineer in India, who entered into an arranged marriage at 16 and with her husband, Talib (b.1947), left for Britain in 1974. She started making curries for local restaurants to stave off boredom in the kitchen of her Derby home, and in 1987 had a breakthrough when she convinced **Asda** to put her dishes into a taste test. Since then, Warsi's enterprise, named after her two sons, Sadiq and Abid, has put her at the top table of the curry industry and by 2000 she was the wealthiest Asian businesswoman in Britain, with a firm employing 1,100 people and producing 1.8 million ready meals a week.

SA *(beer)*

The Welsh bitter beer from **Brains** brewery is affectionately known to its aficionados as "Skull Attack," but the letters actually stand for "Special Ale" (rather than coming from the brewery's formal name of SA Brain & Co., as popularly explained). The beer is exported to the USA under the name "Traditional Welsh Ale."

Saab *(automobiles)*

The name of the company, founded in Trollhättan, Sweden, in 1937, is an acronym of Svenska Aeroplan AB ("Swedish Airplane Company"), indicating its origin as an airplane manufacturer rather than an auto builder. It produced its first cars in the 1940s, while other countries were engaged in World War II, and brought out its prototype in 1947. In 1965 the name was officially shortened to Saab AB. In 1968 the company merged with the truck builders **Scania** to become Saab-Scania AB.

Saatchi & Saatchi *see* **Cordiant**

Sabena *(airline)*

The Belgian airline was set up in 1923 by SNETA (Société Nationale pour l'Étude des Transports Aériens, "National Society for the Study of Air Transport") as the Société Anonyme Belge d'Exploitation de la Navigation Aérienne ("Belgian Limited Company for the Exploitation of Air Navigation"), and its present name is the acronym of this. The first official flight made by a Sabena aircraft was on May 23, 1923, when a Handley-Page single-engined airplane flew mail and goods from Brussels, Belgium, to Lympne, Kent, England, via Ostend.

Sabra *(liqueur)*

The Israeli chocolate orange liqueur was originally made in the 1960s from the sabra cactus that grows in Israel and around the south and eastern Mediterranean. "Sabra" is also a punning nickname for a native-born Israeli, who is said to be like the plant, prickly on the outside but sweet inside.

Saccone & Speed *(wine and liquor stores)*

The name of the British chain begins with James Speed, who set up as a wine and liquor merchant in Gibraltar in 1839, dealing mainly with Royal Navy personnel and the garrison as his main customers. A year later Jerome Saccone also started in the same business, being at first Speed's big rival, but later his great friend. By the turn of the century the two merchants had merged their businesses, and so Saccone & Speed was born, expanding the trade to the Navy by opening up offices in other countries in the British Empire.

Safeway *(supermarkets)*

The company owes its origins to the enterprise of two American families. In 1915 S.M. Skaggs, a Baptist minister, built a small grocery store in American Falls, Idaho, with the aim of rendering a Christian service to his neighbors, mostly hard-pressed grain farmers. Skaggs' six sons followed him into the business, and the eldest, Marion Barton Skaggs, extended the original store to a Western chain, Skaggs United Stores, that by 1926 had 428 units in 10 states. That same year, Skaggs merged with a Southern California chain of 322 stores originally known as the Sam Seelig stores that had adopted the Safeway name in 1925 following a contest to choose a new name. The resulting Safeway Stores expanded rapidly, so that in 1927 they had 915 stores and by 1931 3,527. Skaggs ran the company until 1934, when he passed control to Lingan A. Warren. Skaggs retired as company chairman in 1941, after which there were no longer any members of the Skaggs family in Safeway. The UK Safeway supermarket chain arose in 1962 as a subsidiary of the American company, but became an independent operation in 1987, by which time it had 133 stores.

Saga *(leisure)*

Saga Leisure started life as a travel business for pensioners, but now offers everything from insurance services to share dealing and home shopping. It was founded in 1951 by Sidney de Haan (1919-2002), a British hotelier in Folkestone, Kent, to provide affordable vacation tours for the over-50s, allowing them to maximize vacation savings by offering off-season accommodation. It soon became popular, and grew into a full-service management company. In 1979 it expanded to the USA, opening Saga International Holidays with headquarters in Boston, Massachusetts. The name itself implies extended adventure and achievement beyond the limits of a traditional working life.

Sagbag *(seating)*

The informal chair or seat, marketed by **Habitat** in the 1970s, consists of a large bag filled with polystyrene granules which mold themselves ("sag") to the form of the sitter. The name was entered in the *Trade Marks Journal* of December 18, 1974, the description specifying that the seating was "not for medical or surgical purposes."

Sage *(computer software)*

The British firm was founded in 1981 in Newcastle upon Tyne, northeast England, by Graham Wylie, David Goldman, Paul Muller, and Phil Lever. The four men held an impromptu board meeting in a local pub to decide a name, and took it from a wall poster showing different sorts of herbs. At the same time the name suggested wisdom, as a welcome bonus. Sage now has a staff of over 1,000 and claims to be the world's largest supplier of PC-based accounting software.

Sainsbury's *(food stores)*

John James Sainsbury (1844-1928) was born in Lambeth, London, England, the son of a frame and ornament maker. His first job, at age 14, was in a grocer's shop in Lambeth, after which he gained experience working with provision merchants and oil merchants. In 1869 he married Mary Ann Staples (1849-1927), the daughter of a north London dairyman, and the couple opened a dairy shop at 173 Drury Lane, selling butter, milk, eggs, and later, cheese. Their business thrived, and by 1876 they had opened another shop, in Kentish Town. They moved there as a family and opened a bacon store and depot nearby. Soon other stores were added to these two, with 14 branches in London by 1891, mostly in traditional market streets. The business was built up into a chain of supermarkets by his grandson, Alan John Sainsbury (1902-1998), company chairman from 1956 to 1967 and president to his death. By 1997 there were over 300 Sainsbury supermarkets throughout the UK, and the original shop in Drury Lane was in use as a Sainsbury store until 1958.

St Ivel *(dairy products)*

The British name is ostensibly that of a saint or place. In fact it is fictional, representing an imaginary monk who supposedly lived near the Yeo River that runs through the town of Yeovil, Somerset. The name was invented around 1900 as an advertising gimmick by a Mr. Barrett, director of the firm of Aplin and Barrett, then based in Yeovil. His creation was not entirely random, as "Ivel" is an old name of the Yeo and itself gave the name of the town. (The river name later dropped its second syllable.) St Ivel products are now marketed by **Unigate**, who have one of their main centers in Yeovil.

Saint Luis Rey *(cigars)*

The brand of Havana cigars was created in the 1950s by British importers Michael de Keyser and Nathan Silverstone, who named their creation after the popular American movie *The Bridge of San Luis Rey* (1944), based on Thornton Wilder's 1927 novel. (By good fortune, there was a Cuban town called San Luis Obispo.) The cigars are made at the **Romeo and Juliet** factory, and should not be confused with the San Luis Rey brand, made in Cuba for the German market.

St Margaret *(hosiery)*

The hosiery is made by the British firm of Corah, founded at the Globe Inn, Silver Street, Leicester, in 1815. It was here that Nathaniel

Corah first started out as a hosiery factor, as the Globe Inn was a recognized rendezvous for stockingers with goods to sell. The business grew, and the firm finally moved to a site near St. Margaret's church, in the northeast of the city, where in 1865 the foundation stone for a large factory and warehouse was laid. The site gave the company its brand name, which was first used that same year.

St Michael *(clothing and foods)*

The brand name, used for products made or prepared to **Marks & Spencer**'s own specifications, is based on that of Michael Marks, the company's founder. The firm had established a direct relationship with Corah, makers of **St Margaret** hosiery, and sought a saint's name to match this. Various possibilities were considered, among them "St Joan," but the final choice was made by Simon Marks in honor of his father.

Sally Line *(shipping line)*

The shipping line's parent company, Rederiaktebolaget Sally, is based in the Åland Islands (Ahvenanmaa), Finland, where it was founded and named by Algot Johansson in 1937 when he merged his various companies into one. He gave the name in honor of the Finnish writer Sally Salminen (1906-1976), who came from Åland and who gained popularity in Scandinavia (although by then living in the USA) following the publication of her novel *Katrina* (1936).

Salmson *(automobiles)*

The Société des Moteurs Salmson of Billancourt, near Paris, France, began life by manufacturing liquid-cooled aero engines. Émile Salmson had been experimenting with a seven-cylinder radial unit as early as 1909, and in World War I his engines figured strongly in military aircraft. When a demand for these slumped after the war, however, Salmson took out a license to build cars instead. The firm's sports cars were followed by luxury models in the 1920s and 1930s, but the company faltered after World War II and the last Salmson left the factory in 1957.

Salters *(scales)*

The British firm's roots go back to Richard Salter, who set up as a "spring maker" in Bilston, Staffordshire, in about 1760. Some time after 1770 he moved to West Bromwich, where his business was ultimately taken over by his nephew, George Salter (1780-1849), originally a bayonet maker. It was he who effectively established the present business, which until quite recently was called after him as "Geo. Salter & Co." The present company of Salter Industrial Measurement Ltd. is still based in West Bromwich, although in George Street, not the High Street, where George Salter had made his spring balances.

Salvarsan *(anti-syphilis drug)*

The former proprietary name for arsphenamine derives from Latin *salvare*, "to save," German *Arsenik*, "arsenic," and the chemical suffix "-an." It was the invention in 1907 of the German bacteriologist Paul Ehrlich, and the name was registered by Farbwerke, formerly Meister, Lucius & Brüning, of **Hoechst**, in the US Patent Office *Official Gazette* of August 23, 1910, with a note of filing on February 23, 1909. The arsenic compound was also known as "606," as it resulted from the 606th experiment, and this name was registered as a trademark in September 1911.

Salyrgan *(diuretic)*

The proprietary name for the drug mersalyl, a powerful diuretic formerly used in the treatment of edema, appears to be loosely based on the generic name, itself blending "mercury" and "salicyl." It was originally in German use, and was entered by H.A. Metz Laboratories, Inc., of New York, in the US Patent Office *Official Gazette* of June 10, 1924 for: "Preparations for the treatment of spirochetal and other infectious diseases and as a diuretic," with a claim of use since about April 11, 1924. A later entry by Farbwerke, formerly Meister, Lucius & Brüning, of **Hoechst**, Germany, was made in the *Trade Marks Journal* of October 15, 1924.

La Samaritaine *(department store)*

The Paris, France, department store was founded in 1870 by Ernest Cognacq (1839-1928), taking its name from a pump under the Pont-Neuf that drew water from the Seine to supply the Louvre until 1813 and that was decorated with a figure of the biblical woman of Samaria (French, *la Samaritaine*) giving Jesus water at the well (John 4:7).

Samsonite *(luggage)*

The company takes its name from the biblical hero Samson, famous for his strength. The name "Samsonite Streamlite" was entered by Shwayder Bros., Inc., of Denver, Colorado, in the US Patent Office *Official Gazette* of February 21, 1939: "For trunks, suitcases, and traveling bags," with a claim of use since April 18, 1938. The company stresses the robustness of its products: "These cases may look sleek and satin-smooth, but they're also tough and durable" (magazine ad insert, March 2000).

Samsung *(electronics)*

The Korean company was founded under its present name in Taegu, now in South Korea, by Byung Chull-Lee in 1938. His business originally exported dried fish, vegetables, and fruit to Manchuria and Peking (Beijing), but a flour mill was then set up and a confectionery factory built. In 1948 Lee moved his head office to Seoul and founded the Samsung Corporation with the aim of entering the manufacturing industry. The electronics side of the company, for which it is now best known, followed the establishment of the Samsung Electronics Co. in 1969. Samsung successes include the digital clock radio (1978), PC (1983), mobile phone (1988), DVD player (1997), and high-definition TV (1998).

Samuel, H *see* **H. Samuel**

Samuel French *(publishers)*

The British publishers of acting editions of plays was founded in London in 1830 by an actor, Thomas Lacy. In 1872 the business was bought by Samuel French, who moved to London that year after setting up a similar enterprise in 1854 in New York. The firm still has British and American branches and thrives on amateur dramatic societies, who have a constant demand for play texts.

Samuel Smith *(beer)*

When John Smith of Tadcaster, Yorkshire, England, died in 1879, he left the business to his two sons, William and Samuel, whose fraternal relations were hardly cordial. Samuel Smith died the following year, however, leaving a son, also named Samuel. Pursuing his family feud beyond the grave, William Smith refused to take his nephew into the business, and instead built a new brewery in 1884, leaving his old and derelict premises to Samuel Smith. It is not clear exactly when the old brewery was resurrected, but it is known that Samuel Smith III (son of the spurned Samuel) operated it until he died in 1927. So it is really this last "Sam Smith" who gave his name to the present company, and to the beer it brews, rated among the best in Britain.

San Miguel *(beer)*

The best-known brand of Spanish beer outside Spain takes its name from the Filippino brewing company who set up a plant in Lerida, Catalonia, in 1956. The brewery itself, the first in South-East Asia, was established in 1890 next to the colonial mansion of the Spanish governor-general of the Philippines in Manila as La Fábrica de Cerveza de San Miguel ("The St. Michael Brewery").

Sanatogen *(tonic wine)*

The name was entered in the US Patent Office *Official Gazette* of June 14, 1898 by the German company Bauer Cie. of Berlin for "dietetic albuminous preparations," with a note of use since October 25, 1897. The meaning was undoubtedly intended to be "health-giving," based on Latin *sanitas*, "health," and the Greek element "-gen" found in such chemical names as "oxygen." The wine has also been associated with the anagrammatically named British firm of Genatosan, of Loughborough, Leicestershire, who entered "Sanatogen Tonic Wine" in the *Trade Marks Journal* of March 1, 1939. Sanatogen is now produced by **Whiteway**.

Sandeman *(port)*

Familiar for its trademark of a silhouetted, cloaked, and hatted figure ("The Don"), the House of Sandeman was founded in 1790 in London, England, by George G. Sandeman (1765-1841), a member of an old Scottish family. He traded for some time at Tom's Coffee House in Cornhill, and after a short time decided to specialize in sherry and port. By 1792 he was representing the sherries of James Duff of Cadiz, and shipped his first port, the true first vintage Sandeman, that same year. In 1809 one of the firm's partners, James Gordon, began shipping sherries from Cadiz under the Sandeman name, and Sandeman madeira from Portugal followed. By now George Sandeman was established in St. Swithin's Lane, where the firm's head offices remained until 1969. The "Don" trademark was acquired by Sandeman in 1928. The figure is intended to represent a blend of port and sherry, with the cloak that of a Portuguese student and the wide-brimmed hat of the kind worn by a typical Spanish *caballero* of Jerez.

Sanders, Colonel *see* Colonel Sanders

Sandersons *(wallpaper)*

The British firm was founded by Arthur Sanderson (1829-1882), who in 1860 set himself up in London as an importer of luxury French wallpapers. It was not until 1879 that he began to manufacture his own papers, by hand and machine, but by the mid-1880s, when the business was in the hands of his three sons, John, Arthur Bengough, and Harold, Sandersons had both a factory in Chiswick and a showroom in Berners Street, in the heart of London. It is not certain what sparked Arthur Sanderson's initial interest in wallpapers, and little is known of his career before 1860, but his name has become synonymous with artistic wallpaper, typically with a floral or William Morris design.

Sandoz *(pharmaceuticals)*

The Swiss company originated in Basel as the Chemische Fabrik Kern u. Sandoz ("Kern and Sandoz Chemical Works"), set up in 1876 by the color chemist Alfred Kern (1850-1893) and the merchant Édouard Sandoz (1853-1928). The Sandoz name was always to the fore, but 1895 the firm became the joint-stock company Chemische Fabrik vormals Sandoz ("Chemical Works formerly Sandoz"). In 1911, however, the Sandoz Chemical Co. was established in Bradford, Yorkshire, England, and in 1919 the Sandoz Chemical Works, Inc., was formed in New York. Sandoz merged with **Wander** in 1967, with **Gerber** in 1994, and famously with **Ciba-Geigy** in 1996 to create **Novartis** and the world's second largest pharmaceutical company.

Sanforized *(preshrunk fabric)*

The name is based on that of Sanford Lockwood Cluett (1874-1968), director of engineering and research at the US company of **Cluett**, Peabody Inc. of Troy, New York. Sanford Cluett had invented the patented process named for him, basically by pushing back (compressing) a fabric that had been pulled out when it was under tension in the various stages of manufacture: weaving, bleaching, dyeing, and printing. The name was entered in the US Patent Office *Official Gazette* of September 30, 1930 and the *Trade Marks Journal* of May 24, 1939.

Sanibin *(refuse receptacle)*

The type of hygienically secure trashcan derives its name rather obviously from a contraction of "sanitary bin." It was entered by its British manufacturers, Robert Bailey and Son, of Stockport, Cheshire, in the *Trade Marks Journal* of March 16, 1921.

Sanitas *(disinfectants)*

The British business of this name was set up as a private company in 1876 by the chemist Charles Thomas Kingzett (1852-1935), noted for his research into ozone and the oxidation of terpenes and essential oils. In World War I it was one of the chief government contractors for the supply of disinfectants in bulk and also for that of larvicides for the destruction of mosquitos and other insects in Mesopotamia and elsewhere. The name is simply Latin for "health."

Sanka *(decaffeinated coffee)*

Decaffeinated coffee was first made in 1903 by Ludwig Roselius, a German importer of coffee to France, who named his product from the French phrase *sans caffeine*, "without caffeine." The name was entered by the Société Anonyme Fabriques de Produits de Chimie Organique ("Organic Chemistry Products Co. Ltd.") of Laire, France, in the US Patent Office *Official Gazette* of August 14, 1923 for: "Teas and coffees; tea and coffee extracts, both dry and liquid, and tea and coffee substitutes," with a claim of use since March 19, 1910. Sanka Coffee Corporation, New York, then entered the name in the *Gazette* of October 18, 1933, and General Foods (*see* **Bird's**) in that of December 17, 1952. Roselius was also the creator of **HAG**.

Sanocrysin *(drug for treating tuberculosis)*

The drug, a colorless crystalline complex salt of gold, formerly used in the treatment of tuberculosis, is of Danish origin. Its name, from

Latin *sanus*, "healthy," Greek *khrusos*, "gold," and the chemical suffix "-in," was entered in the US Patent Office *Official Gazette* of March 10, 1925 as a "medicine for phthisis," with a claim of use since March 16, 1924.

Sansoni *(publishers)*

The Italian publishing house was founded in Florence in 1873 by Giulio Cesare Sansoni (1837-1885). In 1976 it merged with Rizzoli (*see* **RSC Editori**).

Santobrite *(wood preservative)*

The preparation of sodium pentachlorophenate, used as a fungicide, wood preservative, insecticide, etc., takes its name from its manufacturers, the **Monsanto** Chemical Company, who entered it in the US Patent Office *Official Gazette* of June 2, 1936, with a claim of use since April 2, 1936.

Sanyo *(electrical and electronic goods)*

The Japanese company Sanyo Electric, based in Osaka, was founded in 1947 by Toshio Iue with a name meaning "three oceans" (*san*, "three," and *yo*, "ocean"). The Atlantic (*taiseiyo*), Pacific (*taiheiyo*), and Indian (*indoyo*) oceans are the three principal oceans of the world, providing access to most countries.

Sara Lee *(foods, knitwear, and household products)*

The American company was incorporated in 1941 as the South Street Company and went through various name changes before becoming the Consolidated Grocers Corporation in 1945 and Consolidated Foods Corporation in 1954. In 1956 the company purchased a frozen bakery business, Kitchens of Sara Lee, founded in 1935 by Charles Lubin, who named it after his eight-year-old daughter. In 1985, following further expansion, the entire corporation took the name Sara Lee in order to promote its frozen food brand.

Saran *(cling film)*

The proprietary name for polyvinyl chloride (PVC) was entered by the **Dow** Chemical Company, its manufacturers, in the US Patent Office *Official Gazette* of November 26, 1940 for: "Thermoplastic synthetic resins comprising polymers and co-polymers derived from vinylidene chloride," with a claim of use since August 21, 1940. The name itself (stressed on the second syllable) appears to be arbitrary. A report in the *Textile Colorist* for February 1948 announced that Dow's Plastic Sales Division had "formally released its trademark right to the name 'saran' permitting it to become the descriptive name of the product." In the UK, however, the name was entered by Dow in the *Trade Marks Journal* of November 26, 1958 for: "Wrapping (packaging) materials included in Class 16 in the form of films." The product is also known as "Saran Wrap."

Sarson's *(vinegar)*

Englishman Thomas Sarson first made vinegars in 1794. The business stayed in the family thoughout the 19th century, when the special brand "Sarson's Virgin Vinegar" was introduced. The firm is now owned by **Nestlé**.

Sasha *(dolls)*

The name is that of the Swiss designer Sasha Morgenthaler (1893-1975), who first made toys for her three children in the 1920s, mainly in the form of animals and dolls. She sought to create dolls with lively expressions, but production problems hampered the realization of her program. An old friend took over the business in 1988, moving its base to the USA, but died in 1993. The following year the business was acquired by Franz and Marianne Götz of Götz-Puppenfabrik, Rodental, Germany.

Satchwell *(heating controls)*

Familiar in Britain from the heat control knob on many household radiators, the name is that of Leonard Satchwell (1888-1962), born near Nuneaton, Warwickshire, the son of a Nonconformist minister. After working for several years for an engineering company, Satchwell set up a business in 1921 to make unbreakable power resistors, used for varying the speeds of trams (streetcars) and trolleybuses. He called his venture the Rheostatic Company, and it operated from a converted cowshed on the Slough Trading Estate, with a staff of just six. In 1927 the enterprise manufactured the world's first commercially available thermostat, used to control electric heaters. At the end of the 1920s, the Rheostatic Company expanded into larger premises on the Farnham Road, Slough, where the business remains today, and in 1937 became a limited company. It was only in 1962, the year of its founder's death, that the Rheostatic Co. Ltd. was commemoratively renamed Satchwell Control Systems Ltd.

Saunders-Roe *see* **Avro**

Sauza *(tequila)*

The best-selling brand of tequila takes its name from Don Cenobio Sauza, who went to Tequila, Mexico, in 1858 to work in the liquor industry. In 1870 he rented the Antigua Cruz distillery to begin distilling for himself, and in 1873 bought it. Sauza was the first tequila to be exported to the USA, in the same year that Sauza bought the distillery.

Savage *(rifles)*

Arthur William Savage (1857-1938) was born in Kingston, Jamaica. He immigrated to the USA in 1886, became a naturalized subject in 1895, and in 1893 founded the Savage Arms Co. in Utica, New York. Savage's specialty was the improvement of magazine rifles, but he was also the inventor of a dirigible torpedo. His name was entered by the Savage Arms Co., of Frankfort, New York, in the US Patent Office *Official Gazette* of August 18, 1914 for "Rifles, Pistols, and Cartridges," with a claim of use since January 1, 1906.

Savlon *(skin antiseptic)*

The proprietary name for chlorhexidine with cetrimide appears to take its name from its British manufacturers, Avlex, a subsidiary of **ICI**, but perhaps with an intentional suggestion of French *savon*, "soap." The name was entered in the *Trade Marks Journal* of December 1, 1954.

Savory & Moore *(drugstore, or chemist's)*

In 1798 Thomas Field Savory, a London, England, apothecary's apprentice, opened a chemist's shop (drugstore) at 143 New Bond Street, where the resulting firm of Savory & Moore had its head office until the early 1980s. Savory's shop was patronized by the aristocracy, and became well known for its sale of Seidlitz powders. On Savory's death the business passed to his nephew, John Savory, a founder of the Royal Pharmaceutical Society. Little is known about the Mr. Moore who was Savory's partner, although he appears to have been involved in the business at an early stage, if not right from the start. The firm's head office is now in Curzon Street, not far from its place of origin almost 200 years ago.

Saxa *(salt)*

The name was first in used in 1907, and entered in the *Trade Marks Journal* of May 27, 1908. It presumably derives from Latin *saxum*, "rock," alluding to rock salt as a term for common salt in its natural mineral form.

Saxby's *(pies and sausages)*

The English firm, famous for its Melton Mowbray pies, was founded in 1904 by two brothers, Herbert W. Saxby (1870-1953) and Edward E. Saxby (1873-1966), who had worked together in the food trade since leaving school. They set up shop in Wellingborough, Northamptonshire, making pies above the shop and sausages and cooked meats at the rear. Although initially simply a retail pork butcher's shop, the hard work of the "two-men-and-a-boy" enterprise paid off, so that in 1912 the brothers bought a small factory just behind the shop, taking on a staff of 20. In 1920 the manufacturing side of the business had grown to such an extent that a new factory was built, and it is that same factory, with a staff of 80 in its bakery department in 1987, and 55 in the butchery department, that now produces a whole range of pies and puddings. The firm remains in family hands today.

Saxin *(artificial sweetener)*

The name, based on "saccharin," was originally entered by "Henry Solomon Wellcome … manufacturing chemist" (*see* **Wellcome**) in the *Trade Marks Journal* of July 28, 1897 for: "Chemical substances prepared for use in medicine and pharmacy, but not including those prepared for use in the cure of corns and warts and not including any goods of a like kind to any of these excluded goods." In a much later entry in the *Journal* of August 19, 1964, the definition has narrowed and altered to "Flavourings and essences, none being essential oils; and sweetening materials included in Class 30."

Sazerac *(cocktail)*

According to *Webster's Third New International Dictionary*, the cocktail consists of "bourbon, absinthe flavoring, bitters, and sugar stirred with ice, strained, and flavored with a twist of lemon peel when served." The name comes from the Sazerac Coffee Bar, on Exchange Alley, New Orleans, where the cocktail became popular in the 1850s. It is now manufactured by the company of the same name.

Scaldis *see* **Bush**

Scalextric *(model racing car systems)*

The range of models so named was launched in around 1950 by a British firm called Minimodels. They were originally called "Scalex," as they were built to no specific scale ("scale x"), but when an electrical system was introduced in 1957 the name was adapted by adding the "-tric" of "electric." The name was entered in the *Trade Marks Journal* of January 30, 1957.

Scania *(trucks and buses)*

The Swedish company originated from the factory set up in the 1890s in the town of Malmö by the English bicycle manufacturers **Humber**. At first the works was known as Swedish Humber Aktiebolaget, but just before the turn of the 20th century its split from the parent company to diversify into vacuum cleaners, paper machinery, and the like, and for these new activities took the name Maskinfabriks Aktiebolaget Scania, the latter being the latinized form of the name Skåne, that of the southern county of Sweden of which Malmö is the capital. (This itself derives from Scandia, the Roman name of what is now Scandinavia, the European peninsula occupied by Norway and Sweden.) Production soon exapanded to the manufacture of motorcycles and automobiles, and in 1902 Scania produced their first truck. In 1968 Scania merged with **Saab** to form Saab-Scania Aktiebolaget.

Scenicruiser *(coaches)*

The name of the luxury **Greyhound** coaches equipped for long-distance travel derives from a blend of "scenic" and "cruiser." It was entered by Greyhound in the US Patent Office *Official Gazette* of January 13, 1959.

Schering-Plough *(drugs)*

The first part of the name is that of the German company of Schering, who began to export drugs from Berlin to the United States in 1894 and established a branch in New York in 1929. The second part names Abe Plough, who in 1908, as a teenager in Memphis, Tennessee, borrowed $125 from his father, mixed up a batch of cotton-seed oil, carbolic acid, and camphor, and sold it to druggists as "antiseptic healing oil." In 1915 he bought the stock of the bankrupt Memphis Drug Company, mostly cases of "Chill Tonic Oxidine," supposedly a cure for chills, and sold it for $34,000 in Louisiana and Texas. In 1920 he bought the St. Joseph Company of Chattanooga, Tennessee, makers of aspirin, and targeted the children's aspirin market. Further company purchases followed until 1971, when he merged his business with Schering. The original Schering company is still active in Germany and competes against Schering USA outside the United States.

Schermuly *(pistols and rockets)*

The name is that of William Schermuly (1857-1929), the English inventor of a type of line-carrying rocket fired from a pistol, used in lifesaving at sea. The name was entered by the Schermuly Pistol Rocket Apparatus Ltd., of Newdigate, Surrey, in the *Trade Marks Journal* of July 30, 1947 for: "Pyrotechnic articles, cartridges, and apparatus for firing rockets," although the apparatus itself was already in use in the 1920s.

Schick *(electric razors)*

The razors owe their origin to Jacob Schick (1877-1937), a US Army veteran, who during a mining expedition to British Columbia in 1911-14 became vexed at having to heat a pot of water every morning to shave in subzero temperatures. To dispense with this nuisance, he designed a manual razor that could be used without soap and water. On returning home, Schick sent prototypes of his "dry razor" to several manufacturers, but all rejected it. Undaunted, he worked on plans for an electrically powered razor, and eventually introduced it in 1931. It was not the first electric razor, as they had been patented as early as 1900 in the United States, but it was the first to be successfully manufactured. Fortuitously, Schick's name is the German word for "style" or "elegance" (French *chic*).

Schirmer *(music publishers)*

There are two American firms of this name, respectively G. Schirmer, Inc. and E.C. Schirmer. The former takes its name from Gustav Schirmer (1829-1893), who immigrated to

New York from Germany in 1837 and in 1854 became manager of the Kerksieg & Bruesing Co., which he renamed G. Schirmer. The Schirmer Library of Musical Classics, with their distinctive yellow covers, is known worldwide. The latter company was founded in Boston in 1914 by Ernest Charles Schirmer (1865-1958) and began by publishing the choral repertory of university glee clubs.

Schlitz (beer)

The American brewing business was founded in 1849, when August Krug started a brewery in a disused restaurant in Milwaukee. On his death in 1856, the firm was taken over by the brewery's young bookkeeper, Joseph Schlitz (1831-1875), who married Krug's widow and in 1874 renamed the business after himself. Tragically, Schlitz died the following year on the way to Germany to visit relatives when the steamer *Schiller* went down in the Irish Sea. Until 1949 Milwaukee was the only place in the United States where Schlitz brewed beer. "The beer that made Milwaukee famous" has not been brewed in the city since 1982, however, when the brewery was taken over by **Stroh's**.

Schlumberger (oil)

The name of the American oil-well testing company is that of the French brothers Conrad Schlumberger (1878-1936) and Marcel Schlumberger (1884-1953), born in Guebwiller, northeastern France. As the region was then under German control, the brothers moved to Paris to avoid being made German citizens. There Conrad taught at the École Supérieure des Mines from 1907 until 1923, when he resigned his professorship of physics to join his brother Marcel in developing applications of physics for use in mining and petroleum geology. In 1913 Conrad developed the first geophysical method of detecting a nonmagnetic ore deposit. After World War I Conrad had perfected a resistance-measuring device and together with Marcel began measuring the shapes of subsurface mineral deposits for mining companies. The company dates its founding from this year, 1919, and extended the use of their techniques worldwide. The name is properly pronounced in the French fashion, "Shloom-bear-zhay," but is usually known to oilmen as "Slumber-Jay."

Schneider (beer)

The German family of G. Schneider & Sohn have been bottling wheat beer for six generations and are said to have been first active in the trade in 1607. They began as lessees of the Royal Court brewery in Munich, but have been brewing in their own right since 1872.

Scholl (footcare products)

The name is that of Dr. William Mathias Scholl (1882-1968), born in La Porte, Indiana. As a child, he enjoyed making things from leather, and at 15 designed and sewed a complete harness set for the biggest horse on his father's farm. But the horizons of farm life were narrow, and Scholl made his way to Michigan City, where he found work as a shoemaker's apprentice. Soon he had his own shoe shop in nearby Armour, Indiana, where he noticed that many of his customers had misshapen feet, due to the crudely made shoes of the day. Scholl visited local libraries to study the anatomy of the human foot and anatomy in general, and at 18 enrolled at the Harvey Medical College (now Loyola University), Chicago, continuing his work in the shop when he could. He graduated a doctor of medicine in 1904, and started his own business that year as a manufacturer of orthopedic foot appliances, working from a single rented room in West Madison Street, Chicago. His venture steadily grew, so that he was able to move to bigger and better premises, and in 1906 he formally registered his enterprise as The Scholl Manufacturing Company. Dr. Scholl's footcare products are today marketed by **Schering-Plough**.

Schott (music publishers)

The German music publishers take their name from the clarinetist Bernhard Schott (1748-1809), who founded the firm in Mainz in 1780. His sons Johann Andreas (1781-1840) and Johann Joseph (1782-1855) developed the list and absorbed a number of other firms, so that in the 19th century B. Schott Söhne, as it came to be known, was a flourishing business. Schott of London became a separate British concern in 1914 but Schott of Mainz resumed control in 1980.

Schrader (air valves)

George H.F. Schrader of New York invented a new type of air valve for use on pneumatic tires in the late 19th century, and the name "Schrader Universal" was entered in the US Patent Office *Official Gazette* of April 30, 1895, with a note of use since February 12, 1895.

Schroder *(bank)*

The English merchant bank was founded in London in 1804 by Henry Schroder, of the Hamburg, Germany, merchant family of this name. Schroders were one of the first international houses to gain a foothold in London banking, and Henry Schoder soon developed a large business in the acceptance of bills. In 1962 the firm merged with Helbert, Wagg & Co, a merchant bank established in London in around 1800, to become J. Henry Schroder Wagg and Co. Ltd.

Schweppes *(tonic water)*

The name is that of Jean Jacob Schweppe (1740-1821), born a farmer's son in Witzenhausen, Germany. Jacob's parents entrusted him to the care of a tinker when he was about 12 years old, but the boy showed such skill with the pots and pans that the tinker returned him to his family, recommending he be apprenticed to a silversmith. This was done, and the same thing happened: the silversmith suggested Jacob work for a jeweler. This in turn was arranged, and Jacob was so successful in his new trade that he decided to seek a post in Geneva, Switzerland. It is not known exactly when he went there, but he was certainly in Geneva by 1765, and by 1786 had qualified as a master jeweler. Meanwhile, Schweppe had not been idle in other spheres of activity. He keenly followed the scientific experiments of his day, and was especially interested to see if it was possible to make gases combine with water. As the constituents of natural mineral water were known, might it not be possible to combine them artificially? Schweppe's experiments proved that it was, and by 1788 he was selling his bottled mineral water commercially. He took on partners and set up his business in Geneva in 1790, went to London to continue on his own in 1792, and took three English partners in 1798. The following year he retired, returning to Geneva to pursue his interests privately. The firm he founded added a lemonade product in 1835, but the tonic water, for which it became famous, did not arrive until 1870, and a decade later was being sold around the world. In 1969 the company merged with **Cadbury** to form Cadbury Schweppes.

Schwinn *(bicycles)*

Ignaz Schwinn (1860-1948) spent most of his early years as an itinerant machinist in northern Germany. In the 1880s, Schwinn was working at a Frankfurt machine shop that supplied parts to Heinrich Kleyer, a bicycle maker. The two became friends, and Kleyer eventually hired Schwinn as his designer and works manager. Schwinn was keen to set up his own company, and moved to Chicago in 1891. Four years later he joined with Adoph Arnold, president of a local meatpacking house, to form Arnold, Schwinn and Co. With Schwinn providing the technical knowhow, and Arnold looking after the management side, the bicycle-making business was a success, selling 25,000 in their first year. Schwinn bought out his partner in 1908 and remained the active head of the firm for the rest of his life.

SCi *(computer games)*

As a young girl, Jane Cavanagh (b.1957), whose father ran a small electronics company in Hardley, Hampshire, England, was more interested in circuit boards than dollhouses. She first showed entrepreneurial flair at age 17 when she hit on a way of making money by repainting car bodies. This resourcefulness and her early exposure to technology led her to spot the potential of the computer games market. The opportunity came when she persuaded FIL, a division of the French conglomerate **Thales**, to finance the launch of her own company. She called it SCI, for Sales Curve Interactive, because she saw it as primarily a sales and marketing organization for foreign companies, and began by distributing computer games from a base in south London. Her enterprise boomed, and by the end of the century Cavanagh was the most successful woman in the British computer games industry.

Scientology *(religious system)*

Scientology, from Latin *scientia*, "knowledge," and "-ology," is a religious system founded in 1954 (as the "Church of Scientology") by the American science-fiction writer L. Ron Hubbard (1911-1986). It is based on the seeking of self-knowledge and spiritual fulfillment through graded courses of study and training, and its name was entered by Hubbard in the US Patent Office *Official Gazette* of September 1, 1970, with a note of first use on November 21, 1951.

Scleroscope *(measuring instrument)*

The Scleroscope determines the hardness of metal or some other material by measuring the height of rebound of a small diamond-tipped hammer dropped onto the material from a fixed height. Its name, from the Greek elements "sclero-" ("hard") and "-scope" ("viewing"), was entered by the Shore Instrument and Mfg. Company, Inc., New York, in the US Patent Office *Official Gazette* of August 29, 1961. The instrument dates from the early 20th century as the invention of the American manufacturer Albert F. Shore.

Scoline *(anesthetic)*

The proprietary name for the drug succinylcholine, used as a muscle relaxant and local anesthetic, derives its name from letters in the generic name. It was entered by **Allen & Hanbury**, of London, England, in the *Trade Marks Journal* of January 30, 1952.

Scophony *(television system)*

The dated television system, using an optical and mechanical method of picture scanning, appears to derive its name from the Greek-based "-scope" element meaning "to look at" (as in "telescope," etc.) and "-phony" meaning "sound" (as in "telephony"). It was originally entered by Scophony Ltd., of London, England, in the *Trade Marks Journal* of April 20, 1932 for: "Philosophical instruments, scientific instruments and apparatus for useful purposes; instruments and apparatus for teaching."

Scotch *(adhesive tapes)*

The brand name, reserved for products by **3M**, has no direct association with Scotland except as recounted in the following story. A fashion arose in the 1920s for having cars painted in two tones, and 3M had evolved a 2-inchwide masking tape for use by auto manufacturers when painting such cars. This expensive procedure continued until an employee, Richard Drew (1886-1956), hit on the idea of restricting the adhesive coating to just one quarter of a strip of each side of the tape instead of covering the whole two inches This was duly done, but the tape had a tendency to fall off, so that auto manufacturers and garage proprietors were as dissatisfied as before. When the 3M salesman called at one garage, the painter told him, "Take this Scotch tape back to those bosses of yours and tell them to put adhesive all over it, not just on the edges!" (He meant "Scotch" in its slang sense of "miserly," alluding to the legendary thriftiness of the Scots.) 3M thus reverted to the full coating, and when the salesman next called, and was asked if he was "still selling that Scotch tape," he was pleased to reply that he was not. The colloquialism caught on, and "Scotch" was entered by 3M (then still the Minnesota Mining & Manufacturing Co.) in the US Patent Office *Official Gazette* of October 16, 1945, with a claim of use since January 1928. *See also* (1) **Scotchgard**; (2) **Scotchlite**.

Scotchgard *(textile finish)*

The waterproof grease- and stain-resistant finish for textiles, suedes, leather, and other materials is manufactured by **3M**, the makers of **Scotch** tape. Hence the name, with the second element based on "guard," entered by the then Minnesota Mining and Manufacturing Company of St. Paul, Minnesota, in the US Patent Office *Official Gazette* of May 1, 1956: "For chemical composition for application to various surfaces to repel grease and oil therefrom." *Cp.* **Scotchlite**.

Scotchlite *(light-reflecting material)*

The light-reflecting material, containing a layer of minute glass lenses and used on signs, road vehicles, etc., is manufactured by **3M**, the makers of **Scotch** tape. Hence the name, with the second element representing "light," entered by the then Minnesota Mining and Manufacturing Company of St. Paul, Minnesota, in the US Patent Office *Official Gazette* of May 4, 1941, with a claim of use since December 1, 1939. A later registration in the *Trade Marks Journal* of June 17, 1970 was for: "Sign faces made of or incorporating plastics embedded with light reflective substances." *Cp.* **Scotchgard**.

Scott *(motorcycles)*

The British motorcycles owe their name to Alfred Scott (d.1923), who originally developed his water-cooled two-stroke engine for use on boats. He launched his first motorcycle in 1908, but production finally petered out in the 1960s.

Scott, Bowater *see* **Bowater-Scott**

Scotties *(paper tissues)*

The tissues are made and marketed by **Bowater-Scott** and take their name from the Scott brothers who founded the original business. The name was entered in the *Trade Marks Journal* of February 21, 1979.

Scottish Courage *see* **Courage**

Scott's *("Emulsion")*

The man behind the so-called "emulsion" was Alfred Bowne Scott, a New York manufacturing chemist, who established his business with his cousin Samuel Wood Bowne as partner in 1874. Together they produced their "emulsion," or cod liver oil, and the preparation first came to England exactly ten years later, in 1884, where it was manufactured at a laboratory in Farringdon Street, London. Subsequently the firm of Scott & Bowne Ltd. acquired a factory in Southall, and went on to produce a wide range of pharmaceuticals. In 1978 the business was acquired by **Beecham**.

Scott's *("Porage Oats")*

Little is known about the Scottish firm of A. & R. Scott which was formed into a limited company in 1887, except that it manufactured Midlothian Biscuits and had premises in the Kingston Dock area of Glasgow. The concern also produced Scott's Midlothian Oatflour and Scott's Improved Oatcakes. In 1909 the business was transferred to Colinton, Edinburgh, and the mills there must have been producing "Porage Oats" at about this time. The spelling "porage" instead of the now standard "porridge" was formerly quite common, although it was not used for the breakfast food of today but for the original soup ("pottage") of meat or vegetables thickened with barley or flour. No doubt the firm chose the spelling for purposes of distinctiveness. They capitalized on it in their promotional material, one 1954 ad beginning: "Porage or Porridge? What's the difference? Spell it either way; it means a fine hot breakfast. But there *is* a difference. There's something *extra special* about PORAGE (spelt

like this on every Scott's pack) because Scott's Porage is made from genuine Scottish oats."

Scovill *(household goods)*

Scovill make a range of products, running from electric knives to corn poppers, snap fasteners to door chimes. They started out as Abel Porter & Company, a button-manufacturing business founded by Abel Porter in Waterbury, Connecticut, in 1804. His successors, the Scovill brothers, bought the company and moved it into brass casting and rolling. Scovill were associated exclusively with brass until the mid-1960s, when they expanded into other areas, mainly by purchasing other companies.

Scrabble *(board game).*

The game was the invention in 1931 of Alfred M. Butts (1900-1993), an architect of Rhinebeck, New York, who devised it when out of work during the Depression. First, he constructed it as a game of lettered tiles to be placed on a squared board to make a crossword. Then, unsure of what to do next, he called it "It" and invited some friends to play. They liked the game, and he tried to market it. But there were no sales. Butts refined the rules, changed the name to "Lexico," and tried again. Then he called it "Alph", and then "Criss-Crosswords." Still no one was interested, with the exception of James Brunot (d.1984), a government social worker, to whom Butts introduced the game in 1939. Ten years later, Brunot and his wife, Helen, risked buying the rights to the game to sell under a new name, "Scrabble." It did quite well for a time, but the Brunots were on the brink of bankruptcy when Jack Strauss, chairman of **Macy's**, came across the game on holiday and decided to market it. Sales now took off. The Brunots sold the rights and made their fortune, but they did not forget the real inventor and made sure he received a few cents in royalties from every sale. Alfred Butts never needed to work again. The name was entered by the Production and Marketing Corporation of Newtown, Connecticut, in the US Patent Office *Official Gazette* of January 10, 1950, with a claim of use since December 1, 1948, and later in the *Trade Marks Journal* of July 21, 1954, the year **Spear's** introduced the game to Britain. According to the dictionary, "scrabble" means "scratch, scrape, or paw with the hands or feet," and it seems Brunot thought this an apt description of a player "scrabbling" to select letters and fit a word on to the board.

Scribner *(publishers)*

The publishing house of Charles Scribner's Sons takes its name from Charles Scribner (1821-1871), born in New York City the son of a successful merchant. He attended New York University in 1837 and then moved to the College of New Jersey (now Princeton University), where he graduated in 1840. After a physical breakdown caused him to abandon his law studies with a New York attorney, he organized a publishing company with a local dry goods merchant, Isaac D. Baker, in 1846, calling the business Baker & Scribner. Initially the firm's list comprised mainly philosophical and theological works, especially Presbyterian books, progressing subsequently to reprints and translations of various British and continental European literary works. In 1850, just as the firm was becoming established, Baker died suddenly, and Scribner continued under his own name. After his own death the business was managed successively by his three sons, John Blair Scribner (1850-1879), Charles Scribner (1854-1930), and Arthur Hawley Scribner (1859-1932). Charles Scribner, the second son, was in control from 1879 to 1930, and it was during his lengthy (and dictatorial) presidency that the house gained fame for its publication of many leading American and British writers, such as Henry James, Theodore Roosevelt, Ernest Hemingway, R.L. Stephenson, Rudyard Kipling, and J.M. Barrie. The business became Charles Scribner's Sons in 1878. Charles Scribner, Jr. (1921-1995), the founder's great-grandson, was head of the firm from 1952 through 1984 and personal editor of Hemingway's works. The family name, meaning "writer" (Old French *escrivain*), is nicely apt for a publisher.

Sea Legs *(anti-sea sickness tablets)*

The name is refreshingly obvious for a medicinal preparation: "Sea Legs" will help you find (and keep) your sea legs. The product contains meclozine, an antihistamine used to prevent motion sickness. The name was entered in the *Trade Marks Journal* of January 21, 1981.

Seaby's *(coins and medals)*

The Englishman who gave his name to the London numismatists was Herbert "Bert" Allen Seaby (1898-1979), born in Reading the son of an art lecturer. As a boy he became interested in coins when given a set of Maundy money one birthday. He quit school in 1914 and entered the Royal Engineers at a time when volunteers were required for service in World War I. After the war he obtained a position in London with **Spinks**. He was with them seven years, but cherished the ambition of setting up his own business, which he eventually did in 1926, in premises in Oxford Circus House, above the Underground (subway) station. He named his firm B.A. Seaby Ltd., retaining his pet name "Bert" for the "B." In 1933 he moved to new premises in Great Portland Street, by which time his business was already expanding rapidly. At first he issued lists of coins for sale by duplicating them on the office copying machine, but from 1936 he published printed lists, with this in turn becoming a monthly magazine, *Seaby's Coin and Medal Bulletin*, after World War II. The company now has its head office in Margaret Street, London.

Seagram *(liquor)*

The Canadian company, now the largest producer and marketer of distilled spirits in the world, owes its name to Joseph E. Seagram (1841-1919), son of an English family who had emigrated to Canada in 1837. Joseph married into a grain-milling family who ran a distilling plant in Waterloo, Ontario, and in 1883 he had done well enough to buy his relatives out. His first whiskey, marketed that same year, was a great success, and was effectively the cornerstone on which he built his "empire" before he died. In 1928 the firm of Joseph E. Seagram & Sons was purchased by the Distillers Corporation, headed by Samuel Bronfman, the son of a Russian family who had gone to Canada in the last quarter of the 19th century. The new company was renamed Distillers Corporation-Seagram, Ltd., and it grew rapidly during the later years of the Prohibition era and during the 1930s. Although by then the company headquarters were in the Seagram Building, New York, Bronfman moved them back to Waterloo, Canada, in 1971, the year of his death, by way of a tribute to Seagram himself, who had started it all. The concern then passed to Bronfman's son, Peter F. Bronfman (1929-1996), and in 1975 it became The Seagram Co.

In 1998 Seagram bought **Polygram** and become the world's largest music company.

Sealy *(mattresses)*

The name is that of Sealy, Texas, where in 1884 a mattress business was launched by Daniel Haynes. He himself called his product the Haynes mattress, but customers began to refer to it as "the mattress from Sealy" and, finally, "the Sealy mattress." When Haynes sold out to a group of investors in 1906, the name of the firm was officially changed to the Sealy Mattress Company.

Sears *(department stores and footwear)*

John George Sears (1870-1916) was born in Northampton, England, the son of a leather seller. On leaving school, he was apprenticed to a local clicker (foreman shoemaker), and rose to the position of foreman himself before setting up as a shoe manufacturer in 1891, when he took over his father's unstable business. He was soon joined by his brother, William Thomas Sears, and they traded as partners under the name of J. Sears (True-Form) Boot Company. The business became a public limited company in 1912, with its name eventually changing to Sears Holdings Ltd. in 1955 and then simply Sears plc in 1985. The original activity subsequently grew to be the biggest store group in the UK.

Sears, Roebuck *(mail order and department stores)*

The Chicago-based company takes its name from Richard Warren Sears (1864-1914), born in Stewartville, Minnesota, the son of a blacksmith. He spent his boyhood in various small towns and attended high school but never graduated. When he was 14 his father bought a farm, but the elder Sears suffered from mental and physical illness and the running of the farm fell to the son. Two years later his father died, and Richard became the family breadwinner. He learned telegraphy, and in due course became a stationmaster and telegraph agent in North Redwood, Minnesota. Opportunity knocked for Sears in 1886, when he left his job at the railroad station to start the R.W. Sears Watch Company in Minneapolis. But only a year later he moved the business to Chicago, where he took on Alvah C. Roebuck (1864-1948) from Indiana as a watch assembler and repairer. In 1891 the partners started a mail-order business as Sears, Roebuck and Company, sending out catalogs to potential customers, and at first advertising almost exclusively watches and jewelry. The following year the catalog had expanded to include a whole range of goods, from furniture and guns to clothing and baby carriages. Growth in the last decade of the 19th century was spectacularly swift, so that in 1900 the company became the largest mail-order firm in the USA, overtaking their great rivals, **Montgomery Ward**.

Sebastiani *(wines)*

Italian immigrant Samuele Sebastiani (1874-1944) arrived in San Francisco in 1895 to raise artichokes and cabbages. He wanted to move into the wine business, however, so soon moved to nearby Sonoma County. Here he helped haul cobblestones from the local quarries to San Francisco, where they were being used to pave the city's streets. By 1904 he had saved enough to purchase a redwood vat, a rudimentary press, and a supply of Zinfandel grapes. The following year he bought a portion of northern California's oldest vineyards, originally planted in 1825 by the Franciscan fathers. Sebastiani built up a lucrative business selling wine in bulk to bottlers throughout the United States. It was his son, August Sebastiani, who modernized the winery after World War II and introduced the company's famous varietal wines.

Seccotine *(adhesive)*

The adhesive of this name seems to have been invented in the latter half of the 19th century in Germany, where it was patented by an Irishman, John Stevenson, one of the founders in 1878 of the Northern Ireland firm of McCaw, Stevenson & Orr, the original manufacturers. The name itself was apparently suggested by Italian *secco*, "dry," rather than Latin *siccus*, and was entered in the *Trade Marks Journal* of December 18, 1894.

Secker & Warburg *(publishers)*

The British publishing house was founded in 1910 by Martin Secker (1882-1978), who had entered the publishing trade two years earlier. He made his name with works by writers such as Compton Mackenzie, Hugh Walpole, and Francis Brett Young, and published all the works of D.H. Lawrence until his death in

1930. Fredric John Warburg (1898-1981), earlier joint managing director of **Routledge**, bought Secker's firm in 1936 and changed its name to Martin Secker & Warburg Ltd., with himself as chairman. Secker cut all ties with the firm in 1938 and in 1951 Warburg joined **Heinemann**. Secker & Warburg is now an imprint of **Random House**.

Seconal *(sedative)*

The proprietary term for the drug secobarbital, used as a sedative and hypnotic, derives from a blend of "*secon*dary" and "*allyl*" and was entered by **Eli Lilly** in the US Patent Office *Official Gazette* of July 23, 1935: "For products of secondary amyl allyl barbituric acid and the sodium salts thereof ... useful as hypnotics."

Securicor *(security services)*

The ubiquitous British security services company began its career in 1935 as a small private guard business called Night Watch Services. Contracts were at first hard to come by, and at the outbreak of World War II it had just 12 patrol guards. After the war its luck changed following a move into industrial security and the return into the jobs market of hundreds of soldiers. In 1953, as Night Guards Ltd., and employing nearly 200 guards, it changed its name to Securicor, a contraction (or possibly corruption) of "Security Corps." It subsequently entered the "cash-in-transit" business, as well as parcels delivery and detective work, and later added mobile communications to its portfolio.

Sedobrol *(sedative)*

The drug presumably bases the first half of its name on "sedative." It was entered by John Henry Land of Coalville, Leicestershire, England, in the *Trade Marks Journal* of January 22, 1913.

Sedormid *(sedative)*

The name of the sedative and hypnotic drug appears to be based on the roots of "sedative" and "dormant." It was entered by **Hoffmann-La Roche** in the *Trade Marks Journal* of May 9, 1928 and the US Patent Office *Official Gazette* of May 14, 1929.

Seeing Eye *(guide dogs)*

The American organization that provides guide dogs for blind people was founded in 1929 by Mrs. Dorothy Harrison Eustis, the first such dog being a German shepherd bitch named Buddy, assigned to guide Morris Frank, a young blind man in Tennessee. The name is biblical in origin—"The hearing ear, and the seeing eye, the Lord hath made even both of them" (Proverbs 20:12)—and was entered in the US Patent Office *Official Gazette* of August 26, 1930, with a claim of use since March 30, 1929.

Sega *(electronic games)*

The Japanese company was formed in 1951 by David Rosen, a Californian expatriate, when he began importing US arcade machines to Japan, and the machines still remain a core part of the company's business today. Rosen called his enterprise "Service Game," but in 1965 this was shortened to "Sega." In 1989 Sega launched its "Mega Drive" home video system and has made its name and fortune in the highly lucrative field of electronic games.

Seiko *(watches)*

The Japanese company dates from 1881, when Kintaro Hattori started selling clocks in Tokyo's Ginza district under the name K. Hattori & Co. In 1892, together with a handful of workers, Hattori opened a factory to make clocks in Tokyo, and in 1913 his firm launched Japan's first wristwatch. In 1924 the Seiko brand was introduced, based on a personal name, and in 1938 a new factory opened, producing over a million watches a day.

Seitz *(filters)*

The filter so named, made of asbestos fibers compressed into a disk, is mainly used for sterilizing liquids that cannot be subjected to heat. The filters date from the 1920s and take their name from their German inventor. As noted in the entry of the name by Republic Filters, Inc., of Paterson, New Jersey, in the US Patent Office *Official Gazette* of April 4, 1944: "The trade-mark is a facsimile of the signature of Mr. Seitz, the late inventor of the basic construction of the filtering apparatus manufactured and sold by applicant."

Selectasine *(color-printing process)*

The name of the color-printing process, which uses a single silk screen for each of the colors, appears to derive from "select" and a suffix designed to suggest a blend of "single" and "screen" (or even "single," "silk," and "screen.") It was entered in the US Patent Office *Official Gazette* of January 29, 1918 for: "Method of delineating or reproducing pictures and designs."

Selectric *(typewriters)*

The make of electric typewriter derives its name from a blend of "select" and "electric," entered by **IBM** in the US Patent Office *Official Gazette* of September 29, 1964, with a note of first use on July 21, 1961, and in the *Trade Marks Journal* of November 8, 1967. The model itself was introduced by IBM in the summer of 1961 and had a "golfball" for its printing element in place of the conventional typebars and and movable carriage.

Selfridges *(department store)*

The London, England, department store takes its name from Harry Gordon Selfridge (1858-1947), born in Ripon, Wisconsin, the son of the owner of a dry-goods business. He quit school at 14 to become a junior bank clerk, but applied at the same time to join the navy. He was rejected, however, as he was not quite tall enough. At 17 Harry joined Field, Leiter & Co. (later **Marshall Field**), the Chicago mail-order firm, and in 1886 became manager of the retail department. His work took him all over the world, and this increased his ambition to start his own business. In 1904 he retired from the company with a small fortune, and indulged in his hobbies of travel, reading, and collecting wild orchids. But he still wanted to start up a business. In 1906 he went to England to survey the commercial scene. He found several well-established stores in London, but optimistically felt there was room for one more. He secured a site on the north side of Oxford Street and put the architects and builders to work. In 1909 the business of Selfridge & Co. opened, with 130 departments and all kinds of facilities for the customer, such as a rest room, roof garden, and special free information service by telephone. Selfridge remained an American citizen until 1937, when he was naturalized a British subject. He would surely have approved the founding of Miss Selfridge in 1966 as a chain of youth-oriented fashion shops.

Sellotape *(adhesive tapes)*

The name is sometimes used generically for any "sticky tape" but properly belongs to the British company who first marketed it in 1937. The name, entered by Adhesive Tapes Ltd. in the *Trade Marks Journal* of November 9, 1949, is based on that of **Cellophane**, but with the initial "C" changed to "S" for purposes of trademark registration. A familiar US equivalent is **Scotch** tape.

Selsyn *(motor system)*

The name, deriving from "self-synchronizing," was entered by the General Electric Company (*see* **Thales**) in the US Patent Office *Official Gazette* of April 27, 1926 for "Electrical apparatus for transmitting and receiving motion," with a claim of use since April 1921. In its simplest form, a Selsyn motor is an interlocking system that forces two motors to run exactly together. Such a system came to have a particular application in cinematography, especially in special-effects work, when projector and camera must run synchronically together. The name is now used generically for any similar system.

Semtex *(explosive)*

The pliable, odorless, plastic explosive, familiar from the 1980s from its use by terrorists, probably takes its name from the Czech village of Semtín, near the factory where it was manufactured, and the first syllable of "explosive."

Sensodyne *(toothpaste)*

The toothpaste is designed for sensitive teeth. Hence the first part of the name. The second part denotes the power (as in "dynamic") of the product to eliminate the pain of such sensitivity. The name was entered in the *Trade Marks Journal* of April 11, 1962.

Sensurround *(film projection system)*

The name is that of a system of special effects used to enhance the physical impact of a disaster movie or similar "action" film. It was developed by **Universal Pictures** in 1974 to magnify the tremor scenes in *Earthquake* (1974) by adding air vibrations to the sound track during the dubbing process. The vibrations then "blast" the body and ears of the audience to create the illusion of participation in the scene on the screen. The name itself is a blend of "sense" and "surround" and was entered by MCA Systems, Inc., of Universal City, California, in the US Patent Office *Official Gazette* of April 6, 1976: "For electronic apparatus for generating special effects, including simulated earthquake effects, in motion picture theaters," with a note of first use on September 3, 1974.

Sephadex *(gel)*

The proprietary name for a preparation of dextran, used as a gel in chromatography, electrophoresis, and other separation techniques, is presumably a blend of "separation" and "dextran." It was entered by Aktiebolaget Pharmacia of Sweden in the *Trade Marks Journal* of September 16, 1959 for: "Polymers being chemical compounds for industrial use in the purification of chemical substances." *Cp.* **Sepharose.**

Sepharose *(gel)*

The proprietary name for a preparation of agarose, used as a gel in chromatography, electrophoresis, and other separation techniques, is presumably a blend of "separation" and "agarose." It was entered by Aktiebolaget Pharmacia of Sweden in the *Trade Marks Journal* of November 10, 1960 for: "Polymers being chemical compounds for industrial use in the purification of chemical substances." *Cp.* **Sephadex.**

Sequestrene *(sequestering agent)*

The proprietary name for preparations of ethylenediamine tetra-acetic acid and its salts, used as sequestering agents, and especially one containing sequestered iron for use on iron-deficient soils, derives its name from "sequestration" and the chemical suffix "-ene." (In chemistry, sequestering agents effectively remove ions from a solution.) The name was entered by the Alrose Chemical Co., Inc., of Cranston, Rhode Island, in the US Patent Office *Official Gazette* of February 8, 1949, with a claim of use since January 16, 1948.

Serax *(tranquilizer)*

The proprietary name for the drug oxazepam, given to relieve anxiety states and control the withdrawal symptoms of alcoholism, is presumably of arbitrary origin. It was entered by **American Home Products** in the US Patent Office *Official Gazette* of August 27, 1957.

Serpasil *(sedative)*

The proprietary name for the drug reserpine, used to treat hypertension and as a sedative,

derives from the generic name, itself based on the name of the tropical shrub *Rauvolfia serpentina* (*see* **Raudixin**). It was entered by Ciba Ltd. (*see Ciba-Geigy*) in the *Trade Marks Journal* of April 29, 1953 and the US Patent Office *Official Gazette* of October 20, 1953.

Serpent's Tail *(publishers)*

The British publishing house, noted for its cult, unconventional profile, was founded in 1986 by Pete Ayrton, a former philosophy lecturer and translator, with the aim of publishing contemporary literature in paperback. The figure of a serpent with a tail in its mouth (a uroboros) is a symbol of eternity, and was adopted by the firm as its logo. According to the firm's own statement, it "represents the two fundamental attributes of time – imminent annihilation and rising hope."

Setlers *(antacid)*

The preparation contains calcium carbonate and magnesium hydroxide to settle an upset stomach. Hence the name, entered in the *Trade Marks Journal* of November 28, 1962.

Seuil *(publishers)*

The French publishing house Éditions du Seuil was founded in 1935 by Jean Bardet and Paul Flamand (1909-1998) as an enterprise born of the Catholic intellectual Resistance. Their aim was to take a different direction in publishing and explore new territories in the field of human sciences, especially linguistics and semiology, as well as the avant-garde in literature. Hence its name, from French *le seuil*, "the threshold."

7-Up *(soft drink)*

The drink was invented in 1920 by Charles L. Griggs of Price's Branch, Missouri. He originally called it "Howdy," but aiming to improve on it, devised another drink under the name of "Bib-Label Lithiated Lemon-Lime Soda." The drinks were tasty but the sales were bad, so he tried to think up a snappier name. The story goes that after six tries he came up with "7-Up," although another account takes the the name from the seven-ounce bottle in which the drink was sold. "Seven-up" already existed in any case as the name of a card game in which the trump card is a turned-up card and there is a fixed total of seven points to win. The name (as "Seven Up") was entered in the

US Patent Office *Official Gazette* of November 13, 1928 and (as "Seven-up") in the *Trade Marks Journal* of June 24, 1953.

Sevin *(insecticide)*

The proprietary name for carbaryl, an insecticide used to protect crops, appears to be of arbitrary origin. It was entered by **Union Carbide** in the *Trade Marks Journal* of April 9, 1958.

Shaklee *(natural health products)*

The American purveyors of nutritional, household, and personal care products take their name from Dr. Forrest Shaklee, who in 1956 set up a business in Oakland, California, to promote the food supplements he had developed and that he dispensed from his chiropractic clinic. Business boomed almost instantly, and despite subsequent setbacks has remained essentially healthy ever since.

Shanks, Armitage *see* **Armitage Shanks**

Sharp *(electronics)*

The Japanese manufacturers of camcorders and palmtops were founded in 1915 by Tokuji Hayakawa, the inventor three years earlier of a snap buckle that he called the "Tokubijo" (from own his name and Japanese *bijogane*, "buckle"). He set the firm up to produce another invention, a new type of automatic (propelling) pencil that he called "Ever-Sharp," meaning a pencil that never needed to be sharpened since one merely advanced the lead in the casing. The company progressed to the commercial production of crystal radio sets in 1925, colour televisions in 1960, microwave ovens in 1962, and electronic calculators in 1964. It also shortened its name to simply "Sharp."

Sharps *(toffee)*

The British confectionery name is that of Edward Sharp (1864-1931), born a papermaker's son in Maidstone, Kent. Sharp began his first job at age 12, working at the mill with his father and grandfather. He was then apprenticed to a local grocer, and afterwards joined a local grocery chain. In 1886 he set up on his own account as a grocer and provision merchant in Maidstone, with premises in Week Street. Two years later he married Clara Betts, a butcher's daughter who had learned a number of con-

fectionery recipes from a friend in Jersey. These recipes helped supplement Edward Sharp's grocery lines, and in 1889 he decided to expand the confectionery side of his business. This activity prospered, and a new type of creamy nougat that he made was "recast" by his works manager as a creamy toffee. This was the original Sharps "Kreemy" toffee, made at the turn of the 20th century. In 1913 Sharps moved to a new factory in Maidstone called the "Kreemy Works," and the company produced both "Kreemy" toffee and the higher quality "Super-Kreem", the latter launched in 1919 and promoted by a character called "Sir Kreemy Knut."

Sharwood's *(chutney and curry powder)*

Englishman James Allen Sharwood first became familiar with curry in India in the 1880s, when he was introduced to the spice house of P. Vencatachellum in Madras. He began importing curry powder to his native London in 1889, and gradually extended his range of special foods to include mango chutney, initially importing it in small quantities from Bombay. Sharwood was a great traveler, especially in continental Europe and India, and wherever he went he was on the lookout for good quality food or ingredients to import to England. In this way he added such delicacies as sherry olives from Spain, crystallized fruits from France, and tomatoes from Italy to make a fine tomato purée. Today Sharwood's is the main supplier of Indian and Chinese food to leading British supermarkets. In 1963 Sharwood's was bought by **Rank Hovis McDougall**.

Sheaffer *(pens)*

Walter A. Sheaffer (1867-1946), the son of a jeweler in Bloomfield, Iowa, became a printer's devil at the age of 12. He then worked as a grocery clerk and a peanut vendor befor returning to become a partner in his father's store in 1888. He was still running a jewelry store 20 years later, when he patented a lever-operated fountain pen. At first, Sheaffer regarded his invention as a sideline, but the growing demand for his writing instruments forced him to start a separate pen company in 1912. In 1938 Sheaffer stepped down as president of his firm to devote more time to politics and other interests.

Sheba *(petfood)*

The British brand of cat food, first marketed

in 1985, was named for the biblical Queen of Sheba, associated with opulence and luxury (1 Kings 10, 2 Chronicles 9). Sheba is a popular pet cat name for the same reason, with a coincidental suggestion of "she" for the conventional gender of a cat.

Sheed & Ward *(publishers)*

The Catholic publishing house takes its name from Francis Joseph Sheed (1897-1981), born in Sydney, Australia, the son of a draftsman, and his English wife Maisie Ward (1889-1975), whom he met in London, England, while working for the Catholic Evidence Guild, a group of street preachers founded in 1919. The couple married in 1926 and set up their publishing business that year with financial help from Maisie's family. A New York branch of their house opened in 1933 but passed to the publishing firm of Andrews & McMeel in 1973.

Sheep Dip *(whisky)*

The British brand of vatted malt dates from 1974, when a Gloucestershire publican had special labels put on a reasonable malt whisky that his local customers jokingly ordered as "that there sheep dip." It is now exported to over half a dozen countries. "Sheep dip" has long been a colloquial name for any supposedly (or actually) inferior whiskey or "rotgut."

Sheetrock *(plasterboard)*

The type of plasterboard, made from gypsum layered between sheets of heavy paper, has a name combining "sheet" and "rock" that was entered for "Plaster Wall-Board" by the U.S. Gypsum Co., of Chicago, in the US Patent Office *Official Gazette* of November 29, 1921, with a claim of use since August 28, 1917, and by the same company in the *Trade Marks Journal* of November 5, 1924 for: "Plaster in sheets, for use as wall boards in building or decoration."

Shell *(petroleum)*

The British company traces its origins to the first half of the 19th century, when a Jewish dealer, Marcus Samuel, set up a curio shop in East Smithfield, London. His children had fastened seaside shells to their empty lunch boxes on returning from a holiday, and Samuel made up a number of such boxes and labeled them with the names of the resorts where the shells had been found. He then began importing fancy polished shells to meet the more sophisticated demands of his lady customers. His shop soon became known as the Shell Shop, and business expanded so rapidly that by 1830 Samuel had built up an international trade in oriental curios and copra, as well as shells. In 1878 his son, also Marcus Samuel (1853-1927), took over his father's business and started a sideline of handling consignments of kerosene. In 1892 he began operating tankers sailing to the Far East and set up oil depots, then oil wells and refineries in Borneo. In 1897 he formed a separate company for his oil interests, Shell Transport and Trading (*see* **Hill Samuel**), and was soon contracting for petroleum supplies in several countries. His company adopted the scallop as its trademark in 1904 and in 1907 merged with the Royal Dutch Petroleum Company to form **Royal Dutch/Shell**.

Shell-Mex *(petroleum)*

The name began its association with the asphaltic bitumen supplied by **Shell** refineries in the early 1920s. The second part of the name comes from the interests in the Mexican Eagle Oil Company sold to **Royal Dutch/Shell** after World War I by the **Pearson** group, who had set up Highways Construction Ltd in 1913 with the aim of using bitumen as the basis for road asphalt. The name survives today in Shell-Mex House in the Strand, London, opened in 1933.

Shepherd Neame *(beer)*

Britain's oldest brewery, in Faversham, Kent, dates from 1698, when it was started by Captain Richard Marsh. On his death, in *c*.1727, it passed to his widow, Mary, and in due course to his daughter, Sylvester, who ran it singlehanded until her own early death at the age of 24 in 1741, when it was acquired by Samuel Shepherd, a local landowner, already active as a maltster. He was joined by his sons, Julius and John, the business now being known as the Faversham Steam Brewery. Various partners came and went, so that the firm was known as Shepherd and Hilton, then Shepherd and Mares, and when John Mares died in 1864, the Shepherd then in place was joined by 28-year-old Percy Beale Neame (d.1913). By 1877 Neame was in sole control, and was eventually joined by his sons Harry, Arthur, and Alick. Harry ran the business on his own until 1925, when he was joined by his son Jasper and in

1931 by his youngest son, Laurie. Jasper died in 1961 and at the end of the 20th century the firm was in the hands of his son, Robert "Bobby" Neame (b.1934). Shepherd Neame is famous for its "Bishops Finger" beer, named after a former type of local signpost.

Sherwin-Williams *(paint)*

Henry Alden Sherwin (1842-1916) was a partner in a Cleveland, Ohio, paint-manufacturing company, and Edward Porter Williams (1843-1903) a shareowner in a Kent, Ohio, glass factory, when their respective companies began doing business with each other in the 1860s and the two men met. They shared an ambition to do something bigger, and when Sherwin described his wish to develop a ready-mixed paint process, William agreed to back him. Sherwin soon came up with an appropriate formula, and in 1873 the duo began manufacturing their revolutionary kind of paint. The new product caught on and made the men's fortunes. In 1905 the firm that they founded adopted its famous "Cover the Earth" trademark, although it exported little of its product at the time.

Shinola *(boot polish)*

The name of the polish, from "shine" and the "-ola" suffix as in **Pianola**, is familiar to many from the phrase "not to know shit from Shinola," denoting a state of innocence or ignorance. It was entered in the US Patent Office *Official Gazette* of September 8, 1903, with a note of use since January 1, 1900.

Shippams *(meat paste)*

The British company traces its origins to 1786, when Charles Shippam opened a grocery shop in Westgate, Chichester, Sussex. Shippam had ten children. Four of them were boys, and three of these followed him into the grocery trade while the fourth, George, started up a tea and grocery business of his own in North Street. George Shippam had a son, Charles Shippam (1828-1897), who began his career as a pork butcher in East Street, Chichester. At first his products included "fine home cured and York hams." By 1855 he was describing himself as a "pork butcher and bacon curer and maker of the celebrated Chichester sausage."

(The sausages were made until 1968, when they were discontinued.) It was in 1892 that Charles Shippam first ventured into potted meats, the product for which the firm is famous today. At first the meats were sold in earthenware pots, and it was only after Shippam's death that the familiar glass jars were introduced. The company is still based in Chichester, with Charles' original pork butcher's premises incorporated into the present factory. In 1995, after 20 years of American ownership, Shippams was acquired by **Grand Metropolitan**. The company's personnel manager at this time was John Shippam, Charles Shippam's great-great-great-grandson.

Shiseido *(cosmetics)*

The company was founded in 1872 by Yushin Fukuhara, a former chemist with the Japanese navy, as a Western-style pharmacy in Tokyo's fashionable shopping street of Ginza, taking its name from a passage in the *I Ching* celebrating the beauties of the Earth. At first it was a solely pharmaceutical business, but in 1897 diversified into cosmetics with the launch of *Eudermine*, a rose-scented skin freshener that soon came to be known as *eau rouge* for its bright magenta color. Its first perfume, *Hanatsubaki*, went on the market in 1916 and in 1923 the company opened a network of chainstores that would eventually cover Japan. Overseas expansion followed, and in 1965 Shiseido Cosmetics America was founded. The launch of *Zen* perfume that year was its first product for overseas markets.

Shorts *(aircraft)*

The British firm of Short Bros., manufacturers in the 1930s of the Empire and Sunderland flying boats and in World War II of the Stirling bomber, derive their name from Hugh Oswald Short (1883-1969), born in Stanton-by-Dale, Derbyshire, an engineer's son, and his brothers Horace (1872-1917) and Eustace (1875-1932). All three trained as engineers and in 1908, in a factory on the Isle of Sheppey, Kent, formed the firm of Short Bros., Aeronautical Engineers, where they began to build aircraft. In 1913 they moved to more suitable premises at Rochester, on the Medway River, where one of their main lines of development in World War I was seaplanes. In World War II the government took over the company when Oswald Short and his general manager, Arthur Gouge, refused to build Lancaster bombers. This was the only time in the war that a firm in the aircraft industry had to be nationalized. Short Bros. should not be confused with Short Brothers the British shipbuilders, founded in Sunderland in 1850 by John Young Short (1844-1900). In 1865 he was joined by his brothers George, Thomas, and Joseph, and their firm was known as George Short until 1871, when they became Short Brothers.

Showerings (cider)

Famous for its **Babycham** perry, the British firm of Showerings goes back to the 17th century, when the family were shoemakers and innkeepers in the Somerset town of Shepton Mallet. They acquired the Ship Inn in Kilvert Street in 1843, and it was on that site that the present firm developed and that it remains today. In its current form, Showerings was founded in 1932 by the four Showering brothers, Herbert, Arthur, Ralph, and Francis, all great-grandsons of the shoemaker Francis Showering. The Showerings appear not to have exploited the aptness of their family name for their sparkling drinks.

Shredded Wheat (breakfast cereal)

Shredded Wheat, the first ready-to-eat breakfast cereal, was originally made by Henry D. Perky in Denver, Colorado, in 1893, a year before the appearance of John Harvey **Kellogg's** corn flakes. His idea for the food is said to have come from seeing fellow dyspepsia sufferers in a Nebraska hotel eating whole boiled wheat with milk for breakfast. Perky decided that such wheat would be more easily assimilated in "shredded" form. After marketing his product locally, Perky founded the Natural Foods Company in 1895 and started to produce the cereal commercially at Worcester, Massachusetts. In 1929 the National Biscuit Co. (now **Nabisco**) acquired the Canadian Shredded Wheat Co., including the British operation established in 1908, the Shredded Wheat Co. of England. In 1956 the name of the British company, which had remained a part of the National Biscuit Co., was changed to Nabisco Foods Ltd. Meanwhile, back in 1924, the name "Shredded Wheat" had been registered, but with the passing of the Trade Marks Act of 1938, which banned the registration of

descriptive words, an action was taken against the Shredded Wheat Co. to have the name removed from the Register. This action succeeded, with the result that the National Biscuit Co. entered the name "Welgar" (from *Wel*wyn *Gar*den City, Hertfordshire, the location of its head office) in the *Trade Marks Journal* of December 10, 1941. This same action naturally opened the way for competitors to produce their own brand of Shredded Wheat. The name has thus become common property in the UK, and packets of cereal will state, in addition to the words "Shredded Wheat," the name or trademark of the manufacturers, so that consumers will know which brand they are buying. Hence the note by the *Oxford English Dictionary* against the entry for the name that it is "often written with capital initials as if a proprietary term." (It is currently a trademark used by **Nestlé** on their brand of Shredded Wheat marketed in the UK.) In the USA, Nabisco held the name until 1993, when it passed to **Kraft**.

Sidgwick & Jackson (publishers)

The British firm was founded in 1908 by Frank Sidgwick (d.1939) and Robert Cameron Jackson (1882-1917). Sidgwick had earlier been a partner of a publishing house in Stratford-upon-Avon, and brought many of his publications with him when the new business was started up in Adam Street, London. Jackson had had similar publishing experience with **Hutchinson** and **Dent**. Sidgwick has gone down in publishing history as the man who turned down many subsequently famous names, especially in the early years. He published Rupert Brooke, for example, but in 1911 rejected the poems of Siegfried Sassoon. Jackson was killed in action in France in World War I, leaving Sidgwick devastated and obliged to carry on alone. Sidgwick & Jackson is now an imprint of **Macmillan**.

Siebel Systems (computer software)

The Silicon Valley firm was started in 1993 by Thomas Siebel (b.1952), a lawyer's son raised in Chicago, who developed an interest in software while studying history at the University of Illinois. On graduating, he joined the computing company **Oracle**, and devised a system to personalize service so that when a customer phoned a company, the operator taking the call had access to all the necessary information from different departments, such as billing, sales, and shipping. But Oracle's chief executive, Larry Ellison, was not interested in commercializing the software Siegel had developed, so he went his own way. By 2000, Siebel Systems was America's fastest-growing company, with 22,000 people, including contractors, working worldwide, selling, installing, and customizing software.

Siemens *(electrical equipment)*

The name goes back to four German brothers, famous for their contributions to the electrical and steel industries. They were Ernst Werner von Siemens (1816-1892), Karl Wilhelm Siemens, later Sir Charles William Siemens (1823-1883), Karl von Siemens (1829-1906), and Friedrich Siemens (1826-1904). It was Ernst, the eldest brother, who founded the original firm when he started up a telegraph construction factory in Berlin in 1847, taking as partners his cousin, Johann Georg Siemens (1805-1879), and Johann Georg Halske (1814-1890), a mechanic. The second brother, Karl Wilhelm Siemens, went to London in 1843 and decided to settle in England as an inventor. In 1859 he married the sister of a Scottish engineering professor and adopted British citizenship, at the same time anglicizing his first names to Charles William. He was particularly interested in cable laying, and in 1863 started up a factory at Charlton, Kent, to make cables. The electric lighting side of the business, for which Siemens is best known today, was not begun until the late 1870s. The original Siemens factory in Berlin was seriously damaged by British and American bombers in World War II, and after the war its reconstruction in Munich was supervised by Hermann von Siemens (1885-1986), grandson of the founder. In 1966 all constituent companies were merged into the newly created Siemens AG.

Signal Companies *(automotive and aerospace engineering)*

The American company was incorporated in 1928 as the Signal Oil and Gas Company to continue the business of the Signal Gas Company. It soon became involved in the production side of the petroleum industry, and adopted its present generally prestigious name in 1968.

Signet *see* **Ratners**

Silastic *(silicone rubber)*

The name, a blend of "silicon" and "elastic," was entered by the **Dow** Corning Corporation in the US Patent Office *Official Gazette* of December 2, 1947, with a claim of use since July 1942, and in the *Trade Marks Journal* of May 12, 1965.

Silentnight *(beds)*

Tom Clarke (d.1993) was wondering what to do with himself after leaving the navy in 1945 when his mother-in-law said to him, "Look, lad, what about opening a shop as a mattress repairer?" Tom did so, with his £100 gratuity, and built the Lancashire-based business into Britain's biggest bed maker. The company is now run by professional managers, but Clarke's two sons, Peter (b.1949) and John (b. 1952), are nonexecutive directors. The name perhaps intentionally evokes the familiar Christmas carol.

Silly Putty *(toy)*

The "putty" that can be stretched, shattered, and bounced if appropriately manipulated had its genesis in World War II, when Rob Roy McGregor and Earl Warrick, two scientists working for **Corning** Glass, sought a way of making synthetic rubber with silicone. In an experiment, they added boric acid to a fluid called "Corning 200" resembling petroleum. They heated it overnight, and next day found a strange substance that they could mold, stretch, and bounce around the laboratory, but that was useless as rubber. They kept some as a curiosity, however, and filed a patent for it in 1943 as a method of "treating dimethyl silicone polymer with boric oxide." A little later, James Wright of General Electric (*see* **Ediswan**) was also trying to figure out how to make synthetic rubber from silicone. The company claims that he likewise mixed up boric acid with silicone and got something unusual. When someone asked what use it had, a chemist said you could drop it on the floor and say, "Golly, look at it bounce!" General Electric sent out samples worldwide asking if anyone could think of way of using it, but no one could. But they also patented it, and the putty occasionally surfaced at parties, when people played around with it. One day, Ruth Fallgatter, owner of a toy store in New Haven, Connecticut, hired Peter Hodgson, an advertising copywriter, to produce a catalog that included the putty. Hodgson decided that it was an interesing product. He bought a large consigment from General Electric, cut it into one-ounce lumps, put it into plastic eggs, and introduced it at the 1950 International Toy Fair under its present name (which he registered as a trademark in 1952), but there was no immediate interest from the experts. He then tried the **Neiman-Marcus** department stores and **Doubleday** bookshops. A *New Yorker* writer saw the eggs in a Doubleday store, wrote about them in its "Talk of the Town" column, and within three days Hodgson received orders for over 750,000 eggs. Over 230 million have been sold since, and at his death in 1976 Hodgson was worth $140 million. A UK equivalent was the more memorably named "Potty Putty," with "potty" in its British sense of "crazy."

Silver Cross *(baby carriages)*

The British company takes its name from Silver Cross Street, Leeds, Yorkshire, the location of its first factory. The firm itself was founded in 1877 in Hunslet, Leeds, by William Wilson, who had already had experience making springs for baby carriages. The business was long known by the family name but in 1988 adopted the name of its famous brand, becoming Silver Cross Ltd. The name happens to be descriptively appropriate for certain models of baby carriage, which have a silver metal chassis.

Silvikrin *(hair dressing and shampoo)*

The name dates back before World War II, although the shampoo so called was first marketed only in 1960. The second part of the name derives from Latin *crinis*, "hair." The first part is of uncertain origin, although the manufacturers, **Beecham**, are aware that it has led some to suppose that the product is designed for gray or silver hair. Latin *silva*, "wood," seems an unlikely source. The name was first entered in the *Trade Marks Journal* of September 3, 1924.

Simca *(automobiles)*

The French car derives its name acronymically from the Société industrielle de mécanique et carrosserie automobiles ("Automobile Engineering and Bodywork Company"), a firm founded in 1934 by Italian-born Henri Théodore Pigozzi (1898-1964) to expand his activities as a distributor of **Fiat** cars in France. The first Simcas were thus Fiats. Only in 1951 did Simca produce a car that markedly differed from a Fiat in the form of the "Aronde" model. (The name means "Arrow.") Simca were taken over by **Chrysler** in 1963 to become Chrysler-Simca.

Simmerstat *(thermostatic control)*

The name is that of a thermostatic control that regulates the temperature of the hotplates or grill of an electric cooker. It is a blend of "simmer" and "thermostat" and was entered by Sun-Vic Controls Ltd., of London, England, in the *Trade Marks Journal* of September 7, 1938.

Simmons *(bedding products)*

When Zalmon G. Simmons (1828-1910), owner of a prosperous store in Kenosha, Wisconsin, was owed money by a struggling inventor in the 1860s, he agreed to accept the man's patent for a woven-wire bedspring instead of cash, even though the inventor warned that it was too costly to be profitably mass-produced. Simmons showed the prototype to a friend, who figured out how to reduce production costs, and in 1870 began to manufacture the bedspring. Soon after, Simmons complemented it with a line of brass bedsteads. Other bedding products were gradually added, and the famous "Beautyrest" mattress was introduced in 1925 by Simmons' son, Zalmon G. Simmons, Jr.

Simon, Norton *see* Norton Simon

Simon & Schuster *(publishers)*

The American publishing house takes its name from Richard Leo Simon (1899-1960) and Max Lincoln Schuster (1897-1970). Simon was born in New York City, the son of a wholesale milliner, and early in life became a pianist and organist. He was educated at the Ethical Culture School and then enrolled at Columbia University, where he graduated with a bachelor of arts degree in 1920. Schuster, born in Kalusz, Austria, of American parents, was brought to the United States at seven weeks old and began his career by helping his father sell newspapers. At age 16 he enrolled in the Pulitzer School of Journalism at Columbia and began writing articles for periodicals. After graduating from Columbia in 1917 with a bachelor of literature degree, he became a reporter for the Washington, DC, bureau of the New Republic News Service, later the United Press. The two men met in 1921, when Simon was selling pianos and had an office in the same building as Schuster's. A personal and professional friendship followed, and two years later they decided to form a publishing house. In January 1924 they pooled $4,000 and opened an office for business. Their first publication, in April, was *The Cross-Word Puzzle Book*. It sold half a million copies by year's end and during the following decade, 1.5 million copies of the firm's crossword puzzle books were sold, making expansion possible. In 1998 Simon & Schuster was acquired by **Pearson**.

Simonds *(beer)*

William Simonds was a maltster who began brewing in Reading, England, in about 1769. His son William Blackall Simonds (1761-1834) inherited the business in 1782, when it owned four public houses. Using inherited money and his wife's dowry, William Simonds opened a new brewhouse in Broad Street, Reading, and in 1789 commissioned the famous architect, Sir John Soane, to design another in Bridge Street. He retired in 1816 by which time his son, Blackall Simonds, was managing the business. The company went on to acquire several other breweries, and remained in the Simonds family until 1953, when the last Simonds chairman died. In 1960 the business merged with **Courage**.

Simpson *(menswear)*

The British firm, famous for **Daks** men's trousers and suits, was founded in London in 1894 by Simeon Simpson (1878-1932), a bespoke tailor who aimed to make high-quality ready-to-wear-garments on a commercial scale. He called his firm S. Simpson, and gradually built up the business so that by the time his second son, Alexander, joined him in 1917 the concern was one of the leading tailors in the country, with retail outlets in many stores. The company's flagship store, Simpson of Piccadilly, opened in 1936 and regularly supplied clothing to royalty and celebrities until losses compelled its closure in 1999.

Sinclair *(oil)*

The name is that of Harry Ford Sinclair

(1876-1956), born in Wheeling, West Virginia, the son of a pharmacist. In 1882 his family moved to Independence, Kansas, where he enrolled at the University of Kansas in 1897 to study pharmacy. After receiving a certificate in 1898, he took over his father's drugstore, but soon lost the business. In 1901 he began a new career in the oil industry of Kansas and Oklahoma, selling lumber for oil derricks and buying and selling oil leases. In 1904 a drilling syndicate he had organized enabled him to become an independent producer, and he brought in his first well the following year in the Indian Territory. By 1912 he was involved in 62 venture companies, and in 1916 founded the Sinclair Oil and Refining Corporation. By the time of Sinclair's retirement in 1949, the Sinclair Oil Corporation was valued at $700 million and had retail outlets in areas covering 85 percent of the population of the United States.

Singer *(automobiles)*

There have been no cars of this name built since 1970, so they are increasingly rarely seen on the road. The name is still familiar in Britain, however, and is that of George Singer (1847-1909), who founded a bicycle-making business in Coventry, Warwickshire, in 1876. Like similar ventures, the firm went on to produce motorcycles and tricycles before manufacturing its first car in 1905. After Singer's death, the company was re-formed as Singer & Co. (1909) Ltd., although the date was dropped three years later. Singer stopped making motorcycles after World War I.

Singer *(sewing machines)*

The machines get their name from Isaac Merritt Singer (1811-1875), born in Pittstown or in nearby Schaghticoke, New York, the son of a German immigrant cooper originally named Reisinger. When he was 12 he ran away from his family and went to Rochester, New York, to live with an older brother. He stayed there seven years, working at odd jobs and picking up a sporadic education. In 1830 he discovered the theater, and worked as an actor or advance man when he could and as a laborer, mechanic, or cabinetworker when theater jobs were in short supply. In 1839, while working for his brother who was a contractor on the Lockport and Illinois Canal, he invented a rock drill. He sold the patent for $2,000 and used the money to finance his own theater company. In 1844 his troupe collapsed, however, and he returned to the life of a mechanic. His next invention was a mechanical device for carving woodblock type. He went to Boston to sell it to type manufacturers, and when negotiating with one such firm took an interest in his client's other business, which was running a sewing-machine repair shop. Sewing machines were nothing new, but they were as yet fairly basic, and able to sew only very slowly, a few stitches at a time. Singer set out to make a more efficient model, and completed it in 1850. Despite claims that he had infringed the patents of several existing manufacturers, Singer's machine sold so well that it virtually made his fortune overnight. In 1867 the resulting company opened its first plant outside America, in Glasgow, Scotland. After five marriages that produced 24 children, Singer died on his estate near Torquay, Devonshire, England.

Singha *(beer)*

The lager beer so called, produced by the Boon Rawn Brewery Co., Thailand, is named after a mythical creature resembling a lion (Sanskrit *simha*, Punjabi *singh*). The brewery itself was established in the 1930s.

Siporex *(cement)*

The name is of Swedish and apparently arbitrary origin and was entered by the Internationella Siporex Aktiebolaget in the *Trade Marks Journal* of July 27, 1938 for: "Slates, bricks, blocks, beams, piles, pillars, posts, tiles, pipes, drains and shaped pieces, all made of cement or concrete for use in building or construction."

Sir Robert McAlpine *(construction)*

The British construction company evolved from the Victorian firm set up by a Scottish bricklayer, Robert McAlpine (1847-1934), created 1st Baronet McAlpine in 1918. The business was essentially "made" by his son, William Hepburn McAlpine, and developed by his grandson, Robert Edwin McAlpine (1907-1990), who went straight into the family concern on quitting school at age 18. Some of London's best-known postwar buildings, such as the National Theatre and the Shell Centre, arose when Lord McAlpine of Moffat (as he became) was director of London projects for the company.

Sirdar *(woolen goods and knitwear)*

The British firm was founded at the turn of the 20th century and took its name from Lord Kitchener ("of Khartoum"), the military hero of the day, who was appointed Sirdar of Egypt in 1892. His title was a word of Indian origin meaning "leader."

Six Continents *see* **Bass**

606 *see* **Salvarsan**

Skechers *(footwear)*

Michael Greenberg (b.1963) was still in college when his father, Robert Greenberg (b.1940), who owned a womenswear shop called L.A. Gear, started importing canvas sneakers in 1983. Greenberg copied the shoe and named it after the shop. The brand took off, and Michael dropped out of junior college to join the business in 1983. Sales soared, making L.A. Gear the USA's third-largest sneaker vendor, behind **Nike** and **Reebok**. But the brand then went out of fashion and stocks tumbled. A way out was needed with a new venture. In 1992 Robert made his move, and Skechers was born with a name suggesting a cross between "sketch" and "sneaker", with a further hint of "skeeter" or "skitter." Working out of the first floor of a beachfront house in Manhattan Beach, California, father and son got going. Business boomed, and in 2001 Skechers sneakers, sandals, and loafers were hitting the street in New York, London, and Amsterdam, with stores in London, Paris, and Oberhausen, Germany.

Skee-Ball *(game)*

The name, from "ski" and "ball," is that of an indoor game in which balls set rolling down an alley strike a hump to leap in the air (as if on skis) on to the target. The game first became popular in the USA in the 1920s.

Sketchley *(dry cleaners)*

The name is not that of the British company's founder. The business, with branches in many towns and cities, owes its origin to Alfred Ernest Hawley. He was born into a family with a background in the wool-dyeing trade, and in 1885, at the age of 24, himself set up a dyeing works in Hinckley, Leicestershire. For the actual process of dyeing, Hawley used the waters of the local Sketchley brook, adopting its name for the "Sketchley Fast Black" dyeing process that he later introduced for cotton hose. He ran his business under his own name, as A.E. Hawley & Co. In due course the brook's name came to be given to the factory, as the Sketchley Dye Works, with "Sketchley Dry Cleaning" used for the new process of cleaning by spirit some time after Hawley introduced it in 1889. It was not until 1951 that Hawley's name was eventually dropped when the company name was changed to Sketchley in turn. So although Sketchley can be an English surname, it was not so in this instance, even if many High Street shoppers mistakenly take it for one when they see it over the dry-cleaning shops.

SKF *see* **Volvo**

Ski *(yogurt)*

The brand of yogurt was launched in the UK in 1963, at a time when yogurt itself was regarded as a rather exotic, "healthy" food. "The name, of course, was crucial. Skiing was not, at that point, even a middle-class pastime – it was the preserve of the upper classes. It was, of course, also redolent of tanned, healthy, Scandinavian, Swiss and Germanic types who ate exciting things like fondue, pickled herrings and... yogurt" (*Sunday Business*, May 7, 2000). For a quarter of a century, Ski was the biggest yogurt brand in the UK.

Skiatron *(cathode ray tube)*

The type of cathode ray tube, in which the electron beam produces a dark trace, derives its name from Greek *skia*, "shadow," and the second part of "electron." The name was entered by **Scophony** Ltd in the *Trade Marks Journal* of June 26, 1946 and the US Patent Office *Official Gazette* of November 21, 1953, the latter with a claim of use since August 1, 1942.

Skidoo *(snowmobile)*

The make of motorized toboggan was the invention in 1957 of the Canadian engineer Joseph-Armand **Bombardier**. Its name, based on "ski" but also suggesting "skidoo" in the sense "leave quickly," was entered by Bombardier Ltd. in the Canadian *Trade Marks Journal* of July 23, 1969.

Skippers *(sardines)*

The name was long familiar in Britain for the Norwegian brisling canned by the firm of Angus Watson & Co., founded by Angus Watson (1874-1961), born in Ryton, near Newcastle upon Tyne, the son of a sanitary pipe manufacturer. After a private education, he gained a post as a junior clerk and made rapid progress, developing good business relations with W.H. Lever, the future Lord Leverhulme, who gave the name of **Unilever**. Watson founded his cannery in Newcastle itself in 1903, importing the fish from Norway. The name alluded to the skipper who is the master of a fishing vessel, depicted in the portrait of an "Old Salt" that became the company's trademark. At the same time, "skipper" is a fish name in its own right (for the saury, which is also edible.) The sitter for the portrait was William Duncan Anderson, an old naval hero who posed for atmospheric portraits in London. Watson subsequently added "Sailor" salmon to his "Skippers," and later, in 1911, "My Lady" canned fruits. The name "Skipper" was first entered in the *Trade Marks Journal* of June 12, 1907.

Škoda *(automobiles)*

After studying engineering in Germany, the Czech industrialist and engineer Emil von Škoda (1839-1900) became chief engineer at a small machine factory in Pilsen. Three years later he bought and rapidly expanded it, building his own railroad connection to the main Vienna-Cheb line in 1886 and adding an arms factory in 1890 to produce a newly invented machine gun for the Austrian army. In 1899 he incorporated his growing collection of machine shops, forges, and tool-and-die shops in Pilsen as the Škoda Works. The cars followed much later, in the 20th century, together with other types of transport and machinery, from trolleybuses to steam turbines. Škoda's son Karl (1879-1929) was director of the firm from 1909.

Skol *(beer)*

The lager beer, produced in the UK by **Carlsberg-Tetley**, derives its name from the Scandinavian drinking toast (Danish and Norwegian *skaal*, Swedish *skål*), itself from Old Scandinavian *skál*, "bowl."

Skytrain *(airline service)*

The low-cost, "no-frills" transatlantic passenger air service, introduced in the UK in the 1970s by Laker Airways Ltd., founded by Freddie Laker (b.1922) in 1966, derives its name obviously enough from "sky" and "train." The name was entered in the US Patent Office *Official Gazette* of May 23, 1978: "For air passenger services—namely, the transportation of passengers by air." The business failed in 1982, but Laker founded a new company, Laker Airways, Inc., in 1995.

Slazenger *(sports equipment)*

The founder of the British firm was Ralph Slazenger (1845-1910), born a tailor's son in Warrington, Lancashire, the son of a Jewish immigrant tailor and umbrella maker. Quitting school in 1859, Ralph learned tailoring under his father. On his father's death in 1872 he began to expand the business beyond the two existing Warrington shops, and by 1877 he was advertising himself as "J.S. Moss & Son." At the Market Street shop, however, he announced himself as "Slazenger et Fils, Importer of French Fancy Goods." In 1881 "Slazenger et Fils" registered as gaiter and leggings manufacturers, and this was the effective founding of the present firm. Ralph ran this side of the business, while his brother, Isaac, ran the tailoring department in Market Street. Another brother, Albert, was the traveling salesman, and he and Ralph can be regarded as the cofounders of the company. All the brothers were unmarried and lived with their mother, Eliza, who acted as their accountant. There was thus no "Son" and no "Fils." In 1885 Ralph and Albert moved their business to London, with Ralph dropping his adopted name of Moss and reverting to Slazenger. Ralph subsequently renounced his Jewish religion, and even altered his birthplace to Lymm, Cheshire, five miles from Warrington, which he apparently regarded as not so "genteel." By 1890 the brothers were making sports equipment proper, including lawn tennis rackets, cricket bats, and football boots.

Sleepeezee *(beds and bedding)*

W. Howard Price founded his British firm of bedding manufacturers, Howard Price Ltd., soon after World War I. In the late 1920s he began making beds which could be used as everyday furniture when not in use. One such bed was the "Sleepeezee," marketed as a "luxurious comfortable divan, readily converted into a bed which is no less attractive." It was covered in exotic, striped ticking, and also had a box compartment in which the bedclothes

could be stored. The dual-purpose bed was so popular that the company renamed themselves after it. The name itself, a respelled "sleep easy," happens to be punningly "full of Es." The name was entered in the *Trade Marks Journal* of February 19, 1941.

Sleeperette *(reclining seat)*

The name was entered by **Pan American** Airways in the US Patent Office *Official Gazette* of July 11, 1950 for a seat designed "for transportation of passengers by aircraft." The name was subsequently applied generally to any sleeper or seat that converts into a bed, on any form of transport.

Slimcea *see* **Procea**

Slinky *(toy)*

The toy, popular in the 1960s, consists of a flexible helical spring that can be set to "somersault" down stairs or steps in a "U" shape. It was the creation of marine engineer Richard James, who one day in 1945 was sitting in his office at the Cramp Shipyard, Philadelphia, when a torsion spring fell off a shelf and "walked" over a pile of books. He and his wife, Betty, borrowed $500, used it to make 400 springs, dreamed up the name "Slinky" for the product's slithering, sinuous motion, and launched it at **Gimbel's** of New York. All 400 sold out in 90 minutes, and the Jameses knew they had an instant appeal to the small boy or small girl in every American. By the end of the 20th century, over 250 millions Slinkys had been made. The name was entered by James Industries, Inc., of Germantown, Philadelphia, in the *Trade Marks Journal* of February 11, 1948.

Slipperette *(slipper)*

The type of slipper or slipper-shaped foot covering, made of soft fabric and often distributed to airline passengers, takes its name fairly obviously from "slipper" and the diminutive suffix "-ette." It was entered in the US Patent Office *Official Gazette* of December 29, 1931: "For footwear—namely, rectangular bags of knitted or crotcheted fabric adapted to be worn on the feet as low socks."

Sloan's *("Liniment")*

Earl Sawyer Sloan (1848-1923) was born in Zanesfield, Ohio, the son of a veterinary surgeon, the family having immigrated from Ireland to the United States in the 17th century. Leaving school young, Sloan worked buying and selling horses, thus largely following in the footsteps of his father, who had purchased horses for combat use in the Civil War. After some years thus occupied, however, he devoted more and more time to making the liniment or skin embrocation to which he gave his name, basing it on a formula devised by his father. The preparation sold well, so that in 1888 he gave up the horses (for whom the liniment had been originally prepared) and concentrated on the commercial manufacture of "Sloan's Liniment" in Boston. As a result of his remedy and reputation he became known as "Dr. Sloan," and adopted the title, although never formally qualifying in medicine. A British branch of Dr. Earl S. Sloan, Inc. was established in 1913.

Slovignac (brandy)

The Czech brand of brandy was originally established before World War II by the Tauber brothers in Prague. The brand name, now owned by the Seliko firm in Olomouc, was introduced in 1955 and is presumably a blend of "Czechoslovak" and "cognac."

Smarties (chocolates)

The multicolored candy-covered milk-chocolate buttons, made by **Rowntree Mackintosh**, take their name from their bright or showy appearance. They were launched in 1937 and their name was entered in the *Trade Marks Journal* of November 8, 1939 and the US Patent Office *Official Gazette* of January 26, 1965, with a note of first use on April 17, 1950.

Smedley (canned foods)

Englishman Samuel W. Smedley grew up in Evesham, Worcestershire, before World War I and on leaving school joined a local fruit grower's business. He was keen to market the fruit commercially, so set up a stall in London's Covent Garden market, selling produce from Evesham. He then opened a depot in Wisbech, Cambridgeshire, and one morning acquired the whole of the gooseberry market in that town, so that he was nicknamed the "Gooseberry King." During World War I he was kept busy by the government making jam for the troops. After the war, Smedley saw a future in preserving fruit, and visited the United States to

study methods there. By 1924 the firm of S.W. Smedley & Co. had started fruit-bottling in Wisbech, and the following year Smedley set up a full canning and bottling company, Wisbech Produce Canners Ltd. He in turn sent his son Wallace to the United States to study development in the canning business. Father and son made a good partnership, and were joined by Samuel's friend, Robert Barlow, founder of The **Metal Box** Co. In 1953 Samuel Smedley retired. Subsequently Smedley joined forces with HP Foods (makers of **HP Sauce**) to become Smedley-HP Foods in 1972. But in 1981 the company sold off its fruit and vegetable canning interests to another firm, TKM Foods, so that HP Foods reverted to its old name. The Smedley name continues, however, on its canned fruit and vegetable produce.

Smedley, John *see* **John Smedley**

Smell-O-Vision (film projection technique)

The process involved the releasing of odors that corresponded to the particular events of a film through tubing that ran to each seat in the movie theater. The system was sponsored by Mike Todd, Jr., son of the promoter of **Todd-AO**, and used for a single feature film, *Scent of Mystery* (1959). The name itself was patterned on those of other production techniques, such as **Vistavision**, and was entered for a similar technique involving "scent-emitting stickers" with television film in the US Patent Office *Official Gazette* of December 16, 1986.

Smirnoff (vodka)

The well-known Russian name is that of Pyotr Arsenyevich Smirnov (1831-1898), the son of poor rural serfs, who was sent to Moscow as a teenager to work as a servant for his wine merchant uncle, Ivan. In 1862 he produced his first bottles of vodka in a distillery across the Moskva River from the Kremlin. He then broadened his range to include fruit brandies and wines, and these gained a favorable reputation among the Muscovite nobility. In 1877 Smirnov was invited to become the official supplier to the Czarist court, and he rose overnight from the lowly position of "Moscow merchant of the 3d order" to the nobility when he was awarded the order of St. Vladimir by Czar Alexander III. His company expanded, with branches in London, Paris, and New York, and employed more than 25,000 people. On his death, the business was continued by his son, also named Pyotr, but he died in 1910, aged 40, and management of the company then passed to his own sons, Vladimir and Nikolai. Following the 1917 Russian Revolution, the Smirnov distillery and company were nationalized and Vladimir was imprisoned and condemned to death. The sentence was never carried out, however, and he escaped to Poland, then to France, where he gallicized his name and opened another distillery. Almost bankrupt, he was saved by Rudolph Kunett, a fellow Russian exile born Rudolf Semyonovich Kunetsky, whose family had been grain suppliers to the Smirnoff distilleries. Kunett took Smirnoff's vodka formula to the United States, and in 1934 opened a small distillery in Connecticut. Sales did not really take off, however, until after World War II, when Kunett sold the formula and distillery to **Heublein**.

On the advent of glasnost, Boris Smirnov (b.1957), Pyotr Smirnov's great-grandson, emerged to claim back the name as a trademark, but Heublein's lawyers soon saw him off. In 1991, however, Smirnoff's US manufacturers discovered that vodka was being made under the family label in Krasnodar in the south of Russia by Boris and Andrei Smirnov, the latter being the son of Viktor Smirnov, the adopted son of Pyotr Smirnov, Jr. The company took the Smirnovs to court but the case was thrown out. Smirnoff responded by opening a distillery in St. Petersburg, aiming to establish the US-owned brand in Russia and put the Smirnovs out of business. But Smirnov then launched a counteraction against Smirnoff in the USA, claiming its advertising was misleading because it suggested the drink had links with the Smirnov family. In 1999, an American court dismissed Boris Smirnov's claim for a percentage of Smirnoff's universal sales since 1939, which would have netted him a vast $1.2 billion. At the turn of the 21st century, Heublein was selling 500,000 bottles of Smirnoff worldwide every day in around 150 countries, while production at the Smirnov distillery was peaking at a million bottles a month. Smirnoff's best-selling Red Label vodka commemorates the Smirnovskaya Vodka No. 21, which Pyotr Smirnov had supplied to the Czar's armed forces, and its name appears in Russian on the label. The Smirnoff name was entered in the US Patent Office *Official Gazette* of April 26, 1948, with a claim of use since 1914, and by W. & A. Gilbey Ltd. (*see* **Gilbey's**) in the *Trade Marks Journal* of April 15, 1959.

Smith, John *see* **John Smith**

Smith, Samuel *see* **Samuel Smith**

Smith, Tom *see* **Tom Smith**

Smith, W.H *see* **W.H. Smith**

Smith & Nephew *(home healthcare)*

Well known for its **Elastoplast** adhesive plasters, the British firm takes its name from its founder, Thomas James Smith (1825-1896) and his nephew, Horatio Nelson Smith (1874-1960). Thomas was a chemist and apothecary who in 1856 went to Hull, Yorkshire, from Grantham, Lincolnshire, to set up his first business. He began to sell a superior type of cod liver oil, pleasant and palatable, unlike the former kind, which had a disagreeable fishy taste and smell. Increasing orders came for his oil, and his business expanded. By 1883, when he won an award as a refiner and blender of cod liver oil, Smith was well established in Hull. All this time a bachelor, he was living with his sister, Amelia Jane Smith, and was thinking who could succeed him in the business. His nephew, Horatio, had stayed with his uncle and aunt since he had been a small boy, and the three were on close terms. When he was 16, Horatio quit school and took a job with a firm of wholesale drapers and woolen manufacturers in Dewsbury, Yorkshire. In 1896 he received a letter from Aunt Amelia asking if he would like to join his uncle in the cod liver oil business. He accepted, and joined the firm that same year, when it was first known as Smith & Nephew. It was Horatio who developed the surgical dressings side of the business.

Smith & Wesson *(firearms)*

The names are those of Horace Smith (1808-1893) and Daniel Baird Wesson (1825-1906). After serving an apprenticeship with his brother, Wesson, born in Worcester, Massachusetts, engaged in the making of firearms. His long association with Smith, from 1853 to 1855 and from 1857 to 1873, was profitable for both men. In 1854 they patented a new type of repeating pistol, and in 1857 the famous Smith and Wesson revolver. In the latter year they organized the Smith & Wesson Company in Springfield, Massachusetts, to manufacture the new type of pistol. Smith retired in 1873, after which Wesson worked alone until 1883, then brought two of his sons into the business. In 1986 the company passed to British owners, Tomkins plc. The Smith & Wesson name was entered in the US Patent Office *Official Gazette* of May 16, 1893, with a note of use since 1857. *See also* **Magnum**.

Smith Brothers *(cough drops)*

The American cough drop empire associated with the brothers William Smith (1830-1913) and Andrew Smith (*c*.1836-1894) traces its origin to the decade before the Civil War, when their father, James Smith, a restaurant owner in Poughkeepsie, New York, obtained a formula for cough drops from an itinerant peddler and began to make them as a sideline to his main business. By 1852 he was advertising his product as "highly recommended for coughs, colds, hoarseness, sore throats, whooping cough, asthma, etc., etc." When James Smith died in 1866, his sons took over both businesses. Their cough drops became so popular that unscrupulous competitors tried to capitalize on the product by selling confections under names such as "Schmitt Brothers," "Smyth Brothers," and even "Smythe Sisters." Clearly, something had to be done, and to protect their product, the Smiths registered their portraits as trademarks and had them affixed to the glass bowls in which their drops were displayed at general stores and apothecary shops. By pure chance, the word "Trade" appeared under the picture of William, and the word "Mark" under Andrew, so that the brothers came to be affectionately known as "Trade" and "Mark."

Smith Kendon *("travel sweets")*

The name of the British firm became associated with **Altoids** peppermint lozenges and "Skels" sugar-free pastilles. The company traces its origins to the firm of Smith & Co., founded in London in 1780 by one William Smith. The present name dates from 1848, when the firm was registered as a limited company. At that time, the controlling directors were brothers Kenneth and Donald Smith, and the second word of the company name is simply a combination of the first syllables of the brothers' first names. Donald Smith retired as chairman in 1978, and Smith Kendon later became part of the **Callard & Bowser** group.

Smith-Corona *(typewriters)*

The history of the Smith-Corona typewriter really begins with the inventor and engineer Alexander Brown, who in the mid-1880s was hired by Lyman Smith (1850-1910) and Wilbert Smith (1852-1937) to make improvements in one of the shotguns being manufactured in their factory at Syracuse, New York. After completing the project, Brown asked the brothers if they would like to make a typewriter he had designed. They were interested, and in 1886 Brown's double keyboard machine was completed. It proved to be such a success that within a few months the two men had dropped gunmaking to specialize in typewriters. In 1893 Lyman and Wilbert Smith joined with six other manufacturers to form the Union Typewriter Co. They pulled out of this firm ten years later, however, and together with their two other brothers, Hurlbut and Monroe Smith, started a new typewriter company in Syracuse. In 1926 the Smith company merged with another New York firm, the Corona Typewriter Co., and the two names were linked above the keyboard of their typewriters from then on.

SmithKline Beecham *(pharmaceuticals)*

The US firm of SmithKline dates from 1830, when John K. Smith set up a drugstore in Philadelphia, Pennsylvania, selling pills to his own recipe. His younger brother George joined him, and they formed John K. Smith and Co. In 1875 their business was renamed Smith, Kline and Co., ten years after Marlon Kline joined the firm as their 19-year-old bookkeeper. He was a promising entrepreneur, and soon moved into sales. In 1891 the company absorbed the firm of French, Richards and Co., adding perfumes, liniments, and tonics to its growing range of home remedies. In 1989 SmithKline Beckham, as it had become, merged with British **Beecham** to become SmithKline Beecham. *See also* **Glaxo**.

Smiths *(potato crisps, or chips)*

It was Frank Smith, a young English wholesale grocer's assistant, who put the common name Smith on the snack map. In 1920 he decided to start making crisps (chips), using a French recipe that he had for thinly sliced potatoes cooked in oil. He set up his enterprise in Cricklewood, north London, with just £10,000 of capital. His product proved a great success, and his twopenny bags of Smith's Potato Crisps with their blue twist of salt soon caught the imagination of the public. At first the whole process of making the crisps was entirely manual, with a team of cooks slicing, frying, draining, and stacking the crisps ready for packing. In 1939, however, the hand-slicing of potatoes was superseded by an automatic machine process. Smiths is now part of the **Nabisco** group, and produces a whole range of snacks as well as its staple crisps.

Smucker's *(jellies and jams)*

America's leading maker of jellies and preserves owes its origin to Jerome Smucker (1858-1948), an apple cider maker in Orville, Ohio, who began selling apple butter in 1897. At first his product was bought only by local farmers, but soon city dwellers were asking for it, and Smucker was obliged to enlarge his original mill. Although the J.M. Smucker Co. still makes apple butter, its best-selling products are now strawberry jam and grape jelly, with a recent shift into portable snacks. (Two popular lines are Smucker's Uncrustables, as peanut butter and jelly sandwiches, and Smucker's Snackers, combining peanut butter and jelly with crackers.) By 2001, the family enterprise was into its fourth generation, with brothers Timothy and Richard Smucker as chairman and president respectively.

Smythson *(stationery and leather goods)*

The prestigious British firm, the holder of three royal warrants, dates from 1887, when Frank Smythson (1847-1929) opened a stationery shop at 133 Bond Street, London. He introduced featherweight paper in 1892 and was soon producing diaries for royalty and the aristocracy. On his death, the firm was taken over by his nephew, Ralph, and when Ralph died in 1940 it passed in turn to his widow, Nellie Smythson, née Jutton. In 1998 Smythson were bought out by **John Menzies**.

Snapple *(natural fruit drinks)*

The Snapple Beverage Corporation was set up in Brooklyn, New York, in 1972 by health-food-store owner Arnold Greenberg and window washers Leonard Marsh and Hyman Golden. It was originally called Unadulterated Food Products but in 1980 changed to the present, snappier name, from the carbo*nated apple soda* that was part of their original line. In 1994 the brand was bought by **Quaker Oats**, sold by them in 1997 to Triarc Beverages, and in 2000 acquired by **Cadbury Schweppes**.

SNIA *(chemicals)*

The Italian company was founded in 1917 by Riccardo Gualino (1879-1964) as the Società di Navigazione Italo-Americana ("Italo-American Navigation Company"). Following the fall in demand for freightage at the end of World War I, it made its name as a major Italian manufacturer of synthetic fibers. It subsequently diversified into bioengineering.

Snickers *(candy bar)*

The name of the **Mars** product, a bar of peanut butter nougat, topped with caramel and roasted peanuts and covered in milk chocolate, is said to derive from that of a horse owned by the Mars family, itself doubtless so called because of its distinctive snickering or whinnying. At the same time the name happens to suggest "snicker-snack," i.e. "snack." Snickers were launched in 1930 and until 1990 were marketed in the UK as "Marathon," a name based on that of the manufacturer and having a similar classical allusion, as well as suggesting a "long-distance" type of candy. (At the time of the rebranding, the strapline "All that's changed is the name" was printed on the packaging along the side of the bar.) The Snickers name was entered in the *Trade Marks Journal* of July 19, 1933.

Sno-Cat *(snowcat)*

The vehicle now usually known generically as a snowcat was designed in the USA in the 1930s for traveling over snow. It does this by means of caterpillar tracks. Hence the name, entered in the US Patent Office *Official Gazette* of September 10, 1946, with a claim of use since September 1, 1941. A rider states: "No claim is made to the exclusive use of the word 'Sno' apart from the mark."

Snowcem *(paint)*

The cement-based paint, used for covering external walls, is usually white. Hence the first part of the name, which was entered by The Cement Marketing Co. Ltd. in the *Trade Marks Journal* of September 20, 1939.

Soamin *(drug to treat skin diseases)*

The proprietary name for sodium *p*-aminophenylarsonate derives from letters in the generic name. It was entered by "Henry Solomon Wellcome, trading as Burroughs, Wellcome and Co." (*see* **Wellcome**) in the *Trade Marks Journal* of May 13, 1908 for: "Chemical substances prepared for use in Medicine and Pharmacy," and in the US Patent Office *Official Gazette* of January 19, 1909.

Sobelair *(airline)*

The Belgian airline, a subsidiary of **Sabena**, has an acronymic name like that of its parent, in this case *Société belge* de transport par *air* ("Belgian Air Transport Society").

Sobranie *(tobacco and cigarettes)*

The British firm was founded in 1879 to blend and manufacture so-called "Balkan" cigarettes and tobacco, taking a name that is the Bulgarian word for "parliament." The company's interests were taken over by **Gallaher** in 1980. The name was entered (misprinted "Sobraine") for cigarettes manufactured by Isaiah Redstone in the *Trade Marks Journal* of September 19, 1923, while "Balkan Sobranie" was entered in the *Journal* of December 19, 1923.

Socony *see* **Mobil**

Soda Stream *(home carbonation machine)*

The domestic device for making tonic and soda water was the invention in 1903 of George Gilbey, a member of the **Gilbey's** distillers family. It was initially aimed at the aristocracy and well-to-do, with their love of gin and tonic or Scotch and soda, but after World War I found a wider market not only in upper-class homes but also in hospitals, convenience stores, and clubs. The machine stayed in the hands of the Gilbey family until the early 1960s, when a group of entrepreneurs bought the rights. At the height of its popularity in the late 1970s and early 1980s, the Soda Stream (originally Sodastream) was thought to be in one in three British households. By then the business was owned by **Kenwood**, but in 1985 was acquired by **Cadbury Schweppes**. The machines are still manufactured today (in Israel), although only 24,000 were sold in the UK in 2000.

Sohio *see* **Standard Oil**

Sol *(beer)*

The Mexican beer, brewed by the Cervecería Moctezuma of Monterey, has a name that is Spanish for "sun," with reference to the sun worship practiced by the Aztecs.

Solacet *(dyes)*

The range of azo-dyestuffs, containing sulphate ester groups and formerly used for the direct dyeing of artificial fabrics, derive their name from the first elements of "soluble" and "acetate." The name was entered by the British Dyestuffs Corporation Ltd. in the *Trade Marks Journal* of May 17, 1939 for: "Water soluble dyes for cellulose acetate silk."

Soledon *(dyes)*

The range of water-soluble vat dyes take their name from a blend of "soluble" and "Caledon," the latter being the name of an earlier range of dyes. The name was entered by Scottish Dyes Ltd. in the *Trade Marks Journal* of December 24, 1924, and by **ICI** in the US Patent Office *Official Gazette* of December 22, 1964.

Solignum *(wood preservative)*

The name was first used in 1894 and was entered by the British firm of Major and Co. Ltd. in the *Trade Marks Journal* of October 17, 1900 for "preparations for the destruction of weeds, vermin, and insects." The second part of the name is undoubtedly Latin *lignum*, "wood." The first part, given the function of the product, is perhaps taken from Greek *sozein*, "to save," rather than Latin *sol*, "sun."

Solochrome *(dyes)*

The name of the range of synthetic dyestuffs, used in chemical analysis in color tests for different metals (especially aluminum), was entered by the British Dyestuffs Corporation Ltd. in the *Trade Marks Journal* of April 23, 1924. The name appears to derive from "solo" (in the sense "single," perhaps referring to the individual metals) and "chrome" (in the sense "color").

Solpadeine *(analgesic)*

The drug contains paracetamol, codeine, and

457   Soma • Sotheby's

caffeine. Hence its name, as a dis*solv*able preparation of *par*acetamol and co*deine*. The name was entered in the *Trade Marks Journal* of April 26, 1967.

Soma *(analgesic)*

The drug used to relieve pain and as a muscle relaxant takes its name from the fictional perfect drug described by Aldous Huxley in *Brave New World* (1932): "There is always *soma*, delicious *soma*, half a gramme for a half-holiday, a gramme for a week-end, two grammes for a trip to the gorgeous East, three for a dark eternity on the moon." Huxley himself took the name from *soma*, the plant with intoxicating juice used in ancient Indian religious ceremonies and personified as a god.

Somastic *(coating material)*

The asphalt-based material, used for coating oil pipelines, derives its name from the initials of **Standard Oil** and "mastic." The name was entered by Standard Oil of California in the US Patent Office *Official Gazette* of July 8, 1930.

Soneryl *(sedative)*

The proprietary name for the drug butobarbitone, a sedative and hypnotic, is of French and apparently arbitrary origin (although Latin *somnus*, "sleep," may have suggested the first element). It was entered by Établissements Poulenc Frères, of Paris, in the US Patent Office *Official Gazette* of September 18, 1923, and by **May & Baker** in the *Trade Marks Journal* of May 3, 1933.

Sonifier *(sonicator)*

The make of sonicator (a device for treating samples with ultrasound) derives its name from the root of "sonic" and the agent ending "-ifier." It was entered by Branson Instruments, Inc., of Stamford, Connecticut, in the US Patent Office *Official Gazette* of August 1, 1961: "For electrical generators of ultrasonic energy, ultrasonic energy transducers and electrically powered processing systems for the same," with a note of first use on October 19, 1960.

Sony *(consumer electronics)*

The Japanese company was founded in Tokyo in 1946 by Masaru Ibuka (1908-1997), whose Japan Precision Instruments Company had supplied electronic devices in World War II, and Akio Morita (1921-1999), an applied sciences instructor. The company was known as the Tokyo Tsushin Kogyo KK ("Tokyo Communications Industry Co."), and clearly a shorter name was desirable. At first the founders thought of "TTK," but there already existed a TKK, the short name of Tokyo Kyuko KK ("Tokyo Express Co."), which could cause confusion. (KK in these names stands for Kabushiki Kaisha, "Joint-Stock Company.") Earlier they had used "Tape-corder" for their tape recorder, and "Soni," from English "sonic," for its tape. But this name would probably be mispronounced in English as "so-nigh." Even so, the "son" base from Latin *sonus*, "sound," was good, and a "y" added to this would give "Sonny," a word meaningful to Morita as he referred to himself and his partner as "sonny boys." However, this raised a further problem: "Sonny" in Japanese would suggest *son-ni*, "at a loss." The spelling was therefore finally adjusted to "Sony", rhyming with "bony" rather than "bunny." The name was first used in 1955 for Japan's first all-transistor radio and passed to the company as a whole in 1958. Sony launched the first all-transistor television in 1960, the **Trinitron** TV in 1967, the **Betamax** VTR in 1975. the **Walkman** personal stereo in 1979, and the video camera in 1996.

Sorbo *(sponge rubber)*

The make of sponge rubber has a name apparently based on "absorb" that was entered by the Leeson Sponge and Rubber Co. Ltd. in the *Trade Marks Journal* of August 15, 1917. (In the *Journal* of May 7, 1919, the name of the manufacturers is given as "Sorbo Sponge Rubber Products Ltd.")

Soreen *(malt loaf)*

The present British product dates from 1959, when **Warburtons** bought Imperial Bakeries, who were already marketing goods under the name. The origin of the name itself is obscure, although "-een" is probably a form of "-ine." The "Sor-" could come from "sorghum," a type of grass used for grain.

Sotheby's *(fine art auctioneers and valuers)*

Christie's and Sotheby's have long been major rivals in the auctioneering world. The forerunner of Sotheby's was founded in London, England, in 1744 by Samuel Baker, a bookseller and auctioneer of "Literary Properties." On his death in 1778 his estate was divided equally between his partner, George Leigh, and a nephew, John Sotheby, whose successors moved the business to 13 Wellington Street in 1818 and ran the company for over 80 years. The last member of the family to be actively involved with the firm was Samuel Leigh Sotheby (1805-1861). From then until World War I Sotheby's was not an art auctioneering company but a book auctioneering concern, and it was only when the firm moved to 34-35 New Bond Street in 1917 that it began to become a serious challenger to Christie's. In 1964 Sotheby's acquired the Parke-Bernet Galleries, New York, its US counterpart, to become Sotheby Parke Bernet, and in 1974 it added the Dutch equivalent, Mak van Waay. In 1983 Sotheby's itself passed to A. Alfred Taubman, an American businessman and art patron, and took its present name.

Southern Comfort *(whiskey liqueur)*

"The Grand Old Drink of the South" was introduced to the market in the 1860s by M.W. Heron, a New Orleans bartender, who is said to have coined the name to console those of his customers who were still smarting from defeat in the recent Civil War. It was the Mississippi River that launched the nationwide fame of Southern Comfort, carrying enthusiastic reports of the drink hundreds of miles upriver. By the 1890s, Heron was bottling the liqueur spirit for general sale, having bought his own bar on Beale Street in the more northerly Mississippi port of Memphis. The name was entered in the US Patent Office *Official Gazette* of July 24, 1934 and the *Trade Marks Journal* of November 12, 1947.

Southland *(convenience stores)*

The American corporation dates from 1927, when the Consumers Ice Company of Dallas, Texas, famous for its ice-cold watermelons, joined with four other Texas companies to form the Southland Ice Company. The new firm's director was Joe C. Thompson (1901-1961), who had spent his summers as a high school student in World War I loading blocks of ice on to horse-drawn wagons for Consumers Ice and who had come up with the idea

of chilling watermelons and selling them off the ice docks. Southland started the Tote'm Stores from their ice docks, changing the name in 1946 to 7-Eleven (the hours when they were open).

Spackle *(surfacing compound)*

The compound is used to fill cracks in plaster in order to provide a smooth surface before painting. The name is of German origin and may be a blend of "sparkle" and German *Spachtel*, "putty knife," "mastic." It was entered in the US Patent Office *Official Gazette* of February 7, 1928 for: "A surfacing compound for filling imperfection so as to bring up to a smooth and level surface areas that are to be painted or decorated."

Spalding *(sporting goods)*

The name is that of Albert Goodwill Spalding (1850-1915), a professional baseball player born in Byron, Illinois, whose sporting career began in 1865, when Rockford, Illinois, businessmen formed a new baseball club, the Forest Citys, and asked him to join as pitcher. Spalding soon rose to fame as a professional pitcher, playing for the Boston Red Stockings in the National Association from 1871 to 1875, and managing the Chicago National League, the White Stockings, from 1876 to 1877. In 1876, the year he moved to Chicago, Spalding and his younger brother James founded the company A.G. Spalding and Brother to manufacture and sell baseball equipment. The business later diversified into other sports and marketed its goods internationally.

Spam *(canned meat)*

The name was first used in 1937 by the product's US manufacturers, **Hormel**, for their newly marketed cans of luncheon meat. A cash prize of $100 was offered for the best suggestion of a name, and at first "Brunch" was offered, and seriously considered. "Spam," for "*sp*iced h*am*" (or "*s*houlder of *p*ork and h*am*") was then proposed by the New York radio actor Kenneth Daigneau, brother of a Hormel vice-president, and was declared the easy winner. It is sometimes said that Daigneau had already devised the name and was simply waiting for a product to attach to it. The name was entered in the US Patent Office *Official Gazette* of October 26, 1937, with a claim of use since May

11, 1937, and in the *Trade Marks Journal* of July 5, 1939.

Spandex *(synthetic fiber)*

The artificial fiber with high stretch qualities was introduced in 1958 by **Du Pont** for use in swimwear, lingerie, and hosiery. The name, based on "expand," was entered as a generic name in the *Federal Register* of February 10, 1959 and (by **Monsanto**) as a trademark in the *Trade Marks Journal* of February 7, 1968.

Spansules *(sustained-release capsules)*

When swallowed, the capsules of this name release a drug steadily over a number of hours, instead of instantly. Hence the name, from a blend of "span" and "capsule," entered by Smith, Kline & French Laboratories (now **SmithKline Beecham**), of Philadelphia, Pennsylvania, in the US Patent Office *Official Gazette* of March 2, 1954: "For capsules containing multiples of specially coated globules ... and providing for the gradual release of a medicament in the gastro-intestinal tract." *See also* **Contac.**

Spar *(food stores)*

The chain of food stores is of Dutch origin and was founded in The Hague in 1932 by a food wholesaler, A.J.M. van Well. As his trading device, van Well chose the symbol of a fir tree, the Dutch for which is *spar*. Hence the name, which the company itself has promoted by linking it with the (unrelated) Dutch word *sparen*, "savings." Spar International was formed in 1948 and stores soon began to open in other European countries, so that by 1980 there were almost 4,000 in the UK.

Sparine *(sedative)*

The proprietary name of the antipsychotic drug promazine hydrochloride is perhaps of arbitrary origin. It was entered in the US Patent Office *Official Gazette* of October 2, 1956, with a note of first use on December 21, 1955, and in the *Trade Marks Journal* of December 12, 1956.

Sparklets *(carbon dioxide capsules)*

The small bulbs of carbon dioxide, used to carbonate the water in a siphon and so provide the "sparkle" for a drink, were originally manufactured by the British firm of Aerators Ltd., founded in Edmonton, London, in 1896, who entered the name in the *Trade Marks Journal* of December 23, 1896. In 1920 the business was taken over by the British Oxygen Co. (*see* **BOC**), who moved their engineering business to the site.

Spear & Jackson *(handsaws)*

The English company traces its history to 1774, when one John Love, a Sheffield draper, ran a business as a steel founder and refiner in Castle Street, Sheffield. Two years later a record mentions that he supplied a local sawmill with "two dozens of mill webbes eache with 28 teeth." In 1784 John Spear was taken into partnership and the firm became Love & Spear. In 1814 Samuel Jackson was apprenticed to Spear, and became his partner in 1830, when the name of the business became Spear & Jackson. After Spear's death in 1851 the firm was carried on by Jackson, who was then joined by his brother Robert. The business was taken over by **Neill** Tools Ltd. in 1985.

Spear's *(board games)*

The full name of the British company that makes **Scrabble** and other board games is J.W. Spear & Sons plc. Not much is known about the early days of the firm, but it is on record that Jacob Spear set up a business making games and novelties in Eldon Street, London, in 1878. In 1886 he moved his activity to Nürnberg, Germany, the "toy capital" of Europe. He had six sons, one of whom subsequently became a partner. Spear remained in Nürnberg while his son represented the firm in London, assembling and selling games made partly by his father and partly by other manufacturers. In 1899 another son, Carl, built a large factory in Nürnberg, and this town remained the center of the business, with Britain its best customer. A British factory was subsequently opened at Enfield, Middlesex, in 1932. Spears introduced Scrabble in 1954 and in 1969 acquired the worldwide rights for the game outside the United States, Canada, and Australia. The company is still based in Enfield and in the hands of the Spear family.

Speclettes *(spectacles)*

The spectacles, fashionable in the 1930s, are so designed that they fold at the bridge. Their name derives from "specs" (spectacles) and a French-style diminutive ending "-lette(s)."

Specsavers *(opticians)*

Britain's biggest private optical retailer is owned by Douglas Perkins (b.1943) and his wife Mary (b.1944), who met on an opticians' course at the University of Wales and built up one chain before selling it in 1980. The firm, based in Guernsey, Channel Islands, specializes in "buy-one-get-one-free" spectacles. Hence the name.

Spectris *see* **Fairey**

Speed Gun *(vehicle speed calculator)*

The hand-held device for estimating the speed of a moving vehicle is so called because it is pointed at the vehicle like a gun. The name was entered by CMI, Inc., of Minturn, Colorado, in the US Patent Office *Official Gazette* of August 1, 1972 , with a note of first use on December 10, 1970.

Speedwalk *(moving walkway)*

The moving walkway for conveying passengers, as at an airport or railroad station, has a name of obvious origin entered by Passenger Belt Conveyors, Inc., of Akron, Ohio, in the US Patent Office *Official Gazette* of September 4, 1956, with a note of first use on March 29, 1954. *Cp.* **Travolator.**

Speedwriting *(shorthand system)*

The form of shorthand, using the letters of the alphabet instead of special symbols, was devised in the USA around 1924 by Emma B. Dearborn, who entered its name in the US Patent Office *Official Gazette* of August 8, 1927 ("Printed Lessons and Examination Sheets Issued from Time to Time"), with a claim of use since December 29, 1924. The name has an exact equivalent in the word for "shorthand" in some languages, such as Chinese *sùjì* and (though now dated) Russian *skoropis'*.

Sperling & Kupfer *(publishers)*

The Italian publishing house was founded in Milan in 1899 by the German H.O. Sperling, who already ran his own firm in Stuttgart. In 1911 he added the name of his partner, R. Kupfer. In 1970 the business was bought by the Italian T.M. Barbieri (1938-1994), who remained chairman until his death. In 1995 the company was acquired by **Montadori.**

Sperring's *(newsagents)*

The British firm was founded in the mid-1930s by Thomas Sperring, who owned a newsagent's shop in Bitterne, Southampton. He died in the late 1960s, and although the firm continued in the hands of his son, it was sold by him in the 1980s to the American company Circle K Corporation, of Phoenix, Arizona, and now trades in Britain as Circle K (UK) Ltd. The Sperring name has now disappeared from the facias of the many High Street stores in the chain, and Sperring's Newsmarkets are now Circle K Convenience Stores.

Sperry Rand *(computers)*

Elmer Ambrose Sperry (1860-1930) was born in Cortland, New York, the son of a farmer turned drayman and carpenter. At school he was interested in mechanical things, and when barely out of his teens invented an improved type of dynamo and a new kind of arc lamp. In 1880 he set up the Sperry Electric Company in Chicago, following this by founding other companies with electrically-based production processes and manufactures. His most famous invention was the gyroscopic compass, manufactured by the Sperry Gyroscope Company that he founded in 1910. James H. Rand was a New York City bank cashier who developed a business index system in the closing years of the 19th century. In 1915 his son, also named James H. Rand, organized the American Kardex Company to manufacture his invention, a visible record control system ("Kardex"). In 1927 the Rand Kardex Corporation, as it had become, merged with the **Remington** Typewriter Company to form Remington Rand, Inc., and from that year began to prosper as a manufacturer of business machines and systems. In 1955 Sperry joined with Remington Rand to form the Sperry Rand Corporation, who in 1979 sold its shaver business to the marketing executive Victor Kiam (1926-2001) in a leveraged buyout, leading to the formation of Remington Products Ltd. In 1986 Sperry merged with **Burroughs** to form **Unisys.**

Spillers *(pet foods)*

The British company is named for Joel Spiller (1804-1853), an ironmonger's son who in 1829 set up in Bridgwater, Somerset, as a "Corn Factor and Dealer." His business did well, for the corn trade was vigorous then, with good harvests. In 1840 Spiller went into partnership with Samuel Woolcott Browne, a banker in the town, and the two men built a substantial warehouse on the West Quay, with their office in Castle Street. Soon after, they decided to build their own mill, using steam power. After the Corn Laws were repealed in 1846, Spiller and Browne expanded their business and built more mills in Somerset and Cardiff, South Wales. While inspecting work on the Cardiff site, Spiller grazed his shin. The wound turned septic, and he died aged only 49. Browne continued alone, retiring in 1864, by which time Spillers was making ship's biscuits. It was not until the 1930s, however, that the firm's pet foods became prominent, and that names such as **Winalot** and "Shapes" became popular as dog biscuits. Finally, in 1978, Spillers closed all its bakeries and its three mills and began to concentrate entirely on pet foods. *See also* **Turog.**

Spinks *(coins and medals)*

Spink & Son Ltd. traces its origins back to 1666, when John Spink, on completion of a nine-year apprenticeship, set up as a goldsmith in the City of London. He was joined four years later by his cousin, Elwes Spink, and the two men became established dealers in plate and jewelry. By 1703 the partnership had been so successful that larger premises were needed, and a move was made from Lombard Street to Gracechurch Street, where the firm remained for more than 100 years. From that date on the family business followed the spread of London to the west, moving first to a shop near Piccadilly Circus, then in the 1920s to the present site in King Street, off St. James's Square. Members of the Spink family remain with the company today.

Spirella *(corsets and fashionwear)*

In 1900, or soon after, an American engineer, Marcus Beeman, became concerned that there was no flexible support that could be inserted in women's corsets. By bending a piece of wire backward and forward in a series of "S" shapes he accordingly devised a spiral stay which he called the "Spirella flexible stay." Two of his associates were impressed with the device and began designing corsets on an anatomical basis, incorporating the new stay. A few years

later, one of the two partners, a Mr. Kincaid, went to England and in 1909 set up the Spirella Company of Great Britain. The name of the company and its original product is thus based on "spiral," and it was entered in the *Trade Marks Journal* of September 1, 1909.

Spirograph *(toy)*

The toy marketed by **Hasbro** uses interlocking plastic cogs and toothed rings of different sizes to draw intricate curved patterns. Hence the name, from Latin *spira,* "coil" (English "spiral") and the Greek-derived "-graph" meaning "to write." A spirograph is also a medical instrument recording respiratory movements, but here "spiro-" represents Latin *spirare,* "to breathe." The name was entered in the *Trade Marks Journal* of May 13, 1964.

Spode *(china)*

Josiah Spode (1754-1827) was the most successful china manufacturer of his day. He was born in Stoke-on-Trent, England, the son of an identically named potter who had begun manufacturing independently in the year of his son's birth. The younger Josiah learned the trade of a potter in his father's workshops and went on to produce porcelain in 1800 and stone china in 1805, with a factory founded in the former year. In around 1813 William Copeland became a partner in the business, which from then on was known as Spode & Copeland. After Josiah Spode's death the whole business passed to Copeland's son, William T. Copeland, and continued under various combinations of the name Copeland to the present time. The factory amalgamated with **Wedgwood** in 1964 but continued to manufacture under the name of Spode.

Spong *(coffee mills)*

The British firm was founded in north London by James Osborn Spong, born in 1839 near Northampton the son of a Congregational minister. On leaving school he set up in 1856 as a varnish maker, gradually increasing the range of his products until by the 1890s he was selling a number of labor-saving appliances and gadgets, including meat mincers, sausage machines, and knife cleaners. It was coffee mills, however, that seem to have been a particular interest of his. Some were commercial models, rather than domestic, and one, the "Monster"

Mincer, weighed over half a ton. After 1900 the firm's activities moved to High Holborn, London, and James Spong's son, James William Spong, joined his father in the business. Today the company headquarters are in Basildon, Essex, and although coffee mills remain one of the firm's principal products, it also manufactures a number of other domestic appliances for kitchen use.

Spork *(cutlery)*

The name of a type of combined spoon and fork (and sometimes knife) is a Carrollian portmanteau creation ("spoon" and "fork") that was entered by the Van Brode Milling Co., Inc., of Clinton, Massachusetts, in the US Patent Office *Official Gazette* of April 11, 1970, and by D. Green and Company, of Sutton, Surrey, England, in the *Trade Marks Journal* of December 22, 1976. The word itself is already recorded in generic use in the early years of the 20th century.

Sprague-Dawley *(rats)*

The inbred strain of rats, much used in laboratories, takes its name from the American scientist who established it, R.W. Dawley (1897-1949), and the maiden name of his wife, née Sprague. The name was entered by the Mogul Corporation in the US Patent Office *Official Gazette* of January 3, 1978.

Spratt's *(dog food)*

Before the mid-19th century, people mostly fed their pets on scraps and "leftovers" from the dining table, and dogs often had nothing more nutritious than musty ship's biscuits. This concerned James Spratt (*c.*1809-1880), a dog-loving electrician who lived in Holborn, London. He felt his dogs deserved better food, and that they would benefit by it. He therefore set to work to devise a "dog cake" which would be both inexpensive and nourishing. His experiments showed that a blend of wheatmeal, vegetable matter, and meat fibrin was best for the purpose. He fed it to his dogs, who enjoyed it and lived active and healthy lives on it. He patented the food, and in 1860 opened a shop in High Holborn to make and sell it to dog owners. In 1866 he took as his assistant a youngster named Charles Cruft (1852-1939), who rose to be general manager and who 20 years later organized the first Cruft's Dog Show. The popularity of Spratt's dog food spread, and by the year of his death the firm had moved to a new factory in Bermondsey to make "Meat Fibrine Dog Cake" and "Puppy Biscuit" in large quantities. Spratt's dog biscuits were marketed until World War II.

Springer *(publishers)*

The major German scientific publishing house Springer Verlag was founded in 1842 by Julius Springer (1817-1877). A descendant was Axel Springer (1912-1985), founder in 1945 of the newspaper publishing concern Axel Springer Verlag, who by the time of his death controlled the largest press empire in Europe. *See also* **Pergamon**.

Springs Mills *(bed linen)*

The American company takes its name from Leroy Springs, who became president early in the 20th century when his father-in-law, Samuel White, resigned rather than obey a summon to New York to meet with bankers. The story goes that White told his board of directors that he had gone North of the Mason-Dixon line only to chase Yankees, not to take orders from them. Captain White had organized the original Fort Mill cotton-spinning plant in South Carolina in 1887, and the company has been based at Fort Mill ever since.

Sprüngli *(chocolates)*

The Swiss firm, not to be confused with **Lindt** & Sprüngli, is one of the oldest establishments of its kind in the world. It was founded in Zürich in 1836 by David Sprüngli, and is still in family hands today, managed by the sixth generation of Sprünglis. At the age of 60, David Sprüngli acquired the Vogel confectionery business in Martgasse from the widow Vogel, whose shop had been in existence since 1720, and together with his 20-year-old son, Rudolf, founded Confiserie Sprüngli. In 1859, the shop relocated to Paradeplatz. By 1870 the chocolate side of the business had outgrown the general confectionery, so production moved from Zürich to Werdmühle. In 1892, Rudolf Sprüngli divided the two sides of the business between his two sons: Johann Rudolf Sprüngli took over the chocolate factory (the Lindt & Sprüngli of today), while David Robert Sprüngli continued the confectionery business in the Paradeplatz.

Spry *(vegetable fat)*

The cooking fat was introduced in the USA by the Dutch firm of Jurgens (*see* **Unilever**) in 1936 as a counter to **Procter & Gamble**'s popular **Crisco**. Its name represents the standard English word, in its senses of "smart," "brisk," "lively and healthy." The names "Sprybake" and "Spryfry" were entered in the *Trade Marks Journal* of March 6, 1968.

Spyker *(automobiles)*

The Dutch engineers Jacobus Spijker and his younger brother Hendrik first produced cars at Trompenburg in 1900, changing the spelling of their name to aid foreign sales. Many fine cars, including taxis, were produced until 1927, when a rash attempt at expansion caused the company's downfall.

SQ *(audio equipment)*

The abbreviation of "stereophonic-quadraphonic," used for a system of quadraphonic recording and reproduction, was entered by **CBS** in the US Patent Office *Official Gazette* of November 20, 1973: "For pre-recorded phonograph records, and pre-recorded tapes," with a note of first use on June 10, 1971.

Squibb *(pharmaceuticals)*

The name of Squibb is one of the oldest and best known in the pharmaceutical industry. It is that of Edward Robinson Squibb (1819-1900), born in Wilmington, Delaware. After Squibb's mother died in 1831, the family moved to Philadelphia. In 1837 he became a pharmacist's apprentice, and five years later entered Jefferson Medical College, receiving his doctor of medicine degree in 1845. That same year Squibb set up his own medical practice, and two years later joined the US Navy as a surgeon, where he witnessed the sorry state of medicine and pharmacy as practiced on navy ships. In 1851 the navy assigned Squibb to the Brooklyn Naval Hospital, New York, where he set up a laboratory for the production of pharmaceuticals. His first main product was chloroform, and on the basis of this he built up a substantial company, which in due course passed to his sons. In 1905 the business was sold to Theodore Weicker, a German chemist, who kept the family name. Squibb is now known not only for drugs but also for bubblegum and perfume. The company headquarters remain in New York.

Staedtler *(pencils)*

The German city of Nürnberg has long been famous for its pencils, and records of 1662 show that Friedrich Staedtler was making them there then. He was not, however, the founder of the present company, who was a descendant, Johann Sebastian Staedtler, a craftsman who in 1835 applied for an independent concession to make pencils in Nürnberg. This was granted the same year, after he had passed the master craftsman examinations. Having left the family business to set up in this way, Staedtler established a factory and soon had a flourishing concern, transferring it to his three sons in 1855, on his retirement. Staedtler pencils subsequently became familiar under their different brand names, such as "Luna," "Camel," and "Mars," and in Germany today the company, still based in Nürnberg, has the official name of Staedtler Mars GmbH & Co.

Stagecoach *(public transport)*

The seeds of the British bus and coach company were sown in 1976, when Scottish businesswoman Ann Gloag (b.1942) and her husband Robin set up a caravan (trailer) hire business in Perth. In 1980, Ann and her brother, Brian Souter (b.1954), founded a small private bus service punningly named Gloagtrotter, operating between Scotland and London and undercutting existing companies. Their vehicles were really coaches rather than buses, however, and they felt a change of name would be appropriate. "Stagecoach" was an obvious choice, and a colorful promotion was mounted to tie the name in with a Wild West image. The gimmicks were successful, and Stagecoach attracted much welcome free publicity. The name was proposed by Souter's elder brother, David, who had worked in marketing: "I made up the name. I had been involved in publicity in London and they came to me for ideas. We were talking about licences for stage carriage, and I was trying to get away from the bus image. We wanted to be coach, better than a bus, because we were offering more of a service, like feeding people, and showing videos" (Christian Wolmar, *Stagecoach*, 1999).

Stag's Breath *(whisky liqueur)*

The liqueur has been produced by Meikles of Scotland, a small Speyside family firm, since 1989. It takes its name from one of the fictional whiskies in Compton Mackenzie's amusing novel *Whisky Galore* (1947), a retelling of the story of the SS *Politician*, shipwrecked in 1941 off the northwest coast of Scotland while bound for the USA with a cargo of whisky and other luxury goods.

Stainer & Bell *(music publishers)*

The British firm of music publishers was founded in 1907 by a group of young composers who devised the name simply for its euphony. There was thus neither a Mr. Stainer nor a Mr. Bell behind the business, although the former name evokes the English composer John Stainer (1840-1901) and the latter has an obvious musical resonance.

Stakis *(hotels)*

The British hotel chain owes its name to Reo Stakis (1913-2001), born in Cyprus the son of a farmer. His mother made lace for sale in Britain. When money was tight, the family decided to send their 15-year-old heir to Britain to sell their wares door-to-door. For the next ten years, young Reo traveled up and down the country selling his mother's needlework. All this time, he was eating out, and he soon found that the warmest hopsitality was in Scotland. By the late 1930s, Stakis had resolved to open his own restaurant, but his plans were thwarted by the outbreak of war. In 1947, he finally realized his ambition, and a steakhouse opened in Hope Street, Glasgow. It did well, and during the 1960s he opened more restaurants and his first casino. The hotels followed, together with more casinos, until by 1960 there were 26 hotels in Scotland. Expansion south of the border to England followed, and in 1999 the chain was sold to **Ladbrokes**, by which time the business was employing around 14,000 people.

Staley *(foods and starches)*

The American corn refiners, based in Decatur, Illinois, in the heart of the Midwest farm belt, have not always been located in this state. They take their name from August Eugene Staley, a North Carolina farm boy, who began making cream corn starch in a Baltimore loft in 1898. In 1906 he moved closer to the source of the raw material he was using, bought two buildings and 40 acres left by a former Decatur corn milling firm, and started grinding corn. In 1922 he opened the first United States soybean processing plant. The company's food prod-

ucts now include fruit drinks, "Gold 'n Soft" margarine, and Staley waffle and pancake syrups.

Standard *(automobiles)*

The Standard Motor Company was founded in Coventry, Warwickshire, England, in 1903 by Reginald Walter Maudslay (1871-1934), a civil engineer. At Maudslay's request, his consulting engineer, Alex Craig, designed "a car to be composed purely of those components whose principles have been tried and tested and accepted as reliable standards." ("In fact," added Maudslay, "I will name my car the Standard car.") The first car of this name, a single-cylinder six-horsepower model, never went into production, and the first to be actually built was the two-cylinder 12/15 horsepower Standard, presented at the Crystal Palace Motor Show in 1904. In 1908 the company displayed the Union Jack on the car, the first time this had happened, as a symbol of its all-British manufacture. The flag, a "standard on a Standard," was incorporated in the car's logo in 1931. Standard also made power units for SS Cars Ltd (*see* **Jaguar**), thus prompting the idea that these initials stood for "Standard Special" rather than "Swallow Sidecar." In 1944 Standard purchased the goodwill of the **Triumph** Company, and the last Standard car, an "Ensign," was manufactured in 1963.

Standard Brands *(food and liquor)*

The US corporation came into being in 1929 when **Fleischmann** joined forces with the Royal Baking Company, founded in 1863 by two druggists in Fort Wayne, Indiana, and Chase & Sanborn, founded also in 1863 in Boston, Massachusetts, by two tea and coffee merchants, Caleb Chase and James Sanborn. In 1879 the latter became the first American company to pack roasted coffee in sealed cans.

Standard Chartered *(bank)*

The British bank was incorporated in 1969 as the Standard and Chartered Banking Group to effect the merger of two British overseas banks: The Standard Bank and The Chartered Bank. The Standard Bank was established in 1862 as The Standard Bank of British South Africa and gradually set up offices in other African countries. The Chartered Bank was incorporated by royal charter in 1853 as The

Chartered Bank of India, Australia and China, opening branches in the Far East in subsequent years.

Standard Life *(insurance)*

Britain's second largest life insurance company was founded in 1825 and by the end of the century had offices in countries all over the world. Its name indicated that the ideal client, a "standard" life, was a healthy adult living in the UK with temperate habits and a secure occupation free of any hazards.

Standard Oil *(oil)*

The famous American name arose from the industrial empire of John D. Rockefeller (1839-1937) and his associates, which came to control almost all oil production, processing, marketing, and transportation in the United States. The company's origins date from 1863, when Rockefeller joined Maurice B. Clark and Samuel Andrews in a Cleveland refining business. Two years later, Rockefeller bought out Clark and brought in Henry M. Flagler. By 1870, the firm of Rockefeller, Andrews, and Flagler was operating the largest refineries in Cleveland, and these and related businesses became the property of the new Standard Oil Company, incorporated in Ohio in 1870. In 1882, the Standard Oil Company and its affiliated companies were combined in the Standard Oil trust, created by an agreement signed by nine trustees, including Rockefeller. On the terms of the agreement, companies could be purchased, created, dissolved, merged, or divided, so that eventually the trustees controlled some 40 corporations. In 1899 Standard Oil Company (New Jersey) was incorporated as a holding company, and all assets and interests formerly grouped in the trust were transferred to the New Jersey company. In 1906 the US government brought suit against Standard Oil Company (New Jersey) for excessive concentration of economic power, and in 1911 the company was ordered to divest itself of all its major holdings, amounting to 33 companies in all. After dissolution of the Standard Oil empire, eight companies retained "Standard Oil" in their names, although by the close of the 20th century the name had almost passed into history.

The fates of the eight were as follows. In 1931 Standard Oil Company of New York (1)

merged with Vacuum Oil Company to form Socony-Vacuum, which in 1966 became **Mobil** Oil Corporation. Standard Oil (Indiana) (2) absorbed Standard Oil of Nebraska (3) in 1939 and Standard Oil of Kansas (4) in 1948 and was renamed **Amoco** Corporation in 1985. Standard Oil of California (5) acquired Standard Oil of Kentucky (6) in 1961 and was renamed **Chevron** Corporation in 1984. Standard Oil Company (New Jersey) (7) changed its name to **Exxon** Corporation in 1972. **British Petroleum** (BP) completed the purchase of Standard Oil Company (Ohio) (Sohio) (8) in 1987.

Other companies that were at one time part of the trust include **Atlantic Richfield**, Buckeye Pipe Line Company (Ohio), **Chesebrough-Pond's** Inc., Pennzoil Company, and Union Tank Car Company (New Jersey). The standard thus rose and ruled for over a century, but ultimately fell.

Stanfords *(mapsellers and publishers)*

Britain's most famous map shop, in Long Acre, London, takes its name from Edward Stanford (1827-1904), the London-born son of a tailor and draper, who began his career as a printer. In 1852 he set up a partnership with T.W. Saunders in London as a firm of publishers, booksellers, mapsellers, and stationers. The partnership was mutually dissolved the following year, however, and Stanford began publishing and selling maps on his own account. In 1860 he acquired the bookselling business of C.H. Law, in 1874 the plates and stock of the mapmaker John Arrowsmith, and in 1877 the stationery business of Staunton & Sons. In 1887 Stanford was obliged by illness to hand over the business to his son, also Edward, who in 1893 was appointed "Geographer to the Queen." The present shop opened in 1901, and soon became a Mecca for travelers to all parts of the globe.

Stanley *(automobiles)*

The Stanley Motor Company owed its origin to American twin brothers, Francis Edgar Stanley (1849-1918) and Freelan Oscar Stanley (1849-1940), born in Kingfield, Maine, the sons of a farmer. Both brothers began their careers as teachers, but in 1885 established a shop in Lewiston, Maine, to manufacture dry plates. In 1889 they sold the operation and set up a new factory for the Stanley Dry Plate Company in Watertown, Massachusetts, a Boston suburb. The twins became interested in motor carriages after seeing one near Boston in 1896, and began the construction of several prototype steam cars. The Stanley Motor Company itself was founded in 1901. It was sold off in 1917, when the brothers had reached the age of 68, and by the time it closed in 1924 had made a total of some 14,000 steamers.

Stanley *(tools)*

The Stanley knife with its sharp, replaceable blade, used for trimming carpets, cutting cardboard, and the like, gets its name from Frederick T. Stanley, who in 1831, together with his brother, William T. Stanley, set up a business in New Britain, Connecticut, to make house hardware and fittings. By 1842 the two men had added wrought-iron bolts, door and chest handles, and coffin handles to their products. In 1854 August and Timothy Stanley set up a partnership with Thomas Conklin, a steel rule maker, and the resulting merger was known as the Stanley Rule and Level Company. The firm gradually extended its range of tools over the years, making a number of acquisitions. It was not until 1934, however, that the famous Stanley knife was introduced, and two years later Stanley set up a British branch of the company in Sheffield. By now the organization was known simply as Stanley Tools. In 1938 it introduced another well-known product, the **Phillips** screwdriver, designed for use with the screws of the same name.

Stanley Gibbons *(stamp dealers)*

Edward Stanley Gibbons (1840-1913) was born in Plymouth, England, the son of a pharmaceutical chemist. The year of his birth was the one when the first adhesive postage stamps were issued in Britain, and it was only natural that Gibbons, as he grew up, should acquire a typical boy's interest in stamps. He quit school at 15, getting a job as a junior bank clerk, but the sudden death of his elder brother, William, obliged him to abandon banking and return to the family business. He pursued his interest in stamps, his father giving him a special desk in the shop for his hobby. Soon the stamps took over, and within three years Gibbons had moved to a room over the shop and set up the embryonic firm of E. Stanley Gibbons. When

his father died in about 1862, Gibbons became the owner of the chemist's shop. He disposed of it, and devoted himself entirely to trading in stamps. In 1865 he produced his first price list, the prototype of the now well established Gibbons Catalogue, and by 1870 he had published his first stamp albums. In 1874 he moved his activity from Plymouth to London, taking a house on Clapham Common. This was not so convenient for business, however, so in 1876 he moved to Gower Street, where he stayed for the rest of his working life. He retired early, in 1890, and sold the business (for £25,000) to a spare-time dealer, Charles Phillips, and it was he, not Gibbons, who moved the firm to its world-famous address, 391 Strand, where it remains today.

Stanley Leisure *(betting agents)*

The British bookmaker owes its origin to Leonard Steinberg, who set up the business in 1958 after inheriting an illegal betting shop from his father at the age of 18. (The name is based on his own.) The growth of racketeering in Northern Ireland, where the enterprise began, prompted Steinberg to move Stanley Leisure to Liverpool in 1977. The following year, **Ladbrokes** sold 109 betting shops to Stanley Leisure, and in 2000 the company bought Regency Bookmakers, bringing its total number of betting shops to 660.

Staples *(office supplies)*

Thomas Stemberg was writing a business plan for a new venture when his typewriter ribbon broke. It was Fourth of July weekend 1985, and the local stationer was closed. In his frustration, Stemberg conceived the idea of setting up a superstore for office supplies where small businesses and consumers could obtain the products they used at the same discount prices only available to the large corporations that purchased in large quantities. In 1986 the first Staples office supply superstore opened in Brighton, Massachusetts, and by 2001 Stemberg had a network of 1,307 stores in North America and Europe. Staples is now based in Framingham, Massachusetts, and looking to open even more superstores. The name evokes the term for essential or economically important products.

Starbucks *(coffee shops)*

The first Starbucks coffee shop was opened

in 1971 by three college students in Pike Place Market, Seattle, Washington, the city's famous open-air farmers' market. They were aware of the exotic appeal of coffee, as a drink and drug imported from foreign lands, and accordingly sought an appropriate nautical name and logo. They took the name from Captain Starbuck, the coffee-loving first mate of the *Pequod* in Herman Melville's classic novel *Moby-Dick* (1851), while the company logo is a two-tailed siren, a creature of strength and power found in medieval adventure stories. By 1990 there were 84 Starbucks stores, and in 1992 it became the first specialty coffee company to go public. In 2001 there were 4,435 Starbucks cafés worldwide, the largest being opened in Seoul, South Korea, in 1999.

Staropramen *(beer)*

The Czech beer has been produced in the brewery of this name in the Smichov district of Prague since 1869. The name itself means "old spring."

Start-rite *(children's footwear)*

The history of the name begins with James Smith, who in 1792 started making ladies' shoes in the Upper Market in Norwich, England. His business was later taken over by one Charles Winter before passing into the hands of Willis & Southall in 1865. The firm still specialized in footwear for women, but soon after World War I began to develop children's lines. In 1921 the name "Startrite" was created by Quant & Son for a patent design of children's shoes and later sold to Willis & Southall, who entered it in the *Trade Marks Journal* of June 12, 1929.

State Express *(cigarettes)*

The brand name was registered at the time of the formation of **Ardath** by its founder, Albert Levy. He took it from the Empire State Express, then the world's fastest train, which ran from Buffalo to New York City in the "Empire State" of New York. When traveling on this train, Levy noticed that the locomotive number was 999. This inspired the numerical combinations used by him for various brands of cigarettes, one being **Three Fives**.

Stationery Office *(publishers)*

The British publishing house was founded in 1786, in the reign of George III, as His Majesty' Stationery Office (HMSO), providing print-ing, stationery, and office supplies to government departments. It grew into a publisher of material sponsored by the English parliament and other official bodies, changing the first word of its name to "Her" in the reign of a queen, and took its present name in 1996 on becoming part of the private sector. It is now also involved in commercial publishing.

Statler *(hotels)*

The man behind the first US hotel chain owned by an individual was Ellsworth Milton Statler (1863-1928), born in Somerset County, Pennsylvania, the son of a German Reformed pastor. The family moved to Bridgeport, Ohio, in 1868, and in 1872, aged only nine, Statler joined his two older brothers in securing employment at a glass factory in Wheeling, West Virginia, across the river. At age 13 Statler became a bellboy in Wheeling's McClure House, a hotel catering to travelers and salesmen. Promotions followed, so that by age 17 he was leasing the hotel's billiard room and had installed a railroad discount ticket office in the lobby. He then purchased a private bowling club in Wheeling, and in 1895 expanded operations to Buffalo, New York, where he opened a restaurant. When Buffalo hosted the Pan American exposition in 1900, Statler build a huge temporary hotel, offering lodging and meals at a flat rate. In 1908 Statler erected the Hotel Statler in Buffalo, and other hotels gradually followed, the grandest being the 2,200-room Pennsylvania Hotel, built in New York City in 1919.

Staybrite *(stainless steel)*

The make of stainless steel is so called because it was designed to "stay bright" and not tarnish. The name was entered by Firth-Vickers Stainless Steels Ltd., of Sheffield, England, in the *Trade Marks Journal* of July 7, 1937, but the steel itself was available at least ten years earlier.

Stead & Simpson *(footwear)*

The British stores take their name from the firm founded in Leeds in 1834 by Edmund Stead and Edward Simpson. The two men had set up together as leather merchants and curriers. Their business of tanning and dressing leather soon began to expand, and by 1860 they had opened a factory in Daventry and another in Leicester as well as moving to larger premises in Leeds itself. On moving, it occurred to the partners that they could start up the manufacture of boots and shoes, which until then had traditionally been the trade of bespoke shoemakers. They did so, and found a ready market for their shoes. In the early 1870s the firm opened its first retail branches in the north of England, mainly as outlets for the factories. By the mid-1980s Stead & Simpson had over 200 branches, but the company ceased manufacturing shoes in 1973. The firm itself now has its head office in Leicester, not Leeds.

Steiner *(cosmetics)*

The founder of the British company was H.D. Steiner, born in the opening years of the 20th century in London the son of a Central European hairdresser who ran a business in Muswell Hill. The son learned much about his father's profession, but had no wish to follow in his footsteps, instead setting his sights on a career as a violinist. He was a gifted performer on the instrument as a child, and Jascha Heifetz, the noted violinist, recommended the boy be sent to the Moscow Conservatoire to pursue his ambition. However, Henry Steiner was killed in a road accident, leaving his wife to run the salon, so the son abandoned his musical plans and entered the world of hairdressing after all. In the 1930s he opened a new salon in London's West End, where word of his skill soon spread, with many aristocrats and celebrities becoming his clients. The premises were destroyed in World War II, and after it Mr. Steiner opened a further salon nearby, where the company remains today.

Steinway *(pianos)*

The pianos take their name from a German cabinetmaker, Heinrich Engelhard Steinweg (1797–1871), born in Wolfshagen in the duchy of Brunswick, whose workshop was the kitchen of his home in the small town of Seesen, near Hanover. According to family legend he made his first piano there in 1825. In 1850, together with his wife, his three daughters, and four of his six sons, Steinweg immigrated to the United States, where he anglicized his name to Henry E. Steinway. In 1853 he set up a business as a piano manufacturer in a rented loft in downtown Manhattan, naming his firm Steinway & Sons. The concern was well established by this time, since Steinway (when still Steinweg) had made nearly 500 pianos in Germany before leaving the country. It therefore continued to prosper in the United States without much difficulty, and many famous pianists performed on the instrument in New York's Steinway Hall, named for him. Steinway produced his first grand piano in 1856 and the first upright in 1862. The company opened a British branch in London in 1875.

Stelazine *(antipsychotic)*

The proprietary name for the drug trifluoperazine, used as an antipsychotic and antiemetic, is of uncertain origin, although "-azine" must derive from the generic name. It was entered by Smith, Kline & French Laboratories Ltd. (now **SmithKline Beecham**), of London, England, in the *Trade Marks Journal* of July 23, 1958.

Stella Artois *(beer)*

Belgium's best-known lager beer takes its name from Sebastian Artois, who in 1708 became master brewer of the Horn brewery, founded in Leuven in 1366. (Hence the picture of a horn on the label.) He intended it as a Christmas brew. Hence Latin *stella*, "star," referring to the wise men. In 1988 Artois merged with the Jupiler brewery to form Interbrew, which after taking over **Labatt** in 1995 and expansion into Eastern Europe is now one of the largest brewing groups in the world.

Stellite *(alloy)*

The cobalt-based alloy, used for its hardness and resistance to heat, was invented by the US metallurgist Elwood Haynes (1857–1925) and patented in 1907. Its name, presumably based on English "steel" rather than Latin *stella*, "star" (an alloy of cobalt chromium can be substituted for mild tempered steel), was entered by the Haynes Stellite Co. in the US Patent Office *Official Gazette* of October 3, 1916.

Stelna *(corned beef)*

The corned beef was launched in the early 20th century as a by-product of meat extract manufacture by the makers of **Bovril**, taking its name from the company's beef-processing factory at Santa Elena, Argentina. It was later sold as "Bovril Corned Beef," with a wider market in the USA than in Britain.

Stena *(transport and travel)*

The Swedish firm, operating ferry services between many countries of Western Europe, was founded in 1962 by Sten Allan Olsson, who in 1939 had already established Sweden's leading metal-recycling company, Stena Metal Group. In 1996 **P&O** and Stena merged their ferry operations across the English Channel on routes between England and France and Belgium.

Stents *(dental composition)*

The name of the substance used in dentistry for taking an impression of the teeth derives from the English dentist Charles Stent (1807-1885). It was entered by Caroline Stent of 5, Coventry Street, London, England, in the *Trade Marks Journal* of February 15, 1899 for: "A composition, sold in tablet form, specially intended for taking impressions of the gums and for like dental purposes."

Stephens *(ink)*

Stephens' ink was long familiar to generations of British schoolchildren until ballpoints replaced dip pens and fountain pens. The name is that of Henry Charles Stephens (1841-1918), born a surgeon's son in Lambeth, London. It was in fact Stephens' father who first manufactured ink on a commercial scale and who gained fame for the "blue-black writing fluid" that he began to produce in the 1830s. On his father's death in 1864, Henry Charles became manager of the family firm, which had now expanded to include wood stains and gums. Stephens rapidly expanded the business worldwide, and his famous "blot" trademark and outsize Stephens wall thermometers became as familiar abroad as on British railroad station platforms. Stephens' great-granddaughter is the novelist Evelyn Anthony (b.1928).

Sterling *(household remedies)*

Sterling Drug dates from 1901, when William Erhard Weiss, a pharmacist, joined up with a friend, Albert H. Diebold, to form the the Neuralgyline Company in Wheeling, West Virginia. Their product was a pain reliever called Neuralgine, which made them enough money to acquire another drug business, Sterling Remedy, in 1909. They adopted Sterling as the corporate name in 1917 and heavily promoted aspirin when the courts ruled that the name did not belong exclusively to **Bayer** (*see* **Aspro**).

Sterling *(sub-machine gun)*

The gun takes its name from its British manufacturers, the Sterling Armament Company Ltd., of London, who entered it in the *Trade Marks Journal* of May 21, 1975. The gun itself dates from at least the 1950s.

Sterno *(fuel)*

The fuel for cooking stoves, marketed in the form of solidified alcohol in containers, derives its name from its manufacturers, S. Sternau & Co., of New York, who entered it in the US Patent Office *Official Gazette* of May 11, 1915. The name was subsequently entered by the **Colgate-Palmolive** Co., of New York, in the *Trade Marks Journal* of July 30, 1969.

Stetson *(hats)*

John Batterson Stetson (1830-1906) was born in Orange, New Jersey, the son of a hatter. He learned the hat trade from an early age as an apprentice in his father's shop, but as time went on saw little future in his family's small business. When he was nearly 30 he accordingly moved to Philadelphia and set up his own hat business. He contracted tuberculosis, however, so sold his enterprise and attempted to regain his health by traveling West. He eventually arrived in the Rocky Mountains, where he was so impressed by the wide-brimmed hats worn by cowboys that he resolved to make them himself when he returned home in 1865. His styles caught the public fancy, and he had to open a fully-fledged factory to cope with the demand. By the time of his death, Stetson's Philadelphia plant was employing 3,500 workers who turned out 2 million hats a year. The name was entered by the John B. Stetson Co., Philadelphia, in the US Patent Office *Official Gazette* of March 6, 1906.

Steuben *(glass)*

The Steuben Glass Company was founded in 1903 at **Corning**, New York, by Frederick Carder (1863-1963), born in Kingswinford, Staffordshire, England, the son of a potter. He quit school at the age of 14 to work in the pottery, but soon left it to pursue a broader career in art. A visit in 1878 to the studio of a local glass carver, John Northwood, attracted him to work in glass, and two years later he joined the firm of Stevens and Williams in Brierley Hill as a designer and draftsman. In due course he became chief designer, and meanwhile studied in night art classes. In 1902 he was sent by the local council to survey the state of glassmaking in Austria and Germany, and in 1903 to Corning, New York, where he met Thomas G. Hawkes, owner of a glass-cutting firm. Hawkes convinced Carder to leave England, and that same year Carder did so, emigrating with his family and starting the Steuben Glass Works. The company took its name from Steuben County, in which Corning is located, the name itself being that of Frederick William, Freiherr von Steuben (1730-1794), the German officer who served the cause of US independence by converting the revolutionary army into a disciplined fighting force. The name was entered by the Corning Glass Works, of Corning, New York, in the US Patent Office *Official Gazette* of March 16, 1920, with a claim of use since about Jan 1, 1904, and the note: "No claim being made to the exclusive use of the word 'Steuben' apart from the mark as shown in the drawing."

Stevengraph *(silk picture)*

The type of small picture made of brightly colored woven silk, produced in the 19th century, takes its name from its inventor, Thomas Stevens (1828-1888), a ribbon weaver of Coventry, England. The name was entered by the firm he founded, Thomas Stevens (Coventry) Ltd., in the *Trade Marks Journal* of July 4, 1928 for: "Woven labels of cotton, or in which cotton predominates."

Steyr-Puch *(automobiles)*

The first part of the name is that of the Austrian city of Steyr, where Josef Werndl set up as a gunsmith in 1864. The Österreichische Waffenfabriksgesellchaft ("Austrian Weapon Manufacturing Company"), as it became, was noted as the makers of the Mannlicher sporting rifle and other weapons, and as Steyr Werke A.G. it also turned to the manufacture of motorcycles. An experimental automobile followed in 1910, and in 1920 the first Steyr cars left the factory. The second part of the name is that of Johann Puch, who began to make motorcycles in the town of Graz in 1899. He progressed to automobiles in 1906, but in 1920 the Puch Werke merged with Austro-**Daimler**.

The Austro-Daimler-Puchwerke then amalgamated with Steyr in 1934 to form Steyr-Daimler-Puch A.G. The name Steyr-Puch was subsequently used for **Fiat** cars destined for the Austrian market.

Stiffel *(lamps)*

As a boy, young Theodopholous "Ted" A. Stiffel (1899-1971), the son of a shirt manufacturer in Memphis, Tennessee, enjoyed playing the violin, as well as tinkering with machines, and after graduating from high school he left Memphis to study the violin in Chicago. He joined the Marines in World War I, and intended to resume his musical studies after completing his tour of duty, but by the end of the war he had lost his ambition to be a concert performer and instead took a job at the Western Electric Company's office in Chicago. His restless temperament was not suited to routine office work, however, so he sought a more rewarding outlet for his talents. He eventually found it with the Nellie Kaplan Co., Chicago, a manufacturer of domestic lamps. In 1932, after several years with the firm, Stiffel struck out on his own, founding the T.A. Stiffel Company in a small basement on Chicago's near North Side. He concentrated on making simply designed functional floor lamps, and demands for his product gradually grew so that by the end of World War II the firm had built up a profitable business, selling 90 percent of its lamps through **Montgomery Ward** stores.

Stillson *(pipe wrench)*

The wrench with jaws that tighten when pressure is increased on the handle takes its name from Daniel Chapman Stillson (1830-1899), its American inventor in 1869. It was originally manufactured by his employers, the Walworth Company of New York.

Stilton *(cheese)*

Stilton cheese takes its name from the village of Stilton, Cambridgeshire (formerly Huntingdonshire), England, although it has never been made there. Rather, it was the innkeeper at the Bell Inn, Stilton, on the Great North Road on the route to London, who originally bought the creamy blue cheese from a farmer's wife in Melton Mowbray, Leicestershire. The name now has the status of a "protected designation of origin," and since 1969 has been restricted to cheese made by members of the Stilton Cheese Makers Association in the counties of Leicestershire, Derbyshire, and Nottinghamshire, with only seven creameries licensed to produce it. The name was accordingly entered by the chairman of the association, based in Melton Mowbray, in the *Trade Marks Journal* of February 5, 1969.

Stokely *(foods)*

Widowed at the age of 38 and with nine children to support, Anna Stokely (1852-1916) determined to keep her family's farm going at French Broad, Tennessee, with the help of her five sons. They could see the potential in canning what they grew, and in 1898 Anna Stokely, together with her second and third sons, James Stokely (1875-1922) and John Stokely (1876-1919), established a small cannery. In only six years they were selling 50,000 cases of canned produce annually, and by 1933, when the family-run firm acquired the **Van Camp** Company, their enterprise had become a major national food packer.

Stolichnaya *(vodka)*

The name of the variety of Russian vodka is the adjectival form of *stolitsa*, "capital," meaning that it originates from Moscow. It was entered in the US Patent Office *Official Gazette* of February 25, 1969 by "V/O Sojuzplodoimport," the abbreviated Russian title of the All-Union Association for Fruit Import of the Ministry of Foreign Trade of the USSR.

Stones *("Original Green Ginger Wine")*

Joseph Stone (1809-1896) was born in London, England, the son of a grocer and tea dealer trading from premises in High Holborn. At 17, he was apprenticed to the Finsbury Distillery to learn about the distilling business, leaving to set up as a wine and spirit merchant in about 1830, with premises in Crown Street, Finsbury. In due course he acquired the right to retail some of the Finsbury Distillery products under his own name, so that "Bishop & Pell's Original Green Ginger Wine" was relabeled as "Stone's Original Green Ginger Wine." (Bishop and Pell were the names of partners who ran the Finsbury Distillery: brothers George and James Bishop together with Bennett Pell.) Stone's name thus became associated with the wine in the 1830s, and about ten years later the bottle

labels also included the coat of arms of the City of London, one of the very few products to do so.

Stork *(margarine)*

The margarine of this name was introduced to Britain in 1920 by the Dutch firm of Jurgens (*see* **Unilever**). The name itself was registered in 1900, and was adopted from the bird that is a favorite subject in Dutch (and German) folklore, in which it is said to bring babies and also good luck to the houses where it nests.

Stoudt's *(beer)*

The name is that of Carol Stoudt, owner of a microbrewery in Adamstown, Pennsylvania, started in 1987. The stylized portrait on the bottle bears a passing resemblance to the maker of the beer, who as she is a woman should perhaps properly be called a "brewster" rather than a brewer.

Stouffer's *(frozen foods)*

After graduating from the Wharton School of Business, Vernon B. Stouffer (1901-1974) set out to make a career in transportation, first founding a bus company, then a trucking firm. Both ventures ended in failure, however, and in 1924 Stouffer went to work in the luncheonette run by his parents in downtown Cleveland, Ohio. He realized that a single outlet restricted their business potential, so went ahead and opened a chain of restaurants, forming the Stouffer Corporation in 1929. He continued to expand his business, and in 1954 introduced frozen versions of his most popular dishes for the retail grocery market. In 1967 Stouffer Corporation merged with **Litton** Industries, and in 1973 it was acquired from Litton by **Nestlé**.

Stratovision *(television broadcasting system)*

The name is that of a system whereby television programs are broadcast over a wide area by retransmission from a circling aircraft. Hence the name, a blend of "stratosphere" and "television," entered in the US Patent Office *Official Gazette* of May 14, 1946.

Strega *(liqueur)*

The orange-flavored Italian herb liqueur was introduced by the Alberti family in Benevento, southern Italy, in 1860. Its name is Italian for "witch," in allusion to a local tale that tells of maidens who dress up as witches and mix a "witch's brew." (The label depicts an old hag with a broomstick and a group of classical-style figures dancing in a glade.) The name was entered by "the firm trading as Ditta Giuseppe Alberti" in the *Trade Marks Journal* of January 19, 1910. ("Ditta" actually means "firm.")

Strepsils *(throat lozenges)*

The antibacterial lozenges, made by **Crookes** Healthcare (now owned by **Boots**), have a name suggesting a remedy for a throat afflicted by a streptococcal infection. The "-sil" suffix, as in the similar **Prontosil**, is perhaps from Latin *silere*, "to be still," "to rest" (the source of English *silent*), implying a soothing medicine. The name was entered in the *Trade Marks Journal* of May 20, 1959.

Strimmer *(grass trimmer)*

The electrically powered grass trimmer operates by means of a nylon cutting cord rotating at high speed on a spindle, instead of a cutting blade. Its name is probably a blend of "string," referring to the cord, and "trimmer," although an origin in "grass trimmer" itself is also possible. The name was entered by **Black & Decker** in the *Trade Marks Journal* of May 4, 1978.

Stroh's *(beer)*

In 1848, Bernhard Stroh (1822-1882) immigrated to South America from his native Germany, where his family had started brewing in the late 1700s at Kirn, near Bad Kreuznach. After only a brief stay, he moved to Detroit, where he used his meager savings to establish a small brewery in 1850, making lager beer in copper kettles. His most popular product was a Bohemian-style beer that was brewed over a direct fire. At the time of Stroh's death, when the business was taken over by his eldest son, Bernhard Stroh, Jr., the brewery was the biggest in Michigan. At the end of the 20th century, still a family-run business, it was the fourth largest brewing company in the USA.

Studebaker *(automobiles)*

Clement Studebaker (1831-1901) was born in Pinetown, Pennsylvania, the son of a farmer and blacksmith. In 1836 the family moved to Ashland, Ohio, where Clement studied spo-

radically at school while working in his father's blacksmith's shop. In 1850 Studebaker moved to South Bend, Indiana, where he found work as a teacher. His experience as a blacksmith drew him to return to the craft, however, and in 1852 he and his older brother, Henry, set up their own blacksmithing shop, H. & C. Studebaker. The business boomed and grew, and in 1857 the Milburn Wagon Company subcontracted with Studebaker to produce wagons for the US army. John Mohler Studebaker joined his brothers the following year and bought out Henry, who retired to a prosperous life on the farm. Clement continued to build the business up, and by 1870 two more brothers had joined, Peter E. Studebaker and Jacob F. Studebaker. That same year the firm established its first branch office at St. Joseph, Missouri, and the Studebaker Brothers Manufacturing Company was incorporated. The brothers began to experiment with automobiles in 1897, and by 1902 had built electric cars. The Studebaker Corporation absorbed the original firm in 1911 and merged with **Packard** in 1954. US production ceased in 1963, and the Canadian operation followed suit in 1966.

Sturmey-Archer *(bicycle gears)*

Henry Sturmey was an English schoolmaster from Somerset with a basic knowledge of engineering who came to evolve a three-speed gear for bicycles together with a London bicycle dealer named Arthur Pellant. His invention came to the attention of Frank Bowden, founder of the **Raleigh** Cycle Company, who was keen to manufacture such a gear. In the closing years of the 19th century Bowden became acquainted with James Archer, who had independently developed his own three-speed gear on similar lines. Bowden realized the commercial potential of a combination of the two inventions, and in 1902 took out a patent for the new Sturmey-Archer three-speed gear. A special workshop was set up in the Raleigh factory to manufacture the gear, and Archer was appointed foreman to sort out any teething problems. In 1903 the gear was first sold to an appreciative cycling public, who especially liked the freewheel facility in all three gears, something that had previously been available only in the higher gear of the old two-speed gears. A separate subsidiary company, the Sturmey-Archer Gear Co., was then set up to continue making the gears, which today (as hub gears) are still produced by Raleigh.

Stüssy (fashionwear)

The US fashion label was launched in 1982 by Shaun Stüssy (b.1954), originally as a surfboard design imprint. The company expanded into apparel in 1985, when it soon set the tone for street fashion, introducing skatewear, workwear, military chic, and preppy elements. By the 1990s, Stüffy's gear had achieved worldwide renown, bringing revenues of over $20 million.

Stutz (automobiles)

Harry Clayton Stutz (1876-1930) was born near Ansonia, Ohio, a farmer's son. After completing his public school education, Stutz moved to Dayton, Ohio, working first for the Davis Sewing Machine Company, then for **NCR**. In 1897 he opened his own machine shop and repair busines in Dayton, and in 1898 built his own two-horsepower automobile. A second auto followed in 1900, and on the basis of this production, the Stutz Manufacturing Company was established to build single-cylinder gasoline engines. In 1902 Stutz moved to Indianapolis, where in 1910 he formed the Stutz Auto Parts Company to manufacture the transaxle he had developed. In 1911 Stutz helped the Empire Motor Car Company design their new car, and inspired by the first Indianapolis 500-mile race, designed and built his own car in five weeks. That same year he organized the Ideal Motor Car Company to manufacture his designs, and production soon began, leading to the "Bearcat," probably the most famous of all American sports cars. In 1913 the Stutz Auto Parts Company and the Ideal Motor car Company were merged to form the Stutz Motor Car Company of Indiana, with Stutz as president. The firm lost its founder in 1919, when Stutz left to set up another marque, the HCS, but it was much less successful. Stutz went out of business in 1938, although the name remained in such high regard that a "new" Stutz company was set up in 1970 to build cars. There was no real link with the classic concern, however.

Stuyvesant, Peter *see* **Peter Stuyvesant**

Stylophone (musical instrument)

The Stylophone is a battery-operated instrument played by drawing an attached "stylus" along a keyboard of metal touchplates, producing a distinctive buzzing tone. Its name, combining "stylo-" and "-phone" and overall based on "xylophone," was entered by Moviecol Enterprises Ltd. in the *Trade Marks Journal* of June 26, 1968. A subsequent registration in the US Patent Office *Official Gazette* of April 29, 1969 is "for electronic organs," with a note of first use on January 24, 1968.

Stypven (blood coagulant)

The medical preparation consists of the dried and purified venom of the Russell's viper used in solution as a local hemostatic and blood coagulant. The name combines the first syllables of "styptic" and "venom," and was entered by Burroughs **Wellcome** of New York in the US Patent Office *Official Gazette* of January 20, 1948, with a claim of use since 1937.

Styrofoam (plastic)

The light plastic material, used for making disposable items (typically drinking beakers), insulation, and packing materials, takes its name from a blend of "polystyrene" and "foam." It was inadvertently created by the US chemical engineer Ray McIntire (1918-1996), an employee of the **Dow** Chemical Company, while he was trying to develop a rubberlike polymer to be used as a flexible insulator. Dow entered the name in the US Patent Office *Official Gazette* of July 11, 1950: "For irregular solid masses of irregular synthetic resinous material and granular masses of the same material comminuted."

Subaru (automobile)

The Japanese car has a name denoting the Pleiades cluster of stars in the Taurus constellation. Six stars in the cluster are visible to the naked eye, and here they represent the six companies that merged to form Fuji Heavy Industries in 1953. They are represented pictorially on the company's logo. The first Subaru car left the factory in 1958.

Subbuteo (table football)

The popular British game dates from 1947 as the creation of Peter Adolph, a birdwatcher from Tunbridge Wells, Kent, who originally wanted to call it "The Hobby." This name was not acceptable for registration purposes, however, so instead he took the Latin name of the hobby hawk, *Falco subbuteo*, and adopted the second word by default. The suggestion of "boot" in the name is thus fortuitous but apt. The name was entered in the *Trade Marks Journal* of April 14, 1948.

Suchard *(chocolate)*

Philippe Suchard (1797-1884) began his career as a chocolate maker in 1815, when he was apprenticed to his elder brother, a confectioner in Berne, Switzerland. In 1824 he went to the United States, and on his return a year later opened a candy business in Neuchâtel. Soon after, he set up a chocolate factory, powered by a water wheel, in Serrières. He worked with a single assistant, turning out between 55 and 65 lbs. of chocolate a day. Suchard's firm was thus one of the first to make chocolate in Switzerland.

Sugar Puffs *(breakfast cereal)*

The brand of breakfast cereal coated with sugar and flavored with honey is made by **Quaker Oats** and has a name denoting its sweetness and lightness. The name itself was entered in the *Trade Marks Journal* of May 1, 1957. It was not original, however, and "sugar puff" was a term in use as early as the 18th century for a type of light pastry made with sugar.

Sulfasuxidine *(antiseptic)*

The proprietary name for the drug succinyl-sulfathiazone is made up of "sulfa-," "sux-" (representing "succ-," ultimately from Latin *succinum*, "amber"), and the chemical suffix "-idine." It was entered by Sharp & Dohme, Inc., of Philadelphia, in the US Patent Office *Official Gazette* of January 6, 1942: "For pharmaceutical preparations useful as bactericides and as antiseptics," and in the *Trade Marks Journal* of May 26, 1943 for: "Pharmaceutical substances for human use and for veterinary use … consisting wholly of sulphur compounds."

Sun Alliance *(insurance)*

The British insurance company originated as the Sun Fire Office, founded in London in 1710. Its symbol, a smiling sun, with multiple rays like a starfish, can still be seen today on the walls of some 18th-century English houses, meaning they were insured with the Sun. In 1958 the company merged with Alliance Assurance, founded in 1824, and other mergers followed. In 1996 the resultant Sun Alliance company merged with **Royal Insurance** to form Royal and SunAlliance (RSA).

Sunbeam *(automobiles)*

The bright and cheerful name was originally given to the bicycles first produced by John Marston in Wolverhampton, England, in 1887. (He was a descendant of the founder of Marston & Co., a firm set up in 1790.) He launched his first automobile in 1899 and in 1905 his firm became the Sunbeam Motor Car Company. Motorcycles were added to the output in 1912, but in 1920 Sunbeam lost its independence when the company joined the Anglo-French alliance of Sunbeam, **Talbot** and **Darracq** (STD), and this new company was taken over in 1935 by the Rootes Brothers. From then on the cars were sold as Sunbeam-Talbot, but the latter name was dropped in 1954. The last Sunbeam motorycle, designed by **BSA**, left the works in 1957.

Sunbeam *(household appliances)*

The US company dates back to 1893, when John K. Stewart and Thomas J. Clark made mechanical horse clippers in Chicago. By 1897 they had expanded into sheep-shearing machines and flexible shafts for grinders and drills, and were incorporated as the Chicago Flexible Shaft Company. In 1910 they made their first appliance, an electric iron, and soon branched out into other appliances, which they advertised in the 1920s under the generally favorable name "Sunbeam." It was not until 1946, however, that the name was adopted for the company.

Sunlight *(soap)*

Sunlight was the first branded soap, produced in England in 1885 by William Lever (who gave the name of **Unilever**). Orginally all of Lever's soaps, made for him by different manufacturers, were branded "Sunlight." But when Lever transferred his business in 1888 to the purpose-built site and model village called Port Sunlight, south of Liverpool, he concentrated on his own brand of "Sunlight" soap. The name obviously evokes radiant health and cleanliness, qualities associated with a good soap, but the selection of the apparently straightforward name had its agonizing moments. The following account, in Lever's own words (of around 1916), is given in Beable 1, 1926 (*see* Bibliography, p. 565).

"I began to think about soap, and I thought: 'Now, I must have a trade mark, and the greater success I make of the soap the more they will try to copy my trade mark'—I had just enough sense for that. I went to the best Trade Mark and Patent Agent in Liverpool whose name—Mr. W.P. Thompson—had been given me. I walked into his office and said I wanted a trade mark for soap, and asked what he would advise. 'Of course,' I said, 'it must be a name I can uphold in the law courts if an imitator comes along.' He wrote down half a dozen names on a half sheet of paper ... but none of them appealed to me, yet amongst them was SUNLIGHT.

But really, at the first blush, none of those names appealed to me. I had big ideas of some sort of name—I did not know what—but it was going to be such a marvel, and when I saw it written down in cold ink—the names that were possible—names that you could register and fight for, names that did not describe the article, that were neither geographical nor descriptive, did not refer to quality, and got over all the obstacles that the Trade Marks Law has very properly put in front of us—none of them appealed to me. I put the list in my pocket and went away feeling disappointed. Every time I had a few minutes to spare I had this list out and looked at it. Then, suddenly, I didn't know how, after three or four days it flashed across me that SUNLIGHT was the one. It was on this paper; Mr. Thompson had simply given me names that were typical, SUNLIGHT along with the other half-dozen. When that occurred to me I had to go straight off to Liverpool and ask him to register it at once: I was all in a tremble to have it registered, for fear somebody else had got it. And a marvellous thing it is, that the word SUNLIGHT was not only capable of being registered in England, but we have never yet gone to a country where it could not be registered. I don't think I could say that of any other name I could have tumbled on. Fancy a name that can be registered everywhere and that nobody had forestalled."

Sünner (beer)

The German beer owes its origin to Christian Sünner, who founded the Cologne brewery that bears his name in 1830. Today, after five generations, Sünner is the oldest family concern still making its own beer in Cologne.

Sunny Jim see **Force**

Suntory (whisky)

The name of the Japanese whisky was entered in the *Trade Marks Journal* of December 21, 1960 by the Kabushiki Kaisha Kotobukiya, of Osaka. It is a simplified form of the name of Shinjiro Torii, who in the early years of the 20th century produced a port-style sweet wine

called "Akadama" ("Red Stone," the name of a secret medicine made into red pills and used for stomach pains). He felt he could establish a whisky market in Japan, and in 1921 employed a young chemist, Masataka Taketsuru (*see* **Nikka**), to set up a distillation project. Torii sought a "Scottish-style" site for a distillery and eventually found one at Yamazaki, where three rivers converge. The factory was built in 1923 and the first whisky marketed there in 1929. The blend now known as "Suntory White" was introduced in 1929 as "Shirofuda." It was soon known as "White Label," the English equivalent, and the name stuck.

Supadriv (screwdriver)

The type of cross-head screwdriver, with extra ridges between the arms of the cross, has a name entered in the *Trade Marks Journal* of January 11, 1978, that presumably denotes a "super" **Pozidriv**, as an improved version of the latter.

Surgicenter (surgical unit)

The unit where minor operations are performed on outpatients derives its name as a shortening of "surgical center," entered by Surgicenter, Inc., of Phoenix, Arizona, in the US Patent Office *Official Gazette* of June 15, 1971: "For providing facilities for doctors to perform surgical operations on patients," with a note of first use on February 12, 1970.

Surtitle (screened caption)

The term for a caption projected on a screen above the stage during the performance of an opera is registered as proprietary in Canada, and "Surtitles" is entered in the Canadian *Trade Marks Journal* of July 20, 1983 for: "Projection of translations of spoken text and song to stage locations during live artistic performances." The device, its name based on "subtitles," was invented in 1983 by John Leberg as part of a move to popularize opera generally.

Sutton's (seeds)

The English firm arose from the small business started in Reading, Berkshire, in 1806 by John Sutton (1777-1863), a corn merchant who traded in agricultural seeds and corn and in grasses for pastures. It was not until his son, Martin Hope Sutton, joined the firm, however, that it began to expand to be eventually the major concern it is today. Martin Sutton was a botanist, and was particularly interested in supplying high-quality seeds that would give a pure stock and germinate readily. Royal recognition for the firm came in 1858, when Queen Victoria requested Martin Sutton supply seeds to the royal household. The company's head office and seed testing laboratory remained in Reading until the mid-1960s, when Sutton Seeds moved to new premises in Torquay, Devon.

Suze (liqueur)

The yellow, gentian-based aperitif takes its name from its French manufacturers, the Distillerie de la Suze, of Maisons-Alfort, near Paris, who entered it in the Trade Marks Journal of April 5, 1961. The brand first appeared in 1889 and is now owned by **Pernod Ricard**.

Suzuki (motorcycles)

Japanese engineer Michio Suzuki was born in 1887 in the village of Hamamatsu, where the company that bears his name is still based today. In 1909 Suzuki set up on his own account, building silk looms. Business boomed, as the silk industry was important to Japan. But Suzuki was seeking other outlets for his enterprise, and in 1937 he built a prototype motorcycle engine, at the same time signing an agreement to produce the **Austin** Seven automobile under licence. World War II put paid to any further development in that direction, and after it Suzuki was obliged to seek other markets, which he found in the form of heaters, agricultural machinery, and related products. Suzuki was a keen fisherman, and was accustomed to cycling to his favorite fishing haunts. This gave him the idea of introducing a motorized bicycle, to take the effort out of such trips. In 1951 work accordingly began on a two-stroke clip-on unit that could be fitted to any bicycle. It went on sale in 1952, under the name "Power Free," and soon led to the manufacture of conventional motorcycles, so that by 1957 Suzuki was second only to **Honda** in the Japanese market. Its range soon increased to include both sportsbikes and roadbikes, and by the end of the century Suzuki enjoyed world fame for its motorcycles.

Swan (beer)

The Australian brewing company was built in Perth, Western Australia, in 1857 and takes its name from the Swan River there. In 1928 they took over the rival Emu brewery in the same city.

Swan (electric kettles)

The earliest electric kettles had their heating element underneath the kettle. Swan was the first firm to manufacture a kettle with the element inside it. A kettle of this type was developed in the 1920s by one Leslie Large, who worked as an electrical engineer for Bulpitt & Sons in Birmingham, England. At this time the firm already made "Swan" products, taking the name from Swansea tinplate. The name subsequently became directly associated with the firm's kettles. It was almost descriptively apt, since the kettle's curved spout resembled a swan's long neck and the rear electric plug its short tail. The name was entered in the Trade Marks Journal of March 16, 1932.

Swan (electric lights) see **Ediswan**

Swan & Edgar (department store)

The British department store in London's Regent Street arose from the partnership formed in the early years of the 19th century between John Swan and William Edgar. Edgar had a haberdashery stall in St. James's Market. He met Swan, and the two set up shop in the Ludgate area, moving in around 1812 to Piccadilly then to Regent Street. Swan died in 1821, leaving Edgar to carry on the firm alone. It flourished under him, with a brand-new shop front appearing on the Piccadilly premises in 1841. When Queen Victoria visited the store, Edgar attended to her personally. The store finally closed in 1982 after being taken over by the **Debenham** Group.

Swan Hunter (shipbuilders)

The British builders of the Mauretania, the outstanding ship of the **Cunard** Line, launched in 1906, took their name from C.S. Swan, manager of a shipyard at Wallsend, Northumberland, and George Burton Hunter (1845-1937), born in the seaport of Sunderland, Co. Durham, the son of a shipwright. The merger came about in 1880 by way of a partnership formed with Swan's widow following her husband's tragic death. The firm was originally known as C.S. Swan and Hunter, then in 1903 Swan, Hunter & Wigham Richardson Ltd., and now simply Swan Hunter.

Swan Vestas *(matches)*

The matches now produced by the British firm of **Bryant & May** date back to 1883, when the Liverpool firm of Collard & Co. introduced a new match brand called "Swan." The name itself was probably chosen to suggest elegance and neatness, and could be attractively illustrated on the label. In 1895, The Diamond Match Co. in the USA acquired Collard, and although continuing to produce "Swan" matches, introduced a different match in 1897 called "Swan White Pine Vestas." The latter word was aimed at a market in which the traditional "wax vestas" were declining. Hence "White Pine," meaning that the new matches had a wooden stem, not a wax one. When Bryant & May amalgamated with Diamond Match in 1901 they took over the Liverpool production of "Swan Vestas," as they were popularly called, and the name was officially shortened thus in 1906. Wax vestas themselves, taking their name from Vesta, the Roman goddess of the hearth, ceased to be produced in the late 1930s. The name "Swan Vestas" was entered in the *Trade Marks Journal* of August 12, 1908.

Swanson *(TV dinners)*

Carl A. Swanson (1876-1949) emigrated to America from his native Sweden in 1896. Three years later, he had saved enough money to buy a share in food wholesaling company in Omaha, Nebraska. Swanson eventually acquired his partners' interests in the firm, and turned the business into a wholesale food processor, at first concentrating on three main products: butter, eggs, and turkey. By the early 1940s, he had become a millionaire, and was dubbed "the US Turkey King" by *Fortune* magazine. After his death, the business passed to his sons, Gilbert and Clarke, who anticipated the trend toward convenience foods by introducing their first TV dinner in 1953. In 1955 the Swansons sold their business to the **Campbell** Soup Co. C.A. Swanson & Sons entered the name "TV Dinner" in the US Patent Office *Official Gazette* of July 17, 1954: "For frozen Turkey Dinner, Including Turkey, Dressing, Giblet Gravy, Sweet Potatoes, and Green Peas."

Swatch *(watches)*

The idea of a cheap, reliable, mass-produced plastic watch was conceived in the early 1980s by Nicolas G. Hayek (b.1928), a Lebanese-born Swiss engineer, who began manufacturing them in Biel, Switzerland, in 1983. The name is short for "Swiss watch," and the watches themselves soon became fashionable and collectable items. The name was entered in the *Trade Marks Journal* of July 20, 1988.

Sweet & Maxwell *(law publishers)*

The names behind the British publishing house are those of Stephen Sweet (d.1841) and Alexander Maxwell (1776-1849). Sweet started his business as a seller of law books in Chancery Lane, London, in 1799. A year later, Maxwell founded a separate business at the corner of Fetter Lane. Both men sold law books, but did not initially publish them. In 1811 Maxwell moved to 21 Bell Yard, near the Inns of Court, and it was probably this proximity that encouraged him to begin publishing books on law as well as selling them. The present company came about when the businesses of W. Maxwell & Son and S. Sweet & Son merged in 1889. It is now part of the Thomson Organization (*see* **Thomson Travel**).

Swift *(bicycles)*

Bicycle-making in Britain may be said to date from 1859, when James Starley (1831-1881) and others began manufacturing sewing machines in Cheylesmore, Coventry, Warwickshire. In 1863 the European Sewing Machine Co. was set up to take over Starley's business, and this in turn was taken over by the Coventry Sewing Machine Co. in 1867. In 1868, the latter company began the manufacture of bicycles, basing their model on the "Velocipede" then being made in France. In 1869, the firm changed its name to The Coventry Machinists Co., and the production of bicycles was gradually stepped up. In 1886, one of the firm's models was named "Swift," perhaps partly as a tribute to the "Velocipede," whose name means literally "swift-footed" (Latin *velox*, "swift," and *pes*, *pedis*, "foot"). In 1896 the firm itself adopted the name, as the Swift Cycle Co. In 1900, like other bicycle makers, the firm progressed to the manufacture of automobiles, and in 1918, after World War I, when the factory was requisitioned by the government to turn out munitions and aircraft engines, the company was further renamed as Swift of Coventry Ltd. Its last car appeared in 1931, when the company closed.

Swift *(meatpackers)*

The man behind the familiar name is Gustavus F. Swift (1839-1903), born near Sandwich, Cape Cod, Massachusetts, the son of a farmer. After a patchy schooling, at 14 Swift was already a butcher's assistant. In 1855 he began to buy cattle at the Brighton Market and drive them to Eastham for sale, a journey taking ten days. In 1862 he moved with his newlywed wife to Barnstable, Massachusetts, where he opened a small livestock slaughtering house and retail butcher's shop. In 1872 he became a partner of James A. Hathaway, a Boston meat dealer, and three years later, as cattle buyer for the firm, organized his own meatpacking company in Chicago, where the center of the cattle market had shifted. It is this year, 1875, that the company now regards as that of its founding. Swift himself went on to perfect the refrigerated railroad car, and in 1877 shipped the first refrigerated railroad carload of fresh meat from Chicago to the East. The business he founded developed into the huge slaughtering operation that inspired *The Jungle* (1906), Upton Sinclair's muckraking novel of the Chicago stockyards.

Switch *(payment system)*

The computerized payment system, enabling goods to be paid for by debit card using EFT-POS (electronic funds transfer at point of sale), was launched in the UK in 1988 by the Midland Bank (*see* **HSBC**), **National Westminster** Bank, and the Royal Bank of Scotland. The name uses "switch" in the sense of the computer term referring to a program variable that activates or deactivates a particular function of a program. In simpler terms, the name can be thought of as describing the way the specified amount is "switched" or transferred from the user's bank account to that of the retailer.

Swoe *(hoe)*

The make of long-handled hoe has an angled trapezoidal blade and can be used in two directions. Its name, perhaps a shortening of "swung hoe," was entered in the *Trade Marks Journal* of February 17, 1954 and the US Patent Office *Official Gazette* of February 11, 1986.

Syalon *(ceramic)*

The hard, strong, light, ceramic material, used in high-temperature environments such as gas turbines and auto engines, derives its name from its constituents: *si*licon, *al*umina, and *oxy*nitrides. The name was entered in the *Trade Marks Journal* of december 3, 1986.

Sylphon *(bellows)*

The name, that of a type of concertina-like metal bellows, looks meaningful but is apparently arbitrary. It was entered in the US Patent Office *Official Gazette* of April 3, 1906 for: "Heat-regulators for use on boilers, furnaces, and stoves," in the *Gazette* of July 25, 1916 for: "A hollow expansible and contractible corrugated tubular metal device," and by the Fulton Sylphon Company, of Knoxville, Tennessee, in the *Trade Marks Journal* of August 2, 1933 for: "Valves, hot and cold water mixers and dampers all being parts of steam boilers."

Symington's *(soups and stays)*

The British firm takes its name from William Symington (1809-1898), who in 1827 came from Scotland to Market Harborough, Leicestershire, and set up as a tea dealer in Adam and Eve Street. His business did well, and by 1840 he had acquired a shop in Church Street, where he started to perfect a method of preparing peas to make pea flour for pea soup. This was the essential launch of what today is still the company's best-known product. Symington's younger brother, James, followed quite a different path. He came to Market Harborough in 1841 as a draper and staymaker. At first he was in partnership with William, but he then set up on his own account. His sons, Robert and William Henry Symington, carried on the business of staymaking and ultimately opened a corset factory where, under different management in the early years of the 20th century, the famous **Liberty** bodice was first made.

Sympatex *(synthetic fabric)*

Described by its German manufacturers, Sympatex Technologies GmbH, of Wuppertal, as a "lightweight, ultra-thin, non-porous polyester membrane that is totally waterproof, totally windproof, and highly breathable," Sympatex was invented at one of the Akzo Nobel research laboratories in the Netherlands in the 1980s, the technology that produced it being originally developed for kidney dialysis filtration systems. The name, perhaps implying a "*sympa*thetic *tex*ture," was entered in the

Trade Marks Journal of November 26, 1986 for: "Woven and knitted fabrics, pile fabrics, fleeces, composite fabrics, all being textile piece goods."

Synclavier *(synthesizer)*

The name for certain digital synthesizers derives from a combination of the first syllable of "synthesizer" itself and "clavier" (in the sense "keyboard"). It was entered in the US Patent Office *Official Gazette* of February 27, 1979: "For electronic musical synthesizer and an electronic musical instrument controlled by a clavier and a control panel," with a note of first use on November 9, 1977.

Syntocinon *(labor-inducing drug)*

The proprietary name for a synthetic preparation of oxytocin, a hormone causing increased contraction of the womb during labor, is based on the generic name, with "syn-" (in the sense "synthetic") replacing the "oxy-" of "oxytocin" and with an added "-on." It was entered in the *Trade Marks Journal* of September 7, 1955 and the US Patent Office *Official Gazette* of September 18, 1956.

Syrette *(injection unit)*

The disposable injection unit consists of a collapsible tube with an attached hypodermic needle and a single dose of a drug, typically morphine. Its name, from "syringe" and the diminutive suffix "-ette," was entered by **Squibb** in the US Patent Office *Official Gazette* of September 9, 1941, and the *Trade Marks Journal* of August 12, 1953.

T. Eaton *(department stores)*

T. Eaton Co. Ltd. was founded in Toronto, Canada, in 1869 by Timothy Eaton (1834-1907), born near Ballymena, Ireland, who had emigrated to Canada in around 1854. The chain developed into one of the largest department stores in North America, with branches in Winnipeg and Montreal, but in 1997 the firm obtained bankruptcy protection after a string of losses, obliging it to close unprofitable outlets and reorganize its debts under a new chief executive officer.

Tabasco *(sauce)*

The hot, red sauce, made from the fruit of a capsicum pepper, takes its name from the state of Tabasco, southeastern Mexico, where that pepper grows. It originated in the United States, however, on Avery Island, Louisiana, home to the McIlhenny family, where the business started just after the American Civil War, when Edmund McIlhenny, a prosperous banker, had to get out of town fast when the Yankees took New Orleans. While he was looking for work, the story goes that an old soldier on his way back from fighting in Mexico gave him a pocketful of peppers. McIlhenny planted the peppers, and they flourished. Mulched together, with the addition of vinegar and salt, the legendary Tabasco was born. The name was entered by Edward Avery McIlhenny in the *Trade Marks Journal* of September 3, 1902, with the note: "Mark has been used in respect of the said Goods by the applicant and his predecessors in business since five years before the 13th August 1875."

Tabloid *(medicinal pills)*

The name, from "tablet" and the suffix "-oid" meaning "having the form of," was entered by Burroughs, **Wellcome** & Co. in the *Trade Marks Journal* of April 23, 1884 for: "Chemical substances not included in Class I, used in Medicine and Pharmacy," and in the US Patent Office *Official Gazette* of October 18, 1904 for: "Drugs and chemicals for human and veterinary use." The designation was essentially associated with a new type of tablet in compressed form, and this sense of the word led to its general adoption as a term for anything in condensed or "potted" form, and especially for a popular newspaper, with news and pictures in a concentrated and easily digested format. In 1900 to 1905, annoyed at the usurpation of their term, Wellcome took a strong stand against firms selling goods under descriptions that infringed their registered trademarks. The culmination of this legal battle was the case against Thompson & Capper (1903-4), which was largely won by Wellcome's tenacity in insisting on the validity of "Tabloid" as a nondescriptive trademark. In the ruling of Mr. Justice Byrne:

The word Tabloid has become so well-known ... in consequence of the use of it by the Plaintiff firm in connection with their compressed drugs that I think it has acquired a secondary sense in which it has been used and may legitimately be used so long as it does not interfere with their trade rights. I think the word has been so applied generally with reference to the notion of a compressed form or dose of anything.

Reports on Patent and Trade Mark Cases, XXI (November 20-December 14, 1903)

Taco Bell *(fast-food chain)*

The US company, famous for its Mexican food, traces its origin to 1952, when Glen W. Bell, Jr., founded Bell's Hamburger Stand in San Bernardino, California. Two years later, he became the partner in the three-unit Taco-Tia chain. He broke with his partner, however, in the hope of franchising a more lucrative taco chain. The result was his creation in 1962 of Taco Bell. Within a decade, Taco Bell outstripped several taco competitors to dominate the market, with 673 units by 1975. In 1978 the chain was taken over by PepsiCo (*see* **Lay's**) and by 1990 had 3,500 outlets.

Tae-Bo *(fitness regime)*

The combination of karate, boxing, and ballet was the invention of the former US tae kwon do champion Billy Blanks (b.1956). Interviewed in *The Times* (May 19, 2001) he glossed the pseudo-oriental name thus: "You see T stands for Total (totally commit yourself to what you're doing), A for Awareness (of what's going on at all times), E for Excellence (at your own level, not at the teacher's level), B for Body (you need that to achieve the first three) and O for Obedience (to yourself be true)."

Tagamet *(antihistamine)*

The proprietary name of the antihistamine drug cimetidine, used to treat stomach acidity and peptic ulcers, is apparently of arbitrary origin (although "-met" is also in the generic name). It was entered in the *Trade Marks Journal* of December 4, 1974 and the US Patent Officie *Official Gazette* of September 16, 1975, the latter with a note of first use on June 17, 1974.

Taittinger *(champagne)*

The firm was originally established in Reims, France, by Jacques Fourneaux under his own name in 1743. He was succeeded by his son, Jérôme Fourneaux, adviser to the young widowed Nicole Barbe Clicquot, and he blended all the **Veuve Clicquot** wines between 1805 and 1810. In 1932 the house was purchased by Pierre Taittinger from Lorraine, and he changed the firm's name to Établissements Taittinger Mailly & Cie., who entered it in the *Trade Marks Journal* of April 6, 1949.

Takadiastase *(enzyme preparation)*

The preparation, usually obtained as a powder by growing a mold on wheat bran, is mainly used as a starch digestant. The enzyme was developed by the Japanese-born biochemist and industrialist Jokichi Takamine *(1854-1922)*, who named it partly after himself, partly for its similarity to diastase. In 1890 he was called to the United States to devise a practical application of the enzyme for the distilling industry, and the production of Takadiastase for medicinal use was taken over by Parke, Davis & Co., with whom Takamine was associated for the rest of his career. The Takamine Ferment Company, New York, entered the name (as "Taka-diastase") in the US Patent Office *Official Gazette* of November 6, 1928: "For koji, moyashi, diastase, ferments, and converting agents," with a claim of use since 1895. The same form of the name was subsequently entered in the *Trade Marks Journal* of March 9, 1955.

Talbot *(automobiles)*

The British firm of Clément-Talbot Ltd., founded in 1903 to import Clément cars from France, derived the second half of its name from its main sponsor, Charles Henry John Chetwyd-Talbot, 20th Earl of Shrewsbury (1860-1921). By 1906 the cars were being assembled in the UK and the resulting Talbots were regarded as essentially British vehicles, not French Cléments. The name was familiar for the **Sunbeam**-Talbot from the 1930s, after the Rootes Group had gained control of the Sunbeam Motor Car Company, but the Talbot half of the name was dropped from 1954. The name resurfaced, however, in the late 1970s, when it was used for British cars produced by the European interests of the **Chrysler** Corporation, and an advertisement in the *Sunday Telegraph* of July 15, 1979, headed "Today Chrysler Has a New Name," began as follows:

The new name is Talbot, a proud name to stand beside its partners, Peugeot and Citroën. A name better able to represent its new European role. Talbot will be the new name for your Chrysler dealer and for the cars he sells. ... WHY THE CHANGE? WHAT'S THE DIFFERENCE? A year ago the whole of Chrysler's European operations were bought by P.S.A. Peugeot-Citroën—which became Europe's biggest car manufacturer. The benefits of the group are the resources of production, research and financial backing. Resources that mean it can support three famous brands with totally separate personalities, different cars, different dealer networks. Real choice for the motoring public.

Talisker (whisky)

The name is that of a house about six miles from the village of Carbost on the island of Skye in the Hebrides, Scotland, where a distillery was founded in the early 1830s. The name was entered by "Roderick Kemp & Co., Talisker Distillery, Skye" in the *Trade Marks Journal* of May 9, 1883.

Talwin (analgesic)

The proprietary name of pentazocine or pentazocine hydrochloride, an analgesic drug often used in childbirth, is apparently of arbitrary origin. It was entered in the US Patent Office *Official Gazette* of January 26, 1965, with a note of first use on July 31, 1964, and in the *Trade Marks Journal* of February 17, 1965.

Tamagotchi (toy)

The electronic toy, which has to be looked after by its owner as if it were a "pet," was first introduced in Japan in late 1996 by the Japanese firm **Bandai**. Its name amounts to "cute little egg," from Japanese *tamago*, "egg." Bandai received orders for at least 70 million of the cyberpets during 1997, but the craze soon faded.

Tampax (sanitary napkins)

In 1921 **Smith & Nephew** introduced a disposable sanitary napkin called "Dr. White's." Although rudimentary, it at least stayed put and was disposable, qualities that had been lacking in earlier pads. But clearly something more sophisticated was possible, and a prototype Tampax was invented in 1931 by Dr. Earle Haas of Colorado, whose wife, a nurse, hated sanitary pads. It was this that spurred him on to devise a disposable napkin. Within a month of his patent being granted, he was contacted by a Denver physician, Gertrude Tenderich, and she and a syndicate of backers bought the rights for $32,000. They formed the Tampax Corporation and Tenderich made the first napkins herself at home using a sewing machine

and a hand-operated compressor. The name of the product blends "tampon" and a phonetically respelled "packs," referring to the application of the product and to the packs in which it is sold. The name was entered in the US Patent Office *Official Gazette* of 29 March, 1932 and the *Trade Marks Journal* of February 13, 1935.

Tan Sad (baby carriages)

The manufacturing company's leading product was formerly a motorcycle pillion seat called the "Tandem Saddle," a name shortened to "Tan Sad." This subsequently passed to the baby carriage. In its original use, the name also gave *tan-sad* as the general French word for a motorcycle pillion seat.

Tandy (electronics)

Based in Fort Worth, Texas, Tandy owes its name to Charles David Tandy (1918-1978), born in Brownsville, Texas, the son of a leather merchant. He grew up in Fort Worth, where he attended public schools. He enrolled at Rice University in 1935 but dropped out and went to work for his father at Hinckley-Tandy Leather Company. He then spent a year at Harvard Business School before entering the US Navy, where he rose to the rank of lieutenant-commander. When he returned from service in 1947, he assumed management of the leathercraft division at his father's firm, and three years later opened two retail stores than handled only leathercraft. Soon there was a nationwide chain of leathercraft and hobby stores. In the 1950s Tandy made a big effort to break out of the leather business. This was finally realized in 1963 when he bought a small chain of electronics stores in Boston named Radio Shack. He sorted out their financial problems, advertised widely, and by 1973 had raised the number of Radio Shack stores from 172 in 1968 to 2,294. The introduction in 1977 of personal computers sealed the success of the Tandy Corporation, as the business had now become, and in 1979 Radio Shack sold over 100,000 TR-80 units.

Tangle Foot (beer)

The "deceptively drinkable" brand of English beer produced by the Badger Brewery (*see* **Hall & Woodhouse**) has a name whose origin is recounted on the label on the bottle: "Many years ago, the Head Brewer invited his staff to sample his latest creation and coin a name for it. So successful was the sampling that several tankards of the ale were consumed. On rising to go, the Head Brewer experienced a sudden loss of steering, and so unwittingly fell on a name for this legendary ale."

Tanglefoot *(flypaper)*

It was formerly usual for druggists to make their own flypaper. One day in the summer of 1886, Otto and William Thum, clerking in their father's drugstore at Grand Rapids, Michigan, decided they would make flypaper for all the drugstores in the city, and accordingly, without parental approval, launched their enterprise in the rear of the store. They soon evolved an effective formula, and patented it in 1887, calling their product "Tanglefoot" for the way the sticky surface tangled the feet of the flies when it caught them. Their firm was later incorporated as the O. & W. Thum Co., a name that continued until 1924, when thanks to the fame of their product it was renamed as The Tanglefoot Co.

Tannoy *(public address system)*

The company of this name traces its origin to 1922, when an English engineer, Guy Fountain, was looking for a way to simplify the charging process required by lead-acid accumulators used to power radio receivers. He eventually produced a chemical rectifier using two different metals in a solution. One of the metals was a lead alloy and the other was tantalum, and when Fountain began to market the materials he coined the name "Tannoy" from a blend of "tantalum" and "alloy." The name was entered by "Guy Rupert Fountain, trading as the Tulsemere Manufacturing Co." in the *Trade Marks Journal* of April 18, 1928.

Tanqueray *(gin)*

Charles Tanqueray, of Huguenot stock, first made gin in Finsbury, north London, England, in 1830. Unlike many other distillers he did not aim at the mass market, for gin by then was beginning to acquire a social cachet that it had formerly lacked. In particular, Tanqueray saw his gin as a drink worthy to be kept in the blue Bristol glass decanters fashionable in respectable homes. In 1898 his business merged with **Gordon's** and transferred to the latter's premises in Clerkenwell.

Taper-Lock *(machine part)*

The Taper-Lock is a type of tapered bush designed to be inserted into a pulley, sprocket, or the like, so it can be mounted rigidly on a shaft. The name was entered by the Dodge Manufacturing Corporation, Mishawaka, Indiana, in the US Patent Office *Official Gazette* of May 31, 1954: "For machine elements to be mounted on shafts and bushings therefor."

Tapis Saint-Maclou *(carpet stores)*

The French chain of carpet stores was founded in 1963 by Gonzague Mulliez. A few months earlier, as a young man of 22, Mulliez was hitch-hiking across the United States when he was offered a lift by two young ladies. They asked him what he was doing. He replied that he was looking for ideas to start a company back in France. The two women then asked him to meet their husbands, who were in the carpet industry. The experience inspired Mulliez to start in the same line. Today there are 165 Tapis Saint-Maclou stores and the company is now the largest in France. The name means "Saint-Maclou Carpets," after the Normandy village where the company is based.

Tappan *(microwave ovens)*

William J. Tappan (1860-1937) of Mansfield, Ohio, began his business career in 1881, selling coal and wood-burning stoves. The small firm, originally called the Ohio Valley Foundry but later the Eclipse Stove Co., expanded steadily. In 1920 Tappan came across an Illinois company also called the Eclipse Stove Co., so the respective concerns agreed to rechristen themselves, using their family names. As the Tappan Co, the Ohio company continued to grow, diversifying into other products and eventually into the now familiar Tappan microwave ovens.

Tarantulle *(cotton fabric)*

The name of the cotton fabric was entered by **Tootal** Broadhurst Lee Co., of Manchester, England, in the *Trade Marks Journal* of September 3, 1890 and the US Patent Office *Official Gazette* of March 16, 1915. The initial "T" of the name is perhaps for "Tootal," while the second part presumably relates to "tulle." The name as a whole was perhaps intended to suggest "tarantella," as if a light enough fabric to be worn for this whirling dance. It is no longer manufactured.

Tarmac *(road-making materials)*

The ultimate source of the name, or rather the second half of it, is John Loudon McAdam (1756-1856), the Scottish engineer who was general surveyor of roads in England from 1827 and who introduced improved roads built of crushed stone, and thus the word "macadam" to the English language as a term for broken stones used for surfacing roads. In 1901, when the search was on for even better road conditions, Edgar Hooley, county surveyor of Nottingham, noticed that a patch of road near an ironworks in Denby, Derbyshire, was quite dustless and unrutted by traffic. On inquiring the reason, he was told the road had been accidentally covered in tar when a barrel fell off a passing dray and, in order to simplify matters, the tar had been covered with waste blast-furnace slag from the ironworks. This gave Hooley an idea, and by April the following year he had obtained a patent for a method of mixing slag with tar. He called the material "Tarmac," combing "tar" with a short form of "macadam," and the name was entered in the *Trade Marks Journal* of July 1, 1903. The name has subsequently come to be used for any made-up road surface or area, largely as a result of the runways built in World War II as part of the large airfield construction program ordered by the British government.

Tarom *(airline)*

The major Romanian airline was founded in 1954 and takes its name acronymically from *Transporturile Aeriene Româ*ne ("Romanian Air Transport").

Tartan *(synthetic surfacing)*

The synthetic resin material used for surfacing running tracks, ramps, and the like, derives its name from the standard word for the Scottish woolen cloth and its characteristic checked pattern. It was entered in the US Patent Office *Official Gazette* of January 14, 1964, with a note of first use on August 28, 1962, and in the *Trade Marks Journal* of October 22, 1969.

Tarvia *(road-surfacing material)*

The road-surfacing and binding material so known is made of tar. Hence its name, from "tar" and Latin *via*, "road," entered in the US Patent Office *Official Gazette* of July 23, 1912 for: "Pitch prepared from natural or manufac-tured bituminous oils and tars for road and pavement construction, roofing, waterproofing, and insulating," with a claim of use since June 1, 1903.

Taser *(stun weapon)*

The small gunlike device, firing electrified darts or barbs to stun or temporarily paralyze an attacker, was patented in 1974 by Taser Systems Inc., of Los Angeles. It derives its name from the acronym of *Tele-Active Shock Electronic Repulsion*, based on "laser" and in turn apparently suggested by letters in "*Tom Swift's electric rifle*." Tom Swift was the inventive boy-hero of a long series of scientific romances for children, created by the American publisher Edward L. Stratemeyer and beginning with *Tom Swift and His Motor Cycle* (1910) and *Tom Swift and His Electric Rifle* (1911).

Taslan *(synthetic yarn)*

The name is used not only for the yarn, but for the process that produces it by special bulking and texturing. The name itself is probably arbitrary, although the second element suggests Latin *lana*, "wool." (Taslan can be woven and knitted into fabrics.) It was entered by **Du Pont** in the *Trade Marks Journal* of March 31, 1954 and the US Patent Office *Official Gazette* of July 13, 1954, with a note of use since January 4, 1954.

Tate & Lyle *(sugar and Golden Syrup)*

Henry Tate (1819-1899) was born in Chorley, Lancashire, England, the son of a Unitarian minister. He quit school at 13 and was apprenticed to an elder brother who was a grocer in Liverpool. In 1839 Tate acquired his own grocery business in that city, and did so well that he soon opened further shops. In 1858 he decided to improve his prospects by specializing in sugar refining, taking as partner one John Wright. But the partnership dissolved in 1869 and on his own he set up the firm of Henry Tate & Sons, Sugar Refiners. His company expanded when it moved to London in 1876 to open a new refinery. Meanwhile Abram Lyle (1820-1891) was a shipowner in Greenock on the Clyde River, Scotland, where he had become a partner in a sugar refinery. In 1881 he moved to London and there set up his own business as Abram Lyle and Sons, Sugar Refiners. The following year he first marketed his best-known product, Lyle's Golden Syrup. His business and Tate's merged only in 1921, however, and it remains uncertain whether the two men ever met, despite their almost parallel careers. Tate became very wealthy, and in 1896 endowed the founding of London's famous Tate Gallery, which contains several pictures from his private collection.

Tatra (automobiles)

The origins of the European car lie in the railroad rolling stock produced in Nesselsdorf, Moravia, in the mid-19th century. The first car, known as the President, was launched in 1897. When the borders of Central Europe were redrawn after World War I, Nesselsdorf became Kopřivnice, Czechoslovakia (now Czech Republic), and in 1923 the names of the cars was changed from Nesselsdorfer to Tatra, after the highest mountain range of the Central Carpathians.

Tavener's (fruit drops)

Known as Tavener Rutledge until 1988, the British company takes its name from William Henry Tavener (b.1864) and George Rutledge (b.1878). Tavener was born near Lisburn, Northern Ireland, and was apprenticed to the grocery trade before coming over to Liverpool at the age of 20 to seek his commercial fortune. By 1885 he had started his own grocery business, and had begun to make sauces and pickles, progressing to boiled sweets in 1889. Rutledge was also an Ulsterman, and also originally a grocer's apprentice. He in turn crossed the Irish Sea to Liverpool when he was 16, and set up three shops of his own before joining forces with Tavener's son, Herbert, to form the partnership of Tavener Rutledge & Co. in 1922. The business became a private limited company in 1933. The fruit drops were first made the following year, and were the company's sole product during World War II.

Taylor (wine)

In around 1880, Walter Taylor (1858-1934) moved from Tioga County, New York, to the region of New York's Finger Lakes, where he used his skill as a carpenter to supply barrels to local winemakers. Within a few months he had established his own vineyard, where as well as growing Catawba grapes he also produced table wines and dessert ports. In due course he was joined in the business by his sons. When the Eighteenth Amendment came into effect, the Taylors switched to selling sparkling white grape juice accompanied by detailed booklets on "How not to turn the juice into wine." The drink was a hit with bars and consumers but not with the Federal Bureau of Inland Revenue, who ordered it off the market. In 1977, following the death of Taylor's last surviving son, the winery was purchased by the **Coca-Cola** Company.

TCP (antiseptic)

The story goes that the disinfectant and germicidal solution was invented by one Theodore Cadwallader Parry and that it takes its name from his initials. More scientifically, however, the letters come from the solution's main constituent, *tri*chloro*p*henylmethyliodisalycil. The name was entered by the original manufacturers, British Alkaloids Ltd., in the *Trade Marks Journal* of August 22, 1934.

Teacher's (whisky)

William Teacher (1811-1876) was born in Glasgow, Scotland, and at the early age of seven joined his widowed mother in her work at a spinning mill near the city. At 11, William was apprenticed to a tailor, but five years later he was back in the spinning industry. By 1830, however, he was employed in a small grocery business in Glasgow. The shop soon set aside a special area for the sale of alcoholic drinks, and by the time Teacher took over the business in 1836 the groceries had disappeared from the shelves altogether. By 1851 he was listed as a wine and whisky merchant, and he and his sons, Adam and William, had begun to blend their own whisky and sell it in a number of "dram shops" in Glasgow. In 1884 the company, now known as Wm. Teacher & Sons, introduced its famous "Highland Cream" brand, the one primarily associated with the Teacher's name today. The last of the family to be associated with the firm was Teacher's great-grandson, Ronald McNairn Teacher, who died in 1976.

Teasmade (automatic teamaker)

Automatic teamakers, placed by the bedside for a refreshing drink on awaking, have existed since 1902, when the first of its kind was invented by Frank Clarke, a gunsmith of Birmingham, England. But it was a cumbersome machine, and was not improved on until 1936, when Brenner Thornton devised a more sophisticated model that eliminated the precarious balancing acts of the original. **Goblin** Electrical Appliances purchased Thornton's invention in 1937 and began manufacturing it. It proved difficult to register the name, however, as it was technically descriptive if understood as "tea's made" (though not as "tea's maid"). The Goblin chairman of the day suggested "Cheerywake" as an alternative, but this was fortunately outvoted by the rest of the board. In order to extricate themselves from the dilemma, the firm distributed the product through leading department stores such as **Harrods** and **Selfridges** until the time came when these stores accredited Goblin as the manufacturers of the appliance. The name was eventually entered in the *Trade Marks Journal* of January 26, 1938: "*Goblin Teasmade* ... Time controlled and electric water heating and tea making apparatus. The British Vacuum Cleaner & Engineering Company Limited ... Fulham, London, S.W.6; manufacturers."

Te Bheag *(whisky)*

The "old-style" blend of Scotch whisky was created in 1976 as a partner to **Poit Dubh**, the vatted malt produced by the same small company Praban na Linne ("Shebeen of the Pool"), on the Scottish island of Skye. The name is Gaelic for "Little One."

Tebilized *(crease-resistant)*

The patent method of treating cotton and linen fabrics by a finishing process that prevents shrinking and creasing takes its name from the initials of the British firm that invented the process, **Tootal** Broadhurst Lee Co. Ltd., who entered it in the US Patent Office *Official Gazette* of December 7, 1937 and the *Trade Marks Journal* of March 28, 1945.

Technicolor *(color cinematography process)*

The color processes so named originated with the work of Herbert T. Kalmus (1881-1963) and Donald E. Comstock, who formed the Technicolor Motion Picture Corporation in Boston, Massachusetts, in 1915. The name, blending "technical" and "color," was patented by Comstock in 1917 and entered in the US

Patent Office *Official Gazette* of December 3, 1929. (The "Techni-" is said to pay tribute to the Massachusetts Institute of Technology, where Kalmus and Comstock had studied.) The first motion picture using the new two-color additive system was *The Gulf Between* (1917), while the first three-color movie was the Disney animated short *Flowers and Trees* (1931). The process was used for the first time in a feature film in *Becky Sharp* (1934). Kalmus's wife Natalie (1883-1965) was adviser on all Technicolor movies from 1933. The British sometimes misspell the name as "Technicolour."

Tecla *(artificial pearl)*

The name was entered by Isaac Blumenthal, of Hendon, Middlesex, England, in the *Trade Marks Journal* of September 9, 1908 for: "Imitation or reconstructed pearls, imitation or reconstructed rubies, imitation emeralds, and imitation or reconstructed sapphires." The name itself appears to be arbitrary, unless it is an anagram of French (now also English) *éclat*, "brilliance," "radiance."

Teepol *(detergent)*

The type of detergent for cleaning fabrics and ceramics was originally manufactured by the British company Technical Products Ltd., of London, who entered it in the *Trade Marks Journal* of December 9, 1942. The name seems to derive from "TP" (the firm's initials) with the "-ol" suffix meaning "oil." It was entered by the **Shell** Union Oil Corporation, San Francisco, in the US Patent Office *Official Gazette* of July 10, 1945.

Tefal *(nonstick kitchenware)*

In 1954, Frenchman Marc Grégoire used **Teflon** to lubricate fishing tackle. Realizing the material's potential, he founded the Tefal Company in 1955 to manufacture nonstick kitchenware. The name was entered in the *Trade Marks Journal* of August 31, 1960.

Teflon *(nonstick plastic material)*

On April 6, 1938, a **Du Pont** scientist, Roy J. Plunkett, was conducting research into refrigerants when he found that a cylinder of tetrafluorethylene that he had stored in a cold box no longer contained the gas. On cutting it open, he was instead surprised to discover a waxy substance that slid and slithered around without adhering to the walls of the cylinder. Thus Teflon was born, deriving its name from letters in "*tetrafluoroethylene*," with the final "-on" patterned on words such as "nylon" and "rayon." The name was entered in the US Patent Office *Official Gazette* of October 23, 1945 and the *Trade Marks Journal* of May 5, 1954. *See also* (1) **Gore-Tex**; (2) **Tefal**.

Telechron *(clocks)*

The clocks so named were the invention of Henry Ellis Warren (1872-1957), born in Boston, Massachusetts, the son of a businessman. On graduating from the Massachusetts Institute of Technology with a degree in electrical engineering in 1894, he went to work for the Saginaw Valley Traction Company. When it failed, he and a friend, Henry Loring, took it over and revived it. Warren was meanwhile pursuing a hobby of modifying old clocks to run on electricity. In 1916 he realized his most important invention, a "master clock," in the form of an accurate pendulum clock that ran on the same dial as an electric clock driven by the power system. In 1919 he set up the Warren Clock Company to manufacture it, by which time he had also designed the first of the simple, reliable motor-driven household clocks that his company marketed under the name "Telechron" (Greek for "time at a distance"). By 1925, some 30 million people were using Telechron clocks. The Warren Clock Company became a part of General Electric in 1948 and was sold to the **Timex** Company in 1978.

Teleplayer *(video recorder and player)*

The device for recording and playing back videotape has a name derived from "television" and "player" that was entered in the US Patent Office *Official Gazette* of November 23, 1971, with a note of first use on March 24, 1970.

Teleprompter *(television prompting device)*

The device is essentially the US equivalent of the British **Autocue**. The name combines the Greek element "tele-" (meaning "at a distance") and "prompter" and was entered in the US Patent Office *Official Gazette* of February 10, 1953, with a claim of use since September 1, 1950. Unlike the British name, the US name is no longer proprietary.

Teletel *(viewdata system)*

The name (properly "Télétel") is that of the viewdata system operated by the French government. It combines the first elements of "television" and "telephone" and was entered in the *Trade Marks Journal* of August 4, 1989, but was in use at least ten years before this.

Teletex *(data processing system)*

The name of the date processing and communications system, using interconnected computer terminals, dates from the 1970s and probably derives from a blend of "telex" and "text." It was entered by **Siemens** in the *Trade Marks Journal* of May 16, 1979.

Teletype *(teleprinter)*

The early form of teleprinter originated in the USA at the turn of the 20th century. The name, a blend of "tele-" (in the sense "at a distance") and "type(writer)," was entered by the Morkrum-Kleinschmidt Corporation, of Chicago, in the US Patent Office *Official Gazette* of May 26, 1925.

Teletypesetter *(typesetting machine)*

The machine first appeared in the 1920s as an apparatus for the casting and setting of type in response to telegraphed signals recorded on perforated tape. Its name, an obvious blend of "tele-" (meaning "at a distance") and "typesetter," was entered in the US Patent Office *Official Gazette* of March 17, 1931.

Telex *(telegraphic system)*

The system of telegraphy in which printed messages are are transmitted and received by teleprinters derives its name from the first elements of "teleprinter" and "exchange." A "teleprinter exchange service" opened in London, England, in 1932. The word was formerly written with a capital "T," leading many to suppose it was a registered trademark, but the *Oxford English Dictionary* points out:

> Despite the frequent use of a capital initial, *telex* ... is not a proprietary term. The names of some specific products (radio equipment, hearing aids, etc.) of the Telex Corporation are registered as trade marks, however.

Telidon *(viewdata system)*

The name of the viewdata system operated by the Canadian government derives somewhat esoterically from "tele-" and Greek *idon*, "seeing," the aorist participle of *horan*, "to see." The name replaced the earlier Videotex in 1978.

Ten *(concierge services)*

The concept of a concierge services firm came to Alex Cheatle (b.1970) when visiting San Francisco in 1999. On his return to his native Britain, with no business plan, no office, and no money, he and a colleague, Andrew Long (b.1975), launched Ten, ostensibly standing for "Time Energy Network" but also implying a "ten-out-of-ten" service. The pair found plenty of people willing to give them a go, and the word soon spread. Individual members pay £1,500 a year for a personal lifestyle manager, who will arrange everything from dog walking to wedding planning. If you can't find anyone to let the builder in, Ten UK will arrange for someone to be there, and even find a reliable builder. By 2001, Ten DE had been launched in Germany, with Cheatle and Long setting their sights on France and the USA.

Tencel *(artificial fiber)*

The cellulosic fiber, obtained from wood pulp using recyclable solvents, has a name apparently of arbitrary origin (although the second part suggests "cellulose") entered by **Courtaulds** in the *Trade Marks Journal* of November 1, 1967.

Tenneco *(oil and natural gas)*

The American company was formed in 1943 as the Tennessee division of the Chicago Corporation to build a natural gas pipeline from Texas to West Virginia. Soon after World War II, the division was sold, and the new company was incorporated in 1947 as the Tennessee Gas and Transmission Company. This name was abbreviated as now in 1966.

Tennent *(beer)*

The Scottish brewery dates its founding from 1556, the year when Robert Tennent, born in about 1530, was known to be a member of Glasgow's Incorporation of Maltmen. From 1632 successive members of the Tennent family entered the Incorporation, including those who gave their names to the later title of J. & R. Tennent Ltd. These were John Tennent (1732-1827) and his younger brother Robert Tennent (1749-1826), who first traded under their joint name in 1769, as brewers in the Dry-

gate, Glasgow. In 1885 the firm gained fame as Scotland's first lager brewers, and this date now appears on their cans.

Tergal *(polyester fiber)*

The artificial fiber or fabric is of French origin. Its name derives from the first elements of French *téréphthalique*, "terephthalic" (*see* **Terylene**), and *gallique*, "Gallic," and was entered by the manufacturers, Société Rhodiacéta, of Paris, in the *Trade Marks Journal* of December 22, 1954, and the US Patent Office *Official Gazette* of April 26, 1955. *Cp.* **Terital**.

Terital *(polyester fiber)*

The natural or synthetic (usually polyester) fiber or fabric, also used as a floor covering, is of Italian origin. Its name derives from the first syllable of Italian *tereftalico*, "terephthalic" (*see* **Terylene**), and the first half of *italiano*, "Italian," and was entered by the manufacturers, Società Rhodiatoce, of Milan, in the US Patent Office *Official Gazette* of June 4, 1963. *Cp.* **Tergal**.

Terramycin *(antibiotic)*

The name, a brand name for oxytetracycline, derives from Latin *terra*, "earth," and "-mycin," an element relating to antibiotics derived from fungi (as in "streptomycin"), from Greek *mykēs*, "fungus." (Oxytetracycline is specifically produced by cultures of the bacterium *Streptomyces rimosus*.) The name was entered by **Pfizer** in the US Patent Office *Official Gazette* of May 5, 1953 and the *Trade Marks Journal* of May 11, 1954.

Terrapin *(prefabricated building)*

The make of prefabricated building, usually having a single floor and designed for temporary use, apparently derives its name from the freshwater turtle so called, although there may may in fact be a punning reference to a building that is "pinned" to the ground (Latin *terra*). The name was entered by the British manufacturer, Harry Collett Bolt, of London, in the *Trade Marks Journal* of September 21, 1949, and for "Terrapin Minihouses" by Terrapin Ltd., of London, in the *Journal* of July 25, 1962.

Terrot *(motorcycles)*

Charles Terrot first began manufacturing motorcycles in the French city of Dijon in 1902.

The range of machines expanded to include racing bikes, and in the late 1920s the business moved to a large new factory that was one of the most modern in Europe. Terrot became part of the **Peugeot** group in the 1950s, but production ceased in the 1960s. The models are still popular with collectors and restorers today.

Terry's *(chocolate)*

The origin of the British company lies with Joseph Terry (1793-1850), a York apothecary, who in 1823 joined the partnership formed in 1767 by two men named respectively Bayldon and Berry, founders of a business importing citrus peel, and manufacturers of candy at a site near the northern entrance to York. Using his pharmaceutical skills, Terry developed his range of confectionery and by 1840 was distributing his products to 75 towns throughout Britain. His sons, Joseph, Robert, and John, took over the business shortly after their father's death, naming their partnership Joseph Terry & Sons. They did not manufacture chocolate until 1886, however, when they built a new factory for the purpose south of the city. The Terry family were fully involved in the running of the company down to World War II, and are still senior members today.

Terylene *(artificial fiber)*

The synthetic fiber was first produced in the 1940s by **ICI** and takes its name from a reversal of elements in its chemical formula, poly*ethylene tere*phthalate. It was the invention of the British chemist John Rex Whinfield (1901-1966), who in the 1930s discovered how to condense terephthalic acid and ethylene glycol to yield a substance that could be drawn into a fiber. Whinfield filed a patent for his discovery in 1941, but it was suppressed for security reasons in World War II and was not published until 1946. Its name was entered by ICI in the *Trade Marks Journal* of April 23, 1947 and in the US Patent Office *Official Gazette* of September 27, 1949. **Dacron**, manufactured by **Du Pont**, is the US equivalent.

Tesa *(medical adhesive tape)*

The **Beiersdorf** product was introduced in 1936 as a new type of transparent adhesive film, taking its name from letters in the name of a company employee, Elsa Tesmer. The name is generic in some countries.

Tesco *(supermarkets)*

The name of the British food stores conceals the two men who lie behind them, John (originally Jacob) Cohen (1898-1979) and T.E. Stockwell. The latter's initials form the "Tes-" of the name, and Jack (as he was usually known) Cohen's surname provides the "-co," which is thus not "Company," as might be supposed. After serving in the Royal Flying Corps in World War I, Cohen, the son of an immigrant Polish-Jewish tailor, used the £30 given him on demobilization to set up as a market trader in London's East End. Within a short time he was trading in a different market in and around London each day of the week. One of the main products he sold was tea, and he established the name "Tesco" for his business because T.E. Stockwell, a partner in the firm of Torring & Stockwell, was his main tea supplier. London's suburbs were expanding rapidly in the 1930s, and in 1931 Cohen founded Tesco Stores Ltd. to take advantage of this retailing potential. By the start of World War II there were 100 Tesco grocery stores in and around London, and by the mid-1990s there were over 500 across Britain. The name has been humorously (or cynically) interpreted by some as an acronym of "To Eclipse **Sainsburys** with Cutprice Offers." In 1994, Tesco in fact outbid Sainsburys to acquire the William Low chain of 57 supermarkets in Scotland.

Testa *(advertising agency)*

The Italian firm was founded in Turin in 1946 by the graphic artist Armando Testa (1917-1992). It has conducted a number of notable campaigns, and has taken a hold in other countries, where it specializes in the field of communication.

Tetley *(beer)*

England's leading brewery of bitter beer was founded by Joshua Tetley in Leeds, Yorkshire, in 1822. The company merged with **Carlsberg** in 1993 to become Carlsberg-Tetley.

Tetley *(tea)*

The British name is that of two brothers, Joseph Tetley (1811-1889) and Edward Tetley (b.1816), who in 1837 set up a partnership in Huddersfield, Yorkshire, to deal in tea. In 1856 they moved south to London, as that was increasingly the center of the expanding world tea trade. Subsequently only Joseph was left in London to establish the firm of Joseph Tetley & Co., Wholesale Tea Dealers, with premises first in Cullum Street, near Mincing Lane, then in Fenchurch Street. In 1952 Tetley's was the first firm to market tea bags for home retail consumption and by 1999 was the world's second biggest tea brand.

Tetra Pak *(food packaging)*

The familiar plastic-coated paperboard cartons for milk and other liquids were the invention in 1951 of the Swiss entrepreneur Dr. Ruben Rausing, who chose the original tetrahedral shape that gave the name because it used a small amount of material to enclose a large volume. It was awkward to handle, however, and was superseded by several other configurations, including the "Tetra Brik." These were developed by the inventor's son, Gad Anders Rausing (1922-2000), who bought the rights to the product in 1965 and together with his brother, Hans, built up the business into the world's largest food packaging group. It later merged with **Alfa-Laval** to become Tetra-Laval. The name was entered by Aktiebolaget Tetra Pak, of Lund, Sweden, in the US Patent Office *Official Gazette* of June 16, 1953.

Tetralin *(solvent)*

The proprietary name for tetrahydronaphthalene, a liquid used as a solvent for hydrocarbons, especially varnishes and lacquers, derives its name from a combination of "tetra-" and the "-lin" of "naphthaline," a former spelling of "naphthalene." It was entered by **Du Pont** in the US Patent Office *Official Gazette* of January 18, 1944.

Tetris *(computer game)*

The game was the invention in 1985 of the Russian computer scientist Aleksei Pazhitnov, who devised it on his ageing microcomputer to stave off boredom at work in a computer laboratory at the Academy of Sciences, Moscow. He based his game on the old Roman puzzle called *pentamino*, in which players had to arrange 12 pieces in five squares into a perfect rectangle. He reduced the five (Greek *penta-*) squares to four (*tetra-*), and the game caught on like wildfire in the computer labs. Pazhitnov copied the game onto disks and it was eventually smuggled out of the USSR into Hungary,

where it was seized on by such video game giants as **Nintendo** and **Atari**, who bought up the rights and quickly turned it into the most popular computer game in the world.

Teva *(footwear)*

In 1983, Mark Thatcher (b.1950), a whitewater-rafting guide and former African oil explorer, invented a new style of footwear by attaching an ankle strap to sandals. His "sports sandals," made of nylon webbing with neoprene rubber thongs and **Velcro** fixings, were launched the following year under the name Teva, Hebrew for "nature," and were soon taken up by outdoor types and the public generally.

Texaco *(oil and petrochemicals)*

The name is an abbreviation of The *Texa*s *Co*mpany, as which the corporation was founded in 1902 by Joseph S. Cullinan (1860-1937), a former **Standard Oil** field worker, and Arnold Schlaet (1859-1946), a New York investment manager. Their original intention was to buy and refine oil in Texas and sell it at a profit to Standard Oil Company in the North, but they soon expanded into oil production in the Spindletop field. The present abbreviated name was adopted in 1959.

Texas Instruments *(watches and calculators)*

The American corporation began life as Geophysical Service, Inc. (GSI), a company founded in 1930 by two scientists, Clarence Karcher and Eugene McDermott, to carry out oil exploration in Texas. When World War II slowed oil exploration, the company was contracted to manufacture submarine-detecting equipment, and after the war they decided to stay in the electronic business, renaming themselves Texas Instruments accordingly. In the 1950s the company was the first to make transistors cheap enough to be commercially useful in radio. Their greatest success came in the 1970s, when they applied the same principle to calculators, quartering their retail price from $45 in 1974 to $10 in 1980.

Thales *(electronics)*

The French company traces its origins to the American electrical engineer Elihu Thomson (1853-1937), born in Manchester, England, the son of a mechanic, whose family immigrated to Philadelphia, Pennsylvania, in 1858. He went on to teach chemistry and mechanics at the Central High School in that city, and with a fellow teacher, Edwin J. Houston (1847-1914), born in Alexandria, Virginia, designed an arc lighting system that won financial backing and that led to the founding in 1880 of the American Electric Company in New Britain, Connecticut. In 1882 a group from Lynn, Massachusetts, bought a controlling interest in the company and moved it to Lynn. Thomson went with the company, which was renamed the Thomson-Houston Electric Company. In 1892 Thomson-Houston merged with the Edison Electric Light Company (*see* **Ediswan**) to form the General Electric Company (not to be confused with the British **GEC**), while the following year the Compagnie Française Thomson-Houston (CFTH) was established in France. In 1918 the Compagnie Générale de Télégraphie Sans Fil ("General Wireless Company") (CSF) was set up to take a controlling interest in the Société Française Radioélectrique ("French Radioelectric Society") (SFR), which had been developing wireless technologies since 1910. In 1957 CSF took over SFR completely, at the same time diversifying into electron tubes, semiconductors, radio transmitters, and professional television. In 1966 Thomson-Houston merged with Hotchkiss-Brandt, a company itself formed as a merger between **Hotchkiss** and Brandt (a home appliances and armaments manufacturer founded in 1926), to become Thomson-Brandt. In 1968 Thomson-Brandt merged with CSF to become Thomson CSF, a name that was retained until 2000, when the company rebranded itself as Thales (pronounced "Tallis"), after the 6th-century BC Greek philosopher and mathematician. *See also* **RCA**.

Thames and Hudson *(publishers)*

The British publishing house, noted for its quality illustrated books on art and design, was founded in 1949 with offices in both London and New York, the aim being to attract English-speaking readers on both sides of the Atlantic. Hence the significant name, that of the rivers on which London and New York respectively stand. The "east-west" theme is repeated in the firm's colophon, which represents two dolphins, one facing left (west), the other right (east).

Theakston *(beer)*

The British brewery was established by the Theakston family in the small town of Masham, Yorkshire, in 1827. One member, Paul Theakston, fell out with other family members over the sale of the brewery and set up his own brewing business in the same town in 1992 as the wryly named Black Sheep Brewery. Theakston, famous for its **Old Peculier** brand, is now owned by Scottish **Courage**.

Thermalite *(building material)*

The type of cellular concrete for making building blocks, of light density and high insulation value, derives its name from "thermal" and the commercial suffix "-ite." It was entered in the *Trade Marks Journal* of August 3, 1949 for: "Concrete products included in Class 19."

Thermit *(welding agent)*

The powdered mixture of aluminum and iron oxide, used in welding and for incendiary bombs, was invented in 1895 by the German chemist Hans Goldschmidt (1861-1923) and named for the great heat it produces on combustion, from Greek *thermos*, "hot," and the commercial suffix *-it*. The name was entered by Goldschmidt AG, of Essen, Germany, in the *Trade Marks Journal* of October 10, 1906. The English equivalent name, "thermite," is not a registered trademark.

Thermo-Fax *(document-copying process)*

The name became current in the 1950s for a type of overhead projector using copies made by a process described in the US Patent Office *Official Gazette* of March 17, 1953: "For electrically operated machine employing infrared light source for producing copies of printed or pictorial matter by means of heat-sensitive paper." The name, deriving from "thermo-" ("heat") and "facsimile" (modern "fax"), had a claim of use since November 1949. It was subsequently entered by **3M** in the *Trade Marks Journal* of April 18, 1956 for "Reproducing (copying) apparatus for office use."

Thermogene *(medicated cotton wool)*

The name derives from French *thermogène*, "thermogenic," meaning "produced by heat," and the product was originally made by Vandenbroeck & Cie., of Brussels, Belgium, who entered it for "absorbent wadding" in the US Patent Office *Official Gazette* of March 18, 1902. The material was soon produced in England by "Thomas Other Windsor, trading as the Thermogène Co., Invermay, Lucastes Avenue, Hayward's Heath, Sussex; manufacturer," who entered the name in the *Trade Marks Journal* of November 22, 1905.

Thermolactyl *(material for thermal underwear)*

The material was the invention in the 1950s of the three French brothers Despature, who used it for their **Damart** underwear. "Thermo-" is from the Greek meaning "warm," while "lactyl" is a chemical radical derived from lactic acid used in the manufacturing process. The name was entered in the *Bulletin Officiel de la Propriété Industrielle: Marques de Fabrique* of April 26, 1956, the US Patent Office *Official Gazette* of December 29, 1959, and the *Trade Marks Journal* of October 31, 1962.

Thermopane *(double-glazed window)*

The name of the openable double-glazed window unit derives from the Greek element "thermo-," meaning "warm," and English "pane." It was entered in the US Patent Office *Official Gazette* in 1941: "For multiple glass sheet glazing units," with a claim of use since May 1, 1931.

Thermos *(vacuum flask)*

The name, a straight borrowing of Greek *thermos*, "hot," was devised in 1904 by a resident of Munich, Germany, who had won a competition to name a new type of domestic vacuum flask developed by Reinhold Burger. In 1907 a group of English businessmen secured the patent rights to manufacture the flask for marketing in the British Empire, South America, and certain other countries, and accordingly formed the company of Thermos Ltd., at the same time entering the name in the *Trade Marks Journal* of March 20, 1907. In 1963, however, the name became legally generic in the United States as the result of an application made against the King-Seeley Thermos Co. by the relatively small company of Aladdin Industries. The English Thermos Co. was shaken by the decision, as were various other companies whose brand names were in danger of becoming generic (notably

Formica), and ever since it has made increasingly strenuous efforts to protect the name.

Thomas Cook *(travel agents)*

Thomas Cook (1808-1892) was born in Melbourne, Derbyshire, England, and was raised by his mother after his father died when he was only four. He went to work at age 10, and at 14 was a wood turner. For four years from 1828 he served as a "Baptist missionary," traveling around the Midland counties of England. He then set up as a cabinetmaker in Market Harborough, Leicestershire, in 1831. Cook became increasingly supportive of the temperance cause, and in 1842 devised a method of transporting a large number of people by train from Leicester to Loughborough, Leicestershire, to attend a temperance meeting, with 570 passengers paying a shilling each for their fare. This was not quite the first railway excursion, but it prompted Cook to plan others. His trips became increasingly adventurous and lengthy, traveling to North Wales in 1845, for example, and to Scotland the following year. By 1855 he had crossed the English Channel, arranging with different railway companies to take his travelers to continental Europe via Newhaven and Harwich. In 1865 he moved his head office from Leicester to London. The following year he organized the first tour to the United States. In 1871 the firm of Thomas Cook & Son was formed, and from then on "Cook's tours" were an established feature of the British tourist scene.

Thomas Hardy *see* **Eldridge Pope**

Thomas Pink *(shirts)*

The British firm of this name was founded in London in 1984 by an Irishman, James Mullen, together with his brothers, Peter and John, and vigorous marketing soon established it as Britain's leading luxury shirt brand. The name is that of an 18th-century Mayfair tailor who reputedly made the best hunting coats. By 2001, the company had 17 stores in the UK and three in New York, as well as outlets in Boston, Washington, and San Francisco, and another planned in Dallas.

Thomas's *("English Muffins")*

In 1876 Samuel Bath Thomas (1855-1919), an English baker, immigrated from his native Plymouth, Devonshire, to the United States.

He worked at a number of menial jobs before at last saving enough money to start his own bakery business in 1880 in New York City, selling gluten bread, raisin bread, and English muffins. New Yorkers quickly developed a taste for his goods, especially the English muffins, and Thomas was soon selling them to restaurants. The business then branched out into retail food stores, so that by the time of his death, Thomas's bakery was selling English muffins throughout the New York area. In 1970 the S.B. Thomas Co., as it then was, became a subsidiary of **Bestfoods**.

Thompson, J. Walter *see* **J. Walter Thompson**

Thomson CSF *see* **Thales**

Thomson-Houston *see* **Thales**

Thomson Travel *(travel agents)*

The name is that of newspaper proprietor Roy Herbert Thomson, 1st Baron Thomson of Fleet (1894-1976), who launched the travel company that bears his name in 1971. He was born a Canadian in Toronto, the son of a barber and hotel maid and the great-great-grandson of a Scot who had emigrated to Canada in 1773. He quit school at 14 and after learning bookkeeping for a year became a clerk and salesman for the next 10 years. In 1920 he failed at being a farmer in Saskatchewan, in 1925 at dealing in automobile parts in Toronto, and in 1928 at selling radio parts in Ottawa. In 1931 he founded a radio station at North Bay, north of Ontario. This was the effective start of his "media empire," so that by 1944 he owned eight radio stations and several newspapers. In 1967 he acquired *The Times* of London, having already gained control of the *Sunday Times* in 1959. Thomson became a British citizen in 1963 and was made Baron Thomson the following year. In 2000, Thomson Travel passed to Preussag, Germany's biggest tour operator, already owners of **Lunn Poly** and the UK airline Britannia.

Thorazine *(tranquilizer)*

The proprietary name for the drug chlorpromazine derives from letters in the full chemical name: 2-chlor*o*-N, N-dimethyl-10-H-phe-no*thia*zine-10-propanamine. It was entered by Smith, Kline & French Laboratories (*see*

SmithKline Beecham) in the US Patent Office *Official Gazette* of March 9, 1954 and the *Trade Marks Journal* of September 20, 1972.

Thorn EMI *(electronics)*

The first half of the name is that of Jules Thorn (1899-1980), born in Austria. His first job was in the gas industry, and his first post in Britain, where he arrived as a young man, was as the representative of an Austrian gas mantle company. His real career began in 1926, when he became a distributor of electric lamps and radio valves. Two years later he formed the Electric Lamp Service Co. In 1931 he opened his first radio rental shop in Twickenham, Middlesex, and the following year he started a factory in Angel Road, Edmonton, to make electric lamps. In 1936 his company was renamed Thorn Electrical Industries Ltd., and it gradually increased in commercial profitability so that eventually in 1961, after a string of acquisitions, the company was the biggest producer of radio and television sets in the UK. By the year of his death the Thorn empire had become truly international, with subsidiaries in many countries of the world. The second half of the company name is that of **EMI**, which was taken over by Thorn in 1979. *See also* **Virgin**.

Thornton's *(chocolates)*

The brand of quality chocolates takes its name from Joseph William Thornton, who in 1911 opened his first candy store in Sheffield, England, intending it to be the best. A second shop was opened in 1913 and Thornton began to make candy by hand on its premises. On his death in 1919 his son, Norman, continued the business, and when joined by his brother, Stanley, in 1921 opened further stores and developed the business generally. A factory was opened in Sheffield in the mid-1930s, and by 1950 the firm owned around 30 stores. By 1988 this number had risen to 176, and the company remains in family ownership today.

Thorotrast *(colloidal solution)*

The colloidal solution of thorium dioxide, formerly used as a contrast medium in radiography, derives its name from a blend of "thorium" and "contrast." It was entered by the Heyden Chemical Corporation, New York, in the US Patent Office *Official Gazette* of April 5, 1932: "For medicinal preparation finding its application in the photography by X-rays for medicinal and similar purposes." (The awkward English was presumably a rendering of the original German. The name was actually devised by A. Weiser in an article in the *Wiener medizinische Wochenschrift*, October 25, 1930.)

Three Castles *(tobacco and cigarettes)*

The name for the tobacco was suggested to **Wills**, its original manufacturers, by a Mr. Waterston of Edinburgh, Scotland. He took the name from a line in the first chapter of W.M. Thackeray's novel *The Virginians* (1857-9): "There's no sweeter tobacco comes from Virginia, and no better brand than the Three Castles." Thackeray had apparently invented the name for use in his novel. Wills introduced the tobacco of this name in 1877, following it a year later with "Three Castles" cigarettes.

Three Fives *(cigarettes)*

The name is a brand of **State Express** cigarettes, appearing on the pack in numerical form ("555") as well as in words. It goes back to the original Empire State Express train in which Albert Levy, founder of the manufacturers, **Ardath**, used to travel. One one occasion he noticed that the locomotive number was 999. This prompted him to choose similar three-number names for his cigarettes, so he duly registered "111," "222," etc. up to "999." The whole series of names was in use until the 1950s, with "555," or "Three Fives," the most successful. It is also the only State Express brand sold in the UK.

3i *(business finance)*

The British institution was formed in 1945 by the leading banks and the Bank of England as the Industrial and Commercial Finance Corporation Ltd. (ICFC) with the aim of supplying long-term finance to small and medium-sized businesses, a sector previous starved of investment capital. In 1973 ICFC merged with a sister body, Finance Corporation for Industry Ltd. (FCI), also set up in 1945, as subsidiaries of a new holding company, Finance for Industry Ltd. (FFI). In 1983 a new simplified orgaanization was planned and a new name sought for it. Both "Finance for Industry" and its abbreviation, "FFI," were considered, but were rejected as being not sufficiently descriptive and as suggesting a government

body. Eventually the title "Investors in Industry" was generally approved, but in abbreviated form, although not as "III" but as "3i." The lowercase letter enabled the organization's logo to show a stylized eye replacing the dot of the "i."

3M *(adhesive tapes)*

The American company dates from 1902, when it was set up to exploit carborundum in Two Harbors, Minnesota, by five local citizens (a doctor, a lawyer, a merchant, and two railroad executives) as the Minnesota Mining and Manufacturing Company. The name was something of a misnomer, since the intention of the founders was simply to mine carborundum, not to manufacture it. Only in 1905 did the company begin to manufacture its first product, sandpaper, and shortly after ceased mining until 1930, when the name could be said to be accurate. Further confusion is caused since the name suggests the company is associated with Minnesota iron mining, which is not the case. This misunderstanding has not been helped by 3M employees themselves, who call their company as "The Mining." 3M has now diversified widely, one of its best-known products being **Scotch** tape.

Three Nuns *(tobacco)*

The origin of the brand name is uncertain. It is known that a brand so called was originally manufacturered some time before 1892 by J. and F. Bell, whose products were acquired by Stephen Mitchell & Son of Glasgow, Scotland, in 1904. Mitchells themselves amalgamated with **Wills** in 1957, and the name now belongs to the latter company. James Bell, the original producer, is said to have had the name suggested to him by his second son, Hope, as suitable for a tobacco that was smaller and lighter than a popular brand of strong tobacco at that time called "Thick Black." The precise reasoning behind this name has been lost, although nuns are certainly more "ethereal" than strong "Thick Black."

Thunderbird *(automobiles)*

The American car of this name was introduced by **Ford** at the Detroit Motor Show on February 10, 1954. It was still only a wooden model, but it attracted many potential purchasers. The first actual "T-bird" rolled off the line on September 9, 1954. The name derives from the mythical bird believed by Native American tribes to cause thunder. In 1959 Thunderbird became a separate marque within Ford.

Thyssen *(iron and steel)*

The vast German industrial empire had its beginnings in the firm of Thyssen & Co. established at Mülheim in 1871 by August Thyssen (1842-1926), a self-made millionaire nicknamed "Rockefeller of the Ruhr" who had founded his first rolling mill at Duisburg in 1867. In 1926, Fritz Thyssen (1873-1951) inherited his father's fortune and industrial empire and combined the family holdings into a trust, Vereinigte Stahlwerke AG ("United Steelworks Co."), which on his death passed to his wife, Amelia zur Helle Thyssen (*c.*1878-1965). In 1953 August Thyssen-Hütte AG ("August Thyssen Iron and Steelworks Co.") was founded as one of the successor companies of Vereinigte Stahlwerke, adopting the shorter name Thyssen AG in 1977.

Tia Maria *(coffee-flavored liqueur)*

The name is Spanish for "Aunt Mary." The romantic (and possibly romanticized) story behind the name runs something as follows. In 1655 the Spanish grandees who had taken possession of Jamaica were forced to flee before the invading forces of Cromwell's British expedition. Maria, a young servant girl employed by one such fleeing family, had time to salvage only a few of her mistress's possessions, including a pair of black pearl earrings at one time owned by Queen Isabella of Spain and an ancient recipe for a home-made cordial. In due course, Maria married a gallant British officer (of course), and became the mother of a large family. When Maria's eldest daughter in turn married, her mother gave her the pearl earrings and the fading parchment recipe. The resulting cordial was named "Tia Maria" (perhaps better rendered "Dame Maria" or "Goodwife Maria" than "Aunt Mary") in memory of the servant girl's loyalty and devotion to the family. Some 300 years later the recipe was rediscovered and adapted to make the coffee-flavored liqueur based on rum that now bears the name, which was entered in the *Trade Marks Journal* of September 29, 1948 and the US Patent Office *Official Gazette* of August 31, 1954. *Cp.* **Tio Pepe**.

Tiffany's *(department store)*

The famous New York store, on Fifth Avenue, derives its name from Charles Lewis Tiffany (1812-1902), born in Killingly, Connecticut, the son of a cotton goods manufacturer. He attended a local school in Danielsonville and later spent two years at the Plainfield (Connecticut) Academy. When he was 15, his father made him the manager of a general store near the family's mill, and Tiffany worked there for the next ten years, acquiring schooling at odd intervals. He eventually joined his father in the office of his firm, now known as C. Tiffany & Son, and seemed to have a secure future. Trips to New York, however, had persuaded him that a richer market awaited him there, and in 1837 he went to the city with a friend, John B. Young, and opened a fancy goods store on lower Broadway. He soon made his name, and his business became Tiffany, Young, and Ellis in 1841 and then Tiffany & Company in 1853, by which time he had branched out into manufacturing jewelry. His name is now a byword for elegance. It became popularly known in the English-speaking world on the publication in 1958 of Truman Capote's novel *Breakfast at Tiffany's*, about a light-hearted but amoral New York playgirl, Holly Golightly. Tiffany's does not usually serve breakfasts, although it did in 1987 to mark the publication of a book on the company's history by Jacqueline Kennedy Onassis.

Tiger *(beer)*

The well-known Asian lager beer is brewed in Singapore by Asia Pacific Breweries, founded in 1931. It takes its name from the fierce and proud animal that is a native of the forests of Asia and that gave the term "tiger economy" for the dynamic economy of Singapore and other small East Asian countries. The beer's slogan, "Time for a Tiger," even gave the title of a 1954 novel by Anthony Burgess.

Tilley *(lamps)*

The name of the portable kerosene lamp, in which air pressure is used to supply the burner with fuel, appears to originate with John Tilley, the British inventor of a hydropneumatic blowpipe in 1813. The firm of W.H. Tilley was later set up in London, producing gas pressure lamps. In World War I, Frederick Tilley started to use kerosene as a lamp fuel in pressurized containers, and the Tilley Lamp Co. Ltd. was set up in Hendon, London, soon after the war. The company subsequently entered the name in the *Trade Marks Journal* of March 17, 1948 for: "Lighting and heating lamps employing liquid fuel." *See also* **Coleman**.

Timberland *(fashionwear)*

In 1952, aiming to set up his own company, Nathan Swartz bough a half interest in The Abington Shoe Company, Massachusetts. Three years later he bought the remaining interest and, together with his sons, set out to make boots and shoes suitable for rugged outdoor wear. In 1973, the Timberland name was created by a local advertising firm headed by a Swartz family neighbor for the waterproof boot that Swartz had developed, and in due course was adopted for the company itself. Casual boots and shoes were added at the end of the decade, and when Nathan's son Sidney took over in the 1980s, clothing and women's footwear were introduced. At the turn of the 21st century, based in Stratham, New Hampshire, the business was in the hands of Jeffrey Swartz, Nathan's grandson.

Times Furnishing *(furniture)*

The British firm was founded at a time when *The Times* newspaper was selling an encyclopedia in instalments. The name "Times" was thus adopted on fairly arbitrary grounds, the newspaper itself being long established and of high repute. Some years later, an Indian maharajah wote to *The Times* to say how much he admired the newspaper and asking if he could have a list of their furniture. His innocent act created a potentially tricky legal situation. Fortunately for the Jacobs brothers, who had started the furniture business, they had been using the name "Times" for 25 years, the statutory period of recognition, so were under no obligation to change it. Instead, they merely agreed to modify it to The Times Furnishing Co. Their firm was taken over by **Great Universal Stores** in 1968.

Time Warner *(publishers)*

Time Inc. was founded in 1922 by Yale University graduates Henry R. Luce (1898-1967) and Briton Hadden (1898-1929), and the first issue of *Time*, the world's first weekly news magazine, appeared on March 3, 1923. Luce was born in Tengchow, China, the son of a missionary, while Hadden came from Brooklyn, New York, a stockbroker's son. The men first met at the Hotchkiss School, and after attending Yale together were officers in the US Army Artillery. At boot camp they had discussed the possibility of starting a new kind of publication. They wrote prospectuses for potential backers and planned to call their magazine *Time* for its up-to-date, timely coverage of the week's events. Once the magazine was established the business grew to include other periodicals: *Fortune* (1930), *Life* (1936), *Sports Illustrated* (1954), *Money* (1972), *People* (1974), and *Discover* (1980). Time-Life Books was launched in 1960. In 1989 Time Inc. merged with Warner Communications Inc., a descendant of the **Warner Brothers**, to form Time Warner Inc., which in 2000 was in turn acquired by **AOL**.

Timex *(watches)*

The American company originated as the United States Time Corporation. Soon after World War II, however, the company's president, Joakim Lehmkuhl, decided the business needed a new basic product name which might eventually replace the corporate name. After considering many possible names he chose "Timex" as it was product-related and "had a scientific overtone."

Timotei *(shampoo)*

The origins of the shampoo lie in a Finnish deodorant named after the timothy grass, itself named for Timothy Hanson, the American farmer who introduced it to Carolina from New York around 1720. Neill O'Touria, a local **Unilever** manager in Finland, saw the marketing potential of a mild and natural brand and transferred the formula to shampoo. In 1975 he launched it in Sweden, where it was an immediate success. A year later, Unilever took it back to Finland and from there to the rest of Europe.

Timothy White *(houseware stores)*

The formerly familiar British name is that of Timothy White (1825-1908), who in the mid-1840s left his home town of Rickmansworth, Hertfordshire, and went to Portsmouth to seek his commercial fortune. In 1848 he opened an oil and drysaltery business in Commercial Road, Portsmouth, to meet the demands of a growing community round the naval dockyard. He gradually extended his range of goods to include both drugs and basic household essentials, and a few years later opened a warehouse in Chandos Street, at the same time setting up another retail shop in Palmerston Road, Southsea. Further branches in the south of England followed. By 1928 the company had about 100 stores, and in 1935 Timothy White gained control of the Taylor Drug Company (founded in 1888, and named for Miss Taylor, the fiancée of its founder, W.B. Mason), so that it for many years it was known as Timothy White & Taylor. In 1971 Timothy White was acquired by **Boots**, and although the stores kept their original name for several years, they had all been renamed as Boots stores by the mid-1980s.

Timpson *(footwear)*

The British firm takes its name from William Timpson (1849-1929), born in Rothwell, Northamptonshire, the youngest of six children of a silkweaver. He had little formal education, and by the age of eight was making leather bootlaces. At the age of ten or 11 he went by train to Manchester, where his elder brother Charles lived, and started delivering boots for him. He then returned to Rothwell to learn the art of shoemaking before again going to Manchester to form a partnership with his brother-in-law, Walter Joyce. He was still only 16. Four years later he opened his own shop in Oldham Street, Manchester, but poor health and increasing deafness forced him into virtual retirement at the early age of 31. The firm he had founded continued to grow, however, and became a public company in 1926. Timpson was taken over by United Drapery Stores in the 1960s, but family control was regained in 1983 by John Timpson, the founder's great-grandson, who sold off the shoeshops to **Olivers** and bought out the repair business, which he built up with the help of his son, James.

Tinkertoy *(toys)*

The child's construction toy of fitting parts derives its name from "tinker" (both "mender of metal utensils" and "adjust amateurishly") and "toy." It was entered by its original manufacturer, Charles H. Pajeau of Chicago, Illinois, in the US Patent Office *Official Gazette*

of February 3, 1914, with a claim of use since June 12, 1913. The full name and address are spelled out in a subsequent registration in the *Trade Marks Journal* of December 22, 1915: "Charles Hamilton Pajeau, McCormick Building, 332, South Michigan Avenue, Chicago, County of Cook, State of Illinois, United States of America."

Tintometer *(colorimeter)*

The apparatus for determining an exact shade of color was named (from "tint" and "-ometer") in the late 19th century by the English brewer James W. Lovibond (1833-1918). The name was entered by The Tintometer, Ltd. (*sic*, no "Co."), in the *Trade Marks Journal* of August 17, 1966.

Tio Pepe *(sherry)*

The name is Spanish for "Uncle Joe." The fino brand of sherry dates from 1849, when it was named after José de la Pena, the uncle of Manuel María González Angel, who shipped his first sherry from Spain to England in 1835, the year that **Gonzalez Byass** regards as that of its founding. The name was entered in the *Trade Marks Journal* of September 15, 1886.

Tipp-Ex *(correction fluid)*

The type of correction fluid, enabling a writer or typist to erase errors by "whiting out" the text, derives its name from German *tippen*, "to type," and Latin *ex*, "out." The product was invented in 1959 by Wolfgang Dabisch, of Eltville am Rhein, near Wiesbaden, and originally took the form of a white paper strip, to be inserted between the type and the text. One then typed the same characters on the strip as those to be erased under it, so that they were literally "typed out." (English speakers ignorant of German often assume that the name refers to the tip of the small brush with which the fluid is applied.) The name was entered in the *Warenzeichenblatt: Eingetragene Zeichen* ("Trade Marks Journal: Registered Marks") of August 14, 1962, and in the *Trade Marks Journal* of August 23, 1972 for: "Erasers (stationery); inks, paper, foil and fluids, all for correcting errors in handwriting and typing."

Tiptree *see* **Wilkin's**

Tissot *(watches)*

The Swiss name is that of Charles-Félicien

Tissot (1804-1873) and his son and partner Charles-Émile Tissot (1830-1910). Charles-Émile began his apprenticeship with a watchmaker when he was only 12. In 1848 he left for the United States to study the commercial scene in general and watchmaking in particular, staying to attend the Exhibition of Industry and Arts in New York in 1853. That year he returned to Switzerland and reported favorably to his father on the American commercial outlook, and on the boom that seemed likely to occur before the end of the century. Father and son thus together founded the Charles-Félicien Tissot et Fils watch factory at Le Locle, near La Chaux de Fonds not far from the French border. On the death of Tissot *père* the name of the firm was changed to Charles Tissot-Favre and subsequently simply Charles Tissot.

Tizer *(sparkling soft drink)*

Fred Pickup began his business at New Moston, Manchester, England, in 1907, when he sold ginger beer, originally in stone flasks but later in glass bottles. In 1920 he produced a distinctive red fizzy drink which he called "Pickup Appetizer." It was renamed "Tizer" in 1924, and the company grew steadily, so that from the 1930s it was *the* sparkling drink for young Britons. The name was entered in the *Trade Marks Journal* of October 22, 1924.

TNT *(transport)*

The international transport company owes its origin to Peter Abeles (1924-1999), born in Vienna into a Hungarian Jewish family and educated in Budapest. His early ventures were in the Hungarian scrap industry. In 1947 he left Hungary for Switzerland, but two years later emigrated to Australia. There he clubbed together with a fellow Hungarian to buy two trucks and in 1950 founded Alltrans. It went well, but it was the merger with Thomas Nationwide Transport to create TNT that gave Abeles the chance to operate internationally, and in the 1980s he built up TNT to become the largest transport company in the world.

Toastmaster *(toasters)*

In 1920 the Waters-Genter Company, of Minneapolis, began marketing a toaster called the "Strite Automatic," naming it after Charles Strite, inventor of the "pop-up" toaster. Around four years later, the company's adver-

tising agent, the Mitchell Advertising Agency, coined the name "Toastmaster" for the toaster, and this was registered in 1925. It was a doubly effective name, since the toaster not only "mastered the toast" but also presided at a meal, like a toastmaster at a banquet. Max McGraw purchased the capital stock of Waters-Genter in 1925 and four years later the business and its trademark were acquired by the McGraw Electric Company (later McGraw-Edison). The name has since been extended to other electrical products.

Tobler *(chocolate)*

The name is that of Johann Jakob Tobler (1830-1905), born in Appenzell, Switzerland, the son of a farmer. He became an apprentice confectioner at the age of 14, and for the next 17 years worked as a journeyman in France and Germany, at the same time changing his German name of Johann to French Jean. On returning to Switzerland in 1865 he originally settled in Vevey, where Henri **Nestlé** started his firm. In 1868 he opened a *confiserie* in the Länggasse district of Berne, where he sold mainly specialties that he had made himself, using chocolate coatings supplied by other manufacturers. Soon he was selling so much chocolate that he was obliged to make that, too. Eventually, in 1899, he and his sons founded the Fabrique de Chocolat de Berne, Tobler & Cie. The firm, famed for its **Toblerone** bars, merged with **Suchard** in 1970 to form Jacob Suchard Tobler.

Toblerone *(chocolate bars)*

The chocolate bars now so known were first made by **Tobler** in 1899. This explains the main part of the name but not its modification, which is based on Italian *torrone*, a kind of nougat. The name was devised in 1908 by the firm's production manager, Emil Baumann, and was patented the following year. The bar's distinctive triangular shape, together with its practical serrations, making it easy to break or bite off each portion, are intended to suggest the peaks of Swiss mountains.

Tobralco *(cotton fabric)*

The name derives acronymically from that of the manufacturers, **Tootal** Broadhurst Lee Co. Ltd., who entered it in the *Trade Marks Journal* of September 26, 1917 for: "Textile fabrics (not included in other Classes) made from substances covered by Class 50, but not including Incandescent Gas Mantles and not including any goods of a like kind."

Todd-AO *(film projection process)*

The wide-screen film projection process took its name from the US stage and film producer Mike Todd *(c.1907-1958)*, born Avrom Hirsch Goldbogen in Minneapolis, Minnesota, the son of an Orthodox Jewish rabbi. In 1918 Todd moved with his family to Chicago, where he launched himself into a series of occupations. In 1928 he established a Los Angeles company that soundproofed Hollywood stages for the new "talkies." In the 1930s Todd's attention turned to show business, producing a number of stage plays. Not surprisingly, his interest then passed to the movie theater, and in the early 1950s he became involved in the development of the three-camera **Cinerama** film process. He went on to work with scientists at the American Optical Company on a system that would produce the same wide-screen effect with a single camera. The result, developed by Dr. Brian O'Brien, was Todd-AO, the initials being those of "American Optical." Todd sold his interest in the Todd-AO process as its first film, *Oklahoma!*, was released in 1955. The name was entered in the US Patent Office *Official Gazette* of November 29, 1955, with a note of: "Use since August 1953 on motion picture camera equipment."

Tofranil *(antidepressant)*

The proprietary name for the drug imipramine appears to be arbitrary in origin. It was entered by J.E. Geigy *(see* **Ciba-Geigy***)* of Basle, Switzerland, in the *Trade Marks Journal* of June 4, 1958, and by the Geigy Chemical Corporation, of Ardsley, New York, in the US Patent Office *Official Gazette* of September 16, 1958.

Toidey *(toilet-training device)*

The device is is a form of seat clipped or strapped on to an ordinary lavatory seat in order to train young children to use the toilet. Its name, perhaps a combination of "toilet" and "tidy," was entered (as "Little Toidey") in the US Patent Office *Official Gazette* of December 9, 1924 for: "Water-Closet Seats for Infants, Attachable to Ordinary Water-Closet Seats,"

and (as "Toidey") by Gertrude A. Muller of The Toidey Company in the *Gazette* of March 6, 1956.

Tolly Cobbold *(beer)*

The British brewery name is that of two men. Thomas Cobbold (1680-1752) built a brewery in Harwich, Essex, in 1723. Because the water was so brackish, however, the business was moved to Ipswich, Suffolk, in 1746, where in 1896 the handsome Cliff Brewery was built on Cliff Quay, by the Orwell River. By the 19th century the interests of the Cobbold family, who still ran the brewery, had extended into banking, and members of the family were partners of several local banks. One of them was that of Bacon, Cobbold & Tollemache (now long absorbed into **Lloyds** bank). The Tollemaches became brewers in 1888 when two brothers of the name bought a brewery in Ipswich, trading separately from the Cobbolds. The concept of a merger between the two companies was increasingly discussed from the 1930s, and it eventually took place in 1957, with the combined production taking place at the Cliff Brewery. A pet form of the surname Tollemache was adopted for the joint business of Tolly Cobbold, with the formal company name, however, registered as Tollemache & Cobbold Breweries Ltd. The Cliff Brewery was closed in 1989 as it was operating uneconomically, but was saved by a management buyout in 1990, when the Cobbold name was revived.

Tom Parker *(dairies)*

The Hampshire, England, company, which provides milk for a wide region of southern England, was founded in 1928 by Thomas Parker (1896-1982), born into a farming family at Bentworth, near Alton, Hampshire. He helped his father on the farm as a boy, and longed to leave school to take up farming full-time. In 1919 his family moved to Fareham, and it was there that Parker took over half his father's rented farm of 500 acres. In 1928 he started his dairy business, delivering milk daily to homes in Fareham. His enterprise thrived, and eventually covered the neighboring counties of West Sussex and Surrey, as well as the large county of Hampshire itself. Later in his life, Tom Parker was introduced to Prince Charles, who asked him what he did. "I'm the local milkman," said Tom.

Tom Smith *(Christmas crackers)*

Tom Smith was originally a London, England, candymaker. In 1840, on holiday in Paris, he was struck by the way in which the French sold sugared almonds, wrapping them in colored paper with twists at the end. On returning to London, Smith arranged to import quantities of sugared almonds from France and wrap them in the French way, at the same time enclosing mottoes. The confection sold well, but the mottoes were not very popular, so Smith substituted small toys. He noticed that the sweets sold particularly well at Christmas, and to give the packets an added sparkle he decided to include a cracker "snap" in each wrapping. After several experiments, Smith created a cracker strip that gave a good sharp snap when two people pulled it. His Christmas "crackers" sold well, and in increasing quantities, so that today Tom Smith & Co. Ltd. makes over 50 million crackers annually at its factory in Norwich, with both mottoes and little toys.

Tommy Hilfiger *(fashionwear)*

US designer Tommy Hilfiger (b.1952) began his career in 1969 as a vendor of hippie fashions. In 1985 he launched his self-named brand of preppy gear and the following year, still relatively unknown, ran a $3 million ad campaign which declared: "The 4 Great American Designers for Men Are: R— L—, P— E—, C— K—, T— H—" (meaning **Ralph Lauren**, Perry Ellis, **Calvin Klein** and, of course, himself). By the end of the decade, Hilfiger's sales were at $25 million a year. His company does not make anything itself but commissions its products through licensing agreements with other companies.

Toni *(home perm)*

"Which twin has the Toni?" The famous slogan was created in 1946 by Irving Harris, brother of Richard N. Harris (known as "Wishbone" Harris from his fondness for this part of a chicken), for whom the name was invented by a friend. In the 1930s Harris ran a beauty business called Noma Inc. in Saint Paul, Minnesota. (Its name came from one of the firm's products, chemically activated hair-curling pads that needed *no ma*chines to generate heat for setting the curls.) Harris was trying to de-

velop a method by which women could have a good, cheap permanent wave at home instead of having to sit for hours in a beauty salon. His first entry into this market, called "Rol-Wav," was a failure because it was too cheap. He therefore worked on a better-class product at a higher price. This was "Toni." Harris's friend allegedly chose the name because Harris himself was a graduate of Yale, a "tony" university, meaning one with "tone" or "class." (The word is less familiar to the British, and even Harris said he had never heard of it.) The name was first used in 1944, and its subsequent popular (though apparently unwarranted) association with the female name Toni was in the event no bad thing.

Toni & Guy *(hair stylists)*

Brothers Toni and Guy Mascolo set up their first hairdressing salon in Clapham, London, England, in 1963. The business expanded rapidly when the the brothers created a franchise system to satisfy staff who wanted their own salons, and by 2001 there were 143 franchises in the UK and Ireland, and more than 100 in the USA and elsewhere. The company markets haircare products under the name TiGi.

Tonka *(toys)*

In 1947, the Mound Metalcraft Company, a business making garden tools in a small schoolhouse basement near Lake Minnetonka in Mound, Minnesota, produced its first toy trucks. They went down well with young purchasers and their families, and by the end of the year the firm had turned out 37,000 metal trucks. It later expanded its output to include other vehicles and toy play sets, and adopted the name of its original trucks, taken from Lake Minnetonka, whose own name is Siouan for "big water." In 1991, Tonka Corp. was taken over by **Hasbro**.

Tootal *(menswear)*

The name of the British firm derives from Edward Tootal (1799-1873), but he was almost certainly not its founder. This was a man named Robert Gardner (*c.*1780-1866), born in Sunderland, near Lancaster, who set up in Manchester in 1799 as a textile merchant. Tootal was born near Wakefield, Yorkshire, and appears to have become a partner in Gardner's business in 1842. What happened to Gardner after that is not clear, and the next record of the firm's name is as Atkinson, Tootal & Co. In 1859 it became Tootal, Broadhurst and Lee, the latter names being those of Tootal's nephew, Henry Tootal Broadhurst (1822-1896), and Henry Lee (1817-1904), whose eldest son, Harold Lee (1852-1936), became chairman in 1894. Tootal retired in 1856, becoming director of the London and North-Eastern Railway Company, having apparently pursued his railroad interests when still an active partner in the textile firm. Today Tootal Group plc remain with their headquarters in Manchester. *See also* (1) **Tarantulle**; (2) **Tebilized**; (3) **Tebralco**.

Tootsie Roll *(sweet, or candy bar)*

The name, presumably from "tootsie" as a nickname for a girl or woman (or sweetheart), was entered by The Sweets Company of America, Inc., of New York, in the US Patent Office *Official Gazette* of April 7, 1925, with a claim of use since September 1908.

Top-siders *(casual shoes)*

The name of the shoe presumably refers both to its literal top side of canvas, as distinct from its rubber sole, and to its implicit "classiness." Since the shoes were worn on board sailboats, there was also an allusion to the topside that is the upper deck of a ship. The name was entered in the US Patent Office *Official Gazette* of April 13, 1937: "For boots and shoes made of a combination of rubber or rubber substitute in combination with either fabric or leather or both."

Tornegus *(cheese)*

The English cheese was first made in 1989 by James Aldridge (1939-2001), a former garage mechanic and scaffolder, from an unpasteurized Somerset Caerphilly. He named his creation from "tor", a local Somerset word for a hill, and "negus," signifying a flavored wine, although his cheese was not actually produced in the West Country but in his model dairy, Eastside Cheese, at Oxted, Surrey, near London. The enterprise met with disaster in 1998, however, when a single case of *E. coli* poisoning was found to be have been caused by a batch of Caerphilly cheese despatched to Aldridge. All seven tons were seized for inspection by the Department of Health and then

destroyed. Aldridge's business was in ruins, and he never revived his masterpiece.

Torras *(chocolate)*

Spain's largest chocolate producers, based in Gerona, were founded in 1890 by Señora Dolores Torras, who was soon making around 220 lbs. of chocolate a day. In 1924 the company was bought by the Costa family, and later passed to the Sans family. Torras is best known for its *chocolate a la piedra*, or stone-ground solid-block drinking chocolate.

Toshiba *(electrical and electronic goods)*

The Japanese company was incorporated in 1939 as the Tokyo Shibaura Electric Company in the merger of Shibaura Engineering Works, founded in 1875 to produce telegraphic equipment and taking its name from what is now the region of Tokyo where the present company is based, and the Tokyo Electric Company, founded in 1890 to make electric light bulbs. The name Toshiba, adopted in 1978, is thus an acronym of "*To*kyo *Shiba*ura."

Total *(petroleum)*

The French petroleum company was founded in 1924 on the initiative of the French government to exploit oil fields in the Middle East. It was originally known as the Compagnie Française des Pétroles (CFP) ("French Petroleum Company"), but adopted the name "Total" for its major products in 1954, selecting a name that denoted global scope and full commitment, as well as a word that is identical in many languages. In 1985 it changed the company name to TOTAL CFP and in 1991 to TOTAL. In 1998 it took over **Petrofina** to become TOTALFINA and then **Elf Aquitaine** to become TotalFina Elf.

Touch-Tone *(push-button telephone)*

Telephones with push buttons rather than a dial are now the norm, but this was not the case when the name was entered by **AT&T** in the US Patent Office *Official Gazette* of June 19, 1962. When touched (pushed), the buttons produce tones that correspond to the numbers.

Tower Records *(superstores)*

North America's first music superstore chain was founded in the 1950s by Russ Solomon, who started by selling Glen Miller and Elvis Presley hits in his father's Tower Drugstore in

Sacramento, California. The first large store opened in San Francisco in 1968, but it was only in the 1980s that Tower spread across the United States. The business grew to be one of the biggest retailers of music, books (especially "zines") and street fashionwear, living up to its lofty name.

Townsend Thoresen (ferries)

The British name was tragically highlighted in 1987 as a result of the disaster in which the Townsend Thoresen car ferry *Herald of Free Enterprise* capsized off Zeebrugge, Belgium, with the loss of 189 lives. The first half of the name is that of Captain Stuart Townsend (1888-1968), who in 1928 started the first ferry service across the English Channel designed specifically for motorists, using a chartered coaster adapted to take 15 cars and just 12 passengers. His venture operated on a fairly small scale until the 1950s, and he lost control of the business when it became a public company in 1956. The operation still continued modestly, so that even in 1965 Townsend Ferries, as it then was, ran only a single ship between Dover, England, and Calais, France. The second half of the name derives from the Norwegian firm of Thoresen Car Ferries, which had started a ferry service between Southampton, England, and Le Havre and Cherbourg, France, in 1964, and which was acquired by Townsends in 1969. The company now operates as **P&O** Continental Ferries.

Toyota (automobiles)

The name goes back to the Japanese inventor Sakichi Toyoda (1894-1952), who in 1929 sold the patent for an automatic loom he had designed to a British company of weaving machine manufacturers in Oldham, Lancashire. They paid him £10,000, and he promptly turned it over to his son, Kiichiro Toyoda, who was building an automobile. This was the embryo of the Toyota Motor Corporation, formed in 1933 as a division of the Toyoda Automatic Loom Works, now a subsidiary. The Toyota Motor Company was actually founded in 1937, a year after the prototype car had been created. The Toyoda family were superstitious. Spelled "Toyoda," their name needed ten strokes of the Japanese pen, but as "Toyota" it needed only eight, and eight is a lucky number for the Japanese. They therefore adopted the altered spelling. Toyota, based in Toyota City, Japan, now has assembly plants and distributors in most major countries of the world.

Toys "R" Us (toy chain)

The chain and its quirky name (the "R" is actually reversed) were the brainchild of Charles Lazarus (b.1923), born in Washington, DC. In 1948 he opened a baby furniture store in Washington, then extended his stock to include first toys for babies then toys for older children. In 1957 he opened Washington's first toy supermarket. New outlets were added in other cities, so that by the 1990s there were 700 Toys "R" Us stores in the USA and the chain was the country's largest toy retailer. Kids "R" Us clothing stores came in 1983, and Babies "R" Us, stocking everything for infants, in 1996.

Trabant (automobiles)

The popular but small and smelly East German car was first produced in Zwickau in 1959, shortly after the Soviet Union launched Sputnik, the first artificial satellite. "Trabant" is essentially the equivalent German name, meaning "satellite," "bodyguard" (and coincidentally "kiddie"). From 1959 through 1990, 150,000 "Trabbis" a year were built, but the last left the factory in 1991 when the newly reunified Germany introduced tax laws banning cars that polluted the atmosphere.

Transformers (toys)

The toys, originally manufactured as "Diakrons" by the Takara Toys Corp., Japan, are model robots that can be transformed into other kinds of toys (such as a motor vehicle or gun) by manipulating their component pieces. The name was entered by **Hasbro** in the US Patent Office *Official Gazette* of July 10, 1984, with a note of first use on October 4, 1982, and in the *Trade Marks Journal* of November 9, 1988, the latter for: "Toys, robots, all being changeable in form, but none utilising computer programs and/or transformers."

Transtainer (mobile crane)

The mobile gantry crane derives its name from "trans-" ("across") and "container." The name was entered by the Pacific Coast Engineering Co., of Alameda, California, in the US Patent Office *Official Gazette* of July 21, 1964, with a note of first use on June 15, 1960.

Transverter *(electric transformer and converter)*

The device for converting alternating current (AC) into high-voltage direct current (DC) , and vice versa, takes its name from a blend of "transformer" and "converter." It was entered in the US Patent Office *Official Gazette* of May 16, 1916.

Transworld *see* **Corgi**

Traquair *(beer)*

Beer from the castle in the village of Traquair, south of Edinburgh, Scotland, is first mentioned in 1566. The brewery was revived in 1965 by the 20th Laird ("Lord") of Traquair, Peter Maxwell Stuart, and was subsequently managed by his daughter, Lady Catherine.

Travellers Fare *(railroad caterers)*

The name was adopted in 1973 for the catering outlets of **British Railways** (BR). They were actually owned by British Transport Hotels, but became a free-standing division of that body in 1982. In 1988, when the group had 270 catering units at 140 stations, many operating under brand names such as "Casey Jones" (after the railroad folk hero) and (punningly) "Upper Crust," it was sold to BR, who retained the freehold of the station sites. In 1992 BR in turn sold it to the Compass Group, itself formed in 1987 as a buy-out of the contract catering arm of **Grand Metropolitan**. The name obviously puns on "fare" in the sense of both "payment for travel on public transport" and "range of food."

Travolator *(moving sidewalk)*

The moving sidewalk, found mainly at railroad stations, airports, shopping malls, and the like, was developed by **Otis** in the 1950s, taking its name from a blend of "travel" and "escalator." The name was entered (as "Trav-o-lator") in the *Trade Marks Journal* of February 26, 1958 and the US Patent Office *Official Gazette* of May 19, 1959, the latter with a note of first use on July 28, 1955.

Traxcavator *(excavator)*

The mechanical excavator moves on endless steel bands of tracks. Hence its name, a triple blend of "tracks," "tractor," and "excavator," entered in the US Patent Office *Official Gazette* of April 30, 1940: "For excavating, grading and loading machinery—namely high shovels, tractor shovels, tractor loaders, bull-dozers, graders, and the like," with a claim of use since January 22, 1940. The name was subsequently entered by the **Caterpillar** Tractor Co., of San Leandro, California, in the *Trade Marks Journal* of February 22, 1956.

Trebor *(candy)*

The British company dates from 1907, when Robert Robertson got together with three other young men to start a venture making boiled sweets to sell to retailers in London's East End. The premises they leased were a row of small terraced houses named Trebor Villas in Forest Gate, London. Although the rent was high, they felt the name was propitious, for "Trebor" spelled "Robert" backwards, and this was doubly appropriate for Robert Robertson. At first the firm was called Robertson and Woodcock, but in 1921 adopted its brand name. The company, now based in Woodford Green, Essex, has preserved the original nameplate saying "Trebor Villas," although the houses themselves no longer exist. Their own name presumably reversed that of their builder or owner. The name was entered in the *Trade Marks Journal* of January 22, 1919.

Trevira *(polyester fiber)*

The name of the artificial fiber or fabric was entered by its German manufacturers, Farbwerke **Hoechst**, in the US Patent Office *Official Gazette* of November 24, 1959: "For table linen and bed linen; net, lace, woven and mesh fabrics; textile ribbons; textile trimmings; carpets and rugs; mats; curtains; flags; and felt." A subsequent registration followed in the *Trade Marks Journal* of December 21, 1960. The name itself looks meaningful but appears to be arbitrary.

Trex *(vegetable cooking fat)*

The cooking fat was introduced by Joseph **Bibby** during the 1930s. The name itself is of disputed origin, but may be a shortening of a proposed longer name. The name was entered in the *Trade Marks Journal* of May 18, 1938.

Tri-Ang *(toys)*

The British toys owe their name to Lines Brothers Ltd, a business set up in 1919 by Walter Lines (1882-1972) and his brothers W.J. and A.E. Lines, who began their career in their father's toy company, G. & J. Lines Ltd, of which Walter became managing director in 1908. The brothers broke away from the company after service in World War I, partly because their father thought that the rocking horses he made were the end of the toy business and would not increase their salaries. Walter Lines built the company up until in the 1960s it had more than a third of the toy trade in Britain. The business went bankrupt in 1971, however, and was split up and sold off by the receivers. "Tri-Ang" derived from "triangle," and represented the three brothers. The name was entered in the *Trade Marks Journal* of May 13, 1931, and evolved from their first trademark, "Triangtois," registered in 1924.

Tricel *(artificial fiber)*

The textile fiber takes its name from the *cell*-ulose *tri*acetate from which it is made. The name was entered by the material's manufacturers, British **Celanese** Ltd., in the *Trade Marks Journal* of December 22, 1954 for: "Raw or partly prepared artificial fibrous textile materials not being yarns or threads," and the US Patent Office *Official Gazette* of November 20, 1956: "For staple fibres made wholly or partially of cellulose derivatives."

Tricker *(footwear)*

The Northampton, England, company of R.E. Tricker Ltd.takes its name from the maiden name of the wife of the firm's founder, Joseph Barltrop. Both he and Miss Tricker's father were shoemakers, and they decided to start up their business when Barltrop married in 1829. He chose her name rather than his own because he felt that "Barltrop" was rather awkward for trading purposes. The firm began its life in Walthamstow, London, and moved to Northampton only in the late 19th century. The company continues in the hands of the Barltrop family today.

Tricotine *(fabric)*

The worsted fabric with a double twill derives its name from "tricot" (in the sense "knitted fabric," from French *tricoter*, "to knit") and the commercial suffix "-ine." It was entered in the US Patent Office *Official Gazette* of October 27, 1914 for: "Woolen, Worsted, Silk, Mohair and Cotton Piece Goods and Piece Goods Made of a Combination of Two or More of Those Fibers."

Tricouni *(climbing-boot nail)*

The former name of the climbing-boot nail with a serrated edge apparently derived from a combination of "tri-," "co-," and "uni-," as if a "three-in-one" device. The nail was invented in around 1914 by a Swiss climber, F. Genecand, and the name was entered by Tricouni, S.A., of Geneva, Switzerland, in the *Trade Marks Journal* of October 3, 1934.

Tridione *(analgesic)*

The proprietary name of the drug trimethadone (troxidone) derives from "tri-" and the suffix "-dione" (used to indicate the presence of two carbonyl groups, as also in "menadione"). It was entered in the US Patent Office *Official Gazette* of February 24, 1948: "For anticonvulsant intended for use in treatment of the petit mal triad and other convulsive disorders," and by **Abbott** Laboratories, of North Chicago, in the *Trade Marks Journal* of February 25, 1948 for: "Therapeutic compounds being alkyl derivatives of diketo oxazolidine."

Trilby *(footwear)*

The former proprietary name derives from the heroine of George du Maurier's novel *Trilby* (1894), whose feet were much admired. ("They were astonishingly beautiful feet, such as one only sees in pictures and statues.") It was entered for "boots, shoes and lasts" by the manufacturers, S. Weil & Co. of New York, in the US Patent Office *Official Gazette* of April 16, 1895. "Trilby" later became associated with a type of men's soft hat, though not as a proprietary name.

Trilene *(analgesic)*

The proprietary name for a medicinal grade of trichloroethylene, used as an analgesic and light anesthetic, is a shortening of the chemical name. It was entered by **ICI** in the *Trade Marks Journal* of February 13, 1935.

Trimphone *(telephone)*

The Trimphone, introduced in the 1960s, was a lightweight, narrow-fronted telephone set with a "warbler" in place of a bell. The name alludes to the appearance of the phone rather than its function or its distinctive ringing tone, and was entered by the British Post Office in the *Trade Marks Journal* of September 26, 1973.

Trinitron *(television)*

The award-winning color television was launched by **Sony** in 1967. Its invention was a breakthrough that circumvented US patents by firing the three electronic beams needed to produce a color picture through a single gun, and then focusing them through one lens. Its name alluded to this innovative process, from "trini-" (three) and "electron."

Triplex *(safety glass)*

The name was first used in Paris, France, in 1909 for a nonshattering glass constructed of three layers, i.e., as a "sandwich" of glass containing celluloid. The nonsplintering quality of the glass was discovered by accident six years earlier, when a French chemist, Édouard Bénédictus, dropped a glass flask that had contined a solution of nitrocellulose and found that it did not break. The name itself, entered in the *Trade Marks Journal* of November 28, 1923 (with use claimed from August 2, 1912), represents Latin *triplex*, "triple," "threefold," while the company's trademark "XXX" is a "triple X."

Triscuit *(crackers)*

The name arose in the United States in the early 20th century for a make of savory cracker. The name puns on "biscuit" (literally "twice cooked") as if denoting a cracker that had been baked three times. It was entered by The Natural Food Company in the US Patent Office *Official Gazette* of March 27, 1906 and later by the **Shredded Wheat** Company in the *Trade Marks Journal* of March 23, 1932.

Triumph *(automobiles and motorcycles)*

The Triumph Cycle Company was founded in Coventry, Warwickshire, England, in 1897 by an immigrant German, Siegfried Bettmann (1863-1951), who had teamed up with a fellow German settler, Mauritz Schulte, to make bicycles. Bettmann had originally set himself up in business under the style of S. Bettmann & Co., but did not formally register his company. He then realized that sales would improve with a more obviously British trademark, and so chose the name "Triumph." The firm's motorcyles brought it greater fame from 1902, but it did not progress to the production of cars until 1923. In 1939, after increasing financial difficulties, the business went into receivership, but the Triumph name was kept alive in World War II and after the war was taken over by the **Standard** Motor Company to form the Triumph Motor Company (1945) Ltd. In 1961 Triumph was acquired by Leyland Motors (*see* **BL**) but the famous marque was abandoned in 1983. The name was bought by millionaire John Bloor, however, who had made his fortune from house building, and in 1990 production of the motorcycle resumed at a new factory built by him in Hinckley, Leicestershire. (The familiar Triumph logo, with the foot of the "R" extended below to curl up and back as the bar of the "H," was subtly amended in the revived name.) *See also* **Norton**.

Triumph *(foundation garments)*

The company that in 1953 came to be Triumph International, as Europe's largest maker of foundation garments, was founded in 1886 by Johann Gottfried Spiesshofer, a German corset-maker, and Michael Braun, a merchant, in a small workshop at Heubach, near Schwäbisch-Gmünd. Business gradually built up, and Spiesshofer was joined by his son, Fritz, and by Braun's two sons, Kurt and Herbert. By 1939 there were 20 plants aside from the one in Heubach producing brassières, corselets, and girdles. The firm had already registered the name "Triumph" in 1902, partly as a general sign of superiority, but also partly to denote that the corset, a once unmentionable garment, could now be called by name.

Trivial Pursuit *(board game)*

The commercially packaged quiz game was created in 1979 when two Canadians, photo editor Chris Haney and sportswriter Scott Abbott, bought their eighth game of **Scrabble**, having worked through seven previous sets, and began to wonder how many other people had bought multiple copies of the game. The realization of a potential market led them to devise their own game, and as their job was reporting news it was natural for them to be interested in current affairs, and to present this from the time-honoured angles of "who, what, when, where, and why." They originally planned to call the game "Trivia Pursuit," but Haney's wife jokingly called it "Trivial Pursuit" and this was the name adopted. Sales were initially discouraging, but a breakthrough came when the game was taken up by the American company

Selchow and Righter, who gave it a major pro-
motion at the 1983 New York Toy Fair. The
name was entered in the Ottawa *Trade Marks
Journal* of March 3, 1982, the US Patent Office
Official Gazette of February 8, 1983, and the
Trade Marks Journal of August 15, 1984.

Trojan *(condom)*

The name presumably alludes to the people
of ancient Troy, popularly regarded as heroic
and romantic (although they lost the Trojan
War). It was first registered as a proprietary
term in the USA on April 26, 1927, and was entered in the US Patent Office *Official Gazette*
of April 17, 1951: "For Prophylactic Membra-
neous Articles for the Prevention of Contagious
Diseases."

Tromexan *(anticoagulant)*

The anticoagulant drug, a white crystalline
powder, is said to be so called from an Egyptian name for dicoumarol, the compound from
which it is derived. The name was entered in
the *Trade Marks Journal* of June 22, 1949 and
the US Patent Office *Official Gazette* of August
14, 1951.

Tropicana *(chilled fruit juices)*

The chilled fruit-juice packs were the brainchild of Anthony T. Rossi (1900-1993), born in
Messina, Italy, as one of eight children. His
first job as a teenager was as a trolley conductor. He then served three years in the military,
after which he decided to head for America. At
age 21, knowing no English, Rossi departed
from Messina with two suitcases and $30 and
sailed alone from Naples to New York. There
he worked at a relative's machine shop, and was
soon earning enough to buy a used car. Meanwhile, as a side business, he was also a wholesaler of fresh eggs to grocers and bakeries, and
in 1928 he opened his own grocery store, Au-
rora Farms, in Jackson Heights, Queens. He
then opened a supermarket, but soon after decided to take up farming in a warmer climate.
In 1941 Rossi started a tomato farm near
Bradenton, Florida, and at the same time set up
a small business in Miami, shipping Florida citrus fruit in gift boxes. The latter enterprise did
well, and led him to found a company called
Fruit Industries Inc. in 1947. Rossi now decided to focus on northern cities, with luxury
hotels such as New York's Waldorf-Astoria. He

packed his fruit salads and juices in ice for their
journey, and in 1949 pioneered the concept of
fresh chilled orange juice as a product. Business
flourished, and soon Fruit Industries overtook
the original fruit gift box business. Within the
year, Rossi changed the company name to
Tropicana Products Inc., and under his direction it evolved into an integrated self-sufficient
business, making its own containers and organizing its own transportation.

Trubenized *(stiffened)*

The originator of a process for producing
shirt collars that do not need to be starched was
the US engineer Benjamin Liebowitz, who in
the 1920s developed the idea of textile "spot
welding." This involved the insertion of an interlining of cotton with acetate yarns into a collar and fusing the resulting three plies together
by means of a solvent and pressure. The result
was a collar that retained its porosity and permeability, which was important for washing
and wearing. At the time, Dr. Liebowitz was
working for his father's firm, S. Liebowitz &
Sons, but the new fusing technique was judged
to be sufficiently important to justify the formation of a separate company. This was called
the Essley Shirt Co., taking its name from *S.
Lie*bowitz. Benjamin Liebowitz found the constraints of running a business rather tiresome,
however, so set up a licensing arrangement for
his process by agreement with his family. This
was the Trubenizing Process Corporation,
which would soon produce the Trubenized
semistiff collar. The name is thus based on a
blend of "true" and the first syllable of "Benjamin." The name is no longer proprietary in
the USA but was entered in the US Patent
Office *Official Gazette* of December 26, 1933
"for dress and negligee shirts and collars" and
(as "Trubenised") by Trubenising Ltd. of London, England, in the *Trade Marks Journal* of
July 26, 1939.

Truman *(beer)*

The origins of the English company are
rather obscure, but it is known that in 1666
Joseph Truman, a member of the family already involved in brewing, set up his own business, leasing a brewhouse in Brick Lane, London, in 1679. He left his brewery to his sons,
Joseph Truman, who retired in 1730, and Benjamin Truman. It was the latter, later Sir Ben-

jamin, who effectively shaped the future destiny of the company.

Trussardi *(fashionwear)*

The name of the Italian fashion house became famous through Nicola Trussardi (1942-1999), born in Bergamo, who transformed the family firm, founded in 1910, into a company of international repute.

Trusthouse Forte *see* **Forte**

Tsingtao *(beer)*

The light beer takes its name from the city and port of Tsingtao (now more usually spelled Qingdao) in eastern China, where it is brewed. The name dates from the turn of the 20th century, and was entered by the China National Cereals, Oils and Foodstuffs Import and Export Corporation, of Peking, in the US Patent Office *Official Gazette* of October 27, 1981.

Tsuru *(whisky)*

The Japanese blend of whisky is produced by the **Nikka** company and takes its name from its founder, Masataka Take*tsuru*. Japanese *tsuru* means "crane." Hence the depiction of this bird on the packaging.

Tuborg *(beer)*

The brewery in Copenhagen, Denmark, takes its name from Tuborg, to the north of Copenhagen, where it was founded in 1873 by a group of bankers. The firm's main beer is "Grøn Tuborg," launched in 1880 as Denmark's first Pilsner and so called from its green label.

Tuck, Raphael *see* **Raphael Tuck**

Tucker *(automobiles)*

The name behind the futuristic Tucker Torpedo car, launched in 1947, is that of Preston Thomas Tucker (1903-1956), born in Capac, Michigan, the son of a railroad engineer. Tucker's father died when the boy was two, and his family subsequently moved to Lincoln Park, Michigan, near Detroit. At age 13 Tucker found work as an office boy at **Cadillac**, then later became a car salesman in a number of cities. In 1929 he befriended Harry Miller, an engine designer, and in 1935 the two men formed a partnership, Miller and Tucker, Inc., to produce racing cars and engines. The business soon folded, but Tucker was determined to pursue his interest in automobile construction. In 1933 he bought a house in Ypsilanti, Michigan, where he set up a machine shop. In 1940 he named his enterprise Tucker Aviation, but later changed the name to Ypsilanti Machine and Tool Company. When World War II ended, Tucker was determined to build the most advanced car America had ever seen. The result was the Tucker Torpedo, which boasted a 150-horsepower engine and could do 130 mph. Tucker soon ran into major financial difficulties, however, and in 1948, after a year of glory, his factory closed. Only 51 Tucker cars were built, all by hand, and the 49 that still exist have become prized collectors' items.

Tudric *(pewter)*

The type of pewter appears to derive its name from a blend of "Tudor" and "Cymric." It was devised by Arthur **Liberty**, who from 1894 produced silver in an Art Nouveau version of the Celtic style which he called "Cymric" (from Welsh *Cymru*, "Wales"), and from 1903 a new type of pewter which he called "Tudric." The name was entered by "Liberty & Co. (Cymric) Limited, 16, Hilton Street, Birmingham; manufacturers of pewter wares" in the *Trade Marks Journal* of February 7, 1922.

Tuinal *(sedative)*

The proprietary name for a combination of the two barbiturate drugs quinalbarbital and amilobarbital, used as a sedative and hypnotic, is of uncertain origin. "Tuin-" may represent "two in (one)," while the "-al" is as in **Amytal** and **Seconal**. The name was entered by **Eli Lilly** in the *Trade Marks Journal* of May 25, 1949.

Tullamore Dew *(whiskey)*

The Tullamore Dew Co. had its origins in the distillery founded in Tullamore, Co. Offaly, Ireland, by one Michael Molloy in 1829. On his death in 1857, the business passed to his nephew, Bernard Daley, who in turn passed it on to his son, Captain Bernard Daley. Deciding his life lay outside the whiskey industry, the latter Daley promoted the distillery's engineer, Daniel E. Williams, to the post of general manager. Williams eventually bought into the company, which gained fame for its Tullamore Dew blend. "Dew" was ostensibly a pun on Williams' initials, but "dew" is also a slang term for whiskey in general (and "mountain dew" for whiskey illicitly distilled in the mountains). The advertising slogan, "Give every man his Dew," soon became one of the best known in Ireland.

Tungar *(rectifier)*

The name of the low-voltage discharge tube filled with argon and having a heated cathode of thoriated tungsten, used as a rectifier, derives from a blend of "tungsten" and "argon." It was entered by the General Electric Company (*see* **Ediswan**) in the US Patent Office *Official Gazette* of December 4, 1917, with a claim of use since October 1916.

Tunnock's *("Caramel Wafers")*

The caramel, wafer, and chocolate bars, popular in Scotland and one of the top ten best-selling products in the UK, originated in Uddingston, South Lanarkshire, where Thomas Tunnock first opened a bakery in 1890. The bar was not produced until 1952, however, when Thomas's son, Archie, began to experiment with dry wafers and caramel. Today, Archie's son, Boyd, carries on the family tradition and is expanding production at the factory to keep up with growing demand in export markets.

Tupperware *(food containers)*

The name derives from that of Earl S. Tupper (1907-1983), born in Berlin, New Hampshire, the son of a farmer. Soon after his birth the family moved to a farm in Massachusetts, where he enjoyed buying and selling vegetables. After graduating from high school in 1926, Tupper turned his hobby into a mail-order business for household items such as combs and toothbrushes. His self-taught skills led him to **Du Pont**, where he worked as an engineer in the 1930s. In 1938 he left Du Pont to form the Tupper Plastic Company, and began producing Tupperware there in 1942. Within a few years he had made his fortune, and Tupperware Home Parties had become an American institution. Tupper's plastic products were unique in that they had airtight lids, and the concept of selling the containers through private sales parties added to their mystique. By 1983 Tupperware was being distributed by around 250,000 dealers, and included toys and indoor garden equipment. In 1958 Tupper sold his company to the **Rexall** Drug Company, Los Angeles, for over $9 million. He remained active as chairman of the board until 1973. The name was entered in the US Patent Office *Official Gazette* of June 12, 1956, with a note of first use on March 3, 1950, and subsequently by Rexall in the *Trade Marks Journal* of August 23, 1961.

Turog *(flour)*

The brown flour of this name was introduced by **Spillers** in 1903. At first it was named "Twrog," after a legendary Welsh saint (said to have given the name of the village of Maentwrog, "Twrog's stone," in northwest Wales), but the spelling was later simplified to "Turog." The name was entered in the *Trade Marks Journal* of May 10, 1905.

Turtle Wax *(car polish)*

The name was devised by Benjamin Hirsch, the founder of Turtle Wax Inc. of Chicago. After setting up a business to sell a car polish called "Plastone," Hirsch was one day driving in the States when he stopped at a place named Turtle Creek. There, the story goes, he rested by a stream and was struck by the appearance of his reflection in the water. Thinking of a polish in which one could similarly see one's own reflection, he was inspired to choose a new name for his product, "Turtle Wax." The unusual name has resulted in supplies of turtles being offered to the company on several occasions. A former president of the company, Carl Schmid, used to refuse such offers politely and point out that the "turtles" in Turtle Wax have the same relationship to the product as horses do to horseradish sauce.

Tutti Frutti *(chewing gum)*

The make of chewing gum with a mixed fruit flavoring takes its name from Italian *tutti frutti*, "all fruits," adopted generally in English for a type of ice cream containing (or flavored with) mixed fruits. The name was entered by the **American Chicle** Company in the US Patent Office *Official Gazette* of October 21, 1924, with a claim of use since October 1882.

TVP *(vegetarian food)*

The initials stand for "textured vegetable protein," meaning protein foods that are derived from vegetables but given a texture that resembles meat. The abbreviation was entered:

"For unflavored and meat and poultry flavored vegetable protein food" in the US Patent Office *Official Gazette* of March 18, 1969, with a note of "first use on or before May 2, 1966," and by the Archer Daniels Midland Company of Decatur, Illinois, in the *Trade Marks Journal* of May 21, 1975 for: "Foods prepared from soya bean derivatives and included in Class 9."

TVR *(automobiles)*

The British company owes its origin to Trevor Wilkinson (b.1923), a special car builder of Blackpool who decided to produce cars in greater numbers. The first "Wilkinson special" took shape in 1949, but it was not until 1954 that the first TVR-badged model appeared. The letters come from "Trevor." Financial problems obliged Wilkinson to leave the company in 1962 but the remains of the business were bought by Arthur and Martin Lilley in 1965 and although passing subsequently into other hands, the firm has flourished ever since.

TWA *(airline)*

The American airline was formed in 1930 in the amalgamation of divisions of Western Air Express, founded in 1925, and Transcontinental Air Transport, founded in 1928. In 1934 Western Air Express became independent again, and was subsequently known as Western Air Lines, but TWA continued as a transcontinental airline, with extensive routes in the United States and to Europe, the Caribbean, and the Middle East. TWA was known as Transcontinental & Western Air, Inc., until 1950, when it became Trans World Air Lines, Inc.

Tween *(emulsifier)*

The proprietary name for various derivatives of fatty esters of sorbitan, used as emulsifiers and surfactants, appears to be of arbitrary origin. It was entered in the US Patent Office *Official Gazette* of July 8, 1941 and the *Trade Marks Journal* of March 16, 1949.

Twentieth Century–Fox *(motion pictures)*

The first half of the familiar name represents the Twentieth Century Company founded in 1933 by the American movie mogul Darryl F. Zanuck (1902-1979), formerly head of production at **Warner Brothers**, and Joseph M. Schenk, until then head of **United Artists**. Two years later they merged with Fox Film Corporation, founded in 1913 by William Fox (1879-1952), a Hungarian-born movie pioneer originally named Wilhelm Fried who had been brought to the United States as a child. Fox at first called his company Box Office Attractions but it was renamed after him two years later.

Twiglets *(snacks)*

The crisp, knobbly, wholewheat "stick snacks," so called from their resemblance to little twigs, were introduced by **Jacobs** in 1920. The snacks come in various flavors, but the basic flavoring is **Marmite**. The name was entered in the *Trade Marks Journal* of June 15, 1932.

Twinings *(tea)*

Britain's oldest tea and coffee business, still in family hands, was founded by Thomas Twining (1675-1741), who was brought from Painswick, Gloucestershire, to London by his father in 1684 to be apprenticed as a weaver. When his brother, Daniel, died in 1695, Thomas was apprenticed to his brother's former master, John Dowse. In 1706 he set up in business on his own account, buying Tom's Coffee House at Devereux Court, Temple Bar. Coffee houses were becoming increasingly popular in London then, so in order to attract new business Twining began to serve tea as a sideline. His business flourished, and his reputation as a tea merchant and blender soon spread. In 1716 he opened the Golden Lion in the Strand as one of the first tea and coffee houses. The present company of R. Twining & Co. Ltd. was registered in 1904 with the name of Thomas's grandson, Richard Twining (1749-1824), who was instrumental in getting an act of parliament passed that would cut the hitherto heavy duties on tea. Consumption of tea increased considerably as a result, so that Twining and other tea merchants benefitted greatly. In 1964 Twinings became part of the British Foods Group, and by the end of the 1980s was producing over 120 blends of teas and coffees and exporting tea worldwide.

Twinkies *(cupcakes)*

The small, finger-shaped sponge cakes with

a white cream filling are said to have a name suggested in the 1930s by Jimmy Dewar on seeing a St. Louis billboard advertising "Twinkle Toe" shoes. The name "Twinkie" was entered in the *Trade Marks Journal* of October 21, 1936.

Twix *(cookie bar)*

The chocolate-coated caramel bar made by **Mars** was launched in the UK in 1968 and in the USA in 1979. Its name is said to derive from a shortening of "twin biscuits," although it also suggests a snack, something that can be enjoyed "betwixt and between" meals. In continental Europe the Twix is known as "Raider," perhaps because it is so tasty that the eater is tempted to "raid" the local candy store to eat another. The name was entered in the *Trade Marks Journal* of September 22, 1965.

Two Guys *(discount stores)*

The American chain of this name was founded by two brothers, Herbert and Sidney Hubschman, who opened their store in an empty diner in Harrison, New Jersey, in 1947. They began in the discount business by selling cut-price televisions, refrigerators, and washing machines, calling their store "Two Guys from Harrison." The name stuck for several years, until their business spread beyond New Jersey, and they shortened it to "Two Guys." The original name had been based on a competitor's comment on the Hubschmans when he found out they were underselling him by 25 percent. "Those two bastards from Harrison," he called them, and the appellation, judiciously modified, was adopted for the corporate name. Sidney left the company in 1963 and Herbert died in 1964.

Twydale *(turkeys)*

Twydale Turkeys, now part of the British agricultural division of **Bibby's**, takes its name from the founder of the firm, Raymond Twiddle, who in 1956 hatched seven turkeys from 11 eggs on his poultry farm at Kilham, near Driffield, Yorkshire. Within a few years his technological improvements had paid dividends, so that he went on to employ over 500 people in farms and factories in the Driffield area, producing more than 3 million birds a year. He respelled his name to blend in with typical Yorkshire valley names, such as Wharfedale and Wensleydale. (The name Twiddle ac-

tually means "Tweeddale," so his adaptation is etymologically valid as well as commercially justifiable.)

Twyfords *(bathroom furniture)*

The English firm traces its history back to about 1690, when Josiah Twyford (1640-1729) was known to have been a potter in Stoke-on-Trent, Staffordshire, the central town of the Potteries. His employer was John Philip Elers, who had developed certain secret processes in his pottery-making. Twyford was able to discover them by pretending to be quite uninterested in every operation at which he assisted. After mastering Elers' processes, Twyford set up his own factory south of Hanley, a nearby Potteries town. There he made red and white stoneware, which was much in demand locally. By the end of the 19th century Twyfords was manufacturing wash basins and one-piece pedestal closets (toilet units), and exporting to America, continental Europe, and Russia. One of the best-known pedestal models was the **Unitas**.

Tylenol *(analgesic)*

The proprietary name for paracetamol is presumably of arbitrary origin. It was entered in the US Patent Office *Official Gazette* of September 18, 1956: "For pediatric analgesic-antipyretic," with a note of first use on January 19, 1955.

Tylose *(cosmetic medium)*

The proprietary and presumably arbitrary name for various esters or ethers of cellulose, used as a medium in pharmaceutical and cosmetic products, was entered by the German firm of Kalle & Co., of Biebrich-am-Rhein, now a suburb of Wiesbaden, in the *Trade Marks Journal* of April 1, 1936, and the US Patent Office *Official Gazette* of August 18, 1936, the latter with a claim of use since December 16, 1931.

Ty-Phoo *(tea)*

The British brand of tea was first produced in 1903 by a Birmingham grocer, John Sumner, as "Ty-Phoo Tipps." The first word was a meaningless oriental-style creation, perhaps suggested by "typhoon." The second was a printer's misprint for "tips," meaning the top leaves and buds of the tea plant that are picked to be dried, crushed, and infused in boiling water to make the drink. *(Cp.* **PG Tips***.)* The firm of Sumner's Ty-Phoo Tea Ltd., incorporated in 1905, became Ty-Phoo Tea in 1941. Today the name usually appears with a raised dot replacing the hyphen *(i.e. as* "Ty•Phoo"*)*. The name was entered in the *Trade Marks Journal* of September 26, 1928.

Tyrozets *(antiseptic throat lozenges)*

The lozenges, first on the market in 1949, have a name alluding to two of the ingredients, *tyro*thricin (an antibiotic) and ben*zoc*aine (a local anesthetic). The middle "-oz-" also suggests "lozenge" itself, while the final "-ets" perhaps refers to the manufacture of the lozenge by tabl*et*ing rather than molding. The name was entered in the *Trade Marks Journal* of November 3, 1948.

UDS *(oil and gas)*

The story of Ultramar Diamond Shamrock (UDS) began in Amarillo, Texas, in 1929, when an immigrant Irishman, John Sheerin, started an oil venture, naming it for the plant that was his native emblem. Four years later, the Shamrock Oil and Gas Company was founded, a small refinery was built, and a gasoline service station was opened at Amarillo. In 1935, with the backing of Alfred Meyer (1877-1965), German-born US president of Caracas Petroleum, a small group of British financiers and mining men formed the Ultramar Exploration Company in London, England, the principal aim being to raise finance to fund the development of oil fields in Venezuela. Hence the name, Spanish for "overseas." (In 1940 the company name was changed to Ultramar Company Ltd., emphasizing the change to an investment holding company whose activities were now carried out by subsidiaries.) In 1987, Diamond Shamrock was formed in San Antonio, Texas, and in 1996 merged with Ultramar as UDS, which the following year acquired **Total** Petroleum (North America) Ltd.

Ugh *(boot)*

The type of soft, sheepskin boot, of Australian origin, probably derives its name not from the exclamation of disgust but from a series of cartoon characters called Ugh (pronounced "Ug"). The name was entered in the *Official Journal of Patents, Trade Marks and Designs* of June 1, 1972.

Ugli *(fruit)*

The hybrid citrus was first produced in Jamaica by crossing the Seville orange, the grapefruit, and the tangerine. The name, reflecting the fruit's unprepossessing appearance, something like a large, wrinkled, discolored grapefruit, was entered in the *Trade Marks Journal* of December 7, 1938.

Uhu *(adhesive)*

The synthetic resin-based adhesive was formulated in 1932 by August Fischer (d.1940) and his eldest son Hugo (d.1964) in Bühl, southwestern Germany. Their chemical company already produced goods with brand names based on birds, such as "Pelikan" and "Schwan," and for this new product they selected "Uhu," meaning "eagle owl," a bird of prey found in the nearby Black Forest, its own name based on its cry.

Ulay *see* **Olay**

Ultralente *(insulin)*

The name of the form of insulin implies that it is absorbed into the body more slowly after its introduction than **Lente**. The name is of Danish origin. It was registered in Denmark in 1952 and entered in the US Patent Office *Official Gazette* of July 21, 1959: "For preparation for the treatment of diabetes."

Ultramar *see* **UDS**

Ultrasuede *(synthetic fabric)*

The name of the synthetic nonwoven fabric resembling suede implies that it is "beyond" suede, or an improvement on it. It was entered by **Springs Mills**, Inc., of Fort Mill, South Carolina, in the US Patent Office *Official Gazette* of March 13, 1973, with a note of first use on November 24, 1971.

U-Matic *(video and television format)*

The name of the 1970s videocassette format, and of equipment designed to accept it, derives from "U," referring to the shape of the tape path around the drum and heads of the machine, and a shortening of "automatic." It was entered in the *Trade Marks Journal* of June 7, 1972 and the US Patent Office *Official Gazette* of April 17, 1973, the latter with a claim of first use on August 2, 1971.

Umbro *(sportswear)*

Harold C. Humphreys quit school at 13 and in 1920 started a small sports goods workshop in Wilmslow, Cheshire, England. His brother Wallace joined him, the enterprise grew, and Humphrey Brothers Ltd. was founded. The business capitalized on the exposure it received in England through football clubs, and adopted the present name for its sportswear from letters in "H*umphrey Bro*thers."

Uncle Ben's *(rice)*

The original Uncle Ben is a semilegendary figure who is said to have been a rich farmer from Texas. He made his name locally through the fine quality of the rice he delivered for milling, so that "rice like Uncle Ben's" became a catchphrase, something like "the real McCoy." In 1943 the firm of Uncle Ben's, Inc., was set up in the United States to market high quality rice. The name was adopted from that of the famous Uncle Ben of Texas. However, the portrait on the rice packets is not of Uncle Ben. It is of one Frank Brown, the maître d' (head waiter) at a restaurant frequented by Gordon L. Harwell, first president of Converted Rice Inc., as the firm was originally known. Frank Brown was Harwell's personal friend and his partner, and he agreed to pose as a portrait for "Uncle Ben."

Underberg *(digestif)*

The herbal digestif, familiar in restaurants, is designed to aid digestion in the way that brandies and other liquors do. Hence the phrase "After a good meal" on the tiny 2cl. bottles. The name is that of Hubert Underberg, who founded his company in Rheinberg, Germany, in 1846 on the day he got married. The business is still run by the family, and Christiane, wife of Emil Underberg, company chief in the late 20th century, was the model for the "herb girl" in the firm's publicity material.

Underseal *(waterproof coating)*

The name of the rubberized underbody coating for vehicles was entered by the US manufacturers, Minnesota Mining and Manufacturing Company, now **3M**, in the US Patent Office *Official Gazette* of September 14, 1948.

Underwood *(deviled ham)*

William Underwood (1787-1864), a British-born tinsmith, opened a cannery in Massachusetts in 1821. At first he faced resistance from American consumers, who regarded domestically canned foods as inferior to the established English products. Underwood countered such opposition by printing "England" on his labels, thus giving the impression that the products were imported. With customer confidence restored, the William Underwood Co. expanded quickly and diversified into a wide range of foods. It was William's grandson, Henry Oliver Underwood, who decided to concentrate on the more profitable items and trim down the rest. One of the bestsellers was the firm's deviled ham, which Henry advertised by using the company's famous "red devil" trademark that had been appearing on Underwood cans since 1867.

Underwood *(typewriters)*

In 1895 Franz Xavier Wagner and W.F. Helmond designed a new kind of typewriter. The model they produced was shown to John T. Underwood (1857-1937), born in London, England, but immigrating to the United States in 1873, where in 1882 he succeeded to his father's business as a manufacturer of carbon papers, inks, and typewriter ribbons. Underwood realized at once that here, for the first time, was a machine on which the typist could see every letter as it was being typed. He thus keenly supported promotion of the new model, and on March 29, 1895, the Wagner Typewriting Company was formed, the first machines being manufactured by the firm of Lambert and Edgar. However, Lambert and Edgar made only 500 machines before the need to expand was so great that they moved to new premises on Hudson Street, New York City, and the Wagner Typewriting Company began production themselves, changing the name to the Underwood Typewriter Company in 1896. The change to visible writing was such a success that sales increased beyond expectation and in May 1898 the manufacturing plant was moved to Bayonne, New Jersey. Following various mergers, the company name was changed to Underwood Corporation in 1945 and control of the business subsequently passed to **Olivetti**. Underwood himself was president of the company from 1896 through 1927.

Uneeda *(crackers)*

The classic brand name was proposed by Chicago lawyer Adolphus W. Green to the newly formed National Biscuit Company (the future **Nabisco**) for their soda crackers. Following the rejection of such names as "Hava Cracker," "Usa Cracker," "Taka Cracker," and the like, "Uneeda Biscuit" first appeared in advertising in 1899. The name is said to have given that of Uneeda, West Virginia, although here there may have been an equal hint at "Uneeda post office."

Unibroue *(beer)*

Canada's largest microbrewery dates from 1990, when André Dion and Serge Racine set up Unibroue, Inc. (as if "Unibrew"), to acquire 75 percent of the outstanding shares in La Brasserie Massawippi, Inc., a failing brewery in Lennoxville, Quebec. The following year they purchased the remaining shares in La Brasserie Massawippi and it became a Unibroue subsidiary. In 1993 they moved their brewing activity from Lennoxville to Chambly, near Montreal, Quebec, and began exporting to the USA and Europe. In 1995 they set up Unibrew USA, Inc., as an American subsidiary, and Unibroue sprl as a European one.

Unigate *(food and dairy products)*

In 1889 Charles Maggs (d.1898), a rope and twine manufacturer in Melksham, Wiltshire, England, started a butter factory. (The town's Anglo-Saxon name appropriately means "homestead where milk is produced.") In 1896 he became the first chairman of a newly-formed wholesale firm, Wilts United Dairies. The company thrived, and soon after the outbreak of World War I became the core of a new large dairy combine formed in 1915 as United Dairies Ltd., with Joseph Maggs (1875-1964), one of Charles's 11 sons, as chairman from 1922. In 1959 United Dairies acquired another large dairy firm, **Cow & Gate**, to become Unigate, with Leonard Maggs (1890-1959), the youngest of Joseph's sons, as its first chairman. The company subsequently became one of the world's largest food corporations.

Unilever *(detergents)*

The man behind the British company name is William Hesketh Lever (1851-1925), subsequently Lord Leverhulme. He was born in Bolton, Lancashire, the son of a retail grocer. His mother wanted him to become a doctor, but he quit school at 16 to enter the family business, becoming his father's partner at 21. Until about 1885 he was in business as a wholesale grocer, apparently independently from his father, and from the 1880s onwards devoted his special attention to making **Sunlight** Soap, which he was obliged to manufacture himself as no one else could do this to his satisfaction. Demand for the soap grew so rapidly that in 1889 it was manufactured at a new factory on the Mersey River named Port Sunlight. The following year Lever Bros. was made a limited company, the "Bros." representing Lever himself and his brother, James Darcy Lever, who very much took a back seat in the business. The firm became a public company in 1894. The modern company Unilever is the result of a merger in 1929 between the firms of Margarine Unie NV (in the Netherlands) and Margarine Union Ltd. (in the UK). The two companies, bonded together with identical boards, were formed in 1927 in a merger between the Dutch firms of Van den Bergh, set up by Simon Van den Bergh (1819-1907) as a family business to trade in butter in the 1850s, and Jurgens, founded by Anton Jurgens (1805-1880) and his brother Johannes for the same purpose in 1854. The "Uni-" thus represents the unifying of the two great concerns, while the rest of the name is that of Lever Bros., who joined Margarine Union at the same time, having initially been in competition with it. Today Unilever is fully multinational.

Union Carbide *(chemicals and petrochemicals)*

The American company was formed in 1917 as Union Carbide and Carbon Corporation on the acquisition of four earlier companies: Linde Air Products Company, established in 1907, National Carbon Company, founded in 1899, Pret-O-Lite Company, formed in 1913, and Union Carbide Company, dating from 1898. It adopted its present name, based on this last, in 1957.

Uniqlo *(fashionwear)*

The Japanese company, its name short for Unique Clothing Warehouse, was founded in the 1980s by Tadashi Yanai (b.1950) to sell "cheap 'n' chic" **Gap**-style casualwear for a third of the price. By the end of the century there were 519 Uniqlo stores in Japan and in 2001 the company opened the first of its projected 50 stores in the UK.

Uniroyal *(rubber, plastic, and chemical products)*

The firm was founded in 1892 as the United States Rubber Company, later usually known as US Rubber. In 1917 four tire companies that US Rubber had bought began selling their products under the US Royal brand, and by 1940 US Royal controlled 30 percent of both the new and replacement tire markets. High feelings about the US involvement in Vietnam and the racial disturbances in Little Rock, Arkansas, in 1957 led to demonstrations against the company in some Latin American countries. The "nationalist" name US Rubber was thus changed in 1967 to Uniroyal, which was usable anywhere.

Unisys *(computers)*

The American company was formed in 1986 from the merger of Sperry Corporation, formerly **Sperry Rand**, with **Burroughs** Corporation, its new name being an acronym of "*uni*versal computer *sy*stems."

Unitas *(toilet fittings)*

The name was first registered by **Twyfords** in 1884 for a toilet basin made in one piece, i.e. with an integral bowl and trap, as distinct from the earlier basins, manufactured with separate pan and trap. Hence the name, representing Latin *unitas,* "unity." Twyford exported washbasins and toilet fittings to Russia, among other European countries, and by a linguistic quirk the name came to give the standard Russian word for a toilet bowl, *unitaz,* partly influenced by the existing Russian word *taz,* "bowl."

United Artists *(motion pictures)*

The American corporation was formed in 1919 by the comedy star Charlie Chaplin, the film star Mary Pickford, her equally famous actor husband, Douglas Fairbanks, and the pioneer film director D.W. Griffith. These were thus the "united artists." Their sole purpose in setting up the company was to distribute the films they made as independent producers.

United Brands *(food products)*

The American corporation was formed in 1970 in the merger of United Fruit Company, founded in 1899 in the merger of the Boston Fruit Company and other companies producing and marketing bananas, and AMK Corporation, the holding company for the meatpackers John Morrell and Company, and itself having its beginnings in a bottle-cap company called American Seal-Kap, whose initial letters gave AMK.

Universal Music *see* **Polygram**

Universal Pictures *(motion pictures)*

The American motion picture studio arose from the Independent Motion Picture Company set up in New York City in 1909 by Carl Laemmle (1867-1939), a film exhibitor turned producer. As Laemmle made his millions, he felt a more ambitious title would be appropriate, so in 1912 renamed his company Universal Studios and moved it to Los Angeles, where in 1915 he opened Universal City Studios. During the next decade, Universal City Studios operated as the largest filmmaking business in the world, justifying its new name. In 1966 Universal Pictures was formed as the feature film production division of Universal City Studios.

Unix *(computer operating system)*

The multiuser operating system, originally designed for use with minicomputers, bases its name on that of the earlier **Multics** system, but with "Uni-" instead of "Multi-," with reference to the relative compactness of the new system, and "-ix" instead of "-ics." The system was designed and implemented at Bell Laboratories (*see* **Bell System**) and the name was entered in the US Patent Office *Official Gazette* of October 29, 1985, with a note of first use on December 14, 1972. *See also* **Linux**.

Unocal *(petrochemicals)*

The American corporation was founded in 1890 as the Union Oil Company of California with the union of three "wildcatter" companies: the Hardison & Stewart Oil Company, the Sespe Oil Company, and the Torrey Canyon Oil Company. It adopted its present acronymic name in 1983, when the company was reorganized.

Unwins *(wine and liquor merchants)*

The British company dates its founding from 1843. The choice of this year seems odd, however, as it was actually started in 1879 by Stephen Unwin, member of a family engaged as seedsmen and printers. He leased a shop in Parkway, London, that year, but in 1895 sold out to one Jason Gurney. In 1906 Gurney then sold Unwins to M.A. Wetz, and the company has remained in the hands of the Wetz family ever since. Unwins now has its head office in Dartford, Kent.

UPI *(news agency)*

The American-based news agency, one of the largest in the world, was formed in 1958 from the merger of the United Press (UP), founded in 1907, with the International News Service (INS), set up by William Randolph Hearst to provide news to morning newspapers.

Upjohn *(drugs)*

The American makers of "Cheracol" cough syrup, which can be bought over the counter, and "Mitrin," used for treating arthritis, which cannot, take their name from William E. Upjohn (1853-1932), himself a doctor's son, born in Richland Township, Michigan. In 1885 he patented a process for making pills which readily dissolved in the body, and the following year, together with his brother Henry, another doctor, founded the Upjohn Pill and Granule Co. in Kalamazoo, Michigan. The company grew steadily, adding newer and better drugs to its range, and is still based in Kalamazoo today. In 1996 Upjohn merged with the Swedish company Pharmacia to become Pharmacia & Upjohn.

Upmann *see* **H. Upmann**

UPS *(express collection and delivery service)*

The American company owes its origin to James E. Casey (1888-1983), born in Candelaria, Nevada, the son of a part-time prospector and innkeeper. After working as a delivery boy for a department store and as a messenger for the American District Telegraph Company, in 1907 he and a teenage friend, Claude Ryan, began a messenger service in Seattle, calling it the American Messenger Company. They were soon known for their fast and reliable service and in 1913, after merging with a rival, Evert McCabe's Motorcycle Delivery Service, renamed their business Merchants' Parcel Deliv-

ery (MPD). In 1917 Ryan resigned as director of MPD but Casey stayed with the company. In 1919 MPD purchased the Motor Parcel Delivery Company in Oakland, California. Because a San Francisco company already had the name of Merchants' Parcel Delivery, the new branch was called United Parcel Service. That name was used for other West Coast branches that opened subsequently, and in 1925 the Seattle headquarters followed its branches by officially changing its name to United Parcel Service (UPS).

Uralite *(building material)*

The asbestos-based building material has a name of uncertain origin, entered by the British Uralite Company, of London, in the *Trade Marks Journal* of August 30, 1899 for: "Compounds of asbestos and silica, being manufactures for building and decoration."

Urecholine *(stimulant drug)*

The drug used to stimulate bowel or bladder muscle activity contains a form of choline chloride. Hence its name, from "urea" and "choline," entered by **Merck** in the US Patent Office *Official Gazette* of April 29, 1941: "For medicinal preparation for the treatment of disorders of the peripheral circulatory system and for stimulation of the para-sympathetic nervous system."

USAir *(airline)*

USAir Group, Inc., was established in 1983 as the holding company for the American airline incorporated in 1937 as All American Aviation. The airline was renamed All American Airways in 1948, Allegheny Airlines in 1953, and USAir in 1979. The name rather obviously but neatly enough combines "US" (or "USA") and "air."

Ushers *(beer)*

Thomas Usher (1792-1891) acquired a small brewery in Back Street, Trowbridge, Wiltshire, in 1824. His business did well, despite competition from the many households which brewed their own liquor. The British firm became a limited company in 1889, as Ushers Wiltshire Brewery Ltd., and the Usher family retained their link with the business until 1941, when the grandson of the founder retired. By the 1960s the firm's activity had expanded to such an extent that "Wiltshire" was dropped from the name. It was then taken over by **Watney's** but in 1980 the name Ushers Brewery was restored as it was the family name that people associated with the beer. A management buyout in 1991 finally restored the firm's independence.

Usquaebach *(whisky)*

The name of the US-based brand of Scotch whisky is based on a spelling mistake in a 1768 London auctioneer's list in an attempt at "usquebaugh," itself an Elizabethan anglicization of the Gaelic term for whisky, *uisge beatha*, "water of life." The blend has been marketed by the Twelve Stone Flagons company in Pittsburgh since 1969.

US Steel *see* **USX**

USX *(steel and oil)*

The USX Corporation was incorporated in 1986 to oversee the the operations formerly directed by the United States Steel Corporation (US Steel), founded in 1901 as America's first billion-dollar company, and the biggest steelmaker in the United States. "X" was the New York stock exchange ticker symbol for US Steel., just as "S" is **Sears, Roebuck** and "T" is **AT&T**. Such symbols usually relate to the company name, although in the case of US Steel it probably represents an X-shaped steel structure.

UTET *(publishers)*

The Italian publishing group was formed in Turin in 1854 in the merger of Giuseppe Pomba and other printing firms and is now one of Italy's oldest and most prodigious companies of its kind. The letters are the initials of Unione tipografico-editrice torinese, "Turin Printing and Publishing Union."

Utilidor *(conduit system)*

The Canadian system of enclosed conduits for carrying water and sewage in regions of permafrost derives its name from "utility" and the "-dor" suffix as in "cuspidor" and "humidor" (itself perhaps meant to suggest Greek *dōron*, "gift," although not having this sense in the ordinary words). The name was entered by Ric-Wil, Inc., of Barberton, Ohio, in the US Patent Office *Official Gazette* of April 15, 1969: "For prefabricated conduits used in under-ground services," with a note of use "as least as early as" April 30, 1950.

Vacutainer *(container for blood samples)*

The name, a blend of "vacuum" and "container," is that of an evacuated container in the form of a test tube sealed with a bung and used with a double-ended hypodermic needle for the collection of samples of blood. It was entered in the US Patent Office *Official Gazette* of August 13, 1946, with a claim of use since September 25, 1944.

Valderma *(antiseptic soap and cream)*

The name was originally entered by Dae Health Laboratories in the *Trade Marks Journal* of May 15, 1940. The meaning is approximately "healthy skin," from Latin *valere*, "to be well," and Greek *derma*, "skin."

Valentine's *(greeting cards and calendars)*

The Scottish company, based in Dundee, was founded in 1825 by John Valentine, born in Dundee in 1792 the son of a maltster. The premises where Valentine set up as an engraver of wooden blocks for linen printing were in Overgate, and he was joined there five years later by his son, James, who became his partner. James Valentine had been trained as a portrait painter, and he designed a series of illustrated envelopes. These were essentially the forerunners of the picture postcard. It was James Valentine, too, who realized the commercial advantages of photography in his business, and who began to print pictures of well-known scenes and local views. It was only in 1897, when the government gave permission for people to write on the reverse of cards sent through the mail, that Valentine's started producing the picture postcards for which it is now well known. Birthday cards and other types of greeting cards, including Valentine cards (appropriately enough), followed in the 1920s. In 1963, on becoming a subsidiary of **Waddington's**, Valentine's withdrew from their long-established postcard business and moved into giftwrap, tags, and ribbons. In 1980, Waddington's then sold the company to **Hallmark**.

Valium *(tranquilizer)*

The proprietary name for the drug diazepam, used to relieve anxiety and as a muscle relaxant, perhaps derives from Latin *valere*, "to be strong," "to be healthy." Valium was first marketed in the USA in 1960 and its name was entered by **Hoffmann-La Roche** in the US Patent Office *Official Gazette* of October 10, 1961 and by Roche Products Ltd. in the *Trade Marks Journal* of January 10, 1962.

Vallecchi *(publishers)*

The Italian publishing house was founded in Florence in 1913 by Attilio Vallecchi (1880-1946), editor of the Futurist review *Lacerba*, started that same year by the writer Giovanni Papini and the painter and writer Ardegno Soffini and running until 1915.

Valpack *(travel bag)*

Although now often found in this form, the original name of the soft, zip-up travel bag was Val-A-Pak, entered in the US Patent Office *Official Gazette* of October 30, 1934: "For Hand Bags." The name itself presumably derives from a blend of "valise" and "pack."

Valrhona *(chocolate)*

The French company was set up in 1922 in the Rhône valley (*vallée du Rhône*). Hence the name.

Van Camp *(baked beans)*

One day in 1890, Frank Van Camp, son of Gilbert Van Camp (1817-1901), was eating his lunch in the warehouse of his father's Indianapolis cannery when he absently set a tomato down on a can of pork and beans. Noticing the unusual combination, Frank had the idea of mixing the beans with the tomato. The result was so tasty that he had no trouble convincing his father to market his serendipitous discovery. The Van Camps' new product was such a success that soon other manufacturers were baking beans in tomato sauce, while the family company went on to become the biggest producer of pork and beans in the United States.

Van der Hum *(liqueur)*

The South African equivalent of curaçao, made by various producers, is said to have a whimsical name equivalent to "Whatsitsname." ("Van der" names are typically South African, as for the explorer Laurens van der Post, while the "Hum" denotes hesitation.) A genuine surname may be involved, however:

The most famous South African liqueur is undoubtedly Van der Hum with its tangerine flavour, and it has remained popular since the early days of [Dutch] settlement at the Cape [in the 17th century]. According to tradition the name is derived from a sea captain, Van der Hum, who had a special liking for this liqueur.

J.D. Opperman, *Spirit of the Vine* (1968)

Van Heusen *(shirts)*

The company was founded in 1922 in Boston, Massachusetts, by John Manning Van Heusen (1869-1931) and C.L. Harding, with the business extended soon after to the UK as Van Heusen International. After World War I, the company mainly marketed semistiff collars, which were welcomed by many men after the rigors of earlier dress, with formal high collars worn for most activities and occasions, even when playing tennis. In 1928 the firm changed its name to Harding, Tilton and Hartley, the first of these being the name of the cofounder, and the last that of the general manager from 1923. In 1952 the British name of the firm became the British Van Heusen Company Ltd. The American songwriter Jimmy Van Heusen (1913-1990), born Edward Chester Babcock, adopted the name of the shirtmaker.

Van Houten *(cocoa)*

Coenraad Johannes Van Houten (1801-1887) was a Dutchman employed in his father's Amsterdam chocolate mill in the early 19th century, a "chocolate mill" being one where cocoa beans were ground. Van Houten had the idea of removing part of the fat, or cocoa butter, from the raw cocoa by mechanical means, thus enabling cocoa to be produced in powder form, as distinct from the former blocks or cakes of cocoa used for making chocolate drinks. Such blocks were often virtually insoluble, and the resulting drink was often almost indigestible. With the cocoa butter removed, the cocoa would be immediately soluble and the drink tastier. The removed cocoa butter, too, could be used as one of the basic ingredients from which chocolate itself could be made. The process of extracting the cocoa butter was evolved gradually, and in 1828 Van Houten was granted a royal patent for his invention, which that year resulted in the first production of "powdered chocolate." The company is now based in Norderstedt, Germany, having undergone several takeovers and mergers.

Van Nostrand Reinhold *(publishers)*

David Van Nostrand (1811-1886) was born in

New York City the son of a wealthy merchant. After graduating in 1826 with a good classical knowledge, he was taken on by John P. Haven, a prominent publisher and bookseller on Broadway, where he worked for the next six years, becoming Haven's partner in 1832. In 1834 Van Nostrand and a friend, William R. Dwight, set up their own publishing and bookselling business, dealing chiefly in religious books. The firm was hit by the panic of 1837, however, and forced to close. In around 1848 Van Nostrand opened a bookstore back on Broadway, opposite Haven's shop. He not only sold books but published trade editions of books issued elsewhere. This was the start of the D. Van Nostrand Company, which in 1969 was purchased by **Litton** Industries and merged with the Reinhold Publishing Corporation, thus creating the Van Nostrand Reinhold Company, which later became part of the worldwide Thomson Organization (*see* **Thomson Travel**).

Vanden Plas *(automobiles)*

The British cars trace their origins to Belgium, where a carriage-maker in Antwerp in the 1880s was Guillaume Van den Plas. The carriages inevitably progressed to car bodies, although further advances were halted by the German occupation of Belgium in World War I. Meanwhile the British importer Captain Teho Masui of Westminster, London, decided to change the name of his firm in 1913 to Vanden Plas (England) Ltd. in order to build Van den Plas car bodies under license. When war broke out, this company was taken over by the Aircraft Manufacturing Co. of Hendon and became committed to manufacturing airplanes. After the war, Vanden Plas was resuscitated, moved to London in 1923, and eventually, after a further spell making aircraft in World War II, became a subsidiary of **Austin** in 1946. The name then transferred to the automobiles themselves, with the Austin Princess of 1947 becoming the Vanden Plas Princess and finally, from 1974, just the Vanden Plas. The last model of the marque was made in 1980.

Vanitory *(vanity unit)*

The proprietary name for a type of vanity unit, as a washbasin set into a flat top with cupboards underneath, derives from a blend of "vanity" and "lavatory" and was entered in the US Patent Office *Official Gazette* of March 13, 1951 and the *Trade Marks Journal* of July 16, 1958.

Variac *(autotransformer)*

The make of autotransformer, in which the ratio of the input and output voltages can be varied, derives its name from "variable" and the suffix "-ac," which may itself represent the regular abbreviation "ac" ("alternating current"). The name was entered by the General Radio Company, Cambridge, Massachusetts, in the US Patent Office *Official Gazette* of December 26, 1933 and the *Trade Marks Journal* of February 16, 1938, the latter for: "Electrical transformers (not being machines)."

Varig *(airline)*

Brazil's principal airline, based in Rio de Janeiro, was founded by Otto Ernst Meyer in 1927 and has an acronymic Portuguese name representing *Viação Aérea Rio Grandense* ("Rio Grande Air Transport").

Varityper *(typewriter)*

The kind of typewriter with variable type has a name of obvious origin that was entered in the US Patent Office *Official Gazette* of October 16, 1928 and (as "Vari-typer") by the Ralph C. Coxhead Corporation of Newark, New Jersey, in the *Trade Marks Journal* of January 11, 1956.

Vaseline *(petroleum jelly)*

There are two accounts of the origin of the name, both linked with the product's original manufacturer in around 1870, the US chemist Robert A. Chesebrough, of the subsequent **Chesebrough-Pond's**. The first and generally accepted account tells how Chesebrough devised the word from German *Wasser*, "water," and Greek *elaion*, "oil," thinking that petroleum was produced by the decomposition of water in the earth. The second story, much more homely, tells how one day, while working in his laboratory and finding no beaker to hand, Chesebrough tossed out the flowers his wife had brought him from their vase and filled it with petroleum jelly. When he had perfected the process, there were several vases of jelly in the laboratory, and they inspired the name, with "vase" adding "-line" as a generally popular suffix for medical products. Standard dictionaries normally give the first origin. The name was entered by Chesebrough Manufacturing Company Consolidated in the *Trade Marks Journal* of August 3, 1927 for: "Petroleum Jelly and Disinfectant Soap for Veterinary use." (The *Oxford English Dictionary* notes that the name was "introduced by R.A. Chesebrough in 1872.")

Vat 69 *(whisky)*

The blend of whisky was originally produced in 1882 by William Sanderson & Son of Leith, Scotland, a firm of wine and liquor merchants who had moved into whisky blending in the 1860s. Sanderson was keen to find a good blend to market and produced 100 different whiskies to be tested, each in numbered casks. The unanimous choice of his associates was the whisky from vat number 69, and the name accordingly suggested itself.

Vaux *(beer)*

In about 1804 Cuthbert Vaux, in partnership with one W. Story, set up in business as a brewer in Moor Street, Sunderland, England. The partnership lasted until 1837, when the business continued under Vaux alone as C. Vaux & Sons on a slightly different site. Vaux died in 1878 at what must have been a very advanced age. By this date his sons, John Story Vaux and Colonel Edwin Vaux, had been in charge of the business for some time. The former died in 1881, only three years after his father, and subsequently his own two sons, Major Cuthbert Vaux and Colonel Ernest Vaux, joined the firm and continued in partnership with their uncle. In 1898 the business became a limited company. Vaux Breweries Ltd. remain in Sunderland today as one of Britain's largest regional brewers.

Vauxhall *(automobiles)*

The British firm of Vauxhall Motors Ltd. has long been based at Luton, Bedfordshire. The very first cars of the name, however, were produced in 1903 in the Vauxhall district of south London, where in 1857 the Scottish engineer Alexander Wilson had founded the Vauxhall Ironworks. The auto business moved to Luton in 1904. Vauxhall itself takes its name from the "hall" or manor of a Norman soldier called Falkes, who by pure coincidence had in his day been Lord of the Manor of Luton.

Veeto *(depilatory cream)*

The name was originally registered as "Veet" in 1922 by a British firm called Tokalon Ltd., who took it from French *vite*, "quick," referring to the cream's rapid removal of unwanted hair. In 1961 the product passed to Dae Health Laboratories, and they added "O," ostensibly standing for "odorless" but also as a common tradename suffix. "Veet 'O'" was thus entered in the *Trade Marks Journal* of October 18, 1961. Veeto was subsequently marketed by **Reckitt & Colman** and the name entered in the *Journal* of June 6, 1973.

Veganin *(analgesic)*

The proprietary analgesic, containing aspirin, paracetamol, and codeine phosphate, has a name suggesting "vegetable" or "vegetate," although it may well be arbitrary. It was entered by the German chemical company of Gödecke & Co. of Berlin in the *Trade Marks Journal* of June 23, 1926.

Vegeburger *(savory cake)*

The Vegeburger resembles a hamburger in appearance but instead is made with vegetable protein, soya, and the like, instead of meat. The name, combining "vegetable" and "burger," was entered (originally as "Vege-burger") in the US Patent Office *Official Gazette* of June 29, 1976, with a note of first use on March 28, 1955.

Vegemite *(savory spread)*

The product is essentially an Australian equivalent of **Marmite**. Hence its name, blending "vegetable" and "Marmite," entered in the *Australian Official Journal of Trade Marks* of November 30, 1923.

Veg-O-Matic *(food cutter)*

The kitchen gadget of this name, combining "vegetable" and "automatic," was one of the many handy inventions of the Popeil Brothers, a firm founded in New York City in 1938 by Samuel J. Popeil (1915-1984), a garment worker's son, and his younger brother Raymond. The Veg-O-Matic was a small plastic device that could slice, dice, and wedge fruits and vegetables. Similar products from the same stable were the Dial-O-Matic, Chop-O-Matic, and Mince-O-Matic, used for chopping, grating, shredding and ripple-cutting. Samuel

Popeil's most profitable invention was the **Pocket Fisherman.**

Velcro *(fabric fastener)*

The name derives from French *velours croché*, "hooked velvet," referring to the tiny hooks on one strip of nylon which grip the tiny loops on another strip when the two are pressed together. The form of "touch-and-close" fastening, as it is commercially known, was first manufacturered around 1957 by George de Mestral, a Swiss engineer, who was inspired to create an alternative to the zip by the burrs from burdock weed that stuck to his clothes and to his dog's ears when he was out hunting. On examining the burrs under a microscope, de Mestrel saw that they bristled with tiny hooks which caught in the loops of clothing and in hair. The reference to "velvet" in the name may seem misleading, but is explained by the entry in the *Trade Marks Journal* of November 30, 1960: "Narrow fabrics in imitation of velvet being textile smallwares for use as fasteners or fastenings for clothing."

Velocette *(motorcycles)*

The British make of motorcycle first appeared on the roads in 1913. It was manufactured by the Veloce Motor Company, founded in 1904 by John Goodman, a German immigrant to England originally named Johannes Gutemann, and taking its name from Latin *velox, velocis,* "swift," with a suggestion of "velocipede" as an early form of bicycle. The marque survived until 1971.

Velox *(photographic paper)*

The brand of **Kodak** photographic paper can be developed under artificial light, so speeding up the process. Hence the name, as the Latin word for "swift." Paper of this type was invented by L.H. Baekeland of **Bakelite** fame, who in 1899 sold his Velox company and rights to George **Eastman**.

Venos *(cough mixture)*

The British proprietary medicine takes its name from Sir William Veno (1866-1933), born in Castle Douglas, Scotland, founder of the Veno Drug Company, Manchester. A major holding in the company was acquired by **Beecham** in 1928.

Vent-Axia *(air-extraction units)*

The British company originally manufactured "Axia" fans, so called as they were axial, i.e. rotated on an axis instead of moving to and fro. The present name was adopted in 1936, with "Vent-" from "ventilation." The name was entered in the *Trade Marks Journal* of May 6, 1936.

Ventile *(water-repellent fabric)*

The closely woven water-repellent cotton fabric has a name based on "ventilate," referring to its ability to let the skin "breathe." It was entered in the *Trade Marks Journal* of October 25, 1961, but the name was already in use in the mid-1950s.

Ventolin *(inhalant)*

The name is used for various preparations of salbutamol, a drug that relieves symptoms of asthma, chronic bronchitis, and emphysema. It is probably based on "ventilate," and was entered in the *Trade Marks Journal* of August 7, 1968 and the US Patent Office *Official Gazette* of April 18, 1978.

Verel *(synthetic fiber)*

The name of the synthetic acrylic fiber is probably of arbitrary origin. It was entered in the US Patent Office *Official Gazette* of October 2, 1956, and by **Eastman Kodak** in the *Trade Marks Journal* of October 24, 1956, the latter for: "Raw or partly prepared synthetic fibres."

Veridian *(aeronautics and information technology)*

The US company was formed in 1997 on the merger of Calspan SRL and Veda International, taking its name from the Latin element *veri-,* "true" (as in English *verity*), reflecting the company's integrity in its markets. The suggestion of Latin *viridis,* "green," "blooming," "vigorous," is an incidental bonus.

Vernons *(football pools)*

The British firm derives its name from that of its founder, Vernon Sangster (1899-1986). His father, Edmund Sangster, had started a football pool business in Preston, Lancashire, in 1923, and Vernon followed by setting up his own organization in Liverpool in 1926. Prior to this, Vernon Sangster had served with the Manchester Regiment in World War I, while in World War II he oversaw the various wartime activities of Vernons, which included the manufacture of generators and catering equipment for the forces. From modest beginnings, his enterprise developed into a million-pound business by the time of his death. The company was inherited by Vernon Sangster's son, Robert Sangster (b.1936), who sold it off in 1988 to concentrate on breeding racehorses.

Veronal (sedative)

The sedative and sleep-inducing drug, generically known as barbital, derives its name from the Italian city of Verona. The name is ingeniously explained by Ivor Brown in A Word in Edgeways (1953) as a literary allusion to the drug that Friar Laurence gives to Juliet in Shakespeare's Romeo and Juliet, on the grounds that the play is set in Verona and that the drug promises her "a cold and drowsy humor" and a "borrow'd likeness of shrunk death" from which, 42 hours later, she will "awake as from a pleasant sleep" (Act IV, scene i). More prosaically, the name was created by the drug's inventor, the German chemist Emil Fischer (1852-1919), who was in Verona at the time of his research.

Versace (fashionwear)

The Italian fashion house takes its name from Gianni Versace (1946-1997), born in Calabria, where he initially worked with his dressmaker mother. He then moved to Milan, where in 1978 he started his own business, Giannni Versace SpA, his distinctive designs coming to the fore in the 1980s and 1990s. Following his death in Miami, Florida, at the hands of a spree killer, his business was taken over by his sister, Donatella.

Versene (water-softening agent)

The proprietary name for a preparation containing ethylenediamine tetra-acetic acid, or a similar chelating agent, is apparently of arbitrary origin. It was entered by the Martin-Dennis Company, of Newark, New Jersey, in the US Patent Office Official Gazette of August 29, 1944 for: "Water softening agents in powdered and liquid form with or without detergents," and by the Bersworth Chemical Company, of Framingham, Massachusetts, in the Trade Marks Journal of November 14, 1951 for: "Chemical products used in industry."

Vespa (motorscooters)

The Italian firm of **Piaggio** first produced the scooters of this name in 1946. The word is Italian for "wasp," referring not to the engine's buzzing sound but to the rear end of the original model. The company rather went in for insect names, producing a three-wheeler car called "Ape" ("Bee") and an outboard motor called "Moscone" ("Bluebottle"). The name was entered in the Trade Marks Journal of March 22, 1950. Vespa midget cars were also produced from 1957 to 1961.

Veuve Clicquot (champagne)

The firm dates its founding from 1772, when Philippe Clicquot Muiron opened a trading house in Reims, France, dealing mainly in fabrics and banking, with modest transactions in champagne. In 1799 Clicquot's son, François, married Nicole Barbe Ponsardin (1777-1866), a baron's daughter, and the couple began trading in wine. After his early death in 1805 the business was carried on by his young widow, who renamed it Veuve ("Widow") Clicquot-Ponsardin, a name entered in the Trade Marks Journal of June 9, 1926, by "Bertrand de Mun & Cie., successeurs de Veuve Clicquot-Ponsardin." Hence the English nickname "the Widow" for Veuve Clicquot champagne. On Mme. Clicquot's own death the company passed to her former chief partner, Édouard Werlé, and it remained in the hands of the Werlé family until 1987, when it became part of the LVMH conglomerate (see **Moët et Chandon**).

VIA Rail Canada (railway system)

Canada's state-owned passenger railway system was estsblished in 1978 as a crown corporation independent of Canadian National Railways (CNR) and the Canadian Pacific Railway (CPR). "VIA" was already in use as a brand name by CNR from 1976, representing either English "via" (i.e. traveling through) or its source, Latin via, "way." In the latter case, "VIA Rail" is thus an inversion of "railway."

Viagra (anti-impotence drug)

The "wonder drug" to treat male impotence, technically a pyrazolopyramidinone antianginal agent called sildenafil citrate, was launched by **Pfizer** in 1998 and has a name of arbitrary origin. It was entered in the Trade Marks Journal of May 1, 1996, and happens to suggest a blend of "virile" and "Niagara," as if referring to the increased blood flow that the drug produces.

> The makers of Viagra threatened a pub chain with legal action for naming an alcoholic drink after its anti-impotence drug. The JD Wetherspoon group has now renamed its cocktail Niagra after a letter from Pfizer.
>
> (News item, *The Times*, August 22, 2000)

Vibram *(rubber soles)*

The type of tough, heavily-patterned rubber used, without nails, for the soles of climbing and walking boots takes its name from *Vitale Bram*ini, the Italian climber who invented it in the 1930s. The name was entered by the manufacturers, Vibram SpA., of Albizzate, Italy, in the *Trade Marks Journal* of November 24, 1976 for: "Soles, heels, heel-tips, cork-heels and intersoles for shoes."

Vibroseis *(oil-locating system)*

The system for locating oil or gas underground operates (without the use of explosives) by measuring the reflected sound waves produced by a large vibrator that repeatedly strikes the ground. Hence the name, from the first elements of "vibrator" and "seismic," entered in the *Trade Marks Journal* of August 23, 1961 for: "Instruments and apparatus for use in detecting the presence of oil by seismic vibrations," and in the US Patent Office *Official Gazette* of July 3, 1962: "For electrical and electronic apparatus for seismic exploration for oil," with a note of first use on or about February 22, 1961.

Vici *(shoe leather)*

The type of chrome-tanned kid leather used for boots and shoes perhaps derives its name from Latin *vici*, "I conquered," denoting its superiority. It was entered in the US Patent Office *Official Gazette* of October 13, 1891 for: "Kid, goat, and similar light weight leathers."

Vickers *(armaments and aircraft)*

The British company traces its origins to 1828, when Naylor, Hutchinson, Vickers and Co. were established as a steel firm in Sheffield. In 1867 the firm of Vickers, Sons & Co. Ltd. was incorporated, headed by the brothers Thomas Edward Vickers (1833-1915) and Albert Vickers (1838-1919), sons of Edward Vickers (1804-1897), a miller. In 1897 Vickers combined its business with Maxim, making the Vickers Maxim machine gun, and soon after moved into aviation, producing such well-known aircraft as the Vickers Vimy, Wellington, Spitfire, Viscount, and VC10. Its aircraft division merged in 1960 with two other companies to form the British Aircraft Corporation, which was nationalized in 1977 and became part of British Aerospace. In 1980 Vickers merged with **Rolls-Royce**.

Vick's *(seeds)*

The name is that of James Vick (1818-1882), born in Chichester, Sussex, England, the son of a keen gardener. (His principal occupation is unknown.) Vick moved with his family to New York City in 1833, where he learned the printing trade, then in 1837 accompanied his parents to Rochester, New York, where he set type for various newspapers. In 1849, having inherited his father's horticultural interests, Vick began to write for the *Genesee Farmer*, a journal founded in 1831 to disseminate views about agricultural improvement. He became coeditor of the *Farmer*'s horticultural department in 1850, and five years later bought the journal. Further journalistic enterprise followed, but Vick was already interested in the seed trade, and offered a selection of French flower seeds to *Farmer* readers in 1856. In 1856 he bought a racecourse about two miles out of Rochester and converted it into a garden center. Here he started selling seeds by mail order, and by 1870 was receiving more than 300 orders a day. After Vick's death, the flourishing business was continued by his son, James Vick, Jr., who made seeds and images of flowers available wherever Americans enjoyed mail-order service.

Vicks *("VapoRub")*

The founder of the firm (subsequently **Richardson-Merrell**) that came to make Vicks VapoRub was Lunsford Richardson (1854-1919), born a farmer's son near Raleigh, North Carolina. He became a pharmacist and set up a store in Greensboro, where in the 1890s he developed new products, including Vick's VapoRub, which used a new drug, menthol, in what was for its day a novel treatment for colds. The name for the product was suggested to him by a magazine advertisement for "**Vick's** Seeds." That suited him well, as he wanted a short name that was easy to remember. Moreover, it happened to be the name of his brother-in-law, Dr. Joshua Vick. In 1905

Richardson sold his wholesale drug business and founded the Vick Family Remedies Company, which handled nothing but the 21 Vick's products that he had developed by this time. He later discarded all the products except one, Vick's VapoRub. The second word of the name referred to the way the heat of a person's body vaporized the menthol of the product (long known as simply "Vick" in the UK) after it had been rubbed on the chest.

Victor *see* **Victrola**

Victor Value *(grocery stores)*

The British grocery stories, formerly one of the leading food chains in the south of England, took their name from Victor Cohen, an importer of toys from Germany who moved into the grocery trade on the rise of Nazism in the 1930s. By 1950 there were over 40 Victor Value stores in London and the Home Counties. Victor's son, Alex Cohen (1903-2000), who inherited the business from his father, retired after the chain was taken over by **Tesco** in 1968.

Victory V *(lozenges)*

The name owes its origin to Edward Smith, a Scottish doctor who in the mid-19th century compounded a lozenge designed not only to relieve coughs and colds but also to settle upset stomachs. So great was the demand for the lozenge in Bolton, Lancashire, England, where Dr. Smith worked, that he stepped up production and put the pastille on the market as the "Cough No More Lozenge." In the process of expansion Smith took over the bankrupt pharmaceuticals factory in Nelson, Lancashire, belonging to Thomas Fryer, and installed his younger brother there as manager. Back in Bolton, both brothers were seeking a more succinct name for their lozenges. One day, seeing a mill called the "Victory Spinning Mill," Edward reportedly turned to his brother and said: "There's your name, William – Victory. How well it goes with Nelson." He then named his product "Victory Chlorodyne Lozenges," which was really a misnomer, as they contained no chlorodyne. Aware of the anomaly, and also of the possibility that the supposed chlorodyne might attract stamp duty, Smith dropped the word "Chlorodyne" from the name and changed it to "Linseed Liquorice V Lozenge Victory," putting "Victory" last to make it pro-

prietary. In 1911 this was finally shortened to "Victory-V Lozenges." The name in its present form was entered in the *Trade Marks Journal* of August 1, 1951, and the lozenges are now made by Ernest Jackson & Co. of Crediton, Devon.

Victrola *(phonographs)*

The phonographs, launched in 1906 as disk machines with an enclosed speaker horn and encased in an attractive wood cabinet, took their name from their manufacturers, the Victor Talking Machine Co., founded in 1901 by Eldridge Reeves Johnson (1867-1945), and itself so called because its instruments would play "Victor" records. The latter part of the name was probably based on that of the **Pianola**, the automatic piano that had appeared nine years earlier. Names based in turn on "Victrola" were "Radiola," an electric-recording phonograph, introduced in 1925, and "Electrola," an electrically operated phonograph. (*See also* **Motorola**.) "Victrola" was entered in the US Patent Office *Official Gazette* of January 9, 1906 and the *Trade Marks Journal* of May 9, 1906. *See also* **HMV**.

Vileda *(cleaning cloths)*

The company of this name is a German subsidiary of Bondina Ltd., itself a subsidiary of Carl Freudenberg GmbH, who market its products worldwide. The name is a phonetic representation of German *wie Leder*, "like leather." The reference is to the company's principal product, a synthetic chamois window cloth and car cloth, which is claimed to clean like real chamois leather. The name was entered in the *Trade Marks Journal* of April 28, 1954.

Vilene *(backing material)*

The name of the backing or interlining for clothing material was entered by the Viledon Co. Ltd. of London, England, in the *Trade Marks Journal* of February 9, 1954 for: "Lining and stiffening materials for clothing, all being textile piece goods." The name itself appears to be arbitrary, as does that of the company.

Vim *(detergent)*

The British detergent was put on the market by Lever Brothers (later **Unilever**) in 1904, initially with some misgiving about the choice of name, which according to a contemporary report was "thought to be too reminiscent of certain processed meat products." The name represents English "vim," in the colloquial sense "force," "vigor," and had already been entered by Lever in the *Trade Marks Journal* of April 6, 1894 for "all goods included in Class 48."

Vimto *(soft drink)*

The British firm of J.N. Nichols was founded at the turn of the 20th century by John Noel Nichols (d.1966), a Manchester trader. His main business was trading herbs and spices, but in 1908 he developed a cordial, which he sold to local herbalist outlets. The retailers added water and sold it to customers as a health tonic. The drink itself was at first called "Vimtonic," as a tonic that gave one "vim," but the name was subsequently shortened as now and entered in the *Trade Marks Journal* of February 12, 1913, as a "medicinal preparation for humans." By the 1950s Vimto had become the firm's main product, and in 1969 J.N. Nichols (Vimto) Ltd. began bottling their own version of it.

Vincent-HRD *(motorcycles)*

Philip Conrad Vincent was born in Argentina, where his English father owned a ranch, in 1908. He was sent to England for his education, and while at Harrow School developed an interest in motorcycles. On leaving school, he was keen to exploit this commercially, and persuaded his father to put up the money to buy the motorcycle makers HRD, founded in 1924 by Howard R. Davies (hence the name). In 1927, Philip Vincent accordingly came along with £400 and bought the name and its brief, but so far successful, history. The new Vincent-HRD company was set up in Stevenage, Hertfordshire, and produced many interesting models until 1955, when despite full order books, Vincent decided to cease production in the light of rising costs. The company was taken over in 1959, with Vincent himself beset by illness and financial problems. He died in 1979, but the name lives on.

Vinolia *(toilet soaps)*

The British company of this name, noted for its high-class toilet soaps, toilet preparations, and perfumery, was founded in London as Blondeau et Cie. in 1899. Soon after, it adopted the product name, originally entered in the *Trade Marks Journal* of June 20, 1888 for: "Chemical substances prepared for use in medicine and pharmacy; substances prepared as remedies for human skin diseases," and presumably based on Latin *vinum*, "wine," and *oleum*, "oil." The firm was acquired by Lever Bros. (*see* **Unilever**) in 1906.

Vinylite *(vinyl resin)*

The name, from "vinyl" and the chemical suffix "-ite," was entered by the Carbide & Carbon Chemicals Corporation, New York, in the US Patent Office *Official Gazette* of May 28, 1929: "For artificial resins in powder form or in form of plates or sheets and molding mixtures containing such resins," and in the *Trade Marks Journal* of September 25, 1929 for: "Synthetic resin sold in slabs, sheets, bars and tubes for industrial purposes and moulding materials made of synthetic resin." The resin itself was formerly used in the manufacture of phonograph records.

Virago *(publishers)*

The British publishing house was founded in 1972 by Carmen Callil (b.1938) to specialize in books by or about women. The name was a clever piece of public relations, taking "virago" as an abusive term for a shrewish woman in its original sense of a manlike (Latin *vir*, "man") and vigorous woman, and equally evoking the name given by Adam to Eve in the Vulgate (Latin) version of Genesis 2:23, retained in Wyclif's translation of 1388: "This schal be clepid virago, for she is takun of man." Calill remained chairman until 1995. According to an article by Adrienne Blue in *Ms.* (April 1984):

> The name Virago, which in my two dictionaries is defined as "a noisy, domineering woman" and "a shrew," was chosen because of its original meaning, " a heroic woman," and because the founders knew it would shock a little.

Virazole *(antiviral drug)*

The proprietary name for ribavirin, a synthetic ribonucleoside that inhibits the replication of both DNA and RNA in viruses, derives from a blend of "virus" and "azole." The name dates from the 1970s.

Virgin *(travel and entertainment)*

The story of Virgin is one of English teenage entrepreneurship. At age 15 Richard Branson (b.1950) became editor of a school magazine,

Student. In the mid-1960s he spotted the growth in pop music sales and began selling cut-price records through *Student*, but when a postal strike threatened sales by this method set about finding a shop. He settled for a former shoe shop in London's Oxford Street and used his charm and cheek to persuade the owner to let him occupy it free until a paying tenant came along. The scheme worked and a year later he opened a recording studio in an Oxfordshire country house. In 1972 Virgin released its first record, Mike Oldfield's *Tubular Bells*. Branson chose the name because when he and his friends started their publishing venture they were virgin businessmen. Virgin Atlantic Airlines followed in 1984, but in 1992 Branson sold Virgin Music to **Thorn EMI**.

Virol *(malt food tonic)*

The English tonic food of this name was first produced experimentally in 1899 at the London factory of **Bovril** Ltd., with the name itself entered in the *Trade Marks Journal* of June 7, 1899. As the demand for the product grew, Bovril formed a separate company, Virol Ltd., in the early 1900s. In 1920 the Virol factory was moved to larger, more modern premises at Perivale, Middlesex. After World War II Virol changed hands more than once. Cavenham Foods took over Bovril, and so Virol, in 1971, but in 1977 sold off Virol to Jenks Brothers of High Wycombe, Buckinghamshire, who in 1979 sold it to **Optrex**. The name itself arose in the "classical" period of trade name creation, and thus might be supposed to derive from Latin *vir*, "man," and the common "-ol" suffix meaning "oil" (Latin *oleum*). Latin *vir* means not only "man as opposed to woman" but also "man as opposed to boy," and this distinction seems to support the import of the name, as Virol was widely advertised as a suitable "tonic" for childen. ("Virol—Growing Boys Need It," "Virol—Anæmic Girls Need It.") But the fact that Virol was first made on the premises of Bovril, as an alternate product to Bovril itself, suggests that the name may have been actually suggested by "Bovril," of which it is in fact a near anagram.

VISA *(credit card)*

The credit card, originally known as "Bank-Americard," was first issued on a statewise basis by the Bank of America (*see* **BankAmerica**) in California in 1959. Licensing in other states began in 1966, and in 1977 the name was changed to "Visa," entered in the US Patent Office *Official Gazette* of May 17, 1977: "For financial services involving the use of plastic cards by cardholders and merchant and banking outlets for payment to merchants, loans to cardholders, or transfer of cardholder funds," and in the *Trade Marks Journal* of July 27, 1977 for: "Printed cards related to banking and to credit services." The name itself, now usually spelled in capital letters, denotes admittance to certain financial services, just as a passport visa grants admission of the holder to a particular country.

Visking *(tubing)*

The type of seamless cellulose tubing, used on the one hand as a membrane in dialysis and on the other as an edible casing for sausages, was originally manufactured by the Visking Corporation of Chicago, who entered the name in the *Trade Marks Journal* of July 29, 1931 and the US Patent Office *Official Gazette* of April 15, 1941. *See also* **Visqueen**.

VI-Spring *(beds and mattresses)*

The British company, based in Plymouth, Devon, dates from 1901, when it bought the patent to spring mattresses. Its name alludes to the six (Roman VI) coils of wire present in every spring.

Visqueen *(sheeting)*

The durable polyethylene sheeting, used in various building applications and in the manufacture of waterproof domestic articles, bases its name punningly on its US manufacturers, **Visking**. It was entered in the US Patent Office *Official Gazette* of July 27, 1948, with a claim of use since May 1, 1946, and in the *Trade Marks Journal* of March 11, 1953.

Vistavision *(film projection system)*

The wide-screen film process was developed by **Paramount** in the 1950s in response to **Twentieth Century–Fox**'s **CinemaScope**, but without anamorphic lenses for the camera and projector. (It used film running through the camera horizontally rather than vertically, thereby creating a frame with an area twice the normal size.) The process was first used for Michael Curtiz's *White Christmas* (1954). The name, combining "vista" and "vision," was entered in the US Patent Office *Official Gazette* of January 25, 1955.

Vitaglass *(glass)*

The type of glass that transmits most of the ultraviolet rays of sunlight, which ordinary glass does not, derives its name from Latin *vita*, "life." Sunlight, in moderation, is essential for the body to produce vitamin D. The name (first as simply "Vita") was entered by the British chemist Francis Everard Lamplough of King's Norton, Birmingham, in the *Trade Marks Journal* of July 29, 1925.

Vitagraph *(motion pictures)*

The early American film studio was established in 1899 by J. Stuart Blackton and Albert E. Smith in New York City, basing its name on the projector they had developed from the earlier "Vitascope." The name itself is based on Latin *vita*, "life," and the Greek "-graph" element meaning "writing." After a long and successful career, the studio was taken over by **Warner Brothers** in 1925. *Cp.* **Vitaphone**.

Vitallium *(alloy)*

The name is that of an alloy of cobalt, chromium, and molybdenum that has a high resistance to abrasion, corrosion, and heat, making it suitable for use in surgery, dentistry, and engineering. The name itself is of uncertain origin (a connection with Latin *vita*, "life," is possible). It was entered in the US Patent Office *Official Gazette* of June 18, 1935, with a claim of use since July 8, 1934, and subsequently by Austenal Laboratories, New York, in the *Trade Marks Journal* of August 1, 1951.

Vitamizer *(food blender)*

The Australian appliance for blending cooking ingredients, or for reducing raw fruit and vegetables to liquid form, has a name suggesting the process releases or enhances the vitamins present in the food. It was entered "for food and drink mixing machines" by the manufacturers, Semak Electrics Pty, Ltd., in the *Australian Official Journal of Patents* (Canberra) of May 16, 1950.

Vitaphone *(film sound-recording process)*

The "sound-on-disc" system for motion pictures, in which the sound track was recorded on discs and played in synchronization with the projection of the film, was first widely used for what is generally recognized to be the first "talkie," *The Jazz Singer* (1927), starring Al Jolson. The system itself was developed by **Western Electric**, the research facility of Bell Telephone (*see* **Bell System**). In 1926, Western Electric formed the Vitaphone Company with **Warner Brothers**. The name combines Latin *vita*, "life," and the Greek "-phone" element meaning "sound." *Cp.* **Vitagraph**.

VitBe *(bread)*

The British make of wholewheat (wheatgerm) bread derives its name from "Vitamin B," which is readily present in such bread.

Vitello *(margarine)*

The margarine was introduced in Germany by the Dutch firm of Van den Bergh (*see* **Unilever**) in 1898. It was actually based on a patent taken out by a German chemist named Bergenau, who had discovered that if he added yolk of egg to margarine, the resulting substance turned brown and frothed when used for frying just like butter. In fact, it was the nearest approach to butter yet made. Hence the name, from Latin *vitellus*, "yolk of egg." The patent was declared void in 1906, but the margarine gained such popularity that it became the near-generic German term for margarine itself.

Vitreosil *(vitreous silica)*

The proprietary name for vitreous silica, derived as a blend of these two words, was entered by the British manufacturers, The Thermal Syndicate Ltd., of Wallsend, Northumberland, in the *Trade Marks Journal* of December 15, 1909 for: "Fused silica articles included in Class 15 in the form of tubes, plates, basins ... and other shapes for chemical, electrical, ornamental and other similar purposes."

Vitrolite *(opal glass)*

The name of the make of opal glass (a type of semitranslucent white glass) derives from Latin *vitrum*, "glass" and "-lite" denoting a mineral (rather than a respelled "light") and was entered by **Pilkington** Brothers Ltd. of Liverpool, England, in the *Trade Marks Journal* of February 1, 1939

Vittel *(mineral water)*

The mineral water is obtained from springs near the town of Vittel in the Vosges department of France. Hence the name, entered by the Société Générale des Eaux Minérales de Vittel in the *Trade Marks Journal* of May 26, 1909.

Vivendi *(water supply and multimedia)*

The French company was formed in 1998 on the merger of the Compagnie Générale des Eaux ("General Water Company"), founded in 1853 to irrigate the countryside and supply water to towns and cities, and Havas (*see* **Agence France-Presse**). According to company publicity, the new name "symbolizes the vivacity and mobility of an international company working in locally-based activities that improve everyday life." Possibly its creators had in mind the Latin tag *vivendi causa*, "source of life," as water is generally said to be.

Viyella *(textiles)*

The British-made fabric, a twilled mixture of cotton and wool, was originally manufactured by the firm of William Hollins near Matlock, Derbyshire. The firm's factory was located on the valley road called the Via Gellia, known to local people as "the Vi Jella," and this colloquial pronunciation influenced the form of the trade name, which was entered in the *Trade Marks Journal* of June 6, 1894 for: "Yarns of wool, worsted or hair." The Via Gellia itself was named for Philip Gell of Hopton Hall, Wirksworth, who built the road in 1792. (The name was patterned on those of ancient Roman roads in Britain, such as the Via Devana that ran across central England.) Viyella International became one of the three largest textile firms in Britain by the end of the 1960s, and shortly after was acquired by **ICI**. In 1986, after a series of mergers, it was bought by **Coats Patons** to become Coats Viyella.

Vladivar *(vodka)*

The name of the brand of British vodka, produced by the Vladivar Vodka Company, of Glasgow, Scotland, evokes the familiar Russian first name "Vladimir," the two *v*s matching the first letter of "vodka." The name was entered in the *Trade Marks Journal* of January 10, 1962.

Vlasic *(pickles)*

In 1923 Joseph Vlasic (b.1904), then still a teenager, acquired a small milk run in Detroit and built it up into a large wholesale milk company. In 1937, by now a food wholesaler, he was approached by the owner of a small pickle plant and asked to handle a new home-style pickle he had developed. Vlasic agreed, but only on condition he label them with his own name. His products sold well, especially among Detroit's Polish community, and his company went on to become the nation's largest manufacturer of pickles. In 1978, headed by Joseph's son, Robert J. Vlasic, the firm merged with the **Campbell** Soup Company.

Vocalion *(phonograph)*

The phonograph of this name was produced by the **Aeolian** Co. in the early years of the 20th century as a cabinet model with a so-called "Graduola" tone control. The name is obviously based on "vocal."

Vodafone *(cellular telephones)*

Britain's first commercial cellphone service was launched in 1985 by **Racal**, its name combining "voice," "data," and a respelled "phone." In 1988 it was floated as a separate company, Racal Telecom, which in 1991 became the Vodafone Group. The name was entered in the *Trade Marks Journal* of September 3, 1986.

Voisin *(automobiles)*

Best known for his aircraft, Gabriel Voisin (1880-1973) built his first experimental automobile with his brother Charles (1882-1912) in 1899, seven years before they founded the first aircraft manufacturing business in France. Charles was killed in a road accident four years later, and their aircraft concern halted. After World War I, Gabriel set up again, returning to motor vehicles in 1919. The company passed to the aeroengine manufacturers Gnome et Rhône in the 1930s, and by the end of the 1950s the Voisin name had been phased out.

Voit *(balls)*

William Voit (1880-1946) worked as a salesman for a number of rubber companies in California before forming his own business, the W.J. Voit Rubber Co., in 1924. His earliest product was camelback, a material used in recapping automobile tires. Aiming to expand his business, Voit developed a multicolored inflatable rubber beach ball in 1927. The new product became an instant hit with California beachgoers, and sales soared. They were punctured in the stock market crash, however, obliging Voit to try another tack. In 1932 he introduced a rubber athletic ball, followed soon after by rubber basketballs and footballs. By the time of his death, Voit was providing balls and other rubber athletic goods to thousands of school, colleges, and public playgrounds in America.

Volkswagen *(automobiles)*

This is the famous "people's car" (the meaning of the German name) that Adolf Hitler ordered to be mass produced in 1937. The original manufacturing company set up that year was the Gesellschaft zur Vorbereitung des deutschen Volkswagens ("Company for the Development of the German People's Car"), operated by the Deutsche Arbeitsfront ("German Labor Front"), a Nazi organization. The site for the works was 50 miles east of Hanover, near Fallersleben, and was named in 1938 as Stadt des KdF-Wagens ("Town of the Strength-through-Joy Car"), after the German Labor Front slogan. (The town that grew around the works was named Wolfsburg in 1946 by the British government, reviving the locality's original name, and the Volkswagen-Werke were temporarily renamed Wolfsburger-Werke.) The prototype of the Volkswagen, called the "Volksauto," had already been built by **NSU** in 1934 to a design by Ferdinand **Porsche** as a small, air-cooled, rear-engined vehicle. Eventually, after various mergers and takeovers, Volkswagen produces not only the "VW" but the **Audi** and the **NSU**.

Volvo *(automobiles)*

The first Swedish car of this name made its test run from Stockholm to Göteborg in 1926 and was produced by a company set up by two engineers, Assar Gabrielsson (1891-1962), born in Korsberga, and Gustaf Larson (1887-1968), born near Örebro. The name is Latin for "I roll," although this did not originally apply to the car but to the ball bearings made by the Göteborg firm where the two men worked, SKF (Svenska Kullagerfabriken, "Swedish Ball-Bearing Works"), founded in 1907. The story goes that the pair met up and elected to start their own automotive business over a crawfish dinner at Stockholm's Sturehof restaurant in 1924, the plan being that all the main components would be of their own design, but produced under contract by outside suppliers. The

name is obvious enough for ball bearings but is also suitable for a vehicle that "rolls" or runs on wheels along the road.

Vono *(beds and bedding)*

The British firm was founded around 1920 by a family named Vaughan, and the product name is apparently a phonetic development of this. The name was originally entered in the *Trade Marks Journal* of September 29, 1909.

Vosene *(medicated shamppo)*

The British product was first marketed by a retired London fishmonger who had moved to Bury, Lancashire, in 1946, and the company that manufactured it was originally called Vosemar Ltd. The precise origin of the name remains uncertain, although it appears the company was named after the product, not the other way around. It is possible the fishmonger was named Vos. Vosene was acquired by **Beecham** in 1955. The name was entered in the *Trade Marks Journal* of March 26, 1941.

Vosper Thornycroft *(shipbuilders)*

John Isaac Thornycroft (1843-1928) was born in Rome, Italy, the son of an English sculptor. His father was also an amateur engineer, and his studio was equally a workshop, containing model railway engines. Young John began his career in this workshop, where after making smaller craft he constructed a steam launch, the *Nautilus*. In 1862 his father sent him to work as a draftsman at a shipyard in Jarrow, northeastern England, after which he studied natural philosophy and engineering at Glasgow University, graduating in engineering science. In 1866 Thornycroft's father helped him set up a shipyard at Chiswick, on the Thames near London, where in 1871 he built the first small high-speed boat of which there is any record, the *Miranda*. The shipyard's expanding manufacture of destroyers and torpedo craft obliged it to move from Chiswick to Woolston, Southampton, in 1906. In 1966 John I. Thornycroft & Co. Ltd. merged with Vosper Ltd. as Vosper Thornycroft (UK) Ltd. The latter name emerged from Wilson, Vosper & Coltart, a Liverpool firm of ships' store and export merchants, represented subsequently by Dennis Forwood Vosper, Baron Runcorn of Heswall (1916-1968), a former Conservative cabinet minister. *See also* **David Brown**.

Vuitton, Louis *see* Louis Vuitton

Vynide *(plastic fabric)*

The form of plastic, used as a substitute for leather in upholstery, clothing, and the like, seems to have a name suggesting "vinyl." It was described as "leather cloth" when entered by its manufacturers, **ICI**, in the *Trade Marks Journal* of June 16, 1943.

W. H. Allen *(publishers)*

Little that is known about William Houghton Allen, who gave his name to the British firm. He was probably born in about 1790, and seems to have been a stationer and bookseller in Leadenhall Street, London, in the 1840s. In the London Post Office Directory of 1851 he is described as being a "general stationer and publisher," so that he must have founded his business by then. Allen probably came from Kent, for in Sevenoaks parish church there is a marble plaque placed by his widow to Lieutenant Colonel Augustine Allen, fifth son of William Houghton Allen "of this parish," who died in 1869.

W. H. Smith *(newsagents, stationers, and booksellers)*

The ubiquitous British chain store was founded by Henry Walton Smith, a London Custom House official, who in 1792 opened a newsagent's shop in Mayfair and set up a "newswalk," the equivalent of a modern newspaper delivery route. Sadly, he died that same year, aged 54, but not before his wife had given birth to a son, William Henry Smith (1792-1865). William's mother kept the business going, and after her own death, in 1816, William took it over, together with his elder brother, Henry Edward Smith. William became the dominant partner, and when the partnership dissolved in 1828, he continued the business alone, as a wholesale newsagents and stationers. In 1846 his son, also William Henry Smith (1825-1891), joined him on reaching the age of 21, and the firm of W.H. Smith & Son was created. It was William Henry, Jr., who set up the well-known W.H. Smith railway bookstalls, the first of which opened at Euston Station, London, in 1848.

W. W. Norton *(publishers)*

William Warder Norton (1891-1945) was born in Springfield, Ohio, the son of a patent lawyer. He attended local public schools and on graduating from St. Paul's School in Concord, Ohio, entered Ohio State University in Columbus, Ohio, to study mechanical engineering. Norton left college after his junior year to become foreign sales manager of Kilbourne & Jacobs, a manufacturing company in Columbus. After several years there he moved to Philadelphia, where he became a manager at Harrisons & Crossfield, a British-based export-import firm. In 1916 he moved to New York City to open a new company office there. In time Norton became interested in establishing a publishing division of the People's Institute, an adult-education school of which he was a trustee, and in 1923 the People's Institute Publishing Company was formally established. In 1926 Norton became a fulltime publisher, changing the name of the firm to W.W. Norton & Company, Inc. The firm grew steadily and today remains a major publisher of quality trade books and textbooks.

Waddington's *(board and card games)*

Not much is known about John Waddington who gave his name to the British company. He apparently started a printing business in Leeds in the late 19th century, having as partner Wilson Garrett, actor-manager at the Grand Theatre, Leeds. A company was formed as Waddington's Ltd. to print theater posters and related theater advertising. Nor is it certain when the firm was founded, but an advertisement describing Waddington's as printers appears in the theatrical publication *Yorkshire Harlequin* of January 5, 1898. There then seems to have been some sort of disagreement between Waddington and Garrett, so that the two men split up, with Waddington setting up his own printing business. He ran into financial difficulties, however, and had to be rescued by his local bank manager. In 1905 a private limited company was formed as John Waddington Ltd. But there were again problems with debts, and Waddington resigned in 1913. The business was put on its feet again by Victor Watson (1878-1943), the lithographic foreman, and all went well from then on. In 1933 Waddington's introduced one of its most popular card games, **Lexicon**, and this was the start of the company's games division. *See also* **Monopoly**.

Wade *(pottery)*

The British company of George Wade & Son Ltd., based in Stoke-on-Trent, Staffordshire, in the heart of the Potteries, takes its name not from Colonel Sir George Wade (1891-1986), its former chairman, but from the George Wade who was probably his great-uncle, and who in about 1830 purchased the pottery business started in 1810 near Chesterton, north of Newcastle-under-Lyne, by Henry Hallen. There were three Wade factories originally, operating as George Wade & Son Ltd., J. & A. Wade (later A.J. Wade), and Wade & Co. (later Wade Heath & Co.). These were all run by Sir George Wade's uncles, George and Albert Wade, and it seems that the first of these was the son of the founder.

Wadham Stringer *(automobile mechanics)*

Wadham Stringer is the trading name in the south of England of the Wadham **Kenning** Motor Group, which trades as Kenning in the north, with the group itself formed in 1987 after its parent company, T.K.M., had acquired the Kenning Motor Group the previous year. Harold Wadham purchased his bicycle business in Waterlooville, Hampshire, in the closing years of the 19th century. In 1905 he was joined by his brother, Wilfred, and the motor business began. Expansion followed, and by 1920 Wadham brothers had premises along much of the south coast. Meanwhile in Melksham, Wiltshire, Frederick C. Stringer and his father were also rapidly expanding their identical business, and similarly came to occupy south coast sites. In due course the two firms became public companies, trading respectively as Wadham (Holdings) Ltd. and Stringer Motors Ltd. In 1968 the two businesses took the logical step of merging, thus forming Wadham Stringer Ltd. The combined organization now covers much of the south of England and the Midlands.

Wadworth *(beer)*

In 1875, 22-year-old English brewer Henry Alfred Wadworth purchased the old Northgate brewery in Devizes, Wiltshire. He already had six years of brewing experience behind him, both as an apprentice at a London brewery and as the manager of a small brewery in Long Street, Devizes. He formed a partnership with his lifelong friend and brother-in-law John Smith Bartholomew and in 1885 built a new brewery on the site of a sweet-water well only 100 yards from the original. Wadworth had no male issue, but Bartholomew did, and after his death in 1923 the business passed to his son, John Bartholomew, who ran the brewery as managing director to 1929, then as chairman following Wadworth's death that year after a fall from his horse. John C. Bartholomew, grandson of John Smith Bartholomew, succeeded his father in 1952, and at the close of the 20th century his own son, Charles Bartholomew, was both chairman and managing director.

Wah Wah *(electronic musical device)*

The name is that of a device attached to an electric guitar that can produce a "wah-wah" effect. It was entered in the US Patent Office *Official Gazette* of September 2, 1969: "For musical auxiliary amplification and attenuation tone devices, consisting of a pedal and an electronic circuitry housing for use with electronic musical instruments," with a note of first use on April 3, 1967.

Waitrose *(supermarkets)*

In 1904, three assistants at a London, England, grocery store decided to open their own shop at 263 Acton Hill, West London. They were Wallace Wyndham Waite (1881-1971), Arthur Rose (1881-1949), and David Taylor. The latter left soon after, and from 1908 Waite and Rose traded under their combined names as Waitrose. They gradually opened other branches of their business, until by the outbreak of World War I there were as many as 25. Some shops had to be sold during the war, but trade picked up after it, although Rose had to quit the business in 1923 on medical advice, leaving Waite to continue alone. Waite clearly wanted his grocery stores to be more than routine corner shops, and he named one of them "The Marble Palace of Pure Food" and another punningly "Pro Bono Pimlico," after the London district where it was located. The stores sold a variety of foods, including some "own-label" products and a good selection of cheeses. In 1937 Waitrose was acquired by the **John Lewis** Partnership, with Waite remaining as managing director until his retirement in 1940.

Walgreen *(drugs)*

The American company operates the country's largest retail drug chain. It takes its name from Charles Rudolph Walgreen (1873-1939), born near Galesburg, Illinois, the son of a Swedish immigrant farmer. The family moved to Dixon, Illinois, in 1887. Walgreen's involvement with drugs came about as the result of an accident. While working in a shoe factory in Dixon he cut off the top joint of a middle finger. Despite his injury, Walgreen went on playing baseball, preventing his hand from healing properly. His doctor therefore arranged for him to apprentice at a local drugstore in the hope of keeping him off the diamond. Walgreen stayed with the job for a year and a half, when he was fired (or quit) during a disagreement with the owner. Anxious to see more of the world, Walgreen moved to Chicago in 1893, where he quickly found work in a drugstore. He was encouraged to set up his own business, and after serving in Cuba in the Spanish-American War, he eventually did so, purchasing a drugstore on Chicago's south side in 1901. His aim was to make products that were better and cheaper than anyone else's. His shop technically became a chain with the purchase of a second Chicago store in 1909. After that, numbers grew steadily, so that by the time of his death there were around 500 stores.

Walker, Johnnie *see* **Johnnie Walker**

Walker Books *(publishers)*

Walker Books, one of Britain's leading children's book publishers, was founded in 1980 by Sebastian Walker (1942-1991). His grandfather made the family fortune in machine tools, and Walker himself began his career in an Ealing, London, factory making milling machines. He then moved into publishing, but left **Cape** to set up his own firm in a former bedding factory in southeast London, choosing the lucrative youth market. Walker sold many of his books in **Sainsbury** supermarkets, and his authors and illustrators benefit from the trust fund that he set up in 1990 to own half the company. All his life he resisted takeover attempts from companies such as **Pearson** and **Simon & Schuster**.

Walkers *(potato crisps, or chips)*

The Englishman behind the name is Henry Walker, a pork butcher from Mansfield, Nottinghamshire, who in the 1880s took over a pork butchery business established in Leicester in 1820. Walker and his son saw their shop do good trade in the High Street, and in 1912 they moved to larger premises in Cheapside. From then on, the Walkers continued steadily as butchers, opening further shops, until World War II, when there were problems, mainly through meat rationing. Things were not much better after the war, since meat supplies continued to be restricted. In 1948, when Walkers' shops were sold out by 10 o'clock each morning, and the meat factory was working at half capacity, the managing director, R.E. Gerrard, began looking for another way of using his work force. There were two possibilities: ice cream or potato chips. The first was ruled out, as there could have been serious health problems if meat and dairy products were manufactured together. The crisps were therefore chosen, and in 1949 production began on the empty upper floor of the firm's premises in Oxford Street, Leicester. The beginnings were modest, with the potatoes cut by hand and cooked in an ordinary fish and chip shop frier. But the Leicester public approved. Since then, Walkers potato crisps have gained national popularity. The company's main factory remains in Leicester.

Walkman *(personal stereo)*

The personal stereo was launched by **Sony** in 1979 and so called because it could be played while walking (or bicycling) along the street or riding in public transport. The device was the inspiration of Sony's founder, Akio Morita, who wanted to find a way his children and their friends could listen to loud music without using deafening boom boxes that disturbed their neighbors. He asked his engineers to build a small radio and cassette player that could be attached to people's heads. That way they could take their music with them and listen to it without annoying others. The Sony staff were dubious, as there was no demand for little radios that people could attach to their heads. But Morita insisted, and the Walkman stormed the market. Sony's American agents told their parent company that the name did not make sense, and the stereo was launched in the USA as the "Soundabout." The British agreed that it was a meaningless name, but chose to call it a "Stowaway." As a result, when tourists started bringing home-grown Walkmans back from Japan, a serious brand identity crisis developed. Within a few months, Sony had decided that a Walkman should be a Walkman worldwide, and the name gained universal acceptance. It was entered in the *Trade Marks Journal* of March 25, 1981 and the US Patent Office *Official Gazette* of December 20, 1983.

Walk-Over *(footwear)*

When the Geo. E. Keith Company, of Brockton, Massachusetts, was founded in 1874, much of the firm's original output went to jobbers, who in turn sold the shoes to retailers, either under their own name or that of the retailer. George E. Keith realized that this was not a good way to win customer loyalty to his products, so dropped the jobber in favor of producing footwear himself. What could he call his specialty shoe? He did not want to use his own name, as there were already a number of Keiths in the footwear business. The solution came in the summer of 1898, when the international yacht races were on. Arriving home from the factory one day, Keith told his wife of the difficulty he was having in choosing an appropriate name. His wife was reading a newspaper, which carried a prominent headline, "American Boat Has a Walk-Over," referring to the yacht race. She suggested that "Walk-Over" might be an apt name, and Keith gratefully adopted it.

Wall Drug *(pharmacy)*

The company that grew from a small Depression-era pharmacy into an internationally famous multimillion-dollar business owes its existence to Ted E. Hustead (1902-1999), an entrepreneur from Nebraska who moved to the small town of Wall, South Dakota, where he opened a tiny drugstore in 1931. Trade was at first slow, until in 1936 his wife, Dorothy, suggested he put up a sign out of town advertising free ice water at Wall Drug. The trick worked, and people came flocking, the customers in turn spreading the store's fame worldwide by posting signs stating the number of miles to Wall Drug.

Wallabees *(footwear)*

Wallabees are an American type of rubber-soled, soft, moccasin-style suede shoes first in vogue in the late 1960s. The name, apparently based on "wallaby" (the kangaroo-like animal), was entered in the US Patent Office *Official Gazette* of February 18, 1969, with a note of first use in April 1968, and in the *Trade Marks Journal* of April 7, 1971.

Wallace *(whisky liqueur)*

The liqueur takes its name from the Scottish national hero Sir William Wallace (*c.*1270-1305), whose famous victory over the English in 1297 at the battle of Stirling Bridge took place only a few miles from The Wallace Malt Liqueur Co.'s distillery at Deanston, Perthshire.

Wallace Arnold *(coach tours)*

Two men are involved in the English company name, Wallace Cunningham and Arnold Crowe, who ran a bus company business in Leeds before World War I. The present company, however, dates its origins from 1926, when Robert Barr, the Leeds owner of a trucking line who ran several sightseeing buses and organized trips to local beauty spots, bought the original enterprise set up by the two partners. Wallace Arnold Tours is still based in Leeds today.

Wallace Heaton *(photographers)*

The name is that of Wallace Evans Heaton (1876-1957), a Yorkshireman who qualified as a chemist (druggist) in 1899 and who began his career as an assistant to a chemist in Brighton, Sussex. The business had a photographic department, and Heaton felt that this side of the shop could pay dividends. In 1902, back in Yorkshire, he bought a drugstore in Sheffield. It, too, had a photographic department, and Heaton decided to put his plan into action. He advertised in the *Amateur Photographer* and his photographic business boomed. In 1909 he acquired another small firm that consisted of three retail shops in Rotherham, Worksop, and Retford. In 1918 his business was incorporated as Wallace Heaton Ltd., and the following year its founder moved south from Sheffield to New Bond Street, London.

Wall's *(ice cream and sausages)*

The British name is ultimately that of Richard Wall (1775-1836), who in 1790 was apprenticed to Edmund Cotterill, a pork butcher who had started trading in St. James's

Market, London, in 1786. In 1797 Wall became a partner in the business, and its sole owner in 1807. In 1834 he moved it to Jermyn Street. In 1870 the butchery business became known as Thomas Wall & Son, taking its name from Wall's grandson, Thomas Wall (1846-1930), who completed his apprenticeship that year. He was the real "architect" of the present company. The ice cream did not appear until 1922, partly as a result of falling meat sales in summer months. The original aim had been to sell ice cream to retailers, but shopkeepers were not keen to buy in quantity, and early sales were disappointing. So Wall's decided to sell direct to the public, and in 1922 ten tricycles set off with a new slogan, "Stop me and buy one." The venture into factory-produced ice cream was a great success, and in 1923 **Lyons** entered into competition. The brand later passed to **Unilever**, who in 1994 sold it to the Irish firm of Kerry Foods.

Wal-Mart *(discount stores)*

The American stores take their name from Samuel Moore Walton (1918-1992), born in Kingfisher, Oklahoma, the son of a farm mortgage broker. When Sam was five, his family moved to Missouri, where they lived at various rural locations until 1926. In that year they moved to Columbia, where Sam attended Hickman High School. In 1936 he enrolled in the University of Missouri, graduating in 1940 with a degree in economics. He trained in a **J.C. Penney** management program in Iowa, and in 1945 opened his first five-and-dime in Newport, Arkansas. In 1950 he moved to Bentonville, Arkansas, where he and his brother, James, ran a regional chain of Ben Franklin dime stores. In 1962 Walton approached Franklin with regard to a new type of discount store. They rejected his proposal, so he decided to go ahead himself, opening his first Wal-Mart in nearby Rogers later that same year. By 1985 *Forbes* magazine was describing Walton as "the richest man in America." In 1990 the same magazine listed his family fortune at $12.5 billion, and in 1991 at $18.5 billion. "Mr. Sam" is said to have commented: "It's just paper—all I own is a pickup truck and a little Wal-Mart stock."

Walpamur *(paints)*

The name is a contraction of the original British firm, The Wall Paper Manufacturers Ltd., formed in 1899. The company began to manufacture paints in 1906 as a subsidiary activity to making wallpaper, and following the success of the paint side of the business, the company name was changed to Walpamur in 1915. In 1975 the name was changed completely to Crown Decorative Products, since it was felt that "Walpamur" was associated too closely with the original water-based wall paints, whereas the company was now producing emulsion paints. Moreover, the firm's prime name of "Crown" had become widely familiar for its paints. Although the "-mur" of "Walpamur" is made up of letters in "Manufacturers," it equally suggests French *mur*, "wall," and this may have been the intention.

Wanamaker *(menswear stores)*

The American stores take their name from John Wanamaker (1838-1922), born in what is now the Gray's Ferry area of Philadelphia, Pennsylvania, the son of a brickmaker. At age 14 he began to work as an errand boy for the Troutman and Hayes bookstore. Four years later he became a clerk in Tower Hall, then the most prominent clothing store in the city. Following the collapse of his health, he served as the first fulltime paid secretary of the Young Men's Christian Association, and in 1859 founded the Bethany Sunday School. He resigned as YMCA secretary in 1861 and teamed up with his brother-in-law, Nathan Brown, to form the clothing firm of Brown and Wanamaker. The partnership ended with Brown's death in 1868, and the following year he founded John Wanamaker & Co. He now needed suitable premises for his store and found it in the freight depot of the Pennsylvania Railroad, which he bought in 1875. His store consisted of different shops under a single roof and so was a genuine "department store" and one of the largest in the country. Wanamaker opened a store in New York City in 1896 but it closed in 1954.

Wander *(health foods)*

The Swiss company traces its origins to 1865, when the chemist Georg Wander, together with a partner, Albert Lohner, set up a "technical and analytical" chemistry laboratory in Berne. His original work was to investigate the nutritional values of barley malt. In 1897 the business passed to his son, Albert Wander (1867-1950), and it was he who in 1904 introduced one of the firm's best-known products, **Ovaltine**. Wander became a limited company in 1908 but in 1967 was purchased by **Sandoz**.

Wang *(computers)*

Wang Laboratories, Inc., based in Cambridge, Massachusetts, takes its name from An Wang (1920-1990), born in Shanghai, China, the son of a teacher. He studied electrical engineering at Chiao-t'ung University, Shanghai, and after graduating in 1940 was an instructor at the university for one year, then went to work for the Chinese government as an engineer at the Central Radio Work in Kueis-lin. In 1945 the Chinese government sent Wang to the United States in a technical apprentice program. He studied applied physics at Harvard University, and on graduating with a doctorate in 1948 carried out work in the Harvard Computational Laboratory, gaining increasing recognition for his invention of the computer core memory, the small doughnut-shaped ring of iron that stored computer data and that was the forerunner of the microchip. He sold the patent for his invention to **IBM**, and this gave him the funds to set up his own company in 1951 in Boston, Massachusetts, to develop custom-made electronic components. His activity increased, and in 1954 Wang moved his enterprise to Cambridge, Massachusetts, incorporating his business the following year. It was not until 1964, however, that his company really took off, on the introduction of a desktop computer. This enabled Wang to make a successful switch to the production of word-processing systems and, in due course, personal computers, although Wang PCs were not IBM-compatible until 1989.

Warburtons *(bread and rolls)*

The British bakery takes its name from Thomas Warburton, who with his wife, Ellen, and the financial backing of his brother, George, set up a small grocery shop in Bolton, Lancashire, in 1870. At first business prospered, but by 1875 the grocery trade had slumped, with supplies hard to come by. Ellen suggested to her husband that they bake some bread and offer it for sale. Thomas was initially appalled, since no self-respecting housewife would buy bread but would bake it herself. Ellen was de-

termined, however, and the next day they baked four loaves and six flour cakes and put them in the window. They sold out within the hour. The following day they doubled production, and again sold out. Within two weeks they were baking fulltime, the shop was renamed "Warburtons The Bakers," and business boomed. Thomas's nephew Henry joined the enterprise in 1880 and gradually expanded the baking facilities, so that by 1915 a purpose-built bakery was operating. By the end of the 20th century Warburtons had seven bakeries and was Britain's leading independent bakery group.

Warfarin *(rat poison)*

The chemical compound, originally known as compound 42, was named in 1948 by the American biochemist Karl Link (1901-1978), who based the name on the initials of the Wisconsin Alumni Research Foundation (WARF), to which he assigned his patents, and the last four letters of "coumarin," the substance responsible for the fragrant odor of sweet clover, used in medicine as an anticoagulant. Warfarin became the most effective rat poison following field tests by US government and private agencies undertaken for its approval in 1950.

Warne *(publishers)*

Frederick Warne (1825-1901) was born in Westminster, London, England, a builder's son. He quit school at 14, and joined his brother, William Henry Warne, and his brother-in-law, George **Routledge**, in the bookselling business which the latter had started in 1836. In 1851 Warne became a partner of Routledge in his publishing business that had by then developed, and in 1858 this became known as Routledge, Warne & Routledge when Routledge's son, Robert Warne Routledge, also became a partner. In 1865 Warne set up his own publishing business in Bedford Street, off the Strand, where he took his cue from Routledge and aimed to popularize good literature. He retired in 1895, leaving the business in the hands of his three sons. Frederick Warne is now a division of **Penguin** Books.

Warner *(silks and fabrics)*

The English firm of Warner Fabrics traces its history back to the late 17th century, when William Warner (d.1712) was a scarlet dyer in

Spitalfields, Stepney (now in London). The present company of Warner & Sons Ltd., however, was founded in 1870 by Warner's descendant, Benjamin Warner (1828-1908), born in Wanstead, Essex, the son of a weaver and engineer who worked on Jacquard looms. Benjamin's father died when he was only 11, so he was taken from school to help his mother run the business. At first this seems to have been weaving and harness-making, but Warner soon added designing to his skills and in 1870, together with two partners, he set up a small silk-weaving factory in east London, with a warehouse and weaving factory subsequently established in Newgate Street. The partnership gradually dissolved, with one partner leaving in 1874 and the other in 1891, whereupon Warner took his two sons into the business in their place. A wholesale company throughout its history, Warner is now part of **Wickes**.

Warner Brothers *(motion pictures)*

The famous name derives from that of four brothers, the sons of a Polish couple originally named Eichelbaum who immigrated to the United States in about 1890. Their first names were Harry Morris (1881-1958), Albert (1887-1967), Samuel Louis (1887-1927), and Jack Leonard (1892-1978). They landed up in Youngstown, Ohio, where Samuel got a job as a projectionist at a local cinema. When the owner went broke, Sam persuaded his father to buy the projector. The family set up a traveling show: Sam worked the projector, Jack sang and performed in blackface, and their 13-year-old sister Rose played the piano. In 1905 the brothers opened a nickelodeon in New Castle, Pennsylvania, and from this moved to making and distributing movies. Their first notable production was *My Four Years in Germany* (1917). In 1918, the year the company regards as that of its foundation, they established studios in Hollywood, and in 1923 they incorporated as Warner Brother Pictures, with Harry as president. In 1966 Warner Brothers merged with Seven Arts Productions to form Warner Bros.-Seven Arts. Finally, after successful diversification into records and music publishing, among other activities, the company became Warner Communications in 1971, and this in turn merged with Time Inc. in 1989 to form **Time Warner**, Inc., the largest communications and media conglomerate in the United States.

Warner-Lambert *(drugs)*

The American makers of such diversified health products as **Listerine** mouthwash, Clorets breath fresheners, and **Schick** razor blades, are a company resulting from several mergers. The first half of the name is that of William R. Warner Co., named for its founder, a Philadelphia pharmacist who invented the sugar-coated pill some time before the American Civil War. The second half of the name comes from one of the many companies acquired by Warner from the early 1950s. In this case it was the Lambert Pharmacal (earlier Pharmaceutical) Company, named for Jordan W. Lambert, who developed Listerine in 1879. Warner judged the product so important that the firm changed its name to Warner-Lambert Pharmaceutical Co. in 1955 and to Warner-Lambert in 1970. In 1960 Warner-Lambert bought **American Chicle** and in 1970 the prescription drug maker Parke, Davis & Co.

Warninks *(liqueur)*

Warninks advocaat, made with eggs, sugar, and brandy, originated with Wed. H. Warnink in Amsterdam, Holland, in 1616. Today the firm is the largest producer of advocaat in the Netherlands.

Wartburg *(automobiles)*

When the German Democratic Republic (East Germany) came into existence in 1949, the Russians annexed many of the factories in the auto-manufacturing cities of Chemnitz, Eisenach, and Zwickau. As a result, EMW cars rolled out of the former **BMW** works at Eisenach. In 1956, the Wartburg model was created, so called after the famous castle of this name that stands on a hill overlooking Eisenach.

Wastemaster *(waste disposal unit)*

The name, combining "waste" and "master," was entered by the disposal unit's manufacturers, the Lockley Machine Co., in the US Patent Office *Official Gazette* of November 5, 1946: "For electrically driven garbage grinders," with a claim of use since June 14, 1945.

Water Pik *(dental irrigator)*

The device cleans the teeth by directing a jet of water at them. Hence the name, with "Pik" representing "pick," as a tool used to free and clear debris. The name was entered by the Aqua-Tec Corporation, of Fort Collins, Colorado, in the US Patent Office *Official Gazette* of October 15, 1963: "For readily portable oral hygiene appliance utilizing a pulsed jet of water for massaging the gums and cleaning spaces adjacent to the teeth," with a note of first use on October 14, 1961.

Waterbury *(watches)*

The name of the low-priced watch or clock is that of the Waterbury Watch Company, of Waterbury, Connecticut, who entered the words "The Waterbury" in the US Patent Office *Official Gazette* of May 6, 1884, with a note of filing the application on July 21, 1883. The timepieces themselves were subsequently made and marketed with great success by Robert H. **Ingersoll**.

Waterman *(pens)*

Lewis Edson Waterman (1837-1901) was an American insurance salesman who had the misfortune to lose the sale of a large policy to a customer when, at the very moment of signing, his fountain pen discharged its contents over the application form. This embarrassing incident determined him to devise a practical pen in which the flow of ink could be controlled. After much research and experimentation, Waterman at last came up in 1884 with a "three fissure feed," which incorporated a system allowing ink and air to pass in opposite directions at the same time. That same year he began manufacturing such pens in a tobacconist's shop on the corner of Fulton Street and Nassau Street, New York, and that was the germ from which the sophisticated Waterman pens of today evolved.

Waterstone *(bookstores)*

The British bookstore chain takes its name from Timothy Waterstone (b.1940), the son of the chairman of a small tea company, who on completing his education at Cambridge University at first followed his father's business to India but then caught typhoid and returned home to join Allied Breweries as a management trainee. He was promoted to be marketing manager of the wine and liquor division, but in 1975 left to run the book distribution business of **W.H. Smith**. He was made chairman of that company's North American operation, based in the USA, but a clash of aims and personalities lost him the post in 1981. Back in London, he opened a bookshop, the first of a chain of 30 by the end of the 1980s. In 1989 W.H. Smith bought the company, with Waterstone remaining as chief executive until 1993. In 1998 Waterstone was acquired by the newly formed **HMV** Media, who merged it with the HMV music stores and **Dillons** bookstores. In 2001 Waterstone himself was planning to make a new bid for control of his company, which by then had 220 outlets.

Wates *(houses)*

The British construction company takes its name from Edward Wates, who in 1901 joined forces with his three brothers to build and sell just two houses in Purley, Surrey. The venture was a success, and led the four to reinvest in similar projects, until in 1909 they staked all their capital on the construction of 50 houses in Streatham, nearer London. A further development followed in a neighboring area, Norbury, and after World War I the brothers had sufficient capital to launch a major development of 1,000 houses in Streatham Vale. Edward Wates's three sons, Norman, Ronald, and Allan, saw the business expand to become one of the largest family-owned firms in the country.

Watneys *(beer)*

The name behind the British **Red Barrel** beer is that of James Watney (1800-1884), the son of a clergyman in Mitcham, Surrey. He began his career in the milling trade, and became the manager of Wandsworth flour mills. In 1837 he took a quarter share in the Stag Brewery, Pimlico, founded in 1641 by William Greene. The firm has been involved in several mergers and acquisitions since then, notably with Mann's Albion Brewery in 1959, so that the brewery was known for many years as Watney Mann, but the basic Watney name has remained one of the best-known to the British beer drinker, if only through such advertising slogans as "What we want is Watney's." The company is now part of Scottish **Courage**, and its Mortlake, London, brewery is used by **Anheuser-Busch** to brew **Budweiser**.

Weatherometer *(weather-resistance testing device)*

The device subjects substances to simulated

weather conditions in order to evaluate their weather-resistance. The name, an obvious combination of "weather" and "-ometer" (in the sense "measurer") was entered by the Atlas Electric Devices Co., of Chicago, Illinois, in the US Patent Office *Official Gazette* of June 11, 1929: "For Apparatus for Testing the Effect of Weather Upon the Surfaces of Objects," with a claim of use since December 3, 1926.

Weatings *(wheat residue)*

The animal feed consists of the residue of the milling of wheat, also known as "the sharps" or "the middlings" (because midway between bran and flour). The name, a blend of a respelled "wheat" and "middlings," was entered by M.M.A., Ltd., of London, England, in the *Trade Marks Journal* of September 30, 1931 for: "Fine wheat offals (for food)."

Webb's City *(drugstore)*

At one time the world's largest drugstore, Webb's City in St. Petersburg, Florida, took its name from James Earl "Doc" Webb (1899-1982), born in Nashville, Tennessee, of mixed Scottish, Irish, and English descent. In his teens he worked around drugstores, and earned his title of "Doc" in Knoxville, where he developed a venereal disease compound known as "Webb's 608." At age 26 Webb decided to go into business for himself, and opened a small drugstore in St. Petersburg. By shrewd purchasing and spectacular promotions, he managed to lure the public to his store, so that sales passed $1 million in 1936, $2 million in 1939, and $30 million in the 1960s. The name "Webb's City" denoted the citylike nature of the business, with separate operations in various "stores" carried on under one roof. In the early 1970s, however, St. Petersburg went into economic decline, and in 1974 Doc Webb sold his original stock holdings. By 1979 the company was bankrupt, and "The World's Most Unusual Drugstore" closed its doors for the last time.

Webley *(revolver)*

The name is that of the British manufacturers, Webley & Scott, Ltd., of Birmingham, originally P. Webley & Son, who entered it in the *Trade Marks Journal* of March 24, 1920 and the US Patent Office *Official Gazette* of January 16, 1923. The revolver itself dates from the late 19th century.

Webster's *(beer)*

The familiar English beer brand "Yorkshire Bitter" is brewed by a firm that traces its origin to Samuel Webster (1813-1872), born in Halifax, Yorkshire. In 1838 Webster acquired a small brewery business in Ovenden Wood, near Halifax, and supplied beer to the local inns. In 1845 he bought his first public house, the Lane Ends Inn, across the Wheatley Valley. His business gradually grew, with further breweries acquired, until on his death the firm was carried on by Webster's three sons. One of these, Isaac Webster, became chairman when the business was organized as a public limited company in 1889. The full name of the company, still based on Ovenden Wood, is now Samuel Webster & Wilson's Ltd. The latter name is the result of a merger in 1985 between Samuel Webster and Wilson Ltd., the second brewery having been acquired in 1865 in Newton Heath, Manchester, by Henry Charles Wilson.

Wedgwood *(pottery)*

Josiah Wedgwood (1730-1795) is the Englishman who gave his name to the quality pottery, with its typical classical decorations in white or blue. He was born in Burslem, Staffordshire, the 13th and youngest child of a potter. Josiah's father died when he was only eight, and the boy's schooling ceased so that he could work in the pottery of his eldest brother, Thomas, to whom he was apprenticed when he was 14. After a period working with another noted potter, Thomas Whieldon, he established a factory in 1759 in Burslem where he would soon make his characteristic cream-colored earthenware. Later, in 1769, his new factory in Etruria first produced its famous Greek-style vases. Today Josiah Wedgwood & Sons Ltd. manufactures a whole range of fine chinaware. The name was entered by Godfrey Wedgwood, "trading under the Firm of Josiah Wedgwood and Sons," in the *Trade Marks Journal* of August 2, 1876, and in the US Patent Office *Official Gazette* of December 4, 1906: "Particular description of goods.—Porcelain, stoneware, and earthenware, including Jasper."

Weejuns *(loafers)*

The moccasin-style casual shoes were introduced by **Bass** in 1936. They were based on a Norwegian slipper moccasin that the Basses had noticed were popular on the French Riviera. Hence their name, a casual corruption of "Norwegian." Weejuns first went on sale in men's fittings only at Rogers Peet of New York at $12 a pair, with women's fittings following the next year. They became a fad on college campuses from the 1960s, forcing Bass to expand their production facilities. The name was entered in the US Patent Office *Official Gazette* of June 11, 1957, with a note of first use on April 17, 1936.

Weetabix *(breakfast cereal)*

The cereal is in the form of thick crumbly biscuits made of wheat. Hence its name, entered in the US Patent Office *Official Gazette* of March 3, 1936 and the *Trade Marks Journal* of August 17, 1938. Based in Kettering, Northamptonshire, the British firm made their first wheat cereal breakfast biscuits in the 1930s. At first the cereal was sold only to local shops. Soon demand grew, and a sales forces was recruited to distribute Weetabix all over the country. By 1970 the business had become the largest British-owned breakfast cereal manufacturer.

Weidenfeld & Nicolson *(publishers)*

The British publishing house was founded by Arthur George Weidenfeld (b.1919), later Baron Weidenfeld, and Nigel Nicolson (b.1917). Weidenfeld was born and raised in Vienna, the son of a lecturer turned banker. He was studying to be a diplomat when the Nazis turned their attention to Austria, and in 1938 he escaped to Britain with less than £1 in his pocket. During World War II he worked for the BBC, both in the monitoring service and as a news commentator. Nicolson, son of the writers Harold Nicolson and Victoria ("Vita") Sackville-West, was educated at Eton and Oxford and served in the Tunisian and Italian campaigns as a Grenadier Guards captain in World War II. The two men formed their partnership in 1948, helped by a contract with **Marks & Spencer** for the mass supply of cheap books. Weidenfeld & Nicolson is now a division of Orion Publishing, founded in 1992

Weight Watchers *(dieting organization)*

Weight Watchers International, Inc., was founded in 1963 by Jean Nidetch, a 39-year-old American homemaker who had failed to become thin by conventional means and who was tired of always being asked when her baby was due. By 1968 Weight Watchers had 87 US franchises, and by the 1990s there were Weight Watchers clubs in 24 countries. The name was not original, and "Weight Watcher" was entered by the Low Calorie Candy Co. in the US Patent Office *Official Gazette* of February 28, 1961 "for dessert and pie mixes sold in combination packages," with a claim of first use on February 1, 1960. The organization entered its name in the *Trade Marks Journal* of October 25, 1967.

Weihenstephan *(beer)*

The world's oldest brewery, on a hillside near Freising, north of Munich, Germany, dates from the 8th century, when Benedictine monks established a community dedicated to St. Stephen on the hill and began to grow hops. ("Weihenstephan" means literally "Holy Stephen.") The first specific reference to brewing on the site is from 1040, and the present firm dates its foundation from that year. The monastery was destroyed by wars, rebuilt, closed by Napoleon, then acquired by the royal family of Bavaria. The brewery is now owned by the state, and in part occupies the former monastic buildings.

Welch's *(grape juice)*

In 1869 Dr. Thomas B. Welch (1825-1903), a New Jersey dentist who was also a devout Methodist and ardent prohibitionist, decided to find a nonalcoholic substitute for communion wine. Using the abundance of grapes around his hometown of Vineland (named for its vineyards), he eventually came up with what he called "Dr. Welch's Unfermented Wine." His fellow Methodists would have none of it, however, saying that wine was an essential ingredient of the communion ceremony, and that to replace it with anything else would be not far short of heretical. Disappointed, Welch redirected his energy into the prohibition cause. Then in 1892 his youngest son, Dr. Charles Welch, also a dentist, decided to test "Dr. Welch's Unfermented Wine" as a commercial product. Changing its name to the more attractive "Welch's Grape Juice," he introduced the beverage at the Columbian Exposition in Chicago, giving out free samples to millions of fairgoers. The drink caught on in a big way, and by 1897 "Welch's Grape Juice" had become a familiar sight at soda fountains alongside root beer and sarsaparilla. Needless to say, the Eighteenth Amendment provided a huge boost to the already popular drink, but Dr. Thomas B. Welch, its original creator, did not live long enough to see it.

Weldmesh *(wire mesh)*

The type of wire mesh is formed by welding together two series of parallel wires crossing at right angles. Hence the name, entered by the British Reinforced Concrete Engineering Co. Ltd., of Stafford, in the *Trade Marks Journal* of April 24, 1935 for: "Screens, partitions, guards, frames, sieves and seatings, all made of welded steel wire."

Welgar *see* **Shredded Wheat**

Wellcome *(pharmaceuticals)*

Henry Solomon Wellcome (1853-1936) was born in a log cabin in Almond, Wisconsin, the son of a farmer and itinerant missionary to the Dakota Indians. As a boy he began to take a keen interest in pharmacy and decided to devote his life to it. On qualifying as a pharmacist at the Philadelphia College of Pharmacy he served apprenticeships with various firms until in 1880 he went to England. There he set up a partnership in London with another American pharmacist, Silas M. Burroughs (1846-1895), as Burroughs, Wellcome & Co. At first the venture was an agency for the manufacturing of a new type of compressed tablet, called a **Tabloid**. Soon they began to manufacture their own pharmaceutical products, including the "Tabloids" themselves. After Burroughs' death, Wellcome became the sole proprietor, and in 1924 the name of the company was changed to The Wellcome Foundation Ltd. On his own death Wellcome bequeathed all the company shares to trustees, as The Wellcome Trust, to fund research in medicine and related subjects. *See also* **Glaxo**.

Wells, Fargo *(express transport and banking)*

The famous paired name is that of Henry A. Wells (1805-1878) and William George Fargo (1818-1881). On March 18, 1852, having already helped found the **American Express** Company, they and other investors established Wells, Fargo & Company to handle the banking and express business prompted by the California Gold Rush. Initially they provided services between California and the eastern United States, but later for other parts of the West and for Latin America. They are best known for the stagecoach lines that evolved in the 1850s from the original transportation business. In 1905 the banking operations of Wells Fargo (*sic*, without a comma) were separated from the express operations and merged with the Nevada National Bank to form the Wells Fargo Nevada National Bank. Eventually, in 1968, Wells Fargo & Company was incorporated as a holding company for Wells Fargo Bank, National Association, a descendant of the original firm. Other companies have also possessed rights at various times to use the Wells Fargo name.

Welsbach *(gas mantle and lamp)*

The name is that of the Austrian chemist and engineer Carl Auer Freiherr von Welsbach (1858-1929), born in Vienna, who invented the incandescent gas mantle in 1885. His invention gave gas light a new lease of life, and was in wide use by 1900, including for industrial and street lighting. The name was entered by the Welsbach Corporation, Philadelphia, Pennsylvania, in the US Patent Office *Official Gazette* of July 21, 1964.

Wendy Wool *(hand-knit yarn)*

The British-made wool of the name is produced by the West Yorkshire company of Carter & Parker Ltd. It is named for Wendy Darling, the little girl heroine of J.M. Barrie's children's play Peter Pan, first performed in 1904. The company's founder, Arthur Carter, was a friend of Barrie's, and asked him if he could adopt the name Wendy as he admired Barrie's works. At the same time he wanted to find a new name to replace the former somewhat unoriginal name of "Paragon." Barrie agreed to this on condition a royalty on knitting patterns be paid to the Great Ormond Street Hospital for Sick Children, London. The name Wendy was adopted in the mid-1920s. (The copyright has now lapsed.)

Wendy's *(hamburgers)*

Wendy's International, America's third largest hamburger chain, was founded by R. David Thomas (b.1932), born in Atlantic City,

New Jersey. He never knew his natural parents, and was adopted by a family who were constantly on the move in search of work. He tried his hand at a succession of menial jobs, joined the army at 18, and at age 24, in Fort Wayne, Indiana, helped start a barbecue restaurant and run one of the first Kentucky Fried Chicken franchises (*see* **Colonel Sanders**). He became vice president of the barbecue franchise chain by 1958, and ten years later sold them back to Kentucky Fried Chicken. All this time Thomas was restless, seeking the chance to start his own chain of hamburger places. In 1969 he opened his first outlet in Columbus, Ohio, naming it after his youngest daughter, eight-year-old Wendy. (She was born Melinda Lou Thomas, but her siblings called her "Wendy" because they could not pronounce "Melinda.") By 1976 he had 207 US outlets, and by 1996 almost 5,000 worldwide.

Wesson *(oil)*

In 1899 David Wesson (1861-1934), a brilliant American chemist, discovered a new refining process for cottonseed oil, enabling it to be used for cooking. Southern Oil Co., a Georgia food manufacturer, moved quickly to buy the right to the process, and in 1900 began marketing the oil under the trade name Wesson Oil. It made Wesson wealthy, but he was a modest man and eschewed the high-profile commercial status it accorded him.

West, John *see* **John West**

Western Air Lines *(airline)*

The American airline was incorporated in 1925 as Western Air Express to operate as a mail carrier for the federal government. On May 23, 1926 it began the first scheduled passenger service in the United States, on a route between Salt Lake City, Utah, and Los Angeles, via Las Vegas, Nevada. Two years later a regular service was inaugurated between Los Angeles and Oakland, California. In 1930 Western became part of **TWA** but recovered its independence in 1934. The company was renamed Western Air Lines in 1941 and in 1947 was acquired by **Delta** Air Lines.

Western Electric *(telecommunications)*

The US company was founded by Elisha Gray (1835-1901) and Enos N. Barton (1844-1916) as a shop making telegraph equipment in Cleveland in 1869. That same year, Gray and Barton, as it was known, was moved by the founders to Chicago, where together with other investors representing **Western Union** they incorporated it as the Western Electric Manufacturing Company in 1872. Western Electric soon became Western Union's main supplier of electrical equipment, but in 1881 the Bell Telephone Company (*see* **Bell System**) bought a controlling interest in the business. In 1882 Western Electric was reincorporated as the Western Electric Company and became a part of Bell and so of the future **AT&T**.

Western Union *(telecommunications)*

The US company was formed in 1851 as the New York and Mississippi Printing Telegraph Company. Five years later, following the acquisition of several other independent lines, the firm was reorganized to become the Western Union Telegraph Company, the name denoting a westward-looking stance. By the end of 1861, Western Union had replaced the Pony Express with a transcontinental telegraph line.

Westinghouse *(electrical appliances)*

The American company was founded in 1886 by George Westinghouse (1846-1914), born in Central Bridge, New York, the son of a farmer. In 1856 his father moved the family to Schenectady, New York, where he formed G. Westinghouse & Company to manufacture agricultural implements. Its machine shop gave young George useful experience in mechanical experimentation. His first invention was a rotary engine, which he devised before he was 15. Following a military career in the army and navy he wasted no time in resuming civilian life. He entered the sophomore class at Union College in 1865 but dropped out soon after. In 1869 he patented the first of his major inventions, the railroad air brake, and three years later organized the Westinghouse Air Brake Company to manufacture it. He also devised automatic railroad signal equipment and was one of the organizers of the Union Switch & Signal Co. in 1882. His abiding interest, however, was in electricity, and in particular in the problems involved in transmitting electrical current over long distances. He settled on alternating current (AC) to effect this, as against the direct current (DC) that was then in use. Alternating current was actually the brainchild of Nikola Tesla, but Westinghouse paid Tesla $1 million for his patents and in 1886 organized the Westinghouse Electric Company to manufacture and market AC systems. In 1945 the company became the Westinghouse Electric Corporation.

Weyerhaeuser *(timber and construction)*

The name is that of Frederick Weyerhaeuser (1834-1914), born in Niedersaulheim, Germany, the son of a prosperous farmer. He completed his education at a local Lutheran school by the age of 14 but then, following his father's death in 1846, was obliged to work on the family farm to support his siblings and his widowed mother. The family emigrated to the United States in 1852, when he was 18. After a while working as a brewer's apprentice in Pennsylvania, he moved to Illinois, where he got a job in a sawmill and lumber yard. When his boss's business failed in the panic of 1858, Weyerhaeuser bought the yard at a sheriff's auction. He gradually built up a thriving lumber activity, buying up sawmills and timberlands, and in 1891 moved his family to St.Paul, where his near neighbor was James J. Hill (1838-1916), the Canadian-born railroad developer. In 1901 Hill sold Weyerhaeuser 900,000 acres in Washington for $6 an acre, and that was the birth of the Weyerhaeuser Timber Co.

Wham-O *see* **Frisbee**

Whatman *(paper)*

The high-quality paper, used for drawings, engravings, and the like, takes its name from James Whatman (1702-1759), the English papermaker who invented wove paper in 1756 at Turkey Mill, near Maidstone, Kent. After his death, Turkey Mill was managed by his widow for three years until his son, also James (1741-1798), was old enough to take charge. In 1769 the mill was described as the largest paper mill in England, where the best writing paper was made. The name "J. Whatman" was entered by W. and R. Balston, of Springfield, Maidstone, Kent, in the *Trade Marks Journal* of November 8, 1876. A century on, as Whatman Ltd., of Springfield Mill, Maidstone, Kent, the firm entered "Whatman" in the *Journal* of April 28, 1976. The word has been adopted by some foreign languages as a term for paper of this type, such as Russian *vatman*.

Wheaties *(breakfast cereal)*

The breakfast cereal made of wheat was originally manufactured by the Washburn Crosby Company, of Minneapolis, Minnesota, who entered its self-descriptive name in the US Patent Office *Official Gazette* of March 25, 1925. *See also* **General Mills**.

Whiffle *see* **Wiffle**

Whirlpool *(household appliances)*

The American corporation began its life in 1911 as the Upton Machine Company, set up in St. Joseph, Michigan, by two brothers, Fred and Lou Upton, to make a hand-operated washing machine. In 1929 the brothers merged the operations with the Nineteen Hundred Washer Company, losing their name in the process. In 1947 Nineteen Hundred marketed a washing machine under a new name, "Whirlpool," and by 1950 the machine had done well enough to prompt the company to adopt the name itself.

Whitaker *(publishers)*

The British publishers of the familiar annual *Whitaker's Almanack* owe their name to Joseph Whitaker (1820-1895), born in London a silversmith's son. At the age of 14 he was apprenticed to a Fleet Street bookseller, a Mr. Barritt. In 1843 he joined John William Parker of the Strand, a printer who had earlier been superintendent of the Cambridge University Press. Whitaker next became the London agent of the Oxford bookseller and publisher, J.H. & J. Parker (no relation), opening a branch at 377 Strand. Here in 1849 he started the *Penny Post*, the first penny monthly church magazine, and embarked on a career as what was effectively a religious publisher. In 1858 he broadened his range to found the *Bookseller*, a journal for booksellers and publishers, still published today as a trade journal, and in 1868 he issued the first edition of *Whitaker's Almanack*, with 36,000 copies subscribed before publication. J. Whitaker & Sons remained independent until 1999, when it was acquired by BPI, US subsidiary of the Dutch group VNU. *Whitaker's Almanack* was sold to the **Stationery Office** in 1997.

Whitbread *(beer)*

Samuel Whitbread (1720-1796) was born in Cardington, Bedfordshire, England, the eighth of nine children. At 14 he was sent to London to be apprenticed to a brewer. He did so well that in 1742 he formed a partnership with Godfrey and Thomas Shewell at the Goat Brewhouse, London, trading as Godfrey Shewell & Co. The business expanded and moved to new premises in Chiswell Street in 1750, where beer was brewed continuously until 1976. In 1761 Shewell left the partnership and Whitbread remained as sole proprietor. The company chairman from 1984 through 1992, Samuel Whitbread (b.1937), was the great-great-great-great-grandson of the founder, and was named after him. Whitbread's head offices are still in Chiswell Street, but in 2000 the company sold off its brewing interests to Interbrew of Belgium in order to become simply a hotels and leisure group.

White Castle (hamburger chain)

The chain had its origins in three hamburger stands in downtown Wichita, Kansas, owned by Walter Anderson. In 1921 Edgar W. Ingram (1880-1966), the originator of American fast food, became a partner in the business when he realized that its operation and profits could be greatly expanded. Hamburgers at that time had a dubious reputation, with a general public bias against ground beef. When Ingram began his campaign to promote the hamburger sandwich, therefore, he gave his company a name, White Castle System, that evoked cleanliness and quality: "White" implied purity, and "Castle" strength and permanence. The first White Castle diner actually had the appearance of a "white castle," with white-painted cement blocks and a tower and battlements.

The White Company (mail-order bedlinen)

The idea for the company came to British journalist Chris Rucker in 1993, when she and her husband, Nick Wheeler, were staying with his sister, Susie, who had just bought a house. The conversation turned to decorating and kitting out her home. Everyone commented on how they prefered white linen and towels, and how difficult it was to find a full range of "white" under one roof. Wheeler suggested that mail order would offer a national market without the overheads of retail premises. Rucker agreed, and in 1994 resigned from her job as assistant health and beauty editor at *Harpers &*

Queen magazine to put her plan into action. Advertising by press and letter brought hundreds of inquiries, and The White Company has since gone from strength to strength, so that by 2001 it had 270,000 people on its mailing list and was processing up to 1,300 orders a day. A London store opened soon after. The name perhaps partly puns on the title of Arthur Conan Doyle's novel *The White Company* (1894).

White Horse (whisky)

The blend of whisky takes its name from the White Horse coaching inn in the Canongate, Edinburgh, where it was first sold. It was originally known as "Mackie's," after Mackie & Co., the firm established by James Logan Mackie in 1861. (The actual founder of the firm in 1742 was a Mr. Johnston. The Mackies had been maltsters from the 17th century, however, even though the family became involved in distilling much later.) The blend was named "White Horse" in 1890 by the company's second head, Peter J. Mackie (1855-1924), James Logan Mackie's nephew. The inn itself is said to be named after the white horse ridden by Mary, Queen of Scots (Mary Stuart) (1542-1587), from her palace at Holyrood House to Edinburgh Castle, although a white horse has long been a traditional symbol of victory. White Horse Distillers Ltd., who produce the whisky (in Glasgow, not Edinburgh), were so named in the year of Peter Mackie's death.

White Rock (mineral waters)

The brand of sparkling mineral water takes its name from the springs at Waukesha, Wisconsin, so called in 1871 by the owner of the property, H.M. Colver, with reference to the natural magnesan rock basin from which they flowed. Towards the end of the century "White Rock" began to be used as the name of a table water that was soon being exported to Europe. The White Rock Mineral Springs Company gained ownership and operation of the springs in 1913.

White Stuff (skiwear)

The British company was born from a casual attempt by two friends, George Treves and Sean Thomas, to raise cash while skiing in the French Alps in 1986. The two skibums were sitting in a bar after a hard day on the slopes and discussing the cheap and nasty T-shirts they saw all around them. They knew style was everything, and saw a gap for their enterprise. They called themselves "Boys from the White Stuff," punning on the title of Alan Bleasdale's TV play *The Boys from the Black Stuff* (1982). ("White stuff "is snow, while in the TV title "black stuff" is **Tarmac**.) The pair enlisted the help of a design student friend, Kate Tregoning, to draft a "splash" design, then bought hundreds of cheap T-shirts and sweatshirts and shipped them out to the Alps. Skiers snapped them up, enabling the two to return home and start production fulltime. Their first shop opened in London in 1991 and by 2000 they had built up a lucrative mail-order company, with ski clothes stocked at more than 70 outlets, including **Harrods**.

Whiteley's *(department store)*

Britain owes its first modern department store to William Whiteley (1831-1907), born the son of a corn factor in Agrigg, near Wakefield, Yorkshire. Inspired by seeing so much merchandise under one roof at the Great Exhibition of 1851, he opened a shop selling ribbons, lace, and fancy goods in Westbourne Grove, London, in 1863. By 1872 he had bought up premises all along the street and stocked so many lines that he styled himself "The Universal Provider." In 1896, when Hyde Park was opened to bicycle riders, he bought 500 bicycles and sold out in a day. In 1907 he was shot dead in his office by a man who claimed to be his illegitimate son. A new Whiteley's store was opened in Queen's Road (now Queensway) in 1911, and extended in 1925. Two years later it was bought by Gordon **Selfridge** but then came under control of the United Drapery Stores Group, who closed it as "unviable" in 1981.

Whiteway's *(cider)*

The British company was founded in the 1890s by Henry Whiteway (1853-1932), born near Totnes, Devon, into a farming family. Devon farmers regularly made their own cider, and Henry's family was no exception. He went further than most, however, for he progressed to making cider commercially, building a factory near the London and South-Western Railway at Whimple, near Exeter. In 1904 the firm became a private company as Henry Whiteway

& Co. Ltd., and a branch was opened in London. Whiteway retired in the 1920s, and in 1924 the company went public under the name of Whiteway's Cyder Co. Ltd. The company's headquarters are still at Whimple (where Whiteway's wife had been raised), and their commercial name is familiar as "Whiteway's of Whimple." The business is still in the hands of the Whiteway family.

Whitman's *(candies)*

In 1842 Stephen F. Whitman (1823-1888) opened a small candy shop on Market Street, Philadelphia, one of the city's main commercial thoroughfares. As the popularity of his candy spread, Whitman began to market it in elaborately decorated packages with names like "The Fussy Package for Fastidious Folks." The famous "Whitman's Sampler" first appeared in 1912, when Walter Sharp, the firm's president, came across an embroidered sampler made by his grandmother and realized its potential as a candy box. The slogan, "Give Whitman's Chocolates—it's the thoughtful thing to do," was first used in 1933.

Whitworths *(dried fruit)*

The British firm, based in Irthlingborough, Northamptonshire, arose as a family flour-milling business in 1886. It then expanded to supply all kinds of baking requisites, including dried apricots, raisins, and currants, and soon became a household name for its dried fruit. Following a buyout in 1997, however, Whitworths trimmed down its operations and sold off its cake-making business.

Whyte & Mackay *(whisky)*

Noted for their "Special Reserve" blend, the Scottish firm, based in Glasgow, takes its name from James Whyte and Charles Mackay, who formed a partnership in 1882. The company and its sales expanded steadily through the late 19th century and well into the 20th. In 1960 White & Mackay merged with McKenzie Brothers of Dalmore, and in 1993 acquired the Invergordon Distillery.

Wickes *(furniture and home improvement)*

The American company introduced its first supermarket-style lumber and building materials store in 1954, and from the early 1960s has also marketed furniture. The name behind the business is that of two brothers, Henry and Edward Wickes, who in 1854 opened a machine shop in Saginaw, Michigan, to manufacture gangsaws for the local lumber industry. In 1874 they started making steam boilers for sawmills, and in 1890 they bought a graphite mine in northern Mexico and began selling graphite to manufacturers of paint and pencils. The brothers' descendants continued and expanded the activities, operating as three separate companies, respectively, for machinery, graphite, and boiler-making. In 1947 the three businesses merged to form the Wickes Corporation. The company's headquarters remained in Saginaw until 1972, when they moved to San Diego, California.

Wiffle (ball)

The lightweight, hollow, plastic ball, used by children to play baseball, or a variant of it, was originally developed for golf practice. It takes its name from a respelling of "whiffle," meaning a slight movement ("whiff") of air. "Wiffle" was entered in the US Patent Office *Official Gazette* of January 22, 1957: "For simulated or auxiliary pliable plastic baseball and a game played therewith," with a note of first use on February 5, 1954, and in the *Gazette* of November 16, 1965: "For bats and a device for tossing a ball." Earlier, "Whiffle" was entered in the *Gazette* of November 17, 1931: "For game apparatus of the type having ball receiving and discharging mechanism."

Wigfalls (electrical stores)

The English High Street name is that of Henry Wigfall (c.1873-1955), who began his career hiring out and repairing bicycles in Sheffield in the closing years of the 19th century. His business was a success, and he opened a shop to provide more efficient service. He was planning to open another, but World War I intervened, and his son, who was his partner, was called up for military service. After the war Wigfall took to selling bicycles, as well as renting them out, and in the 1920s added furniture and then radios to the range of goods sold, with further shops opening elsewhere in the north of England. In the 1930s Wigfalls shops sold clothing and shoes, but after World War II the emphasis was more on electrical goods, especially radios and televisions. The Wigfall head office remains in Sheffield today.

Wiggins Teape (paper)

Sometime at the start of the 18th century the firm of Hathaway & Edwards were paper merchants at "The Sign of the Nag's Head" in Northumberland Avenue, London, England, and this was the beginning of the present Wiggins Teape Group. The British company dates its founding to 1761, however, when offices under the name Edwards & Jones were purchased in Aldgate, London. At some stage a Mr. Wiggins and a Mr. Teape must have joined the firm, since in 1889 the partnership of Wiggins, Teape, Carter & Barlow became a private company under the name Wiggins Teape & Co. Ltd. It was converted into a public company in 1919 as Wiggins Teape & Co. (1919) Ltd., and this subsequently became the parent company of the group.

Wild Turkey (whiskey)

The name of the brand of straight Kentucky bourbon ostensibly refers to the wild bird from which the domesticated turkey is derived. It was entered by Austin Nichols & Co., Inc., of Brooklyn, New York, in the US Patent Office *Official Gazette* of April 26, 1949, with a claim of use since May 29, 1942, and by Five Mills Ltd., of London, England, in the *Trade Marks Journal* of March 20, 1968.

Wiley (publishers)

The American publishing house John Wiley and Sons owes its origin to Charles Wiley (1782-1826), who opened a bookshop on Reade Street, New York City, in 1807. By 1814 he was publishing reprints of works by European authors, but the business was beset by financial difficulties and on Wiley's death it was taken over by his son John. John's own son, Charles Wiley, became a partner in 1865, as did his son William H. Wiley in 1875. The firm took its current name in 1876. In the mid-1990s W. Bradford Wiley II, great-great-great-grandson of the founder, was the chairman of the company

Wilkin's (preserves)

Familiar for its "Tiptree" jam, the British company takes its name from its founder, Arthur Charles Wilkin (1835-1913), born at Tiptree, near Colchester, Essex, a farmer's son. After working as an office boy in London and as a helper on various farms he returned to his native Essex in 1859 to join his father on the family farm, renting ten acres from him to grow mangold seed. Further agricultural and horticultural experience followed, when he experimented with different kinds of nursery and market gardening. By the mid-1860s, when he married, Wilkin had taken over his parents' farm and it was at about this time that he first began growing fruit. He was soon supplying strawberries to London jam makers, and in 1883 he decided to start making his own jam with the fruit that he grew. He took two friends as partners, and in 1885 formed a small company to make strawberry jam, initially in the farmhouse kitchen, but soon in a barn on the farm. He called his venture the Britannia Fruit Preserving Company. Business increased, with a proper jam factory soon built by the railway. Eventually in 1905, the year of Wilkin's 70th birthday, the name of the company became Wilkin & Sons Ltd., as it has remained ever since. The business is still based in Tiptree today.

Wilkinson *(hardware stores)*

James Kemsey Wilkinson (1906-1997) was born in Birmingham, England, the ninth child of William Wilkinson, who ran a family ironmonger business (hardware store) in the city. After attending Aston Grammar School, "JK," as he was known, joined Evans and Matthews, an old-fashioned store of finishing ironmongers in Bull Street, Birmingham. He harbored a dream of farming in Canada but instead moved to Leicester in 1924 to learn more of the hardware trade with Pochins in Granby Street. In 1928 he had risen to be manager of a store in the **Timothy White** group, working in their outlets in Chichester, Portsmouth, and Plymouth. While staying the latter city he met his future wife, Mary Cooper, his landlady's daughter. In 1930 the couple opened their own hardware store at 151 Charnwood Street, Leicester, living separately until they married in 1934. A second branch was opened in neighboring Wigston Magna in 1933 and by 1919 there were seven stores. Expansion continued through World War II, slowly at first, but by 2001 there were 187 stores. Popularly known as "Wilko," the company is now based in Worksop, Nottinghamshire, and is owned by Tony Wilkinson (b.1938).

Wilkinson Sword *(razor blades and gardening tools)*

The British company traces its origins to 1772, when Henry Nock (1741-1804), a gunmaker, started his business in Ludgate Hill, London. One of his apprentices was James Wilkinson, who not only married his daughter but eventually became his partner, inheriting the firm on Nock's death. In 1825 Wilkinson's son, Henry (d.1861), took over the business, still that of gunmaking, and started to make swords. The manufacture of military accoutrements naturally followed, and business boomed in the war-ridden years that succeeded, with first the Crimean War, then the Boer War, and finally World War I. In 1887 the name of Wilkinson & Son was changed to Wilkinson Sword to denote the firm's new specialty. (The company still makes swords today, although only for ceremonial purposes, or as collectors' items.) The much more familiar razor blades followed as a logical development in the 1920s, and gardening tools were introduced at around the same time.

William H. Brown *(estate agents, or realtors)*

William H. Brown (1869-1935) was born in Lincolnshire, England, and began his working life as a farmer at his home in the village of Ruskington, near Sleaford. He was keen to expand his activities, and in the early 1890s set himself up as an auctioneer, operating from a small wooden hut in the farmyard. Business grew, and by the turn of the century he had opened an office in the village. Between 1911 and 1919 he was joined by his two sons, Fred and Albert, with the three men becoming partners and operating as William H. Brown & Sons. A third son, Herbert, joined them later. By the 1930s the firm had diversified, and in 1933 it divided into two distinct businesses. William and Herbert Brown continued as auctioneers, valuers, and estate agents, while Fred ran the fertilizer, hay, corn, and straw side of the business, trading as F.W. Brown & Co. (later Brown Butlin). Albert had meantime left to devote himself to farming. The company is still in the hands of the Brown family, and is still based in Sleaford, although now operating as estate agents nationwide.

William Hill *(bookmakers)*

William Hill (1903-1971) was born in Birmingham, England, the son of a coach painter. As a teenager he followed his father's trade for a while, but soon became fascinated by betting and horseracing. Although his bets were rarely successful, he decided nevertheless to become a bookmaker himself. At first he visited pubs in the Midlands, collecting bets by bicycle. This activity offered limited scope, however, so he decided to set himself up on the racecourses themselves. Lacking experience, he initially lost much of his capital, but gradually came to gain headway and make a profit. In 1929 he went to London, operating at first not on the racecourse but at different greyhound tracks. Then he extended his activities to the Northolt Park racecourse, where his profits enabled him to keep and race horses on his own. In 1934 he opened a credit office for his clients, taking a single room in Jermyn Street. By 1939 he needed new premises, and found them in Park Lane, at the same time forming the private company of William Hill (Park Lane) Ltd. Further expansion followed, and in 1966 Hill reluctantly began taking bets on elections.

Wills *(cigarettes and tobacco)*

Familiar for their **Woodbine** cigarettes, the British firm of W.D. & H.O. Wills has a name that represents William Day Wills (1797-1865) and Henry Overton Wills (1800-1871), the sons of another Henry Overton Wills (1761-1826), who first appeared on the scene in 1786 as a partner in the Bristol tobacco business of Wills, Watkins & Co. By the end of the 19th century, the small family business had become the biggest tobacco manufacturers in Britain. In 1901 the Wills business joined with other tobacco firms to form the **Imperial Tobacco** Co.

Willys-Overland *(automobiles)*

The cars take their name from John North Willys (1873-1935), born in Canandaigua, New York, the son of a brick and tile maker. His first major venture was a retail and wholesale bicycle business, but he soon realized that the rise of the automobile would effectively kill the bicycle industry. He made a move accordingly, and in 1901 began selling cars on a small scale. In 1906 Willys established the American Motor Car Sales Company in Elmira, New York, and three years later purchased the failing Pope-

Toledo automobile works, moving the renamed Willys-Overland into its large factory in Toledo, Ohio. Production increased rapidly, so that from 1912 to 1918 Willys-Overland ranked second to **Ford** in output. As with many other companies, sales dropped dramatically during the Great Depression, and the firm went into receivership in 1933. It survived, however, thanks to financing secured from Toledo banks and business leaders, and in World War II became world-famous for the **Jeep**. The Willys name died out in 1963 when the company's name was changed to the **Kaiser**-Jeep Corporation. (In Russian military vocabulary at that time the Jeep actually came to be known as the *villis*.)

Wimpey *(houses)*

The British company was founded in 1880 by George Wimpey (1855-1913), born in Hammersmith, London. It was there that at the age of 25 Wimpey set up a stoneworking business, taking as partner a stonemason, Walter Tomes. Their yard was in Hammersmith Grove, close to the railway. By 1889 the two men were carrying out work for Hammersmith Council, and by 1893, when Wimpey became the sole owner of the business, his reputation as a builder and contractor was already established. Now called George Wimpey & Co., the firm soon received its first important commission: the construction of Hammersmith Town Hall in 1896. From then on the company flourished and expanded to be Britain's biggest housebuilder.

Wimpy *(hamburgers and restaurants)*

The name is that of J. Wellington Wimpy, a character often portrayed eating a hamburger in Elzie C. Segar's "Popeye" cartoon strip. The Wimpy hamburger first made its appearance in Chicago in the mid-1930s, the name of the manufacturing firm being Wimpy Grills, Inc. The Wimpy went to Britain in the mid-1950s, when Wimpy Bars selling and serving Wimpies started up in various towns and other strategic sites, such as by main roads. The actual first Wimpy Bar in the UK opened in 1954 at what was then the **Lyons** Corner House in London's Oxford Street, and ever since J. Lyons have had the monopoly of sales everywhere outside the United States. The name was entered in the US Patent Office *Official Gazette* of May 21, 1935, with use claimed from September 12, 1934.

Winalot *(dog biscuits)*

The **Spillers** product was originally formulated as a greyhound food, so that when the name was first used in 1927 it implied that a dog fed on the biscuits would "win a lot" of races and hence prizes. The name was entered in the *Trade Marks Journal* of July 27, 1927.

Wincarnis *(tonic wine)*

The British wine of this name originated as "Coleman's Liebig's Extract of Meat & Malt Wine," sold in the 1880s by William Coleman at his chemist's shop (drugstore) in Norwich, Norfolk. After World War I, when Coleman's business had passed into other hands, the name of the wine was changed to "Wincarnis," a blend of "wine" and Latin *carnis*, "of meat." This name was originally entered in the *Trade Marks Journal* of April 26, 1899. In 1968 Coleman & Co. Ltd. were acquired by **Reckitt** & **Colman**, and from around 1975 the business was one of importing, bottling, and distributing wines. "Liebig's Extract of Meat" also produced **Oxo**.

Winchester *(rifle)*

The proprietary name of a type of breech-loading, side-action, repeating rifle derives from its developer, the American small-arms manufacturer Oliver F. Winchester (1810-1880), born in Boston, Massachusetts. After an early career as a master builder and shirt manufacturer, in 1856 Winchester purchased the Volcanic Repeating Arms Company of New Haven, Connecticut. The following year he reorganized the firm as the New Haven Arms Company, with himself as president, and in 1867 as the Winchester Repeating Arms Company. His new rifle was based on the lever-action model patented in 1860 by Benjamin T. Henry, and this was the forerunner of the famous Winchester 73, a favorite weapon of settlers in the American West. "Winchester" is now a tradename for the firearms produced by the original makers of the rifle.

Windows *(computer operating system)*

The GUI (graphical user interface) operating system for personal computers was introduced by **Microsoft** in 1983. The name was based on "window" in its computing sense for a framed area on a display screen for viewing information.

Windsurfer *(sailboard)*

Driving home one day, American aeronautical engineer James Drake conceived the idea of adding a sail to a surfboard and so create a new type of sport. He put the notion to his friend Hoyle Schweitzer, a businessman and keen surfer, and together they developed the invention. They originally used fiberglass for the board, but the cheaper and more durable polythene was later employed. **Du Pont** were so pleased by the novel use of their material that they published an article about the sailboard, which boosted sales. In 1973 Schweitzer bought out Drake, set up Windsurfer International Inc., of Santa Monica, California, to sell the product, and entered the name "Windsurfer" in the US Patent Office *Official Gazette* of August 20, 1974: "For sailboats comprising a surf board type hull and a sail." The name gave the general word "windsurfer" for a person who takes part in windsurfing.

Winnebago *(campers)*

The make of motor vehicle with insulated panels, used for living accommodation when traveling long distances or camping, takes its name from its manufacturers, based in Forest City, the seat of Winnebago County, Iowa. (The county name comes from the Native American people who formerly inhabited eastern Wisconsin but who now live mainly in southern Wisconsin and Nebraska.) The vehicle first appeared in the 1960s and its name was entered in the US Patent Office *Official Gazette* of November 17, 1970 for: "Motor Homes, Travel Trailers, House Trailers, Camper Coaches," (etc.), with a note of first use in April 1959.

Winsor & Newton *(artists' materials)*

The English firm was established in 1832 when the two founders were in their late 20s. They were William Winsor (d.1865) and Henry Charles Newton (d.1882). Both men shared an interest in painting, with Winsor the more artistically gifted of the two, whereas Newton had the scientific knowledge that would be important in the development of their products. They set up their business in Rathbone Place, London, and at first aimed to improve the quality of artists' watercolors. In 1837 they introduced Chinese white, a durable opaque paint which earlier had not been available to artists using watercolors. Other innovations followed, and after more than one change of premises they finally built a special steam-powered factory in 1844 at Kentish Town, where it was known as the North London Colour Works. The company later made its headquarters at Wealdstone, west London, where it was transferred from Kentish Town in 1938.

Winton *(automobiles)*

Alexander Winton (1860-1932) was born in Grangemouth, Scotland, the son of a maker of farm implements. After attending elementary school in his home town and a spell as an apprentice in shipyards on the Clyde River, Winton went to the United States, where for a few years he worked as an engineer on an ocean vessel. He then settled in Cleveland, Ohio, where he set up a bicycle repair shop. By 1891 he was making bicycles, but soon, like many others in the business, progressed to automobile manufacturing, and in 1897 he founded the Winton Motor Carriage Co. His first car, a two-seater buggy, appeared the following year, and things went so well that by the turn of the century Winton was the largest American gas-driven car producer. He subsequently turned to the manufacture of luxury cars, but production began to decline in the 1920s and the last Winton auto was built in 1924.

Wippells *(clergy and church suppliers)*

The Wippells were an English Westcountry farming family, with the firm's founder, Joseph Wippell, born in 1810 in the village of Cadeleigh, near Tiverton, Devon. The family moved to Exeter when he was only a year old, and his father set up a grocery business there in Fore Street. In about 1830 he purchased a drapery and wool merchant's business in the High Street, and by 1851 Joseph Wippell had developed this to include clerical tailoring and the making of materials and accessories for church requirements. In 1879 Wippell took his eldest son, Henry Hugh Wippell, into partnership with the business then styled J. Wippell & Co. Further related activities followed, such as metalwork, stonework, and the making of stained glass windows. Even school desks were added. Today the company, still based in Exeter, offers a comprehensive range of products and services for ecclesiastical and clerical use.

Wisdom *(toothbrushes)*

The toothbrushes of this name were introduced by the British firm **Addis** in 1938 as a completely new design, with a cranked plastic handle and a head trimmed flat lengthwise, curved widthwise, and filled with nylon bristles. The name, referring to wisdom teeth, was suggested by the advertising agency Graham & Gillies, and has since been reserved by Addis solely for toothbrushes and dental products.

Wittamer *(chocolates)*

The noted Belgian chocolates take their name from Henri Wittamer, a master baker who founded his business in 1910. The enterprise flourished and expanded over the years under Wittamer's son, Henri-Gustave Wittamer, and his grandson, Henri-Paul (known as Paul) Wittamer. In 1985 Paul's sister Myriam started an outside catering and gourmet service, securing valuable contracts at the United Nations and European Union headquarters in Brussels.

Wolf *(garden tools)*

The name came directly from that of August Wolf, a German village blacksmith from Betzdorf, near Cologne, who in 1922 decided to start a business making ironware by hand, including garden tools. He appointed his son, Gregor, as the salesman for his enterprise, and it was the latter who devised the first main product of the business, a new kind of hoe that could be pulled rather than simply used for "chopping." The Wolf "pulling hoe" was first marketed in 1926, and the firm went on to produce other tools for various garden jobs. Gregor Wolf died in 1967, four years after the company opened its first British factory, at Ross-on-Wye, Herefordshire.

Wolseley *(automobiles)*

Irish-born Frederick York Wolseley (1837-1899) emigrated to Australia in 1854 and worked in New South Wales for five years. In 1867 he produced a working model of mechanical sheep shears, but did not produce an actual machine for another five years. He then needed an engineer to test the reliability of his equipment, and the man he found to do this was Herbert **Austin**, who had gone from Britain to Australia to gain experience. Austin returned to England in 1893 and became general manager of the Wolseley Sheep Shearing Machine Company which had meanwhile moved from Australia to Birmingham. It was not a success as a commercial venture, however, and in 1894 Wolseley resigned. After his death Austin, who had now begun to make cars experimentally, came to an agreement with **Vickers** Sons & Maxim, Wolseley's owners, to form a subsidiary company making cars with the Wolseley name. In this manner the car that became familiar under one name was originally manufactured by the man whose cars became famous under another name, his own. The final car to be sold as a Wolseley was the Six in 1972, with its six-cylinder engine.

Wolsey *(knitwear)*

The British company began its life as a cottage industry set up to make hosiery in Leicester, England, in 1755. The founder was Ann Wood (1726-1813) and her sons, Henry and Thomas. In 1842 the firm Ann Wood & Sons was joined as partner by a Scottish wholesale and retail wool merchant and hosier, Robert Walker. Before long, Walker had become the sole proprietor of the business, and was producing hosiery and underwear under his Scottish "Thistle" trademark. In due course Walker's sons and grandsons followed him in the firm, now known as Robert Walker & Sons. In 1920 the firm merged with one of its competitors, W. Tyler & Co., and the resulting public company was registered under the name of Wolsey, adopted earlier in 1897 by Theodore and Ralph Walker for a new brand of "unshrinkable" woolens. The reference was only indirectly to "wool." The name really related to the English churchman and statesman Cardinal Wolsey (c.1474-1530), who was buried in Leicester Abbey, now only 400 yards from the company's headquarters. On his death, Wolsey was found to be wearing a woolen undergarment made by the abbey's Augustine canons.

Wonderbra *(brassiere)*

The type of padded, underwired, "push-up" bra, making a more pronounced breast shape, was introduced in 1968 by **Gossard**. It was an instant bestseller and remained an object of desire for many young women for many years, gaining particular popularity from 1994, in the wake of adverse publicity for artificial breast implants. The name may partly pun on German *wunderbar*, "wonderful."

Woodbine *(cigarettes)*

The British tobacco firm of **Wills** introduced their popular brand of cheap cigarettes in 1888, and by the end of the following year they made up half of the sales of all their cigarette output, although at this time cigarettes as a whole made up less than 1 percent of their total tobacco production. The name comes from the fragrant climbing plant, also known as honeysuckle, and "Wild Woodbine Cigarettes" was entered in the *Trade Marks Journal* of January 6, 1886. "Woodbine" alone followed in the *Journal* of September 11, 1907 for: "Tobacco whether manufactured or unmanufactured."

Woodward's *("Gripe Water")*

"Woodward's Celebrated Gripe Water" is still sold in the UK to counter a baby's "gripes," as they were once called, otherwise an attack of colic, cramps, or wind. The preparation owes its name to William Woodward (1828-1912), born in Stamford, Lincolnshire. On completing his education at Stamford Grammar School, William was apprenticed at 14 to a pharmacist in Boston, Lincolnshire, who owned a druggist shop and business in that town. In 1849 Woodward went to London, obtaining a position there as an assistant to a pharmacist in Fetter Lane. A year later he went to Nottingham, where he bought an old-fashioned pharmacy in the Market Place and set up a business supplying a whole range of drugs, chemicals, dyes and other products to local workers and residents. That same year, 1851, he first made his "Gripe Water," selling it by the ounce to individual customers and by the gallon to doctors and hospitals. It became his specialty, and in 1876, a year before he retired, Woodward registered the name. Today his particular brand is not made in Nottingham, but in Dundee, Scotland, while the firm of W. Woodward Ltd. became part of the London International Group plc.

Woolworths *(department stores)*

The familiar name is that of Franklin Winfield Woolworth (1852-1919), born into a farming family in Rodman, New York. He attended common schools in Great Bend, New York, and when he was 16 spent a few months studying commerce at a college in Watertown, New York. At the age of 21 he found a job in Watertown working as an unpaid clerk with the merchants Augsbury & Moore. In 1878 he helped launch the store's first five-cent counter. This was a promotional gimmick that gave him an idea for his own store, and on February 22, 1879 Frank opened his first venture, "The Great Five Cent Store," in Utica, New York. Everything was sold for five cents, mainly small domestic items and "bits and bobs," or what were known as "notions." His first store failed because of its unfavorable location, but only ten days later he tried again, this time on a site in Lancaster, Pennsylvania. There he sold a wider range of goods, but still all for five cents or less. The store did good business, and Frank then introduced 10-cent goods, keeping the 5-cent objects on one side of the store and the more expensive items on the other. He called his business "Woolworth's 5¢ and 10¢ Store," and soon opened branches elsewhere. In 1880 he opened a store in Scranton, Pennsylvania, putting the firm's name above it in gold letters on a red background, F.W. WOOLWORTH Co. It was not until 1905, however, that he finally formed F.W. Woolworth & Co. as the founding of the chain proper. In November 1909 Frank Woolworth opened his first British store, in Liverpool, and "Woolies" soon became as much a British institution as an American. In 1997 Woolworths announced the closing of its 400 F.W. Woolworth five-and-dime stores, long a familiar fixture in US downtowns, and in 1999, aiming to shed the "five-and-dime" image, renamed itself Venator, Latin for "hunter." In 2001, however, directors realized their error in picking such a dated name, and changed the name to Foot Locker, reflecting the company's metamophosis into a giant sports and sneaker concern with more than 3,500 stores in 14 countries.

Workmate *(portable workbench)*

South African Ronald Price Hickman left his job as head of design for **Lotus** Cars in the UK in order to explore ideas of his own. He was a do-it-yourself enthusiast, and one day inadvertently cut a chair in half while using it to saw a piece of plywood. He realized that there could be a use for a versatile workbench that was both portable and foldable, so that it could be taken where it was needed and easily stored. He ex-

perimented with various prototypes and by chance had two narrow beams to hand for the work surface when he made the first one. This gave him the idea of using parallel beams for the work surface, with one beam moving at an angle to form the vice, rather than the usual attachments to the side. When eight different companies rejected his invention, Hickman decided to manufacture it himself. He set up a workshop in an old brewery and was soon making 14,000 annually. In 1972 **Black & Decker** approached him, as one of the original rejecting companies, and a deal was struck. By the end of the 20th century, over 55 million Workmate workbenches had been sold, and Hickman had become a tax exile in Jersey, Channel Islands.

Worth *(fashionwear)*

The House of Worth, with its un-French name, is a byword in French fashion for style and elegance. Its English creator was Charles Frederick Worth (1825-1895), born in Bourne, Lincolnshire, the son of a solicitor (lawyer). At the age of 12 he started work with a London draper and a year later began a seven-year apprenticeship with **Swan & Edgar**, selling shawls and dress materials. He left for Paris in 1845, and was taken on at Maison Gagelin, where he sold mantles and shawls. In 1850 he opened a dress-making department at the store, and in 1858 went into partnership with a Swedish businessman, Otto Bobergh, opening his own house. He went on to dress both society and the demi-monde until his death, after which his business was continued by his sons, Gaston Worth (1853-1924) and Jean-Philippe Worth (1856-1926). The name Worth is now associated as much with cosmetics as with dress.

Worthington *(beer)*

William Worthington (1722-1800), born in Orton-on-the-Hill, near Atherstone, Leicestershire, England, set up his brewing business in the High Street, Burton-on-Trent, in 1744, soon working up a good trade. After successive acquisitions and mergers, the business had grown to such proportions that in 1889 it was one of the largest brewing concerns in Britain, and in that year was formed into a limited company as Worthington & Co. Ltd. In 1927 Worthington merged with **Bass**, the other famous

Burton brewery, but continued to brew and operate independently. The brewery has since been demolished, but the name lives on in a national bitter brand and in the pale ale Worthington "White Shield."

WPP *(advertising)*

The world's biggest advertising agency owes its existence to the British entrepreneur Martin Sorrell (b.1945), whose first employment was with Glendinning, a marketing consultancy. He then worked with Mark McCormack, a sports promoter, and from 1977 through 1986 was finance director of Saatchi & Saatchi (*see* **Cordiant**). He then left to invest in WPP (Wire and Plastic Products), a small manufacturer of supermarket baskets, and used it as a vehicle to build his advertising empire, buying **J. Walter Thompson**, **Ogilvy & Mather**, and **Young & Rubicam**.

Wrangler *(jeans)*

Britons tend to associate this name with a quarreler, or more academically with a first-class mathematical scholar at Cambridge University, not realizing that it is an American word for a cowboy or ranch hand. The name was entered by **Blue Bell**, Inc., of Greensboro, North Carolina, in the US Patent Office *Official Gazette* of December 16, 1947: "For Western style dungarees and pants," with a claim of use since January 19, 1929. It was entered by the British manufacturers, Kilgour & Walker Ltd., of Aberdeen, Scotland, in the *Trade Marks Journal* of October 16, 1963.

Wren's *(shoe polish)*

The British name is that of William Wren, who in 1884 first devised a new type of wax shoe polish as a more convenient way of cleaning shoes than the previous primitive and messy blacking. It is said that Mrs. Wren first made the new polish in her back kitchen copper, using a mixture of beeswax and turpentine. The advantages of the wax polish over the earlier oily blacking soon became known, and Wren set up a factory in Greyfriars Street, Northampton, to make the polish in quantity. In 1887 his factory first produced a brown-colored shoe cream for the then fashionable brown boots worn by colonial troops when they came to Britain for Queen Victoria's Diamond Jubilee, and his financial success was assured from then

on. The Wren family's interest in the business lasted until the 1920s. Today Wren shoe polish is marketed by **Reckitt**.

Wright's *("Coal Tar Soap")*

William Valentine Wright (1826-1877) was trained as a pharmacist in Ipswich, Suffolk, England, before going to London and taking a position in a chemist's shop (drugstore) in Oxford Street. In 1848 he became a partner in a pharmacy in Old Fish Street Hill, trading as Curtis & Wright. It was in about 1863 that he introduced his "Coal Tar Soap," so named to distinguish it from other tar soaps of the day, since it contained all the antiseptic ingredients of coal tar without the coloring matter that made the other soaps unpleasant for toilet use. Today the soap is manufactured by Wright, Layman & Umney, part of the London International Group. The name of the firm combines the three partners who formed it in 1876: Charles Wright (William Wright's son), Charles Layman, and Charles Umney. Ironically, William Wright died an untimely death from the skin disease erysipelas.

Wrigley's *(chewing gum)*

The familiar name is that of William Wrigley, Jr. (1861-1932), born in Philadelphia, who began his working life at age 13 riding from town to town in Pennsylvania to sell his father's soap. In 1891 he went to Chicago as a soap distributor and there started offering baking powder as a gimmick with each box of soap. In 1892 he began selling baking powder as a sideline, offering chewing gum as a premium. The gum soon proved more popular than the baking powder, however, so he dropped both soap and baking powder and switched for good to making and selling gum. He still used the gimmicks, but this time they were in the form of giving away the gum itself. On one occasion he sent sample sticks of gum to all 1 million subscribers listed in United States telephone books, and every year he sent more than 750,000 children two sticks of gum on their second birthday. By 1910 his "Spearmint" gum, introduced in 1893, was the best-selling gum in America. In 1911 Wrigley took over Zeno Manufacturing, the company that made his gum, and established the Wm. Wrigley Jr. Company. Today Wrigley's gum is as popular as ever, and the initials "P.K." that appear on the packets are a tribute to Wrigley's son, Philip Knight Wrigley (1894-1977), who ran the company after his father's death until the 1960s, when his own son, also William Wrigley (d.1999), took over the presidency.

Wurlitzer *(electric organs and pianos)*

Rudolph Wurlitzer (1831-1914) arrived in America from his native Germany in 1853 with no money, no friends, and just a few words of English. He was determined to make his mark, however, and gradually built up his savings in a series of jobs until in 1856 he had $700. How should he invest this? The answer came following a visit to a Cincinnati music store. When he asked the store's owner why the musical instruments were so expensive, the man explained that they were imported from Europe through a number of middlemen. Wurlitzer was convinced there was money to be made if he could cut out the middlemen and import European instruments direct to dealers in the Midwest. He sent his precious $700 to relatives back in Germany with a request to buy as many instruments of different types as possible. They duly arrived, and by the end of 1856 Wurlitzer was ready to launch his business. Before long his entire stock of instruments was depleted, and he had to order more from his relatives. As the demand for his products continued to grow, Wurlitzer reasoned that he could lower the cost of his instruments still further by making them himself. In 1861 he set up a plant in Cincinnati and began producing a variety of band and orchestra instruments. By 1890 Wurlitzer's original venture had blossomed into a national corporation, while he himself had become specially interested in the production of automatic music machines. He sold the world's first coin-operated electric organ in 1892, and at the turn of the 20th century produced an electric piano. The legendary "Mighty Wurlitzer" did not follow until after 1910, however, when the Wurlitzer Company acquired the Hope-Jones Organ Company of Elmira, New York, founded in 1907 by Robert Hope-Jones (1859-1914), an immigrant English organ builder. The Wurlitzer name was entered in the US Patent Office *Official Gazette* of March 23, 1926 and the *Trade Marks Journal* of May 12, 1926.

Wyborowa *(vodka)*

The brand of Polish vodka, made from high-grade rye, has a name meaning "select." Hence the full label name, *Wódka Wyborowa*, "Choice Vodka."

Xansa *(IT services)*

The British company, formerly the FI Group, specializes in business consulting, IT, and outsourcing. It was founded in 1962 by Steve Shirley (b.1933), now Dame Stephanie Shirley, who at the age of of six immigrated to Britain with her German father, Arnold Buchtal. (On taking British nationality he changed his name from Buchtal to Brooke to honor the English World War I poet Rupert Brooke.) The company rebranded itself in 2001, and in a press release of March 29 that year explained the motives and rationale for the name change and the procedure involved:

> Several thousand new names are registered each week and 98% of the names in the English Dictionary [*sic*] have already been registered as dot coms. So the company sought a new brand name that was unique, could be used in chosen worldwide markets and represented the brand values. The two month process involved extensive linguistic, domain name and registration checks. The name finally chosen was Xansa. The name is easy to say and read in all major market places and has clear phonetic links with "Answer." The other inspiration has been the Sanskrit word SANSKAR which, among its many meanings, also refers to culture and values which are internalised from past experiences and determine future actions.

The "Sanskrit word" equates with Hindi *sanskar*, whose prime definition in the *Allied Chambers Transliterated Hindi–Hindi–English Dictionary* (1993) is "completing, accomplishing, perfecting."

Xerox *(photocopiers)*

The American company was founded in 1906 as the Haloid Company, taking this name from the halides or silver compounds used in the photographic process. In 1958 it became the Haloid Xerox Company, and in 1961 the Xerox Corporation. The name "Xerox" alludes to the xerographic process (from Greek *xēros*, "dry") for making photographic copies onto plain, uncoated paper, which unlike a conventional photographic process does not use liquids or chemical developers but an electrically charged surface. Xerography itself was invented in the USA by Chester F. Carlson in 1938, and the company sold its first commercial xerographic copier in 1960. The name was entered in the *Trade Marks Journal* of August 19, 1952 and the US Patent Office *Official Gazette* of May 12, 1953, the latter with a claim of use since June 22, 1949.

Xylonite *see* **British Xylonite**

Y Lolfa *see* **Lolfa**

Yahoo! *(Internet search engine)*

The following ad appeared in *The Times* of May 18, 2000:

> What did you do in 1994? David Filo and Jerry Yang surfed. And in surfing they came across some pretty cool websites. So they bookmarked them. When that became unwieldy, they created an on-line directory. Suddenly, people began using it to navigate the web. A lot of people. Yahoo! was born. They moved out of the trailer and the rest, as they say, is history.

The text does not mention that at the time Filo (b.1966) and Yang (b.1969), a Taiwanese immigrant who came to California at the age of ten, were two electrical engineering graduate students at Stanford University. Nor does it give the source of the name. Cynics claim it is an acronym of "Yet Another Hierarchical Officious Oracle," but Filo and Wang jokingly say they regarded themselves as yahoos (philistines). "Yahoo!" is also, of course, an exclamation of joy or excitement, as one could well make on coming across a wonderful website.

Yahtzee *(game)*

The game, played with dice and scoresheet, was originally known as "the yacht game," and involves trying for a particular category of points on the scorepad within three throws. In ascending order, the top five scores are "Full House" (28), obtained with three dice of one number and two (a pair) of another, "Four of a Kind" (29), with four dice of one number, "Little Straight" (30), a throw of 1-2-3-4-5, "Big Straight" (30), a throw of 2-3-4-5-6, and "Yacht" (50), five of a kind. The name was entered by the E.S. Lowe Company, Inc., of New York, in the US Patent Office *Official Gazette* of January 1, 1957, for "poker dice games," and in the *Trade Marks Journal* of April 8, 1970 for: "Boxed games; dice, boards, counters and cards (other than ordinary playing cards), all for games."

Yakult *(milk drink)*

The fermented milk drink, containing a lactic acid, was invented in 1930 by Minoru Shi-

rota (1899-1982), a Japanese microbiologist at Kyoto University, who also founded the company of the name, taking it from the Esperanto for "yogurt." The company is based in Tokyo and the drink was launched on the European market in 1994. The name was entered in the *Trade Marks Journal* of May 6, 1970.

Yale *(locks)*

The locks take their name from Linus Yale, Jr. (1821-1868), born in Salisbury, New York, the son of a locksmith, general mechanic, and inventor. His education was influenced by his father's metalworking and lockmaking shop, but his interests were artistic rather than mechanical and he began his career as a portrait painter. His deeeeper interest in locks followed in around 1840, when his father began to manufacture bank locks in Newport, New York. Linus Yale's first major achievement was the Yale Infallible Bank Lock, which he brought out in 1851. He subsequently opened a shop in Shelburne Falls, Massachusetts, where he produced the Yale Magic Bank Lock and the Yale Double Treasury Bank Lock. By about 1862 Yale had introduced the combination lock. His most important invention, however, was the cylinder lock, in which the serrations ("teeth") on the edge of the key raise pin tumblers to just the right height, allowing the cylinder of the lock to revolve and so withdraw the bolt. Yale locks like these, and many similar makes, are familiar in thousands of front and back doors today. In 1868 Linus Yale, together with his partner, John Henry Towne, and his partner's son, Henry Robinson Towne, founded the Yale Lock Manufacturing Company in Stamford, Connecticut, but sadly Linus died on Christmas Day that year, aged 47. The name was entered by The Yale and Towne Manufacturing Company (Incorporated) in the *Trade Marks Journal* of April 15, 1885.

Yamaha *(organs and motorcycles)*

The motorcycle marque takes its name from the Japanese engineer Torakusu Yamaha (1851-1916), who at the age of 20 left home for Nagasaki to embark on a ten-year apprenticeship to an English clockmaker. He soon developed a high degree of expertise, and at the age of 30 took up another apprenticeship in a medical equipment shop at Osaka. In 1883 he was sent to carry out a repair job for the Hamamatsu

Hospital, and decided that Hamamatsu was the place for him to make his home, and that he could make a living there with his background of work on clocks and his growing knowledge of complicated machinery. In 1887, Yamaha was called to repair an organ owned by the Hamamatsu Elementary School. He did so, to the joy of the children, and decided to make a harmonium of his own. His first attempt was a failure, but a second harmonium in 1888 was a success, and together with a partner, Kisaburo Kawai, Yamaha set up an organ-making business. Pianos were added in 1900, and the company flourished. It continued to produce musical instruments under its next two presidents, Chiyomaru Amano and Kaichi Kawakami, and it was the fourth president, Kawakami's son Genichi, who in 1955 decided to diversify the company's interests to the manufacture of motorcycles. The first model, the YA1, nicknamed *Akatonbo* ("Red Dragonfly"), was a near relative of the German **DKW**.

Yardley *(toiletries)*

William Yardley (1756-1824) was an English maker of swords, buckles, and spurs. In 1801 his daughter, Hermina, married William Cleaver, who had inherited a soapmaking business founded by his father in London. When Cleaver ran into financial difficulties, his father-in-law took over the business. The firm in due course passed to Yardley's grandson, Charles, but he died young, leaving no one in the family to continue the business. It was therefore taken over by a senior partner, Thomas Exton Gardiner. Eventually, in 1890, the firm became a limited company, even though there were now no Yardleys involved in it. It was only in the early 20th century that Gardiner's sons turned from soapmaking to the production of perfumes. They also aimed to stress the name itself by putting "Yardley" on the soap they made. Until then they had simply made the soap in twopenny cakes and sold them to chemists, who then put their own name on. Thus the Yardley name, associated by many with its "Old English Lavender" perfume, passed from swords to soaps. In 1998 the company called in the receivers and its brand name and cosmetics range were acquired by the German group Wella.

Yarg *(cheese)*

The cow's-milk cheese, sold in a wrapping of (edible) nettle leaves, was first produced in Cornwall, England, in 1983 by a couple named Gray, who based it on an old recipe found in an attic. The name is simply a reversal of their surname.

Yellow Pages *(classified telephone directory)*

The name was originally in US use in the early 20th century for an index printed on yellow paper. It then came to be used specifically for the classified section of a telephone directory, at first included with the main directory, but later published separately. In the UK the name is a registered trademark of British Telecommunications plc and was entered in the *Trade Marks Journal* of June 29, 1983.

Y-Fronts *(men's or boys' briefs)*

The name is descriptive of the inverted Y-shaped tape on the front of the briefs, which were first experimentally produced in 1934 by the US firm of Coopers Inc. under the factory name of "Brief Style 1001." One day in 1938, Charlie Oliver, managing director of the Scottish firm of **Lyle & Scott**, saw a pair of Y-Fronts in the windows of **Simpson** of Piccadilly, London. He took a pair home, tried them on, and liked them. That same year an agreement was signed between Lyle & Scott and Coopers for the UK franchise. Not surprisingly, World War II hampered early promotion of the new-style briefs, but after the war the garment soon caught on and sales gradually rose. The name was entered in the *Trade Marks Journal* of June 17, 1953 with a description referring to "pants and vests," although vests (undershirts) obviously have no "Y-front."

Yorkshire Relish *(sauce)*

The English savory sauce of this name was first produced in the 19th century by Goodall, Backhouse & Co., a firm of drysalters and general merchants of Leeds, Yorkshire, who entered it in the *Trade Marks Journal* of January 13, 1877.

Young & Rubicam *(advertising agency)*

Young & Rubicam began in Philadelphia in 1923, founded by John Orr Young (1886-1976), a marketing man, and Raymond Rubicam (1892-1978), a copywriter at N.W. Ayer and Son, then regarded as America's largest agency. Their enterprise was literally founded on a shoestring, as the agency's first account was a device for making shoelaces at home. Their first major client was Postum (*see* **Post Toasties**), which helped to establish their reputation, and in 1926 Y&R moved to New York, where unlike other agencies it actually grew during the depression.

Younger's *(beer)*

Younger is a well-known brewing name in Scotland. George Younger (1722-1788) was born in Alloa, Clackmannan, into a family who originally came from Fife. The earliest mention of George Younger is as simply "a brewer" in 1745. It is known that he bought a malt kiln in 1762, and that in 1764 he set up his first brewery in Bank Street, Alloa, where it became known as the Meadow Brewery. After his death, the business continued in his family until it was formed as a limited company, George Younger & Sons Ltd., in 1897. Brewing meanwhile had been transferred from the Meadow Brewery, which was incapable of meeting the increased demand for Younger's beer, to larger premises at the Candleriggs Brewery, also in Alloa. In 1960 Younger's was taken over by Northern Breweries and assimilated into the **Bass** group. Another famous Younger's name is that of William Younger, who founded the Abbey Brewery at Holyrood, Edinburgh, in 1749. It closed in 1986 and production moved to **McEwan's** Fountain Brewery. This Younger's is now part of Scottish **Courage**.

Young's *(beer)*

The English firm's origins go back to 1831, when Charles A. Young and his business partner, Anthony F. Bainbridge, purchased the Ram Brewery in Wandsworth, London. Subsequently Young's son, Charles F. Young, entered the partnership together with Herbert Bainbridge, who was either the son or nephew of Anthony Bainbridge. The partnership was dissolved in 1884, however, leaving the younger Young to carry on alone. His business traded as Young & Co., and was incorporated as a limited company, Young & Co.'s Brewery Ltd., in 1890. The company is still in the hands of the Young family, and still brews at the Ram Brewery, with a prize ram as its trademark and "Ram Rod" as one of its beer brands.

Yo-Yo *(toy)*

The toy in the form of a reel wound and unwound on a string was first mass-produced in the USA by Louis Marx in 1929, and was introduced to the UK three years later, when the name was entered by Henry Clement Conlin, of Vancouver, British Columbia, Canada, in the *Trade Marks Journal* of March 2, 1932. The yo-yo is said to have originated from a Filipino jungle fighting weapon recorded in the 16th century, its name being Tagalog for "come back." *See also* **Duncan**.

Yuban *(coffee)*

The coffee now marketed by General Foods (*see* **Bird's**) was originally sold at the turn of the 20th century by John Arbuckle of Brooklyn, New York. At Christmas, Arbuckle would serve his special blend of coffee at a dinner party for his friends, referring to the repast as his "Yuletide Banquet." Hence, goes the story, the name "Yuban." But there is a more prosaic explanation of the name. On green coffee shipments, the bags containing the beans for Arbuckle's special blend were marked

A B

N Y

for "Arbuckle Brothers, New York." When a brand name came to be chose, an attempt was made to create a name out of these letters. Combinations such as "Bany" and "Naby" were regarded as unsuitable, as was "Yban," until someone suggested adding "u" to it. Thus "Yuban" was created.

Yves Saint Laurent *(fashionwear)*

The famous French fashion house, colloquially known as YSL, was founded by Yves Saint Laurent (b.1936), born in Oran, Algeria. Studying in Paris at the age of 17, he entered a competition sponsored by the International Wool Secretariat and won first prize for a cocktail dress. Soon after, he was hired by **Dior**, and when Christian Dior himself died in 1957, took over the house. After introducing a number of controversial designs, Saint Laurent was called up in 1960 to serve in the Algerian war, but on returning some months later following discharge through illness, found that his post as head designer at Dior had been taken over by Marc Bohan. With business partner Pierre Berger, Saint Laurent accordingly set up his own house in 1961. In 1999 it was taken over by **Gucci**.

Zagato *(automobile bodywork)*

The Italian bodywork designer Ugo Zagato (1892-1968) set up his famous *carrozzeria* (body factory) in Milan in 1919. Its heyday was in the 1950s and 1960s, when it created superb sporting bodywork for such well-known automobile names as **Ferrari**, **Alfa Romeo**, **Fiat**, **Maserati**, **Aston Martin**, **Bristol**, and **Lancia**. Brothers Elio and Gianni Zagato opened a new factory in 1962 and eventually expanded into areas such as electric and armored cars.

Zamboni *(ice-rink resurfacing machine)*

The machine takes its name from its American inventor, Frank J. Zamboni, who set up a business to manufacture it in Paramount, California, in the early 1960s. The name was entered in the US Patent Office *Official Gazette* of February 16, 1965, with a claim of first use in July 1962, and in the *Trade Marks Journal* of April 3, 1968.

Zam-Buk *(antiseptic ointment)*

The ointment is said to take its name from a former ingredient known as "Zambuci oil," although it may actually be random. (An ad in the Australian Sunday newspaper *Truth* for December 21, 1902 runs: "*Zam-buk.* Name carries no meaning. The ointment carries a blessing.") It was originally the formula of a medical officer in the Indian Civil Service, and the name was entered by the Bile Bean Manufacturing Company of Leeds, England, in the *Trade Marks Journal* of November 23, 1904 for: "Chemical substances prepared for use in medicine and pharmacy, but not including gelatine capsules." The name was subsequently adopted in Australia and New Zealand as a slang term for a first aider, and specifically for a member of the St. John's Ambulance Brigade attending a sporting event, when the ointment would routinely form part of their equipment.

Zantac *(anti-ulcer drug)*

The name is that of the drug known generically as ranitidine, developed in the late 20th century. The name itself probably derives from "antacid" prefixed by the letter "Z." The name was entered in the *Trade Marks Journal* of July 3, 1974.

Zanussi *(electrical appliances)*

The familiar name, primarily associated with refrigerators and washing machines, is that of Antonio Zanussi, an Italian who in 1916 first set up a workshop in Pordenone, northeastern Italy, to make wood-burning kitchen stoves. By 1934 his venture had progressed to the manufacture of commercial catering equipment in a specially built factory, and by 1951, five years after he had been succeeded by his son, Lino Zanussi, the firm had expanded to produce both gas and electric cookers. Refrigerators followed in a new factory three years later, and washing machines were introduced in 1958. Lino Zanussi was killed in an air crash in Spain in 1968, thus severing the company link with the Zanussi family. Since 1984 Zanussi has been under the control of the Swedish company **Electrolux.**

Zeal *(thermometers)*

Giles Henry Zeal (1860-1938) was born in London, England, the son of an umbrella maker. In 1879 he took up an apprenticeship with a clinical thermometer blower, and two years later set himself up as an "outsider" blower, working for other firms. In 1888 he began to produce his own clinical thermometers, and in 1901 patented his "Repello" model. Many people disliked having to shake the mercury down to reset the thermometer after use. The "Repello" had a flexible glass bulb at the top, which one simply squeezed to force the mercury down from the maximum. It proved to be very popular, and was regarded in the trade as superior to all other clinical thermometers. In 1920 Zeal expanded his business into other types of thermometers, and later into measuring instruments for the brewing and distilling trades. Zeal's clinical thermometer was long familiar in domestic use, however, and his sons took the firm into new expansion, making it one of the largest manufacturers of thermometers in Europe.

Zebrite *(grate polish)*

The polish of this name was originally introduced by **Reckitt** in 1890 under the name "Zebra," so called because it was sold in a black-and-white wrapper, resembling the stripes of the animal. The name was changed to "Zebrite" in 1952 in order to indicate the nature of the product ("bright") while retaining the black-and-white wrapper of the original. The name was entered in the *Trade Marks Journal* of October 15, 1982.

Zegna *(menswear)*

The Italian company was founded at Trivero, northwestern Italy, by Angelo Zegna in 1908. Two years later his son, Ermenegildo, took over and expanded the business, modernizing the machinery and increasing production. Clothing manufacture was added to the original cloth and fabrics in the 1960s. In 1998, Ermenegildo (Gildo) Zegna (b.1956) and his cousin, Paolo (b.1957), took over the running of Zegna following the retirement of Paolo's father, Aldo, and his brother, Angelo, Gildo's father, while Gildo's sister, Anna (b.1957), took charge of the company's image and global communications. In 2000, when Zegna had 337 stores worldwide, the company launched a womenswear brand, Agnona.

Zeiss *(optical instruments)*

The name is that of Carl Zeiss (1816-1888), born in Weimar, Germany, who after completing his early education in Weimar became an apprentice to the engineer Dr. Frederick Koerner. As part of his training, Zeiss was required to travel widely, and he visited Vienna, Berlin, Stuttgart, and Darmstadt to study his trade. In 1846 he set up a business of his own, an optical workshop in Jena, where he produced magnifying glasses and microscopes. He took on Ernest Abbe (1840-1905), a physics and mathematics lecturer at the University of Jena, to advise him on advances in optical theory and in 1875 made him his partner. In 1880 Zeiss began an association with the chemist Friedrich Otto Schott (1851-1935), who developed many new kinds of optical glass, and this led to the establishment of the famous Jena glassworks in 1884. After World War II, US forces evacuated the board of management and most of the staff of the Carl Zeiss firm to West Germany, where it was reestablished.

Zeneca *see* ICI

Zephiran *(antiseptic)*

The proprietary name for an antiseptic preparation of benzalkonium chloride is presumably of arbitrary origin. It was entered by **Bayer** in the *Trade Marks Journal* of July 17, 1935, and by I.G. Farbenindustrie (*see* **IG Farben**) in the US Patent Office *Official Gazette* of January 28, 1936: "For antiseptic and disinfectant."

Zhiguli *see* Lada.

Zil *(automobiles)*

The car that was a perquisite of office for the upper echelons of the former Soviet government was produced by a Moscow automobile factory founded in 1916 as the Aktsionernoe mashinostroitel'noe obshchestvo (AMO) ("Joint-Stock Engineering Company"). In 1918 it was nationalized, and in the 1930s renamed Zavod imeni Stalina (ZiS) ("Factory Named after Stalin"). The Zis was a copy of the American **Packard** and was a luxury car. In 1956, following the disgrace of Stalin, the factory was renamed Zavod imeni Likhachëva (ZiL) ("Factory Named after Likhachëv"), referring to its former managing director, Ivan Alekseevich Likhachëv (1896-1956), and this gave the name of the Zil (sometimes wrongly said to stand for Zavod imeni Lenina, "Factory Named after Lenin").

Zimmer *(walking frame)*

The make of walking frame for elderly or disabled people is manufactured by Zimmer Orthopaedic Ltd. of London, England, who entered the name in the *Trade Marks Journal* of April 11, 1951 and the US Patent Office *Official Gazette* of April 16, 1957. The name itself comes from Mongolian *zhima*, the word for a sledge drawn by a *zho*, a hybrid of a yak and a cow, which was guided by a man walking at the rear holding an upright frame.

Ziploc *(plastic bags)*

The respelling of "zip lock" as the name of a type of plastic bag with an airtight fastening of two interlocking strips was entered by the **Dow** Chemical Company in the US Patent Office *Official Gazette* of February 17, 1970, with a note of filing on September 9, 1968.

Zipper *(slide fastener)*

Slide fasteners were the invention in 1893 of Whitcomb L. Judson of Chicago, and were originally designed for use on boots and shoes. In 1923 B.G. Work of **Goodrich** coined the name "Zipper" for the slide fastener that had just been adopted for closing the firm's overshoes, the name denoting the audible "zip" when the fastener was opened or closed. The name was registered as a trademark in the USA in April 1925, but specifically in its application to "boots made of rubber and fabric." The term then passed generically to a similar fastener on any item of clothing or object. Goodrich naturally objected to this purloinment of their name, and appealed to the courts to have it protected. Their rights to the trademark were sustained, but only with regard to their boots. Thus "Zipper Boots" became the name for boots with a zip manufactured by the B.F. Goodrich Co., but "zipper" became a common noun for a zip fastener. ("Zip" in this last sense derives from the Goodrich name.) *See also* **Zippo**.

Zippo *(cigarette lighters)*

The familiar lighter was the invention of George G. Blaisdell (1895-1978), born in Bradford, Pennsylvania, the son of an oil equipment manufacturer. After two years in military school, young George entered his father's Blaisdell Machinery Company as an apprentice, and soon showed an aptitude for machining and engineering. He eventually took over the business, but in 1920 sold it and, with his brother, started an oil drilling enterprise under the name of the Blaisdell Oil Company. He was always looking out for new opportunities, and found one by chance when he attended a function at the Bradford Country Club in 1931 and saw an elegant young man lighting a cigarette with a clumsy and unsightly lighter that hardly matched its owner's suavity. George is said to have remarked, "You're all dressed up—why don't you get a lighter that looks decent?" "Because it works," came the reply. The simple answer so impressed George that he applied for the US distribution rights for the cheap Austrian lighter. Sales were disappointing, however, and George decided to design a lighter of his own. He rented a small workshop above a garage in Bradford and set about remodeling the Austrian original. The result was the Zippo, launched in 1933, and the name was entered by the Zippo Manufacturing Company, of Bradford, Pennsylvania, in the US Patent Office *Official Gazette* of July 10, 1934: "For pocket lighter of the pyrophoric type," and by Miriam Barcroft Blaisdell, "trading as Zippo Manufacturing Company," in the *Trade Marks Journal* of March 16, 1938.

There was no special significance in the choice of the name 'Zippo'. Shortly before the time of Blaisdell's invention the Talon Company of Pennsylvania had introduced to the market its slide fastener under the name 'Zipper'. Blaisdell's imag-

ination was caught by the modern sound of this name, which seemed to him to represent all that was new and progressive; so he named his lighter 'Zippo', simply because it sounded right to him. 67 years later it has become almost a generic name for a lighter.

(Avi R. Baer and Alexander Neumark, *Zippo: An American Legend*, 1999)

Zovirax *(antiviral drug)*

The proprietary name for acyclovir, a drug chiefly used in the treatment of herpes and Aids, is apparently partly based on the generic name, in which the final element represents "viral." It was entered by the **Wellcome** Foundation in the *Trade Marks Journal* of September 6, 1978.

Zubes *(lozenges)*

The British throat lozenges apparently date from before World War I, since when they have been made by a series of manufacturers. The name is perhaps based on "tubes," referring to the bronchial passages, with the "z" of "lozenge" replacing the "t." A familiar 1960s slogan was actually "Zubes are good for your tubes." The name was entered in the *Trade Marks Journal* of February 22, 1928.

Zubrovka *(vodka)*

The Russian brand of vodka is flavored with bison grass. Hence the name, from Russian *zubr*, "bison." There is a counterpart in Polish "Zubrówka." The grass itself is so called because it was originally grazed by herds of European bison. (It still is, in the Białowieski National Park, northeastern Poland.)

Zucchi *(fabrics)*

The Italian company had its origins in the workshop set up at Casorezzo, near Milan, by Vincenzo Zucchi in 1920. The business flourished and expanded in the 1950s thanks to the acquisition of similar firms, and in 1986 acquired the important household linen specialty from the **Marzotto** group.

Zug *(waterproof leather)*

The make of waterproofed leather, used in particular for the uppers of climbing boots, presumably derives its name from the Swiss canton of Zug, noted for its forests and mountains. It was entered by its Scottish manufacturers, W. & J. Martin, of Glasgow, in the

Trade Marks Journal of September 6, 1899. The name is no longer proprietary.

Zwemmer *(publishers)*

The London, England, art book publishers were established in 1916 by the Dutchman Anton Zwemmer (1892-1979), when he opened what was originally a foreign-language bookshop in Charing Cross Road. In the 1920s he developed it into a specialist art bookshop that played an important role in disseminating modern art in Britain. One of Zwemmer's first successful publications was Herbert Read's study of the sculptor Henry Moore, *Henry Moore: An Appreciation* (1934), and their list soon became an important catalog of scholarly works on art, architecture, and related subjects. The family also owned the Zwemmer Gallery next door, where the British public first had an opportunity to purchase the works of Picasso and become acquainted with Dalí. In 1985 the business was sold to a fine arts company, Philip Wilson, who continued to trade under the Zwemmer name.

Zyklon *(insecticide)*

The insecticidal fumigant, familiar as "Zyklon B" in World War II, when it was used by the Germans as a lethal gas, consists of hydrogen cyanide adsorbed on (or released from) a carrier in the form of small tablets. The name is identical to the German word for "cyclone," but this may not be the actual meaning. (The first two letters could in fact come from *Zyanid*, "cyanide.") It was originally entered by the Deutsche Gesellschaft für Schädlingsbekämpfung ("German Pest Control Company") of Frankfurt in the US Patent Office *Official Gazette* of November 9, 1926 for: "Apparatus for measuring the quantities of substances which generate poisonous gases—for instance, hydrocyanic acid."

Advertising Slogans

The following is a selection of slogans naming a particular product or service, together with date of first use, where known.

Abbey National: Get the Abbey habit (late 1970s)

Aetna: Aetna, I'm glad I met ya

All-Bran: Join the "regulars" with Kellogg's All-Bran

Aluminum Company of America: What next from Alcoa!

American Express: American Express? That'll do nicely, sir (1970s)

Amplex: Someone isn't using Amplex (1950s)

Amtrak: All Aboard Amtrak

Anadin: Nothing acts faster than Anadin (1960s)

Apple: Why every kid should have an Apple after school

AT&T: AT&T. The right choice

Babycham: I'd love a Babycham (1955)

Badedas: Things happen after a Badedas bath (1966)

Band-Aid: I'm stuck on Band-Aid because Band-Aid is stuck on me

Barratt: Walk the Barratt way (early 1940s)

Bayer: Bayer works wonders

Beechcraft: The world is smaller when you fly a Beechcraft

Bell & Howell: Bell & Howell brings out the expert in you (automatically!)

Benetton: United colors of Benetton (late 1980s)

Betty Crocker: You and Betty Crocker can bake someone happy

Bic: Flick your Bic (1975)

Bigelow: A title on the door rates a Bigelow on the floor

Birds Eye: Better buy Birds Eye

Bissell: Put your sweeping reliance on a Bissell appliance

Bisto: Ahh Bisto! (1919)

Boeing: Capability has many faces at Boeing

Borden: If it's Bordens, it's got to be good

Bournvita: Sleep sweeter, Bournvita (1960s)

Bovril: Bovril… prevents that sinking feeling (1920)

Budweiser: Where there's life there's Bud (1959)

Buick: When better cars are built, Buick will build them

Bulova: America runs on Bulova time

Burger King: Burger King—the home of the whopper (1981)

BVDs: Next to myself I like BVD's best (*c*.1920)

Calvin Klein: You know what comes between me and my Calvins? Nothing! (1980)

Camel: I'd walk a mile for a Camel (early 1900s)

Campbell's: Stir up the Campbell's … soup is good food

Canada Dry: Emigrate to Canada Dry (for the sake of your Scotch) (1980)

Canon: Canon meets tomorrow's challenges today

Carling: I bet he drinks Carling Black Label (1990)

Castlemaine XXXX: Australians wouldn't give a XXXX for anything else (1986)

Castrol: Castrol. Liquid engineering (1977)

Celanese: Add a fiber from Celanese and good things get better

Cessna: More people buy Cessna twins than any other

Champion: To feel new power, *instantly*, install new Champions now and every 10,000 miles

Chanel: Every woman alive wants Chanel No. 5

Chef Boy-ar-dee: Thank goodness for Chef Boy-ar-dee

Chock Full O'Nuts: Chock Full O'Nuts is that heavenly coffee (1950s)

Chrysler: You get the goods things first from Chrysler Corp.

Cinzano: When you mix with Cinzano, you mix with the best

Clairol: Clairol is going to make someone beautiful today

Coca-Cola: Drink Coca-Cola

Coke: Things go better with Coke (1963); Coke is it (1982)

Coleman: Light, heat and cook the Coleman way

Colman: C'mon Colman's, light my fire (1979)

Contac: Give your cold to Contac

Courage: Take Courage (1966)

Craven "A": For your throat's sake, smoke Craven "A" (1920s)

Crisco: Crisco'll do you proud every time

Cyril Lord: This is luxury you can afford by Cyril Lord (early 1960s)

Dacron: America lives in Dacron

Danskin: Danskins are not just for dancing

Deere: Nothing runs like a Deere

Del Monte: The man from Del Monte says "yes" (1985)

Delta: Delta is ready when you are

Dictaphone: Dictate to the Dictaphone

Dodge: We are Dodge, an American Revolution

Double Diamond: A Double Diamond works wonders (1952)

Dunlop: Around the world on Dunlops

Eastman: If it isn't an Eastman, it isn't a Kodak

Enos: First thing every morning renew your health with Eno's (1927)

Esso: The Esso sign means happy motoring (1950s)

Eversharp: Give Eversharp and you give the finest

Evinrude: Evinruding is rowboat motoring

Ex-Lax: Keep "regular" with Ex-Lax (1934)

Firestone: The name that's known is Firestone—all over the world

Flit: Don't get bit, get Flit

Force: High o'er the fence leaps Sunny Jim / "Force" is the food that raises him (1903)

Ford: Ford has a better idea

Formica: The surprise of Formica products

Galliano: Fond of things Italiano? Try a sip of Galliano

Gallo: It's time for a change to Gallo

Gillette: Good mornings begin with Gillette (c.1952)

Glaxo: Glaxo builds bonny babies (1913)

Goodyear: More people ride on Goodyear tires than on any other brand

Gordon's: It's got to be Gordon's (1977)

Grant's: We'll wait. Grant's 8

Guinness: Guinness is good for you (1929); My goodness, my Guinness (1935)

Gulf Oil: Gulf makes things run better

Haig: Don't be vague—ask for Haig (c. 1936)

Harp: Harp puts out the fire (c.1976)

Heineken: Heineken refreshes the parts other beers cannot reach (1975)

Heinz: Beanz meanz Heinz (c.1967)

Hellmann's: Bring out the Hellmann's and bring out the best

Holiday Inns: Holiday Inn is Number One in people pleasin'

Honda: Honda ... we make it simple; Follow the leader, he's on a Honda

Hoover: Give her a Hoover and you give her the best

Horlicks: Horlicks guards against night starvation (1930s)

Hovis: Don't say brown—say Hovis (mid-1930s)

Hush Puppies: Anything goes with Hush Puppies

Hyatt: Feel the Hyatt touch

IBM: A little IBM can mean a lot of freedom

Ivory: Ivory is kind to everything it touches

Jantzen: The season belongs to Jantzen

Jeep: Only in a Jeep

Kelly Services: Kelly can do

Kinney: Kiddies' feet are safe in Kinney's hands

Kit-Kat: Have a break, have a Kit-Kat (c.1955)

Knirps: You can't k-nacker a K-nirps (1981)

Kodak: There are no game laws for those who hunt with a Kodak

Kruschen: I've got that Kruschen feeling (1920s)

Libby: Look to Libby's for perfection

Litton: Nobody knows more about microwave cooking than Litton

Lockheed: Look to Lockheed for leadership

Lucky Strike: Have you tried a Lucky lately?

Lucozade: Lucozade aids recovery (c.1986)

Lux: Nine out of ten screen stars use Lux toilet soap for their priceless smooth skins (1927)

Macleans: Did you Maclean your teeth today? (1934)

Macy's: No one is in debt to Macy's

Marlboro: Come to where the flavor is. Come to Marlboro Country (mid-1950s)

Mars: A Mars a day helps you work, rest and play (c.1960)

Mazola: Mazola makes eating good sense

Merrill Lynch: Merrill Lynch is bullish on America

McDonald's: Nobody can do it like McDonald's can (1970s)

Minolta: Only from the mind of Minolta

Mr Kipling: Mr Kipling does make exceedingly good cakes (early 1970s)

Mumm: Mumm's the word for champagne

Munsingwear: Don't say underwear, say Munsingwear

Nestlé: Nestle's makes the very best

Noilly Prat: Don't stir without Noilly Prat

Noxzema: Beautiful skin begins with Noxzema

Omo: Omo adds brightness to whiteness (late 1950s)

Orange: The future's bright, the future's Orange (1996)

Oxo: Oxo gives a meal man-appeal (1958)

Pan American: Pan Am makes the going great

Parker: It's a mark of distinction to own a Parker Pen

Pears: Good morning! Have you used Pears' soap?

Penguin (cookies): P-P-P-Pick up a Penguin (1960)

Penguin (publishers): For the best in paparbacks, look for the Penguin

Pepsi Cola: Come alive—you're in the Pepsi generation (1964)

Pepsodent: You'll wonder where the yellow went / When you brush your teeth with Pepsodent: (1950s)

Persil: Persil washes whiter (1970s)

Philip Morris: If every smoker knew what Philip Morris smokers know, they'd all change to Philip Morris

Phillips': To fly high in the morning, take Phillips at night

Phyllosan: Phyllosan fortifies the over-forties (late 1940s)

Pillsbury: The freshest ideas are baking at Pillsbury

Piper: More people have bought Pipers than any other plane in the world

Piper-Heidsieck: Pop goes the Piper

Player's: Player's please (1927)

Quaker Oats: Quaker Oats. It's the right thing to do

P&O: Run away to sea with P&O

Palmolive: Doctors prove Palmolive's beauty results

Paramount: If it's a Paramount picture, it's the best show in town

Phillips Petroleum: Go *first class* ... go Phillips 66

Porsche: Porsche 968: The next evolution

Ralston Purina: If Purina chows won't make your hens lay, they are roosters

Revlon: The most unforgettable women in the world wear Revlon

Rolls-Royce: At 60 miles an hour the loudest noise in this new Rolls-Royce comes from the electric clock (1958)

Saab: We don't make compromises. We make Saabs

Sara Lee: Nobody doesn't like Sara Lee

Schlitz: When you're out of Schlitz, you're out of beer

Schweppes: Schh... you-know-who (1960s)

Seagram: Say Seagram's and be sure

Sears, Roebuck: Shop at Sears and save

7-Up: Freshen up with 7-Up (1962)

Sharp: From sharp minds come Sharp products

Sharp's: Sharp's the word for toffee (1927)

Shell: You can be sure of Shell (*c*.1931); That's Shell—that was! (late 1930s)

Singer (sewing machines): Make it yourself on a Singer

Smuckers: With a name like Smuckers it has to be good (*c*.1960)

Spandex: Nothing but Spandex makes you look so female

Standard Oil: You *expect* more from Standard and you *get* it

Stetson: Step out with a Stetson (1930s)

Stork: Can you tell Stork from butter? (*c*.1956)

Teacher's: No Scotch improves the flavor of water like Teacher's

Tetley (tea): Tetley make tea-bags make tea (1970s)

Tizer: Drink Tizer, the appetizer (1920s)

Toni: Which twin has the Toni—and which twin has the expensive perm? (1951)

Toyota: Get your hands on a Toyota... you'll never let go

Vicks: At the first sneeze, Vicks VapoRub

Volkswagen: Nothing else is a Volkswagen

Waterman: All write with a Waterman Ideal Fountain Pen... all wrong if you don't

Watneys: What we want is Watneys (1940s)

Wheaties: Had your Wheaties today?

White Horse: You can take a White Horse anywhere (1969)

Wurlitzer: Wurlitzer means music to millions

Yamaha: Yamaha—the way it should be

Zubes: Zubes are good for your tubes (1960s)

Appendix:
The Naming of Nylon

The naming of nylon was hardly straightforward. The synthetic fiber was originally code-named "Fiber 66" and test-marketed as "Exton." At first meaningful names were considered, such as "Duparooh," an acronysm of "Du Pont pulls a rabbit out of a hat." A similar proposal was "Dupron," short for "Du Pont pulls rabbit out of nitrogen (or nature, or nozzle, or naphtha)." "Duponese," "Pontella," and "Lustrol" were also suggested. One offering was "Wacara," for the name of nylon's inventor, Wallace Carothers. Another was "Klis," as an inverted "silk." Further candidates of around 350 included: "Amidarn," "Amiray," "Amoray," "Amido Silk," "Artex," "Ceron," "Duamex," "Dualin," "Dusilk," "Extra," "Eidaise," "Eidu," "Ekastra," "Filosel," "Linex," "Lamiam," "Longduray," "Lastica," "Lastrapon," "Mertal," "Mouran," "Moursheen," "Nepon," "Novasilk," "Nyzara," "Pantex," "Pontex," "Poya," "Ramex," "Ramisil," "Rayamide," "Supralin," "Silpon," "Syntex," "Silf," "Silmon," "Siltra," "Silkex," "Silpnex," "Tane," "Tensheer," "Terikon," and "Wiralene."

In the end, it seemed desirable to have a name that hinted at the product's *new*ness while categorizing it as a fabric by a suggestion of (natural) cott*on* or (artificial) ray*on*. "Nulon" was thus considered for a time. The "u" was then replaced by an "i" giving "nilon." But this could be pronounced as "neelon," "nillon," or "nighlon," and the pronunciation must be unambiguous. The spelling was thus finally amended to "nylon," and Du Pont's vice president Leonard Yerkes wrote the Executive Committee on September 1, 1938: "The name Nylon has been selected ... we feel it is the best suggested and should be satisfactory ... Permission to register as trade-marks other names denoting products made from NYLON will be requested of your Committee from time to time" (quoted in Stephen Fenichell, *Plastic: The Making of a Synthetic Century*, 1996).

The name is thus generic and not a registered name or trademark. It does not combine the names "*N*ew *Yo*rk" and "*Lon*don," nor was it inspired by the "Trylon" (the tapering tower symbolizing the New York World's Fair), nor is it an acronym of "*N*ow *You* *L*ousy *O*ld *N*ipponese," jibing at the Japanese silk trade, nor, similarly, is it a reversal of "nolyn," sounding like Japanese *norin*, "agriculture and forestry" (from *nogyo*, "agriculture," and *ringyo*, "forestry"). Having raised Japanese hackles, Yerkes wrote to the Fiber Supply and Demand Adjustment Association of Japan: "I adopted the word 'nylon' because it was plain, easy to pronounce and easy to memorize. Please rest assured ... when we state that the word 'nylon' positively contains no malicious implications."

Bibliography

Adburgham, Alison. *Shopping in Style*. London: Thames & Hudson, 1979.

Arnold, Oren. *What's In a Name: Famous Brand Names*. New York: Julian Messner, 1979.

Ayto, John. *The Glutton's Glossary: A Dictionary of Food and Drink Terms*. London: Routledge, 1980.

Baren, Maurice. *How It All Began*. Otley: Smith Settle, 1992.

_____. *How It All Began Up the High Street*. London: Michael O'Mara, 1996.

_____. *How Household Names Began*. London: Michael O'Mara, 1997.

_____. *Victorian Shopping*. London: Michael O'Mara, 1998.

Bati, Anwer. *The Cigar Companion*. Toronto: Macmillan, 3d ed., 1998.

Beable, William H. *Romance of Great Businesses*, 2 vols. London: Heath Cranton, 1926.

Beeching, Wilfred A. *Century of the Typewriter*, new ed. Bournemouth: British Typewriter Museum Publishing, 1990.

Binney, Ruth, ed. *The Origins of Everyday Things*. London: Reader's Digest, 1998.

Boddewyn, J. "The Names of U.S. Industrial Corporations: A Study in Change" in: Kelsie B. Harder, comp. *Names and Their Varieties*. Lanham, MD: University Press of America, 1986.

Bowman, John S., ed. *The Cambridge Dictionary of American Biography*. Cambridge: Cambridge University Press, 1995.

Bradley, Ian Campbell. *Enlightened Entrepreneurs*. London: Weidenfeld and Nicolson, 1987.

Brazendale, Kevin, gen. ed. *The Encyclopedia of Classic Cars*. Enderby: Bookmart, 1999.

Brown, Gordon. *Classic Spirits of the World*. London: Prion, 1995.

Buckley, Martin, and Chris Rees. *The World Encyclopedia of Cars*. New York: Hermes House, 2000.

Button, Henry, and Andrew Lampert. *The Guinness Book of the Business World*. Enfield: Guinness Superlatives, 1976.

Callan, Georgina O'Hara. *The Thames and Hudson Dictionary of Fashion and Fashion Designers*. London: Thames and Hudson, 1998.

Campbell, Hannah. *Why Did They Name It..?* New York: Ace Books, 1964.

Carter, E.F., ed. *Dictionary of Inventions and Discoveries*. Stevenage: Robin Clark, 1978.

Coady, Chantal. *The Chocolate Companion*. London: Apple Press, 1995.

The Compact Oxford English Dictionary, 2d ed. Oxford: Clarendon Press, 1991.

Curwen, Henry. *A History of Booksellers*. London: Chatto and Windus, 1873.

Daly, Steven, and Nathaniel Wice. *alt.culture*. London: Fourth Estate, 1995.

Davis, William. *The Innovators*. London: Genesis Productions, 1987.

Day, Lance, and Ian McNeil, eds. *Biographical Dictionary of the History of Technology*. London: Routledge, 1996.

Donnachie, Ian. *A History of the Brewing Industry in Scotland*. Edinburgh: John Donald, 1979.

Dyson, James. *20th Century Icons: Design*. Bath: Absolute Press, 1999.

Edwards, Graham, and Sue Edwards. *The Language of Drink*. Stroud: Alan Sutton, 1988.

The Food Makers: A History of General Foods Ltd. Banbury: General Foods, 1972.

The Food Trade Directory of Trade Marks and Brand Names. London: Food Trade Review, 1959.

Fox, Stephen. *The Mirror Makers*. London: William Heinemann, 1990.

Fragrance and Fashion. Enderby: Silverdale Books, 2000.

Fucini, Joseph J., and Suzy Fucini. *Entrepreneurs: The Men and Women Behind Famous Brand Names and How They Made It*. Boston: G.K. Hall, 1985.

Garraty, John A., and Mark C. Carnes, gen. eds. *American National Biography*. 24 vols. New York: Oxford University Press, 1999.

Glennon, Lorraine, ed. in chief. *Our Times: The Illustrated History of the 20th Century*. Atlanta: Turner Publishing, 1995.

Glover, Brian. *The World Encyclopedia of Beer*. London: Anness Publishing, 1997.

Grunfeld, Nina. *The Royal Shopping Guide*. London: Pan Books, 1984.

Hart, Susannah, and John Murphy, eds. *Brands: The New Wealth Creators*. London: Macmillan, 1998.

Heald, Tim. *By Appointment: 150 Years of the Royal Warrant and its Holders*. London: Queen Anne Press, 1989.

Healey, Tim. *Unforgettable Ads*. London: Reader's Digest, 1992.

Henshaw, Peter. *The Encyclopedia of the Motorcycle*. Broxbourne: Regency Publishing, 2000.

Hillman, David, and David Gibbs. *Century Makers*. London: Weidenfeld & Nicolson, 1998.

Horton, Chris, ed. *Encyclopedia of the Car*. Hoo: Grange Books, 1998.

Jackson, Kenneth T., ed. *The Encyclopedia of New York City*. New Haven: Yale University Press, 1995.

Jackson, Michael. *Great Beer Guide*. London: Dorling Kindersley, 2000.

Jakle, John A., and Keith A. Sculle. *Fast Food: Roadside Restaurants in the Automobile Age*. Baltimore: Johns Hopkins University Press, 1999.

Jeremy, David J., ed. *Dictionary of Business Biography*. 5 vols. London: Butterworths, 1984-6.

Kay, William. *The Battle for the High Street*. London: Piatkus, 1987.

_____. *Tycoons: Where They Came From and How They Made It*. London: Piatkus, 1985.

Klein, Naomi. *No Logo*. London: Flamingo, 2000.

Krueger, John R. "Beer Brand Names in the United States" in: Kelsie B. Harder, comp. *Names and Their Varieties*. Lanham, MD: University Press of America, 1986.

Lambert, I.E. *The Public Accepts: Stories Behind Famous Trade-Marks, Names, and Slogans*. Albuquerque: University of New Mexico Press, 1941.

Lazell, H.G. *From Pills to Penicillin: The Beecham Story*. London: Heinemann, 1975.

Lee, Laura. *The Name's Familiar*. Gretna, LA: Pelican, 1999.

Mahoney, Tom, and Leonard Stone. *The Great Merchants: America's Foremost Retail Institutions and the People Who Made Them Great*, updated and enlarged ed. New York: Harper & Row, 1974.

McDowall, R.J.S. *The Whiskies of Scotland*, 3d ed. London: John Murray, 1975.

Mencken, H.L. *The American Language*, 4th ed. New York: Alfred A. Knopf, 1936.

Merriam Webster's Biographical Dictionary. Springfield, MA: Merriam-Webster, 1995.

Messadié, Gérald. *Les Grandes Inventions de l'humanité*. Paris: Bordas, 1988.

Millard, Patricia. *British Made?* Havant: Kenneth Mason, 1969.

Millington, Neil. *Cigars*. London: PRC Publishing, 1998.

Morton, Ian, and Judith Hall. *Medicines: The Comprehensive Guide*, 4th ed. London: Bloomsbury, 1995.

Moskowitz, Milton, Michael Katz, and Robert Levering, eds. *Everybody's Business: The Irreverent Guide to Corporate America*. San Francisco, CA: Harper & Row, 1980.

Murray, Jim. *Classic Irish Whiskey*. London: Prion Books, 1997.

The New Encyclopædia Britannica, 15th ed., 32 vols. Chicago: Encyclopædia Britannica, 2002.

Nicholas, Tim. *Car Badges of the World*. London: Cassell, 1970.

Nightingale MultiMedia. *The 100 Best Companies to Work For in the UK*. London: Hodder & Stoughton, 1997.

Opie, Robert. *Remember When: A Nostalgic Trip Through the Consumer Era*. London: Mitchell Beazley, 1999.

Pavitt, Jane, ed. *brand. new*. London: V&A Publications, 2000.

Porter, Roy, and Marilyn Ogilvie, consultant eds. *The Hutchinson Dictionary of Scientific Biography*, 3d ed. 2 vols. Oxford: Helicon, 2000.

Pringle, Hamish, and William Gordon. *Brand Manners*, Chichester: John Wiley, 2001.

Proffitt, Michael, ed. *Oxford English Dictionary Additions Series*, vol. 3. Oxford: Clarendon Press, 1997.

Reader, W.J. *Fifty Years of Unilever*. London: Heinemann, 1980.

Richmond, Lesley, and Bridget Stockford. *Company Archives*. Brookfield, VT: Gower, 1986.

Robertson, Patrick. *The Shell Book of Firsts*, rev. ed. London: Ebury Press/Michael Joseph, 1983.

Room, Adrian. *Dictionary of Trade Name Origins*. London: Routledge & Kegan Paul, 1982.

_____. *Corporate Eponymy*. Jefferson, NC: McFarland, 1992.

The Royal Warrant Holders Who's Who. London: Royal Warrant Holders Association, 1921.

Schreuders, Piet. *Paperbacks U.S.A.* Amsterdam: Loeb, 1971.

Seth, Andrew, and Geoffrey Randall. *The Grocers: The Rise and Rise of the Supermarket Chains*. London: Kogan Page, 1999.

Simpson, John, and Edmund Weiner, eds. *Oxford English Dictionary Additions Series*, vols. 1 and 2. Oxford: Clarendon Press, 1993.

Soboleva, T.A., and A.V. Superanskaya. *Tovarnyye znaki* ("Trade Marks"). Moscow: Nauka, 1986.

Steiner, Rupert. *My First Break*. London: News International, 1998.

Stevenson, Tom. *Christie's World Encyclopedia of Champagne & Sparkling Wine*. Bath: Absolute Press, 1998.

Stiling, Marjorie. *Famous Brand Names, Emblems and Trademarks*. North Pomfret, VT: David & Charles, 1980.

Tambini, Michael. *The Look of the Century*, rev. ed. London: Dorling Kindersley, 1999.

Taylor, Michael J.H. *The World's Commercial Airlines*. Hoo: Grange Books, 1998.

Turner, Barry, ed. *The Writer's Handbook 2002*. London: Macmillan, 2001.

Urdang, Laurence, and Janet Braunstein. *Every Bite a Delight and Other Slogans*. Detroit: Visible Ink, 1992.

Van Dulken, Stephen. *Inventing the 20th Century:*

100 Inventions That Shaped the World. London: The British Library, 2000.

Walton, Stuart, and Norma Miller. *The Cook's Practical Encyclopedia of Spirits & Liqueurs.* London: Anness Publishing, 1997.

Weinreb, Ben, and Christopher Hibbert, eds. *The London Encyclopaedia*, rev. ed. London: Macmillan, 1993.

What's Behind the Name? Household Names That Rose to Fame and Fortune: London: Reader's Digest, 1986.

Whyte, Andrew. *101 Great Marques.* London: Octopus Books, 1985.

Wilson, Charles. *The History of Unilever.* London: Cassell; vols. 1 and 2, 1954; vol. 3, 1968.

Wilson, Hugo. *The Ultimate Motorcycle Book.* London: Dorling Kindersley, 1993.

Index